山东调查年鉴

SHANDONG SURVEY YEARBOOK

2007

国家统计局山东调查总队　编

Compiled by NBS Survey Office in Shandong

《山东调查年鉴—2007》编辑委员会

主　　任：宋志中

副 主 任：段连芳　谭　杰　赵兴成　刘同星

委　　员：（以姓氏笔划为序）

王庆国　王洪卫　王象永　仝义贵　刘　敏　刘传云

杜敏杰　宋义贵　宋秀娟　张向春　李承法　李常良

杨晓福　孟庆斌　范坤文　姜宏济　胡宗明　黄成海

寇祖传

主　　编：谭　杰

副 主 编：刘同星　宋秀娟　李方平

责任编辑：纪　文　丁瑞虎

编　　辑：（以姓氏笔划为序）

马明霞　刘永奇　孙瑞玲　张立新　张燕丽　李东法

杨延斌　杨志东　陈晓林　林雪梅　金立娟　胡东香

赵学功　郭　琦　崔　刚　景　虹　游海涛　董　岩

英文编译：丁瑞虎　刘明霞　翟文佳

封面设计：陈　刚

Shandong Survey Yearbook—2007

EDITORIAL BOARD AND STAFF

序　言

沐浴改革的春风，韵和时代的节拍。2006年3月，国家统计局山东调查总队正式揭牌成立。山东调查总队是根据国务院办公厅《关于印发国家统计局直属调查队管理体制改革方案的通知》精神，在整合原省城市社会经济调查队、农村社会经济调查队和企业调查队的基础上组建的正厅级专职调查机构，隶属国家统计局，实行垂直管理。除继续承担农产量、市场价格、城乡居民收入、有关企业等调查任务外，同时增加了国家宏观调控和国民经济核算所需重要统计信息的调查任务，肩负着为中央和地方服务的双重使命。依法独立行使统计调查、统计分析、统计监督的职能，独立向国家统计局上报调查资料，并对上报调查资料的真实性负责。国家统计局直属调查队管理体制改革的主要目的就是整合内部资源，增强中央统计的权威性。

站在新起点，实现新发展。国家统计局山东调查总队成立一年多来，在国家统计局的正确领导下，以服务经济社会发展为己任，以科学发展观为统领，根植齐鲁大地，心系山东发展，积极推进科学统计、依法统计、阳光统计，努力以调查质量立队、以优质服务强队、以团结实干兴队，认真履行信息、咨询、监督职责，数据质量有了新提高，服务水平有了新提升，取得了改革和发展的新突破，受到各级领导和社会各界的充分肯定和广泛好评。

一分耕耘，一分收获。《山东调查年鉴》的出版发行是山东调查总队贯彻落实科学发展观，坚持以人为本，服务党政决策、服务社会公众的又一重要成果。《山东调查年鉴》是总队成立以后出版发行的第一本综合性调查资料。编辑过程中，我们始终坚持高标准，力求做到较强的专业性和科学性，是一本党政部门、企事业单位、教学研究机构和社会公众所需的重要工具书。内容包括市场物价、居民生活、城乡发展、企业集团、农产量等调查数据资料。全书采用中英文对照模式，既能满足国内需要又符合涉外要求。全书真实反映了山东农业、市场价格、城乡居民生活、县域经济发展、城市综合实力、企业集团等方面的基本情况，对了解和分析山东经济社会发展具有重要参考价值。

改革刚刚起步，未来就在脚下。国家统计局山东调查总队将继续围绕国家宏观调控和山东省委、省政府的中心工作，坚定信心，奋力拼搏，努力做好各项工作，谱写山东统计调查事业的新篇章，为建设“大而强，富而美”的社会主义新山东做出应有的贡献。

国家统计局山东调查总队　总队长

二00七年九月

PREFACE

Bathing the reform spring breeze and rhyming the time beat. NBS Survey Office in Shandong was uncovered the sign to be established in March, 2006. NBS Survey Office in Shandong is specialty investigation organization of leading roles of departments or equivalents which was set up by combining provincial city social economy investigation team, the countryside social economy investigation team and the enterprise investigation team, according to "plan notice about NBS subordinate investigation team management organizational reform" which was Print and distributed by State Council office, NBS Survey Office in Shandong is subordinated to NBS, and implemented by the vertical management. Except continuing to undertake investigation duties for the agricultural production quantity, the market price, the city and countryside inhabitant receive and the related enterprise, NBS Survey Office in Shandong increases the investigation duties of important statistical information about the national macroeconomic regulation and control and the national economy calculation, shoulders the dual missions about serving for the central committee and the place. Independently exercises function for the statistical investigation, the statistical analysis, the statistical surveillance according to law, independently reports the investigation materials to NBS, is responsible to investigation material. The main purpose of NBS subordinate investigation team management organizational reform is combining interior resources, enhancing central statistics authority.

Standing on a new origin and realizing a new development. NBS Survey Office in Shandong is established for more than a year, under NBS correct leadership, take serving the economic society development as own duty, take the science development view as commands, rooted in the Qilu earth, tied Shandong develops, advances the science statistics positively, the legal statistics ,the sunlight statistics, sets up the team as the investigation quality, strengthens team by the high-quality service, prospers the team by uniting to practice, fulfilled responsibility about the information, the consultation, the surveillance earnestly, the data quality has the new enhancement, the service level has the new promotion, has obtained new breakthrough of the reform and the development, is received the widespread high praise and full affirmation from leaders and the social.

No pains, no gains. "Shandong survey Yearbook" is the important achievement that NBS Survey Office in Shandong implements and realizes science development view, persists human as foundation, service party politics decision-making and society public. "Shandong survey Yearbook" is the first comprehensive investigation material which we have established and published since NBS Survey Office in Shandong was established. In the edition process, we always persisted the high standard, endeavour it strong professional and scientific, "Shandong survey Yearbook" is important reference book which party politics departments, the enterprises and institutions, the teaching development facilities and the social public need. The content includes the market price, the inhabitant lives, enterprise group, agricultural production and city and countryside development investigation data materials and so on. The entire book uses the Chinese and English model. Both can meet the domestic need and touch on foreign request. The entire book had really reflected Shandong agriculture, the market price, the city and countryside inhabitant life, county economy development, city synthesis strength, enterprise group basic situations and so on, to understood and analyzes the Shandong economic society development to have the important reference value.

The reform just starts, the future is under foot. NBS Survey Office in Shandong will continue to revolve the national macroeconomic regulation and control with the Shandong provincial party committee, provincial government's main task, will firm confidence, strive for success furiously, complete each work diligently, compose the new chapter of Shandong investigation enterprise, contribute to new socialism Shandong which will be "big and strong, rich and beautiful".

NBS Survey Office in Shandong Director Song Zhishen

September.2007

国家统计局山东调查总队

国家统计局山东调查总队是国家统计局派驻山东的正厅级政府统计调查机构，参照公务员管理，承担国家统计局部署和地方党委、政府及有关部门委托的各项统计调查、分析研究工作。由国家统计局垂直管理，并依法独立行使统计调查、统计分析、统计监督的职权，独立向国家统计局上报调查结果。

▲国家统计局山东调查总队隆重揭牌正式成立

国家统计局山东调查总队是根据国务院办公厅关于国家统计局直属调查队管理体制改革的决定和中组部、中编办及国家发改委、人事部、财政部、国家统计局等部门的文件精神，在原山东省农村社会经济调查队、山东省城市社会经济调查队、山东省企业调查队基础上整合组建的。2006 年 3 月 22 日由国家统计局和山东省人民政府在济南举行了成立暨揭牌仪式。总队机关内设办公室、综合处、法规制度处、农业调查处、农村住户调查处、城镇住户调查处、工业调查处、服务业调查处、统计监测处、生产投资价格处、居民消费价格处、商业和投资建筑业调查处、专项调查处、人事教育处（含老干部管理）、财务管理处、纪检监察室、机关党委等 17 个处室。下辖 17 个市级调查队和 42 个县级调查队。

▲山东调查总队在成立当年就被评为省直文明机关。省直机关工委领导亲自到山东调查总队，为文明机关揭牌。

国家统计局山东调查总队建队以来，秉承原三支调查队的优良传统，整合人才资源，锐意创新，确立了“以调查质量立队、以优质服务强队、以团结实干兴队”的工作理念，建立了多层次的统计调查网络，在全省 17 市 42 个县（市、区）设置各类样本观测点 3 万余个，利用先进的现代化信息采集和远程通讯传输交换网络，充分发挥科学、准确、快捷的优势，从农业、工业、建筑业、服务业、投资、价格、城乡居民生活等方面，全方位、多角度反映和监测山东经济社会发展中的新变化、新情况和新问题，成为活跃在统计战线上的“轻骑兵”，得到各级党政领导的充分肯定和社会各界的高度评价。

统计是认识社会的手段和管理经济的重要工具。国家统计局山东调查总队坚持求真务实，脚踏实地，运用抽样调查、重点调查、典型调查等科学的调查方法，依托完善的调查网络，圆满完成国家和各级地方政府赋予的各项调查任务，提供了大量真实可靠的统计调查数据资料。承担的主要调查任务有：农产量抽样调查；农民收入抽样调查和农村全面小康实现程度监测工作；城镇居民收支抽样调查；居民消费、工业品、房地产、固定资产投资、农产品等各类价格调查；企业景气抽样调查和企业集团统计；有关服务业（主要是12个行业服务业）抽样调查；有关商业投资、建筑业方面的抽样调查；规模以下工业抽样调查；县域经济和城市基本情况全面统计；根据经济社会中的难点、热点和部门需要开展专题、专项调查；参与实施重大国情国力普查（如经济普查、农业普查、人口普查等）。

▲总队领导班子

作为领导宏观决策的参谋和助手，国家统计局山东调查总队根据掌握的丰富资料，为国家和地方党委、政府决策提供了翔实的统计分析和调研报告，充分发挥了统计调查的职能作用。建队伊始，国家统计局山东调查总队就牢固树立"立足山东、反映山东、服务山东、宣传山东"的宗旨，向省委、省政府报送分析报告近200篇，其中多篇被省领导批示，向省委、省政府两个办公厅报送经济社会信息600余条，信息采用量居省直部门前三位。山东调查总队已成为山东省委、省政府决策的重要"参谋部"、"智囊团"，成为服务社会公众的重要信息窗口。

作为统计战线的新生力量，国家统计局山东调查总队充分发挥快速反应机制的优势和特点，建立了为各级党政部门和社会各界双向服务体系，强化多主题调查的综合功能，承担了各种类型的委托调查。先后承担

▲宋志申总队长赴齐河县调研夏粮生产情况（收割小麦样本）

▲国家统计局山东调查队系统队长会议

完成了未成年人思想道德建设及大学生思想政治教育状况调查、城镇居民购房意向调查、党风廉政建设民意调查、城市农民工生活质量状况调查、城镇居民和企业金融需求调查、39 个县 1260 个行政村基本情况调查、全省国内旅游调查、“文明山东”测评指标体系构建、电视观众满意度调查、全省快递业调查、城市环保群众满意情况调查、山东省职工队伍状况抽样调查等，为有关部门管理和决策提供了准确的依据，受到社会各界的广泛好评。

作为社会经济发展重大问题研究部门，国家统计局山东调查总队拥有一批精通统计、经济、社会、计算机、市场研究和经济形势分析的权威人士，建立课题招标制度，设立专项课题经费，有计划地组织、承担国家、省及有关部门的重大社会经济科研项目研究工作。建队不到 2 年，总队先后组织重大课题项目近 10 项，主要研究成果有《PPI 与 CPI 关联的理论与实证分析》、《山东房价与商品房空置率、居民收入关系研究》、《农村劳动力有序流动和转移问题研究》、《不同地区新农村建设的目的模式调查与研究》、《国际市场价格对国内市场的影响研究》、《加速城镇化进程对资源和环境的影响研究》、《山东粮食供求平衡问题研究》、《山东现代服务业发展问题研究》、《山东城乡协调发展问题研究》等。其中 3 项成果获国家统计局优秀课题成果特等奖；《PPI 与 CPI 关联的理论与实证分析》、《山东房价与商品房空置率、居民收入关系研究》连续获 2006、2007 年度山东省软科学优秀成果一等奖。组织系统内课题研究项目 30 余项。

“为经济社会又好又快发展服务是统计调查工作第一要务”，国家统计局山东调查总队全体干部职工在总队党组的带领下，坚持在优质服务中体现调查总队的价值，发挥自身优势，以可靠的信誉、快捷的调查、准确的数据、科学的分析为国家宏观调控，为社会各界提供全方位的优质服务。

NBS Survey Office in Shandong

NBS Survey Office in Shandong is specialty investigation organization of leading roles of departments or equivalents which is accredited by NBS, is managed as officials. Undertake each statistical investigation and analysis research works which were deployed by NBS and local party committee, the government and the department concerned. By vertical management of NBS, Independently exercises function for the statistical investigation, the statistical analysis, the statistical surveillance according to law, independently reports the investigation result to NBS.

NBS Survey Office in Shandong was set up by combining provincial city social economy investigation team, the countryside social economy investigation team and the enterprise investigation team, according to "plan notice about NBS subordinate investigation team management organizational reform" which was Print and distributed by State Council office. NBS Survey Office in Shandong was uncovered the sign to be established on March 22, 2006 by NBS and Shandong province government in Jinan. institution is set up by the office, the synthesis office, the laws and regulations system office, the agriculture investigation office, the countryside inhabitant investigation office, the city inhabitant investigation office, the industry investigation office, service industry investigation office, the statistical monitor office, the production investment price office, the inhabitant expend price office, the trade and the investment architecture industry investigation office, the special accent investigation office, the human affairs training office (including old cadre),the financial administrative office, the disciplinary inspection monitor office, the institution party committee and so on 17 offices, Governs 17 city investigation teams and 42 county investigation teams.

Since NBS Survey Office in Shandong is constructed, receives fine tradition of the original three investigation teams, adjust human resources, firmly innovates, establishes the work idea for "set up the team by the investigated quality, strength team by the high-quality service, prosper the team by united doing", has established the multi-level statistical investigation network, establishes 30,000 sample observation points,17 cities, 42 counties (cities, areas) in entire province, uses advanced modernized information gathering and the long-distance communication transmission exchange network, displays scientific, accurate, quick superiority fully, from agricultural, industry, architecture industry, service industry, investment, price, aspects city and countryside inhabitant life and so on, Omni-directional, the multiple perspectives reflects and monitors the new change, the new situation and the new question for the Shandong economic society and develop, becomes "the light cavalry" which enlivens in the statistical front, obtains full affirmation and strong approval the all levels of party politics leadership and the social.

The statistics is the method of knowing the social and the important tool of managing economy. NBS Survey Office in Shandong persists true, conscientious, uses sample investigation, key investigation, type investigation methods and so on, depends on the consummation investigation network, completes each investigation task which NBS and all levels of local authority entrust with, has provided the massive real reliable statistical investigation data materials. Undertaking the main investigation duties includes: sample investigation for agricultural production quantity; the sample investigation for the farmer receives and monitor work for the countryside comprehensive well-off realization degree; sample investigation for cities inhabitant revenue and expenditure; the inhabitant expends, the industrial product, the real estate, the investment in the fixed assets, the agricultural product and so on each kind of price investigations; the enterprise booming sample investigation and the enterprise group count; the sample investigation for the related service industry (mainly including 12 profession service industries); sample investigation for related business investment, architecture industry aspect; sample investigation for scale following industry; comprehensive statistics for county territory economy and city basic situation; the topic and special investigation according to difficulty, the hot spot in the economic society and the department need; Participates in general surveys for significant national condition and national strength (for example economical general survey, agricultural general survey, census and so on).

As the staff officer and the assistant for the leadership macroscopic decision-making, NBS Survey Office in

Shandong by grasping rich materials, has provided the full and accurate statistical analysis and investigation reports for NBS and the local party committee, the government decision-making, has fully displayed the statistical investigation function. Beginning for constructing the team, NBS Survey Office in Shandong sets up the objective reliably for "bases Shandong, reflects Shandong, serves Shandong, propagandizes Shandong", sends near 200 analysis reports to the provincial party committee and the provincial government, in which many are make written comments by the leaders, sends 600 economic society information to two office for the provincial party committee and provincial government, the quantity of the used information occupies first three directly under the provincial party committee department. NBS Survey Office in Shandong has become important "the general staff", "the brain trust" for the Shandong provincial party committee and the provincial government decision-making, become the important information window for servicing society public.

As new strength of the statistical front, NBS Survey Office in Shandong displays rapid reaction mechanism superiority and the characteristic fully, has established bidirectional service system for all levels of party politics departments and social, strengthens the multi-subject investigation comprehensive function, undertakes each kind of type authorized investigation. Successively has completed the investigation for the minor thought moral reconstruction and the university student thought political education condition situation, the intention investigation for buying homes of the cities inhabitant, the poll investigation for party spirit cultivation and clean government, the investigation for the city peasant laborer quality of life condition, finance demand investigation for the cities inhabitant and the enterprises, the basic situation investigation of 39 counties 1260 administrative villages, domestic traveling investigation in entire province, target system construction for Shandong cultured and civilized city evaluation, degree of satisfaction investigation for the television viewers, express industry investigation in entire province, the populace satisfies investigation for the city environmental protection, Shandong Province staff troop condition sample investigation and so on, has provided the accurate basis for the department concerned management and the decision-making, received widespread high praise from the social.

As research department for major issue of the social economy development, NBS Survey Office in Shandong has one batch of authoritative source about familiar statistics, the economical, social, the computer, the marketing research and the economic situation analysis, establishes the topic tender system, sets up the special topic funds, has organized and undertake significant social economy scientific research item research work of NBS, the province and concerned department. Since near 2 years, successively organized near 10 important issue projects, the main research results have "PPI And CPI Connection Theory And Real diagnosis Analysis", "Shandong House price And Commodity apartment Vacancy rate, Inhabitant Receive Relational Research", "Question Research for Rural labor force Order Flowing And Shift", "Investigation And Research for Different Area New Rural reconstruction Goal Pattern", "Research for World market price Influence to Domestic market", "Research for Acceleration Urbanization Advancement Influence to Resources And Environment", "Question Research for Shandong Grain Balance between supply and demand", "Question Research for Shandong Modern Service industry Development", "question Research for Shandong city and countryside coordinated development" and so on.3 achievements attain NBS outstanding topic achievement special award; "PPI And CPI Connection Theory And Real diagnosis Analysis" and "Shandong House price And Commodity apartment Vacancy rate, Inhabitant Receive Relational Research" attain Shandong Province soft sciences outstanding achievement first award in 2006, 2007 continuously. Organized system topic research project more than 30 terms.

"Serves is the first important matter counts of the statistics and investigation work for the economic society good and quick development", all cadre staff for NBS Survey Office in Shandong is under the unit party group's leadership, persist manifesting the investigation team the value in the high-quality service, display own superiority, take the reliable prestige, the quick investigation, the accurate data, the science analysis to provide the Omni-directional high-quality service for the national macroeconomic regulation and control and the society.

目 录

CONTENTS

一、城市主要社会经济指标

Main Social Economy Target of Various Cities

二、县（市、区）主要社会经济指标

Main Social Economy Target of Various Counties (City,Area)

三、主要农产品产量调查资料

Investigation Material on Output of Major Farm Products

四、城镇居民生活调查资料

Investigation Material of City and Town Residential Life

五、农村居民生活调查资料
Investigation Material of Rural Residential Life

六、生产价格调查资料
Investigation Material of Production Prices

九、企业景气调查资料

Investigation Material of Business Climate

大 事 记

1

城市主要社会经济指标

Main Social Economy Target of Various Cities

编辑单位：统计监测处　　Editorial Unit: the Statistical Monitoring Office

编　　委：仝义贵　　Editorial Board: Tong Yigui

责任编辑：李东法　郭　琦　　Executive Editor-in-Chief: Li Dongfa Guo Qi

校　　对：李东法　郭　琦　　Proofreader: Li Dongfa Guo Qi

电　　话：86197886　　Telephone: 86197886

简要说明

一、本篇资料反映了全省17个省辖市城市主要经济发展情况。包括人口、综合经济、农业、工业、财政、交通运输、文教、劳动保障、环境等方面的年度数据。

二、本篇资料来源于2006年度城市社会经济基本情况统计年报资料。

Brief Introduction

Ⅰ.This material reflects 17 cities main economy development situation in the entire province. Includes year data for population, synthesis economy, agriculture, industry, finance, transportation, culture and education, work safeguard, environment.

Ⅱ.This material originates from annual report material for the city social economy basic situation statistics in 2006.

1-1 济南市城市基本情况
City Basic Situation of Jinan
2006

指标名称	Index	计量单位	Prickle	全市 Total City	市辖区 Districts under City
年末总人口（公安户籍口径）	Total Year-end Population(Census Requirements of Public Security)	万人	10 000 persons	603.35	352.29
年末单位从业人员数	Employed Persons at Year-end in Units	万人	10 000 persons	101.26	81.89
第一产业（农、林、牧、渔业）	Primary Industry(Farming, Forestry, Animal Husbandry and Fishery)	万人	10 000 persons	0.11	0.08
第二产业	Secondary Industry	万人	10 000 persons	49.38	38.14
第三产业	Tertiary-industry	万人	10 000 persons	51.77	43.67
行政区域土地面积	Area of Administrative Land	平方公里	sq.km.	8177	3257
其中：建成区面积	Among: Developed Areas	平方公里	sq.km.		305
地区生产总值（当年价格）	Gross Regional Product(Current Year's Prices)	万元	10 000 yuan	21850856	16593093
第一产业增加值	Value Added of Primary Industry	万元	10 000 yuan	1451210	461092
第二产业增加值	Value Added of Secondary Industry	万元	10 000 yuan	10017754	7272065
其中：工业增加值	Among: Value Added of Industry	万元	10 000 yuan	8615053	6177715
第三产业增加值	Value Added of Tertiary Industry	万元	10 000 yuan	10381892	8859936
人均地区生产总值	Per Gross Regional Product	元	yuan	36394	47398
地区生产总值增长率	Growth Rate of Gross Regional Product	%	percentage	15.7	13
地方财政一般预算内收入	Local Financial Budgetary Revenue	万元	10 000 yuan	1284388	1065454
地方财政一般预算内支出	Local Financial Budgetary Expenditure	万元	10 000 yuan	1469762	1112104
年末耕地总资源	Total Areas of Year-end Cultivated Land	千公顷	1 000 ha.	345	
蔬菜产量	Output of Vegetables	吨	ton	7104258	
水果产量	Output of Fruits	吨	ton	437136	
肉类总产量	Output of Meat	吨	ton	429510	
奶类产量	Output of Milk	吨	ton	268329	
水产品产量	Output of Aquatic Product	吨	ton	36649	
规模以上工业企业数	Sum of State-owned and Non-state-owned Industrial Enterprises above Designated Size	个	unit	1856	1036
规模以上工业总产值（当年价）	Gross Industrial Output Value of State-owned and Non-state-owned Industrial Enterprises above Designated Size (Current Year's Prices)	万元	10 000 yuan	26192494	19080262
私人汽车拥有量	Possession of Private Vehicles	辆	unit	309504	
公路客运量	Passenger Traffic of Highway	万人	10 000 persons	5541	
公路货运量	Freight Traffic of Highway	万吨	10 000 tons	8784	
境内等级公路里程	Expressway and Class Ⅰ to Ⅳ Highways	公里	km.	9833	
境内高速公路里程	Expressway and Class Ⅰ to Ⅳ Freeway	公里	km.	194	

1-1 续表 1 continued

指标名称	Index	计量单位	Prickle	全市 Total City	市辖区 Districts under City
全年用电量	Annual Electricity Consumption	万千瓦时	10 000 kw·m	1716323	1373424
其中：工业用电	Among: Industrial Electricity consumption	万千瓦时	10 000 kw·m	1154855	922579
居民生活用电	Resident Electricity Consumption	万千瓦时	10 000 kw·m	268969	195833
社会消费品零售总额	Total Retail Sales of Consumer Goods	万元	10 000 yuan	9393436	7497837
货物进口额（海关数）	Value of Imports(Customs Numbers)	万美元	10 000 U.S. dollars	194981	
货物出口额（海关数）	Value of Exports(Customs Numbers)	万美元	10 000 U.S. dollars	243949	
海外游客人数（含一日游游客）	Sum of Overseas Visitors (Including One-day Visitors)	人	person	135940	
小学毕业生升学率	Primary School Rate of Admission into Higher Level of Education	%	percentage	100	100
初中毕业生升学率	Junior Middle School Rate of Admission into Higher Level of Education	%	percentage	94	100
专利申请授权量	Authorization Quantity of Applying for Patents	项	unit	3104	
其中：发明	Among: Inventions	项	unit	275	
基本养老保险参保人数	Number of People Participated in Basic Pension Insurance	人	person	1054054	848874
基本医疗保险参保人数	Number of People Participated in Basic Medical Insurance	人	person	826207	711228
失业保险参保人数	Number of People Participated in Unemployment Insurance	人	person	666671	548364
城镇居民最低生活保障人数	Number of Participated in Minimum Standard of Living for City Residents	人	person	67395	55245
环境污染治理投资总额	Total Investment of Environmental Pollution Government	万元	10 000 yuan	442928	
城市环境基础设施建设本年完成投资额	Investment Cost of Urban Environment in Frastructure Construction Completed This Year	万元	10 000 yuan	382538	
三废综合利用产品产值	Output Value of Products Made from Utilization of Waste Gas, Water &Solid Wastes	万元	10 000 yuan	91840	
工业固体废物综合利用率	Ratio of Industrial Solid Wastes	%	percentage	93.65	
烟尘控制区总面积	Total Area of Soot Control Zones	平方公里	sq.km.	270	
环境噪声达标区总面积	Area of Environmental Noise Meeting National Standard	平方公里	sq.km.	196	

1-2 青岛市城市基本情况
City Basic Situation of Qingdao
2006

指标名称	Index	计量单位	Prickle	全市 Total City	市辖区 Districts under City
年末总人口（公安户籍口径）	Total Year-end Population(Census Requirements of Public Security)	万人	10 000 persons	749.38	271
年末单位从业人员数	Employed Persons at Year-end in Units	万人	10 000 persons	129.47	76.65
第一产业（农、林、牧、渔业）	Primary Industry(Farming, Forestry, Animal Husbandry and Fishery)	万人	10 000 persons	0.58	0.24
第二产业	Secondary Industry	万人	10 000 persons	84.68	46.12
第三产业	Tertiary-industry	万人	10 000 persons	44.21	30.29
行政区域土地面积	Area of Administrative Land	平方公里	sq.km.	11175	1411
其中：建成区面积	Among: Developed Areas	平方公里	sq.km.		227
地区生产总值（当年价格）	Gross Regional Product(Current Year's Prices)	万元	10 000 yuan	32065800	17840270
第一产业增加值	Value Added of Primary Industry	万元	10 000 yuan	1839500	226549
第二产业增加值	Value Added of Secondary Industry	万元	10 000 yuan	16771700	9502699
其中：工业增加值	Among: Value Added of Industry	万元	10 000 yuan	15274900	8785975
第三产业增加值	Value Added of Tertiary Industry	万元	10 000 yuan	13454600	8111022
人均地区生产总值	Per Gross Regional Product	元	yuan	38892	64538
地区生产总值增长率	Growth Rate of Gross Regional Product	%	percentage	15.7	17.6
地方财政一般预算内收入	Local Financial Budgetary Revenue	万元	10 000 yuan	2259904	1706532
地方财政一般预算内支出	Local Financial Budgetary Expenditure	万元	10 000 yuan	2367875	1629050
年末耕地总资源	Total Areas of Year-end Cultivated Land	千公顷	1 000 ha.	415	
蔬菜产量	Output of Vegetables	吨	ton	6051239	
水果产量	Output of Fruits	吨	ton	827755	
肉类总产量	Output of Meat	吨	ton	842578	
奶类产量	Output of Milk	吨	ton	572926	
水产品产量	Output of Aquatic Product	吨	ton	1250041	
规模以上工业企业数	Sum of State-owned and Non-state-owned Industrial Enterprises above Designated Size	个	unit	4567	1580
规模以上工业总产值（当年价）	Gross Industrial Output Value of State-owned and Non-state-owned Industrial Enterprises above Designated Size (Current Year's Prices)	万元	10 000 yuan	51846820	30424759
私人汽车拥有量	Possession of Private Vehicles	辆	unit	340912	
公路客运量	Passenger Traffic of Highway	万人	10 000 persons	22332	
公路货运量	Freight Traffic of Highway	万吨	10 000 tons	32047	
境内等级公路里程	Expressway and Class Ⅰ to Ⅳ Highways	公里	km.	13836	
境内高速公路里程	Expressway and Class Ⅰ to Ⅳ Freeway	公里	km.	525	

1-2 续表 1 continued

指标名称	Index	计量单位	Prickle	全市 Total City	市辖区 Districts under City
全年用电量	Annual Electricity Consumption	万千瓦时	10 000 kw • m	2153519	1373706.21
其中：工业用电	Among: Industrial Electricity consumption	万千瓦时	10 000 kw • m	1437082	909340.06
居民生活用电	Resident Electricity Consumption	万千瓦时	10 000 kw • m	383802	233090.28
社会消费品零售总额	Total Retail Sales of Consumer Goods	万元	10 000 yuan	10066708	5690563
货物进口额（海关数）	Value of Imports(Customs Numbers)	万美元	10 000 U.S. dollars	1564991	
货物出口额（海关数）	Value of Exports(Customs Numbers)	万美元	10 000 U.S. dollars	2346552	
海外游客人数（含一日游游客）	Sum of Overseas Visitors (Including One-day Visitors)	人	person	854462	
小学毕业生升学率	Primary School Rate of Admission into Higher Level of Education	%	percentage	100	100
初中毕业生升学率	Junior Middle School Rate of Admission into Higher Level of Education	%	percentage	100	100
专利申请授权量	Authorization Quantity of Applying for Patents	项	unit	3124	
其中：发明	Among: Inventions	项	unit	244	
基本养老保险参保人数	Number of People Participated in Basic Pension Insurance	人	person	1715592	1135874
基本医疗保险参保人数	Number of People Participated in Basic Medical Insurance	人	person	1928277	1431747
失业保险参保人数	Number of People Participated in Unemployment Insurance	人	person	1081058	725855
城镇居民最低生活保障人数	Number of Participated in Minimum Standard of Living for City Residents	人	person	41780	36213
环境污染治理投资总额	Total Investment of Environmental Pollution Government	万元	10 000 yuan	566252	
城市环境基础设施建设本年完成投资额	Investment Cost of Urban Environment in Frastructure Construction Completed This Year	万元	10 000 yuan	485974	
三废综合利用产品产值	Output Value of Products Made from Utilization of Waste Gas, Water &Solid Wastes	万元	10 000 yuan	54603	
工业固体废物综合利用率	Ratio of Industrial Solid Wastes	%	percentage	97.05	
烟尘控制区总面积	Total Area of Soot Control Zones	平方公里	sq.km.	393	
环境噪声达标区总面积	Area of Environmental Noise Meeting National Standard	平方公里	sq.km.	318	

1-3 淄博市城市基本情况
City Basic Situation of Zibo
2006

指标名称	Index	计量单位	Prickle	全市 Total City	市辖区 Districts under City
年末总人口（公安户籍口径）	Total Year-end Population(Census Requirements of Public Security)	万人	10 000 persons	418.13	276.53
年末单位从业人员数	Employed Persons at Year-end in Units	万人	10 000 persons	57.1	44.8
第一产业（农、林、牧、渔业）	Primary Industry(Farming, Forestry, Animal Husbandry and Fishery)	万人	10 000 persons	0.36	0.08
第二产业	Secondary Industry	万人	10 000 persons	38.67	30.68
第三产业	Tertiary-industry	万人	10 000 persons	18.07	14.04
行政区域土地面积	Area of Administrative Land	平方公里	sq.km.	5965.2	2977.8
其中：建成区面积	Among: Developed Areas	平方公里	sq.km.		195.7
地区生产总值（当年价格）	Gross Regional Product(Current Year's Prices)	万元	10 000 yuan	16451600	13268417
第一产业增加值	Value Added of Primary Industry	万元	10 000 yuan	627200	310680
第二产业增加值	Value Added of Secondary Industry	万元	10 000 yuan	10790600	8820184
其中：工业增加值	Among: Value Added of Industry	万元	10 000 yuan	10030000	8374309
第三产业增加值	Value Added of Tertiary Industry	万元	10 000 yuan	5033800	4137553
人均地区生产总值	Per Gross Regional Product	元	yuan	37039	48058
地区生产总值增长率	Growth Rate of Gross Regional Product	%	percentage	15.8	15.9
地方财政一般预算内收入	Local Financial Budgetary Revenue	万元	10 000 yuan	806969	666149
地方财政一般预算内支出	Local Financial Budgetary Expenditure	万元	10 000 yuan	1010541	792196
年末耕地总资源	Total Areas of Year-end Cultivated Land	千公顷	1 000 ha.	158.65	
蔬菜产量	Output of Vegetables	吨	ton	1923700	
水果产量	Output of Fruits	吨	ton	550600	
肉类总产量	Output of Meat	吨	ton	151200	
奶类产量	Output of Milk	吨	ton	91800	
水产品产量	Output of Aquatic Product	吨	ton	28000	
规模以上工业企业数	Sum of State-owned and Non-state-owned Industrial Enterprises above Designated Size	个	unit	2559	2102
规模以上工业总产值（当年价）	Gross Industrial Output Value of State-owned and Non-state-owned Industrial Enterprises above Designated Size (Current Year's Prices)	万元	10 000 yuan	35625150	29630892
私人汽车拥有量	Possession of Private Vehicles	辆	unit	183714	
公路客运量	Passenger Traffic of Highway	万人	10 000 persons	21990	
公路货运量	Freight Traffic of Highway	万吨	10 000 tons	5864	
境内等级公路里程	Expressway and Class Ⅰ to Ⅳ Highways	公里	km.	9160.9	
境内高速公路里程	Expressway and Class Ⅰ to Ⅳ Freeway	公里	km.	148	

1-3 续表 1 continued

指标名称	Index	计量单位	Prickle	全市 Total City	市辖区 Districts under City
全年用电量	Annual Electricity Consumption	万千瓦时	10 000 kw・m	2610793	2320491
其中：工业用电	Among: Industrial Electricity consumption	万千瓦时	10 000 kw・m	2314720	2066423
居民生活用电	Resident Electricity Consumption	万千瓦时	10 000 kw・m	153888	127726
社会消费品零售总额	Total Retail Sales of Consumer Goods	万元	10 000 yuan	4998126	3993481
货物进口额（海关数）	Value of Imports(Customs Numbers)	万美元	10 000 U.S. dollars	125150	
货物出口额（海关数）	Value of Exports(Customs Numbers)	万美元	10 000 U.S. dollars	250884	
海外游客人数（含一日游游客）	Sum of Overseas Visitors (Including One-day Visitors)	人	person	52385	
小学毕业生升学率	Primary School Rate of Admission into Higher Level of Education	%	percentage	100	100
初中毕业生升学率	Junior Middle School Rate of Admission into Higher Level of Education	%	percentage	91.46	100
专利申请授权量	Authorization Quantity of Applying for Patents	项	unit	1018	
其中：发明	Among: Inventions	项	unit	127	
基本养老保险参保人数	Number of People Participated in Basic Pension Insurance	人	person	656991	612534
基本医疗保险参保人数	Number of People Participated in Basic Medical Insurance	人	person	777565	707471
失业保险参保人数	Number of People Participated in Unemployment Insurance	人	person	421466	338133
城镇居民最低生活保障人数	Number of Participated in Minimum Standard of Living for City Residents	人	person	36820	29779
环境污染治理投资总额	Total Investment of Environmental Pollution Government	万元	10 000 yuan	197284	
城市环境基础设施建设本年完成投资额	Investment Cost of Urban Environment in Frastructure Construction Completed This Year	万元	10 000 yuan	107186	
三废综合利用产品产值	Output Value of Products Made from Utilization of Waste Gas, Water &Solid Wastes	万元	10 000 yuan	143462.8	
工业固体废物综合利用率	Ratio of Industrial Solid Wastes	%	percentage	81.89	
烟尘控制区总面积	Total Area of Soot Control Zones	平方公里	sq.km.	211.5	
环境噪声达标区总面积	Area of Environmental Noise Meeting National Standard	平方公里	sq.km.	136.6	

1-4 枣庄市城市基本情况
City Basic Situation of Zaozhuang
2006

指标名称	Index	计量单位	Prickle	全市 Total City	市辖区 Districts under City
年末总人口（公安户籍口径）	Total Year-end Population(Census Requirements of Public Security)	万人	10 000 persons	371.97	213.28
年末单位从业人员数	Employed Persons at Year-end in Units	万人	10 000 persons	35.41	25.46
第一产业（农、林、牧、渔业）	Primary Industry(Farming, Forestry, Animal Husbandry and Fishery)	万人	10 000 persons	0.34	0.05
第二产业	Secondary Industry	万人	10 000 persons	19.72	14.51
第三产业	Tertiary-industry	万人	10 000 persons	15.35	10.9
行政区域土地面积	Area of Administrative Land	平方公里	sq.km.	4563	3069
其中：建成区面积	Among: Developed Areas	平方公里	sq.km.		105
地区生产总值（当年价格）	Gross Regional Product(Current Year's Prices)	万元	10 000 yuan	7599500	4247900
第一产业增加值	Value Added of Primary Industry	万元	10 000 yuan	684800	357200
第二产业增加值	Value Added of Secondary Industry	万元	10 000 yuan	4828200	2759800
其中：工业增加值	Among: Value Added of Industry	万元	10 000 yuan	4457200	2573800
第三产业增加值	Value Added of Tertiary Industry	万元	10 000 yuan	2086500	1130900
人均地区生产总值	Per Gross Regional Product	元	yuan	21045	20928
地区生产总值增长率	Growth Rate of Gross Regional Product	%	percentage	16.4	15.2
地方财政一般预算内收入	Local Financial Budgetary Revenue	万元	10 000 yuan	370044	247878
地方财政一般预算内支出	Local Financial Budgetary Expenditure	万元	10 000 yuan	514969	345467
年末耕地总资源	Total Areas of Year-end Cultivated Land	千公顷	1 000 ha.	230	
蔬菜产量	Output of Vegetables	吨	ton	5460928	
水果产量	Output of Fruits	吨	ton	219630	
肉类总产量	Output of Meat	吨	ton	239480	
奶类产量	Output of Milk	吨	ton	23763	
水产品产量	Output of Aquatic Product	吨	ton	43581	
规模以上工业企业数	Sum of State-owned and Non-state-owned Industrial Enterprises above Designated Size	个	unit	1086	741
规模以上工业总产值（当年价）	Gross Industrial Output Value of State-owned and Non-state-owned Industrial Enterprises above Designated Size (Current Year's Prices)	万元	10 000 yuan	13346779	8829537
私人汽车拥有量	Possession of Private Vehicles	辆	unit	111060	
公路客运量	Passenger Traffic of Highway	万人	10 000 persons	7696	
公路货运量	Freight Traffic of Highway	万吨	10 000 tons	5268	
境内等级公路里程	Expressway and Class Ⅰ to Ⅳ Highways	公里	km.	5391	
境内高速公路里程	Expressway and Class Ⅰ to Ⅳ Freeway	公里	km.	115	

1-4 续表 1 continued

指标名称	Index	计量单位	Prickle	全市 Total City	市辖区 Districts under City
全年用电量	Annual Electricity Consumption	万千瓦时	10 000 kw • m	821091	471480
其中：工业用电	Among: Industrial Electricity consumption	万千瓦时	10 000 kw • m	681941	396442
居民生活用电	Resident Electricity Consumption	万千瓦时	10 000 kw • m	60931	36208
社会消费品零售总额	Total Retail Sales of Consumer Goods	万元	10 000 yuan	2044219	1083506
货物进口额（海关数）	Value of Imports(Customs Numbers)	万美元	10 000 U.S. dollars	5835	
货物出口额（海关数）	Value of Exports(Customs Numbers)	万美元	10 000 U.S. dollars	41570	
海外游客人数（含一日游游客）	Sum of Overseas Visitors (Including One-day Visitors)	人	person	17000	
小学毕业生升学率	Primary School Rate of Admission into Higher Level of Education	%	percentage	100	100
初中毕业生升学率	Junior Middle School Rate of Admission into Higher Level of Education	%	percentage	77.1	93.3
专利申请授权量	Authorization Quantity of Applying for Patents	项	unit	275	
其中：发明	Among: Inventions	项	unit	9	
基本养老保险参保人数	Number of People Participated in Basic Pension Insurance	人	person	357260	219126
基本医疗保险参保人数	Number of People Participated in Basic Medical Insurance	人	person	383340	283445
失业保险参保人数	Number of People Participated in Unemployment Insurance	人	person	305179	223885
城镇居民最低生活保障人数	Number of Participated in Minimum Standard of Living for City Residents	人	person	62843	49740
环境污染治理投资总额	Total Investment of Environmental Pollution Government	万元	10 000 yuan	128649	
城市环境基础设施建设，本年完成投资额	Investment Cost of Urban Environment in Frastructure Construction Completed This Year	万元	10 000 yuan	45029	
三废综合利用产品产值	Output Value of Products Made from Utilization of Waste Gas, Water &Solid Wastes	万元	10 000 yuan	45429	
工业固体废物综合利用率	Ratio of Industrial Solid Wastes	%	percentage	96.15	
烟尘控制区总面积	Total Area of Soot Control Zones	平方公里	sq.km.	125	
环境噪声达标区总面积	Area of Environmental Noise Meeting National Standard	平方公里	sq.km.	90	

1-5　东营市城市基本情况
City Basic Situation of Dongying
2006

指标名称	Index	计量单位	Prickle	全市 Total City	市辖区 Districts under City
年末总人口（公安户籍口径）	Total Year-end Population(Census Requirements of Public Security)	万人	10 000 persons	181.82	82.13
年末单位从业人员数	Employed Persons at Year-end in Units	万人	10 000 persons	34.82	26.16
第一产业（农、林、牧、渔业）	Primary Industry(Farming, Forestry, Animal Husbandry and Fishery)	万人	10 000 persons	0.43	0.05
第二产业	Secondary Industry	万人	10 000 persons	21.86	17.14
第三产业	Tertiary-industry	万人	10 000 persons	12.53	8.97
行政区域土地面积	Area of Administrative Land	平方公里	sq.km.	7923	3294
其中：建成区面积	Among: Developed Areas	平方公里	sq.km.		90
地区生产总值（当年价格）	Gross Regional Product(Current Year's Prices)	万元	10 000 yuan	14503100	10820637
第一产业增加值	Value Added of Primary Industry	万元	10 000 yuan	532700	135456
第二产业增加值	Value Added of Secondary Industry	万元	10 000 yuan	11701300	9003481
其中：工业增加值	Among: Value Added of Industry	万元	10 000 yuan	11150300	8671641
第三产业增加值	Value Added of Tertiary Industry	万元	10 000 yuan	2269100	1681700
人均地区生产总值	Per Gross Regional Product	元	yuan	74048	112326
地区生产总值增长率	Growth Rate of Gross Regional Product	%	percentage	17	19.7
地方财政一般预算内收入	Local Financial Budgetary Revenue	万元	10 000 yuan	480975	352452
地方财政一般预算内支出	Local Financial Budgetary Expenditure	万元	10 000 yuan	618612	411129
年末耕地总资源	Total Areas of Year-end Cultivated Land	千公顷	1 000 ha.	195	
蔬菜产量	Output of Vegetables	吨	ton	2124262	
水果产量	Output of Fruits	吨	ton	95980	
肉类总产量	Output of Meat	吨	ton	214607	
奶类产量	Output of Milk	吨	ton	90557	
水产品产量	Output of Aquatic Product	吨	ton	450010	
规模以上工业企业数	Sum of State-owned and Non-state-owned Industrial Enterprises above Designated Size	个	unit	580	232
规模以上工业总产值（当年价）	Gross Industrial Output Value of State-owned and Non-state-owned Industrial Enterprises above Designated Size (Current Year's Prices)	万元	10 000 yuan	24646693	14628036
私人汽车拥有量	Possession of Private Vehicles	辆	unit	144202	
公路客运量	Passenger Traffic of Highway	万人	10 000 persons	2908	
公路货运量	Freight Traffic of Highway	万吨	10 000 tons	6134	
境内等级公路里程	Expressway and Class Ⅰ to Ⅳ Highways	公里	km.	7297	
境内高速公路里程	Expressway and Class Ⅰ to Ⅳ Freeway	公里	km.	145	

1-5 续表 1 continued

指标名称	Index	计量单位	Prickle	全市 Total City	市辖区 Districts under City
全年用电量	Annual Electricity Consumption	万千瓦时	10 000 kw • m	1160359	780725
其中：工业用电	Among: Industrial Electricity consumption	万千瓦时	10 000 kw • m	1072344	737057
居民生活用电	Resident Electricity Consumption	万千瓦时	10 000 kw • m	42245	17872
社会消费品零售总额	Total Retail Sales of Consumer Goods	万元	10 000 yuan	1735253	1292051
货物进口额（海关数）	Value of Imports(Customs Numbers)	万美元	10 000 U.S. dollars	75915	
货物出口额（海关数）	Value of Exports(Customs Numbers)	万美元	10 000 U.S. dollars	112083	
海外游客人数（含一日游游客）	Sum of Overseas Visitors (Including One-day Visitors)	人	person	4692	
小学毕业生升学率	Primary School Rate of Admission into Higher Level of Education	%	percentage	100	100
初中毕业生升学率	Junior Middle School Rate of Admission into Higher Level of Education	%	percentage	89.98	100
专利申请授权量	Authorization Quantity of Applying for Patents	项	unit	1048	
其中：发明	Among: Inventions	项	unit	53	
基本养老保险参保人数	Number of People Participated in Basic Pension Insurance	人	person	170702	91898
基本医疗保险参保人数	Number of People Participated in Basic Medical Insurance	人	person	441892	365159
失业保险参保人数	Number of People Participated in Unemployment Insurance	人	person	89349	51607
城镇居民最低生活保障人数	Number of Participated in Minimum Standard of Living for City Residents	人	person	8632	4468
环境污染治理投资总额	Total Investment of Environmental Pollution Government	万元	10 000 yuan	264296	
城市环境基础设施建设本年完成投资额	Investment Cost of Urban Environment in Frastructure Construction Completed This Year	万元	10 000 yuan	175123	
三废综合利用产品产值	Output Value of Products Made from Utilization of Waste Gas, Water &Solid Wastes	万元	10 000 yuan	105646	
工业固体废物综合利用率	Ratio of Industrial Solid Wastes	%	percentage	90.83	
烟尘控制区总面积	Total Area of Soot Control Zones	平方公里	sq.km.	127	
环境噪声达标区总面积	Area of Environmental Noise Meeting National Standard	平方公里	sq.km.	90	

1-6 烟台市城市基本情况
City Basic Situation of Yantai
2006

指标名称	Index	计量单位	Prickle	全市 Total City	市辖区 Districts under City
年末总人口（公安户籍口径）	Total Year-end Population(Census Requirements of Public Security)	万人	10 000 persons	649.98	178.91
年末单位从业人员数	Employed Persons at Year-end in Units	万人	10 000 persons	84.72	44.85
第一产业（农、林、牧、渔业）	Primary Industry(Farming, Forestry, Animal Husbandry and Fishery)	万人	10 000 persons	0.63	0.3
第二产业	Secondary Industry	万人	10 000 persons	52.23	28.98
第三产业	Tertiary-industry	万人	10 000 persons	31.86	15.57
行政区域土地面积	Area of Administrative Land	平方公里	sq.km.	13746	2726
其中：建成区面积	Among: Developed Areas	平方公里	sq.km.		179
地区生产总值（当年价格）	Gross Regional Product(Current Year's Prices)	万元	10 000 yuan	24057504	9633348
第一产业增加值	Value Added of Primary Industry	万元	10 000 yuan	2160143	376722
第二产业增加值	Value Added of Secondary Industry	万元	10 000 yuan	14622422	5782124
其中：工业增加值	Among: Value Added of Industry	万元	10 000 yuan	13362622	5066807
第三产业增加值	Value Added of Tertiary Industry	万元	10 000 yuan	7274939	3474502
人均地区生产总值	Per Gross Regional Product	元	yuan	37075	54230
地区生产总值增长率	Growth Rate of Gross Regional Product	%	percentage	17	21.91
地方财政一般预算内收入	Local Financial Budgetary Revenue	万元	10 000 yuan	1124217	526623
地方财政一般预算内支出	Local Financial Budgetary Expenditure	万元	10 000 yuan	1436891	686594
年末耕地总资源	Total Areas of Year-end Cultivated Land	千公顷	1 000 ha.	425	
蔬菜产量	Output of Vegetables	吨	ton	2754669	
水果产量	Output of Fruits	吨	ton	3609160	
肉类总产量	Output of Meat	吨	ton	438269	
奶类产量	Output of Milk	吨	ton	240221	
水产品产量	Output of Aquatic Product	吨	ton	2032641	
规模以上工业企业数	Sum of State-owned and Non-state-owned Industrial Enterprises above Designated Size	个	unit	3073	1049
规模以上工业总产值（当年价）	Gross Industrial Output Value of State-owned and Non-state-owned Industrial Enterprises above Designated Size (Current Year's Prices)	万元	10 000 yuan	51960256	18069985
私人汽车拥有量	Possession of Private Vehicles	辆	unit	333382	
公路客运量	Passenger Traffic of Highway	万人	10 000 persons	9142	
公路货运量	Freight Traffic of Highway	万吨	10 000 tons	13744	
境内等级公路里程	Expressway and Class Ⅰ to Ⅳ Highways	公里	km.	13142	
境内高速公路里程	Expressway and Class Ⅰ to Ⅳ Freeway	公里	km.	425	

1-6 续表 1 continued

指标名称	Index	计量单位	Prickle	全市 Total City	市辖区 Districts under City
全年用电量	Annual Electricity Consumption	万千瓦时	10 000 kw • m	1979402	657023
其中：工业用电	Among: Industrial Electricity consumption	万千瓦时	10 000 kw • m	1546279	455778
居民生活用电	Resident Electricity Consumption	万千瓦时	10 000 kw • m	206031	78131
社会消费品零售总额	Total Retail Sales of Consumer Goods	万元	10 000 yuan	6979595	2798028
货物进口额（海关数）	Value of Imports(Customs Numbers)	万美元	10 000 U.S. dollars	627777	
货物出口额（海关数）	Value of Exports(Customs Numbers)	万美元	10 000 U.S. dollars	879877	
海外游客人数（含一日游游客）	Sum of Overseas Visitors (Including One-day Visitors)	人	person	239690	
小学毕业生升学率	Primary School Rate of Admission into Higher Level of Education	%	percentage	100	100
初中毕业生升学率	Junior Middle School Rate of Admission into Higher Level of Education	%	percentage	89	93.89
专利申请授权量	Authorization Quantity of Applying for Patents	项	unit	1173	
其中：发明	Among: Inventions	项	unit	107	
基本养老保险参保人数	Number of People Participated in Basic Pension Insurance	人	person	1027659	498072
基本医疗保险参保人数	Number of People Participated in Basic Medical Insurance	人	person	1002599	474980
失业保险参保人数	Number of People Participated in Unemployment Insurance	人	person	720030	334911
城镇居民最低生活保障人数	Number of Participated in Minimum Standard of Living for City Residents	人	person	17008	7601
环境污染治理投资总额	Total Investment of Environmental Pollution Government	万元	10 000 yuan	511122	
城市环境基础设施建设本年完成投资额	Investment Cost of Urban Environment in Frastructure Construction Completed This Year	万元	10 000 yuan	353117	
三废综合利用产品产值	Output Value of Products Made from Utilization of Waste Gas, Water &Solid Wastes	万元	10 000 yuan	46379	
工业固体废物综合利用率	Ratio of Industrial Solid Wastes	%	percentage	88.18	
烟尘控制区总面积	Total Area of Soot Control Zones	平方公里	sq.km.	339	
环境噪声达标区总面积	Area of Environmental Noise Meeting National Standard	平方公里	sq.km.	264	

1-7 潍坊市城市基本情况
City Basic Situation of Weifang
2006

指标名称	Index	计量单位	Prickle	全市 Total City	市辖区 Districts under City
年末总人口（公安户籍口径）	Total Year-end Population(Census Requirements of Public Security)	万人	10 000 persons	855.29	146.21
年末单位从业人员数	Employed Persons at Year-end in Units	万人	10 000 persons	69.61	27.47
第一产业（农、林、牧、渔业）	Primary Industry(Farming, Forestry, Animal Husbandry and Fishery)	万人	10 000 persons	0.5	0.08
第二产业	Secondary Industry	万人	10 000 persons	38.83	16.72
第三产业	Tertiary-industry	万人	10 000 persons	30.28	10.67
行政区域土地面积	Area of Administrative Land	平方公里	sq.km.	16005	1630
其中：建成区面积	Among: Developed Areas	平方公里	sq.km.		122.8
地区生产总值（当年价格）	Gross Regional Product(Current Year's Prices)	万元	10 000 yuan	17208800	4471475
第一产业增加值	Value Added of Primary Industry	万元	10 000 yuan	2118100	193119
第二产业增加值	Value Added of Secondary Industry	万元	10 000 yuan	10006300	2558218
其中：工业增加值	Among: Value Added of Industry	万元	10 000 yuan	9165100	2359190
第三产业增加值	Value Added of Tertiary Industry	万元	10 000 yuan	5084400	1720138
人均地区生产总值	Per Gross Regional Product	元	yuan	19677	30798
地区生产总值增长率	Growth Rate of Gross Regional Product	%	percentage	16.5	9.2
地方财政一般预算内收入	Local Financial Budgetary Revenue	万元	10 000 yuan	885497	343514
地方财政一般预算内支出	Local Financial Budgetary Expenditure	万元	10 000 yuan	1149828	401743
年末耕地总资源	Total Areas of Year-end Cultivated Land	千公顷	1 000 ha.	780.51	
蔬菜产量	Output of Vegetables	吨	ton	9589947	
水果产量	Output of Fruits	吨	ton	1064042	
肉类总产量	Output of Meat	吨	ton	1196528	
奶类产量	Output of Milk	吨	ton	235823	
水产品产量	Output of Aquatic Product	吨	ton	644211	
规模以上工业企业数	Sum of State-owned and Non-state-owned Industrial Enterprises above Designated Size	个	unit	4119	856
规模以上工业总产值（当年价）	Gross Industrial Output Value of State-owned and Non-state-owned Industrial Enterprises above Designated Size (Current Year's Prices)	万元	10 000 yuan	34046982	9154808
私人汽车拥有量	Possession of Private Vehicles	辆	unit	442930	
公路客运量	Passenger Traffic of Highway	万人	10 000 persons	6924	
公路货运量	Freight Traffic of Highway	万吨	10 000 tons	9016	
境内等级公路里程	Expressway and Class Ⅰ to Ⅳ Highways	公里	km.	19433	
境内高速公路里程	Expressway and Class Ⅰ to Ⅳ Freeway	公里	km.	205	

1-7 续表 1 continued

指标名称	Index	计量单位	Prickle	全市 Total City	市辖区 Districts under City
全年用电量	Annual Electricity Consumption	万千瓦时	10 000 kw • m	1979470	654117
其中：工业用电	Among: Industrial Electricity consumption	万千瓦时	10 000 kw • m	1542350	535506
居民生活用电	Resident Electricity Consumption	万千瓦时	10 000 kw • m	232711	47204
社会消费品零售总额	Total Retail Sales of Consumer Goods	万元	10 000 yuan	5736374	1699019
货物进口额（海关数）	Value of Imports(Customs Numbers)	万美元	10 000 U.S. dollars	132758	
货物出口额（海关数）	Value of Exports(Customs Numbers)	万美元	10 000 U.S. dollars	385846	
海外游客人数（含一日游游客）	Sum of Overseas Visitors (Including One-day Visitors)	人	person	43052	
小学毕业生升学率	Primary School Rate of Admission into Higher Level of Education	%	percentage	100	100
初中毕业生升学率	Junior Middle School Rate of Admission into Higher Level of Education	%	percentage	80	80
专利申请授权量	Authorization Quantity of Applying for Patents	项	unit	1370	
其中：发明	Among: Inventions	项	unit	46	
基本养老保险参保人数	Number of People Participated in Basic Pension Insurance	人	person	1101977	401919
基本医疗保险参保人数	Number of People Participated in Basic Medical Insurance	人	person	881608	376765
失业保险参保人数	Number of People Participated in Unemployment Insurance	人	person	636939	223654
城镇居民最低生活保障人数	Number of Participated in Minimum Standard of Living for City Residents	人	person	36746	18631
环境污染治理投资总额	Total Investment of Environmental Pollution Government	万元	10 000 yuan	248693	
城市环境基础设施建设本年完成投资额	Investment Cost of Urban Environment in Frastructure Construction Completed This Year	万元	10 000 yuan	135491	
三废综合利用产品产值	Output Value of Products Made from Utilization of Waste Gas, Water &Solid Wastes	万元	10 000 yuan	52639	
工业固体废物综合利用率	Ratio of Industrial Solid Wastes	%	percentage	93.5	
烟尘控制区总面积	Total Area of Soot Control Zones	平方公里	sq.km.	288	
环境噪声达标区总面积	Area of Environmental Noise Meeting National Standard	平方公里	sq.km.	219	

1-8 济宁市城市基本情况
City Basic Situation of Jining
2006

指标名称	Index	计量单位	Prickle	全市 Total City	市辖区 Districts under City
年末总人口（公安户籍口径）	Total Year-end Population(Census Requirements of Public Security)	万人	10 000 persons	811.83	107.83
年末单位从业人员数	Employed Persons at Year-end in Units	万人	10 000 persons	61.46	15.9
第一产业（农、林、牧、渔业）	Primary Industry(Farming, Forestry, Animal Husbandry and Fishery)	万人	10 000 persons	0.19	0.06
第二产业	Secondary Industry	万人	10 000 persons	31.6	7.22
第三产业	Tertiary-industry	万人	10 000 persons	29.67	8.62
行政区域土地面积	Area of Administrative Land	平方公里	sq.km.	11194	1043
其中：建成区面积	Among: Developed Areas	平方公里	sq.km.		58
地区生产总值（当年价格）	Gross Regional Product(Current Year's Prices)	万元	10 000 yuan	14560939	3318966
第一产业增加值	Value Added of Primary Industry	万元	10 000 yuan	1870600	143100
第二产业增加值	Value Added of Secondary Industry	万元	10 000 yuan	8034400	2003300
其中：工业增加值	Among: Value Added of Industry	万元	10 000 yuan	7409700	1808000
第三产业增加值	Value Added of Tertiary Industry	万元	10 000 yuan	4655939	1172566
人均地区生产总值	Per Gross Regional Product	元	yuan	18563	30961
地区生产总值增长率	Growth Rate of Gross Regional Product	%	percentage	16.5	17.8
地方财政一般预算内收入	Local Financial Budgetary Revenue	万元	10 000 yuan	815526	323103
地方财政一般预算内支出	Local Financial Budgetary Expenditure	万元	10 000 yuan	1140286	400857
年末耕地总资源	Total Areas of Year-end Cultivated Land	千公顷	1 000 ha.	546	
蔬菜产量	Output of Vegetables	吨	ton	9104880	
水果产量	Output of Fruits	吨	ton	235348	
肉类总产量	Output of Meat	吨	ton	753522	
奶类产量	Output of Milk	吨	ton	91603	
水产品产量	Output of Aquatic Product	吨	ton	309189	
规模以上工业企业数	Sum of State-owned and Non-state-owned Industrial Enterprises above Designated Size	个	unit	1999	402
规模以上工业总产值（当年价）	Gross Industrial Output Value of State-owned and Non-state-owned Industrial Enterprises above Designated Size (Current Year's Prices)	万元	10 000 yuan	18274757	5516282
私人汽车拥有量	Possession of Private Vehicles	辆	unit	263361	
公路客运量	Passenger Traffic of Highway	万人	10 000 persons	6856	
公路货运量	Freight Traffic of Highway	万吨	10 000 tons	13996	
境内等级公路里程	Expressway and Class Ⅰ to Ⅳ Highways	公里	km.	13086	
境内高速公路里程	Expressway and Class Ⅰ to Ⅳ Freeway	公里	km.	183	

1-8 续表 1 continued

指标名称	Index	计量单位	Prickle	全市 Total City	市辖区 Districts under City
全年用电量	Annual Electricity Consumption	万千瓦时	10 000 kw・m	1527709	574899
其中：工业用电	Among: Industrial Electricity consumption	万千瓦时	10 000 kw・m	1262085	509370
居民生活用电	Resident Electricity Consumption	万千瓦时	10 000 kw・m	132223	29746
社会消费品零售总额	Total Retail Sales of Consumer Goods	万元	10 000 yuan	4996049	1521879
货物进口额（海关数）	Value of Imports(Customs Numbers)	万美元	10 000 U.S. dollars	84526	
货物出口额（海关数）	Value of Exports(Customs Numbers)	万美元	10 000 U.S. dollars	150017	
海外游客人数（含一日游游客）	Sum of Overseas Visitors (Including One-day Visitors)	人	person	127326	
小学毕业生升学率	Primary School Rate of Admission into Higher Level of Education	%	percentage	99.86	100
初中毕业生升学率	Junior Middle School Rate of Admission into Higher Level of Education	%	percentage	78	100
专利申请授权量	Authorization Quantity of Applying for Patents	项	unit	824	
其中：发明	Among: Inventions	项	unit	22	
基本养老保险参保人数	Number of People Participated in Basic Pension Insurance	人	person	694958	238400
基本医疗保险参保人数	Number of People Participated in Basic Medical Insurance	人	person	624918	190600
失业保险参保人数	Number of People Participated in Unemployment Insurance	人	person	614593	185900
城镇居民最低生活保障人数	Number of Participated in Minimum Standard of Living for City Residents	人	person	47834	14787
环境污染治理投资总额	Total Investment of Environmental Pollution Government	万元	10 000 yuan	255325	
城市环境基础设施建设本年完成投资额	Investment Cost of Urban Environment in Frastructure Construction Completed This Year	万元	10 000 yuan	133132	
三废综合利用产品产值	Output Value of Products Made from Utilization of Waste Gas, Water &Solid Wastes	万元	10 000 yuan	103393	
工业固体废物综合利用率	Ratio of Industrial Solid Wastes	%	percentage	91.65	
烟尘控制区总面积	Total Area of Soot Control Zones	平方公里	sq.km.	281	
环境噪声达标区总面积	Area of Environmental Noise Meeting National Standard	平方公里	sq.km.	270	

1-9　泰安市城市基本情况
City Basic Situation of Taian
2006

指标名称	Index	计量单位	Prickle	全市 Total City	市辖区 Districts under City
年末总人口（公安户籍口径）	Total Year-end Population(Census Requirements of Public Security)	万人	10 000 persons	551.7	160.9
年末单位从业人员数	Employed Persons at Year-end in Units	万人	10 000 persons	49.39	18.76
第一产业（农、林、牧、渔业）	Primary Industry(Farming, Forestry, Animal Husbandry and Fishery)	万人	10 000 persons	0.3	0.09
第二产业	Secondary Industry	万人	10 000 persons	30.77	6.82
第三产业	Tertiary-industry	万人	10 000 persons	18.32	11.85
行政区域土地面积	Area of Administrative Land	平方公里	sq.km.	7762	2087
其中：建成区面积	Among: Developed Areas	平方公里	sq.km.		97
地区生产总值（当年价格）	Gross Regional Product(Current Year's Prices)	万元	10 000 yuan	10181800	3946787
第一产业增加值	Value Added of Primary Industry	万元	10 000 yuan	1162800	285762
第二产业增加值	Value Added of Secondary Industry	万元	10 000 yuan	5722200	1470083
其中：工业增加值	Among: Value Added of Industry	万元	10 000 yuan	5035400	1235666
第三产业增加值	Value Added of Tertiary Industry	万元	10 000 yuan	3296800	2190942
人均地区生产总值	Per Gross Regional Product	元	yuan	18872	24675
地区生产总值增长率	Growth Rate of Gross Regional Product	%	percentage	16.5	20.3
地方财政一般预算内收入	Local Financial Budgetary Revenue	万元	10 000 yuan	516879	228522
地方财政一般预算内支出	Local Financial Budgetary Expenditure	万元	10 000 yuan	780580	281687
年末耕地总资源	Total Areas of Year-end Cultivated Land	千公顷	1 000 ha.	316	
蔬菜产量	Output of Vegetables	吨	ton	7074585	
水果产量	Output of Fruits	吨	ton	554213	
肉类总产量	Output of Meat	吨	ton	411140	
奶类产量	Output of Milk	吨	ton	285044	
水产品产量	Output of Aquatic Product	吨	ton	78600	
规模以上工业企业数	Sum of State-owned and Non-state-owned Industrial Enterprises above Designated Size	个	unit	1168	396
规模以上工业总产值（当年价）	Gross Industrial Output Value of State-owned and Non-state-owned Industrial Enterprises above Designated Size (Current Year's Prices)	万元	10 000 yuan	14944778	3133696
私人汽车拥有量	Possession of Private Vehicles	辆	unit	122807	
公路客运量	Passenger Traffic of Highway	万人	10 000 persons	4608	
公路货运量	Freight Traffic of Highway	万吨	10 000 tons	6083	
境内等级公路里程	Expressway and Class Ⅰ to Ⅳ Highways	公里	km.	12150	
境内高速公路里程	Expressway and Class Ⅰ to Ⅳ Freeway	公里	km.	208	

1-9 续表 1 continued

指标名称	Index	计量单位	Prickle	全市 Total City	市辖区 Districts under City
全年用电量	Annual Electricity Consumption	万千瓦时	10 000 kw · m	988159	385301
其中：工业用电	Among: Industrial Electricity consumption	万千瓦时	10 000 kw · m	802108	271455
居民生活用电	Resident Electricity Consumption	万千瓦时	10 000 kw · m	103321	40206
社会消费品零售总额	Total Retail Sales of Consumer Goods	万元	10 000 yuan	3182087	1122410
货物进口额（海关数）	Value of Imports(Customs Numbers)	万美元	10 000 U.S. dollars	29779	
货物出口额（海关数）	Value of Exports(Customs Numbers)	万美元	10 000 U.S. dollars	68753	
海外游客人数（含一日游游客）	Sum of Overseas Visitors (Including One-day Visitors)	人	person	125972	
小学毕业生升学率	Primary School Rate of Admission into Higher Level of Education	%	percentage	99.72	100
初中毕业生升学率	Junior Middle School Rate of Admission into Higher Level of Education	%	percentage	85.32	88.13
专利申请授权量	Authorization Quantity of Applying for Patents	项	unit	448	
其中：发明	Among: Inventions	项	unit	37	
基本养老保险参保人数	Number of People Participated in Basic Pension Insurance	人	person	478260	246791
基本医疗保险参保人数	Number of People Participated in Basic Medical Insurance	人	person	479432	314623
失业保险参保人数	Number of People Participated in Unemployment Insurance	人	person	453167	142117
城镇居民最低生活保障人数	Number of Participated in Minimum Standard of Living for City Residents	人	person	31488	12172
环境污染治理投资总额	Total Investment of Environmental Pollution Government	万元	10 000 yuan	130021	
城市环境基础设施建设本年完成投资额	Investment Cost of Urban Environment in Frastructure Construction Completed This Year	万元	10 000 yuan	118163	
三废综合利用产品产值	Output Value of Products Made from Utilization of Waste Gas, Water &Solid Wastes	万元	10 000 yuan	153221	
工业固体废物综合利用率	Ratio of Industrial Solid Wastes	%	percentage	93.64	
烟尘控制区总面积	Total Area of Soot Control Zones	平方公里	sq.km.	165	
环境噪声达标区总面积	Area of Environmental Noise Meeting National Standard	平方公里	sq.km.	89	

1-10 威海市城市基本情况
City Basic Situation of Weihai
2006

指标名称	Index	计量单位	Prickle	全市 Total City	市辖区 Districts under City
年末总人口（公安户籍口径）	Total Year-end Population(Census Requirements of Public Security)	万人	10 000 persons	249.83	62
年末单位从业人员数	Employed Persons at Year-end in Units	万人	10 000 persons	38.57	20.25
第一产业（农、林、牧、渔业）	Primary Industry(Farming, Forestry, Animal Husbandry and Fishery)	万人	10 000 persons	0.25	0.03
第二产业	Secondary Industry	万人	10 000 persons	25.01	14.21
第三产业	Tertiary-industry	万人	10 000 persons	13.31	6.01
行政区域土地面积	Area of Administrative Land	平方公里	sq.km.	5698	769
其中：建成区面积	Among: Developed Areas	平方公里	sq.km.		92
地区生产总值（当年价格）	Gross Regional Product(Current Year's Prices)	万元	10 000 yuan	13685270	4350330
第一产业增加值	Value Added of Primary Industry	万元	10 000 yuan	1165787	217114
第二产业增加值	Value Added of Secondary Industry	万元	10 000 yuan	8495900	2491980
其中：工业增加值	Among: Value Added of Industry	万元	10 000 yuan	7931200	2276380
第三产业增加值	Value Added of Tertiary Industry	万元	10 000 yuan	4023583	1641236
人均地区生产总值	Per Gross Regional Product	元	yuan	54860	70947
地区生产总值增长率	Growth Rate of Gross Regional Product	%	percentage	15.9	18.8
地方财政一般预算内收入	Local Financial Budgetary Revenue	万元	10 000 yuan	701079	280045
地方财政一般预算内支出	Local Financial Budgetary Expenditure	万元	10 000 yuan	882819	365806
年末耕地总资源	Total Areas of Year-end Cultivated Land	千公顷	1 000 ha.	178.91	
蔬菜产量	Output of Vegetables	吨	ton	1072071	
水果产量	Output of Fruits	吨	ton	690455	
肉类总产量	Output of Meat	吨	ton	110417	
奶类产量	Output of Milk	吨	ton	229898	
水产品产量	Output of Aquatic Product	吨	ton	2600010	
规模以上工业企业数	Sum of State-owned and Non-state-owned Industrial Enterprises above Designated Size	个	unit	1762	410
规模以上工业总产值（当年价）	Gross Industrial Output Value of State-owned and Non-state-owned Industrial Enterprises above Designated Size (Current Year's Prices)	万元	10 000 yuan	31662034	7061095
私人汽车拥有量	Possession of Private Vehicles	辆	unit	128519	
公路客运量	Passenger Traffic of Highway	万人	10 000 persons	4586	
公路货运量	Freight Traffic of Highway	万吨	10 000 tons	5535	
境内等级公路里程	Expressway and Class Ⅰ to Ⅳ Highways	公里	km.	6521.8	
境内高速公路里程	Expressway and Class Ⅰ to Ⅳ Freeway	公里	km.	36.4	

1-10 续表 1 continued

指标名称	Index	计量单位	Prickle	全市 Total City	市辖区 Districts under City
全年用电量	Annual Electricity Consumption	万千瓦时	10 000 kw • m	618877	290677
其中：工业用电	Among: Industrial Electricity consumption	万千瓦时	10 000 kw • m	422252	198198
居民生活用电	Resident Electricity Consumption	万千瓦时	10 000 kw • m	94506	41531
社会消费品零售总额	Total Retail Sales of Consumer Goods	万元	10 000 yuan	3312068	1198517
货物进口额（海关数）	Value of Imports(Customs Numbers)	万美元	10 000 U.S. dollars	350417	
货物出口额（海关数）	Value of Exports(Customs Numbers)	万美元	10 000 U.S. dollars	601076	
海外游客人数（含一日游游客）	Sum of Overseas Visitors (Including One-day Visitors)	人	person	204866	
小学毕业生升学率	Primary School Rate of Admission into Higher Level of Education	%	percentage	100	100
初中毕业生升学率	Junior Middle School Rate of Admission into Higher Level of Education	%	percentage	95.19	97.86
专利申请授权量	Authorization Quantity of Applying for Patents	项	unit	755	
其中：发明	Among: Inventions	项	unit	22	
基本养老保险参保人数	Number of People Participated in Basic Pension Insurance	人	person	483660	172601
基本医疗保险参保人数	Number of People Participated in Basic Medical Insurance	人	person	483142	218677
失业保险参保人数	Number of People Participated in Unemployment Insurance	人	person	316238	116721
城镇居民最低生活保障人数	Number of Participated in Minimum Standard of Living for City Residents	人	person	1407	629
环境污染治理投资总额	Total Investment of Environmental Pollution Government	万元	10 000 yuan	256738	
城市环境基础设施建设本年完成投资额	Investment Cost of Urban Environment in Frastructure Construction Completed This Year	万元	10 000 yuan	236515	
三废综合利用产品产值	Output Value of Products Made from Utilization of Waste Gas, Water &Solid Wastes	万元	10 000 yuan	17891	
工业固体废物综合利用率	Ratio of Industrial Solid Wastes	%	percentage	90	
烟尘控制区总面积	Total Area of Soot Control Zones	平方公里	sq.km.	159.7	
环境噪声达标区总面积	Area of Environmental Noise Meeting National Standard	平方公里	sq.km.	107.1	

1-11 日照市城市基本情况
City Basic Situation of Rizhao
2006

指标名称	Index	计量单位	Prickle	全市 Total City	市辖区 Districts under City
年末总人口（公安户籍口径）	Total Year-end Population(Census Requirements of Public Security)	万人	10 000 persons	282.4	121.26
年末单位从业人员数	Employed Persons at Year-end in Units	万人	10 000 persons	17.98	11.25
第一产业（农、林、牧、渔业）	Primary Industry(Farming, Forestry, Animal Husbandry and Fishery)	万人	10 000 persons	0.11	0.09
第二产业	Secondary Industry	万人	10 000 persons	8.26	4.76
第三产业	Tertiary-industry	万人	10 000 persons	9.61	6.4
行政区域土地面积	Area of Administrative Land	平方公里	sq.km.	5310	1915
其中：建成区面积	Among: Developed Areas	平方公里	sq.km.		61
地区生产总值（当年价格）	Gross Regional Product(Current Year's Prices)	万元	10 000 yuan	5058700	2997900
第一产业增加值	Value Added of Primary Industry	万元	10 000 yuan	738900	337400
第二产业增加值	Value Added of Secondary Industry	万元	10 000 yuan	2515600	1587000
其中：工业增加值	Among: Value Added of Industry	万元	10 000 yuan	2200700	1325500
第三产业增加值	Value Added of Tertiary Industry	万元	10 000 yuan	1804200	1073500
人均地区生产总值	Per Gross Regional Product	元	yuan	18718	24696
地区生产总值增长率	Growth Rate of Gross Regional Product	%	percentage	16.9	16.6
地方财政一般预算内收入	Local Financial Budgetary Revenue	万元	10 000 yuan	207609	167075
地方财政一般预算内支出	Local Financial Budgetary Expenditure	万元	10 000 yuan	326714	216880
年末耕地总资源	Total Areas of Year-end Cultivated Land	千公顷	1 000 ha.	168	
蔬菜产量	Output of Vegetables	吨	ton	1246995	
水果产量	Output of Fruits	吨	ton	190787	
肉类总产量	Output of Meat	吨	ton	161150	
奶类产量	Output of Milk	吨	ton	5952	
水产品产量	Output of Aquatic Product	吨	ton	679300	
规模以上工业企业数	Sum of State-owned and Non-state-owned Industrial Enterprises above Designated Size	个	unit	725	272
规模以上工业总产值（当年价）	Gross Industrial Output Value of State-owned and Non-state-owned Industrial Enterprises above Designated Size (Current Year's Prices)	万元	10 000 yuan	7163311	4561439
私人汽车拥有量	Possession of Private Vehicles	辆	unit	79622	
公路客运量	Passenger Traffic of Highway	万人	10 000 persons	5445	
公路货运量	Freight Traffic of Highway	万吨	10 000 tons	2950	
境内等级公路里程	Expressway and Class Ⅰ to Ⅳ Highways	公里	km.	5413	
境内高速公路里程	Expressway and Class Ⅰ to Ⅳ Freeway	公里	km.	140	

1-11 续表 1 continued

指标名称	Index	计量单位	Prickle	全市 Total City	市辖区 Districts under City
全年用电量	Annual Electricity Consumption	万千瓦时	10 000 kw • m	550371	356583
其中：工业用电	Among: Industrial Electricity consumption	万千瓦时	10 000 kw • m	421437	264182
居民生活用电	Resident Electricity Consumption	万千瓦时	10 000 kw • m	52654	31710
社会消费品零售总额	Total Retail Sales of Consumer Goods	万元	10 000 yuan	1450617	888566
货物进口额（海关数）	Value of Imports(Customs Numbers)	万美元	10 000 U.S. dollars	207675	
货物出口额（海关数）	Value of Exports(Customs Numbers)	万美元	10 000 U.S. dollars	183819	
海外游客人数（含一日游游客）	Sum of Overseas Visitors (Including One-day Visitors)	人	person	75665	
小学毕业生升学率	Primary School Rate of Admission into Higher Level of Education	%	percentage	100	100
初中毕业生升学率	Junior Middle School Rate of Admission into Higher Level of Education	%	percentage	73	81
专利申请授权量	Authorization Quantity of Applying for Patents	项	unit	231	
其中：发明	Among: Inventions	项	unit	4	
基本养老保险参保人数	Number of People Participated in Basic Pension Insurance	人	person	219123	126844
基本医疗保险参保人数	Number of People Participated in Basic Medical Insurance	人	person	174898	102758
失业保险参保人数	Number of People Participated in Unemployment Insurance	人	person	122302	79066
城镇居民最低生活保障人数	Number of Participated in Minimum Standard of Living for City Residents	人	person	13829	8018
环境污染治理投资总额	Total Investment of Environmental Pollution Government	万元	10 000 yuan	102136	
城市环境基础设施建设本年完成投资额	Investment Cost of Urban Environment in Frastructure Construction Completed This Year	万元	10 000 yuan	56463	
三废综合利用产品产值	Output Value of Products Made from Utilization of Waste Gas, Water &Solid Wastes	万元	10 000 yuan	47612	
工业固体废物综合利用率	Ratio of Industrial Solid Wastes	%	percentage	98.24	
烟尘控制区总面积	Total Area of Soot Control Zones	平方公里	sq.km.	96	
环境噪声达标区总面积	Area of Environmental Noise Meeting National Standard	平方公里	sq.km.	47	

1-12 莱芜市城市基本情况
City Basic Situation of Laiwu
2006

指标名称	Index	计量单位	Prickle	全市 Total City	市辖区 Districts under City
年末总人口（公安户籍口径）	Total Year-end Population(Census Requirements of Public Security)	万人	10 000 persons	124.86	124.86
年末单位从业人员数	Employed Persons at Year-end in Units	万人	10 000 persons	14.42	14.42
第一产业（农、林、牧、渔业）	Primary Industry(Farming, Forestry, Animal Husbandry and Fishery)	万人	10 000 persons	0.01	0.01
第二产业	Secondary Industry	万人	10 000 persons	9.6	9.6
第三产业	Tertiary-industry	万人	10 000 persons	4.81	4.81
行政区域土地面积	Area of Administrative Land	平方公里	sq.km.	2246	2246
其中：建成区面积	Among: Developed Areas	平方公里	sq.km.		55
地区生产总值（当年价格）	Gross Regional Product(Current Year's Prices)	万元	10 000 yuan	2919800	2919800
第一产业增加值	Value Added of Primary Industry	万元	10 000 yuan	195500	195500
第二产业增加值	Value Added of Secondary Industry	万元	10 000 yuan	1924000	1924000
其中：工业增加值	Among: Value Added of Industry	万元	10 000 yuan	1805900	1805900
第三产业增加值	Value Added of Tertiary Industry	万元	10 000 yuan	800300	800300
人均地区生产总值	Per Gross Regional Product	元	yuan	23430	23430
地区生产总值增长率	Growth Rate of Gross Regional Product	%	percentage	16.2	16.2
地方财政一般预算内收入	Local Financial Budgetary Revenue	万元	10 000 yuan	192572	192572
地方财政一般预算内支出	Local Financial Budgetary Expenditure	万元	10 000 yuan	282419	282419
年末耕地总资源	Total Areas of Year-end Cultivated Land	千公顷	1 000 ha.	63	
蔬菜产量	Output of Vegetables	吨	ton	1364031	
水果产量	Output of Fruits	吨	ton	100891	
肉类总产量	Output of Meat	吨	ton	58584	
奶类产量	Output of Milk	吨	ton	3082	
水产品产量	Output of Aquatic Product	吨	ton	8438	
规模以上工业企业数	Sum of State-owned and Non-state-owned Industrial Enterprises above Designated Size	个	unit	238	238
规模以上工业总产值（当年价）	Gross Industrial Output Value of State-owned and Non-state-owned Industrial Enterprises above Designated Size (Current Year's Prices)	万元	10 000 yuan	6468459	6468459
私人汽车拥有量	Possession of Private Vehicles	辆	unit	54295	
公路客运量	Passenger Traffic of Highway	万人	10 000 persons	2168	
公路货运量	Freight Traffic of Highway	万吨	10 000 tons	2116	
境内等级公路里程	Expressway and Class Ⅰ to Ⅳ Highways	公里	km.	3161	
境内高速公路里程	Expressway and Class Ⅰ to Ⅳ Freeway	公里	km.	97	

1-12 续表 1 continued

指标名称	Index	计量单位	Prickle	全市 Total City	市辖区 Districts under City
全年用电量	Annual Electricity Consumption	万千瓦时	10 000 kw • m	694104	694104
其中：工业用电	Among: Industrial Electricity consumption	万千瓦时	10 000 kw • m	631891	631891
居民生活用电	Resident Electricity Consumption	万千瓦时	10 000 kw • m	26762	26762
社会消费品零售总额	Total Retail Sales of Consumer Goods	万元	10 000 yuan	945046	945046
货物进口额（海关数）	Value of Imports(Customs Numbers)	万美元	10 000 U.S. dollars	24947	
货物出口额（海关数）	Value of Exports(Customs Numbers)	万美元	10 000 U.S. dollars	97379	
海外游客人数（含一日游游客）	Sum of Overseas Visitors (Including One-day Visitors)	人	person	1101	
小学毕业生升学率	Primary School Rate of Admission into Higher Level of Education	%	percentage	100	100
初中毕业生升学率	Junior Middle School Rate of Admission into Higher Level of Education	%	percentage	75	75
专利申请授权量	Authorization Quantity of Applying for Patents	项	unit	476	
其中：发明	Among: Inventions	项	unit	9	
基本养老保险参保人数	Number of People Participated in Basic Pension Insurance	人	person	180946	180946
基本医疗保险参保人数	Number of People Participated in Basic Medical Insurance	人	person	137757	137757
失业保险参保人数	Number of People Participated in Unemployment Insurance	人	person	135411	135411
城镇居民最低生活保障人数	Number of Participated in Minimum Standard of Living for City Residents	人	person	7239	7239
环境污染治理投资总额	Total Investment of Environmental Pollution Government	万元	10 000 yuan	41922	
城市环境基础设施建设本年完成投资额	Investment Cost of Urban Environment in Frastructure Construction Completed This Year	万元	10 000 yuan	20718	
三废综合利用产品产值	Output Value of Products Made from Utilization of Waste Gas, Water &Solid Wastes	万元	10 000 yuan	46596	
工业固体废物综合利用率	Ratio of Industrial Solid Wastes	%	percentage	80.64	
烟尘控制区总面积	Total Area of Soot Control Zones	平方公里	sq.km.	61	
环境噪声达标区总面积	Area of Environmental Noise Meeting National Standard	平方公里	sq.km.	34	

1-13　临沂市城市基本情况
City Basic Situation of Linyi
2006

指标名称	Index	计量单位	Prickle	全市 Total City	市辖区 Districts under City
年末总人口（公安户籍口径）	Total Year-end Population(Census Requirements of Public Security)	万人	10 000 persons	1022.73	194.47
年末单位从业人员数	Employed Persons at Year-end in Units	万人	10 000 persons	55.67	23.01
第一产业（农、林、牧、渔业）	Primary Industry(Farming, Forestry, Animal Husbandry and Fishery)	万人	10 000 persons	0.74	0.07
第二产业	Secondary Industry	万人	10 000 persons	23.15	11.8
第三产业	Tertiary-industry	万人	10 000 persons	31.78	11.14
行政区域土地面积	Area of Administrative Land	平方公里	sq.km.	17194	1761
其中：建成区面积	Among: Developed Areas	平方公里	sq.km.		116
地区生产总值（当年价格）	Gross Regional Product(Current Year's Prices)	万元	10 000 yuan	14048600	4455300
第一产业增加值	Value Added of Primary Industry	万元	10 000 yuan	1786500	175200
第二产业增加值	Value Added of Secondary Industry	万元	10 000 yuan	7308300	2728900
其中：工业增加值	Among: Value Added of Industry	万元	10 000 yuan	6332000	2433200
第三产业增加值	Value Added of Tertiary Industry	万元	10 000 yuan	4953800	1551200
人均地区生产总值	Per Gross Regional Product	元	yuan	14400	24560
地区生产总值增长率	Growth Rate of Gross Regional Product	%	percentage	16.3	19.4
地方财政一般预算内收入	Local Financial Budgetary Revenue	万元	10 000 yuan	582719	334233
地方财政一般预算内支出	Local Financial Budgetary Expenditure	万元	10 000 yuan	991680	414140
年末耕地总资源	Total Areas of Year-end Cultivated Land	千公顷	1 000 ha.	726	
蔬菜产量	Output of Vegetables	吨	ton	6004651	
水果产量	Output of Fruits	吨	ton	1619079	
肉类总产量	Output of Meat	吨	ton	626770	
奶类产量	Output of Milk	吨	ton	69822	
水产品产量	Output of Aquatic Product	吨	ton	110084	
规模以上工业企业数	Sum of State-owned and Non-state-owned Industrial Enterprises above Designated Size	个	unit	2542	904
规模以上工业总产值（当年价）	Gross Industrial Output Value of State-owned and Non-state-owned Industrial Enterprises above Designated Size (Current Year's Prices)	万元	10 000 yuan	18704258	9899973
私人汽车拥有量	Possession of Private Vehicles	辆	unit	318404	
公路客运量	Passenger Traffic of Highway	万人	10 000 persons	9510	
公路货运量	Freight Traffic of Highway	万吨	10 000 tons	10904	
境内等级公路里程	Expressway and Class Ⅰ to Ⅳ Highways	公里	km.	18871	
境内高速公路里程	Expressway and Class Ⅰ to Ⅳ Freeway	公里	km.	282	

1-13 续表 1 continued

指标名称	Index	计量单位	Prickle	全市 Total City	市辖区 Districts under City
全年用电量	Annual Electricity Consumption	万千瓦时	10 000 kw・m	1596763	928995
其中：工业用电	Among: Industrial Electricity consumption	万千瓦时	10 000 kw・m	1308198	793896
居民生活用电	Resident Electricity Consumption	万千瓦时	10 000 kw・m	160821	69291
社会消费品零售总额	Total Retail Sales of Consumer Goods	万元	10 000 yuan	5547080	2343701
货物进口额（海关数）	Value of Imports(Customs Numbers)	万美元	10 000 U.S. dollars	60074	
货物出口额（海关数）	Value of Exports(Customs Numbers)	万美元	10 000 U.S. dollars	167805	
海外游客人数（含一日游游客）	Sum of Overseas Visitors (Including One-day Visitors)	人	person	20466	
小学毕业生升学率	Primary School Rate of Admission into Higher Level of Education	%	percentage	100	100
初中毕业生升学率	Junior Middle School Rate of Admission into Higher Level of Education	%	percentage	74	90
专利申请授权量	Authorization Quantity of Applying for Patents	项	unit	840	
其中：发明	Among: Inventions	项	unit	45	
基本养老保险参保人数	Number of People Participated in Basic Pension Insurance	人	person	622001	219345
基本医疗保险参保人数	Number of People Participated in Basic Medical Insurance	人	person	549839	208990
失业保险参保人数	Number of People Participated in Unemployment Insurance	人	person	401518	132151
城镇居民最低生活保障人数	Number of Participated in Minimum Standard of Living for City Residents	人	person	71065	25316
环境污染治理投资总额	Total Investment of Environmental Pollution Government	万元	10 000 yuan	283323	
城市环境基础设施建设本年完成投资额	Investment Cost of Urban Environment in Frastructure Construction Completed This Year	万元	10 000 yuan	189588	
三废综合利用产品产值	Output Value of Products Made from Utilization of Waste Gas, Water &Solid Wastes	万元	10 000 yuan	72689	
工业固体废物综合利用率	Ratio of Industrial Solid Wastes	%	percentage	98.66	
烟尘控制区总面积	Total Area of Soot Control Zones	平方公里	sq.km.	246	
环境噪声达标区总面积	Area of Environmental Noise Meeting National Standard	平方公里	sq.km.	197	

1-14 德州市城市基本情况
City Basic Situation of Dezhou
2006

指标名称	Index	计量单位	Prickle	全市 Total City	市辖区 Districts under City
年末总人口（公安户籍口径）	Total Year-end Population(Census Requirements of Public Security)	万人	10 000 persons	557.85	59.2
年末单位从业人员数	Employed Persons at Year-end in Units	万人	10 000 persons	36.67	10.87
第一产业（农、林、牧、渔业）	Primary Industry(Farming, Forestry, Animal Husbandry and Fishery)	万人	10 000 persons	0.38	0.01
第二产业	Secondary Industry	万人	10 000 persons	16.7	6.23
第三产业	Tertiary-industry	万人	10 000 persons	19.59	4.63
行政区域土地面积	Area of Administrative Land	平方公里	sq.km.	10356	539
其中：建成区面积	Among: Developed Areas	平方公里	sq.km.		44
地区生产总值（当年价格）	Gross Regional Product(Current Year's Prices)	万元	10 000 yuan	10033800	2393400
第一产业增加值	Value Added of Primary Industry	万元	10 000 yuan	1407300	75500
第二产业增加值	Value Added of Secondary Industry	万元	10 000 yuan	5595100	1472500
其中：工业增加值	Among: Value Added of Industry	万元	10 000 yuan	5040000	1297600
第三产业增加值	Value Added of Tertiary Industry	万元	10 000 yuan	3031400	845400
人均地区生产总值	Per Gross Regional Product	元	yuan	18071	40429
地区生产总值增长率	Growth Rate of Gross Regional Product	%	percentage	16.4	21.8
地方财政一般预算内收入	Local Financial Budgetary Revenue	万元	10 000 yuan	357291	107978
地方财政一般预算内支出	Local Financial Budgetary Expenditure	万元	10 000 yuan	636011	161578
年末耕地总资源	Total Areas of Year-end Cultivated Land	千公顷	1 000 ha.	536	
蔬菜产量	Output of Vegetables	吨	ton	4887585	
水果产量	Output of Fruits	吨	ton	573617	
肉类总产量	Output of Meat	吨	ton	591705	
奶类产量	Output of Milk	吨	ton	127981	
水产品产量	Output of Aquatic Product	吨	ton	100676	
规模以上工业企业数	Sum of State-owned and Non-state-owned Industrial Enterprises above Designated Size	个	unit	2320	297
规模以上工业总产值（当年价）	Gross Industrial Output Value of State-owned and Non-state-owned Industrial Enterprises above Designated Size (Current Year's Prices)	万元	10 000 yuan	15485588	3834650
私人汽车拥有量	Possession of Private Vehicles	辆	unit	213942	
公路客运量	Passenger Traffic of Highway	万人	10 000 persons	5445	
公路货运量	Freight Traffic of Highway	万吨	10 000 tons	4568	
境内等级公路里程	Expressway and Class Ⅰ to Ⅳ Highways	公里	km.	19794	
境内高速公路里程	Expressway and Class Ⅰ to Ⅳ Freeway	公里	km.	210	

1-14 续表 1 continued

指标名称	Index	计量单位	Prickle	全市 Total City	市辖区 Districts under City
全年用电量	Annual Electricity Consumption	万千瓦时	10 000 kw • m	1092352	266535
其中：工业用电	Among: Industrial Electricity consumption	万千瓦时	10 000 kw • m	845688	204939
居民生活用电	Resident Electricity Consumption	万千瓦时	10 000 kw • m	126666	20497
社会消费品零售总额	Total Retail Sales of Consumer Goods	万元	10 000 yuan	3282617	551761
货物进口额（海关数）	Value of Imports(Customs Numbers)	万美元	10 000 U.S. dollars	19500	
货物出口额（海关数）	Value of Exports(Customs Numbers)	万美元	10 000 U.S. dollars	63200	
海外游客人数（含一日游游客）	Sum of Overseas Visitors (Including One-day Visitors)	人	person	18108	
小学毕业生升学率	Primary School Rate of Admission into Higher Level of Education	%	percentage	100	100
初中毕业生升学率	Junior Middle School Rate of Admission into Higher Level of Education	%	percentage	40.2	67.15
专利申请授权量	Authorization Quantity of Applying for Patents	项	unit	299	
其中：发明	Among: Inventions	项	unit	11	
基本养老保险参保人数	Number of People Participated in Basic Pension Insurance	人	person	370048	122336
基本医疗保险参保人数	Number of People Participated in Basic Medical Insurance	人	person	358628	160765
失业保险参保人数	Number of People Participated in Unemployment Insurance	人	person	236156	101102
城镇居民最低生活保障人数	Number of Participated in Minimum Standard of Living for City Residents	人	person	45259	11680
环境污染治理投资总额	Total Investment of Environmental Pollution Government	万元	10 000 yuan	205109	
城市环境基础设施建设本年完成投资额	Investment Cost of Urban Environment in Frastructure Construction Completed This Year	万元	10 000 yuan	171594	
三废综合利用产品产值	Output Value of Products Made from Utilization of Waste Gas, Water &Solid Wastes	万元	10 000 yuan	28945	
工业固体废物综合利用率	Ratio of Industrial Solid Wastes	%	percentage	96.81	
烟尘控制区总面积	Total Area of Soot Control Zones	平方公里	sq.km.	111	
环境噪声达标区总面积	Area of Environmental Noise Meeting National Standard	平方公里	sq.km.	116	

1-15 聊城市城市基本情况
City Basic Situation of Liaocheng
2006

指标名称	Index	计量单位	Prickle	全市 Total City	市辖区 Districts under City
年末总人口（公安户籍口径）	Total Year-end Population(Census Requirements of Public Security)	万人	10 000 persons	572.82	103.68
年末单位从业人员数	Employed Persons at Year-end in Units	万人	10 000 persons	34.5	10.76
第一产业（农、林、牧、渔业）	Primary Industry(Farming, Forestry, Animal Husbandry and Fishery)	万人	10 000 persons	0.12	0.01
第二产业	Secondary Industry	万人	10 000 persons	14.2	3.29
第三产业	Tertiary-industry	万人	10 000 persons	20.18	7.46
行政区域土地面积	Area of Administrative Land	平方公里	sq.km.	8715	1254
其中：建成区面积	Among: Developed Areas	平方公里	sq.km.		59
地区生产总值（当年价格）	Gross Regional Product(Current Year's Prices)	万元	10 000 yuan	8413300	1414080
第一产业增加值	Value Added of Primary Industry	万元	10 000 yuan	1388400	178704
第二产业增加值	Value Added of Secondary Industry	万元	10 000 yuan	4919500	701500
其中：工业增加值	Among: Value Added of Industry	万元	10 000 yuan	4534500	606500
第三产业增加值	Value Added of Tertiary Industry	万元	10 000 yuan	2105400	533876
人均地区生产总值	Per Gross Regional Product	元	yuan	15347	13714
地区生产总值增长率	Growth Rate of Gross Regional Product	%	percentage	17.34	16.02
地方财政一般预算内收入	Local Financial Budgetary Revenue	万元	10 000 yuan	336419	138696
地方财政一般预算内支出	Local Financial Budgetary Expenditure	万元	10 000 yuan	599786	190329
年末耕地总资源	Total Areas of Year-end Cultivated Land	千公顷	1 000 ha.	548.65	
蔬菜产量	Output of Vegetables	吨	ton	8266282	
水果产量	Output of Fruits	吨	ton	390758	
肉类总产量	Output of Meat	吨	ton	497941	
奶类产量	Output of Milk	吨	ton	46458	
水产品产量	Output of Aquatic Product	吨	ton	70318	
规模以上工业企业数	Sum of State-owned and Non-state-owned Industrial Enterprises above Designated Size	个	unit	1268	281
规模以上工业总产值（当年价）	Gross Industrial Output Value of State-owned and Non-state-owned Industrial Enterprises above Designated Size (Current Year's Prices)	万元	10 000 yuan	14323026	1901904
私人汽车拥有量	Possession of Private Vehicles	辆	unit	334180	
公路客运量	Passenger Traffic of Highway	万人	10 000 persons	3165	
公路货运量	Freight Traffic of Highway	万吨	10 000 tons	1891	
境内等级公路里程	Expressway and Class Ⅰ to Ⅳ Highways	公里	km.	12561	
境内高速公路里程	Expressway and Class Ⅰ to Ⅳ Freeway	公里	km.	135	

1-15 续表 1 continued

指标名称	Index	计量单位	Prickle	全市 Total City	市辖区 Districts under City
全年用电量	Annual Electricity Consumption	万千瓦时	10 000 kw • m	1408654	174444
其中：工业用电	Among: Industrial Electricity consumption	万千瓦时	10 000 kw • m	1205489	119402
居民生活用电	Resident Electricity Consumption	万千瓦时	10 000 kw • m	113468	25212
社会消费品零售总额	Total Retail Sales of Consumer Goods	万元	10 000 yuan	2717967	607757
货物进口额（海关数）	Value of Imports(Customs Numbers)	万美元	10 000 U.S. dollars	38464	
货物出口额（海关数）	Value of Exports(Customs Numbers)	万美元	10 000 U.S. dollars	61079	
海外游客人数（含一日游游客）	Sum of Overseas Visitors (Including One-day Visitors)	人	person	12904	
小学毕业生升学率	Primary School Rate of Admission into Higher Level of Education	%	percentage	97.25	100
初中毕业生升学率	Junior Middle School Rate of Admission into Higher Level of Education	%	percentage	74.23	99
专利申请授权量	Authorization Quantity of Applying for Patents	项	unit	484	
其中：发明	Among: Inventions	项	unit	43	
基本养老保险参保人数	Number of People Participated in Basic Pension Insurance	人	person	389784	119394
基本医疗保险参保人数	Number of People Participated in Basic Medical Insurance	人	person	346965	128784
失业保险参保人数	Number of People Participated in Unemployment Insurance	人	person	270600	93590
城镇居民最低生活保障人数	Number of Participated in Minimum Standard of Living for City Residents	人	person	51932	10079
环境污染治理投资总额	Total Investment of Environmental Pollution Government	万元	10 000 yuan	90434	
城市环境基础设施建设本年完成投资额	Investment Cost of Urban Environment in Frastructure Construction Completed This Year	万元	10 000 yuan	65351	
三废综合利用产品产值	Output Value of Products Made from Utilization of Waste Gas, Water &Solid Wastes	万元	10 000 yuan	40886	
工业固体废物综合利用率	Ratio of Industrial Solid Wastes	%	percentage	100	
烟尘控制区总面积	Total Area of Soot Control Zones	平方公里	sq.km.	156	
环境噪声达标区总面积	Area of Environmental Noise Meeting National Standard	平方公里	sq.km.	177	

1-16 滨州市城市基本情况
City Basic Situation of Binzhou
2006

指标名称	Index	计量单位	Prickle	全市 Total City	市辖区 Districts under City
年末总人口（公安户籍口径）	Total Year-end Population(Census Requirements of Public Security)	万人	10 000 persons	373.16	63.07
年末单位从业人员数	Employed Persons at Year-end in Units	万人	10 000 persons	34.87	9.45
第一产业（农、林、牧、渔业）	Primary Industry(Farming, Forestry, Animal Husbandry and Fishery)	万人	10 000 persons	0.09	0.02
第二产业	Secondary Industry	万人	10 000 persons	22.65	6.11
第三产业	Tertiary-industry	万人	10 000 persons	12.13	3.32
行政区域土地面积	Area of Administrative Land	平方公里	sq.km.	9445	1042
其中：建成区面积	Among: Developed Areas	平方公里	sq.km.		67
地区生产总值（当年价格）	Gross Regional Product(Current Year's Prices)	万元	10 000 yuan	8336700	1784485
第一产业增加值	Value Added of Primary Industry	万元	10 000 yuan	972100	118748
第二产业增加值	Value Added of Secondary Industry	万元	10 000 yuan	5148200	1054029
其中：工业增加值	Among: Value Added of Industry	万元	10 000 yuan	4717500	937729
第三产业增加值	Value Added of Tertiary Industry	万元	10 000 yuan	2216400	611708
人均地区生产总值	Per Gross Regional Product	元	yuan	22398	28294
地区生产总值增长率	Growth Rate of Gross Regional Product	%	percentage	17.5	14.2
地方财政一般预算内收入	Local Financial Budgetary Revenue	万元	10 000 yuan	451216	164245
地方财政一般预算内支出	Local Financial Budgetary Expenditure	万元	10 000 yuan	646732	206415
年末耕地总资源	Total Areas of Year-end Cultivated Land	千公顷	1 000 ha.	378	
蔬菜产量	Output of Vegetables	吨	ton	2199172	
水果产量	Output of Fruits	吨	ton	862837	
肉类总产量	Output of Meat	吨	ton	320555	
奶类产量	Output of Milk	吨	ton	108180	
水产品产量	Output of Aquatic Product	吨	ton	375352	
规模以上工业企业数	Sum of State-owned and Non-state-owned Industrial Enterprises above Designated Size	个	unit	1106	192
规模以上工业总产值（当年价）	Gross Industrial Output Value of State-owned and Non-state-owned Industrial Enterprises above Designated Size (Current Year's Prices)	万元	10 000 yuan	16689159	3819463
私人汽车拥有量	Possession of Private Vehicles	辆	unit	189877	
公路客运量	Passenger Traffic of Highway	万人	10 000 persons	3029	
公路货运量	Freight Traffic of Highway	万吨	10 000 tons	4432	
境内等级公路里程	Expressway and Class Ⅰ to Ⅳ Highways	公里	km.	13066	
境内高速公路里程	Expressway and Class Ⅰ to Ⅳ Freeway	公里	km.	69	

1-16 续表 1 continued

指标名称	Index	计量单位	Prickle	全市 Total City	市辖区 Districts under City
全年用电量	Annual Electricity Consumption	万千瓦时	10 000 kw・m	1041990	371144
其中：工业用电	Among: Industrial Electricity consumption	万千瓦时	10 000 kw・m	897685	321074
居民生活用电	Resident Electricity Consumption	万千瓦时	10 000 kw・m	73201	21631
社会消费品零售总额	Total Retail Sales of Consumer Goods	万元	10 000 yuan	2085748	584067
货物进口额（海关数）	Value of Imports(Customs Numbers)	万美元	10 000 U.S. dollars	112008	
货物出口额（海关数）	Value of Exports(Customs Numbers)	万美元	10 000 U.S. dollars	158264	
海外游客人数（含一日游游客）	Sum of Overseas Visitors (Including One-day Visitors)	人	person	5886	
小学毕业生升学率	Primary School Rate of Admission into Higher Level of Education	%	percentage	99	95
初中毕业生升学率	Junior Middle School Rate of Admission into Higher Level of Education	%	percentage	45	52
专利申请授权量	Authorization Quantity of Applying for Patents	项	unit	222	
其中：发明	Among: Inventions	项	unit	15	
基本养老保险参保人数	Number of People Participated in Basic Pension Insurance	人	person	265832	93673
基本医疗保险参保人数	Number of People Participated in Basic Medical Insurance	人	person	214305	93875
失业保险参保人数	Number of People Participated in Unemployment Insurance	人	person	163960	61520
城镇居民最低生活保障人数	Number of Participated in Minimum Standard of Living for City Residents	人	person	26623	3553
环境污染治理投资总额	Total Investment of Environmental Pollution Government	万元	10 000 yuan	76504	
城市环境基础设施建设本年完成投资额	Investment Cost of Urban Environment in Frastructure Construction Completed This Year	万元	10 000 yuan	45750	
三废综合利用产品产值	Output Value of Products Made from Utilization of Waste Gas, Water &Solid Wastes	万元	10 000 yuan	71124	
工业固体废物综合利用率	Ratio of Industrial Solid Wastes	%	percentage	99.03	
烟尘控制区总面积	Total Area of Soot Control Zones	平方公里	sq.km.	126	
环境噪声达标区总面积	Area of Environmental Noise Meeting National Standard	平方公里	sq.km.	88	

1-17 菏泽市城市基本情况
City Basic Situation of Heze
2006

指标名称	Index	计量单位	Prickle	全市 Total City	市辖区 Districts under City
年末总人口（公安户籍口径）	Total Year-end Population(Census Requirements of Public Security)	万人	10 000 persons	905.2	145.96
年末单位从业人员数	Employed Persons at Year-end in Units	万人	10 000 persons	34.44	12.89
第一产业（农、林、牧、渔业）	Primary Industry(Farming, Forestry, Animal Husbandry and Fishery)	万人	10 000 persons	0.48	0.04
第二产业	Secondary Industry	万人	10 000 persons	8.53	4.4
第三产业	Tertiary-industry	万人	10 000 persons	25.43	8.45
行政区域土地面积	Area of Administrative Land	平方公里	sq.km.	12194	1415
其中：建成区面积	Among: Developed Areas	平方公里	sq.km.		54.54
地区生产总值（当年价格）	Gross Regional Product(Current Year's Prices)	万元	10 000 yuan	5396000	1058173
第一产业增加值	Value Added of Primary Industry	万元	10 000 yuan	1664400	195842
第二产业增加值	Value Added of Secondary Industry	万元	10 000 yuan	2477200	451664
其中：工业增加值	Among: Value Added of Industry	万元	10 000 yuan	2096300	374770
第三产业增加值	Value Added of Tertiary Industry	万元	10 000 yuan	1254400	410667
人均地区生产总值	Per Gross Regional Product	元	yuan	6652	7434
地区生产总值增长率	Growth Rate of Gross Regional Product	%	percentage	17.1	17.4
地方财政一般预算内收入	Local Financial Budgetary Revenue	万元	10 000 yuan	300355	107978
地方财政一般预算内支出	Local Financial Budgetary Expenditure	万元	10 000 yuan	692541	193211
年末耕地总资源	Total Areas of Year-end Cultivated Land	千公顷	1 000 ha.	694	
蔬菜产量	Output of Vegetables	吨	ton	6863874	
水果产量	Output of Fruits	吨	ton	564390	
肉类总产量	Output of Meat	吨	ton	558083	
奶类产量	Output of Milk	吨	ton	49747	
水产品产量	Output of Aquatic Product	吨	ton	110505	
规模以上工业企业数	Sum of State-owned and Non-state-owned Industrial Enterprises above Designated Size	个	unit	1068	183
规模以上工业总产值（当年价）	Gross Industrial Output Value of State-owned and Non-state-owned Industrial Enterprises above Designated Size (Current Year's Prices)	万元	10 000 yuan	6420448	1373012
私人汽车拥有量	Possession of Private Vehicles	辆	unit	237488	
公路客运量	Passenger Traffic of Highway	万人	10 000 persons	4614	
公路货运量	Freight Traffic of Highway	万吨	10 000 tons	3419	
境内等级公路里程	Expressway and Class Ⅰ to Ⅳ Highways	公里	km.	17329	
境内高速公路里程	Expressway and Class Ⅰ to Ⅳ Freeway	公里	km.	166	

1-17 续表 1 continued

指标名称	Index	计量单位	Prickle	全市 Total City	市辖区 Districts under City
全年用电量	Annual Electricity Consumption	万千瓦时	10 000 kw • m	579846	193487
其中：工业用电	Among: Industrial Electricity consumption	万千瓦时	10 000 kw • m	317971	135892
居民生活用电	Resident Electricity Consumption	万千瓦时	10 000 kw • m	160505	24650
社会消费品零售总额	Total Retail Sales of Consumer Goods	万元	10 000 yuan	2752473	638189
货物进口额（海关数）	Value of Imports(Customs Numbers)	万美元	10 000 U.S. dollars	9277	
货物出口额（海关数）	Value of Exports(Customs Numbers)	万美元	10 000 U.S. dollars	55936	
海外游客人数（含一日游游客）	Sum of Overseas Visitors (Including One-day Visitors)	人	person	2989	
小学毕业生升学率	Primary School Rate of Admission into Higher Level of Education	%	percentage	98.29	99.03
初中毕业生升学率	Junior Middle School Rate of Admission into Higher Level of Education	%	percentage	66.92	100
专利申请授权量	Authorization Quantity of Applying for Patents	项	unit	236	
其中：发明	Among: Inventions	项	unit	23	
基本养老保险参保人数	Number of People Participated in Basic Pension Insurance	人	person	420482	122172
基本医疗保险参保人数	Number of People Participated in Basic Medical Insurance	人	person	356096	128900
失业保险参保人数	Number of People Participated in Unemployment Insurance	人	person	258111	78526
城镇居民最低生活保障人数	Number of Participated in Minimum Standard of Living for City Residents	人	person	54128	14813
环境污染治理投资总额	Total Investment of Environmental Pollution Government	万元	10 000 yuan	92202	
城市环境基础设施建设本年完成投资额	Investment Cost of Urban Environment in Frastructure Construction Completed This Year	万元	10 000 yuan	58971	
三废综合利用产品产值	Output Value of Products Made from Utilization of Waste Gas, Water &Solid Wastes	万元	10 000 yuan	25599	
工业固体废物综合利用率	Ratio of Industrial Solid Wastes	%	percentage	100	
烟尘控制区总面积	Total Area of Soot Control Zones	平方公里	sq.km.	140	
环境噪声达标区总面积	Area of Environmental Noise Meeting National Standard	平方公里	sq.km.	128	

2

县（市、区）主要社会经济指标

Main Social Economy Target of Various Counties(City,Area)

编辑单位：统计监测处
编　　委：仝义贵
责任编辑：马明霞　刘永奇
校　　对：马明霞　刘永奇
电　　话：81912100

Editorial Unit: the Statistical Monitoring Office
Editorial Board: Tong Yigui
Executive Editor-in-Chief: Ma Mingxia Liu Yongqi
Proofreader: Ma Mingxia Liu Yongqi
Telephone:81912100

简要说明

一、本篇资料反映了全省各县（市、区）的主要经济发展情况。包括农业、工业、财政、金融、运输邮电、外经外贸、固定资产投资、文教卫生、人民生活、人口及劳动力等方面的年度数据。

二、本篇资料来源于2006年县（市）社会经济基本情况年报资料。

Brief Introduction

Ⅰ.This material reflects various counties (cities, areas) main economical development situation in entire province. Includes year data for agriculture, industry, finance, banking, transportation post and telecommunications, foreign economics and foreign trade, investment in the fixed assets, hygiene education, people′s life, population and labor force.

Ⅱ.This material originates from annual report material for the county (city) the social economy basic situation in 2006.

2-1 分县（市、区）主要社会经济指标
Main Social Economy Target of Various Counties (City, Area) 2006

地　区	Area	乡（镇）个数（个） Village (Town) Amount (unit)	村民委员会个数（个） Residents' Committee (unit)	自来水受益村（个） Benefital Village From Running Water (unit)	通电话的村（个） Accessible Village by Calls (unit)	通有线电视的村（个） Accessible Village by CATV (unit)	年末总户数（户） Year-end Total Households (household)	乡村户数（户） Rural Households (household)	年末总人口（万人） Total Population at Year-end (10 000 persons)	乡村人口（万人） Rural Population (10 000 persons)
济南市	**Jinan**									
历下区	Lixia	1	19	19	19	19	157617	8392	58.8	3
市中区	Shizhong	2	77	77	77	77	182288	38211	56.9	13
槐荫区	Huaiyin	2	92	49	92	30	124644	29500	36.7	10.1
天桥区	Tianqiao	2	120	120	120	120	168939	43000	50.4	13.3
历城区	Licheng	12	598	598	598	598	249215	156100	86.3	53.8
长清县	Changqing	6	590	514	590	463	162591	122000	56.3	43.5
平阴县	Pingyin	7	337	315	337	337	124566	82300	36.7	28.9
济阳县	Jiyang	8	852	368	852	356	151871	117800	53.6	47.8
商河县	Shanghe	10	962	646	962	427	160857	130800	60.7	52.6
章丘市	Zhangqiu	14	908	842	908	908	295599	243472	99.9	82.5
青岛市	**Qingdao**									
市南区	Shinan	0	0	0	0	0	162126	0	52.4	0
市北区	Shibei	0	1	1	1	1	177809	448	47.5	0.1
四方区	Sifang	0	0	0	0	0	131378	0	39.1	0
黄岛区	Huangdao	0	162	161	162	162	81089	49051	31.6	15.6
崂山区	Laoshan	0	139	139	139	139	70383	65461	21.9	18.1
李沧区	Licang	0	0	0	0	0	106774	0	29.5	0
城阳区	Chengyang	0	9	9	9	9	161669	136460	49	38.6
胶州市	Jiaozhou	18	811	801	811	790	238718	192100	77.8	63
即墨市	Jimo	23	1033	1025	1031	1031	334416	293900	110	94.3
平度市	Pingdu	30	1785	1644	1785	1678	420214	369965	135.7	119.5
胶南市	Jiaonan	17	972	968	972	972	265308	216273	81.7	67.6
莱西市	Laixi	15	861	833	861	861	243436	187092	72.4	61.6
淄博市	**Zibo**									
淄川区	Zichuan	17	403	403	403	403	229968	171804	67.3	49.5
张店区	Zhangdian	8	158	158	158	158	232800	76952	71	22.5
博山区	Boshan	11	209	209	209	209	162204	90854	46.5	26.1
临淄区	Linzi	9	414	414	414	414	190500	114125	59.9	38

2-1 续表 1 continued

地 区	Area	乡（镇）个数（个） Village (Town) Amount (unit)	村民委员会个数（个） Residents' Committee (unit)	自来水受益村（个） Benefital Village From Running Water (unit)	通电话的村（个） Accessible Village by Calls (unit)	通有线电视的村（个） Accessible Village by CATV (unit)	年末总户数（户） Year-end Total Households (household)	乡村户数（户） Rural Households (household)	年末总人口（万人） Total Population at Year-end (10 000 persons)	乡村人口（万人） Rural Population (10 000 persons)
周村区	Zhoucun	4	200	200	200	200	106791	49667	31.9	15.3
桓台县	Huantai	11	335	335	335	335	155700	124994	49.5	40.9
高青县	Gaoqing	9	759	621	759	510	103766	93510	36.3	31.7
沂源县	Yiyuan	13	626	561	626	626	195086	162883	55.8	47.7
枣庄市	**Zaozhuang**									
市中区	Shizhong	6	98	98	98	98	153494	60900	50.3	21.3
薛城区	Xuecheng	9	237	137	237	132	138869	90600	47.4	31
峄城区	Yicheng	7	343	343	343	69	117808	82000	36.6	30.8
台儿庄区	Taierzhuang	6	206	72	206	206	106006	70900	30.2	24.3
山亭区	Shanting	10	255	237	255	239	133314	122000	48.9	45.1
滕州市	Tengzhou	21	1157	1021	1157	1126	436360	338000	158.7	125.7
东营市	**Dongying**									
东营区	Dongying	4	201	201	201	201	207513	44300	61.1	13.8
河口区	Hekou	6	178	178	178	178	75476	23000	21	6
垦利县	Kenli	7	333	333	333	333	83591	58264	22.3	17.6
利津县	Lijin	9	512	512	510	470	89600	77500	29.5	26.6
广饶县	Guangrao	10	553	553	553	529	150112	125400	48.7	42.1
烟台市	**Yantai**									
芝罘区	Zhifu	5	80	80	80	80	238223	35000	69.5	8.3
福山区	Fushan	9	272	193	272	272	149848	91680	41.3	25.2
牟平区	Mouping	13	608	516	608	608	179264	143178	47.1	37.8
莱山区	Laishan	5	118	115	118	108	63061	46800	21	12.2
长岛县	Changdao	8	40	40	40	40	15976	9600	4.3	2.7
龙口市	Longkou	11	631	631	631	631	221265	167900	63	47.3
莱阳市	Laiyang	18	784	435	784	784	276653	231800	87.1	74.2
莱州市	Laizhou	16	1018	1018	1018	1018	276581	240479	86	71.6
蓬莱市	Penglai	12	584	553	584	584	163080	148200	44.5	39.4
招远市	Zhaoyuan	14	724	503	724	724	206800	160700	56.3	44.8
栖霞市	Qixia	15	953	479	953	953	246408	196374	62.8	54.5
海阳市	Haiyang	14	732	706	732	732	246052	216126	66.6	58.6
潍坊市	**Weifang**									
潍城区	Weicheng	8	212	210	212	155	113495	50500	37	17.3
寒亭区	Hanting	10	375	300	375	375	108602	82500	35.3	27.4

2-1 续表 2 continued

地 区	Area	乡（镇）个数（个）Village (Town) Amount (unit)	村民委员会个数（个）Residents' Committee (unit)	自来水受益村（个）Benefital Village From Running Water (unit)	通电话的村（个）Accessible Village by Calls (unit)	通有线电视的村（个）Accessible Village by CATV (unit)	年末总户数（户）Year-end Total Households (household)	乡村户数（户）Rural Households (household)	年末总人口（万人）Total Population at Year-end (10 000 persons)	乡村人口（万人）Rural Population (10 000 persons)
坊子区	Fangzi	8	220	208	220	219	73930	54500	24.4	18.8
奎文区	Kuiwen	11	65	65	65	65	98488	21500	35.3	6.8
临朐县	Linqu	18	937	834	937	937	275496	217565	85	76.6
昌乐县	Changle	16	892	379	892	868	182686	147200	59.5	51.5
青州市	Qingzhou	21	1053	1018	1053	1053	261238	215000	89.8	74.4
诸城市	Zhucheng	23	1337	1077	1337	1337	319941	261100	107	88.4
寿光市	Shouguan	17	1002	1002	1002	1002	312656	257899	107.4	89.6
安丘市	Anqiu	23	1388	545	1388	1266	310239	263651	104.8	92.3
高密市	Gaomi	20	994	723	994	662	268537	223000	86.6	75.6
昌邑市	Changyi	15	814	740	814	612	208035	179290	67.9	59.1
济宁市	**Jining**									
市中区	Shizhong	0	0	0	0	0	130965	0	40.6	0
任城区	Rencheng	12	559	520	559	395	170189	157376	65.9	58.2
微山县	Weishan	13	523	364	523	174	178861	155738	69.9	60.1
鱼台县	Yutai	10	392	209	392	392	124116	98340	45.6	39.5
金乡县	Jinxiang	13	651	625	651	651	178219	137500	61.4	53.8
嘉祥县	Jiaxiang	15	714	714	714	560	219537	190435	79.8	71.1
汶上县	Wenshang	14	493	321	493	300	195868	176057	74.2	68.4
泗水县	Sishui	11	591	427	591	351	186206	156800	60.3	54.5
梁山县	Liangshan	14	687	201	686	170	199177	176600	73.5	63.9
曲阜市	Qufu	12	392	369	392	305	186675	145451	64.2	52.1
兖州市	Yanzhou	10	492	492	492	473	179889	116900	60.9	43
邹城市	Zoucheng	14	869	748	869	759	334049	231447	113.2	82.5
泰安市	**Taian**									
泰山区	Taishan	3	137	137	137	98	225608	56604	63.4	18.7
岱岳区	Daiyue	16	700	515	700	356	284350	263000	97.5	87.4
宁阳县	Ningyang	12	566	476	566	566	228600	185385	80.7	68.3
东平县	Dongping	14	716	337	716	302	222398	186800	77.6	68.9
新泰市	Xintai	18	888	840	888	587	403001	300400	136.2	96.3
肥城市	Feicheng	14	589	589	589	550	291307	204275	96.3	72.1
威海市	**Weihai**									
环翠区	Huancui	14	339	331	339	339	188315	87300	62	22.8
文登市	Wendeng	17	827	800	827	827	252132	193800	64.1	48.8

2-1 续表 3 continued

地区	Area	乡（镇）个数（个） Village (Town) Amount (unit)	村民委员会个数（个） Residents' Committee (unit)	自来水受益村（个） Benefital Village From Running Water (unit)	通电话的村（个） Accessible Village by Calls (unit)	通有线电视的村（个） Accessible Village by CATV (unit)	年末总户数（户） Year-end Total Households (household)	乡村户数（户） Rural Households (household)	年末总人口（万人） Total Population at Year-end (10 000 persons)	乡村人口（万人） Rural Population (10 000 persons)
荣成市	Rongcheng	19	853	853	853	853	239041	167400	66.4	39.8
乳山市	Rushan	15	601	506	600	592	214294	183100	57.4	47.6
日照市	**Rizhao**									
东港区	Donggang	10	585	474	585	320	231000	168917	68.7	49.8
岚山区	Lanshan	9	417	379	417	368	132786	121538	41.7	38
五莲县	Wulian	12	632	336	632	632	174375	138900	51	42.5
莒　县	Juxian	21	1260	376	1260	960	384045	309419	110.1	95.6
莱芜市	**Laiwu**									
莱城区	Laicheng	11	758	679	758	281	330018	223936	95.7	66.7
钢城区	Gangcheng	4	213	213	213	79	99440	63693	29.1	19.2
临沂市	**Linyi**									
兰山区	Lanshan	11	413	195	413	413	259743	137312	90	45.9
罗庄区	Luozhuang	8	135	135	135	135	145119	98211	42.8	32.3
河东区	Hedong	12	475	324	475	472	182755	176200	61.6	57.9
沂南县	Yinan	17	600	422	600	346	298829	267740	91	82.7
郯城县	Tancheng	17	674	411	674	674	263402	244445	98.6	89.1
沂水县	Yishui	19	1063	633	1063	1063	362771	325769	110.9	98.7
苍山县	Cangshan	21	1056	271	1056	673	317168	296200	118.9	109.6
费　县	Feixian	18	563	427	563	431	285953	257500	93.2	86.5
平邑县	Pingyi	16	738	695	738	738	292663	263900	99.3	89.4
莒南县	Junan	18	758	602	758	730	348463	239721	99.3	71
蒙阴县	Mengyin	11	451	442	451	451	176088	147096	53.2	45.7
临沭县	Linshu	12	300	271	300	300	193581	174261	63.8	56.9
德州市	**Dezhou**									
德城区	Decheng	14	340	310	340	340	186893	63200	59.2	22.7
陵　县	Lingxian	13	990	486	990	990	169289	123006	56.9	46.7
宁津县	Ningjin	11	856	609	856	856	134859	101700	46.1	39.6
庆云县	Qingyun	9	381	280	381	381	83251	69206	30.2	25.7
临邑县	Linyi	12	859	430	859	827	144652	107137	53	42.5
齐河县	Qihe	14	1014	226	1014	1014	173470	140600	61.5	51
平原县	Pingyuan	11	878	298	878	878	131207	105800	45.1	37.5
夏津县	Xiajin	14	507	356	507	492	138335	127841	49.9	44.7
武城县	Wucheng	8	393	393	393	393	103162	93300	37.5	31.3

2-1 续表 4 continued

地区	Area	乡（镇）个数（个） Village (Town) Amount (unit)	村民委员会个数（个） Residents' Committee (unit)	自来水受益村（个） Benefital Village From Running Water (unit)	通电话的村（个） Accessible Village by Calls (unit)	通有线电视的村（个） Accessible Village by CATV (unit)	年末总户数（户） Year-end Total Households (household)	乡村户数（户） Rural Households (household)	年末总人口（万人） Total Population at Year-end (10 000 persons)	乡村人口（万人） Rural Population (10 000 persons)
乐陵市	Leling	16	1089	860	1089	225	180187	143000	67.1	55.2
禹城市	Yucheng	11	1008	570	1008	1008	135801	114200	51.4	42.2
聊城市	**Liaocheng**									
东昌府区	Dongchangfu	10	1017	699	1017	720	278408	184822	103.6	69.4
阳谷县	Yanggu	15	857	285	857	642	218788	181917	76	68.1
莘　县	Shenxian	20	1153	648	1153	599	269954	239827	97.5	88.8
茌平县	Chiping	14	819	719	819	819	180738	133000	57.8	49.3
东阿县	Donge	9	559	42	559	545	131227	101018	42	37.2
冠　县	Guanxian	17	756	496	756	328	209541	187700	74.5	68.5
高唐县	Gaotang	9	635	424	635	635	162363	110500	47.9	37.9
临清市	Linqing	12	436	436	436	400	213432	156300	73.2	56.5
滨州市	**Binzhou**									
滨城区	Bincheng	15	716	619	715	715	201923	91700	63.1	30.9
惠民县	Huimin	14	1282	1051	1282	1282	161982	151700	63.1	54
阳信县	Yangxin	9	857	743	857	372	124853	110200	44.1	37.9
无棣县	Wudi	11	593	593	593	326	138830	113000	44.2	37.1
沾化县	Zhanhua	10	440	440	440	440	126708	99800	38.7	33.9
博兴县	Boxing	10	448	448	448	448	146996	120400	48.1	40.5
邹平县	Zouping	16	858	759	858	858	203331	176100	72	62.4
菏泽市	**Heze**									
牡丹区	Mudan	24	742	91	742	167	409739	258593	145.5	100.7
曹　县	Caoxian	27	1175	100	1175	208	387130	293496	149.7	127.7
单　县	Shanxian	20	502	338	502	280	304854	275300	118.8	107
成武县	Chengwu	12	476	391	476	473	184718	152607	64.7	55.4
巨野县	Juye	16	885	169	881	370	260635	223613	95.5	80.3
郓城县	Yuncheng	21	1037	105	1037	108	316547	275839	111.3	97.4
鄄城县	Juancheng	16	418	78	418	175	218013	187566	80.9	69.9
定陶县	Dingtao	11	362	86	362	143	166798	140962	63.3	52.8
东明县	Dongming	13	398	37	398	132	209395	153965	75.5	60.6

2-2 续表 continued

地　区	Area	年末单位从业人员数（人） Total Employed Persons at Year-end in Unis(person)	第二产业（人） Secondary Industry (person)	第三产业（人） Tertiary Industry (person)	乡村从业人员数（人） Rural Laborers (person)	农林牧渔业（人） Farming, Forestry, Animal Husbandry and Fishery (person)	第一产业增加值（万元） Value Added of Primary Industy (10 000 yuan)	农业（万元） Farming (10 000 yuan)	第二产业增加值（万元） Value Added of Secondary Industry (10 000 yuan)	第三产业增加值（万元） Value Added of Tertiary Industry (10 000 yuan)
济南市	**Jinan**									
历下区	Lixia	228861	78449	150292	17674	1848	914	699	850140	2903274
市中区	Shizhong	144246	35702	108509	71000	32300	21887	6189	470320	2016304
槐荫区	Huaiyin	85153	37340	47607	49200	18900	19566	13556	410518	689023
天桥区	Tianqiao	132414	49841	80633	76000	18000	21223	12726	436844	1422593
历城区	Licheng	161539	98732	62233	307500	150400	202743	129423	3021817	1305793
长清县	Changqing	91715	70289	20339	215000	99100	194759	135563	811882	421491
平阴县	Pingyin	48175	28687	12188	148800	80400	136914	81894	567404	236221
济阳县	Jiyang	38770	19138	19530	267900	96900	233055	180005	602391	253092
商河县	Shanghe	57097	38730	18067	269100	161200	263770	174294	193255	136836
章丘市	Zhangqiu	98111	57901	40055	471042	136168	356379	223689	1382639	895807
青岛市	**Qingdao**									
市南区	Shinan	156830	31145	125685	0	0	0	0	401406	2360841
市北区	Shibei	44009	14271	29481	1204	0	0	0	599400	1193600
四方区	Sifang	50970	32046	18717	0	0	0	0	539047	501248
黄岛区	Huangdao	161186	130120	31006	87592	14585	34029	4232	3224468	1441728
崂山区	Laoshan	51508	33805	17652	105456	23155	57118	3110	1314944	831577
李沧区	Licang	56193	39291	16578	0	0	1002	132	1075500	534018
城阳区	Chengyang	185142	163747	20126	207637	33163	134400	9981	2617900	1248000
胶州市	Jiaozhou	147764	118966	28524	328000	95030	253446	112169	2042100	1190384
即墨市	Jimo	146038	111991	33441	562000	164000	305297	112507	1951500	1324700
平度市	Pingdu	81229	44252	35209	670573	368829	480183	353122	1547400	1025406
胶南市	Jiaonan	171561	130628	40633	343452	132183	305503	93168	2095573	1032621
莱西市	Laixi	97532	72800	21600	341845	181826	268402	143897	1116600	956900
淄博市	**Zibo**									
淄川区	Zichuan	68959	46326	22579	258479	68992	40889	26733	1421978	733518
张店区	Zhangdian	225639	151357	73797	124067	30285	16201	13676	2134433	1557581
博山区	Boshan	44261	29498	14763	141367	44555	48252	29598	1103520	530001
临淄区	Linzi	79538	58326	21212	223147	119742	159739	128377	3117397	778213
周村区	Zhoucun	52733	37141	15486	86794	23302	45619	29249	786386	584678
桓台县	Huantai	53594	39529	13956	230888	100008	103860	74021	1217007	433223

2-2 续表 1 continued

地 区	Area	年末单位从业人员数（人）Total Employed Persons at Year-end in Unis(person)	第二产业（人）Secondary Industry (person)	第三产业（人）Tertiary Industry (person)	乡村从业人员数（人）Rural Laborers (person)	农林牧渔业（人）Farming, Forestry, Animal Husbandry and Fishery (person)	第一产业增加值（万元）Value Added of Primary Industy (10 000 yuan)	农业（万元）Farming (10 000 yuan)	第二产业增加值（万元）Value Added of Secondary Industry (10 000 yuan)	第三产业增加值（万元）Value Added of Tertiary Industry (10 000 yuan)
高青县	Gaoqing	44676	34448	7878	178666	115431	106055	74964	266013	156730
沂源县	Yiyuan	58942	35919	23023	288474	193751	106605	60862	487396	306295
枣庄市	**Zaozhuang**									
市中区	Shizhong	74967	46130	28820	102500	36600	39029	23305	761030	328760
薛城区	Xuecheng	56784	30530	26208	180300	83800	67370	46491	702520	264440
峄城区	Yicheng	23923	12987	10578	176100	82100	82282	66319	329400	152300
台儿庄区	Taierzhuang	19919	9167	10385	153200	75900	90678	65313	377300	153800
山亭区	Shanting	17129	5118	11916	240700	139200	77885	45134	235500	160400
滕州市	Tengzhou	161405	93021	65581	742000	395900	327637	245603	2422450	1026719
东营市	**Dongying**									
东营区	Dongying	42845	21236	21548	64300	47300	75338	36640	693909	392569
河口区	Hekou	20039	13510	6467	42200	26000	55749	19024	307274	112048
垦利县	Kenli	22807	12838	9706	63600	39900	83330	33308	818762	114913
利津县	Lijin	16556	6872	9566	149700	90200	130209	73682	409079	125021
广饶县	Guangrao	27328	7596	16281	229500	125000	183705	134802	1469978	347466
烟台市	**Yantai**									
芝罘区	Zhifu	168587	63801	89661	42200	11600	39427	4927	816995	846672
福山区	Fushan	174129	140776	33260	131298	65826	185790	66180	3272857	953739
牟平区	Mouping	42547	23188	18731	192394	123760	134905	83045	733362	404957
莱山区	Laishan	109100	79860	27431	66900	24900	16600	7617	476126	311382
长岛县	Changdao	5095	1233	3586	12800	1225	133979	184	29272	78832
龙口市	Longkou	75473	48663	26042	250500	102500	220135	98250	2577603	1210600
莱阳市	Laiyang	73767	40017	33662	374500	207600	258426	156485	1130133	562754
莱州市	Laizhou	85618	56772	28124	372420	186059	330890	140453	1655838	828211
蓬莱市	Penglai	50141	29860	20257	211900	128200	180768	102889	1300878	558765
招远市	Zhaoyuan	78574	55640	22544	206100	111500	137706	91940	1645347	669616
栖霞市	Qixia	40478	16592	23786	273289	221133	254618	222050	519695	348886
海阳市	Haiyang	45473	18012	3124	319824	187128	266899	91370	580856	347547
潍坊市	**Weifang**									
潍城区	Weicheng	40834	18280	22467	85400	29800	51417	22361	358729	211917
寒亭区	Hanting	29777	15408	14287	166600	65200	76445	32951	347554	173861
坊子区	Fangzi	45953	34147	11386	103500	47300	30644	16030	309321	142153

2-2 续表 2 continued

地 区	Area	年末单位从业人员数（人） Total Employed Persons at Year-end in Unis(person)	第二产业（人） Secondary Industry (person)	第三产业（人） Tertiary Industry (person)	乡村从业人员数（人） Rural Laborers (person)	农林牧渔业（人） Farming, Forestry, Animal Husbandry and Fishery (person)	第一产业增加值（万元） Value Added of Primary Industy (10 000 yuan)	农业（万元） Farming (10 000 yuan)	第二产业增加值（万元） Value Added of Secondary Industry (10 000 yuan)	第三产业增加值（万元） Value Added of Tertiary Industry (10 000 yuan)
奎文区	Kuiwen	72527	35568	36909	33300	5800	7658	1029	346483	205764
临朐县	Linqu	55581	28751	26272	410786	153177	165493	93382	406810	236587
昌乐县	Changle	44636	21447	23024	236900	111000	166512	124165	441193	227310
青州市	Qingzhou	66891	35459	30067	297100	168700	191049	163742	1134380	451048
诸城市	Zhucheng	108818	69619	38135	432700	213600	303417	163120	1586296	600830
寿光市	Shouguan	92775	50947	41412	432649	235467	438371	323696	1754184	919969
安丘市	Anqiu	69087	33859	35152	480400	292650	246237	204886	571595	332223
高密市	Gaomi	88913	57209	31029	372800	165800	223303	148409	1029799	327566
昌邑市	Changyi	35313	14196	21100	301014	147310	204761	125016	882922	327024
济宁市	**Jining**									
市中区	Shizhong	101460	36429	65031	0	0	0	0	427400	607400
任城区	Rencheng	20067	4101	15507	333472	164440	146200	77000	644100	352800
微山县	Weishan	36869	16537	20077	362116	175379	169500	42472	667300	513300
鱼台县	Yutai	24382	9050	15216	220625	149318	150785	90195	255788	198926
金乡县	Jinxiang	24771	5276	19409	301400	172000	243383	192715	270000	225800
嘉祥县	Jiaxiang	34159	8550	21465	416492	207615	129970	71151	514800	240900
汶上县	Wenshang	29008	9316	19692	387476	147262	151430	96227	344900	216500
泗水县	Sishui	20500	5683	14657	273600	142100	151906	84083	253604	171124
梁山县	Liangshan	35519	11199	21700	324400	189000	179902	141569	411300	176798
曲阜市	Qufu	50320	22459	27861	287550	150897	132833	67418	726000	636400
兖州市	Yanzhou	42282	17092	25190	237900	113876	208363	118521	1242845	607323
邹城市	Zoucheng	164097	130201	33323	216466	114134	221274	103513	1993000	950400
泰安市	**Taian**									
泰山区	Taishan	128953	71059	57855	85368	39892	42145	19657	723900	1370151
岱岳区	Daiyue	35995	16052	19044	479100	266700	243630	176671	382100	179200
宁阳县	Ningyang	54017	29672	24254	353547	180711	206777	142359	509800	277200
东平县	Dongping	40611	19081	21442	356400	226700	158015	82545	516000	228000
新泰市	Xintai	140987	110475	30246	593250	133783	249051	143359	1981740	709588
肥城市	Feicheng	93370	68849	22899	361100	128433	263195	198898	1608700	572700
威海市	**Weihai**									
环翠区	Huancui	200723	143658	56763	101500	31400	217114	22033	2491980	1641236
文登市	Wendeng	67234	41327	25414	302400	127000	300115	59100	2247841	1095358

2-2 续表 3 continued

地 区	Area	年末单位从业人员数（人） Total Employed Persons at Year-end in Unis(person)	第二产业（人） Secondary Industry (person)	第三产业（人） Tertiary Industry (person)	乡村从业人员数（人） Rural Laborers (person)	农林牧渔业（人） Farming, Forestry, Animal Husbandry and Fishery (person)	第一产业增加值（万元） Value Added of Primary Industry (10 000 yuan)	农业（万元） Farming (10 000 yuan)	第二产业增加值（万元） Value Added of Secondary Industry (10 000 yuan)	第三产业增加值（万元） Value Added of Tertiary Industry (10 000 yuan)
荣成市	Rongcheng	69369	38309	29955	198900	85800	433466	60997	2516511	1204920
乳山市	Rushan	48328	26793	20977	262900	114300	215092	102714	1320993	636594
日照市	**Rizhao**									
东港区	Donggang	91525	37996	52563	257300	130500	148300	33311	621700	779000
岚山区	Lanshan	36001	20881	13745	200772	120099	127200	62686	501700	225400
五莲县	Wulian	50198	31309	18789	236300	129600	112734	61919	425300	231666
莒 县	Juxian	50783	20685	29790	556218	368771	247842	180364	500300	309858
莱芜市	**Laiwu**									
莱城区	Laicheng	87968	40394	43789	384321	213845	160200	124705	931300	572700
钢城区	Gangcheng	51310	35749	15532	112000	52101	35300	28917	992700	180700
临沂市	**Linyi**									
兰山区	Lanshan	147859	59440	88191	256600	100800	55985	35209	1480600	1015200
罗庄区	Luozhuang	64564	53629	10757	182250	66688	38593	19279	870287	312665
河东区	Hedong	21939	7461	14202	280400	137000	89075	57793	378100	214825
沂南县	Yinan	34611	14747	19821	488804	305972	162779	122007	389000	267000
郯城县	Tancheng	30787	6661	23256	533449	316283	182543	124628	613300	416200
沂水县	Yishui	46329	16620	28181	572668	366487	186400	125880	728600	480988
苍山县	Cangshan	34814	8762	25828	613509	367800	263400	225053	454000	478200
费 县	Feixian	34636	11267	22221	503600	282000	161000	124984	674000	403000
平邑县	Pingyi	49771	17214	31717	525400	338000	174622	116111	575482	395897
莒南县	Junan	37197	11391	25025	375000	206200	178300	116900	508800	442900
蒙阴县	Mengyin	33156	13389	19758	257203	139704	143673	94655	322578	294877
临沭县	Linshu	36336	15631	20401	345735	210567	103794	56562	466800	268400
德州市	**Dezhou**									
德城区	Decheng	108615	62279	46259	115200	51100	70658	33293	346242	330400
陵 县	Lingxian	27336	12325	14897	230871	153600	157200	90394	440800	239500
宁津县	Ningjin	18743	6874	11716	172400	102300	122941	61369	459890	261913
庆云县	Qingyun	13389	3708	9646	122458	79350	62600	37822	215300	201700
临邑县	Linyi	26646	9682	16894	228200	159244	157765	96610	540026	308010
齐河县	Qihe	36881	16668	20176	263500	201700	171100	111711	554100	285000
平原县	Pingyuan	27978	14748	13069	204400	140200	143100	107523	418600	234200
夏津县	Xiajin	18058	2655	13403	232267	163858	131781	85500	393021	231263

2-2 续表 4 continued

地 区	Area	年末单位从业人员数（人） Total Employed Persons at Year-end in Unis(person)	第二产业（人） Secondary Industry (person)	第三产业（人） Tertiary Industry (person)	乡村从业人员数（人） Rural Laborers (person)	农林牧渔业（人） Farming, Forestry, Animal Husbandry and Fishery (person)	第一产业增加值（万元） Value Added of Primary Industy (10 000 yuan)	农业（万元） Farming (10 000 yuan)	第二产业增加值（万元） Value Added of Secondary Industry (10 000 yuan)	第三产业增加值（万元） Value Added of Tertiary Industry (10 000 yuan)
武城县	Wucheng	30041	12995	15928	164400	109300	89500	61206	467700	226000
乐陵市	Leling	28533	10435	17701	276500	221400	146600	93250	401200	267500
禹城市	Yucheng	32509	14528	16341	227300	109000	155110	79491	470428	286911
聊城市	**Liaocheng**									
东昌府区	Dongchangfu	107888	34625	73125	370100	247900	178700	124321	700800	539600
阳谷县	Yanggu	46226	19651	26179	399237	167102	187989	124185	487700	200600
莘 县	Shenxian	33110	2950	29997	526531	377393	253591	199367	459400	254000
茌平县	Chiping	49730	29568	19997	279000	216000	186991	144775	734428	164864
东阿县	Donge	31436	11680	19756	201960	138375	96800	67868	422500	129500
冠 县	Guanxian	38950	17527	21423	360208	194400	200867	149281	359800	183100
高唐县	Gaotang	60385	42131	18236	202700	133100	139518	113522	884700	197100
临清市	Linqing	44069	21994	22075	330300	211200	143941	115123	741400	275900
滨州市	**Binzhou**									
滨城区	Bincheng	123200	76000	46001	181900	108200	118748	75527	1054029	611708
惠民县	Huimin	33300	11500	21583	309100	199400	145616	125579	448218	193923
阳信县	Yangxin	19600	6000	13418	189900	107600	96402	54125	261745	107747
无棣县	Wudi	27400	13000	14360	225400	127900	165528	91060	608408	173609
沾化县	Zhanhua	15000	4100	10701	186800	139900	153796	100215	329998	187485
博兴县	Boxing	30400	11800	18452	221400	137100	116091	82941	639397	300218
邹平县	Zouping	185000	158300	26501	344700	133100	166570	111720	2113198	474403
菏泽市	**Heze**									
牡丹区	Mudan	117380	39421	77631	504506	232895	195858	148165	475046	387081
曹 县	Caoxian	43076	9238	32532	671700	386600	225642	152332	303604.5	143409.5
单 县	Shanxian	37810	6048	31078	556800	286200	245630	172410	271914	131313.8
成武县	Chengwu	32567	11988	20136	272018	154458	146890	100984	215569.1	64969.2
巨野县	Juye	41141	13268	27728	405362	262320	172703	137423	256603.5	109806.5
郓城县	Yuncheng	37566	3329	34061	503024	312043	231174	165459	332402.1	127780
鄄城县	Juancheng	28233	5466	22133	383075	223781	156156	110374	151076.9	101346.7
定陶县	Dingtao	32610	12987	19427	298508	178927	144021	99023	153157.2	71469.4
东明县	Dongming	33805	9133	23745	253829	154185	146342	113833	338475.7	92081.6

2-3 续表 continued

地区	Area	地方财政一般预算收入（万元） Local Financial Budgetary Revenue (10 000 yuan)	地方财政一般预算支出（万元） Local Financial Expenditure (10 000 yuan)	各项税收（万元） Every Kind Tax Revenue (10 000 yuan)	年末金融机构各项存款余额（万元） Deposit Balance of Financial Institution at Year-end (10 000 yuan)	城乡居民储蓄存款余额（万元） Urban and Rural Household Savings Deposits (10 000 yuan)	年末金融机构各项贷款余额（万元） Loans Balance of Financial Institution at Year-end (10 000 yuan)	农业机械总动力（万千瓦特） Total Power of Agricultural Machinery (10 000 kw)	有效灌溉面积（公顷） Effective Irrigated Area (hectare)	粮食作物播种面积（公顷） Grain Crops Sown Area (hectare)
济南市	**Jinan**									
历下区	Lixia	105636	73789	409723	5865396	1596798	6398867	1	197	749
市中区	Shizhong	92023	66798	814867	1860561	470368.3	1915979.4	45	3879	8952
槐荫区	Huaiyin	39417	56939	116228	3466781	898774	3714285	9.3	3511	4985
天桥区	Tianqiao	51092	62316	151006	1346633	854016	919274	13.2	5486	10270
历城区	Licheng	116718	148022	693844	1686767	1197914	801599	151.7	24660	45627
长清县	Changqing	29126	57936	55376	603001	458785	353102	40.8	22350	56906
平阴县	Pingyin	26009	54551	48279	407130	269635	185889	39.6	15960	38225
济阳县	Jiyang	32026	61303	63178	302603	223976	183173	79.2	49660	72042
商河县	Shanghe	22725	53203	26763	283198	206028	132065	82	60610	91446
章丘市	Zhangqiu	138174	188601	161588	1256479	916322	1391874	102	70770	114217
青岛市	**Qingdao**									
市南区	Shinan	152007	114978	607145	0	0	0	0	0	0
市北区	Shibei	82022	95552	358591	0	0	0	0	0	0
四方区	Sifang	44660	51062	174092	0	0	0	0	0	0
黄岛区	Huangdao	61574	74657	563005	2301182	788865	2450653	12.8	640	1815
崂山区	Laoshan	145981	159027	539502	3203747	1189196	2286634	2.7	721	295
李沧区	Licang	72283	82221	254707	0	0	0	0	0	0
城阳区	Chengyang	86246	137686	306732	1986463	971959	1823696	34.6	3302	649
胶州市	Jiaozhou	110830	143895	181977	1257469	896618	622172	91.6	49410	69758
即墨市	Jimo	119677	157088	206847	1731630	1284942	983461	102.2	54590	91202
平度市	Pingdu	93180	138797	110281	1256069	1055013	613035	261.8	127520	189519
胶南市	Jiaonan	154035	193574	237267	1072228	756808	715117	60.3	43070	54013
莱西市	Laixi	73409	105471	91735	912961	727864	555285	87.3	56670	90607
淄博市	**Zibo**									
淄川区	Zichuan	72730	89119	144638	1611185	1076504	708800	29.4	7905	27003
张店区	Zhangdian	102378	99387	577246	4496010	2140868	3628104	20.3	7720	15839
博山区	Boshan	51316	62759	96616	1016638	713544	833229	19.4	4420	9393.5
临淄区	Linzi	120019	140151	536539	2320168	1508342	1158466	74	30060	46984.1
周村区	Zhoucun	50107	55817	78603	976059	644148	666130	17.8	9400	14380

2-3 续表 1 continued

地 区	Area	地方财政一般预算收入（万元） Local Financial Budgetary Revenue (10 000 yuan)	地方财政一般预算支出（万元） Local Financial Expenditure (10 000 yuan)	各项税收（万元） Every Kind Tax Revenue (10 000 yuan)	年末金融机构各项存款余额（万元） Deposit Balance of Financial Institution at Year-end (10 000 yuan)	城乡居民储蓄存款余额（万元） Urban and Rural Household Savings Deposits (10 000 yuan)	年末金融机构各项贷款余额（万元） Loans Balance of Financial Institution at Year-end (10 000 yuan)	农业机械总动力（万千瓦特） Total Power of Agricultural Machinery (10 000 kw)	有效灌溉面积（公顷） Effective Irrigated Area (hectare)	粮食作物播种面积（公顷） Grain Crops Sown Area (hectare)
桓台县	Huantai	71145	103374	148616	1042793	598200	1058880	56.8	25253	46876
高青县	Gaoqing	28068	45048	49696	369924	234897	263524	55.4	33200	50590
沂源县	Yiyuan	41607	69923	74711	530046	350316	350791	34.9	10321	11951
枣庄市	**Zaozhuang**									
市中区	Shizhong	54510	69262	112996	1575302	802410	1049327	18	7710	12152
薛城区	Xuecheng	39216	60230	149439	712908	456737	333918	21.5	17030	33341
峄城区	Yicheng	14012	31625	33313	174799	120326	148473	22.3	20160	37311
台儿庄区	Taierzhuang	20220	36691	32259	194137	127061	164678	26.1	22580	44917
山亭区	Shanting	10090	31812	16232	157511	122731	124004	29.1	14560	26524
滕州市	Tengzhou	122166	169502	320722	1382340	976478	1050660	92	66873	108854
东营市	**Dongying**									
东营区	Dongying	81088	91427	66856	4844864	2361509	2140197	25.8	16526.7	10638
河口区	Hekou	36129	46273	32502	880267	690204	267177	19.1	13450	4310
垦利县	Kenli	38078	55578	75939	751232	462300	690272	37	27367	13475
利津县	Lijin	20703	48083	45439	314721	191018	287622	35	37280	23985
广饶县	Guangrao	69742	103822	117630	1109097	555787	1778821	79.7	52680	65330
烟台市	**Yantai**									
芝罘区	Zhifu	71041	88533	262040	5854967	2720636	6096366	7.4	684	0
福山区	Fushan	48001	56600	463862	1880438	856258	1167754	38.8	9036	6238
牟平区	Mouping	41590	64059	28000	1058666	756767	540114	59.4	24990	30776
莱山区	Laishan	48750	52416	75281	753831	339714	395021	16.9	4030	4158
长岛县	Changdao	5040	14659	3528	149658	109235	42431	9.7	20	78
龙口市	Longkou	160016	177379	391017	2131716	1470011	2245276	73.3	19647	18131
莱阳市	Laiyang	65369	80366	85132	1020416	759974	613435	92	55606	70854
莱州市	Laizhou	105307	124011	178435.2	1875017	1376853	572524	115.1	57920	87163
蓬莱市	Penglai	86206	106573	128967	1127534	802884	808661	70.1	22030	22304
招远市	Zhaoyuan	96880	117320	147062	1400161	910162	708900	65.6	36000	44549
栖霞市	Qixia	25496	56242	17560	669423	560120	263823	109	29276	43778
海阳市	Haiyang	53280	73747	56384	817305	513552	265502	70.2	35530	57930
潍坊市	**Weifang**									
潍城区	Weicheng	44036	37427	69715	662533	383000	438300	16	11490	15603

2-3 续表 2 continued

地 区	Area	地方财政一般预算收入（万元） Local Financial Budgetary Revenue (10 000 yuan)	地方财政一般预算支出（万元） Local Financial Expenditure (10 000 yuan)	各项税收（万元） Every Kind Tax Revenue (10 000 yuan)	年末金融机构各项存款余额（万元） Deposit Balance of Financial Institution at Year-end (10 000 yuan)	城乡居民储蓄存款余额（万元） Urban and Rural Household Savings Deposits (10 000 yuan)	年末金融机构各项贷款余额（万元） Loans Balance of Financial Institution at Year-end (10 000 yuan)	农业机械总动力（万千瓦特） Total Power of Agricultural Machinery (10 000 kw)	有效灌溉面积（公顷） Effective Irrigated Area (hectare)	粮食作物播种面积（公顷） Grain Crops Sown Area (hectare)
寒亭区	Hanting	46399	50042	61322	380922	310743	284184	70.7	30030	41734
坊子区	Fangzi	30338	39279	51274	303857	216827	174724	17.4	7920	25733
奎文区	Kuiwen	68800	48126	114205	713408	392102	544562	2.3	1154	1560
临朐县	Linqu	21623	52588	40361	693492	561902	347052	39.4	17340	60842
昌乐县	Changle	42019	62330	56581	556760	425471	472276	53.3	36180	48427
青州市	Qingzhou	64578	96937	210655	1397430	1106363	675802	116.2	47550	78961
诸城市	Zhucheng	121168	145116	167840	1290195	898653	1242206	102.3	95615	118282
寿光市	Shouguan	126600	153153	296468	2065648	1458919	1585236	121.9	75118	83875
安丘市	Anqiu	34160	66068	68344	844920	650676	553042	144.9	65460	75576
高密市	Gaomi	71368	92897	121414	860000	641376	720830	108.4	66950	108696
昌邑市	Changyi	60467	78496	98750	1087392	817439	675471	153.1	58240	81510
济宁市	**Jining**									
市中区	Shizhong	23666	30068	36387.8	637550	407750	316268	0	0	0
任城区	Rencheng	52096	66356	126000	824186	555165	503956	76.9	40640	58732
微山县	Weishan	60066	75001	145630	657285	373790	209360	56.9	24670	47141
鱼台县	Yutai	14532	38850	24190	271928	213151	139139	112	36240	35188
金乡县	Jinxiang	13626	40901	11173	481794	402904	208584	70.5	52651	10213
嘉祥县	Jiaxiang	25506	58316	42488	464225	394520	302037	67.3	54209	66330
汶上县	Wenshang	20018	55600	46024	399800	322900	163700	67	50180	63128
泗水县	Sishui	15369	37321	11107	282979	237402	143307	25.6	18970	34125
梁山县	Liangshan	14065	44650	9841	508799	420778	215270	77.3	49650	74685
曲阜市	Qufu	65892	85697	64811	688545	466923	323857	54.9	35320	59714.3
兖州市	Yanzhou	108783	129873	192800	975122	678003	670896	52.3	36991	48139
邹城市	Zoucheng	154566	173220	472800	1912576	1117600	2200358	56.4	58315	83327
泰安市	**Taian**									
泰山区	Taishan	48860	58513	259063	2887663	1567826	924507	11.3	8022	8747
岱岳区	Daiyue	26026	53081	39341	559738	446762	352576	68.4	50127	71934
宁阳县	Ningyang	36006	71594	56623	548086	395263	363526	66.2	41890	79988
东平县	Dongping	31158	70904	20891	447248	367837	294997	74.8	45223	95674
新泰市	Xintai	131212	218000	174738	1583573	1169832	1752585	70.3	58122	73772
肥城市	Feicheng	103153	138395	168807	1473472	888518	1281340	72.5	49237	81419

2-3 续表 3 continued

地 区	Area	地方财政一般预算收入（万元） Local Financial Budgetary Revenue (10 000 yuan)	地方财政一般预算支出（万元） Local Financial Expenditure (10 000 yuan)	各项税收（万元） Every Kind Tax Revenue (10 000 yuan)	年末金融机构各项存款余额（万元） Deposit Balance of Financial Institution at Year-end (10 000 yuan)	城乡居民储蓄存款余额（万元） Urban and Rural Household Savings Deposits (10 000 yuan)	年末金融机构各项贷款余额（万元） Loans Balance of Financial Institution at Year-end (10 000 yuan)	农业机械总动力（万千瓦特） Total Power of Agricultural Machinery (10 000 kw)	有效灌溉面积（公顷） Effective Irrigated Area (hectare)	粮食作物播种面积（公顷） Grain Crops Sown Area (hectare)
威海市	**Weihai**									
环翠区	Huancui	127581	95259	229846	4431316	2139701	3165827	42.8	11730	12818
文登市	Wendeng	150007	177061	124993	1329216	1062354	659513	121.8	50549	60391
荣成市	Rongcheng	182158	231674	132528	1833092	1341912	1236597	150	52140	43669
乳山市	Rushan	88869	108278	64337	949469	720295	576776	83.2	45110	45393
日照市	**Rizhao**									
东港区	Donggang	68588	42868	63393	682700	396700	589000	48	10428	28388
岚山区	Lanshan	39470	30043	35843	363100	193600	433800	51.6	11545	27131
五莲县	Wulian	18541	45057	41531	542859	368248	232119	54.1	26670	36501
莒 县	Juxian	21993	64777	39254	683100	496900	389600	95.2	48200	77728.5
莱芜市	**Laiwu**									
莱城区	Laicheng	37920	77902	35577	3176440	1174385	1708237	62.2	23750	39743
钢城区	Gangcheng	35938	48155	33535	959400	396100	1166900	18.2	3587	7659
临沂市	**Linyi**									
兰山区	Lanshan	80541	100035	317528	4030900	2036713	3621100	82.9	12090	28479
罗庄区	Luozhuang	32308	45348	124081	929732.9	476581.3	1070005	20.7	7440	19278
河东区	Hedong	18733	47162	33000	621428.6	466740.1	539060	92	21220	45783
沂南县	Yinan	20530	59264	27997	519484	421867	249397	54.6	39927	77865
郯城县	Tancheng	35200	67130	45009	507192	440838	324740	63.6	45490	96605
沂水县	Yishui	44268	89236	61301	764491	618454.3	371839	79	50880	66221
苍山县	Cangshan	22619	70265	16125	550854	438601	288266	72.4	42560	103480
费 县	Feixian	30013	67441	37500	485600	394000	519300	51.9	31210	67766
平邑县	Pingyi	28860	64962	29910	461224	356355	314528	57.4	34530	53777
莒南县	Junan	30021	70844	37183	584178	485798	387473	75.3	41930	67894
蒙阴县	Mengyin	13975	39369	28641	330265	274205	199665	66	9870	27822
临沭县	Linshu	23000	49029	40481	425790	301066	306218	57.1	24260	55445
德州市	**Dezhou**									
德城区	Decheng	53861	75444	93937	2726946	1321264	2053681	25.7	19570	31740
陵 县	Lingxian	18669	43279	24501	353246	272865	394038	104	49950	98300
宁津县	Ningjin	17561	39600	20781	497686	386627	327640	151.8	41980	60613
庆云县	Qingyun	8009	23468	10465	153352	114912	129347	42	19060	43291

2-3 续表 4 continued

地 区	Area	地方财政一般预算收入（万元）Local Financial Budgetary Revenue (10 000 yuan)	地方财政一般预算支出（万元）Local Financial Expenditure (10 000 yuan)	各项税收（万元）Every Kind Tax Revenue (10 000 yuan)	年末金融机构各项存款余额（万元）Deposit Balance of Financial Institution at Year-end (10 000 yuan)	城乡居民储蓄存款余额（万元）Urban and Rural Household Savings Deposits (10 000 yuan)	年末金融机构各项贷款余额（万元）Loans Balance of Financial Institution at Year-end (10 000 yuan)	农业机械总动力（万千瓦特）Total Power of Agricultural Machinery (10 000 kw)	有效灌溉面积（公顷）Effective Irrigated Area (hectare)	粮食作物播种面积（公顷）Grain Crops Sown Area (hectare)
临邑县	Linyi	50014	70164	60041	433437	344802	333151	161.5	43750	92558
齐河县	Qihe	48989	71601	65092	402682	299069	349374	150	51790	124819
平原县	Pingyuan	27059	55235	33608	436684	339301	437353	97.9	43570	72319
夏津县	Xiajin	15678	38983	26410	333111	261674	308137	79.4	46260	34565
武城县	Wucheng	15809	34055	16140	355169	286768	315564	51.6	37640	38534
乐陵市	Leling	16260	41328	19340	413988	340203	366237	80.3	38860	91170
禹城市	Yucheng	31265	56720	41101	394787	261466	403066	57.4	44750	92529
聊城市	**Liaocheng**									
东昌府区	Dongchangfu	33039	67673	104022	2038800	1251300	1730500	146	69820	105501
阳谷县	Yanggu	16246	46886	27461	609903	510597	478527	118.8	58930	85236
莘 县	Shenxian	15479	53725	25389	465139	412655	306419	210.2	73910	106274
茌平县	Chiping	50066	88969	166911	607036	352296	595925	67.5	65000	88516
东阿县	Donge	16471	39923	45334	383876	262735	243794	101	40060	68310
冠 县	Guanxian	12939	43589	22106	429708	341300	325875	110	71390	88013
高唐县	Gaotang	50467	74448	50520	509339	309807	478304	87.7	56150	69413
临清市	Linqing	36055	61867	65018	780350	589048	652201	106	54530	73443
滨州市	**Binzhou**									
滨城区	Bincheng	105428	74595	126174	1567400	797295	1183286	48.7	31970	41831
惠民县	Huimin	10068	43476	19536	334279	256024	215492	91.9	59950	69700
阳信县	Yangxin	9521	32454	17942	220315	157933	124608	60.7	24830	66475
无棣县	Wudi	48008	72199	62975	405849	267232	486739	68.3	37010	53064
沾化县	Zhanhua	22128	46525	32080	298069	205661	256667	35.2	31670	25378
博兴县	Boxing	57059	75353	87529	787697	463228	576351	106.7	41760	55879
邹平县	Zouping	140187	170310	262486	1147202	584135	1690048	85.2	56430	86653
菏泽市	**Heze**									
牡丹区	Mudan	38798	85825	154996	1625307.7	1019768.2	1277112.7	129.5	70090	117683
曹 县	Caoxian	27007	75528	44290	477158.5	387610.8	305182.7	177.9	72120	165491
单 县	Shanxian	26216	73848	31870	436101.3	374154.3	303183.3	189.6	64470	109405
成武县	Chengwu	17966	46269	22383	294257.9	247076.6	241678.7	76.1	40000	74480
巨野县	Juye	22224	62024	25752	460313.7	363085	503509.8	165.4	48400	62573

2-3 续表 5 continued

地 区	Area	地方财政一般预算收入（万元）Local Financial Budgetary Revenue (10 000 yuan)	地方财政一般预算支出（万元）Local Financial Expenditure (10 000 yuan)	各项税收（万元）Every Kind Tax Revenue (10 000 yuan)	年末金融机构各项存款余额（万元）Deposit Balance of Financial Institution at Year-end (10 000 yuan)	城乡居民储蓄存款余额（万元）Urban and Rural Household Savings Deposits (10 000 yuan)	年末金融机构各项贷款余额（万元）Loans Balance of Financial Institution at Year-end (10 000 yuan)	农业机械总动力（万千瓦特）Total Power of Agricultural Machinery (10 000 kw)	有效灌溉面积（公顷）Effective Irrigated Area (hectare)	粮食作物播种面积（公顷）Grain Crops Sown Area (hectare)
郓城县	Yuncheng	36007	80471	46117	625374.5	523056.2	528837.1	130.5	74330	122728
鄄城县	Juancheng	17300	52885	23545	343325.9	285416	210862	99.2	45500	84663
定陶县	Dingtao	14561	42856	21941	275230.3	223458.4	258794	61.9	38270	71840
东明县	Dongming	31096	65449	50936	427848.9	289312.4	345944	80.2	40730	91843

2-4 续表 continued

地 区	Area	油料播种面积（公顷）Oil-bearing Crops Sown Area (hectare)	棉花播种面积（公顷）Cotton Sown Area (hectare)	蔬菜播种面积（公顷）Vegetable Sown Area (hectare)	粮食总产量（吨）Output of Grain(ton)	油料产量（吨）Output of Oil-bearing Crops(ton)	棉花产量（吨）Output of Fruits(ton)	水果产量（吨）Output of Meat(ton)	肉类总产量（吨）Output of Milk (ton)	蔬菜产量（吨）Output of Vegetables (ton)
济南市	**Jinan**									
历下区	Lixia	0	0	89	4500	0	0	62	144	2372
市中区	Shizhong	92	114	541	40212	328	144	8695	9779	15135
槐荫区	Huaiyin	0	0	2052	31461	0	0	2944	2558	89108
天桥区	Tianqiao	390	790	1318	60204	939	1043	1952	11586	71100
历城区	Licheng	935	243	13150	248438	3777	406	118455	57959	900883
长清县	Changqing	4983	356	10244	338039	14612	287	43890	44068	891084
平阴县	Pingyin	2851	2676	8408	226126	9642	3118	101950	53832	588535
济阳县	Jiyang	4017	5446	32904	473320	19599	6415	56670	62887	1690608
商河县	Shanghe	133	13385	28727	638686	700	16277	47917	83751	1200407
章丘市	Zhangqiu	2707	8397	24503	618145	7641	9393	56520	102241	1653645
青岛市	**Qingdao**									
市南区	Shinan	0	0	0	0	0	0	0	0	0
市北区	Shibei	0	0	0	0	0	0	0	0	0
四方区	Sifang	0	0	0	0	0	0	0	0	0
黄岛区	Huangdao	964	0	263	10458	4005	0	2553	1315	10689
崂山区	Laoshan	270	0	412	2076	795	0	8217	6457	15099
李沧区	Licang	0	0	70	0	0	0	431	1708	3548
城阳区	Chengyang	37	7	2126	3523	137	18	12465	6821	96335

2-4 续表 1 continued

地区	Area	油料播种面积（公顷）Oil-bearing Crops Sown Area (hectare)	棉花播种面积（公顷）Cotton Sown Area (hectare)	蔬菜播种面积（公顷）Vegetable Sown Area (hectare)	粮食总产量（吨）Output of Grain(ton)	油料产量（吨）Output of Oil-bearing Crops(ton)	棉花产量（吨）Output of Fruits(ton)	水果产量（吨）Output of Meat(ton)	肉类总产量（吨）Output of Milk (ton)	蔬菜产量（吨）Output of Vegetables (ton)
胶州市	Jiaozhou	8660	100	27980	368877	34839	130	67642	94841	1146620
即墨市	Jimo	21162	0	14009	458593	88246	0	25308	124469	695247
平度市	Pingdu	31109	3352	50668	1323421	154642	3802	296633	283375	2282593
胶南市	Jiaonan	20308	3	13818	304278	97783	4	216338	115544	657709
莱西市	Laixi	19172	0	21953	568040	91450	0	195320	208166	1143399
淄博市	**Zibo**									
淄川区	Zichuan	603	185	1053	98975	1226	186	6032	5871	36261
张店区	Zhangdian	194	287	501	98786	866	645	2454	7004	15792
博山区	Boshan	189.6	0	2357.1	34794	507	0	18465	17138	162750
临淄区	Linzi	4.7	37.7	10447.5	335812	8	50	7969	27504	1041985
周村区	Zhoucun	286	123	8429	70865	569	84	8609	6839	288059
桓台县	Huantai	66.2	848.9	2733	397428	348	1013	2028	16459	318892
高青县	Gaoqing	225	15942	4246	345153	1031	16103	27603	33299	174739
沂源县	Yiyuan	3029	216	5691	53293	9230	278	477401	37104	278304
枣庄市	**Zaozhuang**									
市中区	Shizhong	3616	24	6655	70756	13928	33	8441	12962	219509
薛城区	Xuecheng	4841	165	10369	210890	16686	204	11692	28733	430799
峄城区	Yicheng	4366	845	21273	232662	16042	863	29665	16087	1176536
台儿庄区	Taierzhuang	963	593	12230	294316	3249	761	10500	21011	715795
山亭区	Shanting	6123	726	5147	163729	25418	1075	99600	22845	177406
滕州市	Tengzhou	11140	497	54128	825212	56483	503	59332	137842	2740883
东营市	**Dongying**									
东营区	Dongying	133	10464	5762	64788	531	14146	5581	47021	366057
河口区	Hekou	860	13882	293	23225	2329	14721	28163	16479	9067
垦利县	Kenli	311	24297	2226	67189	818	28697	10989	22950	48948
利津县	Lijin	431	35319	7041	121317	1951	40755	29368	51609	401473
广饶县	Guangrao	7	16104	19440	477760	27	21737	20479	72859	1288217
烟台市	**Yantai**									
芝罘区	Zhifu	47	0	964	0	187	0	5222	563	35347
福山区	Fushan	3644	0	2015	33411	12080	0	83047	14945	116980
牟平区	Mouping	12346	0	3348	162682	36330	0	397362	92048	128941
莱山区	Laishan	1101	0	1550	18655	2519	0	15209	3936	70430
长岛县	Changdao	0	0	0	440	0	0	785	250	0
龙口市	Longkou	3210	0	4154	130016	9333	0	401089	43866	212921

2-4 续表 2 continued

地　区	Area	油料播种面积（公顷）Oil-bearing Crops Sown Area (hectare)	棉花播种面积（公顷）Cotton Sown Area (hectare)	蔬菜播种面积（公顷）Vegetable Sown Area (hectare)	粮食总产量（吨）Output of Grain(ton)	油料产量（吨）Output of Oil-bearing Crops(ton)	棉花产量（吨）Output of Fruits(ton)	水果产量（吨）Output of Meat(ton)	肉类总产量（吨）Output of Milk (ton)	蔬菜产量（吨）Output of Vegetables (ton)
莱阳市	Laiyang	21789	0	22617	402431	85128	0	246835	67492	959351
莱州市	Laizhou	14190	305	6164	553045	57200	598	257085	71248	334978
蓬莱市	Penglai	10969	0	2675	151832	51200	0	552347	38163	128400
招远市	Zhaoyuan	14228	0	1244	277904	67901	0	265881	35512	38946
栖霞市	Qixia	16884	0	4825	266126	61289	0	1143650	35938	215002
海阳市	Haiyang	18440	0	7213	350057	78000	0	240648	34534	513373
潍坊市	**Weifang**									
潍城区	Weicheng	104	82	939	90078	289	109	22838	14616	45254
寒亭区	Hanting	71	5547	3419	252754	269	6153	99857	24592	220460
坊子区	Fangzi	979	543	1024	129448	3801	744	4491	13528	46143
奎文区	Kuiwen	40	27	266	7996	115	104	369	881	13283
临朐县	Linqu	3865	145	6210	298557	10347	150	231625	110995	228874
昌乐县	Changle	7447	1125	14299	280396	35755	1414	62965	104494	690014
青州市	Qingzhou	20	110	21822	403442	30	129	104934	69073	1108664
诸城市	Zhucheng	13982	2097	21960	708204	63424	3485	75262	334133	893535
寿光市	Shouguan	33	9981	51939	546899	83	10906	112269	123971	3490237
安丘市	Anqiu	9974	3549	35185	436834	38552	4316	112106	71265	1530043
高密市	Gaomi	13491	5355	12438	636038	69378	6987	103892	190751	665159
昌邑市	Changyi	4246	10670	12548	495423	16583	11570	124654	133362	655947
济宁市	**Jining**									
市中区	Shizhong	0	0	0	0	0	0	0	0	0
任城区	Rencheng	1777	692	18363	444010	7822	1174	24300	38340	918047
微山县	Weishan	892	556	9612	323725	3391	550	1915	46503	343680
鱼台县	Yutai	0	13042	24150	292928	0	15632	6233	27636	88042
金乡县	Jinxiang	100	42174	61311	77093	399	58545	19000	54978	1858190
嘉祥县	Jiaxiang	1845	22045	28231	420507	7127	27051	11626	59000	1215422
汶上县	Wenshang	12041	13897	20729	408977	36091	15802	20218	86409	794859
泗水县	Sishui	14402	1543	17944	199302	61255	3658	49612	72376	638716
梁山县	Liangshan	6740	14013	13378	453940	34547	19446	39539	65834	791548
曲阜市	Qufu	3399.5	1288.9	10000.5	382228	11583	1475	21833	102066	278186
兖州市	Yanzhou	5751	1342	20779	373432	30047	2168	6837	110994	833076
邹城市	Zoucheng	14891	1091	12846	565150	67477	2107	34235	89366	552724
泰安市	**Taian**									
泰山区	Taishan	39	5	4035	57678	98	6	10446	6138	138595

2-4 续表 3 continued

地 区	Area	油料播种面积（公顷）Oil-bearing Crops Sown Area (hectare)	棉花播种面积（公顷）Cotton Sown Area (hectare)	蔬菜播种面积（公顷）Vegetable Sown Area (hectare)	粮食总产量（吨）Output of Grain(ton)	油料产量（吨）Output of Oil-bearing Crops(ton)	棉花产量（吨）Output of Fruits(ton)	水果产量（吨）Output of Meat(ton)	肉类总产量（吨）Output of Milk (ton)	蔬菜产量（吨）Output of Vegetables (ton)
岱岳区	Daiyue	6515	711	47898	508511	25796	635	244573	58183	2502326
宁阳县	Ningyang	16209	1480	20836	548352	75185	1625	42398	72593	1030616
东平县	Dongping	4147	4474	10849	593309	14721	6711	27725	38734	419816
新泰市	Xintai	15688	247	19528	464082	50594	538	94968	159140	1057896
肥城市	Feicheng	2096	1483	33919	559321	6372	2851	134103	76352	1925336
威海市	**Weihai**									
环翠区	Huancui	4869	0	1840	66760	19185	0	63347	8437	80864
文登市	Wendeng	20400	0	4120	366221	70319	0	124159	46403	212970
荣成市	Rongcheng	22208	0	6887	260676	80995	0	148668	29110	375585
乳山市	Rushan	19290	0	8135	269771	74650	0	354281	26467	402652
日照市	**Rizhao**									
东港区	Donggang	10447	0	1605	164487	42026	0	44402	20802	54677
岚山区	Lanshan	10208	0	2268	171097	51906	0	35460	21359	133309
五莲县	Wulian	12674	532	4765	206846	43681	418	61136	39356	262929
莒 县	Juxian	19762.8	598.8	14199.9	488550	80804	614	36878	74800	776700
莱芜市	**Laiwu**									
莱城区	Laicheng	3546	627	30512	214724	9480	880	52816	44551	1094085
钢城区	Gangcheng	2574	24	4497	37665	5822	42	46316	11744	232927
临沂市	**Linyi**									
兰山区	Lanshan	3012	88	2096	151143	10326	129	30388	32363	57730
罗庄区	Luozhuang	851	1	1162	96944	3231	2	2100	17950	59290
河东区	Hedong	3076	144	5893	257620	13239	234	16316	33336	267083
沂南县	Yinan	17424	2154	13807	392685	69990	3487	58669	95835	745472
郯城县	Tancheng	6084	1341	16687	656499	26483	2212	25784	47512	856815
沂水县	Yishui	18919	2293	16670	410853	74449	2780	303858	69942	549963
苍山县	Cangshan	14451	1068	46033	584251	58699	1201	87690	39209	2053295
费 县	Feixian	23109	1561	10617	380160	102597	2061	210282	67548	600369
平邑县	Pingyi	16639	418	13778	319705	64714	503	145926	64957	451603
莒南县	Junan	28071	51	3440	386550	131792	112	165880	98099	122000
蒙阴县	Mengyin	9419	1265	2593	184496	33721	1959	556822	23055	115864
临沭县	Linshu	24155	198	4123	300691	122808	290	15363	52112	125167
德州市	**Dezhou**									
德城区	Decheng	158	4666	18268	213951	510	8246	26496	33385	1011981
陵 县	Lingxian	67	13811	6119	664667	200	51074	51888	67546	234922

2-4 续表 4 continued

地 区	Area	油料播种面积（公顷）Oil-bearing Crops Sown Area (hectare)	棉花播种面积（公顷）Cotton Sown Area (hectare)	蔬菜播种面积（公顷）Vegetable Sown Area (hectare)	粮食总产量（吨）Output of Grain(ton)	油料产量（吨）Output of Oil-bearing Crops(ton)	棉花产量（吨）Output of Fruits(ton)	水果产量（吨）Output of Meat(ton)	肉类总产量（吨）Output of Milk (ton)	蔬菜产量（吨）Output of Vegetables (ton)
宁津县	Ningjin	547	13533	11287	395200	1947	17100	30115	40195	485100
庆云县	Qingyun	10	2206	2149	242267	31	2693	32558	14251	86243
临邑县	Linyi	113	2005	10900	620027	429	2689	19218	75817	569095
齐河县	Qihe	2022	6501	12649	861526	10492	9879	29726	81869	607433
平原县	Pingyuan	1494	11277	10727	483619	8466	15167	22633	62039	707400
夏津县	Xiajin	2441	37995	4770	227205	10504	54711	50322	25377	194535
武城县	Wucheng	297	21583	6389	260349	1368	27626	2827	17793	172549
乐陵市	Leling	135	11369	7848	607496	603	15395	293948	65290	243377
禹城市	Yucheng	140	6674	10119	697918	650	9761	13886	83261	574950
聊城市	**Liaocheng**									
东昌府区	Dongchangfu	2732	5579	21257	654106	11354	6443	21842	58955	1154556
阳谷县	Yanggu	7680	3448	30860	543555	32117	3791	30900	112674	1498012
莘 县	Shenxian	8221	5728	36845	655262	49449	9738	31000	118363	2073940
茌平县	Chiping	4414	6192	21926	578600	14687	7180	70001	59940	1024215
东阿县	Donge	151	2724	6801	416764	651	3333	16452	27114	337136
冠 县	Guanxian	15438	11931	21785	500082	56549	14555	158900	59662	883013
高唐县	Gaotang	5697	17115	16086	441461	20366	18096	30146	44371	779263
临清市	Linqing	1891	16755	11998	448898	4900	21591	31517	16860	516147
滨州市	**Binzhou**									
滨城区	Bincheng	57	18488	9620	252937	118	23750	52811	19459	445268
惠民县	Huimin	2461	29705	13094	470419	7242	37183	121521	46283	805071
阳信县	Yangxin	7	5802	3462	407071	9	6894	205500	60541	181302
无棣县	Wudi	172	27720	410	286866	237	36446	160310	52875	11313
沾化县	Zhanhua	193	27040	1382	156000	570	33800	272851	30193	74056
博兴县	Boxing	72	14122	4184	402880	318	17480	10383	50121	318228
邹平县	Zouping	330	14132	8664	606350	1028	18654	39461	61083	363934
菏泽市	**Heze**									
牡丹区	Mudan	4731	11119	16265	643374	15324	12341	50077	70553	627561
曹 县	Caoxian	11125	23431	7159	853369	39757	24954	29378	79725	194498
单 县	Shanxian	12073	26538	34687	586985	50038	33699	225054	112124	1537360
成武县	Chengwu	203	26032	22128	413488	657	31406	23960	51238	761635
巨野县	Juye	3128	58374	23476	336694	13507	68789	76659	40182	756678
郓城县	Yuncheng	20051	33137	31991	662907	75752	38456	70652	71467	1266293

2-4 续表 5 continued

地 区	Area	油料播种面积（公顷）Oil-bearing Crops Sown Area (hectare)	棉花播种面积（公顷）Cotton Sown Area (hectare)	蔬菜播种面积（公顷）Vegetable Sown Area (hectare)	粮食总产量（吨）Output of Grain(ton)	油料产量（吨）Output of Oil-bearing Crops(ton)	棉花产量（吨）Output of Fruits(ton)	水果产量（吨）Output of Meat(ton)	肉类总产量（吨）Output of Milk (ton)	蔬菜产量（吨）Output of Vegetables (ton)
鄄城县	Juancheng	15176	9631	12242	442315	65180	9127	38522	38525	471966
定陶县	Dingtao	2972	13702	14087	385407	9803	16511	20730	63024	835708
东明县	Dongming	18780	23591	12906	466864	50546	27982	29358	31245	412175

2-5 续表 continued

地 区	Area	水产品产量（吨）Total Aquatic Products (ton)	工业企业数（个）Number of Enterprises (unit)	工业总产值（现价）（万元）Gross Industrial Output (Value) (10 000 yuan)	内资企业（万元）Domestic Company (10 000 yuan)	港澳台商投资企业（万元）Enterprises Invested by Hong Kong, Macao and Taiwan (10 000 yuan)	外商投资企业（万元）Foreign Invested Enterprise (10 000 yuan)	产品销售收入（万元）Product Sale Income (10 000 yuan)	产品销售税金及附加（万元）Tax and Extra Charges on Sales of Products (10 000 yuan)	利润总额（万元）Total Profits (10 000 yuan)
济南市	Jinan									
历下区	Lixia	0	90	2317831	2207300	31715	78816	2267711	57965	12268
市中区	Shizhong	0	71	2165238	2016511	3304	145423	2294303	10888	96015
槐荫区	Huaiyin	3400	111	967924	926031	24509	17384	897095	4269	29990
天桥区	Tianqiao	1520	106	844160	777140	18852	48168	777645	5341	1606
历城区	Licheng	4200	263	7155868	6943344	200593	11931	7109474	238451	382686
长清县	Changqing	755	161	2239454	1653616	419484	166354	2109277	19484	121003
平阴县	Pingyin	1770	135	1562436	1341656	91020	129760	1402466	11074	108110
济阳县	Jiyang	7700	178	1615610	1430096	139879	45635	1540269	27691	108605
商河县	Shanghe	8100	139	414054	414054	0	0	372545	4030	17269
章丘市	Zhangqiu	8900	371	3786849	3097642	193372	495835	3364718	24456	249280
青岛市	Qingdao									
市南区	Shinan	0	59	1212366	1149572	18376	44418	1236393	3134	33
市北区	Shibei	0	105	1022937	844954	11491	166492	961849	165338	63157
四方区	Sifang	0	134	1712714	1359102	70397	283215	1823574	7395	72463
黄岛区	Huangdao	45873	332	10232551	6124103	801206	3307242	9888753	23087	439561
崂山区	Laoshan	90010	168	4008603	3054603	88000	866000	4001649	70742	185000
李沧区	Licang	0	134	5129943	4525678	150372	453893	5495804	42326	-10979
城阳区	Chengyang	310371	677	6850985	2959147	169968	3721870	6279686	22109	221067
胶州市	Jiaozhou	143170	556	5762063	2944415	481075	2336573	5527533	137709	234624

2-5 续表 1 continued

地 区	Area	水产品产量（吨） Total Aquatic Products (ton)	工业企业数（个） Number of Enterprises (unit)	工业总产值（现价）（万元） Gross Industrial Output Value (10 000 yuan)	内资企业（万元） Domestic Company (10 000 yuan)	港澳台商投资企业（万元） Enterprises Invested by Hong Kong, Macao and Taiwan (10 000 yuan)	外商投资企业（万元） Foreign Invested Enterprise (10 000 yuan)	产品销售收入（万元） Product Sale Income (10 000 yuan)	产品销售税金及附加（万元） Tax and Extra Charges on Sales of Products (10 000 yuan)	利润总额（万元） Total Profits (10 000 yuan)
即墨市	Jimo	307137	612	5807891	2867511	401462	2538918	5219948	43850	377808
平度市	Pingdu	13000	486	3769129	1947263	1343396	478470	3625481	23753	247820
胶南市	Jiaonan	317340	697	5316248	4241408	115435	959405	4814623	26135	227593
莱西市	Laixi	11255	548	3425650	1951473	476391	997786	3183531	19904	132528
淄博市	**Zibo**									
淄川区	Zichuan	922	491	5626268	5097228	133922	395118	5417763	32651	379901
张店区	Zhangdian	968	422	7508183	6623149	157220	727814	6753275	48159	464905
博山区	Boshan	1006	352	2367671	2136332	123832	107507	2267021	9396	109430
临淄区	Linzi	1000	425	11518534	10500317	51009	967208	11642178	130030	475638
周村区	Zhoucun	355	349	2576224	2143245	74791	358188	2600006	10129	147554
桓台县	Huantai	3205	271	4132746	3440628	222169	469949	3954660	26615	237449
高青县	Gaoqing	17200	100	700057	572480	123237	4340	733600	10283	22262
沂源县	Yiyuan	2846	94	1150501	1064124	26054	60323	1061607	8977	106095
枣庄市	**Zaozhuang**									
市中区	Shizhong	3850	236	2567702	2218426	40656	308620	2395385	20282	149628
薛城区	Xuecheng	1556	203	2273152	2099795	6820	166537	2089460	16514	81735
峄城区	Yicheng	3105	112	1011556	975993	15854	19709	1021566	18003	90551
台儿庄区	Taierzhuang	6810	123	1261078	1225772	34517	789	1200491	16772	91110
山亭区	Shanting	13910	49	424562	353000	71562	0	417186	3737	29708
滕州市	Tengzhou	14350	363	5808731	5491284	143060	174387	5641642	50086	358715
东营市	**Dongying**									
东营区	Dongying	52230	86	1782242	1728147	32402	21693	1646203	12457	117513
河口区	Hekou	120000	60	985313	941435	27300	16578	959297	8778	60869
垦利县	Kenli	101895	101	2921510	2906183	8969	6358	2915437	24460	296189
利津县	Lijin	90120	111	1838562	1829588	0	8974	1826928	20419	68718
广饶县	Guangrao	85750	135	5254830	4512528.2	671392.8	70909	5148020	36089	374952
烟台市	**Yantai**									
芝罘区	Zhifu	237545	206	4224249	3246505	232881	744863	3767649	30129	282188
福山区	Fushan	192620	454	9037742	1352834	462955	7221953	8489499	46918	417696
牟平区	Muping	123156	108	2382128	1562777	177085	642266	2370323	11628	158441

2-5 续表 2 continued

地区	Area	水产品产量（吨）Total Aquatic Products (ton)	工业企业数（个）Number of Enterprises (unit)	工业总产值（现价）（万元）Gross Industrial Output Value (10 000 yuan)	内资企业（万元）Domestic Company (10 000 yuan)	港澳台商投资企业（万元）Enterprises Invested by Hong Kong, Macao and Taiwan (10 000 yuan)	外商投资企业（万元）Foreign Invested Enterprise (10 000 yuan)	产品销售收入（万元）Product Sale Income (10 000 yuan)	产品销售税金及附加（万元）Tax and Extra Charges on Sales of Products (10 000 yuan)	利润总额（万元）Total Profits (10 000 yuan)
莱山区	Laishan	25880	251	1251629	585018	94441	572170	1384526	2824	111806
长岛县	Changdao	260988	19	64775	26883	21409	16483	66464	52	1478
龙口市	Longkou	242013	324	10057587	6878384	922799	2256404	9877835	42668	812440
莱阳市	Laiyang	38000	304	4097457	2441104	729115	927238	4257303	11801	296519
莱州市	Laizhou	298740	364	5233197	3946945	276984	1009268	5242186	12090	478605
蓬莱市	Penglai	265000	240	5559880	4387848	679779	492253	5448384	13298	585256
招远市	Zhaoyuan	16700	340	6135255	4741304	738071	655880	6226292	46759	543213
栖霞市	Qixia	4000	209	1299800	1041830	62364	195606	1278409	5624	69821
海阳市	Haiyang	327812	206	1452913	1006205	160450	286258	1274174	3397	90630
潍坊市	**Weifang**									
潍城区	Weicheng	207	219	2208885	2059769	14954	134162	1625264	3530	54314
寒亭区	Hanting	30687	195	1285852	1204994	21919	58939	1262156	9865	75852
坊子区	Fangzi	810	158	1247423.5	1045740.3	120817.9	80865.3	1270495.9	1802.9	55837
奎文区	Kuiwen	80	67	1512615	1149443	233480	129692	1484541	4906	48134
临朐县	Linqu	9300	294	1304674	1147100	56832	100742	1264443	11307	35072
昌乐县	Changle	645	264	1257769	778044	286668	193057	1270658	3272.8	40017.9
青州市	Qingzhou	530	500	3577657	3110874	86460	380323	3504720	104605	165789
诸城市	Zhucheng	12830	492	5742351	3952115	40590	1749646	5811953	23405	268425
寿光市	Shouguan	477030	554	5656111	3776568	176638	1702905	6387838	39140	447459
安丘市	Anqiu	16900	360	1612962	1279081	132851	201030	1586287	9480	60476
高密市	Gaomi	8510	524	3466869	3139361	58469	269039	3567022	14941	187898
昌邑市	Changyi	80180	361	3447493	3244219	123514	79760	3363539	18628	149221
济宁市	**Jining**									
市中区	Shizhong	0	118	950747	778760	90457	81530	1103096	4688	16437
任城区	Rencheng	37355	207	1729314	1673696.9	44947.1	10670	1695105	14451	129508
微山县	Weishan	169948	164	1162817	1162817	0	0	1187326	33053	190000
鱼台县	Yutai	42000	118	466400	449826	0	16574	469573	2396	37708
金乡县	Jinxiang	3560	144	619944	551427	665	67852	575805	8735	27256
嘉祥县	Jiaxiang	4660	169	1041448	1012219	20114	9115	1043558	17964	52444
汶上县	Wenshang	2662	180	569897	562287	7610	0	595823	5466	51911

2-5 续表 3 continued

地区	Area	水产品产量（吨） Total Aquatic Products (ton)	工业企业数（个） Number of Enterprises (unit)	工业总产值（现价）（万元） Gross Industrial Output Value (10 000 yuan)	内资企业（万元） Domestic Company (10 000 yuan)	港澳台商投资企业（万元） Enterprises Invested by Hong Kong, Macao and Taiwan (10 000 yuan)	外商投资企业（万元） Foreign Invested Enterprise (10 000 yuan)	产品销售收入（万元） Product Sale Income (10 000 yuan)	产品销售税金及附加（万元） Tax and Extra Charges on Sales of Products (10 000 yuan)	利润总额（万元） Total Profits (10 000 yuan)
泗水县	Sishui	3540	137	656644	533474	0	123170	640417	8753	53033
梁山县	Liangshan	23619	162	969700	956688	0	13012	1048874	21314	82212
曲阜市	Qufu	835	160	1075939	1016541	11386	48012	1070789	12212	82836
兖州市	Yanzhou	1720	184	2765736	1902826	12703	850207	2714668	9113	317032
邹城市	Zoucheng	18855	208	4830360	3422875	1432	1406053	4934169	64932	491342
泰安市	**Taian**									
泰山区	Taishan	750	218	9437396	9227711	75995	133690	2188944	12963	112890
岱岳区	Daiyue	4201	178	650331	599531	0	50800	677170	5220	32392
宁阳县	Ningyang	2160	183	1165206	1132647	11616	20943	1115814	18638	85424
东平县	Dongping	67056	175	1126247	1087349	29062	9836	1121278	18004	68156
新泰市	Xintai	5500	236	5104165	4189221	324653	590291	4813334	71377	387394
肥城市	Feicheng	2610	190	4522658	3432701	620392	469565	3778257	71793	194893
威海市	**Weihai**									
环翠区	Huancui	529783	410	7061095.1	4605896	352901.4	2102297.7	6425767	25266	353859
文登市	Wendeng	450227	457	8941753	5541536	64505	3335712	8202190	41292	400918
荣成市	Rongcheng	1260000	551	10989526	7117407	118794	3753325	9231159	69696	437667
乳山市	Rushan	360000	344	4669661	3613308	227290	829063	4466064	29603	188757
日照市	**Rizhao**									
东港区	Donggang	166700	129	1038513	946046	11617	80850	836899	11211	27311
岚山区	Lanshan	308481	59	1771290	1393719	22596	354975	1775295	2902	224118
五莲县	Wulian	11229	152	1392744	1339714	29130	23900	1373583	2454	55932
莒县	Juxian	12150	301	1209128	1121394	16091	71643	1186192	4610	50447
莱芜市	**Laiwu**									
莱城区	Laicheng	7673	130	2640000	2640000	0	0	2170300	13883	97900
钢城区	Gangcheng	363	63	3695700	3695700	0	0	4813361	36351	243981
临沂市	**Linyi**									
兰山区	Lanshan	3020	412	4818121	3010064	29649	1778408	4694021	11585	300057
罗庄区	Luozhuang	1966	254	3227893	2768757	307286	151850	3318301	14788	187165
河东区	Hedong	3498	187	554922	378688	103304	72930	524963	1810	21473

2-5 续表 4 continued

地区	Area	水产品产量（吨） Total Aquatic Products (ton)	工业企业数（个） Number of Enterprises (unit)	工业总产值（现价）（万元） Gross Industrial Output Value (10 000 yuan)	内资企业（万元） Domestic Company (10 000 yuan)	港澳台商投资企业（万元） Enterprises Invested by Hong Kong, Macao and Taiwan (10 000 yuan)	外商投资企业（万元） Foreign Invested Enterprise (10 000 yuan)	产品销售收入（万元） Product Sale Income (10 000 yuan)	产品销售税金及附加（万元） Tax and Extra Charges on Sales of Products (10 000 yuan)	利润总额（万元） Total Profits (10 000 yuan)
沂南县	Yinan	3079	145	500671	426434	14633	59604	491933	3281	19230
郯城县	Tancheng	10150	200	1261777	1196380	27534	37863	1275718	20614	94052
沂水县	Yishui	10096	159	1318232	1163304	77100	77828	1290026	4277.7	51246
苍山县	Cangshan	21600	121	691990	618115	18782	55093	678463	5539	42045
费　县	Feixian	13000	245	1310803	1203693	63239	43871	1304355	8659	85094
平邑县	Pingyi	11857	231	1132868	1103032	5065	24771	1068712	17202.7	61376
莒南县	Junan	8658	172	922598	691634	9546	221418	885622	2506	51270
蒙阴县	Mengyin	16960	140	672567	599117	59438	14012	657243	10773	27150
临沭县	Linshu	6156	158	1111437	1001920	40090	69427	1071565	7261.7	36008
德州市	**Dezhou**									
德城区	Decheng	5104	262	3834650	3173527	153631	507492	3639218	14213	313114
陵　县	Lingxian	18151	134	1150888	1118416	22350	10122	1140303	11534	73917
宁津县	Ningjin	1038	248	1145772	1132639	0	13133	1138328	11969	75768
庆云县	Qingyun	2800	141	560340	558216	2124	0	582310	1891	44184
临邑县	Linyi	20714	226	1472996	1394879	50	78067	1467676	20974	108279
齐河县	Qihe	23740	185	1374724	1346946	3614	24164	1368185	11351	92380
平原县	Pingyuan	8912	161	1173036	1063291	105780	3965	1161868	10301	87999
夏津县	Xiajin	497	246	1114566	1100939	2248	11379	1107510	13243	67940
武城县	Wucheng	2330	306	1130814	838022	6762	286030	1122517	44710	72255
乐陵市	Leling	3400	163	1174968	1174968	0	0	1145456	9851	79612
禹城市	Yucheng	14000	213	1352833	1290814	8741	53278	1359418	10791	94543
聊城市	**Liaocheng**									
东昌府区	Dongchangfu	14406	281	1901904	1666244	3516	232144	1597441	5679	76953
阳谷县	Yanggu	7850	119	1521648	1479448	2412	39788	1496640	8667	103745
莘　县	Shenxian	3250	105	1071347	1028961	0	42386	1068514	6672.1	61770
茌平县	Chiping	10200	123	2146246	2007328	1612	137306	2100850	4753	193197
东阿县	Donge	15997	90	940269	936807	662	2800	928649	8185	89351
冠　县	Guanxian	3725	114	1105750	1105750	0	0	1102800	15502	55535
高唐县	Gaotang	8250	186	3114048	3024149	0	89899	3145674	8154	177865
临清市	Linqing	6480	250	2521814	2386050	68456	67308	2507920	21772	165284

2-5 续表 5 continued

地 区	Area	水产品产量（吨） Total Aquatic Products (ton)	工业企业数（个） Number of Enterprises (unit)	工业总产值（现价）（万元） Gross Industrial Output Value (10 000 yuan)	内资企业（万元） Domestic Company (10 000 yuan)	港澳台商投资企业（万元） Enterprises Invested by Hong Kong, Macao and Taiwan (10 000 yuan)	外商投资企业（万元） Foreign Invested Enterprise (10 000 yuan)	产品销售收入（万元） Product Sale Income (10 000 yuan)	产品销售税金及附加（万元） Tax and Extra Charges on Sales of Products (10 000 yuan)	利润总额（万元） Total Profits (10 000 yuan)
滨州市	**Binzhou**									
滨城区	Bincheng	30995	191	3391647	3059852	265693	66102	3209914	24163	192686
惠民县	Huimin	21972	152	710822	685667	23134	2021	679632	11117	20680
阳信县	Yangxin	22131	113	543918	388712	48345	106861	463071	1305	6392
无棣县	Wudi	131722	115	1603349	1429101	467	173781	1632250	12298	145476
沾化县	Zhanhua	123600	106	770961	719473	31366	20122	749986	2767	19289
博兴县	Boxing	33090	159	1906408	1479894	413983	12531	1877760	18519	75781
邹平县	Zouping	11842	270	7762055	7755167	0	6888	7883837	17293	448597
菏泽市	**Heze**									
牡丹区	Mudan	11020	161	1395887.8	1214299.8	28957.8	152630.2	1120436	6154	38733
曹 县	Caoxian	15126	162	861115.6	741650.9	53481.3	65983.4	844214	4636	25771
单 县	Shanxian	10000	122	585623.1	549706	31535.9	4381.2	550574	6338	23892
成武县	Chengwu	17561	94	557364.7	547401.4	1881.9	8081.4	488065	7154	21733
巨野县	Juye	7296	128	642162.8	606125	18437.5	17600.3	651293	2970	20495
郓城县	Yuncheng	14800	155	754301.3	730553.3	17077.2	6670.8	760169	7826	24006
鄄城县	Juancheng	9598	98	317674.8	258077.7	0	59597.1	291429	1602	5375
定陶县	Dingtao	9030	66	327169.7	218707.4	101061.1	7401.2	336986	854	16951
东明县	Dongming	16074	57	1096590.7	1091391.5	0	5199.2	1098614	7542	38272

2-6 续表 continued

地 区	Area	境内公路里程（公里） Length of Highway (km)	高等级公路（公里） First-class Highway (km)	民用汽车拥有量（辆） Number of Civil Motor Vehicles (unit)	个人汽车（辆） Personal Motor Vehicles (unit)	邮政业务总量（万元） Business Volume of Post (10 000 yuan)	电信业务总量（万元） Business Volume of Telecom-munication (10 000 yuan)	本地电话年末用户（户） Number of Local Telephone Subscr-ibers at Year-end (household)	全年用电量（万千瓦时） Annual Electricity Consumption (10 000 kw·m)	工业用电量（万千瓦时） Industrial Electricity Consumption (10000 kw·m)
济南市	**Jinan**									
历下区	Lixia	140	33	23368	16336	26136	30865	159325	78756	47323

2-6 续表 1 continued

地 区	Area	境内公路里程（公里） Length of Highway (km)	高等级公路（公里） First-class Highway (km)	民用汽车拥有量（辆） Number of Civil Motor Vehicles (unit)	个人汽车（辆） Personal Motor Vehicles (unit)	邮政业务总量（万元） Business Volume of Post (10 000 yuan)	电信业务总量（万元） Business Volume of Telecom-munication (10 000 yuan)	本地电话年末用户（户） Number of Local Telephone Subscribers at Year-end (household)	全年用电量（万千瓦时） Annual Electricity Consumption (10 000 kw・m)	工业用电量（万千瓦时） Industrial Electricity Consumption (10 000 kw・m)
市中区	Shizhong	160	40	58643	38240	4315	5933	199398	51272	26134
槐荫区	Huaiyin	151.6	34	31700	27800	183	3838	200050	88614.5	75496.4
天桥区	Tianqiao	144.6	30	68648	25963	32322	54799	167215	47843	32044
历城区	Licheng	1536.8	1470.1	23580	16020	4845	12057	247360	609558	517550
长清县	Changqing	494.2	261.4	19297	19025	1749	6000	132225	44839	24952
平阴县	Pingyin	1000.3	636.3	7670	5330	1913	4880	111264	101903	86710
济阳县	Jiyang	1543.5	76.9	7566	5492	1527.7	10018.9	134984	31677.3	14719.3
商河县	Shanghe	1543.5	0	2689	1988	1662	10150	122462	48519	35550
章丘市	Zhangqiu	2823	261.4	66996	44553	5713	16637	343856	198572	150894
青岛市	**Qingdao**									
市南区	Shinan	0	0	0	0	0	0	0	146205	106863
市北区	Shibei	0	0	0	0	0	0	0	35825	24600
四方区	Sifang	0	0	0	0	0	0	0	143502	93240
黄岛区	Huangdao	400	195	29714	17045	3601	43560	189815	202692	142848
崂山区	Laoshan	379.5	0	10650	10650	2574.7	0	0	89152	44892
李沧区	Licang	0	0	0	0	0	0	0	325900	271375
城阳区	Chengyang	1126.1	187.5	46595	23625	4520.9	54000	266300	199573	143800
胶州市	Jiaozhou	1650	206	36135	23600	6097	81801	275082	165719	125499
即墨市	Jimo	1929	35	55850	45000	6532	52237	466926	170032	104402
平度市	Pingdu	2320.4	250.4	42167	20181	6120	62085.7	407000	176046.7	75300.4
胶南市	Jiaonan	1186	140.7	44356	25922	4813	36474	298480	155583	122148
莱西市	Laixi	1745	135	33663	23818	4600	30000	357591	127689	92717
淄博市	**Zibo**									
淄川区	Zichuan	1254	98.1	32089	20388	4372.7	30270	233341	487729	367054
张店区	Zhangdian	915.1	138	50414	28447	7432.9	84999	402407	782800	666256
博山区	Boshan	732.8	43.3	16782	11060	3772.8	13300	181521	220021	149629
临淄区	Linzi	622	62.8	43765	27874	7896.7	36468	186518	686309	623769
周村区	Zhoucun	662	53.2	18895	11257	2716	23455	115600	107574	88763
桓台县	Huantai	480	47.9	16470	10747	3392	18180	165079	151646	129016
高青县	Gaoqing	509	18.8	8139	6286	1347	9523	97515	59502	50026

2-6 续表 2 continued

地 区	Area	境内公路里程（公里） Length of Highway (km)	高等级公路（公里） First-class Highway (km)	民用汽车拥有量（辆） Number of Civil Motor Vehicles (unit)	个人汽车（辆） Personal Motor Vehicles (unit)	邮政业务总量（万元） Business Volume of Post (10 000 yuan)	电信业务总量（万元） Business Volume of Telecom-munication (10 000 yuan)	本地电话年末用户（户） Number of Local Telephone Subscribers at Year-end (household)	全年用电量（万千瓦时） Annual Electricity Consumption (10 000 kw·m)	工业用电量（万千瓦时） Industrial Electricity Consumption (10 000 kw·m)
沂源县	Yiyuan	1570	0	9708	6986	2567	13820	124931	135469	119136
枣庄市	**Zaozhuang**									
市中区	Shizhong	240.8	73.5	40205	28537	2878.2	107709	195984	202668	169118
薛城区	Xuecheng	274.1	123.5	16716	13602	1143.7	57852.4	117865	86428	67972
峄城区	Yicheng	229.4	18.6	13160	11308	975.6	27585.8	73712	57209	50114
台儿庄区	Taierzhuang	209.1	19.3	19801	15512	911.3	23084.1	69772	73467	66515
山亭区	Shanting	523.8	9.2	17526	14915	977.4	26350.1	85667	51708	42723
滕州市	Tengzhou	708.7	86.4	35376	30567	4648.5	159763	323278	349611	285499
东营市	**Dongying**									
东营区	Dongying	1106	23.3	93514	55134	7230	177344	280734	79603	71405
河口区	Hekou	1511.2	38.3	3625	0	2033	1808	50800	20350	9768
垦利县	Kenli	1786.1	14	9644	6520	1514	3325	66386	58953	42715
利津县	Lijin	732	27.4	4423	3792	1029	2336	55257	45132	33536
广饶县	Guangrao	1576	110.5	46093	39089	2194.4	21187	146823	274469	252006
烟台市	**Yantai**									
芝罘区	Zhifu	178	78	156793	92534	9942	97634	399984	214053	193053
福山区	Fushan	674	308	37536	14146	4465.8	26356	186664	239548	200922
牟平区	Muping	1356	24	18848	13211	3504	7335	171469	68746	39703
莱山区	Laishan	141.7	28.7	12416	8241	6612	6907.7	108000	58466	31532
长岛县	Changdao	93	25	2018	982	1207	1967	19777	6209	1511
龙口市	Longkou	1331	165	58149	35908	4975	30400	384950	581454	540749
莱阳市	Laiyang	1810	241	23118	15891	4193	42188	384487	114131	83557
莱州市	Laizhou	1933	243	32075	22752	5650	38477.1	370614	204254	140138
蓬莱市	Penglai	951.2	267	19678	14917	4063	21675	170315	125573	92403
招远市	Zhaoyuan	1108	78.1	23568	15756	4400	33640	219646	164845	134362
栖霞市	Qixia	688.3	81.8	14800	5630	4368	15926.7	187700	82847	60381
海阳市	Haiyang	653.2	104	14919	10700	2712	9528	211032	45787	24570
潍坊市	**Weifang**									
潍城区	Weicheng	283.3	56.3	31026	20041	2568	58062	165640	46080	23561
寒亭区	Hanting	1093	217	46872	26100	1574	15340	150872	83800	54921

2-6 续表 3 continued

地　区	Area	境内公路里程（公里） Length of Highway (km)	高等级公路（公里） First-class Highway (km)	民用汽车拥有量（辆） Number of Civil Motor Vehicles (unit)	个人汽车（辆） Personal Motor Vehicles (unit)	邮政业务总量（万元） Business Volume of Post (10 000 yuan)	电信业务总量（万元） Business Volume of Telecommunication (10 000 yuan)	本地电话年末用户（户） Number of Local Telephone Subscribers at Year-end (household)	全年用电量（万千瓦时） Annual Electricity Consumption (10 000 kw・m)	工业用电量（万千瓦时） Industrial Electricity Consumption (10 000 kw・m)
坊子区	Fangzi	277	85	21644	14680	1725.2	15018	107291	50638.1	40196.9
奎文区	Kuiwen	77.7	33.4	42508	27391	5632	53210	193100	49643	43410
临朐县	Linqu	1678	254	27732	13263	2962	31200	230000	82840	60242
昌乐县	Changle	689	57	26711	12447	1955.9	27210	165677	90316	67537
青州市	Qingzhou	1645	252.6	51272	24828	5804	40186	263758	140461	99635
诸城市	Zhucheng	2759	240.7	51484	36908	4171	47474	325680	194135	155021
寿光市	Shouguang	3148	362	65732	46875	9040	52100	380600	337967	297786
安丘市	Anqiu	1049	118	48515	17855	3405.9	41250	271198	106631	76494
高密市	Gaomi	1528.8	57	60989	45228	3003	40500	253000	184844	148538
昌邑市	Changyi	1718.3	268.3	49293	24509	5715	30728	218936	167410	124789
济宁市	**Jining**									
市中区	Shizhong	87	50	6623	4557	5721	91411	130911	5092164	138170
任城区	Rencheng	882.4	40.6	12850	11050	6259	6780	132100	141973.9	124429.1
微山县	Weishan	980	3	9735	7869	2230	12641	131000	62566	57477
鱼台县	Yutai	865	0	42783	4465	1229	7708	83783	25710	12359
金乡县	Jinxiang	1302	40.7	6499	6008	2430	14579	110000	56181	26474
嘉祥县	Jiaxiang	1320	70	5445	4723	1896.5	14079	203756	47215	46454.4
汶上县	Wenshang	1363	116	4769	190	1622	9353	131928	34967	21282
泗水县	Sishui	518	76	3320	3298	1560	4264	95500	64671	53894
梁山县	Liangshan	1186	0	8230	6687	1600	15035	126243	34729	22901
曲阜市	Qufu	733	68.7	7358	5762	2642	14926	121568	64203	38212
兖州市	Yanzhou	1089	294.3	27848	5425	3739	15719	239252	161401	104962
邹城市	Zoucheng	3197	198.1	63446	20117	3962	21841	444953	571690	562211
泰安市	**Taian**									
泰山区	Taishan	499.6	69.5	60317	21924	6200	79004	433409	243836	236151
岱岳区	Daiyue	2492.4	149.2	8834	8642	2367	6369	186127	58655.4	42630
宁阳县	Ningyang	2288.5	64.7	4746	3966	2686	14294	134821	96463	73640
东平县	Dongping	2170.7	0	6120	2850	1750	9300	138492	97030	80010
新泰市	Xintai	2915.7	95.5	49594	34985	4367	70907	311230	336292	258000
肥城市	Feicheng	2218.9	36.6	26859	9588	4562	32897	246821	315089	261200

2-6 续表 4 continued

地 区	Area	境内公路里程（公里） Length of Highway (km)	高等级公路（公里） First-class Highway (km)	民用汽车拥有量（辆） Number of Civil Motor Vehicles (unit)	个人汽车（辆） Personal Motor Vehicles (unit)	邮政业务总量（万元） Business Volume of Post (10 000 yuan)	电信业务总量（万元） Business Volume of Telecom-munication (10 000 yuan)	本地电话年末用户（户） Number of Local Telephone Subscribers at Year-end (household)	全年用电量（万千瓦时） Annual Electricity Consumption (10 000 kw·m)	工业用电量（万千瓦时） Industrial Electricity Consumption (10 000 kw·m)
威海市	**Weihai**									
环翠区	Huancui	821.2	237.4	79904	53229	11840	84905	412136	290677	198198
文登市	Wendeng	1980	131.9	59571	44128	8378	51667	411429	106576	74552
荣成市	Rongcheng	2019	86.9	66931	58898	9336	41658	418049	159756	114449
乳山市	Rushan	1680	122.7	27428	20308	4455	38545	245000	61868	35053
日照市	**Rizhao**									
东港区	Donggang	160	100	108023	80006	9400	54000	144126	222199	146192
岚山区	Lanshan	1249.9	25	10184	5920	868	9746	80304	181239	163236
五莲县	Wulian	1215	0	34359	32939	3075	11425	105000	73643	57000
莒 县	Juxian	753	39	8360	7200	4462	17723	176500	120198	97118
莱芜市	**Laiwu**									
莱城区	Laicheng	2495	21	45468	24695	8313.6	43460.4	321675	339000	239613
钢城区	Gangcheng	344.1	60.9	21397	11096	1829	10942.1	76469	355088	349898
临沂市	**Linyi**									
兰山区	Lanshan	1232.4	38.5	74600	56200	4637	117909	420700	280924	212011
罗庄区	Luozhuang	521.6	59.1	6097	5866	654	20100	120301	565498	511997
河东区	Hedong	1139	93	48162	41868	1021	16681.5	136191	82573	59888
沂南县	Yinan	1302	53.7	9654	4533	3130.4	17030.3	150563	51976	38560
郯城县	Tancheng	2184.9	164	12317	9311	2284.2	20979.1	171413	177332	153363
沂水县	Yishui	2342.7	0	13053	9522	3677.4	22937.3	316000	94553	75511
苍山县	Cangshan	2082.3	53.5	20713	16227	3154.7	13156	269800	68156	45276
费 县	Feixian	2378	398	29183	5681	2947.6	16080	146011	56794.4	43377
平邑县	Pingyi	2142.7	546	9550	5516	2189.4	19310.5	252289	64874	44763
莒南县	Junan	1207	0	13505	8077	2817	17299	175305	68113	51626
蒙阴县	Mengyin	1481	41.1	11167	7861	1578	10846	109660	35367	18456
临沭县	Linshu	1203.5	0	8745	6480	2427.4	18722.9	125049	60655	47983
德州市	**Dezhou**									
德城区	Decheng	1072	105	38151	9500	5532.4	6641	176229	230069	211450
陵 县	Lingxian	2438	51	4585	3435	2354.2	8500	112029	41746	28615
宁津县	Ningjin	1386	0	4511	3642	2294	9860	96699	52614	33437

2-6 续表 5 continued

地 区	Area	境内公路里程（公里）Length of Highway (km)	高等级公路（公里）First-class Highway (km)	民用汽车拥有量（辆）Number of Civil Motor Vehicles (unit)	个人汽车（辆）Personal Motor Vehicles (unit)	邮政业务总量（万元）Business Volume of Post (10 000 yuan)	电信业务总量（万元）Business Volume of Telecom-munication (10 000 yuan)	本地电话年末用户（户）Number of Local Telephone Subscribers at Year-end (household)	全年用电量（万千瓦时）Annual Electricity Consumption (10 000 kw·m)	工业用电量（万千瓦时）Industrial Electricity Consumption (10 000 kw·m)
庆云县	Qingyun	878	0	2383	1656	1508	4250	56403	20990	10515
临邑县	Linyi	1993	35	4995	2674	2285.9	11230	101111	72106	49848
齐河县	Qihe	2683.2	68.6	4530	3915	2017	13067	148200	121352	91921
平原县	Pingyuan	2458	41	4081	3000	2264.1	12640	102350	150244	138530
夏津县	Xiajin	1644.2	32.6	3969	2742	2193.1	10058	88246	80765	52342
武城县	Wucheng	1800.8	15.5	6118	1623	2499	6900	75473	30366	20776
乐陵市	Leling	1705	0	2336	2100	2450.4	4749	99000	44193	20982
禹城市	Yucheng	2618	53	3283	1930	1817	7900	94973	103765	84719
聊城市	**Liaocheng**									
东昌府区	Dongchangfu	2026	150	63000	29576	8777	26575	267600	210837	155004
阳谷县	Yanggu	2165.8	52.1	2819	1376	3999.8	12015	140250	59871	39524
莘 县	Shenxian	2738	45.1	720	520	4146	12990	100426	39302	30500
茌平县	Chiping	1967	171	34339	28503	2555	12006	97834	659064	645264
东阿县	Donge	1692	27	6930	3590	2284	3873	79287	92446	77827
冠 县	Guanxian	2178	44	10900	6540	3378	9726	108325	61608	37170
高唐县	Gaotang	2123.4	63.7	28600	25476	1835	13193	110993	108309	95034.1
临清市	Linqing	1415	13.3	10878	2000	3844	18083	224725	159023	115000
滨州市	**Binzhou**									
滨城区	Bincheng	2007.7	86	82121	75646	6876	36175	115006	371144	321074
惠民县	Huimin	1805.5	57.8	7081	5767	1852	7751	148000	40938	24197
阳信县	Yangxin	1155.6	18.4	4754	4138	855	10021	113714	25023	13907
无棣县	Wudi	1746.7	3.1	4200	1500	1773	8518	130979	92073	76872
沾化县	Zhanhua	1984.6	0	2100	1200	1193	9042	90300	52246	43467
博兴县	Boxing	1464.1	322.7	75971	71205	302	612	144246	73186	54672
邹平县	Zouping	2252.8	50.6	36547	30421	3655	36241	200500	387290	363496
菏泽市	**Heze**									
牡丹区	Mudan	714.2	268.6	52136	40164	7981.5	82287.9	329789	193487	135892
曹 县	Caoxian	951.1	273.9	51816	48691	2065.3	28092.9	228425	61534	27486
单 县	Shanxian	884	305.2	25180	22644	1946.3	23099	197898	45493	15493

2-6 续表 6 continued

地区	Area	境内公路里程（公里） Length of Highway (km)	高等级公路（公里） First-class Highway (km)	民用汽车拥有量（辆） Number of Civil Motor Vehicles (unit)	个人汽车（辆） Personal Motor Vehicles (unit)	邮政业务总量（万元） Business Volume of Post (10 000 yuan)	电信业务总量（万元） Business Volume of Telecommunication (10 000 yuan)	本地电话年末用户（户） Number of Local Telephone Subscribers at Year-end (household)	全年用电量（万千瓦时） Annual Electricity Consumption (10 000 kw·m)	工业用电量（万千瓦时） Industrial Electricity Consumption (10 000 kw·m)
成武县	Chengwu	503.1	138.4	21432	19534	1339.8	13520.5	110135	33094	11456
巨野县	Juye	661.3	145.8	30351	24654	2019.5	19748.9	136123	41329	14602
郓城县	Yuncheng	852.7	223.7	39135	36084	2334	26544.6	201045	89594	51779
鄄城县	Juancheng	523.4	87.1	39645	37879	1494.9	14279.6	106241	20966	7913
定陶县	Dingtao	375.4	112.3	18842	17126	1307.2	13612.9	91715	32075	13449
东明县	Dongming	490.4	406.5	21730	19245	1930.7	15058.7	92089	62274	39826

2-7 续表 continued

地区	Area	社会消费品零售总额（万元） Total Retail Sales of Consumer Goods (10 000 yuan)	限额以上批发和零售业商品销售总额（万元） Total Sales Above Designated Size (10 000 yuan)	出口总额（万美元） Total Exports (USD 10 000)	当年实际使用外资金额（万美元） Foreign Investment Actually Used in This Year (USD 10 000)	城镇固定资产投资完成额（万元） Investment of Construction in Urban Area (10 000 yuan)	普通中学数（所） Number of Regular Secondary Schools (unit)	小学数（所） Number of Primary Schools (unit)	普通中学专任教师数（人） Fulltime Teachers of Regular Secondary Schools (person)	小学专任教师数（人） Fulltime Teachers of Primary Schools (person)
济南市	**Jinan**									
历下区	Lixia	2263010	3257722	29634	14260	526557	23	38	2408	2199
市中区	Shizhong	1353273	1486903	30913	4095	498730	22	51	2834	2063
槐荫区	Huaiyin	1255394	1245026	12112	4185.9	272326	13	47	1015	1623
天桥区	Tianqiao	953968	239002	33009	4015	591024	22	53	1344	1847
历城区	Licheng	1226869	1865774	78634	19837.9	1664016	25	102	2529	3149
长清县	Changqing	445323	40516	8512	2457	1145526	20	87	2023	2231
平阴县	Pingyin	289628	164531	16019	579	327857	19	53	1634	1653
济阳县	Jiyang	304243	78799	3492	4275	473584	20	79	1682	2629
商河县	Shanghe	259846	16030	3731	411	167006	25	83	1740	2521
章丘市	Zhangqiu	992904	221557	49261	35009	1646270	38	186	4377	4932
青岛市	**Qingdao**									
市南区	Shinan	1442714	4703788	322905	6915	664127	11	31	829	1677
市北区	Shibei	1263907	143356	58513	6898	676917	12	40	650	1716

2-7 续表 1 continued

地 区	Area	社会消费品零售总额（万元） Total Retail Sales of Consumer Goods (10 000 yuan)	限额以上批发和零售业商品销售总额（万元） Total Sales Above Designated Size (10 000 yuan)	出口总额（万美元） Total Exports (USD 10 000)	当年实际使用外资金额（万美元） Foreign Investment Actually Used in This Year (USD 10 000)	城镇固定资产投资完成额（万元） Investment of Construction in Urban Area (10 000 yuan)	普通中学数（所） Number of Regular Secondary Schools (unit)	小学数（所） Number of Primary Schools (unit)	普通中学专任教师数（人） Fulltime Teachers of Regular Secondary Schools (person)	小学专任教师数（人） Fulltime Teachers of Primary Schools (person)
四方区	Sifang	627626	617548	47101	5063	445437	7	31	528	1433
黄岛区	Huangdao	519154	1047426	381600	82800	2012632	10	32	1305	1318
崂山区	Laoshan	443223	125462	191474	14300	1111507	16	33	977	915
李沧区	Licang	862001	456663	106189	18296	679602	11	29	880	1331
城阳区	Chengyang	531938	450211	421243	54000	1662462	16	70	2134	2079
胶州市	Jiaozhou	873629	147774	228220	55000	1679715	31	121	3238	3943
即墨市	Jimo	1055180	626000	206431	80788	1811357	54	191	4705	5094
平度市	Pingdu	974460	518670	60994	35298	1314630	58	210	5454	5803
胶南市	Jiaonan	769124	388278	125500	42005	1638499	33	98	4094	4031
莱西市	Laixi	703752	118782	90486	32687	1301924	42	104	3448	2877
淄博市	**Zibo**									
淄川区	Zichuan	791326	269954	37461	1564	834061	41	77	3437	2884
张店区	Zhangdian	1477120	846595	70713	20634	1266186	45	54	2984	2634
博山区	Boshan	541011	76396	26223	1062	582949	30	24	2180	1557
临淄区	Linzi	710127	384580	38160	5836	859033	35	62	3544	2397
周村区	Zhoucun	473897	160486	29617	2349	688318	16	32	1540	1265
桓台县	Huantai	504500	109538	30938	4533	754571	22	49	2242	1685
高青县	Gaoqing	127060	16611	7221	865	156587	13	44	1270	1248
沂源县	Yiyuan	373123	34837	10524	110	155419	25	71	2647	2326
枣庄市	**Zaozhuang**									
市中区	Shizhong	312907	210829	12695	1929	347396	28	65	2320	2260
薛城区	Xuecheng	252828	76554	2618	1243	421179	20	80	2161	2591
峄城区	Yicheng	161377	2867	4028	1156	110118	18	68	1397	1548
台儿庄区	Taierzhuang	168460	2290	2552	809	86660	16	62	1138	1358
山亭区	Shanting	187934	12650	2561	1007	99830	24	152	1641	2868
滕州市	Tengzhou	960713	269858	17116	4184	623511	69	325	6508	7295
东营市	**Dongying**									
东营区	Dongying	1132266	659563	20016	3260	1210007	13	24	786	806
河口区	Hekou	119141	14569	3209	1462	570987	14	22	1088	876
垦利县	Kenli	87087	70076	15273	1353	473122	9	32	972	816

2-7 续表 2 continued

地区	Area	社会消费品零售总额（万元） Total Retail Sales of Consumer Goods (10 000 yuan)	限额以上批发和零售业商品销售总额（万元） Total Sales Above Designated Size (10 000 yuan)	出口总额（万美元） Total Exports (USD 10 000)	当年实际使用外资金额（万美元） Foreign Investment Actually Used in This Year (USD 10 000)	城镇固定资产投资完成额（万元） Investment of Construction in Urban Area (10 000 yuan)	普通中学数（所） Number of Regular Secondary Schools (unit)	小学数（所） Number of Primary Schools (unit)	普通中学专任教师数（人） Fulltime Teachers of Regular Secondary Schools (person)	小学专任教师数（人） Fulltime Teachers of Primary Schools (person)
利津县	Lijin	131359	15516	8807	897	244520	19	47	1542	1125
广饶县	Guangrao	224756	146594.5	38731	7500	666292	22	68	3124	2356
烟台市	**Yantai**									
芝罘区	Zhifu	1827582	1854358	54042	21507	1481476	26	48	2743	1803
福山区	Fushan	517628	1044462	350442	49849	3290331	23	72	2016	1590
牟平区	Muping	385992	122539	43853	12654	307108	24	35	2565	1883
莱山区	Laishan	252471	37927	53016	19507	949010	8	21	657	500
长岛县	Changdao	66304	2395	3007	267	41263	4	9	229	178
龙口市	Longkou	796007	606055	64090	49700	1823290	44	101	4209	2203
莱阳市	Laiyang	706931	172870	51099	22545	522276	38	122	4371	3137
莱州市	Laizhou	827441	368976	54570.4	27885	1215092	50	118	3694	2274
蓬莱市	Penglai	432110	156220	32730	28915	957558	25	83	1927	1367
招远市	Zhaoyuan	485548	339783	60844	20872	966357	36	72	2962	1908
栖霞市	Qixia	425594	100642	16674	5500	167508	33	83	3212	2312
海阳市	Haiyang	441333	67334	32971	10918	425579	35	103	2930	2660
潍坊市	**Weifang**									
潍城区	Weicheng	445539	757116.5	11498	3296	344566	14	54	1205	1671
寒亭区	Hanting	186225	198974	9251	4383	410877	18	69	1354	1500
坊子区	Fangzi	144958	119227	15049	3806	196111	12	60	1144	1049
奎文区	Kuiwen	311266	724107	13435	3506	350227	19	49	1688	1661
临朐县	Linqu	360849	119609	8625	4567	427276	44	188	3917	4057
昌乐县	Changle	340860	161856	13390	4801	201998	31	97	3134	2896
青州市	Qingzhou	617069	407241	11771	4579	618035	45	168	3787	4114
诸城市	Zhucheng	622028	423092	50154	5766	915328	59	174	4980	5090
寿光市	Shouguang	691723	289552	74127	8197	1194277	49	207	7230	5033
安丘市	Anqiu	480998	165111	26114	4114	511338	53	185	5489	4442
高密市	Gaomi	511816	252886	48801	5359	511266	45	110	3804	3807
昌邑市	Changyi	471212	105612	20264	4193	346658	40	101	2462	2970
济宁市	**Jining**									

2-7 续表 3 continued

地 区	Area	社会消费品零售总额（万元） Total Retail Sales of Consumer Goods (10 000 yuan)	限额以上批发和零售业商品销售总额（万元） Total Sales Above Designated Size (10 000 yuan)	出口总额（万美元） Total Exports (USD 10 000)	当年实际使用外资金额（万美元） Foreign Investment Actually Used in This Year (USD 10 000)	城镇固定资产投资完成额（万元） Investment of Construction in Urban Area (10 000 yuan)	普通中学数（所） Number of Regular Secondary Schools (unit)	小学数（所） Number of Primary Schools (unit)	普通中学专任教师数（人） Fulltime Teachers of Regular Secondary Schools (person)	小学专任教师数（人） Fulltime Teachers of Primary Schools (person)
市中区	Shizhong	843893	770711.8	6500	1061	395000	23	32	2265	1432
任城区	Rencheng	284868	263183	8400	389	371814	31	77	2174	2017
微山县	Weishan	275580	54841	2740	174	186771	36	124	2476	3012
鱼台县	Yutai	209353	11623	2607	219	114671	20	77	1788	1983
金乡县	Jinxiang	245102	69495.5	18635	581	91907	28	126	2521	2199
嘉祥县	Jiaxiang	259844	23777	5423	705	163892	33	187	3718	3740
汶上县	Wenshang	240360	65254	2524	703	160000	33	156	2260	2942
泗水县	Sishui	216840	45198	11092	1017	86556	26	90	1921	2425
梁山县	Liangshan	244533	125769	2560	284	176902	33	137	2428	3232
曲阜市	Qufu	489508	58722	7014	5164	262540	32	97	2796	2595
兖州市	Yanzhou	538171	135845	11026	10002	736959	28	73	2461	1886
邹城市	Zoucheng	754871	500489	22563	31087	2265350	39	207	4564	5637
泰安市	**Taian**									
泰山区	Taishan	680865	556636	48906	51453	446032	29	64	2756	1851
岱岳区	Daiyue	441545	264781	8493	13010	425070	37	130	2898	3801
宁阳县	Ningyang	378954	65826	5329	8854	473011	27	67	2941	2917
东平县	Dongping	275060	73732	2042	6010	342173	28	120	2924	3005
新泰市	Xintai	726502	135600	69662	36149	987800	51	197	4858	5020
肥城市	Feicheng	679161	235035	63516	32230	1034338	28	142	4390	4518
威海市	**Weihai**									
环翠区	Huancui	1198517	1117877	402673	49601	2277815	24	44	2750	1853
文登市	Wendeng	805506	270770	71108	21205	1116000	30	47	4898	3645
荣成市	Rongcheng	839506	195972	90686	41007	1507559	35	52	5165	3080
乳山市	Rushan	468539	162157.3	36610	18729	839747	26	42	2852	2003
日照市	**Rizhao**									
东港区	Donggang	622000	287181	49000	2063	710861	30	105	2425	2235
岚山区	Lanshan	192391	16911	60644	1925	342329	14	63	1687	1326
五莲县	Wulian	193755	31336	8430	1232	58955	25	109	2020	1901
莒 县	Juxian	368296	127496	12828	1104	253505	54	217	4316	4201
莱芜市	**Laiwu**									

2-7 续表 4 continued

地 区	Area	社会消费品零售总额（万元） Total Retail Sales of Consumer Goods (10 000 yuan)	限额以上批发和零售业商品销售总额（万元） Total Sales Above Designated Size (10 000 yuan)	出口总额（万美元） Total Exports (USD 10 000)	当年实际使用外资金额（万美元） Foreign Investment Actually Used in This Year (USD 10 000)	城镇固定资产投资完成额（万元） Investment of Construction in Urban Area (10 000 yuan)	普通中学数（所） Number of Regular Secondary Schools (unit)	小学数（所） Number of Primary Schools (unit)	普通中学专任教师数（人） Fulltime Teachers of Regular Secondary Schools (person)	小学专任教师数（人） Fulltime Teachers of Primary Schools (person)
莱城区	Laicheng	726900	165419	27710	4160	810005	43	165	4787	4750
钢城区	Gangcheng	218800	746355.1	2830	1748.8	206831	16	45	1058	1058
临沂市	**Linyi**									
兰山区	Lanshan	1667142	1267281	43799	45800	1126124	42	104	5425	3655
罗庄区	Luozhuang	235383	311952.4	20116	8200	376382	15	46	2130	1902
河东区	Hedong	189496	124081	12200	1162	523585	20	104	2248	2132
沂南县	Yinan	283238	14476	4180	1333	137836	33	164	4207	3684
郯城县	Tancheng	420467	47138	5239	1517	238421	44	205	3461	3458
沂水县	Yishui	445867	35496.7	14671	1565.3	326990	43	204	5280	4054
苍山县	Cangshan	420380	253406	5002	1468	193100	49	255	4152	4184
费 县	Feixian	338028	35508	12473	1812	331668	41	178	4027	3208
平邑县	Pingyi	397911	53655.2	5679	300	144876	37	206	3232	3716
莒南县	Junan	425000	55912	18749	1583	279794	39	147	3404	3740
蒙阴县	Mengyin	254482	78812	3672	605	97612	18	145	2125	2111
临沭县	Linshu	218354	44778	11679	802	207707	28	112	2510	2426
德州市	**Dezhou**									
德城区	Decheng	535761	252911	32427	2638	764095	31	108	2454	2171
陵 县	Lingxian	256400	17698	2014	790	438868	22	141	1649	2592
宁津县	Ningjin	264100	88107	3628	276	351492	23	99	1993	1868
庆云县	Qingyun	205231	39608	1680	388	306031	15	55	1529	1304
临邑县	Linyi	303892	97877	4371	979	453479	18	90	1925	2938
齐河县	Qihe	259164	91667	1906	180	334691	23	126	2387	2696
平原县	Pingyuan	243431	70185	1201	1318	391572	9	90	1027	2577
夏津县	Xiajin	218664	95329	613	40	381477	21	148	1771	2491
武城县	Wucheng	223146	88489	1394	2513	363973	19	67	1639	1571
乐陵市	Leling	274663	70668	5312	814	392683	25	118	2396	3029
禹城市	Yucheng	287291	73391	8675	113	456695	20	109	2069	2139
聊城市	**Liaocheng**									
东昌府区	Dongchangfu	607757	166454	2369	122	298847	38	141	3054	3618
阳谷县	Yanggu	319295	56827.5	6474	166	260224	29	143	2868	3271

2-7 续表 5 continued

地 区	Area	社会消费品零售总额（万元） Total Retail Sales of Consumer Goods (10 000 yuan)	限额以上批发和零售业商品销售总额（万元） Total Sales Above Designated Size (10 000 yuan)	出口总额（万美元） Total Exports (USD 10 000)	当年实际使用外资金额（万美元） Foreign Investment Actually Used in This Year (USD 10 000)	城镇固定资产投资完成额（万元） Investment of Construction in Urban Area (10 000 yuan)	普通中学数（所） Number of Regular Secondary Schools (unit)	小学数（所） Number of Primary Schools (unit)	普通中学专任教师数（人） Fulltime Teachers of Regular Secondary Schools (person)	小学专任教师数（人） Fulltime Teachers of Primary Schools (person)
莘 县	Shenxian	388531	20092	2496	559	103704	43	238	3292	3911
茌平县	Chiping	251260	46327	3382	506	404757	24	98	2260	2287
东阿县	Donge	183730	39152	1421	353	269687	20	78	1463	1565
冠 县	Guanxian	277683	15538	1820	156	163407	26	113	2240	2376
高唐县	Gaotang	281662	60254	9806	2251.3	343146	17	83	2558	2536
临清市	Linqing	408049	25442	20120	429	298847	30	97	2318	2555
滨州市	**Binzhou**									
滨城区	Bincheng	584067	407467.7	41596	2273	897000	28	89	2642	2619
惠民县	Huimin	253017	59731.1	706	259	461000	24	123	1753	2398
阳信县	Yangxin	139149	34805.9	10310	1258	416000	21	80	1535	1733
无棣县	Wudi	208899	84432	2669	1538	721000	24	77	1827	1889
沾化县	Zhanhua	187838	256568.6	673	1552	604000	19	66	1509	1575
博兴县	Boxing	260554	86425.4	8632	1127	750000	25	79	1906	2251
邹平县	Zouping	452224	204898.3	93678	7200	1110000	25	72	2804	2732
菏泽市	**Heze**									
牡丹区	Mudan	638189	773331	15111	1518	790616	66	248	5182	6871
曹 县	Caoxian	379565	39389	17965	795	320816	60	326	3923	6943
单 县	Shanxian	338938	45239	3264	1213	316927	57	197	3895	4970
成武县	Chengwu	184800	19782	821	262	182949	40	160	2929	3847
巨野县	Juye	270521	18338	6363	502	386845	39	177	3096	4357
郓城县	Yuncheng	319239	36408	3602	716	319857	63	271	4354	6673
鄄城县	Juancheng	228189	27068	4303	769	260555	34	165	2461	3771
定陶县	Dingtao	181354	34142	2300	645	206556	24	133	2412	3069
东明县	Dongming	211678	41739	2208	670	294612	36	165	2622	3388

2-8 续表 continued

地 区	Area	普通中学在校学生数（人） Students Enrollment of Regular Secondary Schools (person)	小学在校学生数（人） Students Enrollment of Primary Schools (person)	专业技术人员数（人） Professionals Counts (person)	农业技术人员（人） Agricultural Technique Workers (person)	农业科技与服务单位个数（个） Number of Agricultural Science, Technology and Service (unit)	全年专利申请数（件） Whole Year Patented Claim Number (unit)	公共图书馆图书总藏量（千册） Total Books Reserved in Public Libraries (1000 volumes)	医院、卫生院数（所） Number of Hospital (unit)	医院、卫生院床位数（床） Beds of Hospitals (bed)
济南市	**Jinan**									
历下区	Lixia	20423	37125	22130	116	6	2401	100	46	4358
市中区	Shizhong	36240	34145	23453	45	13	1004	45	33	3246
槐荫区	Huaiyin	8810	21947	8243	54	20	1063	41	20	4853
天桥区	Tianqiao	13569	29529	4221	37	4	1160	50	2	304
历城区	Licheng	34030	48504	15300	538	11	1660	350	37	1832
长清县	Changqing	24085	39038	14400	640	64	219	80	13	823
平阴县	Pingyin	21863	23174	8653	628	64	130	30.1	14	941
济阳县	Jiyang	27118	32234	20079	390	36	160	91.3	10	599
商河县	Shanghe	26285	38422	7324	318	109	60	24	17	884
章丘市	Zhangqiu	77222	54725	32499	802	136	596	429	38	4321
青岛市	**Qingdao**									
市南区	Shinan	12505	26810	0	0	0	1750	124	18	2491
市北区	Shibei	8421	21262	5452	0	0	593	100	3	759
四方区	Sifang	8654	19361	0	0	0	1503	120	28	3216
黄岛区	Huangdao	13802	23306	26969	170	13	752	190	9	1001
崂山区	Laoshan	10330	12524	13675	170	23	995	112	14	1091
李沧区	Licang	13447	21391	6340	0	0	463	300	45	1797
城阳区	Chengyang	22046	35265	23600	4706	31	679	1183.8	11	1806
胶州市	Jiaozhou	41581	59024	34100	6980	81	124	170	26	3827
即墨市	Jimo	66572	69037	67789	10511	134	1023	460	44	4520
平度市	Pingdu	67072	93913	37110	734	140	171	342	38	2477
胶南市	Jiaonan	42874	56766	41367	629	78	726	386	24	2161
莱西市	Laixi	30817	38815	32882	6826	91	61	320	37	2672
淄博市	**Zibo**									
淄川区	Zichuan	44376	41124	17716	360	52	264	75	33	2445
张店区	Zhangdian	44709	46146	52042	355	32	1046	850	30	3450
博山区	Boshan	27939	23653	12077	157	20	285	134	30	2605
临淄区	Linzi	41766	37111	11235	306	54	368	129	15	1721
周村区	Zhoucun	19899	19996	20985	201	32	275	134	10	1009
桓台县	Huantai	30968	30161	20082	236	63	337	102	20	1583
高青县	Gaoqing	17204	22102	5176	135	89	110	91	13	482

2-8 续表 1 continued

地 区	Area	普通中学在校学生数（人） Students Enrollment of Regular Secondary Schools (person)	小学在校学生数（人） Students Enrollment of Primary Schools (person)	专业技术人员数（人） Professionals Counts (person)	农业技术人员（人） Agricultural Technique Workers (person)	农业科技与服务单位个数（个） Number of Agricultural Science, Technology and Service (unit)	全年专利申请数（件） Whole Year Patented Claim Number (unit)	公共图书馆图书总藏量（千册） Total Books Reserved in Public Libraries (1000 volumes)	医院、卫生院数（所） Number of Hospital (unit)	医院、卫生院床位数（床） Beds of Hospitals (bed)
沂源县	Yiyuan	43573	36470	20753	1502	67	123	131	15	790
枣庄市	**Zaozhuang**									
市中区	Shizhong	39535	39172	7984	224	47	178	451	31	3037
薛城区	Xuecheng	39415	40815	9522	195	56	88	92	19	1692
峄城区	Yicheng	21819	27753	7086	264	55	120	61	10	587
台儿庄区	Taierzhuang	21162	21200	6443	210	140	21	52	8	561
山亭区	Shanting	32077	40994	8860	158	80	29	9	12	571
滕州市	Tengzhou	122783	122592	56780	1358	267	168	240	43	3493
东营市	**Dongying**									
东营区	Dongying	7545	15666	6215	87	41	1507	1736	46	4409
河口区	Hekou	8579	18164	5905	330	12	175	168	18	722
垦利县	Kenli	12772	14182	6694	125	18	218	73	8	710
利津县	Lijin	18565	21085	6237	408	45	126	83	11	806
广饶县	Guangrao	33948	30222	14564	822	76	286	216	22	1701
烟台市	**Yantai**									
芝罘区	Zhifu	34192	40452	39300	153	11	719	25	20	1620
福山区	Fushan	23974	20558	4319	142	73	447	172	24	999
牟平区	Muping	30254	20333	9906	215	59	142	166	19	1221
莱山区	Laishan	8677	7875	2031	66	6	179	2000	11	290
长岛县	Changdao	2495	2631	2370	153	3	7	67	10	201
龙口市	Longkou	44603	37571	25848	1271	52	828	1090	29	3569
莱阳市	Laiyang	53295	34516	13424	1204	148	291	256.6	40	2895
莱州市	Laizhou	59740	39731	13320	2677	64	408	192.4	39	2588
蓬莱市	Penglai	25385	22247	25537	1821	98	360	332	22	1640
招远市	Zhaoyuan	38713	28899	12870	742	73	416	150	19	1269
栖霞市	Qixia	43815	28167	28855	612	85	59	130	19	1415
海阳市	Haiyang	41890	29081	13529	559	87	38	119	20	1267
潍坊市	**Weifang**									
潍城区	Weicheng	14754	26662	3601	52	10	232	0	17	1125
寒亭区	Hanting	14901	22712	15189	1600	82	84	68.5	17	1143
坊子区	Fangzi	13161	15901	9928	2012	16	145	10	7	659
奎文区	Kuiwen	26203	34486	10780	98	7	249	101	21	3367

2-8 续表 2 continued

地区	Area	普通中学在校学生数（人）Students Enrollment of Regular Secondary Schools (person)	小学在校学生数（人）Students Enrollment of Primary Schools (person)	专业技术人员数（人）Professionals Counts (person)	农业技术人员（人）Agricultural Technique Workers (person)	农业科技与服务单位个数（个）Number of Agricultural Science, Technology and Service (unit)	全年专利申请数（件）Whole Year Patented Claim Number (unit)	公共图书馆图书总藏量（千册）Total Books Reserved in Public Libraries (1000 volumes)	医院、卫生院数（所）Number of Hospital (unit)	医院、卫生院床位数（床）Beds of Hospitals (bed)
临朐县	Linqu	44529	47668	31900	12500	130	173	158	20	1313
昌乐县	Changle	41099	36478	13788	4610	140	156	92	22	1683
青州市	Qingzhou	48752	67201	39250	7100	126	153	340	31	3031
诸城市	Zhucheng	67193	85115	60100	11940	108	324	264	29	3509
寿光市	Shouguang	90381	93349	50138	12855	84	381	250	38	3580
安丘市	Anqiu	76117	65348	34892	10010	140	147	138	26	1932
高密市	Gaomi	44239	61176	26585	595	85	292	155	26	1786
昌邑市	Changyi	32136	51760	18709	4308	87	118	192	27	1705
济宁市	**Jining**									
市中区	Shizhong	37760	30453	5209	0	0	212	362	36	5810
任城区	Rencheng	32123	33069	8710	780	22	126	100	15	822
微山县	Weishan	49631	50764	9765	291	113	21	50	24	1116
鱼台县	Yutai	24388	33190	7416	2559	46	0	56	13	528
金乡县	Jinxiang	33583	42676	10700	586	86	72	88	12	1240
嘉祥县	Jiaxiang	33583	42676	10700	586	86	72	88	12	1240
汶上县	Wenshang	48753	68000	17610	1291	112	124	20	16	1038
泗水县	Sishui	27584	34528	9449	988	106	11	13	16	735
梁山县	Liangshan	50841	35663	11100	260	107	113	110	24	1120
曲阜市	Qufu	27460	37367	16973	334	51	140	110	18	1246
兖州市	Yanzhou	28422	30343	9162	818	85	128	810	32	2706
邹城市	Zoucheng	95893	69101	29829	960	375	608	494	57	5205
泰安市	**Taian**									
泰山区	Taishan	36386	36898	5295	145	18	420	1221	42	5396
岱岳区	Daiyue	39091	57775	13385	377	133	213	2	26	1042
宁阳县	Ningyang	41649	37209	15525	681	102	94	39	20	1373
东平县	Dongping	37009	41432	13268	1352	65	53	40	20	1314
新泰市	Xintai	99048	60033	55517	1637	130	632	428	70	5190
肥城市	Feicheng	68837	33898	34699	812	196	518	386	51	3088
威海市	**Weihai**									
环翠区	Huancui	41029	38521	23873	767	43	861	232.3	21	3054
文登市	Wendeng	54215	52714	15621	936	119	348	397	31	3391
荣成市	Rongcheng	58005	58524	12392	1082	130	343	323	35	2995

2-8 续表 3 continued

地区	Area	普通中学在校学生数（人）Students Enrollment of Regular Secondary Schools (person)	小学在校学生数（人）Students Enrollment of Primary Schools (prson)	专业技术人员数（人）Profession-als Counts (person)	农业技术人员（人）Agricultural Technique Workers (person)	农业科技与服务单位个数（个）Number of Agricultural Science, Technology and Service (unit)	全年专利申请数（件）Whole Year Patented Claim Number (unit)	公共图书馆图书总藏量（千册）Total Books Reserved in Public Libraries (1000 volumes)	医院、卫生院数（所）Number of Hospital (unit)	医院、卫生院床位数（床）Beds of Hospitals (bed)
乳山市	Rushan	35744	21189	9765	354	76	64	280	19	2603
日照市	**Rizhao**									
东港区	Donggang	32523	41916	22900	540	58	236	95.4	11	774
岚山区	Lanshan	19605	27402	9626	412	36	84	0	8	535
五莲县	Wulian	30660	34996	9022	298	61	182	83.8	17	1049
莒　县	Juxian	60973	69012	17822	281	115	128	117.4	27	1560
莱芜市	**Laiwu**									
莱城区	Laicheng	62929	62698	26651	1390	118	416	200	36	2643
钢城区	Gangcheng	12930	18264	12120	46	5	49	4	7	1404
临沂市	**Linyi**									
兰山区	Lanshan	60828	84229	44805	512	60	868	172	48	6864
罗庄区	Luozhuang	28983	31429	9017	33	14	188	0	12	880
河东区	Hedong	33804	43198	6162	512	89	137	0	14	867
沂南县	Yinan	53689	67596	12690	838	56	32	80	34	1753
郯城县	Tancheng	64415	73649	12877	693	98	64	203	37	1876
沂水县	Yishui	61601	61533	19119	887	138	101	165	25	2169
苍山县	Cangshan	71946	74817	15219	602	118	81	98	26	1504
费　县	Feixian	56016	57958	16821	758	109	43	136	22	1993
平邑县	Pingyi	59641	74183	10542	673	119	41	50	23	1425
莒南县	Junan	72170	79067	15959	318	122	60	363	24	1898
蒙阴县	Mengyin	27507	38797	14625	568	196	28	138	16	1047
临沭县	Linshu	38363	49341	12340	393	92	72	144	18	1133
德州市	**Dezhou**									
德城区	Decheng	30359	40126	15666	835	29	240	56	16	2792
陵　县	Lingxian	30190	34396	7502	282	92	18	48	14	729
宁津县	Ningjin	29183	27339	10923	3195	15	44	50	13	695
庆云县	Qingyun	23030	18957	5329	206	40	43	3	9	505
临邑县	Linyi	28406	30908	6823	300	43	28	80	15	1055
齐河县	Qihe	28534	36455	8445	1400	135	16	104	16	826
平原县	Pingyuan	35182	29525	11542	173	49	10	165	13	698
夏津县	Xiajin	23084	28820	7465	291	59	19	31	16	504
武城县	Wucheng	25919	25126	4486	295	45	52	100	11	438

2-8 续表 4 continued

地 区	Area	普通中学在校学生数（人）Students Enrollment of Regular Secondary Schools (person)	小学在校学生数（人）Students Enrollment of Primary Schools (person)	专业技术人员数（人）Professionals Counts (person)	农业技术人员（人）Agricultural Technique Workers (person)	农业科技与服务单位个数（个）Number of Agricultural Science, Technology and Service (unit)	全年专利申请数（件）Whole Year Patented Claim Number (unit)	公共图书馆图书总藏量（千册）Total Books Reserved in Public Libraries (1000 volumes)	医院、卫生院数（所）Number of Hospital (unit)	医院、卫生院床位数（床）Beds of Hospitals (bed)
乐陵市	Leling	42797	43087	8920	259	23	38	8	18	686
禹城市	Yucheng	28107	30772	19283	530	13	25	160	13	814
聊城市	**Liaocheng**									
东昌府区	Dongchangfu	36289	63063	13031	601	101	318	186	41	4601
阳谷县	Yanggu	51071	54204	12518	245	136	154	25	29	1186
莘 县	Shenxian	72223	76706	12860	330	158	36	32	26	1365
茌平县	Chiping	37845	29018	12704	78	87	72	130	22	1019
东阿县	Donge	27329	24057	8523	233	48	20	48	19	1010
冠 县	Guanxian	24759	37366	7940	274	52	41	60	18	1150
高唐县	Gaotang	23827	23925	11550	328	81	218	100	20	833
临清市	Linqing	40462	43945	13453	140	5	226	50	26	1578
滨州市	**Binzhou**									
滨城区	Bincheng	36527	39742	22430	1831	85	133	1220	26	1068
惠民县	Huimin	32550	38075	8592	197	69	19	120	22	1235
阳信县	Yangxin	23577	28748	6437	451	67	11	100	11	630
无棣县	Wudi	24332	26796	5760	701	59	18	155	17	1043
沾化县	Zhanhua	26331	21321	11009	1003	35	12	98	13	506
博兴县	Boxing	25718	41020	9044	646	33	148	180	20	906
邹平县	Zouping	44583	60082	10946	160	80	96	357	25	2431
菏泽市	**Heze**									
牡丹区	Mudan	95477	127760	35518	1475	81	296	184.8	63	3024
曹 县	Caoxian	100596	138782	16267	1315	57	148	47.8	36	2464
单 县	Shanxian	77518	98803	17846	1362	60	38	88	29	1492
成武县	Chengwu	45334	51767	11010	1537	73	28	10.2	23	773
巨野县	Juye	62553	82704	14213	842	89	25	85	32	1551
郓城县	Yuncheng	81942	124802	17824	1465	64	44	101.5	29	1511
鄄城县	Juancheng	62507	67765	9617	1385	57	6	22.4	19	934
定陶县	Dingtao	48370	48181	11293	1173	88	29	47.1	26	996
东明县	Dongming	49517	72032	12469	1373	42	32	35.1	24	1076

2-9 续表 continued

地 区	Area	医院、卫生院卫生技术人员数（人） Medical Technical Personnal of Hospitals (person)	医生（人） Doctor (person)	城镇在岗职工年平均人数（人） Annual Average Number of Fully-employed Workers in Town (person)	城镇在岗职工工资总额（万元） Total Wages of Fully-employed Workers in Town (10 000 yuan)	农村居民人均纯收入（元） Annual Per Capita Net Income (yuan)	农民人均住房面积（平方米） Per Capita Living Floor Space of Rural Residents (sq.m)	农民文化娱乐消费比重（%） Proportion of Farmer Cultural Entertainment Expense (Percentage)	农村彩电普及率（%） Adoption Rate of Rural Colour TV (Percentage)	农村恩格尔系数（%） Rural Engel's Coefficient (Percentage)
济南市	**Jinan**									
历下区	Lixia	4178	1399	222147	594335	7018	56	10	100	29.91
市中区	Shizhong	4901	4880	132128	374372.2	6133	50	7.5	100	35.5
槐荫区	Huaiyin	5528	2203	74010	144764.9	6277	38	7.34	100	27.1
天桥区	Tianqiao	343	159	127355	204804	5933	35	7.6	100	38.24
历城区	Licheng	2584	1085	161539	424975	6040	48	9.7	100	38.1
长清县	Changqing	1370	530	88482	117624	5725	41	4.2	99.8	34.2
平阴县	Pingyin	1423	826	42141	52014	4725	31	3.62	100	36.9
济阳县	Jiyang	1328	412	34501	45120	4703	22	3.72	100	35
商河县	Shanghe	1054	401	28830	32988.7	4412	30	3.8	100	39.8
章丘市	Zhangqiu	5027	2628	98314	180167.4	6564	38	13.2	100	34.6
青岛市	**Qingdao**									
市南区	Shinan	3564	1512	148522	551075	0	0	0	0	0
市北区	Shibei	1007	388	42817	119856	0	0	0	0	0
四方区	Sifang	3600	1421	53534	129464	0	0	0	0	0
黄岛区	Huangdao	1041	496	111820	230557	7363	32	7.11	100	34.9
崂山区	Laoshan	1217	534	54329	137793	7599	36	6.25	100	36.7
李沧区	Licang	1992	851	55222	110999.9	0	0	0	0	0
城阳区	Chengyang	1790	918	166915	372432.7	6806	33	12.6	100	34
胶州市	Jiaozhou	4345	2830	141239	257804	6544	37	4.6	98	34.7
即墨市	Jimo	4896	1822	138711	251925	6478	28	3.1	100	39.9
平度市	Pingdu	3406	1529	75030	135065.8	6250	27	6.3	98.9	39.1
胶南市	Jiaonan	3462	1020	128969	216152	6470	28	6.6	100	36.3
莱西市	Laixi	3505	2244	97532	182056	6259	32	4.7	100	34.1
淄博市	**Zibo**									
淄川区	Zichuan	2606	1086	62652	136180	5951	33	13	100	32.34
张店区	Zhangdian	3995	1642	224370	493952	7003	42	7.25	100	30.3
博山区	Boshan	2502	996	44579	75038.7	5669	32	4	100	41.5
临淄区	Linzi	1859	854	80584	207574	6371	41	5.88	99	36.9

2-9 续表 1 continued

地 区	Area	医院、卫生院卫生技术人员数（人） Medical Technical Personnal of Hospitals (person)	医生（人） Doctor (person)	城镇在岗职工年平均人数（人） Annual Average Number of Fully-employed Workers in Town (person)	城镇在岗职工工资总额（万元） Total Wages of Fully-employed Workers in Town (10 000 yuan)	农村居民人均纯收入（元） Annual Per Capita Net Income (yuan)	农民人均住房面积（平方米） Per Capita Living Floor Space of Rural Residents (sq.m)	农民文化娱乐消费比重（%） Proportion of Farmer Cultural Entertainment Expense (Percentage)	农村彩电普及率（%） Adoption Rate of Rural Colour TV (Percentage)	农村恩格尔系数（%） Rural Engel's Coefficient (Percentage)
周村区	Zhoucun	1089	472	52195	80169	6265	35	6	99	29.8
桓台县	Huantai	1765	802	53022	92494	6202	30	3.32	100	34
高青县	Gaoqing	577	279	19636	27919.4	4303	36	5.02	96	34
沂源县	Yiyuan	1327	711	56950	75947	4281	27	6	85	37.1
枣庄市	**Zaozhuang**									
市中区	Shizhong	3003	1981	71591	136075	5413	31	5.5	99	40
薛城区	Xuecheng	1898	981	54653	84625	4920	28	4.6	94	44
峄城区	Yicheng	844	411	22139	28732	4609	27	4.6	92	36.9
台儿庄区	Taierzhuang	882	477	19878	23388	4303	31	4	84	38
山亭区	Shanting	828	458	16770	18877	3646	25	2	92	43.9
滕州市	Tengzhou	5050	2594	153908	278807	5097	35	3.9	92.3	37.4
东营市	**Dongying**									
东营区	Dongying	7188	2810	33589	60155	5193	36	7.38	99	34.94
河口区	Hekou	883	488	18067	35281.9	5006	26	3.7	99	34.8
垦利县	Kenli	756	327	22144	45478	5001	27	8.6	100	35.3
利津县	Lijin	781	442	16234	28038	4931	35	3.04	98	35.67
广饶县	Guangrao	1875	868	26676	55659	5380	32	3.78	99	27.7
烟台市	**Yantai**									
芝罘区	Zhifu	1830	1751	40444	82228	7050	35	14.6	100	37
福山区	Fushan	1321	721	165556	413751.2	6652	33	7.54	100	65.7
牟平区	Muping	1797	595	41821	67114	6235	23	2.7	100	37.02
莱山区	Laishan	430	256	65798	157547	6575	30	12.87	98	36
长岛县	Changdao	236	98	5305	9561.6	7052	28	6.3	100	38
龙口市	Longkou	3909	2089	110334	261203	6941	29	11.86	100	39.18
莱阳市	Laiyang	3634	1251	69308	136471	5815	29	18.2	100	41.78
莱州市	Laizhou	2901	1291	83859	176575	6320	31	17.9	100	31.4
蓬莱市	Penglai	1587	1085	42498	71110	6569	21	3	107	30
招远市	Zhaoyuan	1973	945	68019	149910	6475	24	5.6	100	35.56
栖霞市	Qixia	1813	819	36987	54646	4866	24	15	100	40.7
海阳市	Haiyang	1410	712	40482	62630	5368	31	12.41	100	47.5

2-9 续表 2 continued

地　区	Area	医院、卫生院卫生技术人员数（人） Medical Technical Personnal of Hospitals (person)	医生（人） Doctor (person)	城镇在岗职工年平均人数（人） Annual Average Number of Fully-employed Workers in Town (person)	城镇在岗职工工资总额（万元） Total Wages of Fully-employed Workers in Town (10 000 yuan)	农村居民人均纯收入（元） Annual Per Capita Net Income (yuan)	农民人均住房面积（平方米） Per Capita Living Floor Space of Rural Residents (sq.m)	农民文化娱乐消费比重（%） Proportion of Farmer Cultural Entertainment Expense (Percentage)	农村彩电普及率（%） Adoption Rate of Rural Colour TV (Percentage)	农村恩格尔系数（%） Rural Engel's Coefficient (Percentage)
潍坊市	**Weifang**									
潍城区	Weicheng	1021	397	40937	61402	5929	30	9.8	100	36
寒亭区	Hanting	1031	504	29102	43884	5932	33	8.1	100	36
坊子区	Fangzi	762	403	43703	63490	5671	36	13.1	100	34.7
奎文区	Kuiwen	3244	1215	76393	128569	5921	40	9.7	100	37.3
临朐县	Linqu	2269	1133	52335	59753	4546	28	16.6	95	32.7
昌乐县	Changle	1706	910	41354	53953	5022	26	14.6	100	35
青州市	Qingzhou	2609	1125	61324	90960	5183	38	12.5	100	34.1
诸城市	Zhucheng	3889	1678	99365	170914	6060	33	5.6	100	37.6
寿光市	Shouguang	3949	1901	77326	138074	6017	36	13.15	100	26.9
安丘市	Anqiu	2286	1059	63705	75015.2	4651	27	17.55	92	41.96
高密市	Gaomi	2318	1048	87762	113986	5422	31	9.3	100	48.8
昌邑市	Changyi	1436	732	34976	47463	5784	29	7	100	40.1
济宁市	**Jining**									
市中区	Shizhong	6815	3385	88974	175074	0	0	0	0	0
任城区	Rencheng	930	422	19702	38455	4952	32	20	98.5	48
微山县	Weishan	1172	346	36224	95855	4455	26	5.39	99	36.59
鱼台县	Yutai	886	346	24259	27724	4550	26	5.32	97	40.6
金乡县	Jinxiang	1687	701	24847	25654	4769	38	18.9	83	36
嘉祥县	Jiaxiang	1476	1308	26302	31147	4255	32	10.8	85	41.9
汶上县	Wenshang	1380	555	26873	33708	4266	19	14	65	42.9
泗水县	Sishui	1088	474	20175	23117.7	4057	27	15.51	74.3	34.3
梁山县	Liangshan	1500	630	31332	31306	4052	29	13.6	70	42
曲阜市	Qufu	1758	675	66150	92614	4800	35	11.66	95	40.44
兖州市	Yanzhou	2724	1015	39696	71972	6058	31	3.6	89.2	39.3
邹城市	Zoucheng	6103	1963	152988	410457	5198	32	15.3	97	44
泰安市	**Taian**									
泰山区	Taishan	5263	2157	124065	213080	5104	22	15.5	99	42
岱岳区	Daiyue	1618	756	35644	39712	4330	31	4.3	91	45
宁阳县	Ningyang	2199	1055	53434	61404	4048	33	5.6	100	32.9

2-9 续表 3 continued

地 区	Area	医院、卫生院卫生技术人员数（人） Medical Technical Personnal of Hospitals (person)	医生（人） Doctor (person)	城镇在岗职工年平均人数（人） Annual Average Number of Fully-employed Workers in Town (person)	城镇在岗职工工资总额（万元） Total Wages of Fully-employed Workers in Town (10 000 yuan)	农村居民人均纯收入（元） Annual Per Capita Net Income (yuan)	农民人均住房面积（平方米） Per Capita Living Floor Space of Rural Residents (sq.m)	农民文化娱乐消费比重（%） Proportion of Farmer Cultural Entertainment Expens (Percentage)	农村彩电普及率（%） Adoption Rate of Rural Colour TV (Percentage)	农村恩格尔系数（%） Rural Engel's Coefficient (Percentage)
东平县	Dongping	1950	921	40884	45689	3596	43	2.4	95	37.61
新泰市	Xintai	6338	2718	140718	238189	5469	36	8.5	99	37
肥城市	Feicheng	3938	2012	96052	151249.9	5251	32	19	97.5	40
威海市	**Weihai**									
环翠区	Huancui	2622	1166	199061	390255	7366	42	5.34	98	35.34
文登市	Wendeng	3308	1674	67052	129261	6786	31	8.6	100	33.8
荣成市	Rongcheng	3041	1579	68229	133998.4	7376	35	6.5	99	35.98
乳山市	Rushan	2412	829	47023	82582	6035	33	7.73	99.33	39.93
日照市	**Rizhao**									
东港区	Donggang	951	593	80983	141500	4609	45	10.68	80	40.99
岚山区	Lanshan	518	217	33753	56828	5001	33	8.9	66	38.3
五莲县	Wulian	1465	647	48158	47183	4480	25	9.45	91	37.05
莒 县	Juxian	1719	727	46700	52800	4505	36	18.4	93	39.6
莱芜市	**Laiwu**									
莱城区	Laicheng	3844	2098	114005	178798	5174	39	18	95.2	38.6
钢城区	Gangcheng	1353	600	50554	141219	5310	28	5.2	87.3	36.9
临沂市	**Linyi**									
兰山区	Lanshan	5509	2965	130925	266008	4995	37	11.5	98.18	31.53
罗庄区	Luozhuang	749	409	61627	104096	4218	34	12.2	100	34.02
河东区	Hedong	1011	414	17347	31150	4026	38	5.9	98	42
沂南县	Yinan	1490	767	33498	42861	3960	26	15.13	98.74	42.86
郯城县	Tancheng	1541	712	30040	40801.8	4126	30	9.2	92	36.4
沂水县	Yishui	2367	1030	45420	60692	4015	23	15.2	87.2	40.9
苍山县	Cangshan	1637	639	33254	41232	3980	27	9.5	96	39.5
费 县	Feixian	1252	619	32817	44912	3955	26	19.3	91.1	41.9
平邑县	Pingyi	1715	829	46659	64292.7	4017	28	15.14	90.63	40.06
莒南县	Junan	1578	699	36450	47601.7	3982	31	16.45	88	39.9
蒙阴县	Mengyin	1225	539	29894	38942	4021	28	16.8	93	44.4
临沭县	Linshu	1256	607	29439	40162	4014	25	10.96	83.89	46.17
德州市	**Dezhou**									

2-9 续表 4 continued

地 区	Area	医院、卫生院卫生技术人员数（人） Medical Technical Personnal of Hospitals (person)	医生（人） Doctor (person)	城镇在岗职工年平均人数（人） Annual Average Number of Fully-employed Workers in Town (person)	城镇在岗职工工资总额（万元） Total Wages of Fully-employed Workers in Town (10 000 yuan)	农村居民人均纯收入（元） Annual Per Capita Net Income (yuan)	农民人均住房面积（平方米） Per Capita Living Floor Space of Rural Residents (sq.m)	农民文化娱乐消费比重（%） Proportion of Farmer Cultural Entertainment Expense (Percentage)	农村彩电普及率（%） Adoption Rate of Rural Colour TV (Percentage)	农村恩格尔系数（%） Rural Engel's Coefficient (Percentage)
德城区	Decheng	3239	546	107087	154114	4639	34	3.44	100	40
陵 县	Lingxian	1392	626	27501	28929	4243	35	6	100	34
宁津县	Ningjin	1269	536	18531	20464	4410	32	4.2	85	38
庆云县	Qingyun	544	213	12725	12798	4148	27	2.8	78	70
临邑县	Linyi	1327	1100	26067	35433	4290	30	6.1	98.5	40.6
齐河县	Qihe	1812	1089	40826	49349	4403	38	10	96	39.2
平原县	Pingyuan	1056	494	27782	29617	4251	28	8.7	97	30
夏津县	Xiajin	987	635	15463	19776	4162	30	10.3	98	40
武城县	Wucheng	923	388	18235	32695	4218	32	8.3	80	40
乐陵市	Leling	1397	937	27526	26711	4191	24	4.5	95	40
禹城市	Yucheng	1218	508	30021	39723	4313	26	6	78	40
聊城市	**Liaocheng**									
东昌府区	Dongchangfu	4574	1764	100540	172137	3814	43	2.26	85	35.4
阳谷县	Yanggu	2012	798	40399	41502.2	3817	36	4.1	85	36
莘 县	Shenxian	2307	1219	26603	30205.5	3878	41	4.8	93	47
茌平县	Chiping	1328	580	37721	54551	4042	28	2	91	32.6
东阿县	Donge	1237	485	25433	31779	3896	35	5	93	33
冠 县	Guanxian	1305	554	23217	26767	3840	30	10.4	85	45.7
高唐县	Gaotang	1012	490	58030	74529	4331	36	13.5	100	35.68
临清市	Linqing	2216	909	40938	53888	3951	27	8.7	69	39.4
滨州市	**Binzhou**									
滨城区	Bincheng	2426	1200	118778	191751	4418	42	18.07	90	31.82
惠民县	Huimin	1759	901	29003	29489	4114	29	9.64	96	29.01
阳信县	Yangxin	919	322	16290	16067	3780	39	8.62	88	30.08
无棣县	Wudi	939	398	23312	30342	4058	30	6.48	82	28.77
沾化县	Zhanhua	640	190	13238	16935	4226	32	15.56	82	32.92
博兴县	Boxing	1394	556	27778	41590	4665	36	7.7	100	30.49
邹平县	Zouping	2461	1366	141501	231820	5226	28	4.54	100	32.76
菏泽市	**Heze**									

2-9 续表 5 continued

地 区	Area	医院、卫生院卫生技术人员数（人） Medical Technical Personnal of Hospitals (person)	医生（人） Doctor (person)	城镇在岗职工年平均人数（人） Annual Average Number of Fully-employed Workers in Town (person)	城镇在岗职工工资总额（万元） Total Wages of Fully-employed Workers in Town (10 000 yuan)	农村居民人均纯收入（元） Annual Per Capita Net Income (yuan)	农民人均住房面积（平方米） Per Capita Living Floor Space of Rural Residents (sq.m)	农民文化娱乐消费比重（%） Proportion of Farmer Cultural Entertainment Expens (Percentage)	农村彩电普及率（%） Adoption Rate of Rural Colour TV (Percentage)	农村恩格尔系数（%） Rural Engel's Coefficient (Percentage)
牡丹区	Mudan	5347	1925	112604	155459.4	3540	30	3.18	75	37.11
曹 县	Caoxian	3880	1365	42428	37757.6	3404	29	2.56	80.9	38.24
单 县	Shanxian	2487	692	35775	35161.6	3444	24	1.44	71.5	45.12
成武县	Chengwu	1617	607	31170	27537.1	3549	26	3.5	76.6	41.28
巨野县	Juye	2336	942	38819	35154.5	3515	23	2.23	69	41.16
郓城县	Yuncheng	2599	1040	35912	37011.6	3504	25	3.14	68	39.88
鄄城县	Juancheng	1151	623	27386	26249.3	3403	20	2.43	64	42.08
定陶县	Dingtao	1475	725	29173	29408.1	3512	23	2.61	85.1	43.83
东明县	Dongming	1290	841	29778	37492.6	3520	23	2.23	75	40.31

2-10 续表 continued

地 区	Area	各种社会福利收养性单位数（个） Number of Social Welfare Institutions (unit)	各种社会福利收养性单位床位数（床） Beds of Social Welfare Institutions (bed)	参加基本养老保险的职工数（人） Staff Involved in Endowment Insurance (person)	参加基本医疗保险的职工数（人） Staff Involved in Medical Insurance (person)	城镇居民最低生活保障人数（人） Cities Inhabitant Lowest Social Security Population (person)	参加农村合作医疗的人数（人） Population of Participates in the Rural Cooperatives Medical Service (person)	刑事案件立案件数（件） Number of Criminal Case Put on Record (unit)
济南市	**Jinan**							
历下区	Lixia	4	66	124214	66794	9314	10371	287
市中区	Shizhong	3	70	107994	61535	10846	80971	4626
槐荫区	Huaiyin	2	180	96000	45000	11999	47072	246
天桥区	Tianqiao	2	69	129600	51500	15646	69639	4015
历城区	Licheng	16	686	93074	53286	3966	463000	362
长清县	Changqing	11	554	38487	16036	3484	389431	2213
平阴县	Pingyin	9	619	37277	30212	1728	235757	1034
济阳县	Jiyang	8	349	32415	17026	4400	360815	214
商河县	Shanghe	12	421	30298	17675	2462	462062	1015
章丘市	Zhangqiu	31	3031	84629	68340	3904	775300	1623

2-10 续表 1 continued

地 区	Area	各种社会福利收养性单位数（个） Number of Social Welfare Institutions (unit)	各种社会福利收养性单位床位数（床） Beds of Social Welfare Institutions (bed)	参加基本养老保险的职工数（人） Staff Involved in Endowment Insurance (person)	参加基本医疗保险的职工数（人） Staff Involved in Medical Insurance (person)	城镇居民最低生活保障人数（人） Cities Inhabitant Lowest Social Security Population (person)	参加农村合作医疗的人数（人） Population of Participates in the Rural Cooperatives Medical Service (person)	刑事案件立案件数（件） Number of Criminal Case Put on Record (unit)
青岛市	**Qingdao**							
市南区	Shinan	20	1758	345000	315900	4907	0	5835
市北区	Shibei	36	2621	101000	989000	11855	0	362
四方区	Sifang	28	2169	122430	120500	9412	0	256
黄岛区	Huangdao	6	265	179740	150670	590	150125	1779
崂山区	Laoshan	9	458	106161	53827	610	165640	1142
李沧区	Licang	18	1160	109763	103245	8131	0	2548
城阳区	Chengyang	16	734	102135	124195	729	342788	1922
胶州市	Jiaozhou	19	2700	167099	87578	753	585508	2303
即墨市	Jimo	54	2748	180870	131000	1483	930382	3106
平度市	Pingdu	122	3600	121483	110625	694	1060177	2451
胶南市	Jiaonan	214	2400	153898	111445	1662	646775	2175
莱西市	Laixi	44	2596	99561	70837	975	587421	1893
淄博市	**Zibo**							
淄川区	Zichuan	21	1105	80585	43727	5104	260620	3010
张店区	Zhangdian	12	774	346682	503710	5046	201312	6237
博山区	Boshan	10	633	85537	63582	6697	150879	2780
临淄区	Linzi	28	850	59736	57458	2747	345300	2049
周村区	Zhoucun	8	372	53481	41227	2746	152854	1486
桓台县	Huantai	12	572	47654	38312	366	380370	1493
高青县	Gaoqing	9	650	26070	23271	446	136620	424
沂源县	Yiyuan	15	700	48334	44687	5937	257546	1332
枣庄市	**Zaozhuang**							
市中区	Shizhong	6	703	123125	106447	25003	165810	1171
薛城区	Xuecheng	12	1525	42875	143612	5198	209940	968
峄城区	Yicheng	7	1992	19968	11271	4566	215000	670
台儿庄区	Taierzhuang	6	1646	15107	11020	2022	44200	714
山亭区	Shanting	10	1835	18051	11095	12951	82400	258
滕州市	Tengzhou	18	4539	138134	99895	13103	877519	3761
东营市	**Dongying**							
东营区	Dongying	9	1007	13749	17054	3293	136813	956

2-10 续表 2 continued

地 区	Area	各种社会福利收养性单位数（个）Number of Social Welfare Institutions (unit)	各种社会福利收养性单位床位数（床）Beds of Social Welfare Institutions (bed)	参加基本养老保险的职工数（人）Staff Involved in Endowment Insurance (person)	参加基本医疗保险的职工数（人）Staff Involved in Medical Insurance (person)	城镇居民最低生活保障人数（人）Cities Inhabitant Lowest Social Security Population (person)	参加农村合作医疗的人数（人）Population of Participates in the Rural Cooperatives Medical Service (person)	刑事案件立案件数（件）Number of Criminal Case Put on Record (unit)
河口区	Hekou	8	749	9697	9668	1167	64215	183
垦利县	Kenli	9	719	12355	19800	716	147612	266
利津县	Lijin	8	728	19220	12590	1949	234210	92
广饶县	Guangrao	10	1320	50560	39820	1427	353228	469
烟台市	**Yantai**							
芝罘区	Zhifu	14	1585	110328	109631	4471	63809	3295
福山区	Fushan	10	615	88636	88325	1964	159337	644
牟平区	Muping	13	921	70096	46500	667	200263	1754
莱山区	Laishan	4	700	27076	10848	499	101937	435
长岛县	Changdao	3	66	4717	9089	231	13500	49
龙口市	Longkou	16	2205	83297	102996	1290	414862	618
莱阳市	Laiyang	19	1633	55528	89284	1045	223000	1240
莱州市	Laizhou	17	2500	100125	116918	1051	574493	1434
蓬莱市	Penglai	16	1300	68595	74851	475	277000	832
招远市	Zhaoyuan	16	1940	68060	72766	854	315490	1226
栖霞市	Qixia	14	487	36780	30899	3425	385000	309
海阳市	Haiyang	13	570	40138	41038	927	321362	895
潍坊市	**Weifang**							
潍城区	Weicheng	6	428	48744	40604	4517	159840	244
寒亭区	Hanting	10	731	44318	27116	1145	245695	170
坊子区	Fangzi	6	435	41858	32666	7786	140500	133
奎文区	Kuiwen	2	160	34214	34658	4985	36599	294
临朐县	Linqu	18	1528	76236	50838	1788	502500	287
昌乐县	Changle	15	1600	58610	44493	2894	459455	375
青州市	Qingzhou	21	1271	104050	70772	2765	685036	411
诸城市	Zhucheng	19	2310	117891	108157	3564	864159	569
寿光市	Shouguang	20	2649	99534	96232	744	787104	538
安丘市	Anqiu	15	2102	84900	49742	1593	791160	443
高密市	Gaomi	18	2135	89759	63656	2850	593815	518
昌邑市	Changyi	6	580	69540	47390	1862	420433	291

2-10 续表 3 continued

地　区	Area	各种社会福利收养性单位数（个） Number of Social Welfare Institutions (unit)	各种社会福利收养性单位床位数（床） Beds of Social Welfare Institutions (bed)	参加基本养老保险的职工数（人） Staff Involved in Endowment Insurance (person)	参加基本医疗保险的职工数（人） Staff Involved in Medical Insurance (person)	城镇居民最低生活保障人数（人） Cities Inhabitant Lowest Social Security Population (person)	参加农村合作医疗的人数（人） Population of Participates in the Rural Cooperatives Medical Service (person)	刑事案件立案件数（件） Number of Criminal Case Put on Record (unit)
济宁市	**Jining**							
市中区	Shizhong	2	100	24813	17163	12856	0	1866
任城区	Rencheng	12	1420	38958	20200	1505	435159	2045
微山县	Weishan	26	1533	34920	27840	3200	120000	201
鱼台县	Yutai	10	1040	28509	17876	1187	100694	609
金乡县	Jinxiang	15	1817	32326	21268	2030	90354	1413
嘉祥县	Jiaxiang	15	1580	40600	20836	3145	679200	163
汶上县	Wenshang	14	1120	34100	20515	2582	509110	163
泗水县	Sishui	13	1185	31410	19259	3641	86730	114
梁山县	Liangshan	16	500	45039	24000	2059	98255	1140
曲阜市	Qufu	15	1563	74855	26000	2180	467147	210
兖州市	Yanzhou	14	1838	100372	41896	6585	336769	1098
邹城市	Zoucheng	22	4217	172635	185566	5817	694343	2272
泰安市	**Taian**							
泰山区	Taishan	7	1000	157591	192203	10577	141067	298
岱岳区	Daiyue	22	1360	48300	21746	1595	688813	1028
宁阳县	Ningyang	12	1870	60914	30673	21192	579000	946
东平县	Dongping	14	1872	48393	23263	1936	579254	764
新泰市	Xintai	32	3188	182756	170063	7788	924836	933
肥城市	Feicheng	24	1680	146479	41484	4840	618219	203
威海市	**Weihai**							
环翠区	Huancui	13	1038	197508	218677	629	155600	1998
文登市	Wendeng	18	3694	100446	90145	399	408744	301
荣成市	Rongcheng	25	3640	103684	102895	223	339500	906
乳山市	Rushan	15	2106	83646	94520	156	362330	250
日照市	**Rizhao**							
东港区	Donggang	10	497	27428	18824	2061	400450	2698
岚山区	Lanshan	8	477	17233	14063	1096	323450	858
五莲县	Wulian	14	1315	44250	39612	1624	313909	468
莒　县	Juxian	20	850	29600	33000	4000	842000	1539
莱芜市	**Laiwu**							
莱城区	Laicheng	18	2004	128820	83579	11902	597472	1479

2-10 续表 4 continued

地 区	Area	各种社会福利收养性单位数（个） Number of Social Welfare Institutions (unit)	各种社会福利收养性单位床位数（床） Beds of Social Welfare Institutions (bed)	参加基本养老保险的职工数（人） Staff Involved in Endowment Insurance (person)	参加基本医疗保险的职工数（人） Staff Involved in Medical Insurance (person)	城镇居民最低生活保障人数（人） Cities Inhabitant Lowest Social Security Population (person)	参加农村合作医疗的人数（人） Population of Participates in the Rural Cooperatives Medical Service (person)	刑事案件立案件数（件） Number of Criminal Case Put on Record (unit)
钢城区	Gangcheng	5	469	52126	54178	725	164795	664
临沂市	**Linyi**							
兰山区	Lanshan	14	1300	240384	100673	2132	81532	4626
罗庄区	Luozhuang	7	878	29967	24638	2409	231200	1014
河东区	Hedong	10	1687	23315	19293	201	415000	1763
沂南县	Yinan	18	2156	43993	35889	7752	701275	1432
郯城县	Tancheng	12	560	44718	40886	2884	82200	2397
沂水县	Yishui	20	1896	55031	41900	4450	919834	1356
苍山县	Cangshan	22	3963	43939	39853	9746	897700	2608
费 县	Feixian	20	835	26900	22249	4456	695379	1555
平邑县	Pingyi	16	3080	43829	37092	6746	700584	1601
莒南县	Junan	18	1075	46708	46064	3735	709896	1119
蒙阴县	Mengyin	12	1341	35938	30342	3184	133000	920
临沭县	Linshu	12	1333	38649	34758	3065	24255	1267
德州市	**Dezhou**							
德城区	Decheng	10	643	122336	160765	11680	112653	1834
陵 县	Lingxian	13	915	23959	17502	3882	55860	1188
宁津县	Ningjin	18	1179	22574	17245	2673	386028	535
庆云县	Qingyun	9	457	12681	8293	1988	226927	759
临邑县	Linyi	11	1061	26253	24129	3546	418464	1112
齐河县	Qihe	30	1431	35015	29832	2750	442006	964
平原县	Pingyuan	13	560	27129	22112	2100	323700	917
夏津县	Xiajin	14	942	19730	15115	3230	17995	664
武城县	Wucheng	9	719	20971	13225	3917	274614	441
乐陵市	Leling	18	1013	27012	24110	3663	473335	1602
禹城市	Yucheng	11	1056	32438	26300	4206	375569	1103
聊城市	**Liaocheng**							
东昌府区	Dongchangfu	18	1210	119394	128784	10006	559779	335
阳谷县	Yanggu	17	1010	30263	20589	4851	32800	659
莘 县	Shenxian	23	714	34743	22516	10058	19800	1037
茌平县	Chiping	16	1400	40509	31053	5981	405821	664

2-10 续表 5 continued

地 区	Area	各种社会福利收养性单位数（个） Number of Social Welfare Institutions (unit)	各种社会福利收养性单位床位数（床） Beds of Social Welfare Institutions (bed)	参加基本养老保险的职工数（人） Staff Involved in Endowment Insurance (person)	参加基本医疗保险的职工数（人） Staff Involved in Medical Insurance (person)	城镇居民最低生活保障人数（人） Cities Inhabitant Lowest Social Security Population (person)	参加农村合作医疗的人数（人） Population of Participates in the Rural Cooperatives Medical Service (person)	刑事案件立案件数（件） Number of Criminal Case Put on Record (unit)
东阿县	Donge	10	420	28938	20949	3360	305505	44
冠　县	Guanxian	17	487	34002	22568	5487	27215	621
高唐县	Gaotang	12	1117	45618	40519	3316	305679	148
临清市	Linqing	15	760	63275	59987	8575	382391	221
滨州市	**Binzhou**							
滨城区	Bincheng	14	1596	93673	93875	3553	342240	2464
惠民县	Huimin	15	1300	25751	15089	5167	0	1247
阳信县	Yangxin	9	268	12932	11564	3224	308725	829
无棣县	Wudi	12	960	20903	17724	5392	296164	668
沾化县	Zhanhua	15	1200	13904	8175	4975	287972	526
博兴县	Boxing	14	282	39348	24270	3331	359092	1150
邹平县	Zouping	19	2100	59321	43608	981	502585	1620
菏泽市	**Heze**							
牡丹区	Mudan	23	2730	122172	76478	14842	800000	4973
曹　县	Caoxian	26	1760	36871	36974	6567	0	2246
单　县	Shanxian	20	3656	46979	29831	6150	880000	3705
成武县	Chengwu	12	1300	29240	20460	3802	40000	1225
巨野县	Juye	16	1760	43918	29658	4535	0	1142
郓城县	Yuncheng	21	1650	50441	34076	3732	30000	1982
鄄城县	Juancheng	16	3000	24908	24341	5070	0	770
定陶县	Dingtao	13	1772	29094	20992	4202	500000	962
东明县	Dongming	13	2630	36859	26828	5184	580000	973

2-11 续表 continued

地区	Area	行政区域土地面积（平方公里） Area of Administrative Land (sq.km.)	森林面积（公顷） Forest Area (hectare)	年末耕地总资源（公顷） Total Resources of Year-end Cultivated Land (hectare)	常用耕地面积（公顷） Commonly Used Cultivated Area (hectare)	水浇地（公顷） Irrigated Field (hectare)	工业废水排放量达标率（%） Success Rate of Industrial Waste Withdrawal (percentage)	工业烟尘排放量达标率（%） Success Rate of Industry Mist and Dust Withdrawal (percentage)	污水处理厂数（座） Number of Sewage Treatment Plants (unit)
济南市	**Jinan**								
历下区	Lixia	100.9	645	499	473	197	98.66	90.9	0
市中区	Shizhong	280.2	4533.3	6410	5116	2150	100	100	0
槐荫区	Huaiyin	151.5	0	5542	3511	1931	100	100	0
天桥区	Tianqiao	249	1218	7928	7357	2813	100	100	0
历城区	Licheng	1298.5	56987	32041	31368	16162	99	100	0
长清县	Changqing	1178	34987	42214	37330	20700	100	100	1
平阴县	Pingyin	827	18209.8	29445	27623	16959	97	96	1
济阳县	Jiyang	1076	18368	67614	64951	54397	100	100	1
商河县	Shanghe	1162.9	16310.1	71314	68250	68250	25	77	0
章丘市	Zhangqiu	1855	23735	81447	76050	70777	100	100	2
青岛市	**Qingdao**								
市南区	Shinan	30	0	0	0	0	100	100	1
市北区	Shibei	28.6	0	0	0	0	100	100	1
四方区	Sifang	34.6	0	0	0	0	100	100	1
黄岛区	Huangdao	273.2	7192.4	2419	2323	609	100	100	2
崂山区	Laoshan	389.3	22133	875	836	640	98	100	3
李沧区	Licang	98	0	73	73	0	100	100	1
城阳区	Chengyang	553.2	11466.7	4013	3963	2334	100	100	1
胶州市	Jiaozhou	1313	29050	55223	54626	49410	100	100	2
即墨市	Jimo	1780	27484	73808	73297	25271	100	100	1
平度市	Pingdu	3175.6	69458.7	157488	156886	144660	100	100	2
胶南市	Jiaonan	1802	64800	51292	51227	25041	100	100	1
莱西市	Laixi	1522	35754	70116	69542	57067	100	100	1
淄博市	**Zibo**								
淄川区	Zichuan	999	19527	16548	16420	3612	100	100	1
张店区	Zhangdian	360	4696	9061	8971	7103	100	100	4
博山区	Boshan	682	27868.2	7302.1	7224.1	1192.5	100	100	1
临淄区	Linzi	668	7625	32663	32663	29808.7	96.53	100	6
周村区	Zhoucun	263	2356	10573	10573	9400	100	100	1
桓台县	Huantai	499	5664	26104.3	26104.3	25253	100	100	1

2-11 续表 1 continued

地 区	Area	行政区域土地面积（平方公里） Area of Administrative Land (sq.km.)	森林面积（公顷） Forest Area (hectare)	年末耕地总资源（公顷） Total Resources of Year-end Cultivated Land (hectare)	常用耕地面积（公顷） Commonly Used Cultivated Area (hectare)	水浇地（公顷） Irrigated Field (hectare)	工业废水排放量达标率（%） Success Rate of Industrial Waste Withdrawal (percentage)	工业烟尘排放量达标率（%） Success Rate of Industry Mist and Dust Withdrawal (percentage)	污水处理厂数（座） Number of Sewage Treatment Plants (unit)
高青县	Gaoqing	831	19698	42238	42238	41279	100	100	1
沂源县	Yiyuan	1636	73333	14192	14126	6385	100	100	1
枣庄市	**Zaozhuang**								
市中区	Shizhong	373.9	9480	15396	10014	4917	89.79	100	1
薛城区	Xuecheng	507.8	9512	28245	21918	17305	96.75	69.23	1
峄城区	Yicheng	635	10063	38463	28497	17305	91.01	48.4	0
台儿庄区	Taierzhuang	533.3	11400	33836	28499	22708	96.24	98.84	0
山亭区	Shanting	1018.9	43834	38077	24367	14971	92.89	44.48	0
滕州市	Tengzhou	1494.2	19554	77136	77080	71082	96.13	95	1
东营市	**Dongying**								
东营区	Dongying	1155	11305.7	20832	18766	15400	98.88	100	1
河口区	Hekou	2139	9350	20260	18817	12428	100	100	1
垦利县	Kenli	2204	11940	31815	31682	29062	100	100	1
利津县	Lijin	1287	10840	52557	43420	42331	90.08	100	0
广饶县	Guangrao	1138	18613	58599	56638	48018	99.2	100	1
烟台市	**Yantai**								
芝罘区	Zhifu	169	6430	703	684	684	100	100	1
福山区	Fushan	707	19702	13331	13331	1706	97.5	100	1
牟平区	Muping	1588	71884	36365	36365	24990	100	100	0
莱山区	Laishan	258	7105.8	7945	7945	2970	100	100	1
长岛县	Changdao	56.1	3133	438	295	0	88	92	1
龙口市	Longkou	893	42387	19647	19647	17634	100	100	2
莱阳市	Laiyang	1731.5	32254	76698	75783	24778	90.98	99.68	1
莱州市	Laizhou	1878.1	45575.7	76844	67770	46120	100	100	1
蓬莱市	Penglai	1128.6	44666.7	35075	35075	22030	100	100	4
招远市	Zhaoyuan	1433	44783.7	39419	39419	31313	100	100	1
栖霞市	Qixia	2016	78874	50724	50216	27325	100	100	1
海阳市	Haiyang	1887	37069	68019	56757	22104	100	100	1
潍坊市	**Weifang**								
潍城区	Weicheng	272.3	4940.3	12560	11518	10532	90	100	0
寒亭区	Hanting	872	6989	35873	33095	27787	100	100	1
坊子区	Fangzi	345.5	2983.6	16180	15360	6678	100	100	1

2-11 续表 2 continued

地 区	Area	行政区域土地面积（平方公里） Area of Administrative Land (sq.km.)	森林面积（公顷） Forest Area (hectare)	年末耕地总资源（公顷） Total Resources of Year-end Cultivated Land (hectare)	常用耕地面积（公顷） Commonly Used Cultivated Area (hectare)	水浇地（公顷） Irrigated Field (hectare)	工业废水排放量达标率（%） Success Rate of Industrial Waste Withdrawal (percentage)	工业烟尘排放量达标率（%） Success Rate of Industry Mist and Dust Withdrawal (percentage)	污水处理厂数（座） Number of Sewage Treatment Plants (unit)
奎文区	Kuiwen	77.3	228	1631	1154	1154	100	100	1
临朐县	Linqu	1834	53888	58168	49237	29981	100	100	1
昌乐县	Changle	1101	22215.5	61510	51487	30629	100	100	1
青州市	Qingzhou	1569	25433.4	76754	60732	46867	100	100	1
诸城市	Zhucheng	2182.7	44086.3	119938	103540	95610	100	100	2
寿光市	Shouguang	2180	16372	100528	88311	71454	100	100	2
安丘市	Anqiu	1928	43404	106926	93907	45322	100	100	1
高密市	Gaomi	1603	32757	95622	88504	88504	100	100	2
昌邑市	Changyi	1812.2	18047.7	84524	67549	56609	100	100	2
济宁市	**Jining**								
市中区	Shizhong	39	70	0	0	0	96.7	99.2	1
任城区	Rencheng	881.1	1650	54368	53882	33407	99.3	99.5	1
微山县	Weishan	1780	7214	30631	26586	22903	99.45	99.13	1
鱼台县	Yutai	654.2	2335	39896	37697	12324	75	35	1
金乡县	Jinxiang	886.5	9371.8	54816	52651	51672	99.09	11.36	0
嘉祥县	Jiaxiang	973	14933	57707	57707	51442	100	99.6	1
汶上县	Wenshang	877.2	16000	54743	54743	47529	100	100	1
泗水县	Sishui	1070	25353	44047	41272	14150	100	100	1
梁山县	Liangshan	962.7	8880	64437	54808	49650	100	100	0
曲阜市	Qufu	896	15674.7	43043	42862	35812	99.25	100	1
兖州市	Yanzhou	648.2	19633.3	39597	36991	34510	99.8	100	1
邹城市	Zoucheng	1618.7	31356	62883	62704	35606	100	100	1
泰安市	**Taian**								
泰山区	Taishan	375.7	23159	8727	8635	8628	98.04	81.7	1
岱岳区	Daiyue	1750	49011.8	63168	60283	50127	96.73	90	0
宁阳县	Ningyang	1124.3	20730	67670	58379	41770	100	99.16	1
东平县	Dongping	1340.4	17554	61464	60237	44718	88	79	1
新泰市	Xintai	1933	469333	64157	64157	59734	99.59	99.51	2
肥城市	Feicheng	1277.3	32644.6	59079	58620	45237	100	100	1
威海市	**Weihai**								
环翠区	Huancui	731	26187.2	13780	13660	4296	100	100	3
文登市	Wendeng	1645	52696	55700	51581	25419	100	100	1

2-11 续表 3 continued

地 区	Area	行政区域土地面积（平方公里） Area of Administrative Land (sq.km.)	森林面积（公顷） Forest Area (hectare)	年末耕地总资源（公顷） Total Resources of Year-end Cultivated Land (hectare)	常用耕地面积（公顷） Commonly Used Cultivated Area (hectare)	水浇地（公顷） Irrigated Field (hectare)	工业废水排放量达标率（%） Success Rate of Industrial Waste Withdrawal (percentage)	工业烟尘排放量达标率（%） Success Rate of Industry Mist and Dust Withdrawal (percentage)	污水处理厂数（座） Number of Sewage Treatment Plants (unit)
荣成市	Rongcheng	1392	39189	54921	52604	22884	100	100	4
乳山市	Rushan	1668	39068	54509	46037	27353	100	100	1
日照市	**Rizhao**								
东港区	Donggang	1030	27207	27832	27758	3965	100	100	2
岚山区	Lanshan	759	22714	24491	23959	7892	28	85	1
五莲县	Wulian	1443	45068	40923	39887	12841	100	100	1
莒 县	Juxian	1952.4	54422	71922	69294	61527	100	100	1
莱芜市	**Laiwu**								
莱城区	Laicheng	1734	43399.6	51821	43076	23750	99.5	99.77	1
钢城区	Gangcheng	512	19528.1	12832	10318	3565	99.93	99.99	0
临沂市	**Linyi**								
兰山区	Lanshan	657	13651.8	19006	18882	1748	100	100	1
罗庄区	Luozhuang	370.6	4688	11244	10861	2116	100	100	1
河东区	Hedong	727.6	12837	31976	31818	6712	96	93	0
沂南县	Yinan	1774	46079	87749	67073	36666	97	96	1
郯城县	Tancheng	1306.6	32000	66573	65588	22426	100	100	0
沂水县	Yishui	2434.8	61241	100503	75310	15635	100	100	1
苍山县	Cangshan	1800	23933	104120	92050	41926	100	100	1
费 县	Feixian	1897.6	64183	74374	62168	13300	96	98	0
平邑县	Pingyi	1824.8	43935	61656	55262	13551	100	100	1
莒南县	Junan	1752	46091	68693	65014	21586	99	98	1
蒙阴县	Mengyin	1601.6	50667	46412	30222	11853	100	100	1
临沭县	Linshu	1038.1	19030	54910	52129	17237	100	100	1
德州市	**Dezhou**								
德城区	Decheng	352.7	8313.8	23142	22920	22323	100	100	2
陵 县	Lingxian	1213	16313	62219	62219	60219	60	60	1
宁津县	Ningjin	833	12111	48201	48092	47985	85	89	1
庆云县	Qingyun	502	7500	24312	24312	23213	100	100	1
临邑县	Linyi	1016	9322	52076	52076	52076	99.5	100	1
齐河县	Qihe	1554.5	53110.7	69185	67852	66598	100	100	1
平原县	Pingyuan	1047	16855	50453	50176	50175	100	100	1
夏津县	Xiajin	872	8826.5	54476	54476	54476	98	58	0

2-11 续表 4 continued

地 区	Area	行政区域土地面积（平方公里） Area of Administrative Land (sq.km.)	森林面积（公顷） Forest Area (hectare)	年末耕地总资源（公顷） Total Resources of Year-end Cultivated Land (hectare)	常用耕地面积（公顷） Commonly Used Cultivated Area (hectare)	水浇地（公顷） Irrigated Field (hectare)	工业废水排放量达标率（%） Success Rate of Industrial Waste Withdrawal (percentage)	工业烟尘排放量达标率（%） Success Rate of Industry Mist and Dust Withdrawal (percentage)	污水处理厂数（座） Number of Sewage Treatment Plants (unit)
武城县	Wucheng	748	11183	37867	37640	35563	100	95	0
乐陵市	Leling	1172	27216.3	62993	62993	62993	100	100	1
禹城市	Yucheng	990	24967	52638	52638	52638	100	100	1
聊城市	**Liaocheng**								
东昌府区	Dongchangfu	1254	15898	76958	76958	68893	97.19	93.29	1
阳谷县	Yanggu	1065	11093	66687	62426	61491	100	98	1
莘 县	Shenxian	1416	24155	85271	81106	81106	85	100	0
茌平县	Chiping	1120	20973	68100	68100	67616	100	100	1
东阿县	Donge	799	20342	46567	46455	44887	100	100	1
冠 县	Guanxian	1161	20677	79392	74666	74666	100	100	1
高唐县	Gaotang	949	20779	59145	59093	57408	100	100	1
临清市	Linqing	960	12569	66530	57988	57988	100	100	1
滨州市	**Binzhou**								
滨城区	Bincheng	1041	16000	41096	41096	35498	95.45	99.59	3
惠民县	Huimin	1357	38000	75155	75155	66372	97.4	97.49	1
阳信县	Yangxin	792.5	13734	42305	42022	37625	84.03	96.68	1
无棣县	Wudi	1998	13965.2	54476	52039	37010	100	100	1
沾化县	Zhanhua	2114	22020	57148	55151	40315	88.9	97.6	1
博兴县	Boxing	901	12000	44682	44682	44295	90.65	98.97	2
邹平县	Zouping	1250	20657	63340	63105	61305	98.06	99.5	1
菏泽市	**Heze**								
牡丹区	Mudan	1415.3	25331.8	80183	78776	75096	100	99.97	1
曹 县	Caoxian	1969	37529.1	103680	103680	102930	99.26	97.63	0
单 县	Shanxian	1702	27973.3	99265	91960	84174	99.46	98.13	0
成武县	Chengwu	949.4	8387.9	48956	48956	48280	97.93	100	0
巨野县	Juye	1303.4	22241	76448	76448	76148	98.11	100	0
郓城县	Yuncheng	1642.6	32759.2	102491	99173	86797	100	100	0
鄄城县	Juancheng	1041	24385	64899	55931	55872	99.05	98.87	0
定陶县	Dingtao	845.9	15892	49876	49876	49763	98.75	99.34	0
东明县	Dongming	1370	22716	68118	53731	49982	99.23	99.56	0

3

主要农产品产量调查资料

Investigation Material on Output of Major Farm Products

简要说明

农业生产调查。主要包括国家抽中县的农作物播种面积、种植业产品产量、畜牧业产品产量、农业中间消耗等抽样调查。调查网点有：319个农作物综合面积（包括小麦、玉米）调查村，80个棉花面积调查村，150个小麦产量调查村，150个玉米产量调查村，80个棉花产量调查村，90个猪存栏出栏量调查村，95个牛存栏出栏量调查村，95个羊存栏出栏量调查村，95个禽存栏出栏量调查村，247个农业中间消耗调查村。

抽样调查取得的数据，经过数据质量评估和国家统计局核实后，均作为全省法定统计数据对外发布使用。

Brief Introduction

Agricultural production investigation. Mainly includes crops sown area, crop production volume of output, animal husbandry volume of output, agricultural middle consumption of counties that pulled out by NBS. Investigation point includes: 319 investigation villages of crops synthesis area (including wheat, corn), 80 investigation villages of cotton area,150 investigation villages of wheat output, 150 investigation villages of corn output, 80 investigation villages of cotton output, 90 investigation villages of pig amounts of livestock and leave, 95 investigation villages of cow amounts of livestock and leave, 95 investigation villages of sheep amounts of livestock and leave, 95 investigation villages of fowls amounts of livestock and leave, 247 investigation villages of agricultural middle consumption.

After the data quality is appraised and the checking of NBS, The data of sample investigation is announced and used as legal statistical data.

3-1 历年粮食棉花播种面积
Grain Cotton Sown Area During All Previous Years

单位：千公顷 unit :1 000 hectares

年份 Year	粮食作物 Grain Crops	夏粮 Summer Grain Crops	#小麦 Wheat	秋粮 Autumn Grain Crops	#玉米 Corn	棉花 Cotton
1949	10976	3727	3583.8	7248.53	949.07	457
1952	11702	4090	3923.93	7612.33	996.8	697
1957	11494	4378	4147.87	7116.2	1373	774
1962	9920	3548	3294.8	6371.93	927.2	377
1965	9940	3925	3725.4	6014.87	1356.47	683
1970	9345	3540	3435.4	5804.4	1329	701
1975	9205	3853	3771.2	5352.67	1799.13	630
1978	8808	3758	3714.07	5049.8	2134.6	627
1979	8735	3755	3721.2	4980.13	2136.2	543
1980	8475	3697	3668.47	4777.47	2142.73	737
1981	8150	3531	3509.93	4619.33	2200.73	938
1982	7685	3352	3343.2	4333.13	2167.27	1339
1983	7795	3594	3587	4201.07	2191.53	1500
1984	7833	3810	3802.73	4023.07	2070.2	1712
1985	7984	3959	3952.07	4025.47	2087.53	1170
1986	8448	4229	4217.93	4218.93	2243.8	1010
1987	8215	4018	4004.4	4197.2	2314.53	1222
1988	8094	4062	4051.93	4031.8	2323.67	1403
1989	8058	3998	3991.43	4060.61	2398.07	1323
1990	8152	4152	4147.19	4000.33	2405.25	1409
1991	8088	4201	4197.45	3887.55	2535.91	1563
1992	7919	4132	4129.71	3786.8	2345.86	1489
1993	8213	4158	4156.03	3397.57	2439.8	760
1994	8014	4056	4048.96	3957.9	2454.6	793
1995	8132	4013	4010.87	4118.18	2694.84	666
1996	8237	4035	4031.64	4202.4	2826.65	482
1997	8083	4041	4037.59	4041.94	2626.83	396
1998	8133	3983	3981.95	4149.23	2781.89	414
1999	8099.25	4007.49	4006.75	4091.76	2768.17	365.78
2000	7772.4	3960.8	3960	3811.5	2615.7	543.8
2001	7153.5	3547.1	3545.7	3606.4	2505.2	735.4
2002	6912.61	3398.66	3397.48	3513.95	2530.07	664.89
2003	6415.41	3106.1	3105.13	3309.3	2405.89	881.69
2004	6313.88	3106.67	3105.7	3207.21	2455.05	1059.21
2005	6711.73	3279.93	3278.67	3431.81	2731.44	846.26
2006	6797.45	3355.46	3354.52	3441.99	2753.59	929.75

3-2 历年粮食棉花总产量

Grain Cotton Ultimate Output During All Previous Years

单位：万吨 unit:10 000 tons

年份 Year	粮食作物 Grain Crops	夏粮 Summer Grain Crops	#小麦 Wheat	秋粮 Autumn Grain Crops	#玉米 Corn	棉花 Cotton
1949	870.0	232.5	221.5	637.5	88.0	8.1
1952	1199.0	336.0	320.5	863.0	122.0	16.9
1957	1126.0	356.0	337.0	770.0	181.0	17.4
1962	910.0	212.5	198.5	697.5	101.0	3.9
1965	1332.0	364.0	347.5	968.0	237.0	19.9
1970	1464.5	329.5	318.5	1135.0	287.5	27.3
1975	2170.5	668.5	656.0	1502.0	491.0	24.1
1978	2288.0	809.0	803.5	1479.0	612.0	15.4
1979	2472.0	963.5	957.0	1508.5	730.0	16.7
1980	2384.0	770.0	766.0	1614.0	825.5	53.7
1981	2313.0	873.0	870.0	1440.0	794.0	67.5
1982	2375.0	826.5	824.0	1548.5	848.0	96.0
1983	2700.0	1201.5	1200.0	1498.5	822.0	122.5
1984	3040.0	1280.0	1278.5	1760.0	993.3	172.5
1985	3137.7	1497.8	1496.1	1639.9	937.7	106.2
1986	3250.0	1564.5	1562.4	1685.5	1016.5	94.1
1987	3393.7	1477.3	1474.1	1916.4	1170.2	124.4
1988	3225.0	1442.3	1440.1	1782.7	1149.4	113.7
1989	3249.9	1582.0	1580.6	1667.9	1124.0	102.5
1990	3570.4	1663.0	1661.4	1907.4	1252.1	102.8
1991	3917.0	1891.0	1889.8	2026.0	1383.8	135.1
1992	3589.3	1878.8	1878.3	1710.5	1150.8	67.7
1993	4100.0	2025.0	2024.3	2075.0	1390.9	41.0
1994	4091.1	2035.3	2033.1	2055.8	1401.5	55.9
1995	4245.0	2063.0	2061.9	2182.0	1543.0	47.1
1996	4332.7	2054.4	2053.7	2278.3	1614.0	37.2
1997	3852.2	2243.0	2241.3	1609.2	1106.0	35.4
1998	4264.8	2025.0	2024.5	2239.8	1610.4	41.3
1999	4269.0	2117.9	2117.7	2151.1	1551.4	39.2
2000	3837.7	1860.2	1860.0	1977.5	1467.5	59.0
2001	3720.6	1655.4	1655.2	2065.2	1532.4	78.1
2002	3292.7	1547.3	1547.1	1745.4	1316.0	72.2
2003	3435.5	1565.3	1565.0	1870.2	1411.0	87.7
2004	3516.7	1585.0	1584.6	1931.7	1499.2	109.8
2005	3917.4	1801.1	1800.5	2116.3	1735.4	84.6
2006	4048.8	1890.1	1889.8	2158.6	1761.3	102.3

3-3 历年粮食棉花单位面积产量

Per Unit of Area Output of Grain Cotton During All Previous Years

单位：公斤/公顷 unit:kg / hectare

年份 Year	粮食作物 Grain Crops	夏粮 Summer Grain Crops	#小麦 Wheat	秋粮 Autumn Grain Crops	#玉米 Corn	棉花 Cotton
1949	795	630	615	885	930	180
1952	1035	825	825	1140	1230	240
1957	990	810	810	1080	1320	225
1962	915	600	600	1095	1095	105
1965	1350	930	930	1620	1755	300
1970	1575	930	930	1965	2160	390
1975	2355	1740	1740	2805	2730	390
1978	2595	2160	2160	2925	2865	248
1979	2835	2565	2580	3030	3420	308
1980	2820	2085	2085	3375	3855	728
1981	2835	1725	2490	3120	3615	720
1982	3090	2475	2475	3585	3915	720
1983	3465	3345	3345	3570	3750	818
1984	3885	3375	3375	4380	4800	1005
1985	3930	3780	3780	4080	4500	908
1986	3840	3705	3705	3990	4530	930
1987	4125	3675	3675	4560	5055	1020
1988	3990	3555	3555	4425	4950	825
1989	4035	3960	3960	4110	4680	780
1990	4380	4005	4005	4770	5205	729
1991	4845	4500	4500	5205	5760	864
1992	4533	4547	4548	4517	4906	455
1993	4992	4870	4871	5117	5701	539
1994	5105	5018	5021	5194	5710	705
1995	5220	5140	5141	5299	5726	707
1996	5260	5092	5094	5421	5710	773
1997	4766	5550	5551	3981	4211	894
1998	5244	5084	5084	5398	5789	996
1999	5271	5285	5285	5257	5604	1072
2000	4938	4697	4697	5188	5610	1085
2001	5201	4667	4668	5726	6117	1062
2002	4763	4553	4554	4967	5202	1086
2003	5355	5039	5040	5651	5865	994
2004	5570	5102	5102	6023	6106	1036
2005	5837	5491	5492	6167	6353	1000
2006	5956	5633	5634	6271	6396	1100

3-4 历年主要畜禽存出栏和畜产品产量

Main Poultry Stock , Offtake and Livestock Product Output During All Previous Years

单位：万头、万只、万吨 unit:10 000 heads 10 000 heads 10 000 tons

年份 Year	猪 Pig		牛 Cattle		羊 Sheep		家禽 Fowl		肉类总产量 Meat Total Output	禽蛋产量 Fowl Eggs Output	奶类产量 Milk Output
	存栏 Stock	出栏 Offtake	存栏 Stock	出栏 Offtake	存栏 Stock	出栏 Offtake	存栏 Stock	出栏 Offtake			
1978	1992.1	901.2	227.6	4.6	756.4	142.4	6766		60.8	22.5	6.83
1979	2117.6	1047.5	221.5	6.7	925.8	228.6	7204		65.18	23.67	6.95
1980	2112.5	1241.6	217.8	8.8	1041.3	377.5	7997		90.1	25.62	6.8
1981	1901.1	1296.8	213.7	11.5	1025.6	460.7	8075		96.26	29.47	5.24
1982	1726.2	1213.2	213.6	10.6	989.5	521.6	9115		94.98	34.3	8.77
1983	1562.7	1159.2	222.1	18.9	901.8	616.3	10216.8		94.54	41.07	11.43
1984	1681.5	1284	232.6	18.4	753.9	519.1	14688.9		104.38	62.28	13.34
1985	1812.8	1482.6	258	27.6	783.3	558.3	16548.2	8283.1	128.62	72.5	13.26
1986	1668.9	1681.2	292.5	32.3	985.3	617.6	15120.7	9234.5	141.78	69.66	15.81
1987	1547	1514	344.6	49.8	1404.1	842.1	16916.3	11397.3	141.02	79.14	17.28
1988	1688.6	1619.6	416	69	1436.4	1219	21582.1	15904	171.47	102.97	19.53
1989	1604.1	1845.4	472.4	82.8	1491.3	1348.4	20471.3	16701.2	195.63	109.43	21.24
1990	1576.7	1936.2	511.8	110.1	1528.1	1416.4	23974.6	22769	221.61	124.25	22.53
1991	1599.4	1983.5	501.4	119.5	1591.2	1348.7	24136.8	30792.7	241.49	149.14	23.65
1992	1602.6	2046	531.9	140.9	1655.2	1366.1	25810.8	33467.9	250.67	154.3	25.17
1993	1603.7	2092.9	603	177.1	1703.5	1411	27188.7	42837.3	286.61	184.07	28.05
1994	1701.5	2185.7	681.3	213.1	1799.8	1668.2	35118.6	64716.7	338.77	240.75	32.45
1995	1718.1	2453	714.1	248.4	1866.1	2034.1	34613.8	71286.5	394.42	247.15	36.98
1996	1723.6	2500.9	740.1	272.4	1877.2	2051.8	37485	73508	405.52	267.3	41.14
1997	2209.7	2801.1	811.9	334.5	2038.6	2269.3	41833	82549	460.64	294.3	45.82
1998	2485.9	3123.2	911.8	354.9	2322	2518.9	48484	91299	497.9	321.98	53.98
1999	2560.5	3248.1	977.3	391.1	2536.2	2838.8	53332	100246	524.49	349.06	61.29
2000	2660.34	3426.78	1008.61	413.8	2784.73	3014.91	58558	109168	560.15	366.22	70.47
2001	2769.41	3594.69	1006.85	461.8	2904.47	3210.88	61589.23	119102.29	595.44	379.04	90.43
2002	2882.96	3803.18	1018.93	488.12	3039.45	3358.58	65231.51	126352.58	626.99	399.41	116.76
2003	2975.21	4016.16	1040.17	509.11	3133.67	3466.05	67431.01	135818.96	662.11	424.69	148.38
2004	3058.19	4330.24	997.76	530.6	3286.77	3641.44	69690.94	146834.98	696.53	432.87	188.68
2005	3070.33	4546.88	970.52	546.68	3260.21	3810.92	66953.11	173684.05	736.93	441.83	220.97
2006	2778.51	4681.63	818.24	560.64	2918.1	3840.39	63839.62	180868.37	762.94	430.52	238.65

3-5 全省粮食生产情况

Whole Province Grain Production Situation Table

指标名称	index	播种面积（千公顷）Sowing Area (1 000 hectares)	产量（万吨）Output (10 000 tons)	每公顷产量（千克）Output Per Hectare (kg)
全年粮食	**Annual Grain**	**6797.45**	**4048.77**	**5956.3**
其中：夏收粮食	Among:Summer Grain	3355.46	1890.13	5633.0
秋收粮食	Autumn Grain	3441.99	2158.64	6271.49
一、谷物	**Cereal**	**6279.12**	**3774.02**	**6010.4**
（一）稻谷	Rice	125.68	106.61	8482.7
其中：籼稻	Among:Indica Rice	0.00	0.00	0.0
粳稻	Japonica Rice	0.00	0.00	0.0
糯稻	Glutinous Erce	0.00	0.00	0.0
1、早稻	Early Season Rice	0.00	0.00	0.0
2、中稻和一季晚稻	Semilate Rice and a Season Late Rice	125.68	106.61	8482.7
3、双季晚稻	Two Seasons Late Rice	0.00	0.00	0.0
（二）小麦	Wheat	3354.52	1889.79	5633.6
其中：硬粒小麦	Smong:Flint Wheat	1493.51	915.24	6128.1
软粒小麦	Miller Wheat	0.00	0.00	0.0
1、冬小麦	Winter Wheat	3353.84	1889.65	5634.3
2、春小麦	Spring Wheat	0.68	0.14	2058.8
（三）玉米	Corn	2753.59	1761.28	6396.3
（四）谷子	Millet	25.54	9.30	3641.3
（五）高粱	Jowar	14.18	5.00	3526.1
（六）其它谷物	Other Cereal	5.61	2.04	3636.4
其中：大麦	Among: Barley	0.24	0.09	3750.0
燕麦	Oats	0.00	0.00	0.0
荞麦	Buck Wheat	0.00	0.00	0.0
二、豆类	**Beans**	**236.13**	**65.61**	**2778.6**
其中：大豆	Among :Soybean	224.03	62.12	2772.8
绿豆	Urad	8.07	1.74	2156.1
红小豆	Red Bean	0.92	0.22	2391.3
三、薯类（折粮）	**Tubers**	**282.20**	**209.14**	**7411.1**

3-6 全省农作物播种面积
Whole Province Sown Areas of Farm Crops

计量单位：千公顷 unit:1 000 hectares

指标名称	index	2006	2005	比上年增减（%） Add or Subtract Compare with Last Year
全年农作物播种面积	**Total Sown Area**	**10727.93**	**10736.06**	**-0.1**
一、粮食	**Grain**	**6797.45**	**6711.73**	**1.3**
其中：夏收粮食	Among:Summer Grain	3355.46	3279.93	2.3
（一）谷物	Cereal	6279.12	6178.08	1.6
1. 稻谷	Rice	125.68	119.80	4.9
2. 小麦	Wheat	3354.52	3278.67	2.3
其中：硬粒小麦	Among:Flint Wheat	1493.51	1001.14	49.2
①冬小麦	Winter Wheat	3353.84	3273.97	2.4
②春小麦	Spring Wheat	0.68	4.70	-85.5
3. 玉米	Corn	2753.59	2731.44	0.8
4. 谷子	Millet	25.54	28.71	-11.0
5. 高粱	Jowar	14.18	13.89	2.1
6. 其他谷物	Other Cereal	5.61	5.57	0.7
其中：大麦	Among:Barley	0.24	0.18	33.3
（二）豆类	Beans	236.13	251.71	-6.2
其中：大豆	Among:Soybean	224.03	238.69	-6.1
绿豆	Urad	8.07	9.11	-11.4
红小豆	Red Bean	0.92	1.06	-13.2
（三）薯类（折粮）	Tubers	282.20	281.94	0.1
二、油料	**Oil-bearing Crops**	**870.31**	**899.81**	**-3.3**
其中：花生	Among:Peanuts	857.90	884.81	-3.0
油菜籽	Rapeseeds	10.66	12.41	-14.1
芝麻	Sesame	1.54	1.77	-13.0
向日葵	Sunflower	0.03	0.23	-87.0
三、棉花	**Cotton**	**929.75**	**846.26**	**9.9**
四、麻类合计	**Fiber Crops**	**0.45**	**0.68**	**-33.8**
其中：黄红麻	Among:Jute and Ambary Hemp	0.39	0.58	-32.8
大麻（线麻）	Cannabis Sativa	0.02	0.07	-71.4
五、糖料	**Sugar Crops**	**0.01**	**0.002**	**400.0**
（二）甜菜	Beetroots	0.01	0.002	400.0
六、烟叶	**Tobacco**	**33.41**	**34.59**	**-3.4**
其中：烤烟	Among:Flue-cured Tobacco	32.76	33.88	-3.3
七、药材	**Medicinal Materials**	**32.05**	**32.32**	**-0.8**
八、蔬菜（含菜用瓜）	**Vegetables**	**1738.19**	**1847.69**	**-5.9**
九、瓜果类	**Melon and Fruit**	**267.85**	**291.96**	**-8.3**
其中：西瓜	Among:Watermelon	212.28	232.74	-8.8
甜瓜	Muskmelon	39.19	40.48	-3.2
草莓	Strawberry	11.80	12.69	-7.0
十、其它作物	**Other Crops**	**58.46**	**71.02**	**-17.7**
其中：青饲料	Among:Greenfeed	3.65	5.24	-30.3
十一、耕地面积	**Cultivated Land**	**6326.00**	**6339.38**	**-0.2**
十二、非耕地上的播种面积	**Sown Area on Noncultivated Land**	**95.00**	**96.00**	**-1.0**

3-7 全省畜牧业主要产品生产情况

Main for Entire Province Animal Husbandry Product Production Situation

指标名称	index	计量单位	unit	2005	2006	2006年比2005年增减（+、-）Add or Subtract, 2006 Compared with 2005	
						绝对数 Absolute Number	% Percentage
一、主要畜、禽存栏情况	The Situation for Main Livestock,Birds and Beasts Amount of Livestock on Hand						
猪	Hogs	万头	10 000 heads	3070.33	2778.51	-291.82	-9.5
#能繁殖的母猪	Sow Which can Reproduce	万头	10 000 heads	393.82	362.58	-31.24	-7.9
牛	Cattle and Buffaloes	万头	10 000 heads	970.52	818.24	-152.28	-15.7
羊	Goats and Sheep	万只	10 000 heads	3260.21	2918.1	-342.11	-10.5
家禽	Fowl	万只	10 000 heads	66953.1	63839.62	-3113.49	-4.7
二、主要畜、禽出栏情况	The Situation for Leaving the Pen of the Main Livestock,the Birds and Beasts						
猪	Hogs	万头	10 000 heads	4546.88	4681.63	134.75	3.0
牛	Cattle and Buffaloes	万头	10 000 heads	546.68	560.64	13.96	2.6
羊	Goats and Sheep	万只	10 000 heads	3810.92	3840.39	29.47	0.8
家禽	Fowl	万只	10 000 heads	173684.0	180868.37	7184.32	4.1
三、主要畜产品产量情况	Main Output of Livestock Product						
肉类总产量	Pork	万吨	10 000 tons	736.93	762.94	26.01	3.5
#猪肉	Beet	万吨	10 000 tons	363.64	380.68	17.04	4.7
牛肉	Mutton	万吨	10 000 tons	80.72	81.08	0.36	0.4
羊肉	Fowl Meat	万吨	10 000 tons	36.36	36.64	0.28	0.8
禽肉	Fowl Eggs Products	万吨	10 000 tons	244.98	254.80	9.83	4.0
禽蛋产量	Milk Products	万吨	10 000 tons	441.83	430.52	-11.31	-2.6
牛奶产量	Milk Products	万吨	10 000 tons	187.07	215.80	28.73	15.4
绵羊毛产量	Sheep Wool Products	万吨	10 000 tons	2.16	1.80	-0.35	-16.4

3-8 调查县农用生产资料准备情况

Preparation Situation of Capital Goods for Agriculture on Investigation County

2006

指标名称	name of index	单位	unit	需求量 Demand Level	可供量 Supply Level	可供量比重% Percentage of Supply Level
一、化肥	**Chemical Fertilizer**	**吨**	**ton**	**3231148**	**3202427**	**99.1**
（1）氮	Nitrogen	吨	ton	1338288	1333180	99.6
（2）磷	Phosphorus	吨	ton	659850	603377	91.4
（3）钾	Potassium	吨	ton	180636	185948	102.9
（4）复合肥	Compound Fertilizer	吨	ton	1013344	1042057	102.8
（5）其 它	Other	吨	ton	39030	37865	97.0
二、农药	**Pesticide**	**公斤**	**kg**	**12627881**	**12993267**	**102.9**
三、农用薄膜	**Agricul Tural Film**	**吨**	**ton**	**81852**	**93551**	**114.3**
其中：地膜	Among:Mulch Film	吨	ton	33285	34120	102.5
四、柴油	**Diesel Oil**	**吨**	**ton**	**317833**	**314987**	**99.1**
五、种子	**Seed**					
粮食种子	Grain Seed	吨	ton	254723	258008	101.3
棉花种子	Cotton Seed	吨	ton	12470	12756	102.3
油料种子	Seed of Oil Bearing Materials	吨	ton	49937	53849	107.8

3-9 分市粮食生产情况

Grain Production Situation by City

2006

地 区	Area	播种面积（公顷） Sown Area（hectare）	总产量 绝对数（吨） Absolute Number（ton）	Total Cutput 比上年增减（%） Add or Subtract Compare with Last Year
全省总计	**Total**	**6797450**	**40487721**	**3.4**
济南市	Jinan	443419	2679131	3
青岛市	Qingdao	497858	3039266	-1.8
淄博市	Zibo	223016	1435105	9.1
枣庄市	Zaozhuang	263099	1797565	12.6
东营市	Dongying	120528	767314	18.2
烟台市	Yantai	385959	2346639	8.4
潍坊市	Weifang	752468	4331772	2.6
济宁市	Jining	580723	3951352	12.9
泰安市	Taian	411534	2731253	8.1
威海市	Weihai	162271	963428	1.4
日照市	Rizhao	173037	1045519	4.2
莱芜市	Laiwu	50262	266865	6
临沂市	Linyi	710417	4122868	6.3
德州市	Dezhou	780453	5274257	18.9
聊城市	Liaocheng	684706	4238728	5.7
滨州市	Binzhou	398980	2582523	9.3
菏泽市	Heze	900706	4791403	16.8

3-10 分市小麦生产情况

Wheat Production Situation by City

2006

地 区	Area	播种面积（公顷） Sown Area（hectare）	总产量 绝对数（吨） Absolute Number（ton）	Total Cutput 比上年增减（%） Add or Subtract Compare with Last Year
全省总计	**Total**	**3354520**	**18897900**	**5**
济南市	Jinan	201787	1169006	5.6
青岛市	Qingdao	254143	1548928	4.6
淄博市	Zibo	106652	645307	8.9
枣庄市	Zaozhuang	139680	903663	7.7
东营市	Dongying	52438	327100	17
烟台市	Yantai	171423	900985	14.7
潍坊市	Weifang	366807	2175453	10.5
济宁市	Jining	310327	1966760	11
泰安市	Taian	200203	1239183	14.2
威海市	Weihai	82815	448466	2.2
日照市	Rizhao	82450	422877	7.7
莱芜市	Laiwu	17862	80168	17
临沂市	Linyi	327189	1713338	5.6
德州市	Dezhou	409394	2645894	26.6
聊城市	Liaocheng	367966	2193004	4.1
滨州市	Binzhou	201208	1229517	10.9
菏泽市	Heze	636157	3354582	16.6

3-11 分市玉米生产情况
Corn Production Situation by City
2006

地 区	Area	播种面积（公顷）Sown Area（hectare）	总产量 绝对数（吨）Absolute Number（ton）	Total Cutput 比上年增减（%）Add or Subtract Compare with Last Year
全省总计	**Total**	**2753585**	**17612805**	**1.5**
济南市	Jinan	188434	1231231	1.7
青岛市	Qingdao	216217	1372166	-7.2
淄博市	Zibo	105501	752412	10.5
枣庄市	Zaozhuang	97459	728862	18.5
东营市	Dongying	54863	387118	24.2
烟台市	Yantai	172904	1222076	5.6
潍坊市	Weifang	348938	1992792	-3
济宁市	Jining	184289	1368495	20.7
泰安市	Taian	167075	1218393	6.3
威海市	Weihai	61203	419153	0.2
日照市	Rizhao	53320	351559	6.2
莱芜市	Laiwu	25963	142115	7.7
临沂市	Linyi	223707	1377483	13.1
德州市	Dezhou	351232	2528805	27.9
聊城市	Liaocheng	290502	1935819	8.5
滨州市	Binzhou	186848	1313827	7.5
菏泽市	Heze	215499	1250682	19.2

3-12 分市棉花生产情况
Cotton Production Situation by City
2006

地 区	Area	播种面积（公顷）Sown Area（hectare）	总产量 绝对数（吨）Absolute Number（ton）	Total Cutput 比上年增减（%）Add or Subtract Compare with Last Year
全省总计	**Total**	**929753**	**1023100**	**20.9**
济南市	Jinan	31407	37083	4.5
青岛市	Qingdao	3462	3954	-2.2
淄博市	Zibo	17639	18359	-8.3
枣庄市	Zaozhuang	2850	3439	17.5
东营市	Dongying	103456	123551	18.4
烟台市	Yantai	305	598	2.2
潍坊市	Weifang	39256	46100	-5.4
济宁市	Jining	111684	150011	3.7
泰安市	Taian	8400	12366	-16.2
威海市	Weihai			
日照市	Rizhao	1131	1032	2
莱芜市	Laiwu	693	976	88.1
临沂市	Linyi	10615	14728	23
德州市	Dezhou	131619	214292	6.1
聊城市	Liaocheng	69472	84727	4.7
滨州市	Binzhou	137009	174207	14.8
菏泽市	Heze	225555	263265	5.9

3-13 分市油料生产情况
Oil Bearing Materials Production Situation by City
2006

地 区	Area	播种面积（公顷）Sown Area（hectare）	总产量 Total Cutput	
			绝对数（吨）Absolute Number（ton）	比上年增减（%）Add or Subtract Compare with Last Year
全省总计	**Total**	**870305**	**3582387**	**-1.5**
济南市	Jinan	16108	57238	0.3
青岛市	Qingdao	101682	471897	-7.1
淄博市	Zibo	4597	13802	-3.4
枣庄市	Zaozhuang	31049	131799	2.3
东营市	Dongying	1742	5656	-1.9
烟台市	Yantai	116848	461167	0.6
潍坊市	Weifang	54355	238779	-1.6
济宁市	Jining	61839	278013	-6.3
泰安市	Taian	44694	172766	-0.1
威海市	Weihai	66767	245149	-0.3
日照市	Rizhao	53729	222530	4.1
莱芜市	Laiwu	6505	16183	-7
临沂市	Linyi	165210	712049	5.3
德州市	Dezhou	7425	35200	-14
聊城市	Liaocheng	46224	190073	-6.3
滨州市	Binzhou	3292	9522	1
菏泽市	Heze	88239	320564	-7.6

3-14 分市蔬菜生产情况
Vegetable Production Situation by City
2006

地 区	Area	播种面积（公顷）Sown Area（hectare）	总产量 Total Cutput	
			绝对数（吨）Absolute Number（ton）	比上年增减（%）Add or Subtract Compare with Last Year
全省总计	**Total**	**1738186**	**83093182**	**-3.5**
济南市	Jinan	121968	7104258	1.3
青岛市	Qingdao	131083	6051239	4.5
淄博市	Zibo	28287	1923753	-43.1
枣庄市	Zaozhuang	109802	5460928	3.9
东营市	Dongying	35062	2124262	1.4
烟台市	Yantai	56769	2754669	-4.5
潍坊市	Weifang	182091	9589947	-7.2
济宁市	Jining	237215	9104880	-11.5
泰安市	Taian	137065	7074585	1.7
威海市	Weihai	20982	1072071	4.2
日照市	Rizhao	23065	1246995	-1.2
莱芜市	Laiwu	35825	1364031	-6.4
临沂市	Linyi	136899	6004651	3.7
德州市	Dezhou	98758	4887585	-10.3
聊城市	Liaocheng	167558	8266282	8.2
滨州市	Binzhou	40816	2199172	-11.6
菏泽市	Heze	174941	6863874	-1.5

3-15　分市肉类总产量
Meat Production by City

单位：万吨　　unit:10 000 tons

地 区	Area	2006	比上年增减（%） Add or Subtract Compare with Last Year
全省总计	**Total**	**762.94**	**3.5**
济南市	Jinan	42.95	2.1
青岛市	Qingdao	84.26	2.8
淄博市	Zibo	15.12	-10.6
枣庄市	Zaozhuang	23.95	5.7
东营市	Dongying	21.46	16.1
烟台市	Yantai	43.83	22.5
潍坊市	Weifang	119.65	-7.6
济宁市	Jining	75.35	-12.5
泰安市	Taian	41.11	-2.4
威海市	Weihai	11.04	-4.4
日照市	Rizhao	16.12	0.9
莱芜市	Laiwu	5.86	-10.9
临沂市	Linyi	62.68	-4.8
德州市	Dezhou	59.17	1.3
聊城市	Liaocheng	49.79	-19.9
滨州市	Binzhou	32.06	-2.4
菏泽市	Heze	55.81	6.1

3-16　分市禽蛋产量
Fowls Egg Production by City

单位：万吨　　unit:10 000 tons

地 区	Area	2006	比上年增减（%） Add or Subtract Compare with Last Year
全省总计	**Total**	**430.52**	**-2.6**
济南市	Jinan	49.64	0.5
青岛市	Qingdao	36.85	-4.6
淄博市	Zibo	9.79	-35.2
枣庄市	Zaozhuang	11.53	6
东营市	Dongying	12.48	14.9
烟台市	Yantai	32.72	0.8
潍坊市	Weifang	28.85	-22.7
济宁市	Jining	47.77	-13.2
泰安市	Taian	21.07	-3.7
威海市	Weihai	10.58	10.7
日照市	Rizhao	11.8	-3.2
莱芜市	Laiwu	3.23	-12.3
临沂市	Linyi	23.51	-11.8
德州市	Dezhou	33	-26.9
聊城市	Liaocheng	23.28	-23.4
滨州市	Binzhou	15.7	-23.3
菏泽市	Heze	33.73	1.8

3-17 分市奶类产量
Milk Production by City

单位：万吨　　unit:10 000 tons

地区	Area	2006	比上年增减（%） Add or Subtract Compare with Last Year
全省总计	**Total**	**238.65**	**8**
济南市	Jinan	26.83	16.9
青岛市	Qingdao	57.29	12.7
淄博市	Zibo	9.18	-12.3
枣庄市	Zaozhuang	2.38	19.9
东营市	Dongying	9.06	9.5
烟台市	Yantai	24.02	12.1
潍坊市	Weifang	23.58	-4.7
济宁市	Jining	9.16	22.5
泰安市	Taian	28.5	37.5
威海市	Weihai	22.99	13.9
日照市	Rizhao	0.6	6.4
莱芜市	Laiwu	0.31	81.5
临沂市	Linyi	6.98	-9.1
德州市	Dezhou	12.8	-0.2
聊城市	Liaocheng	4.65	13.5
滨州市	Binzhou	10.82	16.5
菏泽市	Heze	4.97	15.5

3-18 分市园林水果生产情况
Gardens Fruit Production Situation by City

单位:吨　　unit:ton

地区	Area	2006	比上年增减（+、-） Add or Subtract Compare with Last Year	
			绝对数 Absolute Number	% Percentage
全省总计	**Total**	**12588158**	**573391**	**4.8**
济南市	Jinan	439055	12641	3
青岛市	Qingdao	827755	90455	12.3
淄博市	Zibo	550561	26153	5
枣庄市	Zaozhuang	219230	919	0.4
东营市	Dongying	95980	15308	19
烟台市	Yantai	3609160	315101	9.6
潍坊市	Weifang	1064042	-117455	-9.9
济宁市	Jining	235348	-6756	-2.8
泰安市	Taian	554213	6401	1.2
威海市	Weihai	690455	116333	20.3
日照市	Rizhao	190787	-11661	-5.8
莱芜市	Laiwu	100891	2743	2.8
临沂市	Linyi	1619079	114385	7.6
德州市	Dezhou	573617	-86020	-13
聊城市	Liaocheng	390758	-42442	-9.8
滨州市	Binzhou	862837	183481	27
菏泽市	Heze	564390	-46195	-7.6

4

城镇居民生活调查资料

Investigation Material of City and Town Residential Life

编辑单位：城镇住户调查处　Editorial Unit: the City Inhabitant Investigation Office
编　　委：姜宏济　Editorial Board: Jiang Hongji
责任编辑：张立新　Executive Editor-in-Chief: Zhang Lixin
校　　对：张立新　Proofreader: Zhang Lixin
电　　话：86129461　Telephone: 86129461

简要说明

一、本资料反映山东城镇居民2006年度生活状况，包括家庭基本情况、人口就业情况、居民收支情况、居住及耐用消费品拥有情况、消费性支出情况等。

二、城镇居民消费性支出包括八大类：食品、衣着、设备用品及服务、医疗保健、交通和通讯、娱乐文教服务、居住、杂项商品和服务。

三、本部分数据来源于全省27个调查市、县共计3000户城镇居民家庭的抽样调查汇总资料。

四、资料数据缺少部分是由于制度方法变动，指标口径不一致，数据无法获取造成的。

五、年人均指标是按全部家庭人口进行平均的。如，年人均工资及补贴收入是职工工资及补贴收入总额按全部家庭人口的平均数，而不是按职工人数计算的职工平均工资。其他指标类同。

六、表26《全省城市居民主要指标情况表》是由17个地级市加权汇总得到的资料。

七、表27《全省县城居民主要指标情况表》是由20个调查县（市）加权汇总得到的资料。

Brief Introduction

Ⅰ.This material reflects Shandong province city inhabitant living condition in 2006, including the family basic situation, the population employment situation, the inhabitant revenue and expenditure situation, the housing and the durable consumable commodity situation, the consumption disbursement situation and so on.

Ⅱ. City inhabitant consumption disbursement includes eight big kinds: Food, attire, equipment thing and service, medical health care, transportation and communication, entertainment culture and education service, housing, miscellaneous commodity and service.

Ⅲ. This part of data originates from the investigated and compiled materials including total 3000 households city inhabitant family sample of 27 investigation cities(counties)in the entire province.

Ⅳ. The lacked part of material data is as the system method is changed, the target caliber is inconsistent and the data is unable to gain.

Ⅴ. The year average per (person) target is carrying on averaging according to the complete family population. For example, the year average per (person) wages and the subsidy income is average data from the staff wages and the subsidy total income divided by the complete family population, but is not average wages according to the staff population. Other targets are similar.

Ⅵ. Table 26 "City Inhabitant Major Targets Situation Table in Entire Province" is a material which is weighted and compiled to obtain by materials of 17 cities.

Ⅶ. Table 27 "County Inhabitant Major Targets Situation Table in Entire Province" is a material which is weighted and compiled to obtain by materials of 20 counties.

4-1 全省主要指标情况表
Leading Indicator Table of Whole Province

单位：元/人

unit：yuan/person

类别	Classification	2004	同比增长% Increase Compared with Last Year	2005	同比增长% Increase Compared with Last Year	2006	同比增长% Increase Compared with Last Year
一、期初手存现金	**Cash in Hand at Term-beginning**	**513**	**-0.2**	**395**	**-23.1**	**473**	**19.8**
二、家庭总收入	**Total Income**	**1018**	**12.5**	**11608**	**13.9**	**13223**	**13.9**
其中：可支配收入	Disposable Income	9438	12.4	10745	13.8	12192	13.5
（一）工薪收入	Income of Wages and Salaries	8327	12.2	9027	8.4	10442	15.7
1.工资及补贴收入	Wages and Subsidies	8189	11.8	8853	8.1	10272	16.0
2.其他劳动收入	Other Income	138	43.1	174	25.5	170	-2.2
（二）经营净收入	Net Business Income	300	31.6	492	64.1	558	13.4
（三）财产性收入	Income from Properties	117	6.4	152	30.0	221	45.3
（四）转移性收入	Income from Transfer	1443	10.9	1937	34.2	2002	3.3
三、出售财物收入	**Income from Properties Sale**	**24**	**-12.0**	**27**	**15.0**	**83**	**206.8**
四、借贷收入	**Income from Lending**	**5619**	**50.3**	**5317**	**-5.4**	**6499**	**22.2**
五、家庭总支出	**Total Expenditure**	**9026**	**8.9**	**9889**	**9.6**	**11717**	**18.5**
（一）消费支出	Consumption Expenditure	6674	10.0	7457	11.7	8468	13.6
其中：服务性消费支出	Consumption Expenditure	1689	15.5	1816	7.5	2120	16.7
1.食品	Food	2311	12.6	2513	8.7	2712	7.9
2.衣着	Clothing Material	829	4.9	926	11.7	1091	17.8
3.家庭设备用品及服务	Household Appliances and Services	457	-0.8	503	10.1	526	4.6
4.医疗保健	Health Care and Medical Services	484	9.1	579	19.5	624	7.8
5.交通和通信	Transport and Communications	801	25.5	902	12.6	1176	30.3
6.教育文化娱乐服务	Recreation,Education and Cultural Services	983	5.5	1040	5.8	1202	15.6
7.居住	Residence	602	9.0	752	25.0	838	11.5
8.杂项商品和服务	Miscellaneous Goods and Services	206	2.7	242	17.5	299	23.6
（二）购房与建房支出	Buying and Building House Expenditure	496	-16.0	475	-4.1	937	97.2
（三）转移性支出	Transferred Expenditure	1174	14.4	1162	-1.1	1352	16.4
（四）财产性支出	Propetry Expenditure	3	-37.4	10	245.8	8	-20.2
（五）社会保障支出	Social Security Expenditure	679	13.4	784	15.5	951	21.3
六、借贷支出	**Expenditure for Savings and Lending**	**6834**	**51.0**	**6910**	**1.1**	**7910**	**14.5**
七、期末手存现金	**Cash in Hand at Term-end**	**483**	**-8.3**	**541**	**12.0**	**649**	**20.0**

4-2 全省城镇居民家庭人口就业情况
Whole Province Employment Situation of Urban Households

类别	Classification	单位	unit	总计 Total	最低10% Lowest Income Household	更低5% of which: Lower	低10% Low Income Household	较低20% Lower Middle Income Household	中间20% Middle Income Household	较高20% Upper Middle Income Household	高10% High Income Household	最高10% Highest Income Household	更高5% of which: Higher
家庭类型（世代层次）（构成）	**Family Type**	**%**	**percentage**	**100.00**	**100.00**	**100.00**	**100.00**	**100.00**	**100.00**	**100.00**	**100.00**	**100.00**	**100.00**
1.单身户	Single	%	percentage	0.75	0.00	0.00	0.65	0.42	0.78	0.07	2.23	2.35	3.09
2.一对夫妇户	One Couple	%	percentage	20.40	5.00	6.14	7.98	11.64	20.28	22.75	36.59	50.94	56.00
3.两代人单亲	Two Generations Single	%	percentage	1.05	1.68	0.58	0.91	1.16	0.86	1.68	0.00	0.41	0.31
4.两代人一个小孩	Two Generations with One Child	%	percentage	64.31	62.87	55.04	68.46	69.12	69.67	67.42	55.12	40.84	36.51
5.两代人两个小孩	Two Generations with Two Children	%	percentage	5.45	14.41	15.38	8.80	7.24	3.86	2.81	1.13	1.12	1.27
6.两代人多个小孩	Two Generations with Many Children	%	percentage	0.10	0.35	0.72	0.00	0.30	0.00	0.00	0.00	0.00	0.00
7.与父母	with Parents	%	percentage	1.43	2.01	2.15	1.51	0.88	0.51	2.00	2.18	1.95	1.32
8.三代人	Three Generations	%	percentage	4.67	10.70	14.28	9.94	6.86	2.34	2.17	0.94	1.09	0.52
9.其他	Others	%	percentage	1.84	2.99	5.72	1.76	2.37	1.70	1.10	1.81	1.30	0.98
一、家庭人口数	**Number of Household Population**	**人/户**	**person/ household**	**2.91**	**3.26**	**3.34**	**3.16**	**3.05**	**2.85**	**2.82**	**2.61**	**2.47**	**2.41**
（一）有收入者人数	Number of Persons with Income	人/户	person/ household	2.05	1.83	1.73	2.03	2.07	2.05	2.11	2.09	2.11	2.08
1.就业人口数	Number of Employed Persons	人/户	person/ household	1.71	1.57	1.39	1.77	1.77	1.70	1.74	1.68	1.59	1.56
①国有经济单位职工人数	Staff and Workers of State Owned Units	人/户	person/ household	1.07	0.74	0.60	0.93	1.03	1.08	1.19	1.24	1.21	1.13
②城镇集体经济单位职工人数	Staff and Workers of Collective Owned Units	人/户	person/ household	0.13	0.17	0.15	0.18	0.17	0.11	0.13	0.05	0.05	0.03
③其他各种经济类型单位职工	Staff and Workers of Other Units	人/户	person/ household	0.28	0.34	0.30	0.36	0.35	0.28	0.24	0.21	0.15	0.17
④城镇个体经营者人员数	Number of Urban Individual Operators	人/户	person/ household	0.08	0.14	0.14	0.12	0.07	0.08	0.06	0.04	0.10	0.16
⑤城镇个体被雇人员数	Number of Urban Individual Employed Persons	人/户	person/ household	0.07	0.13	0.14	0.12	0.11	0.07	0.05	0.02	0.02	0.02
⑥离退休再就业人员数	Number of Retirees Employed Again	人/户	person/ household	0.02	0.01	0.01	0.02	0.01	0.02	0.01	0.04	0.04	0.04
⑦其他就业人员数	Number of Other Employed Persons	人/户	person/ household	0.06	0.05	0.05	0.06	0.04	0.07	0.07	0.08	0.02	0.02
2.离退休人数	Number of Retirees	人/户	person/ household	0.30	0.16	0.21	0.19	0.24	0.31	0.34	0.38	0.51	0.51
3.其他有收入者人数	Number of Other Persons with Income	人/户	person/ household	0.04	0.10	0.13	0.07	0.05	0.04	0.02	0.02	0.01	0.01
（二）无收入者人数	Number of Persons without Income	人/户	person/ household	0.86	1.43	1.62	1.13	0.99	0.80	0.71	0.52	0.37	0.33
二、期末家庭人口数	**Terminal Number of Household Population**	**人/户**	**person/ household**	**2.90**	**3.25**	**3.32**	**3.16**	**3.05**	**2.86**	**2.82**	**2.61**	**2.46**	**2.39**
三、非家庭人口在家用餐人次数	**Number of Non-household Members Eating at Home**	**人次/户**	**person·time /household**	**5.92**	**3.74**	**3.89**	**4.42**	**4.98**	**5.23**	**5.90**	**8.97**	**10.67**	**11.82**
四、家庭人口在外用餐人次数	**Number of Household Members Eating Outside**	**人次/户**	**person·time /household**	**11.71**	**9.19**	**7.01**	**10.04**	**10.57**	**10.65**	**13.68**	**13.18**	**15.73**	**19.19**
五、负担系数	**Dependency Coefficient**	**人/就业者**	**person/ employment**	**1.70**	**2.08**	**2.40**	**1.79**	**1.72**	**1.68**	**1.62**	**1.55**	**1.55**	**1.54**

4-3 全省城镇居民家庭现金收支

Whole Province Cash Income and Expenditure of Urban Households

单位：元/人

unit:yuan/person

类别	Classification	总计 Total	最低10% Lowest Income Household	更低5% of which: Lower	低10% Low Income Household	较低20% Lower Middle Income Household	中间20% Middle Income Household	较高20% Upper Middle Income Household	高10% High Income Household	最高10% Highest Income Household	更高5% of which: Higher
一、期初手存现金	**Cash in Hand at Term-beginning**	**473**	**352**	**316**	**367**	**420**	**450**	**527**	**629**	**685**	**788**
二、家庭总收入	**Total Income**	**13223**	**4629**	**3828**	**6886**	**9094**	**12420**	**16657**	**21523**	**31715**	**37132**
其中：可支配收入	Disposable Income	12192	4242	3494	6348	8349	11352	15306	19961	29646	34949
（一）工薪收入	Income of Wages and Salaries	10442	3715	2914	5740	7549	10095	13479	17050	21821	24032
1.工资及补贴收入	Wages and Subsidies	10272	3568	2770	5608	7426	9923	13340	16814	21423	23357
2.其他劳动收入	Other Income	170	148	144	132	122	172	139	236	399	675
（二）经营净收入	Net Business Income	558	305	203	365	321	568	478	548	2103	3753
（三）财产性收入	Income from Properties	221	41	38	49	85	148	303	259	1081	1542
1.利息收入	Interest Income	38	8	8	7	16	19	55	34	200	303
2.股息与红利收入	Divident and Bonus	100	13	1	22	25	75	121	120	562	848
3.保险收益	Insurance Profit	6	0	0	1	7	6	9	2	11	6
4.其它投资收入	Other Investment Income	10	0	1	2	3	3	18	1	70	117
5.出租房屋收入	Income from Housing Renting	58	20	29	9	33	43	84	101	186	170
6.知识产权收入	Intellectual Property Income	4	0	0	0	0	0	0	0	52	97
7.其他财产性收入	Other Property Income	5	0	0	9	1	2	17	1	0	0
（一）转移性收入	Income from Transfer	2002	567	673	731	1140	1609	2396	3666	6709	7806
1.养老金或离退休金	Retirement Pension	1617	389	445	520	913	1357	1949	3004	5424	6173
2.社会救济收入	Social Relief	10	26	43	15	16	3	6	1	3	4
3.辞退金	Dismissal Fund	0	0	0	0	0	0	0	0	0	0
4.赔偿收入	Compensation	10	5	8	0	0	0	1	87	16	21
5.保险收入	Insurance Income	9	12	11	21	4	4	6	23	4	3
其中：失业保险金	Unemployment Insurance Benefits	7	12	11	19	4	3	4	5	3	2
6.赡养收入	Alimony Income	57	39	71	46	41	32	89	50	136	148
7.捐赠收入	Contribution Income	219	59	55	92	116	138	257	348	914	1299
8.亲友搭伙费	Fund for relatives or Friends Eat-ing Regularly in	3	0	1	0	0	2	2	21	0	0
9.提取住房公积金	Housing Accumulation Fund	22	0	0	0	1	4	33	54	129	43
10.记帐补贴	Account Subsidies	38	33	34	29	35	35	43	49	51	54
11.其他转移性收入	Other Transfer Income	18	3	5	8	13	34	10	29	33	60
三、出售财物收入	**Income from Properties Sale**	**83**	**8**	**13**	**3**	**6**	**130**	**9**	**338**	**321**	**15**
1.出售住房收入	Income from Housing Sale	73	1	2	0	0	112	2	332	291	2

4-3 续表 1 continued

类别	Classification	总计 Total	最低10% Lowest Income House-hold	更低5% of which: Lower	低10% Low Income House-hold	较低20% Lower Middle Income House-hold	中间20% Middle Income House-hold	较高20% Upper Middle Income House-hold	高10% High Income House-hold	最高10% Highest Income House-hold	更高5% of which: Higher
2.出售其他物品收入	Income from Other Items Sale	10	7	11	3	6	18	7	6	30	12
四、借贷收入	**Income from Lending**	**6499**	**1964**	**1707**	**2598**	**4019**	**5847**	**8788**	**11191**	**17027**	**18931**
1.提取储蓄存款	Money Drawn from Bank	5957	1729	1514	2564	3849	5496	7795	10206	15317	17275
2.借入款	Borrowing Money	280	209	170	25	137	90	468	633	812	967
3.收回借出款	Loans Recalled	53	6	2	0	15	15	57	182	261	351
4.收回储蓄性保险本	Principal of Insurance Like Savings	12	4	4	4	1	2	37	19	28	28
5.兑售有价证券	Exchanging or Selling Marketable Securities	6	2	0	0	0	0	2	0	68	139
6.收回投资本金	Investment Principal	3	4	9	0	1	3	5	1	5	4
7.住房贷款	Housing Loan	172	1	1	0	0	220	416	133	498	116
8.汽车贷款	Car Loan	0	0	0	0	0	0	0	0	0	0
9.教育贷款	Education Loan	0	0	0	0	0	0	0	0	0	0
10.其他贷款	Other Loans	3	0	0	0	4	3	0	2	13	16
11.其他借贷收入	Other Income from Lending	13	11	7	6	12	19	9	15	26	35
五、家庭总支出	**Total Expenditure**	**11717**	**4898**	**4285**	**6225**	**8237**	**10817**	**14630**	**18668**	**27490**	**30456**
（一）消费支出	Consumption Expenditure	8468	3903	3501	4991	6541	8198	10046	12635	18179	20768
其中：服务性消费支出	Consumption Expenditure for Services	2120	881	768	1134	1498	2056	2725	3496	4360	5049
1.食品	Food	2712	1646	1475	1978	2337	2757	3089	3474	4579	4982
2.衣着	Clothing	1091	445	332	627	865	1080	1399	1614	2083	2232
3.家庭设备用品及服务	Household Appliances and Services	526	192	213	269	378	452	634	936	1303	1416
4.医疗保健	Health care and Medical Services	624	256	245	393	409	678	768	918	1320	1368
5.交通和通信	Transport and Communications	1176	358	304	461	891	994	1267	1798	3839	4526
6.教育文化娱乐服务	Recreation,Education and Cultural Services	1202	518	455	605	853	1184	1588	2056	2259	2607
7.居住	Residence	838	378	377	531	621	780	912	1350	2006	2643
8.杂项商品和服务	Miscellaneous Goods and Services	299	110	101	128	188	274	390	490	789	994
（二）购房与建房支出	Expenditure for Housing Purchase and Building	937	124	0	18	120	450	1633	2157	4049	4101
1.购房	Housing Purchase	918	124	0	18	107	450	1572	2102	4049	4101
2.建房	Housing Building	19	0	0	0	13	0	61	55	0	0
（三）转移性支出	Expenditure for Transfer	1352	522	492	708	874	1157	1680	2451	3397	3679
1.交纳的个人收入税	Individual Income Tax	41	5	9	3	10	26	47	93	214	265

4-3 续表 2 continued

类别	Classification	总计 Total	最低10% Lowest Income Household	更低5% of which: Lower	低10% Low Income Household	较低20% Lower Middle Income Household	中间20% Middle Income Household	较高20% Upper Middle Income Household	高10% High Income Household	最高10% Highest Income Household	更高5% of which: Higher
2.捐赠支出	Contribution Expenditure	797	301	266	468	574	690	954	1323	1962	2068
3.购买彩票	Buying Lotteries	7	1	0	5	7	7	10	6	11	15
4.赡养支出	Alimony Expenditure	382	183	182	185	208	341	507	792	816	838
其中：在外就学子女费用	Expenditure for Chindren's Education	229	141	130	146	130	201	264	495	452	380
5.各种非储蓄性保险支出	Expenditure for Various Non-saving Insurance	58	15	17	27	37	44	78	98	174	209
其中：车辆保险支出	Expenditure for Vehicle Insurance	14	0	0	1	6	3	16	24	85	121
6.其他转移性支出	Other Transfer Expenditure	67	17	18	19	37	49	84	139	221	284
（四）财产性支出	Expenditure for Properties	8	0	0	1	1	4	10	6	61	44
1.非生产性利息支出	Expenditure for Nonproductive Interest	3	0	0	1	1	3	5	2	19	37
2.其他	Others	5	0	0	0	1	1	4	4	42	6
（五）社会保障支出	Expenditure for Social Security	951	349	291	507	701	1007	1261	1419	1804	1864
1.个人交纳的养老基金	Pension Fund	405	202	164	292	352	470	500	518	503	515
2.个人交纳的住房公积金	Housing Accumulation Fund	381	89	79	115	218	362	555	656	996	1069
3.个人交纳的医疗基金	Medical Fund	107	34	25	69	88	111	140	153	185	179
4.个人交纳的失业基金	Unemployment Fund	40	18	16	22	31	38	47	64	81	74
5.其他社会保障支出	Other Social Security Expenditure	19	6	8	9	12	26	20	28	40	27
六、借贷支出	**Expenditure for Lending**	**7910**	**1613**	**1185**	**3115**	**4770**	**7364**	**10684**	**14009**	**21255**	**25071**
1.存入储蓄款	Money Deposited in Bank	7269	1502	1127	2969	4475	6715	9988	12781	18898	21861
2.借出款	Lending Money	70	4	2	3	21	30	166	83	266	407
3.归还借款	Money Returned to the Borrower	112	29	18	62	29	117	106	124	535	661
4.储蓄性保险支出	Expenditure for Insurance Like Savings	139	39	26	46	107	152	154	186	403	539
5.购买有价证券	Buying Marketable Securities	35	1	0	4	2	48	15	105	169	292
6.其它投资支出	Other Investment	26	0	0	2	9	74	2	77	35	5
7.归还住房贷款	Housing Loan Returned	234	27	0	20	106	195	243	636	862	1165
8.归还汽车贷款	Car Loan Returned	1	0	0	0	0	0	0	0	8	0
9.归还教育贷款	Education Loan Returned	0	0	0	0	0	0	0	0	3	3
10.归还其他贷款	Other Loans Returned	6	0	0	2	10	3	1	0	37	73
11.其他借贷支出	Other Expenditure for Lending	17	11	12	8	12	30	8	17	38	63
七、期末手存现金	**Cash in Hand at Term-end**	**649**	**360**	**326**	**535**	**500**	**671**	**749**	**912**	**1099**	**1282**

4-4 全省城镇居民家庭食品消费支出

Whole Province Consumption Expenditure for Food of Urban Households

单位：元/人 unit:yuan/person

类别	Classification	总计 Total	最低10% Lowest Income Household	更低5% of which: Lower	低10% Low Income Household	较低20% Lower Middle Income Household	中间20% Middle Income Household	较高20% Upper Middle Income Household	高10% High Income Household	最高10% Highest Income Household	更高5% of which: Higher
消费支出	**Consumption Expenditure**	**8468**	**3903**	**3501**	**4991**	**6541**	**8198**	**10046**	**12635**	**18179**	**20768**
其中：服务性消费支出	Consumption Expenditure for Services	2120	881	768	1134	1498	2056	2725	3496	4360	5049
一、食品	**Food**	**2712**	**1646**	**1475**	**1978**	**2337**	**2757**	**3089**	**3474**	**4579**	**4982**
（一）粮油类	Grain and Oil	349	320	320	333	338	357	349	371	409	422
1.粮食	Grain	224	208	210	219	220	229	218	234	252	255
(1)大米	Rice	40	32	36	36	36	45	42	46	48	46
(2)面粉	Flour	37	45	53	41	34	38	35	33	37	39
(3)其他粮食	Other Grain	13	10	12	11	10	14	14	14	17	19
(4)粮食制品	Grain Products	134	121	110	130	139	133	127	140	151	151
2.淀粉及薯类	Starches and Tubers	24	22	23	21	23	23	25	24	28	30
3.干豆类及豆制品	Dried Beans and Bean Products	33	30	31	30	31	33	34	36	45	45
4.油脂类	Oil or Fat	69	60	56	62	64	72	72	77	84	93
(1)食用植物油	Vegetable Oil	69	60	56	62	64	72	72	77	84	93
(2)食用动物油	Animal Fats	0	0	0	0	0	0	0	0	0	0
（二）肉禽蛋水产品类	Meat,Poultry,Eggs and Aquatic Products	686	432	390	516	633	699	777	840	1047	1100
1.肉类	Meat	347	224	201	278	334	358	383	400	496	508
(1)猪肉	Pork	185	135	127	161	183	189	195	204	239	245
(2)牛肉	Beef	22	12	10	15	21	25	24	27	30	33
(3)羊肉	Mutton	22	14	14	18	19	23	25	28	32	33
(4)其他肉	Other Meat	4	2	1	2	3	5	5	3	4	3
(5)肉制品	Meat Products	115	61	48	83	107	117	134	139	191	194
2.禽类	Poultries	75	57	46	61	78	73	81	85	94	93
(1)鸡	Chicken	29	24	21	25	32	29	31	32	31	30
(2)鸭	Duck	2	0	0	1	1	2	2	5	3	3
(3)其他禽类	Other Poultries	1	0	0	0	1	1	1	1	1	1
(4)禽制品	Poultry Products	43	32	24	35	44	42	48	48	59	59
3.蛋类	Eggs	90	85	83	84	88	88	90	96	106	111
(1)鲜蛋	Fresh Eggs	84	82	80	81	84	81	83	89	95	101
(2)蛋制品	Eggs Products	6	3	3	3	5	7	8	7	11	10
4.水产品类	Aquatic Products	174	66	61	92	133	179	223	258	350	388
(1)鱼	Fish	67	38	36	46	57	70	80	86	106	115
(2)虾	Shrimp	41	14	13	21	33	40	53	60	84	92
(3)其他水产品	Other Aquatic Products	45	9	8	16	30	50	63	67	101	119
(4)水产制品	Aquatic Finished Products	22	5	4	9	13	20	27	44	60	62
（三）蔬菜类	Vegetables	239	172	167	189	221	246	269	291	318	329
1.鲜菜	Fresh Vegetables	218	160	156	176	204	224	246	262	284	293

4-4 续表 1 continued

类别	Classification	总计 Total	最低10% Lowest Income Household	更低5% of which: Lower	低10% Low Income Household	较低20% Lower Middle Income Household	中间20% Middle Income Household	较高20% Upper Middle Income Household	高10% High Income Household	最高10% Highest Income Household	更高5% of which: Higher
2.干菜	Dry Vegetables	11	5	5	7	9	13	12	15	17	18
3.菜制品	Vegetable Products	10	6	6	6	8	10	11	14	17	18
（四）调味品	Flavoring	33	26	26	27	30	35	35	38	47	50
（五）糖烟酒饮料类	Carbohydrate,Tobacco, Liquor and Beverages	273	166	145	194	234	289	282	375	486	497
1.糖类	Carbohydrate	23	14	14	16	18	24	25	31	44	45
2.烟草类	Tobacco	83	50	49	62	74	96	79	107	138	155
3.酒类	Liquor	106	73	59	81	92	106	108	144	190	183
(1)白酒	White Spirit	67	51	44	53	57	65	65	96	117	106
(2)果酒	Wine	6	2	2	3	5	5	5	10	17	21
(3)啤酒	Beer	31	20	13	24	28	33	34	35	53	54
(4)其他酒	Others	2	1	0	1	1	2	3	3	4	2
4.饮料	Beverages	61	29	23	35	50	62	70	93	114	114
(1)碳酸饮料	Carbonated Beverages	7	4	3	5	5	7	8	10	12	11
(2)果蔬饮料	Fruit Beverages	8	4	3	6	7	7	10	13	12	11
(3)瓶装饮用水	Bottled Beverages	9	3	2	4	7	10	12	14	21	20
(4)茶叶	Tea	26	12	11	13	23	28	28	41	53	56
(5)咖啡可可粉	Coffee Cocoa Powder	2	0	0	1	1	2	3	3	4	2
(6)其他饮料	Other Beverages	8	5	3	5	7	9	10	13	12	13
（六）干鲜瓜果类	Dried and Fresh Melons and Fruits	251	134	114	171	220	254	299	339	411	433
1.鲜果	Fresh Fruits	152	78	65	101	132	155	184	207	247	257
2.鲜瓜	Fresh Melons	44	26	21	32	39	43	52	55	70	75
3.干果	Dried Fruits	11	5	5	7	9	11	15	17	18	20
4.瓜果制品	Melon and Fruit Products	6	3	2	5	5	6	7	7	10	11
5.坚果及果仁	Nuts	38	23	20	26	35	38	42	52	67	70
（七）糕点、奶及奶制品	Cake,Milk and Products	254	156	125	195	230	259	287	334	368	382
1.糕点	Cake	77	49	42	60	72	80	83	91	120	117
2.奶及奶制品	Milk and Products	177	107	83	135	159	179	204	243	247	265
(1)鲜乳品	Fresh Milk	125	80	62	98	117	129	143	165	164	168
(2)奶粉	Milk Power	14	6	5	13	10	15	15	24	20	24
(3)酸奶	Yogurt	21	11	10	12	16	21	28	29	40	47
(4)其他奶制品	Others	16	9	7	12	15	14	18	25	23	26
（八）其他食品	Other Foods	77	35	26	45	59	92	85	105	146	159
其中：半成品	Semi-finished Products	7	5	4	5	7	6	8	8	12	13
（九）饮食服务	Catering Services	549	204	162	309	372	527	705	781	1348	1610
1.食品加工服务费	Proceeding Services	1	1	1	1	1	1	3	1	1	1
2.在外饮食	Outward Dinner	548	203	161	309	371	526	703	780	1347	1609
(1)购自食堂	Food from Dining Room	71	40	34	57	64	75	74	104	110	136
(2)购自饮食业	Food from Catering Trade	471	162	126	251	303	445	617	675	1226	1459
(3)在亲友家搭伙支出	Expenditure for Relatives or Friends Eating Regularly in	5	1	1	1	4	5	12	1	11	14

4-5 全省城镇居民家庭食品消费数量

Whole Province Consumption Amount for Food of Urban Households

单位：千克/人 unit:kg/person

类别	Classification	总计 Total	最低10% Lowest Income House-hold	更低5% of which: Lower	低10% Low Income House-hold	较低20% Lower M-iddle Inc-ome Hou-sehold	中间20% Middle Income House-hold	较高20% Upper M-iddle Inc-ome Hou-sehold	高10% High Income House-hold	最高10% Highest Income House-hold	更高5% of which: Higher
粮食	**Grain**	**72.95**	**76.53**	**79.81**	**76.54**	**71.96**	**73.42**	**68.87**	**71.75**	**75.40**	**75.66**
(1)大米	Rice	12.66	10.24	11.75	11.60	11.49	14.09	12.93	14.57	14.77	13.75
(2)面粉	Flour	16.85	22.22	26.21	19.81	15.75	16.63	15.41	14.04	14.94	15.83
(3)其他粮食	Other Grain	3.89	3.44	4.02	3.48	3.22	4.28	4.20	4.25	5.01	5.50
(4)粮食制品	Grain Products	39.54	40.62	37.83	41.65	41.49	38.41	36.34	38.90	40.69	40.58
淀粉及薯类	**Starches and Tubers**	**9.82**	**10.10**	**10.89**	**9.57**	**9.71**	**9.33**	**9.81**	**10.03**	**11.20**	**12.06**
油脂类	**Oil or Fat**	**6.24**	**6.16**	**5.88**	**6.12**	**5.76**	**6.45**	**6.27**	**6.44**	**7.13**	**7.86**
(1)食用植物油	Vegetable Oil	6.23	6.15	5.87	6.11	5.75	6.44	6.25	6.42	7.11	7.85
(2)食用动物油	Animal Fats	0.02	0.01	0.00	0.01	0.01	0.01	0.02	0.02	0.02	0.00
肉类	**Meat**	**22.98**	**15.94**	**14.49**	**18.99**	**22.44**	**23.85**	**24.76**	**25.58**	**31.42**	**31.83**
(1)猪肉	Pork	14.42	10.99	10.35	12.84	14.52	14.80	14.93	15.55	18.05	18.37
(2)牛肉	Beef	1.25	0.72	0.62	0.83	1.21	1.42	1.36	1.51	1.77	1.91
(3)羊肉	Mutton	1.21	0.79	0.81	0.94	1.06	1.26	1.38	1.50	1.77	1.80
(4)其他肉	Other Meat	0.27	0.12	0.10	0.11	0.24	0.39	0.36	0.23	0.31	0.21
(5)肉制品	Meat Products	5.83	3.32	2.62	4.27	5.40	5.98	6.73	6.78	9.51	9.54
禽类	**Poultries**	**5.10**	**4.26**	**3.49**	**4.49**	**5.42**	**4.92**	**5.28**	**5.56**	**5.84**	**5.67**
(1)鸡	Chicken	2.60	2.44	2.07	2.42	2.95	2.46	2.55	2.64	2.52	2.46
(2)鸭	Duck	0.14	0.03	0.03	0.05	0.09	0.14	0.20	0.36	0.22	0.21
(3)其他禽类	Other Poultries	0.04	0.02	0.02	0.02	0.04	0.04	0.05	0.05	0.07	0.07
(4)禽制品	Poultry Products	2.31	1.77	1.37	2.00	2.33	2.27	2.48	2.51	3.03	2.92
蛋类	**Eggs**	**16.50**	**16.27**	**15.79**	**15.82**	**16.36**	**16.23**	**16.17**	**17.35**	**18.88**	**19.72**
(1)鲜蛋	Fresh Eggs	15.85	15.90	15.45	15.46	15.86	15.46	15.38	16.57	17.66	18.69
(2)蛋制品	Eggs Products	0.66	0.37	0.33	0.37	0.50	0.77	0.79	0.78	1.22	1.03
水产品类	**Aquatic Products**										
(1)鱼	Fish	6.48	4.43	4.22	5.07	6.01	6.64	7.03	7.45	10.15	8.85
(2)虾	Shrimp	1.54	0.69	0.64	0.87	1.29	1.58	1.93	2.13	2.84	2.94
(3)其他水产品	Other Aquatic Products	3.11	1.10	1.06	1.69	2.50	3.69	3.93	4.00	5.45	6.23
鲜菜	**Fresh Vegetables**	**107.00**	**92.70**	**91.30**	**98.46**	**104.56**	**106.94**	**112.14**	**116.41**	**125.00**	**127.41**
干菜	**Dry Vegetables**	**0.40**	**0.22**	**0.19**	**0.28**	**0.32**	**0.50**	**0.44**	**0.51**	**0.58**	**0.53**
酒类	**Liquor**	**10.15**	**8.34**	**6.60**	**8.68**	**9.62**	**10.47**	**10.47**	**10.32**	**14.78**	**14.98**
(1)白酒	White Spirit	2.80	2.96	2.89	2.61	2.64	2.84	2.46	3.01	3.80	3.56
(2)果酒	Wine	0.23	0.10	0.08	0.20	0.23	0.21	0.21	0.30	0.53	0.61
(3)啤酒	Beer	6.97	5.24	3.61	5.80	6.66	7.27	7.57	6.81	10.19	10.56
(4)其他酒	Others	0.14	0.03	0.02	0.07	0.10	0.14	0.23	0.20	0.26	0.26
碳酸饮料	**Carbonated Beverages**	**1.44**	**0.93**	**0.57**	**1.06**	**1.07**	**1.51**	**1.58**	**2.21**	**2.50**	**2.41**
果蔬饮料	**Fruit Beverages**	**1.40**	**0.85**	**0.62**	**1.01**	**1.20**	**1.23**	**1.61**	**2.49**	**2.02**	**1.89**
瓶装饮用水	**Bottled Beverages**	**16.93**	**7.27**	**6.87**	**8.34**	**13.23**	**18.73**	**22.82**	**23.33**	**28.54**	**29.69**
茶叶	**Tea**	**0.28**	**0.20**	**0.20**	**0.21**	**0.29**	**0.30**	**0.28**	**0.34**	**0.40**	**0.42**
咖啡可可粉	**Coffee Cocoa Powder**	**0.04**	**0.01**	**0.01**	**0.03**	**0.02**	**0.04**	**0.05**	**0.05**	**0.09**	**0.03**
鲜果	**Fresh Fruits**	**47.22**	**29.24**	**25.45**	**36.24**	**43.70**	**49.12**	**54.48**	**58.38**	**65.20**	**65.85**
鲜瓜	**Fresh Melons**	**27.96**	**21.20**	**17.68**	**24.25**	**25.86**	**27.72**	**30.85**	**32.75**	**37.73**	**41.42**
干果	**Dried Fruits**	**0.86**	**0.46**	**0.50**	**0.63**	**0.75**	**0.90**	**1.09**	**1.16**	**1.16**	**1.25**
瓜果制品	**Melon and Fruit Products**	**0.51**	**0.26**	**0.21**	**0.47**	**0.41**	**0.55**	**0.58**	**0.61**	**0.82**	**0.90**
坚果及果仁	**Nuts**	**3.45**	**2.53**	**2.37**	**2.83**	**3.47**	**3.40**	**3.47**	**4.21**	**4.89**	**5.12**
糕点	**Cake**	**6.80**	**5.12**	**4.52**	**5.97**	**6.54**	**6.99**	**7.04**	**7.82**	**9.06**	**8.71**
奶及奶制品	**Milk and Products**										
(1)鲜乳品	Fresh Milk	28.31	18.83	14.59	22.71	26.26	29.29	31.83	36.68	36.07	36.74
(2)奶粉	Milk Power	0.34	0.23	0.14	0.38	0.25	0.30	0.48	0.44	0.34	0.39
(3)酸奶	Yogurt	3.72	2.30	1.95	2.11	3.01	3.57	4.56	5.02	7.08	8.40

4-6 全省城镇居民家庭非食品消费支出

Whole Province Consumption Expenditure for Non-food of Urban Households

单位：元/人 unit:yuan/person

类别	Classification	总计 Total	最低10% Lowest Income Household	更低5% of which: Lower	低10% Low Income Household	较低20% Lower Middle Income Household	中间20% Middle Income Household	较高20% Upper Middle Income Household	高10% High Income Household	最高10% Highest Income Household	更高5% of which: Higher
非食品类	**Non-food**	**5757**	**2257**	**2027**	**3013**	**4204**	**5441**	**6957**	**9161**	**13600**	**15785**
二、衣着	**Clothing**	**1091**	**445**	**332**	**627**	**865**	**1080**	**1399**	**1614**	**2083**	**2232**
㈠服装	Garments	777	304	218	411	602	768	1020	1172	1519	1633
1.男士服装	Men's Clothing	326	130	94	176	263	327	414	471	644	697
2.女士服装	Women's Clothing	397	145	103	195	290	377	539	637	807	869
3.童装	Children's Clothing	54	29	22	40	49	63	66	64	68	67
㈡衣着材料	Clothing Material	12	7	5	9	12	12	11	12	19	18
㈢鞋类	Footwear	243	104	84	168	202	244	297	343	438	465
㈣其他衣着用品	Other Clothing	50	26	21	33	42	46	61	74	93	97
㈤衣着加工服务费	Clothing Proceeding Services	9	4	4	6	7	10	10	12	15	19
三、家庭设备用品及服务	**Household Facilities, Articles and Services**	**526**	**192**	**213**	**269**	**378**	**452**	**634**	**936**	**1303**	**1416**
㈠耐用消费品	Durable Consumer Goods	276	71	97	102	198	224	349	521	743	811
1.家具	Furniture	97	40	70	19	55	54	106	218	380	351
⑴成套家具	Furniture Sets	33	29	57	2	26	9	25	49	169	197
⑵其他家具	Others	64	12	13	17	29	45	80	168	211	154
2.家庭设备	Household Facilities	179	31	27	83	143	170	244	303	364	461
⑴洗衣机	Washing Machines	21	1	0	15	17	26	27	22	36	51
⑵电风扇	Electric Fans	3	2	1	4	3	3	3	3	6	7
⑶电冰箱	Refrigerators	27	8	14	12	14	23	38	52	70	62
⑷冰柜	Freezer	3	0	0	0	2	3	4	8	8	8
⑸微波炉	Microwave Ovens	4	1	0	0	5	4	7	6	7	8
⑹空调器	Air Conditioner	49	5	6	18	42	48	81	62	85	137
⑺电炊具	Electric Cookers	8	2	1	5	7	8	8	14	14	16
⑻淋浴热水器	Water Heaters	22	3	0	10	21	19	25	46	46	64
⑼排油烟机	Lampblack Exhausters	8	0	0	4	4	10	11	15	22	23
⑽吸尘器	Vacuam Cleaner	1	0	0	0	1	2	0	1	2	3
⑾消毒碗柜	Sterilized Cabinet	0	0	0	0	0	0	0	0	0	0
⑿洗碗机	Dishwasher	0	0	0	0	0	0	0	0	0	0
⒀饮水机	Drinking Machine	4	0	0	1	1	4	6	16	10	15
⒁取暖器	Heater	4	2	2	3	6	3	2	5	9	15
⒂其他	Others	25	6	3	11	19	19	32	54	50	53

4-6 续表 1 continued

类别	Classification	总计 Total	最低10% Lowest Income Household	更低5% of which: Lower	低10% Low Income Household	较低20% Lower Middle Income Household	中间20% Middle Income Household	较高20% Upper Middle Income Household	高10% High Income Household	最高10% Highest Income Household	更高5% of which: Higher
(二)室内装饰品	Interior Decorations	21	4	5	8	9	16	21	62	72	70
1.纺织装饰品	Textile Decorations	9	2	3	2	5	8	10	30	24	22
2.装饰灯具	Decorative Lamps	5	1	1	2	1	4	4	19	18	22
3.其他装饰品	Others	7	1	1	4	3	5	7	13	30	26
(三)床上用品	Bed Articles	44	13	13	17	34	39	55	82	104	118
(四)家庭日用杂品	Grocery for Daily Use	161	95	85	113	126	160	178	239	303	308
1.厨、餐、茶具	Kitchenware,Tea-things and Tab-leware	27	13	8	13	19	26	29	41	68	66
2.家用工具	Household Tools	3	1	1	1	1	4	3	5	5	3
3.家居清洁用品	Household Cleaning Products	27	18	17	21	22	26	29	41	41	42
4.其他日用杂品	Other Grocery for Daily Use	105	62	59	78	83	104	118	152	190	197
(五)家具材料	Furniture Materials	4	2	3	0	0	1	9	10	14	18
(六)家庭服务	Household Service	20	8	9	29	10	11	21	21	67	91
1.家政服务	Household Service	8	3	5	3	2	3	9	9	49	72
2.加工维修服务费	Proceeding Upkeep	12	5	5	26	8	9	13	12	18	19
四、医疗保健	**Health Care and Personal Articles**	**624**	**256**	**245**	**393**	**409**	**678**	**768**	**918**	**1320**	**1368**
(一)医疗器具	Medical Appliances	7	1	0	0	6	5	4	8	42	12
(二)保健器具	Health Care Appliances	14	2	0	8	10	14	20	23	30	36
(三)药品费	Drugs Charges	313	153	154	240	221	355	381	399	552	546
(四)滋补保健品	Nutritious and Health Articles	82	7	5	16	31	56	117	160	338	461
(五)医疗费	Medical Charges	197	92	85	126	134	233	230	317	338	282
(六)其他	Others	11	2	1	2	7	15	17	11	21	31
五、交通和通讯	**Transportation and Communication**	**1176**	**358**	**304**	**461**	**891**	**994**	**1267**	**1798**	**3839**	**4526**
(一)交通	Transportation	704	161	140	166	499	514	659	1117	3054	3678
1.家庭交通工具	Transportation Facility	399	60	65	56	300	258	258	612	2185	2589
(1)摩托车	Motorcycles	4	9	11	0	2	5	4	3	2	0
(2)自行车	Bicycles	14	11	6	12	14	15	16	16	17	11
(3)助力车	Motorbikes	52	40	47	44	48	66	51	63	51	56
(4)家用汽车	Automobiles	328	0	0	0	235	169	186	529	2114	2522
(5)其他交通工具	Others	1	0	0	1	2	2	1	1	1	0
2.车辆用燃料及零配件	Fuels and Parts	75	31	15	23	50	68	87	140	206	274
(1)燃料	Fuels	65	25	11	19	44	59	77	125	166	216
(2)零配件	Parts	8	6	4	4	5	6	8	12	27	50
(3)其他	Others	2	0	0	0	1	2	2	3	14	8

4-6 续表 2 continued

类别	Classification	总计 Total	最低10% Lowest Income Household	更低5% of which: Lower	低10% Low Income Household	较低20% Lower Middle Income Household	中间20% Middle Income Household	较高20% Upper Middle Income Household	高10% High Income Household	最高10% Highest Income Household	更高5% of which: Higher
3.交通工具服务支出	Expenditure for Transportation Facility Services	69	13	8	16	46	43	82	99	300	416
(1)维修费	Mending Cost	18	10	8	13	16	18	16	23	46	72
(2)车辆使用税费	Tax Payment of Automobile Use	40	1	0	2	24	18	43	63	228	315
(3)其它车辆使用费用	Other Cost of Automobile Use	10	2	1	1	5	7	23	13	27	29
4.交通费	Transportation Costs	161	56	51	70	103	145	233	267	362	399
(1)飞机	Airplane	11	0	1	0	4	2	27	19	35	45
(2)火车	Train	25	6	8	6	17	20	34	49	66	70
(3)长途汽车	Coaches	33	18	17	20	24	35	47	47	49	52
(4)市内公共交通	Incity Public Traffic	45	17	14	23	32	46	57	71	95	93
(5)出租汽车费	Taxis Charges	41	11	9	15	21	38	61	70	107	130
(6)其他交通费	Other Transportation Costs	6	2	3	5	5	4	6	11	10	9
(二)通信	Communication	472	196	165	295	392	480	608	681	785	847
1.通信工具	Communication Facility	108	25	14	67	85	118	148	141	190	227
(1)电话机	Fixed Phones	2	1	0	1	1	3	2	3	3	3
(2)移动电话	Mobile Phones	104	24	13	65	83	114	144	137	183	218
(3)寻呼机	Pagers	0	0	0	0	0	0	0	0	0	0
(4)传真机	Faxes	0	0	0	0	0	0	0	0	1	2
(5)其他通信工具	Other Communication Facility	1	0	0	1	1	1	1	1	3	4
2.通信服务	Communication Service	364	171	151	228	307	362	460	540	595	620
(1)电信费	Costs of Telecommunications Services	351	168	148	222	296	342	444	522	577	602
(2)邮费	Costs of Postal Services	2	0	1	1	1	2	3	5	4	5
(3)其他	Others	11	3	2	5	9	18	13	13	14	13
六、教育文化娱乐服务	**Education,Culture and Recreation Articles**	**1202**	**518**	**455**	**605**	**853**	**1184**	**1588**	**2056**	**2259**	**2607**
(一)文化娱乐用品	Culture and Recreation Articles	355	121	113	162	232	335	472	566	870	1082
1.彩色电视机	Color TV Sets	48	15	22	15	39	46	51	60	157	260
2.影碟机	Video Disc Players	3	1	2	1	4	2	1	10	5	5
3.录放像机	Video Recorders	2	0	0	0	3	0	0	10	0	0
4.家用电脑	Computers	105	29	17	48	60	106	136	184	264	325
(1)整机电脑	Entire Computers	93	28	16	45	49	98	121	161	236	293
(2)计算机外部设备	External Equipment of Computer	6	0	0	1	4	4	8	17	13	18
(3)各种零配件及耗材	Various Spare Parts	6	1	0	2	8	4	8	6	15	13

4-6 续表 3 continued

类别	Classification	总计 Total	最低10% Lowest Income Household	更低5% of which: Lower	低10% Low Income Household	较低20% Lower Middle Income Household	中间20% Middle Income Household	较高20% Upper Middle Income Household	高10% High Income Household	最高10% Highest Income Household	更高5% of which: Higher
5.组合音响	Hi-Fi Stereo Component System	1	0	0	1	1	0	1	1	1	0
6.录音机	Tape Recorders	3	0	0	2	2	3	4	5	3	7
7.摄像机	Pickup Cameras	9	0	0	0	2	10	14	5	49	69
8.照相机	Cameras	26	0	0	8	7	16	51	63	70	94
9.钢琴	Pianos	4	0	0	0	0	0	21	0	0	0
10.其他中高档乐器	Other Medium and Top Grade Music Instruments	3	2	5	1	2	0	4	8	14	1
11.健身器材	Body Building Equipment	5	13	25	1	7	2	5	4	8	8
12.电子辞典	Electronic Dictionary	4	1	1	4	3	4	4	9	8	8
13.音像制品及软件	Audio-visual Products and Software	6	2	1	3	5	6	9	12	11	12
14.体育用品	Sports Goods	2	0	0	0	1	2	1	2	5	7
15.书报杂志	Books, Newspapers and Magazines	44	18	14	25	30	43	57	68	99	108
16.纸张文具	Paper and Stationery	19	12	10	14	16	22	22	22	23	25
17.其他文娱用品	Other Culture and Recreation Articles	71	27	16	38	51	72	91	104	152	152
㈡文化娱乐服务	Culture and Recreation Services	215	52	40	72	124	204	287	444	528	581
1.参观游览	Visit	36	4	3	12	19	37	50	73	96	92
2.健身活动	Body Building Activities	9	0	0	1	2	6	17	23	34	41
3.团体旅游	TeamTour	101	7	2	15	46	96	138	258	276	307
4.其它文娱活动	Other Culture and Recreation Activities	59	38	33	37	48	56	71	80	103	125
5.文娱用品修理服务费	Service Charges for Recreation and Culture Articles Mending	9	3	2	8	8	9	10	11	19	16
㈢教育	Education	633	345	301	372	497	645	829	1046	862	945
1.教材	Teaching Materials	37	30	23	22	33	43	40	58	39	36
⑴课本及参考书	Text Books and Reference Books	30	27	21	20	28	35	31	37	35	30
⑵教育软件	Teaching Software	3	1	0	0	1	1	4	14	1	1
⑶其它教材	Other Teaching Material	4	2	2	2	4	6	6	7	4	5
2.教育费用	Education Costs	595	315	278	350	464	602	788	988	822	909
⑴非义务教育学杂费	Tuition Fee for Noncompulsory Education	226	132	119	128	180	227	267	392	354	452
⑵义务教育学杂费	Tuition Fee for Compulsory Education	67	89	91	66	60	72	69	55	45	47
⑶托幼费	Child-care Fee	50	37	30	47	48	41	58	62	67	50
⑷成人教育费	Adult Education Expenses	79	5	6	32	37	73	124	209	137	134
⑸家教费	Family Education Expenses	13	4	4	5	9	13	24	28	14	6
⑹培训班	Training Fee	93	32	16	49	69	110	134	129	128	123
⑺学校住宿费	Accommodation Expenses at School	9	6	5	3	7	13	12	17	7	5
⑻其他	Others	59	10	8	19	55	53	102	95	72	91
七、居住	**Residence**	**838**	**378**	**377**	**531**	**621**	**780**	**912**	**1350**	**2006**	**2643**

4-6 续表 4 continued

类别	Classification	总计 Total	最低10% Lowest Income Household	更低5% of which: Lower	低10% Low Income Household	较低20% Lower Middle Income Household	中间20% Middle Income Household	较高20% Upper Middle Income Household	高10% High Income Household	最高10% Highest Income Household	更高5% of which: Higher
㈠住房	Housing	218	30	23	76	98	165	211	509	881	1443
1.租赁房房租	House Rent	18	15	14	13	12	18	21	11	43	53
2.自有房租金折算	Private House Convert to House Rent	0	0	0	0	0	0	0	0	0	0
3.住房装潢支出	Decoration Expenses	138	2	1	13	43	81	123	405	682	1166
4.维修用建筑材料	Construction Material for Mending	47	13	8	39	29	56	53	70	104	179
5.其他	Others	15	1	0	10	14	10	14	24	52	45
㈡水电燃料及其他	Water, Electricity,Fuel and Others	573	331	338	432	492	571	637	775	1002	1066
1.水	Water	45	30	28	35	40	45	48	60	72	72
2.电	Electricity	196	119	117	141	174	193	225	257	326	340
3.燃料	Fuels	135	138	152	124	136	130	132	142	154	168
(1)煤炭	Coal	44	79	90	59	53	39	30	21	23	30
(2)液化石油气	Liquefied Petroleum Gas	42	41	46	33	40	46	45	45	38	28
(3)管道煤气	Pipeline Gas	36	16	13	30	32	33	39	51	66	68
(4)其他燃料	Other Fuels	13	2	2	3	10	11	19	25	27	42
4.其他	Others	197	44	41	132	142	203	231	316	450	486
㈢居住服务费	Charges of Residence Service	47	17	16	23	31	45	64	65	123	134
1.物业管理费	Property Management Fees	18	8	6	12	11	14	21	33	46	49
2.维修服务费	Charges of Mending Services	11	2	1	4	11	14	11	8	32	52
3.其它	Others	18	6	8	7	8	16	32	24	45	33
八、杂项商品和服务	**Miscellanecus Commodities and Services**	**299**	**110**	**101**	**128**	**188**	**274**	**390**	**490**	**789**	**994**
㈠杂项商品	Miscellanecus Commodities	205	76	72	87	131	188	264	311	569	721
1.金银珠宝饰品	Jewellerys	47	17	27	4	15	39	60	55	229	361
2.手表	Watches	4	0	0	0	1	2	4	9	20	8
3.理发美容用具	Haircut and Cosmetology Articles	3	0	0	3	1	3	3	4	7	8
4.化妆品	Cosmetics	94	33	25	48	72	85	126	159	186	209
5.其他杂品	Other Miscellanecus Commodities	58	26	20	32	41	58	71	84	128	136
㈡服务	Services	95	34	29	41	57	86	126	179	219	273
1.旅馆住宿费	Accommodation Expenses at Inn	8	2	4	2	6	6	13	22	14	18
2.理发洗澡费	Washing and Haircut Service Charges	25	13	11	16	21	25	35	32	42	44
3.美容费	Cosmetology Service Charges	19	2	1	3	7	20	29	40	50	65
4.其他服务	Other Services	42	17	13	21	23	36	50	85	114	146

4-7 全省城镇居民非食品消费数量

Whole Province Consumption Amount for Non-food of Urban Households

类别	Classification	单位	unit	总计 Total	最低10% Lowest Income Household	更低5% of which: Lower	低10% Low Income Household	较低20% Lower Middle Income Household	中间20% Middle Income Household	较高20% Upper Middle Income Household	高10% High Income Household	最高10% Highest Income Household	更高5% of which: Higher
服装	Garments	件/人	unit/person	7.99	5.09	4.06	6.00	7.30	8.25	9.26	9.89	11.37	12.06
1.男士服装	Men's Clothing	件/人	unit/person	3.06	1.98	1.60	2.35	2.85	3.15	3.45	3.71	4.44	4.83
2.女士服装	Women's Clothing	件/人	unit/person	3.75	2.29	1.80	2.65	3.29	3.81	4.45	4.99	5.63	5.82
3.童装	Children's Clothing	件/人	unit/person	1.18	0.82	0.66	1.00	1.16	1.29	1.36	1.19	1.30	1.40
鞋类	Footwear	双/人	pair/person	3.17	2.49	2.20	2.94	3.05	3.25	3.30	3.58	3.85	4.00
洗衣机	Washing Machines	台/百户	unit/100 households	4.44	0.48	0.00	5.16	4.44	5.04	4.68	4.92	5.76	7.56
电风扇	Electric Fans	台/百户	unit/100 households	6.24	5.28	3.84	8.04	6.84	5.16	6.00	4.68	8.40	10.92
电冰箱	Refrigerators	台/百户	unit/100 households	3.48	1.08	1.80	2.40	2.16	3.12	4.68	5.04	7.68	5.88
冰柜	Freezer	台/百户	unit/100 households	0.72	0.00	0.00	0.00	0.36	0.72	1.08	1.44	1.44	0.96
微波炉	Microwave Ovens	台/百户	unit/100 households	2.04	0.60	0.00	0.36	2.40	1.68	3.48	1.56	2.76	3.12
空调器	Air Conditioner	台/百户	unit/100 households	5.40	0.72	0.96	2.88	5.28	5.52	7.80	6.24	8.16	13.32
电炊具	Electric Cookers	台/百户	unit/100 households	8.04	3.36	1.68	6.60	8.04	8.52	8.28	10.32	10.56	13.44
淋浴热水器	Water Heaters	台/百户	unit/100 households	5.16	1.08	0.00	2.16	5.88	4.68	6.12	7.80	7.92	10.32
排油烟机	Lampblack Exhausters	台/百户	unit/100 households	3.36	0.12	0.00	2.04	2.28	4.44	4.08	3.84	7.20	7.92
吸尘器	Vacuam Cleaner	台/百户	unit/100 households	0.72	0.00	0.00	0.12	0.96	1.32	0.12	1.20	0.72	0.96
消毒碗柜	Sterilized Cabinet	台/百户	unit/100 households	0.12	0.00	0.00	0.00	0.00	0.24	0.12	0.00	0.24	0.48
洗碗机	Dishwasher	台/百户	unit/100 households	0.00	0.00	0.00	0.00	0.00	0.00	0.12	0.00	0.00	0.00
饮水机	Drinking Machine	台/百户	unit/100 households	2.64	0.72	0.00	1.68	1.32	3.84	2.16	4.68	5.28	6.48
取暖器	Heater	台/百户	unit/100 households	2.40	1.80	1.20	2.16	1.92	2.64	1.44	2.64	5.64	6.60
摩托车	Motorcycles	辆/百户	unit/100 households	0.24	0.72	0.96	0.00	0.24	0.36	0.24	0.36	0.12	0.00
自行车	Bicycles	辆/百户	unit/100 households	13.92	15.24	10.56	13.80	14.52	12.84	15.00	10.92	13.80	8.28
助力车	Motorbikes	辆/百户	unit/100 households	7.80	7.44	9.36	7.68	7.80	9.60	7.08	7.56	6.00	6.12

4-7 续表 1 continued

类别	Classification	单位	unit	总计 Total	最低10% Lowest Income Household	更低5% of which: Lower	低10% Low Income Household	较低20% Lower Middle Income Household	中间20% Middle Income Household	较高20% Upper Middle Income Household	高10% High Income Household	最高10% Highest Income Household	更高5% of which: Higher
家用汽车	Automobiles	辆/百户	unit/100 households	1.20	0.00	0.00	0.00	0.84	0.72	1.08	2.16	5.40	6.36
电话机	Fixed Phones	部/百户	unit/100 households	3.60	3.96	1.32	2.28	3.12	4.80	2.52	3.84	5.16	5.28
移动电话	Mobile Phones	部/百户	unit/100 households	26.04	9.48	6.00	24.48	24.12	27.48	32.52	26.52	32.64	35.16
传真机	Faxes	部/百户	unit/100 households	0.00	0.00	0.00	0.00	0.00	0.00	0.00	0.00	0.24	0.48
彩色电视机	Color TV Sets	台/百户	unit/100 households	4.92	1.80	2.28	4.08	4.56	5.64	5.28	4.20	8.40	11.88
影碟机	Video Disc Players	台/百户	unit/100 households	1.68	0.96	1.92	0.84	2.52	0.96	0.96	3.48	2.64	3.24
录放像机	Video Recorders	台/百户	unit/100 households	0.12	0.00	0.00	0.00	0.24	0.00	0.00	0.96	0.00	0.00
整机电脑	Entire Computers	台/百户	unit/100 households	5.40	1.80	1.20	3.00	3.12	6.12	7.32	7.20	9.36	10.32
组合音响	Hi-Fi Stereo Component System	台/百户	unit/100 households	0.24	0.00	0.00	0.48	0.24	0.24	0.24	0.72	0.24	0.00
录音机	Tape Recorders	台/百户	unit/100 households	2.40	0.72	0.00	1.92	2.64	2.64	3.24	2.64	2.04	3.48
摄像机	Pickup Cameras	架/百户	unit/100 households	0.48	0.00	0.00	0.00	0.12	0.60	0.72	0.24	2.28	3.24
照相机	Cameras	架/百户	unit/100 households	3.24	0.00	0.00	1.32	1.08	2.04	5.76	6.72	7.20	7.92
钢琴	Pianos	架/百户	unit/100 households	0.12	0.00	0.00	0.00	0.00	0.00	0.48	0.00	0.00	0.00
其他中高档乐器	Other Medium and Top Grade Music Instruments	件/百户	unit/100 households	0.72	0.48	0.96	0.36	0.60	0.36	0.84	1.68	1.56	0.48
健身器材	Body Building Equipment	件/人	unit/100 households	0.00	0.00	0.00	0.00	0.00	0.00	0.00	0.00	0.01	0.01
电子辞典	Electronic Dictionary	部/人	unit/100 households	0.01	0.01	0.00	0.00	0.01	0.01	0.01	0.02	0.01	0.01
水	Water	吨/人	ton/person	18.54	12.40	11.74	15.14	16.66	18.38	19.86	25.24	27.85	26.93
电	Electricity	度/人	kwh/person	360.17	216.18	212.19	257.91	317.84	355.60	415.51	472.74	598.80	622.15
煤炭	Coal	千克/人	kg/person	98.28	171.52	185.33	139.08	116.36	87.33	66.20	44.87	43.45	51.78
液化石油气	Liquefied Petroleum Gas	千克/人	kg/person	10.09	9.94	11.41	7.95	9.49	11.59	10.68	11.18	8.80	7.05
管道煤气	Pipeline Gas	立方米/人	cu.m/person	24.84	10.29	7.81	20.95	21.20	24.80	26.90	36.16	44.94	46.13
手表	Watches	只/人	unit/person	0.03	0.01	0.00	0.02	0.02	0.03	0.03	0.05	0.05	0.06

4-8 全省城镇居民家庭非现金收入

Whole Province Non-cash Income of Urban Households

单位：元/人 unit:yuan/person

类别	Classification	总计 Total	最低10% Lowest Income Household	更低5% of which: Lower	低10% Low Income Household	较低20% Lower Middle Income Household	中间20% Middle Income Household	较高20% Upper Middle Income Household	高10% High Income Household	最高10% Highest Income Household	更高5% of which: Higher
非现金（实物与服务）收入总计	**Total Non-cash(material objects and services) income**	**593**	**350**	**249**	**439**	**525**	**572**	**693**	**784**	**979**	**927**
一、食品	**Food**	**145**	**83**	**81**	**94**	**113**	**129**	**158**	**164**	**392**	**406**
㈠粮油类	Grain and Oil	38	25	23	28	34	37	41	38	77	76
1.粮食	Grain	13	10	10	11	13	13	14	9	23	22
2.淀粉及薯类	Starches and Tubers	1	0	0	0	1	0	1	1	1	2
3.干豆类及豆制品	Dried Beans and Bean Products	0	0	0	0	0	0	0	1	1	0
4.油脂类	Oil or Fat	24	15	13	18	21	23	26	28	52	52
㈡肉禽蛋水产品类	Meat,Poultry,Eggs and Aquatic Products	35	21	22	22	26	33	40	34	91	85
1.肉类	Meat	13	10	9	11	10	10	16	13	27	27
2.禽类	Poultries	2	1	2	1	2	2	2	2	3	3
3.蛋类	Eggs	5	3	4	3	6	5	6	4	15	19
4.水产品类	Aquatic Products	15	7	8	7	8	16	17	14	46	36
㈢蔬菜类	Vegetables	3	2	3	2	2	3	3	2	9	12
㈣调味品	Flavoring	1	0	0	1	1	1	1	1	2	2
㈤糖烟酒饮料类	Carbohydrate,Tobacco,Liquor and Beverages	31	14	11	17	23	24	35	33	111	103
1.糖类	Carbohydrate	0	0	0	0	0	0	1	0	1	1
2.烟草类	Tobacco	5	0	0	2	4	3	3	7	26	14
3.酒类	Liquor	22	13	10	14	16	18	25	21	67	65
4.饮料类	Beverages	4	1	1	2	3	2	5	4	17	22
㈥干鲜瓜果类	Dried and Fresh Melons and Fruits	9	3	4	3	6	6	10	14	28	29
㈦糕点、奶及奶制品	Cake,Milk and Products	13	8	7	7	12	12	15	14	30	34
1.糕点	Cake	3	1	2	1	3	3	4	4	10	14
2.奶及奶制品	Milk and Products	10	7	6	6	9	8	11	10	20	20
㈧其他食品	Other Foods	6	6	6	7	3	4	4	5	18	26
㈨饮食服务	Catering Services	10	3	4	6	6	9	10	22	27	40
1.食品加工服务费	Proceeding Services	0	0	0	0	0	0	0	1	0	1
2.在外饮食	Outward Dinner	10	3	4	6	6	9	10	21	26	39
二、衣着	**Clothing**	**15**	**11**	**7**	**8**	**12**	**12**	**16**	**22**	**36**	**51**
㈠服装	Garments	12	9	6	6	10	9	14	16	29	42
㈡衣着材料	Clothing Material	0	0	0	0	0	0	0	1	1	1

4-8 续表 1 continued

类别	Classification	总计 Total	最低10% Lowest Income House-hold	更低5% of which: Lower	低10% Low Income House-hold	较低20% Lower Middle Income Househ-old	中间20% Middle Income House-hold	较高20% Upper Middle Income House-hold	高10% High Income House-hold	最高10% Highest Income House-hold	更高5% of which: Higher
㈢鞋类	Footwear	2	1	1	1	1	2	2	4	4	5
㈣其他衣着用品	Other Clothing	1	0	0	0	0	0	0	1	1	2
㈤衣着加工服务费	Clothing Proceeding Services	0	0	0	0	0	0	0	0	0	0
三、家庭设备用品及服务	**Household Facilities,Articles and Services**	**9**	**3**	**2**	**10**	**6**	**6**	**15**	**12**	**18**	**22**
㈠耐用消费品	Durable Consumer Goods	5	1	0	7	3	4	8	7	6	10
㈡室内装饰品	Interior Decorations	0	0	0	0	0	0	1	1	1	0
㈢床上用品	Bed Articles	2	0	1	0	1	1	3	2	5	4
㈣家庭日用杂品	Grocery for Daily Use	2	2	1	2	2	1	3	3	6	8
㈤家具材料	Furniture Materials	0	0	0	0	0	0	0	0	0	0
㈥家庭服务	Household Service	0	0	0	0	0	0	0	0	0	0
四、医疗保健	**Health Care and Personal Articles**	**14**	**2**	**2**	**3**	**10**	**12**	**13**	**22**	**56**	**75**
㈠医疗器具	Medical Appliances	0	0	0	0	0	0	0	0	0	0
㈡保健用品	Health Care Appliances	0	0	0	0	0	0	0	3	3	2
㈢药品费	Drugs Charges	3	0	0	1	1	2	1	3	19	36
㈣滋补保健品	Nutritious and Health Articles	1	0	0	0	1	1	1	2	6	11
㈤医疗费	Medical Charges	2	1	1	0	3	5	0	3	5	3
㈥其他	Others	7	1	1	2	4	5	9	11	24	23
其中:医疗基金	among:medical fund	4	1	1	1	3	4	6	4	11	12
五、交通和通讯	**Transportation and Communication**	**3**	**1**	**3**	**0**	**3**	**2**	**2**	**5**	**10**	**18**
㈠交通	Transportation	1	1	2	0	2	1	0	0	5	10
㈡通信	Communication	2	0	0	0	2	1	2	4	5	9
六、教育文化娱乐服务	**Education, Culture andRecreation Articles**	**23**	**2**	**3**	**13**	**6**	**11**	**47**	**54**	**47**	**65**
㈠文化娱乐用品	Culture and Recreation Articles	4	1	1	9	1	2	8	1	8	15
㈡文化娱乐服务	Culture and Recreation Services	18	0	0	4	5	9	38	53	34	41
㈢教育	Education	1	1	1	0	0	0	2	0	4	8
七、居住	**Residence**	**3**	**1**	**1**	**4**	**2**	**3**	**5**	**4**	**4**	**7**
㈠住房	Housing	0	0	0	0	0	0	0	0	0	0
㈡水电燃料及其他	Water, Electricity,Fuel and Others	3	1	1	4	1	3	5	4	4	7
㈢居住服务费	Charges of Residence Service	0	0	0	0	2	0	0	0	0	0
八、杂项商品和服务	**Miscellanecus Commodities and Services**	**382**	**246**	**151**	**306**	**373**	**396**	**438**	**502**	**417**	**283**
㈠杂项商品	Miscellanecus Commodities	9	1	0	1	2	1	6	19	74	26
㈡服务	Services	373	245	151	305	371	395	431	483	343	256

4-9 全省城镇居民家庭年末耐用品百户拥有量

Whole Province Number of Durable Consumer Goods Owned by Per 100 Urban Households at the Year-end

类别	Classification	单位	unit	总计 Total	最低10% Lowest Income Household	更低5% of which: Lower	低10% Low Income Household	较低20% Lower Middle Income Household	中间20% Middle Income Household	较高20% Upper Middle Income Household	高10% High Income Household	最高10% Highest Income Household	更高5% of which: Higher
1.成套家具	Furniture Sets	套	set	93.47	89.33	79.65	94.55	93.67	93.99	92.72	95.10	95.27	93.92
2.摩托车	Motorcycles	辆	unit	46.63	44.07	37.14	56.18	54.85	50.35	41.63	39.79	29.07	38.16
3.自行车	Bicycles	辆	unit	168.16	178.50	171.86	188.81	177.26	164.72	161.00	150.45	151.98	135.55
4.助力车	Motorbikes	辆	unit	25.07	19.77	18.87	21.84	28.92	27.05	26.93	25.05	17.93	18.06
5.家用汽车	Automobiles	辆	unit	6.15	3.06	1.96	3.44	3.69	4.65	9.46	6.20	14.75	19.20
6.洗衣机	Washing Machines	台	unit	95.09	82.09	76.81	87.53	91.78	96.16	100.84	100.69	106.38	107.95
7.电风扇	Electric Fans	台	unit	168.11	180.76	179.54	172.56	183.53	161.29	160.79	158.86	152.37	148.32
8.电冰箱	Refrigerators	台	unit	92.09	70.86	66.70	85.18	89.53	92.53	99.34	102.83	103.22	105.79
9.冰柜	Freezer	台	unit	14.90	8.91	11.02	10.61	13.03	12.30	18.36	17.37	26.99	28.96
10.彩色电视机	Color TV Sets	台	unit	120.40	109.93	111.05	110.67	119.88	119.14	123.16	129.05	133.09	141.95
11.影碟机	Video Disc Players	台	unit	66.95	57.31	49.45	66.21	69.18	67.53	67.13	67.92	71.24	71.34
12.录音机	Tape Recorders	台	unit	53.49	40.19	37.30	46.94	53.04	55.75	57.80	60.12	56.71	57.82
13.录放像机	Video Recorders	台	unit	18.57	7.93	8.41	11.16	16.41	20.21	22.68	22.76	27.96	23.50
14.家用电脑	Computers	台	unit	52.71	19.30	15.57	33.26	46.92	54.93	67.58	68.49	74.98	81.46
15.组合音响	Hi-Fi Stereo Component System	套	set	24.22	14.10	16.10	19.95	23.70	25.45	23.85	31.18	33.08	35.44
16.摄像机	Pickup Cameras	架	unit	6.44	3.06	0.95	1.74	2.41	7.93	7.30	11.78	14.62	17.56
17.照相机	Cameras	架	unit	58.30	30.29	29.51	41.92	49.28	55.32	72.00	77.55	88.27	85.31
18.钢琴	Pianos	架	unit	3.45	0.34	0.00	0.53	.1.96	3.18	5.83	5.72	7.08	10.37
19.其他中高档乐器	Other Medium and Top Grade Music Instrument	件	piece	9.86	5.85	7.01	7.31	6.65	11.11	15.72	7.17	12.62	16.28
20.微波炉	Microwave Ovens	台	unit	46.32	17.02	14.06	26.51	37.37	50.31	58.03	61.41	75.16	82.35
21.空调器	Air Conditioner	台	unit	82.03	35.89	26.68	56.10	76.12	82.34	97.62	105.87	121.16	130.37
22.取暖器	Heater	台	unit	30.90	24.85	25.23	23.34	26.74	32.66	35.24	39.14	34.88	34.30
23.电炊具	Electric Cookers	台	unit	96.60	65.85	57.50	92.34	86.70	101.96	112.17	94.52	117.82	117.43
24.淋浴热水器	Water Heaters	台	unit	73.97	45.83	45.41	62.01	68.02	79.04	80.83	86.88	95.46	99.90
25.排油烟机	Lampblack Exhausters	台	unit	88.87	67.88	64.61	82.59	85.95	90.77	97.01	95.90	98.68	99.94
26.消毒碗柜	Sterilized Cabinet	台	unit	6.88	2.79	0.69	2.39	4.04	6.16	9.44	12.45	13.86	14.34
27.洗碗机	Dishwasher	台	unit	1.38	1.75	1.67	0.40	0.88	1.39	2.24	0.87	1.99	1.13
28.饮水机	Drinking Machine	台	unit	68.43	47.99	45.67	51.33	64.34	71.42	78.46	79.92	82.01	81.85
29.吸尘器	Vacuam Cleaner	台	unit	17.95	4.91	5.58	8.82	14.57	17.81	22.48	26.13	33.77	37.97
30.健身器材	Body Building Equipment	套	set	6.59	2.11	2.69	3.59	3.83	4.79	6.91	14.63	16.56	22.29
31.普通电话	Common Phones	部	unit	90.77	86.44	85.47	89.05	90.48	89.04	92.75	94.69	93.98	93.96
32.移动电话	Mobile Phones	部	unit	164.30	113.69	100.64	144.87	163.65	166.46	181.90	183.26	185.55	195.31
33.传真机	Faxes	部	unit	1.23	0.91	0.00	0.52	0.87	0.97	1.72	1.36	2.67	4.14

4-10 全省城镇居民家庭年末住房情况
Whole Province Housing Situation of Urban Households at the Year-end

类别	Classification	单位	unit	总计 Total	最低10% Lowest Income Household	更低5% of which: Lower	低10% Low Income Household	较低20% Lower Middle Income Household	中间20% Middle Income Household	较高20% Upper Middle Income Household	高10% High Income Household	最高10% Highest Income Household	更高5% of which: Higher
家庭居住人口数	Number of Household Residents	人/户	person/household	2.91	3.21	3.24	3.18	3.07	2.84	2.80	2.63	2.54	2.48
现住房总建筑面积	Total Housing Construction Area	平米/人	sq.m/household	29.29	24.11	22.83	25.63	28.40	29.52	31.03	33.63	35.40	37.10
现住房屋总使用面积	Total Housing used Area	平米/人	sq.m/household	22.56	18.64	17.68	19.73	21.78	22.83	23.96	25.84	27.20	28.37
房屋产权（构成）	Property Right of House	%	percentage	100.00	100.00	100.00	100.00	100.00	100.00	100.00	100.00	100.00	100.00
租赁公房	Public House for Renting	%	percentage	3.26	7.97	10.36	3.45	2.98	2.52	1.51	3.11	3.65	3.70
租赁私房	Private House for Renting	%	percentage	1.42	3.02	2.33	1.36	1.53	1.40	1.10	0.91	0.63	0.53
原有私房	Original Private House	%	percentage	9.03	19.98	22.33	13.29	10.68	8.52	3.98	2.78	5.86	6.12
房改私房	Reformed Private House	%	percentage	64.58	52.48	52.38	58.75	59.41	67.63	71.08	71.06	70.31	71.11
商品房	Commercial House	%	percentage	20.39	13.93	10.65	21.67	24.51	18.94	21.52	20.41	17.55	15.84
其他	Others	%	percentage	1.31	2.62	1.95	1.47	0.88	0.98	0.80	1.73	2.00	2.70
住宅建筑式样（构成）	Architectural Style of House	%	percentage	100.00	100.00	100.00	100.00	100.00	100.00	100.00	100.00	100.00	100.00
单栋住宅	Single House	%	percentage	0.98	1.96	2.29	0.00	1.04	1.33	0.77	0.65	0.90	0.47
四居室	House with Four Rooms	%	percentage	3.27	2.34	1.25	1.64	1.54	3.25	6.16	4.15	3.28	5.05
三居室	House with Three Rooms	%	percentage	44.67	25.65	22.25	39.43	44.23	42.45	50.78	53.51	56.60	54.31
二居室	House with Two Rooms	%	percentage	39.45	45.72	52.14	42.63	39.59	43.02	35.66	35.62	32.47	35.30
一居室	House with One Room	%	percentage	2.04	3.27	2.91	2.42	2.51	1.91	1.65	1.71	0.57	0.53
普通楼房	Common Building	%	percentage	3.16	4.02	4.62	3.08	2.41	3.97	2.39	3.58	3.41	3.00
平房及其他	Bungalow and Others	%	percentage	6.42	17.05	14.54	10.81	8.67	4.07	2.60	0.78	2.76	1.33
装修状况（构成）	Finishing Situation	%	percentage	100.00	100.00	100.00	100.00	100.00	100.00	100.00	100.00	100.00	100.00
有装修	Fit Up	%	percentage	52.85	25.69	24.46	43.66	51.49	53.44	59.59	63.97	71.14	77.05
未装修	Non-fit Up	%	percentage	47.15	74.31	75.54	56.34	48.51	46.56	40.41	36.03	28.86	22.95

4-10 续表 1 continued

类别	Classification	单位	unit	总计 Total	最低10% Lowest Income House-hold	更低5% of which: Lower	低10% Low Income House-hold	较低20% Lower Middle Income Househ-old	中间20% Middle Income House-hold	较高20% Upper Middle Income House-hold	高10% High Income House-hold	最高10% Highest Income House-hold	更高5% of which: Higher
最近一次装修花费	Finishing Cost Last Time	元/户	yuan/household	8071	2360	2390	4387	6546	7425	9869	13427	14557	17708
现有住房按市场价估计值	Marketable Estimated Value of Current House	元/户	yuan/household	136929	89658	93130	101183	123529	129786	149876	177205	210894	221165
租赁房房租	House Rent	元/户	yuan/household	141	17	21	9	4	683	4	5	10	11
自有房房租折算	Obversion of Owned-house Rent	元/户	yuan/household	295	215	212	289	275	297	320	328	351	390
购房总金额	Total Amount of Purchasing House	元/户	yuan/household	53241	34246	32928	47320	49568	53693	55496	64873	72878	81670
购房实际支出金额	Realistic Amount of Purchasing House	元/户	yuan/household	48824	31637	30541	44307	46090	49440	50690	59574	63926	71776
饮水情况（构成）	Situation of Drinking Water	%	percentage	100.00	100.00	100.00	100.00	100.00	100.00	100.00	100.00	100.00	100.00
自来水	Tap Water	%	percentage	79.37	91.90	93.20	89.24	83.89	80.73	71.89	69.46	65.99	60.94
矿泉水	Mineral Spring Water	%	percentage	10.60	1.53	1.51	4.20	6.17	9.69	15.42	19.67	21.25	23.37
纯净水	Pured Water	%	percentage	8.80	5.00	3.91	4.37	8.17	8.50	12.15	9.39	12.76	15.68
井、河水	Well Waterand River Water	%	percentage	1.19	1.58	1.39	2.19	1.77	1.08	0.45	1.28	0.00	0.00
其他	Others	%	percentage	0.04	0.00	0.00	0.00	0.00	0.00	0.09	0.19	0.00	0.00
用水情况（构成）	Situation of Drinking Water	%	percentage	100.00	100.00	100.00	100.00	100.00	100.00	100.00	100.00	100.00	100.00
独用自来水	Individual Tap-water	%	percentage	91.05	87.04	88.47	90.72	90.20	91.36	92.22	92.84	93.01	91.93
公用自来水	Public Tap-water	%	percentage	7.51	10.37	9.45	6.55	7.67	7.34	7.33	6.25	6.99	8.07
井、河水	Well Water and River Water	%	percentage	1.44	2.59	2.08	2.73	2.13	1.30	0.45	0.91	0.00	0.00
其他	Others	%	percentage	0.00	0.00	0.00	0.00	0.00	0.00	0.00	0.00	0.00	0.00
卫生设备（构成）	Health Equipment	%	percentage	100.00	100.00	100.00	100.00	100.00	100.00	100.00	100.00	100.00	100.00
无卫生设备	Non-health Equipment	%	percentage	1.99	5.81	4.79	3.50	1.80	1.03	1.18	0.83	1.19	0.70
有厕所浴室	Lavatory with Bathroom	%	percentage	63.94	47.76	48.25	57.48	60.24	64.93	69.01	72.76	76.85	81.65
有厕所无浴室	Lavatory without Bathroom	%	percentage	31.43	38.51	41.21	33.94	35.01	33.16	28.78	25.66	19.80	17.18
公用	Public	%	percentage	2.65	7.92	5.75	5.08	2.95	0.88	1.03	0.76	2.17	0.47
取暖设备（构成）	Heating Equipment	%	percentage	100.00	100.00	100.00	100.00	100.00	100.00	100.00	100.00	100.00	100.00

4-10 续表 2 continued

类别	Classification	单位	unit	总计 Total	最低10% Lowest Income Household	更低5% of which: Lower	低10% Low Income Household	较低20% Lower Middle Income Household	中间20% Middle Income Household	较高20% Upper Middle Income Household	高10% High Income Household	最高10% Highest Income Household	更高5% of which: Higher
无取暖设备	No Heating Equipment	%	percentage	4.76	10.10	11.13	6.48	4.81	4.61	2.78	2.86	2.88	2.63
空调设备	Air Conditioner	%	percentage	18.01	10.06	8.64	10.32	17.46	18.14	20.83	26.58	22.36	16.73
暖气	Heater	%	percentage	59.58	41.73	38.11	54.15	57.86	61.21	67.47	61.98	67.86	74.95
其他	Others	%	percentage	17.65	38.11	42.12	29.06	19.86	16.04	8.92	8.58	6.90	5.69
炊用燃料使用情况（构成）	Fuel of Cooking	%	percentage	100.00	100.00	100.00	100.00	100.00	100.00	100.00	100.00	100.00	100.00
管道煤气	Pipelined Gas	%	percentage	44.15	27.69	26.51	35.15	40.00	42.16	48.49	58.83	63.20	72.67
液化石油气	Liquefied Petroleum Gas	%	percentage	49.26	52.23	53.42	54.66	53.31	53.11	48.77	38.07	34.43	26.35
煤	Coal	%	percentage	5.33	18.52	17.53	8.37	5.78	3.25	1.61	1.98	1.35	0.98
其他	Others	%	percentage	1.26	1.56	2.55	1.82	0.91	1.48	1.12	1.12	1.03	0.00
通信设备使用情况	Communication Equipment	%	percentage										
(1)无电话（构成）	Non-telephone	%	percentage	100.00	100.00	100.00	100.00	100.00	100.00	100.00	100.00	100.00	100.00
无	No	%	percentage	0.60	2.25	1.14	0.44	0.97	0.00	0.36	0.22	0.23	0.47
有	Have	%	percentage	99.40	97.75	98.86	99.56	99.03	100.00	99.64	99.78	99.77	99.53
(2)固定电话	Hand-free Telephone	部/百户	unit/100 households	90.77	86.44	85.47	89.05	90.48	89.04	92.75	94.69	93.98	93.96
(3)移动电话	Mobile Telephone	部/百户	unit/100 households	164.30	113.69	100.64	144.87	163.65	166.46	181.90	183.26	185.55	195.31
(4)使用互联网	Use Internet	条/百户	piece/100 households	32.52	8.89	4.78	17.13	29.46	34.84	42.13	42.67	49.10	47.46
除了现住房，还有几处其他住房	Other Houses Besides Current House	套/户	set/household	0.11	0.09	0.09	0.09	0.10	0.11	0.12	0.13	0.16	0.19
①出租房	Houseforren	套/户	set/household	0.05	0.05	0.05	0.02	0.04	0.06	0.05	0.06	0.08	0.12
使用面积	Areaforuse	平方米/户	sq.m/household	3.58	2.92	2.80	1.44	3.31	3.70	3.41	3.93	7.24	11.67
②偶尔居住房	House for Occasionally Living	套/户	set/household	0.03	0.02	0.01	0.03	0.03	0.02	0.04	0.04	0.03	0.02
使用面积	Area for Use	平方米/户	sq.m/household	2.37	1.24	0.34	2.17	2.04	1.83	3.51	2.21	3.53	1.50
③其它用途房	House for Other Use	套/户	set/household	0.03	0.02	0.03	0.04	0.03	0.03	0.02	0.03	0.05	0.06
使用面积	Area for Use	平方米/户	sq.m/household	1.75	1.08	2.06	2.12	1.63	1.20	1.19	2.04	4.43	3.28

4-11 分调查市县城镇居民家庭人口就业情况

类别	Classification	单位	unit	济南 Jinan	青岛 Qingdao	淄博 Zibo
家庭类型（世代层次）（构成）	**Family Type**	**%**	**percentage**	**100.00**	**100.00**	**100.00**
1.单身户	Single	%	percentage	1.90	0.69	0.67
2.一对夫妇户	One Couple	%	percentage	20.43	22.38	26.39
3.两代人单亲	Two Generations Single	%	percentage	2.45	1.08	0.67
4.两代人一个小孩	Two Generations with One Child	%	percentage	62.83	63.26	66.94
5.两代人两个小孩	Two Generations with Two Children	%	percentage	3.85	2.29	1.33
6.两代人多个小孩	Two Generations with Many Children	%	percentage	0.00	0.00	0.00
7.与父母	with Parents	%	percentage	1.25	3.10	0.67
8.三代人	Three Generations	%	percentage	6.54	4.81	2.00
9.其他	Others	%	percentage	0.75	2.38	1.33
一、家庭人口数	**Number of Household Population**	**人/户**	**person/ household**	**2.88**	**2.84**	**2.77**
㈠有收入者人数	Number of Persons with Income	人/户	person/ household	2.11	2.20	2.02
1.就业人口数	Number of Employed Persons	人/户	person/ household	1.66	1.59	1.55
⑴国有经济单位职工人数	Staff and Workers of State Owned Units	人/户	person/ household	1.33	0.91	1.00
⑵城镇集体经济单位职工人数	Staff and Workers of Collective Owned Units	人/户	person/ household	0.07	0.10	0.11
⑶其他各种经济类型单位职工	Staff and Workers of Other Units	人/户	person/ household	0.14	0.31	0.13
⑷城镇个体经营者人员数	Number of Urban Individual Operators	人/户	person/ household	0.03	0.08	0.05
⑸城镇个体被雇人员数	Number of Urban Individual Employed Persons	人/户	person/ household	0.05	0.07	0.10
⑹离退休再就业人员数	Number of Retirees Employed Again	人/户	person/ household	0.00	0.05	0.03
⑺其他就业人员数	Number of Other Employed Persons	人/户	person/ household	0.04	0.08	0.11
2.离退休人数	Number of Retirees	人/户	person /household	0.37	0.55	0.45
3.其他有收入者人数	Number of Other Persons with Income	人/户	person/ household	0.08	0.06	0.03
㈡无收入者人数	Number of Persons Without Income	人/户	person/ household	0.77	0.65	0.75
二、期末家庭人口数	**Terminal Number of Household Population**	**人/户**	**person/ household**	**2.87**	**2.84**	**2.77**
三、非家庭人口在家用餐人次数	**Number of Non-household Members Eating at Home**	**人次/户**	**person · time /household**	**6.33**	**3.40**	**1.84**
四、家庭人口在外用餐人次数	**Number of Household Members Eating Outside**	**人次/户**	**person · time /household**	**13.69**	**9.60**	**3.71**
五、负担系数	**Dependency Coefficient**	**人/就业者**	**person/ employment**	**1.73**	**1.79**	**1.79**

Employment Situation of Urban Households by City and County

枣庄 Zaozhuang	东营 Dongying	烟台 Yantai	潍坊 Weifang	济宁 Jining	泰安 Taian	威海 Weihai	日照 Rizhao	莱芜 Laiwu	临沂 Linyi	德州 Dezhou
100.00	**100.00**	**100.00**	**100.00**	**100.00**	**100.00**	**100.00**	**100.00**	**100.00**	**100.00**	**100.00**
0.00	0.00	0.00	2.00	0.00	0.33	2.00	0.00	0.00	0.00	1.92
21.42	15.00	24.50	21.00	25.58	16.67	17.58	21.29	17.00	15.00	20.42
1.00	0.00	0.00	0.00	2.00	0.00	1.00	0.00	2.00	2.00	1.75
66.58	80.00	68.00	67.00	59.33	67.67	71.42	71.64	74.00	64.00	57.92
9.00	2.00	1.00	7.00	4.08	7.33	3.00	5.07	2.00	10.00	3.17
0.00	0.00	0.00	0.00	0.00	0.00	0.00	0.00	0.00	1.00	0.00
2.00	0.00	0.00	1.00	1.00	2.00	2.00	0.00	2.00	0.00	0.00
0.00	1.00	6.00	1.00	4.00	6.00	0.00	2.00	3.00	7.00	10.83
0.00	2.00	0.50	1.00	4.00	0.00	3.00	0.00	0.00	1.00	4.00
2.87	**2.88**	**2.84**	**2.83**	**2.85**	**3.00**	**2.80**	**2.87**	**2.89**	**3.05**	**2.97**
2.07	1.91	2.14	2.08	2.10	2.18	1.98	1.92	1.99	2.06	2.07
1.92	1.66	1.76	1.79	1.72	1.89	1.68	1.75	1.83	1.70	1.83
1.26	1.22	0.83	1.03	1.21	0.93	0.53	1.01	1.37	0.94	1.13
0.08	0.16	0.22	0.22	0.11	0.31	0.26	0.15	0.10	0.11	0.09
0.40	0.08	0.31	0.35	0.20	0.33	0.55	0.38	0.30	0.31	0.38
0.07	0.03	0.12	0.05	0.04	0.15	0.12	0.15	0.00	0.16	0.14
0.05	0.02	0.13	0.03	0.04	0.07	0.17	0.04	0.00	0.17	0.05
0.01	0.01	0.02	0.00	0.06	0.01	0.03	0.00	0.00	0.00	0.02
0.06	0.14	0.14	0.11	0.05	0.08	0.01	0.02	0.06	0.01	0.02
0.14	0.23	0.36	0.28	0.37	0.26	0.25	0.15	0.15	0.27	0.19
0.02	0.02	0.02	0.01	0.01	0.04	0.05	0.03	0.01	0.09	0.05
0.80	0.97	0.70	0.75	0.75	0.82	0.82	0.94	0.90	0.99	0.90
2.86	**2.88**	**2.84**	**2.83**	**2.83**	**3.00**	**2.80**	**2.89**	**2.89**	**3.05**	**2.98**
2.62	**6.98**	**8.67**	**6.03**	**0.35**	**8.07**	**8.60**	**9.18**	**4.24**	**9.19**	**8.07**
3.85	**7.92**	**20.11**	**8.01**	**1.39**	**23.64**	**15.80**	**15.51**	**6.88**	**15.99**	**22.79**
1.49	**1.73**	**1.61**	**1.58**	**1.66**	**1.59**	**1.67**	**1.64**	**1.58**	**1.79**	**1.62**

4-11 续表 1

类别	Classification	单位	unit	聊城 Liaocheng	滨州 Binzhou	菏泽 Heze
家庭类型（世代层次）（构成）	**Family Type**	%	**percentage**	**100.00**	**100.00**	**100.00**
1.单身户	Single	%	percentage	5.04	0.00	0.00
2.一对夫妇户	One Couple	%	percentage	23.70	17.58	10.00
3.两代人单亲	Two Generations Single	%	percentage	1.34	3.00	0.00
4.两代人一个小孩	Two Generations with One Child	%	percentage	44.29	65.50	62.75
5.两代人两个小孩	Two Generations with Two Children	%	percentage	7.98	1.17	14.25
6.两代人多个小孩	Two Generations with Many Children	%	percentage	0.00	0.00	0.00
7.与父母	with Parents	%	percentage	3.03	1.00	3.25
8.三代人	Three Generations	%	percentage	10.17	7.00	5.75
9.其他	Others	%	percentage	4.45	4.75	4.00
一、家庭人口数	**Number of Household Population**	人/户	**person/household**	**2.90**	**2.89**	**3.18**
㈠有收入者人数	Number of Persons with Income	人/户	person/household	1.93	1.95	1.99
1.就业人口数	Number of Employed Persons	人/户	person/household	1.48	1.69	1.75
⑴国有经济单位职工人数	Staff and Workers of State Owned Units	人/户	person/household	1.07	1.20	1.36
⑵城镇集体经济单位职工人数	Staff and Workers of Collective Owned Units	人/户	person/household	0.07	0.06	0.10
⑶其他各种经济类型单位职工	Staff and Workers of Other Units	人/户	person/household	0.07	0.21	0.20
⑷城镇个体经营者人员数	Number of Urban Individual Operators	人/户	person/household	0.01	0.12	0.05
⑸城镇个体被雇人员数	Number of Urban Individual Employed Persons	人/户	person/household	0.14	0.06	0.01
⑹离退休再就业人员数	Number of Retirees Employed Again	人/户	person/household	0.04	0.02	0.00
⑺其他就业人员数	Number of Other Employed Persons	人/户	person/household	0.09	0.02	0.02
2.离退休人数	Number of Retirees	人/户	person/household	0.35	0.21	0.17
3.其他有收入者人数	Number of Other Persons with Income	人/户	person/household	0.09	0.05	0.07
㈡无收入者人数	Number of Persons Without Income	人/户	person/household	0.97	0.94	1.19
二、期末家庭人口数	**Terminal Number of Household Population**	人/户	**person/household**	**2.90**	**2.86**	**3.17**
三、非家庭人口在家用餐人次数	**Number of Non-household Members Eating at Home**	人次/户	**person・time/household**	**3.68**	**6.55**	**5.94**
四、家庭人口在外用餐人次数	**Number of Household Members Eating Outside**	人次/户	**person・time/household**	**5.03**	**15.72**	**10.57**
五、负担系数	**Dependency Coefficient**	人/就业者	**person/employment**	**1.96**	**1.71**	**1.82**

continued

文登 Wendeng	诸城 Zhucheng	青州 Qingzhou	微山 Weishan	临清 Linqing	费县 Feixian	利津 Lijin	武城 Wucheng	东阿 Donga	巨野 Juye
100.00	**100.00**	**100.00**	**100.00**	**100.00**	**100.00**	**100.00**	**100.00**	**100.00**	**100.00**
4.00	0.00	0.00	0.00	0.00	0.00	0.00	0.00	2.00	0.00
30.00	4.00	25.67	32.67	42.00	14.33	10.83	26.00	18.00	17.17
4.00	0.00	0.00	2.00	0.00	0.00	0.00	2.00	2.00	2.00
48.67	78.00	54.33	46.00	26.00	71.17	85.17	60.00	52.00	54.83
8.00	2.00	4.92	9.33	12.00	8.00	0.00	8.00	12.00	16.00
0.00	0.00	0.00	0.00	0.00	0.00	0.00	0.00	0.00	2.00
3.33	4.00	0.00	0.00	2.00	0.00	2.00	0.00	4.00	0.67
0.00	6.00	9.08	6.00	14.00	6.00	0.00	4.00	8.00	5.33
2.00	6.00	6.00	4.00	4.00	0.50	2.00	0.00	2.00	2.00
2.65	**3.14**	**3.01**	**2.85**	**2.88**	**3.02**	**2.89**	**2.88**	**3.01**	**3.08**
1.62	2.05	2.13	2.01	2.10	1.98	1.82	1.78	2.04	1.95
1.12	1.78	1.66	1.77	1.62	1.87	1.70	1.58	1.88	1.76
0.27	0.72	0.56	1.19	1.08	1.87	0.98	1.14	1.26	1.60
0.23	0.00	0.06	0.10	0.22	0.00	0.18	0.12	0.18	0.06
0.21	0.82	0.65	0.40	0.06	0.00	0.41	0.00	0.30	0.04
0.24	0.20	0.15	0.02	0.12	0.00	0.06	0.20	0.10	0.00
0.15	0.04	0.18	0.03	0.04	0.00	0.02	0.12	0.04	0.04
0.00	0.00	0.02	0.02	0.10	0.00	0.00	0.00	0.00	0.02
0.02	0.00	0.04	0.02	0.00	0.00	0.05	0.00	0.00	0.00
0.47	0.26	0.38	0.24	0.48	0.08	0.08	0.20	0.16	0.16
0.03	0.01	0.10	0.00	0.00	0.02	0.04	0.00	0.00	0.03
1.03	1.09	0.89	0.84	0.78	1.04	1.07	1.10	0.97	1.13
2.66	**3.14**	**3.00**	**2.82**	**2.88**	**3.02**	**2.90**	**2.88**	**3.00**	**3.04**
5.31	**18.48**	**10.43**	**9.08**	**6.84**	**3.20**	**3.47**	**5.56**	**7.79**	**8.06**
6.70	**11.25**	**19.21**	**12.32**	**33.47**	**5.92**	**12.20**	**10.72**	**15.33**	**10.81**
2.37	**1.76**	**1.81**	**1.61**	**1.78**	**1.61**	**1.70**	**1.82**	**1.60**	**1.75**

4-12 分调查市县城镇居民现金收支（一）

单位：元/人

类别	Classification	济南 Jinan	青岛 Qingdao	淄博 Zibo	枣庄 Zaozhuang
一、期初手存现金	**Cash in Hand at Term-beginning**	**546**	**791**	**512**	**395**
二、家庭总收入	**Total Income**	**16831**	**16645**	**14591**	**12096**
其中：可支配收入	Disposable Income	15340	15328	13794	11020
㈠工薪收入	Income of Wages and Salaries	13762	12003	10779	10177
1.工资及补贴收入	Wages and Subsidies	13385	11677	10360	10158
2.其他劳动收入	Other Income	377	326	419	19
㈡经营净收入	Net Business Income	176	874	625	624
㈢财产性收入	Income from Properties	211	98	195	326
1.利息收入	Interest Income	30	18	8	8
2.股息与红利收入	Divident and Bonus	95	0	98	319
3.保险收益	Insurance Profit	0	18	0	0
4.其它投资收入	Other Investment Income	0	2	12	0
5.出租房屋收入	Income from Housing Renting	83	58	76	0
6.知识产权收入	Intellectual Property Income	0	0	0	0
7.其他财产性收入	Other Property Income	3	2	0	0
㈣转移性收入	Income from Transfer	2681	3669	2992	968
1.养老金或离退休金	Retirement Pension	2144	3315	2813	724
2.社会救济收入	Social Relief	17	37	13	17
3.辞退金	Dismissal Fund	0	0	0	1
4.赔偿收入	Compensation	34	4	0	0
5.保险收入	Insurance Income	35	10	7	4
其中：失业保险金	of which:UnemploymentInsurance Benefits	35	9	7	1
6.赡养收入	Alimony Income	46	45	47	10
7.捐赠收入	Contribution Income	331	153	92	130
8.亲友搭伙费	Fund for relatives or FriendsEating Regularly in	3	1	1	19
9.提取住房公积金	Housing AccumulationFund	18	54	0	23
10.记帐补贴	Account Subsidies	31	27	15	13
11.其他转移性收入	Other Transfer Income	21	24	3	27
三、出售财物收入	**Income from Properties Sale**	**38**	**18**	**88**	**209**
1.出售住房收入	Income from Housing Sale	4	0	84	202
2.出售其他物品收入	Income from Other Items Sale	34	18	4	7
四、借贷收入	**Income from Lending**	**10187**	**3668**	**9301**	**4814**
1.提取储蓄存款	Money Drawn from Bank	9170	3077	8957	3783
2.借入款	Borrowing Money	901	268	246	76
3.收回借出款	Loans Recalled	36	15	42	2
4.收回储蓄性保险本	Principal of Insurance Like Savings	8	0	3	0
5.兑售有价证券	Exchanging or Selling Marketable Securities	56	0	0	0
6.收回投资本金	Investment Principal	0	0	5	0
7.住房贷款	Housing Loan	0	255	48	953
8.汽车贷款	Car Loan	0	0	0	0
9.教育贷款	Education Loan	0	0	0	0
10.其他贷款	Other Loans	1	0	0	0
11.其他借贷收入	Other Income from Lending	14	53	0	0

Cash Income and Expenditure of Urban Households by City and County

unit:yuan/person

东营 Dongying	烟台 Yantai	潍坊 Weifang	济宁 Jining	泰安 Taian	威海 Weihai	日照 Rizhao	莱芜 Laiwu	临沂 Linyi
637	**716**	**461**	**508**	**339**	**600**	**316**	**298**	**472**
18737	**16045**	**12705**	**13009**	**12623**	**15042**	**12085**	**13319**	**13199**
16742	14374	11846	12111	11966	13975	11040	11588	12355
15331	11800	9627	10263	10277	11570	10226	12443	10477
15182	11419	9472	10227	10270	11499	10212	12406	10377
149	381	155	36	7	71	14	37	100
303	1512	833	164	519	833	458	0	978
357	263	223	266	466	328	156	47	381
131	68	68	49	78	65	12	9	32
41	107	130	71	190	50	101	12	113
28	6	4	0	21	0	7	0	0
0	12	9	90	0	133	9	0	0
3	65	12	45	177	80	23	26	236
153	0	0	0	0	0	0	0	0
0	5	0	11	0	0	3	0	0
2747	2470	2023	2315	1362	2310	1245	829	1363
1815	2117	1463	1757	1054	1686	821	717	988
0	1	12	0	1	25	12	0	6
0	0	0	0	0	0	0	0	0
223	0	5	0	0	0	1	0	0
0	8	0	0	4	17	0	0	8
0	3	0	0	0	17	0	0	8
187	98	81	114	35	125	66	0	15
119	82	400	394	208	381	309	84	133
3	8	0	0	0	0	9	0	0
347	44	0	0	0	23	0	0	33
51	72	57	33	57	46	19	28	79
2	41	5	17	3	7	8	0	102
36	**7**	**494**	**3**	**10**	**4**	**710**	**2**	**15**
31	0	488	0	0	0	704	0	0
5	7	6	3	10	4	6	2	15
7910	**8779**	**5361**	**9910**	**5751**	**4961**	**5523**	**8349**	**8072**
7515	8712	5174	9682	5612	4481	4672	7963	6919
82	6	100	11	34	441	362	282	508
25	26	86	206	22	39	374	76	49
45	1	0	7	70	0	0	1	69
0	5	0	0	0	0	2	0	0
0	0	0	4	1	0	3	0	0
243	0	0	0	0	0	0	25	525
0	0	0	0	0	0	0	0	0
0	0	0	0	0	0	0	0	0
0	25	0	0	0	0	0	2	3
0	3	0	0	11	0	110	0	0

4-12 续表 1

类别	Classification	德州 Dezhou	聊城 Liaocheng	滨州 Binzhou	菏泽 Heze
一、期初手存现金	**Cash in Hand at Term-beginning**	**310**	**408**	**631**	**381**
二、家庭总收入	**Total Income**	**11205**	**11011**	**13107**	**8919**
其中：可支配收入	Disposable Income	10257	10474	11726	8137
㈠工薪收入	Income of Wages and Salaries	9509	8280	11136	7767
1.工资及补贴收入	Wages and Subsidies	9485	8092	10983	7616
2.其他劳动收入	Other Income	24	188	153	151
㈡经营净收入	Net Business Income	404	37	493	117
㈢财产性收入	Income from Properties	180	15	249	156
1.利息收入	Interest Income	42	1	66	9
2.股息与红利收入	Divident and Bonus	83	1	166	71
3.保险收益	Insurance Profit	4	0	0	0
4.其它投资收入	Other Investment Income	19	0	8	0
5.出租房屋收入	Income from Housing Renting	31	13	9	6
6.知识产权收入	Intellectual Property Income	0	0	0	0
7.其他财产性收入	Other Property Income	0	1	0	69
㈣转移性收入	Income from Transfer	1112	2678	1229	879
1.养老金或离退休金	Retirement Pension	804	2526	954	641
2.社会救济收入	Social Relief	18	0	2	2
3.辞退金	Dismissal Fund	0	0	0	0
4.赔偿收入	Compensation	0	0	0	0
5.保险收入	Insurance Income	84	0	40	0
其中：失业保险金	of which:UnemploymentInsurance Benefits	0	0	40	0
6.赡养收入	Alimony Income	30	34	40	55
7.捐赠收入	Contribution Income	122	29	133	154
8.亲友搭伙费	Fund for relatives or FriendsEating Regularly in	0	0	0	0
9.提取住房公积金	Housing AccumulationFund	0	0	3	0
10.记帐补贴	Account Subsidies	54	79	56	27
11.其他转移性收入	Other Transfer Income	1	10	1	0
三、出售财物收入	**Income from Properties Sale**	**19**	**18**	**4**	**7**
1.出售住房收入	Income from Housing Sale	0	12	0	0
2.出售其他物品收入	Income from Other Items Sale	19	6	4	7
四、借贷收入	**Income from Lending**	**4300**	**1646**	**9160**	**2405**
1.提取储蓄存款	Money Drawn from Bank	3998	1583	8179	2136
2.借入款	Borrowing Money	263	60	749	216
3.收回借出款	Loans Recalled	18	0	163	38
4.收回储蓄性保险本	Principal of Insurance Like Savings	0	0	10	11
5.兑售有价证券	Exchanging or SellingMarketable Securities	0	0	0	4
6.收回投资本金	Investment Principal	0	0	59	0
7.住房贷款	Housing Loan	0	2	0	0
8.汽车贷款	Car Loan	0	0	0	0
9.教育贷款	Education Loan	0	0	0	0
10.其他贷款	Other Loans	2	0	0	0
11.其他借贷收入	Other Income from Lending	20	1	0	0

continued

文登 Wendeng	诸城 Zhucheng	青州 Qingzhou	微山 Weishan	临清 Linqing	费县 Feixian	利津 Lijin	武城 Wucheng	东阿 Donga	巨野 Juye
383	**258**	**547**	**722**	**211**	**220**	**217**	**276**	**148**	**230**
11645	**11719**	**10320**	**11341**	**8869**	**8502**	**12939**	**7330**	**7559**	**8070**
11019	11177	9752	10554	8337	7892	12054	7137	7049	7477
5765	8800	6887	9550	6178	7824	11401	5447	6487	6716
5491	8654	6817	9550	6117	7721	11401	5440	6486	6688
274	145	71	0	61	103	0	7	1	28
1572	966	743	10	606	0	422	828	197	0
286	39	262	95	34	64	283	50	34	197
43	6	144	11	12	39	0	16	17	26
243	22	80	73	14	4	279	2	11	9
0	0	0	0	8	0	0	0	0	69
0	0	0	0	0	21	3	0	0	76
0	11	38	8	0	0	0	0	6	13
0	0	0	0	0	0	0	0	0	0
0	0	0	2	0	0	0	31	0	4
4022	1914	2427	1687	2051	614	834	1005	841	1157
3244	1205	1731	1127	1961	314	463	686	486	739
0	0	19	0	2	0	0	0	0	0
0	0	0	0	0	0	0	0	0	0
0	0	3	0	0	4	0	0	0	0
20	0	2	0	2	0	0	10	0	0
20	0	0	0	0	0	0	0	0	0
1	29	125	87	53	16	65	45	55	135
734	666	520	415	4	187	298	222	252	240
0	0	0	0	0	0	0	0	0	0
0	0	0	0	0	40	0	0	0	0
23	14	26	58	31	8	0	42	40	37
0	0	1	0	0	45	8	0	7	6
19	**1**	**5**	**0**	**3**	**3**	**1**	**4**	**4**	**11**
8	0	0	0	0	0	0	0	0	0
11	1	5	0	3	3	1	4	4	11
10378	**3598**	**4258**	**4582**	**3949**	**1037**	**10084**	**4194**	**4111**	**4906**
9784	3546	3866	3422	3949	963	7920	3996	4000	4771
535	0	363	1158	0	70	266	160	100	57
19	0	28	1	0	0	35	21	11	0
40	0	0	0	0	4	0	17	0	0
0	0	0	0	0	0	0	0	0	0
0	0	0	0	0	0	6	0	0	26
0	0	0	0	0	0	1798	0	0	0
0	0	0	0	0	0	0	0	0	0
0	0	0	0	0	0	0	0	0	0
0	0	0	0	0	0	46	0	0	0
0	51	0	0	0	0	14	0	0	52

4-13 分调查市县城镇居民现金收支（二）

单位：元/人

类别	Classification	济南 Jinan	青岛 Qingdao	淄博 Zibo	枣庄 Zaozhuang
五、家庭总支出	**Total Expenditure**	**15981**	**15180**	**13707**	**9942**
㈠消费支出	Consumption Expenditure	10713	11945	9545	6304
其中：服务性消费支出	Consumption Expenditure for Services	2918	3047	2867	1376
1.食品	Food	3335	4352	2784	2152
2.衣着	Clothing	1111	1413	1097	1021
3.家庭设备用品及服务	Household Appliances and Services	595	801	469	361
4.医疗保健	Health care and Medical Services	931	782	809	510
5.交通和通信	Transport and Communications	1782	1424	1251	626
6.教育文化娱乐服务	Recreation,Education and Cultural Services	1450	1640	1725	867
7.居住	Residence	1134	1170	1075	495
8.杂项商品和服务	Miscellaneous Goods and Services	376	363	335	272
㈡购房与建房支出	Expenditure for HousingPurchase and Building	2465	665	1737	1288
1.购房	Housing Purchase	2465	665	1699	1288
2.建房	Housing Building	0	0	38	0
㈢转移性支出	Expenditure for Transfer	1468	1268	1660	1291
1.交纳的个人收入税	Individual Income Tax	130	21	17	11
2.捐赠支出	Contribution Expenditure	724	646	1136	821
3.购买彩票	Buying Lotteries	8	20	14	3
4.赡养支出	Alimony Expenditure	493	263	393	365
其中：在外就学子女费用	Expenditure for Chindren's Education	283	133	157	234
5.各种非储蓄性保险支出	Expenditure for Various Non-saving Insurance	47	125	80	52
其中：车辆保险支出	Expenditure for Vehicle Insurance	25	19	3	0
6.其他转移性支出	Other Transfer Expenditure	66	194	21	40
㈣财产性支出	Expenditure for Properties	6	33	0	7
1.非生产性利息支出	Expenditure for Non－productive Interest	6	5	0	7
2.其他	Others	1	28	0	0
㈤社会保障支出	Expenditure for Social Security	1329	1269	764	1052
1.个人交纳的养老基金	Pension Fund	476	410	317	435
2.个人交纳的住房公积金	Housing Accumulation Fund	702	631	301	438
3.个人交纳的医疗基金	Medical Fund	81	129	101	129
4.个人交纳的失业基金	Unemployment Fund	65	39	26	41
5.其他社会保障支出	Other Social Security Expenditure	5	60	20	8
六、借贷支出	**Expenditure for Lending**	**11004**	**4714**	**9947**	**6854**
1.存入储蓄款	Money Deposited in Bank	10126	3965	8896	6740
2.借出款	Lending Money	31	1	80	10
3.归还借款	Money Returned to the Borrower	100	62	202	39
4.储蓄性保险支出	Expenditure for Insurance Like Savings	234	160	187	4
5.购买有价证券	Buying Marketable Securities	29	4	86	0
6.其它投资支出	Other Investment	1	3	166	1
7.归还住房贷款	Housing Loan Returned	461	489	325	58
8.归还汽车贷款	Car Loan Returned	0	0	0	0
9.归还教育贷款	Education Loan Returned	0	4	0	0
10.归还其他贷款	Other Loans Returned	4	11	0	0
11.其他借贷支出	Other Expenditure for Lending	19	15	7	1
七、期末手存现金	**Cash in Hand at Term-end**	**636**	**1224**	**844**	**720**

Cash Income and Expenditure of Urban Households by City and County

unit: yuan/person

东营 Dongying	烟台 Yantai	潍坊 Weifang	济宁 Jining	泰安 Taian	威海 Weihai	日照 Rizhao	莱芜 Laiwu	临沂 Linyi
16643	**12946**	**11297**	**10192**	**10645**	**13648**	**11801**	**10852**	**12447**
10698	10316	8816	7151	8566	10505	8897	7638	8795
2844	2368	2120	1624	2371	2297	1904	1787	1984
2706	3578	2733	2543	2486	3085	2619	2567	2539
1768	1769	1146	968	964	1672	1136	965	1122
1003	328	348	715	619	811	551	572	536
698	1112	579	429	596	749	527	435	373
1057	1067	1554	643	1351	1168	2169	1034	1826
1799	1202	1223	895	1531	1174	939	1237	1113
1272	753	974	761	639	1327	634	634	978
396	508	258	196	380	519	322	195	308
2156	219	600	35	333	892	493	457	1508
2155	218	600	35	333	892	493	457	1508
1	1	0	0	0	0	0	0	0
1976	894	1089	2151	1193	1234	1403	1143	1388
140	86	10	11	47	14	18	93	44
1096	410	560	1512	815	583	865	386	908
1	5	4	6	8	6	9	3	2
539	264	360	455	239	489	431	516	315
227	38	211	340	53	333	258	377	248
165	32	79	31	0	110	41	110	99
15	5	23	0	0	14	29	20	64
35	97	75	137	84	32	40	35	21
10	5	0	0	0	11	1	4	35
10	0	0	0	0	0	1	3	5
0	5	0	0	0	11	0	1	30
1804	1512	792	854	553	1007	1008	1610	721
767	863	434	315	172	405	398	694	357
694	438	219	331	232	418	417	598	269
230	141	108	93	92	141	112	194	69
102	54	29	36	34	42	57	85	26
11	15	2	79	22	2	23	40	0
10082	**11607**	**7176**	**12800**	**7656**	**6313**	**6298**	**10629**	**8869**
9464	11342	5998	12351	7092	5652	4902	10481	8060
51	24	104	186	50	9	16	90	328
40	27	369	7	93	116	79	19	142
317	115	182	162	208	306	290	12	105
0	0	0	30	13	118	20	0	0
0	24	0	0	0	0	10	1	46
180	70	432	56	199	108	845	26	176
0	0	0	0	0	0	16	0	0
0	0	0	0	0	0	0	0	0
0	0	20	8	0	0	0	0	0
31	4	71	0	0	4	120	0	11
595	**993**	**547**	**441**	**422**	**648**	**526**	**486**	**442**

4-13 续表 1

类别	Classification	德州 Dezhou	聊城 Liaocheng	滨州 Binzhou	菏泽 Heze
五、家庭总支出	**Total Expenditure**	**9954**	**8564**	**12880**	**7860**
(一)消费支出	Consumption Expenditure	7229	6765	7989	5946
其中：服务性消费支出	Consumption Expenditure for Services	2081	1728	1895	1345
1.食品	Food	2298	2100	2454	2194
2.衣着	Clothing	941	752	906	910
3.家庭设备用品及服务	Household Appliances and Services	413	649	603	401
4.医疗保健	Health care and Medical Services	436	604	416	338
5.交通和通信	Transport and Communications	903	744	1207	605
6.教育文化娱乐服务	Recreation,Education and Cultural Services	1338	975	1331	839
7.居住	Residence	668	716	841	443
8.杂项商品和服务	Miscellaneous Goods and Services	233	226	230	216
(二)购房与建房支出	Expenditure for HousingPurchase and Building	374	0	1916	52
1.购房	Housing Purchase	340	0	1916	0
2.建房	Housing Building	34	0	0	52
(三)转移性支出	Expenditure for Transfer	1539	1345	1685	1113
1.交纳的个人收入税	Individual Income Tax	81	4	96	7
2.捐赠支出	Contribution Expenditure	824	933	974	621
3.购买彩票	Buying Lotteries	5	2	11	8
4.赡养支出	Alimony Expenditure	455	292	526	406
其中：在外就学子女费用	Expenditure forChindren's Education	290	225	314	199
5.各种非储蓄性保险支出	Expenditure for Various Non-saving Insurance	156	27	30	2
其中：车辆保险支出	Expenditure forVehicle Insurance	8	0	25	0
6.其他转移性支出	Other Transfer Expenditure	18	87	49	68
(四)财产性支出	Expenditure for Properties	0	0	61	0
1.非生产性利息支出	Expenditure for Non－productive Interest	0	0	60	0
2.其他	Others	0	0	1	0
(五)社会保障支出	Expenditure for Social Security	813	453	1230	748
1.个人交纳的养老基金	Pension Fund	405	123	574	349
2.个人交纳的住房公积金	Housing Accumulation Fund	229	180	424	293
3.个人交纳的医疗基金	Medical Fund	128	66	185	86
4.个人交纳的失业基金	Unemployment Fund	48	11	46	14
5.其他社会保障支出	Other Social Security Expenditure	2	73	0	7
六、借贷支出	**Expenditure for Lending**	**5519**	**3339**	**9390**	**3291**
1.存入储蓄款	Money Deposited in Bank	5138	3095	8064	2903
2.借出款	Lending Money	104	7	273	28
3.归还借款	Money Returned to the Borrower	7	10	141	19
4.储蓄性保险支出	Expenditure for Insurance Like Savings	8	6	213	124
5.购买有价证券	Buying Marketable Securities	34	0	263	157
6.其它投资支出	Other Investment	25	35	1	0
7.归还住房贷款	Housing Loan Returned	176	169	348	56
8.归还汽车贷款	Car Loan Returned	0	0	0	0
9.归还教育贷款	Education Loan Returned	2	0	0	0
10.归还其他贷款	Other Loans Returned	0	6	88	0
11.其他借贷支出	Other Expenditure for Lending	25	9	0	3
七、期末手存现金	**Cash in Hand at Term-end**	**359**	**1060**	**645**	**564**

continued

文登 Wendeng	诸城 Zhucheng	青州 Qingzhou	微山 Weishan	临清 Linqing	费县 Feixian	利津 Lijin	武城 Wucheng	东阿 Donga	巨野 Juye
9682	**7914**	**8782**	**13505**	**7064**	**6768**	**11775**	**6136**	**6717**	**6984**
6815	6837	6852	7186	5458	4705	6997	4958	4688	5132
1654	1444	1704	2075	1150	1094	1586	1072	1150	1352
2147	2109	2165	2325	1999	1682	2273	1626	1732	1852
840	1016	793	965	623	700	955	569	629	693
335	569	437	690	357	362	494	410	226	278
751	369	675	375	514	208	391	326	525	305
911	779	1025	699	418	453	646	453	441	648
414	1106	733	1437	623	828	1357	684	534	545
1226	721	845	417	773	391	672	798	445	508
191	169	180	279	150	82	210	91	157	302
754	127	484	3382	0	298	2075	0	66	0
754	127	484	0	0	298	2075	0	66	0
0	0	0	3382	0	0	0	0	0	0
1511	446	921	2214	1105	1165	1843	1031	1494	1298
1	24	18	7	1	3	24	5	2	3
792	353	576	1718	1022	784	1231	622	880	576
4	2	2	3	2	1	7	2	7	0
651	61	286	460	69	344	324	384	522	687
414	0	235	269	50	296	128	346	501	662
40	0	19	0	2	6	14	5	35	7
39	0	12	0	0	0	0	0	0	0
23	7	21	26	9	28	243	13	49	25
0	0	0	0	1	1	0	1	0	0
0	0	0	0	1	0	0	1	0	0
0	0	0	0	0	1	0	0	0	0
602	504	524	723	501	599	861	146	468	554
271	268	307	300	231	291	311	72	202	329
203	145	130	302	140	229	417	0	170	160
118	77	65	110	96	65	64	71	72	46
6	13	22	11	21	3	69	2	22	16
3	0	0	0	13	10	0	1	1	4
12051	**7433**	**5674**	**1934**	**5635**	**2718**	**11272**	**5448**	**4932**	**5947**
11281	7070	5305	1611	5619	2468	9984	5188	4575	5669
3	134	32	187	0	2	14	0	79	16
243	76	126	30	7	6	602	123	268	45
348	55	84	97	10	100	119	113	4	28
0	0	0	0	0	0	207	0	0	93
0	0	0	10	0	0	214	0	3	1
133	21	122	0	0	125	130	25	0	0
0	0	0	0	0	0	0	0	0	0
0	0	0	0	0	0	0	0	0	0
23	77	4	0	0	14	0	0	0	0
19	0	1	0	0	3	0	0	4	95
661	**228**	**679**	**1221**	**335**	**273**	**193**	**220**	**177**	**291**

4-14 分调查市县城镇居民食品消费支出（一）

单位：元/人

类别	Classification	济南 Jinan	青岛 Qingdao	淄博 Zibo	枣庄 Zaozhuang	东营 Dongying	烟台 Yantai
消费支出	Consumption Expenditure	10713	11945	9545	6304	10698	10316
其中：服务性消费支出	Consumption Expenditurefor Services	2918	3047	2867	1376	2844	2368
一、食品	**Food**	**3335**	**4352**	**2784**	**2152**	**2706**	**3578**
㈠粮油类	Grain and Oil	387	440	338	321	319	423
1.粮食	Grain	219	268	218	211	224	228
⑴大米	Rice	44	66	32	33	43	78
⑵面粉	Flour	31	33	36	17	39	69
⑶其他粮食	Other Grain	12	19	14	10	12	22
⑷粮食制品	Grain Products	132	149	136	152	130	58
2.淀粉及薯类	Starches and Tubers	28	31	14	20	15	33
3.干豆类及豆制品	Dried Beans and Bean Products	40	38	44	31	24	39
4.油脂类	Oil or Fat	100	103	62	59	56	123
⑴食用植物油	Vegetable Oil	100	103	62	59	55	123
⑵食用动物油	Animal Fats	0	0	0	0	0	0
㈡肉禽蛋水产品类	Meat,Poultry,Eggsand Aquatic Products	761	1338	561	578	607	1204
1.肉类	Meat	398	526	345	318	344	493
⑴猪肉	Pork	217	252	183	149	185	251
⑵牛肉	Beef	22	30	21	46	20	43
⑶羊肉	Mutton	25	27	18	14	17	45
⑷其他肉	Other Meat	1	7	5	0	2	18
⑸肉制品	Meat Products	132	210	117	109	120	136
2.禽类	Poultries	86	96	54	81	78	84
⑴鸡	Chicken	26	43	12	42	24	53
⑵鸭	Duck	2	5	0	1	11	8
⑶其他禽类	Other Poultries	0	3	0	0	1	2
⑷禽制品	Poultry Products	57	46	41	39	42	20
3.蛋类	Eggs	94	109	67	84	76	126
⑴鲜蛋	Fresh Eggs	86	97	63	81	70	115
⑵蛋制品	Eggs Products	7	12	4	3	6	11
4.水产品类	Aquatic Products	184	606	96	94	109	501
⑴鱼	Fish	66	183	35	62	43	162
⑵虾	Shrimp	60	120	20	19	38	105
⑶其他水产品	Other Aquatic Products	47	223	20	6	19	153
⑷水产制品	Aquatic Finished Products	11	81	21	7	9	82
㈢蔬菜类	Vegetables	256	336	265	192	261	413
1.鲜菜	Fresh Vegetables	236	303	249	169	245	381

Consumption Expenditure for Food of Urban Households by City and County

unit：yuan/person

潍坊 Weifang	济宁 Jining	泰安 Taian	威海 Weihai	日照 Rizhao	莱芜 Laiwu	临沂 Linyi	德州 Dezhou	聊城 Liaocheng	滨州 Binzhou	菏泽 Heze	文登 Wendeng	诸城 Zhucheng	青州 Qingzhou	微山 Weishan
8816	7151	8566	10505	8897	7638	8795	7229	6765	7989	5946	6815	6837	6852	7186
2120	1624	2371	2297	1904	1787	1984	2081	1728	1895	1345	1654	1444	1704	2075
2733	**2543**	**2486**	**3085**	**2619**	**2567**	**2539**	**2298**	**2100**	**2454**	**2194**	**2147**	**2109**	**2165**	**2325**
444	279	340	301	309	443	372	349	306	345	278	263	219	337	300
328	182	227	188	211	320	239	232	191	227	167	171	146	221	190
34	33	33	37	54	51	43	29	34	35	33	51	27	18	29
53	35	32	40	32	42	30	40	45	34	39	51	38	36	20
14	7	7	10	7	9	8	12	24	9	14	9	17	5	8
227	108	155	100	118	219	158	151	88	149	80	61	64	163	133
21	24	12	24	25	20	22	19	22	35	38	7	28	35	40
33	29	30	26	23	36	52	37	28	29	21	15	18	27	36
63	44	71	62	50	67	59	61	65	53	53	71	27	54	34
62	44	71	62	50	67	59	61	65	53	53	71	27	54	34
0	0	0	0	0	0	0	0	0	0	0	1	0	0	0
610	612	569	838	675	715	604	538	503	584	485	626	521	512	614
307	312	330	350	338	429	331	287	258	319	234	300	293	286	285
189	150	184	182	221	226	171	134	131	168	142	171	167	164	155
3	24	17	20	12	28	29	8	11	2	2	11	11	31	14
8	48	15	19	15	21	32	24	19	15	19	10	13	11	16
0	1	0	1	0	3	6	12	4	0	0	0	1	0	2
107	90	114	128	89	151	93	109	93	133	71	108	101	80	99
80	64	67	56	56	77	99	94	71	74	91	25	68	53	93
22	0	22	16	33	35	52	13	28	21	39	11	16	18	57
1	5	0	0	0	1	0	0	0	0	0	2	0	0	1
0	0	0	1	1	0	1	0	0	0	0	0	0	0	0
58	58	45	39	22	41	46	81	42	52	52	12	52	35	35
84	80	86	87	82	93	90	80	109	86	91	81	68	97	93
76	74	83	76	76	90	82	74	107	77	87	79	64	92	71
8	6	3	11	6	3	8	6	3	9	4	2	4	5	23
138	156	86	345	199	115	84	76	64	106	69	219	92	76	142
47	88	42	71	83	58	45	40	39	40	34	71	47	28	118
46	33	22	82	43	30	19	23	11	30	25	53	23	30	12
32	15	5	119	69	13	11	7	7	20	7	70	15	9	6
13	19	18	73	4	14	10	5	7	16	4	26	7	8	6
234	207	223	216	194	252	234	232	219	216	183	185	157	187	175
219	187	209	197	172	222	198	214	204	201	172	176	139	169	154

4-14 续表 1 continued

类别	Classification	临清 Linqing	费县 Feixian	利津 Lijin	武城 Wucheng	东阿 Donga	巨野 Juye
消费支出	**Consumption Expenditure**	**5458**	**4705**	**6997**	**4958**	**4688**	**5132**
其中：服务性消费支出	Consumption Expenditurefor Services	1150	1094	1586	1072	1150	1352
一、食品	**Food**	**1999**	**1682**	**2273**	**1626**	**1732**	**1852**
(一)粮油类	Grain and Oil	308	273	336	247	231	252
1.粮食	Grain	208	199	240	160	141	147
(1)大米	Rice	25	29	22	19	20	24
(2)面粉	Flour	57	32	37	51	43	46
(3)其他粮食	Other Grain	24	12	13	19	19	6
(4)粮食制品	Grain Products	101	126	169	71	59	70
2.淀粉及薯类	Starches and Tubers	17	14	14	21	16	31
3.干豆类及豆制品	Dried Beans and Bean Products	19	30	20	27	25	17
4.油脂类	Oil or Fat	65	30	62	39	49	57
(1)食用植物油	Vegetable Oil	65	30	62	39	49	57
(2)食用动物油	Animal Fats	0	0	0	0	0	1
(二)肉禽蛋水产品类	Meat,Poultry,Eggsand Aquatic Products	480	500	505	427	423	469
1.肉类	Meat	298	288	298	221	236	220
(1)猪肉	Pork	180	193	176	88	119	119
(2)牛肉	Beef	39	18	4	17	3	7
(3)羊肉	Mutton	22	22	9	38	16	54
(4)其他肉	Other Meat	0	1	5	16	4	2
(5)肉制品	Meat Products	56	55	105	62	94	38
2.禽类	Poultries	51	68	58	54	61	81
(1)鸡	Chicken	20	34	20	1	25	44
(2)鸭	Duck	0	2	1	0	0	0
(3)其他禽类	Other Poultries	0	0	0	0	0	0
(4)禽制品	Poultry Products	31	33	37	53	35	37
3.蛋类	Eggs	93	79	69	99	78	106
(1)鲜蛋	Fresh Eggs	91	76	65	98	77	104
(2)蛋制品	Eggs Products	1	2	5	1	1	2
4.水产品类	Aquatic Products	39	66	79	52	49	61
(1)鱼	Fish	26	44	34	24	32	43
(2)虾	Shrimp	5	5	18	1	7	10
(3)其他水产品	Other Aquatic Products	2	5	15	12	2	6
(4)水产制品	Aquatic Finished Products	5	11	13	15	8	3
(三)蔬菜类	Vegetables	216	160	214	172	152	149
1.鲜菜	Fresh Vegetables	198	145	200	160	142	141

4-15 分调查市县城镇居民食品消费支出（二）

Consumption Expenditure for Food of Urban Households by City and County

单位：元/人

类别	Classification	济南 Jinan	青岛 Qingdao	淄博 Zibo	枣庄 Zaozhuang
2.干菜	Dry Vegetables	11	22	4	15
3.菜制品	Vegetable Products	9	11	12	8
㈣调味品	Flavoring	41	59	31	21
㈤糖烟酒饮料类	Carbohydrate,Tobacco,Liquor and Beverages	321	456	271	229
1.糖类	Carbohydrate	25	38	16	18
2.烟草类	Tobacco	103	136	79	73
3.酒类	Liquor	111	156	113	82
(1)白酒	White Spirit	63	60	84	59
(2)果酒	Wine	5	16	5	4
(3)啤酒	Beer	43	72	23	19
(4)其他酒	Others	1	8	1	0
4.饮料	Beverages	82	126	62	56
(1)碳酸饮料	Carbonated Beverages	7	14	4	2
(2)果蔬饮料	Fruit Beverages	10	11	8	4
(3)瓶装饮用水	Bottled Beverages	15	17	13	9
(4)茶叶	Tea	37	66	25	30
(5)咖啡可可粉	Coffee Cocoa Powder	2	6	2	1
(6)其他饮料	Other Beverages	11	12	10	10
㈥干鲜瓜果类	Dried and Fresh Melons and Fruits	297	426	230	208
1.鲜果	Fresh Fruits	169	263	149	126
2.鲜瓜	Fresh Melons	57	53	38	34
3.干果	Dried Fruits	9	26	11	6
4.瓜果制品	Melon and Fruit Products	7	14	2	3
5.坚果及果仁	Nuts	55	70	31	38
㈦糕点、奶及奶制品	Cake,Milk and Products	301	333	254	221
1.糕点	Cake	81	110	67	91
2.奶及奶制品	Milk and Products	221	223	187	130
(1)鲜乳品	Fresh Milk	144	145	157	84
(2)奶粉	Milk Power	33	14	4	17
(3)酸奶	Yogurt	26	40	13	9
(4)其他奶制品	Others	17	25	13	20
㈧其他食品	Other Foods	78	115	164	36
其中：半成品	Semi-finished Products	10	10	2	9
㈨饮食服务	Catering Services	894	850	669	346
1.食品加工服务费	Proceeding Services	1	2	0	1
2.在外饮食	Outward Dinner	893	849	668	345
(1)购自食堂	Food from Dining Room	129	83	50	36
(2)购自饮食业	Food from Catering Trade	748	753	617	309
(3)在亲友家搭伙支出	Expenditure for relatives or Friends Eating Regularly in	16	12	1	0

4-15 续表 1

类别	Classification	东营 Dongying	烟台 Yantai	潍坊 Weifang	济宁 Jining
2.干菜	Dry Vegetables	9	27	9	11
3.菜制品	Vegetable Products	8	5	7	9
(四)调味品	Flavoring	30	38	34	31
(五)糖烟酒饮料类	Carbohydrate,Tobacco,Liquor and Beverages	225	376	286	235
1.糖类	Carbohydrate	25	35	23	22
2.烟草类	Tobacco	58	112	105	70
3.酒类	Liquor	91	120	97	91
(1)白酒	White Spirit	59	47	61	62
(2)果酒	Wine	5	5	4	5
(3)啤酒	Beer	26	55	30	24
(4)其他酒	Others	1	13	3	0
4.饮料	Beverages	51	109	61	52
(1)碳酸饮料	Carbonated Beverages	9	11	7	7
(2)果蔬饮料	Fruit Beverages	13	13	5	3
(3)瓶装饮用水	Bottled Beverages	8	21	9	3
(4)茶叶	Tea	19	52	28	31
(5)咖啡可可粉	Coffee Cocoa Powder	2	4	1	0
(6)其他饮料	Other Beverages	2	9	11	8
(六)干鲜瓜果类	Dried and Fresh Melons and Fruits	288	359	272	246
1.鲜果	Fresh Fruits	171	256	157	127
2.鲜瓜	Fresh Melons	60	55	56	54
3.干果	Dried Fruits	11	24	4	4
4.瓜果制品	Melon and Fruit Products	7	6	5	4
5.坚果及果仁	Nuts	39	18	50	57
(七)糕点、奶及奶制品	Cake,Milk and Products	257	316	256	234
1.糕点	Cake	60	70	108	68
2.奶及奶制品	Milk and Products	197	245	148	167
(1)鲜乳品	Fresh Milk	125	181	118	153
(2)奶粉	Milk Power	9	21	5	2
(3)酸奶	Yogurt	24	35	14	2
(4)其他奶制品	Others	39	9	11	10
(八)其他食品	Other Foods	103	55	57	63
其中：半成品	Semi-finished Products	0	2	3	9
(九)饮食服务	Catering Services	616	393	540	636
1.食品加工服务费	Proceeding Services	0	6	6	1
2.在外饮食	Outward Dinner	616	388	534	635
(1)购自食堂	Food from Dining Room	108	104	128	10
(2)购自饮食业	Food from Catering Trade	500	283	406	625
(3)在亲友家搭伙支出	Expenditure for relatives or Friends Eating Regularly in	8	1	0	0

continued

泰安 Taian	威海 Weihai	日照 Rizhao	莱芜 Laiwu	临沂 Linyi	德州 Dezhou	聊城 Liaocheng	滨州 Binzhou	菏泽 Heze	文登 Wendeng	诸城 Zhucheng	青州 Qingzhou	微山 Weishan	临清 Linqing	费县 Feixian
8	13	8	14	11	11	8	7	7	5	8	3	9	10	5
6	7	13	17	25	8	7	7	4	3	10	15	13	8	10
28	35	23	32	33	32	37	26	32	37	30	28	28	32	24
243	296	344	242	237	214	190	230	220	212	263	220	166	226	167
17	34	26	13	24	23	19	29	21	15	23	20	14	14	21
62	91	132	49	72	64	50	83	80	88	66	53	71	69	31
115	120	130	123	97	77	81	73	91	79	143	101	53	64	93
82	67	91	72	66	46	56	50	70	52	108	66	42	39	76
3	10	14	4	8	3	4	2	5	2	4	3	4	4	1
29	41	24	43	21	27	20	20	16	22	31	32	7	21	14
1	1	1	2	2	0	0	0	0	3	0	0	0	0	2
48	50	57	57	44	50	41	46	29	30	30	46	27	79	22
8	6	5	8	8	5	3	6	5	5	7	9	6	3	2
8	12	5	10	8	10	12	5	6	7	8	6	5	3	2
2	10	6	18	8	8	4	7	3	13	2	3	2	1	2
21	10	23	17	10	17	17	22	7	4	13	21	14	39	9
1	3	2	1	1	1	0	3	1	0	1	1	0	0	1
9	10	17	4	9	10	5	4	8	0	1	6	1	33	6
211	326	190	225	234	218	231	231	208	169	176	210	182	173	142
120	206	122	147	137	128	136	127	125	121	107	121	100	90	91
42	54	27	37	50	31	38	49	44	22	32	37	33	22	22
2	14	9	12	17	7	19	8	11	4	21	5	13	19	12
5	9	4	4	5	7	6	6	3	1	5	4	7	4	6
42	43	28	25	26	44	32	41	24	21	9	43	28	37	11
233	313	254	247	240	178	212	227	261	241	263	219	197	163	173
63	82	85	67	90	59	46	77	84	19	126	65	95	62	63
170	231	169	180	151	120	166	150	177	222	137	154	102	101	110
91	159	110	119	114	83	123	101	138	155	106	117	53	92	82
11	11	24	14	16	9	14	6	9	30	5	6	6	1	14
51	32	22	35	9	16	15	19	20	11	9	9	35	5	10
17	30	13	12	11	12	15	24	10	27	17	23	8	2	4
84	100	54	43	61	33	100	35	81	108	2	65	31	55	59
9	13	4	10	7	7	5	8	16	5	0	8	12	18	0
554	660	577	368	523	503	302	560	445	306	478	387	633	344	184
1	0	1	1	1	1	1	1	1	1	1	1	1	0	2
553	660	576	368	522	503	302	559	444	305	477	385	632	344	182
9	131	86	59	125	25	2	169	111	22	101	26	159	1	3
545	530	482	261	397	478	299	390	333	283	376	359	472	343	172
0	0	9	47	0	0	0	0	0	0	0	0	0	0	7

4-15 续表 2 continued

类别	Classification	利津 Lijin	武城 Wucheng	东阿 Donga	巨野 Juye
2.干菜	Dry Vegetables	7	5	4	3
3.菜制品	Vegetable Products	7	7	6	4
㈣调味品	Flavoring	22	28	27	23
㈤糖烟酒饮料类	Carbohydrate,Tobacco,Liquor and Beverages	237	118	183	203
1.糖类	Carbohydrate	22	8	18	19
2.烟草类	Tobacco	76	36	39	84
3.酒类	Liquor	95	55	109	75
(1)白酒	White Spirit	82	40	91	56
(2)果酒	Wine	2	0	2	3
(3)啤酒	Beer	11	14	15	15
(4)其他酒	Others	1	1	1	0
4.饮料	Beverages	43	18	18	26
(1)碳酸饮料	Carbonated Beverages	9	0	4	2
(2)果蔬饮料	Fruit Beverages	5	1	4	6
(3)瓶装饮用水	Bottled Beverages	5	1	2	10
(4)茶叶	Tea	20	4	4	5
(5)咖啡可可粉	Coffee Cocoa Powder	1	0	2	1
(6)其他饮料	Other Beverages	3	11	2	2
㈥干鲜瓜果类	Dried and Fresh Melons and Fruits	202	144	138	172
1.鲜果	Fresh Fruits	117	86	73	95
2.鲜瓜	Fresh Melons	44	22	23	36
3.干果	Dried Fruits	1	4	5	6
4.瓜果制品	Melon and Fruit Products	13	0	8	7
5.坚果及果仁	Nuts	27	31	29	28
㈦糕点、奶及奶制品	Cake,Milk and Products	245	150	186	179
1.糕点	Cake	62	53	49	56
2.奶及奶制品	Milk and Products	183	97	137	123
(1)鲜乳品	Fresh Milk	97	86	106	95
(2)奶粉	Milk Power	25	2	14	13
(3)酸奶	Yogurt	30	2	11	8
(4)其他奶制品	Others	30	7	7	7
㈧其他食品	Other Foods	122	64	31	21
其中：半成品	Semi-finished Products	4	0	1	3
㈨饮食服务	Catering Services	390	277	361	385
1.食品加工服务费	Proceeding Services	1	0	3	0
2.在外饮食	Outward Dinner	389	277	358	384
(1)购自食堂	Food from Dining Room	9	0	11	39
(2)购自饮食业	Food from Catering Trade	381	277	346	342
(3)在亲友家搭伙支出	Expenditure for relatives or Friends Eating Regularly in	0	0	0	4

4-16 分调查市县城镇居民食品消费数量

Consumption Amount for Food of Urban Households by City and County

单位：千克/人 unit:kg/person

类别	Classification	济南 Jinan	青岛 Qingdao	淄博 Zibo	枣庄 Zaozhuang	东营 Dongying	烟台 Yantai	潍坊 Weifang
粮食	**Grain**	**65.98**	**80.72**	**70.02**	**69.47**	**68.77**	**70.60**	**93.55**
(1)大米	Rice	13.83	19.65	10.39	10.53	14.43	23.27	11.36
(2)面粉	Flour	12.71	12.73	15.67	7.53	16.77	28.68	23.40
(3)其他粮食	Other Grain	3.60	5.87	4.03	3.59	4.01	6.04	4.81
(4)粮食制品	Grain Products	35.84	42.46	39.94	47.81	33.57	12.61	53.98
淀粉及薯类	**Starches and Tubers**	**11.56**	**11.09**	**5.57**	**9.52**	**5.43**	**14.23**	**7.80**
油脂类	**Oil or Fat**	**7.93**	**8.79**	**5.03**	**5.92**	**4.29**	**10.43**	**4.94**
(1)食用植物油	Vegetable Oil	7.92	8.79	5.02	5.92	4.27	10.39	4.92
(2)食用动物油	Animal Fats	0.00	0.00	0.00	0.00	0.02	0.04	0.02
肉类	**Meat**	**25.04**	**33.83**	**22.23**	**18.93**	**23.06**	**33.82**	**22.22**
(1)猪肉	Pork	16.67	18.33	14.06	10.78	13.71	20.42	16.24
(2)牛肉	Beef	1.26	1.84	1.29	2.65	1.05	2.51	0.20
(3)羊肉	Mutton	1.30	1.69	0.89	0.90	0.95	2.55	0.49
(4)其他肉	Other Meat	0.04	0.55	0.45	0.01	0.13	1.30	0.02
(5)肉制品	Meat Products	5.77	11.41	5.54	4.59	7.21	7.03	5.27
禽类	**Poultries**	**5.08**	**6.47**	**3.38**	**5.82**	**5.63**	**6.27**	**4.75**
(1)鸡	Chicken	2.23	3.56	1.01	3.81	1.93	4.32	1.86
(2)鸭	Duck	0.20	0.37	0.03	0.05	0.84	0.65	0.06
(3)其他禽类	Other Poultries	0.00	0.28	0.02	0.00	0.08	0.12	0.00
(4)禽制品	Poultry Products	2.64	2.26	2.32	1.95	2.77	1.18	2.82
蛋类	**Eggs**	**16.49**	**20.22**	**12.01**	**15.14**	**13.27**	**23.85**	**15.48**
(1)鲜蛋	Fresh Eggs	15.88	18.64	11.52	14.82	12.65	22.61	14.67
(2)蛋制品	Eggs Products	0.61	1.57	0.49	0.32	0.61	1.24	0.81
水产品类	**Aquatic Products**							
(1)鱼	Fish	6.29	13.00	3.77	8.40	4.01	13.39	4.98
(2)虾	Shrimp	2.01	4.44	0.65	0.75	1.53	3.91	1.60
(3)其他水产品	Other Aquatic Products	1.90	15.22	1.23	0.52	1.43	8.94	2.96
鲜菜	**Fresh Vegetables**	**115.83**	**108.42**	**117.37**	**94.56**	**103.63**	**153.86**	**106.40**
干菜	**Dry Vegetables**	**0.24**	**0.99**	**0.14**	**0.58**	**0.25**	**0.90**	**0.37**
酒类	**Liquor**	**12.68**	**16.41**	**8.45**	**8.30**	**6.45**	**16.11**	**9.32**
(1)白酒	White Spirit	2.34	2.45	3.23	2.43	1.48	2.78	2.70
(2)果酒	Wine	0.22	0.49	0.21	0.16	0.15	0.29	0.13
(3)啤酒	Beer	10.08	12.84	4.92	5.71	4.78	12.21	6.35
(4)其他酒	Others	0.03	0.62	0.10	0.00	0.05	0.84	0.14
碳酸饮料	**Carbonated Beverages**	**1.54**	**2.85**	**0.74**	**0.59**	**1.68**	**1.99**	**1.44**
果蔬饮料	**Fruit Beverages**	**1.70**	**2.14**	**1.35**	**0.69**	**2.08**	**2.11**	**1.00**
瓶装饮用水	**Bottled Beverages**	**26.88**	**16.85**	**18.27**	**21.54**	**3.84**	**47.01**	**13.25**
茶叶	**Tea**	**0.49**	**0.58**	**0.27**	**0.18**	**0.17**	**0.37**	**0.38**
咖啡可可粉	**Coffee Cocoa Powder**	**0.03**	**0.10**	**0.06**	**0.02**	**0.04**	**0.08**	**0.01**
鲜果	**Fresh Fruits**	**45.68**	**59.80**	**52.90**	**42.81**	**45.22**	**69.27**	**52.83**
鲜瓜	**Fresh Melons**	**36.72**	**24.59**	**24.01**	**24.30**	**32.94**	**27.53**	**33.93**
干果	**Dried Fruits**	**0.59**	**1.54**	**1.09**	**0.56**	**0.74**	**1.34**	**0.33**
瓜果制品	**Melon and Fruit Products**	**0.60**	**1.14**	**0.18**	**0.25**	**0.63**	**0.43**	**0.47**
坚果及果仁	**Nuts**	**4.88**	**4.46**	**2.75**	**3.39**	**3.21**	**1.19**	**4.35**
糕点	**Cake**	**5.13**	**8.88**	**6.27**	**8.37**	**4.43**	**6.60**	**9.45**
奶及奶制品	**Milk and Products**							
(1)鲜乳品	Fresh Milk	25.04	32.24	34.12	14.86	29.48	48.09	29.35
(2)奶粉	Milk Powder	0.38	0.53	0.13	0.30	0.22	0.62	0.08
(3)酸奶	Yogurt	4.30	6.21	2.31	1.05	3.96	4.70	2.59

4-16 续表 1

类别	Classification	济宁 Jining	泰安 Taian	威海 Weihai	日照 Rizhao	莱芜 Laiwu	临沂 Linyi	德州 Dezhou	聊城 Liaocheng
粮食	**Grain**	**77.18**	**74.40**	**46.49**	**66.41**	**98.87**	**81.00**	**78.90**	**75.49**
⑴大米	Rice	11.40	10.16	11.43	17.36	15.28	14.06	9.21	11.55
⑵面粉	Flour	16.32	15.02	17.44	14.16	19.35	14.09	17.70	21.73
⑶其他粮食	Other Grain	2.41	2.16	2.62	2.20	2.58	2.58	3.99	7.32
⑷粮食制品	Grain Products	47.06	47.06	15.00	32.69	61.65	50.27	48.00	34.89
淀粉及薯类	**Starches and Tubers**	**11.41**	**3.96**	**9.10**	**11.44**	**8.40**	**7.62**	**8.04**	**11.37**
油脂类	**Oil or Fat**	**4.70**	**6.10**	**5.28**	**4.47**	**5.60**	**5.44**	**5.56**	**7.36**
⑴食用植物油	Vegetable Oil	4.65	6.09	5.27	4.46	5.58	5.42	5.56	7.36
⑵食用动物油	Animal Fats	0.05	0.01	0.01	0.01	0.02	0.02	0.00	0.01
肉类	**Meat**	**18.97**	**21.43**	**22.75**	**22.81**	**27.97**	**22.65**	**19.42**	**17.17**
⑴猪肉	Pork	10.85	14.32	14.92	16.88	17.84	13.56	10.59	9.83
⑵牛肉	Beef	1.32	1.01	1.06	0.64	1.60	1.55	0.49	0.61
⑶羊肉	Mutton	2.41	0.77	0.97	0.77	1.10	1.69	1.32	1.01
⑷其他肉	Other Meat	0.05	0.01	0.04	0.01	0.26	0.53	0.99	0.31
⑸肉制品	Meat Products	4.35	5.31	5.76	4.51	7.17	5.32	6.03	5.41
禽类	**Poultries**	**4.80**	**4.22**	**3.35**	**3.69**	**5.14**	**6.68**	**5.24**	**5.26**
⑴鸡	Chicken	0.02	2.07	1.56	2.49	3.06	4.04	1.19	2.83
⑵鸭	Duck	0.36	0.00	0.03	0.06	0.10	0.03	0.00	0.05
⑶其他禽类	Other Poultries	0.03	0.00	0.02	0.04	0.00	0.04	0.02	0.01
⑷禽制品	Poultry Products	4.39	2.15	1.74	1.11	1.98	2.58	4.02	2.38
蛋类	**Eggs**	**14.97**	**15.96**	**15.18**	**14.26**	**17.02**	**16.33**	**15.33**	**21.23**
⑴鲜蛋	Fresh Eggs	14.43	15.69	14.22	13.72	16.70	15.44	14.61	20.84
⑵蛋制品	Eggs Products	0.54	0.26	0.96	0.55	0.32	0.89	0.72	0.39
水产品类	**Aquatic Products**								
⑴鱼	Fish	9.25	4.81	6.51	8.79	5.51	4.40	4.39	4.53
⑵虾	Shrimp	1.30	0.73	3.49	2.24	1.08	0.86	0.85	0.41
⑶其他水产品	Other Aquatic Products	0.96	0.46	11.63	6.02	0.84	0.97	0.67	0.39
鲜菜	**Fresh Vegetables**	**92.54**	**112.52**	**81.99**	**83.87**	**111.98**	**95.31**	**107.99**	**123.80**
干菜	**Dry Vegetables**	**0.51**	**0.18**	**0.24**	**0.36**	**0.79**	**0.49**	**0.26**	**0.23**
酒类	**Liquor**	**8.38**	**9.99**	**13.03**	**10.21**	**12.39**	**8.78**	**8.76**	**6.61**
⑴白酒	White Spirit	1.98	3.55	2.72	3.92	3.81	2.47	1.69	2.25
⑵果酒	Wine	0.18	0.17	0.29	0.27	0.16	0.44	0.19	0.29
⑶啤酒	Beer	6.22	6.23	9.94	5.95	8.35	5.76	6.87	4.06
⑷其他酒	Others	0.00	0.04	0.06	0.07	0.08	0.11	0.01	0.01
碳酸饮料	**Carbonated Beverages**	**1.41**	**1.59**	**1.35**	**1.44**	**1.82**	**1.56**	**1.02**	**0.60**
果蔬饮料	**Fruit Beverages**	**0.66**	**1.61**	**1.51**	**0.94**	**2.06**	**1.15**	**1.56**	**2.50**
瓶装饮用水	**Bottled Beverages**	**0.54**	**0.82**	**39.16**	**2.38**	**48.20**	**10.89**	**24.56**	**1.30**
茶叶	**Tea**	**0.22**	**0.38**	**0.09**	**0.29**	**0.24**	**0.13**	**0.17**	**0.17**
咖啡可可粉	**Coffee Cocoa Powder**	**0.01**	**0.02**	**0.03**	**0.04**	**0.02**	**0.02**	**0.02**	**0.01**
鲜果	**Fresh Fruits**	**44.42**	**42.06**	**45.86**	**38.15**	**50.91**	**45.47**	**45.19**	**50.90**
鲜瓜	**Fresh Melons**	**35.01**	**28.27**	**22.79**	**14.83**	**22.69**	**32.45**	**26.36**	**31.12**
干果	**Dried Fruits**	**0.25**	**0.09**	**0.83**	**0.94**	**0.95**	**1.61**	**0.54**	**1.52**
瓜果制品	**Melon and Fruit Products**	**0.39**	**0.51**	**0.69**	**0.31**	**0.37**	**0.51**	**0.65**	**0.58**
坚果及果仁	**Nuts**	**4.59**	**4.17**	**3.28**	**2.79**	**2.60**	**2.51**	**4.52**	**3.08**
糕点	**Cake**	**6.03**	**5.78**	**4.97**	**7.15**	**6.04**	**8.89**	**5.16**	**4.68**
奶及奶制品	**Milk and Products**								
⑴鲜乳品	Fresh Milk	51.04	27.24	26.34	16.38	26.18	22.77	16.72	29.06
⑵奶粉	Milk Power	0.05	0.27	0.24	0.44	0.55	0.50	0.34	0.38
⑶酸奶	Yogurt	0.39	12.16	4.23	2.69	6.66	1.58	2.65	3.40

continued

滨州 Binzhou	菏泽 Heze	文登 Wendeng	诸城 Zhucheng	青州 Qingzhou	微山 Weishan	临清 Linqing	费县 Feixian	利津 Lijin	武城 Wucheng	东阿 Donga	巨野 Juye
71.10	**62.82**	**64.40**	**52.25**	**72.45**	**68.29**	**90.75**	**71.50**	**73.87**	**71.03**	**60.30**	**55.00**
10.93	10.95	16.98	8.42	5.80	9.21	7.47	10.58	6.81	5.84	6.05	7.69
15.65	18.95	23.32	19.48	18.23	10.44	27.85	14.90	16.80	25.38	22.86	23.83
2.98	4.71	2.62	4.52	1.48	2.55	7.67	5.13	4.65	6.46	5.94	1.90
41.55	28.20	21.48	19.83	46.93	46.10	47.76	40.89	45.61	33.36	25.45	21.58
14.67	**14.69**	**1.51**	**13.16**	**14.69**	**17.74**	**6.63**	**6.13**	**5.78**	**10.10**	**9.38**	**14.61**
4.79	**5.42**	**6.82**	**3.00**	**5.68**	**3.50**	**7.18**	**2.94**	**6.95**	**5.52**	**6.16**	**6.29**
4.76	5.41	6.72	3.00	5.68	3.50	7.18	2.84	6.90	5.52	6.16	6.22
0.03	0.01	0.10	0.00	0.00	0.00	0.00	0.10	0.05	0.00	0.00	0.06
19.89	**15.87**	**25.46**	**20.16**	**21.15**	**17.06**	**19.33**	**21.65**	**21.24**	**15.38**	**16.32**	**16.38**
12.55	11.57	16.02	13.87	14.30	11.09	13.29	15.93	13.22	6.83	9.87	10.02
0.13	0.12	0.54	0.65	1.94	0.78	2.32	1.01	0.15	0.98	0.22	0.45
0.81	1.10	0.42	0.71	0.63	0.84	1.23	1.12	0.42	1.89	0.85	3.04
0.00	0.00	0.00	0.08	0.00	0.10	0.03	0.07	0.32	1.37	0.24	0.09
6.40	3.08	8.47	4.86	4.28	4.25	2.46	3.51	7.13	4.30	5.14	2.78
4.52	**7.08**	**1.93**	**4.07**	**3.71**	**6.95**	**3.37**	**4.49**	**3.70**	**4.37**	**4.95**	**6.84**
1.86	4.10	0.83	1.51	1.73	5.03	2.13	2.60	1.83	0.12	2.75	4.89
0.00	0.04	0.12	0.00	0.00	0.08	0.02	0.12	0.03	0.00	0.02	0.01
0.00	0.01	0.01	0.00	0.00	0.00	0.00	0.00	0.01	0.00	0.00	0.01
2.66	2.93	0.98	2.55	1.98	1.84	1.21	1.76	1.82	4.25	2.19	1.92
15.17	**17.33**	**16.53**	**13.30**	**17.54**	**16.35**	**18.57**	**13.76**	**12.92**	**19.95**	**14.33**	**20.85**
14.28	16.78	16.30	12.80	17.03	13.30	18.44	13.49	12.44	19.82	14.21	20.50
0.89	0.56	0.23	0.50	0.52	3.05	0.13	0.27	0.48	0.12	0.12	0.35
4.47	4.11	7.90	5.28	3.42	14.24	2.91	4.90	4.46	2.92	4.13	5.84
1.27	0.94	1.70	0.85	1.12	0.73	0.17	0.21	0.76	0.03	0.27	0.47
1.50	0.28	9.42	1.56	1.11	0.59	0.13	0.33	1.51	1.35	0.12	0.70
109.37	**106.70**	**94.63**	**80.68**	**96.85**	**93.52**	**116.81**	**81.43**	**97.35**	**110.45**	**96.13**	**88.27**
0.12	**0.33**	**0.14**	**0.18**	**0.09**	**0.40**	**0.30**	**0.16**	**0.29**	**0.19**	**0.12**	**0.15**
7.02	**6.55**	**7.72**	**11.05**	**11.41**	**3.79**	**6.43**	**7.38**	**6.25**	**5.27**	**7.53**	**7.71**
2.40	2.11	1.93	4.98	3.73	1.70	1.68	3.76	3.69	2.11	3.46	3.21
0.13	0.26	0.11	0.21	0.13	0.31	0.07	0.07	0.15	0.02	0.12	0.20
4.47	4.18	5.36	5.86	7.50	1.78	4.68	3.27	2.37	3.10	3.93	4.30
0.01	0.00	0.33	0.00	0.05	0.00	0.00	0.27	0.04	0.05	0.02	0.00
1.74	**0.90**	**1.08**	**1.66**	**2.55**	**1.15**	**0.40**	**0.59**	**1.64**	**0.07**	**0.70**	**0.31**
1.03	**1.08**	**1.45**	**1.96**	**0.98**	**1.06**	**0.43**	**0.37**	**1.01**	**0.26**	**0.60**	**1.02**
13.58	**1.18**	**9.06**	**0.94**	**12.90**	**1.03**	**0.37**	**0.64**	**14.20**	**0.19**	**1.03**	**59.03**
0.26	**0.09**	**0.05**	**0.21**	**0.34**	**0.08**	**0.36**	**0.12**	**0.27**	**0.04**	**0.09**	**0.05**
0.04	**0.02**	**0.00**	**0.01**	**0.01**	**0.01**	**0.00**	**0.01**	**0.02**	**0.00**	**0.05**	**0.03**
39.80	**41.85**	**32.18**	**39.35**	**49.58**	**36.47**	**33.57**	**33.45**	**37.74**	**35.03**	**29.24**	**32.93**
39.37	**38.42**	**14.20**	**21.89**	**18.76**	**23.51**	**25.31**	**17.66**	**31.81**	**21.43**	**19.37**	**33.77**
0.65	**0.88**	**0.23**	**2.59**	**0.51**	**1.58**	**1.53**	**1.25**	**0.05**	**0.37**	**0.62**	**0.39**
0.47	**0.29**	**0.07**	**0.42**	**0.36**	**0.57**	**0.32**	**0.63**	**1.18**	**0.02**	**0.83**	**0.65**
3.79	**2.95**	**1.68**	**0.49**	**4.78**	**3.12**	**3.25**	**0.99**	**3.30**	**4.22**	**3.62**	**3.46**
6.30	**8.78**	**1.54**	**10.16**	**6.45**	**6.93**	**5.43**	**7.36**	**5.87**	**6.00**	**5.17**	**6.59**
20.31	33.35	38.49	25.18	30.09	11.16	23.90	18.49	16.97	20.92	27.81	20.97
0.14	0.21	0.53	0.16	0.13	0.13	0.03	0.67	0.50	0.06	0.75	0.33
2.76	4.73	2.60	1.70	1.50	6.42	0.65	1.83	5.03	0.31	1.72	1.48

4-17 分调查市县城镇居民非食品消费支出（一）

单位：元/人

类别	Classification	济南 Jinan	青岛 Qingdao	淄博 Zibo	枣庄 Zaozhuang	东营 Dongying	烟台 Yantai	潍坊 Weifang
非食品类	**Non-food**	**7378**	**7593**	**6761**	**4153**	**7992**	**6738**	**6083**
二、衣着	**Clothing**	**1111**	**1413**	**1097**	**1021**	**1768**	**1769**	**1146**
㈠服装	Garments	806	921	790	703	1306	1382	819
1.男士服装	Men's Clothing	330	385	326	319	543	555	346
2.女士服装	Women's Clothing	420	507	423	330	703	693	414
3.童装	Children's Clothing	56	29	41	54	60	135	59
㈡衣着材料	Clothing Material	14	9	16	22	11	1	11
㈢鞋类	Footwear	246	346	246	228	375	312	254
㈣其他衣着用品	Other Clothing	35	127	37	58	67	64	46
㈤衣着加工服务费	Clothing Proceeding Services	9	9	7	10	8	10	15
三、家庭设备用品及服务	**Household Facilities,Articles and Services**	**595**	**801**	**469**	**361**	**1003**	**328**	**348**
㈠耐用消费品	Durable Consumer Goods	315	348	254	149	532	176	175
1.家具	Furniture	106	95	70	29	301	28	63
⑴成套家具	Furniture Sets	21	15	4	0	101	11	0
⑵其他家具	Others	85	79	66	29	200	17	63
2.家庭设备	Household Facilities	209	253	184	121	231	147	112
⑴洗衣机	Washing Machines	22	24	18	15	21	19	21
⑵电风扇	Electric Fans	4	2	2	2	4	2	4
⑶电冰箱	Refrigerators	37	41	30	26	35	19	10
⑷冰柜	Freezer	6	4	0	5	4	4	0
⑸微波炉	Microwave Ovens	3	8	6	0	8	2	4
⑹空调器	Air Conditioner	69	66	46	36	34	12	6
⑺电炊具	Electric Cookers	6	9	11	1	3	22	6
⑻淋浴热水器	Water Heaters	29	28	24	21	33	19	21
⑼排油烟机	Lampblack Exhausters	6	13	11	6	21	12	6
⑽吸尘器	Vacuam Cleaner	1	2	1	0	0	1	0
⑾消毒碗柜	Sterilized Cabinet	0	0	0	0	0	3	0
⑿洗碗机	Dishwasher	0	0	0	0	0	0	0
⒀饮水机	Drinking Machine	3	3	5	1	2	5	0
⒁取暖器	Heater	3	7	2	0	0	1	0
⒂其他	Others	20	44	28	9	65	27	36
㈡室内装饰品	Interior Decorations	18	40	18	1	114	21	7
1.纺织装饰品	Textile Decorations	4	11	8	0	68	14	3
2.装饰灯具	Decorative Lamps	7	8	3	0	26	4	0
3.其他装饰品	Others	6	21	7	0	19	3	4
㈢床上用品	Bed Articles	43	67	48	46	84	22	29
㈣家庭日用杂品	Grocery for Daily Use	187	293	131	158	248	108	132
1.厨、餐、茶具	Kitchenware,Tea-things and Tableware	35	53	14	13	54	26	33
2.家用工具	Household Tools	1	3	4	0	0	0	6
3.家居清洁用品	Household Cleaning Products	29	52	18	47	17	14	21

Consumption Expenditure for Non-food of Urban Households by City and County

unit:yuan/person

济宁	泰安	威海	日照	莱芜	临沂	德州	聊城	滨州	菏泽	文登	诸城	青州
Jining	Taian	Weihai	Rizhao	Laiwu	Linyi	Dezhou	Liaocheng	Binzhou	Heze	Wendeng	Zhucheng	Qingzhou
4608	**6080**	**7419**	**6279**	**5072**	**6256**	**4931**	**4665**	**5535**	**3752**	**4668**	**4728**	**4687**
968	**964**	**1672**	**1136**	**965**	**1122**	**941**	**752**	**906**	**910**	**840**	**1016**	**793**
706	691	1253	815	672	758	684	537	658	653	607	750	576
276	319	539	292	242	324	286	214	227	333	305	367	277
388	331	649	417	363	385	337	298	371	268	281	330	268
42	40	65	106	67	50	60	26	60	51	21	52	31
14	15	8	13	15	4	9	14	9	3	7	13	16
207	199	353	252	238	309	212	162	213	184	171	224	170
24	50	49	43	35	47	29	30	21	64	49	24	23
17	10	8	14	6	4	7	8	6	8	6	4	8
715	**619**	**811**	**551**	**572**	**536**	**413**	**649**	**603**	**401**	**335**	**569**	**437**
362	434	461	262	361	282	228	313	409	221	144	352	223
150	208	274	80	98	121	53	130	224	25	17	134	86
135	153	143	0	28	77	14	62	0	14	0	69	0
15	54	131	80	70	44	39	68	224	11	17	65	86
213	226	187	182	263	161	175	182	186	196	128	218	137
40	16	23	27	43	28	14	7	17	31	3	4	17
3	5	1	1	7	3	3	4	2	5	0	1	2
19	60	40	17	9	32	27	33	16	11	44	21	31
0	9	1	22	4	0	0	0	0	0	0	0	0
1	1	10	9	14	3	2	4	0	4	0	27	3
63	37	30	61	124	21	72	40	112	58	23	98	32
3	6	13	10	5	1	10	3	11	14	13	19	9
50	15	35	8	13	38	10	15	12	37	6	20	11
10	15	14	3	11	6	17	11	0	0	12	13	5
0	1	0	3	2	1	3	1	0	1	0	0	0
0	0	0	0	0	0	0	0	0	0	0	0	0
0	0	0	0	0	0	0	0	0	0	0	0	0
0	13	8	0	3	4	0	25	1	1	4	1	17
2	20	1	4	4	5	7	0	1	12	0	0	1
22	29	11	17	26	20	12	39	13	22	23	14	9
20	5	52	16	24	30	15	35	37	14	18	39	5
9	1	27	2	12	11	9	15	24	3	0	31	3
8	1	11	2	2	15	2	8	4	3	1	5	0
2	3	14	11	9	4	3	12	9	7	18	3	2
71	40	74	47	40	39	22	52	51	45	59	75	27
232	131	184	196	140	157	139	171	92	111	108	91	113
32	20	34	38	28	32	22	16	15	16	18	35	11
0	0	0	11	4	10	5	2	1	1	10	0	0
24	24	35	22	19	47	26	20	20	12	27	19	11

4-17 续表 1 continued

类别	Classification	微山 Weishan	临清 Linqing	费县 Feixian	利津 Lijin	武城 Wucheng	东阿 Donga	巨野 Juye
非食品类	**Non-food**	**4861**	**3459**	**3023**	**4724**	**3331**	**2957**	**3280**
二、衣着	**Clothing**	**965**	**623**	**700**	**955**	**569**	**629**	**693**
㈠服装	Garments	702	394	370	667	390	421	495
1.男士服装	Men's Clothing	270	162	194	244	121	160	230
2.女士服装	Women's Clothing	357	210	145	341	247	224	217
3.童装	Children's Clothing	75	22	31	82	22	37	48
㈡衣着材料	Clothing Material	20	15	4	12	9	11	8
㈢鞋类	Footwear	200	144	169	195	122	167	165
㈣其他衣着用品	Other Clothing	33	62	154	76	43	26	21
㈤衣着加工服务费	Clothing Proceeding Services	10	9	4	4	5	5	4
三、家庭设备用品及服务	**Household Facilities,Articles and Services**	**690**	**357**	**362**	**494**	**410**	**226**	**278**
㈠耐用消费品	Durable Consumer Goods	476	148	167	240	213	85	111
1.家具	Furniture	161	63	38	100	29	31	53
⑴成套家具	Furniture Sets	73	0	0	0	15	0	0
⑵其他家具	Others	87	63	38	100	14	31	53
2.家庭设备	Household Facilities	315	84	129	140	185	55	59
⑴洗衣机	Washing Machines	13	5	17	0	11	9	6
⑵电风扇	Electric Fans	4	4	1	1	4	5	3
⑶电冰箱	Refrigerators	18	31	0	14	72	0	0
⑷冰柜	Freezer	0	0	0	0	0	0	0
⑸微波炉	Microwave Ovens	12	0	3	0	7	0	5
⑹空调器	Air Conditioner	178	23	46	106	16	15	0
⑺电炊具	Electric Cookers	25	5	5	3	3	0	11
⑻淋浴热水器	Water Heaters	36	0	29	0	0	0	13
⑼排油烟机	Lampblack Exhausters	4	0	5	3	12	0	0
⑽吸尘器	Vacuam Cleaner	0	0	0	0	0	0	0
⑾消毒碗柜	Sterilized Cabinet	0	0	0	0	0	0	0
⑿洗碗机	Dishwasher	0	0	0	0	0	0	0
⒀饮水机	Drinking Machine	2	0	2	3	0	0	1
⒁取暖器	Heater	0	3	7	0	8	0	3
⒂其他	Others	23	14	15	9	50	25	18
㈡室内装饰品	Interior Decorations	33	16	23	17	8	7	16
1.纺织装饰品	Textile Decorations	11	12	7	17	3	3	3
2.装饰灯具	Decorative Lamps	5	1	4	0	2	2	12
3.其他装饰品	Others	17	3	13	0	3	2	1
㈢床上用品	Bed Articles	44	33	32	34	26	17	26
㈣家庭日用杂品	Grocery for Daily Use	124	141	132	197	159	111	120
1.厨、餐、茶具	Kitchenware,Tea-things and Tableware	19	30	18	37	19	11	15
2.家用工具	Household Tools	0	2	2	0	0	0	0
3.家居清洁用品	Household Cleaning Products	25	48	14	14	18	22	16

4-18 分调查市县城镇居民非食品消费支出（二）

Consumption Expenditure for Non-food of Urban Households by City and County

单位：元/人 unit:yuan/person

类别	Classification	济南 Jinan	青岛 Qingdao	淄博 Zibo	枣庄 Zaozhuang	东营 Dongying	烟台 Yantai	潍坊 Weifang
4.其他日用杂品	Other Grocery for Daily Use	122	186	95	98	178	68	71
㈤家具材料	Furniture Materials	0	20	3	0	3	0	0
㈥家庭服务	Household Service	32	34	15	7	23	2	6
1.家政服务	Household Service	19	17	3	0	13	1	1
2.加工维修服务费	Proceeding Upkeep	13	17	13	6	10	1	5
四、医疗保健	**Health Care and Personal Articles**	**931**	**782**	**809**	**510**	**698**	**1112**	**579**
㈠医疗器具	Medical Appliances	3	14	31	1	2	9	0
㈡保健器具	Health Care Appliances	5	14	18	12	45	25	32
㈢药品费	Drugs Charges	537	292	305	344	372	466	350
㈣滋补保健品	Nutritious and Health Articles	75	183	70	38	108	394	57
㈤医疗费	Medical Charges	302	254	373	97	165	202	139
㈥其他	Others	9	26	11	18	6	16	1
五、交通和通讯	**Transportation and Communication**	**1782**	**1424**	**1251**	**626**	**1057**	**1067**	**1554**
㈠交通	Transportation	1246	724	737	293	551	368	1057
1.家庭交通工具	Household Means of Transportation	784	258	398	124	250	17	678
(1)摩托车	Motorcycles	2	0	0	0	0	0	0
(2)自行车	Bicycles	14	6	17	15	24	11	23
(3)助力车	Motorbikes	46	0	20	107	24	7	40
(4)家用汽车	Automobiles	722	252	360	0	194	0	607
(5)其他交通工具	Others	0	0	0	2	7	0	7
2.车辆用燃料及零配件	Fuels and Parts	107	70	77	24	40	36	127
(1)燃料	Fuels	87	61	68	20	32	35	114
(2)零配件	Parts	19	2	7	4	7	1	9
(3)其他	Others	1	7	2	0	1	0	4
3.交通工具服务支出	Expenditure for Transportation Facility Services	107	79	84	20	100	41	121
(1)维修费	Mending Cost	18	14	25	18	27	6	36
(2)车辆使用税费	Tax Payment of Automobile Use	79	48	44	0	64	32	70
(3)其它车辆使	Other Cost of Automobile	9	17	15	2	8	4	16
4.交通费	Transportation Costs	247	317	178	125	162	273	131
(1)飞机	Airplane	24	24	12	2	9	32	29
(2)火车	Train	25	27	33	29	13	30	25
(3)长途汽车	Coaches	23	16	37	54	55	37	19
(4)市内公共交	Incity Public Traffic	102	168	34	21	26	85	19
(5)出租汽车费	Taxis Charges	72	71	57	19	57	66	34
(6)其他交通费	Other Transportation Costs	1	11	6	0	3	22	6
㈡通信	Communication	536	700	514	333	506	699	497
1.通信工具	Communication Facility	117	179	136	74	147	121	146
(1)电话机	Fixed Phones	2	2	6	0	3	0	1
(2)移动电话	Mobile Phones	113	174	129	73	141	121	140
(3)寻呼机	Pagers	0	0	0	0	0	0	0

4-18 续表 1

类别	Classification	济宁 Jining	泰安 Taian	威海 Weihai	日照 Rizhao	莱芜 Laiwu	临沂 Linyi	德州 Dezhou
4.其他日用杂品	Other Grocery for Daily Use	177	88	114	125	89	69	85
㈤家具材料	Furniture Materials	10	0	0	9	1	12	0
㈥家庭服务	Household Service	20	10	41	20	6	17	9
1.家政服务	Household Service	3	5	31	10	2	6	3
2.加工维修服务费	Proceeding Upkeep	17	5	9	10	5	11	7
四、医疗保健	**Health Care and Personal Articles**	**429**	**596**	**749**	**527**	**435**	**373**	**436**
㈠医疗器具	Medical Appliances	7	8	2	4	2	3	2
㈡保健器具	Health Care Appliances	24	3	73	4	3	10	5
㈢药品费	Drugs Charges	252	251	288	350	263	249	182
㈣滋补保健品	Nutritious and Health Articles	13	96	176	40	70	25	23
㈤医疗费	Medical Charges	133	237	209	107	92	85	214
㈥其他	Others	0	0	0	22	5	1	10
五、交通和通讯	**Transportation and Communication**	**643**	**1351**	**1168**	**2169**	**1034**	**1826**	**903**
㈠交通	Transportation	253	853	583	1719	623	1328	416
1.家庭交通工具	Household Means of Transportation	90	555	239	1220	354	992	185
⑴摩托车	Motorcycles	8	15	39	0	15	0	0
⑵自行车	Bicycles	14	9	2	9	1	23	21
⑶助力车	Motorbikes	67	61	0	34	33	71	95
⑷家用汽车	Automobiles	0	470	198	1176	305	896	66
⑸其他交通工具	Others	2	1	0	1	0	2	3
2.车辆用燃料及零配件	Fuels and Parts	9	81	53	180	73	133	56
⑴燃料	Fuels	6	78	42	165	68	108	38
⑵零配件	Parts	2	2	11	12	4	13	18
⑶其他	Others	1	0	0	3	0	12	0
3.交通工具服务支出	Expenditure for Transportation Facility Services	22	87	76	160	37	110	31
⑴维修费	Mending Cost	12	14	15	17	21	16	17
⑵车辆使用税费	Tax Payment of Automobile Use	0	46	55	120	14	80	10
⑶其它车辆使	Other Cost of Automobile	10	26	6	23	3	13	4
4.交通费	Transportation Costs	132	130	215	159	159	93	143
⑴飞机	Airplane	0	0	19	1	2	0	11
⑵火车	Train	36	38	32	26	13	9	56
⑶长途汽车	Coaches	33	28	50	28	51	33	33
⑷市内公共交通	Incity Public Traffic	32	26	58	47	34	12	3
⑸出租汽车费	Taxis Charges	28	37	46	47	54	37	38
⑹其他交通费	Other Transportation Costs	3	1	10	9	4	2	3
㈡通信	Communication	390	498	585	451	410	498	487
1.通信工具	Communication Facility	79	126	142	73	79	104	105
⑴电话机	Fixed Phones	7	1	2	5	2	2	3
⑵移动电话	Mobile Phones	72	125	138	69	77	101	100
⑶寻呼机	Pagers	0	0	0	0	0	0	0

continued

聊城 Liaocheng	滨州 Binzhou	菏泽 Heze	文登 Wendeng	诸城 Zhucheng	青州 Qingzhou	微山 Weishan	临清 Linqing	费县 Feixian	利津 Lijin	武城 Wucheng	东阿 Donga	巨野 Juye
134	55	82	53	37	91	80	61	98	146	122	78	88
12	1	4	0	0	0	0	5	4	0	0	0	0
67	14	7	6	11	68	13	15	3	5	3	6	5
39	3	2	0	2	12	5	0	0	0	0	0	2
27	11	5	6	9	56	8	15	3	5	3	5	3
604	**416**	**338**	**751**	**369**	**675**	**375**	**514**	**208**	**391**	**326**	**525**	**305**
9	0	0	0	0	8	0	8	0	0	1	1	0
48	4	5	11	13	4	3	0	1	2	0	7	1
204	246	228	219	184	371	179	280	136	233	230	231	131
86	25	31	72	88	26	1	29	9	16	10	10	15
248	122	74	449	84	266	192	192	57	25	85	276	157
9	18	0	0	0	0	0	5	4	115	0	0	1
744	**1207**	**605**	**911**	**779**	**1025**	**699**	**418**	**453**	**646**	**453**	**441**	**648**
454	845	264	413	340	633	255	177	163	262	146	155	289
293	542	101	127	97	324	124	74	73	77	81	58	147
0	19	0	0	0	13	37	0	0	0	0	0	0
12	9	20	14	24	17	25	13	12	7	9	21	15
54	109	80	0	70	114	62	56	60	70	73	37	132
223	405	0	113	0	178	0	0	0	0	0	0	0
4	0	2	0	3	1	0	5	0	0	0	0	0
28	125	32	99	94	127	23	20	13	34	9	31	39
21	103	24	93	72	113	14	12	9	30	9	29	23
6	21	8	6	22	12	9	6	4	3	0	1	16
1	1	0	0	0	2	0	1	0	0	0	0	0
31	50	18	116	58	90	6	10	27	26	15	17	13
10	6	17	30	1	35	6	8	17	26	15	17	12
16	42	0	86	26	36	0	2	10	0	0	0	0
5	2	1	0	31	20	0	0	0	0	0	0	1
102	128	112	71	91	92	101	72	50	126	41	49	90
0	12	0	0	12	24	7	0	0	0	0	0	0
13	18	32	7	14	33	7	17	11	3	5	1	36
43	52	39	14	19	21	57	26	17	67	14	6	45
24	14	16	40	16	7	7	20	21	25	6	0	5
20	32	23	10	30	6	19	7	1	28	9	7	4
2	0	1	1	0	2	4	2	0	4	7	36	0
291	362	341	498	439	392	444	241	290	384	307	285	360
92	64	83	120	110	101	98	27	24	62	104	58	21
2	0	0	1	0	1	1	0	0	1	0	0	0
88	62	83	119	110	99	95	27	23	61	104	58	19
0	0	0	0	0	0	0	0	0	0	0	0	0

4-19 分调查市县城镇居民非食品消费支出（三）

单位：元/人

类别	Classification	济南 Jinan	青岛 Qingdao	淄博 Zibo	枣庄 Zaozhuang	东营 Dongying	烟台 Yantai	潍坊 Weifang
(4)传真机	Faxes	0	1	0	0	0	0	0
(5)其他通信工具	Other Communication Facility	2	2	1	1	3	0	6
2.通信服务	Communication Service	420	520	378	259	358	578	351
(1)电信费	Costs of Telecommunication	412	491	362	243	334	529	345
(2)邮费	Costs of Postal Services	4	2	4	2	2	3	2
(3)其他	Others	4	27	13	14	22	46	5
六、教育文化娱乐服务	**Education,Culture and Recreation Articles**	**1450**	**1640**	**1725**	**867**	**1799**	**1202**	**1223**
(一)文化娱乐用品	Culture and Recreation Articles	385	493	459	289	462	325	307
1.彩色电视机	Color TV Sets	32	109	38	62	99	34	32
2.影碟机	Video Disc Players	3	5	5	7	2	3	3
3.录放像机	Video Recorders	0	0	0	0	0	0	0
4.家用电脑	Computers	114	114	143	72	61	62	83
(1)整机电脑	Entire Computers	95	90	130	66	49	58	76
(2)计算机外部设备	External Equipment of Computer	10	15	3	1	10	0	0
(3)各种零配件	Various Spare Parts	9	9	10	5	3	4	6
5.组合音响	Hi-Fi Stereo Component System	2	1	0	0	0	0	0
6.录音机	Tape Recorders	3	1	8	10	2	1	2
7.摄像机	Pickup Cameras	10	22	33	0	0	9	0
8.照相机	Cameras	39	39	24	31	28	28	18
9.钢琴	Pianos	11	0	24	0	0	0	0
10.其他中高档乐器	Other Medium and Top Grade Music Instruments	3	2	2	2	52	1	0
11.健身器材	Body Building Equipment	0	1	0	8	0	5	0
12.电子辞典	Electronic Dictionary	4	3	8	3	0	2	5
13.音像制品及软件	Audio-visual Productsand Software	23	9	3	7	5	0	2
14.体育用品	Sports Goods	3	2	4	1	2	2	1
15.书报杂志	Books,Newspapers and Magazines	51	68	44	35	58	93	43
16.纸张文具	Paper and Stationery	20	16	26	17	20	19	25
17.其他文娱用品	Other Culture and Recreation Articles	67	101	95	33	132	67	94
(二)文化娱乐服务	Culture and Recreation Services	252	382	299	158	295	292	139
1.参观游览	Visit	43	54	58	38	69	63	19
2.健身活动	Body Building Activities	12	7	8	2	12	105	0
3.团体旅游	Team Tour	112	233	141	54	180	74	61
4.其它文娱活动	Other Culture and Recreation Activities	75	84	74	38	24	48	32
5.文娱用品修理服务费	Service Charges for Recreation and Culture Articles Mending	11	5	17	26	10	3	26
(三)教育	Education	813	765	967	421	1042	585	777
1.教材	Teaching Materials	47	49	32	47	34	72	23
(1)课本及参考书	Text Books and Reference Books	41	39	24	41	27	47	17
(2)教育软件	Teaching Software	1	2	3	0	4	10	0
(3)其它教材	Other Teaching Material	5	8	6	7	3	15	6
2.教育费用	Education Costs	766	716	934	373	1008	513	754

Consumption Expenditure for Non-food of Urban Households by City and County

unit:yuan/person

济宁 Jining	泰安 Taian	威海 Weihai	日照 Rizhao	莱芜 Laiwu	临沂 Linyi	德州 Dezhou	聊城 Liaocheng	滨州 Binzhou	菏泽 Heze	文登 Wendeng	诸城 Zhucheng	青州 Qingzhou
0	0	0	0	0	0	0	0	0	0	0	0	0
0	1	2	0	0	1	2	2	2	0	0	0	1
311	372	443	377	331	394	382	198	298	258	379	329	291
302	370	436	365	313	390	376	194	292	255	375	327	278
3	2	2	3	1	1	3	1	2	1	2	1	1
7	0	4	9	18	4	3	3	4	3	2	1	12
895	**1531**	**1174**	**939**	**1237**	**1113**	**1338**	**975**	**1331**	**839**	**414**	**1106**	**733**
389	464	412	320	366	310	393	314	376	231	100	546	194
45	121	21	22	56	33	33	24	104	33	22	42	15
1	0	1	0	0	4	3	5	0	3	0	0	1
0	12	0	0	0	12	0	0	0	0	0	0	0
240	92	106	88	163	87	73	122	115	77	19	126	74
234	70	83	83	147	78	44	115	112	74	17	124	68
3	17	14	0	12	4	23	2	2	1	0	1	6
3	5	9	5	4	5	6	5	1	3	2	1	0
0	0	0	1	0	0	7	1	0	3	0	0	0
0	0	12	0	1	0	13	2	7	0	0	0	3
0	0	28	0	0	10	68	0	19	0	0	0	0
0	76	28	49	28	17	16	9	8	0	0	37	9
0	0	53	0	0	0	0	0	0	0	0	0	0
0	0	5	2	0	1	19	0	0	7	0	0	0
1	1	7	0	30	0	30	49	0	0	0	49	0
0	1	3	1	1	12	1	10	1	11	0	0	1
3	6	4	5	3	6	13	4	3	6	1	19	4
0	0	5	0	1	2	1	0	3	2	0	0	1
52	43	44	52	21	45	37	29	35	21	24	76	19
6	18	19	23	12	20	15	14	13	22	12	40	15
41	94	75	76	50	60	65	46	68	47	22	157	53
223	310	232	153	170	210	219	258	132	113	82	134	107
60	9	15	53	13	16	25	61	18	4	16	78	10
0	0	8	0	0	1	12	0	9	1	0	0	1
24	211	115	46	135	112	127	143	53	43	0	3	37
132	77	91	54	19	74	50	51	48	62	61	51	54
7	13	2	0	2	7	4	2	4	2	5	1	5
283	757	530	466	701	593	727	402	823	495	232	425	431
22	16	65	23	30	22	38	16	94	71	3	10	20
20	10	64	21	26	15	37	14	92	65	1	0	20
0	2	0	0	1	7	0	0	2	0	0	3	0
2	3	0	2	3	1	1	2	0	6	2	7	0
261	742	465	443	671	570	689	387	729	425	229	415	411

4-19 续表 1 continued

类别	Classification	微山 Weishan	临清 Linqing	费县 Feixian	利津 Lijin	武城 Wucheng	东阿 Donga	巨野 Juye
(4)传真机	Faxes	0	0	0	0	0	0	0
(5)其他通信工具	Other Communication Facility	2	0	1	0	0	0	2
2.通信服务	Communication Service	345	215	266	321	204	228	339
(1)电信费	Costs of Telecommunicati	345	211	254	318	202	218	331
(2)邮费	Costs of Postal Services	1	1	1	0	0	1	5
(3)其他	Others	0	2	11	3	1	9	3
六、教育文化娱乐服务	**Education,Culture andRecreation Articles**	**1437**	**623**	**828**	**1357**	**684**	**534**	**545**
(一)文化娱乐用品	Culture and Recreation Articles	399	253	278	479	175	198	169
1.彩色电视机	Color TV Sets	141	10	23	14	0	11	29
2.影碟机	Video Disc Players	6	0	4	0	0	2	0
3.录放像机	Video Recorders	0	0	0	0	0	0	0
4.家用电脑	Computers	123	153	144	177	96	102	30
(1)整机电脑	Entire Computers	122	150	136	142	96	102	24
(2)计算机外部设备	External Equipment of Computer	0	1	4	2	0	0	1
(3)各种零配件	Various Spare Parts	1	2	4	33	0	0	5
5.组合音响	Hi-Fi Stereo Component System	0	0	0	0	0	0	0
6.录音机	Tape Recorders	6	0	0	0	0	0	0
7.摄像机	Pickup Cameras	30	0	0	0	0	0	0
8.照相机	Cameras	29	0	38	51	0	0	0
9.钢琴	Pianos	0	0	0	0	0	0	0
10.其他中高档乐器	Other Medium and Top Grade Music Instruments	0	0	0	0	0	3	3
11.健身器材	Body Building Equipment	1	0	0	0	0	0	0
12.电子辞典	Electronic Dictionary	0	0	1	14	0	0	3
13.音像制品及软件	Audio-visual Productsand Software	2	1	1	3	0	0	4
14.体育用品	Sports Goods	1	1	0	2	0	0	1
15.书报杂志	Books,Newspapers and Magazines	17	16	9	53	34	26	35
16.纸张文具	Paper and Stationery	15	18	9	28	23	11	19
17.其他文娱用品	Other Culture and Recreation Articles	28	54	48	137	22	42	45
(二)文化娱乐服务	Culture and Recreation Services	214	60	46	118	88	68	80
1.参观游览	Visit	3	7	1	93	2	15	22
2.健身活动	Body Building Activities	0	0	0	1	0	0	0
3.团体旅游	Team Tour	148	12	43	21	25	25	15
4.其它文娱活动	Other Culture and Recreation Activities	59	34	1	1	59	21	28
5.文娱用品修理服务费	Service Charges for Recreation-and Culture Articles Mending	5	7	1	2	2	6	15
(三)教育	Education	824	309	503	760	421	268	297
1.教材	Teaching Materials	34	38	26	47	10	0	58
(1)课本及参考书	Text Books and Reference Books	32	36	23	5	10	0	51
(2)教育软件	Teaching Software	1	2	1	42	0	0	0
(3)其它教材	Other Teaching Material	0	1	2	1	0	0	7
2.教育费用	Education Costs	790	271	478	712	411	268	239

4-20 分调查市县城镇居民非食品消费支出（四）

Consumption Expenditure for Non-food of Urban Households by City and County

单位：元/人 unit:yuan/person

类别	Classification	济南 Jinan	青岛 Qingdao	淄博 Zibo	枣庄 Zaozhuang	东营 Dongying	烟台 Yantai	潍坊 Weifang
(1)非义务教育学杂费	Tuition Fee for Noncompulsory Education	324	283	313	111	452	133	344
(2)义务教育学杂费	Tuition Fee for Compulsory Education	63	53	64	40	71	62	91
(3)托幼费	Child-care Fee	92	40	63	33	58	63	60
(4)成人教育费	Adult Education Expenses	86	93	127	30	164	51	70
(5)家教费	Family Education Expenses	11	59	19	6	14	25	2
(6)培训班	Training Fee	94	90	149	119	217	141	128
(7)学校住宿费	Accommodation Expenses at School	7	29	13	0	16	11	5
(8)其他	Others	90	70	186	35	16	27	54
七、居住	**Residence**	**1134**	**1170**	**1075**	**495**	**1272**	**753**	**974**
(一)住房	Housing	389	300	302	71	815	89	184
1.租赁房房租	House Rent	54	41	35	8	2	7	5
2.自有房租金折算	Private House Convert to House Rent	0	0	0	0	0	0	0
3.住房装潢支出	Decoration Expenses	227	230	170	50	596	58	129
4.维修用建筑材料	Construction Material for Mending	97	18	47	8	117	23	44
5.其他	Others	11	11	50	4	101	0	6
(二)水电燃料及其他	Water, Electricity,Fuel and Others	695	771	720	374	391	632	738
1.水	Water	55	53	39	39	69	60	53
2.电	Electricity	252	292	224	160	142	231	210
3.燃料	Fuels	154	200	149	103	49	154	107
(1)煤炭	Coal	56	37	34	13	0	26	29
(2)液化石油气	Liquefied Petroleum Gas	54	53	59	14	5	68	14
(3)管道煤气	Pipeline Gas	32	66	21	59	41	61	64
(4)其他燃料	Other Fuels	12	44	34	16	3	0	0
4.其他	Others	234	226	308	72	131	187	369
(三)居住服务费	Charges of Residence Service	50	99	54	50	66	33	52
1.物业管理费	Property Management Fees	18	29	23	6	34	14	14
2.维修服务费	Charges of Mending Services	16	10	12	5	7	15	21
3.其它	Others	16	60	19	39	25	4	16
八、杂项商品和服务	**Miscellanecus Commodities and Services**	**376**	**363**	**335**	**272**	**396**	**508**	**258**
(一)杂项商品	Miscellanecus Commodities	235	285	230	197	285	314	177
1.金银珠宝饰品	Jewellerys	48	70	43	93	75	16	45
2.手表	Watches	2	7	3	1	2	1	3
3.理发美容用具	Haircut and Cosmetology Articles	5	8	6	0	4	1	1
4.化妆品	Cosmetics	111	110	98	41	77	258	65
5.其他杂品	Other Miscellanecus Commodities	69	90	81	62	127	39	63
(二)服务	Services	141	78	105	76	111	194	81
1.旅馆住宿费	Accommodation Expenses at Inn	12	1	5	6	13	5	11
2.理发洗澡费	Washing and Haircut Service Charges	20	29	20	23	19	88	21
3.美容费	Cosmetology Service Charges	30	21	25	15	18	61	17
4.其他服务	Other Services	79	26	55	31	61	40	32

4-20 续表 1

类别	Classification	济宁 Jining	泰安 Taian	威海 Weihai	日照 Rizhao	莱芜 Laiwu	临沂 Linyi	德州 Dezhou
⑴非义务教育学杂费	Tuition Fee for Noncompulsory Education	120	262	84	94	244	293	320
⑵义务教育学杂费	Tuition Fee for Compulsory Education	34	42	59	106	53	59	75
⑶托幼费	Child-care Fee	28	81	50	83	18	55	39
⑷成人教育费	Adult Education Expenses	11	158	88	27	203	70	141
⑸家教费	Family Education Expenses	10	12	0	23	3	12	8
⑹培训班	Training Fee	42	103	136	57	84	57	99
⑺学校住宿费	Accommodation Expenses at School	0	2	8	6	19	14	0
⑻其他	Others	17	83	41	47	47	11	6
七、居住	**Residence**	**761**	**639**	**1327.41**	**634**	**634**	**978**	**668**
㈠住房	Housing	265	157	361	77	179	232	79
1.租赁房房租	House Rent	12	9	4	1	4	13	3
2.自有房租金折算	Private House Convert to House Rent	0	0	0	0	0	0	0
3.住房装潢支出	Decoration Expenses	213	131	148	42	68	212	48
4.维修用建筑材料	Construction Material for Mending	37	3	210	21	102	3	21
5.其他	Others	3	15	0	14	4	4	7
㈡水电燃料及其他	Water, Electricity,Fuel and Others	462	436	875	522	423	685	565
1.水	Water	36	37	61	56	35	56	39
2.电	Electricity	196	176	227	177	157	221	166
3.燃料	Fuels	120	100	77	182	114	161	85
⑴煤炭	Coal	49	52	0	44	41	64	27
⑵液化石油气	Liquefied Petroleum Gas	0	9	21	56	44	74	22
⑶管道煤气	Pipeline Gas	69	39	56	11	24	17	36
⑷其他燃料	Other Fuels	2	1	0	72	5	6	0
4.其他	Others	110	123	511	106	117	247	274
㈢居住服务费	Charges of Residence Service	34	46	91	35	32	61	24
1.物业管理费	Property Management Fees	3	12	9	28	14	29	11
2.维修服务费	Charges of Mending Services	3	9	77	7	5	5	4
3.其它	Others	28	25	6	0	13	27	9
八、杂项商品和服务	**Miscellanecus Commoditiesand Services**	**196**	**380**	**519**	**322**	**195**	**308**	**233**
㈠杂项商品	Miscellanecus Commodities	141	292	395	193	129	227	144
1.金银珠宝饰品	Jewellerys	33	166	77	28	28	51	9
2.手表	Watches	0	1	13	1	1	25	1
3.理发美容用具	Haircut and Cosmetology Articles	1	2	3	4	3	3	1
4.化妆品	Cosmetics	52	77	193	111	67	103	78
5.其他杂品	Other Miscellanecus Commodities	56	44	109	49	29	45	56
㈡服务	Services	55	89	124	129	67	81	89
1.旅馆住宿费	Accommodation Expenses at Inn	2	13	11	22	3	9	21
2.理发洗澡费	Washing and Haircut Service Charges	29	17	43	19	18	24	25
3.美容费	Cosmetology Service Charges	3	8	37	12	19	26	9
4.其他服务	Other Services	20	50	32	76	27	22	34

continued

聊城 Liaocheng	滨州 Binzhou	菏泽 Heze	文登 Wendeng	诸城 Zhucheng	青州 Qingzhou	微山 Weishan	临清 Linqing	费县 Feixian	利津 Lijin	武城 Wucheng	东阿 Donga	巨野 Juye
107	167	197	40	9	162	406	177	289	333	236	95	128
147	59	61	87	141	41	212	43	47	125	63	110	49
40	77	21	35	22	18	6	20	20	73	0	5	18
31	174	18	40	18	44	120	11	7	59	17	50	10
5	0	3	5	2	0	24	1	0	5	1	3	1
29	149	106	22	36	57	5	9	62	46	54	3	18
8	6	8	0	21	10	15	7	21	0	2	0	1
20	98	10	0	168	78	0	3	33	72	37	2	13
716	**841**	**443**	**1226**	**721**	**845**	**417**	**773**	**391**	**672**	**798**	**445**	**508**
163	116	59	552	155	282	74	97	42	138	158	21	134
15	3	1	14	0	31	0	0	0	0	25	7	13
0	0	0	0	0	0	0	0	0	0	0	0	0
137	94	35	123	57	109	69	69	9	39	33	0	62
9	19	17	415	93	139	5	11	12	2	71	7	49
2	0	5	0	5	3	0	17	20	97	29	7	10
478	697	363	607	538	536	335	657	332	526	616	408	338
33	27	32	60	45	49	24	41	20	22	33	34	23
121	172	180	167	157	144	130	141	119	144	136	134	168
86	81	94	205	83	219	119	325	95	55	301	99	121
15	21	40	115	25	143	58	265	36	25	233	23	56
13	53	42	88	32	70	57	43	45	30	41	18	65
58	7	11	1	26	6	3	18	1	0	0	58	0
0	0	2	0	0	0	0	0	13	0	27	0	0
238	418	56	175	252	124	62	149	98	304	146	141	26
74	28	22	67	28	27	7	19	18	7	24	16	36
56	26	19	3	17	4	7	7	2	4	3	12	2
5	1	2	64	5	22	0	5	1	4	22	0	33
12	0	0	0	6	1	0	8	15	0	0	4	1
226	**230**	**216**	**191**	**169**	**180**	**279**	**150**	**82**	**210**	**91**	**157**	**302**
92	164	145	158	142	105	228	64	34	180	73	129	142
2	31	1	26	48	4	63	4	4	45	12	29	2
1	3	0	1	6	1	14	0	1	2	0	0	1
1	2	0	0	1	0	2	0	2	0	0	0	0
55	67	108	83	54	62	81	39	24	86	22	64	68
33	60	36	48	33	38	69	21	3	48	38	36	71
134	66	70	33	27	75	50	86	48	30	19	28	160
0	11	10	0	0	11	12	14	6	5	0	2	24
19	8	20	23	10	21	25	33	9	20	19	16	28
12	13	18	2	17	1	7	0	3	0	0	0	5
102	34	22	8	0	41	7	38	30	4	0	10	102

4-21 分调查市县城镇居民非食品消费数量

类别	Classification	单位	unit	济南 Jinan	青岛 Qingdao	淄博 Zibo
服装	Garments	件/人	piece/person	8.99	6.96	7.61
1.男士服装	Men's Clothing	件/人	piece/person	3.59	2.91	3.18
2.女士服装	Women's Clothing	件/人	piece/person	4.11	3.59	3.52
3.童装	Children's Clothing	件/人	piece/person	1.29	0.47	0.90
鞋类	Footwear	双/人	pair/person	2.96	3.11	3.06
洗衣机	Washing Machines	台/百户	unit/100 households	5.04	4.44	6.00
电风扇	Electric Fans	台/百户	unit/100 households	6.72	4.20	6.00
电冰箱	Refrigerators	台/百户	unit/100 households	4.56	5.76	3.96
冰柜	Freezer	台/百户	unit/100 households	1.20	0.96	0.00
微波炉	Microwave Ovens	台/百户	unit/100 households	1.80	3.48	2.64
空调器	Air Conditioner	台/百户	unit/100 households	7.20	6.00	6.72
电炊具	Electric Cookers	台/百户	unit/100 households	8.28	9.96	10.68
淋浴热水器	Water Heaters	台/百户	unit/100 households	5.52	8.04	3.96
排油烟机	Lampblack Exhausters	台/百户	unit/100 households	2.76	5.52	3.36
吸尘器	Vacuam Cleaner	台/百户	unit/100 households	0.96	1.56	0.72
消毒碗柜	Sterilized Cabinet	台/百户	unit/100 households	0.00	0.48	0.00
洗碗机	Dishwasher	台/百户	unit/100 households	0.00	0.24	0.00
饮水机	Drinking Machine	台/百户	unit/100 households	2.28	3.96	3.96
取暖器	Heater	台/百户	unit/100 households	3.00	5.76	2.64
摩托车	Motorcycles	辆/百户	unit/100 households	0.24	0.00	0.00
自行车	Bicycles	辆/百户	unit/100 households	12.00	5.76	17.28
助力车	Motorbikes	辆/百户	unit/100 households	6.48	0.00	2.64
家用汽车	Automobiles	辆/百户	unit/100 households	2.04	0.72	1.32
电话机	Fixed Phones	部/百户	unit/100 households	2.76	5.76	8.64
移动电话	Mobile Phones	部/百户	unit/100 households	29.40	34.32	26.64
传真机	Faxes	部/百户	unit/100 households	0.00	0.24	0.00
彩色电视机	Color TV Sets	台/百户	unit/100 households	4.20	6.24	6.00
影碟机	Video Disc Players	台/百户	unit/100 households	1.56	2.76	2.04
录放像机	Video Recorders	台/百户	unit/100 households	0.24	0.00	0.00
整机电脑	Computers	台/百户	unit/100 households	5.04	5.04	7.32
组合音响	Hi-Fi Stereo Component System	台/百户	unit/100 households	0.48	0.48	0.00
录音机	Tape Recorders	台/百户	unit/100 households	2.76	0.72	3.36
摄像机	Pickup Cameras	架/百户	unit/100 households	0.48	1.20	1.32
照相机	Cameras	架/百户	unit/100 households	4.32	5.52	2.64
钢琴	Pianos	架/百户	unit/100 households	0.24	0.00	0.72
其他中高档乐器	Other Medium and Top Grade Music Instruments	件/百户	piece/100 households	0.72	0.48	0.72
健身器材	Body Building Equipment	件/人	piece/person	0.00	0.00	0.00
电子辞典	Electronic Dictionary	部/人	unit/person	0.01	0.00	0.01
水	Water	吨/人	ton/person	18.52	20.72	13.76
电	Electricity	度人	kwh/person	459.92	524.32	416.28
煤炭	Coal	千克/人	kg/person	113.85	84.02	70.80
液化石油气	Liquefied Petroleum Gas	千克/人	kg/person	9.06	9.35	20.10
管道煤气	Pipeline Gas	立方米/人	cu.m/person	19.61	51.35	15.77
手表	Watches	只/人	unit/person	0.03	0.04	0.05

Consumption Amount for Non-food of Urban Households by City and County

枣庄 Zaozhuang	东营 Dongying	烟台 Yantai	潍坊 Weifang	济宁 Jining	泰安 Taian	威海 Weihai	日照 Rizhao	莱芜 Laiwu	临沂 Linyi
8.40	9.27	9.72	8.55	8.42	6.70	12.90	7.66	6.62	8.21
3.34	3.21	3.08	3.28	3.14	2.79	5.04	2.40	2.14	3.17
3.86	5.02	4.44	3.92	4.55	3.04	6.21	3.48	3.28	3.90
1.20	1.04	2.20	1.36	0.72	0.87	1.65	1.79	1.20	1.15
3.24	3.52	2.91	3.08	2.62	2.96	3.37	3.52	3.15	3.97
3.96	3.00	3.00	3.00	5.04	3.96	3.96	5.04	6.96	6.00
3.96	11.04	2.52	3.00	3.00	8.04	0.96	4.08	12.00	6.96
3.00	5.04	2.52	0.96	2.04	6.00	5.04	2.04	0.96	5.04
0.96	0.96	0.96	0.00	0.00	2.04	0.96	5.04	0.96	0.00
0.00	3.00	0.96	2.04	0.96	0.96	3.00	3.96	3.00	2.04
6.00	3.00	1.44	0.96	6.96	5.04	2.04	6.96	6.96	3.00
2.04	3.00	16.56	5.04	3.00	8.04	11.04	7.92	6.96	2.04
3.96	5.04	6.00	3.96	9.00	3.96	8.04	2.04	5.04	9.96
3.00	5.04	5.52	3.00	6.00	3.00	6.00	1.08	6.00	2.04
0.00	0.00	0.96	0.00	0.00	0.96	0.00	2.04	0.96	0.96
0.00	0.00	0.96	0.00	0.00	0.00	0.00	0.00	0.00	0.00
0.00	0.00	0.00	0.00	0.00	0.00	0.00	0.00	0.00	0.00
2.04	3.00	3.00	0.00	0.96	3.00	5.04	0.00	5.04	3.00
0.96	0.00	1.44	0.00	3.00	2.04	0.96	3.00	3.00	0.96
0.00	0.00	0.00	0.00	0.96	0.96	2.04	0.00	0.96	0.00
12.00	26.04	8.52	15.00	15.96	9.96	3.00	10.92	2.04	27.96
12.96	3.96	0.96	6.96	9.96	9.00	0.00	5.04	5.04	12.96
0.00	0.96	0.00	3.00	0.00	0.96	0.96	3.96	0.96	3.96
0.96	3.00	0.48	2.04	2.04	3.96	3.00	3.00	6.00	5.04
15.96	35.04	22.56	30.96	17.04	33.00	30.00	15.96	21.00	32.04
0.00	0.00	0.00	0.00	0.00	0.00	0.00	0.00	0.00	0.00
6.96	3.96	3.48	5.04	3.00	8.04	2.04	3.00	3.96	3.00
3.96	2.04	2.04	2.04	0.96	0.00	0.96	0.00	0.00	3.00
0.00	0.00	0.00	0.00	0.00	0.96	0.00	0.00	0.00	0.96
3.96	2.04	3.48	3.96	12.00	3.00	5.04	3.96	6.96	6.00
0.00	0.00	0.00	0.00	0.00	0.96	0.00	0.96	0.00	0.00
8.04	3.96	1.44	0.96	0.00	0.00	12.00	0.96	2.04	0.00
0.00	0.00	0.48	0.00	0.00	0.00	2.04	0.00	0.00	0.96
3.96	3.00	3.96	3.96	0.00	6.96	3.00	7.08	3.00	2.04
0.00	0.00	0.00	0.00	0.00	0.00	0.96	0.00	0.00	0.00
0.96	3.96	0.48	0.00	0.00	0.00	2.04	0.96	0.00	0.96
0.00	0.00	0.00	0.00	0.00	0.00	0.00	0.00	0.01	0.00
0.01	0.00	0.00	0.01	0.00	0.00	0.01	0.00	0.00	0.02
19.41	38.34	21.23	17.61	17.53	14.17	21.27	20.11	17.36	25.45
295.18	277.54	423.70	385.33	387.83	326.27	414.76	327.76	291.45	401.59
53.14	0.17	42.09	48.03	140.99	155.40	0.00	95.13	56.48	110.63
3.02	4.20	11.88	2.89	0.14	3.48	3.80	9.43	11.96	17.30
53.27	40.99	37.62	55.05	69.00	19.27	21.90	2.12	17.91	5.71
0.02	0.03	0.01	0.04	0.00	0.03	0.04	0.01	0.03	0.03

4-21 续表 1

类别	Classification	单位	unit	德州 Dezhou	聊城 Liaocheng	滨州 Binzhou
服装	Garments	件/人	piece/person	8.81	8.07	9.57
1.男士服装	Men's Clothing	件/人	piece/person	3.32	2.73	2.95
2.女士服装	Women's Clothing	件/人	piece/person	3.79	4.37	4.76
3.童装	Children's Clothing	件/人	piece/person	1.71	0.97	1.85
鞋类	Footwear	双/人	pair/person	2.99	14.28	2.98
洗衣机	Washing Machines	台/百户	unit/100 households	5.04	3.43	3.00
电风扇	Electric Fans	台/百户	unit/100 households	6.96	2.04	3.96
电冰箱	Refrigerators	台/百户	unit/100 households	3.00	9.12	2.04
冰柜	Freezer	台/百户	unit/100 households	0.00	6.00	0.00
微波炉	Microwave Ovens	台/百户	unit/100 households	0.96	0.00	0.00
空调器	Air Conditioner	台/百户	unit/100 households	9.00	3.00	12.96
电炊具	Electric Cookers	台/百户	unit/100 households	8.04	5.04	15.96
淋浴热水器	Water Heaters	台/百户	unit/100 households	3.00	3.00	2.04
排油烟机	Lampblack Exhausters	台/百户	unit/100 households	8.04	6.12	0.00
吸尘器	Vacuam Cleaner	台/百户	unit/100 households	0.96	4.08	0.00
消毒碗柜	Sterilized Cabinet	台/百户	unit/100 households	0.00	0.96	0.00
洗碗机	Dishwasher	台/百户	unit/100 households	0.00	0.00	0.00
饮水机	Drinking Machine	台/百户	unit/100 households	0.00	0.00	2.04
取暖器	Heater	台/百户	unit/100 households	6.96	3.00	2.04
摩托车	Motorcycles	辆/百户	unit/100 households	0.00	0.00	0.96
自行车	Bicycles	辆/百户	unit/100 households	21.00	0.00	12.00
助力车	Motorbikes	辆/百户	unit/100 households	14.04	11.16	15.96
家用汽车	Automobiles	辆/百户	unit/100 households	0.96	8.04	2.04
电话机	Fixed Phones	部/百户	unit/100 households	3.96	0.96	2.04
移动电话	Mobile Phones	部/百户	unit/100 households	26.04	4.08	20.04
传真机	Faxes	部/百户	unit/100 households	0.00	28.32	0.00
彩色电视机	Color TV Sets	台/百户	unit/100 households	6.00	0.00	8.04
影碟机	Video Disc Players	台/百户	unit/100 households	2.04	0.00	0.00
录放像机	Video Recorders	台/百户	unit/100 households	0.00	4.08	0.00
整机电脑	Computers	台/百户	unit/100 households	3.00	3.00	6.96
组合音响	Hi-Fi Stereo Component System	台/百户	unit/100 households	2.04	0.00	0.00
录音机	Tape Recorders	台/百户	unit/100 households	11.04	7.08	6.96
摄像机	Pickup Cameras	架/百户	unit/100 households	3.00	0.96	0.96
照相机	Cameras	架/百户	unit/100 households	2.04	0.96	0.96
钢琴	Pianos	架/百户	unit/100 households	0.00	0.00	0.00
其他中高档乐器	Other Medium and Top Grade Music Instruments	件/百户	piece/100 households	2.04	0.96	0.00
健身器材	Body Building Equipment	件/人	piece/person	0.01	0.00	0.00
电子辞典	Electronic Dictionary	部/人	unit/person	0.00	0.00	0.00
水	Water	吨/人	ton/person	17.39	0.01	10.15
电	Electricity	度人	kwh/person	309.70	0.01	312.15
煤炭	Coal	千克/人	kg/person	70.07	43.76	36.76
液化石油气	Liquefied Petroleum Gas	千克/人	kg/person	6.55	4.62	9.93
管道煤气	Pipeline Gas	立方米/人	cu.m/person	17.99	32.08	3.71
手表	Watches	只/人	unit/person	0.01	0.03	0.04

continued

菏泽 Heze	文登 Wendeng	诸城 Zhucheng	青州 Qingzhou	微山 Weishan	临清 Linqing	费县 Feixian	利津 Lijin	武城 Wucheng	东阿 Donga	巨野 Juye
7.10	5.00	7.30	7.49	8.34	4.97	4.04	9.00	5.54	6.29	8.43
3.31	2.35	3.14	3.45	2.22	1.78	1.66	2.67	1.55	2.07	3.23
2.69	2.09	3.12	3.11	4.24	2.53	1.61	3.71	3.31	3.45	3.69
1.11	0.56	1.04	0.93	1.88	0.66	0.78	2.61	0.68	0.78	1.51
3.19	2.55	2.76	3.05	2.66	2.99	3.00	3.64	3.10	3.07	3.58
5.04	3.96	2.04	6.96	3.96	2.04	6.00	0.00	2.04	2.04	2.04
9.00	2.04	2.04	9.00	3.96	8.04	2.04	6.00	12.00	14.04	6.00
0.96	6.00	3.96	5.04	2.04	3.96	0.00	2.04	8.04	0.00	0.00
0.00	0.00	0.00	0.00	0.00	0.00	0.00	0.00	0.00	0.00	0.00
2.04	0.00	12.00	2.04	3.96	0.00	2.04	0.00	3.96	0.00	3.96
5.04	2.04	9.96	5.04	18.00	2.04	8.04	14.04	2.04	2.04	0.00
12.96	12.00	14.04	12.96	21.96	6.00	6.00	6.00	3.96	0.00	9.96
9.00	2.04	3.96	3.00	8.04	0.00	9.96	0.00	0.00	0.00	3.96
0.00	3.96	6.00	3.96	2.04	0.00	3.96	2.04	3.96	0.00	0.00
0.96	0.00	0.00	0.00	0.00	0.00	0.00	0.00	0.00	0.00	0.00
0.00	0.00	0.00	0.00	0.00	0.00	0.00	0.00	0.00	0.00	0.00
0.00	0.00	0.00	0.00	0.00	0.00	0.00	0.00	0.00	0.00	0.00
2.04	6.00	2.04	3.96	2.04	0.00	2.04	3.96	0.00	0.00	2.04
5.04	0.00	0.00	2.04	0.00	2.04	3.96	2.04	3.96	0.00	6.00
0.00	0.00	0.00	0.96	2.04	0.00	0.00	0.00	0.00	0.00	0.00
17.04	14.04	18.00	18.00	26.04	12.00	14.04	8.04	8.04	21.96	20.04
12.96	0.00	12.00	17.04	8.04	8.04	9.96	14.04	12.00	6.00	24.00
0.00	2.04	0.00	0.96	0.00	0.00	0.00	0.00	0.00	0.00	0.00
2.04	3.96	0.00	3.96	2.04	0.00	2.04	6.00	0.00	0.00	0.00
24.00	32.04	24.00	33.00	21.96	8.04	8.04	20.04	24.00	24.00	8.04
0.00	0.00	0.00	0.00	0.00	0.00	0.00	0.00	0.00	0.00	0.00
6.96	6.00	3.96	3.00	14.04	2.04	3.96	6.00	0.00	2.04	3.96
0.96	0.00	0.00	0.96	2.04	0.00	3.96	0.00	0.00	2.04	0.00
0.00	0.00	0.00	0.00	0.00	0.00	0.00	0.00	0.00	0.00	0.00
5.04	2.04	6.00	3.96	8.04	9.96	8.04	9.96	6.00	6.00	2.04
0.96	0.00	0.00	0.00	0.00	0.00	0.00	0.00	0.00	0.00	0.00
0.00	0.00	0.00	5.04	8.04	0.00	0.00	0.00	0.00	0.00	0.00
0.00	0.00	0.00	0.00	2.04	0.00	0.00	0.00	0.00	0.00	0.00
0.00	0.00	6.00	0.96	3.96	0.00	3.96	6.00	0.00	0.00	0.00
0.00	0.00	0.00	0.00	0.00	0.00	0.00	0.00	0.00	0.00	0.00
2.04	0.00	0.00	0.00	0.00	0.00	0.00	0.00	0.00	2.04	2.04
0.00	0.00	0.02	0.00	0.01	0.00	0.00	0.00	0.00	0.00	0.00
0.03	0.00	0.00	0.00	0.00	0.00	0.01	0.01	0.00	0.00	0.01
16.90	28.14	23.09	17.76	14.88	15.49	12.58	11.45	15.95	16.82	12.53
323.16	308.89	304.97	256.32	233.89	260.26	217.78	267.48	246.54	236.53	307.53
72.64	337.17	36.47	369.72	84.92	475.00	91.70	73.88	351.44	48.98	105.46
7.52	32.09	5.79	24.88	10.06	7.87	7.67	10.76	7.57	7.64	11.06
6.27	0.45	9.80	2.78	0.80	8.34	0.08	0.00	0.00	28.85	0.00
0.01	0.02	0.01	0.01	0.01	0.00	0.01	0.06	0.00	0.01	0.01

4-22 分调查市县城镇居民非现金收入（一）

单位：元/人

类别	Classification	济南 Jinan	青岛 Qingdao	淄博 Zibo	枣庄 Zaozhuang	东营 Dongying	烟台 Yantai	潍坊 Weifang
非现金（实物与服务）收入总计	**Total Non-cash (material objects and services) income**	**269**	**140**	**350**	**895**	**936**	**1083**	**564**
一、食品	**Food**	**161**	**102**	**58**	**56**	**62**	**191**	**135**
㈠粮油类	Grain and Oil	39	14	19	27	18	43	45
1.粮食	Grain	13	5	7	7	7	14	13
2.淀粉及薯类	Starches and Tubers	1	0	0	1	0	1	0
3.干豆类及豆制品	Dried Beans and Bean Products	0	0	0	0	0	0	0
4.油脂类	Oil or Fat	25	9	11	19	11	28	31
㈡肉禽蛋水产品类	Meat,Poultry,Eggs andAquatic Products	32	32	12	8	18	54	41
1.肉类	Meat	10	10	5	3	8	12	14
2.禽类	Poultries	2	0	0	0	1	2	3
3.蛋类	Eggs	5	4	3	3	0	4	10
4.水产品类	Aquatic Products	16	17	4	2	8	36	14
㈢蔬菜类	Vegetables	5	2	2	1	1	3	5
㈣调味品	Flavoring	1	0	3	0	3	1	2
㈤糖烟酒饮料类	Carbohydrate,Tobacco,Liquor and Beverages	37	27	14	7	10	33	19
1.糖类	Carbohydrate	1	0	0	0	0	0	1
2.烟草类	Tobacco	5	6	4	1	1	5	3
3.酒类	Liquor	21	17	8	4	8	24	11
4.饮料类	Beverages	10	5	2	3	1	4	5
㈥干鲜瓜果类	Dried and Fresh Melons and Fruits	15	7	2	4	6	21	6
㈦糕点、奶及奶制品	Cake,Milk and Products	14	8	4	6	4	23	13
1.糕点	Cake	6	4	1	1	1	7	3
2.奶及奶制品	Milk and Products	7	4	3	5	4	16	10
㈧其他食品	Other Foods	6	11	2	1	1	8	4
㈨饮食服务	Catering Services	14	2	1	2	0	4	0
1.食品加工服务费	Proceeding Services	1	0	0	0	0	0	0
2.在外饮食	Outward Dinner	13	2	0	2	0	4	0
二、衣着	**Clothing**	**21**	**11**	**5**	**7**	**8**	**17**	**9**
㈠服装	Garments	17	7	4	4	8	16	7
㈡衣着材料	Clothing Material	1	0	0	2	0	0	0
㈢鞋类	Footwear	2	1	2	2	0	1	2

Non-cash Income of Urban Households by City and County

unit:yuan/person

济宁 Jining	泰安 Taian	威海 Weihai	日照 Rizhao	莱芜 Laiwu	临沂 Linyi	德州 Dezhou	聊城 Liaocheng	滨州 Binzhou	菏泽 Heze	文登 Wendeng	诸城 Zhucheng	青州 Qingzhou
63	**587**	**225**	**678**	**1777**	**327**	**1395**	**209**	**850**	**1120**	**125**	**182**	**321**
55	**317**	**74**	**240**	**36**	**239**	**157**	**142**	**286**	**148**	**117**	**156**	**231**
17	78	16	48	19	66	39	41	57	51	48	31	55
6	14	6	18	5	25	12	13	14	25	27	7	17
1	1	0	1	1	1	0	0	0	1	0	1	1
0	1	0	0	0	1	0	0	1	0	0	0	1
10	62	10	29	13	38	26	27	42	25	22	23	37
14	83	39	90	9	44	12	19	42	26	41	73	53
3	60	11	13	1	15	2	6	15	13	10	40	14
2	1	2	5	0	3	1	3	1	3	1	4	4
4	11	6	8	0	8	4	6	9	8	4	6	12
5	11	20	64	7	17	5	4	17	3	26	23	23
1	3	3	6	1	4	2	1	5	3	4	4	6
0	1	0	0	0	0	1	0	2	1	0	1	1
16	97	6	49	6	61	17	28	32	26	6	29	50
0	0	0	0	0	0	0	0	0	1	0	0	0
3	3	1	12	0	23	2	2	6	6	0	3	4
10	80	5	34	6	35	14	24	24	16	6	21	42
2	13	0	3	0	3	1	2	3	3	0	6	4
2	10	4	7	1	22	6	4	12	9	5	10	11
5	35	5	16	1	19	18	20	19	14	2	7	18
2	4	3	4	0	6	0	1	2	2	0	5	5
4	31	2	12	1	13	17	19	17	12	2	2	13
0	5	1	5	0	6	4	28	3	18	10	0	2
0	4	0	19	0	16	58	1	114	0	0	0	35
0	0	0	0	0	0	0	0	0	0	0	0	0
0	4	0	19	0	16	58	1	114	0	0	0	35
3	**50**	**9**	**24**	**5**	**16**	**19**	**3**	**13**	**14**	**5**	**6**	**31**
3	43	3	20	4	14	14	2	10	12	5	6	26
0	0	0	0	0	0	2	0	0	0	0	0	0
0	6	6	3	1	2	2	1	2	2	0	0	5

4-22 续表 1 continued

类别	Classification	微山 Weishan	临清 Linqing	费县 Feixian	利津 Lijin	武城 Wucheng	东阿 Donga	巨野 Juye
非现金（实物与服务）收入总计	**Total Non-cash (material objects and services) income**	**75**	**537**	**107**	**425**	**99**	**1022**	**948**
一、食品	**Food**	**74**	**254**	**93**	**233**	**78**	**33**	**131**
(一)粮油类	Grain and Oil	32	62	37	63	37	17	25
1.粮食	Grain	10	15	14	23	19	13	16
2.淀粉及薯类	Starches and Tubers	2	1	0	0	0	0	0
3.干豆类及豆制品	Dried Beans and Bean Products	0	0	0	0	0	0	0
4.油脂类	Oil or Fat	20	47	22	40	18	4	9
(二)肉禽蛋水产品类	Meat,Poultry,Eggs andAquatic Products	21	90	20	70	13	4	16
1.肉类	Meat	4	40	10	36	5	1	9
2.禽类	Poultries	2	24	3	1	1	1	3
3.蛋类	Eggs	4	4	2	8	3	1	2
4.水产品类	Aquatic Products	11	23	5	25	4	0	2
(三)蔬菜类	Vegetables	0	4	1	5	0	0	1
(四)调味品	Flavoring	0	0	0	7	0	0	0
(五)糖烟酒饮料类	Carbohydrate,Tobacco,Liquor and Beverages	10	64	26	44	22	9	32
1.糖类	Carbohydrate	0	1	0	0	0	0	0
2.烟草类	Tobacco	0	3	2	4	0	0	0
3.酒类	Liquor	8	41	23	37	22	9	32
4.饮料类	Beverages	1	19	0	3	0	0	0
(六)干鲜瓜果类	Dried and Fresh Melons and Fruits	1	5	2	20	2	0	4
(七)糕点、奶及奶制品	Cake,Milk and Products	10	28	7	23	3	3	10
1.糕点	Cake	2	9	5	5	1	0	1
2.奶及奶制品	Milk and Products	9	19	2	18	2	3	9
(八)其他食品	Other Foods	0	1	0	2	1	0	1
(九)饮食服务	Catering Services	0	0	0	0	0	0	42
1.食品加工服务费	Proceeding Services	0	0	0	0	0	0	0
2.在外饮食	Outward Dinner	0	0	0	0	0	0	42
二、衣着	**Clothing**	**1**	**14**	**5**	**22**	**2**	**2**	**24**
(一)服装	Garments	0	5	0	17	1	2	24
(二)衣着材料	Clothing Material	0	1	0	0	0	0	0
(三)鞋类	Footwear	1	8	2	5	1	0	0

4-23 分调查市县城镇居民非现金收入（二）

Non-cash Income of Urban Households by City and County

单位：元/人 unit:yuan/person

类别	Classification	济南 Jinan	青岛 Qingdao	淄博 Zibo	枣庄 Zaozhuang	东营 Dongying	烟台 Yantai	潍坊 Weifang
㈣其他衣着用品	Other Clothing	1	4	0	0	0	0	0
㈤衣着加工服务费	Clothing Proceeding Services	0	0	0	0	0	0	0
三、家庭设备用品及服务	**Household Facilities,Articles and Services**	**8**	**13**	**1**	**3**	**1**	**9**	**6**
㈠耐用消费品	Durable Consumer Goods	1	9	0	0	0	4	1
㈡室内装饰品	Interior Decorations	0	1	1	0	0	1	0
㈢床上用品	Bed Articles	2	0	0	2	0	4	2
㈣家庭日用杂品	Grocery for Daily Use	4	3	0	2	0	1	3
㈤家具材料	Furniture Materials	0	0	0	0	0	0	0
㈥家庭服务	Household Service	0	0	0	0	0	0	0
四、医疗保健	**Health Care and Personal Articles**	**32**	**2**	**4**	**0**	**115**	**6**	**2**
㈠医疗器具	Medical Appliances	0	0	0	0	0	0	0
㈡保健用品	Health Care Appliances	2	0	0	0	0	4	0
㈢药品费	Drugs Charges	18	0	2	0	0	0	0
㈣滋补保健品	Nutritious and Health Articles	1	1	2	0	0	2	1
㈤医疗费	Medical Charges	11	0	0	0	0	0	0
㈥其他	Others	0	0	0	0	115	0	1
其中:医疗基金	Medical Foundation	0	0	0	0	11	0	1
五、交通和通讯	**Transportation and Communication**	**7**	**2**	**1**	**1**	**0**	**0**	**11**
㈠交通	Transportation	4	0	0	0	0	0	0
㈡通信	Communication	3	2	1	1	0	0	11
六、教育文化娱乐服务	**Education,Culture andRecreation Articles**	**30**	**2**	**35**	**33**	**19**	**18**	**2**
㈠文化娱乐用品	Culture and Recreation Articles	8	1	1	0	0	2	1
㈡文化娱乐服务	Culture and Recreation Services	19	0	30	33	19	16	0
㈢教育	Education	3	0	4	0	0	0	0
七、居住	**Residence**	**0**	**0**	**2**	**0**	**0**	**1**	**0**
㈠住房	Housing	0	0	0	0	0	0	0
㈡水电燃料及其他	Water, Electricity,Fuel and Others	0	0	2	0	0	1	0
㈢居住服务费	Charges of Residence Service	0	0	0	0	0	0	0
八、杂项商品和服务	**Miscellanecus Commodities and Services**	**10**	**8**	**244**	**795**	**731**	**841**	**400**
㈠杂项商品	Miscellanecus Commodities	8	5	4	0	1	9	93
㈡服务	Services	2	2	240	795	731	832	307

4-23 续表 1

类别	Classification	济宁 Jining	泰安 Taian	威海 Weihai	日照 Rizhao	莱芜 Laiwu	临沂 Linyi	德州 Dezhou
㈣其他衣着用品	Other Clothing	0	1	0	0	0	0	1
㈤衣着加工服务费	Clothing Proceeding Services	0	0	0	0	0	0	0
三、家庭设备用品及服务	**Household Facilities,Articles and Services**	**1**	**20**	**2**	**20**	**0**	**6**	**4**
㈠耐用消费品	Durable Consumer Goods	0	2	0	16	0	0	0
㈡室内装饰品	Interior Decorations	0	1	1	0	0	2	0
㈢床上用品	Bed Articles	0	5	1	2	0	4	0
㈣家庭日用杂品	Grocery for Daily Use	0	12	0	2	0	0	4
㈤家具材料	Furniture Materials	0	0	0	0	0	0	0
㈥家庭服务	Household Service	0	0	0	0	0	0	0
四、医疗保健	**Health Care and Personal Articles**	**2**	**12**	**20**	**6**	**0**	**3**	**204**
㈠医疗器具	Medical Appliances	0	0	0	0	0	0	0
㈡保健用品	Health Care Appliances	0	1	0	0	0	0	0
㈢药品费	Drugs Charges	2	1	5	0	0	1	0
㈣滋补保健品	Nutritious and Health Articles	0	8	2	4	0	2	0
㈤医疗费	Medical Charges	0	2	12	1	0	0	1
㈥其他	Others	0	0	0	0	0	0	202
其中：医疗基金	Medical Foundation	0	0	0	0	0	0	202
五、交通和通讯	**Transportation and Communication**	**0**	**2**	**4**	**0**	**0**	**8**	**3**
㈠交通	Transportation	0	0	0	0	0	8	3
㈡通信	Communication	0	1	4	0	0	0	0
六、教育文化娱乐服务	**Education,Culture and Recreation Articles**	**0**	**59**	**13**	**35**	**0**	**23**	**19**
㈠文化娱乐用品	Culture and Recreation Articles	0	6	2	28	0	1	1
㈡文化娱乐服务	Culture and Recreation Services	0	53	11	7	0	22	17
㈢教育	Education	0	0	0	0	0	0	1
七、居住	**Residence**	**0**	**5**	**0**	**13**	**0**	**2**	**1**
㈠住房	Housing	0	0	0	0	0	0	1
㈡水电燃料及其他	Water, Electricity,Fuel and Others	0	5	0	13	0	2	0
㈢居住服务费	Charges of Residence Service	0	0	0	0	0	0	0
八、杂项商品和服务	**Miscellanecus Commodities and Services**	**2**	**122**	**103**	**341**	**1736**	**31**	**989**
㈠杂项商品	Miscellanecus Commodities	2	1	0	2	3	31	4
㈡服务	Services	0	121	103	339	1733	0	984

continued

聊城 Liaocheng	滨州 Binzhou	菏泽 Heze	文登 Wendeng	诸城 Zhucheng	青州 Qingzhou	微山 Weishan	临清 Linqing	费县 Feixian	利津 Lijin	武城 Wucheng	东阿 Donga	巨野 Juye
0	1	0	0	0	0	0	0	2	0	0	0	0
0	0	0	0	0	0	0	0	0	0	0	0	0
32	**19**	**5**	**1**	**4**	**7**	**0**	**1**	**0**	**72**	**16**	**0**	**5**
30	16	1	0	0	3	0	0	0	71	0	0	0
0	0	0	0	0	1	0	0	0	1	0	0	0
0	3	2	1	4	2	0	1	0	0	16	0	0
2	0	1	0	0	1	0	0	0	0	0	0	5
0	0	0	0	0	0	0	0	0	0	0	0	0
0	0	0	0	0	1	0	0	0	0	0	0	0
30	**14**	**1**	**0**	**0**	**3**	**0**	**6**	**0**	**0**	**0**	**0**	**0**
0	0	0	0	0	0	0	0	0	0	0	0	0
0	0	0	0	0	0	0	0	0	0	0	0	0
4	12	1	0	0	2	0	2	0	0	0	0	0
0	1	0	0	0	1	0	4	0	0	0	0	0
26	2	0	0	0	0	0	0	0	0	0	0	0
0	0	0	0	0	0	0	0	0	0	0	0	0
0	0	0	0	0	0	0	0	0	0	0	0	0
0	**13**	**2**	**0**	**12**	**1**	**0**	**3**	**0**	**7**	**0**	**0**	**2**
0	0	1	0	12	0	0	3	0	0	0	0	2
0	13	0	0	0	1	0	0	0	7	0	0	0
0	**94**	**19**	**0**	**0**	**27**	**0**	**6**	**0**	**74**	**1**	**0**	**5**
0	1	19	0	0	6	0	1	0	5	1	0	0
0	93	0	0	0	21	0	4	0	69	0	0	1
0	0	0	0	0	0	0	0	0	0	0	0	4
1	**10**	**12**	**2**	**2**	**18**	**0**	**6**	**7**	**1**	**0**	**0**	**19**
0	0	0	0	0	0	0	6	0	0	0	0	0
1	10	12	2	2	16	0	0	7	1	0	0	1
0	0	0	0	0	2	0	0	0	0	0	0	19
0	**402**	**921**	**0**	**1**	**3**	**0**	**248**	**1**	**17**	**2**	**987**	**761**
0	3	0	0	1	3	0	1	1	14	2	0	0
0	399	920	0	0	0	0	247	0	3	0	987	761

4-24 分调查市县城镇居民家庭年末耐用消费品百户拥有量

类别	Classification	单位	unit	济南 Jinan	青岛 Qingdao	淄博 Zibo	枣庄 Zaozhuang	东营 Dongying	烟台 Yantai	潍坊 Weifang
1.成套家具	Furniture Sets	套	set	70.53	81.00	90.67	99.00	98.00	81.00	93.00
2.摩托车	Motorcycles	辆	unit	28.46	6.75	45.33	65.00	22.00	33.00	46.00
3.自行车	Bicycles	辆	unit	159.45	27.75	172.67	221.00	170.00	130.50	222.00
4.助力车	Motorbikes	辆	unit	22.67	0.75	21.33	35.00	15.00	14.50	22.00
5.家用汽车	Automobiles	辆	unit	6.80	6.25	9.33	3.00	8.00	6.50	9.00
6.洗衣机	Washing Machines	台	unit	98.99	97.25	97.33	102.00	93.00	91.50	97.00
7.电风扇	Electric Fans	台	unit	138.54	104.75	140.67	209.00	186.00	110.50	168.00
8.电冰箱	Refrigerators	台	unit	96.73	98.50	96.00	89.00	105.00	95.00	95.00
9.冰柜	Freezer	台	unit	14.11	25.25	12.00	5.00	29.00	34.50	18.00
10.彩色电视机	Color TV Sets	台	unit	121.91	124.50	114.67	118.00	132.00	136.00	122.00
11.影碟机	Video Disc Players	台	unit	63.98	55.00	70.67	76.00	76.00	62.50	58.00
12.录音机	Tape Recorders	台	unit	45.09	59.50	57.33	69.00	67.00	61.00	53.00
13.录放像机	Video Recorders	台	unit	21.91	29.75	22.00	17.00	24.00	33.50	26.00
14.家用电脑	Computers	台	unit	64.48	71.25	54.00	47.00	60.00	51.50	39.00
15.组合音响	Hi-Fi Stereo Component System	套	set	27.46	33.75	32.00	25.00	21.00	25.50	24.00
16.摄像机	Pickup Cameras	架	unit	5.04	12.75	12.00	4.00	14.00	9.00	5.00
17.照相机	Cameras	架	unit	62.47	81.75	64.00	53.00	74.00	73.00	75.00
18.钢琴	Pianos	架	unit	3.78	7.75	2.67	3.00	3.00	5.00	0.00
19.其他中高档乐器	Other Medium and Top Grade Music Instruments	件	piece	8.56	8.50	8.00	17.00	20.00	17.00	18.00
20.微波炉	Microwave Ovens	台	unit	57.68	80.75	55.33	29.00	40.00	60.50	61.00
21.空调器	Air Conditioner	台	unit	112.34	89.25	92.67	91.00	119.00	46.50	75.00
22.取暖器	Heater	台	unit	26.95	52.00	26.00	41.00	30.00	44.00	30.00
23.电炊具	Electric Cookers	台	unit	80.10	76.25	107.33	87.00	75.00	94.00	115.00
24.淋浴热水器	Water Heaters	台	unit	82.87	88.00	78.00	82.00	99.00	90.50	86.00
25.排油烟机	Lampblack Exhausters	台	unit	88.41	96.00	96.00	86.00	100.00	98.50	99.00
26.消毒碗柜	Sterilized Cabinet	台	unit	5.79	8.25	14.00	2.00	12.00	10.50	4.00
27.洗碗机	Dishwasher	台	unit	2.02	2.00	2.00	0.00	1.00	1.50	0.00
28.饮水机	Drinking Machine	台	unit	59.19	68.25	90.67	78.00	81.00	75.00	65.00
29.吸尘器	Vacuam Cleaner	台	unit	16.12	48.25	20.67	11.00	25.00	31.00	24.00
30.健身器材	Body Building Equipment	套	set	5.04	8.75	8.00	7.00	13.00	5.50	4.00
31.普通电话	Common Phones	部	unit	83.88	95.75	94.00	84.00	94.00	84.50	99.00
32.移动电话	Mobile Phones	部	unit	162.72	187.00	152.00	162.00	215.00	163.00	183.00
33.传真机	Faxes	部	unit	0.76	4.25	1.33	0.00	2.00	0.00	0.00

Number of Durable Consumer Goods Owned by Per 100 Urban Households at the Year-end by City and County

济宁	泰安	威海	日照	莱芜	临沂	德州	聊城	滨州	菏泽	文登	诸城	青州
Jining	Taian	Weihai	Rizhao	Laiwu	Linyi	Dezhou	Liaocheng	Binzhou	Heze	Wendeng	Zhucheng	Qingzhou
94.00	149.00	78.00	87.00	100.00	91.00	90.00	94.95	100.00	108.00	94.00	116.00	100.00
20.00	81.00	22.00	78.00	74.00	51.00	33.00	30.30	47.00	49.00	52.00	96.00	91.00
233.00	163.00	126.00	134.00	147.00	208.00	212.00	183.84	184.00	200.00	146.00	204.00	171.00
31.00	20.00	7.00	6.00	15.00	34.00	39.00	44.44	44.00	47.00	6.00	40.00	30.00
0.00	4.00	8.00	9.00	10.00	12.00	2.00	2.02	7.00	0.00	10.00	10.00	10.00
101.00	94.00	84.00	82.00	97.00	99.00	94.00	96.97	96.00	99.00	56.00	98.00	94.00
198.00	171.00	88.00	138.00	145.00	204.00	168.00	261.62	224.00	163.00	88.00	178.00	189.00
101.00	94.00	99.00	91.00	98.00	94.00	83.00	89.90	88.00	83.00	98.00	94.00	82.00
6.00	10.00	21.00	24.00	15.00	10.00	17.00	8.08	17.00	14.00	14.00	18.00	12.00
120.00	126.00	139.00	108.00	118.00	110.00	120.00	118.18	118.00	126.00	128.00	124.00	118.00
66.00	68.00	59.00	63.00	75.00	75.00	69.00	70.71	75.00	64.00	36.00	74.00	67.00
50.00	50.00	80.00	35.00	67.00	55.00	52.00	42.42	86.00	39.00	48.00	94.00	39.00
17.00	17.00	19.00	7.00	29.00	19.00	8.00	9.09	16.00	9.00	12.00	20.00	9.00
64.00	58.00	54.00	38.00	71.00	46.00	52.00	41.41	50.00	42.00	28.00	54.00	41.00
25.00	19.00	18.00	17.00	25.00	29.00	18.00	18.18	18.00	21.00	4.00	30.00	15.00
7.00	5.00	7.00	8.00	12.00	2.00	5.00	3.03	2.00	2.00	0.00	12.00	2.00
62.00	69.00	62.00	50.00	67.00	46.00	53.00	42.42	58.00	41.00	30.00	84.00	40.00
3.00	6.00	3.00	5.00	6.00	3.00	1.00	0.00	2.00	2.00	0.00	2.00	3.00
10.00	5.00	16.00	9.00	10.00	10.00	5.00	6.06	14.00	5.00	4.00	12.00	8.00
42.00	46.00	52.00	35.00	54.00	45.00	36.00	32.32	36.00	33.00	24.00	58.00	21.00
106.00	73.00	27.00	59.00	64.00	80.00	110.00	82.83	101.00	95.00	16.00	78.00	56.00
36.00	38.00	23.00	20.00	29.00	32.00	25.00	19.19	33.00	38.00	18.00	48.00	17.00
96.00	123.00	90.00	95.00	94.00	58.00	151.00	84.85	205.00	103.00	52.00	140.00	113.00
71.00	82.00	92.00	37.00	88.00	66.00	67.00	42.42	88.00	58.00	66.00	92.00	78.00
85.00	96.00	97.00	87.00	96.00	88.00	86.00	98.99	95.00	67.00	78.00	102.00	78.00
6.00	7.00	3.00	8.00	11.00	9.00	4.00	2.02	3.00	5.00	0.00	8.00	3.00
3.00	2.00	1.00	3.00	2.00	1.00	0.00	1.01	0.00	1.00	0.00	4.00	0.00
57.00	65.00	88.00	25.00	89.00	86.00	80.00	54.55	72.00	41.00	94.00	60.00	59.00
21.00	10.00	36.00	15.00	19.00	9.00	12.00	4.04	12.00	8.00	10.00	10.00	10.00
15.00	9.00	7.00	2.00	7.00	11.00	9.00	6.06	2.00	3.00	2.00	18.00	2.00
95.00	87.00	89.00	94.00	94.00	91.00	90.00	100.00	100.00	89.00	92.00	100.00	92.00
145.00	198.00	175.00	143.00	176.00	155.00	161.00	125.25	160.00	157.00	140.00	192.00	152.00
1.00	3.00	4.00	2.00	0.00	1.00	0.00	2.02	0.00	0.00	2.00	0.00	1.00

4-24 续表 1 continued

类别	Classification	单位	unit	微山 Weishan	临清 Linqing	费县 Feixian	利津 Lijin	武城 Wucheng	东阿 Donga	巨野 Juye
1.成套家具	Furniture Sets	套	set	96.00	60.00	82.00	94.00	104.00	82.00	110.00
2.摩托车	Motorcycles	辆	unit	28.00	54.00	46.00	36.00	46.00	48.00	62.00
3.自行车	Bicycles	辆	unit	232.00	222.00	184.00	182.00	226.00	212.00	182.00
4.助力车	Motorbikes	辆	unit	36.00	58.00	12.00	64.00	30.00	16.00	62.00
5.家用汽车	Automobiles	辆	unit	0.00	0.00	2.00	0.00	4.00	0.00	2.00
6.洗衣机	Washing Machines	台	unit	104.00	86.00	88.00	92.00	96.00	80.00	94.00
7.电风扇	Electric Fans	台	unit	282.00	190.00	214.00	240.00	240.00	238.00	252.00
8.电冰箱	Refrigerators	台	unit	84.00	68.00	88.00	86.00	64.00	70.00	72.00
9.冰柜	Freezer	台	unit	4.00	6.00	6.00	10.00	10.00	6.00	6.00
10.彩色电视机	Color TV Sets	台	unit	124.00	116.00	112.00	110.00	116.00	108.00	130.00
11.影碟机	Video Disc Players	台	unit	84.00	62.00	70.00	76.00	64.00	66.00	66.00
12.录音机	Tape Recorders	台	unit	42.00	34.00	44.00	54.00	32.00	34.00	28.00
13.录放像机	Video Recorders	台	unit	12.00	4.00	14.00	6.00	12.00	2.00	8.00
14.家用电脑	Computers	台	unit	50.00	20.00	36.00	62.00	22.00	40.00	58.00
15.组合音响	Hi-Fi Stereo Component System	套	set	20.00	20.00	10.00	22.00	26.00	22.00	18.00
16.摄像机	Pickup Cameras	架	unit	6.00	0.00	0.00	4.00	0.00	0.00	8.00
17.照相机	Cameras	架	unit	54.00	20.00	36.00	40.00	20.00	38.00	22.00
18.钢琴	Pianos	架	unit	0.00	0.00	4.00	0.00	0.00	2.00	6.00
19.其他中高档乐器	Other Medium and Top Grade Music Instruments	件	piece	8.00	2.00	2.00	4.00	0.00	2.00	10.00
20.微波炉	Microwave Ovens	台	unit	36.00	12.00	32.00	24.00	22.00	22.00	42.00
21.空调器	Air Conditioner	台	unit	106.00	42.00	60.00	92.00	68.00	72.00	66.00
22.取暖器	Heater	台	unit	32.00	18.00	10.00	18.00	4.00	2.00	28.00
23.电炊具	Electric Cookers	台	unit	172.00	58.00	98.00	162.00	56.00	60.00	100.00
24.淋浴热水器	Water Heaters	台	unit	90.00	22.00	22.00	66.00	40.00	20.00	48.00
25.排油烟机	Lampblack Exhausters	台	unit	86.00	26.00	84.00	82.00	44.00	80.00	46.00
26.消毒碗柜	Sterilized Cabinet	台	unit	16.00	0.00	4.00	12.00	4.00	2.00	2.00
27.洗碗机	Dishwasher	台	unit	0.00	0.00	2.00	0.00	0.00	2.00	2.00
28.饮水机	Drinking Machine	台	unit	54.00	28.00	70.00	72.00	98.00	32.00	96.00
29.吸尘器	Vacuam Cleaner	台	unit	16.00	2.00	8.00	8.00	4.00	8.00	6.00
30.健身器材	Body Building Equipment	套	set	10.00	4.00	0.00	6.00	2.00	0.00	2.00
31.普通电话	Common Phones	部	unit	86.00	96.00	88.00	80.00	96.00	80.00	94.00
32.移动电话	Mobile Phones	部	unit	152.00	100.00	110.00	186.00	132.00	162.00	162.00
33.传真机	Faxes	部	unit	0.00	0.00	0.00	2.00	2.00	0.00	2.00

4-25　分调查市县城镇居民住房情况（一）

Housing Situation of Urban Households at the Year-end by City and County

类别	Classification	单位	unit	济南 Jinan	青岛 Qingdao	淄博 Zibo
家庭居住人口数	Number of Household Residents	人/户	person/household	2.87	2.84	2.76
现住房总建筑面积	Total Housing Construction Area	平米/人	sq.m/household	26.34	23.73	34.02
现住房屋总使用面积	Total Housing used Area	平米/人	sq.m/household	19.98	17.55	26.43
房屋产权（构成）	Property Right of House	%	percentage	100.00	100.00	100.00
租赁公房	Public House for Renting	%	percentage	8.31	11.00	1.33
租赁私房	Private House for Renting	%	percentage	2.27	2.00	2.00
原有私房	Original Private House	%	percentage	5.79	14.00	4.00
房改私房	Reformed Private House	%	percentage	69.27	52.25	52.00
商品房	Commercial House	%	percentage	13.35	20.00	40.00
其他	Others	%	percentage	1.01	0.75	0.67
住宅建筑式样（构成）	Architectural Style of House	%	percentage	100.00	100.00	100.00
单栋住宅	Single House	%	percentage	0.00	1.75	0.67
四居室	House with Four Rooms	%	percentage	1.76	2.00	6.67
三居室	House with Three Rooms	%	percentage	29.22	19.75	56.00
二居室	House with Two Rooms	%	percentage	55.67	63.25	34.00
一居室	House with One Room	%	percentage	3.78	5.75	0.67
普通楼房	Common Building	%	percentage	3.27	5.25	1.33
平房及其他	Bungalow and Others	%	percentage	6.30	2.25	0.67
装修状况（构成）	Finishing Situation	%	percentage	100.00	100.00	100.00
有装修	Fit up	%	percentage	54.16	66.50	66.67
未装修	Non-fit Up	%	percentage	45.84	33.50	33.33
最近一次装修花费	Finishing Cost Last Time	元/户	yuan/household	7542	16156	9602
现有住房按市场价估计值	Marketable Estimated Value of Current House	元/户	yuan/household	170842	284503	130678
租赁房房租	House Rent	元/户	yuan/household	13	1645	10
自有房房租折算	Obversion of Owned-House Rent	元/户	yuan/household	463	126	281
购房总金额	Total Amount of Purchasing House	元/户	yuan/household	57108	72468	69013
购房实际支出金额	Realistic Amount of Purchasing House	元/户	yuan/household	47473	67564	66573
饮水情况(构成)	Situation of Drinking Water	%	percentage	100.00	100.00	100.00
自来水	Tap Water	%	percentage	89.67	76.75	54.00
矿泉水	Mineral Spring Water	%	percentage	5.04	17.75	35.33
纯净水	Pured Water	%	percentage	5.29	5.50	10.67
井、河水	Well Waterand River Water	%	percentage	0.00	0.00	0.00
其他	Others	%	percentage	0.00	0.00	0.00

4-25　续表 1

类别	Classification	单位	unit	枣庄 Zaozhuang	东营 Dongying	烟台 Yantai
家庭居住人口数	Number of Household Residents	人/户	person/household	2.89	2.91	2.84
现住房总建筑面积	Total Housing Construction Area	平米/人	sq.m/household	26.82	29.82	25.63
现住房屋总使用面积	Total Housing used Area	平米/人	sq.m/household	22.32	23.08	18.77
房屋产权（构成）	Property Right of House	%	percentage	100.00	100.00	100.00
租赁公房	Public House for Renting	%	percentage	2.00	0.00	2.50
租赁私房	Private House for Renting	%	percentage	2.00	0.00	0.50
原有私房	Original Private House	%	percentage	5.00	0.00	7.00
房改私房	Reformed Private House	%	percentage	69.00	87.00	61.00
商品房	Commercial House	%	percentage	20.00	8.00	28.50
其他	Others	%	percentage	2.00	5.00	0.50
住宅建筑式样（构成）	Architectural Style of House	%	percentage	100.00	100.00	100.00
单栋住宅	Single House	%	percentage	0.00	0.00	0.00
四居室	House with Four Rooms	%	percentage	3.00	8.00	4.00
三居室	House with Three Rooms	%	percentage	36.00	61.00	37.50
二居室	House with Two Rooms	%	percentage	43.00	22.00	52.00
一居室	House with One Room	%	percentage	3.00	2.00	3.00
普通楼房	Common Building	%	percentage	7.00	3.00	2.50
平房及其他	Bungalow and Others	%	percentage	8.00	4.00	1.00
装修状况（构成）	Finishing Situation	%	percentage	100.00	100.00	100.00
有装修	Fit up	%	percentage	39.00	61.00	71.00
未装修	Non-fit Up	%	percentage	61.00	39.00	29.00
最近一次装修花费	Finishing Cost Last Time	元/户	yuan/household	4774	15007	17207
现有住房按市场价估计值	Marketable Estimated Value of Current House	元/户	yuan/household	76770	160993	159782
租赁房房租	House Rent	元/户	yuan/household	7	7	8
自有房房租折算	Obversion of Owned-House Rent	元/户	yuan/household	256	341	177
购房总金额	Total Amount of Purchasing House	元/户	yuan/household	42029	54580	56180
购房实际支出金额	Realistic Amount of Purchasing House	元/户	yuan/household	35767	48268	54115
饮水情况(构成)	Situation of Drinking Water	%	percentage	100.00	100.00	100.00
自来水	Tap Water	%	percentage	83.00	85.00	60.50
矿泉水	Mineral Spring Water	%	percentage	6.00	12.00	27.50
纯净水	Pured Water	%	percentage	11.00	3.00	12.00
井、河水	Well Waterand River Water	%	percentage	0.00	0.00	0.00
其他	Others	%	percentage	0.00	0.00	0.00

continued

潍坊 Weifang	济宁 Jining	泰安 Taian	威海 Weihai	日照 Rizhao	莱芜 Laiwu	临沂 Linyi	德州 Dezhou	聊城 Liaocheng
2.83	2.93	3.00	2.80	2.82	2.89	3.06	2.98	2.98
29.60	27.74	29.66	27.31	28.68	30.60	33.48	30.38	30.89
22.16	20.88	22.29	20.02	23.08	24.78	25.84	22.83	23.98
100.00	100.00	100.00	100.00	100.00	100.00	100.00	100.00	100.00
4.00	5.00	4.00	2.00	0.00	0.00	0.00	1.00	2.02
0.00	2.00	1.00	0.00	1.00	1.00	1.00	0.00	3.03
1.00	3.00	29.00	3.00	8.00	4.00	24.00	8.00	3.03
77.00	76.00	53.00	64.00	72.00	69.00	61.00	77.00	62.63
18.00	12.00	13.00	30.00	19.00	21.00	14.00	13.00	23.23
0.00	2.00	0.00	1.00	0.00	5.00	0.00	1.00	6.06
100.00	100.00	100.00	100.00	100.00	100.00	100.00	100.00	100.00
0.00	0.00	4.00	0.00	0.00	2.00	5.00	0.00	0.00
5.00	5.00	1.00	2.00	9.00	1.00	2.00	1.00	1.01
47.00	60.00	52.00	63.00	65.00	39.00	49.00	39.00	60.61
44.00	21.00	41.00	34.00	21.00	49.00	33.00	49.00	33.33
2.00	3.00	0.00	0.00	0.00	4.00	1.00	3.00	1.01
0.00	10.00	1.00	0.00	1.00	4.00	3.00	0.00	3.03
2.00	1.00	1.00	1.00	4.00	1.00	7.00	8.00	1.01
100.00	100.00	100.00	100.00	100.00	100.00	100.00	100.00	100.00
67.00	47.00	73.00	81.00	56.00	53.00	41.00	28.00	31.31
33.00	53.00	27.00	19.00	44.00	47.00	59.00	72.00	68.69
9706	6844	8819	16837	7083	4612	4735	3564	1736
124577	91371	147620	192240	137750	88361	166222	134540	119747
9	7	5	1	0	2	0	1	26.28
765	297	381	119	294	236	268	129	187
56104	38711	38316	59633	52637	47053	31748	96847	69185
55644	36175	30493	55409	51875	43018	31367	94187	64951
100.00	100.00	100.00	100.00	100.00	100.00	100.00	100.00	100.00
92.00	91.00	81.00	37.00	100.00	66.00	68.00	78.00	95.96
3.00	1.00	4.00	50.00	0.00	22.00	1.00	2.00	4.04
5.00	7.00	15.00	11.00	0.00	0.00	31.00	20.00	0.00
0.00	1.00	0.00	0.00	0.00	12.00	0.00	0.00	0.00
0.00	0.00	0.00	2.00	0.00	0.00	0.00	0.00	0.00

4-25 续表 2

类别	Classification	单位	unit	滨州 Binzhou	菏泽 Heze	文登 Wendeng
家庭居住人口数	Number of Household Residents	人/户	person/household	2.86	3.17	2.66
现住房总建筑面积	Total Housing Construction Area	平米/人	sq.m/household	29.96	32.09	30.56
现住房屋总使用面积	Total Housing used Area	平米/人	sq.m/household	22.65	24.62	22.23
房屋产权（构成）	Property Right of House	%	percentage	100.00	100.00	100.00
租赁公房	Public House for Renting	%	percentage	0.00	4.00	0.00
租赁私房	Private House for Renting	%	percentage	0.00	3.00	0.00
原有私房	Original Private House	%	percentage	0.00	15.00	2.00
房改私房	Reformed Private House	%	percentage	98.00	61.00	62.00
商品房	Commercial House	%	percentage	2.00	17.00	36.00
其他	Others	%	percentage	0.00	0.00	0.00
住宅建筑式样（构成）	Architectural Style of House	%	percentage	100.00	100.00	100.00
单栋住宅	Single House	%	percentage	0.00	0.00	0.00
四居室	House with Four Rooms	%	percentage	1.00	6.00	2.00
三居室	House with Three Rooms	%	percentage	43.00	52.00	10.00
二居室	House with Two Rooms	%	percentage	52.00	17.00	88.00
一居室	House with One Room	%	percentage	1.00	0.00	0.00
普通楼房	Common Building	%	percentage	0.00	2.00	0.00
平房及其他	Bungalow and Others	%	percentage	3.00	23.00	0.00
装修状况（构成）	Finishing Situation	%	percentage	100.00	100.00	100.00
有装修	Fit up	%	percentage	41.00	34.00	54.00
未装修	Non-fit Up	%	percentage	59.00	66.00	46.00
最近一次装修花费	Finishing Cost Last Time	元/户	yuan/household	3656	3029	8300
现有住房按市场价估计值	Marketable Estimated Value of Current House	元/户	yuan/household	86877	103670	75620
租赁房房租	House Rent	元/户	yuan/household	0	5	0
自有房房租折算	Obversion of Owned-House Rent	元/户	yuan/household	181	262	230
购房总金额	Total Amount of Purchasing House	元/户	yuan/household	49099	50964	52831
购房实际支出金额	Realistic Amount of Purchasing House	元/户	yuan/household	45962	34488	47965
饮水情况（构成）	Situation of Drinking Water	%	percentage	100.00	100.00	100.00
自来水	Tap Water	%	percentage	94.00	90.00	46.00
矿泉水	Mineral Spring Water	%	percentage	4.00	0.00	46.00
纯净水	Pured Water	%	percentage	2.00	2.00	4.00
井、河水	Well Waterand River Water	%	percentage	0.00	8.00	4.00
其他	Others	%	percentage	0.00	0.00	0.00

continued

诸城 Zhucheng	青州 Qingzhou	微山 Weishan	临清 Linqing	费县 Feixian	利津 Lijin	武城 Wucheng	东阿 Donga	巨野 Juye
3.14	3.00	2.80	2.88	3.02	2.86	2.88	3.00	3.04
29.26	27.06	34.98	31.81	27.72	32.28	39.28	33.04	29.92
22.28	20.40	26.76	23.92	21.34	27.82	29.74	24.83	24.33
100.00	100.00	100.00	100.00	100.00	100.00	100.00	100.00	100.00
0.00	5.00	12.00	2.00	0.00	0.00	0.00	0.00	0.00
0.00	1.00	0.00	0.00	0.00	0.00	2.00	4.00	0.00
8.00	13.00	2.00	46.00	2.00	2.00	22.00	0.00	18.00
54.00	61.00	84.00	20.00	82.00	86.00	28.00	60.00	66.00
38.00	20.00	2.00	30.00	2.00	8.00	48.00	34.00	14.00
0.00	0.00	0.00	2.00	14.00	4.00	0.00	2.00	2.00
100.00	100.00	100.00	100.00	100.00	100.00	100.00	100.00	100.00
0.00	0.00	2.00	2.00	2.00	0.00	4.00	0.00	6.00
4.00	1.00	16.00	0.00	4.00	0.00	0.00	2.00	2.00
40.00	36.00	54.00	12.00	60.00	60.00	32.00	68.00	44.00
44.00	40.00	28.00	18.00	30.00	18.00	2.00	18.00	8.00
0.00	2.00	0.00	0.00	0.00	4.00	0.00	0.00	0.00
0.00	3.00	0.00	6.00	0.00	6.00	12.00	6.00	2.00
12.00	18.00	0.00	62.00	4.00	12.00	50.00	6.00	38.00
100.00	100.00	100.00	100.00	100.00	100.00	100.00	100.00	100.00
60.00	53.00	50.00	40.00	34.00	30.00	36.00	20.00	38.00
40.00	47.00	50.00	60.00	66.00	70.00	64.00	80.00	62.00
13180	8688	5054	1594	2048	1820	3300	1180	4172
134400	88473	74480	79500	68300	85149	83412	73732	74240
0	0	3	2	0	0	3	3	0
446	229	69	186	179	358	171	111	137
59815	41319	32089	27560	39189	51682	52014	48611	40138
55738	39223	32089	23664	39189	48145	52014	47706	39998
100.00	100.00	100.00	100.00	100.00	100.00	100.00	100.00	100.00
100.00	94.00	100.00	100.00	100.00	72.00	94.00	100.00	64.00
0.00	0.00	0.00	0.00	0.00	0.00	0.00	0.00	0.00
0.00	6.00	0.00	0.00	0.00	28.00	0.00	0.00	24.00
0.00	0.00	0.00	0.00	0.00	0.00	6.00	0.00	12.00
0.00	0.00	0.00	0.00	0.00	0.00	0.00	0.00	0.00

4-26 分调查市县城镇居民住房情况（二）

类别	Classification	单位	unit	济南 Jinan	青岛 Qingdao	淄博 Zibo
用水情况（构成）	Situation of Drinking Water	%	percentage	100.00	100.00	100.00
独用自来水	Individual Tap-water	%	percentage	95.72	95.25	85.33
公用自来水	Public tap-water	%	percentage	4.28	4.75	14.00
井、河水	Well Waterand River Water	%	percentage	0.00	0.00	0.67
其他	Others	%	percentage	0.00	0.00	0.00
卫生设备（构成）	Health Equipment	%	percentage	100.00	100.00	100.00
无卫生设备	Non-health Equipment	%	percentage	3.27	0.00	0.00
有厕所浴室	Lavatory with Bathroom	%	percentage	72.29	92.75	45.33
有厕所无浴室	Lavatory without Bathroom	%	percentage	20.91	3.25	54.67
公用	Public	%	percentage	3.53	4.00	0.00
取暖设备（构成）	Heating Equipment	%	percentage	100.00	100.00	100.00
无取暖设备	No Heating Equipment	%	percentage	3.02	2.50	4.67
空调设备	Air Conditioner	%	percentage	13.85	43.25	26.67
暖气	Heater	%	percentage	51.13	43.50	59.33
其他	Others	%	percentage	31.99	10.75	9.33
炊用燃料使用情况（构成）	Fuel of Cooking	%	percentage	100.00	100.00	100.00
管道煤气	Pipelined Gas	%	percentage	44.58	61.00	32.00
液化石油气	Liquefied Petroleum Gas	%	percentage	49.87	36.50	63.33
煤	Coal	%	percentage	3.53	2.00	1.33
其他	Others	%	percentage	2.02	0.50	3.33
通信设备使用情况	Communication Equipment	%	percentage			
(1)无电话（构成）	Non-telephone	%	percentage	100.00	100.00	100.00
无	No	%	percentage	0.00	0.50	0.00
有	Have	%	percentage	100.00	99.50	100.00
(2)固定电话	Hand-free Telephone	部/百户	unit/100 households	83.88	95.75	94.00
(3)移动电话	Mobile Telephone	部/百户	unit/100 households	162.72	187.00	152.00
(4)使用互联网	use Internet	条/百户	piece /100 households	36.02	41.00	42.00
除了现住房，还有几处其他住房	Other Houses Besides Current House	套/户	set/household	0.11	0.18	0.14
①出租房	House for Ren	套/户	set/ household	0.05	0.10	0.08
使用面积	Area for Use	平方米/户	sq.m/household	2.47	5.07	6.54
②偶尔居住房	House for Occasionally Living	套/户	set/household	0.04	0.05	0.03
使用面积	Area for Use	平方米/户	sq.m/household	3.36	2.79	2.55
③其它用途房	House for Other Use	套/户	set/household	0.02	0.04	0.03
使用面积	Area for Use	平方米/户	sq.m/household	1.32	1.69	3.63

Housing Situation of Urban Households at the Year-end by City and County

枣庄 Zaozhuang	东营 Dongying	烟台 Yantai	潍坊 Weifang	济宁 Jining	泰安 Taian	威海 Weihai	日照 Rizhao	莱芜 Laiwu	临沂 Linyi	德州 Dezhou
100.00	100.00	100.00	100.00	100.00	100.00	100.00	100.00	100.00	100.00	100.00
90.00	100.00	91.50	99.00	88.00	94.00	99.00	99.00	80.00	94.00	100.00
10.00	0.00	8.50	1.00	11.00	6.00	1.00	1.00	8.00	6.00	0.00
0.00	0.00	0.00	0.00	1.00	0.00	0.00	0.00	12.00	0.00	0.00
0.00	0.00	0.00	0.00	0.00	0.00	0.00	0.00	0.00	0.00	0.00
100.00	100.00	100.00	100.00	100.00	100.00	100.00	100.00	100.00	100.00	100.00
6.00	0.00	0.00	0.00	5.00	0.00	0.00	0.00	3.00	0.00	3.00
39.00	84.00	59.00	57.00	41.00	69.00	75.00	75.00	45.00	62.00	65.00
51.00	12.00	41.00	42.00	53.00	29.00	24.00	25.00	52.00	37.00	28.00
4.00	4.00	0.00	1.00	1.00	2.00	1.00	0.00	0.00	1.00	4.00
100.00	100.00	100.00	100.00	100.00	100.00	100.00	100.00	100.00	100.00	100.00
10.00	0.00	0.00	0.00	15.00	3.00	1.00	0.00	1.00	3.00	3.00
13.00	9.00	17.50	12.00	49.00	10.00	2.00	9.00	10.00	13.00	7.00
55.00	91.00	66.00	78.00	26.00	59.00	93.00	67.00	88.00	65.00	78.00
22.00	0.00	16.50	10.00	10.00	28.00	4.00	24.00	1.00	19.00	12.00
100.00	100.00	100.00	100.00	100.00	100.00	100.00	100.00	100.00	100.00	100.00
78.00	86.00	52.50	78.00	94.00	72.00	70.00	7.00	45.00	15.00	68.00
22.00	12.00	46.50	21.00	5.00	21.00	28.00	84.00	53.00	73.00	23.00
0.00	0.00	0.50	0.00	1.00	7.00	1.00	9.00	2.00	11.00	5.00
0.00	2.00	0.50	1.00	0.00	0.00	1.00	0.00	0.00	1.00	4.00
100.00	100.00	100.00	100.00	100.00	100.00	100.00	100.00	100.00	100.00	100.00
2.00	0.00	0.00	1.00	0.00	2.00	0.00	1.00	0.00	0.00	1.00
98.00	100.00	100.00	99.00	100.00	98.00	100.00	99.00	100.00	100.00	99.00
84.00	94.00	84.50	99.00	95.00	87.00	89.00	94.00	94.00	91.00	90.00
162.00	215.00	163.00	183.00	145.00	198.00	175.00	143.00	176.00	155.00	161.00
26.00	25.00	23.00	20.00	19.00	41.00	37.00	25.00	53.00	31.00	37.00
0.04	0.11	0.09	0.06	0.07	0.29	0.15	0.11	0.02	0.11	0.51
0.00	0.03	0.06	0.02	0.04	0.17	0.08	0.05	0.01	0.07	0.04
0.00	1.22	3.08	0.90	4.71	10.41	4.05	4.37	3.00	5.78	3.15
0.03	0.05	0.03	0.04	0.01	0.06	0.02	0.04	0.01	0.01	0.04
1.41	4.30	1.83	3.47	1.26	4.21	1.00	2.06	0.45	1.13	3.14
0.01	0.03	0.01	0.00	0.02	0.06	0.05	0.02	0.00	0.03	0.43
0.60	2.33	0.42	0.00	1.85	4.55	2.85	2.17	0.00	2.72	3.85

4-26 续表 1

类别	Classification	单位	unit	聊城 Liaocheng	滨州 Binzhou	菏泽 Heze
用水情况（构成）	Situation of Drinking Water	%	percentage	100.00	100.00	100.00
独用自来水	Individual Tap-water	%	percentage	58.59	100.00	88.00
公用自来水	Public tap-water	%	percentage	41.41	0.00	4.00
井、河水	Well Waterand River Water	%	percentage	0.00	0.00	8.00
其他	Others	%	percentage	0.00	0.00	0.00
卫生设备（构成）	Health Equipment	%	percentage	100.00	100.00	100.00
无卫生设备	Non-health Equipment	%	percentage	1.01	0.00	3.00
有厕所浴室	Lavatory with Bathroom	%	percentage	82.83	84.00	76.00
有厕所无浴室	Lavatory without Bathroom	%	percentage	16.16	14.00	17.00
公用	Public	%	percentage	0.00	2.00	4.00
取暖设备（构成）	Heating Equipment	%	percentage	100.00	100.00	100.00
无取暖设备	No Heating Equipment	%	percentage	2.02	0.00	20.00
空调设备	Air Conditioner	%	percentage	43.43	5.00	16.00
暖气	Heater	%	percentage	52.53	82.00	37.00
其他	Others	%	percentage	2.02	13.00	27.00
炊用燃料使用情况（构成）	Fuel of Cooking	%	percentage	100.00	100.00	100.00
管道煤气	Pipelined Gas	%	percentage	76.77	7.00	4.00
液化石油气	Liquefied Petroleum Gas	%	percentage	19.19	92.00	75.00
煤	Coal	%	percentage	3.03	0.00	16.00
其他	Others	%	percentage	1.01	1.00	5.00
通信设备使用情况	Communication Equipment	%	percentage			
⑴无电话（构成）	Non-telephone	%	percentage	100.00	100.00	100.00
无	No	%	percentage	1.01	0.00	1.00
有	Have	%	percentage	98.99	100.00	99.00
⑵固定电话	Hand-free Telephone	部/百户	unit/100 households	100.00	100.00	89.00
⑶移动电话	Mobile Telephone	部/百户	unit/100 households	125.25	160.00	157.00
⑷使用互联网	use Internet	条/百户	piece /100 households	22.22	45.00	25.00
除了现住房，还有几处其他住房	Other Houses Besides Current House	套/户	set/100 households	0.10	0.02	0.03
①出租房	House for Ren	套/户	set/100 households	0.04	0.02	0.01
使用面积	Area for Use	平方米/户	sq.m/household	3.68	1.56	1.04
②偶尔居住房	House for Occasionally Living	套/户	set/100 households	0.05	0.00	0.00
使用面积	Area for Use	平方米/户	sq.m/household	5.35	0.00	0.00
③其它用途房	House for Other Use	套/户	set/100 households	0.01	0.00	0.02
使用面积	Area for Use	平方米/户	sq.m/household	0.61	0.00	1.50

continued

文登 Wendeng	诸城 Zhucheng	青州 Qingzhou	微山 Weishan	临清 Linqing	费县 Feixian	利津 Lijin	武城 Wucheng	东阿 Donga	巨野 Juye
100.00	100.00	100.00	100.00	100.00	100.00	100.00	100.00	100.00	100.00
88.00	100.00	99.00	100.00	100.00	100.00	96.00	94.00	76.00	70.00
4.00	0.00	1.00	0.00	0.00	0.00	4.00	0.00	24.00	10.00
8.00	0.00	0.00	0.00	0.00	0.00	0.00	6.00	0.00	20.00
0.00	0.00	0.00	0.00	0.00	0.00	0.00	0.00	0.00	0.00
100.00	100.00	100.00	100.00	100.00	100.00	100.00	100.00	100.00	100.00
0.00	2.00	4.00	2.00	0.00	4.00	12.00	18.00	2.00	6.00
46.00	56.00	61.00	78.00	26.00	70.00	68.00	48.00	80.00	50.00
54.00	42.00	29.00	16.00	16.00	26.00	18.00	32.00	10.00	42.00
0.00	0.00	6.00	4.00	58.00	0.00	2.00	2.00	8.00	2.00
100.00	100.00	100.00	100.00	100.00	100.00	100.00	100.00	100.00	100.00
52.00	0.00	0.00	2.00	0.00	22.00	8.00	0.00	0.00	16.00
2.00	0.00	8.00	4.00	2.00	6.00	26.00	0.00	0.00	34.00
46.00	88.00	43.00	50.00	26.00	46.00	64.00	40.00	94.00	30.00
0.00	12.00	49.00	44.00	72.00	26.00	2.00	60.00	6.00	20.00
100.00	100.00	100.00	100.00	100.00	100.00	100.00	100.00	100.00	100.00
4.00	26.00	9.00	0.00	18.00	0.00	2.00	0.00	28.00	0.00
90.00	74.00	81.00	86.00	20.00	88.00	94.00	60.00	56.00	70.00
0.00	0.00	9.00	14.00	62.00	12.00	2.00	40.00	16.00	30.00
6.00	0.00	1.00	0.00	0.00	0.00	2.00	0.00	0.00	0.00
100.00	100.00	100.00	100.00	100.00	100.00	100.00	100.00	100.00	100.00
2.00	0.00	0.00	4.00	2.00	2.00	0.00	0.00	2.00	0.00
98.00	100.00	100.00	96.00	98.00	98.00	100.00	100.00	98.00	100.00
92.00	100.00	92.00	86.00	96.00	88.00	80.00	96.00	80.00	94.00
140.00	192.00	152.00	152.00	100.00	110.00	186.00	132.00	162.00	162.00
18.00	54.00	26.00	38.00	20.00	36.00	38.00	8.00	26.00	40.00
0.14	0.06	0.08	0.04	0.08	0.00	0.04	0.02	0.08	0.18
0.04	0.02	0.03	0.02	0.02	0.00	0.00	0.00	0.04	0.04
3.78	2.60	1.88	0.80	0.80	0.00	0.00	0.00	3.20	4.12
0.00	0.00	0.05	0.02	0.04	0.00	0.00	0.02	0.04	0.04
0.00	0.00	4.46	0.78	3.22	0.00	0.00	2.00	3.20	3.80
0.10	0.04	0.00	0.00	0.02	0.00	0.04	0.00	0.00	0.10
6.56	3.70	0.00	0.00	1.00	0.00	0.42	0.00	0.00	6.10

4-27 全省城市居民主要指标情况表

Whole Province Leading Indicator Table of City Households

单位：元/人 unit:yuan/person

类别	Classification	总计 Total	最低10% Lowest Income Household	更低5% of which: Lower	低10% Low Income Household	较低20% Lower Middle Income Household	中间20% Middle Income Household	较高20% Upper Middle Income Household	高10% High Income Household	最高10% Highest Income Household	更高5% of which: Higher
一、家庭总收入	**Total Income**	**13872**	**5011**	**4150**	**7425**	**9839**	**13322**	**17620**	**22647**	**32858**	**38805**
其中：可支配收入	Disposable Income	12758	4559	3723	6824	8987	12135	16178	20927	30755	36389
㈠工薪收入	Income of Wages and Salaries	11016	4113	3383	6225	8220	11081	14221	17998	22229	25279
1.工资及补贴收入	Wages and Subsidies	10824	3920	3192	6077	8066	10910	14066	17745	21784	24438
2.其他劳动收入	Other Income	192	193	192	148	154	171	156	254	444	841
㈡经营净收入	Net Business Income	564	288	189	254	324	496	520	589	2481	4295
㈢财产性收入	Income from Properties	230	39	30	99	78	168	296	415	990	1616
㈣转移性收入	Income from Transfer	2062	571	547	846	1216	1577	2583	3644	7158	7616
二、出售财物收入	**Income from Properties Sale**	**99**	**7**	**12**	**8**	**82**	**67**	**9**	**420**	**389**	**18**
三、借贷收入	**Income from Lending**	**6736**	**2026**	**1792**	**2538**	**4506**	**6001**	**9150**	**12557**	**17181**	**20322**
四、家庭总支出	**Total Expenditure**	**12348**	**5207**	**4728**	**6637**	**9267**	**11242**	**15465**	**20978**	**27793**	**32625**
㈠消费支出	Consumption Expenditure	8932	4165	3782	5345	7151	8706	10611	13527	18989	22296
其中：服务性消费支出	Consumption Expenditure for Services	2246	963	862	1229	1624	2275	2838	3768	4547	5509
1.食品	Food	2845	1803	1650	2079	2571	2923	3144	3796	4571	5072
2.衣着	Clothing	1152	481	370	711	909	1168	1532	1662	2110	2284
3.家庭设备用品及服务	Household Appliances and Services	553	205	217	309	400	478	691	1032	1288	1499
4.医疗保健	Health care and Medical Services	646	247	228	424	442	711	763	1025	1359	1349
5.交通和通信	Transport and Communications	1262	365	299	460	1020	1057	1370	1810	4403	5309
6.教育文化娱乐服务	Recreation,Education and Cultural Services	1285	558	530	692	969	1289	1671	2190	2369	2832
7.居住	Residence	867	399	391	533	640	777	997	1494	2047	2850
8.杂项商品和服务	Miscellaneous Goods and Services	321	107	98	137	200	303	445	517	841	1101
㈡购房与建房支出	Expenditure for Housing Purchase and Building	1008	139	117	7	475	200	1699	3238	3559	4324
㈢转移性支出	Expenditure for Transfer	1372	489	446	719	835	1217	1806	2614	3384	3905
㈣财产性支出	Expenditure for Properties	10	1	0	1	3	5	11	38	39	55
㈤社会保障支出	Expenditure for Social Security	1027	414	383	565	802	1114	1338	1561	1821	2045
五、借贷支出	**Expenditure for Lending**	**8162**	**1698**	**1177**	**3173**	**5031**	**7942**	**11143**	**14246**	**22282**	**25897**

4-28 全省县（市）城居民主要指标情况表

Whole Province Leading Indicator Table of County Households

单位：元/人　　unit:yuan/person

类别	Classification	总计 Total	最低10% Lowest Income Household	更低5% of which: Lower	低10% Low Income Household	较低20% Lower Middle Income Househ-old	中间20% Middle Income Household	较高20% Upper Middle Income Household	高10% High Income Household	最高10% Highest Income Household	更高5% of which: Higher
一、家庭总收入	**Total Income**	**9860**	**3751**	**3065**	**5274**	**7080**	**8875**	**11832**	**15531**	**22240**	**26156**
其中：可支配收入	Disposable Income	9262	3466	2829	5049	6601	8319	11037	14738	21004	25106
㈠工薪收入	Income of Wages and Salaries	7468	2759	2287	4088	5719	7000	9125	11126	15646	16101
1.工资及补贴收入	Wages and Subsidies	7410	2663	2225	4072	5691	6931	9071	11026	15568	15994
2.其他劳动收入	Other Income	58	97	62	17	27	69	54	100	78	107
㈡经营净收入	Net Business Income	527	172	211	657	551	277	924	186	928	1424
㈢财产性收入	Income from Properties	172	51	36	23	46	23	179	576	716	1087
㈣转移性收入	Income from Transfer	1693	769	531	505	765	1576	1604	3643	4950	7543
二、出售财物收入	**Income from Properties Sale**	**5**	**10**	**14**	**2**	**7**	**1**	**5**	**9**	**5**	**9**
三、借贷收入	**Income from Lending**	**5271**	**2154**	**1581**	**1330**	**3508**	**4351**	**6075**	**9479**	**14262**	**17766**
四、家庭总支出	**Total Expenditure**	**8449**	**4137**	**3488**	**4841**	**6382**	**7124**	**9707**	**14002**	**17910**	**21724**
㈠消费支出	Consumption Expenditure	6069	3238	2760	4097	4877	5508	7537	9215	9968	11497
其中：服务性消费支出	Consumption Expenditure for Services	1466	709	548	806	1118	1299	1959	2355	2527	2247
1.食品	Food	2019	1275	1072	1599	1750	1878	2286	2764	3123	3710
2.衣着	Clothing	777	349	319	556	610	789	906	1142	1322	1551
3.家庭设备用品及服务	Household Appliances and Services	386	180	112	209	289	270	530	569	887	1340
4.医疗保健	Health care and Medical Services	511	285	182	349	348	435	677	1039	677	655
5.交通和通信	Transport and Communications	726	373	378	384	565	621	848	1648	975	1049
6.教育文化娱乐服务	Recreation,Education and Cultural Services	772	330	314	502	581	694	1080	1031	1432	1115
7.居住	Residence	689	348	290	345	594	625	1013	799	1152	1774
8.杂项商品和服务	Miscellaneous Goods and Services	189	98	94	153	140	197	197	223	400	302
㈡购房与建房支出	Expenditure for Housing Purchase and Building	570	0	0	0	134	0	0	2077	3856	5743
㈢转移性支出	Expenditure for Transfer	1249	649	528	547	920	1090	1405	1989	2923	3530
㈣财产性支出	Expenditure for Properties	0	0	0	0	0	0	0	0	0	0
㈤社会保障支出	Expenditure for Social Security	561	250	200	197	452	525	765	722	1163	955
五、借贷支出	**Expenditure for Lending**	**6606**	**1713**	**1113**	**1724**	**4173**	**5987**	**8012**	**11193**	**18363**	**21794**

农村居民生活调查资料

Investigation Material of Rural Residential Life

简要说明

一、农村住户调查是按照国家统计局的要求，采取多阶段、随机起点、对称等距的抽样方法抽选调查样本。调查抽样误差在正负3%以内。

二、农村住户调查的主要内容包括：农村居民家庭基本情况、人口与就业情况、生产结构与技术应用情况、总收入和纯收入情况、总支出情况、现金收支情况、生活消费现金支出情况、主要农产品出售情况、食品消费情况、商品购买情况、粮食收支情况等。

三、农村住户调查的调查单位为农村常住户。全省农村住户调查的样本单位包括39个县、420个调查村、4200个调查户，占全省总县数的31%。

四、为保证农村住户调查资料的准确性，国家统计局农村司为调查户设置了现金和实物两本帐，并聘请辅助调查员帮助做好记帐工作。农村住户调查资料实行帐页超级汇总方式，即由县队人员将调查户记的现金帐和实物帐逐户逐笔录入计算机后，直接上报总队，再由总队将分户资料进行汇总生成全省资料。

五、为解决调查户的样本老化等问题，增强抽样调查网点的代表性，更加准确、及时地反映农村社会经济情况，国家统计局对农村住户调查网点实行样本轮换制度，每四年为一个周期。

Brief Introduction

Ⅰ.The countryside inhabitant investigation adopts the sampling method of the multi-stages, the stochastic beginning and the symmetrical equal-space to sample the investigation sample based on NBS request, investigation sampling error is in negative 3%.

Ⅱ.The primary coverage of the countryside inhabitant investigation includes: basic indicators of rural households, population and employment situation, production structure and technical application situation, gross income and net income situation, gross charge situation, cash revenue and expenditure situation, life expense cash disbursement situation, main agricultural product sold situation, food expenditure situation, purchasing commodity situation, grain revenue and expenditure situation and so on.

Ⅲ.Investigation unit for the countryside inhabitant investigation are countryside often inhabitant. The sample units of countryside inhabitant investigation includes 39 counties, 420 investigation villages, 4200 investigation households in the entire province, occupy total county number 31% in entire province.

Ⅳ.In order to guarantee the accuracy of the materials for the countryside inhabitant investigation, NBS Countryside Operation Office give the investigation households to establish two accounts for the cash and material object, and invited the assistant investigators to help complete accounts work. The materials of countryside inhabitant investigation use the super way to compile, namely persons of the county team record the materials of that the cash and the account book into the computers and report these materials to the province team directly, the divided household materials are carried on compiling to produce the entire province materials by the province team.

Ⅴ. In order to solve questions of investigation old households and so on, enhance sample investigation point representation, more accurate, reflect promptly the countryside social economy situation, NBS carry on the system that the investigation points were taken turns, every four years is a cycle.

5-1　农村住户家庭基本情况
Basic Indicators of Rural Households

类别	Classification	单位	Unit	2006	2005	增减 Add or Subtract	增幅 Increase Range
一、调查户数	Number of Households Surveyed	户	household	4200	4200		
（一）调查户从业类型（按总收入比重计算）	Business Types of Households Serveyed (Calculated According to the Proportion of Total Income)						
1.农业户	Households Engaged in Agriculture	户/百户	household/ 100 households	17.43	19.79	-2.36	-11.91
2.农业兼业户	Households Engeged in Agricuture and Other Sectors	户/百户	household/ 100 households	38.43	39.4	-0.98	-2.48
3.非农业兼业户	Households Engaged in Non-agriculture	户/百户	household/ 100 households	36.83	33.62	3.21	9.56
4.非农业户	Households Engeged in Non-agricuture and Other Sectors	户/百户	household/ 100 households	7.31	7.19	0.12	1.66
（二）调查户从业类型（按劳动力比重计算）	Business Types of Households Serveyed (Calculated According to the Proportion of Business Labour Force)						
1.农业户	Households Engaged in Agriculture	户/百户	household/ 100 households	31.64	36.26	-4.62	-12.74
2.农业兼业户	Households Engeged in Agricuture and Other Sectors	户/百户	household/ 100 households	18.45	17.64	0.81	4.59
3.非农业兼业户	Households Engaged in Non-agriculture	户/百户	household/ 100 households	32.4	31.21	1.19	3.81
4.非农业户	Households Engeged in Non-agricuture and Other Sectors	户/百户	household/ 100 households	17.5	14.88	2.62	17.6
（三）户别	Household Types						
1.个体工商户	Households Engaged in Individual Businesses	户/百户	household/ 100 households	6.9	6.88	0.02	0.35
2.干部户	Cadres Households	户/百户	household/ 100 households	10.6	10.64	-0.05	-0.45
3.个体工商和干部户	Households Engaged in Individual Businesses and Cadres Households	户/百户	household/ 100 households	2.45	2.4	0.05	1.98
4.五保户	Five Guaranteed Households	户/百户	household/ 100 households	0.02	0.05	-0.02	-50
5.其他户	Other Types Households	户/百户	household/ 100 households	80.02	80.02		
（四）家庭结构	Household Structure						
1.单身或夫妇	Single and Couples	户/百户	household/ 100 households	10.5	10.17	0.33	3.28
2.夫妇与一个孩子	Couples with One Child	户/百户	household/ 100 households	32.71	32.76	-0.05	-0.15

5-1 续表 1 continued

类别	Classification	单位	Unit	2006	2005	增减 Add or Subtract	增幅 Increase Range
3.夫妇与两个孩子	Couples with Two Children	户/百户	household/ 100 households	30.67	31.26	-0.6	-1.9
4.夫妇与三个以上孩子	Couples with Three Children and More	户/百户	household/ 100 households	7.4	7.76	-0.36	-4.6
5.单亲与孩子	Single-parent with Children	户/百户	household/ 100 households	1.55	1.33	0.21	16.07
6.三代同堂	Three Generations Living under One Roof	户/百户	household/ 100 households	15.12	14.48	0.64	4.44
7.其他	Others	户/百户	household/ 100 households	2.05	2.24	-0.19	-8.51
（五）是否参加专业性合作经济组织	Whether to Participating in Professional Cooperative Economic Organizations						
1.参加的户数	Number of Households Participating in	户/百户	household/ 100 households	3.67	3.64	0.02	0.65
2.未参加的户数	Number of Households Not Participating in	户/百户	household/ 100 households	96.33	96.36	-0.02	-0.02
（六）是否参加合作医疗社会保障	Whether to Participating in the New Type of Rural Cooperative Medical Care						
1.参加的户数	Number of Households Participating in	户/百户	household/ 100 households	80.07	49.57	30.5	61.53
2.未参加的户数	Number of Households Not Participating in	户/百户	household/ 100 households	19.93	50.43	-30.5	-60.48
（七）是否领取最低生活保障	Whether to Receiving the Minimum Livelihood Guarantee						
1.领取的户数	Number of Households Receiving	户/百户	household/ 100 households	0.31	0.07	0.24	333.33
2.未领取的户数	Number of Households Not Receiving	户/百户	household/ 100 households	99.69	99.93	-0.24	-0.24
二、期末生产性固定资产拥有情况	**Ownership of Productive Fixed Assets at Term-end**						
（一）生产性固定资产原值	Original Value of Productive Fixed Assets	元/户	yuan/household	9383.12	9262.74	120.38	1.3
1.农业	Farming	元/户	yuan/household	4840.77	4583.41	257.36	5.62
其中：	Among:						
房屋及建筑物	Houses and Buildings	元/户	yuan/household	1136.64	1213.88	-77.25	-6.36
役畜	Draught Animal	元/户	yuan/household	212.25	248.52	-36.27	-14.59
大中型铁木农具	Large and Middle Scale Lignum Vitae Farm Tool	元/户	yuan/household	284.96	284.37	0.6	0.21
农业机械	Agricultural Machinery	元/户	yuan/household	3026.95	2740.99	285.96	10.43
2.林业	Forestry	元/户	yuan/household	6.83	5.02	1.81	36.05
其中：	Among:						
房屋及建筑物	Houses and Buildings	元/户	yuan/household	2.94	3.49	-0.55	-15.7
役畜	Draught Animal	元/户	yuan/household		0.88	-0.88	-100
大中型铁木农具	Large and Middle Scale Lignum Vitae Farm Tool	元/户	yuan/household	0.98	0.1	0.88	860.47
林业机械	Forestry Machinery	元/户	yuan/household	2.9	0.55	2.36	430.43

5-1 续表 2 continued

类别	Classification	单位	Unit	2006	2005	增减 Add or Subtract	增幅 Increase Range
3.牧业	Animal Husbandry	元/户	yuan/household	937.71	1108.48	-170.77	-15.41
其中：	Among:						
房屋及建筑物	Houses and Buildings	元/户	yuan/household	566	608.99	-42.99	-7.06
产品畜	Draught Animal	元/户	yuan/household	315.33	453.59	-138.26	-30.48
大中型铁木农具	Large and Middle Scale Lignum Vitae Farm Tool	元/户	yuan/household	8.01	6.41	1.6	24.99
牧业机械	Animal Husbandry Machinery	元/户	yuan/household	22.84	21.48	1.36	6.32
4.渔业	Fishing	元/户	yuan/household	86.17	86.17		
其中:	Among:						
房屋及建筑物	Houses and Buildings	元/户	yuan/household	73.93	73.93		
大中型铁木农具	Large and Middle Scale Lignum Vitae Farm Tool	元/户	yuan/household				
渔业机械	Fishery Industry Machinery	元/户	yuan/household	12.24	12.24		
5.采矿业	Mining	元/户	yuan/household	139.26	69.05	70.21	101.69
6.制造业	Manufacturing	元/户	yuan/household	898.83	906.59	-7.75	-0.86
其中：	Among:						
房屋及建筑物	Houses and Buildings	元/户	yuan/household	392.62	373.71	18.9	5.06
生产设备	Production Equipment	元/户	yuan/household	470.12	351.45	118.67	33.77
7.电力煤气与水的生产及供应	Production and Supply of Electric Power and Heat Power	元/户	yuan/household				
8.建筑业	Construction	元/户	yuan/household	97.55	83.5	14.05	16.82
9.交通运输业、仓储和邮政业	Traffic, Transport, Storage and Post	元/户	yuan/household	1414.8	1421.34	-6.54	-0.46
10.批发和零售贸易业	Wholesale and Retail Trade	元/户	yuan/household	561.71	547.08	14.63	2.67
11.住宿和餐饮业	Hotels and Catering Services	元/户	yuan/household	77.74	151.26	-73.52	-48.61
12.居民服务与其他服务业	Services to Households and Other Services	元/户	yuan/household	181.93	137.81	44.12	32.01
13.教育	Education	元/户	yuan/household	15.48	16.79	-1.31	-7.8
14.卫生、社会保障和福利业	Health, Social Security and Social Welfare	元/户	yuan/household	41.95	23.26	18.69	80.35
15.文化、体育和娱乐业	Culture, Sports and Entertainment	元/户	yuan/household	2.83	24.28	-21.45	-88.33
16.其他	Others	元/户	yuan/household	79.56	98.7	-19.13	-19.39
（二）主要生产性固定资产数量	Amount of Major Productive Fixed Assets						
1.房屋及建筑物	Housing and Building	平米/人	sq.m/person	6.64	7.5	-0.86	-11.48
2.汽车	Automobile	辆/百户	unit/100 households	2.95	2.86	0.1	3.33
3.大中型拖拉机	Large and Medium Tractor	台/百户	unit/100 households	3.25	3.29	-0.04	-1.16
4.小型和手扶拖拉机	Small and Walking Tractor	台/百户	unit/100 households	30.77	29.7	1.07	3.61
5.机动脱粒机	Motorized Thresher	台/百户	unit/100 households	2.65	1.91	0.74	38.65
6.收割机	Harvester	台/百户	unit/100 households	1.82	1.61	0.21	13.04
7.农用动力机械	Farm Power Plant	台/百户	unit/100 households	28.4	28.48	-0.08	-0.29

5-1 续表 3 continued

类别	Classification	单位	Unit	2006	2005	增减 Add or Subtract	增幅 Increase Range
8.胶轮大车	Cart with Rubber Tires	台/百户	unit/100 households	15.54	17.04	-1.5	-8.81
9.水泵	Pump	台/百户	unit/100 households	42.64	41.9	0.75	1.78
10.役畜	Draught Animal	头/百户	head/100 households	10.26	12.05	-1.79	-14.82
11.产品畜	Commodity Animal	头/百户	head/100 households	22.93	31.9	-8.98	-28.13
三、期内住户固定资产投资完成额	**Investment in Fixed Assets in the Term**	元/户	**yuan/household**	**2064.24**	**1462.98**	**601.26**	**41.1**
其中：住宅投资完成额	Investment in Housing	元/户	yuan/household	1128.03	786.28	341.74	43.46
四、通过互联网购买商品和服务的总额	**Total Amount of Purchasing Commodity and Service from Internet**	元/人	**yuan/person**	**5.23**	**5.14**	**0.09**	**1.71**
五、期末主要耐用消费品拥有情况	**Ownership of Major Durable Consumer Goods at Term-end**						
1.大型家具	Large Furniture	件/百户	unit/100 households	348.88	336.43	12.45	3.7
2.洗衣机	Washing Machine	台/百户	unit/100 households	49.57	40.9	8.67	21.19
3.电风扇	Electric Fan	台/百户	unit/100 households	180.88	175.5	5.38	3.07
4.电冰箱	Refrigerator	台/百户	unit/100 households	33.62	28.6	5.02	17.57
5.空调机	Air Conditioner	台/百户	unit/100 households	5.12	4.02	1.1	27.22
6.抽油烟机	Lampblack Exhauster	台/百户	unit/100 households	6.74	6	0.74	12.3
7.吸尘器	Vacuam Cleaner	台/百户	unit/100 households	0.52	0.43	0.1	22.22
8.微波炉	Microwave Oven	台/百户	unit/100 households	2.62	2.21	0.4	18.28
9.热水器	Water Heater	台/百户	unit/100 households	19.21	15.38	3.83	24.92
10.自行车	Bicycle	辆/百户	unit/100 households	168.67	169.26	-0.6	-0.35
11.摩托车	Motorcycle	辆/百户	unit/100 households	68.95	65.21	3.74	5.73
12.汽车（生活用）	Automobile	辆/百户	unit/100 households	1.19	1.07	0.12	11.11
13.电话机	Phone	部/百户	unit/100 households	85.9	85.86	0.05	0.06
14.移动电话	Cell Phone	部/百户	unit/100 households	60.67	46.6	14.07	30.2
#接入互联网的	Access to the Internet	部/百户	unit/100 households	1.52	1.5	0.02	1.59
15.寻呼机	Pager	台/百户	unit/100 households		0.43	-0.43	-100
16.彩色电视机	Color TV Set	台/百户	unit/100 households	98.36	90.98	7.38	8.11
#接入有线电视网的	Access to Cable TV Network	台/百户	unit/100 households	51.55	43.1	8.45	19.61
17.黑白电视机	Black/White TV Set	台/百户	unit/100 households	15.14	19.21	-4.07	-21.19
#接入有线电视网的	Access to Cable TV Network	台/百户	unit/100 households	1.93	2.26	-0.33	-14.74
18.录放像机	Video Recorder	台/百户	unit/100 households	3.19	2.95	0.24	8.06
19.摄像机	Pickup Camera	台/百户	unit/100 households	0.26	0.24	0.02	10
20.影碟机	Video Disc Player	台/百户	unit/100 households	55.84	45.05	10.79	23.95
21.组合音响	Hi-Fi Stereo Component System	台/百户	unit/100 households	18.4	14.24	4.17	29.26
22.收录机	Tape Recorder	台/百户	unit/100 households	11.55	12	-0.45	-3.77
23.照相机	Camera	架/百户	unit/100 households	6.86	7	-0.14	-2.04
24.家用计算机	Computer	台/百户	unit/100 households	2.43	2.29	0.14	6.25
#接入互联网的	Access to the Internet	台/百户	unit/100 households	1.07	0.88	0.19	21.62
25.中高档乐器	Medium and Top Grade Music Instruments	件/百户	unit/100 households	0.29	0.26	0.02	9.09

5-2 农村住户居住情况
Living Condition of Rural Households

类别	Classification	单位	Unit	2006	2005	增减 Add or Subtract	增幅 Increase Range
一、期末住房情况	Housing Condition at Term-end						
（一）住房面积	Housing Area	平米/人	sq.m/household	30.69	29.65	1.03	3.48
其中：租用住房面积	of which:Rental Housing Area	平米/人	sq.m/household	0.14	0.05	0.09	202.37
（二）住房价值	Housing Value	元/平米	sq.m/household	306.3	283.85	22.45	7.91
（三）住房类型	Houging Type						
1.楼房面积	Apartment Area	平米/人	sq.m/household	3.55	3.27	0.28	8.57
2.砖瓦平房面积	Brick Bungalow Area	平米/人	sq.m/household	25.4	24.53	0.87	3.53
3.其他	Other Structures	平米/人	sq.m/household	1.47	1.48	-0.01	-0.57
二、期内新建（购）住房情况	Condition of Newly Building (Buying) Housing in the Term						
（一）新建（购）住房面积	Area of Newly Building (Buying) Housing	平米/人	sq.m/household	1.25	1.03	0.22	21.45
（二）新建（购）住房价值	Value of Newly Building (Buying) Housing	元/平米	yuan/sq.m	459.83	369.36	90.47	24.49
（三）新建（购）住房类型	Type of Newly Building (Buying) Housing						
1.楼房面积	Apartment Area	平米/人	sq.m/household	0.41	0.15	0.26	172.79
2.砖瓦平房面积	Brick Bungalow Area	平米/人	sq.m/household	0.84	0.87	-0.03	-3.08
3.其他	Other Types	平米/人	sq.m/household		0.01	-0.01	-100
（四）新建（购）住房结构	Structure of Newly Building Housing						
1.钢筋混泥土结构面积	Reinforced Concrete Structure	平米/人	sq.m/household	0.54	0.41	0.13	32.1
2.砖木结构面积	Brick and Wood Structure	平米/人	sq.m/household	0.71	0.62	0.09	14.46
3.其他	Other Structures	平米/人	sq.m/household				
三、期内新建（购）住房资金来源	Fund Source of Newly Building (Buying) Housing in the Term						
1.自筹	Self-raising Funds	元/人	yuan/person	488.07	336.29	151.78	45.13
2.银行、信用社贷款	Banks, Credit Union Loans	元/人	yuan/person	19.55	12.48	7.06	56.58
3.其他	Others	元/人	yuan/person	65.7	26.41	39.29	148.73
四、期内房屋建设情况	Housing Construction in the Term						
1.期内施工房屋面积	Floor Space under Construction in the Term	平米/户	sq.m/household	4.17	3.38	0.79	23.45
其中：住宅面积	of which:Residental Buildings	平米/户	sq.m/household	3.88	3.08	0.8	26.01
2.期内竣工房屋面积	Floor Space Completed in the Term	平米/户	sq.m/household	4.24	3.62	0.62	17.02
其中：住宅面积	of which:Residental Buildings	平米/户	sq.m/household	4.01	3.27	0.75	22.8
五、居住条件	Living Condition						
（一）住房卫生设备使用情况	Condition of Health Equipment						

5-2　续表 1 continued

类别	Classification	单位	Unit	2006	2005	增减 Add or Subtract	增幅 Increase Range
1.使用水冲式厕所的户数	Having Flushing Toilet	户/百户	household/ 100 households	5.74	5.74		
2.使用旱厕的户数	Having Old Toilet	户/百户	household/ 100 households	93.74	93.74		
3.无厕所的户数	No Toilet	户/百户	household/ 100 households	0.52	0.52		
（二）取暖设备使用情况	Condition of Heating Equipment						
1.使用空调的户数	Having Air Conditioner	户/百户	household/ 100 households	2.45	1.55	0.9	58.46
2.使用暖气的户数	Having Heater	户/百户	household/ 100 households	19.21	18.26	0.95	5.22
3.使用火炕的户数	Having Kang	户/百户	household/ 100 households	35.5	37.33	-1.83	-4.91
4.无取暖设备的户数	No Heating Equipment	户/百户	household/ 100 households	42.83	42.86	-0.02	-0.06
（三）炊事使用的主要能源	Major Source of Cooking						
1.使用液化气的户数	Liquid Natural Gas	户/百户	household/ 100 households	18.5	17.64	0.86	4.86
2.使用煤炭的户数	Coal	户/百户	household/ 100 households	28	29.38	-1.38	-4.7
3.使用柴草的户数	Fuelwood	户/百户	household/ 100 households	51.83	52.1	-0.26	-0.5
4.使用电的户数	Electricity	户/百户	household/ 100 households	1.4	0.48	0.93	195
5.使用沼气的户数	Methane	户/百户	household/ 100 households	0.26		0.26	
6.使用其他燃料的户数	Other Fuels	户/百户	household/ 100 households		0.4	-0.4	-100
（四）饮用水来源情况	Source of Drinking Water						
1.饮用自来水的户数	Tap Water	户/百户	household/ 100 households	57.17	53.67	3.5	6.52
2.饮用深井水的户数	Deep Well Water	户/百户	household/ 100 households	36.36	29.69	6.67	22.45
3.饮用浅井水的户数	Shallow Well Water	户/百户	household/ 100 households	6.4	16.05	-9.64	-60.09
4.饮用江河湖泊水的户数	Rivers and Lakes Water	户/百户	household/ 100 households		0.24	-0.24	-100
5.饮用塘水的户数	Pond Water	户/百户	household/ 100 households				
6.饮用其他水源的户数	Other Water	户/百户	household/ 100 households	0.07	0.36	-0.29	-80
（五）住宅外道路路面状况	Condition of Road Near Residential						
1.水泥或柏油路面的户数	Cement or Asphalt	户/百户	household/ 100 households	46.5	40.29	6.21	15.43
2.沙石或石板等硬质路面的户	Stone, Sand and Gravel or Other Hard Materials	户/百户	household/ 100 households	20.21	19.02	1.19	6.26
3.其他路面的户数	Other Materials	户/百户	household/ 100 households	33.29	40.69	-7.4	-18.2
六、附：期内新建（购）房屋户数	**Household Newly Building Housing**	**户/百户**	**household/ 100 households**	**3.9**	**3.93**	**-0.02**	**-0.61**

5-3 农村住户农业生产结构及生产技术应用情况
Agricultural Production Structure and Technology Application of Rural Households

类别	Classification	单位	Unit	2006	2005	增减 Add or Subtract	增幅 Increase Range
一、土地经营情况	Land Operation						
（一）期初实际经营土地面积	Actually Land Area Operated at Term-beginning	亩/人	mu/person	1.51	1.48	0.03	1.98
1.耕地	Farmland	亩/人	mu/person	1.37	1.36	0.01	0.54
其中：有效灌溉面积	of which:Effective Irrigati-on Area	亩/人	mu/person	1.19	1.13	0.06	5.4
2.山地	Mountain Land	亩/人	mu/person	0.05	0.04	0	6.79
3.园地	Garden Land	亩/人	mu/person	0.08	0.06	0.02	31.1
4.牧草地	Grassland	亩/人	mu/person		0	0	-100
5.养殖水面	Culture Surface	亩/人	mu/person	0.01	0.01	0	0.94
（二）期内增加的经营土地面积	Added Land Area Operated in the Term	亩/人	mu/person	0.06	0.03	0.04	131.77
#耕地	Farmland	亩/人	mu/person	0.05	0.02	0.03	117
（三）期内减少的经营土地面积	Reduced Land Area Operated in the Term	亩/人	mu/person	0.04	0.01	0.03	335.91
#耕地	Farmland	亩/人	mu/person	0.04	0.01	0.03	334.92
（四）期末实际经营的土地面积	Actually Land Area Operated at Term-end	亩/人	mu/person	1.54	1.5	0.03	2.26
1.耕地	Farmland	亩/人	mu/person	1.39	1.38	0.01	0.43
其中：有效灌溉面积	of which:Effective Irrigati-on Area	亩/人	mu/person	1.2	1.14	0.06	5.05
2.山地	Mountain Land	亩/人	mu/person	0.05	0.04	0	6.99
3.园地	Garden Land	亩/人	mu/person	0.09	0.07	0.03	39.19
4.牧草地	Grassland	亩/人	mu/person		0	0	-100
5.养殖水面	Culture Surface	亩/人	mu/person	0.01	0.01	0	0.27
二、土地种植情况	Land Cultivation						
（一）粮食播种面积	Acreage of Grain	亩/人	mu/person	1.99	1.96	0.02	1.15
其中：	Among:						
1.小麦播种面积	Acreage of Wheat	亩/人	mu/person	0.98	0.97	0.01	0.59
2.水稻播种面积	Acreage of Rice	亩/人	mu/person	0.02	0.02	0	-13.04
3.玉米播种面积	Acreage of Corn	亩/人	mu/person	0.93	0.91	0.02	2.69
4.大豆播种面积	Acreage of Beans	亩/人	mu/person	0.02	0.03	-0.01	-31.48
5.薯类播种面积	Acreage of Tubers	亩/人	mu/person	0.03	0.03	0	15.73
（二）经济作物播种面积	Acreage of Economic Crops	亩/人	mu/person	0.64	0.67	-0.03	-4.27
1.棉花播种面积	Acreage of Cotton	亩/人	mu/person	0.31	0.3	0.02	5.92

5-3 续表 1 continued

类别	Classification	单位	Unit	2006	2005	增减 Add or Subtract	增幅 Increase Range
2.油料播种面积	Acreage of Oil	亩/人	mu/person	0.12	0.14	-0.02	-13.29
3.麻类播种面积	Acreage of Flaxen	亩/人	mu/person	0	0	0	2.29
4.糖料播种面积	Acreage of Sugar	亩/人	mu/person	0		0	
5.烟草播种面积	Acreage of Tobacco	亩/人	mu/person	0.01	0	0	22.58
6.蔬菜播种面积	Acreage of Vegetables	亩/人	mu/person	0.17	0.2	-0.03	-14.66
7.瓜类播种面积	Acreage of Melons	亩/人	mu/person	0.03	0.03	0	3.36
8.酱用西红柿播种面积	Acreage of Tomatoes	亩/人	mu/person		0	0	-100
9.打瓜播种面积	Acreage of Sweet Potatoes	亩/人	mu/person				
三、农业生产技术应用情况	**Agricultural Technology Application**						
（一）优质粮食品种播种面积	Acreage of Quality Grain Varieties	亩/人	mu/person	0.6	0.55	0.05	8.24
1.优质小麦面积	Acreage of Quality Wheat	亩/人	mu/person	0.31	0.3	0	1.39
2.优质水稻面积	Acreage of Quality Rice	亩/人	mu/person	0.02	0.01	0.01	100
3.优质玉米面积	Acreage of Quality Corn	亩/人	mu/person	0.27	0.24	0.03	13.41
（二）机耕面积	Mechanical Cultivation Area	亩/人	mu/person	1.34	1.31	0.03	2.05
（三）抛秧面积	Throwing Seedling Area	亩/人	mu/person	0.02	0.01	0.01	229.82
（四）机播面积	Mechanical Seeding Area	亩/人	mu/person	1.24	1.24	0.01	0.6
（五）机收面积	Mechanical Harvesting Area	亩/人	mu/person	0.89	0.89	0	-0.21
（六）机电灌溉面积	Mechanical Irrigation Area	亩/人	mu/person	1.03	1.06	-0.02	-2.28
（七）薄膜覆盖面积	Films Coverage Area	亩/人	mu/person	0.4	0.36	0.04	10.16
（八）温室面积	Greenhouse Area	亩/人	mu/person	0.02	0.02	-0.01	-23.6

5-4 农村住户当年生产经营情况
Production Operations of Rural Households in the Year

类别	Classification	单位	Unit	2006	2005	增减 Add or Subtract	增幅 Increase Range
一、农业	Farming						
（一）谷物产量	Cereal Output	公斤/人	kg/person	804.16	779.14	25.02	3.21
1.普通小麦产量	Ordinary Wheat	公斤/人	kg/person	265.35	257.59	7.76	3.01
2.优质小麦产量	Quality Wheat	公斤/人	kg/person	124.53	115.38	9.16	7.94
3.小麦种子产量	Wheat Seeds	公斤/人	kg/person	5.64	3.83	1.82	47.5
4.普通稻谷产量	Ordinary Rice	公斤/人	kg/person		5.71	-5.71	-100
5.优质稻谷产量	Quality Rice	公斤/人	kg/person	9.76	5.3	4.46	84.04
6.稻谷种子产量	Rice Seeds	公斤/人	kg/person	0.26	0.05	0.21	417.83
7.普通玉米产量	Ordinary Corn	公斤/人	kg/person	292.97	290.26	2.71	0.93
8.优质玉米产量	Quality Corn	公斤/人	kg/person	103.25	99.15	4.09	4.13
9.玉米种子产量	Rice Corn	公斤/人	kg/person	0.99	0.79	0.2	25.68
10.高粱产量	Chinese Sorghum	公斤/人	kg/person	0.54	0.19	0.35	182.04
11.谷子产量	Millet	公斤/人	kg/person	0.31	0.27	0.04	14.78
12.青稞产量	Highland Barley	公斤/人	kg/person				
13.其他谷物产量	Other Cereal	公斤/人	kg/person	0.16	0.46	-0.3	-66.04
14.其他种子产量	Other Seeds	公斤/人	kg/person	0.39	0.16	0.23	150.94
（二）薯类产量	Tubers Output	公斤/人	kg/person	9.46	7.75	1.71	22.11
（三）豆类产量	Beans Output	公斤/人	kg/person	3.94	5.86	-1.93	-32.86
（四）棉花产量	Cotton Output	公斤/人	kg/person	65.41	58.56	6.85	11.71
（五）油料产量	Oil Output	公斤/人	kg/person	37.41	42.04	-4.64	-11.03
#花生产量	of which:Peanut	公斤/人	kg/person	37.08	41.82	-4.74	-11.34
（六）麻类产量	Flaxen Output	公斤/人	kg/person	0.13	0.06	0.07	120.16
（七）糖料产量	Sugar Output	公斤/人	kg/person	0.1		0.1	
（八）烟草产量	Tobacco Output	公斤/人	kg/person	1.46	0.97	0.49	50.88
（九）蔬菜产量	Vegetable Output	公斤/人	kg/person	399.51	394.43	5.08	1.29
（十）瓜果类产量	Melon Output	公斤/人	kg/person	69.62	65.13	4.49	6.9
#西瓜产量	Watermelon Output	公斤/人	kg/person	63.6	57.71	5.89	10.2
（十一）园林水果产量	Fruit Output	公斤/人	kg/person	93.06	86.13	6.94	8.05
#苹果产量	Apple	公斤/人	kg/person	47.75	44.69	3.07	6.86
梨产量	Pear Output	公斤/人	kg/person	5.43	5.52	-0.09	-1.66
葡萄产量	Grape Output	公斤/人	kg/person	9.41	6.95	2.46	35.33
桃产量	Peach	公斤/人	kg/person	11.9	15.2	-3.3	-21.71
杏产量	Apricot Output	公斤/人	kg/person	2.64	1.65	0.99	59.98
枣产量	Jujube Output	公斤/人	kg/person	9.71	6.11	3.61	59.05

5-4 续表 1 continued

类别	Classification	单位	Unit	2006	2005	增减 Add or Subtract	增幅 Increase Range
（十二）中药材（人工种植）产量	Output of Chinese Herbal Medicines(Artificial Cultivation)	公斤/人	kg/person	1.21	1.82	-0.61	-33.28
（十三）农作物副产品产量	Output of Crop By-products	公斤/人	kg/person	216.27	213.58	2.69	1.26
二、林业	**Forestry**						
（一）采集的林产品	Forestry Products			1.31	0.78	0.53	68.28
1.天然林和人工林地采集的果实	Fruit from Natural and Artificial Forest			0.98	0.7	0.28	40.85
#板栗产量	of which:Chestnut Output	公斤/人	kg/person	0.12	0.24	-0.12	-50.11
核桃产量	Walnut Output	公斤/人	kg/person	0.11	0.05	0.06	134.64
花椒产量	Output of Chinese Prickly Ash	公斤/人	kg/person	0.16	0.09	0.08	89.12
2.野生植物、果实	Wild Plant and Fruits			0.32	0.08	0.25	308.85
#柴	Firewood	公担/人	q/person	0.17	0	0.17	7354.79
草	Grass	公担/人	q/person	0.13	0.01	0.12	862.92
（二）竹木采伐量	Output of Bamboo			0.11	0.08	0.02	29.45
#木材	Wood	立米/人	cbm/person	0.11	0.08	0.02	28.02
（三）育种、育苗	Breeding Nursery			3.8	8.31	-4.51	-54.26
1.林木种子产量	Plant Seeds	公斤/人	kg/person	0	0.15	-0.15	-99.57
2.树苗	Sapling	株/人	stem/person	3.8	8.16	-4.36	-53.41
（四）林业副产品	Forestry Borderline Product	任选/人	unit/person	2.28	2.8	-0.53	-18.8
（五）用林产品加工手工业产品	Processes the Handicraft Industry Product with the Forest Product	任选/人	unit/person	0.02	0.03	0	-11.08
三、牧业	**Animal Husbandry**						
（一）畜禽肉产量（出售、自宰）	Output of Livestock and Poultry	公斤/人	kg/person	71.25	68.16	3.09	4.53
1.畜肉产量	Output of Livestock Meat	公斤/人	kg/person	42.87	39.92	2.95	7.39
（1）肉猪头数	Pig	头/人	head/person	0.46	0.39	0.06	15.98
肉猪肉产量	Pork	公斤/人	kg/person	36.71	32.65	4.06	12.44
（2）菜羊只数	Sheep	只/人	head/person	0.07	0.11	-0.04	-36.03
菜羊肉产量	Mutton	公斤/人	kg/person	1.3	1.77	-0.47	-26.39
（3）肉牛头数	Cattle	头/人	head/person	0.03	0.03	-0.01	-16.82
肉牛肉产量	Beef	公斤/人	kg/person	4.77	5.42	-0.65	-11.93
（4）其他牲畜头数	Other Livestock	头/人	head/person	0.02	0	0.02	574.41
其他牲畜肉产量	Meat of Other Livestock	公斤/人	kg/person	0.08	0.08	0	4.1

5-4 续表 2 continued

类别	Classification	单位	Unit	2006	2005	增减 Add or Subtract	增幅 Increase Range
2.家禽肉产量	Output of Poultry Meat	公斤/人	kg/person	28.38	28.24	0.14	0.49
（1）鸡只数	Chicken	只/人	head/person	5.54	7.28	-1.74	-23.89
鸡的肉产量	Chicken Meat	公斤/人	kg/person	11.9	13.46	-1.57	-11.64
（2）鸭只数	Ducks	只/人	head/person	4.97	4.38	0.59	13.5
鸭的肉产量	Ducks Meat	公斤/人	kg/person	16.28	14.56	1.72	11.82
（3）鹅只数	Geese	只/人	head/person	0.1	0.02	0.08	439.63
鹅的肉产量	Geese Meat	公斤/人	kg/person	0.13	0.08	0.05	54.34
（4）其他家禽只数	Other Poultry	只/人	head/person	0.03	0.06	-0.04	-58.48
其他家禽的肉产量	Meat of Other Poultry	公斤/人	kg/person	0.07	0.14	-0.06	-44.88
（二）蛋类产量	Eggs Output	公斤/人	kg/person	23.11	21.54	1.57	7.27
1.鸡蛋产量	Chicken Eggs	公斤/人	kg/person	22.51	21.19	1.31	6.21
2.鸭蛋产量	Duck Eggs	公斤/人	kg/person	0.14	0.35	-0.21	-60.61
3.种蛋产量	Stud Eggs	公斤/人	kg/person	0.46	0	0.46	158711.71
4.其他蛋产量	Other Eggs	公斤/人	kg/person	0	0	0	-47.88
（三）皮产量	Leather Output	张/人		0.09	0.07	0.02	22.1
（四）毛、绒产量	Feather and Cashmere Output	公斤/人	kg/person	0.04	0.01	0.02	168.61
（五）奶类产量	Milk Outout	公斤/人	kg/person	3.9	4.2	-0.3	-7.26
（六）仔、幼、育肥畜、禽产品	Young Animals Product			0.22	0.79	-0.57	-71.95
#仔猪头数	Young Pig	头/人	head/person	0.1	0.27	-0.17	-63.61
架子猪头数	Feeder Pig Number	头/人	head/person	0.01	0.01	0	-41.19
羊羔只数	Young Sheep	只/人	head/person	0.02	0.05	-0.03	-65.64
仔、幼鸭只数	Young Duck	只/人	head/person	0.05	0.05	0	-3.74
仔、幼兔只数	Yonng Rabbit	只/人	head/person	0.05	0.26	-0.22	-82.48
（七）其他牧业产品	Other Animal Husbandry Products			2.35	3.66	-1.32	-35.95
#兔肉产量	Rabbit Meat	公斤/人	kg/person	0.37	0.47	-0.1	-20.87
蚕茧产量	Cocoon	公斤/人	kg/person	1.6	1.5	0.1	6.73
四、渔业	**Fishery**						
（一）海水产品	Seawater Products			4.95	7.93	-2.97	-37.51
#鱼类产量	Fish Output	公斤/人	kg/person	1.26	0.43	0.83	190.8
贝类产量	Cowry Output	公斤/人	kg/person	3.44	7.26	-3.83	-52.7
（二）淡水产品	Fresh Water Products			0.13	0.06	0.08	139.14
#鱼类产量	Fish Output	公斤/人	kg/person	0.13	0.05	0.08	142.69

5-5 农村住户人均总收入与总支出
Per Capita Total Income and Expenditure of Rural Households

类别	Classification	单位	Unit	2006	2005	增减 Add or Subtract	增幅 Increase Range
一、总收入	**Total Income**	元/人	yuan/person	**6188.54**	**5676.98**	**511.56**	**9.01**
（一）工资性收入	Income from Wages and Salaries	元/人	yuan/person	1671.54	1437.57	233.97	16.28
1.在非企业组织中劳动得到收入	Incomes from Working in the Non-business Organizations	元/人	yuan/person	251.28	240.73	10.55	4.38
（1）乡村干部收入	Income of Village Cadres	元/人	yuan/person	133.25	125.86	7.39	5.87
（2）乡村教师收入	Income of Village Teacher	元/人	yuan/person	48.82	43.11	5.72	13.27
（3）行政事业单位等职工收入	Income from Working in Administrative Units	元/人	yuan/person	69.21	71.77	-2.55	-3.56
2.在本乡地域内劳动得到收入	Incomes from Working Inside the Village	元/人	yuan/person	947.35	806.57	140.77	17.45
（1）在企业中劳动得到收入	Incomes from Working in Enterprises	元/人	yuan/person	611.94	522.63	89.3	17.09
a.乡镇企业收入	Township Enterprises	元/人	yuan/person	254.38	230.33	24.05	10.44
b.其他企业收入	Other Enterprises	元/人	yuan/person	357.56	292.31	65.25	22.32
（2）在国家投资基建项目得到收入	Income from Infrastructure ProjectsInvested by the State	元/人	yuan/person	6.55	4.89	1.67	34.12
（3）提供其他劳务收入	Other Labor Income	元/人	yuan/person	328.86	279.05	49.81	17.85
3.外出从业得到收入	Income from Working Somewhere away from Home	元/人	yuan/person	472.91	390.27	82.64	21.18
（1）在乡外县内从业得到收入	In the County but outside the Village	元/人	yuan/person	199.24	169.96	29.28	17.23
（2）在县外省内从业得到收入	In the Province but outside the County	元/人	yuan/person	205.02	163.82	41.2	25.15
（3）在省外国内从业得到收入	In China but outside the Province	元/人	yuan/person	68.43	56.43	12	21.27
（4）在国外从业得到收入	Abroad	元/人	yuan/person	0.22	0.06	0.16	279.85
（二）家庭经营收入	Income from Household Operations	元/人	yuan/person	4174.49	3956.95	217.54	5.5
1.第一产业收入	Income from Primary Industry	元/人	yuan/person	3334.83	3177.37	157.47	4.96
（1）农业收入	Income from Farming	元/人	yuan/person	2382.97	2215.02	167.95	7.58
A.农产品收入	Farming Products	元/人	yuan/person	2323.94	2159.05	164.89	7.64
①粮食收入	Grain	元/人	yuan/person	1004.51	977.43	27.08	2.77
②棉花收入	Cotton	元/人	yuan/person	328.1	279.43	48.67	17.42
③油料收入	Oil	元/人	yuan/person	124.19	132.26	-8.08	-6.11
④麻类收入	Flaxen	元/人	yuan/person	0.58	0.43	0.15	36.27
⑤糖料收入	Sugar	元/人	yuan/person	0.06		0.06	
⑥烟草收入	Tobacco	元/人	yuan/person	12.94	8.16	4.78	58.53
⑦蔬菜收入	Vegetable	元/人	yuan/person	547.22	482.33	64.88	13.45
⑧花卉园艺收入	Flower	元/人	yuan/person	3	2.36	0.64	27.19

5-5 续表 1 continued

类别	Classification	单位	Unit	2006	2005	增减 Add or Subtract	增幅 Increase Range
⑨瓜果收入	Melon	元/人	yuan/person	84.73	69.99	14.73	21.05
⑩园林收入	Garden	元/人	yuan/person	195.13	164.59	30.54	18.56
⑪茶叶和其他饮料收入	Tea and Other Beverages	元/人	yuan/person				
⑫香料收入	Perfume	元/人	yuan/person	0.02	0	0.02	4461.95
⑬中药材收入	Chinese Herbal Medicines	元/人	yuan/person	9.85	9.63	0.22	2.28
⑭其他种植业产品收入	Other Planting Products	元/人	yuan/person	1.78	17.3	-15.52	-89.68
⑮野生植物采集收入	Wild Plant Acquisition	元/人	yuan/person	0.04	0.72	-0.68	-94.21
⑯农作物副产品收入	Crop By-products	元/人	yuan/person	7.35	11.65	-4.31	-36.96
⑰用农产品加工手工业产品收入	Handicraft Products from Farming Product Processing	元/人	yuan/person	3.7	2.33	1.37	58.7
⑱专用农产品收入	Specialized Farm Products	元/人	yuan/person	0.76	0.44	0.32	73.56
B.农业服务性收入	Income from Agricultural Services	元/人	yuan/person	59.03	55.97	3.06	5.47
（2）林业收入	Income from Forestry	元/人	yuan/person	80.28	60.31	19.97	33.1
A.林业产品收入	Forestry Products	元/人	yuan/person	75.81	57.99	17.83	30.75
①采集林产品收入	Forestry Product Acquisition	元/人	yuan/person	4.58	3.32	1.26	37.99
②竹木采伐收入	Bamboo Logging	元/人	yuan/person	58	40.63	17.38	42.77
③育种、育苗收入	Breeding Nursery	元/人	yuan/person	11.32	12.07	-0.75	-6.2
④林业副产品收入	Forestry By-products	元/人	yuan/person	1.25	1.81	-0.55	-30.69
⑤用林产品加工手工业产品收入	Handicraft Products from Forestry Product Processing	元/人	yuan/person	0.66	0.16	0.49	304.37
B.林业服务性收入	Income from Forestry Services	元/人	yuan/person	4.47	2.33	2.14	91.86
（3）牧业收入	Income from Animal Husbandry	元/人	yuan/person	829.71	865.38	-35.67	-4.12
A.牧业产品收入	Animal Husbandry Products	元/人	yuan/person	825.68	857.79	-32.11	-3.74
①成龄家畜收入	Livestock	元/人	yuan/person	398.93	424.2	-25.28	-5.96
#猪收入	Pig	元/人	yuan/person	321.95	340.05	-18.1	-5.32
菜羊收入	Sheep	元/人	yuan/person	16.99	22.07	-5.08	-23
肉牛收入	Cattle	元/人	yuan/person	59.06	61.27	-2.21	-3.6
②成龄家禽收入	Poultry	元/人	yuan/person	181.94	182.79	-0.85	-0.46
③蛋类收入	Eggs	元/人	yuan/person	108.76	111.69	-2.93	-2.62
④皮收入	Leather	元/人	yuan/person	24.15	18.91	5.25	27.77
⑤毛、绒收入	Feather and Cashmere	元/人	yuan/person	1.97	1.49	0.48	32.01
⑥奶类收入	Milk	元/人	yuan/person	6.65	7.36	-0.7	-9.57
⑦仔、幼畜、禽产品收入	Young Livestock and Poultry Products	元/人	yuan/person	41.5	64.38	-22.89	-35.55

5-5 续表 2 continued

类别	Classification	单位	Unit	2006	2005	增减 Add or Subtract	增幅 Increase Range
⑧育肥畜收入	Breeding Livestock	元/人	yuan/person	2.32	1.43	0.89	62.17
⑨其他牧业产品收入	Other Animal Husbandry Products	元/人	yuan/person	54.87	40.13	14.74	36.72
⑩狩猎和捕捉野生动物收入	Hunting and Trapping Wild Animal	元/人	yuan/person	0.59	0.87	-0.27	-31.44
⑪牧业副产品收入	Animal Husbandry By-products	元/人	yuan/person	3.73	4.06	-0.32	-7.97
⑫牧业加工手工业收入	Animal Husbandry Processing	元/人	yuan/person	0.26	0.48	-0.22	-46.34
B.牧业服务性收入	Animal Husbandry Services	元/人	yuan/person	4.03	7.6	-3.57	-46.93
（4）渔业收入	Income from Fishery	元/人	yuan/person	41.87	36.65	5.22	14.25
A.渔业产品收入	Fishery Products	元/人	yuan/person	41.24	36.14	5.1	14.12
①海水产品收入	Seawater Products	元/人	yuan/person	30.76	22.37	8.39	37.5
②淡水产品收入	Fresh Water Products	元/人	yuan/person	0.67	0.41	0.26	63.17
③渔业副产品收入	Fishery By-products	元/人	yuan/person	9.49	13	-3.51	-27.01
④渔业加工手工业产品收入	Fishery Processing	元/人	yuan/person	0.32	0.36	-0.04	-10.15
B.渔业服务性收入	Fishery Services	元/人	yuan/person	0.63	0.51	0.12	23.49
2.第二产业收入	Income from Secondary Industry	元/人	yuan/person	261.92	265.24	-3.32	-1.25
（1）工业收入	Industry	元/人	yuan/person	198.88	209.44	-10.56	-5.04
A.工业产品收入	Industrial Products	元/人	yuan/person	75.24	67.26	7.98	11.86
B.工业服务性收入	Industrial Services	元/人	yuan/person	123.64	142.18	-18.54	-13.04
（2）建筑业收入	Construction	元/人	yuan/person	63.04	55.8	7.25	12.99
①建筑业产品收入	Construction Products	元/人	yuan/person	0.88	1.48	-0.6	-40.6
②建筑业服务性收入	Construction Services	元/人	yuan/person	62.16	54.31	7.85	14.45
3.第三产业收入	Income from Tertiary Industry	元/人	yuan/person	577.74	514.35	63.39	12.32
（1）其他产品收入	Other Products	元/人	yuan/person	2.25	2.25	0	0.16
（2）第三产业服务性收入	Tertiary Industry Services	元/人	yuan/person	575.49	512.1	63.39	12.38
①交通、运输、邮电业收入	Transport, Storage and Post	元/人	yuan/person	175.98	166.45	9.53	5.72
②批零贸易业、饮食业收入	Wholesale, Retail and Catering Trades	元/人	yuan/person	222.32	186.16	36.16	19.42
③社会服务业收入	Social Services	元/人	yuan/person	67.55	54.87	12.68	23.1
④文教卫生业收入	Culture, Education and Health	元/人	yuan/person	34.62	28.2	6.42	22.77
⑤其他行业收入	Other Sectors	元/人	yuan/person	75.02	76.42	-1.4	-1.83
（三）财产性收入	Income from Properties	元/人	yuan/person	127.6	102.8	24.8	24.13
1.利息	Interest	元/人	yuan/person	10.78	9.75	1.03	10.51
2.集体分配股息和红利	Divident and Bonus Distributed by Mass	元/人	yuan/person	0.84	0.63	0.21	33.3

5-5 续表 3 continued

类别	Classification	单位	Unit	2006	2005	增减 Add or Subtract	增幅 Increase Range
3.其他股息和红利	Other Divident and Bonus	元/人	yuan/person	2.47	2.02	0.45	22.4
4.租金（包括农业机械）	Rent (Including Agricultural Machinery)	元/人	yuan/person	11.33	10.36	0.97	9.36
5.出让无形资产净收入	Selling Intangibles	元/人	yuan/person		0.11	-0.11	-100
6.储蓄性保险投资收入	Savings Insurance Investment	元/人	yuan/person	0.83	0.5	0.32	64.18
7.土地征用补偿收入	Compensation for Land Acquisition	元/人	yuan/person	51.61	46.21	5.4	11.69
8.转让承包土地经营权收入	Land Management Rights Transfer	元/人	yuan/person	6.54	2.56	3.98	155.68
9.其他投资收益	Other Investment Profits	元/人	yuan/person	0.46	0.38	0.08	20.51
10.其他	Others	元/人	yuan/person	42.73	30.26	12.47	41.21
（四）转移性收入	Income from Transfers	元/人	yuan/person	214.9	179.66	35.24	19.62
#1.家庭非常住人口寄回和带回收入	Sent Back by Non-permanent Resident	元/人	yuan/person	37.1	34.11	3	8.78
2.城市亲友赠送收入	Presentation from Relatives and Friends in Rural Area	元/人	yuan/person	23.54	21.18	2.36	11.16
3.农村亲友赠送收入	Presentation from Relatives and Friends in Urban Area	元/人	yuan/person	60.6	52.32	8.28	15.82
4.退耕还林还草补贴收入	Subsidies for Returning Farmland to Forest and Grass	元/人	yuan/person	0.17	0.24	-0.07	-30.14
#粮食收入	Grain	元/人	yuan/person	0.03		0.03	
5.粮食直接补贴收入	Direct Subsidies for Grain Planting	元/人	yuan/person	11.34	10.5	0.84	8.03
二、总支出	**Total Expenditure**	**元/人**	**yuan/person**	**5090.48**	**4561.27**	**529.21**	**11.6**
(一)家庭经营费用支出	Expenditure for Household Operations	元/人	yuan/person	1571.69	1496.03	75.66	5.06
1.第一产业生产费用支出	Primary Industry	元/人	yuan/person	1386.6	1314.96	71.64	5.45
（1）农业生产费用支出	Expenditure for Farming Production	元/人	yuan/person	812.97	731.25	81.72	11.18
A.农业生产资料支出	Production Materials of Farming	元/人	yuan/person	687.91	623.63	64.28	10.31
①种籽支出	Seed	元/人	yuan/person	60.4	52.84	7.56	14.31
②饲料支出	Feed	元/人	yuan/person	9.91	12.24	-2.33	-19.05
③其他生产资料支出	Other Production Materials	元/人	yuan/person	617.6	558.55	59.05	10.57
B.农业服务性支出	Farming Services	元/人	yuan/person	125.06	107.62	17.44	16.2
①农业生产雇工工资支出	Wages for Farming Production	元/人	yuan/person	17.02	15.29	1.74	11.36
②其他生产服务支出	Other Production Services	元/人	yuan/person	108.04	92.34	15.7	17
（2）林业生产费用支出	Expenditure for Forestry Production	元/人	yuan/person	15.79	11.33	4.47	39.43
A.林业生产资料支出	Production Materials of Forestry	元/人	yuan/person	13.48	9.83	3.64	37.06

5-5 续表 4 continued

类别	Classification	单位	Unit	2006	2005	增减 Add or Subtract	增幅 Increase Range
①饲料支出	Feed	元/人	yuan/person	0.14	0.86	-0.73	-84.28
②其他生产资料支出	Other Production Materials	元/人	yuan/person	13.34	8.97	4.37	48.7
B.林业服务性支出	Forestry Services	元/人	yuan/person	2.32	1.49	0.82	55.02
①林业生产雇工工资支出	Wages for Forestry Production	元/人	yuan/person	0.9	0.1	0.79	779.02
②其他生产服务支出	Other Production Services	元/人	yuan/person	1.42	1.39	0.03	2.06
(3) 牧业生产费用支出	Expenditure for Animal Husbandry Production	元/人	yuan/person	539.93	557.82	-17.89	-3.21
A.牧业生产资料支出	Production Materials of Animal Husbandry	元/人	yuan/person	524.39	544.54	-20.15	-3.7
①饲料支出	Feed	元/人	yuan/person	421.78	394.39	27.4	6.95
②其他生产资料支出	Other Production Materials	元/人	yuan/person	102.61	150.16	-47.55	-31.66
B.牧业服务性支出	Animal Husbandry Services	元/人	yuan/person	15.54	13.27	2.26	17.04
①牧业生产雇工工资支出	Wages for Animal Husbandry Production	元/人	yuan/person	2.36	1.1	1.25	113.75
②其他生产服务支出	Other Production Services	元/人	yuan/person	13.18	12.17	1.01	8.28
(4) 渔业生产费用支出	Expenditure for Fishery Production	元/人	yuan/person	17.91	14.57	3.34	22.95
A.渔业生产资料支出	Production Materials of Fishery	元/人	yuan/person	7.71	13.55	-5.84	-43.1
①饲料支出	Feed	元/人	yuan/person	5.49	0.22	5.27	2405.13
②其他生产资料支出	Other Production Materials	元/人	yuan/person	2.23	13.34	-11.11	-83.3
B.渔业服务性支出	Fishery Services	元/人	yuan/person	10.2	1.01	9.18	906.28
①渔业生产雇工工资支出	Wages for Fishery Production	元/人	yuan/person	0.01	0.19	-0.18	-97.32
②其他生产服务支出	Other Production Services	元/人	yuan/person	10.19	0.82	9.37	1137.41
2.第二产业生产费用支出	Secondary Industry	元/人	yuan/person	76.59	92.57	-15.98	-17.27
(1) 工业生产费用支出	Expenditure for Industry Production	元/人	yuan/person	69.28	87.82	-18.54	-21.11
A.工业生产资料支出	Production Materials of Industry	元/人	yuan/person	47.48	58.84	-11.36	-19.31
#原料支出	Raw Materials	元/人	yuan/person	45.82	53.77	-7.95	-14.79
燃料支出	Fuel	元/人	yuan/person	0.64	0.57	0.06	11.19
B.工业服务性支出	Industry Services	元/人	yuan/person	21.81	28.98	-7.17	-24.75
①工业生产雇工工资支出	Wages for Industry Production	元/人	yuan/person	7.54	7.44	0.1	1.35
②其他生产服务支出	Other Production Services	元/人	yuan/person	14.26	21.54	-7.27	-33.77

5-5 续表 5 continued

类别	Classification	单位	Unit	2006	2005	增减 Add or Subtract	增幅 Increase Range
（2）建筑业生产费用支出	Expenditure for Construction Production	元/人	yuan/person	7.3	4.75	2.55	53.71
A.建筑业生产资料支出	Production Materials of Construction	元/人	yuan/person	2.7	1.13	1.57	138.16
#原料支出	Raw Materials	元/人	yuan/person	2.03	0.86	1.17	136.3
燃料支出	Fuel	元/人	yuan/person	0.46	0.06	0.4	675.92
B.建筑业服务性支出	Construction Services	元/人	yuan/person	4.6	3.62	0.99	27.27
①建筑业生产雇工工资支出	Wages for Construction Production	元/人	yuan/person	3.5	2.4	1.09	45.46
②其他生产服务支出	Other Production Services	元/人	yuan/person	1.11	1.21	-0.11	-8.79
3.第三产业生产费用支出	Tertiary Industry	元/人	yuan/person	108.5	88.5	20	22.61
（1）交通运输邮电业生产费用支出	Expenditure for Production of Transport, Storage and Post	元/人	yuan/person	24.35	27.35	-3	-10.98
A.交通运输邮电业生产资料支出	Production Materials of Transport,Storage and Post	元/人	yuan/person	16.98	18.41	-1.43	-7.76
#燃料支出	Fuel	元/人	yuan/person	14.3	14.12	0.17	1.21
B.交通运输邮电业服务性支出	Transport, Storage and Post Services	元/人	yuan/person	7.36	8.94	-1.57	-17.6
①交通运输邮电业生产雇工工资支出	Wages for Production of Transport, Storage and Post	元/人	yuan/person	0.62	0.41	0.21	52.25
②其他生产服务支出	Other Production Services	元/人	yuan/person	6.74	8.53	-1.79	-20.95
（2）批零贸易餐饮业生产费用支出	Expenditure for Production of Wholesale, Retail and Catering Trades	元/人	yuan/person	57.37	38.66	18.71	48.39
A.批零贸易餐饮业生产资料支出	Production Materials of Wholesale, Retail and Catering Trades	元/人	yuan/person	29.02	25.48	3.55	13.92
#原料支出	Raw Materials	元/人	yuan/person	25.76	21.9	3.86	17.62
燃料支出	Fuel	元/人	yuan/person	2.22	1.1	1.11	100.66
B.批零贸易餐饮业服务性支出	Wholesale, Retail and Catering Trades Services	元/人	yuan/person	28.35	13.19	15.16	114.99
①批零贸易餐饮业生产雇工工资支出	Wages for Production of Wholesale, Retail and Catering Trades	元/人	yuan/person	6.91	3.68	3.23	87.88
②其他生产服务支出	Other Production Services	元/人	yuan/person	21.44	9.51	11.93	125.47
（3）社会服务业生产费用支出	Expenditure for Production of Social Services	元/人	yuan/person	6.67	8.35	-1.68	-20.13
A.社会服务业生产资料支出	Production Materials of Social Services	元/人	yuan/person	4.57	6.3	-1.73	-27.48
#原料支出	Raw Materials	元/人	yuan/person	3.65	4.72	-1.07	-22.74
燃料支出	Fuel	元/人	yuan/person	0.7	0.97	-0.26	-27.11

5-5 续表 6 continued

类别	Classification	单位	Unit	2006	2005	增减 Add or Subtract	增幅 Increase Range
B.社会服务业服务性支出	Social Services Services	元/人	yuan/person	2.1	2.05	0.05	2.39
①社会服务业生产雇工工资支出	Wages for Production of Social Services	元/人	yuan/person	0.34	0.31	0.03	10.98
②其他生产服务支出	Other Production Services	元/人	yuan/person	1.76	1.75	0.02	0.88
（4）文教卫生业生产费用支出	Expenditure for Production of Culture, Education and Health	元/人	yuan/person	7.34	4.37	2.97	68.08
A.文教卫生业生产资料支出	Production Materials of Culture, Education and Health	元/人	yuan/person	4.48	2.77	1.7	61.46
#原料支出	Raw Materials	元/人	yuan/person	4.37	0.92	3.46	376.93
燃料支出	Fuel	元/人	yuan/person	0.04	0.06	-0.02	-30.73
B.文教卫生业服务性支出	Culture, Education and Health Services	元/人	yuan/person	2.86	1.59	1.27	79.61
①文教卫生业生产雇工工资支出	Wages for Production of Culture, Education and Health	元/人	yuan/person	0.71	0.41	0.3	72.66
②其他生产服务支出	Other Production Services	元/人	yuan/person	2.15	1.18	0.97	82.05
（5）其他行业生产费用支出	Expenditure for Production of Other Secotrs	元/人	yuan/person	12.77	9.76	3.01	30.81
A.其他行业生产资料支出	Production Materials of Other Secotrs	元/人	yuan/person	9.29	4.52	4.77	105.51
#原料支出	Raw Materials	元/人	yuan/person	1.77	2.95	-1.18	-40.08
燃料支出	Fuel	元/人	yuan/person	0.45	0.76	-0.31	-41.3
B.其他行业服务性支出	Other Secotrs Services	元/人	yuan/person	3.48	5.24	-1.76	-33.58
①其他行业生产雇工工资支出	Wages for Production of Other Secotrs	元/人	yuan/person	0.24	3.35	-3.11	-92.97
②其他生产服务支出	Other Production Services	元/人	yuan/person	3.25	1.9	1.35	71.26
（二）购置生产性固定资产支出	Expenditure for Purchase of Productive Fixed Assets	元/人	yuan/person	149.36	117.14	32.22	27.5
（三）建、造生产性固定资产雇工支出	Expenditure for Building of Productive Fixed Assets	元/人	yuan/person	1.8	1.4	0.4	28.5
（四）税费支出	Expenditure for Taxes and Fees	元/人	yuan/person	21.28	34.27	-12.99	-37.9
1.第一产业税	Primary Industry	元/人	yuan/person	0.8	10.81	-10	-92.58
2.第二产业税	Secondary Industry	元/人	yuan/person	1.06	0.86	0.21	24.03
（1）工业生产纳税	Tax of Industry Production	元/人	yuan/person	1.06	0.84	0.22	25.94
（2）建筑业生产纳税	Tax of Construction Production	元/人	yuan/person		0.01	-0.01	-100
3.第三产业税	Tertiary Industry	元/人	yuan/person	3.48	3.07	0.4	13.18
4.其他各种收费	Other Charges	元/人	yuan/person	15.94	19.53	-3.59	-18.39
（五）生活消费支出	Expense on Household Consumption	元/人	yuan/person	3143.8	2735.77	408.03	14.91

5-5 续表 7 continued

类别	Classification	单位	Unit	2006	2005	增减 Add or Subtract	增幅 Increase Range
#服务性支出	Expenditure for Services	元/人	yuan/person	1022.95	880.02	142.93	16.24
1.食品消费支出	Food	元/人	yuan/person	1191.32	1087.65	103.67	9.53
A.食品消费品支出	Consumer Foods	元/人	yuan/person	1004.85	920.96	83.9	9.11
①谷物	Cereal	元/人	yuan/person	245.98	243.57	2.4	0.99
②薯类	Tubers	元/人	yuan/person	4.86	5.58	-0.72	-12.86
③豆类	Beans	元/人	yuan/person	12.81	12.58	0.23	1.81
④食用油	Eatable Oil	元/人	yuan/person	60.17	59.32	0.84	1.42
⑤蔬菜及制品	Vegetable and Products	元/人	yuan/person	101.93	90.69	11.25	12.4
⑥肉、禽、蛋、奶及制品	Meat, Poultry, Egg, Milk and Their Products	元/人	yuan/person	238.63	242.69	-4.06	-1.67
⑦水产品及制品	Aquatic Products	元/人	yuan/person	33.92	33.32	0.61	1.82
⑧烟、酒	Tobacco and Liquor	元/人	yuan/person	156.69	155.93	0.76	0.49
⑨茶叶、饮料	Tea and Beverages	元/人	yuan/person	15.73	13.4	2.33	17.39
⑩其它类食品	Other Foods	元/人	yuan/person	134.14	63.88	70.26	109.99
B.食品消费服务性支出	Services for Foods Consumption	元/人	yuan/person	186.46	166.69	19.77	11.86
①在外饮食	Outward Dinner	元/人	yuan/person	173.27	156.65	16.62	10.61
②食品加工费	Foods Processing	元/人	yuan/person	6.63	7.63	-0.99	-13.04
③其他服务性支出	Other Services	元/人	yuan/person	6.56	2.41	4.15	171.85
2.衣着消费支出	Clothing	元/人	yuan/person	198.12	159.73	38.39	24.03
A.衣着消费品支出	Consumer Clothing	元/人	yuan/person	196.46	157.72	38.74	24.56
①服装	Garments	元/人	yuan/person	126.15	95.21	30.93	32.49
②服装材料	Clothing Material	元/人	yuan/person	10.99	11.11	-0.12	-1.1
③鞋类	Footwear	元/人	yuan/person	48.65	42.31	6.34	14.98
④其他	Others	元/人	yuan/person	10.68	9.09	1.59	17.49
B.衣着消费服务性支出	Services for Clothing Consumption	元/人	yuan/person	1.66	2.01	-0.35	-17.45
①衣着加工费	Clothing Proceeding Services	元/人	yuan/person	1.21	1.27	-0.06	-4.45
②其他服务性支出	Other Services	元/人	yuan/person	0.44	0.74	-0.29	-39.82
3.居住消费支出	Residence	元/人	yuan/person	548.05	445.71	102.35	22.96
A.居住消费品支出	Consumer Residence	元/人	yuan/person	412.37	331.84	80.53	24.27
①建筑生活用房材料	Construction Materials	元/人	yuan/person	249.1	197.47	51.63	26.14
②维修生活用房材料	Repair Materials	元/人	yuan/person	12.84	14.98	-2.14	-14.26
③装修生活用房材料	Decoration Materials	元/人	yuan/person	32.64	24.86	7.78	31.29
④生活用房	Household Housing	元/人	yuan/person	26.35	9.65	16.7	172.99
⑤生活用燃料	Household Fuels	元/人	yuan/person	91.45	84.89	6.57	7.73

5-5 续表 8 continued

类别	Classification	单位	Unit	2006	2005	增减 Add or Subtract	增幅 Increase Range
B.居住消费服务性支出	Services for Residence	元/人	yuan/person	135.68	113.87	21.82	19.16
①建筑、维修生活用房雇工工资	Wages for Housing Construction and Repair	元/人	yuan/person	50.35	43.31	7.03	16.24
②房租	Rent	元/人	yuan/person	3.37	2.17	1.21	55.7
③生活用水	Household Water	元/人	yuan/person	4.04	2.91	1.13	38.67
④生活用电	Household Electricity	元/人	yuan/person	59.95	48.15	11.8	24.51
⑤清洁费、卫生费	Cleaning and Sanitation Costs	元/人	yuan/person	0.28	0.32	-0.04	-11.84
⑥其他服务性支出	Other Services	元/人	yuan/person	17.68	17	0.68	4.02
4.家庭设备、用品消费支出	Household Appliances	元/人	yuan/person	158.73	136.54	22.19	16.25
A.家庭设备用品消费品支出	Consumer Household Appliances	元/人	yuan/person	150.04	127.99	22.05	17.23
①日用品	Goods for Daily Use	元/人	yuan/person	47.87	42.98	4.89	11.38
②床上用品	Bed Articles	元/人	yuan/person	11.96	9.51	2.46	25.84
③室内装饰品	Interior Decorations	元/人	yuan/person	4.97	4.26	0.71	16.73
④家俱类	Furniture	元/人	yuan/person	38.76	31.21	7.56	24.22
⑤机电设备	Electrical Equipment	元/人	yuan/person	46.48	40.04	6.43	16.06
B.家庭设备用品服务性消费支出	Services for Household Appliances	元/人	yuan/person	8.69	8.55	0.14	1.62
①家庭设备修理费	Charges for Household Appliances Repair	元/人	yuan/person	4.09	3.26	0.83	25.57
②日杂用品加工修理费	Charges for Grocery Processing and Repair	元/人	yuan/person	1.54	1.55	-0.01	-0.5
③家政服务费	Charges for Household Services	元/人	yuan/person	0.71	0.81	-0.1	-12.71
④其他服务性支出	Other Services	元/人	yuan/person	2.35	2.93	-0.58	-19.88
5.交通和通讯消费支出	Transport and Communications	元/人	yuan/person	352.19	294.37	57.82	19.64
A.交通和通讯用品支出	Transport andCommunications Goods	元/人	yuan/person	181.74	150.99	30.75	20.36
①交通工具	Transportation Facility	元/人	yuan/person	97.98	85.29	12.69	14.88
②交通工具用燃料	Fuels for Transportation Facility	元/人	yuan/person	36.59	28.58	8.01	28.01
③交通工具用零配件	Parts of Transportation Facility	元/人	yuan/person	6.72	4.62	2.1	45.38
④通讯工具	Communication Facility	元/人	yuan/person	40.13	32.24	7.89	24.48
⑤通讯工具用零配件	Parts of Communication Facility	元/人	yuan/person	0.32	0.26	0.06	22.92
B.交通和通讯服务消费支出	Transport and Communications Services	元/人	yuan/person	170.45	143.38	27.08	18.88
a.交通消费服务支出	Services for Transport	元/人	yuan/person	55.2	45	10.2	22.67
①交通客运费	Passenger Traffic Charges	元/人	yuan/person	37.06	29.37	7.69	26.2
②生活物品货运费	Freight Charges for Living Goods	元/人	yuan/person	0.48	0.63	-0.15	-24.41
③交通工具修理费	Charges for Transportation Facility Repair	元/人	yuan/person	13.53	11.39	2.14	18.83

5-5 续表 9 continued

类别	Classification	单位	Unit	2006	2005	增减 Add or Subtract	增幅 Increase Range
④其他（过路过桥费等）服务性支出	Other Services	元/人	yuan/person	4.14	3.62	0.52	14.38
b.通讯消费服务支出	Services for Communications	元/人	yuan/person	115.25	98.38	16.87	17.15
①邮寄费	Mailing Costs	元/人	yuan/person	0.78	0.88	-0.1	-10.91
②通讯费	Communication Charges	元/人	yuan/person	113.28	96.16	17.11	17.8
③通讯工具修理费	Charges for Communication Facility Repair	元/人	yuan/person	0.65	0.81	-0.16	-19.91
④其他	Others	元/人	yuan/person	0.54	0.53	0.02	2.84
6.文化教育、娱乐消费支出	Recreation, Education and Cultural	元/人	yuan/person	408.84	377.16	31.67	8.4
A.文化教育、娱乐用品消费支出	Culture, Education and Recreation Appliances	元/人	yuan/person	68.92	60.75	8.18	13.46
①文教、娱乐用机电消费品	Electrical Consumer Goods for Culture, Education and Recreation	元/人	yuan/person	38.89	34.21	4.68	13.67
②书、报、杂志	Books, Newspapers and Magazines	元/人	yuan/person	12.46	11.92	0.54	4.53
③纸张、文具	Paper and Stationery	元/人	yuan/person	4.95	4.21	0.75	17.74
④音像制品	Audio-visual Products	元/人	yuan/person	0.96	0.81	0.15	18.39
⑤电脑软件	Software	元/人	yuan/person	0.03	0.03	0	-3.18
⑥体育用品	Sport Goods	元/人	yuan/person	0.27	0.11	0.16	148.07
⑦计算机零配件及耗材	Computer Parts and Materials	元/人	yuan/person	0.09	0.07	0.02	23.67
⑧鲜花	Flower	元/人	yuan/person	0.17	0.15	0.02	15.04
⑨娱乐用品	Recreation Goods	元/人	yuan/person	6.27	4.92	1.35	27.4
⑩其他用品	Other Goods	元/人	yuan/person	4.83	4.32	0.51	11.91
B.教育服务消费支出	Education Services	元/人	yuan/person	311.18	293.27	17.92	6.11
①托儿费	Child-care Fee	元/人	yuan/person	3.67	3.52	0.15	4.21
②幼儿园赞助费	Sponsor Fee for Kindergarten	元/人	yuan/person	2.14	0.77	1.37	178.84
③学杂费	Tuition Fee	元/人	yuan/person	270.09	262.46	7.63	2.91
④入学赞助费	Sponsor Fee for School Entrance	元/人	yuan/person	2.42	2.75	-0.33	-12.15
⑤私立学校就读费	Student Fee for Private Schools Entrance	元/人	yuan/person	1.75	2.08	-0.33	-16.04
⑥成人培训费	Adult Training Expenses	元/人	yuan/person	14.32	6.7	7.62	113.72
⑦教育设备修理费	Repair Charges for Education Equipment	元/人	yuan/person	0.23	0.05	0.18	402.31
⑧其他服务性支出	Other Services	元/人	yuan/person	16.58	14.94	1.64	10.96
C.文化、体育、娱乐服务消费支出	Services for Culture, Sports and Recreation	元/人	yuan/person	28.73	23.15	5.58	24.1
①旅游	Tourism	元/人	yuan/person	4.6	1.91	2.69	140.71
②休闲娱乐费	Recreation Costs	元/人	yuan/person	4.09	3.23	0.86	26.62
③文化、体育、娱乐用品修理费	Repair Charges for Culture, Sports and Recreation Goods	元/人	yuan/person	3.63	3.41	0.22	6.39

5-5 续表 10 continued

类别	Classification	单位	Unit	2006	2005	增减 Add or Subtract	增幅 Increase Range
④其他服务性支出	Other Services	元/人	yuan/person	16.41	14.6	1.81	12.42
7.医疗保健消费支出	Health care	元/人	yuan/person	221.8	188.48	33.33	17.68
A.医疗保健用品	Health Care Appliances	元/人	yuan/person	78	80.27	-2.27	-2.83
(1)医疗卫生用品	Medical Appliances	元/人	yuan/person	74.18	76.58	-2.39	-3.12
①药品	Medicine	元/人	yuan/person	72.23	74.69	-2.46	-3.29
②医疗卫生器械	Medical Equipment	元/人	yuan/person	0.56	1.05	-0.49	-46.53
③其他医疗卫生用品	Other Medical Appliances	元/人	yuan/person	1.39	0.84	0.56	66.38
(2)保健用品	Health Appliances	元/人	yuan/person	3.82	3.69	0.12	3.29
①药品类保健品	Drugs Health Products	元/人	yuan/person	1.72	1.33	0.39	29.65
②保健器材	Health Equipment	元/人	yuan/person	2.09	2.37	-0.27	-11.52
B.医疗保健服务消费支出	Health Care Services	元/人	yuan/person	143.8	108.21	35.6	32.9
①医疗费	Medical Charges	元/人	yuan/person	138.77	103.43	35.34	34.17
②医疗设备修理费	Repair Charges for Medical Equipment	元/人	yuan/person	0.22	0.19	0.02	11.59
③保健费	Health Charges	元/人	yuan/person	1.93	1.51	0.43	28.38
④保健设备修理费	Repair Charges for Health Equipment	元/人	yuan/person	0.02	0.83	-0.81	-97.36
⑤其他服务性支出	Other Services	元/人	yuan/person	2.86	2.25	0.61	27.33
8.其他商品和服务消费支出	Other Goods and Services	元/人	yuan/person	64.75	46.13	18.62	40.35
A.其他商品支出	Other Goods	元/人	yuan/person	28.46	25.23	3.23	12.79
①首饰	Jewelry	元/人	yuan/person	4.46	3.06	1.4	45.87
②手表	Watch	元/人	yuan/person	0.3	0.43	-0.12	-28.47
③化妆品	Cosmetics	元/人	yuan/person	3.91	2.94	0.97	32.89
④迷信、宗教用品	Religious Appliances	元/人	yuan/person	4.24	3.82	0.43	11.19
⑤其他	Others	元/人	yuan/person	15.54	14.99	0.55	3.67
B.其他消费服务支出	Other Services	元/人	yuan/person	36.29	20.9	15.39	73.64
①旅馆住宿费	Hotel Accommodations	元/人	yuan/person	0.45	0.87	-0.42	-47.85
②美容美发	Beauty Salons	元/人	yuan/person	3.9	3.04	0.86	28.45
③殡殓费	Funeral Expenses	元/人	yuan/person	4.19	3.22	0.98	30.33
④生活消费借贷利息	Loan Interest of Household Consumption	元/人	yuan/person	0.53	0.09	0.44	506.98
⑤其他服务性支出	Other Services	元/人	yuan/person	27.21	13.69	13.52	98.79
(六）财产性支出	Expenditure for Properties	元/人	yuan/person	14.74	17.55	-2.81	-15.99
1.宅基地有偿使用费	Paid Use of Land	元/人	yuan/person	4.28	1.58	2.7	171.61
2.承包其他农户转让费	Contract on Other Farmers Transfer	元/人	yuan/person	8.62	14.18	-5.56	-39.21
3.其他	Others	元/人	yuan/person	1.84	1.8	0.05	2.72
(七）转移性支出	Expenditure for Transfers	元/人	yuan/person	187.81	159.11	28.69	18.03
#1.寄给带给家庭非常住人口	Sent to Non-permanent Resident	元/人	yuan/person	57.83	43.42	14.41	33.18
2.赠送农村亲友	Presentation to Relatives and Friends in Rural Area	元/人	yuan/person	54.53	52.86	1.67	3.16
3.赠送城市亲友	Presentation to Relatives and Friends in Urban Area	元/人	yuan/person	9.94	8.69	1.25	14.32

5-6 农村住户人均纯收入构成
Rural Inhabitant Average Per Person Net Income Constitution

类别	Classification	单位	Unit	2006	2005	增减 Add or Subtract	增幅 Increase Range
三、全年纯收入	**Net Income**	**元/人**	**yuan/person**	**4368.33**	**3930.55**	**437.78**	**11.14**
（一）工资性收入	Income from Wages and Salaries	元/人	yuan/person	1671.54	1437.57	233.97	16.28
1.在非企业组织中劳动得到收入	Incomes from Working in the Non-business Organizations	元/人	yuan/person	251.28	240.73	10.55	4.38
（1）乡村干部收入	Income of Village Cadres	元/人	yuan/person	133.25	125.86	7.39	5.87
（2）乡村教师收入	Income of Village Teacher	元/人	yuan/person	48.82	43.11	5.72	13.27
（3）行政事业单位等职工收入	Income from Working in Administrative Units	元/人	yuan/person	69.21	71.77	-2.55	-3.56
2.在本乡地域内劳动得到收入	Incomes from Working inside the Village	元/人	yuan/person	947.35	806.57	140.77	17.45
（1）在企业中劳动得到收入	Incomes from Working in Enterprises	元/人	yuan/person	611.94	522.63	89.3	17.09
a.乡镇企业收入	Township Enterprises	元/人	yuan/person	254.38	230.33	24.05	10.44
b.其他企业收入	Other Enterprises	元/人	yuan/person	357.56	292.31	65.25	22.32
（2）在国家投资基建项目得到收入	Income from Infrastructure Projects Invested by the Stat	元/人	yuan/person	6.55	4.89	1.67	34.12
（3）提供其他劳务收入	Other Labor Income	元/人	yuan/person	328.86	279.05	49.81	17.85
3.外出从业得到收入	Income from Working Somewhere away from Home	元/人	yuan/person	472.91	390.27	82.64	21.18
（1）在乡外县内从业得到收入	in the County but outside the Village	元/人	yuan/person	199.24	169.96	29.28	17.23
（2）在县外省内从业得到收入	in the Province but outside the County	元/人	yuan/person	205.02	163.82	41.2	25.15
（3）在省外国内从业得到收入	in China but outside the Province	元/人	yuan/person	68.43	56.43	12	21.27
（4）在国外从业得到收入	Abroad	元/人	yuan/person	0.22	0.06	0.16	279.85
（二）家庭经营纯收入	Net Income from Household Operations	元/人	yuan/person	2409.78	2258.05	151.74	6.72
1.第一产业纯收入	Net Income from Primary Industry	元/人	yuan/person	1824.97	1727.87	97.1	5.62
（1）农业收入	Net Income from Farming	元/人	yuan/person	1468.23	1376.86	91.37	6.64
（2）林业收入	Net Income from Forestry	元/人	yuan/person	64.23	48.51	15.72	32.4
（3）牧业收入	Net Income from Animal Husbandry	元/人	yuan/person	270.14	281.99	-11.85	-4.2
（4）渔业收入	Net Income from Fishery	元/人	yuan/person	22.37	20.51	1.86	9.06
2.非农产业纯收入	Net Income from Non-agricultural Industries	元/人	yuan/person	584.81	530.17	54.63	10.31
A.第二产业纯收入	Net Income from Secondary Industry	元/人	yuan/person	163.28	152.11	11.17	7.34
①工业收入	Industry	元/人	yuan/person	109.35	102.62	6.73	6.56
②建筑业收入	Construction	元/人	yuan/person	53.93	49.49	4.44	8.97
B.第三产业纯收入	Net Income from Tertiary Industry	元/人	yuan/person	421.53	378.06	43.47	11.5
①交通、运输、邮电业收入	Transport, Storage and Post	元/人	yuan/person	125.07	112.08	12.99	11.59
②批零贸易业、饮食业收入	Wholesale, Retail and Catering Trades	元/人	yuan/person	152.02	134.37	17.65	13.13

5-6 续表 1 continued

类别	Classification	单位	Unit	2006	2005	增减 Add or Subtract	增幅 Increase Range
③社会服务业收入	Social Services	元/人	yuan/person	57.45	43.89	13.55	30.88
④文教卫生业收入	Culture, Education and Health	元/人	yuan/person	26.02	22.61	3.41	15.06
⑤其他行业收入	Other Sectors	元/人	yuan/person	60.97	65.11	-4.13	-6.35
（三）财产性纯收入	Net Income from Properties	元/人	yuan/person	127.6	102.8	24.8	24.13
1.利息	Interest	元/人	yuan/person	10.78	9.75	1.03	10.51
2.集体分配股息和红利	Divident and Bonus Distributed by Mass	元/人	yuan/person	0.84	0.63	0.21	33.3
3.其他股息和红利	Other Divident and Bonus	元/人	yuan/person	2.47	2.02	0.45	22.4
4.租金（包括农业机械）	Rent (including Agricultural Machinery)	元/人	yuan/person	11.33	10.36	0.97	9.36
5.出让无形资产净收入	Selling Intangibles	元/人	yuan/person		0.11	-0.11	-100
6.储蓄性保险投资收入	Savings Insurance Investment	元/人	yuan/person	0.83	0.5	0.32	64.18
7.土地征用补偿收入	Compensation for Land Acquisition	元/人	yuan/person	51.61	46.21	5.4	11.69
8.转让承包土地经营权收入	Land Management Rights Transfer	元/人	yuan/person	6.54	2.56	3.98	155.68
9.其他投资收益	Other Investment Profits	元/人	yuan/person	0.46	0.38	0.08	20.51
10.其他	Others	元/人	yuan/person	42.73	30.26	12.47	41.21
（四）转移性纯收入	Net Income from Transfers	元/人	yuan/person	159.4	132.13	27.27	20.64
1.家庭非常住人口寄回和带回	Sent back by Non-permanent Resident	元/人	yuan/person	37.1	34.11	3	8.78
2.城市亲友赠送	Presentation from Relatives and Friends in Rural Area	元/人	yuan/person	23.54	21.18	2.36	11.16
3.离退休金、养老金	Old-age Pensions	元/人	yuan/person	20.16	17.69	2.47	13.96
4.城市亲友支付赡养费	Alimony Relatives and Friends in Urban Area	元/人	yuan/person	3.8	3.72	0.08	2.07
5.农村亲友支付赡养费	Alimony Relatives and Friends in Rural Area	元/人	yuan/person	5.6	5	0.6	11.92
6.救济金	Relief	元/人	yuan/person	1.57	0.61	0.95	155.37
7.抚恤金	Pensions	元/人	yuan/person	1.73	1.1	0.63	57.22
8.灾款	Disaster Relief	元/人	yuan/person	0.36	0.08	0.29	376.38
9.报销医疗费	Reimbursement for Medical Expenses	元/人	yuan/person	3.21	2.52	0.7	27.63
10.退税	Tax Rebates	元/人	yuan/person	0.12	0.13	-0.01	-7.92
11.退耕还林还草补贴	Subsidies for Returning Farmland to Forest and Grass	元/人	yuan/person	0.17	0.24	-0.07	-30.14
12.无偿扶贫或扶持款	Free of Help Sustain	元/人	yuan/person	1.24	0.94	0.31	32.8
13.得到赔款	Compensation	元/人	yuan/person	13.46	13.88	-0.42	-2.99
14.其他	Others	元/人	yuan/person	47.33	30.94	16.39	52.98
#粮食直接补贴收入	Grain direct subsidy income	元/人	yuan/person	11.34	10.5	0.84	8.03
购置和更新大型农机具补贴收入	Subsidy Income of Purchasing and Renewalling Large-scale Agricultural Tools and Machinery	元/人	yuan/person	1.3	0	1.29	66322.73
良种补贴收入（粮食种植）	Subsidies for Growing Superior Grain Cultivators	元/人	yuan/person	0.9	0.09	0.81	897.61
全年现金纯收入	Cash Income	元/人	yuan/person	4008.25	3553.13	455.11	12.81
全年实物纯收入	Net Income of Material Objects	元/人	yuan/person	360.08	377.41	-17.34	-4.59

5-7 农村住户现金收支情况

Cash Income and Expenditure of Rural Households

类别	Classification	单位	Unit	2006	2005	增减 Add or Subtract	增幅 Increase Range
一、期内现金收入	**Cash Income in the Term**	**元/人**	**yuan/person**	**5636.35**	**5114.45**	**521.9**	**10.2**
（一）工资性收入	Income from Wages and Salaries	元/人	yuan/person	1670.51	1434.64	235.87	16.44
1.在非企业组织中劳动得到收入	Incomes from Working in the Non-business Organizations	元/人	yuan/person	251.17	240.23	10.94	4.55
（1）乡村干部收入	Income of Village Cadres	元/人	yuan/person	133.16	125.45	7.71	6.15
（2）乡村教师收入	Income of Village Teacher	元/人	yuan/person	48.82	43.1	5.72	13.26
（3）行政事业单位等职工收入	Income from Working in Administrative Units	元/人	yuan/person	69.19	71.67	-2.49	-3.47
2.在本乡地域内劳动得到收入	Incomes from Working inside the Village	元/人	yuan/person	946.7	805.69	141.01	17.5
（1）在企业中劳动得到收入	Incomes from Working in Enterprises	元/人	yuan/person	611.54	521.93	89.61	17.17
a.乡镇企业收入	Township Enterprises	元/人	yuan/person	253.99	229.63	24.36	10.61
b.其他企业收入	Other Enterprises	元/人	yuan/person	357.56	292.31	65.25	22.32
（2）在国家投资基建项目得到收入	Income from Infrastructure Projects Invested by the State	元/人	yuan/person	6.55	4.89	1.67	34.12
（3）提供其他劳务收入	Other Labor Income	元/人	yuan/person	328.6	278.87	49.73	17.83
3.外出从业得到收入	Income from Working Somewhere away from Home	元/人	yuan/person	472.64	388.73	83.91	21.59
（1）在乡外县内从业得到收入	in the County but outside the Village	元/人	yuan/person	199.21	168.82	30.38	18
（2）在县外省内从业得到收入	in the Province but outside the County	元/人	yuan/person	204.93	163.52	41.4	25.32
（3）在省外国内从业得到收入	in China but outside the Province	元/人	yuan/person	68.28	56.32	11.96	21.24
（4）在国外从业得到收入	Abroad	元/人	yuan/person	0.22	0.06	0.16	279.85
（二）家庭经营现金收入	Cash Income from Household Operations	元/人	yuan/person	3651.79	3415.49	236.3	6.92
1.第一产业现金收入	Cash Income from Primary Industry	元/人	yuan/person	2812.22	2635.95	176.27	6.69
（1）农业现金收入	Cash Income from Farming	元/人	yuan/person	1865.47	1676.31	189.16	11.28
a.出售农产品收入	Farming Products	元/人	yuan/person	1806.51	1620.41	186.11	11.49
b.农业服务性收入	Income from Agricultural Services	元/人	yuan/person	58.95	55.91	3.05	5.45
①经营水利灌溉系统收入	Operating Irrigation	元/人	yuan/person	3.55	2.65	0.9	33.91
②农产品初加工收入	Processing of Agricultural Products	元/人	yuan/person	10.11	10.01	0.1	0.97
③提供机械和操作人收入	Providing Machinery and Operators	元/人	yuan/person	28.8	30.12	-1.32	-4.39
④其他服务收入	Other Services	元/人	yuan/person	16.49	13.12	3.37	25.72
（2）林业现金收入	Cash Income from Forestry	元/人	yuan/person	73.91	60.23	13.68	22.71
①出售林业产品收入	Forestry Products	元/人	yuan/person	69.55	57.94	11.61	20.04
②林业服务性收入	Income from Forestry Services	元/人	yuan/person	4.35	2.29	2.07	90.44

5-7　续表 1 continued

类别	Classification	单位	Unit	2006	2005	增减 Add or Subtract	增幅 Increase Range
（3）牧业现金收入	Cash Income from Animal Husbandry	元/人	yuan/person	831.21	862.78	-31.57	-3.66
①出售牧业产品收入	Animal Husbandry Products	元/人	yuan/person	827.18	855.23	-28.05	-3.28
②牧业服务性收入	Animal Husbandry Services	元/人	yuan/person	4.03	7.55	-3.52	-46.59
（4）渔业现金收入	Cash Income from Fishery	元/人	yuan/person	41.63	36.63	5.01	13.67
①出售渔业产品收入	Fishery Products	元/人	yuan/person	41	36.12	4.89	13.53
②渔业服务性收入	Fishery Services	元/人	yuan/person	0.63	0.51	0.12	23.49
2.第二产业现金收入	Cash Income from Secondary Industry	元/人	yuan/person	261.92	265.21	-3.28	-1.24
（1）工业收入	Industry	元/人	yuan/person	198.88	209.41	-10.53	-5.03
①出售工业产品收入	Industrial Products	元/人	yuan/person	75.24	67.26	7.98	11.86
②工业服务性收入	Industrial Services	元/人	yuan/person	123.64	142.15	-18.51	-13.02
（2）建筑业收入	Construction	元/人	yuan/person	63.04	55.8	7.25	12.99
①出售建筑业产品收入	Construction Products	元/人	yuan/person	0.88	1.48	-0.6	-40.6
②建筑业服务性收入	Construction Services	元/人	yuan/person	62.16	54.31	7.85	14.45
3.第三产业现金收入	Cash Income from Tertiary Industry	元/人	yuan/person	577.65	514.34	63.32	12.31
（1）出售其他产品收入	Other Products	元/人	yuan/person	2.25	2.25	0	0.16
（2）第三产业服务性现金收入	Tertiary Industry Services	元/人	yuan/person	575.4	512.09	63.31	12.36
a.交通、运输、邮电业收入	Transport, Storage and Post	元/人	yuan/person	175.98	166.45	9.53	5.72
b.批零贸易业、饮食业收入	Wholesale, Retail and Catering Trades	元/人	yuan/person	222.32	186.16	36.16	19.42
c.社会服务业收入	Social Services	元/人	yuan/person	67.55	54.87	12.68	23.1
d.文教卫生业收入	Culture, Education and Health	元/人	yuan/person	34.62	28.2	6.42	22.77
e.其他行业收入	Other Sectors	元/人	yuan/person	74.93	76.4	-1.47	-1.93
（三）财产性收入	Income from Properties	元/人	yuan/person	105.74	89.45	16.29	18.21
1.利息	Interest	元/人	yuan/person	10.78	9.75	1.03	10.51
2.集体分配股息和红利	Divident and Bonus Distributed by Mass	元/人	yuan/person	0.84	0.63	0.21	33.3
3.其他股息和红利	Other Divident and Bonus	元/人	yuan/person	2.47	2.02	0.45	22.4
4.租金（包括农业机械）	Rent (including Agricultural Machinery)	元/人	yuan/person	11.33	10.36	0.97	9.36
5.出让无形资产净收入	Selling Intangibles	元/人	yuan/person		0.11	-0.11	-100
6.储蓄性保险投资收入	Savings Insurance Investment	元/人	yuan/person	0.83	0.5	0.32	64.18
7.土地征用补偿收入	Compensation for Land Acquisition	元/人	yuan/person	51.61	46.21	5.4	11.69
8.转让承包土地经营权收入	Land Management Rights Transfer	元/人	yuan/person	6.54	2.56	3.98	155.68
9.其他投资收益	Other Investment Profits	元/人	yuan/person	0.46	0.38	0.08	20.51
10.其他	Others	元/人	yuan/person	20.87	16.91	3.96	23.4
（四）转移性收入	Income from Transfers	元/人	yuan/person	208.31	174.87	33.44	19.12
1.家庭非常住人口寄回和带回	Sent back by Non-permanent Resident	元/人	yuan/person	37.07	34.04	3.03	8.9

5-7 续表 2 continued

类别	Classification	单位	Unit	2006	2005	增减 Add or Subtract	增幅 Increase Range
2.城市亲友赠送	Presentation from Relatives and Friends in Rural Area	元/人	yuan/person	23.17	20.39	2.78	13.63
3.农村亲友赠送	Presentation from Relatives and Friends in Urban Area	元/人	yuan/person	55.04	48.55	6.49	13.36
4.离退休金、养老金	Old-age Pensions	元/人	yuan/person	20.16	17.69	2.47	13.96
5.城市亲友支付赡养费	Alimony Relatives and Friends in Urban Area	元/人	yuan/person	3.8	3.72	0.08	2.07
6.农村亲友支付赡养费	Alimony Relatives and Friends in Rural Area	元/人	yuan/person	5.6	5	0.6	11.92
7.救济金	Relief	元/人	yuan/person	1.57	0.61	0.95	155.37
8.抚恤金	Pensions	元/人	yuan/person	1.73	1.1	0.63	57.22
9.救灾款	Disaster Relief	元/人	yuan/person	0.36	0.08	0.29	376.38
10.报销医疗费	Reimbursement for Medical Expenses	元/人	yuan/person	3.21	2.52	0.7	27.63
11.退税	Tax Rebates	元/人	yuan/person	0.12	0.13	-0.01	-7.92
12.退耕还林还草补贴	Subsidies for Returning Farmland to Forest and Grass	元/人	yuan/person	0.14	0.24	-0.1	-41.88
13.无偿扶贫或扶持款	Free of Help Sustain	元/人	yuan/person	1.24	0.94	0.31	32.8
14.得到赔款	Compensation	元/人	yuan/person	13.46	13.88	-0.42	-2.99
15.其他	Others	元/人	yuan/person	41.63	25.97	15.66	60.29
#粮食直接补贴收入	Grain direct subsidy income	元/人	yuan/person	11.34	10.5	0.84	8.03
购置和更新大型农机具补贴收入	Subsidy Income of Purchasing and Renewalling Large-scale Agricultural Tools and Machinery	元/人	yuan/person	1.3	0	1.29	66322.73
良种补贴收入（粮食种植）	Subsidies for Growing Superior Grain Cultivators	元/人	yuan/person	0.9	0.09	0.81	897.61
二、非收入现金所得	**Non-Income Cash Proceeds**	**元/人**	**yuan/person**	**833.77**	**781.96**	**51.81**	**6.63**
（一）非借贷性现金所得	Non-lending Cash Proceeds	元/人	yuan/person	141.12	117.64	23.48	19.96
1.保险赔款	Insurance Payments	元/人	yuan/person	3.85	2.69	1.16	43.34
2.出售财物	Property Sales	元/人	yuan/person	45.74	41.34	4.4	10.65
3.出售役畜、产品畜	Draught and Commodity Animal Sales	元/人	yuan/person	7.29	1.49	5.8	389.14
4.彩票中奖所得	Lottery Winners	元/人	yuan/person	0.13	0.1	0.03	26.93
5.调查补贴	Investigation Subsidies	元/人	yuan/person	15.94	13.72	2.22	16.17
6.一次性工伤补贴	One-time Injuries Subsidies	元/人	yuan/person	1.25	2.11	-0.86	-40.86
7.婚、丧、嫁、娶礼金	Gifts of Marriage and Burial	元/人	yuan/person	61.48	52.08	9.4	18.05
8.其他（包括赌博所得）	Others (including Gambling Income)	元/人	yuan/person	5.43	4.1	1.33	32.33
（二）借贷性现金所得	Lending Cash Proceeds	元/人	yuan/person	692.65	664.32	28.33	4.26
1.银行、信用社贷款	Loans from Banks and Credit Union	元/人	yuan/person	67.77	56.93	10.84	19.04
2.借入款	Borrowing	元/人	yuan/person	206.79	210.35	-3.56	-1.69
3.收回借出款	Repayment	元/人	yuan/person	105.5	102.59	2.92	2.85
4.取回存款	Recovered Deposits	元/人	yuan/person	307.96	288.83	19.13	6.62
5.兑换债券（本金）	Converted Bonds	元/人	yuan/person	0.22	0.13	0.09	70.93
6.出售股票	Shares Sales	元/人	yuan/person	0.32		0.32	
7.兑换其他有价证券（本金）	Converted Other securities	元/人	yuan/person	0.52		0.52	

5-7 续表 3 continued

类别	Classification	单位	Unit	2006	2005	增减 Add or Subtract	增幅 Increase Range
8.收回其他投资款	Recovered Other Investments	元/人	yuan/person	0.86	2.25	-1.4	-61.9
9.其他	Others	元/人	yuan/person	2.71	3.24	-0.53	-16.35
三、期内现金支出	**Cash Expenditure in the Term**	元/人	yuan/person	**4711.96**	**4197.12**	**514.85**	**12.27**
(一) 生产费用支出	Expenditure of Production Costs	元/人	yuan/person	1622.43	1518.15	104.28	6.87
1.家庭经营费用支出	Expenditure for Household Operations	元/人	yuan/person	1471.27	1399.61	71.66	5.12
(1) 第一产业生产费用支出	Primary Industry	元/人	yuan/person	1286.21	1218.83	67.37	5.53
A.农业生产费用支出	Expenditure for Farming Production	元/人	yuan/person	773.25	696.58	76.67	11.01
a.购买农业生产资料	Production Materials of Farming	元/人	yuan/person	648.19	588.95	59.24	10.06
b.农业生产雇工工资	Wages for Farming Production	元/人	yuan/person	17.02	15.29	1.74	11.36
c.其他生产服务支出	Other Production Services	元/人	yuan/person	108.04	92.34	15.7	17
#借、贷款利息	Borrowing and lending Interest	元/人	yuan/person	0.95	1.23	-0.28	-22.42
排灌费	Charges for Irrigation and Drainage	元/人	yuan/person	12.84	11.14	1.71	15.35
机耕费	Charges for Farming with Mechines	元/人	yuan/person	35.2	30.31	4.89	16.13
修理费	Repair Charges	元/人	yuan/person	6.46	5.93	0.53	8.94
电费	Electricity Charges	元/人	yuan/person	9.11	7.23	1.88	25.95
B.林业生产费用支出	Expenditure for Forestry Production	元/人	yuan/person	15.79	10.92	4.87	44.61
a.购买林业生产资料	Production Materials of Forestry	元/人	yuan/person	13.48	9.43	4.05	42.95
b.林业生产雇工工资	Wages for Forestry Production	元/人	yuan/person	0.9	0.1	0.79	779.02
c.其他生产服务支出	Other Production Services	元/人	yuan/person	1.42	1.39	0.03	2.06
#借、贷款利息	Borrowing and lending Interest	元/人	yuan/person	0.12	0.2	-0.08	-38.19
修理费	Repair Charges	元/人	yuan/person	0.07	0.03	0.04	151.37
电费	Electricity Charges	元/人	yuan/person	0	0.02	-0.02	-83.04
C.牧业生产费用支出	Expenditure for Animal Husbandry Production	元/人	yuan/person	479.25	496.77	-17.52	-3.53
a.购买牧业生产资料	Production Materials of Animal Husbandry	元/人	yuan/person	463.72	483.49	-19.78	-4.09
b.牧业生产雇工工资	Wages for Animal Husbandry Production	元/人	yuan/person	2.36	1.1	1.25	113.75
c.其他生产服务支出	Other Production Services	元/人	yuan/person	13.18	12.17	1.01	8.28
#借、贷款利息	Borrowing and lending Interest	元/人	yuan/person	0.61	0.82	-0.21	-25.68
畜、禽防疫	Livestock and Poultry Vaccination	元/人	yuan/person	1.84	1.96	-0.11	-5.85
修理费	Repair Charges	元/人	yuan/person	0.24	0.33	-0.09	-26.83
电费	Electricity Charges	元/人	yuan/person	0.71	0.61	0.1	16.02
D.渔业生产费用支出	Expenditure for Fishery Production	元/人	yuan/person	17.91	14.57	3.34	22.95

5-7 续表 4 continued

类别	Classification	单位	Unit	2006	2005	增减 Add or Subtract	增幅 Increase Range
a.购买渔业生产资料	Production Materials of Fishery	元/人	yuan/person	7.71	13.55	-5.84	-43.1
b.渔业生产雇工工资	Wages for Fishery Production	元/人	yuan/person	0.01	0.19	-0.18	-97.32
c.其他生产服务支出	Other Production Services	元/人	yuan/person	10.19	0.82	9.37	1137.41
#借、贷款利息	Borrowing and lending Interest	元/人	yuan/person		0.46	-0.46	-100
修理费	Repair Charges	元/人	yuan/person	0.04	0.04	0	-4.74
电费	Electricity Charges	元/人	yuan/person	9.08	0.29	8.8	3075.29
(2) 第二产业生产费用支出	Secondary Industry	元/人	yuan/person	76.59	92.57	-15.98	-17.27
A.工业生产费用支出	Expenditure for Industry Production	元/人	yuan/person	69.28	87.82	-18.54	-21.11
a.购买工业生产资料	Production Materials of Industry	元/人	yuan/person	47.48	58.84	-11.36	-19.31
b.工业生产雇工工资	Wages for Industry Production	元/人	yuan/person	7.54	7.44	0.1	1.35
c.其他生产服务支出	Other Production Services	元/人	yuan/person	14.26	21.54	-7.27	-33.77
#借、贷款利息	Borrowing and lending Interest	元/人	yuan/person	2.99	0.94	2.06	220.22
修理费	Repair Charges	元/人	yuan/person	0.41	0.82	-0.41	-49.73
电费	Electricity Charges	元/人	yuan/person	3.08	4.47	-1.39	-31.11
B.建筑业生产费用支出	Expenditure for Construction Production	元/人	yuan/person	7.3	4.75	2.55	53.71
a.购买建筑业生产资料	Production Materials of Construction	元/人	yuan/person	2.7	1.13	1.57	138.16
b.建筑业生产雇工工资	Wages for Construction Production	元/人	yuan/person	3.5	2.4	1.09	45.46
c.其他生产服务支出	Other Production Services	元/人	yuan/person	1.11	1.21	-0.11	-8.79
#借、贷款利息	Borrowing and lending Interest	元/人	yuan/person		0	0	-100
修理费	Repair Charges	元/人	yuan/person	0.22	0.38	-0.16	-43.09
电费	Electricity Charges	元/人	yuan/person	0.06	0.07	-0.02	-23.39
(3) 第三产业生产费用支出	Tertiary Industry	元/人	yuan/person	108.47	88.2	20.27	22.98
A.交通运输邮电业生产费用支出	Expenditure for Production of Transport, Storage and Post	元/人	yuan/person	24.35	27.35	-3	-10.98
a.购买交通运输邮电业生产资料	Production Materials of Transport, Storage and Post	元/人	yuan/person	16.98	18.41	-1.43	-7.76
b.交通运输邮电业生产雇工工资	Wages for Production of Transport, Storage and Post	元/人	yuan/person	0.62	0.41	0.21	52.25
c.其他生产服务支出	Other Production Services	元/人	yuan/person	6.74	8.53	-1.79	-20.95
#借、贷款利息	Borrowing and Lending Interest	元/人	yuan/person	0.06	0.09	-0.03	-30.76
修理费	Repair Charges	元/人	yuan/person	3.64	3.69	-0.05	-1.48

5-7 续表 5 continued

类别	Classification	单位	Unit	2006	2005	增减 Add or Subtract	增幅 Increase Range
电费	Electricity Charges	元/人	yuan/person	0.01	0.02	0	-4.74
B.批零贸易餐饮业生产费用支出	Expenditure for Production of Wholesale, Retail and Catering Trades	元/人	yuan/person	57.37	38.66	18.71	48.39
a.购买批零贸易餐饮业生产资料	Production Materials of Wholesale, Retail and Catering Trades	元/人	yuan/person	29.02	25.48	3.55	13.92
b.批零贸易餐饮业生产雇工工资	Wages for Production of Wholesale, Retail and Catering Trades	元/人	yuan/person	6.91	3.68	3.23	87.88
c.其他生产服务支出	Other Production Services	元/人	yuan/person	21.44	9.51	11.93	125.47
#借、贷款利息	Borrowing and Lending Interest	元/人	yuan/person	0.14	0.16	-0.02	-14.23
电费	Electricity Charges	元/人	yuan/person	0.41	0.25	0.16	64.74
C.社会服务业生产费用支出	Expenditure for Production of Social Services	元/人	yuan/person	6.67	8.35	-1.68	-20.13
a.购买社会服务业生产资料	Production Materials of Social Services	元/人	yuan/person	4.57	6.3	-1.73	-27.48
b.社会服务业生产雇工工资	Wages for Production of Social Services	元/人	yuan/person	0.34	0.31	0.03	10.98
c.其他生产服务支出	Other Production Services	元/人	yuan/person	1.76	1.75	0.02	0.88
#借、贷款利息	Borrowing and Lending Interest	元/人	yuan/person	0.14	0.03	0.11	383.96
电费	Electricity Charges	元/人	yuan/person	0.52	0.41	0.11	26.01
D.文教卫生业生产费用支出	Expenditure for Production of Culture, Education and Health	元/人	yuan/person	7.34	4.37	2.97	68.08
a.购买文教卫生业生产资料	Production Materials of Culture, Education and Health	元/人	yuan/person	4.48	2.77	1.7	61.46
b.文教卫生业生产雇工工资	Wages for Production of Culture, Education and Health	元/人	yuan/person	0.71	0.41	0.3	72.66
c.其他生产服务支出	Other Production Services	元/人	yuan/person	2.15	1.18	0.97	82.05
#借、贷款利息	Borrowing and Lending Interest	元/人	yuan/person	0.35	0.02	0.33	1993.46
电费	Electricity Charges	元/人	yuan/person	0.03	0	0.03	1025.71
E.其他行业生产费用支出	Expenditure for Production of Other Secotrs	元/人	yuan/person	12.74	9.47	3.27	34.58
a.购买其他行业生产资料	Production Materials of Other Secotrs	元/人	yuan/person	9.26	4.23	5.03	119.14
b.其他行业生产雇工工资	Wages for Production of Other Secotrs	元/人	yuan/person	0.24	3.35	-3.11	-92.97
c.其他生产服务支出	Other Production Services	元/人	yuan/person	3.25	1.9	1.35	71.26
#借、贷款利息	Borrowing and Lending Interest	元/人	yuan/person	0.3	0.25	0.04	17.57
电费	Electricity Charges	元/人	yuan/person	0.1	0.16	-0.07	-40.72
2.购置生产性固定资产支出	Expenditure for Purchase of Productive Fixed Assets	元/人	yuan/person	149.36	117.14	32.22	27.5

5-7 续表 6 continued

类别	Classification	单位	Unit	2006	2005	增减 Add or Subtract	增幅 Increase Range
（1）购置建筑生产用建筑物材料	Purchase of Building Materials	元/人	yuan/person	13.65	23.26	-9.62	-41.34
（2）购买生产用房	Purchase of Production House	元/人	yuan/person	7.06	1.89	5.17	274.44
（3）购买役畜、产品畜	Purchase of Draught and Commodity Animal	元/人	yuan/person	3.89	6.9	-3	-43.58
（4）购买农林牧渔业机械	Purchase of Agricultural Machinery	元/人	yuan/person	44.84	39.43	5.42	13.74
（5）购买工业机械	Purchase of Industrial Machinery	元/人	yuan/person	28.78	2.14	26.64	1241.88
（6）购买运输机械	Purchase of Transport Machinery	元/人	yuan/person	38.14	35.19	2.95	8.38
（7）购买其他生产性固定资产	Purchase of Other Productive Fixed Assets	元/人	yuan/person	13	8.34	4.66	55.93
3.建、造生产性固定资产雇工支出	Expenditure for Building of Productive Fixed Assets	元/人	yuan/person	1.8	1.4	0.4	28.5
（二）税费支出	Expenditure for Taxes and Fees	元/人	yuan/person	21.03	33.65	-12.62	-37.51
1.第一产业税	Primary Industry	元/人	yuan/person	0.73	10.28	-9.55	-92.89
2.第二产业税	Secondary Industry	元/人	yuan/person	0.9	0.78	0.12	15.86
（1）工业生产纳税	Tax of Industry Production	元/人	yuan/person	0.9	0.77	0.14	17.82
（2）建筑业生产纳税	Tax of Construction Production	元/人	yuan/person		0.01	-0.01	-100
3.第三产业生产纳税	3.Tertiary Industry	元/人	yuan/person	3.47	3.07	0.4	12.88
4.其他各种收费	4.Other Charges	元/人	yuan/person	15.93	19.52	-3.59	-18.41
（三）生活消费支出	Expense on Household Consum -ption	元/人	yuan/person	2867.3	2470.39	396.91	16.07
#服务性支出	Expenditure for Services	元/人	yuan/person	1022.95	880.02	142.93	16.24
1.食品消费支出	Food	元/人	yuan/person	916.49	826.92	89.58	10.83
a.购买食品支出	Purchase of Food	元/人	yuan/person	730.03	660.22	69.81	10.57
①谷物	Cereal	元/人	yuan/person	51.37	45.86	5.51	12.02
②薯类	Tubers	元/人	yuan/person	3.63	3.86	-0.23	-5.98
③豆类	Beans	元/人	yuan/person	10.17	9.53	0.64	6.75
④食用油	Eatable Oil	元/人	yuan/person	38.77	50.07	-11.3	-22.56
⑤蔬菜及制品	Vegetable and Products	元/人	yuan/person	69.22	64.65	4.57	7.07
⑥肉、禽、蛋、奶及制品	Meat, Poultry, Egg, Milk and Their Products	元/人	yuan/person	232.85	236.9	-4.05	-1.71
⑦水产品及制品	Aquatic Products	元/人	yuan/person	33.86	33.07	0.79	2.39
⑧烟、酒	Tobacco and Liquor	元/人	yuan/person	156.58	155.93	0.65	0.41
⑨茶叶、饮料	Tea and Beverages	元/人	yuan/person	15.73	13.4	2.33	17.39
⑩其它类食品	Other Foods	元/人	yuan/person	117.85	46.96	70.89	150.96
b.食品消费服务性支出	Services for Foods Consumption	元/人	yuan/person	186.46	166.69	19.77	11.86
①在外饮食	Outward Dinner	元/人	yuan/person	173.27	156.65	16.62	10.61
②食品加工费	Foods Processing	元/人	yuan/person	6.63	7.63	-0.99	-13.04
③其他服务	Other Services	元/人	yuan/person	6.56	2.41	4.15	171.85
2.衣着	Clothing	元/人	yuan/person	197.11	158.67	38.45	24.23
a.购买衣着支出	Purchase of Clothing	元/人	yuan/person	195.46	156.66	38.8	24.77
①服装	Garments	元/人	yuan/person	126.15	95.21	30.93	32.49
②服装材料	Clothing Material	元/人	yuan/person	9.98	10.05	-0.06	-0.62
③鞋类	Footwear	元/人	yuan/person	48.65	42.31	6.34	14.98

5-7 续表 7 continued

类别	Classification	单位	Unit	2006	2005	增减 Add or Subtract	增幅 Increase Range
④其他	Others	元/人	yuan/person	10.68	9.09	1.59	17.49
b.衣着消费服务性支出	Services for Clothing Consumption	元/人	yuan/person	1.66	2.01	-0.35	-17.45
①衣着加工费	Clothing Proceeding Services	元/人	yuan/person	1.21	1.27	-0.06	-4.45
②其他服务	Other Services	元/人	yuan/person	0.44	0.74	-0.29	-39.82
3.居住	Residence	元/人	yuan/person	548	442.75	105.25	23.77
a.购买居住消费品支出	Purchase of Consumer Residence	元/人	yuan/person	412.32	328.88	83.44	25.37
①购买建筑生活用房材料	Construction Materials	元/人	yuan/person	249.1	197.43	51.67	26.17
②购买维修生活用房材料	Repair Materials	元/人	yuan/person	12.84	14.98	-2.14	-14.26
③装修生活用房材料	Decoration Materials	元/人	yuan/person	32.64	24.86	7.78	31.29
④购买生活用房	Household Housing	元/人	yuan/person	26.35	9.65	16.7	172.99
⑤购买生活用燃料	Household Fuels	元/人	yuan/person	91.4	81.97	9.43	11.5
b.居住消费服务性支出	Services for Residence	元/人	yuan/person	135.68	113.87	21.82	19.16
①建筑、维修生活用房雇工工资	Wages for Housing Construction and Repair	元/人	yuan/person	50.35	43.31	7.03	16.24
②房租	Rent	元/人	yuan/person	3.37	2.17	1.21	55.7
③生活用水	Household Water	元/人	yuan/person	4.04	2.91	1.13	38.67
④生活用电	Household Electricity	元/人	yuan/person	59.95	48.15	11.8	24.51
⑤清洁费、卫生费	Cleaning and Sanitation Costs	元/人	yuan/person	0.28	0.32	-0.04	-11.84
⑥其他	Others	元/人	yuan/person	17.68	17	0.68	4.02
4.家庭设备、用品及服务	Household Appliances	元/人	yuan/person	158.71	136.54	22.17	16.24
a.购买家庭设备、用品支出	Purchase of Household Appliances	元/人	yuan/person	150.03	127.99	22.03	17.21
①日用品	Goods for Daily Use	元/人	yuan/person	47.87	42.98	4.89	11.38
②床上用品	Bed Articles	元/人	yuan/person	11.95	9.51	2.44	25.65
③室内装饰品	Interior Decorations	元/人	yuan/person	4.97	4.26	0.71	16.73
④家俱类	Furniture	元/人	yuan/person	38.76	31.21	7.56	24.22
⑤机电设备	Electrical Equipment	元/人	yuan/person	46.48	40.04	6.43	16.06
b.家庭设备服务消费支出	Services for Household Appliances	元/人	yuan/person	8.69	8.55	0.14	1.62
①家庭设备修理费	Charges for Household Appliances Repair	元/人	yuan/person	4.09	3.26	0.83	25.57
②日杂用品加工修理费	Charges for Grocery Processing and Repair	元/人	yuan/person	1.54	1.55	-0.01	-0.5
③家政服务费	Charges for Household Services	元/人	yuan/person	0.71	0.81	-0.1	-12.71
④其他	Others	元/人	yuan/person	2.35	2.93	-0.58	-19.88
5.交通和通讯	Transport and Communications	元/人	yuan/person	352.19	294.37	57.82	19.64
a.购买交通和通讯用品支出	Purchase of Transport and Communications Goods	元/人	yuan/person	181.74	150.99	30.75	20.36
①交通工具	Transportation Facility	元/人	yuan/person	97.98	85.29	12.69	14.88
②交通工具用燃料	Fuels for Transportation Facility	元/人	yuan/person	36.59	28.58	8.01	28.01

5-7 续表 8 continued

类别	Classification	单位	Unit	2006	2005	增减 Add or Subtract	增幅 Increase Range
③交通工具用零配件	Parts of Transportation Facility	元/人	yuan/person	6.72	4.62	2.1	45.38
④通讯工具	Communication Facility	元/人	yuan/person	40.13	32.24	7.89	24.48
⑤通讯工具用零配件	Parts of Communication Facility	元/人	yuan/person	0.32	0.26	0.06	22.92
b.交通和通讯服务消费支出	Transport and Communications Services	元/人	yuan/person	170.45	143.38	27.08	18.88
①交通服务支出	Services for Transport	元/人	yuan/person	55.2	45	10.2	22.67
交通客运费	Passenger Traffic Charges	元/人	yuan/person	37.06	29.37	7.69	26.2
生活物品货运费	Freight Charges for Living Goods	元/人	yuan/person	0.48	0.63	-0.15	-24.41
交通工具修理费	Charges for Transportation Facility Repair	元/人	yuan/person	13.53	11.39	2.14	18.83
其他（过路过桥费等）	Other Services	元/人	yuan/person	4.14	3.62	0.52	14.38
②通讯服务支出	Services for Communications	元/人	yuan/person	115.25	98.38	16.87	17.15
邮寄费	Mailing Costs	元/人	yuan/person	0.78	0.88	-0.1	-10.91
通讯费	Communication Charges	元/人	yuan/person	113.28	96.16	17.11	17.8
通讯工具修理费	Charges for Communication Facility Repair	元/人	yuan/person	0.65	0.81	-0.16	-19.91
其他	Others	元/人	yuan/person	0.54	0.53	0.02	2.84
6.文化教育、娱乐用品及服务	Recreation, Education,Cultural and Services	元/人	yuan/person	408.84	377.16	31.67	8.4
a.购买文化教育、娱乐用品	Purchase of Culture, Education and Recreation Appliances	元/人	yuan/person	68.92	60.75	8.18	13.46
①文教、娱乐用机电消费品	Electrical Consumer Goods for Culture, Education and Recreation	元/人	yuan/person	38.89	34.21	4.68	13.67
②书、报、杂志	Books, Newspapers and Magazines	元/人	yuan/person	12.46	11.92	0.54	4.53
③纸张、文具	Paper and Stationery	元/人	yuan/person	4.95	4.21	0.75	17.74
④音像制品	Audio-visual Products	元/人	yuan/person	0.96	0.81	0.15	18.39
⑤电脑软件	Software	元/人	yuan/person	0.03	0.03	0	-3.18
⑥体育用品	Sport Goods	元/人	yuan/person	0.27	0.11	0.16	148.07
⑦计算机零配件及耗材	Computer Parts and Materials	元/人	yuan/person	0.09	0.07	0.02	23.67
⑧鲜花	Flower	元/人	yuan/person	0.17	0.15	0.02	15.04
⑨娱乐用品	Recreation Goods	元/人	yuan/person	6.27	4.92	1.35	27.4
⑩其他用品	Other Goods	元/人	yuan/person	4.83	4.32	0.51	11.91
b.教育服务消费	Education Services	元/人	yuan/person	311.18	293.27	17.92	6.11
①托儿费	Child-care Fee	元/人	yuan/person	3.67	3.52	0.15	4.21
②幼儿园赞助费	Sponsor Fee for Kindergarten	元/人	yuan/person	2.14	0.77	1.37	178.84
③学杂费	Tuition Fee	元/人	yuan/person	270.09	262.46	7.63	2.91
④入学赞助费	Sponsor Fee for School Entrance	元/人	yuan/person	2.42	2.75	-0.33	-12.15
⑤私立学校就读费	Student Fee for Private Schools Entrance	元/人	yuan/person	1.75	2.08	-0.33	-16.04
⑥成人培训费	Adult Training Expenses	元/人	yuan/person	14.32	6.7	7.62	113.72
⑦教育设备修理费	Repair Charges for Education Equipment	元/人	yuan/person	0.23	0.05	0.18	402.31

5-7 续表 9 continued

类别	Classification	单位	Unit	2006	2005	增减 Add or Subtract	增幅 Increase Range
⑧其他	Others	元/人	yuan/person	16.58	14.94	1.64	10.96
c.文化、体育、娱乐服务消费	Services for Culture, Sports and Recreation	元/人	yuan/person	28.73	23.15	5.58	24.1
①旅游	Tourism	元/人	yuan/person	4.6	1.91	2.69	140.71
②休闲娱乐费	Recreation Costs	元/人	yuan/person	4.09	3.23	0.86	26.62
③文化、体育、娱乐用品修理费	Repair Charges for Culture, Sports and Recreation Goods	元/人	yuan/person	3.63	3.41	0.22	6.39
④其他	Others	元/人	yuan/person	16.41	14.6	1.81	12.42
7.医疗保健	Health Care	元/人	yuan/person	221.8	188.48	33.33	17.68
a.购买医疗保健用品	Purchase of Health Care Appliances	元/人	yuan/person	78	80.27	-2.27	-2.83
①购买医疗卫生用品	Medical Appliances	元/人	yuan/person	74.18	76.58	-2.39	-3.12
药品	Medicine	元/人	yuan/person	72.23	74.69	-2.46	-3.29
医疗卫生器械	Medical Equipment	元/人	yuan/person	0.56	1.05	-0.49	-46.53
其他医疗卫生用品	Other Medical Appliances	元/人	yuan/person	1.39	0.84	0.56	66.38
②保健用品	Health Appliances	元/人	yuan/person	3.82	3.69	0.12	3.29
药品类保健品	Drugs Health Products	元/人	yuan/person	1.72	1.33	0.39	29.65
保健器材	Health Equipment	元/人	yuan/person	2.09	2.37	-0.27	-11.52
b.医疗保健服务消费支出	Health Care Services	元/人	yuan/person	143.8	108.21	35.6	32.9
①医疗费	Medical Charges	元/人	yuan/person	138.77	103.43	35.34	34.17
②医疗设备修理费	Repair Charges for Medical Equipment	元/人	yuan/person	0.22	0.19	0.02	11.59
③保健费	Health Charges	元/人	yuan/person	1.93	1.51	0.43	28.38
④保健设备修理费	Repair Charges for Health Equipment	元/人	yuan/person	0.02	0.83	-0.81	-97.36
⑤其他	Others	元/人	yuan/person	2.86	2.25	0.61	27.33
8.其他商品和服务	Other Goods and Services	元/人	yuan/person	64.15	45.51	18.64	40.97
a.购买其他商品支出	Purchase of Other Goods	元/人	yuan/person	27.86	24.61	3.25	13.22
①首饰	Jewelry	元/人	yuan/person	4.46	3.06	1.4	45.87
②手表	Watch	元/人	yuan/person	0.3	0.43	-0.12	-28.47
③化妆品	Cosmetics	元/人	yuan/person	3.91	2.94	0.97	32.89
④迷信、宗教用品	Religious Appliances	元/人	yuan/person	4.24	3.82	0.43	11.19
⑤其他	Others	元/人	yuan/person	14.94	14.36	0.58	4.02
b.其他消费服务支出	Other Services	元/人	yuan/person	36.29	20.9	15.39	73.64
①旅馆住宿费	Hotel Accommodations	元/人	yuan/person	0.45	0.87	-0.42	-47.85
②美容美发	Beauty Salons	元/人	yuan/person	3.9	3.04	0.86	28.45
③殡殓费	Funeral Expenses	元/人	yuan/person	4.19	3.22	0.98	30.33
④生活消费借贷利息	Loan Interest of Household Consumption	元/人	yuan/person	0.53	0.09	0.44	506.98
⑤其他服务	Other Services	元/人	yuan/person	27.21	13.69	13.52	98.79
（四）财产性支出	Expenditure for Properties	元/人	yuan/person	14.74	17.55	-2.81	-15.99
1.宅基地有偿使用费	Paid Use of Land	元/人	yuan/person	4.28	1.58	2.7	171.61
2.承包其他农户转让	Contract on Other Farmers Transfer	元/人	yuan/person	8.62	14.18	-5.56	-39.21
3.其他	Others	元/人	yuan/person	1.84	1.8	0.05	2.72

5-7 续表 10 continued

类别	Classification	单位	Unit	2006	2005	增减 Add or Subtract	增幅 Increase Range
（五）转移性支出	Expenditure for Transfers	元/人	yuan/person	186.47	157.38	29.09	18.48
1.寄给带给家庭非常住人口现金	Sent to Non-permanent Resident	元/人	yuan/person	57.76	43.42	14.34	33.03
2.赠送农村亲友	Presentation to Relatives and Friends in Rural Area	元/人	yuan/person	53.58	51.58	2	3.88
3.赠送城市亲友	Presentation to Relatives and Friends in Urban Area	元/人	yuan/person	9.62	8.31	1.31	15.72
4.交纳医疗保险	Medical Insurance	元/人	yuan/person	8.02	7.11	0.91	12.76
5.交纳社会保障基金	Social Security Funds	元/人	yuan/person	14.05	7.18	6.87	95.64
6.购买非储蓄性保险	Non-saving Insurance	元/人	yuan/person	16.79	14.61	2.18	14.94
7.赡养费	Alimony	元/人	yuan/person	9.43	7.48	1.95	26.13
8.其他直接税	Other Direct Taxes	元/人	yuan/person	0.62	1.24	-0.62	-50.37
9.捐赠	Donation	元/人	yuan/person	1.18	1.53	-0.35	-22.99
10.罚款、赔款	Fine and Compensation	元/人	yuan/person	5.91	4.77	1.14	23.8
11.其他	Others	元/人	yuan/person	9.52	10.15	-0.63	-6.23
四、非消费性支出	**Non-consumption Expenditure**	元/人	yuan/person	**931.41**	**848.72**	**82.68**	**9.74**
（一）非借贷性支出	Non-lending Expenditure	元/人	yuan/person	177.45	160.67	16.79	10.45
1.购买彩票	Purchase of Lottery	元/人	yuan/person	0.41	0.91	-0.51	-55.51
2.婚、丧、嫁、娶支出	Expenditure for Marriage and Burial	元/人	yuan/person	170.16	154.08	16.08	10.44
3.交纳党费、团费	Party Membership and League	元/人	yuan/person	0.7	0.45	0.25	56.57
4.迷信、宗教活动捐赠	Donation to Religious Activities	元/人	yuan/person	0.75	1.04	-0.29	-27.85
5.其他	Others	元/人	yuan/person	5.43	4.18	1.25	29.88
（二）储蓄、借贷性支出	Savings and Loan Expenditure	元/人	yuan/person	753.96	688.06	65.9	9.58
1.归还银行、信用社	Repayment to Bank and Credit Union	元/人	yuan/person	34.1	56.82	-22.72	-39.98
2.借出款	Lending Money	元/人	yuan/person	66.06	60.15	5.91	9.82
3.归还借款	Repayment	元/人	yuan/person	132.32	154.2	-21.88	-14.19
4.存款	Deposits	元/人	yuan/person	510.71	399.5	111.21	27.84
5.购债券	Purchase of Notes	元/人	yuan/person	0.1	0.65	-0.55	-84.23
6.购买储蓄性保险	Purchase of Savings Insurance	元/人	yuan/person	7.89	5.3	2.59	48.81
7.购买股票	Purchase of Stock	元/人	yuan/person	1.11	9.16	-8.05	-87.87
8.其他	8.Others	元/人	yuan/person	1.66	2.27	-0.61	-26.69
五、期末金融资产余额	**Balance of Financial Assets at Term-end**	元/人	yuan/person	**4911.94**	**3956.28**	**955.65**	**24.16**
1.手存现金	Cash in Hand	元/人	yuan/person	999.07	867.74	131.34	15.14
2.存款余额	Deposits	元/人	yuan/person	3896.63	3050.63	846	27.73
3.债券价值款	Notes	元/人	yuan/person	5.36	3.25	2.11	64.91
4.股票价值金	Stock	元/人	yuan/person	1.62	4.83	-3.21	-66.44
5.其他金融资产价值	Other Financial Assets	元/人	yuan/person	9.26	29.84	-20.58	-68.98
六、期末债务余额	**Debt at Term-end**	元/人	yuan/person	**261.64**	**258.25**	**3.39**	**1.31**
1.银行、信用社贷款	Bank and Credit Union Loan	元/人	yuan/person	122.45	83.84	38.62	46.07
2.乡村集体组织、企业借款	Rural Collective Organizations and Enterprises Borrowing	元/人	yuan/person	12.77	22.47	-9.7	-43.15
3.个人借（欠）款	Individual Borrowing	元/人	yuan/person	124.26	144.92	-20.67	-14.26
4.其他	Others	元/人	yuan/person	2.16	7.02	-4.86	-69.28

5-8 农村居民出售产品情况
Product Sales of Rural Households

类别	Classification	单位	Unit	2006	2005	增减 Add or Subtract	增幅 Increase Range
一、农业	**Farming**			**1806.51**	**1620.41**	**186.11**	**11.49**
（一）谷物数量	Cereal Amount	公斤/人	kg/person	469.05	417.92	51.13	12.23
金额	Sum	元/人	yuan/person	595.57	530.35	65.23	12.3
#1.出售普通小麦数量	Amount of Ordinary Wheat	公斤/人	kg/person	141.27	125.44	15.82	12.61
出售普通小麦金额	Sum of Ordinary Wheat	元/人	yuan/person	188.71	174.37	14.34	8.22
2.出售优质小麦数量	Amount of Quality Wheat	公斤/人	kg/person	59.84	42.39	17.45	41.17
出售优质小麦金额	Sum of Quality Wheat	元/人	yuan/person	81.28	60.2	21.09	35.03
3.出售小麦种子数量	Amount of Wheat Seed	公斤/人	kg/person	5.22	3.73	1.49	39.89
出售小麦种子金额	Sum of Wheat Seed	元/人	yuan/person	8.04	7.06	0.97	13.76
4.出售普通稻谷数量	Amount of Ordinary Rice	公斤/人	kg/person		4.87	-4.87	-100
出售普通稻谷金额	Sum of Ordinary Rice	元/人	yuan/person		7.96	-7.96	-100
5.出售优质稻谷数量	Amount of Quality Rice	公斤/人	kg/person	6.97	3.9	3.07	78.85
出售优质稻谷金额	Sum of Quality Rice	元/人	yuan/person	12.04	6.6	5.44	82.39
6.出售稻谷种子数量	Amount of Rice Seed	公斤/人	kg/person	0.24		0.24	
出售稻谷种子金额	Sum of Rice Seed	元/人	yuan/person	0.44		0.44	
7.出售普通玉米数量	Amount of Ordinary Corn	公斤/人	kg/person	184.74	179.25	5.5	3.07
出售普通玉米金额	Sum of Ordinary Corn	元/人	yuan/person	217.77	204.38	13.38	6.55
8.出售优质玉米数量	Amount of Quality Corn	公斤/人	kg/person	69.04	57.1	11.94	20.91
出售优质玉米金额	Sum of Quality Corn	元/人	yuan/person	82.69	67.05	15.65	23.34
9.出售玉米种子数量	Amount of Corn Seed	公斤/人	kg/person	0.96	0.78	0.18	22.97
出售玉米种子金额	Sum of Corn Seed	元/人	yuan/person	2.6	1.89	0.71	37.5
10.出售高粱数量	Amount of Chinese Sorghum	公斤/人	kg/person	0.12	0.09	0.02	27.26
出售高粱金额	Sum of Chinese Sorghum	元/人	yuan/person	0.14	0.12	0.02	12.69
11.出售谷子数量	Amount of Millet	公斤/人	kg/person	0.06	0.02	0.04	284.86
出售谷子金额	Sum of Millet	元/人	yuan/person	0.11	0.02	0.09	379.95
12.出售青稞数量	Amount of Highland Barley	公斤/人	kg/person				
出售青稞金额	Sum of Highland Barley	元/人	yuan/person				
13.出售其他谷物数量	Amount of Other Grains	公斤/人	kg/person	0.21	0.2	0.01	4.54
出售其他谷物金额	Sum of Other Grains	元/人	yuan/person	0.22	0.18	0.04	19.65
14.出售其他种子数量	Amount of Other Seeds	公斤/人	kg/person	0.38	0.15	0.23	157.06
出售其他种子金额	Sum of Other Seeds	元/人	yuan/person	1.53	0.51	1.03	203.33
（二）出售薯类数量	Amount of Tubers	公斤/人	kg/person	7.26	4.03	3.23	80.25
出售薯类金额	Sum of Tubers	元/人	yuan/person	17.55	11.35	6.19	54.56
（三）出售豆类数量	Amount of Beans	公斤/人	kg/person	2.05	2.92	-0.87	-29.81
出售豆类金额	Sum of Beans	元/人	yuan/person	5.16	7.27	-2.11	-28.99

5-8 续表 1 continued

类别	Classification	单位	Unit	2006	2005	增减 Add or Subtract	增幅 Increase Range
（四）出售棉花数量	Amount of Cotton	公斤/人	kg/person	60.12	58.05	2.07	3.57
出售棉花金额	Sum of Cotton	元/人	yuan/person	333	284.52	48.47	17.04
（五）出售油料数量	Amount of Oil	公斤/人	kg/person	23.86	25.07	-1.22	-4.85
出售油料金额	Sum of Oil	元/人	yuan/person	83.92	84.02	-0.1	-0.12
（六）出售麻类数量	Amount of Flaxen	公斤/人	kg/person	0.12	0.06	0.07	123.01
出售麻类金额	Sum of Flaxen	元/人	yuan/person	0.57	0.42	0.16	37.78
（七）出售糖料数量	Amount of Sugar	公斤/人	kg/person	0.08		0.08	
出售糖料金额	Sum of Sugar	元/人	yuan/person	0.04		0.04	
（八）出售烟草数量	Amount of Tobacco	公斤/人	kg/person	1.26	0.93	0.32	34.33
出售烟草金额	Sum of Tobacco	元/人	yuan/person	11.37	7.92	3.44	43.43
（九）出售蔬菜数量	Amount of Vegetables	公斤/人	kg/person	344.33	338.87	5.46	1.61
出售蔬菜金额	Sum of Vegetables	元/人	yuan/person	487.21	430.52	56.69	13.17
（十）出售花卉、园艺金额	Sum of Flower and Gardening	元/人	yuan/person	3	2.36	0.64	27.19
（十一）出售瓜类数量	Amount of Melons	公斤/人	kg/person	68.04	62.26	5.78	9.28
出售瓜类金额	Sum of Melons	元/人	yuan/person	82.92	67.3	15.62	23.2
#出售西瓜数量	Amount of Watermelons	公斤/人	kg/person	62.24	55.37	6.87	12.41
出售西瓜金额	Sum of Watermelons	元/人	yuan/person	65.01	52.21	12.8	24.51
（十二）出售园林水果数量	Amount of Fruits	公斤/人	kg/person	76.84	79.69	-2.85	-3.58
出售园林水果金额	Sum of Fruits	元/人	yuan/person	164.27	155.68	8.59	5.51
#1.出售苹果数量	Amount of Apples	公斤/人	kg/person	38.54	40.58	-2.04	-5.03
出售苹果金额	Sum of Apples	元/人	yuan/person	72.71	63.76	8.95	14.04
2.出售梨数量	Amount of Pear	公斤/人	kg/person	4.41	4.45	-0.04	-0.97
出售梨金额	Sum of Pear	元/人	yuan/person	6.39	6.34	0.05	0.8
3.出售葡萄数量	Amount of Grape	公斤/人	kg/person	6.74	7.15	-0.41	-5.77
出售葡萄金额	Sum of Grape	元/人	yuan/person	21.78	18.84	2.95	15.64
4.出售桃数量	Amount of Peaches	公斤/人	kg/person	11.39	14.49	-3.1	-21.4
出售桃金额	Sum of Peaches	元/人	yuan/person	17.4	23.24	-5.84	-25.14
5.出售杏数量	Amount of Apricots	公斤/人	kg/person	2.02	1.58	0.44	28.11
出售杏金额	Sum of Apricots	元/人	yuan/person	3.53	2.81	0.71	25.39
6.出售枣数量	Amount of Jujubes	公斤/人	kg/person	7.81	5.91	1.9	32.17
出售枣金额	Sum of Jujubes	元/人	yuan/person	25.24	24.85	0.39	1.57
7.出售柿子数量	Amount of Persimmon	公斤/人	kg/person	0.74	0.57	0.16	28.4
出售柿子金额	Sum of Persimmon	元/人	yuan/person	1.16	1.08	0.09	8.23
（十三）出售茶叶和其他饮料金额	Sum of Tea and Other Beverages	元/人	yuan/person				
（十四）出售中药材数量	Amount of Chinese Herbal Medicines	公斤/人	kg/person	1.16	1.82	-0.66	-36.36

5-8 续表 2 continued

类别	Classification	单位	Unit	2006	2005	增减 Add or Subtract	增幅 Increase Range
出售中药材金额	Sum of Chinese Herbal Medicines	元/人	yuan/person	9.45	9.9	-0.45	-4.55
（十五）出售其他种植业产品金额	Sum of Other Planting Products	元/人	yuan/person	0.71	17.31	-16.6	-95.88
（十六）出售采集野生植物金额	Sum of Wild Plants	元/人	yuan/person	0.03	0.03	0	-1.42
（十七）出售农作物副产品数量	Amount of Agricultural By-products	公斤/人	kg/person	23.2	23.7	-0.5	-2.1
出售农作物副产品金额	Sum of Agricultural By-products	元/人	yuan/person	7.26	8.67	-1.41	-16.27
（十八）出售手工业产品金额	Sum of Handicrafts	元/人	yuan/person	3.7	2.33	1.37	58.7
（十九）出售专用农产品金额	Sum of Specialized Farm Products	元/人	yuan/person	0.76	0.44	0.32	73.56
二、林业	**Forestry**			**69.55**	**57.94**	**11.61**	**20.04**
（一）出售采集林产品金额	Sum of Forestry Products	元/人	yuan/person	4.4	3.24	1.16	35.7
1.出售天然林和人工林地采集果实	Fruit of Natural Forest and Artificial Forest	元/人	yuan/person	4.1	2.91	1.2	41.23
2.出售采集野生植物和果实金额	Wild Plant and Fruit	元/人	yuan/person	0.3	0.34	-0.04	-12
（二）出售竹木金额	Sum of Bamboo	元/人	yuan/person	51.92	40.66	11.26	27.69
（三）出售育种、育苗金额	Sum of Breeding Nursery	元/人	yuan/person	11.32	12.07	-0.75	-6.2
（四）出售林业副产品金额	Sum of Forestry By-products	元/人	yuan/person	1.25	1.81	-0.55	-30.69
（五）出售林业手工业产品金额	Sum of Handicrafts	元/人	yuan/person	0.66	0.16	0.49	304.37
三、牧业	**Animal Husbandry**			**827.18**	**855.23**	**-28.05**	**-3.28**
（一）出售肉猪及猪肉总重量	Amount of Pigs and Meat	公斤/人	kg/person	36.59	32.56	4.03	12.37
出售肉猪及猪肉总金额	Sum of Pigs and Meat	元/人	yuan/person	320.97	339.54	-18.58	-5.47
（二）出售菜羊及羊肉总重量	Amount of Sheep and Mutton	公斤/人	kg/person	1.28	1.79	-0.51	-28.54
出售菜羊及羊肉总金额	Sum of Sheep and Mutton	元/人	yuan/person	16.73	22.29	-5.56	-24.94
（三）出售肉牛及牛肉总重量	Amount of Cattle and Beef	公斤/人	kg/person	4.68	5.53	-0.85	-15.35
出售肉牛及牛肉总金额	Sum of Cattle and Beef	元/人	yuan/person	58.12	62.93	-4.81	-7.64
（四）出售其他活家畜及自宰畜头数	Amount of Living and Killed Livestock	头/人	head/person	0.01	0.01	0	-13.53
出售其他活家畜及自宰畜肉重量	Amount of Meat of Living and Killed Livestock	公斤/人	kg/person	0.05	0.08	-0.03	-42.99
出售其他活家畜及自宰畜肉金额	Sum of Living and Killed Livestock	元/人	yuan/person	0.52	0.79	-0.27	-34.52
（五）出售家禽总重量	Amount of Livestock	公斤/人	kg/person	28.14	28.2	-0.05	-0.19

5-8 续表 3 continued

类别	Classification	单位	Unit	2006	2005	增减 Add or Subtract	增幅 Increase Range
出售家禽总金额	Sum of Livestock	元/人	yuan/person	180.57	182.69	-2.13	-1.17
（六）出售蛋类的数量	Amount of Eggs	公斤/人	kg/person	22.21	20.7	1.51	7.3
出售蛋类的金额	Sum of Eggs	元/人	yuan/person	105.16	107.95	-2.78	-2.58
（七）出售畜皮数量	Amount of Leather	张/人	Amount/person	0.12	0.07	0.04	59
出售畜皮金额	Sum of Leather	元/人	yuan/person	33.06	19.08	13.98	73.26
（八）出售毛、绒数量	Amount of Feather and Cashmere	公斤/人	kg/person	0.02	0.01	0	8.09
出售毛、绒金额	Sum of Feather and Cashmere	元/人	yuan/person	1.74	1.52	0.23	14.87
（九）出售奶类数量	Amount of Milk	公斤/人	kg/person	3.85	4.16	-0.31	-7.54
出售奶类金额	Sum of Milk	元/人	yuan/person	6.59	7.31	-0.72	-9.91
（十）出售仔、幼、育肥畜禽和小动物	Sum of Young Animals	元/人	yuan/person	43.82	65.81	-22	-33.42
#仔猪数量	Amount of Piglets	只/人	head/person	0.15	0.24	-0.1	-39.53
仔猪金额	Sum of Piglets	元/人	yuan/person	25.06	51.3	-26.25	-51.16
（十一）出售其他牧业产品金额	Sum of Other Animal Husbandry Products	元/人	yuan/person	55.3	39.88	15.42	38.66
1.出售小动物（包括自宰）金额	Sum of Micro-organism	元/人	yuan/person	8.77	7.78	0.99	12.73
2.出售虫类金额	Sum of Worm	元/人	yuan/person	0.21	0.03	0.19	747.11
3.出售其他畜产品金额	Sum of Animal By-products	元/人	yuan/person	46.31	32.07	14.24	44.39
#蚕茧数量	Amount of Silkworm Cocoon	公斤/人	kg/person	1.61	1.49	0.12	7.8
蚕茧金额	Sum of Silkworm Cocoon	元/人	yuan/person	45.57	31.46	14.1	44.83
（十二）出售狩猎和捕捉野生动物	Sum of Hunting and Trapping Wild Animal	元/人	yuan/person	0.59	0.87	-0.27	-31.44
（十三）出售牧业副产品金额	Sum of Animal Husbandry By-products	元/人	yuan/person	3.73	4.06	-0.32	-7.97
（十四）出售牧业手工业产品金额	Sum of Handicrafts	元/人	yuan/person	0.26	0.48	-0.22	-46.34
四、渔业	**Fishery**			**41**	**36.12**	**4.89**	**13.53**
（一）出售水产品金额	Sum of Aquatic Products	元/人	yuan/person	31.19	22.76	8.43	37.06
1.出售海水产品金额	Sum of Seawater Products	元/人	yuan/person	30.53	22.35	8.18	36.58
#鱼类数量	Amount of Fish	公斤/人	kg/person	1.25	0.43	0.82	188.56
鱼类金额	Sum of Fish	元/人	yuan/person	25.5	15.66	9.84	62.81
2.出售淡水产品金额	Sum of Fresh Water Products	元/人	yuan/person	0.67	0.41	0.26	63.48
#鱼类数量	Amount of Fish	公斤/人	kg/person	0.13	0.05	0.08	144.86
鱼类金额	Sum of Fish	元/人	yuan/person	0.67	0.27	0.39	144.88
（二）出售渔业副产品金额	Sum of Fishery By-products	元/人	yuan/person	9.49	13	-3.51	-27.01
（三）出售渔业手工业产品金额	Sum of Handicrafts	元/人	yuan/person	0.32	0.36	-0.04	-10.15

5-9 农村居民购买商品情况
Product Sales of Rural Households

类别	Classification	单位	Unit	2006	2005	增减 Add or Subtract	增幅 Increase Range
一、购买生活消费品情况	**Purchase of Living Consumer Goods**			**1844.35**	**1590.37**	**253.98**	**15.97**
（一）食品类	Food			730.03	660.22	69.81	10.57
1.购买谷物数量	Cereal	公斤/人	kg/person	30.64	27.82	2.83	10.16
金额	Sum	元/人	yuan/person	51.37	45.86	5.51	12.02
2.购买薯类	Tubers	公斤/人	kg/person	0.56	0.63	-0.07	-11.05
金额	Sum	元/人	yuan/person	3.63	3.86	-0.23	-5.98
3.购买豆类	Beans	公斤/人	kg/person	3.51	3.11	0.41	13.05
金额	Sum	元/人	yuan/person	10.17	9.53	0.64	6.75
4.购买食用油	Eatable Oil	公斤/人	kg/person	5.64	8.76	-3.12	-35.59
金额	Sum	元/人	yuan/person	38.77	50.07	-11.3	-22.56
5.购买蔬菜及制品金额	Vegetables and Products	元/人	yuan/person	69.22	64.65	4.57	7.07
（1）购买蔬菜	Vegetables	公斤/人	kg/person	43.18	43.74	-0.56	-1.28
金额	Sum	元/人	yuan/person	63.73	59.32	4.41	7.43
（2）干菜及蔬菜制品金额	Dried Vegetables and Vegetables Product	元/人	yuan/person	5.49	5.32	0.16	3.07
#购买干菜	Dried Vegetables	公斤/人	kg/person	0.42	0.47	-0.05	-10.88
金额	Sum	元/人	yuan/person	2.85	2.82	0.04	1.32
6.购买肉、禽、蛋、奶及其制品金额	Meat, Poultry, Egg, Milk and Products	元/人	yuan/person	232.85	236.9	-4.05	-1.71
#（1）购买猪肉	Pork	公斤/人	kg/person	8.38	7.86	0.52	6.63
金额	Sum	元/人	yuan/person	92.57	97.62	-5.06	-5.18
（2）购买牛肉	Beef	公斤/人	kg/person	0.25	0.29	-0.03	-10.79
金额	Sum	元/人	yuan/person	4.12	4.32	-0.21	-4.79
（3）购买羊肉	Mutton	公斤/人	kg/person	0.33	0.33	0.01	1.99
金额	Sum	元/人	yuan/person	5.94	5.54	0.4	7.22
（4）购买鸡	Chicken	公斤/人	kg/person	2.19	2.44	-0.25	-10.13
金额	Sum	元/人	yuan/person	18.81	21.91	-3.1	-14.16
（5）购买鸭	Duck	公斤/人	kg/person	0.03	0.04	-0.01	-21.68
金额	Sum	元/人	yuan/person	0.35	0.42	-0.07	-16.25
（6）购买鲜鸡蛋	Fresh Hen's Eggs	公斤/人	kg/person	9.6	9.2	0.4	4.38
金额	Sum	元/人	yuan/person	47.81	50.32	-2.51	-4.99
（7）购买鲜鸭蛋	Fresh Duck's Eggs	公斤/人	kg/person	0.11	0.1	0.01	11.55
金额	Sum	元/人	yuan/person	0.57	0.57	0	0.68
（8）购买鲜奶	Fresh Milk	公斤/人	kg/person	4.87	4.15	0.71	17.13
金额	Sum	元/人	yuan/person	16.91	13.78	3.14	22.76

5-9 续表1 continued

类别	Classification	单位	Unit	2006	2005	增减 Add or Subtract	增幅 Increase Range
7.购买水产品及制品金额	Aquatic Products	元/人	yuan/person	33.86	33.07	0.79	2.39
#（1）购买海水鱼类	Seawaterfish	公斤/人	kg/person	1.83	1.92	-0.09	-4.75
金额	Sum	元/人	yuan/person	13.49	13.37	0.12	0.89
（2）购买海水虾类	Seawater Shrimp	公斤/人	kg/person	0.2	0.2	0	-0.66
金额	Sum	元/人	yuan/person	3.48	3.15	0.33	10.59
（3）购买淡水鱼类	Freshwater Fish	公斤/人	kg/person	1.65	1.6	0.05	3.35
金额	Sum	元/人	yuan/person	10.34	10.19	0.15	1.46
（4）购买淡水虾类	Freshwater Shrimp	公斤/人	kg/person	0.09	0.06	0.03	45.26
金额	Sum	元/人	yuan/person	0.93	0.65	0.28	44.08
8.购买烟、酒金额	Tobacco and Liquor	元/人	yuan/person	156.58	155.93	0.65	0.41
#（1）购买卷烟	Cigarette	盒/人	box/person	25.48	24.41	1.07	4.38
金额	Sum	元/人	yuan/person	70.03	61.72	8.31	13.46
（2）购买啤酒	Beer	公斤/人	kg/person	7.59	9.45	-1.86	-19.64
金额	Sum	元/人	yuan/person	19.88	26.93	-7.04	-26.16
（3）购买白酒	Spirit	公斤/人	kg/person	6.94	7.45	-0.51	-6.9
金额	Sum	元/人	yuan/person	64.79	63.8	0.99	1.55
9.购买茶叶、饮料金额	Tea and Beverages	元/人	yuan/person	15.73	13.4	2.33	17.39
#购买茶叶	Tea	公斤/人	kg/person	0.33	0.3	0.03	8.86
金额	Sum	元/人	yuan/person	10.02	8.68	1.34	15.42
10.购买其他种类食品金额	Other Kinds of Food	元/人	yuan/person	117.85	46.96	70.89	150.96
#（1）购买豆制品	Bean Products	元/人	yuan/person	6.21	4.02	2.19	54.54
（2）购买调味	Sauce Products	元/人	yuan/person	15.25	8.94	6.31	70.6
（3）购买食糖	Sugar	元/人	yuan/person	4.39	2.21	2.18	98.74
（4）购买西瓜	Watermelon	元/人	yuan/person	7	1.5	5.5	366.67
（5）购买其他果用瓜	Other Melon for Fruit	元/人	yuan/person	1.07	0.35	0.72	207.28
（6）购买水果	Fruit	元/人	yuan/person	31.19	12.03	19.16	159.36
（7）购买坚果、果仁及制品	Nut and Products	元/人	yuan/person	5.93	1.69	4.24	250.88
（8）购买糖果	Sweet	元/人	yuan/person	3.39	0.64	2.75	430.06
（9）购买糕点	Cookie	元/人	yuan/person	19.09	4.92	14.17	288.02
（10）购买营养滋补品	Nutrition and Nourishing Food	元/人	yuan/person	4.14	0.21	3.92	1838.37
（二）衣着类	Clothing			195.46	156.66	38.8	24.77
#1.购买服装	Garments	件/人	piece/person	2.74	2.69	0.05	1.81
金额	Sum	元/人	yuan/person	126.15	95.21	30.93	32.49
2.购买鞋类	Shoes	双/人	pair/person	2.52	2.35	0.17	7.09

5-9 续表 2 continued

类别	Classification	单位	Unit	2006	2005	增减 Add or Subtract	增幅 Increase Range
金额	Sum	元/人	yuan/person	48.65	42.31	6.34	14.98
（三）居住类	Residence			412.32	328.88	83.44	25.37
1.购买建筑生活用房材料支出	Construction Materials	元/人	yuan/person	249.1	197.43	51.67	26.17
2.购买生活用房支出	Household Housing	元/人	yuan/person	26.35	9.65	16.7	172.99
3.购买生活用燃料	Household Fuels	元/人	yuan/person	91.4	81.97	9.43	11.5
4.购买生活用水	Household Water	元/人	yuan/person	4.04	2.91	1.13	38.67
5.购买生活用电	Household Electricity	元/人	yuan/person	59.95	48.15	11.8	24.51
（四）家用设备和日用品	Household Equipment and Appliances			150.03	127.99	22.03	17.21
#1.购买洗涤及卫生用品	Cleaning and Sanitation Appliances	元/人	yuan/person	23.17	20.01	3.16	15.78
2.购买厨具、餐具、茶具	Kitchenware, Tea-things and Tableware	元/人	yuan/person	9.9	8.29	1.62	19.54
3.购买家具及做家具材料	Furniture	元/人	yuan/person	38.76	31.21	7.56	24.22
4.购买洗衣机	Washing Machine	元/人	yuan/person	10.84	10.6	0.24	2.25
5.购买缝纫机	Sewing Machine	元/人	yuan/person	0.62	0.42	0.21	49.21
6.购买电风扇	Electric Fan	元/人	yuan/person	1.54	1.32	0.21	16.05
7.购买电冰箱	Refrigerators	元/人	yuan/person	13.02	8.99	4.03	44.89
8.购买空调机	Air Conditioner	元/人	yuan/person	2.2	2.23	-0.04	-1.58
9.购买吸尘器	Vacuam Cleaner	元/人	yuan/person	0.17	0.03	0.14	506.11
10.购买抽油烟机	Lampblack Exhausters	元/人	yuan/person	0.71	0.58	0.13	22.47
11.购买热水器	Water Heaters	元/人	yuan/person	4.02	3.09	0.93	29.94
12.购买微波炉	Microwave Ovens	元/人	yuan/person	0.33	1.5	-1.17	-77.9
13.购买电饭锅	Electric Cookers	元/人	yuan/person	1.8	1.14	0.66	58.57
14.购买液化气炉具	LPG Stoves	元/人	yuan/person	0.73	1.72	-1	-57.77
（五）交通、通讯工具和用品	Transport and Communications			181.74	150.99	30.75	20.36
#1.购买自行车	Bicycle	辆/人	unit/person	0.03	0.04	0	-13.71
金额	Sum	元/人	yuan/person	7.52	8.53	-1	-11.76
2.购买电动自行车	Electric Bicycle	辆/人	unit/person	0.03	0.01	0.02	126
金额	Sum	元/人	yuan/person	57.82	22.88	34.94	152.72
3.购买摩托车	Motorcycle	辆/人	unit/person	0.01	0.01	0	-27.38
金额	Sum	元/人	yuan/person	31.59	46.35	-14.77	-31.86
4.购买汽车（生活用）	Car	辆/人	unit/person		0	0	-100
金额	Sum	元/人	yuan/person		5.43	-5.43	-100
5.购买电话	Telephone	部/人	unit/person	0.02	0.02	0	-19.59
金额	Sum	元/人	yuan/person	1.34	1.68	-0.34	-20.36

5-9 续表3 continued

类别	Classification	单位	Unit	2006	2005	增减 Add or Subtract	增幅 Increase Range
6.购买手机	Cell Phone	部/人	unit/person	0.05	0.04	0.01	31.44
金额	Sum	元/人	yuan/person	38.42	30.29	8.12	26.81
（六）文化、教育、体育、娱乐用品	Cultural, Education, Sport and Recreation Appliance			68.92	60.75	8.18	13.46
#1.购买收录机	Recorder	元/人	yuan/person	0.28	0.25	0.04	14.43
2.购买组合音响	Hi-Fi Stereo Component System	元/人	yuan/person	2.06	1.61	0.45	28.23
3.购买电子游戏机	Electronic Game	元/人	yuan/person	0.06	0.05	0.01	27.5
4.购买黑白电视机	Black/White TV Set	元/人	yuan/person	0.31	0.1	0.21	204.69
5.购买彩色电视机	Color TV Set	元/人	yuan/person	22.68	20.31	2.37	11.65
6.购买录放像机	Video Recorder	元/人	yuan/person	0.22	0.08	0.14	168.16
7.购买影碟机	Video Disc Player	元/人	yuan/person	4.42	3.55	0.87	24.51
8.购买照相机	Camera	元/人	yuan/person	0.42	0.33	0.09	28.18
9.购买家用计算机（电脑）	Computer	元/人	yuan/person	5.31	4.65	0.66	14.1
10.购买家用计算机外部设备	External Equipment of Coomputer	元/人	yuan/person	0.32	0.24	0.08	33.92
11.购买中高档乐器	Medium and Top Grade Music Instruments	元/人	yuan/person	0.3	0.01	0.28	1970.4
12.购买体育健身器材	Body Building Equipment	元/人	yuan/person	0.18	0.11	0.07	59.83
13.购买观赏盆栽植物	Ornamental Plant	元/人	yuan/person	0.21	0.17	0.04	23.39
14.购买宠物	Pet	元/人	yuan/person	0.23	0.23	0	-1.11
（七）医疗卫生、保健用品	Health Care and Medical Appliance			78	80.27	-2.27	-2.83
#购买药品	Medicine	元/人	yuan/person	72.23	74.69	-2.46	-3.29
（八）其他杂项商品	Other Miscellaneous Goods			27.86	24.61	3.25	13.22
二、购买生产资料	**Purchase of Producton Materials**			**1247.58**	**1212.59**	**34.99**	**2.89**
（一）购买农业用种籽	Agricultural Seeds	公斤/人	kg/person	10.48	8.77	1.71	19.47
金额	Sum	元/人	yuan/person	58.26	49.08	9.19	18.72
（二）购买农业用饲料	Agricultural Feed	公斤/人	kg/person	6.56	8.16	-1.6	-19.58
金额	Sum	元/人	yuan/person	9.23	11.68	-2.45	-20.95
（三）购买农业用其他生产资料	Other Agricultural Materials of Production	元/人	yuan/person	580.7	528.2	52.49	9.94
#1.购买化肥	Fertilizer	公斤/人	kg/person	208.23	189.14	19.09	10.09
金额	Sum	元/人	yuan/person	340.93	324.51	16.41	5.06
2.购买农药	Pesticides	元/人	yuan/person	52.32	47.89	4.43	9.24
3.购买薄膜	Film	公斤/人	kg/person	3.77	4.02	-0.25	-6.31
金额	Sum	元/人	yuan/person	44.15	45.13	-0.98	-2.16
4.购买燃料	Fuel	公斤/人	kg/person	10.33	9.68	0.65	6.72
金额	Sum	元/人	yuan/person	45.18	34.5	10.68	30.96

5-9 续表4 continued

类别	Classification	单位	Unit	2006	2005	增减 Add or Subtract	增幅 Increase Range
（四）购买林业用饲料	Forestry Feed	公斤/人	kg/person	0.08	0.63	-0.55	-86.88
金额	Sum	元/人	yuan/person	0.14	0.86	-0.73	-84.28
（五）购买林业用其他生产资料	Other Forestry Materials of Production	元/人	yuan/person	13.34	8.57	4.78	55.74
#1.购买树苗	Sapling	株/人	stem/person	3.14	3.98	-0.84	-21.11
金额	Sum	元/人	yuan/person	5.48	4.73	0.75	15.95
2.购买化肥	Fertilizer	公斤/人	kg/person	2.74	1.32	1.43	108.6
金额	Sum	元/人	yuan/person	4.5	2.11	2.39	113.11
3.购买农药	Pesticides	元/人	yuan/person	1.25	0.56	0.7	126.07
（六）购买牧业用饲料	Animal Husbandry Feed	公斤/人	kg/person	234.55	211.29	23.26	11.01
金额	Sum	元/人	yuan/person	366.31	337.06	29.25	8.68
（七）购买牧业用其他生产资料	Other Animal Husbandry Materials of Production	元/人	yuan/person	97.4	146.43	-49.02	-33.48
#1.购买仔、幼畜	Young Livestock	头/人	head/person	0.15	0.18	-0.03	-17.17
金额	Sum	元/人	yuan/person	22.6	48.83	-26.23	-53.72
2.购买育肥周转畜	Livestock	头/人	head/person	0.01	0.04	-0.03	-66.2
金额	Sum	元/人	yuan/person	6.09	19.34	-13.25	-68.51
3.仔、幼禽	Young Poultry	元/人	yuan/person	31.91	25.58	6.33	24.75
4.仔、幼小动物	Young Animal	元/人	yuan/person	9.32	19.27	-9.95	-51.63
5.购买种蛋	Egg	元/人	yuan/person	15.24	18.95	-3.71	-19.56
金额	Sum	元/人	yuan/person	0.96	0.96	-0.01	-0.53
6.兽药	Animal Medicine	公斤/人	kg/person	3.43	0.18	3.25	1818.48
7.燃料	Fuel	元/人	yuan/person	5.49	0.22	5.27	2405.13
（九）购买渔业用生产资料	Fishery Materials of Production	元/人	yuan/person	2.23	13.34	-11.11	-83.3
#1.购买种苗	Seedling	元/人	yuan/person	0.66	0.51	0.16	30.91
2.购买渔用药	Fish Medicine	元/人	yuan/person	0.03	0.11	-0.07	-67.82
3.购买燃料	Fuel	元/人	yuan/person	0.26	0.16	0.1	60.83
（十）购买工业生产用原料	Industrial Production Materials	元/人	yuan/person	45.82	53.77	-7.95	-14.79
（十一）购买工业用燃料	Industrial Fuel	公斤/人	kg/person	0.51	0.33	0.18	54.66
金额	Sum	元/人	yuan/person	0.64	0.57	0.06	11.19
（十二）购买建筑业生产用原料	Construction Production Raw Materials	元/人	yuan/person	2.03	0.86	1.17	136.3
（十三）购买建筑业生产用燃料	Construction Fuel	公斤/人	kg/person	0.09	0.02	0.08	494.75
金额	Sum	元/人	yuan/person	0.46	0.06	0.4	675.92
（十四）购买交通运输业邮电业燃料	Transport, Storage and Post Fuel	公斤/人	kg/person	3.13	3.58	-0.45	-12.58

5-9 续表 5 continued

类别	Classification	单位	Unit	2006	2005	增减 Add or Subtract	增幅 Increase Range
金额	Sum	元/人	yuan/person	14.3	14.12	0.17	1.21
（十五）购买批零贸易业用原料	Wholesale, Retail Trade Raw Materials	元/人	yuan/person	25.76	21.9	3.86	17.62
（十六）购买批零贸易业用燃料	Wholesale, Retail Trade Fuel	公斤/人	kg/person	2.56	1.02	1.54	150.12
金额	Sum	元/人	yuan/person	2.22	1.1	1.11	100.66
（十七）购买社会服务业用原料	Social Services Raw Materials	元/人	yuan/person	3.65	4.72	-1.07	-22.74
（十八）购买社会服务业用燃料	Social Services Fuel	公斤/人	kg/person	0.57	0.53	0.04	7.63
金额	Sum	元/人	yuan/person	0.7	0.97	-0.26	-27.11
（十九）购买文教卫生业用原料	Culture, Education and Health Raw Materials	元/人	yuan/person	4.37	0.92	3.46	376.93
（二十）购买文教卫生业用燃料	Culture, Education and Health Fuel	公斤/人	kg/person	0.01	0.01	-0.01	-44.07
金额	Sum	元/人	yuan/person	0.04	0.06	-0.02	-30.73
（二十一）购买其他行业用原料	Other Sectors Raw Materials	元/人	yuan/person	1.74	2.66	-0.92	-34.46
（二十二）购买其他行业用燃料	Other Sectors Fuel	公斤/人	kg/person	0.09	0.34	-0.25	-72.52
金额	Sum	元/人	yuan/person	0.45	0.76	-0.31	-41.3
三、购买生产用电	**Purchase of Producton Electricity**	**度/人**	**kwh/person**	**28.96**	**17.28**	**11.68**	**67.58**
金额	Sum	元/人	yuan/person	23.12	13.54	9.58	70.74
四、购买生产性固定资产情况	**Purchase of Productive Fixed Assets**			**149.36**	**117.14**	**32.22**	**27.5**
（一）购买建筑生产用建筑物材料	Purchase of Building Materials	元/人	yuan/person	13.65	23.26	-9.62	-41.34
（二）购买生产用房间数	Purchase of Production House	间/人	room/person	0	0	0	9.69
面积	Area	平方米/人	sq.m/person	0.03	0.01	0.01	96.19
金额	Sum	元/人	yuan/person	7.06	1.89	5.17	274.44
（三）购买役畜	Draught Animal	头/人	head/person	0	0	0	-65.53
金额	Sum	元/人	yuan/person	1.32	3.15	-1.84	-58.26
（四）购买产品畜	Commodity Animal	头/人	head/person	0	0.01	0	-48.01
金额	Sum	元/人	yuan/person	2.57	3.74	-1.17	-31.2
（五）购买农林牧渔业机械支出	Agricultural Machinery	元/人	yuan/person	44.84	39.43	5.42	13.74
（六）购买工业机械支出	Industrial Machinery	元/人	yuan/person	28.78	2.14	26.64	1241.88
（七）购买运输机械支出	Transport Machinery	元/人	yuan/person	38.14	35.19	2.95	8.38

5-10　农村住户人均食品消费情况
Per Capita Food Consumption of Rural Households

类别	Classification	单位	Unit	2006	2005	增减 Add or Subtract	增幅 Increase Range
一、粮食消费量	**Grain Consumption**	**公斤/人**	**kg/person**	**200.57**	**195.82**	**4.75**	**2.43**
（一）谷物消费量	Cereal	公斤/人	kg/person	194.75	190.18	4.57	2.4
#小麦	Wheat	公斤/人	kg/person	153.39	154.03	-0.64	-0.42
稻谷	Rice	公斤/人	kg/person	6.65	5.67	0.98	17.37
玉米	Corn	公斤/人	kg/person	26.45	23.55	2.9	12.32
（二）薯类消费量	Tubers	公斤/人	kg/person	1.16	1.23	-0.07	-5.97
（三）豆类消费量	Beans	公斤/人	kg/person	4.66	4.41	0.25	5.67
二、油脂类消费量	**Oil Consumption**	**公斤/人**	**kg/person**	**8.97**	**9.68**	**-0.71**	**-7.34**
1.植物油	Vegetable Oil	公斤/人	kg/person	7.43	6.94	0.49	6.99
2.动物油	Animal Fat	公斤/人	kg/person	1.54	2.73	-1.2	-43.73
三、烟叶消费量	**Tobacco Consumption**	**公斤/人**	**kg/person**	**0.15**	**0.15**	**0**	**2.87**
四、豆制品	**Bean Products**	**公斤/人**	**kg/person**	**2.46**	**1.62**	**0.84**	**51.98**
五、蔬菜及菜制品消费量	**Consumption of Vegetable and Products**	**公斤/人**	**kg/person**	**77.48**	**72.86**	**4.61**	**6.33**
六、瓜类	**Melons**	**公斤/人**	**kg/person**	**10.89**	**3.64**	**7.25**	**199.2**
1.西瓜	Watermelon	公斤/人	kg/person	10.1	3.09	7.01	226.63
2.其他瓜果	Other Melons	公斤/人	kg/person	0.79	0.55	0.24	44
七、水果类	**Fruits**	**公斤/人**	**kg/person**	**16.79**	**8.66**	**8.13**	**93.86**
八、消费茶叶	**Tea Consumption**	**公斤/人**	**kg/person**	**0.33**	**0.3**	**0.03**	**8.86**
九、坚果消费量	**Nuts Consumption**	**公斤/人**	**kg/person**	**0.99**	**0.34**	**0.65**	**188.48**
十、肉禽及其制品	**Meat, Poultry and Products**	**公斤/人**	**kg/person**	**14.82**	**14.29**	**0.53**	**3.71**
1.猪肉	Pork	公斤/人	kg/person	8.38	7.86	0.52	6.59
2.牛肉	Beef	公斤/人	kg/person	0.27	0.29	-0.01	-4.42
3.羊肉	Mutton	公斤/人	kg/person	0.34	0.33	0.01	3.6
4.家禽	Poultry	公斤/人	kg/person	2.49	2.66	-0.17	-6.39
5.其他肉禽及制品	Other Meat, Poultry and Products	公斤/人	kg/person	3.33	3.15	0.18	5.82
十一、蛋类及蛋制品	**Eggs and Products**	**公斤/人**	**kg/person**	**10.81**	**10.44**	**0.37**	**3.59**
十二、奶和奶制品	**Milk and Products**	**公斤/人**	**kg/person**	**6.3**	**5.78**	**0.52**	**8.99**
十三、水产品	**Aquatic Products**	**公斤/人**	**kg/person**	**4.42**	**4.55**	**-0.13**	**-2.89**
1.鱼类	Fish	公斤/人	kg/person	3.48	3.52	-0.04	-1.13
2.虾、贝、蟹类	Shrimp, Shellfish and Crab	公斤/人	kg/person	0.61	0.67	-0.06	-9.02
3.藻类	Algae	公斤/人	kg/person	0.06	0.05	0.01	24.68
4.其他	Others	公斤/人	kg/person	0.27	0.31	-0.04	-13.7
十四、食糖	**Sugar**	**公斤/人**	**kg/person**	**0.89**	**0.57**	**0.32**	**55.32**
十五、酒	**Liquor**	**公斤/人**	**kg/person**	**14.66**	**17.25**	**-2.58**	**-14.98**
#1.白酒	White Spirit	公斤/人	kg/person	6.94	7.45	-0.51	-6.9
2.啤酒	Beer	公斤/人	kg/person	7.59	9.45	-1.86	-19.64
3.果酒	Wine	公斤/人	kg/person	0.09	0.23	-0.14	-60.87

5-11　农村住户人均粮食收支平衡表
Balance of Per Capita Grain of Rural Households

类别	Classification	单位	Unit	2006	2005	增减 Add or Subtract	增幅 Increase Range
一、期内粮食收入合计	**Grain Income in the Term**	**公斤/人**	**kg/person**	**946.35**	**908.19**	**38.16**	**4.2**
（一）家庭经营生产粮食	Grain of Household Operations	公斤/人	kg/person	817.56	792.75	24.81	3.13
1.谷物	Cereal	公斤/人	kg/person	804.16	779.14	25.02	3.21
#小麦	Wheat	公斤/人	kg/person	395.53	376.79	18.74	4.97
水稻	Rice	公斤/人	kg/person	10.02	11.07	-1.04	-9.44
玉米	Corn	公斤/人	kg/person	397.21	390.2	7.01	1.8
2、薯类	Tubers	公斤/人	kg/person	9.46	7.75	1.71	22.11
3、豆类	Beans	公斤/人	kg/person	3.94	5.86	-1.93	-32.86
（二）购入粮食	Purchase of Grain	公斤/人	kg/person	122.55	114.96	7.6	6.61
1.谷物	Cereal	公斤/人	kg/person	118.48	111.22	7.26	6.53
#小麦	Wheat	公斤/人	kg/person	17.76	17.86	-0.1	-0.57
水稻	Rice	公斤/人	kg/person	5.42	4.57	0.85	18.63
玉米	Corn	公斤/人	kg/person	87.18	81.93	5.25	6.4
2.薯类	Tubers	公斤/人	kg/person	0.56	0.63	-0.07	-11.05
3.豆类	Beans	公斤/人	kg/person	3.51	3.11	0.41	13.05
（三）借入粮食	Loan of Grain	公斤/人	kg/person	3.21	0.01	3.2	28964.02
（四）收回借出粮	Grain Repaid	公斤/人	kg/person	1.49	0.29	1.2	416.18
（五）其他粮食收入	Other Grain Income	公斤/人	kg/person	1.54	0.19	1.35	730.09
二、期内粮食支出合计	**Grain Expenditure in the Term**	**公斤/人**	**kg/person**	**825.8**	**767.68**	**58.12**	**7.57**
（一）主食用粮	Grain as Staple	公斤/人	kg/person	200.57	195.82	4.75	2.43
1.谷物	Cereal	公斤/人	kg/person	194.75	190.18	4.57	2.4
#小麦	Wheat	公斤/人	kg/person	153.39	154.03	-0.64	-0.42
水稻	Rice	公斤/人	kg/person	6.65	5.67	0.98	17.37
玉米	Corn	公斤/人	kg/person	26.45	23.55	2.9	12.32
2.薯类	Tubers	公斤/人	kg/person	1.16	1.23	-0.07	-5.97
3.豆类	Beans	公斤/人	kg/person	4.66	4.41	0.25	5.67
（二）其他生活用粮	Other Living Grain	公斤/人	kg/person	0		0	
（三）出售粮食	Sale of Grain	公斤/人	kg/person	478.36	424.87	53.49	12.59
1.谷物	Cereal	公斤/人	kg/person	469.05	417.92	51.13	12.23
#小麦	Wheat	公斤/人	kg/person	206.33	171.56	34.76	20.26
水稻	Rice	公斤/人	kg/person	7.21	8.77	-1.55	-17.73
玉米	Corn	公斤/人	kg/person	254.75	237.13	17.61	7.43
2.薯类	Tubers	公斤/人	kg/person	7.26	4.03	3.23	80.25
3.豆类	Beans	公斤/人	kg/person	2.05	2.92	-0.87	-29.81

5-11 续表 1 continued

类别	Classification	单位	Unit	2006	2005	增减 Add or Subtract	增幅 Increase Range
（四）种籽用粮食	Grain as Seeds	公斤/人	kg/person	8.98	9.88	-0.89	-9.03
1.小麦	Wheat	公斤/人	kg/person	6.35	7.08	-0.73	-10.33
2.水稻	Rice	公斤/人	kg/person	0.12	0.06	0.06	96.77
3.玉米	Corn	公斤/人	kg/person	2.3	2.46	-0.16	-6.62
4.其他	Others	公斤/人	kg/person	0.22	0.27	-0.06	-20.82
（五）饲料用粮食	Grain as Feed	公斤/人	kg/person	133.91	134.15	-0.25	-0.18
1.小麦	Wheat	公斤/人	kg/person	2.84	3.19	-0.35	-10.92
2.水稻	Rice	公斤/人	kg/person	0.06	0.12	-0.05	-44.98
3.玉米	Corn	公斤/人	kg/person	128.66	127.42	1.24	0.97
4.其他	Others	公斤/人	kg/person	2.34	3.43	-1.09	-31.7
（六）借出粮食	Creditor of Grain	公斤/人	kg/person	1.03	1.96	-0.94	-47.69
（七）归还借粮	Grain Returned	公斤/人	kg/person	2.53	0.01	2.52	25804.91
（八）其他粮食支出	Other Grain Expenditure	公斤/人	kg/person	0.42	1	-0.57	-57.32
三、期末粮食结存实际调查数	**Balance of Grain Surveyed at Term-end**	公斤/人	**kg/person**	**643.15**	**708.93**	**-65.78**	**-9.28**
（一）谷物	Cereal	公斤/人	kg/person	632.72	694.72	-62.01	-8.93
#（1）小麦	Wheat	公斤/人	kg/person	305.01	323.53	-18.52	-5.72
（2）水稻	Rice	公斤/人	kg/person	18.34	18.73	-0.39	-2.09
（3）玉米	Corn	公斤/人	kg/person	308.58	351.44	-42.86	-12.19
（二）薯类	Tubers	公斤/人	kg/person	7.72	11.09	-3.37	-30.39
（三）豆类	Beans	公斤/人	kg/person	2.72	3.12	-0.4	-12.78
四、期末粮食结存用途	**Use of Balance of Grain at Term-end**						
1.计划用于口粮	Plan for Rations	公斤/人	kg/person	205.34	218.62	-13.28	-6.07
2.计划用于种子	Plan for Seeds	公斤/人	kg/person	7.95	8.88	-0.94	-10.55
3.计划用于饲料	Plan for Feed	公斤/人	kg/person	88.59	116.37	-27.79	-23.88
4.计划用于其他用途	Plan for Other Use	公斤/人	kg/person	341.28	365.05	-23.77	-6.51
五、期内生产加工用粮	**Production and Processing of Grain in the Term**	公斤/人	**kg/person**	**38.28**	**45.51**	**-7.23**	**-15.88**
#食品加工用粮	Grain for Food Processing	公斤/人	kg/person	23.16	20.27	2.89	14.26
饲料加工用粮	Grain for Feed Processing	公斤/人	kg/person	14.75	23.47	-8.72	-37.14

5-12 农村住户人口与就业情况
Population and Employment of Rural Households

类别	Classification	单位	Unit	2006	2005	增减 Add or Subtract	增幅 Increase Range
一、农村住户人口状况	**Population of Rural Households**	*	*				
（一）家庭常住人口	Number of Permanent Residents	人	person	15298	15382	-84	-0.55
（二）常住人口与户主关系	Relationship between the Permanent Residentsand the Head of the Household	*	*				
1.户主	the Head of the Household	人	person	4207	4214	-7	-0.17
2.配偶	Spouses	人	person	4122	4129	-7	-0.17
3.子女	Children	人	person	5994	6075	-81	-1.33
4.孙子女	Grandchildren	人	person	407	358	49	13.69
5.父母	Parents	人	person	521	549	-28	-5.1
6.祖父母	Grandparents	人	person	8	8		
7.兄弟姐妹	Brothers and Sisters	人	person	22	28	-6	-21.43
8.其他亲属	Other Relatives	人	person	16	21	-5	-23.81
9.非亲属	Unrelated	人	person	1		1	
（三）家庭常住人口年龄状况	Age of Permanent Residents	*	*				
1.6岁及以下	6Year-old and Under	人	person	667	667		
2.7～15岁	Between7and15Year-old	人	person	1397	1578	-181	-11.47
3.16～18岁	Between16and18Year-old	人	person	1183	1389	-206	-14.83
4.19～22岁	Between19and22Year-old	人	person	1503	1281	222	17.33
5.23～25岁	Between23and25Year-old	人	person	808	794	14	1.76
6.26～30岁	Between26and30Year-old	人	person	730	762	-32	-4.2
7.31～40岁	Between31and40Year-old	人	person	2393	2630	-237	-9.01
8.41～50岁	Between41and50Year-old	人	person	3141	3098	43	1.39
9.51～60岁	Between51and60Year-old	人	person	2451	2262	189	8.36
10.61岁及以上	61Year-old and Above	人	person	1025	921	104	11.29
（四）在校学生人数	Students Enrollment	人	person	2821	2904	-83	-2.86
#7～15岁以下在校学生人数	of which:Between7and15 Year-old	人	person	1390	1569	-179	-11.41
（五）7～15岁非在校学生人数	Non-school Students Between7 and15Year-old	人	person	7	9	-2	-22.22
（六）劳动年龄内丧失劳动能力的人数	People at Working Age and Lost the Ability to Work	人	person	19	19		
（七）参加养老保险的人数	People Participated in Endowment Insurance	人	person	1517	1509	8	0.53
（八）参加医疗保险的人数	People Participated in Medical Insuarance	人	person	9380	6073	3307	54.45
二、农村住户劳动力素质状况	**Labor Force Quality of Rural Households**	*	*				

5-12　续表 1 continued

类别	Classification	单位	Unit	2006	2005	增减 Add or Subtract	增幅 Increase Range
（一）整半劳动力数	Number of Full/Semi Labour Force	人	person	11295	11283	12	0.11
#男劳动力人数	Number of Male Labour Force	人	person	5756	5724	32	0.56
整劳动力	Number of Full Labour Force	人	person	7549	7703	-154	-2
（二）劳动力文化程度	Education of Labor Force						
1.不识字或识字很少	Can Not Read or Read Very Little	人	person	621	613	8	1.31
2.小学程度	Primary School	人	person	1984	2053	-69	-3.36
3.初中程度	Junior High School	人	person	6358	6334	24	0.38
4.高中程度	Senior High School	人	person	1707	1701	6	0.35
5.中专	Secondary School	人	person	460	441	19	4.31
6.大专及以上	Junior College and over	人	person	165	141	24	17.02
（三）劳动力接受培训情况	Training of Labor Force	*	*	1645		1645	
1.受过专业培训的人数	Number of Professionally Trained	人	person	2599	2492	107	4.29
2.未受过专业培训的人数	Number of Non-professionally Trained	人	person	8696	8791	-95	-1.08
（四）参加养老保险的人数	People Participated in Endowment Insurance	人	person	1399	1375	24	1.75
（五）参加医疗保险的人数	People Participated in Medical Insuarance	人	person	7057	4517	2540	56.23
三、农村住户劳动力就业情况	**Employment of Rural Labor Force**	*	*				
就业劳动力人数	Number of Employed Labor Force	人	person	11257	11247	10	0.09
#男劳动力人数	Male Labor Force	人	person	5744	5716	28	0.49
整劳动力人数	Full Labor Force	人	person	7528	7685	-157	-2.04
受专业培训的人数	Professionally Trained	人	person	2591	2486	105	4.22
（一）就业地点	Place of Employment						
1.乡内	in the Village	人	person	9603	9599	4	0.04
2.县内乡外	in the County but outside the Village	人	person	549	587	-38	-6.47
3.省内县外	in the Province but outside the County	人	person	721	680	41	6.03
4.国内省外	in China but outside the Province	人	person	381	380	1	0.26
5.国外	Abroad	人	person	3	1	2	200
（二）行业分布	Sector Employment	*	*				
1.一产业就业劳动力	Primary Industry	人	person	6582	6968	-386	-5.54
（1）农业	Farming	人	person	6378	6763	-385	-5.69
（2）林业	Forestry	人	person	43	12	31	258.33

5-12 续表 2 continued

类别	Classification	单位	Unit	2006	2005	增减 Add or Subtract	增幅 Increase Range
（3）牧业	Animal Husbandry	人	person	127	162	-35	-21.6
（4）渔业	Fishery	人	person	34	31	3	9.68
2.非农产业就业劳动力	Non-agricultural Industries	人	person	4675	4279	396	9.25
A.二产业就业劳动力	Secondary Industry	人	person	2086	1800	286	15.89
①采矿业	Mining and Quarrying	人	person	77	82	-5	-6.1
②制造业	Manufacturing	人	person	1439	1224	215	17.57
③电力煤气及水的生产供应业	Electricity, Gas & Water Production and Supply	人	person	45	46	-1	-2.17
④建筑业	Construction	人	person	525	448	77	17.19
B.三产业就业劳动力	Tertiary Industry	人	person	2589	2479	110	4.44
①交通运输仓储及邮电通讯业	Transport, Storage and Post	人	person	254	250	4	1.6
②批发和零售贸易	Wholesale and Retail Trades	人	person	323	291	32	11
③住宿和餐饮业	Hotels and Catering Services	人	person	157	156	1	0.64
④居民服务和其他服务业	Services to Households and Other Services	人	person	475	491	-16	-3.26
⑤教育	Education	人	person	131	140	-9	-6.43
⑥卫生、社会保障和社会福利业	Health, Social Security and Social Welfare	人	person	107	104	3	2.88
⑦文化、体育和娱乐业	Culture, Sports and Entertainment	人	person	20	15	5	33.33
⑧其他	Others	人	person	1122	1032	90	8.72
（三）年内从事各种行业时间	Time Engaged in Various Sectors in the Year	月	month	107870.5	106645.7	1224.8	1.15
1.从事农业的时间	Engaged in Agriculture	月	month	55796.3	59910.7	-4114.4	-6.87
2.从事非农产业的时间	Engaged in Non-agriculture	月	month	52074.2	46735	5339.2	11.42
（四）本地企业职工人数	Employees in Local Enterprises	人	person	1419	1163	256	22.01
在本地企业工作的时间	Time Working at Local Enterprises	月	month	12474.9	10036	2438.9	24.3

5-13 主要年份农民家庭主要指标

Leading Indicator of Peasant Family in Main Year

年份 Year	调查户数（户） Investigatory Households (household)	调查户常住人口（人） Permanent Resident Population of Investigatory Households (person)	平均每户常住人口（人） Permanent Resident Population of Average Household (person)	平均每户整半劳力（人） Labour Force of Average Household (person)	人均年末生活用房面积（平方米） Year-end Per Capital Living Floor Space (sq.m)
1978	715	4126	5.77	2.54	9.81
1979	732	4138	5.65	2.67	9.91
1980	825	4649	5.64	2.70	10.98
1981	827	4538	5.49	2.63	10.03
1982	1529	7849	5.13	2.54	10.64
1983	1438	7266	5.05	2.85	12.50
1984	1558	7730	4.96	2.86	14.54
1985	4000	18896	4.72	2.84	15.13
1986	4200	19667	4.68	2.85	15.74
1987	4200	19339	4.60	2.86	16.48
1988	4200	19074	4.54	2.86	17.34
1989	4200	18749	4.46	2.85	17.96
1990	4200	18486	4.40	2.82	18.48
1991	4200	18241	4.34	2.77	19.87
1992	4200	17886	4.26	2.75	19.31
1993	4200	17494	4.17	2.77	20.64
1994	4200	17239	4.10	2.76	21.15
1995	4200	17089	4.07	2.78	21.56
1996	4200	16847	4.01	2.68	22.32
1997	4200	16574	3.95	2.65	23.16
1998	4200	16379	3.90	2.64	23.91
1999	4200	16116	3.84	2.60	25.07
2000	4200	15918	3.79	2.60	23.61
2001	4200	15671	3.73	2.54	24.60
2002	4200	15569	3.71	2.58	25.59
2003	4200	15405	3.67	2.62	26.53
2004	4200	15386	3.66	2.67	26.92
2005	4200	15382	3.66	2.69	29.64
2006	4200	15298	3.64	2.69	30.69

注:78年至80年的生活用房面积中包括生产用房。

Notice:Living House Inclues Producing House From 1978 to 1980.

5-13 续表 1 continued

年份 Year	平均每人全年总收入（元） Average General Income Per Capita (yuan)	平均每人全年纯收入（元） Average Net Income Per Capita (yuan)	平均每人全年总支出（元） Average General Expenses Per Capita(yuan)	#购置生产性固定资产 Purchase Production Fixed Assets	#生活消费支出 Personal Consumption Expenses
1978	134.58	114.56	116.57		93.69
1979	184.66	159.81	157.41		128.01
1980	240.98	210.23	204.75		165.34
1981	282.07	251.62	247.90	8.99	202.12
1982	343.99	299.95	296.21	17.87	230.02
1983	500.68	360.64	428.14	22.23	264.38
1984	554.61	394.99	461.31	18.11	287.24
1985	592.50	408.12	521.50	18.71	321.98
1986	644.65	449.27	570.40	14.81	364.56
1987	740.61	517.69	639.75	16.36	406.34
1988	857.76	583.74	780.24	23.72	482.11
1989	939.57	630.56	841.95	21.05	513.10
1990	994.36	680.18	878.27	18.14	547.05
1991	1152.02	764.04	1037.81	29.79	612.99
1992	1241.82	802.90	1121.22	27.81	655.69
1993	1413.69	952.74	1210.98	29.48	724.49
1994	1975.12	1319.73	1671.34	30.01	995.72
1995	2626.96	1715.09	2301.34	56.70	1338.46
1996	3246.92	2086.31	2955.16	68.33	1652.51
1997	3468.72	2292.12	2855.26	84.34	1626.27
1998	3561.87	2452.83	2782.48	93.23	1595.09
1999	3645.89	2549.56	2845.88	97.36	1679.75
2000	3880.98	2659.20	3036.20	107.85	1770.75
2001	4161.97	2804.51	3326.79	101.70	1904.95
2002	4330.42	2953.97	3438.78	92.40	1997.83
2003	4482.15	3150.49	3521.42	83.78	2133.20
2004	5037.52	3507.43	3999.23	107.74	2389.27
2005	5676.98	3930.55	4561.27	117.14	2735.77
2006	6188.54	4368.33	5090.48	149.36	3143.8

5-14 分市主要指标

地区	Area	调查户数（户） Investigatory Households (household)	常住人口（人） Permanent Resident Population (person)	整半劳动力（人） Able-bodied and Semi-ablebodied (farm) Workers (person)	每百劳动力中（人） Among Per One Hundred Labour Forces (Person)					
					1.不识字或识字很少 Non-Literacy or Little-literacy	2.小学程度 Primary School Level	3.初中程度 Junior Middle School Level	4.高中程度 Senior Middle School Level	5.中专 Polytechnic School	6.大专及以上 College and Higher Level
济南市	Jinan	1000	3698	2706	5.36	16.91	54.57	15.66	5.04	2.46
青岛市	Qingdao	900	3073	2324	1.46	12.78	54.43	24.01	4.69	2.62
淄博市	Zibo	800	2654	1919	1.57	15.45	51.42	21.96	6.18	3.43
枣庄市	Zaozhuang	630	2382	1717	4.31	21.14	57.72	10.72	4.43	1.69
东营市	Dongying	500	1719	1248	5.19	20.67	59.11	11.74	2.42	0.87
烟台市	Yantai	1140	3391	2560	1.02	17.05	55.08	19.69	5.2	1.96
潍坊市	Weifang	1260	4387	3217	2.08	16.69	57.63	17.38	4.76	1.46
济宁市	Jining	1350	5149	3790	7.27	17	55.52	15.14	3.06	2.01
泰安市	Taian	690	2379	1852	4.16	17.51	59.21	15.05	3.06	1.02
威海市	Weihai	540	1462	1199	0.17	14.43	58.22	20.27	5.09	1.83
日照市	Rizhao	400	1272	939	2.77	23.75	54.95	14.27	3.19	1.06
莱芜市	Laiwu	570	1691	1302	5.96	20.11	52.74	18.17	1.83	1.18
临沂市	Linyi	5214	18587	13831	5.36	21.76	55.72	12.99	2.73	1.45
德州市	Dezhou	1050	3869	3038	5.6	25.31	56.95	10.5	1.18	0.46
聊城市	Liaocheng	4040	14056	10985	9.36	30.22	43.97	14.62	1.15	0.68
滨州市	Binzhou	710	2491	1898	5.95	21.97	60.27	10.01	1.26	0.53
菏泽市	Heze	950	3843	2825	10.58	19.63	48.82	14.39	4.89	1.68

5-14 续表 1 continued

地区	Area	全年总收入 Annual Total Income	1.工资性收入 Wages Income	#在本乡地域内劳动得到收入 Labour Income in One's Region	#外出从业得到收入 Income from go out Working	2.家庭经营收入 Income from Household Business	3.财产性收入 Property Income	4.转移性收入 Transferred Income
济南市	Jinan	7161.72	2160.03	1130.78	664.64	4532.7	249.78	219.21
青岛市	Qingdao	9463.53	2783.07	1554.25	730.91	6296.66	191.61	192.19
淄博市	Zibo	6717.57	3138.35	2380.74	336.95	3194.97	195.56	188.7
枣庄市	Zaozhuang	6158.14	1741.2	992.65	455.66	4005.87	154.82	256.26
东营市	Dongying	7918.84	1507.33	1069.74	267.47	6134.93	174.62	101.97
烟台市	Yantai	7466.18	2420.34	1600.39	409.26	4476.89	248.58	320.37
潍坊市	Weifang	7885.76	2211.86	1486.51	389.17	5345.15	226.18	102.57
济宁市	Jining	6108.74	1845.56	766.52	850.39	3992.54	143.38	127.26
泰安市	Taian	5764.23	2323.57	1183.92	791.53	3204.97	58.87	176.82
威海市	Weihai	9230.31	3275.96	2354.5	354.62	5473.06	241.96	239.33
日照市	Rizhao	7455.99	1613	664.11	603.02	5538.54	114.01	190.43
莱芜市	Laiwu	6904.05	1632.24	855.79	358.21	4890.35	236.77	144.69
临沂市	Linyi	5667.25	1582.19	945.42	418.1	3883.13	80.47	121.46
德州市	Dezhou	5568.36	1618.84	699.42	859.53	3764.2	95.51	89.81
聊城市	Liaocheng	5480	1373.07	567.41	714.12	3933.09	93.74	80.09
滨州市	Binzhou	5960.1	1472.5	946.01	411.82	4143.03	163.48	181.09
菏泽市	Heze	4558.78	1261.68	366.35	747.96	3150.02	52.48	94.6

5-14 续表 2 continued

地区	Area	全年纯收入 Annual Net Income	1.工资性收入 Wages Income	2.家庭经营纯收入 Income from Household Business	3.财产性收入 Property Income	4.转移性收入 Transferred Income	全年现金纯收入 Annual Cash Net Income
济南市	Jinan	5479.99	2160.03	2912.7	249.78	157.48	4915.87
青岛市	Qingdao	6545.88	2783.07	3406.12	191.61	165.08	6157.34
淄博市	Zibo	5640.54	3138.35	2175.9	195.56	130.73	5437.75
枣庄市	Zaozhuang	4687.3	1741.2	2608.1	154.82	183.19	4200.23
东营市	Dongying	5157.13	1507.33	3391.65	174.62	83.54	4654.81
烟台市	Yantai	6072.48	2420.34	3148.51	248.58	255.05	5639.78
潍坊市	Weifang	5507.8	2211.86	2990.72	226.18	79.04	4806.16
济宁市	Jining	4590.77	1845.56	2506.4	143.38	95.43	4278.28
泰安市	Taian	4641.8	2323.57	2127.32	58.87	132.04	4205.24
威海市	Weihai	6841.59	3275.96	3152.28	241.96	171.4	5823.53
日照市	Rizhao	4645.09	1613	2797.57	114.01	120.51	3932.26
莱芜市	Laiwu	5200.51	1632.24	3226.22	236.77	105.29	4570.7
临沂市	Linyi	4083.4	1582.19	2337.34	80.47	83.4	3584.24
德州市	Dezhou	4279.42	1618.84	2484.57	95.51	80.48	3703.58
聊城市	Liaocheng	3947.73	1373.07	2408.74	93.74	72.18	3359.26
滨州市	Binzhou	4370.48	1472.5	2613.53	163.48	120.97	3692.02
菏泽市	Heze	3480.25	1261.68	2078.38	52.48	87.71	2935.96

5-14 续表 3 continued

地区	Area	全年总支出 Annual Total Expenditures	1.家庭经营费用支出 Household Business Expenditures	2.购置生产性固定资产支出 Expenditures for Purchasing Production Fixed Assets	3.建、造生产性固定资产雇工支出 Employing Expenditures for Building Production Fixed Assets	4.税费支出 Tax and Fee Expenditures	5.生活消费支出 Living Expenditures	6.财产性支出 Property Expenditures	7.转移性支出 Transferred Income
济南市	Jinan	5280.54	1448.49	215.92	6.06	9.68	3415.27	19.01	166.11
青岛市	Qingdao	7198.43	2560.28	147.67	2.15	14.13	4202.95	10.13	261.12
淄博市	Zibo	5030.43	835.94	57.43	2.64	24.35	3751.68	13.16	345.23
枣庄市	Zaozhuan	4549.28	1236.73	128.88	0.02	8.44	2908.49	8.25	258.47
东营市	Dongying	6314.12	2467.88	118.16	0.12	11.59	3507	46.41	162.95
烟台市	Yantai	5031.65	1179.77	84.27	0.25	12.62	3402.45	9.48	342.82
潍坊市	Weifang	6069.72	2096.94	202.04	2.19	16.15	3564.47	13.38	174.55
济宁市	Jining	4564.09	1333.9	143.43	2.84	19.12	2821.25	10.37	233.17
泰安市	Taian	3810.93	926.78	39.96	1.05	5.75	2683.07	6.37	147.95
威海市	Weihai	6777	2079.13	292.92	0.05	8	4004.66	3.34	388.9
日照市	Rizhao	5465.2	2504.57	121.24	1.67	15.44	2629.8	19.8	172.68
莱芜市	Laiwu	4964.87	1517.92	76.7	3.91	7.06	3140.1	8.72	210.46
临沂市	Linyi	4134.11	1382.23	98.37	2.88	13.13	2456.17	24.71	156.61
德州市	Dezhou	3082.76	1034.36	82.91	2.41	26.67	1876.37	6.94	53.09
聊城市	Liaocheng	3926.1	1329.36	88.49	1.12	41.47	2391.81	11.19	62.66
滨州市	Binzhou	4556.08	1273.38	116.48	5.22	34.71	2968.54	26.31	131.44
菏泽市	Heze	3279.61	931.07	97.57	0.19	17.67	2154.87	6.06	72.19

5-14 续表 4 continued

地区	Area	生活消费支出 Living Expenditures	1.食品消费支出 Food Expenditures	2.衣着消费支出 Clothing Expenditures	3.居住消费支出 Residences Expenditures	4.家庭设备、用品消费支出 Household Appliances and Servics	5.交通和通讯消费支出 Transportation and Communications	6.文化教育、娱乐消费支出 Cultural, Education and Recreation Expenditures	7.医疗保健消费支出 Medicine and Medical Services	8.其他商品和服务消费支出 Other Commodities and Services
济南市	Jinan	3415.27	1199.81	198.35	655.85	206.67	420.84	431.27	252.92	49.56
青岛市	Qingdao	4202.95	1540.02	396.71	730.86	236.23	482.5	512.29	217.5	86.85
淄博市	Zibo	3751.68	1297.7	301.84	561.59	212.64	411.37	594.17	310.29	62.06
枣庄市	Zaozhuan	2908.49	1152.44	229.19	418.7	185.58	360.13	307.46	187.1	67.89
东营市	Dongying	3507	1112.23	216.73	740.94	217.31	497.4	450.65	238.9	32.85
烟台市	Yantai	3402.45	1273.91	273.22	453.68	177.57	382.36	465.38	317.74	58.59
潍坊市	Weifang	3564.47	1246.56	258.86	749.76	193.74	415.54	423.77	197.65	78.59
济宁市	Jining	2821.25	1071.46	159.65	478.35	156.72	338.56	402.86	167.1	46.56
泰安市	Taian	2683.07	1113.22	171.82	387.61	225.32	299.74	349.6	112.61	23.16
威海市	Weihai	4004.66	1450.54	387.34	588.63	186.32	397.22	614.5	302.35	77.77
日照市	Rizhao	2629.8	1038.13	233.16	380.39	140.79	314.98	387.42	111.91	23
莱芜市	Laiwu	3140.1	1206.65	160.91	455.2	168.31	385.51	539.04	188.52	35.97
临沂市	Linyi	2456.17	963.23	155.81	421.83	118.98	307.19	336.52	112.85	39.76
德州市	Dezhou	1876.37	753.22	104.74	327.15	152.43	232.62	200.96	82.75	22.51
聊城市	Liaocheng	2391.81	911.75	156.2	452.54	116.29	311.97	274.67	130.61	37.78
滨州市	Binzhou	2968.54	916.89	150.41	768.93	132.65	364.59	343.55	246.07	45.46
菏泽市	Heze	2154.87	954.04	128.2	240.87	79.55	242.71	338.31	131.54	39.65

生产价格调查资料

Investigation Material of Production Prices

编辑单位：生产投资价格处
编　　委：刘　敏
责任编辑：张燕丽　杨延斌　景　虹
校　　对：张燕丽　杨延斌　景　虹
　　　　　金立娟
电　　话：86129832

Editorial Unit: the Production Investment Price Office
Editorial Board: Liu Min
Executive Editor-in-Chief: Zhang Yanli Yang Yanbin Jing Hong
Proofreader: Zhang Yanli Yang Yanbin Jing Hong Jin Lijuan
Telephone: 86129832

简要说明

一、本价格指数资料，反映生产和投资环节的价格变动趋势和变动幅度。主要包括工业品出厂价格指数、原材料购进价格指数、固定资产投资价格指数、房地产价格指数和农产品生产价格指数。

二、价格指数统计由国家统计局城市司组织实施。山东工业产品出厂价格及原材料购进价格指数资料，由国家统计局各市级调查队和省属城调队依据国家统计局统一制定的工业品价格统计调查制度向工业调查企业采集原始数据上报国家统计局山东调查总队后汇总而成；固定资产投资价格，由国家统计局各市级调查队和省属城调队依据国家统计局统一制定的固定资产投资价格统计调查制度向施工单位和建设单位采集原始数据上报国家统计局山东调查总队后汇总而成；房地产价格调查由国家统计局各市级调查队和省属城调队依据国家统计局统一制定的房地产价格统计调查制度向房地产调查企业采集原始数据上报国家统计局山东调查总队后汇总而成。

三、工业产品出厂价格及原材料购进价格指数资料，采用重点调查与典型调查相结合的方法统计，重点调查将全部国有企业和年销售收入500万元以上的非国有企业列为调查对象，采用主观选择的方法选择调查企业；典型调查是把年销售收入500万元以下的非国有企业作为抽样对象，采用随机抽样的调查方法。固定资产投资价格指数资料，采用重点调查与典型调查相结合的方法，调查范围包括抽中的各种经济类型的工业、建筑业企业及建设单位。房地产价格指数资料，采用重点调查与典型调查相结合的方法，调查方式采用报表与走访相结合的方式。

四、农产品生产价格调查的目的是，客观反映农产品生产价格水平和结构变动情况，满足农业和国民经济核算需要，为各级政府制定农业保护与农产品流通政策提供决策依据。

Brief Introduction

Ⅰ. This price index material reflects the price change tendency and scope of the link about produces and invests. Mainly includes ex-factory price indices of industrial products, indices of purchasing prices of raw materials, price index of investment in fixed assets, price indices for real estate.

Ⅱ. The price index statistics is organized to implement by NBS City Municipal Corporation. The materials of ex-factory price indices of industrial products and indices of purchasing prices of raw materials in Shandong are compiled by NBS Survey Office in Shandong after NBS various city level investigation team and Shandong province subordinate city level investigation team gather the primary data from industrial investigation enterprise to report based on NBS industrial product price statistics investigation system; The materials of price index of investment in fixed assets is compiled by NBS Survey Office in Shandong after NBS various city level investigation team and Shandong province subordinate city level investigation team gather the primary data from unit in charge of construction and reconstruction unit to report based on NBS fixed assets price statistics investigation system; The materials of price indices for real estate is compiled by NBS Survey Office in Shandong after NBS various city level investigation team and Shandong province subordinate city level investigation team gather the primary data from investigation enterprise of real estate to report based on NBS real estate price statistics investigation system.

Ⅲ. The materials of ex-factory price indices of industrial products and indices of purchasing prices of raw materials use the unified statistics method of key investigation and typical survey, the key investigation list completely the state-owned enterprises and the non-state-owned enterprises of year sale above 5,000,000 Yuan as the investigation objects, use the subjective choice method choice investigation enterprises; The typical survey take the non-state-owned enterprises of year sale below 5,000,000 Yuan as the sampling objects, use the investigation method of the random sampling. The materials of price index of investment in fixed assets uses use the unified statistics method of key investigation and typical survey, the field of investigation includes each kind of economic type industry, the architecture industry enterprise and the construction unitthat were pulled out. The materials of price indices for real estate uses use the unified statistics method of key investigation and typical survey, the investigation way uses to unify report form with visiting.

Ⅳ. The survey objective of agricultural production price is that reflecting objectively agricultural production price changes in the level and structure, meeting the needs of agriculture and the national accounts , providing the policy basis for making decision of agricultural protection and development of the circulation of agricultural products for all levels of governments.

6-1　2006年工业品出厂价格及原材料购进价格月同比价格指数变动趋势

Ex-factory Price Indices of Industrial Products and Indices of Purchasing Prices of Raw Materials, Fuels and Power by Every Month in 2006

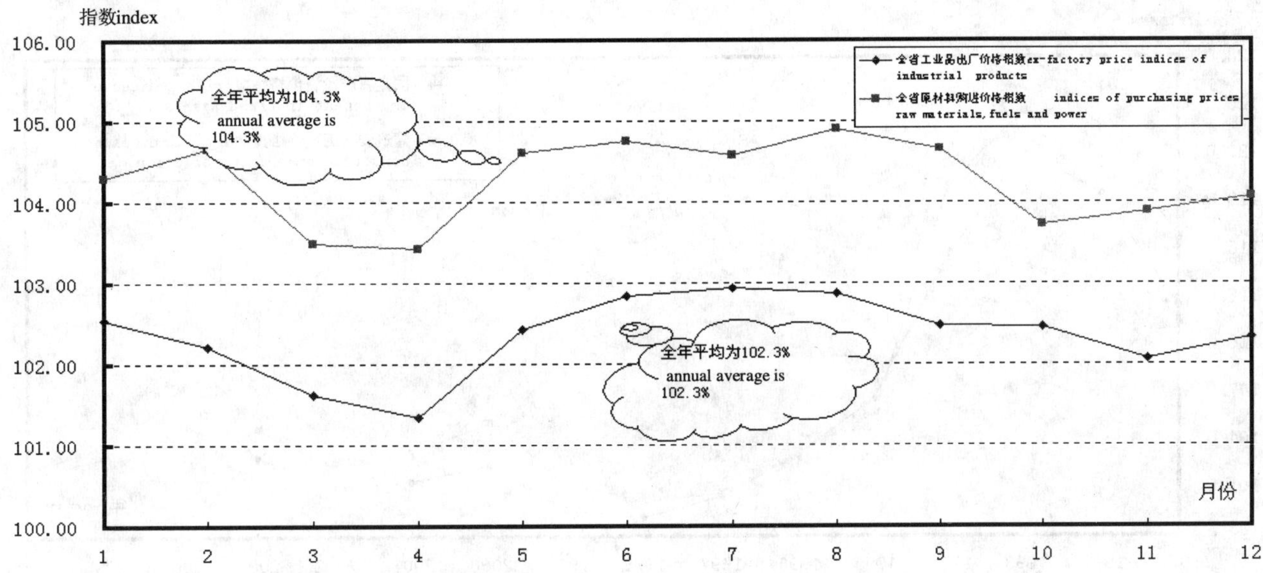

6-2　1990年以来工业品出厂价格及原材料购进价格指数变动趋势

Ex-factory Price Indices of Industrial Products and Indices of Purchasing Prices of Raw Materials, Fuels and Power Since 1990

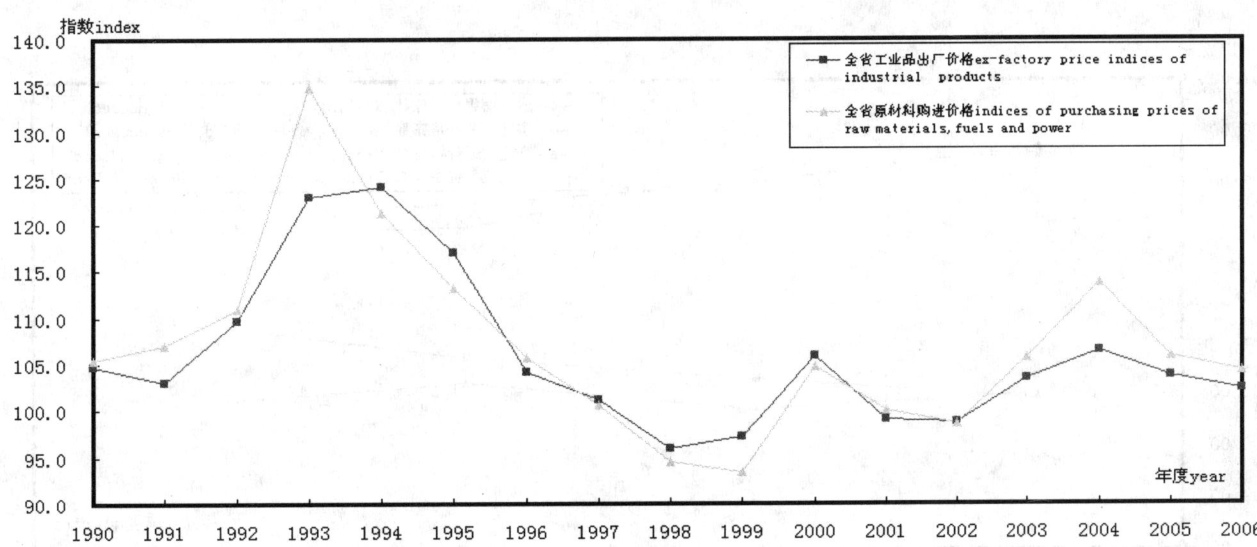

6-3 1991年以来固定资产投资价格指数变动趋势
Price Indices of Investment in Fixed Assets from 1991 to 2006

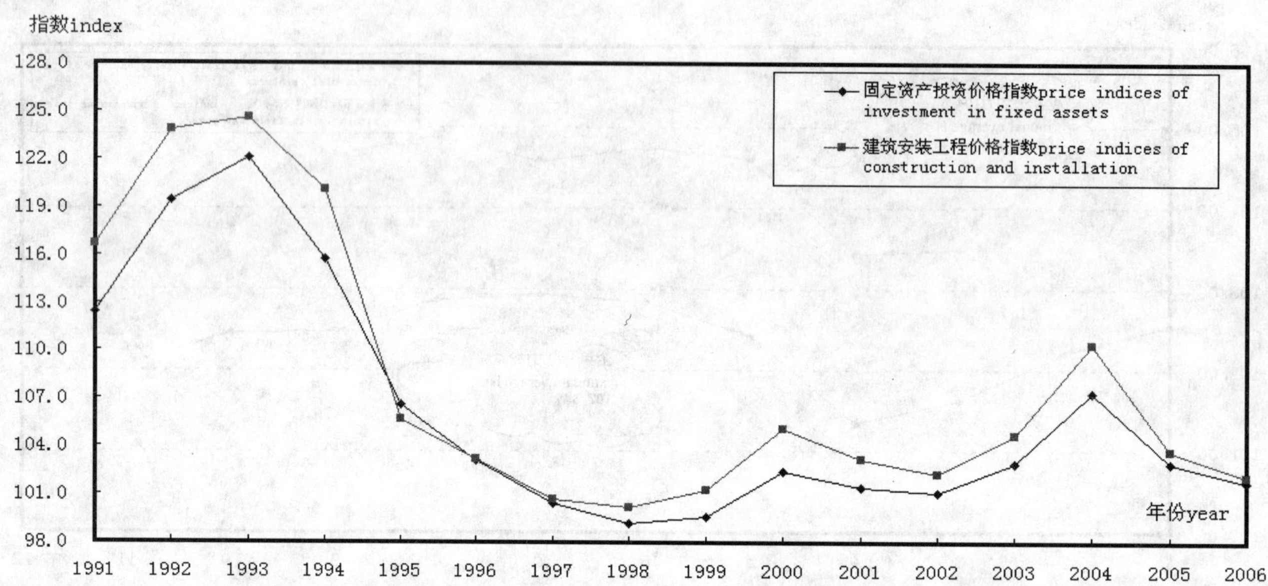

6-4 2006年房地产价格指数变动趋势
Price Indices for Real Estate

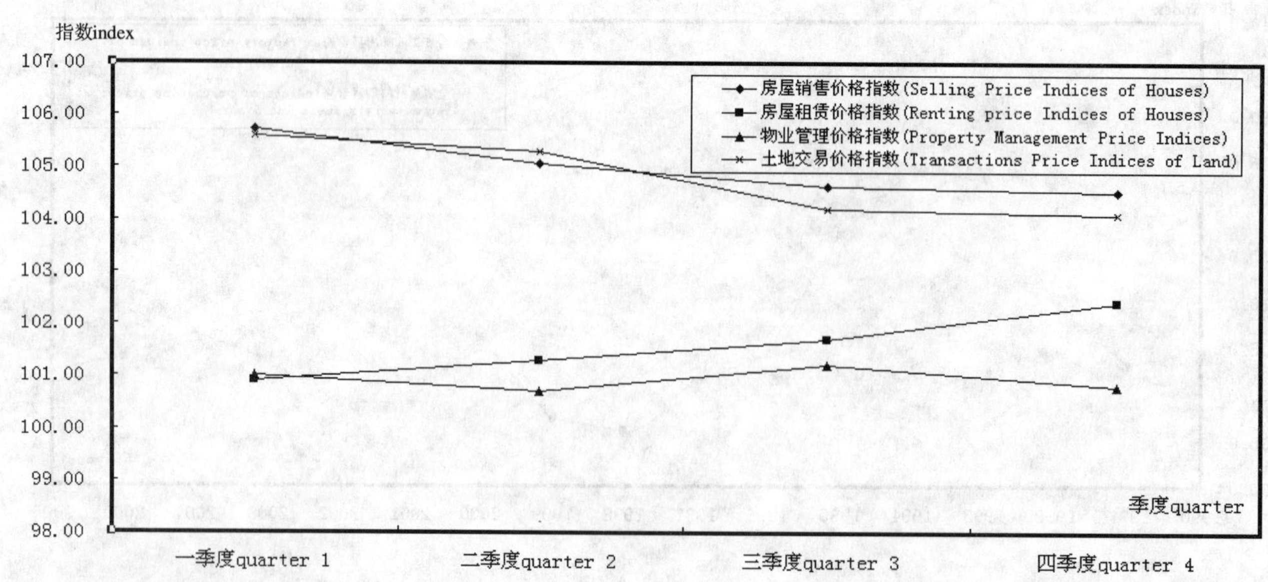

6-5 原材料、燃料、动力购进价格总指数（2006年）

Indices of Purchasing Prices of Raw Materials, Fuels and Power (2006)

类　别	Classification	价格指数（以上年同期价格为100）				
		全年平均 Annual Average	一季度 The First Quarter	二季度 The Second Quarter	三季度 The Third Quarter	四季度 The Forth Quarter
全部原材料	**General Index**	**104.3**	**104.2**	**104.3**	**104.7**	**103.9**
燃料、动力类	Fuels and Energy	109.3	113.2	112.1	109.8	102.2
黑色金属材料类	Ferrous Metals	97.1	97.3	94.2	97.5	99.2
#钢材	Rolled-steel	96.1	97.4	92.8	95.3	99.1
其它	Others	98.0	97.2	95.7	99.8	99.4
有色金属材料和电线类	Non Ferrous Metals	136.1	116.7	127.2	147.2	153.4
化工原料类	Chemical Rqw Materials	103.7	102.1	105.1	103.7	103.9
木材及纸浆类	Wood and Paper Materials	105.1	104.1	104.7	105.6	105.9
建筑材料及非金属矿类	Construction Materials	100.5	100.0	100.6	101.0	100.5
其它工业原材料及半成品类	Other Industrical Raw Materials and Semi-products	102.8	102.2	102.0	103.1	104.0
农副产品类	Farm and Sideline Products	103.2	103.1	103.0	103.6	103.2
纺织原料类	Textile Raw Materials	100.9	101.7	100.5	100.7	100.9

6-6原材料、燃料、动力购进价格指数（2006年）

Indices of Purchasing Prices of Raw Materials, Fuels and Power (2006)

上年=100　　preceding year=100

产品名称	Name of Product	指　数 Indice	产品名称	Name of Product	指　数 Indice
水稻	Rice	101.6	大豆	Soybean	96.1
小麦	Wheat	101.4	赤豆	Bean	84.6
大麦	Barley	99.5	豌豆	Pea	130.3
玉米	Maize	103.4	皮棉	Lint	106.3
高粱	Sorghum	94.3	原棉	Raw Cotton	109.2
黍子	Proso Millet	104.7	棉粕	Cottonseed Meal	116.7
红薯	Sweet Potato	102.4	麻	Flax	100.7
木薯	Cassava	113.7	甜菊干叶	Stevioside Dry Leaves	94.8
花生	Peanut	102.8	烟叶	Tobacco	101.8
葵花籽	Sunflower	100.0	啤酒花	Hops	112.0
芝麻	Sesame	90.0	瓜子	Seeds	109.0
蓖麻	Ricin	101.6	蔬菜类	Vegetables	99.9

6-6 续表 1 continued

产品名称	Name of Product	指 数 Indice	产品名称	Name of Product	指 数 Indice
食用菌	Edible Fungi	104.7	麦杆	Wheat Straw	100.3
水果	Fruit	104.5	米糠	Rice Bran	100.7
茶叶	Tea	104.4	鲜牛奶	Fresh Milk	104.0
中药材	Chinese Herbal Medicines	101.6	蚕茧	Cocoon	125.5
加工用原木	Processing Logs	108.4	麦秸辫	Wheat Straw Braid	121.7
橡胶	Rubber	126.3	无烟煤	Anthracite	102.6
柳条	Wicker	102.9	烟煤	Bituminous Coal	101.2
松油	Terpineol	161.6	洗精煤	Washed Coal	99.4
树枝	Branches	105.0	洗粒级煤	Coal-washing Tablets	99.8
棕榈丝	Palm Wire	108.9	洗混煤	Mixed Coal Washing	95.7
活羊	Live Sheep	98.3	洗中煤	In the Coal Washing	115.8
活牛	Live Cattle	107.9	洗块煤	Wash Lump Coal	109.6
生猪	Pigs	93.0	筛选混末煤	Screening at the End of Coal Mixed	100.6
猪鬃	Bristles	101.6	筛选块煤	Screening of Lump Coal	102.8
家禽	Poultry	98.6	褐煤	Lignite	105.9
鸡蛋	Eggs	99.4	煤泥	Slime	112.4
鸭蛋	Duck	87.2	煤矸石	Gangue	104.6
活兔	Live Rabbits	117.4	天然原油	Natural Oil	114.6
兔皮	Rabbit	133.7	天然气	Natural Gas	113.2
狗皮	Dogskin	106.0	炼钢用铁矿石块	Steelmaking Iron Ore Block	101.1
驴皮	Skin	100.3	炼铁用铁矿石块	Ironmaking Block with Iron Ore	106.7
海产品	Seafood	102.4	铁精矿粉	Iron Concentrate Powder	96.4
贝类	Shellfish	105.7	锰矿石	Manganese Ore	101.0
海产品	Seafood	100.9	锰矿粉	Manganese Ore Powder	98.1
藻类	Algae	100.0	铜精矿	Copper Concentrate	183.2
鲜鱼	Fresh Fish	100.0	铅精矿	Lead Concentrates	133.9
羊毛	Wool	99.6	钴精矿	Cobalt Concentrate	106.0
兔毛	Rabbit Hair	95.9	锑精矿	Sb Concentrate	126.8
牛皮	Kraft	102.2	镁原矿	Magnesium Ore	112.1
羽绒	Eiderdown	100.0	钛原矿	Titanium Ore	120.0
羊皮	Sheepskin	101.6	钛铁矿	Ilmenite	101.0
猪皮	Pigskin	95.9	金精矿	Gold Concentrate	115.3
杂骨	Miscellaneous Bone	93.0	稀土金属	Rare Earth	107.6
棉籽	Cottonseed	108.1	石灰石	Limestone	104.1
菜粕	Rapeseed Meal	99.3	石膏	Gypsum	107.6
麦麸	Wheat Bran	95.9	花岗石荒材	Granite Wood Shortage	101.7

6-6 续表 2 continued

产品名称	Name of Product	指 数 Indice	产品名称	Name of Product	指 数 Indice
大理石荒材	Marble Wood Shortage	98.6	硅微粉	Microsilica	103.0
泽山白荒料	Ze White Stone Mountain	103.7	水晶石	Crystal Stone	100.0
玛瑙红荒材	Agate Red Wood Shortage	100.0	金刚石	Diamond	102.7
西米荒材	Sago Material Shortage	99.7	长石	Feldspar	117.5
硅石	Silica	100.9	白刚玉	White Corundum	102.8
萤石	Fluorite	115.1	地表水	Surface Water	100.0
耐火粘土成品矿	Clay Finished Refractory Ore	101.5	大米	Rice	100.3
活性膨润土	Activity Bentonite	98.8	小麦粉	Wheat Flour	101.2
白云石成品矿	Dolomite Mining Products	92.7	玉米粉	Corn Flour	99.6
硅砂	Silica Sand	101.4	糯米粉	Glutinous Rice Flour	101.9
石英砂	Quartz Sand	101.2	麦芽	Malt	101.6
石渣	Carbide	110.4	豆粕	Soybean Meal	94.1
砂子	Sand	102.0	花生粕	Peanut Meal	95.9
膨润土	Bentonite	107.7	花生油	Peanut Oil	96.9
瓷土	Porcelain Clay	103.5	大豆油	Soybean Oil	100.5
熟料	Clinker	103.7	椰子油	Coconut Oil	92.6
粘土	Clay	109.4	棕榈油	Palm Oil	102.1
矸土	Rock Soil	102.6	桐油	Tung Oil	132.5
沙粉	Sand Powder	105.7	机制甘蔗糖	Cane Sugar Mechanism	125.0
石子	Stone	101.0	机制甜菜糖	Beet Sugar Mechanism	116.8
陶土	Clay	124.2	红糖	Brown Sugar	122.1
高岭土	Kaolin	102.7	液糖	Liquid Sugar	105.7
矸石	Gangue	97.7	鲜冻猪肉	Fresh Frozen Pork	97.9
砂岩	Sandstone	101.9	鲜冻牛肉	Fresh Frozen Beef	101.5
石粉	Powder	100.0	鲜冻羊肉	Fresh Frozen Lamb	108.9
硫铁矿	Pyrite	76.3	鲜冻鸡	Fresh and Frozen Chickens	98.6
磷矿	Phosphorite	118.3	鲜冻兔肉	Fresh Frozen Rabbit Meat	104.2
硼矿	Boron Prospecting	100.0	活鸭	Ducks	87.2
硫精砂	Sulfur Fine Sand	77.0	鲜驴肉	Fresh Donkey Meat	105.5
磷矿粉	Phosphate Fock	109.7	鲜羊肉	Fresh Mutton	103.1
海盐	Sea Salt	75.6	肠衣	Casing	95.8
石棉	Asbestos	100.3	油脂	Oil	101.7
石墨	Graphite	100.1	鱼粉	Fishmeal	111.8
工业原料滑石	Industrial Raw Materials Talc	100.9	淀粉	Starch	104.1
滑石粉	Talc	103.9	蜂蜜	Honey	101.6

6-6 续表 3 continued

产品名称	Name of Product	指 数 Indice	产品名称	Name of Product	指 数 Indice
奶粉	Milk	104.3	晴纶纱	Qingguanmiao	102.0
奶油	Butter	100.0	尼龙布	Nylon Cloth	100.6
消毒鲜牛奶	Disinfection of Fresh Milk	104.2	长毛绒	Plush	107.0
味精	MSG	103.4	腈纶混纺	Acrylic Blended	101.7
柠檬酸	Citric Acid	97.8	棉印染布	Dyeing and Printing of Cotton Cloth	100.9
酵母	Yeast	100.6	混纺印染布	Blended Dyeing Cloth	101.5
精制盐	Refined Salt	101.6	纯毛毛条	Wool Top	98.4
酒精	Alcohol	108.2	混纺毛条	Blended Wool Tops	104.7
白酒	Liquor	100.0	涤纶条	Of Polyester	98.2
浓缩液	Concentrated Liquid	105.6	腈纶毛条	Acrylic Top	99.6
水果汁	Juice	110.1	毛线	Yarn	100.0
固体饮料	Solid Beverage	99.1	毛绒	Stuffed	100.1
复烤烟叶、烟梗	Redrying Tobacco, Tobacco Stems	104.4	纯毛纱	Pure Wool Yarn	101.3
棉纱	Cotton Yarn	103.9	羊绒	Cashmere	98.6
混纺纱	Blended Yarn	98.7	苎麻布	Ramie Cloth	100.0
粘棉纱	Nien Cotton Yarn	102.3	麻线	Thread	106.9
棉短绒	Cotton Linter	108.0	桑蚕丝	Mulberry Silk	122.0
麻纱	Flax Yarn	103.0	桑蚕丝绸（坯绸）	Silkworm Silk (Randgold)	100.3
棉布	Cotton Cloth	102.4	化纤绸（坯绸）	Chemical Fiber Silk (Randgold)	100.3
混纺交织布	Blended Cross Weaving	100.6	桑蚕丝绸（成品绸）	Silkworm Silk (Finished Silk)	100.0
纯化纤布	Pure Chemical Fiber Cloth	101.2	化纤绸（成品稠）	Chemical Fiber Silk (Finished Thick)	107.2
帆布	Canvas	102.1	绉缎坯布	Crepe Satin Fabric	102.4
牛仔布	Denim	102.1	毛（混纺毛）织品	Mao (Mao Blended) Fabric	102.0
PU革基布	PU Leather Fabric	101.6	帘子布	Cord	93.5
涤粘布	Polyester and Viscose Fabrics	100.2	织带	Ribbon	102.0
涤纶布	Polyester Cloth	100.6	网布	Net Cloth	101.5
色织布	Fabric	102.2	轻革	Light Leather	103.2
缝纫线	Sewing Thread	99.9	貂毛皮	Inspector Fur	100.7
棉线	Thread	90.7	山羊毛皮	Goat Fur	92.5
涤纶线	PET Line	100.4	鸭绒	Duck's Down	106.1
粘胶丝线	Viscose Thread	100.0	普通锯材	General Lumber	104.7
坯布	Fabric	106.9	坑木	Pit Prop	105.8
涤棉布	Polyester-cotton Cloth	100.4	铁路用材	Railway Timber	107.3
防粘布	Anti-burn Cloth	108.9	木屑	Sawdust	98.8
防火布	Sharp	96.8	铅笔板	Pencil Board	112.9

6-6 续表 4 continued

产品名称	Name of Product	指 数 Indice	产品名称	Name of Product	指 数 Indice
木薄片	Wood Flakes	101.2	炼厂干气	Dry Gas Refinery	100.0
胶合板	Plywood	102.9	基础油	Base Oil	128.1
纤维板	Fibreboard	104.3	野花石油气	Flowers LPG	113.0
刨花板	Particleboard	105.6	石蜡油	Paraffin Oil	105.0
细木工板	Blockboard	103.7	石油树脂	Petroleum Resin	115.7
木芯板	Wood Veneer	107.0	石油沥青	Asphalt	147.1
杨木旋皮	Poplar Xuan Paper	94.1	乙烯焦油	Ethylene Tar	145.9
机制纸浆	Pulp Mechanism	105.0	焦炭	Coke	99.5
生打纸浆	Pulp Health Fight	100.8	煤焦油	Coal Tar	157.8
硫酸盐漂白浆	Bleached Kraft Pulp	111.0	煅后焦	Calcined Coke	105.5
其他纸浆	Other Pulp	103.1	硫酸	Sulfate	85.3
印刷用纸	Printing Paper	99.5	合成盐酸	Hydrochloric Acid Synthesis	92.2
包装纸板	Wrapping Paper Plate	101.1	硼酸	Boric Acid	97.7
卷烟纸	Cigarette Paper	98.0	氢氟酸	Hydrofluoric Acid	106.1
铝箔衬纸	Making Aluminum Foil Backing Paper	108.1	磷酸	Phosphorylation	96.6
书写纸	Writing Paper	98.3	钾硼氢	Potassium Hydroxide Boron	99.1
彩色包装纸	Color Wrappings	108.5	硬脂酸	Stearic Acid	99.0
普瓦纸	Maciej Paper	101.5	烧碱（氢氧化钠）	Caustic Soda (Sodium Hydroxide)	98.0
有光纸	Bright Paper	106.9	氢氧化钾	Potassium Hydroxide	115.8
版卡纸	Cardboard Edition	100.0	纯碱（碳酸钠）	Soda Ash (Sodium Carbonate)	95.9
白卡纸	White Card	102.5	氢氧化铝	Aluminum Hydroxide	100.1
挂面纸	Noodle Paper	101.0	碳酸钙	Calcium Carbonate	112.7
瓦楞纸箱	Watts Spinulosa Cartons	98.7	泡花碱	Sodium	102.0
水泥包装袋	Cement Packaging Bags	110.3	硫酸盐	Kraft	110.1
各种制印纸板	All Kinds of Printed Cardboard	100.0	硝酸盐	Nitrate	101.5
硅油纸	Silicone Paper	100.0	磷酸盐	Phosphate	96.0
汽油	Gasoline	115.1	硼酸盐	Borate	100.0
煤油	Kerosene	113.8	硅酸盐	Portland	93.6
柴油	Diesel	111.2	氰酸盐	Cyanate Salt	106.5
润滑油	Lubricants	124.5	碳酸盐	Carbonate	99.2
燃料油	Fuel Oil	131.5	氯化物	Chloride	101.9
石蜡	Paraffin	113.9	金属氧化物酸盐	Metal Oxides Permanganate	114.1
溶剂油	Solvent Oil	113.0	其他无机盐	Other Inorganic Salt	100.0
石油焦	Petroleum Coke	105.7	硝酸铵	Ammonium Nitrate	87.3
焦油	Tar	121.0	钠盐	Sodium	63.7
石脑油	Naphtha	107.0	溴化物	Bromide	101.6

6-6 续表 5 continued

产品名称	Name of Product	指 数 Indice	产品名称	Name of Product	指 数 Indice
乙烯	Ethylene	105.8	异氰酸酯	Isocyanate	100.0
丙烯	Propylene	111.9	醋酐	Acetic Anhydride	88.0
纯苯	Merrill	93.8	聚乙烯	Polyethylene	111.0
精甲醇	Fine Methanol	105.2	液氨	Liquid Ammonia	101.2
甲醛	Formaldehyde	102.4	乙醇	Ethanol	107.4
冰醋酸（乙酸）	Glacial Acetic Acid (Acid)	89.5	丙酸	Propionic Acid	121.9
甲苯	Toluene	109.2	已二醇	Has Diol	94.4
苯酚	Phenol	96.0	乙醛	Acetaldehyde	97.1
丁二烯	Butadiene	103.0	二甲基甲酰胺	DMF	82.9
二甲苯	Xylene	105.6	其他	Other	100.9
丙酮	Acetone	92.6	电石（碳化钙）	Calcium Carbide (calcium carbide)	100.5
辛醇	Octanol	117.3	乙炔	Acetylene	96.2
烷基苯	Alkylbenzene	111.0	氯	Chlorine	97.3
环乙烷	Central Ethane	91.7	黄磷	Phosphorus	89.1
苯	Benzene	110.6	赤磷	Red Phosphorous	87.6
丙烷	Propane	103.2	硫磺	Sulfur	89.1
三氯甲烷	Trichloromethane	91.5	氧	Oxygen	99.9
甲胺	Methylamine	97.4	氮	Nitrogen	102.9
对硝基甲苯	On Dinitrotoluene	85.2	双氧水（过氧化氢）	Hydrogen Peroxide (H_2O_2)	105.6
硝基氯化苯	Nitro Chlorobenzene	97.6	漂白粉	Bleaching Powder	100.0
聚醚	Polyether	99.4	碘	Iodine	122.2
季戊四醇	Pentaerythritol	104.2	金属铋	Metal Bismuth	94.0
苯酐	Phthalic Anhydride	123.0	双氯	Diclofenac	92.8
丙烯酸（酯）	Acrylic (ester)	97.8	碳伍	Carbon Kivu	132.8
苯胺	Aniline	97.0	气体二氧化碳	Carbon Dioxide Gas	102.2
乙酯	Ethyl	87.7	氧化物	Oxides	103.1
萘酚	Naphthol	108.0	二氧化物	Dioxide	100.2
邻苯二甲酸酐	Phthalic Anhydride	109.8	硝酸	Nitrate	94.4
二苯甲酮	Benzophenone	86.3	碳酸铵类	Ammonium Carbonate Type	98.5
环已酮	Cyclohexanone	101.2	液氨	Liquid Ammonia	100.6
环已醇	Central Has Alcohol	100.0	硝酸盐	Nitrate	114.3
已二胺	Has Diamine	105.1	氯化钾	Potassium Chloride	98.0
苯乙烯	Styrene	106.7	磷酸铵	Ammonium	92.4
三乙胺	Triethylamine	115.4	敌百虫原粉	Trichlorfon Original Powder	103.6
苯甲酸	Acid	100.4	克百威原粉	Carbofuran Original Powder	99.5
氯乙烯	Vinyl Chloride	96.7	百菌清原粉	Chlorothalonil Original Powder	106.7

6-6 续表 6 continued

产品名称	Name of Product	指 数 Indice	产品名称	Name of Product	指 数 Indice
异丙威原粉	The Original Powder Isoprocarb	99.9	高压聚乙烯塑料	High-pressure Polyethylene Plastic	104.0
甲拌磷	Phorate	99.9	塑料异型材	Plastics Profile	105.5
辛硫磷原油	Crude Oil Phoxim	100.3	醇酸树脂	Alkyd Resin	101.4
阿维菌素	Abamectin	88.0	不饱和聚脂树脂	Unsaturated Polyester Resin	100.5
天然树脂漆	Natural Resin Paint	103.9	聚脂树脂	Polyester Resin	93.5
醇酸树脂漆	Alkyd Resin Paint	100.0	硅单晶片	Monocrystalline Silicon Film	98.3
硝基纤维漆	Nitro Fiber Paint	109.0	氟利昂	Freon	104.1
环氧树脂漆	Epoxy Paint	103.6	顺丁橡胶	BR	107.1
聚氨脂漆	Polyurethane Lacquer	101.0	丁苯橡胶	SBR	111.1
其它漆	Other Chatham	110.1	丁腈橡胶	NBR	100.6
涂料	Coatings	114.2	氯丁橡胶	Neoprene	102.2
涂料用辅助涂料	Assisted Paint Coatings	100.8	硅橡胶	Silastic	98.4
平版胶印油墨	Lithography Offset Printing Ink	105.7	精炼橡胶	Refining Rubber	100.6
水性油墨	Water-based Ink	100.0	聚丙烯酸脂橡胶	Polyacrylic Acid Resin Rubber	106.9
其他油墨类	Like Other Ink	100.0	烟胶	Tobacco Gum	129.8
钛白粉	Titanium Dioxide	101.8	尿醛树脂胶	Urine - formaldehyde Resin Adhesive	102.5
四氧化三铅（红丹）	Lead Oxide (hongdan)	103.9	再生胶	Renewable Plastic	118.9
氧化铁红	Iron Oxide Red	99.9	丁基胶	Butyl Rubber	103.9
颜料中间体	Pigment Intermediates	105.9	涤纶树脂（切片）	Polyester Resin (biopsy)	101.2
活性染料	Reactive	100.0	已内酰胺	Has Lactamase	90.2
分散染料	Disperse Dyes	100.0	丙烯腈	Acrylonitrile	104.4
聚氯乙烯树脂	PVC Resin	99.4	丙纶单体	Polypropylene Monomer	101.1
聚乙烯树脂	Polyethylene Resin	107.2	聚酯	Polyester	102.4
酚醛塑料粉	Phenolic Powder	111.9	聚乙烯醇	PVA	101.9
环氧树脂	Epoxy	102.5	锦纶切片	Nylon Slices	87.9
聚苯乙烯	Polystyrene	102.9	丙烯酰胺	Acrylamide	104.6
聚丙烯	Polypropylene	107.3	精对苯二甲酸	Purified Terephthalic Acid	115.3
有机硅树脂	Silicone Resin	92.6	聚丙烯醇	Polypropylene Alcohol	113.0
酚醛树脂粉	Phenolic Resin Powder	100.9	PET粒子	PET Particles	100.0
交换树脂	Exchange Resin	93.7	尼龙	Nylon	102.2
对氨基苯乙醚	The amino Benzene Ether	117.4	其他催化剂	Other Catalysts	128.8
ＡＢＳ树脂	ABS Resin	100.9	乳化剂	Emulsifier	96.6
塑料树脂	Plastic Resin	97.4	印染助剂	Printing and Dyeing Auxiliaries	97.0
硬树脂	Hard Resin	97.3	粘合剂	Binder	99.0

6-6 续表 7 continued

产品名称	Name of Product	指　数 Indice	产品名称	Name of Product	指　数 Indice
胶粘剂	Adhesive	102.3	硫酸阿托品	Atropine Sulfate	71.3
炭黑	Carbon Black	107.1	曲松钠	Qusong Sodium	84.7
选矿药剂	Beneficiation Pharmacy	105.4	其它	Other	95.8
双面胶半成品	Double-sided Adhesive Semi-finished Products	110.2	化纤用浆粕	Chemical fiber with pulp	104.2
包衣粉	Powder Coating	98.6	粘胶纤维	Viscose Fiber	94.8
分散剂	Dispersant	100.0	醋酸纤维丝束	Cellulose Acetate Tow	145.0
混炼胶	Mix	107.3	锦纶长丝	Nylon Filament	104.8
碳纤维	Carbon Fiber	139.1	锦纶短纤维	Short Fiber Nylon	101.3
表面剂	Surface Agent	100.0	涤纶短纤维	Polyester Staple	103.5
有机合成化学品	Synthetic Organic Chemicals	125.6	涤纶长丝	Polyester Filament	103.1
甘油	Glycerol	100.0	腈纶短纤维	Acrylic Staple Fiber	103.7
松香	Rosin	127.7	腈纶纤维	Acrylic Fibers	100.3
桉叶油	Oil of Folium Eucalypti	100.0	腈纶棉	Acrylic Cotton	126.3
松节油	Turpentine	104.2	丙纶短纤维	Polypropylene Staple Fiber	106.3
炸药	Explosives	106.2	丙纶长丝	PP Filament	99.0
雷管	Detonators	124.5	氨纶丝	Spandex Wire	80.5
导火索	Fuse	112.2	低弹丝	DTY	90.6
萤光粉	Fluorescent Powder	95.8	载重汽车外胎	Truck Tire	112.1
液晶材料	LCD Materials	85.7	轻型载重汽车外胎	Light Truck Tire	101.7
明胶	Gelatin	106.0	轿车外胎	Car Tire	99.9
香精	Flavor	114.6	农用车轮胎外胎	Agricultural Vehicle Tire Tire	107.3
青霉素	Penicillin	100.0	载重汽车内胎	Truck Tubeless	133.1
烟酰胺	Nicotinamide	99.6	轻型车内胎	Light Vehicle Fetal	102.1
麦白霉素	Meleumycinum	100.8	其它橡胶制品	Other Rubber Products	99.8
维生素原粉	Vitamin Original Powder	85.7	胶辊	Cots	109.2
咖啡因	Caffeine	103.2	胶垫	Lining	100.2
维脑路通针用原药	Weinaolutong Needle With the Medicine	96.9	橡胶管	Rubber Tube	102.7
扑热息痛	Paracetamol	101.2	瓶塞	Stopper	120.5
葡萄糖	Glucose	105.3	气球	Balloon	100.0
丙环原料	Propiconazole Raw Materials	100.0	鞋底	Soles	101.8
法莫替丁	Famotidine	97.6	聚氯乙烯薄膜	PVC Film	117.3
注射用甲硝唑粉	Metronidazole Powder for Injection	98.9	聚乙烯薄膜	Polyethylene Film	104.8
克霉唑	Clotrimazole	100.4	聚丙烯制品	Polypropylene Products	103.1
马血清	Ma Serum	100.0	聚脂薄膜	Polyester Film	100.3

6-6 续表 8 continued

产品名称	Name of Product	指 数 Indice	产品名称	Name of Product	指 数 Indice
塑料增强布	Plastic Enhance Cloth	101.9	镜片玻璃	Glass Lenses	90.5
其他塑料制品	Other Plastics	105.2	镀膜玻璃	Coated Glass	101.2
聚丙烯薄膜	Polypropylene Film	100.1	光学玻璃	Optical Glass	102.4
聚氯乙烯电缆料	PVC Cable	101.3	磨砂灯壳	Nubuck Lights Shell	98.6
聚氯乙烯异型材	PVC Profile	100.0	玻璃瓶	Bottles	99.6
聚乙烯管材	Polyethylene Pipes	99.2	玻璃纤维布	Glass Fiber Cloth	101.5
PVC制品	PVC Products	99.8	玻璃纤维纱	Glass Fiber Yarn	101.4
ABS	ABS	103.7	中碱玻璃棉	In the Alkali Glass Wool	98.8
聚乙烯电缆护套	Polyethylene Cable Sheathing	102.6	玻璃纤维润滑剂	Glass Fiber Lubricants	99.3
中纤板	MDF	118.1	玻璃球	Glass Ball	101.2
AGM隔板	AGM Separator	87.9	其他工业电气陶瓷	Other Industrial Electrical Ceramics	100.0
塑料粒子	Plastic Particles	116.0	石棉橡胶板	Asbestos Rubber Plate	96.2
聚丙烯编织袋	Polypropylene Bags	106.2	耐火砖	Firebrick	99.6
聚乙烯编织袋	Polyethylene Bags	117.9	其他耐火材料	Other Refractories	120.8
聚丙烯编织布	Polypropylene Woven	111.5	石墨	Graphite	98.5
泡沫塑料	Foam	101.3	炭素制品	Carbon Products	98.5
组合聚醚	Portfolio Polyether	101.8	玻璃棉管	Glass Wool Tube	97.6
泡沫板材	Bubble Plates	107.9	磨料	Abrasive	107.1
泡沫件	Foam Pieces	93.1	工业硅	Industrial Silicon	105.9
人造革	Leatherette	101.4	石英片	Quartz Tablets	98.2
PUC人造革布	PUC Artificial Leather Cloth	103.4	硅石粉	Silica Powder	111.8
合成革	Synthetic Leather	100.3	生铁	Pig Iron	96.1
铝塑复合带	With Aluminum-plastic Composites	105.0	铁粉	Iron Powder	102.1
塑料包装品	Plastic Packaging Materials	100.1	铁皮	Hut	90.1
普通硅酸盐水泥	Ordinary Portland Cement	100.8	普碳钢坯	Blank Plain Carbon Steel	97.3
矿渣硅酸盐水泥	Slag Portland Cement	98.2	优质碳结钢坯	High-quality Carbon Steel Billet end	90.0
粉煤灰水泥	Fly ash Cement	100.0	钢锭	Ingot	87.5
特种水泥	Special Cement	95.7	钢球	Ball	97.4
混凝土	Suspected Soil Mixed	112.8	合结钢	Astructural Steel	95.2
石灰	Lime	101.0	普通大型钢材	Ordinary Large Steel	98.2
化学石膏	Chemical Gypsum	102.0	普通中型钢材	Ordinary Medium-sized Steel	96.2
釉料	Glaze	104.3	普通小型钢材	Ordinary Small Steel	96.8
平板玻璃	Flat Glass	101.6	优质型钢材	Quality of Steel	96.5
钢化玻璃	Toughened Glass	94.0	线材	Wire	97.7
制镜玻璃	System Mirror Glass	100.0	中厚钢板	In the Thick Plate	95.6

6-6 续表 9 continued

产品名称	Name of Product	指 数 Indice	产品名称	Name of Product	指 数 Indice
薄钢板	Steel Sheet	98.0	紫铜材	Purple Copper	138.3
硅钢片	Silicon Steel Sheet	93.8	黄铜材	Copper Huang	153.9
钢带	Strip	95.6	铅成品材	Lead Finished Wood	100.0
无缝钢管	Seamless Steel Tube	97.5	锡成品材	Tin Finished Wood	174.6
焊接钢管	Welded Steel Pipe	106.1	铝成品材	Aluminum Finished Wood	111.8
低合金钢材	Low Alloy Steel	109.2	铝箔	Aluminum Foil	100.3
钢线	Telegraph	118.1	铝膜	Aluminum	101.4
轴承钢	Bearing Steel	100.8	铝塑型材	APCP Profile	101.2
铁合金	Ferroalloy	93.7	铝塑管	Aluminum-plastic Tube	109.8
铜	Copper	141.1	铝合金型材	Aluminum Profile	109.0
粗铜	Blister Copper	156.7	铝铸件	Aluminum Castings	100.0
铜粉	Copper	171.9	锡青铜带	Tin Bronze Belt	104.2
阴极铜	Copper Cathode	154.6	钨材	W Wood	100.0
铜线	Copper	166.0	钕铁硼	Nd-Fe-B	103.5
铜锭	Copper Ingot	119.9	铁制容器	Metal Containers	121.7
铅	Lead	112.8	钢丝	Wires	99.0
锌	Zinc	144.3	钢丝绳	Wire Rope	100.0
镍	Nickel	119.1	铁丝	Wire	96.9
锡	Tin	93.8	钢绞线	Strand	104.5
氧化铝	Alumina	105.3	铝箔纸	Aluminum Foil Paper	100.0
铝	Aluminum	113.1	油田专用产品	Oilfield Exclusive Products	103.7
镁	Magnesium	96.5	电焊条	Welding Electrodes	97.3
汞	Mercury	163.4	柴油机	Diesel Engine	100.4
海绵钛	Titanium Sponge	122.8	内燃机零部件及配件	Engine Parts and Accessories	91.7
黄金	Gold	117.4	柴油机配件	Diesel Engine Parts	118.9
白银	Silver	105.9	压缩机	Compressor	106.9
铂金	Platinum	112.3	轴承	Bearing	101.2
钨	W	149.0	轴承零配件	Bearing Parts	107.8
钼	Molybdenum	85.9	农用车齿轮	Agricultural Vehicles Gear	92.1
硬质合金	Carbide	100.0	内燃机齿轮	Engine Gear	178.6
铜合金	Copper Alloy	132.1	空调器用压缩机	Air-conditioner Compressor	99.3
铝合金	Aluminum	109.3	铸铁	Cast Iron	98.8
锌合金	Zinc Alloy	152.1	铸钢	Casting	100.7
镍合金	Nickel Alloy	96.1	轻钢龙骨	Metal Frame	68.8
镁合金	Magnesium Alloys	100.8	不锈钢铸件	Stainless Steel Castings	109.5

6-6 续表 10 continued

产品名称	Name of Product	指 数 Indice	产品名称	Name of Product	指 数 Indice
有色铸件	Nonferrous Metal Castings	100.4	显像管	CRT	87.1
锻件	Forging	97.3	晶体管	Transistors	123.8
机车配件	Motorcycle Accessories	117.8	电视机配件	TV Accessories	100.0
汽车配件	Auto Parts	101.6	半导体二极管	Semiconductor Diode	96.8
摩托车配件	Motorcycle Accessories	101.8	半导体三极管	Semiconductor Transistor	100.1
自行车配件	Bicycle Accessories	99.8	半导体器件引线	Semiconductor Devices Lead	148.2
电动自行车	Electric Bicycle	102.2	液晶显示板	LCD Panels	70.4
发电水轮机组	Turbine Power Generation Group	100.0	半导体集成电路	Semiconductor Integrated Circuits	91.0
交流电动机	AC Motor	114.0	模块	Module	103.3
其它各种电动机	All Other Motor	100.6	芯片	Chip	102.9
控制、驱动微电机	Control of Micro-motor Drives	96.9	电子调谐器	Electronic Tuner	100.4
变压器	Transformer	104.7	管座	Control Block	100.0
互感器	Transformer	102.2	电阻	Resistivity	98.3
电容器	Capacitors	100.0	电容器	Capacitors	102.0
变频器	Inverter	100.0	继电器	Relay	103.5
断电器	Broken Electrical Appliances	101.6	电阻、变阻器	Resistance, Rheostat	101.9
开关插座	Switching Sockets	98.2	电路板	Circuit Board	100.2
配电设备及器	Distribution of Equipment and	104.3	摄像头	Cameras	100.0
继电器	Relay	100.0	废钢	Scrap	92.8
电子开关电源	Electronic Switching Power Supply	100.0	其他	Other	122.1
裸铜线	Bare Copper	128.6	废塑料	Waste Plastics	102.2
布电线	Cloth Wires	131.1	废纸	Waste Paper	98.1
漆包铜线	Copper Enameling	134.7	废玻璃	Glass	111.6
线圈	Coil	100.3	煤灰	PFA	109.2
电表配件	Ammeter Accessories	138.4	废油	Waste Oil	109.0
电源设备	Power Equipment	100.0	矿渣	Slag	96.5
蓄电池	Battery	103.4	杂骨	Miscellaneous Bone	65.4
锂电池	Lithium Batteries	101.7	电	Xinhua	102.7
汽车灯泡	Auto Bulb	100.0	热	Heat	104.9
灯头	To Solid	100.9	工业用燃气	Industrial Gas	102.8
电光源玻璃管	Electric Light Source Glass Tube	100.0	工业用天然气	Industrial Gas	108.2
计算机显示终端设备	Computer Display Terminal Equipment	100.0	自来水	Tap Water	109.9
发射管	Launch of	83.3			

6-7 工业品出厂价格总指数及不同分组指数（2006年）
General Ex-factory Price Indices of Industrial Products and Different Groups Index (2006)

类 别	Classification	价格指数（以上年价格为100）				
		全年平均 Annual Average	一季度 The first Quarter	二季度 The Second Quarter	三季度 The Third Quarter	四季度 The Forth Quarter
全部工业品	**General Index**	**102.3**	**102.1**	**102.2**	**102.8**	**102.3**
轻工业	Hight Industry	101.1	100.5	100.3	101.3	102.2
以农产品为原料	Using Agricultural Products as Raw Materials	101.4	100.8	100.3	101.6	102.8
以非农产品为原料	Using Non-agricultural Products as Raw Materials	100.7	100.1	100.2	100.9	101.4
重工业	Heavy Industry	103.7	103.8	104.2	104.3	102.4
采掘	Mining Quarrying	109.0	118.0	113.6	108.5	95.7
原料	Raw Materials	104.9	104.1	105.4	105.8	104.5
加工	Manufacturing	100.9	98.8	100.1	101.6	103.0
生产资料	Means of Production	103.1	103.3	103.3	103.5	102.2
采掘	Mining Quarrying	107.8	116.0	111.9	107.4	96.0
原料	Raw Materials	105.1	104.2	105.6	106.0	104.6
加工	Manufacturing	101.4	100.5	100.8	101.8	102.5
生活资料	Consumer Goods	100.4	99.1	99.2	100.9	102.5
食品	Food	101.0	98.8	98.9	101.8	104.5
衣着	Clothing	101.6	101.7	101.4	101.7	101.5
一般日用品	Articles for Daily Use	100.3	100.6	100.7	100.2	99.8
耐用消费品	Durable Consumer Goods	98.2	96.7	97.3	98.4	100.1
按工业部门分	**By Industrid Department**					
冶金工业	Metallurgical Industry	101.1	96.2	98.6	103.6	106.1
电力工业	Power Industry	102.4	103.2	102.4	101.9	101.9
煤炭及炼焦工业	Coal Industry and Coking Industry	97.6	96.9	95.4	97.7	100.4
石油工业	Petroleum Industry	118.6	130.8	128.3	117.4	98.1
化学工业	Chemical Industry	101.7	100.4	101.2	102.3	103.0
机械工业	Machine Building Industry	100.4	99.6	99.9	100.7	101.4
建筑材料工业	Building Materials Industry	102.2	101.9	102.2	102.4	102.1
森林工业	Timber Industry	100.6	102.0	100.8	99.7	99.8
食品工业	Food Industry	100.9	98.6	98.8	101.8	104.6
纺织工业	Textile Industry	102.4	104.2	102.6	101.7	101.1
缝纫工业	Tailoring Industry	101.3	101.3	101.3	101.6	101.1

6-7 续表 1 continued

类 别	Classification	价格指数（以上年价格为100） 全年平均 Annual Average	一季度 The first Quarter	二季度 The Second Quarter	三季度 The Third Quarter	四季度 The Forth Quarter
皮革工业	Leather Industry	102.4	102.9	102.0	102.3	102.6
造纸工业	Paper Industry	101.1	101.7	101.0	101.0	100.9
文教艺术用品工业	Cultual, Educational Handicrafts Articles	100.9	100.6	101.1	101.3	100.4
其它工业	Other Industry	101.4	100.7	101.7	102.0	101.3
按工业行业分	**By Sector**					
煤炭开采和洗选业	Coal Mining and Dressing	97.8	97.9	95.9	97.5	99.8
#烟煤和无烟煤的开采洗选	Mining and Washing of Bituminous and Anthracite	97.6	98.0	95.8	97.3	99.5
褐煤的开采洗选	Mining and Washing of Lignite	101.9	94.9	95.9	104.5	112.4
石油和天然气开采业	Petrleum and Natural Gas Extraction	121.7	144.3	137.0	119.1	86.3
#天然原油和天然气开采	Extraction of Natural Petroleum and Natual Gas	121.7	144.3	137.0	119.1	86.3
黑色金属矿采选业	Mining and Processing of Ferrous Metal Ores	94.0	93.0	91.3	95.0	96.9
#铁矿采选	Mining and Processing of Iron Ores	94.0	93.0	91.3	95.0	96.9
有色金属矿采选业	Mining nd Processing of Non-ferrous Metal Ores	111.1	107.2	103.2	117.5	116.7
常用有色金属矿采选	Mining and Processing of Frequently Used Non-Ferrous Metal Ores	171.8	130.8	183.9	182.7	189.8
贵金属矿采选	Mining and Processing of Precious MetalOres	110.8	107.0	102.7	117.2	116.3
非金属矿采选业	Mining and Processing of Nonmetal Ores	93.7	95.1	95.0	92.9	91.9
#土砂石开采	Mining of Soil, Sand and Stone	103.2	101.0	103.7	103.0	105.2
采盐	Mining and Processing of Salt Ores	73.6	76.3	75.2	73.7	69.0
石棉及其他非金属矿采选	Mining and Processing of Asbestos and Other Nonmetal Ores	106.7	116.0	109.5	102.0	99.2
农副食品加工业	Processing of Food From Agricultural Products	100.6	97.7	97.7	101.6	105.4
谷物磨制	Polishing of Grain	98.8	96.5	96.2	98.9	103.5
饲料加工	Processing of Feed	100.0	100.7	99.7	99.9	99.8
植物油加工	Processing of Vegetable Oil	99.9	91.5	94.9	102.7	110.6
制糖	Processing of Sugar	117.1	115.7	115.3	123.6	113.9
屠宰及肉类加工	Slaughtering and Processing of Meat	96.1	93.5	89.9	95.8	105.3
水产品加工	Processing of Aquatic Products	102.4	100.5	101.0	104.4	103.7
蔬菜、水果和坚果加工	Processing of Vegetables, Fruits and Nuts	104.5	103.6	104.9	104.8	104.6
其他农副食品加工	Processing of Other Food from Agricultural Products	105.0	104.8	105.2	104.9	105.2
食品制造业	Foodstuff	101.0	100.3	101.2	100.9	101.7
焙烤食品制造	Manufacture of Baking Foodstuff	101.0	100.4	99.5	101.5	102.7
糖果、巧克力及蜜饯制造	Manufacture of Sweet, Chocolate and Candied Fruit	105.1	105.4	103.2	104.7	107.3

6-7 续表 2 continued

类 别	Classification	价格指数（以上年价格为100） 全年平均 Annual Average	一季度 The first Quarter	二季度 The Second Quarter	三季度 The Third Quarter	四季度 The Forth Quarter
方便食品制造	Manufacture of Convenience Food	99.9	97.7	99.2	100.1	102.7
液体乳及乳制品制造	Manufacture of Milk Gel and Dairy Products	102.2	101.3	102.0	102.4	102.9
罐头制造	Manufacture of Cans	109.3	104.1	111.0	114.0	108.0
调味品、发酵制品制造	Manufacture of Condiments and Fermentation Products	99.5	97.7	98.7	98.7	103.1
其他食品制造	Manufacture of Other Foodstuff	99.9	101.4	101.7	99.0	97.5
饮料制造业	Manufacture of Beverages	102.0	101.8	101.8	102.4	101.9
酒精制造	Manufacture of Alcohol	102.1	103.0	101.4	102.0	102.1
酒的制造	Manufacture of Liquor	102.1	102.2	101.8	102.3	101.9
软饮料制造	Manufacture of Soft Drink	101.7	100.6	101.7	102.5	101.8
精制茶加工	Processing of Refined Tea	103.2	99.9	108.9	102.9	101.1
烟草制品业	Manufacture of Tobacco	101.3	100.8	101.1	101.7	101.7
烟叶复烤	Baking of Tobacco	100.0	100.0	100.0	100.0	100.0
卷烟制造	Manufacture of Cigarettes	101.4	100.8	101.2	101.7	101.7
其他烟草制品加工	Manufacture of Other Tobacco Products	100.0	100.0	100.0	100.0	66.7
纺织业	Manufacture of Textile	102.4	104.0	102.6	101.9	101.3
棉、化纤纺织及印染精加工	Processing and Dyeing of Cotton and Chemical Fiber Textile	103.0	104.5	103.2	102.4	101.8
毛纺织和染整精加工	Processing and Dyeing of Wool Textile	98.3	100.5	97.6	97.6	97.6
麻纺织	Flax Textile	102.2	102.9	101.3	101.7	102.8
丝绢纺织及精加工	Processing of Silk Textile	120.6	132.4	125.3	113.3	111.5
纺织制成品制造	Manufacture of Textile Products	99.8	101.3	99.9	99.2	98.6
针织品、编织品及其制品制造	Manufacture of Knitwear and Woven Products	102.5	102.8	102.4	102.8	102.1
纺织服装、鞋、帽制造业	Manufacture of Textile Wearing Apparel, Footware, and Caps	100.7	100.6	100.8	100.9	100.5
纺织服装制造	Manufacture of Textile Wearing Apparel	100.5	100.5	100.7	100.6	100.2
纺织面料鞋的制造	Manufacture of Textile Footware	102.5	100.3	101.5	103.7	104.3
制 帽	Manufacture of Caps	104.7	104.3	103.5	108.7	102.3
皮革、毛皮、羽毛（绒）及其制品业	Manufacture of Leather, Fur, Feather and Related Products	102.3	102.8	101.9	102.2	102.4
皮革鞣制加工	Processing of Leather	101.3	101.8	101.1	101.0	101.1
皮革制品制造	Manufacture of Leather Products	102.9	103.4	102.4	102.8	103.1
毛皮鞣制及制品加工	Manufacture and Processing of Fur Products	101.9	101.0	102.0	101.4	103.3
羽毛（绒）加工及制品制造	Manufacture and Processing of Feather Products	96.6	94.6	98.0	97.5	96.3
木材加工及木、竹、藤、棕、草制品业	Processing of Timber, Manufacture of Wood, Bamboo	100.7	102.6	101.1	99.5	99.6
锯材、木片加工	Processing of Lumber and Wood Chips	101.4	107.0	99.4	98.9	100.5

6-7 续表 3 continued

类 别	Classification	价格指数（以上年价格为100） 全年平均 Annual Average	一季度 The first Quarter	二季度 The Second Quarter	三季度 The Third Quarter	四季度 The Forth Quarter
人造板制造	Manufacture of Plywood	99.7	100.8	99.9	98.9	99.3
木制品制造	Manufacture of Wood Products	101.3	101.7	102.2	100.9	100.2
竹、藤、棕、草制品制造	Manufacture of Penny, Vines Coir and Grass Products	105.1	111.6	107.9	101.3	99.5
家具制造业	Manufacture of Furniture	100.3	100.7	100.3	100.1	100.2
#木质家具制造	Manufacture of Wood Furniture	100.3	100.7	100.3	100.1	100.2
金属家具制造	Manufacture of Metal Furniture	100.2	98.4	100.4	100.8	101.0
其他家具制造	Manufacture of Other Furniture	100.0	99.8	98.8	99.9	101.3
造纸及纸制品业	Manufacture of Paper and Paper Products	101.2	101.7	101.0	101.0	100.9
纸浆制造	Manufacture of Paper Pulp	110.7	107.3	105.6	115.4	114.3
造纸	Manufacture of Paper	101.1	101.5	101.1	101.0	100.8
纸制品制造	Manufacture of Paper Products	101.1	102.2	100.8	100.7	100.8
印刷业和记录媒介的复制	Printing Reproduction of Recording Media	101.3	101.1	100.8	101.8	101.6
印刷	Printing	101.5	101.2	101.0	102.1	101.8
装订及其他印刷服务活动	Binding and Other Printing Services	100.5	102.2	99.2	100.0	100.5
记录媒介的复制	Copy of Record Media	89.7	87.7	88.2	89.3	93.6
文教体育用品制造业	Manufacture of Articles for Culture, Education and Sport Activity	100.4	100.3	100.9	100.8	99.5
#文化用品制造	Manufacture of Culture Articles	101.7	100.9	102.2	102.0	101.5
体育用品制造	Manufacture of Sport Articles	99.0	99.1	99.4	99.4	98.0
乐器制造	Manufacture of Music Instruments	100.1	100.4	100.3	100.0	99.6
玩具制造	Manufacture of Toys	101.8	101.5	102.5	102.4	100.8
石油加工、炼焦及核燃料加工业	Processing of Petroleum, Coking, Processing of Nuclear Fuel	114.4	116.9	118.6	114.6	107.7
#精炼石油产品的制造	Manufacture of Refined Petroleum Products	116.1	119.7	121.1	115.9	107.8
炼焦	Coking	95.6	85.9	90.1	99.9	106.6
化学原料及化学制品制造业	Manufacture of Raw Chemical Materials and Chemical Products	101.7	99.1	101.3	102.8	103.7
基础化学原料制造	Manufacture of Basic Chemical Material	100.8	95.3	97.4	102.7	107.6
肥料制造	Manufacture of Fertilizers	99.6	100.4	101.4	97.6	98.9
农药制造	Manufacture of Pesticides	101.8	104.8	100.3	100.9	101.0
涂料、油墨、颜料及类似产品制造	Manufacture of Coating,Ink and Paint Products	106.0	106.0	105.3	106.2	106.6
合成材料制造	Manufacture of Synthetic Materials	101.9	95.0	104.2	104.1	104.1
专用化学产品制造	Manufacture of Specialized Chemical Products	102.8	100.6	101.0	105.2	104.5
日用化学产品制造	Manufacture of Daily Used Chemical Products	101.2	101.1	101.3	101.3	101.1

6-7 续表 4 continued

类别	Classification	价格指数（以上年价格为100） 全年平均 Annual Average	一季度 The first Quarter	二季度 The Second Quarter	三季度 The Third Quarter	四季度 The Forth Quarter
医药制造业	Manufacture of Medicines	97.8	100.8	98.1	95.6	96.6
化学药品原药制造	Manufacture of Chemical Original Drug	90.4	99.8	90.2	84.3	87.4
化学药品制剂制造	Manufacture of Chemical Agents	99.2	100.7	100.1	97.8	98.0
中药饮片加工	Processing of Herbal Medicine	101.2	103.0	101.9	100.0	100.0
中成药制造	Manufacture of Proprietary Chinese Medicine	99.7	102.6	99.5	98.2	98.3
兽用药品制造	Manufacture of Veterinary Drugs	99.4	98.7	99.0	99.4	100.4
生物、生化制品的制造	Manufacture of Biotechnology and Biochemical Products	109.1	104.9	110.2	112.6	108.8
卫生材料及医药用品制造	Manufacture of Sanitation Materials and Medical Supplies	100.8	100.5	101.5	100.9	100.4
化学纤维制造业	Manufacture of Chemical Fibers	95.9	95.4	95.5	95.6	97.1
纤维素纤维原料及纤维制造	Manufacture of Cellulose Fibers and Fibers	101.0	93.0	100.1	101.7	109.1
合成纤维制造	Manufacture of Synthetic Fibers	93.8	96.2	93.8	93.3	92.0
橡胶制品业	Manufacture of Rubber	107.4	106.5	106.3	108.6	108.4
轮胎制造	Manufacture of Tire	110.3	108.9	109.1	111.9	111.4
橡胶板、管、带的制造	Manfuacture of Rubber Plates, Pipes and Belts	101.4	100.0	101.0	102.5	102.1
橡胶零件制造	Manufacture of Rubber Parts	101.2	104.4	100.9	100.9	98.6
再生橡胶制造	Manufacture of Renewable Rubber	109.5	104.8	109.4	112.2	111.8
日用及医用橡胶制品制造	Manufacture of Daily Used and Medical Rubber Products	98.7	99.4	99.0	96.9	99.5
橡胶靴鞋制造	Manufacture of Rubber Boots and Shoes	99.8	100.0	98.3	100.2	100.5
其他橡胶制品制造	Manufacture of Other Rubber Products	107.0	102.1	108.8	108.2	108.8
塑料制品业	Manufacture of Plastics	102.4	102.1	101.2	102.9	103.5
#塑料薄膜制造	Manufacture of Plastic Film	101.6	99.8	99.7	103.0	104.0
塑料板、管、型材的制造	Manufacture of Plastic Plates, Piles and Profiles	101.9	104.8	100.8	101.3	100.5
塑料丝、绳及编织品的制造	Manufacture of Plastic Wire, Ropes and Woven Products	105.0	103.3	103.3	106.0	107.2
泡沫塑料制造	Manufacture of Foam	99.4	97.9	98.0	99.0	102.5
塑料人造革、合成革制造	Manufacture of Plastic Leatherette and Synthetic Leather	96.4	98.4	93.8	95.7	97.8
塑料包装箱及容器制造	Manufacture of Plastic Packaging Boxes and Containers	105.0	103.4	104.6	105.9	106.0
日用塑料制造	Manufacture of Daily Used Plastic	102.5	100.8	102.0	102.4	104.8
其他塑料制品制造	Manufacture of Other Plastic Products	99.2	99.4	98.5	99.4	99.4
非金属矿物制品业	Manufacture of Non-metallic Products	101.7	101.3	101.8	102.1	101.5
水泥、石灰和石膏的制造	Manufacture of Cement, Lime and Gypsum	100.0	99.6	100.0	100.3	99.9
水泥及石膏制品制造	Manufacture of Cement and Gypsum	102.9	102.7	101.4	103.5	104.2
砖瓦、石材及其他建筑材料制造	Manufacture of Brick, Stone and Other Construction Materials	102.0	102.3	102.0	102.6	101.0

6-7 续表 5 continued

类 别	Classification	价格指数（以上年价格为100）				
		全年平均 Annual Average	一季度 The first Quarter	二季度 The Second Quarter	三季度 The Third Quarter	四季度 The Forth Quarter
玻璃及玻璃制品制造	Manufacture of Glass and Its Products	99.6	97.2	100.3	100.7	100.2
陶瓷制品制造	Manufacture of Ceramic Products	108.4	108.2	108.9	108.1	108.4
耐火材料制品制造	Manufacture of Refractory Products	97.9	99.3	98.6	97.7	96.2
石墨及其他非金属矿物制品制造	Manufacture of Graphite and Other Non-metallic Mineral Products	101.3	102.2	101.1	101.2	100.6
黑色金属冶炼及压延加工业	Smelting and Pressing of Ferrous Metals	94.7	88.7	92.5	96.6	101.1
炼铁	Ironmaking	94.0	89.6	90.9	96.3	99.3
炼钢	Steelmaking	97.4	95.4	97.5	99.2	97.4
钢压延加工	Smelting and Pressing of Steel	94.0	86.5	91.2	95.8	102.3
铁合金冶炼	Smelting of Alloy Iron	102.7	104.2	104.7	101.2	100.8
有色金属冶炼及压延加工业	Smelting and Pressing of Non-ferrous Metals	118.7	110.8	117.6	123.5	122.7
#常用有色金属冶炼	Smelting of Frequently Used Non-Ferrous Metal	122.7	111.7	118.2	129.2	131.5
贵金属冶炼	Smelting of Precious Metal	127.8	114.4	134.1	136.0	126.5
有色金属合金制造	Non-ferrous Metal Alloy Manufacture	110.0	103.8	111.2	116.3	107.8
有色金属压延加工	Pressing of Non-Ferrous Metal	116.6	110.4	116.3	120.5	119.3
金属制品业	Manufacture of Metal Products	97.2	98.0	94.6	97.0	98.9
结构性金属制品制造	Manufacture of Structural Metal Products	94.3	94.9	93.2	94.2	95.0
金属工具制造	Manufacture of Metal Tools	101.6	103.7	101.6	100.1	101.1
集装箱及金属包装容器制造	Manufacture of Containers and Metal Packaging	93.6	96.8	82.4	94.7	100.4
金属丝绳及其制品的制造	Manufacture of Metal Wire, Ropes and Its Products	101.5	99.1	102.4	103.0	101.6
建筑、安全用金属制品制造	Manufacture of Metal Products for Construction and Safety	100.1	99.9	100.2	98.4	101.8
金属表面处理及热处理加工	Processing of Surface Treatment and Heat Treatment of Metals	104.9	101.5	106.0	107.6	104.4
搪瓷制品制造	Manufacture of Enamel Products	105.3	110.3	106.4	105.7	98.8
不锈钢及类似日用金属制品制造	Manufacture of Stainless Steel and Daily Metal Products	103.5	99.4	105.7	101.1	107.6
其他金属制品制造	Manufature of Other Metal Products	102.5	100.3	104.8	101.9	103.0
通用设备制造业	Manufacture of General Purpose Machinery	100.2	100.9	99.9	99.7	100.2
#锅炉及原动机制造	Manufacture of Boilers and Original Motivation	100.0	99.0	100.0	100.6	100.5
金属加工机械制造	Manufacture of Metal Processing Machinery	98.7	98.9	98.4	98.7	98.9
起重运输设备制造	Manufacture of Handling Equipment	100.6	101.7	98.9	100.2	101.5
泵、阀门、压缩机及类似机械的制造	Manufacture of Pumps, Valves, Compressors	99.8	99.9	99.5	99.6	100.3
轴承、齿轮、传动和驱动部件的制造	Manufacture of Bearings, Gears, Transmission and Drive Components	100.4	102.2	100.3	100.4	98.5
风机、衡器、包装设备等通用设备制造	Manufacture of Fans, Weighing, Packaging Equipment and Other General Equipment	101.6	101.9	102.7	100.0	101.7
通用零部件制造及机械修理	Manufacture of General Components and Mechanical Repair	99.7	101.2	99.1	98.9	99.4

6-7 续表 6 continued

类 别	Classification	价格指数（以上年价格为100）				
		全年平均 Annual Average	一季度 The first Quarter	二季度 The Second Quarter	三季度 The Third Quarter	四季度 The Forth Quarter
金属铸、锻加工	Processing of Metal Casting and Forging	100.3	102.3	99.5	99.2	100.0
专用设备制造业	Manufacture of Special Purpose Machinery	101.7	101.7	101.3	102.1	101.8
矿山、冶金、建筑专用设备制造	Manufacture of Special Equipment for Mining, Metallurgy, Construction	103.8	103.1	103.3	104.1	104.7
化工、木材、非金属加工专用设备制造	Manufacture of Special Equipment for Chemicals, Wood, Non-metallic Processing	98.3	101.6	96.6	97.6	97.4
食品、饮料、烟草及饲料生产专用设备制造	Manufacture of Special Equipment for Food, Beverage, Tobacco and Feed Production	99.7	100.9	98.9	99.6	99.5
印刷、制药、日化生产专用设备制造	Manufacture of Special Equipment for Printing, Pharmaceuticals, Chemicals Production	102.1	103.4	102.1	101.0	101.8
纺织、服装和皮革工业专用设备制造	Manufacture of Special Equipment for Textiles, Clothing and Leather Industry	100.7	100.9	100.4	100.9	100.7
电子和电工机械专用设备制造	Manufacture of Special Equipment for Electronic and Electrical Machinery	95.9	95.7	93.7	98.0	96.3
农、林、牧、渔专用机械制造	Manufacture of Special Equipment for Agriculture, Forestry, Animal Husbandry, Fishery	102.4	101.7	102.7	103.1	102.1
医疗仪器设备及器械制造	Manufacture of Medical Equipment and Instrument	97.7	96.0	97.6	98.3	98.8
环保、社会公共安全及其他专用设备制造	Manufacture of Special Equipment for Environmental, Social Public Safety and Others	104.3	103.2	105.6	105.4	102.9
交通运输设备制造业	Manufacture of Transport Equipment	100.1	99.0	99.7	100.3	101.5
#铁路运输设备制造	Manufacture of Equipment for Railway Transport	106.7	104.6	108.4	107.7	106.2
汽车制造	Manufacture of Automobiles	99.6	98.4	98.8	99.6	101.4
摩托车制造	Manufacture of Motorcycles	100.7	101.1	100.7	100.2	100.6
自行车制造	Manufacture of Bicycles	99.4	100.1	101.9	98.9	96.6
船舶及浮动装置制造	Manufacture of Shipping and Floating Devices	100.3	98.3	100.9	102.1	99.8
电气机械及器材制造业	Manufacture of Electrical Machinery and Equipment	104.9	103.3	104.3	105.8	106.3
电机制造	Manufacture of Electrical Motors	104.3	100.3	102.5	106.6	107.9
输配电及控制设备制造	Manufacture of Power Distribution and Control Equipment	103.4	105.1	102.7	103.8	101.8
电线、电缆、光缆及电工器材制造	Manufacture of Wires, Cables,Fiber-optic Cables and Electrical Equipment	112.9	108.1	113.0	115.7	114.8
电池制造	Manufacture of Electric Cells	106.7	102.0	104.4	106.1	114.3
家用电力器具制造	Manufacture of Household Electrical Apparatus	101.6	101.3	100.9	101.3	102.7
非电力家用器具制造	Manufacture of Household Non-electrical Apparatus	99.7	99.2	98.9	100.1	100.6
照明器具制造	Manufacture of Lighting Devices	103.4	101.4	107.5	104.8	99.8
其他电气机械及器材制造	Manufacture of Other Electrical Machinery and Equipment	100.3	98.9	92.0	105.3	104.9

6-7 续表 7 continued

类　别	Classification	价格指数（以上年价格为100）				
		全年平均 Annual Average	一季度 The first Quarter	二季度 The Second Quarter	三季度 The Third Quarter	四季度 The Forth Quarter
通信设备、计算机及其他电子设备制造业	Manufacture of Communication Equipment,Computers and Other Electronic Equipment	92.7	90.1	91.9	93.6	95.0
通信设备制造	Manufacture of Communication Equipment	93.3	94.1	93.6	94.2	91.1
雷达及配套设备制造	Manufacture of Radar and Auxiliary Equipment	100.1	100.4	100.0	100.0	100.0
广播电视设备制造	Manufacture of Communication Broadcasting and TV Equipment	100.0	100.0	100.0	100.0	100.0
电子计算机制造	Manufacture of Computers	93.7	91.0	93.8	94.7	95.5
电子器件制造	Manufacture of Electronic Devices	101.0	100.4	100.6	100.8	101.9
电子元件制造	Manufacture of Electronic Components	92.6	92.1	92.4	92.8	93.2
家用视听设备制造	Manufacture of Household Audio-visual Equipment	88.8	82.5	86.3	90.8	95.8
其他电子设备制造	Manufacture of Other Electronic Equipment	100.0	100.0	100.0	100.0	100.0
仪器仪表及文化、办公用机械制造业	Manufacture of Measuring Instruments and Machinery for Cultural Activity and Office Work	99.3	99.9	98.3	99.3	99.6
#通用仪器仪表制造	Manufacture of General Measuring Instruments and Machinery	98.4	99.6	96.6	98.3	99.1
专用仪器仪表制造	Manufacture of Special Measuring Instruments and Machinery	100.0	100.0	100.0	100.0	100.0
钟表与计时仪器制造	Manufacture of Watches and Chronographs	99.8	101.7	100.4	99.7	97.3
光学仪器及眼镜制造	Manufacture of Optical Equipment and Glasses	98.5	99.6	99.1	97.8	97.6
文化、办公用机械制造	Manufacture of Machinery for Cultural Activity and Office Work	104.3	100.6	106.0	105.1	105.3
工艺品及其他制造业	Manufacture of Artwork and Other Manufacturing	102.4	101.0	102.2	103.0	103.2
#工艺美术品制造	Manufacture of Artwork	102.4	100.9	102.2	103.0	103.2
日用杂品制造	Manufacture of Groceries for Daily Use	102.0	106.4	103.3	100.2	98.1
废弃资源和废旧材料回收加工业	Recycling and Disposal of Waste	100.0	100.0	100.0	100.0	100.0
#非金属废料和碎屑的加工处理	Non-metal Waste and Fragment Treatment and Processing	100.0	100.0	100.0	100.0	100.0
电力、热力的生产和供应业	Production and Supply of Electric Power and Heat Power	102.4	103.4	102.4	101.9	101.9
电力生产	Production of Electric Power	103.4	104.5	103.1	102.8	103.2
电力供应	Supply of Electric Power	101.6	102.5	101.8	101.2	101.0
热力生产和供应	Production and Supply of Heat Power	104.1	105.8	103.9	103.4	103.2
燃气生产和供应业	Production and Supply of Gas	109.9	110.7	108.1	114.6	106.2
燃气生产和供应业	Production and Supply of Gas	109.9	110.7	108.1	114.6	106.2
水的生产和供应业	Production and Supply of Water	104.6	107.6	105.9	102.8	102.2
#自来水的生产和供应	Production and Supply of Water	104.6	107.6	105.9	102.8	102.2

6-8 工业品出厂价格指数（2006年）
Ex-factory Price Indices of Industrial Products (2006)

上年=100　　preceding year=100

产品名称	Name of Product	指数 Index	产品名称	Name of Product	指数 Index
无烟煤	Anthracite	103.1	井盐	Well Salt	102.5
烟煤	Bituminous Coal	97.1	石墨	Graphite	105.5
洗精煤	Washed Coal	97.0	滑石粉	Talc	95.5
洗混煤	Mixed Coal Washing	97.8	金刚石	Diamond	108.4
筛选块煤	Screening of Lump Coal	98.7	透辉石	Diopside	116.6
褐煤	Lignite	101.9	大米	Rice	101.1
天然原油	Natural Oil	121.9	小麦粉	Wheat Flour	97.9
天然气	Natural Gas	97.7	玉米粉	Corn Flour	103.9
炼钢用铁矿石块矿	Steelmaking Block Iron ore Mine	88.5	麦芽	Malt	99.6
炼铁用铁矿石块矿	Iron ore With Iron ore Block	94.2	配合饲料	Feed	97.8
铁精矿	Iron Concentrate	96.5	混合饲料	Mixed Feed	100.9
球团矿	Pellets	88.0	蛋白饲料	Protein Feed	97.1
铜原矿	Copper ore	136.2	其他饲料	Other Feed	89.5
铜精矿	Copper Concentrate	200.2	预混饲料	Premix	98.9
钴精矿	Cobalt Concentrate	112.6	浓缩饲料	Concentrated Feed	98.8
金原矿	Gold ore	104.6	花生油	Peanut Oil	98.3
金精矿	Gold Concentrate	110.8	棉籽油	Cottonseed Oil	99.4
钼精矿	Molybdenum Concentrate	106.2	大豆油	Soybean Oil	100.6
石灰石	Limestone	103.4	色拉油	Salad Oil	103.3
石膏	Gypsum	108.2	大米油	Rice Oil	102.2
花岗石荒材	Granite Wood Shortage	102.4	保健油	Health Oil	98.5
大理石荒材	Marble Wood Shortage	80.7	毛糠油	Mao Bran Oil	101.1
硅石	Silica	93.8	蓖麻油	Castor Oil	95.0
萤石	Fluorite	103.7	机制甘蔗糖	Cane Sugar Mechanism	114.9
粘土	Clay	106.4	机制甜菜糖	Beet Sugar Mechanism	107.4
白云石成品矿	Dolomite Mining Products	100.0	红糖	Brown Sugar	117.2
硅粉	Silica Fume	101.4	果糖	Fructose	100.0
砂子	Sand	101.0	甜菊糖	Stevioside	95.3
覆膜砂	Coated Sand	97.9	鲜猪肉	Fresh Pork	92.0
硫铁矿	Pyrite	96.3	鲜冻猪肉	Fresh Frozen Pork	92.1
蛇蚊石矿	Snake Tiny Quarry	104.7	鲜冻牛肉	Fresh Frozen Beef	104.4
海盐	Sea Salt	70.6	鲜冻羊肉	Fresh Frozen Lamb	97.3

6-8 续表 1 continued

产品名称	Name of Product	指 数 Index	产品名称	Name of Product	指 数 Index
鲜冻兔肉	Fresh Frozen Rabbit Meat	110.7	桃酥	Crisps	100.4
鲜冻鸡	Fresh and Frozen Chickens	99.8	主食面包	Staple Bread	99.9
鸭及鸭制品	Duck and Duck Products	92.2	花色面包	Flower Color Bread	102.9
香肠	Sausage	99.5	饼干	Biscuits	100.7
火腿	Ham	100.7	米饼	Rice Cake	100.6
熟食	Cooked Food	107.0	膨化小食品	Expanded Small Food	100.1
肠衣	Casing	94.5	薯片	Potato Chips	105.6
虾	Shrimp	118.0	夹心糖果	Sandwich Candy	100.0
冻带鱼段	Paragraph Freeze Hairtail	101.6	牛奶糖果	Milk Candy	108.9
冻鲅鱼	Frozen Strawberries	101.5	果脯	Preserves	104.8
冻章鱼	Freeze Octopus	99.1	挂面	Noodle	99.4
冻鱿鱼	Frozen Squid	101.2	速冻食品	Quick-frozen Food	100.4
冻蟹	Frozen Crab	100.0	方便面	Instant Noodles	102.8
冻鳕鱼片	Frozen Cod Fillets	98.7	奶粉	Milk	101.8
鱼片干	Fish Dry	102.8	消毒鲜牛奶	Disinfection of Fresh Milk	103.6
扇贝	Scallop	103.2	纯牛奶	Pure Milk	101.3
鱼丸	Fish Balls	99.4	酸奶	Yogurt	101.8
鱼排	Rafts	109.4	钙奶	Calcium	101.8
深海鱼油	Fish	99.5	炼乳	Condensed Milk	101.7
珍珠	Pearls	101.6	牛肉罐头	Canned Beef	105.0
速冻蔬菜	Quick-frozen Vegetables	105.6	猪肉罐头	Canned Pork	100.0
净菜	Vegetable	104.6	鲭鱼罐头	Mackerel Canned	113.6
腌菜	Pickles	101.5	贻贝罐头	Mussel Canned	105.9
瓜子系列	Melon Seeds Series	113.9	牡蛎罐头	Canned Oysters	97.7
坚果食品	Nuts Food	97.4	苹果罐头	Apple Canned	104.4
脱水蔬菜	Dehydrated Vegetables	100.7	梨罐头	Canned Pear	100.6
淀粉制品	Starch Products	103.6	桃罐头	Canned Peaches	100.7
粉丝	Fans	107.4	山楂罐头	Hawthorn Canned	101.5
变性淀粉	Modified Starch	100.4	葡萄罐头	Canned Grape	103.3
麦芽糖	Maltose	110.4	蘑菇罐头	Canned Mushrooms	109.3
木糖	Xylose	104.4	笋罐头	Shoot Canned	119.5
豆腐干	Pinch	98.8	味精	MSG	98.5
其它豆制品	Other Soybean Products	100.2	酱油	Soy Sauce	102.2
豆奶粉	Soybean Milk	100.2	酱	Sauce	105.5
再制蛋	Re-egg	100.0	食醋	Vinegar	100.7
蜂制品	Bee Products	100.0	鱼露	Fish Sauce	104.5
蛋糕	Cake	100.9	柠檬酸	Citric Acid	92.8

6-8 续表 2 continued

产品名称	Name of Product	指 数 Index	产品名称	Name of Product	指 数 Index
麦麸酸	Wheat Bran Acid	107.9	色纱	Yarn	99.2
酵母	Yeast	100.5	棉布	Cotton Cloth	101.4
淀粉酶	Amylase	99.6	混纺交织布	Blended Cross Weaving	105.2
糖化酶	Glucoamylase	98.5	纯化纤布	Pure Chemical Fiber Cloth	100.3
鸡精	Jijing	87.0	帆布	Canvas	103.8
其他调味品	Other Spices	102.1	牛仔布	Denim	101.9
冷冻饮品	Frozen Drinks	104.3	ＰＵ革基布	PU Leather Fabric	100.0
精制盐	Refined Salt	106.0	坯布	Fabric	99.2
保鲜剂	Preservative	95.5	涤粘布	Polyester and Viscose Fabrics	102.9
色素	Pigment	100.0	色织坯布	Yarn-dyed Fabric	102.8
添加剂	Additive	98.8	缝纫线	Sewing Thread	103.5
豆糕	Bean Cake	101.1	棉线	Thread	108.8
酒精	Alcohol	102.1	涤纶线	PET Line	102.3
白酒	Liquor	101.3	粘胶丝线	Viscose Thread	106.8
啤酒	Beer	102.4	纯化纤纱	Pure Chemical Fiber Yarn	97.7
黄酒	Rice Wine	102.2	土工布	Geotextiles	90.6
葡萄酒	Wine	102.0	棉印染布	Dyeing and Printing of Cotton Cloth	99.5
果酒	Wine	100.0	混纺印染布	Blended Dyeing Cloth	102.8
碳酸饮料	Carbonated Beverages	98.5	纯化纤印染布	Pure Chemical Fiber Dyeing Cloth	102.9
矿泉水	Mineral Water	100.4	纯毛毛条	Wool Top	103.2
纯净水	Pure Water	100.0	混纺毛条	Blended Wool Tops	103.1
果汁	Juice	105.9	毛线	Yarn	101.9
蔬菜汁	Vegetable Juice	109.9	纯毛纱	Pure Wool Yarn	99.9
果粒饮料	Berry Drinks	100.0	毛混纺毛织品	Mao Blended Worsted Spinning	99.8
乳酸菌饮料	Lactic Acid Bacteria Beverage	100.5	纯毛毛织品	Wool Worsted Spinning	95.8
含乳饮料	Milk Drink	101.7	毛染整加工	Hair Dyeing and Finishing	110.0
固体饮料	Solid Beverage	100.0	苎麻布	Ramie Cloth	112.6
茶饮料	Teas	100.3	麻线	Thread	107.6
其他软饮料	Other Soft Drinks	108.4	麻纱	Flax Yarn	102.0
精制茶	Refining Tea	103.2	桑蚕丝	Mulberry Silk	124.4
复烤烟叶	Tobacco Redried	100.0	桑蚕绢丝	Silkworm Silk	108.9
卷烟	Cigarette	101.4	桑蚕丝绸（坯绸）	Silkworm Silk (randgold)	128.6
片烟	Lamina	100.0	化纤绸（坯绸）	Chemical Fiber Silk (randgold)	99.4
棉纱	Cotton Yarn	103.4	桑蚕丝绸（成品）	Silkworm Silk (finished)	123.0
混纺纱	Blended Yarn	103.8	化纤绸（成品）	Chemical Fiber Silk (finished)	106.3
粘棉纱	Nien Cotton Yarn	102.9	印花丝织品	Silk Printing	104.0
棉短绒	Cotton Linter	128.1	染色丝织品	Silk Dyeing	95.9

6-8 续表 3 continued

产品名称	Name of Product	指 数 Index	产品名称	Name of Product	指 数 Index
毛巾	Towel	99.3	防寒服	Cool Suits	101.5
毛巾被	Towelling Coverlet	98.5	亚麻服装	Flax Clothing	104.8
床单	Sheets	100.6	布鞋	Shoes	102.5
被罩	Galle	102.5	帽	Cap	104.7
枕巾	Pillow	103.1	宠物用品	Pet Supplies	101.9
浴巾	Bath Towel	98.4	轻革	Light Leather	101.3
浴衣	Bathrobe	93.2	羊兰湿皮（加色）	Wet Sheep-skin (and color)	101.7
床上用品套件	Bedding Package	102.7	皮鞋	Shoes	104.6
被套	Bearing	93.2	旅游鞋	Trainers	102.6
棉被	Quilt	98.5	运动鞋	Sports Shoes	100.7
方巾	Hood	110.2	跑鞋	Running Shoes	100.0
枕头套	Pillowcases	101.3	合成革鞋	Synthetic Leather Shoes	106.8
抖蓬	Buffeting Peng	114.0	羊皮夹克	Sheepskin Jackets	106.2
毛毯	Blankets	101.3	牛皮夹克	Leather Jacket	99.3
真丝领带	Silk Tie.	108.3	裘皮大衣	Fur Coat	100.7
帘子布	Cord	91.4	皮衣	Leather	100.1
无纺布	Nonwovens	108.6	皮箱	Suitcase	102.1
其他纺织制成品	Other Textile Made-ups	98.1	牛皮包	Leather Pack	91.0
棉针织产品	Knitted Products	101.2	公文包	Briefcase	104.2
针织绒布类衫裤	Knitting Flannel Shirt and Trousers Category	104.0	书包	Schoolbags	100.8
针织单面汗布类衫裤	Knitting Single Undershirt Cloth Type Shirt and Trousers	101.7	旅行包	Bicycles	103.2
袜子	Socks	98.6	挂包	PTI	98.3
短裤	Shorts	101.5	皮手套	Leather Gloves	99.1
窗帘	Curtains	103.1	羊皮包	Sheepskin Packet	107.6
手套	Gloves	99.9	绵羊毛皮	Sheep Fur	102.9
胸罩	Bra	96.6	裘皮短外衣	Fur Jackets	101.9
收腹裤	54th Pants	96.6	皮围巾	Paper Scarf	99.8
纯羊毛衫	Pure Cardigan	100.0	羽绒服装	Down Clothing	91.0
混纺羊毛衫	Blended Cardigan	95.3	羽绒被	Feather Was	102.2
真丝上衣	Silk T-shirt	126.9	普通锯材	General Lumber	101.8
布服装	Cloth Garment	100.7	木片	Wood	101.4
呢绒服装	Wool Clothing	99.5	胶合板	Plywood	99.6
大衣	Coat	99.9	纤维板	Fibreboard	102.2
T恤	T-shirt	100.2	刨花板	Particleboard	102.7
裙子	Skirt	100.0	饰面板	Decorative Panels	103.1

6-8 续表 4 continued

产品名称	Name of Product	指 数 Index	产品名称	Name of Product	指 数 Index
细木工板	Blockboard	102.3	手工纸	Handmade Paper	101.4
桐木板	Countryside Board	104.0	铜版纸	Coated Paper	100.4
防水板	Waterproof Plate	103.8	瓦楞纸箱	Watts spinulosa Cartons	101.6
木制门窗	Wooden Doors and Windows	103.0	医用包装纸制品	Medical Packaging Products	99.5
地板	Floor	102.2	水泥包装袋	Cement Packaging Bags	109.1
木模	Wood Die	103.6	纸管	Paper Tube	107.6
木包装箱	Wooden Boxes	96.0	卫生巾	Sanitary Napkins	99.5
木筷子	Wooden Chopsticks	107.1	书籍印刷	Printed Books	99.7
木制衣架	Wooden Racks	101.2	报纸印刷	Newspaper Printing	107.0
草制品	Grass Products	105.1	期刊印刷	Journal Printing	101.6
藤制品	40,000	100.0	课本印刷	The Printing of Textbooks	102.5
柳制品	Liu Products	107.7	画册印刷	Pictorial Printing	100.3
桌	Tables	101.1	图片印刷	Photo Printing	100.0
床	Bed	99.1	多色印刷品	Multi-color Print	100.0
柜	Counters	100.8	单色印刷品	Monochrome Print	101.4
组合柜	Portfolio Counters	101.2	练习本	This Practice	102.4
木椅子	Wooden Chairs	100.1	包装装潢用印刷	Tastefully Packaged With Printing	98.4
木沙发	Wood Sofa	100.3	商标标识	Trademark Logo	93.5
藤制家俱	Rattan Furniture	100.6	广告宣传品印刷	Advertising for Printing	100.8
桌	Tables	96.9	票证印刷	Coupons Printing	117.8
椅	Chairs	103.9	扑克牌	Poker	99.4
床	Bed	98.8	其他印刷产品	Other Print Products	100.6
柜	Counters	100.0	书刊装订	Book Binding	101.5
席梦思床垫	Mattress Mattress	99.6	制版	Plate	99.1
皮沙发	Pei Sha	102.2	PS版	PS Plate	103.7
布沙发	Madrid	101.8	光碟	CD	89.7
硫酸盐漂白浆	Bleached Kraft Pulp	110.7	磁带	Tape	98.3
其他纸浆	Other Pulp	106.2	文件夹	Folder	99.7
印刷用纸	Printing Paper	100.6	修正液	Stings	101.7
书写用纸	Writing Paper	102.6	铅笔	Pencil	102.4
生活用纸	Household Paper	102.5	圆珠笔	Pen	105.0
技术配套纸	Supporting Technical Paper	100.1	笔芯	Jupiter	100.0
包装纸板	Wrapping Paper Plate	102.1	毛笔	Brush	92.6
卷烟纸	Cigarette Paper	101.8	其他教学学具	Other Teaching of a	100.0
衬纸	Backing	105.1	可充气球类	Inflatable Balls	101.5

6-8　续表 5 continued

产品名称	Name of Product	指　数 Index	产品名称	Name of Product	指　数 Index
其他球类	Other Sports	84.2	纯碱（碳酸钠）	Soda Ash (sodium carbonate)	91.6
单杠	Horizontal Bar	93.0	泡花碱	Sodium	102.6
双杠	Parallel Bars	89.5	硫酸盐	Kraft	102.8
健身器材	Fitness Equipment	99.9	硝酸盐	Nitrate	103.5
各种护具	Various Mob	96.0	磷酸盐	Phosphate	98.6
钓杆	Fishing Rod	104.5	硅酸盐	Portland	102.4
铰轮	Hinge Round	113.6	碳酸盐	Carbonate	104.9
鼓	Drum	100.0	氯化物	Chloride	98.9
钢琴	Piano	100.1	氟化物	Fluoride	109.3
电子乐器	The Electronic Musical Instrument	100.0	金属氧化物酸盐	Metal Oxides Permanganate	104.8
毛绒玩具	Stuffed Toys	101.8	其他无机盐	Other Inorganic Salt	106.0
汽油	Gasoline	117.2	丙烯	Propylene	113.6
煤油	Kerosene	120.3	纯苯	Merrill	98.3
柴油	Diesel	113.6	精甲醇	Fine Methanol	105.8
润滑油	Lubricants	128.1	甲醛	Formaldehyde	105.5
燃料油	Fuel Oil	121.8	甲苯	Toluene	128.1
石油沥青	Asphalt	116.0	苯酚	Phenol	95.6
溶剂油	Solvent Oil	113.4	甲酸	Formic Acid	98.2
石油液化气	Oil LNG	112.6	二甲苯	Xylene	129.5
石油焦	Petroleum Coke	110.2	苯	Benzene	112.4
白色油	White Oil	100.4	丙烷	Propane	94.6
润滑脂	Grease	112.5	三氯甲烷	Trichloromethane	77.6
焦炭	Coke	94.4	糠醇	Furfuralcohol	94.3
煤焦油	Coal Tar	141.9	糖醛	Uronic	80.1
炼焦沥青	Coking Asphalt	169.3	聚醚	Polyether	92.5
煅后焦	Calcined Coke	99.0	邻苯二甲酸酐	Phthalic Anhydride	130.9
硫酸	Sulfate	77.3	已二胺	Has Diamine	101.5
合成盐酸	Hydrochloric Acid Synthesis	86.8	二氮杂二环	Second Azabicyclo	102.0
氯磺酸	Chlorosulfonic Acid	106.4	乙酸乙脂	Acid Blipid	119.7
氯乙酸	Chloroacetate	80.5	二乙烯苯	Divinylbenzene	90.9
磷酸	Phosphorylation	121.7	乙醇	Ethanol	101.0
溴产品	Bromine Products	92.0	其他有机化学原料	Other Organic Materials	103.6
电瓶酸	Battery Acid	74.2	乙炔	Acetylene	99.4
烧碱（氢氧化钠）	Caustic Soda (sodium hydroxide)	96.4	氯	Chlorine	89.7
氢氧化钾	Potassium Hydroxide	103.6	氧	Oxygen	102.7

6-8 续表 6 continued

产品名称	Name of Product	指数 Index	产品名称	Name of Product	指数 Index
氮	Nitrogen	93.2	立灵水	Li Ling Water	100.0
双氧水(过氧化氢)	Hydrogen Peroxide (H_2O_2)	99.7	敌敌畏	Dichlorvos	102.3
漂白粉	Bleaching Powder	100.4	辛硫磷	Phoxim	100.2
氧化物	Oxides	107.2	农药磷化铝	Pesticide Aluminum Phosphide	100.0
氩气	Argon	100.0	生物原杀虫剂	The Biological Insecticide	95.5
硫脲	Thiourea	94.3	天然树脂漆	Natural Resin Paint	107.8
硫酸铵	Ammonium Sulfate	85.3	醇酸树脂漆	Alkyd Resin Paint	108.2
过硫酸氨	The Ammonia Sulfate	105.6	硝基纤维漆	Nitro Fiber Paint	108.1
尿素	Urea	100.5	过氯乙烯漆	The Vinyl Chloride Paint	117.9
碳酸氢铵	Ammonium Bicarbonate	94.4	丙烯树脂漆	Acrylic Resin Paint	99.2
合成氨	Ammonia	105.9	聚氨脂漆	Polyurethane Lacquer	103.2
液氨	Liquid Ammonia	105.4	其它漆	Other Chatham	104.6
硝酸	Nitrate	87.7	涂料	Coatings	105.4
三聚氰胺	Melamine	93.8	涂料用辅助涂料	Assisted Paint Coatings	99.6
磷肥	Phosphate Fertilizer	113.8	平版胶印油墨	Lithography Offset Printing Ink	94.6
农用氯化钾	Farm KCl	93.0	水性油墨	Water-based Ink	87.1
硫酸钾	Potassium Sulfate	99.4	复合墨	Composite Mexico	97.5
复混肥料	Compound Fertilizer	98.6	塑料印刷油墨	Plastic Printing Ink	101.8
微量元素肥料	Trace Elements Fertilizer	100.0	钛白粉	Titanium Dioxide	103.9
乐果	Rogor	103.3	酞青蓝颜料	Qing-lan Phthalocyanine Pigments	110.2
甲基一六零五	Methyl 1,605	103.2	酞箐兰	Phthalocyanine Qing Lan	107.4
马拉硫磷（马拉松）	Malathion (Marathon)	100.9	陶瓷颜料	Ceramic Pigment	121.1
草甘膦	Glyphosate	99.3	中铬黄	In Chrome Yellow	101.8
达螨虫	Of Mite Pest	100.5	钼铬红	Chromium-Molybdenum	107.4
克百威原粉	Carbofuran Original Powder	98.2	华兰	Westlands	98.8
乙草胺	Acetochlor	105.7	酸性染料	Acid Dye	99.2
辛硫磷	Phoxim	100.3	碱性染料	Alkaline Dye	102.3
水铵硫磷	Water Ammonium Parathion	100.0	分散染料	Disperse Dyes	99.6
残杀威原药	Propoxur Original Drug	100.0	偶氮染料	Azo Dyes	104.6
菊脂杀虫剂	Lipid Insecticide-ju	100.7	色母粒	Masterbatch	100.8
辛硫磷油	Phoxim Oil	101.3	黑碳化硅	Black Silicon Carbide	99.5
异柳磷乳剂	Liu Different Phosphorus Emulsion	100.0	聚氯乙烯树脂	PVC Resin	99.0
甲霜灵	Metalaxyl	95.3	聚乙烯树脂	Polyethylene Resin	114.8
达螨灵	Hope of Mites	100.0	环氧树脂	Epoxy	78.6
阿维菌素	Abamectin	97.7	聚苯乙烯	Polystyrene	107.1

6-8 续表 7 continued

产品名称	Name of Product	指 数 Index	产品名称	Name of Product	指 数 Index
聚丙烯	Polypropylene	108.2	稳定剂	Stabilizer	100.7
有机硅树脂	Silicone Resin	85.9	羧甲基纤维素	Carboxymethyl Cellulose	109.1
酚醛树脂粉	Phenolic Resin Powder	100.4	油化学用品	Oil Supplies	99.6
聚氨脂塑料	Polyurethane Plastic	94.3	皮革化学品	Leather Chemicals	100.3
磺化酚醛树脂	Sulfonated Phenolic Resin	110.3	有机合成化学品	Synthetic Organic Chemicals	113.1
塑料树脂	Plastic Resin	101.5	建筑防水剂	Construction Waterproofing Agent	111.2
硬树脂	Hard Resin	100.1	爆剂冻剂	Blasting Agent Freezing Agent	100.1
高压聚乙烯塑料	High-pressure Polyethylene Plastic	108.0	卷烟专用增塑剂	Cigarette Dedicated Plasticizer	93.1
塑料异型材	Plastics Profile	94.8	炸药	Explosives	106.7
不饱和聚脂树脂	Unsaturated Polyester Resin	102.3	雷管	Detonators	113.0
聚脂树脂	Polyester Resin	104.9	导火索	Fuse	107.7
氟利昂	Freon	81.6	弹药	Ammunition	104.5
处理剂树脂	Treatment Agent Resin	107.3	污水处理药剂	Sewage Treatment Pharmacy	100.0
硫酸二甲脂	Dimethyl Sulfate Fat	93.4	骨胶	Bone Glue	98.8
PVB专用树脂	PVB Resin Dedicated	97.7	明胶	Gelatin	100.0
顺丁橡胶	BR	105.4	清洗溶剂	Cleaning Solvent	100.4
丙烯腈	Acrylonitrile	99.4	食品添加剂	Food Additives	97.7
丙烯酰胺	Acrylamide	110.8	香皂	Soaps	100.0
精对苯二甲酸	Purified Terephthalic Acid	103.6	合成洗衣粉	Synthetic Detergent	100.4
离子交换树脂	Ion Exchange Resins	97.5	甘油	Glycerol	81.2
聚四氟乙烯	PTFE	92.0	护发素	Hair Care -	100.0
脂肪酸	Fatty Acids	85.6	洗面奶	Milk	100.1
石油制品催化剂	Petroleum Products Catalyst	101.7	防晒品	Sunscreen Commodities	100.0
其他催化剂	Other Catalysts	98.1	牙膏	Toothpaste	101.1
塑料增塑剂	Plastic Plasticizer	110.0	香精	Flavor	106.6
橡胶防老剂	Rubber Antioxidant	89.9	香料	Spices	102.7
乳化剂	Emulsifier	102.5	火柴	Matches	100.9
印染助剂	Printing and Dyeing Auxiliaries	102.3	青霉素	Penicillin	102.3
印染增白剂	Dyeing Brightener	96.3	土霉素	Oxytetracycline	80.4
炭黑	Carbon Black	126.4	二氯氟苯	Dichlorofluorobenzene	100.0
发泡剂	Blowing Agent	100.2	乙酰螺旋霉素	Acetylspiramycin	87.7
渗透剂	Osmotica	98.8	葡萄糖酸钙	Calcium Gluconate	97.0
MBS增强剂	MBS Intensifier	103.3	头孢曲松	Ceftriaxone	83.1
亚甲基二酸	Methylene Acid	75.8	头孢呱酮	Cefoperazone	84.9
浸润剂	Infiltration of Agents	92.4	新诺明	Sulfamethoxazole	96.7

6-8 续表 8 continued

产品名称	Name of Product	指 数 Index	产品名称	Name of Product	指 数 Index
其他化学药品原药	Other Former Drug Chemicals	85.9	扑热息痛	Paracetamol	94.6
新诺明	Sulfamethoxazole	98.2	氨茶碱	Aminophylline	99.6
氨苄青霉素	Ampicillin	101.4	气雾剂	Aerosol	93.1
先锋	Vanguard	95.1	胃药	Medications	98.1
罗红霉素	Roxithromycin	96.2	肠炎药	Enteritis Medicine	88.2
布洛芬	Ibuprofen	99.8	利胆酸	Li Acid	100.6
氟哌酸	Norfloxacin	101.8	多酶片	Smuggler	100.1
氧氟沙星	Ofloxacin	100.0	格列齐特	Gliclazide	95.7
丁胺卡那霉素	Amikacin	108.2	美吡达	Glipizide	100.3
青霉素钾	Potassium Penicillin	100.8	痔疮栓	Hemorrhoids Shuan	102.7
环丙沙星	Ciprofloxacin	100.7	注射用盐水	Brine Injection	105.8
冻干硫酸妥布霉素	Freeze-dried Tobramycin Sulfate	100.5	葡萄糖	Glucose	102.4
土霉素片	Oxytetracycline Tablets	96.8	葡萄糖氯化钠注射液	Glucose Sodium Chloride Injection	92.6
依托红霉素片	Relying on Erythromycin Tablets	98.7	防裂霜	Cracking Cream	100.0
诺氟沙星胶囊	Norfloxacin Capsules	100.0	刺五加片	Ciwujia Tablets	100.0
注射用庆大霉素	Gentamicin Injection	99.0	西洋参片	American Ginseng Tablet	101.2
病毒唑	Ribavirin	100.3	六味地黄丸	Liuweidihuang Pill	106.0
感冒药	Cold Medicine.	98.9	养胃丸	Yangwei Pill	106.2
阿奇霉素	Azithromycin	99.1	葛根芩连微丸	Gegenqinlian Pellets	108.7
硫酸奈替米星	Netilmicin Sulfate	83.0	心可舒片	Xinkeshu Tablets	101.8
注射用美洛西林钠	Mezlocillin Sodium for Injection	100.0	黄连上清丸	Huanglianshangqing Pill	99.6
硫酸庆大霉素	Gentamicin Sulfate	96.5	感冒冲剂	Cold Infusion	101.1
利巴韦林针剂	Ribavirin Injections	112.5	板蓝根冲剂	Banlangen Granule	102.9
乙酰螺旋霉素	Acetylspiramycin	100.0	排石冲剂	Paishi Granules	100.0
头孢氨苄胶囊	Cephalexin Capsules	99.1	止咳糖浆	Cough Syrup	100.1
维生素	Vitamin	96.1	银翘解毒冲剂	Yinqiaojiedu Granules	100.0
复合维生素	Compound Vitamin	92.2	银屑冲剂	Yinxie Granules	100.0
维生素注射液	Vitamin Injection	97.6	稳心颗粒	Wenxinkeli	100.0
抗癌药	Anti-cancer Drugs	101.1	复方大青叶合剂	Compound Daqingye Mixture	98.1
降压药	Antihypertensive Agents	89.3	阿胶	Ejiao	107.9
心血管制剂	Cardiovascular Agents	102.1	国公酒	The State Liquor	100.0
脑血管用药	Cerebral Vascular Drug	99.4	阿胶三宝膏	Plaster Ejiao Treble	100.0
阿斯匹林	Aspirin	96.6	胶质药品	Glial Drugs	91.5
安乃近	Analgin	100.9	牛黄解毒片	Niuhuangjiedu Tablets	95.1

6-8 续表 9 continued

产品名称	Name of Product	指 数 Index	产品名称	Name of Product	指 数 Index
丹参片	Salvia Tablets	98.9	化纤用浆粕	Chemical Fiber With Pulp	99.1
消食片	Xiaoshi Tablets	92.7	粘胶纤维	Viscose Fiber	101.9
银杏叶胶囊	Ginkgo Biloba Capsules	91.2	粘胶长丝	Viscose Filament	107.5
复方黄连素片	Film Compound Berberine	102.2	纤维素	Cellulose	92.6
溶栓胶囊	Thrombolysis Capsules	88.7	锦纶长丝	Nylon Filament	94.4
汉桃叶片	Peach Leaf Han	100.0	涤纶短纤维	Polyester Staple	98.8
养阴降压胶囊	Yangyin Buck Capsules	100.0	涤纶长丝	Polyester Filament	100.9
新复方大青叶药片	New Compound Daqingye Pills	100.0	晴纶短纤维	Roy Staple Fiber	102.0
双黄莲注射液	Double Embarrassment Injection	100.0	丙纶短纤维	Polypropylene Staple Fiber	101.2
伤湿止痛膏	Mussels	102.5	丙纶长丝	PP Filament	101.4
麝香痔疮膏	Musk Hemorrhoids Ointment	100.0	氨纶丝	Spandex Wire	69.3
儿童清肺口服液	Children Qingfei Oral Solution	101.1	乙丙短纤维	Short Fiber B C	84.3
肝泰乐粉	Le Powder Zhigantai	105.1	复合短纤维	Short Fiber Composites	105.8
鸡疫苗	Chicken Vaccine	95.0	摩托车外胎	Motorcycle Tire	111.6
猪疫苗	Swine Vaccine	100.0	载重汽车外胎	Truck Tire	107.1
兽用破伤风	Veterinary Tetanus	99.6	轻型载重汽车外胎	Light Truck Tire	114.9
磺胺氯吡嗪钠	Sodium Chloride Pyrazine Sulfa	100.0	轿车外胎	Car Tire	101.4
盐酸强力霉素	Hydrochloric Acid Doxycycline	100.0	农用车轮胎外胎	Agricultural Vehicle Tire Tire	119.4
动物用药粉	Animal Drug Powder	100.5	工程轮胎外胎	Works Tire Tire	113.1
兽用青霉素	Veterinary Penicillin	98.2	载重汽车内胎	Truck Tubeless	126.3
止痢宝	Zhilishen Po	103.8	汽车内胎	Car Tubeless	99.3
氯苯胍片	Film Robenidine	100.0	农用车内胎	Fetal Farm Vehicle	106.2
动物用安基比林	Animal on Kay Than Lin	102.4	手推车外胎	Trolleys Tire	115.7
甲肝疫苗	Hepatitis Avaccine	80.6	自行车外胎	Bicycle Tire	104.9
白蛋白	Albumin	113.1	自行车内胎	Bicycle Inner Tube	107.1
注射丙球	Injection C	88.0	橡胶运输带	Rubber Transport Belt	98.9
惠尔血	Filgrastim	102.4	橡胶胶管	Rubber Hose	103.7
胞磷胆碱钠针	Citicoline Sodium Needle	100.1	工业胶板	Industrial Plastic Sheet	102.9
药棉	Troy	101.4	橡胶三角带	Rubber Triangle Zone	104.4
药用胶囊	Drug Capsules	100.3	其它橡胶制品	Other Rubber Products	99.5
脱脂棉纱	Skim Cotton Yarn	106.8	多契带	With More DMC	92.4
脱脂绷带	Skim Bandage	100.1	橡胶布	Rubber Cloth	100.0
过滤线	Filter Line	100.3	胶辊	Cots	101.0
假牙材料	Dentures Materials	100.0	橡胶密封件	Rubber Seals	102.1

6-8 续表 10 continued

产品名称	Name of Product	指 数 Index	产品名称	Name of Product	指 数 Index
其他橡胶件	Other Pieces of Rubber	100.2	聚丙烯打包带	Packaged With Polypropylene	105.7
插接件	Connectors	105.1	聚氯乙烯包装	PVC Packing	102.8
橡胶护套	Rubber Sheathing	91.3	聚乙烯编织袋	Polyethylene Bags	104.0
胶嘴	Plastic Mouth	115.0	聚乙烯绳	Polyethylene Rope	104.3
再生胶	Renewable Plastic	109.5	聚丙烯编织布	Polypropylene Woven	104.5
工业手套（普通）	Industrial Gloves (ordinary)	98.0	聚乙烯线	Polyethylene Line	101.6
医用手套	Medical Gloves	99.8	机带	Machine Band	100.0
瓶塞	Stopper	100.0	紧密袋	Close Bag	112.4
避孕套	Condoms	98.8	泡沫塑料	Foam	100.2
气球	Balloon	100.0	组合聚醚（海绵）	Portfolio Polyether (sponge)	106.6
橡胶鞋	Rubber Shoes	96.0	泡沫板材	Bubble Plates	98.3
布面胶鞋	Cloth Shoes	103.9	人造革	Leatherette	95.6
橡胶水坝	Rubber Dam	101.0	合成革	Synthetic Leather	103.8
阻燃带	Flame Retardant Belt	107.8	塑料篷布	Plastic Car	106.0
聚氯乙烯薄膜	PVC Film	100.7	塑料周转箱	Plastic flow Box	112.4
聚乙烯薄膜	Polyethylene Film	102.4	塑料桶	Plastic Barrels	103.8
聚脂薄膜	Polyester Film	102.6	塑料瓶	Plastic Bottles	101.3
聚丙烯制品	Polypropylene Products	106.8	塑料塞、盖	Plastic Cypriots, Covered	100.7
塑料食品袋	Plastic Bags of Food	101.7	机器塑料零件	Machinery Plastic Parts	100.0
食品包装用膜	Food Packaging Films	101.0	电子产品用零配件	Electronic Products With Spare Parts	97.0
BOPP薄膜制品	BOPP Film Products	93.9	其它塑料零配件	Other Plastic Parts	100.0
塑料增强布	Plastic Enhance Cloth	100.3	其它塑料日用杂品	Daily Sundry Other Plastic	102.5
塑料袋	Plastic Bags	114.7	安全帽	Helmets	99.2
塑料门窗	Plastic Windows and Doors	100.8	其它制品	Other Products	100.1
聚氯乙烯透明片	PVC Transparent Film	99.5	普通硅酸盐水泥（回转窑）	Ordinary Portland Cement (kiln)	99.3
聚氯乙烯异型材	PVC Profile	97.7	矿渣硅酸盐水泥（回转窑）	Slag Portland Cement (kiln)	100.9
聚乙烯管材	Polyethylene Pipes	105.1	复合硅酸盐水泥	Portland Cement Composites	100.1
铝塑板	APCP Board	126.0	普通硅酸盐水泥（立窑）	Ordinary Portland Cement (kilns)	101.4
PVC制品	PVC Products	101.7	矿渣硅酸盐水泥（立窑）	Slag Portland Cement (kilns)	98.3
ABS型材	ABS Profile	104.6	特种水泥	Special Cement	98.6
PP制品	PP Products	103.3	熟料	Clinker	101.3
PPR制品	PPR Products	110.7	石灰	Lime	99.8
PS板材	PS Plate	101.5	建筑石膏	Building Gypsum	100.0
聚丙烯编织袋	Polypropylene Bags	106.3	钢筋混凝土压力管	Reinforced Concrete Pipe	106.9

6-8 续表 11 continued

产品名称	Name of Product	指数 Index	产品名称	Name of Product	指数 Index
钢筋混凝土排水管	Reinforced Concrete Drain	101.2	玻璃瓶	Bottles	102.3
水泥电杆	Cement Pole	100.6	钢化玻璃制品	Toughened Glass Products	95.4
水泥轨枕	Cement Sleeper	103.9	玻璃管	Glass Tube	99.8
水泥瓦	Cement Tile	102.4	保温瓶	Vacuum Flask	113.6
混凝土	Concrete	100.3	玻璃纤维布	Glass Fiber Cloth	100.2
水泥预制构件	Cement Prefabricated Units	102.8	玻璃纤维纱	Glass Fiber Yarn	100.4
石棉水泥瓦	Asbestos-cement Tile	104.5	其他玻璃纤维制品	Other Fiberglass Products	103.2
加气混凝土制品	Aerated Concrete Products	106.6	玻璃球	Glass Ball	100.0
石膏板	Gypsum Board	100.4	玻璃纤维板	Glass Fibreboard	100.0
粘土砖	Clay Brick	106.1	玻璃钢管材	Fiberglass Pipe	101.7
页岩砖	Shale Brick	101.5	玻璃钢板材	FRP Sheet	75.9
瓦	Watts	98.1	大便器	Astool	100.0
空心砖	Hollow Brick	102.3	洗面器	Wash -	100.9
釉面砖	Glazed Tiles	100.0	高压绝缘子	High Voltage Insulator	103.4
墙砖	Wall	101.3	高压瓷管	High Voltage Ceramic Tube	100.6
地砖	Slabs	101.8	其他工业电气陶瓷	Other Industrial Electrical Ceramics	87.6
陶瓷管道	Ceramic Pipes	104.1	电瓷拉棒	Electric Porcelain Pull rod	100.0
大理石板材	Marble Plate	103.0	陶瓷脱水元件	Ceramic Components Dehydration	100.0
花岗岩板材	Granite Plates	103.9	陶瓷碗	Ceramic Bowl	101.2
油毡	Felt	104.4	陶瓷盘	Ceramic Disc	102.5
保温材料稀土	Insulation Materials RE	97.9	陶瓷杯	Ceramic Cup	102.3
复合保温毡	Composite Thermal Insulation Blankets	100.0	陶瓷酒瓶	Ceramic Bottle	100.2
其它隔热和隔音材料	Noise Insulation and Other Materials	115.3	中餐套具	Chinese Meal Kits	125.3
平板玻璃	Flat Glass	100.2	石棉橡胶板	Asbestos Rubber Plate	100.0
压延玻璃	Calendar Glass	102.6	石棉刹车片	The Asbestos Brake Pads	102.1
钢化玻璃	Toughened Glass	101.0	转炉补炉料	Bof Meeting Burden	134.6
弯型夹层	Bend-dissection	99.0	石棉汽缸垫板	Asbestos Cylinder Pad	106.4
其他玻璃制品	Other Glass Products	98.3	电子管云母片	Mica Tablet Tube	100.5
制镜玻璃	System Mirror Glass	100.2	耐火砖	Firebrick	97.2
镀膜玻璃	Coated Glass	96.9	其他耐火材料	Other Refractories	100.4
药用玻璃瓶	Medicinal Bottles	101.0	耐火浇铸料	Casting Material Refractory	97.9
输液瓶	Infusion Bottle	96.1	坩埚	Crucible	92.2
试剂瓶	Reagents Bottles	114.0	陶纤制品	Tao Fiber Products	97.1
玻璃口杯	Glass Cups	101.3	普通功率石墨电极	Ordinary Power Graphite Electrodes	101.6

6-8 续表 12 continued

产品名称	Name of Product	指 数 Index	产品名称	Name of Product	指 数 Index
高功率石墨电极	High-power Graphite Electrodes	103.7	锌	Zinc	192.8
石墨制品	Graphite Products	99.7	氧化铝	Alumina	102.5
炭素制品	Carbon Products	100.0	铝	Aluminum	111.4
其他制品	Other Products	103.6	黄金及冶炼产品	Gold and Smelting Products	127.8
其它炭素制品	Other Carbon Products	107.5	白银	Silver	127.9
炭棒	Carbon Rod	98.7	金属铈	Metal Cerium	77.7
碳阳极	Carbon Anodes	101.6	金属镧	Metal Lanthanum	79.8
预焙碳阳极	Pre-baked Carbon Anode	103.4	紫铜材	Purple Copper	135.2
磨料	Abrasive	102.3	黄铜材	Copper Huang	126.2
磨具	Abrasives	102.2	铝成品材	Aluminum Finished Wood	107.2
工业硅	Industrial Silicon	101.6	铝合金成品材	Aluminum Finished Wood	113.5
硅胶	Silica Gel	103.7	铝箔	Aluminum Foil	108.5
石粉	Powder	104.0	铝膜	Aluminum	100.0
人造刚石	Just Artificial Stone	100.3	铝塑型材	Apcp Profile	114.4
生铁	Pig Iron	94.0	铝塑板	Apcp Board	111.0
普碳钢坯	Blank Plain Carbon Steel	95.2	钨材	W Wood	100.0
优质碳结钢坯	High-quality Carbon Steel Billet end	100.0	钼材	Mo Wood	80.1
钢锭	Ingot	97.3	钢梁	Steel Beam	100.0
钢球	Ball	100.0	钢结构屋架	Steel Roof Truss	92.0
重轨	Heavy Rail	98.1	电缆桥架	Cable Bridge	102.8
普通大型钢材	Ordinary Large Steel	94.9	线路用钢担	Steel Said Lines	99.0
普通中型钢材	Ordinary Medium-sized Steel	93.9	输变电铁塔	The Power Transmission Tower	99.1
普通小型钢材	Ordinary Small Steel	94.7	钢构件	Steel Components	102.7
优质型钢材	Quality of Steel	98.0	金属网架	Metal Grid	108.7
线材	Wire	97.0	钢结构	Steel	98.9
中厚钢板	In the Thick Plate	91.2	金属栏网级配件	Network-level Metal Accessories Column	120.1
薄钢板	Steel Sheet	89.1	其它金属制品及结构	Other Metal Products and Structural	100.7
钢带	Strip	94.6	H型钢	H-beam	104.7
无缝钢管	Seamless Steel Tube	94.7	各种金属柱、板、杆、棒、架	Various Metal Column Plate, Rod, Bar, -	109.6
焊接钢管	Welded Steel Pipe	91.4	拉线抱箍++拉线抱箍	Guyed Hold Hoop + + Cable Adopt Hoop	94.3
钢层面板	Steel Plate Level	83.9	钢门	Steel Doors	104.7
铁合金	Ferroalloy	102.7	铝合金门	Aluminum Doors	99.5
铜	Copper	156.8	防盗门	Security Doors	100.2
粗铜	Blister Copper	154.0	金属门框架	Metal Door Frame	91.4
铅	Lead	123.0	钢窗	Windows	101.6

6-8 续表 13 continued

产品名称	Name of Product	指 数 Index	产品名称	Name of Product	指 数 Index
铝合金窗	Aluminum Window	100.6	建筑模板	Construction Formwork	106.8
钻头	Bits	102.7	金属电镀	Metal Plating	104.9
铣刀	Cutter	101.8	金属表面喷涂	Spray Metal Surface	98.0
丝锥	Taps	98.7	搪瓷浴盆	Enamel Bathtub	100.0
机刀	Machine Tool	99.2	面盆	Sprinkle	113.7
锯条	Saw Blade	108.7	口杯	Kids	98.8
板手	Plate Hand	99.7	搪瓷碗盘	Tangciwan Disc	101.7
钳	Clamp	111.4	厨房调理设备	Kitchen Conditioning Equipment	103.2
锤	Hammer	104.1	铝壶	Aluminum Pots	116.5
斧头	Axes	102.4	不粘锅	Teflon	100.0
钎具	Abrazing	93.6	不锈钢菜刀	Stainless Steel Kitchen Knife	95.4
锯	Saw	92.7	不锈钢勺	Stainless Steel Spoon	99.9
剪枝剪	Pruning Shear	100.0	不锈钢加热设备	Stainless Steel Heating Equipment	102.9
民用剪刀	Civilian Scissors	100.0	不锈钢西餐具	West Stainless Steel Cutlery	102.8
集装箱	Container	85.6	铝筒	Aluminum Tube	101.0
钢制容器	Steel Containers	100.8	钢锯架	Roll -Frame	110.5
其它钢制容器	Other Steel Containers	97.0	织针	KN	95.6
易拉罐	Apop Can	125.9	电焊条	Welding Electrodes	101.0
水箱	Cisterns	118.8	焊丝	Wire	103.9
油罐	Oil Tank	97.5	链条炉排锅炉	The Chain Grate Boiler	101.5
金属桶	Metal Drums	97.0	热水锅炉	Hot Water Boiler	100.8
金属瓶盖	Metal Bottle	102.3	电站锅炉	Utility Boilers	86.7
无氟压缩机壳体	Shell Fluorine-free Compressors	100.6	卧式燃油（气）锅炉	Horizontal Fuel (gas) Boilers	96.2
钢丝	Wires	101.2	工业锅炉辅助设备	Industrial Boiler Auxiliary Equipment	100.6
钢丝绳	Wire Rope	97.8	柴油机	Diesel Engine	102.4
铁丝	Wire	112.7	汽油机	Gasoline Engine	77.5
元钉	Yuan Nails	99.8	内燃机零部件及配件	Engine Parts and Accessories	99.3
造纸网	Paper Network	100.0	车床	Lathe	100.0
金属网	Metal	99.0	铣床	Milling Machine	95.1
锁制品	Lock Products	102.1	磨床	Grinder	106.3
铸铁管	Cast Iron Pipe	92.1	刨床	Planer	100.6
暖气片	Heating Tablets	108.9	钻床	Driller	98.3
铸铁件	Iron Castings	101.7	镗床	Boring Machine	99.1
弯头管	The Elbow	101.6	数控车床	CNC lathe	103.2
窗帘杆	Curtain Rod	91.0	数控铣床	CNC Milling Machine	103.0

6-8 续表 14 continued

产品名称	Name of Product	指 数 Index	产品名称	Name of Product	指 数 Index
数控加工中心	CNC Machining Center	114.1	其它阀门	Other Valves	100.0
金属锯床及刻线机床	Metal Sawing Machine and Groove Machine	95.5	活塞	Pistons	101.0
机械压力机	Mechanical Press	99.2	气缸	Cylinder	102.0
剪切机	Shearing Machine	100.1	液压马达	Hydraulic Motors	101.3
液压机	Hydraulic Press	89.4	气动元件、附件	Pneumatic Components, Annex	93.2
铸造设备	Foundry Equipment	96.8	法兰盘	Flange	99.6
焊灯	Welding Lights	99.7	轴承	Bearing	101.0
机床附件	Machine Annex	99.0	轴承零配件	Bearing Parts	99.5
其他金属加工机械制品	Other Metal Processing Machinery Products	101.1	工业链条	Industry Chain	111.4
桥式起重机	Bridge Crane	101.0	船用链条	Marine Chain	99.0
汽车起重机	Truck Crane	100.1	摩托车齿轮	Motorcycle Gear	101.6
千斤顶	Jack	98.8	汽车齿轮	Car Gear	97.3
塔式起重机	Tower Crane	100.0	农用车齿轮	Agricultural Vehicles Gear	96.7
起重用葫芦	Lifting use Hyacinth	107.5	工程机械齿轮	Engineering Machinery Gear	100.0
电梯	Elevator	100.1	内燃机齿轮	Engine Gear	98.4
叉车	Forklift	89.2	电炉	EAF	101.9
各种工矿车	Various Mining Trucks	91.8	鼓风机	Blower	93.5
输运机械	Transport Machinery	98.5	离心通风机	Centrifugal Fan	97.9
搅拌机	Mixer	101.6	冷冻设备	Refrigeration Equipment	102.3
机械立体仓库、车库	Machinery Warehouse, Garage	104.8	空调机	Air Conditioners.	105.2
其它起重设备	Other Lifting Equipment	113.1	热交换器	Heat Exchanger	99.5
离心式清水泵	Centrifugal Pump	101.0	制冷、空调设备零件	Refrigeration, Air-conditioning Parts	107.4
深井泵	Deep Well Pump	100.2	其他空调机制冷设备	Other Mechanisms Cold air Conditioning Equipment	100.9
轴流泵	Axial Flow Pump	102.1	列车空调机组	Train air Conditioning Units	97.9
叶片泵	Vane Pump	100.0	风铲	Wind Backhoe	100.8
齿轮泵	Gear Pump	99.7	电钻	Electric Drill	100.0
油泵	Pumps	100.1	风钻	Pneumatic Drills	108.1
液压泵	Hydraulic Pump	99.7	焊机	Welder	90.5
油缸	Fuel Tanks	99.9	包装机械	Packaging Machinery	104.9
潜水泵	Submersible Pump	108.7	地上衡	Land Value	98.6
专用泵	Special Pump	95.3	地中衡	The Value of	101.0
其它泵	Other Pump	100.6	台秤	Taiwan Scale	97.2
气体压缩机	Gas Compressor	97.7	案秤	Weigh-in	96.6
制冷压缩机	Refrigeration Compressors	99.7	减速机械	Mechanical Slowdown	99.8
阀门	Valves	100.1	真空干燥机	Dryer	100.0

6-8 续表 15 continued

产品名称	Name of Product	指 数 Index	产品名称	Name of Product	指 数 Index
分离机	Separators	100.0	挖掘机	Excavator	112.7
过滤机	Filter	100.0	压路机	Roller	107.7
滚子	Roller	100.0	推土机	Bulldozers	97.7
螺钉	Screw	99.0	混凝土搅拌机	Concrete Mixers	99.8
螺栓	Bolt	99.4	沥青混凝土摊铺机	Asphalt Paver	99.8
铆钉	Rivet	96.6	建筑升降机	Construction Lifts	96.9
螺母	Nut	102.1	混凝土配料机	Concrete Batching Machine	100.0
弹簧垫	Spring Pad	100.0	研磨设备	Grinding Equipment	95.9
弹簧	Spring	103.9	水泥设备	Cement Equipment	104.8
机械零部件加工	Mechanical Processing Components	103.1	玻璃机械	Glass Machinery	93.5
标准件	Standard Parts	97.5	其他建筑材料生产专用设备	Other Special Equipment for the Production of Building Materials	99.9
滚珠丝杠	Ball Screw	100.1	炼铁设备	Ironmaking Equipment	91.2
其它通用零部件	Other GM Parts	103.4	炼钢设备	Steel-making Equipment	96.8
油马达	Motor Oil	112.3	化工专用设备	Chemical Special Equipment	98.5
铸铁件	Iron Castings	99.7	橡胶加工机械	Rubber Processing Machinery	97.6
铸钢件	Steel Castings	100.7	塑料挤出机组	Plastics Extrusion Unit	101.2
不锈钢铸件	Stainless Steel Castings	101.0	其它塑料工业设备	Other Plastic Industrial Equipment	100.5
摩擦片	Friction Tablets	94.3	带锯机	Band Saw -	94.4
锻件	Forging	101.0	木工刨铣床	Woodworking Shaver Milling Machine	105.5
粉末冶金制品	Powder Metallurgy Products	100.2	其它木工加工机械	Other Woodworking Machinery Processing	102.0
采煤机械	Mining Machinery	101.1	人造板加工设备	Panel Processing Equipment	108.5
刮板运输机	Scraper Transport Planes	94.9	模具	Mold	91.8
液压支架	Hydraulic Support	97.6	制糖机械	Sugar Machinery	101.5
破碎、筛分机械	Broken Screening Machinery	99.5	食品蒸煮均质机械	Cooking Food Heterogeneity Machinery	100.0
选矿设备	Mineral Processing Equipment	99.8	饮食炊事机械	The Catering Kitchen Machinery	103.7
装载机	Loader	100.3	酿酒设备	Brewers Equipment	104.2
采矿机配件	Mining Machine Accessories	99.4	碾米机	Milling Machine	98.0
油井设备	Wells Equipment	101.7	磨粉机	Milling Machine	101.2
抽油机	Pumping Unit	100.0	榨油机	Press	100.0
泥浆泵	Mud Pump	118.7	清理机械	Cleaning Machinery	100.7
螺杆钻	Screw Drill	101.3	其它粮油加工机械	Other Grain and Oil Processing Machinery	100.0
加重钻杆	Add Drill Pipe	100.5	立式洗猪机	Vertical Pig Washing Machine	103.1
石油专用设备部件	Oil Special Equipment Components	103.8	饲料工业机械	Feed Industrial Machinery	99.1

6-8 续表 16 continued

产品名称	Name of Product	指 数 Index	产品名称	Name of Product	指 数 Index
造纸机	Paper Machine	101.3	牵引床	Traction Bed	100.0
制浆洗浆设备	Pulp Pulp Washing Equipment	108.4	假肢	Prosthetics	100.0
其它造纸设备	Other Papermaking Equipment	99.0	除尘器及净化设备	Precipitator and Purification Equipment	108.9
装钉机械	Sewing Machinery	88.7	其它环境污染防治设备	Other Environmental Pollution Control Equipment.	104.6
胶印机	Offset Press	97.4	钻机	Drill	102.7
造纸印刷用切纸机械	Cutter Mechanical Printing Paper Used	97.9	穿孔机	Piercer	104.2
配页机	Allocation of Page	100.0	公安消防设备	Police Fire Equipment	95.9
日用化工设备	Daily Chemical Equipment	100.0	供水设备	Water Supply Equipment	101.7
药品制剂机械	Drugs Agents Machinery	100.0	内燃机车	Locomotives	94.1
其它制药机械	Other Pharmaceutical Machinery	98.9	硬席卧车	Yingxi Car	99.3
棉纺织机械	Textile Machinery	101.5	货车（标准轨距）	Lorry (standard gauge)	134.5
毛纺织机械	Wool Textile Machinery	100.3	铁水车	Hot Metal Cars	95.8
丝纺织机械	Silk Textile Machinery	100.0	机车配件	Motorcycle Accessories	117.4
染整机械	Dyeing and Finishing Machine	100.0	载货汽车	Truck	100.6
制革机械	Tanning Machinery	104.2	越野汽车	Off-road Vehicle	100.7
清洁、熨烫器具	Clean, Ironing Apparatus	97.0	一般自卸汽车	General Dump Truck	102.9
其他机电专用设备	Other Mechanical and Electrical Appliance	95.9	客车	Bus	101.4
轮式拖拉机	Wheeled Tractor	99.9	轿车	Sedan	95.6
小型拖拉机	Small Tractors	103.0	专用汽车	Special Purpose Vehicle	102.7
农用运输车类	Farm Vehicles Category	104.3	改装汽车	Modified Cars	97.4
机引犁、耙	Machine Primer Plow, Harrow	98.3	汽车车身	Auto Body	98.2
机动脱粒机	Mobile Thresher	100.4	挂车	Trailers	105.3
收割机	Harvesters	100.3	车厢	Compartments	81.8
旋耕机	Rotary Machine	101.7	汽车配件	Auto Parts	99.3
粉碎机	Disintegrator	100.4	汽车修理	Auto Repair	99.5
农机试验设备	Farm Machinery Test Equipment	93.6	二轮摩托车	Two Motorcycle	100.1
农林机械	Agriculture and Forestry Machinery	97.0	三轮摩托车	Three-wheeled Motorcycle	103.8
喷雾机	Spray Machine	103.0	摩托车配件	Motorcycle Accessories	103.0
饲草收割设备	Forage Harvest Equipment	95.7	自行车	Bicycles	99.9
养殖设备	Farming Equipment	97.0	电动自行车	Electric Bicycle	99.2
拖拉机配件	Tractor Accessories	99.3	货轮	Freighter	94.7
消毒设备	Sterilization	97.4	客货轮	Passenger and Cargo Ship	92.6
注射器	Syringe	100.2	拖、驳船	Trailers, Barges	98.0

6-8 续表 17 continued

产品名称	Name of Product	指 数 Index	产品名称	Name of Product	指 数 Index
其它水面工作船	Other Surface Ship Work	100.0	裸铝线	Bare Wire	112.6
机动渔船	Fishing Vessel	102.1	漆包铜线（电磁线）	Enameling Copper (wire)	131.3
船用配套设备	Marine Equipment	93.7	电力电缆	Power Cable	125.6
船舶修理及拆船	Ship Repair and Shipbreaking	100.0	通讯电缆	Communication Cables	108.8
手推车	Trolleys	101.4	架空电缆	Overhead Power Lines	100.0
一般交流发电机	General Alternator	100.0	其它电缆	Other Cable	122.8
各种发电机组	Various Units	100.8	安装电线缆	Installation of Electric Cable	141.4
直流电机	DC Motor	99.3	光缆	Optical Cable	98.5
汽轮发电机	Turbogenerator	97.2	还阳板	Yang Also Plate	100.1
交流电动	Electric Exchange	103.9	其它绝缘制品	Other Insulation Products	92.7
分马力电机	Sub-hp Motor	113.4	线圈	Coil	100.1
其它各种电动机	All Other Motor	102.6	电力金具	With the Power	104.5
电机配件	Electrical Accessories	105.8	蓄电池	Battery	106.4
控制、驱动微电机	Control of Micro-motor Drives。	100.6	原电池（折手电池）	The Original Battery (folded hands battery)	116.8
油泵电机	Pump Motor	100.3	锂电池	Lithium Batteries	107.6
磁电机	Magnetic Motor	98.8	电池配件	Battery Accessories	103.9
洗衣机电机	Washing Machine Motor	109.4	镍镉电池	Nickel-cadmium Batteries	100.0
变压器	Transformer	107.5	蓄电池配件	Battery Accessories	122.8
变频器	Inverter	100.0	家用电冰箱	Household Refrigerators	101.8
稳压电源	Regulated Power Supply	99.2	家用冷藏冷冻箱	Frozen Boxes of Household Refrigeration	102.5
整流器	Adapter	96.8	房间空调器	Room Air Conditioner	103.4
增压器	Supercharger	96.3	中央空调	Central Air conditioning	101.3
断路器	Circuit Breaker	99.7	排油烟机	Pai Fume Machine	100.0
开关柜	Switchgear	103.6	微波炉	Microwave Ovens	100.0
开关设备	Switchgear	105.7	电烤（蒸）箱	Xinhua Roast (steamed) Box	110.4
控制、配电箱（台、柜）	Control and Power Distribution Box (Taiwan, counter)	100.8	电炒锅	Frying	100.0
熔断器	Fuse	116.4	家用洗衣机	Domestic Washing Machines	95.0
真空开关管	The Vacuum Switch	97.8	电热水器	Electric Water Heaters	105.0
避雷针	Lightning Rod.	101.5	洗衣机专用配件	Washing Machines Dedicated Accessories	100.0
开关板	Switch Plate	100.0	燃气用具	Gas Appliances	99.9
电源设备	Power Equipment	100.8	太阳能热水器	Solar Water Heaters	99.6
裸铜线	Bare Copper	132.7	采暖炉	Prime	100.5
钢芯铝绞线	Acsr	130.7	普通照明灯泡	General Lighting the Lamp	95.6
布电线	Cloth Wires	137.8	荧光灯	Fluorescent Lamp	106.2

6-8 续表 18 continued

产品名称	Name of Product	指 数 Index	产品名称	Name of Product	指 数 Index
节能灯	Energy-saving Lamps	98.4	其它计算机外部设备	Other External Computer Equipment	84.7
灯炮头	Lamp Head	93.7	显象管玻壳	Kinescope Glass Bulb	99.7
汞灯	Mercury Lamp	99.8	半导体二极管	Semiconductor Diode	105.3
纳灯	Satisfied That the Lights	99.1	半导体三极管	Semiconductor Transistor	100.3
霓虹灯管	Neon Tube	104.7	半导体专用零件	Semiconductor Parts Dedicated	100.0
民用灯具	Civilian Lamps	99.4	集成电路	IC	99.3
文艺灯具	Theatrical Lighting	100.4	电子调谐器	Electronic Tuner	96.7
装饰用灯	Decorative Lights	102.7	LCD点阵	Dot Matrix LCD	100.0
其它灯具	Other Lamps	89.4	电阻器	Resistor	102.9
荧光灯支架	Fluorescent Lamp Stent	100.0	电容器	Capacitors	91.9
车辆专用照明及电气信号设备	Special Lighting and Electrical Vehicles Signal Equipment	100.6	继电器	Relay	100.0
汽车扬声器	Car Speakers	100.8	电感元件	Inductive Components	95.5
热交换器	Heat Exchanger	100.0	磁芯	Cores	103.4
中频电路	IF Circuit	99.9	电连接器	Electrical Connector	112.2
载波通讯设备	Carrier Communications Equipment	96.0	电路板	Circuit Board	88.8
其它通信设备	Other Communications Equipment	80.9	彩色电视机	Color TV	88.8
数字程控交换机	Digital Program-Controlled Switches	94.7	MP3机	MP3 Machine	100.6
传真机	Fax	101.2	其他	Other	96.3
电话单机	Telephone Single	98.2	漏电保护器	Leakage Protection Device	100.0
移动通信（网）设备	Mobile Communications (network) Equipment	90.6	显示及调节仪表	Instrument Display and Conditioning	100.8
配线分线设备	Wiring-line Equipment	100.8	集中控制装置	Centralized Control Device	88.4
移动电话配件	Mobile Phone Accessories	107.2	调节器	Regulator	100.0
电缆挂钩	Cable Link	100.0	流量计	Flowmeter	95.7
雷达	Radar	100.1	网络闭锁系统	Network Locking System	100.3
卫星广播电视设备	Satellite Radio and Television Equipment	100.0	电度表	Power Meter	99.1
放大器	Amplifiers	100.0	计量标准器具	Measurement Standards Apparatus	93.3
电视机荫罩	Television Mask	106.8	量规	Gauge	99.6
计算机	Computer	93.5	温度计	Thermometer	97.6
PC机	PC	90.4	电化学分析仪器	Electrochemical analysis Apparatus	99.0
网络终端	Network Terminal	100.0	物位仪表	Level Meter	100.3
计算机显示终端设备	Computer Display Terminal Equipment	88.4	物理特性分析仪器	Physical Characteristics of Analytical Instruments	100.0
打印机	Printers	101.5	色谱仪	Chromatography	103.9

6-8 续表 19 continued

产品名称	Name of Product	指 数 Index	产品名称	Name of Product	指 数 Index
天平砝码	Balance Weight	100.0	丝织地毯	Silk Carpets	101.4
金属材料试验机	Metal Material Testing Machine	95.0	黄金首饰	Gold Jewelry	155.3
其他	Other	101.8	头饰	Headwears	99.4
水表	Water Meters	97.0	钻石	Diamonds	100.0
压力表	Pressure Gauge	100.0	工艺玻璃	Glass Technology	91.7
汽车仪器仪表	Automobile Instrument	100.0	工艺蜡烛	Candle Technology	107.9
汽车用计价器	Pricing for Vehicle	97.8	人造花卉	Artificial Flowers	108.9
钟	Bell	100.7	皮件工艺品	Leather Products	105.3
表	Table	108.4	发制品	Hair Products	103.6
钟表配件	Watches Accessories	91.1	镜制品	Mirror Products	101.5
光学计量仪器	Optical Measurement Instruments	95.7	油漆刷	Paint Brush	103.0
自动旋光仪	Automatic Polarimeter	100.0	伞	Umbrella	99.7
激光读取器	Laser Reader	102.6	帐篷	Tents	93.7
成形眼镜	Forming Glasses	100.1	锁、链配件	Lock and Chain Accessories	107.9
投影仪	Projector	105.6	废生铁	Waste Pigiron	103.8
装订机	Binding Machine	100.0	废塑料	Waste Plastics	100.0
油印机	Publishing	93.9	火力发电	Thermal Power	103.4
点钞机	Machines	105.7	水力发电	Hydropower	103.1
削笔机	Cut Pencil Machine	100.0	电	Electricity	101.6
石刻	Rock Carving	100.4	热	Heat	104.1
铜像	Statue	108.3	蒸汽	Steam	106.0
其他木制工艺品	Other Wooden Handicrafts	101.4	燃气生产	Gas Production	116.9
竹藤草工艺品	Handicrafts Bamboo Grass	102.9	煤气供应	Gas Supply	101.0
其他编制品	Other Preparation Materials	107.7	液化气	LNG	119.6
抽纱绣品	Merchants Kit	100.8	天然气	Natural Gas	114.5
刺绣工艺品	Embroidery Handicrafts	96.8	自来水	Tap Water	104.6
羊毛地毯	Wool Carpet	103.3	污水处理	Sewage Treatment	100.0
化纤地毯	Chemical Fiber carpet	100.4	中水处理	reclamed Water Treatment	100.0
壁挂毯	Wall Tapestry	106.0			

6-9 1989～2006年全省工业品出厂价格指数

Ex-factory Price Indices of Industrial Products from 1989 to 2006

上年=100 Preceding Year =100

类 别	classification	1989	1990	1991	1992	1993	1994	1995	1996	1997
全部工业品	**General Index**	**123.8**	**104.7**	**103.0**	**109.7**	**123.0**	**124.2**	**117.0**	**104.1**	**101.2**
轻工业	Hight Industry	121.6	106.5	101.2	103.6	111.0	127.0	117.7	101.7	99.7
以农产品为原料	Using Agricultural Products as Raw Materials	123.7	108.7	102.4	104.5	111.8	131.2	119.5	102.1	99.5
以非农产品为原料	Using Non-agricultural Products as Raw Materials	117.3	101.8	98.5	100.4	108.6	112.9	111.9	100.3	100.2
重工业	Heavy Industry	125.4	103.2	104.3	116.1	135.2	121.5	116.4	106.4	102.6
采掘	Mining Quarrying	132.9	102.4	121.3	132.6	135.2	149.5	128.2	109.5	107.7
原料	Raw Materials	120.7	106.5	105.3	117.2	141.7	118.9	112.6	107.4	105.8
加工	Manufacturing	127.7	100.4	101.4	106.9	126.0	109.1	115.2	103.3	96.9
生产资料	Means of Production	125.3	104.9	104.2	115.0	133.0	121.3	117.9	106.2	101.6
采掘	Mining Quarrying	132.9	102.4	121.3	132.6	136.2	149.5	128.2	109.5	107.7
原料	Raw Materials	121.2	105.7	105.1	114.8	137.1	118.6	115.1	106.9	103.1
加工	Manufacturing	127.1	100.1	101.3	107.6	125.2	110.1	116.7	103.3	97.1
生活资料	Consumer Goods	121.5	107.8	101.1	103.5	111.4	127.9	116.0	101.5	100.7
食品	Food	116.8	106.5	102.4	107.6	115.7	122.7	118.4	102.3	100.8
衣着	Clothing	128.5	113.1	101.7	101.6	107.9	138.7	117.6	100.1	101.0
一般日用品	Articles for Daily Use	118.5	102.4	101.2	101.3	111.1	119.5	110.2	102.7	101.3
耐用消费品	Durable Consumer Goods	112.3	100.3	96.4	102.0	109.9	103.6	110.1	103.2	98.2
按工业部门分	**Classify By Industrid Department**									
冶金工业	Metallurgical Industry	126.1	113.3	108.4	115.2	158.2	99.6	106.2	100.5	97.6
电力工业	Power Industry	129.9	112.0	101.5	111.9	119.5	124.9	105.9	118.9	115.9
煤炭及炼焦工业	Coal Industry and Coking Industry	127.2	91.0	119.0	126.7	131.5	110.5	121.5	117.1	106.2
石油工业	Petroleum Industry	116.8	99.2	103.4	132.9	159.9	158.6	126.4	104.0	112.5
化学工业	Chemical Industry	116.4	97.4	100.9	105.4	108.4	111.8	124.7	102.7	95.9
机械工业	Machine Building Industry	127.8	103.4	100.3	106.8	126.4	107.2	106.2	101.5	98.7
建筑材料工业	Building Materials Industry	126.2	100.6	104.1	105.8	122.6	108.0	112.9	103.9	100.6
森林工业	Timber Industry	120.1	92.5	96.5	100.3	112.9	111.7	109.3	105.8	108.9
食品工业	Food Industry	117.0	104.7	101.8	107.6	115.7	122.7	118.4	102.3	100.8
纺织工业	Textile Industry	127.5	107.3	101.3	99.5	102.9	142.6	116.9	98.9	99.5
缝纫工业	Tailoring Industry	128.3	137.0	107.8	120.4	114.5	120.7	127.7	110.5	99.2
皮革工业	Leather Industry	121.6	102.2	109.6	104.4	115.3	115.0	124.4	104.6	99.8
造纸工业	Paper Industry	122.0	98.4	100.3	99.8	105.3	110.6	132.4	113.4	94.2
文教艺术用品工业	Cultual, Educational Handicrafts Articles	102.1	107.3	109.5	106.0	117.7	113.6	101.6	101.3	96.9
其它工业	Other Industry	128.5	113.0	103.4	114.8	132.9	132.0	136.2	106.1	97.0

6-9 续表 1 continued

类 别	classification	1998	1999	2000	2001	2002	2003	2004	2005	2006
全部工业品	**General Index**	**96.0**	**97.2**	**105.9**	**99.1**	**98.8**	**103.5**	**106.4**	**103.7**	**102.3**
轻工业	Hight Industry	96.1	95.3	99.7	99.3	97.5	101.2	103.3	100.8	101.1
以农产品为原料	Using Agricultural Products as Raw Materials	96.3	95.2	100.2	100.1	97.7	103.2	105.1	100.3	101.4
以非农产品为原料	Using Non-agricultural Products as Raw Materials	95.6	95.8	97.8	97.4	97.1	99.2	101.5	101.3	100.7
重工业	Heavy Industry	95.9	98.8	110.9	99.0	99.7	106.5	110.5	107.3	103.7
采掘	Mining Quarrying	98.1	98.1	139.3	96.8	111.7	111.2	121.3	120.8	109.0
原料	Raw Materials	95.2	100.3	111.3	100.7	97.7	109.1	110.0	107.5	104.9
加工	Manufacturing	95.6	97.3	98.0	98.2	97.8	102.6	107.1	102.3	100.9
生产资料	Means of Production	96.0	98.1	109.5	99.1	98.8	104.6	108.0	105.1	103.1
采掘	Mining Quarrying	98.1	98.1	139.2	96.9	111.9	110.6	121.5	120.4	107.8
原料	Raw Materials	95.3	98.6	109.4	100.5	96.8	108.7	108.8	107.0	105.1
加工	Manufacturing	96.0	97.2	99.1	98.6	97.1	101.9	105.4	101.8	101.4
生活资料	Consumer Goods	96.0	95.7	98.8	99.3	98.5	100.9	102.7	100.1	100.4
食品	Food	97.5	96.9	97.5	100.6	99.4	103.4	105.6	100.0	101.0
衣着	Clothing	94.1	93.8	102.4	101.4	98.4	99.4	102.1	101.2	101.6
一般日用品	Articles for Daily Use	96.6	96.7	98.6	98.4	98.5	99.9	101.0	102.3	100.3
耐用消费品	Durable Consumer Goods	93.6	92.1	94.3	96.1	96.7	96.1	97.0	97.7	98.2
按工业部门分	**Classify By Industrid Department**								0.0	0.0
冶金工业	Metallurgical Industry	94.3	95.2	111.1	99.7	97.5	113.0	117.6	102.6	101.1
电力工业	Power Industry	109.7	102.9	100.4	100.7	100.2	100.2	100.6	103.3	102.4
煤炭及炼焦工业	Coal Industry and Coking Industry	96.6	96.8	97.3	115.0	115.2	102.1	124.8	111.0	97.6
石油工业	Petroleum Industry	95.8	105.2	161.4	92.5	102.2	120.1	116.3	127.2	118.6
化学工业	Chemical Industry	92.2	97.2	102.1	98.6	97.8	102.8	107.7	106.8	101.7
机械工业	Machine Building Industry	96.1	96.2	97.2	97.0	97.2	98.6	101.2	100.4	100.4
建筑材料工业	Building Materials Industry	99.0	98.7	98.1	99.4	99.1	99.4	103.9	100.6	102.2
森林工业	Timber Industry	105.7	99.6	98.1	99.2	95.2	99.5	100.9	101.2	100.6
食品工业	Food Industry	97.4	96.5	97.4	100.6	99.4	103.8	106.4	99.9	100.9
纺织工业	Textile Industry	93.2	94.0	105.8	97.7	92.8	105.7	105.7	99.7	102.4
缝纫工业	Tailoring Industry	100.6	88.8	97.9	100.6	98.5	99.2	102.8	101.4	101.3
皮革工业	Leather Industry	96.4	93.0	100.0	103.2	101.0	99.8	101.2	101.1	102.4
造纸工业	Paper Industry	93.6	95.1	101.6	100.4	97.8	98.7	101.2	101.3	101.1
文教艺术用品工业	Cultual, Educational Handicrafts Articles	88.7	93.7	104.0	100.7	100.8	99.1	100.7	102.4	100.9
其它工业	Other Industry	101.6	99.0	103.3	104.1	99.4	100.2	101.2	102.0	101.4

6-10 分市工业品出厂价格指数（2006年）
Ex-factory Price Indices of Industrial Products by Every City (2006)

类 别	Classification	价格指数（以上年价格为100）								
		济南 Jinan	青岛 Qingdao	淄博 Zibo	枣庄 Zaozhuan	东营 Dongyin	烟台 Yanta	潍坊 Weifang	济宁 Jining	泰安 Taian
全部工业品	**General Index**	**100.2**	**101.1**	**103.0**	**101.9**	**115.6**	**103.0**	**101.1**	**97.7**	**99.4**
轻工业	Hight Industry	99.9	99.6	101.1	102.1	104.7	102.3	101.5	100.9	100.6
以农产品为原料	Using Agricultural Products as Raw Materials	102.5	101.0	101.3	101.4	101.2	102.3	101.3	100.6	101.5
以非农产品为原料	Using Non-agricultural Products as Raw Materials	98.8	98.6	101.0	102.8	110.2	102.4	102.6	101.7	99.7
重工业	Heavy Industry	100.5	103.9	104.6	101.7	117.6	103.6	100.5	95.6	98.8
采掘	Mining Quarrying	99.7	104.7	94.7	99.9	120.7	102.4	71.3	90.0	96.4
原料	Raw Materials	107.4	104.0	107.4	103.0	112.3	111.8	103.4	99.6	99.1
加工	Manufacturing	97.5	103.8	98.6	101.5	110.3	101.5	100.5	104.0	99.5
生产资料	Means of Production	100.1	102.5	103.6	102.3	116.5	103.2	101.2	97.0	99.1
采掘	Mining Quarrying	99.7	104.7	94.8	100.5	120.7	102.4	71.3	90.1	96.0
原料	Raw Materials	107.4	104.1	106.9	103.5	112.3	110.8	102.8	99.8	100.1
加工	Manufacturing	98.2	101.9	101.0	102.7	108.2	101.9	101.7	102.4	99.8
生活资料	Consumer Goods	100.7	99.7	99.5	100.9	100.4	102.4	100.7	100.7	101.2
食品	Food	103.4	101.5	100.1	100.3	99.7	103.2	99.4	100.9	101.1
衣着	Clothing	100.9	102.2	99.1	103.5	106.8	100.5	100.9	100.8	104.9
一般日用品	Articles for Daily Use	98.5	101.8	99.4	101.8	100.7	103.9	102.6	100.5	99.6
耐用消费品	Durable Consumer Goods	98.0	97.2	98.1	100.3	102.9	98.3	103.0	100.3	100.6
按工业部门分	**Classify By Industrid Department**									
冶金工业	Metallurgical Industry	96.0	97.1	98.3	103.0	105.1	107.2	97.3	98.9	98.0
电力工业	Power Industry	101.2	103.3	103.0	102.9	102.9	105.3	101.8	100.5	105.7
煤炭及炼焦工业	Coal Industry and Coking Industry	101.3	112.9	95.9	100.8		101.4	93.5	90.8	95.7
石油工业	Petroleum Industry	116.9	112.8	117.4		120.0	94.6	116.4	116.7	113.0
化学工业	Chemical Industry	100.3	100.0	102.0	105.0	110.5	101.0	97.0	99.0	98.0
机械工业	Machine Building Industry	98.0	100.3	99.5	102.8	110.0	101.4	101.0	105.3	100.1
建筑材料工业	Building Materials Industry	100.2	102.3	101.1	101.7	103.8	101.7	101.4	102.7	100.1
森林工业	Timber Industry	99.5	99.7	103.7	101.3	103.6	100.9	102.0	100.9	102.8
食品工业	Food Industry	103.3	100.7	101.6	100.1	99.4	102.6	99.2	100.6	101.1
纺织工业	Textile Industry	104.4	100.7	102.2	108.8	104.9	102.8	104.6	104.7	100.8
缝纫工业	Tailoring Industry	99.7	102.0	99.1	103.8	99.9	100.2	100.9	100.8	104.8
皮革工业	Leather Industry	104.0	101.6	101.1	100.1	108.3	104.6	100.1	101.2	107.7
造纸工业	Paper Industry	99.0	98.9	101.5	99.0	99.5	99.5	100.1	99.3	102.3
文教艺术用品工业	Cultual, Educational Handicrafts Articles	100.9	100.5	100.5	100.6	104.6	102.2	103.1	100.1	90.7
其它工业	Other Industry	102.9	104.8	101.9	102.2	108.8	112.1	101.1	101.4	104.1

6-10 续表 1 continued

类别	Classification	价格指数（以上年价格为100）							
		威海 Weihai	日照 Rizhao	莱芜 Laiwu	临沂 Linyi	德州 Dezhou	聊城 Liaocheng	滨州 Binzhou	菏泽 Heze
全部工业品	**General Index**	**103.7**	**101.2**	**94.7**	**102.4**	**101.5**	**104.8**	**107.4**	**103.8**
轻工业	Hight Industry	103.6	101.6	101.2	101.8	101.1	101.5	103.0	99.8
以农产品为原料	Using Agricultural Products as Raw Materials	101.5	101.7	100.9	101.3	101.1	101.5	103.2	99.6
以非农产品为原料	Using Non-agricultural Products as Raw Materials	104.9	101.3	103.3	102.9	101.3	101.0	99.8	100.4
重工业	Heavy Industry	103.9	100.6	93.6	103.2	102.2	107.6	117.1	110.6
采掘	Mining Quarrying	102.5	113.4	88.2	101.9	98.1	100.0	71.9	
原料	Raw Materials	101.8	99.9	96.5	102.4	102.3	107.7	124.9	108.5
加工	Manufacturing	104.5	100.7	92.6	104.2	102.1	107.5	100.8	119.4
生产资料	Means of Production	105.5	101.6	94.5	103.3	101.9	105.6	108.5	106.7
采掘	Mining Quarrying	102.5	113.4	88.2	101.5	98.1	100.0	71.9	
原料	Raw Materials	101.9	102.5	98.0	102.6	102.3	107.9	122.9	108.4
加工	Manufacturing	106.0	101.1	93.8	103.7	101.7	105.0	103.1	105.1
生活资料	Consumer Goods	100.0	100.4	99.2	100.8	100.8	100.7	103.8	99.1
食品	Food	99.0	100.5	98.8	100.9	100.1	100.4	104.9	98.3
衣着	Clothing	102.0	100.1	100.6	99.9	101.2	100.1	100.6	101.6
一般日用品	Articles for Daily Use	100.1	99.9	98.7	100.8	102.6	103.1	100.4	101.0
耐用消费品	Durable Consumer Goods	101.0	101.1	95.1	102.1	103.3	100.5		97.5
按工业部门分	**Classify By Industrid Department**								
冶金工业	Metallurgical Industry	103.0	98.0	91.8	105.4	101.2	112.7	124.3	144.6
电力工业	Power Industry	98.4	101.8	102.7	102.3	101.8	104.5	103.3	103.1
煤炭及炼焦工业	Coal Industry and Coking Industry		93.5	104.2	100.4	98.1			99.3
石油工业	Petroleum Industry	157.1	159.8		115.3	107.6	102.4	129.2	118.1
化学工业	Chemical Industry	107.4	102.4	109.5	100.2	101.1	98.2	104.4	100.0
机械工业	Machine Building Industry	101.6	101.1	97.4	104.4	101.6	108.8	107.3	109.1
建筑材料工业	Building Materials Industry	119.8	102.5	93.1	105.2	101.0	97.6	101.3	100.1
森林工业	Timber Industry	100.3	102.7		101.7	103.4	102.7	99.9	99.0
食品工业	Food Industry	99.1	99.9	98.6	101.3	100.2	99.0	105.4	98.5
纺织工业	Textile Industry	114.1	107.5	102.6	102.7	101.4	103.0	102.2	101.4
缝纫工业	Tailoring Industry	101.1	100.1	100.3	99.9	101.3	100.1	101.1	102.5
皮革工业	Leather Industry	102.7		106.2	99.7	102.6	100.9	105.4	98.9
造纸工业	Paper Industry	104.7	106.4	99.2	99.5	102.5	101.8	111.0	98.6
文教艺术用品工业	Cultual, Educational Handicrafts Articles	105.6	104.5	98.5	103.7	102.1	104.9	100.0	103.5
其它工业	Other Industry	98.7	100.3	106.5	102.0	102.0	103.8	100.7	105.8

6-11 固定资产投资价格指数（2006年）
Price Index of Investment in Fixed Assets (2006)

类 别	Classification	价格指数（以上年同期为100）				
		全年平均 Annual Average	一季度 The first Quarter	二季度 The Second Quarter	三季度 The Third Quarter	四季度 The Forth Quarter
固定资产投资	**Investment in Fixed Assets**	**101.8**	**100.1**	**101.8**	**102.5**	**102.9**
建筑安装、装饰工程	Construction and Installation	102.1	99.5	102.4	103.1	103.6
人工费	Manpower Cost Price Index	109.0	106.9	108.3	110.2	110.7
工程管理人员	Engineering Management Staff	109.6	107.6	108.6	110.9	111.2
工程技术人员	Engineering Technology Staff	108.8	106.9	107.4	109.9	111.1
普通工人	Common Worker	109.0	106.8	108.4	110.1	110.6
材料费	Materials Price Index	100.1	97.0	100.6	101.0	101.9
钢材	Rolled-steel	97.2	92.3	98.3	98.9	99.4
木材	Wood	102.7	101.5	102.9	102.9	103.7
水泥	Cement	101.4	100.5	100.4	101.5	103.1
地方建筑材料	Local Building Materials	103.7	102.6	104.3	103.9	103.8
化工材料	Chemical Raw Materials	107.0	107.7	109.1	105.4	105.8
电料	Electrical Materials and Appliances	103.7	102.5	102.5	104.3	105.6
其他材料	Other Materials	103.5	103.3	104.8	103.0	102.8
机械费	Machinery Fee	103.9	102.9	104.0	105.1	103.9
（一）土石方及筑路机械	Cubic Meter of Earth and Stone and Road Machinery	103.9	103.2	103.9	105.2	103.2
（二）打桩机械	Piling Machinery	102.4	101.2	102.7	102.2	103.3
（三）起重机械	Hauling-up Machinery	102.5	101.8	102.4	102.9	103.1
（四）运输机械	Transport Machinery	103.6	103.8	102.4	104.5	103.6
（五）混凝土及砂浆机械	Concrete and Mortar Machinery	103.3	103.7	103.5	103.0	102.9
（六）加工机械	Processing Machinery	103.8	102.7	105.1	103.2	104.0
（七）泵类机械	Pump Machinery	104.2	104.0	105.0	104.1	103.6
（八）船舶机械	Shipping Machinery	111.4	102.9	113.5	111.9	117.4
（九）其他机械	Other Machinery	101.8	101.1	101.8	102.0	102.1
设备、工器具购置	Pruchase of Equipment, Tools and Instruments	100.6	100.0	99.9	101.0	101.4
其他费用	Others	103.4	103.5	103.9	103.3	103.0
土地取得费	Land Fee	104.1	103.8	105.3	105.3	101.9
前期工程费	Front-end Engineering Fee	102.5	102.7	103.5	102.1	101.6
施工工作费	Working Fee	102.5	102.9	102.5	101.6	103.2
建设单位其他费用	Other Fee About Units Undertaking Projects	104.6	104.6	104.3	104.2	105.3

6-12 固定资产投资调查产品价格指数（2006年）
Price Index of Investment in Fixed Assets (2006)

类 别	Classification	价格指数（以上年同期为100）				
		全年平均 Annual Average	一季度 The first Quarter	二季度 The Second Quarter	三季度 The Third Quarter	四季度 The Forth Quarter
固定资产投资	**Investment in Fixed Assets**	**101.8**	**100.1**	**101.8**	**102.5**	**102.9**
建筑安装、装饰工程	Construction and Installation	102.1	99.5	102.4	103.1	103.6
人工费	Manpower Cost Price Index	109.0	106.9	108.3	110.2	110.7
工程管理人员	Engineering Management Staff	109.6	107.6	108.6	110.9	111.2
工程技术人员	Engineering Technology Staff	108.8	106.9	107.4	109.9	111.1
普通工人	Common Worker	109.0	106.8	108.4	110.1	110.6
材料费	Materials Price Index	100.1	97.0	100.6	101.0	101.9
钢材	Rolled-steel	97.2	92.3	98.3	98.9	99.4
重轨	Heavy Rail	107.6	105.5	109.4	107.7	107.7
重轨	Heavy Rail	107.6	105.5	109.4	107.7	107.7
其他铁道用钢	Other Railroad Steel	97.6	103.7	90.7	94.9	101.0
垫板	Backing Board	100.6	101.8	100.0	100.0	100.4
其他	Others	97.5	104.2	90.2	94.3	101.5
螺纹钢	Deformed Steel Bar	96.0	90.4	96.7	98.7	98.2
中型φ（38-79mm）	Medium-sized	96.4	85.2	98.3	102.2	99.7
小型φ（9-37mm）	Small-sized	96.4	93.7	96.5	97.5	98.1
薄钢板	Sheet Steel	101.5	100.7	105.5	97.8	102.0
镀锌（锡）	Galvanization	101.4	99.3	105.4	97.7	103.3
不锈钢	Stainless Steel	101.0	102.0	108.5	93.5	100.0
其他	Others	101.6	100.8	103.2	100.7	101.8
中厚钢板	Steel Plate	93.4	90.0	99.9	88.0	95.9
普炭	Common Carbon	93.4	86.4	99.4	88.0	99.7
碳结	Carbon Structure	96.1	100.6	102.2		85.6
不锈钢	Stainless Steel	108.7	94.7	100.1	101.1	138.9
大型钢材	Heavy Wall Pipe	101.2	98.5	99.7	101.0	105.8
角钢	Angle	103.3	110.3	106.0	100.4	96.4
工字钢	Double Tee Iron	99.5	96.8	98.7	99.7	102.5
槽钢	U-steel	98.0	97.9	90.0	101.2	103.1
圆钢φ≥80mm	Round Bar Teel	101.9	98.0	99.4	101.3	108.7
异型钢	Deformed Steel	97.6	95.6	87.4	91.1	116.2
中型钢材	Medium-sized Steel	100.1	94.4	101.3	101.0	103.9
角钢	Angle	102.9	102.2	103.1	102.7	103.5
工字钢	Double Tee Iron	99.2	91.8	100.1	98.2	106.7

6-12 续表 1 continued

类别	Classification	价格指数（以上年同期为100） 全年平均 Annual Average	一季度 The first Quarter	二季度 The Second Quarter	三季度 The Third Quarter	四季度 The Forth Quarter
异型钢	Deformed Steel	100.2	98.0	99.5	99.7	103.8
槽钢	U-steel	94.6	95.2	88.6	94.1	100.5
小型钢材	Small-sized Steel	97.8	91.6	100.9	98.3	100.4
扁钢	Flat-rolled Steel	96.0	89.7	99.0	95.3	100.2
角钢	Angle	96.5	90.7	98.4	97.6	99.3
异型钢	Deformed Steel	102.4	98.5	110.4	99.4	101.1
钢筋	Concrete Iron	96.6	91.8	97.9	98.5	98.1
φ6.5mm	φ6.5mm	96.1	92.4	96.2	97.9	97.7
φ8mm	φ8mm	96.9	91.0	98.8	99.1	98.6
优质钢材	High Quality Steel	100.5	91.7	102.4	104.1	103.9
优质钢材	High Quality Steel	100.5	91.7	102.4	104.1	103.9
钢构件	Steel Member	104.0	104.8	103.7	103.4	104.2
桥架	Crane Span Structure	101.9	101.9	104.4	101.5	100.0
屋架	Roof Truss	102.3	107.6	100.4	100.4	100.8
钢梁	Girder Steel	113.0	110.0	108.5	114.7	118.6
钢门窗	Steel Doors and Windows	98.0			95.9	100.0
其他	Others	98.5	99.9	101.0	98.7	94.3
无缝钢管	Seamless Steel Tube	98.2	96.6	97.3	99.5	99.3
一般碳结管	Common Carbon Structure Pipe	98.1	96.4	96.9	99.5	99.4
镀锌管	Ating Steel Pipe	100.2	97.0	100.9	101.9	101.0
其他	Others	96.0	103.3	94.1	91.0	95.7
焊接钢管	Welding Steel Pipe	99.8	97.7	100.9	99.0	101.7
镀锌管	Coating Steel Pipe	101.5	102.6	103.4	97.6	102.2
普通管	Common Steel Pipe	100.3	94.8	101.8	103.4	101.2
输油（气）管	Petroleum（Gas）Pipe Line	100.2	99.8	99.7	99.8	101.5
铸铁管	Castiron Pipe	101.3	102.3	100.8	101.4	100.8
承接式	Adapting	101.5	102.5	101.0	101.5	100.9
法兰式	Flange	100.1	100.0	100.1	100.2	100.3
钢丝绳	Wirerope	100.9	97.3	109.7	98.3	98.0
钢丝绳	Wirerope	100.9	97.3	109.7	98.3	98.0
钢丝	Steel Wire	97.3	96.5	100.1	88.6	104.2
钢丝	Steel Wire	97.3	96.5	100.1	88.6	104.2
钢带	Steel Band	99.0		101.7	96.4	98.7
钢带	Steel Band	99.0		101.7	96.4	98.7
铁丝	Iron Wire	99.4	100.2	99.2	95.9	102.4

6-12 续表 2 continued

类 别	Classification	价格指数（以上年同期为100） 全年平均 Annual Average	一季度 The first Quarter	二季度 The Second Quarter	三季度 The Third Quarter	四季度 The Forth Quarter
铁丝	Iron Wire	99.4	100.2	99.2	95.9	102.4
铁件	Iron Piece	100.4	99.7	99.3	101.1	101.3
铁件	Iron Piece	100.4	99.7	99.3	101.1	101.3
窗纱	Window Screening	102.4	115.4	100.0	97.8	96.4
窗纱	Window Screening	102.4	115.4	100.0	97.8	96.4
螺栓	Screw Bolt	98.7	99.6	101.1	103.5	90.6
螺栓	Screw Bolt	98.7	99.6	101.1	103.5	90.6
脚手架钢材	Scaffold Steel	96.5	96.1	95.6	99.2	95.0
脚手架钢材	Scaffold Steel	96.5	96.1	95.6	99.2	95.0
木材	Wood	102.7	101.5	102.9	102.9	103.7
原木	Log	103.1	101.4	103.2	104.0	103.8
进口	Import	104.5	103.2	100.2	107.2	107.2
国产	Domestic	103.0	101.1	103.4	103.7	103.7
普通锯材	Common Converted Timber	101.9	101.2	102.0	100.8	103.7
进口	Import	100.8	94.2	103.4	99.7	105.7
国产	Domestic	102.1	101.8	102.0	100.9	103.7
特种锯材	Special Type Converted Timber	100.6	102.3	100.0	100.0	100.0
枕木	Crosstie	100.6	102.3	100.0	100.1	100.1
胶合板	Plywood	102.5	101.9	102.9	103.8	101.3
三合	Three-ply Board	102.3	102.2	102.2	102.0	102.8
五合	Five-ply Board	104.7	104.4	105.0	103.9	105.3
其它	Others	101.5	99.2	102.6	105.4	98.8
纤维板	Fibreboard	105.8	105.6	101.8	108.7	107.1
软质	Flexible	109.1	108.9	101.9	115.3	110.3
硬质	Stiff	103.7	105.5	101.7	103.2	104.4
刨花板	Chipboard	104.2	104.0	102.9	101.8	108.1
装饰板	Decorative Plate	102.1	101.1	104.9	100.2	102.3
木质地板	Xylogen Board	102.1	101.1	104.9	100.2	102.3
水泥	Cement	101.4	100.5	100.4	101.5	103.1
硅酸盐水泥	Portland Cement	101.4	100.6	100.4	101.6	103.0
强度等级52.5	Intensity Grade 52.5	100.3	99.8	100.8	101.4	99.3
强度等级42.5	Intensity Grade 42.5	101.7	101.0	100.3	101.6	103.9
特种水泥	Special Type Cement	101.5	104.5	95.7	104.0	101.7
白水泥	White Cement	99.1	101.0	93.7	97.7	104.0
大坝水泥	Dam Cement	105.2	106.8	107.1	105.0	102.0

6-12 续表 3 continued

类 别	Classification	价格指数（以上年同期为100） 全年平均 Annual Average	一季度 The first Quarter	二季度 The Second Quarter	三季度 The Third Quarter	四季度 The Forth Quarter
膨胀水泥	Swelling Cement	100.9	102.6	100.0	100.0	
自应力水泥	Self-stressing Cement	97.7		93.2	100.0	100.0
水泥砖	Cement Brick	100.9	100.3	99.2	102.5	101.8
水泥砖	Cement Brick	100.9	100.3	99.2	102.5	101.8
水泥瓦	Cement Tile	102.5	104.0	99.7	107.3	98.9
水泥瓦	Cement Tile	102.5	104.0	99.7	107.3	98.9
水泥板	Cement Flag	106.8		106.3	99.9	114.2
水泥板	Cement Flag	106.8		106.3	99.9	114.2
水泥排水管	Cement Drain-pipe	100.6	100.0	104.3	94.6	103.6
水泥排水管	Cement Drain-pipe	100.6	100.0	104.3	94.6	103.6
水泥压力管	Cement Pressure Pipes	98.9	96.6	100.0	100.0	
水泥压力管	Cement Pressure Pipes	98.9	96.6	100.0	100.0	
水泥电杆	Cement （Electrical）Pole	100.0		100.0	100.0	100.0
（园锥型）	Circular Cone	100.0		100.0	100.0	100.0
石棉水泥制品	Asbestos Cement Products	105.0	100.0	104.8	115.3	100.0
瓦	Tile	122.5	100.0	144.9	144.9	100.0
管	Pipe	101.7	100.0	106.6	100.0	100.0
地方建筑材料	Local Building Materials	103.7	102.6	104.3	103.9	103.8
砖	Brick	104.7	106.5	105.0	104.4	102.9
粘土砖	Fireclay Brick	104.6	107.2	104.4	104.1	102.6
空心砖	Hollow Brick	105.7	103.1	108.5	106.1	105.1
煤渣砖	Cinder Brick	104.2	106.6	103.7	101.7	104.7
轻体砖	Light Brick	105.1	104.9	105.6	107.5	102.5
瓦	Tile	102.0	101.3	103.2	101.9	101.6
粘土瓦	Fireclay Tile	102.0	101.3	103.2	101.9	101.6
石棉瓦	Asbestos Tile	104.3		104.6	104.0	
中波瓦	Medium Wave Tile	104.3		104.6	104.0	
石灰	Lime	105.4	108.8	103.8	104.5	104.4
生石灰	Shell	106.3	111.4	106.0	103.7	104.1
熟石灰	Hydrated Lime	103.5	102.6	97.8	106.3	107.2
石灰膏	Lime Cream	104.3	101.8	105.9	105.1	104.2
砂子	Sand	106.4	105.8	105.9	107.7	106.4
粒沙	Grain Sand	107.1	106.0	108.7	105.3	108.5
粗沙	Crude Sand	106.4	106.1	105.8	108.6	105.2
细沙	Thin Sand	104.9	104.1	100.9	108.2	106.3

6-12 续表 4 continued

类 别	Classification	价格指数（以上年同期为100）				
		全年平均 Annual Average	一季度 The first Quarter	二季度 The Second Quarter	三季度 The Third Quarter	四季度 The Forth Quarter
石膏板	Gypsum Boards	102.9	102.0	104.2	102.8	102.7
纸面	Gibraltar	103.2	102.1	106.1	103.1	101.6
纤维	Fibre	102.3	101.8	97.5	101.6	108.4
水磨石板材	Waterstone Panel	109.3	114.8	109.5	103.5	
水磨石板材	Waterstone Panel	109.3	114.8	109.5	103.5	
大理石板材	Marble Panel	103.5	102.7	107.8	99.4	104.0
大理石板材	Marble Panel	103.5	102.7	107.8	99.4	104.0
花岗岩板材	Granite Panel	98.6	96.5	99.2	100.0	98.5
花岗岩板材	Granite Panel	98.6	96.5	99.2	100.0	98.5
加气混凝土	Air Entrainment Concrete	106.7	117.5	101.7	103.6	103.9
加气混凝土	Air Entrainment Concrete	106.7	117.5	101.7	103.6	103.9
加气混凝土砌块	Air Entraining Concrete Block	101.6	94.6	102.6	105.2	104.1
加气混凝土砌块	Air Entraining Concrete Block	101.6	94.6	102.6	105.2	104.1
毛石	Ashler	104.3	102.7	102.9	106.2	105.6
毛石	Ashler	104.3	102.7	102.9	106.2	105.6
粉煤灰硅酸盐砌块	Fly Ash Silicate Block	105.2	105.4		102.3	107.9
粉煤灰硅酸盐砌块	Fly Ash Silicate Block	105.2	105.4		102.3	107.9
商品混凝土	Commodity Concrete	100.8	102.0	101.2	98.5	101.4
商品混凝土	Commodity Concrete	100.8	102.0	101.2	98.5	101.4
石子	Cobblestone	104.2	99.4	106.8	106.2	104.3
石子	Cobblestone	104.2	99.4	106.8	106.2	104.3
化工材料	Chemical Raw Materials	107.0	107.7	109.1	105.4	105.8
清漆	Varnish	103.6	102.7	102.5	105.9	103.3
酚醛漆	Phenol Aldehyde Lacquer	105.4	105.1	102.9	108.8	104.7
醇酸漆	Alcohol Acid Lacquer	103.4	101.5	102.4	106.9	102.8
天然树脂漆	Natural Resin Lacquer	100.8	100.0	102.4	100.0	
硝基纤维漆	Nitrocellulose Lacquer	106.1	104.4	107.1		106.7
其他	Others	100.3	100.0	100.0	100.9	
调和漆	Make up Paint	102.9	100.1	103.8	105.3	102.5
酚醛漆	Phenol Aldehyde Lacquer	105.2	107.7	103.2	105.3	104.4
醇酸漆	Alcohol Acid Lacquer	101.4	96.5	101.2	105.6	102.3
硝基纤维漆	Nitrocellulose Lacquer	111.2	117.7			104.7
其他	Others	103.2	102.6	107.0	100.0	
磁漆	Enamel	103.8	106.9	104.6	100.0	103.8
酚醛漆	Phenol Aldehyde Lacquer	107.9	107.9	107.9		107.9

6-12 续表 5 continued

类 别	Classification	价格指数（以上年同期为100） 全年平均 Annual Average	一季度 The first Quarter	二季度 The Second Quarter	三季度 The Third Quarter	四季度 The Forth Quarter
醇酸漆	Alcohol Acid Lacquer	102.3	105.4	102.4	100.0	101.3
耐热漆	Heat Resistant Paint	101.8		103.6		100.0
耐热漆	Heat Resistant Paint	101.8		103.6		100.0
防锈漆	Anticorrosive Paint	106.0	107.2	105.2	106.2	105.3
防锈漆	Anticorrosive Paint	106.0	107.2	105.2	106.2	105.3
沥清漆	Asphalt Varnish	106.6	109.3	121.1	95.9	100.0
沥清漆	Asphalt Varnish	106.6	109.3	121.1	95.9	100.0
乳胶漆	Latex Paint	107.8	106.3	104.9	114.5	105.6
乳胶漆	Latex Paint	107.8	106.3	104.9	114.5	105.6
银粉	Silver Powder	108.2	105.8	107.0	112.0	108.1
银粉	Silver Powder	108.2	105.8	107.0	112.0	108.1
防水粉	Waterproof Powder	102.6	105.4	104.0	100.5	100.5
防水粉	Waterproof Powder	102.6	105.4	104.0	100.5	100.5
炸药	Explosive	106.0	114.6	103.7	104.4	101.4
硝铵炸药	Nitroglycerin	106.3	114.6	104.0	105.3	101.4
其他	Others	107.7		115.3	100.0	
雷管	Detonator	119.2	166.7	103.0	106.4	100.8
雷管	Detonator	119.2	166.7	103.0	106.4	100.8
速凝剂	Flash Setting Admixture	111.9	116.7	111.7	102.6	116.7
速凝剂	Flash Setting Admixture	111.9	116.7	111.7	102.6	116.7
脱模剂	Demoulding Agent	104.3	101.1	102.6	101.1	112.3
脱模剂	Demoulding Agent	104.3	101.1	102.6	101.1	112.3
稀料	Thinner	109.5	114.1	110.4	109.1	104.4
稀料	Thinner	109.5	114.1	110.4	109.1	104.4
粘合剂	Adhesive	101.4	102.8	102.5	100.7	99.4
107	107	102.5	103.6	103.4	98.5	104.6
801	801	103.9	103.3	104.6	103.3	104.4
其他	Others	100.4	100.5	102.0	100.8	98.4
涂料	Coating Material	104.4	103.5	104.5	103.6	106.1
内墙	Interior Wall	104.0	102.4	105.2	102.9	105.3
外墙	Exposed Wall	104.8	105.9	103.2	104.1	105.9
防水	Waterproof	106.5	100.8	102.3	104.5	118.3
汽油	Gasoline	110.9	111.7	114.0	114.0	103.8
汽油	Gasoline	110.9	111.7	114.0	114.0	103.8
柴油	Diesel Oil	111.3	114.2	114.7	108.9	107.6

6-12 续表 6 continued

类 别	Classification	价格指数（以上年同期为100）				
		全年平均 Annual Average	一季度 The first Quarter	二季度 The Second Quarter	三季度 The Third Quarter	四季度 The Forth Quarter
柴油	Diesel Oil	111.3	114.2	114.7	108.9	107.6
煤油	Kerosene	102.0	106.1	100.4	100.0	101.6
煤油	Kerosene	102.0	106.1	100.4	100.0	101.6
机油	Engine Oil	116.6	143.6	107.0	106.1	109.5
机油	Engine Oil	116.6	143.6	107.0	106.1	109.5
黄油	Butter	106.7	120.1	103.5	103.5	99.7
黄油	Butter	106.7	120.1	103.5	103.5	99.7
防腐油	Antiseptic Oil	115.2	108.5	124.3	120.0	108.1
防腐油	Antiseptic Oil	115.2	108.5	124.3	120.0	108.1
软化水	Soften Water	100.4	100.2	100.4		100.4
软化水	Soften Water	100.4	100.2	100.4		100.4
火碱	Caustic Soda	100.0	100.0			100.0
火碱	Caustic Soda	100.0	100.0			100.0
塑料管	Silent Stock Tube	102.4	100.8	102.1	103.3	103.4
pvc硬塑管	pvc Silent Stock Tube	102.0	100.3	100.8	103.9	103.1
塑铝管	Plastics Aluminium Tube	104.0	102.3	104.5	100.0	109.2
Upvc塑料管	Upvc Silent Stock Tube	103.5	101.0	104.0	101.8	107.3
pp-r给水管	pp-r Feedwater Tube	103.4	103.5	104.4	103.6	102.0
泡沫塑料	Polyfoam	111.5	112.5	111.1	111.1	111.1
泡沫塑料	Polyfoam	111.5	112.5	111.1	111.1	111.1
塑料编织袋	Plastic Bag	115.7	120.0	120.0	104.2	118.5
塑料编织袋	Plastic Bag	115.7	120.0	120.0	104.2	118.5
塑料编织布	Plastic Cloth	106.7	113.4	100.0		
塑料编织布	Plastic Cloth	106.7	113.4	100.0		
塑料板	Plastic Plate	105.8	103.0	119.2	99.4	101.7
塑料胶粘带	Plastic Adhesive Tape	101.2		103.5	100.0	100.0
塑料胶粘带	Plastic Adhesive Tape	101.2		103.5	100.0	100.0
塑料存水弯	Plastic Siphon Trap	111.7	100.0	130.4	111.3	105.0
塑料存水弯	Plastic Siphon Trap	111.7	100.0	130.4	111.3	105.0
沥青	Pitch	108.6	113.0	111.4	103.6	106.4
沥青	Pitch	108.6	113.0	111.4	103.6	106.4
电料	Electrical Materials and Appliances	103.7	102.5	102.5	104.3	105.6
绝缘线	Insulated Wire	104.5	104.3	104.2	102.8	106.8
橡胶绝缘线	Rubber Insulated Wire	104.5	104.3	104.2	102.8	106.8
钢芯铝绞线	Steel-cored Aluminium Wire	106.3	100.0	100.0	125.0	100.4

6-12 续表 7 continued

类 别	Classification	价格指数（以上年同期为100）				
		全年平均 Annual Average	一季度 The first Quarter	二季度 The Second Quarter	三季度 The Third Quarter	四季度 The Forth Quarter
钢芯铝绞线	Steel-cored Aluminium Wire	106.3	100.0	100.0	125.0	100.4
裸铜线	Bare Copper Wire	104.2			100.0	108.3
裸铜线	Bare Copper Wire	104.2			100.0	108.3
护套线	Sheath Wire	112.1	106.0	115.1	115.3	112.0
铜芯	Copper Core	111.8	106.0	115.4	115.2	110.4
铝芯	Aluminum Core	123.4	106.7	107.6	122.6	156.7
通讯电缆	Communication Cable	103.2	105.8	103.3	108.2	95.3
长途对称电缆	Long Distance Symmetric Cable	110.0	113.6		106.4	
市内电话电缆	Local Telecommunication Cable	103.0	106.0			100.0
小同轴电缆	Small Coaxial Cable	98.0	83.3	103.3	110.5	94.7
电力电缆	Power Cable	101.9	101.5	99.3	103.6	103.3
电力电缆	Power Cable	101.9	101.5	99.3	103.6	103.3
光缆	Optical Cable	101.6	106.4	100.0		98.3
直埋光缆	Buried Cable	102.4	108.7	100.0		98.3
灯泡	Lamp Bulb	102.8	101.2	102.0	101.9	106.2
普通灯泡	Common Lamp Bulb	102.8	101.2	102.0	101.9	106.2
特种灯泡	Special Type Lamp Bulb	112.4	122.2	112.2	102.8	
灯管	Tube	99.7	102.1	93.5	101.4	101.9
灯管	Tube	99.7	102.1	93.5	101.4	101.9
开关	Circuit Changer	102.2	101.7	102.1	100.5	104.4
开关	Circuit Changer	102.2	101.7	102.1	100.5	104.4
插座	Jack	103.5	101.8	104.1	105.4	102.6
插座	Jack	103.5	101.8	104.1	105.4	102.6
灯具	Lamps and Lanterns	103.4	105.1	102.2	102.5	103.9
灯具	Lamps and Lanterns	103.4	105.1	102.2	102.5	103.9
其他材料	Other Materials	103.5	103.3	104.8	103.0	102.8
平板玻璃	Flat Glass	103.6	100.5	105.9	102.0	106.1
普通平板玻璃	Common Flat Glass	102.6	100.5	101.8	102.1	106.1
彩色平板玻璃	Colour Flat Glass	101.9		103.8	100.0	
磨砂玻璃	Ground Glass	104.9		113.5	101.2	100.0
油毡	Asphalt Felt	110.0	111.7	111.7	110.6	106.2
油毡	Asphalt Felt	110.0	111.7	111.7	110.6	106.2
密封油膏	Sealing Compound	100.9		102.0	100.5	100.1
密封油膏	Sealing Compound	100.9		102.0	100.5	100.1
密封带	Seal Band	95.0	95.0	95.0	95.0	95.0

6-12 续表 8 continued

类 别	Classification	价格指数（以上年同期为100） 全年平均 Annual Average	一季度 The first Quarter	二季度 The Second Quarter	三季度 The Third Quarter	四季度 The Forth Quarter
密封带	Seal Band	95.0	95.0	95.0	95.0	95.0
岩石棉	Rock Wool	103.9		106.6	100.0	105.3
岩石棉	Rock Wool	103.9		106.6	100.0	105.3
玻璃棉	Mineral Wool	100.0	100.0	100.0	100.0	100.0
玻璃棉	Mineral Wool	100.0	100.0	100.0	100.0	100.0
玻璃纤维	Glass Fibre	100.7	100.0	102.9	100.0	100.0
玻璃纤维	Glass Fibre	100.7	100.0	102.9	100.0	100.0
暖气片	Warm Air Chip	104.5	108.3	102.1	105.5	102.0
暖气片	Warm Air Chip	104.5	108.3	102.1	105.5	102.0
散热器	Radiator	108.2	108.0	108.0	108.1	108.6
散热器	Radiator	108.2	108.0	108.0	108.1	108.6
高压悬垂绝缘子	High Tension Suspending Insulator	100.9	100.0	100.0		102.6
高压悬垂绝缘子	High Tension Suspending Insulator	100.9	100.0	100.0		102.6
大便器	W.C.pan	103.3	103.4	108.6	99.6	101.6
蹲式	Squat	101.4	104.7	114.8	90.8	95.3
坐式	Sit	104.3	102.7	103.6	106.4	104.3
小便器	Urinal	105.1	106.2	106.8	107.8	99.7
立式	Vertical	103.8	107.0	106.8	107.8	93.6
挂式	Hang	105.4	105.9			105.0
洗面器	Wash Basin	102.3	103.0	98.5	103.9	103.8
洗面器	Wash Basin	102.3	103.0	98.5	103.9	103.8
水箱	Water Box	102.1	106.3	100.0	100.0	
高水箱	High Water Box	102.1	106.3	100.0	100.0	
浴盆	Bathtub	102.1	106.0	100.0	101.7	100.5
洗涤盆	Wash Basin	100.8	101.4	99.5	102.0	100.3
洗涤盆	Wash Basin	100.8	101.4	99.5	102.0	100.3
釉面砖	Ceramic Glazed Tile	101.4	102.8	102.1	99.8	101.1
彩色	Multicolour	101.6	103.1	102.6	100.0	100.6
白色	White	101.8	102.7	102.7	100.3	101.4
其他	Others	100.2	100.0	100.0	99.2	101.4
马赛克	Mosaic	99.6	100.0	100.0	100.0	98.5
马赛克	Mosaic	99.6	100.0	100.0	100.0	98.5
墙地砖	Wall and Floor Tiles	104.6	102.1	110.6	103.1	102.6
墙地砖	Wall and Floor Tiles	104.6	102.1	110.6	103.1	102.6
琉璃砖	Glazed Brick	104.1	104.5	107.7		100.0

6-12 续表 9 continued

类　别	Classification	价格指数（以上年同期为100）				
		全年平均 Annual Average	一季度 The first Quarter	二季度 The Second Quarter	三季度 The Third Quarter	四季度 The Forth Quarter
琉璃砖	Glazed Brick	104.1	104.5	107.7		100.0
耐火砖	Refractory Brick	109.3	111.1	108.7	108.7	108.7
耐火砖	Refractory Brick	109.3	111.1	108.7	108.7	108.7
石工砖	Rockwork Brick	104.8	100.0	106.1	104.2	108.7
石工砖	Rockwork Brick	104.8	100.0	106.1	104.2	108.7
玛钢件	Malleable Iron Fittings	103.4	103.7	101.5	100.9	107.6
弯头	Angle Head	104.0	103.6	100.7	100.5	111.0
管箍	Coupling	111.7	119.6	107.2	120.0	100.0
水嘴	Water Taps	106.2	100.8	105.8	128.5	89.5
建筑用小五金	Construction Hardware	102.0	102.7	102.9	102.6	99.8
普通合页	Common Hinge	107.8	105.9	104.0	116.9	104.2
钉子	Nail	101.8	102.0	103.1	102.5	99.7
陶瓷水嘴	Ceramic Water Taps	104.0	116.7	100.0	99.5	99.9
铝合金型材	Alloy Profile	99.9	99.5	95.1	101.9	103.1
铝合金窗	Alufer Window	99.9	100.7	94.3	101.7	103.1
铝合金门	Alufer Door	100.2	91.3	103.0	103.0	103.3
塑钢料	Delrin Zippers	102.2	102.1	103.0	103.1	100.5
塑钢窗	Delrin Window	101.9	102.9	102.8	102.1	99.7
塑钢门	Delrin Door	102.4	95.7	103.6	104.8	105.3
仪表	Meter	101.8	104.4	100.1	101.6	100.9
水表	Water Meter	102.6	106.2	100.4	102.9	100.9
电表	Electric Meter	104.0		102.8	106.5	102.7
煤气表	Gasometer	100.0	100.0	100.0	100.0	100.0
压力表	Pressure Meter	107.5	123.6	103.2	101.5	101.5
阀门	Valve	100.0	100.7	100.5	99.5	99.1
安全阀	Relief Valve	101.7	104.1	100.0	101.9	100.7
减压阀	Negative Valve	100.0	100.0	100.0		
截止阀	Stop Valve	99.7	100.0	100.0	100.4	98.4
闸阀	Gate Valves	99.7	100.2	100.9	98.4	99.2
球阀	Ball Check	100.5	100.2	100.5	101.5	99.8
止回阀	Check Valve	101.8	102.8	109.4	95.6	99.3
消火栓	Fire Hydrant	102.4	105.3	100.4	100.6	103.4
消火栓箱	Fire Hydrant Box	102.4	105.3	100.4	100.6	103.4
法兰	Flange	102.1	100.4	101.2	103.5	103.1
法兰	Flange	102.1	100.4	101.2	103.5	103.1

6-12 续表 10 continued

类 别	Classification	价格指数（以上年同期为100）				
		全年平均 Annual Average	一季度 The first Quarter	二季度 The Second Quarter	三季度 The Third Quarter	四季度 The Forth Quarter
电焊条	Electric Welding Rod	102.5	101.0	100.8	108.0	100.2
电焊条	Electric Welding Rod	102.5	101.0	100.8	108.0	100.2
水、电	Water, Electricity	108.1	103.7	107.6	107.0	114.0
水	Water	119.2	104.7	114.3	119.5	138.4
电	Electricity	102.0	103.0	101.8	101.4	101.8
机械费	Machinery Fee	103.9	102.9	104.0	105.1	103.9
土石方及筑路机械	Cubic meter of Earth and Stone and Road Machinery	103.9	103.2	103.9	105.2	103.2
履带式推土机	Crawler Type Bulldozer	103.8	101.3	105.3	105.1	103.4
自行式铲运机	Motor Scraper Application	101.5	103.0	101.1	102.5	99.4
拖式铲运机	Towed Scraper	102.7	98.4	100.3	99.5	112.5
轮胎式装载机	Wheel Loader	104.9	103.7	103.4	109.3	103.0
履带式拖拉机	Caterpillar Tractor	102.9	105.0	100.9	103.0	102.6
履带式单斗挖掘机	Crawler Walking Single-dipper Excavator	104.9	102.7	105.5	106.0	105.5
拉铲挖掘机	Dragline	106.3	106.7	107.7	103.6	107.0
沥青混凝土摊铺机	Asphalt Paver	101.5	100.0	102.9	103.0	100.3
光轮压路机	Smooth-wheel Roller	105.0	108.8	104.0	104.1	103.1
振动压路机	Vibrating Road Roller	101.1	102.5	99.1	100.7	102.4
电动夯实机	Electric Tamper	101.6	102.7	101.9	101.4	100.3
动凿岩机	Hammerdrill	103.8	107.9	102.3	102.9	102.3
平地机	Road Roller	103.2	103.7	100.5	108.3	100.3
打桩机械	Piling Machinery	102.4	101.2	102.7	102.2	103.3
汽车式钻孔机	Wagon Drill	100.0		100.0	100.0	100.0
工程钻机	Engineering Machine	105.7	103.6	104.9	107.4	106.8
轻便钻孔机	Portable Electric Drill	104.9	101.8	107.6	106.7	103.6
锚杆钻孔机	Anchor Drilling Equipment	110.4	100.0	112.5	118.8	
旋挖钻机	Spin Drilling Rig	95.8			91.7	100.0
起重机械	Hauling-up Machinery	102.5	101.8	102.4	102.9	103.1
履带式起重机	Crawler Crane	103.9	101.0	106.1	105.2	103.2
桅杆式起重机	Gin Pole Derrick	100.5	100.0	100.0	101.3	100.5
汽车式起重机	Autocrane	102.8	102.3	102.3	104.4	102.3
龙门式起重机	Gantry Crane	104.8	101.6	101.1	104.1	112.5
塔式起重机	Tower Crane	102.3	101.7	102.4	102.2	102.9
桥式起重机	Overhead Crane	101.4	99.6	100.5	100.5	104.9
其他	Others	104.3	106.6	103.7	104.4	102.3
运输机械	Transport Machinery	103.6	103.8	102.4	104.5	103.6

6-12 续表 11 continued

类 别	Classification	价格指数（以上年同期为100）				
		全年平均 Annual Average	一季度 The first Quarter	二季度 The Second Quarter	三季度 The Third Quarter	四季度 The Forth Quarter
载重汽车	Truck	105.0	108.1	104.1	104.7	103.2
自卸汽车	Dump Truck	103.0	102.0	101.3	104.6	104.0
机动翻斗车	Powered Tipper	102.9	101.6	103.0	100.8	106.4
洒水汽车	Street Sprinkler	106.9	101.1	106.3	115.0	105.1
电动卷扬机	Electric Winch	102.7	102.2	103.2	103.1	102.1
皮带运输机	Belt Roller	103.4	107.8	105.7	101.0	99.1
提升设备	Lifting Device	102.0	103.3	101.4	101.8	101.7
混凝土及砂浆机械	Concrete and Mortar Machinery	103.3	103.7	103.5	103.0	102.9
混凝土搅拌机	Concrete Mixers	102.7	103.8	102.9	102.1	101.9
灰浆拌和机	Mortar Mill	104.4	103.7	103.7	105.3	104.8
泥浆泵	Sludge Pumps	103.0	101.8	101.1	106.8	102.2
混凝土震动器	Concrete Vibrator	103.6	102.9	104.1	102.8	104.5
混凝土喷射机	Concrete Spraying Machines	103.9	106.7	104.2	104.0	100.5
加工机械	Processing Machinery	103.8	102.7	105.1	103.2	104.0
钢筋调直机	Bar Straightener	105.8	102.6	108.5	104.8	107.3
钢筋切断机	Reinforcing Bar Cutting Machine	103.2	102.4	103.9	102.7	103.8
钢筋弯曲机	Reinforcing Steel Crooking Machine	103.0	102.1	103.5	102.1	104.1
预应力钢筋拉伸机	Steel Extension Machine	105.6	108.2	107.3	103.4	103.4
液压挤压机		96.4	99.9	100.0	99.9	85.7
木工圆锯机	Woodworking Machine	103.8	103.4	105.5	103.9	102.5
木工平刨床	Wood Milling Machine	105.4	105.2	106.8	105.0	104.8
型钢剪断机	Section Shears	99.0	98.0	97.8	100.3	99.8
型钢校正机	Bull Press	105.6	116.7	100.0	100.0	
刨边机	Copy Shaper	105.7	104.6	102.5	108.8	106.9
砂轮切割机	Abrasive Cutting Machine	103.3	103.6	103.5	102.4	103.7
石料切割机	Block Cutting Machine	99.8	99.5	100.2	98.5	101.2
电动切割机	Electric Power Tools	103.0	100.8	101.9	103.9	105.1
抛光机	Polishing Machine	104.9	110.8	100.7	101.4	106.6
手提砂轮机	Angle Grinder	104.2	102.3	101.4	107.7	105.3
板料校平机	Roll-type Sheet Bending Machine	100.4	100.0	100.0	105.6	96.2
泵类机械	Pump Machinery	104.2	104.0	105.0	104.1	103.6
单级射流泵	Single Stage Pump	103.9	105.3	101.5	104.6	104.1
潜水泵	Submersible Pumps	104.6	103.2	103.8	104.7	106.9
高压油泵	High Pressure Oil Pump	102.8	104.2	105.0	100.0	102.0

6-12 续表 12 continued

类 别	Classification	价格指数（以上年同期为100）				
		全年平均 Annual Average	一季度 The first Quarter	二季度 The Second Quarter	三季度 The Third Quarter	四季度 The Forth Quarter
船舶机械	Shipping Machinery	111.4	102.9	113.5	111.9	117.4
拖船	Tug Boat	107.6	102.5	110.7	108.1	109.0
驳子	Barge	109.5	105.5	106.1	105.1	121.2
浮吊	Floating Crane	110.1	105.1	103.6	115.1	116.7
混凝土搅拌船	Concrete Mixer Vessel	113.0	100.5	119.3	119.0	
其他机械	Other Machinery	101.8	101.1	101.8	102.0	102.1
交流电焊机	Arcway Welder	101.7	101.4	102.1	101.9	101.6
直流电焊机	Electric Welding Machine	101.0	101.3	101.6	100.6	100.3
对焊机	Welding Machines	101.7	101.0	101.3	102.5	102.0
电渣焊机	Electroslag Surfacing	102.3	101.4	101.7	104.8	101.3
氩弧焊机	Arc Welding Machine	99.9	100.5	99.2	100.0	100.0
点焊机	Spot Welding Machine	101.6	100.1	103.5	102.9	99.9
电动空气压缩机	Motor-operated Air Compressor	102.4	101.4	102.9	102.5	102.6
风动锻纤机	Air Forging Machine	100.0	100.0	100.0	100.0	100.0
电动修钎机	Electric Dresser	100.0			100.0	100.0
平面磨石机	Surface Grinder	104.0	100.0	106.8	109.3	100.0
吹风机	Hair Dryer	92.7	80.0	101.5		96.4
泥浆拌和机	Clay Slip Blunger	104.6	100.2	101.1	102.5	114.6
电锤	Electric Rotary Hammers	101.4	101.1	101.3	101.3	102.1
液压千斤顶	Hydraulic Jack	102.1	100.0	102.2	103.3	103.0
柴油发电机	Diesel Generator	103.5	100.6	101.9	100.8	110.5
设备、工器具购置	Pruchase of Equipment , Tools and Instruments	100.6	100.0	99.9	101.0	101.4
其他费用	Others	103.4	103.5	103.9	103.3	103.0
土地取得费	Obtaining Land Expenditure	104.1	103.8	105.3	105.3	101.9
前期工程费	Preceding Engineering Expenditure	102.5	102.7	103.5	102.1	101.6
施工工作费	Construction Expenditure	102.5	102.9	102.5	101.6	103.2
建设单位其他费用	Other Expenses of Construction Unit	104.6	104.6	104.3	104.2	105.3

6-13 1991～2006年固定资产投资价格指数

Price Index of Investment in Fixed Assets(1991～2006)

上年=100 Preceding Year =100

年份 (Year)	全省固定资产投资 The Entire Province Investm-nt in Fix-ed Assets	建筑安装工程 Constrc-tion and Ins-tallation	人工费 Manpwer Cost Price Index	材料费 Materials Price Ind-ex	钢材 Rolled-Steel	木材 Wood	水泥 Ceme-nt	地方材料 Local Building materials	化工材料 Chemical Raw Materials	电料 Electrical Materials and Appl-iances	其它材料 Other Materials	机械使用费 Machin-ery Fee	设备工器具购置 Purchas-eof Equ-ipment Tools and Inst-ruments	其它费用 Other Fee
1991	112.4	116.6	122.7	120.9	119.6	121.2	118.5	115.4	103.9	101.9	115.3	105.7	105.3	107.1
1992	119.4	123.8	118.7	122.4	117.0	109.4	107.8	110.8	100.4	99.9	113.6	96.5	115.0	106.2
1993	122.1	124.6	142.9	126.5	127.7	121.6	110.4	114.8	101.7	99.7	121.8	92.5	118.8	113.5
1994	115.7	120.1	159.1	119.4	118.9	132.0	107.0	119.5	102.0	100.5	122.6	100.4	107.6	106.0
1995	106.6	105.7	111.4	104.2	99.3	100.1	101.9	111.1	101.4	100.0	107.1	108.2	106.2	113.8
1996	103.1	103.2	112.8	101.0	99.6	99.9	102.1	106.9	101.7	100.1	102.0	104.8	101.6	107.2
1997	100.4	100.7	106.3	100.6	99.3	100.8	101.7	102.3	103.9	101.9	101.7	96.5	98.7	103.5
1998	99.2	100.2	104.7	99.0	97.6	100.9	98.3	101.2	100.4	99.9	100.0	92.5	96.0	102.0
1999	99.6	101.3	105.8	100.1	98.4	102.1	99.8	102.4	101.7	99.7	101.0	100.4	96.2	98.3
2000	102.4	105.1	105.1	106.2	107.4	109.9	98.2	115.2	106.0	100.0	101.6	102.2	97.2	100.4
2001	101.4	103.2	106.6	102.7	101.8	111.4	103.8	106.7	98.7	98.4	98.7	102.2	97.1	102.1
2002	101.1	102.3	103.3	100.5	100.9	106.1	99.3	98.1	100.3	100.6	101.0	107.6	97.3	104.1
2003	102.9	104.7	103.9	106.7	110.9	110.3	101.8	103.0	101.7	100.0	101.1	101.7	98.5	104.2
2004	107.4	110.4	108.0	113.2	120.3	106.4	108.6	108.9	105.1	108.5	104.7	103.4	101.1	106.7
2005	102.9	103.7	109.5	102.4	101.0	103.3	100.0	104.2	110.2	104.8	103.2	102.6	100.8	103.5
2006	101.8	102.1	109.0	100.1	97.2	102.7	101.4	103.7	107.0	103.7	103.5	103.9	100.6	103.4

6-14 房屋销售价格月度指数（2006年）
Selling Price Monthly Indices of Houses(2006)

类别	Classification	价格指数（以上年同期价格为100）												
		全年平均 Annual Average	1月 January	2月 February	3月 March	4月 April	5月 May	6月 June	7月 July	8月 August	9月 September	10月 October	11月 November	12月 December
房屋销售价格总指数	**Selling Price Indices of Houses**	**105.0**	**105.9**	**105.7**	**105.6**	**105.5**	**104.9**	**104.8**	**104.8**	**104.5**	**104.6**	**104.6**	**104.6**	**104.4**
商品房	Commodity Housing	105.1	106.4	106.0	105.8	105.8	104.9	104.5	104.5	104.4	104.5	104.6	104.8	104.4
住宅	Residence Buildings	105.1	106.6	106.1	105.8	105.8	105.0	104.5	104.4	104.4	104.5	104.7	104.8	104.4
经济适用房	Economic Housing	104.0	104.2	106.4	104.4	105.1	105.3	104.3	102.5	104.5	101.8	102.4	102.8	104.3
普通住宅	General Residential Buildings	105.2	107.0	105.9	105.5	105.9	105.0	104.6	104.7	104.5	104.7	104.9	104.9	104.3
多层住宅	Multiayer Buildings	105.1	107.3	105.9	105.8	105.9	104.7	104.4	104.7	103.8	104.5	105.0	105.2	104.5
高层住宅	High-grade Building	105.2	106.5	105.9	105.1	105.8	105.6	104.7	104.9	105.4	105.0	104.8	104.7	104.2
其他住宅	Other Buildings	101.6	103.8	105.6	101.9	101.3	102.4	103.9	100.2	100.4	99.7	102.1	102.5	95.6
高档住宅	Luxury Residential Buildings	106.0	103.7	108.8	112.3	106.2	104.7	104.5	102.8	104.2	106.1	105.6	107.1	106.0
别墅	Villas	103.6	102.7	106.6	100.7	104.3	101.4	102.7	101.3	104.2	105.9	103.2	103.6	106.0
高档公寓	High-grade Apartment	106.7	103.8	109.0	113.3	106.8	106.0	105.1	103.6	104.2	106.2	106.3	109.8	105.9
非住宅	Non-Residential Buildings	104.3	104.0	104.2	105.3	105.3	103.8	104.5	106.0	103.8	104.5	102.5	103.8	103.7
办公楼	Office Buildings	105.0	103.6	105.4	105.1	109.1	103.3	107.0	108.6	102.5	106.0	101.7	105.1	102.9
写字楼	High-grade Office Buildings	105.1	103.9	105.4	105.1	109.1	103.3	107.1	109.0	102.3	106.0	101.7	105.1	103.2
普通办公用房	General Office Buildings	105.2	100.5	105.0	103.4	108.3	104.6	103.5	103.0	110.3	106.8	110.7	105.0	101.4
商业娱乐用房	Business andEnrert-aubnebt Buildings	103.9	104.1	103.5	105.4	103.2	104.1	103.1	104.5	104.6	103.7	103.1	103.2	104.4
其它用房	Other Buildings	103.0	105.3	103.9	103.8	103.1	103.7	103.1	104.1	102.6	102.8	101.1	101.6	100.5
二手房	Private-owned House	104.9	104.8	105.0	105.3	104.8	104.9	105.4	105.5	104.8	104.6	104.7	104.3	104.6
住宅	Residence Buildings	105.2	105.0	105.0	105.4	105.9	105.1	106.4	106.1	105.1	104.9	104.9	104.3	104.7
高层住宅	High-grade Building	105.3	107.6	107.6	104.3	105.4	103.6	102.1	104.9	105.8	105.8	105.7	105.2	105.7
多层住宅	Multiayer Buildings	105.4	104.8	104.7	105.7	106.0	105.5	107.3	106.5	105.1	104.9	104.8	104.2	104.7
其他住宅	Other Buildings	103.1	101.4	102.8	103.2	104.6	103.8	103.1	102.1	102.9	102.9	103.6	103.6	102.9
非住宅	Other Buildings	103.5	103.7	105.1	105.0	100.8	103.8	101.4	102.9	103.4	103.5	104.0	104.3	103.9

6-15 房地产价格指数（2006年）
Price Indices for Real Estate (2006)

类 别	Classification	价格指数（以上年同期价格为100） 全年平均 Annual Average	一季度 The first Quarter	二季度 The Second Quarter	三季度 The Third Quarter	四季度 The Forth Quarter
房屋销售价格总指数	**Selling Price Indices of Houses**	**105.0**	**105.7**	**105.1**	**104.6**	**104.5**
商品房	Commodity Housing	105.1	106.1	105.1	104.5	104.6
住宅	Residence Buildings	105.1	106.2	105.1	104.4	104.6
经济适用房	Economic Housing	104.0	105.0	104.9	102.9	103.2
普通住宅	Common Residence	105.2	106.1	105.2	104.6	104.7
多层住宅	Multiayer Buildings	105.1	106.3	105.0	104.3	104.9
高层住宅	High-grade Building	105.2	105.8	105.4	105.1	104.6
其他住宅	Other Buildings	101.6	103.8	102.5	100.1	100.1
高档住宅	Luxury Residential Buildings	106.0	108.3	105.1	104.4	106.2
别墅	Villas	103.6	103.3	102.8	103.8	104.3
高档公寓	High-grade Apartment	106.7	108.7	106.0	104.7	107.3
非住宅	Non-Residential Buildings	104.3	104.5	104.5	104.8	103.3
办公楼	Office Buildings	105.0	104.7	106.5	105.7	103.2
写字楼	High-grade Office Buildings	105.1	104.8	106.5	105.8	103.3
普通办公用房	General Office Buildings	105.2	103.0	105.5	106.7	105.7
商业娱乐用房	Business and Enrertaubnebt Buildings	103.9	104.3	103.5	104.3	103.6
其它用房	Other Buildings	103.0	104.3	103.3	103.2	101.1
二手房	Private-owned House	104.9	105.0	105.0	105.0	104.5
住宅	Residence Buildings	105.2	105.1	105.8	105.4	104.6
高层住宅	Multiayer Buildings	105.3	106.5	103.7	105.5	105.5
多层住宅	High-grade Building	105.4	105.1	106.3	105.5	104.6
其他住宅	Other Buildings	103.1	102.5	103.8	102.6	103.4
非住宅	Non-Residential Buildings	103.5	104.6	102.0	103.3	104.1
房屋租赁价格总指数	**Renting Price Indices of Houses**	**101.6**	**100.9**	**101.3**	**101.7**	**102.4**
住宅	Residence	102.4	101.6	101.9	102.2	104.0
普通住宅	Common Residence	103.1	101.8	102.2	102.6	105.9
高档住宅	High-grade Building	101.4	100.6	100.5	102.1	102.2
别墅	Villas	100.6	100.0	100.0	101.2	101.0
高档公寓	High-grade Apartment	111.1	106.7	106.7	116.3	114.6
经济适用房	Economic Housing	102.5	102.7	103.2	102.6	101.4
廉租房	Tenement House	100.0	100.0	100.0	100.0	100.0
办公楼	Office	100.5	100.5	100.5	100.5	100.4
写字楼	High-grade Office Buildings	101.0	100.7	101.2	101.2	101.0
普通办公用房	General Office Buildings	100.3	100.4	100.2	100.2	100.2
商业娱乐用房	Commercial Housing	102.0	101.2	101.8	102.3	102.6
工业仓储用房	Workshops and Storehouses	98.9	97.7	99.1	99.4	99.4
工业厂房	Industrial Factory	100.0	100.1	100.0	100.0	100.0
仓库	Storehouse	97.3	94.1	97.9	98.5	98.5
其它	Other	100.5	100.0	100.0	100.3	101.5
物业管理价格总指数	**Property Management Price Indices**	**100.9**	**101.0**	**100.7**	**101.2**	**100.8**
住宅	Residence	101.4	101.8	101.1	101.7	100.9
普通住宅	Common Residence	101.6	101.7	101.5	102.0	101.2
高档住宅	High-grade Building	100.1	100.0	100.1	100.1	100.1
经济适用房	Economic Housing	101.8	105.3	100.0	101.8	100.0
办公楼	Office	99.7	98.9	100.0	100.0	100.0
写字楼	High-grade Office Buildings	99.5	97.8	100.0	100.0	100.0
普通办公用房	General Office Buildings	100.0	100.0	100.0	100.0	100.0
商业娱乐用房	Commercial Housing	100.2	100.0	100.0	100.2	100.7
工业仓储用房	Workshops and Storehouses	100.7	100.0	100.0	101.3	101.3
#工业厂房	Industrial Factory	100.7	100.0	100.0	101.3	101.3
土地交易价格总指数	**Transactions Price Indices of Land**	**104.8**	**105.6**	**105.3**	**104.2**	**104.1**
居住用地	Land for Residential Building Use	105.4	106.0	106.5	103.5	105.4
高档住宅用地	Luxuryr Residential Building	102.9	102.3	103.9	101.9	103.4
普通住宅用地	General Residential Buildings	105.5	106.3	106.6	103.6	105.4
经济适用房用地	Economically Affordable Housing	103.5	103.8	103.2	103.4	103.7
工业仓储用地	Land for Industry Use	103.8	104.9	103.9	102.9	103.4
商业、旅游、娱乐用地	Land for Business Tour and Entertainment	104.8	105.2	104.9	107.1	102.1
其它用地	Land for Other	105.5	107.7	104.5	102.7	107.0

6-16 2001～2006年房地产价格指数
Price Indices for Real Estate（2001～2006）

（上年＝100） (Preceding Year=100)

类　别	Classification	2001	2002	2003	2004	2005	2006
房屋销售价格总指数	**Slling Price Indices of Houses**	**103.8**	**105.5**	**106.7**	**111.5**	**108.5**	**105.0**
商品房	Commodity Housing	104.0	105.2	107.0	112.3	108.5	105.1
住宅	Residence	104.5	105.4	107.4	112.9	109.0	105.1
经济适用房	Economic Housing	103.0	105.2	105.7	109.3	107.5	104.0
普通住宅	Cmmon Residence	104.9	105.3	107.4	113.1	109.2	105.2
多层住宅	Multiayer Buildings	105.1	105.6	107.5	113.6	108.7	105.1
高层住宅	High-grade Building	103.8	104.5	106.6	111.6	110.2	105.2
高档住宅	Luxury Residential Buildings	103.1	106.6	108.6	116.0	109.2	106.0
别墅	Villas	106.5	109.3	112.5	122.2	110.5	103.6
高档公寓	High-grade Apartment	102.8	106.0	107.9	115.1	108.9	106.7
非住宅	Other Buildings	100.9	104.1	105.0	109.2	106.2	104.3
二手房	Private-owned Huse	104.0	108.1	107.9	113.1	108.4	104.9
住宅	Residence Buildings	104.1	108.5	107.9	111.5	108.8	105.2
非住宅	Other Buildings	103.0	106.0	107.7	119.3	107.5	103.5
房屋租赁价格总指数	**Rnting Pice Idices of Huses**	**101.3**	**99.8**	**98.6**	**100.8**	**101.8**	**101.6**
住宅	Residence Buildings	105.3	100.5	99.3	99.4	102.6	102.4
办公楼	Office Bildings	100.9	98.8	100.5	100.8	101.4	100.5
写字楼	High-grade Office Buildings	100.8	93.5	102.2	100.3	102.0	101.0
普通办公用房	General Office Buildings	100.9	100.3	100.0	100.9	101.1	100.3
商业娱乐用房	Business and Enrertaubnebt Buildings	100.2	100.0	96.3	102.1	101.7	102.0
工业仓储用房	Industrial Storage Bildings	96.7	98.5	101.0	100.7	99.7	98.9
工业厂房	Idustrial Fctory	94.7	97.8	102.2	101.2	100.1	100.0
仓库	Sorehouse	99.0	99.3	99.5	100.0	99.1	97.3
土地交易价格总指数	**Tansactions Pice Idices of Lnd**	**105.1**	**103.7**	**105.1**	**106.2**	**106.4**	**104.8**
居住用地	Land for Residential Building Use	104.0	104.0	104.6	110.0	105.7	105.4
高档住宅用地	Luxury rResidential Building	104.0	103.8	125.1	102.4	104.0	102.9
普通住宅用地	General Residential Bildings	104.0	104.1	104.4	110.1	105.7	105.5
工业仓储用地	Land for Industry Use	104.5	102.6	104.2	103.6	104.5	103.8
商业、旅游、娱乐用地	Land for Business Tour and Entertainment	105.9	104.4	108.0	105.9	109.2	104.8
其它用地	Land for Other	107.0	104.5	103.6	101.5	108.7	105.5

6-17 分市房地产价格指数（2006）
Price Indices for Real Estate in Each City(2006)

（上年＝100）　　　　（Preceding Year =100）

类　别	Classification	济南 Jinan	青岛 Qingdao	淄博 Zibo	枣庄 Zaozhuan	东营 Dongying	烟台 Yantai	潍坊 Weifang
房屋销售价格总指数	**Selling Price Indices of Houses**	**104.3**	**106.9**	**104.3**	**104.3**	**102.9**	**105.5**	**106.6**
商品房	Commercial Houses	104.3	107.6	104.3	104.3	102.5	105.6	106.7
住宅	Residence	104.3	107.1	104.5	104.3	103.0	106.5	107.2
经济适用房	Economic Housing		102.6	104.6	104.4	101.5		106.7
普通住宅	Common Residence	104.6	106.3	105.0	104.3	103.6	107.0	107.3
多层住宅	Multiayer Buildings	105.3	105.3	105.1	104.3	103.5	105.6	107.7
高层住宅	High-grade Building	104.3	106.8	104.3	105.2	108.0	107.5	105.3
其他住宅	Other Buildings				103.2	101.1	104.4	
高档住宅	Luxury Residential Buildings	102.9	113.5		104.4	102.6	104.2	105.0
别墅	Villas	108.7			104.4	102.6		105.0
高档公寓	High-grade Apartment	102.9	113.5				104.2	
非住宅	Non-Residential Buildings	103.9	109.8	104.0	104.2	101.7	103.0	103.9
办公楼	Office Buildings	103.9	107.0	103.0		100.8		102.8
写字楼	High-grade Office Buildings	103.8	107.0	103.0		100.8		
普通办公用房	General Office Buildings	104.0	106.1			100.5		102.8
商业娱乐用房	Business and Enrertaubnebt Buil-dings	103.6	111.0	104.3	104.2	102.5	102.9	104.0
其它用房	Other Buildings	104.1				101.1	107.5	
二手房	Private-owned House	104.3	105.9	104.0	104.2	103.7	104.9	106.0
住宅	Residence Buildings	104.3	106.3	104.4	104.2	104.4	104.9	106.0
高层住宅	High-grade Building	104.2	105.5	105.1				
多层住宅	Multiayer Buildings	104.4	106.8	104.7	104.2	105.0	104.9	106.0
其他住宅	Other Buildings	104.7			103.6			
非住宅	Other Buildings	104.2	103.6	102.4	104.1	101.9		
房屋租赁价格总指数	**Renting Price Indices of Houses**	**101.2**	**110.1**	**102.0**	**100.0**	**100.2**	**100.2**	**102.1**
住宅	Residence	100.1	116.4	102.9	100.0	100.2	100.0	103.1
普通住宅	Common Residence	100.1	120.2	104.0	100.0	100.2	100.0	
高档住宅	Luxury Residential Buildings		101.4					
别墅	Villas		100.6					
高档公寓	High-grade Apartment		111.1					
经济适用房	(Economic Housing)		100.0					103.1
廉租房	(Tenement House)	100.0					100.0	
办公楼	(Office)	100.5	100.2	101.1	100.0	100.0	100.1	100.0
写字楼	(High-grade Office Buildings)	101.2	100.2	100.0		100.0	100.4	
普通办公用房	(General Office Buildings)	99.8	100.0	101.3	100.0		100.0	100.0
商业娱乐用房	(Businessand Enrertaubnebt Buildings)	102.3	103.2	102.4	100.0	100.0	100.8	102.3
工业仓储用房	(Industrial Storage Buildings)	103.0	98.9	100.0	100.0		100.0	100.0
工业厂房	Industrial Factory		100.0	100.0	100.0		100.0	100.0
仓库	Storehouse	103.0	95.9		100.0		100.0	
其它	(Other)	100.0		100.0		104.3		
物业管理价格总指数	**Property Management PriceIndices**	**100.1**	**99.8**	**104.5**	**100.0**	**116.7**	**100.0**	**100.0**
住宅	(Residence)	100.0	100.1	105.3	100.0	116.9	100.0	100.0
普通住宅	(Common Residence)	100.0	100.1	105.9	100.0	113.8	100.0	100.0
高层住宅	(High-grade Building)	100.0	100.0	105.0		106.2	100.0	
经济适用房	(Economic Housing)		100.0		100.0	137.2	100.0	
办公楼	(Officebuildings)	100.0	99.0	100.0		100.0	100.0	
写字楼	(High-grade Office Buildings)	100.0	98.7				100.0	
普通办公用房	(General Office Buildings)	100.0	100.0	100.0		100.0	100.0	
商业娱乐用房	(Businessand Enrertaubnebt Buildings)	100.0	100.0	100.0			100.0	
工业仓储用房	(Industrial Storage Buildings)	102.5	100.0					
#工业厂房	Industrial Factory	102.5	100.0					
土地交易价格总指数	**Transactions PriceIndicesof Land**	**104.9**	**103.2**	**104.8**	**105.6**	**101.2**	**105.1**	**105.2**
居住用地	(Land for Residential Building Use)	104.9	103.0	106.5	106.0	100.4	104.9	105.3
高档住宅用地	(Luxuryr Residential Building)		101.7			100.0	102.3	105.0
普通住宅用地	(General Residential Buildings)	104.9	103.0	107.1	106.0	101.1	106.2	106.2
经济适用房用地	Economically Affordable Housing	104.8		101.0				103.3
工业仓储用地	(LandforIndustry Use)	104.7	103.3	103.0	104.3	101.9	103.9	103.0
商业、旅游、娱乐用地	(Landfor Business Tourand Entertainment	105.1	103.0	103.8	103.7	101.0	105.4	107.8
其它用地	(Landfor Other)	105.3	104.4		108.6	100.3		103.2

6-17 续表 1 continued

类 别	Classification	济宁 Jining	泰安 Taian	威海 Weihai	日照 Rizhao	莱芜 Laiwu	临沂 Linyi	德州 Dezhou	聊城 Liaocheng	滨州 Binzhou	菏泽 Heze
房屋销售价格总指数	**Selling Price Indices of Houses**	**105.4**	**105.1**	**101.9**	**103.5**	**106.4**	**104.0**	**104.6**	**104.5**	**104.1**	**101.6**
商品房	Commercial Houses	105.7	105.1	102.6	104.9	107.0	104.1	105.1	103.5	103.9	101.8
住宅	Residence	105.9	105.3	102.6	105.4	107.3	104.1	105.3	103.8	103.9	101.8
经济适用房	Economic Housing	106.1	108.0	100.0		102.9	102.4	100.4	95.0	101.4	
普通住宅	Common Residence	106.0	105.1	102.6	105.4	108.0	104.3	105.4	105.1	104.2	101.8
多层住宅	Multiayer Buildings	106.5	105.2	102.7	105.7	108.6	105.3	105.6	105.3	104.2	101.8
高层住宅	High-grade Building	104.6	103.6	104.1	103.9	104.6	102.0	104.3	103.3		101.2
其他住宅	Other Buildings		102.6				101.2				
高档住宅	Luxury Residential Buildings	103.8	103.5	113.4	104.5		105.8	105.9	103.8		100.0
别墅	Villas	101.9	101.0	91.6	101.3		103.9		103.3		100.0
高档公寓	High-grade Apartment	104.8	103.7	114.9	104.7		106.4	105.9	106.6		100.0
非住宅	Non-Residential Buildings	104.6	104.4	101.8	102.1	106.1	103.5	104.2	101.2	103.7	101.8
办公楼	Office Buildings	103.3		104.5	103.4		99.2	109.5			100.7
写字楼	High-grade Office Buildings	103.3		105.3	103.1		99.2				
普通办公用房	General Office Buildings			104.2	103.4			109.5			100.7
商业娱乐用房	Business and Enrertaubnebt Buil-dings	104.7	104.4	101.5	101.6	106.1	104.3	103.7	101.2	103.7	101.9
其它用房	Other Buildings		103.5	100.0	100.8		103.8	101.3	100.0		
二手房	Private-owned House	103.8	105.0	100.0	101.8	103.8	103.9	103.5	107.3	104.7	101.1
住宅	Residence Buildings	103.7	105.7	100.0	101.9	103.8	104.2	103.6	107.3	104.8	101.1
高层住宅	High-grade Building		107.8	100.0			102.6		108.9		
多层住宅	Multiayer Buildings	103.8	105.5	100.0	102.4	103.8	104.4	103.6	107.3	104.8	101.0
其他住宅	Other Buildings	103.3			100.1		103.0		102.2		101.2
非住宅	Other Buildings	105.5	104.6	100.0	101.6	110.0	103.1	102.7		103.2	101.1
房屋租赁价格总指数	**Renting Price Indices of Houses**	**101.5**	**101.6**	**98.3**	**102.6**	**100.7**	**102.2**	**107.2**	**100.0**	**101.4**	**101.5**
住宅	Residence	100.2	101.6		101.1	101.7	104.6	117.8	100.0	101.6	101.0
普通住宅	Common Residence	100.3	101.6		101.1	101.7	105.5	117.8	100.0	101.4	101.0
高档住宅	Luxury Residential Buildings										
别墅	Villas										
高档公寓	High-grade Apartment										
经济适用房	(Economic Housing)						100.0			101.8	
廉租房	(Tenement House)	100.0									
办公楼	(Office)		101.0		99.1	100.0	101.4	101.9			100.0
写字楼	(High-grade Office Buildings)				98.9	100.0	100.3	128.6			
普通办公用房	(General Office Buildings)		101.0		99.3	99.8	102.2	100.0			100.0
商业娱乐用房	(Businessand Enrertaubnebt Buildings)	102.5	102.0	100.0	106.0	100.8	101.2	106.4	100.0	101.1	103.9
工业仓储用房	(Industrial Storage Buildings)		100.0	95.0	101.1		100.0	100.8		101.4	100.0
工业厂房	Industrial Factory		100.0		100.0		100.0	101.1			
仓库	Storehouse			95.0	105.0		100.0	100.0		101.4	100.0
其它	(Other)							100.9			
物业管理价格总指数	**Property Management PriceIndices**	**100.0**	**100.0**	**100.0**	**106.4**	**100.0**	**102.6**	**102.9**	**100.0**	**100.0**	**101.0**
住宅	(Residence)	100.0	100.0	100.0	109.3	100.0	104.0	103.3	100.0	100.0	101.5
普通住宅	(Common Residence)	100.0	100.0	100.0	111.1	100.0	105.4	103.3	100.0	100.0	102.3
高层住宅	(High-grade Building)	100.0		100.0	101.0		100.0	100.0			100.0
经济适用房	(Economic Housing)						100.0				100.0
办公楼	(Officebuildings)	100.0	100.0		100.0		100.0		100.0		100.0
写字楼	(High-grade Office Buildings)		100.0		100.0		100.0				
普通办公用房	(General Office Buildings)	100.0	100.0		100.0		100.0		100.0		100.0
商业娱乐用房	(Businessand Enrertaubnebt Buildings		100.0		106.5	100.0	100.0	100.0			100.0
工业仓储用房	(Industrial Storage Buildings)								100.0		
#工业厂房	Industrial Factory								100.0		
土地交易价格总指数	**Transactions PriceIndicesof Land**	**103.2**	**108.2**	**114.4**	**109.5**	**105.7**	**114.3**	**101.8**	**101.7**	**104.4**	**103.2**
居住用地	(Land for Residential Building Use)	101.9	106.5	119.2	109.8	103.8	120.9	101.8	101.5	106.5	101.9
高档住宅用地	(Luxuryr Residential Building)				106.6			102.3			
普通住宅用地	(General Residential Buildings)	101.9	106.5	119.2	109.7	103.4	120.9	101.9	101.5	106.5	101.9
经济适用房用地	Economically Affordable Housing					106.4					
工业仓储用地	(LandforIndustry Use)	104.8	110.8	114.1	109.5	106.1	107.0	101.9	100.0	102.6	107.0
商业、旅游、娱乐用地	(Landfor Business Tourand Entertainment)	105.3	108.1	105.0	108.3	105.8	107.2	101.6	107.7		104.8
其它用地	(Landfor Other)	100.0			113.0		122.9	101.7			103.3

6-18 分市分季度房地产价格指数
Quarter Price Indices for Real Estate in Each City

（上年=100） (Preceding Year =100)

类 别	Classification	济南 Jinan 全年平均 Annual Average	一季度 The first Quarter	二季度 The Second Quarter	三季度 The Third Quarter	四季度 The Forth Quarter
房屋销售价格总指数	**Selling Price Indices of Houses**	**104.3**	**105.2**	**103.8**	**104.0**	**104.1**
商品房	Commercial Houses	104.3	105.5	103.7	103.7	104.1
住宅	Residence	104.3	105.6	103.8	103.5	104.3
经济适用房	Economic Housing					
普通住宅	Common Residence	104.6	106.1	104.1	103.5	104.5
多层住宅	Multiayer Buildings	105.3	106.5	105.2	103.4	105.9
高层住宅	High-grade Building	104.3	105.8	103.7	103.5	104.2
其他住宅	Other Buildings					
高档住宅	Luxury Residential Buildings	102.9	102.7	102.1	103.6	103.3
别墅	Villas	108.7		108.7		
高档公寓	High-grade Apartment	102.9	102.7	102.1	103.6	103.3
非住宅	Non-Residential Buildings	103.9	104.8	103.5	104.5	103.0
办公楼	Office Buildings	103.9	104.2	103.4	104.2	103.7
写字楼	High-grade Office Buildings	103.8	104.2	103.4	104.2	103.7
普通办公用房	General Office Buildings	104.0		103.7	104.7	
商业娱乐用房	Business and Enrertaubnebt Buildings	103.6	104.5	103.0	104.7	102.3
其它用房	Other Buildings	104.1			104.1	
二手房	Private-owned House	104.3	104.4	104.1	104.7	104.0
住宅	Residence Buildings	104.3	104.5	104.1	104.8	103.9
高层住宅	High-grade Building	104.2	104.9	104.0	103.8	104.0
多层住宅	Multiayer Buildings	104.4	104.3	104.2	105.1	103.9
其他住宅	Other Buildings	104.7	104.7			
非住宅	Other Buildings	104.2	104.1	104.1	104.1	104.3
房屋租赁价格总指数	**Renting Price Indices of Houses**	**101.2**	**100.1**	**101.6**	**101.9**	**101.3**
住宅	Residence	100.1	100.1	100.1	100.1	100.1
普通住宅	Common Residence	100.1	100.1	100.1	100.1	100.1
高档住宅	Luxury Residential Buildings					
别墅	Villas					
高档公寓	High-grade Apartment					
经济适用房	Economic Housing					
廉租房	Tenement House	100.0	100.0	100.0	100.0	100.0
办公楼	Office	100.5	100.5	100.5	100.5	100.4
写字楼	High-grade Office Buildings	101.2	101.2	101.2	101.3	101.0
普通办公用房	General Office Buildings	99.8	99.8	99.8	99.8	99.8
商业娱乐用房	Business and Enrertaubnebt Buildings	102.3	100.0	103.1	103.7	102.5
工业仓储用房	Industrial Storage buildings	103.0	99.5	103.5	105.4	103.7
工业厂房	Industrial Factory					
仓库	Storehouse	103.0	99.5	103.5	105.4	103.7
其它	Other	100.0	100.0	100.0	100.0	100.0
物业管理价格总指数	**Property Management Price Indices**	**100.1**	**100.0**	**100.0**	**100.1**	**100.1**
住宅	Residence	100.0	100.0	100.0	100.0	100.0
普通住宅	Common Residence	100.0	100.0	100.0	100.0	100.0
高层住宅	High-grade Building	100.0	100.0	100.0	100.0	100.0
经济适用房	Economic Housing					
办公楼	Office Buildings	100.0	100.0	100.0	100.0	100.0
写字楼	High-grade Office Buildings	100.0	100.0	100.0	100.0	100.0
普通办公用房	General Office Buildings	100.0	100.0	100.0	100.0	100.0
商业娱乐用房	Business and Enrertaubnebt Buildings	100.0	100.1	100.0	100.0	100.0
工业仓储用房	Industrial Storage Buildings	102.5			102.5	102.5
#工业厂房	Industrial Factory	102.5			102.5	102.5
土地交易价格总指数	**Transactions Price Indices of Land**	**104.9**	**105.0**	**105.6**	**104.2**	**104.8**
居住用地	Land for Residential Building Use	104.9	104.8	104.7	104.8	105.3
高档住宅用地	Luxury Residential Building					
普通住宅用地	General Residential buildings	104.9	104.9	104.7	104.8	105.3
经济适用房用地	Economically Affordable Housing	104.8	104.8			
工业仓储用地	Land for Industry Use	104.7	104.4	105.3	104.9	104.0
商业、旅游、娱乐用地	Land for Business Tour and Entertainment	105.1	106.6	107.4	101.2	105.0
其它用地	Land for Other	105.3	104.0	106.1	105.7	

6-18 续表 1 continued

类 别	Classification	青岛 Qingdao 全年平均 Annual Average	一季度 The first Quarter	二季度 The Second Quarter	三季度 The Third Quarter	四季度 The Forth Quarter
房屋销售价格总指数	**Selling Price Indices of Houses**	**106.9**	**107.8**	**107.0**	**106.8**	**106.1**
商品房	Commercial Houses	107.6	108.4	108.0	107.5	106.5
住宅	Residence	107.1	107.6	107.7	106.4	106.6
经济适用房	Economic Housing	102.6	103.4	104.2	100.1	
普通住宅	Common Residence	106.3	107.2	106.7	106.2	105.0
多层住宅	Multiayer Buildings	105.3	107.6	105.6	104.0	103.9
高层住宅	High-grade Building	106.8	106.6	107.7	107.4	105.5
其他住宅	Other Buildings					
高档住宅	Luxury Residential Buildings	113.5	111.6	115.4	111.5	115.6
别墅	Villas					
高档公寓	High-grade Apartment	113.5	111.6	115.4	111.5	115.6
非住宅	Non-Residential Buildings	109.8	112.0	109.2	112.0	105.8
办公楼	Office Buildings	107.0	106.5	107.1	109.4	104.8
写字楼	High-grade Office Buildings	107.0	106.5	107.1	109.5	104.9
普通办公用房	General Office Buildings	106.1	100.0	117.4	105.9	103.9
商业娱乐用房	Business and Enrertaubnebt Buildings	111.0	114.6	110.2	113.1	106.3
其它用房	Other Buildings					
二手房	Private-owned House	105.9	106.9	105.3	105.8	105.4
住宅	Residence Buildings	106.3	107.2	105.9	106.3	105.7
高层住宅	High-grade Building	105.5	106.7	103.7	105.6	105.9
多层住宅	Multiayer Buildings	106.8	107.5	107.5	106.8	105.5
其他住宅	Other Buildings					
非住宅	Other Buildings	103.6	105.2	101.9	103.2	104.3
房屋租赁价格总指数	**Renting Price Indices of Houses**	**110.1**	**105.0**	**109.1**	**112.9**	**113.3**
住宅	Residence	116.4	109.4	114.8	120.2	121.2
普通住宅	Common Residence	120.2	111.6	118.4	124.8	126.0
高档住宅	Luxury Residential Buildings	101.4	100.6	100.5	102.1	102.2
别墅	Villas	100.6	100.0	100.0	101.2	101.0
高档公寓	High-grade Apartment	111.1	106.7	106.7	116.3	114.6
经济适用房	Economic Housing	100.0	100.0	100.0	100.0	100.0
廉租房	Tenement House					
办公楼	Office	100.2	97.4	100.0	102.1	101.1
写字楼	High-grade Office Buildings	100.2	96.8	100.0	102.6	101.3
普通办公用房	General Office Buildings	100.0	100.0	100.0	100.0	100.0
商业娱乐用房	Business and Enrertaubnebt Buildings	103.2	103.2	102.5	103.0	104.0
工业仓储用房	Industrial Storage buildings	98.9	95.6	100.0	100.0	100.0
工业厂房	Industrial Factory	100.0	100.0	100.0	100.0	100.0
仓库	Storehouse	95.9	83.6	100.0	100.0	100.0
其它	Other					
物业管理价格总指数	**Property Management Price Indices**	**99.8**	**99.2**	**100.1**	**100.0**	**100.0**
住宅	Residence	100.1	100.0	100.2	100.0	100.0
普通住宅	Common Residence	100.1	100.0	100.2	100.0	100.0
高层住宅	High-grade Building	100.0	100.0	100.0	100.0	100.0
经济适用房	Economic Housing	100.0	100.0	100.0	100.0	100.0
办公楼	Office Buildings	99.0	95.9	100.0	100.0	100.0
写字楼	High-grade Office Buildings	98.7	94.8	100.0	100.0	100.0
普通办公用房	General Office Buildings	100.0	100.0	100.0	100.0	100.0
商业娱乐用房	Business and Enrertaubnebt Buildings	100.0	100.0	100.0	100.0	100.0
工业仓储用房	Industrial Storage Buildings	100.0	100.0	100.0	100.0	100.0
#工业厂房	Industrial Factory	100.0	100.0	100.0	100.0	100.0
土地交易价格总指数	**Transactions Price Indices of Land**	**103.2**	**104.9**	**104.3**	**101.7**	**101.7**
居住用地	Land for Residential Building Use	103.0	104.1	104.5	101.7	101.7
高档住宅用地	Luxury Residential Building	101.7			101.7	
普通住宅用地	General Residential buildings	103.0	104.1	104.5	101.7	101.7
经济适用房用地	Economically Affordable Housing					
工业仓储用地	Land for Industry Use	103.3	105.7	104.0	101.7	101.7
商业、旅游、娱乐用地	Land for Business Tour and Entertainment	103.0	104.2	104.2	101.8	101.7
其它用地	Land for Other	104.4	109.8	104.4	101.7	101.7

6-18 续表 2 continued

类别	Classification	淄博 Zibo				
		全年平均 Annual Average	一季度 The first Quarter	二季度 The Second Quarter	三季度 The Third Quarter	四季度 The Forth Quarter
房屋销售价格总指数	**Selling Price Indices of Houses**	**104.3**	**104.4**	**106.1**	**103.5**	**103.2**
商品房	Commercial Houses	104.3	104.7	106.0	103.4	103.3
住宅	Residence	104.5	104.6	107.0	103.3	103.1
经济适用房	Economic Housing	104.6	103.5	107.2	103.0	
普通住宅	Common Residence	105.0	105.4	107.9	103.4	103.1
多层住宅	Multiayer Buildings	105.1	106.0	107.9	103.3	103.1
高层住宅	High-grade Building	104.3	102.7	106.9	103.9	103.6
其他住宅	Other Buildings					
高档住宅	Luxury Residential Buildings					
别墅	Villas					
高档公寓	High-grade Apartment					
非住宅	Non-Residential Buildings	104.0	105.1	103.3	103.6	103.8
办公楼	Office Buildings	103.0	103.3	101.9	103.8	103.9
写字楼	High-grade Office Buildings	103.0	103.3	101.9	103.8	103.9
普通办公用房	General Office Buildings					
商业娱乐用房	Business and Enrertaubnebt Buildings	104.3	105.7	104.4	103.4	103.7
其它用房	Other Buildings					
二手房	Private-owned House	104.0	102.2	106.7	104.4	102.5
住宅	Residence Buildings	104.4	102.1	107.7	105.1	102.8
高层住宅	High-grade Building	105.1		105.1		
多层住宅	Multiayer Buildings	104.7	102.1	108.6	105.1	102.8
其他住宅	Other Buildings					
非住宅	Other Buildings	102.4	102.5	103.3	102.2	101.5
房屋租赁价格总指数	**Renting Price Indices of Houses**	**102.0**	**105.2**	**102.9**	**100.0**	**100.0**
住宅	Residence	102.9	108.0	103.4	100.0	100.0
普通住宅	Common Residence	104.0	108.0	108.0	100.0	100.0
高档住宅	Luxury Residential Buildings					
别墅	Villas					
高档公寓	High-grade Apartment					
经济适用房	Economic Housing					
廉租房	Tenement House					
办公楼	Office	101.1	103.9	100.0	100.3	100.0
写字楼	High-grade Office Buildings	100.0	100.0	100.0	100.0	100.0
普通办公用房	General Office Buildings	101.3	104.8	100.0	100.3	100.0
商业娱乐用房	Business and Enrertaubnebt Buildings	102.4	105.0	104.7	100.0	100.0
工业仓储用房	Industrial Storage buildings	100.0	100.0	100.0	100.0	100.0
工业厂房	Industrial Factory	100.0	100.0	100.0	100.0	100.0
仓库	Storehouse					
其它	Other	100.0			100.0	
物业管理价格总指数	**Property Management Price Indices**	**104.5**	**109.9**	**108.2**	**100.0**	**100.0**
住宅	Residence	105.3	111.5	109.5	100.0	100.0
普通住宅	Common Residence	105.9	111.8	111.8	100.0	100.0
高层住宅	High-grade Building	105.0	110.0	110.0	100.0	100.0
经济适用房	Economic Housing					
办公楼	Office Buildings	100.0	100.0	100.0	100.0	100.0
写字楼	High-grade Office Buildings					
普通办公用房	General Office Buildings	100.0	100.0	100.0	100.0	100.0
商业娱乐用房	Business and Enrertaubnebt Buildings	100.0	100.0	100.0	100.0	100.0
工业仓储用房	Industrial Storage Buildings					
#工业厂房	Industrial Factory					
土地交易价格总指数	**Transactions Price Indices of Land**	**104.8**	**106.2**	**107.5**	**102.7**	**102.6**
居住用地	Land for Residential Building Use	106.5	106.3	114.6	102.8	102.4
高档住宅用地	Luxury Residential Building					
普通住宅用地	General Residential buildings	107.1	107.6	115.4	102.8	102.4
经济适用房用地	Economically Affordable Housing	101.0	101.9	100.0		
工业仓储用地	Land for Industry Use	103.0	103.0			
商业、旅游、娱乐用地	Land for Business Tour and Entertainment	103.8	108.4	101.4	102.5	102.9
其它用地	Land for Other					

6-18 续表 3 continued

类　别	Classification	枣庄 Zhaozhuang				
		全年平均 Annual Average	一季度 The first Quarter	二季度 The Second Quarter	三季度 The Third Quarter	四季度 The Forth Quarter
房屋销售价格总指数	**Selling Price Indices of Houses**	**104.3**	**104.3**	**103.8**	**103.9**	**105.1**
商品房	Commercial Houses	104.3	104.2	103.7	104.0	105.1
住宅	Residence	104.3	104.2	103.8	104.0	105.2
经济适用房	Economic Housing	104.4	105.7	104.5	103.2	104.0
普通住宅	Common Residence	104.3	104.1	103.7	104.0	105.2
多层住宅	Multiayer Buildings	104.3	104.2	103.7	103.9	105.3
高层住宅	High-grade Building	105.2		104.8	106.1	104.5
其他住宅	Other Buildings	103.2	102.6	104.4		
高档住宅	Luxury Residential Buildings	104.4		104.2	104.6	
别墅	Villas	104.4		104.2	104.6	
高档公寓	High-grade Apartment					
非住宅	Non-Residential Buildings	104.2	104.1	103.6	104.1	105.1
办公楼	Office Buildings					
写字楼	High-grade Office Buildings					
普通办公用房	General Office Buildings					
商业娱乐用房	Business and Enrertaubnebt Buildings	104.2	104.1	103.6	104.1	105.1
其它用房	Other Buildings					
二手房	Private-owned House	104.2	104.7	104.0	103.2	104.7
住宅	Residence Buildings	104.2	104.3	104.4	103.4	104.6
高层住宅	High-grade Building					
多层住宅	Multiayer Buildings	104.2	104.4	104.4	103.4	104.6
其他住宅	Other Buildings	103.6	103.9	103.8	102.8	103.8
非住宅	Other Buildings	104.1	105.1	103.4	103.1	105.0
房屋租赁价格总指数	**Renting Price Indices of Houses**	**100.0**	**100.0**	**100.0**	**100.0**	**100.0**
住宅	Residence	100.0	100.0	100.0	100.0	100.0
普通住宅	Common Residence	100.0	100.0	100.0	100.0	100.0
高档住宅	Luxury Residential Buildings					
别墅	Villas					
高档公寓	High-grade Apartment					
经济适用房	Economic Housing					
廉租房	Tenement House					
办公楼	Office	100.0	100.0	100.0	100.0	100.0
写字楼	High-grade Office Buildings					
普通办公用房	General Office Buildings	100.0	100.0	100.0	100.0	100.0
商业娱乐用房	Business and Enrertaubnebt Buildings	100.0	100.0	100.0	100.0	100.0
工业仓储用房	Industrial Storage buildings	100.0	100.0	100.0	100.0	100.0
工业厂房	Industrial Factory	100.0	100.0	100.0	100.0	100.0
仓库	Storehouse	100.0	100.0	100.0	100.0	100.0
其它	Other					
物业管理价格总指数	**Property Management Price Indices**	**100.0**	**100.0**	**100.0**	**100.0**	**100.0**
住宅	Residence	100.0	100.0	100.0	100.0	100.0
普通住宅	Common Residence	100.0	100.0	100.0	100.0	100.0
高层住宅	High-grade Building					
经济适用房	Economic Housing	100.0	100.0			
办公楼	Office Buildings					
写字楼	High-grade Office Buildings					
普通办公用房	General Office Buildings					
商业娱乐用房	Business and Enrertaubnebt Buildings					
工业仓储用房	Industrial Storage Buildings					
#工业厂房	Industrial Factory					
土地交易价格总指数	**Transactions Price Indices of Land**	**105.6**	**105.0**	**107.4**	**105.8**	**104.3**
居住用地	Land for Residential Building Use	106.0	105.4	107.4	106.3	104.8
高档住宅用地	Luxury Residential Building					
普通住宅用地	General Residential buildings	106.0	105.4	107.4	106.3	104.8
经济适用房用地	Economically Affordable Housing					
工业仓储用地	Land for Industry Use	104.3	103.1		107.4	102.5
商业、旅游、娱乐用地	Land for Business Tour and Entertainment	103.7	104.2		103.8	103.0
其它用地	Land for Other	108.6		108.6		

6-18 续表 4 continued

类 别	Classification	东营 dongying 全年平均 Annual Average	一季度 The first Quarter	二季度 The Second Quarter	三季度 The Third Quarter	四季度 The Forth Quarter
房屋销售价格总指数	**Selling Price Indices of Houses**	**102.9**	**104.6**	**103.1**	**102.1**	**101.8**
商品房	Commercial Houses	102.5	104.2	102.5	101.7	101.7
住宅	Residence	103.0	105.1	102.7	101.7	102.4
经济适用房	Economic Housing	101.5	102.4	101.1	102.2	100.9
普通住宅	Common Residence	103.6	106.9	103.4	101.7	102.3
多层住宅	Multiayer Buildings	103.5	106.4	103.3	101.6	102.7
高层住宅	High-grade Building	108.0	113.0	108.0	109.8	101.1
其他住宅	Other Buildings	101.1	103.4	100.0	100.0	
高档住宅	Luxury Residential Buildings	102.6	104.1	100.9	101.2	104.1
别墅	Villas	102.6	104.1	100.9	101.2	104.1
高档公寓	High-grade Apartment					
非住宅	Non-Residential Buildings	101.7	102.4	102.1	101.9	100.4
办公楼	Office Buildings	100.8	101.9	100.1	100.4	100.6
写字楼	High-grade Office Buildings	100.8	102.2	100.1	100.4	100.6
普通办公用房	General Office Buildings	100.5	102.4	100.0	100.0	100.0
商业娱乐用房	Business and Enrertaubnebt Buildings	102.5	103.5	103.4	102.7	100.3
其它用房	Other Buildings	101.1	102.1	100.0		
二手房	Private-owned House	103.7	105.5	104.5	102.8	102.0
住宅	Residence Buildings	104.4	108.5	105.2	102.0	101.9
高层住宅	High-grade Building					
多层住宅	Multiayer Buildings	105.0	110.9	105.2	102.0	101.9
其他住宅	Other Buildings					
非住宅	Other Buildings	101.9	97.8	102.6	104.8	102.2
房屋租赁价格总指数	**Renting Price Indices of Houses**	**100.2**	**100.3**	**100.0**	**100.2**	**100.3**
住宅	Residence	100.2	100.9	100.0	100.0	100.0
普通住宅	Common Residence	100.2	100.9	100.0	100.0	100.0
高档住宅	Luxury Residential Buildings					
别墅	Villas					
高档公寓	High-grade Apartment					
经济适用房	Economic Housing					
廉租房	Tenement House					
办公楼	Office	100.0			100.0	100.0
写字楼	High-grade Office Buildings	100.0			100.0	100.0
普通办公用房	General Office Buildings					
商业娱乐用房	Business and Enrertaubnebt Buildings	100.0	100.0	100.0	100.0	100.1
工业仓储用房	Industrial Storage buildings					
工业厂房	Industrial Factory					
仓库	Storehouse					
其它	Other	104.3	100.3		106.2	106.4
物业管理价格总指数	**Property Management Price Indices**	**116.7**	**142.1**	**115.6**	**106.6**	**102.3**
住宅	Residence	116.9	142.1	115.6	107.6	102.3
普通住宅	Common Residence	113.8	135.1	116.3	101.4	102.3
高层住宅	High-grade Building	106.2	100.0	112.4	106.2	106.2
经济适用房	Economic Housing	137.2	186.7		125.0	100.0
办公楼	Office Buildings	100.0			100.0	
写字楼	High-grade Office Buildings					
普通办公用房	General Office Buildings	100.0			100.0	
商业娱乐用房	Business and Enrertaubnebt Buildings					
工业仓储用房	Industrial Storage Buildings					
#工业厂房	Industrial Factory					
土地交易价格总指数	**Transactions Price Indices of Land**	**101.2**	**100.8**	**101.0**	**101.5**	**101.4**
居住用地	Land for Residential Building Use	100.4		100.1	100.5	100.7
高档住宅用地	Luxury Residential Building	100.0			100.0	100.0
普通住宅用地	General Residential buildings	101.1		100.1	102.6	100.7
经济适用房用地	Economically Affordable Housing					
工业仓储用地	Land for Industry Use	101.9	101.3	102.4	101.9	102.1
商业、旅游、娱乐用地	Land for Business Tour and Entertainment	101.0	100.0	100.0	102.4	101.6
其它用地	Land for Other	100.3			100.6	100.0

6-18 续表 5 continued

类 别	Classification	烟台 Yantai 全年平均 Annual Average	一季度 The first Quarter	二季度 The Second Quarter	三季度 The Third Quarter	四季度 The Forth Quarter
房屋销售价格总指数	**Selling Price Indices of Houses**	**105.5**	**105.0**	**105.5**	**105.8**	**105.6**
商品房	Commercial Houses	105.6	105.1	105.6	106.2	105.5
住宅	Residence	106.5	106.2	107.0	107.0	105.8
经济适用房	Economic Housing					
普通住宅	Common Residence	107.0	105.9	107.0	108.3	106.7
多层住宅	Multiayer Buildings	105.6	105.1	105.3	105.9	105.9
高层住宅	High-grade Building	107.5	105.7	108.2	109.1	107.0
其他住宅	Other Buildings	104.4	105.1	104.4	104.5	103.3
高档住宅	Luxury Residential Buildings	104.2	107.3	106.6	101.2	101.7
别墅	Villas					
高档公寓	High-grade Apartment	104.2	107.3	106.6	101.2	101.7
非住宅	Non-Residential Buildings	103.0	102.0	101.7	103.6	104.6
办公楼	Office Buildings					
写字楼	High-grade Office Buildings					
普通办公用房	General Office Buildings					
商业娱乐用房	Business and Enrertaubnebt Buildings	102.9	101.9	101.6	103.6	104.6
其它用房	Other Buildings	107.5	107.4	107.7	107.7	107.3
二手房	Private-owned House	104.9	104.5	104.7	104.4	105.9
住宅	Residence Buildings	104.9	104.5	104.7	104.4	105.9
高层住宅	High-grade Building					
多层住宅	Multiayer Buildings	104.9	104.5	104.7	104.4	105.9
其他住宅	Other Buildings					
非住宅	Other Buildings					
房屋租赁价格总指数	**Renting Price Indices of Houses**	**100.2**	**100.0**	**100.0**	**100.4**	**100.4**
住宅	Residence	100.0	100.0	100.0	100.0	100.0
普通住宅	Common Residence	100.0	100.0	100.0	100.0	100.0
高档住宅	Luxury Residential Buildings					
别墅	Villas					
高档公寓	High-grade Apartment					
经济适用房	Economic Housing					
廉租房	Tenement House	100.0	100.0	100.0	100.0	100.0
办公楼	Office	100.1	100.2	100.1	100.1	100.1
写字楼	High-grade Office Buildings	100.4	100.5	100.4	100.4	100.4
普通办公用房	General Office Buildings	100.0	100.0	100.0	100.0	100.0
商业娱乐用房	Business and Enrertaubnebt Buildings	100.8	100.0	100.0	101.5	101.5
工业仓储用房	Industrial Storage buildings	100.0	100.0	100.0	100.0	100.0
工业厂房	Industrial Factory	100.0	100.0	100.0	100.0	100.0
仓库	Storehouse	100.0	100.0	100.0	100.0	100.0
其它	Other					
物业管理价格总指数	**Property Management Price Indices**	**100.0**	**100.0**	**100.0**	**100.0**	**100.0**
住宅	Residence	100.0	100.0	100.0	100.0	100.0
普通住宅	Common Residence	100.0	100.0	100.0	100.0	100.0
高层住宅	High-grade Building	100.0	100.0	100.0	100.0	100.0
经济适用房	Economic Housing	100.0	100.0	100.0	100.0	100.0
办公楼	Office Buildings	100.0	100.0	100.0	100.0	100.0
写字楼	High-grade Office Buildings	100.0	100.0	100.0	100.0	100.0
普通办公用房	General Office Buildings	100.0	100.0	100.0	100.0	100.0
商业娱乐用房	Business and Enrertaubnebt Buildings	100.0	100.0	100.0	100.0	100.0
工业仓储用房	Industrial Storage Buildings					
#工业厂房	Industrial Factory					
土地交易价格总指数	**Transactions Price Indices of Land**	**105.1**	**104.3**	**104.7**	**105.1**	**106.3**
居住用地	Land for Residential Building Use	104.9	102.3	105.3	107.1	
高档住宅用地	Luxury Residential Building	102.3	102.3			
普通住宅用地	General Residential buildings	106.2		105.3	107.1	
经济适用房用地	Economically Affordable Housing					
工业仓储用地	Land for Industry Use	103.9	105.2	101.6	104.5	104.3
商业、旅游、娱乐用地	Land for Business Tour and Entertainment	105.4	106.5	105.4	102.6	107.2
其它用地	Land for Other					

6-18 续表 6 continued

类 别	Classification	潍坊 Weifang 全年平均 Annual Average	一季度 The first Quarter	二季度 The Second Quarter	三季度 The Third Quarter	四季度 The Forth Quarter
房屋销售价格总指数	**Selling Price Indices of Houses**	**106.6**	**108.0**	**107.0**	**105.7**	**105.6**
商品房	Commercial Houses	106.7	108.1	107.2	105.7	105.7
住宅	Residence	107.2	108.9	107.8	106.1	106.0
经济适用房	Economic Housing	106.7	109.3	106.9	105.0	105.4
普通住宅	Common Residence	107.3	109.0	108.0	106.2	106.1
多层住宅	Multiayer Buildings	107.7	109.7	108.5	106.3	106.1
高层住宅	High-grade Building	105.3	105.9	103.3	105.5	106.3
其他住宅	Other Buildings					
高档住宅	Luxury Residential Buildings	105.0	105.3	105.0	104.8	105.0
别墅	Villas	105.0	105.3	105.0	104.8	105.0
高档公寓	High-grade Apartment					
非住宅	Non-Residential Buildings	103.9	103.6	104.3	103.5	104.3
办公楼	Office Buildings	102.8	102.8			
写字楼	High-grade Office Buildings					
普通办公用房	General Office Buildings	102.8	102.8			
商业娱乐用房	Business and Enrertaubnebt Buildings	104.0	103.7	104.3	103.5	104.3
其它用房	Other Buildings					
二手房	Private-owned House	106.0	107.7	105.8	105.5	105.2
住宅	Residence Buildings	106.0	107.7	105.8	105.5	105.2
高层住宅	High-grade Building					
多层住宅	Multiayer Buildings	106.0	107.7	105.8	105.5	105.2
其他住宅	Other Buildings					
非住宅	Other Buildings					
房屋租赁价格总指数	**Renting Price Indices of Houses**	**102.1**	**102.6**	**102.9**	**101.6**	**101.3**
住宅	Residence	103.1	103.3	103.9	103.3	101.7
普通住宅	Common Residence					
高档住宅	Luxury Residential Buildings					
别墅	Villas					
高档公寓	High-grade Apartment					
经济适用房	Economic Housing	103.1	103.3	103.9	103.3	101.7
廉租房	Tenement House					
办公楼	Office	100.0	100.0	100.0	100.0	100.0
写字楼	High-grade Office Buildings					
普通办公用房	General Office Buildings	100.0	100.0	100.0	100.0	100.0
商业娱乐用房	Business and Enrertaubnebt Buildings	102.3	103.2	103.4	101.2	101.5
工业仓储用房	Industrial Storage buildings	100.0	100.0	100.0	100.0	100.0
工业厂房	Industrial Factory	100.0	100.0	100.0	100.0	100.0
仓库	Storehouse					
其它	Other					
物业管理价格总指数	**Property Management Price Indices**	**100.0**	**100.0**	**100.0**	**100.0**	**100.0**
住 宅	Residence	100.0	100.0	100.0	100.0	100.0
普通住宅	Common Residence	100.0	100.0	100.0	100.0	100.0
高层住宅	High-grade Building					
经济适用房	Economic Housing					
办公楼	Office Buildings					
写字楼	High-grade Office Buildings					
普通办公用房	General Office Buildings					
商业娱乐用房	Business and Enrertaubnebt Buildings					
工业仓储用房	Industrial Storage Buildings					
#工业厂房	Industrial Factory					
土地交易价格总指数	**Transactions Price Indices of Land**	**105.2**	**106.6**	**105.3**	**104.5**	**104.5**
居住用地	Land for Residential Building Use	105.3	105.1	105.3	105.6	105.1
高档住宅用地	Luxury Residential Building	105.0		105.3	106.4	103.4
普通住宅用地	General Residential buildings	106.2	105.9	107.3	106.6	105.1
经济适用房用地	Economically Affordable Housing	103.3	103.1	103.4	103.4	103.4
工业仓储用地	Land for Industry Use	103.0	104.7	103.4	101.7	102.2
商业、旅游、娱乐用地	Land for Business Tour and Entertainment	107.8	109.9	107.4	107.3	106.7
其它用地	Land for Other	103.2	105.9	104.9	100.3	101.8

6-18 续表 7 continued

类 别	Classification	济宁 Jining 全年平均 Annual Average	一季度 The first Quarter	二季度 The Second Quarter	三季度 The Third Quarter	四季度 The Forth Quarter
房屋销售价格总指数	**Selling Price Indices of Houses**	**105.4**	**105.7**	**105.3**	**105.7**	**104.7**
商品房	Commercial Houses	105.7	106.2	105.9	106.0	104.7
住宅	Residence	105.9	106.4	106.1	106.1	105.2
经济适用房	Economic Housing	106.1	108.3		106.7	102.6
普通住宅	Common Residence	106.0	106.2	106.1	105.8	105.7
多层住宅	Multiayer Buildings	106.5	106.3	107.3	106.2	106.1
高层住宅	High-grade Building	104.6	105.5	104.1	104.3	104.6
其他住宅	Other Buildings					
高档住宅	Luxury Residential Buildings	103.8			105.7	102.9
别墅	Villas	101.9				101.9
高档公寓	High-grade Apartment	104.8			105.7	103.8
非住宅	Non-Residential Buildings	104.6	105.7	105.0	105.1	103.0
办公楼	Office Buildings	103.3				103.3
写字楼	High-grade Office Buildings	103.3				103.3
普通办公用房	General Office Buildings					
商业娱乐用房	Business and Enrertaubnebt Buildings	104.7	105.7	105.0	105.1	103.2
其它用房	Other Buildings					
二手房	Private-owned House	103.8	103.4	102.2	104.4	105.0
住宅	Residence Buildings	103.7	103.4	102.2	104.4	104.9
高层住宅	High-grade Building					
多层住宅	Multiayer Buildings	103.8	103.4	102.3	104.4	105.2
其他住宅	Other Buildings	103.3		103.7	104.0	101.5
非住宅	Other Buildings	105.5				105.5
房屋租赁价格总指数	**Renting Price Indices of Houses**	**101.5**	**104.0**	**101.6**	**100.4**	**100.0**
住宅	Residence	100.2	100.0	100.0	100.9	100.0
普通住宅	Common Residence	100.3	100.0	100.0	101.2	100.0
高档住宅	Luxury Residential Buildings					
别墅	Villas					
高档公寓	High-grade Apartment					
经济适用房	Economic Housing					
廉租房	Tenement House	100.0	100.0	100.0	100.0	100.0
办公楼	Office					
写字楼	High-grade Office Buildings					
普通办公用房	General Office Buildings					
商业娱乐用房	Business and Enrertaubnebt Buildings	102.5	107.2	102.9	100.0	100.0
工业仓储用房	Industrial Storage buildings					
工业厂房	Industrial Factory					
仓库	Storehouse					
其它	Other					
物业管理价格总指数	**Property Management Price Indices**	**100.0**	**100.0**	**100.0**	**100.0**	**100.0**
住宅	Residence	100.0	100.0	100.0	100.0	100.0
普通住宅	Common Residence	100.0	100.0	100.0	100.0	100.0
高层住宅	High-grade Building	100.0	100.0			
经济适用房	Economic Housing					
办公楼	Office Buildings	100.0				100.0
写字楼	High-grade Office Buildings					
普通办公用房	General Office Buildings	100.0				100.0
商业娱乐用房	Business and Enrertaubnebt Buildings					
工业仓储用房	Industrial Storage Buildings					
#工业厂房	Industrial Factory					
土地交易价格总指数	**Transactions Price Indices of Land**	**103.2**	**104.8**	**101.5**	**102.7**	**103.6**
居住用地	Land for Residential Building Use	101.9		100.9	101.1	103.7
高档住宅用地	Luxury Residential Building					
普通住宅用地	General Residential buildings	101.9		100.9	101.1	103.7
经济适用房用地	Economically Affordable Housing					
工业仓储用地	Land for Industry Use	104.8	104.8	107.1	104.1	103.2
商业、旅游、娱乐用地	Land for Business Tour and Entertainment	105.3			107.1	103.5
其它用地	Land for Other	100.0		100.0		

6-18 续表 8 continued

类　别	Classification	泰安 Taian				
		全年平均 Annual Average	一季度 The first Quarter	二季度 The Second Quarter	三季度 The Third Quarter	四季度 The Forth Quarter
房屋销售价格总指数	**Selling Price Indices of Houses**	**105.1**	**104.9**	**104.4**	**105.7**	**105.4**
商品房	Commercial Houses	105.1	104.7	104.9	105.5	105.4
住宅	Residence	105.3	104.8	105.2	105.9	105.5
经济适用房	Economic Housing	108.0	109.0	107.5	108.4	107.1
普通住宅	Common Residence	105.1	104.4	105.0	105.7	105.5
多层住宅	Multiayer Buildings	105.2	104.4	105.3	105.7	105.5
高层住宅	High-grade Building	103.6				103.6
其他住宅	Other Buildings	102.6		102.6		
高档住宅	Luxury Residential Buildings	103.5	102.7	103.6	104.3	103.3
别墅	Villas	101.0		101.0		
高档公寓	High-grade Apartment	103.7	102.7	104.9	104.3	103.3
非住宅	Non-residential Buildings	104.4	104.3	103.8	104.2	105.1
办公楼	Office Buildings					
写字楼	High-grade Office Buildings					
普通办公用房	General Office Buildings					
商业娱乐用房	Business and Enrertaubnebt Buildings	104.4	104.3	103.8	104.2	105.1
其它用房	Other Buildings	103.5				103.5
二手房	Private-owned House	105.0	105.5	103.2	105.9	105.5
住宅	Residence Buildings	105.7	106.3	105.5	106.6	104.4
高层住宅	High-grade Building	107.8			107.8	
多层住宅	Multiayer Buildings	105.5	106.3	105.5	106.0	104.4
其他住宅	Other Buildings					
非住宅	Other Buildings	104.6	105.6	102.0	104.6	107.6
房屋租赁价格总指数	**Renting Price Indices of Houses**	**101.6**	**101.2**	**101.0**	**101.5**	**102.5**
住宅	Residence	101.6	100.0	100.0	100.9	105.3
普通住宅	Common Residence	101.6	100.0	100.0	100.9	105.3
高档住宅	Luxury Residential Buildings					
别墅	Villas					
高档公寓	High-grade Apartment					
经济适用房	Economic Housing					
廉租房	Tenement House					
办公楼	Office	101.0	103.6	100.0	100.2	100.0
写字楼	High-grade Office Buildings					
普通办公用房	General Office Buildings	101.0	103.6	100.0	100.2	100.0
商业娱乐用房	Business and Enrertaubnebt Buildings	102.0	101.4	101.9	102.6	101.9
工业仓储用房	Industrial Storage buildings	100.0	100.0		100.0	
工业厂房	Industrial Factory	100.0	100.0		100.0	
仓库	Storehouse					
其它	Other					
物业管理价格总指数	**Property Management Price Indices**	**100.0**	**100.0**	**100.0**	**100.0**	**100.0**
住宅	Residence	100.0	100.0	100.0	100.0	100.0
普通住宅	Common Residence	100.0	100.0	100.0	100.0	100.0
高层住宅	High-grade Building					
经济适用房	Economic Housing					
办公楼	Office Buildings	100.0	100.0	100.0	100.0	100.0
写字楼	High-grade Office Buildings	100.0	100.0	100.0	100.0	100.0
普通办公用房	General Office Buildings	100.0	100.0	100.0	100.0	100.0
商业娱乐用房	Business and Enrertaubnebt Buildings	100.0	100.0	100.0	100.0	100.0
工业仓储用房	Industrial Storage Buildings					
#工业厂房	Industrial Factory					
土地交易价格总指数	**Transactions Price Indices of Land**	**108.2**	**118.6**	**104.4**	**100.6**	**109.1**
居住用地	Land for Residential Building Use	106.5	109.2		100.0	110.4
高档住宅用地	Luxury Residential Building					
普通住宅用地	General Residential buildings	106.5	109.2		100.0	110.4
经济适用房用地	Economically Affordable Housing					
工业仓储用地	Land for Industry Use	110.8	129.4	106.7	100.5	106.7
商业、旅游、娱乐用地	Land for Business Tour and Entertainment	108.1	119.3	101.9	101.3	109.8
其它用地	Land for Other					

6-18 续表 9 continued

类 别	Classification	威海 Weihai				
		全年平均 Annual Average	一季度 The first Quarter	二季度 The Second Quarter	三季度 The Third Quarter	四季度 The Forth Quarter
房屋销售价格总指数	**Selling Price Indices of Houses**	**101.9**	**101.6**	**102.5**	**101.8**	**101.8**
商品房	Commercial Houses	102.6	102.1	102.6	102.8	102.7
住宅	Residence	102.6	102.3	102.2	103.2	102.9
经济适用房	Economic Housing	100.0	100.0			
普通住宅	Common Residence	102.6	102.3	102.1	103.1	102.9
多层住宅	Multiayer Buildings	102.7	102.7	102.0	102.2	103.8
高层住宅	High-grade Building	104.1	96.7	104.4	109.4	106.0
其他住宅	Other Buildings					
高档住宅	Luxury Residential Buildings	113.4	96.9	133.0	111.0	107.4
别墅	Villas	91.6				91.6
高档公寓	High-grade Apartment	114.9	96.9	133.0	111.0	112.8
非住宅	Non-Residential Buildings	101.8	100.4	107.6	100.0	101.1
办公楼	Office Buildings	104.5		104.2		105.3
写字楼	High-grade Office Buildings	105.3				105.3
普通办公用房	General Office Buildings	104.2		104.2		
商业娱乐用房	Business and Enrertaubnebt Buildings	101.5	100.4	107.4	100.0	100.0
其它用房	Other Buildings	100.0	100.0	100.0	100.0	100.0
二手房	Private-owned House	100.0	100.0	100.0	100.0	100.0
住宅	Residence Buildings	100.0	100.0	100.0	100.0	100.0
高层住宅	High-grade Building	100.0			100.0	100.0
多层住宅	Multiayer Buildings	100.0	100.0	100.0	100.0	100.0
其他住宅	Other Buildings					
非住宅	Other Buildings	100.0			100.0	100.0
房屋租赁价格总指数	**Renting Price Indices of Houses**	**98.3**	**93.3**	**99.9**	**100.0**	**100.0**
住宅	Residence					
普通住宅	Common Residence					
高档住宅	Luxury Residential Buildings					
别墅	Villas					
高档公寓	High-grade Apartment					
经济适用房	Economic Housing					
廉租房	Tenement House					
办公楼	Office					
写字楼	High-grade Office Buildings					
普通办公用房	General Office Buildings					
商业娱乐用房	Business and Enrertaubnebt Buildings	100.0		100.0	100.0	100.0
工业仓储用房	Industrial Storage buildings	95.0	93.3	93.3	96.6	96.6
工业厂房	Industrial Factory					
仓库	Storehouse	95.0	93.3	93.3	96.6	96.6
其它	Other					
物业管理价格总指数	**Property Management Price Indices**	**100.0**	**100.0**	**100.0**	**100.0**	**100.0**
住 宅	Residence	100.0	100.0	100.0	100.0	100.0
普通住宅	Common Residence	100.0	100.0	100.0	100.0	100.0
高层住宅	High-grade Building	100.0	100.0	100.0	100.0	100.0
经济适用房	Economic Housing					
办公楼	Office Buildings					
写字楼	High-grade Office Buildings					
普通办公用房	General Office Buildings					
商业娱乐用房	Business and Enrertaubnebt Buildings					
工业仓储用房	Industrial Storage Buildings					
#工业厂房	Industrial Factory					
土地交易价格总指数	**Transactions Price Indices of Land**	**114.4**	**106.6**	**137.4**	**104.8**	**108.9**
居住用地	Land for Residential Building Use	119.2	106.7	147.3	103.6	
高档住宅用地	Luxury Residential Building					
普通住宅用地	General Residential buildings	119.2	106.7	147.3	103.6	
经济适用房用地	Economically Affordable Housing					
工业仓储用地	Land for Industry Use	114.1	105.8	131.1	105.5	113.8
商业、旅游、娱乐用地	Land for Business Tour and Entertainment	105.0	107.5			102.4
其它用地	Land for Other					

6-18 续表 10 continued

类 别	Classification	日照 Rizhao				
		全年平均 Annual Average	一季度 The first Quarter	二季度 The Second Quarter	三季度 The Third Quarter	四季度 The Forth Quarter
房屋销售价格总指数	**Selling Price Indices of Houses**	**103.5**	**102.9**	**103.1**	**102.9**	**105.0**
商品房	Commercial Houses	104.9	104.7	104.1	104.0	106.8
住宅	Residence	105.4	105.0	104.5	104.5	107.5
经济适用房	Economic Housing					
普通住宅	Common Residence	105.4	105.2	104.6	104.5	107.4
多层住宅	Multiayer Buildings	105.7	105.6	104.9	104.8	107.5
高层住宅	High-grade Building	103.9	103.1	102.6	103.2	106.8
其他住宅	Other Buildings					
高档住宅	Luxury Residential Buildings	104.5	103.2	103.0	103.6	108.4
别墅	Villas	101.3	102.3	102.0	100.0	100.0
高档公寓	High-grade Apartment	104.7	103.3	103.0	103.9	108.6
非住宅	Non-Residential Buildings	102.1	102.6	102.2	100.8	102.8
办公楼	Office Buildings	103.4	102.5	105.2	103.5	101.7
写字楼	High-grade Office Buildings	103.1	101.1	105.2	103.9	101.7
普通办公用房	General Office Buildings	103.4	106.7		100.0	
商业娱乐用房	Business and Enrertaubnebt Buildings	101.6	102.9	100.8	99.5	103.3
其它用房	Other Buildings	100.8	100.2	101.2	101.6	
二手房	Private-owned House	101.8	100.8	101.8	101.7	102.9
住宅	Residence Buildings	101.9	101.1	101.9	101.7	102.7
高层住宅	High-grade Building					
多层住宅	Multiayer Buildings	102.4	101.5	102.4	102.1	103.6
其他住宅	Other Buildings	100.1	99.8	100.5	100.5	99.6
非住宅	Other Buildings	101.6	100.1	101.5	101.7	103.3
房屋租赁价格总指数	**Renting Price Indices of Houses**	**102.6**	**101.3**	**101.3**	**102.1**	**105.5**
住宅	Residence	101.1	100.0	100.0	100.0	104.2
普通住宅	Common Residence	101.1	100.0	100.0	100.0	104.2
高档住宅	Luxury Residential Buildings					
别墅	Villas					
高档公寓	High-grade Apartment					
经济适用房	Economic Housing					
廉租房	Tenement House					
办公楼	Office	99.1	99.5	97.1	100.0	99.7
写字楼	High-grade Office Buildings	98.9	98.6			99.1
普通办公用房	General Office Buildings	99.3	100.0	97.1	100.0	100.0
商业娱乐用房	Business and Enrertaubnebt Buildings	106.0	103.9	104.1	106.3	109.6
工业仓储用房	Industrial Storage buildings	101.1	101.0	101.1	101.1	101.1
工业厂房	Industrial Factory	100.0	100.0	100.0	100.0	100.0
仓库	Storehouse	105.0	104.6	105.1	105.1	105.1
其它	Other					
物业管理价格总指数	**Property Management Price Indices**	**106.4**	**102.7**	**102.5**	**109.6**	**110.6**
住宅	Residence	109.3	104.1	103.9	114.0	115.3
普通住宅	Common Residence	111.1	105.0	104.7	116.4	118.2
高层住宅	High-grade Building	101.0	100.0	100.0	102.6	101.5
经济适用房	Economic Housing					
办公楼	Office Buildings	100.0	100.0	100.0	100.0	100.0
写字楼	High-grade Office Buildings	100.0	100.0	100.0	100.0	100.0
普通办公用房	General Office Buildings	100.0	100.0	100.0	100.0	100.0
商业娱乐用房	Business and Enrertaubnebt Buildings	106.5	100.0	100.0	111.4	114.4
工业仓储用房	Industrial Storage Buildings					
#工业厂房	Industrial Factory					
土地交易价格总指数	**Transactions Price Indices of Land**	**109.5**	**108.9**	**103.0**	**110.5**	**115.7**
居住用地	Land for Residential Building Use	109.8	107.8	105.3	108.7	117.4
高档住宅用地	Luxury Residential Building	106.6		102.6	110.6	
普通住宅用地	General Residential buildings	109.7	107.8	105.3	108.4	117.4
经济适用房用地	Economically Affordable Housing					
工业仓储用地	Land for Industry Use	109.5	109.5	100.0	110.7	117.8
商业、旅游、娱乐用地	Land for Business Tour and Entertainment	108.3	109.7	104.0	112.7	106.8
其它用地	Land for Other	113.0	110.2	104.5	117.1	120.0

6-18 续表 11 continued

类 别	Classification	莱芜 Laiwu 全年平均 Annual Average	一季度 The first Quarter	二季度 The Second Quarter	三季度 The Third Quarter	四季度 The Forth Quarter
房屋销售价格总指数	**Selling Price Indices of Houses**	**106.4**	**107.5**	**107.2**	**105.2**	**105.9**
商品房	Commercial Houses	107.0	108.1	108.1	105.5	106.5
住宅	Residence	107.3	108.1	109.1	106.4	105.4
经济适用房	Economic Housing	102.9	105.8	103.2	102.4	100.0
普通住宅	Common Residence	108.0	108.5	110.1	107.0	106.3
多层住宅	Multiayer Buildings	108.6	109.0	110.9	107.6	106.9
高层住宅	High-grade Building	104.6	106.2	103.3	104.3	104.6
其他住宅	Other Buildings					
高档住宅	Luxury Residential Buildings					
别墅	Villas					
高档公寓	High-grade Apartment					
非住宅	Non-Residential Buildings	106.1	107.8	104.2	102.0	110.6
办公楼	Office Buildings					
写字楼	High-grade Office Buildings					
普通办公用房	General Office Buildings					
商业娱乐用房	Business and Enrertaubnebt Buildings	106.1	107.8	104.2	102.0	110.6
其它用房	Other Buildings					
二手房	Private-owned House	103.8	105.0	103.3	103.7	103.2
住宅	Residence Buildings	103.8	105.0	103.3	103.7	103.2
高层住宅	High-grade Building					
多层住宅	Multiayer Buildings	103.8	105.0	103.3	103.7	103.2
其他住宅	Other Buildings					
非住宅	Other Buildings	110.0				110.0
房屋租赁价格总指数	**Renting Price Indices of Houses**	**100.7**	**100.5**	**101.3**	**100.7**	**100.3**
住宅	Residence	101.7	100.0	100.0	104.7	102.2
普通住宅	Common Residence	101.7	100.0	100.0	104.7	102.2
高档住宅	Luxury Residential Buildings					
别墅	Villas					
高档公寓	High-grade Apartment					
经济适用房	Economic Housing					
廉租房	Tenement House					
办公楼	Office	100.0	100.0	100.0	100.0	100.0
写字楼	High-grade Office Buildings	100.0	100.0	100.0	100.0	100.0
普通办公用房	General Office Buildings	99.8		99.5	100.0	100.0
商业娱乐用房	Business and Enrertaubnebt Buildings	100.8	100.6	101.5	100.7	100.3
工业仓储用房	Industrial Storage buildings					
工业厂房	Industrial Factory					
仓库	Storehouse					
其它	Other					
物业管理价格总指数	**Property Management Price Indices**	**100.0**	**100.0**	**100.0**	**100.0**	**100.0**
住宅	Residence	100.0	100.0	100.0	100.0	100.0
普通住宅	Common Residence	100.0	100.0	100.0	100.0	100.0
高层住宅	High-grade Building					
经济适用房	Economic Housing					
办公楼	Office Buildings					
写字楼	High-grade Office Buildings					
普通办公用房	General Office Buildings					
商业娱乐用房	Business and Enrertaubnebt Buildings	100.0	100.0			
工业仓储用房	Industrial Storage Buildings					
#工业厂房	Industrial Factory					
土地交易价格总指数	**Transactions Price Indices of Land**	**105.7**	**107.7**	**104.7**	**106.4**	**103.9**
居住用地	Land for Residential Building Use	103.8	104.1	105.6		101.7
高档住宅用地	Luxury Residential Building					
普通住宅用地	General Residential buildings	103.4	104.1	105.6		100.6
经济适用房用地	Economically Affordable Housing	106.4				106.4
工业仓储用地	Land for Industry Use	106.1	108.5	104.7	106.4	104.9
商业、旅游、娱乐用地	Land for Business Tour and Entertainment	105.8	109.9	103.7		103.9
其它用地	Land for Other					

6-18 续表 12 continued

类 别	Classification	临沂 Linyi 全年平均 Annual Average	一季度 The first Quarter	二季度 The Second Quarter	三季度 The Third Quarter	四季度 The Forth Quarter
房屋销售价格总指数	**Selling Price Indices of Houses**	**104.0**	**105.4**	**104.1**	**103.1**	**103.5**
商品房	Commercial Houses	104.1	105.9	104.1	102.9	103.4
住宅	Residence	104.1	106.1	104.0	102.9	103.6
经济适用房	Economic Housing	102.4	107.0	100.2	100.0	102.2
普通住宅	Common Residence	104.3	105.6	104.6	103.2	103.8
多层住宅	Multiayer Buildings	105.3	107.5	104.9	104.1	104.8
高层住宅	High-grade Building	102.0	100.0	103.6	102.2	102.0
其他住宅	Other Buildings	101.2	103.3	102.0	101.0	99.2
高档住宅	Luxury Residential Buildings	105.8	109.0	106.0	105.0	104.2
别墅	Villas	103.9	101.9	104.0	102.7	106.4
高档公寓	High-grade Apartment	106.4	113.4	106.7	105.7	102.1
非住宅	Non-Residential Buildings	103.5	104.0	105.2	103.1	101.8
办公楼	Office Buildings	99.2			98.7	99.6
写字楼	High-grade Office Buildings	99.2			98.7	99.6
普通办公用房	General Office Buildings					
商业娱乐用房	Business and Enrertaubnebt Buildings	104.3	103.7	105.2	104.1	104.2
其它用房	Other Buildings	103.8	105.2	105.4	103.3	101.2
二手房	Private-owned House	103.9	103.9	103.8	103.8	104.1
住宅	Residence Buildings	104.2	104.3	104.1	104.4	104.2
高层住宅	High-grade Building	102.6	102.6			
多层住宅	Multiayer Buildings	104.4	104.6	103.9	104.8	104.4
其他住宅	Other Buildings	103.0	102.5	105.1	101.7	102.6
非住宅	Other Buildings	103.1	103.1	103.2	102.2	103.6
房屋租赁价格总指数	**Renting Price Indices of Houses**	**102.2**	**101.5**	**100.5**	**103.9**	**102.8**
住宅	Residence	104.6	100.0	100.0	110.7	107.7
普通住宅	Common Residence	105.5	100.0	100.0	112.8	109.2
高档住宅	Luxury Residential Buildings					
别墅	Villas					
高档公寓	High-grade Apartment					
经济适用房	Economic Housing	100.0	100.0	100.0	100.0	100.0
廉租房	Tenement House					
办公楼	Office	101.4	101.3	101.3	101.5	101.5
写字楼	High-grade Office Buildings	100.3	100.3	100.3	100.3	100.3
普通办公用房	General Office Buildings	102.2	102.1	102.1	102.4	102.3
商业娱乐用房	Business and Enrertaubnebt Buildings	101.2	103.2	100.7	100.7	100.3
工业仓储用房	Industrial Storage buildings	100.0	100.0	100.0	100.0	100.0
工业厂房	Industrial Factory	100.0	100.0	100.0	100.0	
仓库	Storehouse	100.0	100.0	100.0	100.0	100.0
其它	Other					
物业管理价格总指数	**Property Management Price Indices**	**102.6**	**102.8**	**103.1**	**103.8**	**100.6**
住宅	Residence	104.0	104.3	104.9	106.0	100.9
普通住宅	Common Residence	105.4	105.8	106.6	108.1	101.2
高层住宅	High-grade Building	100.0	100.0	100.0	100.0	100.0
经济适用房	Economic Housing	100.0	100.0	100.0	100.0	100.0
办公楼	Office Buildings	100.0	100.0	100.0	100.0	100.0
写字楼	High-grade Office Buildings	100.0	100.0	100.0	100.0	100.0
普通办公用房	General Office Buildings	100.0	100.0	100.0	100.0	100.0
商业娱乐用房	Business and Enrertaubnebt Buildings	100.0	100.0	100.0	100.0	100.0
工业仓储用房	Industrial Storage Buildings					
#工业厂房	Industrial Factory					
土地交易价格总指数	**Transactions Price Indices of Land**	**114.3**	**123.6**	**109.7**	**111.5**	**112.5**
居住用地	Land for Residential Building Use	120.9	137.7	109.2	117.7	119.1
高档住宅用地	Luxury Residential Building					
普通住宅用地	General Residential buildings	120.9	137.7	109.2	117.7	119.1
经济适用房用地	Economically Affordable Housing					
工业仓储用地	Land for Industry Use	107.0	112.0	109.6	98.3	107.9
商业、旅游、娱乐用地	Land for Business Tour and Entertainment	107.2	102.5	110.8	114.4	101.2
其它用地	Land for Other	122.9			122.9	

6-18 续表 13 continued

类 别	Classification	德州 Dezhou				
		全年平均 Annual Average	一季度 The first Quarter	二季度 The Second Quarter	三季度 The Third Quarter	四季度 The Forth Quarter
房屋销售价格总指数	**Selling Price Indices of Houses**	**104.6**	**104.3**	**103.6**	**105.9**	**104.7**
商品房	Commercial Houses	105.1	104.8	104.3	105.7	105.8
住宅	Residence	105.3	104.9	104.7	105.7	105.8
经济适用房	Economic Housing	100.4	101.0	100.0	100.0	100.0
普通住宅	Common Residence	105.4	105.4	104.7	105.5	106.1
多层住宅	Multiayer Buildings	105.6	105.6	104.8	105.5	106.3
高层住宅	High-grade Building	104.3	104.5	103.2	105.5	104.0
其他住宅	Other Buildings					
高档住宅	Luxury Residential Buildings	105.9	102.2	106.6	109.2	105.6
别墅	Villas					
高档公寓	High-grade Apartment	105.9	102.2	106.6	109.2	105.6
非住宅	Non-Residential Buildings	104.2	104.0	102.0	105.5	105.5
办公楼	Office Buildings	109.5	106.7		111.5	108.0
写字楼	High-grade Office Buildings					
普通办公用房	General Office Buildings	109.5	106.7		111.5	108.0
商业娱乐用房	Business and Enrertaubnebt Buildings	103.7	103.8	102.2	103.9	105.1
其它用房	Other Buildings	101.3		100.0		102.6
二手房	Private-owned House	103.5	103.2	101.9	106.5	102.4
住宅	Residence Buildings	103.6	103.3	101.9	106.7	102.3
高层住宅	High-grade Building					
多层住宅	Multiayer Buildings	103.6	103.3	101.9	106.7	102.3
其他住宅	Other Buildings					
非住宅	Other Buildings	102.7	101.6	104.5	101.1	103.6
房屋租赁价格总指数	**Renting Price Indices of Houses**	**107.2**	**100.0**	**107.0**	**102.1**	**119.5**
住宅	Residence	117.8	100.0	132.3	102.0	137.0
普通住宅	Common Residence	117.8	100.0	132.3	102.0	137.0
高档住宅	Luxury Residential Buildings					
别墅	Villas					
高档公寓	High-grade Apartment					
经济适用房	Economic Housing					
廉租房	Tenement House					
办公楼	Office	101.9	100.0	101.0	100.0	106.7
写字楼	High-grade Office Buildings	128.6		107.1		150.0
普通办公用房	General Office Buildings	100.0	100.0	100.0	100.0	100.0
商业娱乐用房	Business and Enrertaubnebt Buildings	106.4	99.5	102.6	103.0	120.6
工业仓储用房	Industrial Storage buildings	100.8	104.1	99.6	99.7	99.6
工业厂房	Industrial Factory	101.1	105.8	99.4	99.6	99.4
仓库	Storehouse	100.0	100.0	100.0	100.0	100.0
其它	Other	100.9	100.0	100.0	100.0	103.7
物业管理价格总指数	**Property Management Price Indices**	**102.9**	**100.0**	**102.6**	**108.9**	**100.0**
住宅	Residence	103.3	100.0	102.9	110.1	100.0
普通住宅	Common Residence	103.3	100.0	102.9	110.1	100.0
高层住宅	High-grade Building	100.0	100.0			
经济适用房	Economic Housing					
办公楼	Office Buildings					
写字楼	High-grade Office Buildings					
普通办公用房	General Office Buildings					
商业娱乐用房	Business and Enrertaubnebt Buildings	100.0	100.0	100.0	100.0	
工业仓储用房	Industrial Storage Buildings					
#工业厂房	Industrial Factory					
土地交易价格总指数	**Transactions Price Indices of Land**	**101.8**	**100.6**	**102.4**	**101.4**	**102.9**
居住用地	Land for Residential Building Use	101.8	101.1	102.6	100.8	102.8
高档住宅用地	Luxury Residential Building	102.3		102.3		
普通住宅用地	General Residential buildings	101.9	101.1	103.0	100.8	102.8
经济适用房用地	Economically Affordable Housing					
工业仓储用地	Land for Industry Use	101.9	100.0	101.6	102.2	103.8
商业、旅游、娱乐用地	Land for Business Tour and Entertainment	101.6	100.3	102.8	101.7	101.7
其它用地	Land for Other	101.7	101.7			

6-18 续表 14 continued

类 别	Classification	聊城 Liaocheng 全年平均 Annual Average	一季度 The first Quarter	二季度 The Second Quarter	三季度 The Third Quarter	四季度 The Forth Quarter
房屋销售价格总指数	**Selling Price Indices of Houses**	**104.5**	**101.9**	**103.9**	**106.1**	**106.0**
商品房	Commercial Houses	103.5	100.7	102.8	105.3	105.1
住宅	Residence	103.8	100.7	102.9	105.7	106.1
经济适用房	Economic Housing	95.0	94.6	94.9	100.0	91.6
普通住宅	Common Residence	105.1	102.3	104.8	106.1	107.3
多层住宅	Multiayer Buildings	105.3	102.5	105.2	106.2	107.5
高层住宅	High-grade Building	103.3	100.8	101.9	105.1	106.1
其他住宅	Other Buildings					
高档住宅	Luxury Residential Buildings	103.8	101.8	100.0	105.3	105.7
别墅	Villas	103.3	100.0	100.0	105.2	105.4
高档公寓	High-grade Apartment	106.6	102.8		111.3	108.8
非住宅	Non-Residential Buildings	101.2	100.7	102.5	100.0	100.0
办公楼	Office Buildings					
写字楼	High-grade Office Buildings					
普通办公用房	General Office Buildings					
商业娱乐用房	Business and Enrertaubnebt Buildings	101.2	100.7	102.5	100.0	100.0
其它用房	Other Buildings	100.0	100.0			
二手房	Private-owned House	107.3	106.2	106.4	107.8	108.2
住宅	Residence Buildings	107.3	106.2	106.4	107.8	108.2
高层住宅	High-grade Building	108.9	108.2			109.6
多层住宅	Multiayer Buildings	107.3	106.7	105.6	107.8	108.3
其他住宅	Other Buildings	102.2	102.2			
非住宅	Other Buildings					
房屋租赁价格总指数	**Renting Price Indices of Houses**	**100.0**	**100.0**		**100.0**	**100.0**
住宅	Residence	100.0	100.0		100.0	100.0
普通住宅	Common Residence	100.0	100.0		100.0	100.0
高档住宅	Luxury Residential Buildings					
别墅	Villas					
高档公寓	High-grade Apartment					
经济适用房	Economic Housing					
廉租房	Tenement House					
办公楼	Office					
写字楼	High-grade Office Buildings					
普通办公用房	General Office Buildings					
商业娱乐用房	Business and Enrertaubnebt Buildings	100.0	100.0		100.0	100.0
工业仓储用房	Industrial Storage buildings					
工业厂房	Industrial Factory					
仓库	Storehouse					
其它	Other					
物业管理价格总指数	**Property Management Price Indices**	**100.0**	**100.0**	**100.0**	**100.0**	**100.0**
住宅	Residence	100.0	100.0	100.0		
普通住宅	Common Residence	100.0	100.0	100.0		
高层住宅	High-grade Building					
经济适用房	Economic Housing					
办公楼	Office Buildings	100.0	100.0	100.0		
写字楼	High-grade Office Buildings					
普通办公用房	General Office Buildings	100.0	100.0	100.0		
商业娱乐用房	Business and Enrertaubnebt Buildings					
工业仓储用房	Industrial Storage Buildings	100.0	100.0		100.0	100.0
#工业厂房	Industrial Factory	100.0	100.0		100.0	100.0
土地交易价格总指数	**Transactions Price Indices of Land**	**101.7**	**100.6**	**106.1**	**100.0**	**100.0**
居住用地	Land for Residential Building Use	101.5	100.9	104.9	100.0	100.0
高档住宅用地	Luxury Residential Building					
普通住宅用地	General Residential buildings	101.5	100.9	104.9	100.0	100.0
经济适用房用地	Economically Affordable Housing					
工业仓储用地	Land for Industry Use	100.0	100.0	100.0	100.1	
商业、旅游、娱乐用地	Land for Business Tour and Entertainment	107.7		107.7		
其它用地	Land for Other					

6-18 续表 15 continued

类 别	Classification	滨洲 Binzhou 全年平均 Annual Average	一季度 The first Quarter	二季度 The Second Quarter	三季度 The Third Quarter	四季度 The Forth Quarter
房屋销售价格总指数	**Selling Price Indices of Houses**	**104.1**	**103.8**	**104.8**	**104.2**	**103.5**
商品房	Commercial Houses	103.9	103.7	104.8	103.9	103.1
住宅	Residence	103.9	104.6	104.7	103.8	102.7
经济适用房	Economic Housing	101.4	102.2			100.0
普通住宅	Common Residence	104.2	105.3	104.7	103.8	103.1
多层住宅	Multiayer Buildings	104.2	105.3	104.7	103.8	103.1
高层住宅	High-grade Building					
其他住宅	Other Buildings					
高档住宅	Luxury Residential Buildings					
别墅	Villas					
高档公寓	High-grade Apartment					
非住宅	Non-Residential Buildings	103.7	102.4	104.8	104.1	103.6
办公楼	Office Buildings					
写字楼	High-grade Office Buildings					
普通办公用房	General Office Buildings					
商业娱乐用房	Business and Enrertaubnebt Buildings	103.7	102.4	104.8	104.1	103.6
其它用房	Other Buildings					
二手房	Private-owned House	104.7	104.1	105.0	104.9	104.7
住宅	Residence Buildings	104.8	104.1	105.4	104.9	104.7
高层住宅	High-grade Building					
多层住宅	Multiayer Buildings	104.8	104.1	105.4	104.9	104.7
其他住宅	Other Buildings					
非住宅	Other Buildings	103.2		103.2		
房屋租赁价格总指数	**Renting Price Indices of Houses**	**101.4**	**100.3**	**100.6**	**101.8**	**102.8**
住宅	Residence	101.6	100.8	101.8	101.8	101.8
普通住宅	Common Residence	101.4	100.0	101.8	101.8	101.8
高档住宅	Luxury Residential Buildings					
别墅	Villas					
高档公寓	High-grade Apartment					
经济适用房	Economic Housing	101.8	101.8			
廉租房	Tenement House					
办公楼	Office					
写字楼	High-grade Office Buildings					
普通办公用房	General Office Buildings					
商业娱乐用房	Business and Enrertaubnebt Buildings	101.1	100.0	100.0		103.3
工业仓储用房	Industrial Storage buildings	101.4		100.0		102.8
工业厂房	Industrial Factory					
仓库	Storehouse	101.4		100.0		102.8
其它	Other					
物业管理价格总指数	**Property Management Price Indices**	**100.0**	**100.0**	**100.0**	**100.0**	**100.0**
住宅	Residence	100.0	100.0	100.0	100.0	100.0
普通住宅	Common Residence	100.0	100.0	100.0	100.0	100.0
高层住宅	High-grade Building					
经济适用房	Economic Housing					
办公楼	Office Buildings					
写字楼	High-grade Office Buildings					
普通办公用房	General Office Buildings					
商业娱乐用房	Business and Enrertaubnebt Buildings					
工业仓储用房	Industrial Storage Buildings					
#工业厂房	Industrial Factory					
土地交易价格总指数	**Transactions Price Indices of Land**	**104.4**	**103.8**	**102.6**	**105.0**	**106.3**
居住用地	Land for Residential Building Use	106.5	105.4	103.5		110.7
高档住宅用地	Luxury Residential Building					
普通住宅用地	General Residential buildings	106.5	105.4	103.5		110.7
经济适用房用地	Economically Affordable Housing					
工业仓储用地	Land for Industry Use	102.6	102.1	101.6	105.0	101.6
商业、旅游、娱乐用地	Land for Business Tour and Entertainment					
其它用地	Land for Other					

6-18 续表 16 continued

类 别	Classification	菏泽 Heze				
		全年平均 Annual Average	一季度 The first Quarter	二季度 The Second Quarter	三季度 The Third Quarter	四季度 The Forth Quarter
房屋销售价格总指数	**Selling Price Indices of Houses**	**101.6**	**102.0**	**101.3**	**101.2**	**102.1**
商品房	Commercial Houses	101.8	102.1	101.7	101.2	102.3
住宅	Residence	101.8	102.5	101.3	101.0	102.3
经济适用房	Economic Housing					
普通住宅	Common Residence	101.8	102.5	101.3	101.0	102.3
多层住宅	Multiayer Buildings	101.8	102.5	101.3	101.1	102.5
高层住宅	High-grade Building	101.2			100.9	101.4
其他住宅	Other Buildings					
高档住宅	Luxury Residential Buildings	100.0		100.0	100.0	
别墅	Villas	100.0		100.0		
高档公寓	High-grade Apartment	100.0			100.0	
非住宅	Non-Residential Buildings	101.8	101.0	102.6	101.5	102.1
办公楼	Office Buildings	100.7				100.7
写字楼	High-grade Office Buildings					
普通办公用房	General Office Buildings	100.7				100.7
商业娱乐用房	Business and Enrertaubnebt Buildings	101.9	101.0	102.6	101.5	102.4
其它用房	Other Buildings					
二手房	Private-owned House	101.1	101.4	100.2	101.2	101.4
住宅	Residence Buildings	101.1	101.7	100.3	100.9	101.4
高层住宅	High-grade Building					
多层住宅	Multiayer Buildings	101.0	101.7	100.4	101.0	100.8
其他住宅	Other Buildings		101.5	100.1	100.9	102.2
非住宅	Other Buildings	101.1	100.5	100.0	102.3	101.4
房屋租赁价格总指数	**Renting Price Indices of Houses**	**101.5**	**102.2**	**101.5**	**101.5**	**100.9**
住宅	Residence	101.0	104.0	100.0	100.0	100.0
普通住宅	Common Residence	101.0	104.0	100.0	100.0	100.0
高档住宅	Luxury Residential Buildings					
别墅	Villas					
高档公寓	High-grade Apartment					
经济适用房	Economic Housing					
廉租房	Tenement House					
办公楼	Office	100.0	100.0	100.0	100.0	100.0
写字楼	High-grade Office Buildings					
普通办公用房	General Office Buildings	100.0	100.0	100.0	100.0	100.0
商业娱乐用房	Business and Enrertaubnebt Buildings	103.9	102.0	105.0	104.8	103.6
工业仓储用房	Industrial Storage buildings	100.0	100.0			100.0
工业厂房	Industrial Factory					
仓库	Storehouse	100.0	100.0			100.0
其它	Other					
物业管理价格总指数	**Property Management Price Indices**	**101.0**	**100.0**	**100.0**	**101.9**	**101.9**
住宅	Residence	101.5	100.0	100.0	102.9	102.9
普通住宅	Common Residence	102.3	100.0	100.0	104.6	104.6
高层住宅	High-grade Building	100.0		100.0	100.0	100.0
经济适用房	Economic Housing	100.0	100.0	100.0	100.0	100.0
办公楼	Office Buildings	100.0	100.0			
写字楼	High-grade Office Buildings					
普通办公用房	General Office Buildings	100.0	100.0			
商业娱乐用房	Business and Enrertaubnebt Buildings	100.0	100.0	100.0	100.0	100.0
工业仓储用房	Industrial Storage Buildings					
#工业厂房	Industrial Factory					
土地交易价格总指数	**Transactions Price Indices of Land**	**103.2**	**95.9**	**109.7**	**102.4**	**104.8**
居住用地	Land for Residential Building Use	101.9	93.1	111.3	101.0	102.0
高档住宅用地	Luxury Residential Building					
普通住宅用地	General Residential buildings	101.9	93.1	111.3	101.0	102.0
经济适用房用地	Economically Affordable Housing					
工业仓储用地	Land for Industry Use	107.0	101.4		107.0	112.6
商业、旅游、娱乐用地	Land for Business Tour and Entertainment	104.8	101.7	106.1		106.7
其它用地	Land for Other	103.3		103.3		

6-19 农产品生产价格指数（2006年）
Price Index of Farm Products (2006)

类别	Classification	1季度 The First Quarter	上半年 The Firt Half Year	前三季度 The Firt Three Quarters	全年 Annual
农产品生产价格总指数	**General Price Index of Farm Products**	**103.45**	**104.05**	**102.07**	**103.35**
一、农业产品	**Agricultural Products**	**114.93**	**109.99**	**102.73**	**103.18**
（一）谷物及其他作物	Grain and Other Crops	96.13	96.93	97.81	101.12
1、谷物（原粮）	Grain	94.98	95.88	99.77	100.04
#（1）小麦	Wheat	94.73	95.05	96.79	99.02
（2）稻谷	Cice	117.05	107.79	105.93	103.69
（3）玉米	Corn	93.88	96.44	98	100.14
2、薯类	Potato	105.48	107.66	109.55	106.98
3、油料	Oil Bearing Crops	99.07	102.20	101.36	103.83
4、豆类	Beans	76.09	83.55	88.32	91.48
5、棉花（籽棉）	Cotton	112.80	111.28	110.57	101.98
（二）蔬菜、园艺作物	Vegetables and Garden Crop	126.46	113.57	104.61	104.76
#蔬菜	Vegetables	126.70	114.09	104.23	105.29
（三）水果、坚果、饮料和香料	Fruit, Nut ,Drink and Perfume	126.16	115.70	101.1	103.89
#水果、坚果	Fruit, Nut	126.16	115.70	101.1	103.89
（四）中药材	Traditional Chinese Medicine	109.04	0.00	126.35	123.53
二、林业产品	**Forestry Products**	**108.13**	**106.94**	**103.15**	**104.27**
#竹木采运	Bamboo Harvesting	107.80	108.42	105.9	107.23
林产品的采集	Forestry Products Collecting	108.86	104.26	99.41	103.16
三、牧业（畜产品）	**Animal Husbandry Products**	**93.11**	**94.94**	**98.51**	**99.69**
（一）牲畜的饲养	Penkeeping	104.79	103.06	102.25	101.51
#1牛的饲养	Cattle Feeding	104.21	102.75	101.92	100.36
2羊的饲养	Sheep Feeding	108.09	106.69	106.29	106.82
3奶产品	Milk Products	100.25	100.66	98.82	98.75
（二）猪的饲养	Pig Feeding	86.37	91.29	94.08	99.65
（三）家禽	Poultry	94.95	94.58	95.52	98.73
#肉禽（毛重）	Poultry for Eating Meat	98.33	96.17	98.34	99.83
禽蛋	Eggs	91.94	92.93	93.17	97.72
四、渔业	**Fishery Industry**	**103.31**	**108.79**	**108.99**	**111.62**
（一）海水水产品	Seawater Aquatic Product	105.60	110.87	111.2	113.49
#海水鱼类	Seawater Fish	110.50	116.69	116.31	115.53
海水虾蟹类	Seawater Shrimp and Crab	100.00	100.00	100.01	100.98
海水贝类	Seawater Cowry	101.10	110.06	114.6	116.81
（二）内陆水域水产品	Endorheism Aquatic Product	98.66	99.91	100.16	103.23
#淡水鱼类	Freshwater Fish	98.66	99.91	100.16	103.23

消费价格调查资料
Investigation Material of Consumer Price

简要说明

一、目前，山东在流通和消费领域编制的价格指数主要包括居民消费价格指数、商品零售价格指数和农业生产资料价格指数。

二、价格指数统计由国家统计局山东调查总队组织实施，各抽中市县依据国家统计局统一制定的价格统计调查制度向基层采集原始数据汇总后上报。

三、编制居民消费价格、商品零售价格和农业生产资料价格指数采用分层抽样调查方法，即在全省选取不同经济区域以及有代表性的商品作为样本，对市场价格进行经常性的调查，以样本推断总体。目前，全省抽选出调查市、县27个。编制过程分几个步骤：

1．调查市、县和调查点的选择。按照大中小兼顾以及地区分布合理原则，采用划类选择法抽选价格调查市、县。价格调查点的选定是以代表性为原则选择品种齐全、零售额较大的中心市场、农贸市场和服务网点作为价格调查点。

2．代表商品和代表规格品的选择。代表商品是选择那些消费量大、价格变动有代表性的商品，商品集团和服务项目基本上是国家统一规定。代表规格品的确定：一是消费量大；二是价格变动趋势和变动程度有较强的代表性；三是选中的规格品之间，性质相隔要远，价格变动特征的相关性要好；四是选中的工业消费品必须是合格产品，产品包装上有注册商标、产地、规格等级等标识。

3．价格调查方法。采用定点、定时、定人直接到调查点登记调查，同时聘用辅助调查员协助登记调查。对价格变动频繁的每月必须正式调查登记6次，价格比较稳定的每月调查1～2次。

4．权数的确定。居民消费价格指数的计算权数是根据城乡居民家庭消费支出，商品零售价格指数的计算权数是根据全社会商品零售额统计确定的。

Brief Introduction

Ⅰ. At present，Shandong price index in the circulation and the consume domain mainly includes the inhabitant consume price index，the commodity retail price index and the agricultural means of production price index.

Ⅱ. The price index statistics is organized by NBC Survey Office in Shandong, the city(county) that were pulled out gathers primary data after the basic unit and reports based on the price statistics investigation system compiled by NBC.

Ⅲ. Establishes of the inhabitant consumer price index, the commodity retail price index and the agricultural means of production price index use the stratified sampling investigation method, namely as well as select different economic region to take the typical commodity as sample in the entire province, carry on the regular investigation to the market price, deduce overall by sample inference. At present, 27 cities (counties) are the investigation samples in the entire province. The establishment process is divided several steps:

1. Choice of investigation city, county and investigation spot. According to proper attention of the major medium and small both as well as the local distribution reasonable principle, use a kind of trial-and-error method to sample the price investigation city (county). The price investigation spot designation is selecting market centre, the agricultural market fair and servicing point whose commodity are complete and whose retail turnover is big by representation as principle.

2. Choice of typical commodity and represents commodity. Choice of typical commodity is chooses these commodity whose consumption quantities is big and whose price changing is representative, the commodity group and the service project basically are the national unification stipulation. Determination of typical represents commodity: One, the consumption quantity is big; Two, the price changing tendency and the change degree have the strong representation; Three, Select of typical represents commodity, the distance of quality must be far, the characteristic relevance of price changing must be friend with; Four, the selected industry consumable commodity must be the certified product, There are registered trademark, place of production, habitat, specification and rank on the product packing.

3. Price investigation method. Decide the people directly to the investigation spot register and investigate by the fixed point, fixed time and fixed people, simultaneously hire the assists investigator to assist to register and investigate. Must register and investigate 6 times each month officially to commodity whose price changing is frequent, Must register and investigate 1-2 time each month to commodity whose price is quite stable.

4. Weight determination. The computation weight of the inhabitant consume price index is determined according to the city and countryside inhabitant family consume disbursement, computation weight of the commodity retail price index is determined according to the entire society retail commodity turnover.

7-1 1991～2006年全省居民消费和商品零售价格指数
Consumer Price Index and Retail Price Index (1991～2006)

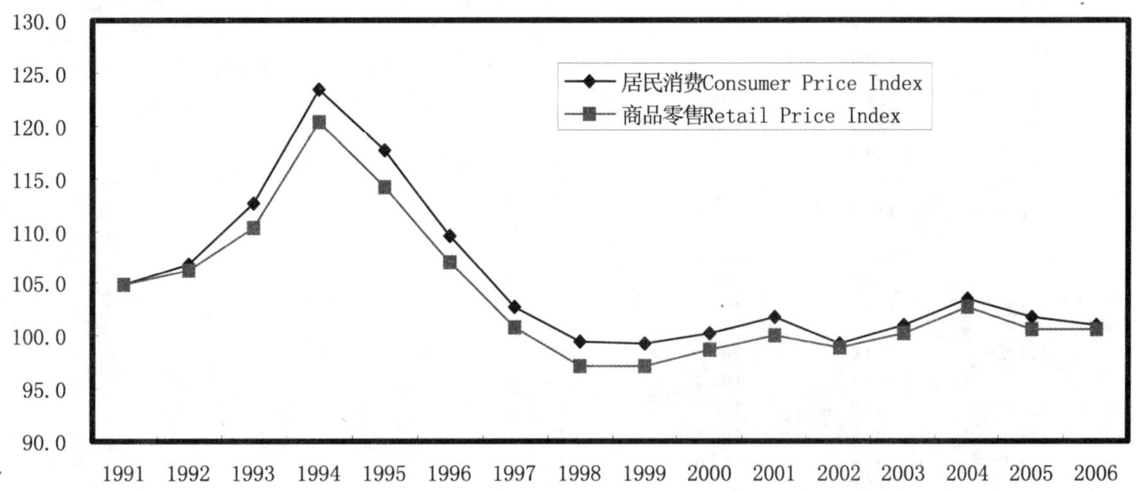

7-2 2006年1～12月全省居民消费和商品零售价格指数
（以上年同期价格为100）
Consumer Price Index and Retail Price Index(1～12,2006)
preceding year=100

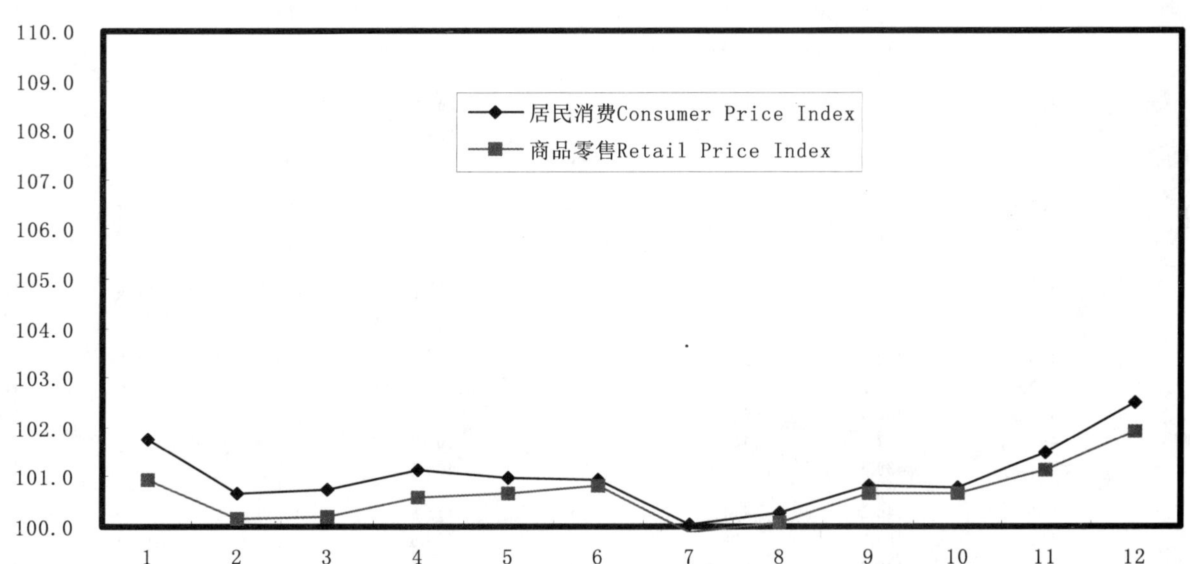

7-3 历年全省居民消费价格总指数
Entire Province Consumer Price Indices from 1953 to 2006

年份 Year	以1950年为100 1950=100	以1952年为100 1952=100	以1957年为100 1957=100	以1965年为100 1965=100	以1970年为100 1970=100	以1978年为100 1978=100	以1990年为100 1990=100	以上年为100 Preceding Year=100
1953	116.9	103.3						103.3
1954	120.9	106.8						103.4
1955	120.8	106.7						99.9
1956	121.7	107.5						100.7
1957	122.9	108.6						101.0
1958	122.4	108.2	99.6					99.6
1959	123.1	108.9	100.2					100.6
1960	123.7	109.4	100.7					100.5
1961	131.5	116.3	107.0					106.3
1962	132.2	116.9	107.6					100.5
1963	130.5	115.4	106.2					98.7
1964	127.6	112.9	103.9					97.8
1965	124.8	110.4	101.6					97.8
1966	123.2	109.0	100.3	98.7				98.7
1967	123.3	109.1	100.4	98.8				100.1
1968	123.1	108.9	100.2	98.6				99.8
1969	123.0	108.8	100.1	98.5				99.9
1970	121.7	107.6	99.0	97.4				98.9
1971	121.6	107.5	98.9	97.3	99.9			99.9
1972	121.6	107.5	98.9	93.3	99.9			100.0
1973	121.4	107.3	98.7	97.1	99.7			99.8
1974	121.3	107.2	98.6	97.0	99.6			99.9
1975	121.5	107.4	98.8	97.2	99.8			100.2
1976	121.7	107.6	99.0	97.4	100.0			100.2
1977	121.5	107.4	98.8	97.2	99.8			99.8
1978	121.9	107.7	99.1	97.5	100.1			100.3
1979	122.8	108.5	99.7	98.2	100.8	100.7		100.7
1980	128.9	113.9	104.7	103.1	105.8	105.7		105.0
1981	131.2	116.0	106.6	105.0	107.7	107.6		101.8
1982	132.4	117.0	107.6	106.0	108.7	108.6		100.9
1983	135.6	119.8	110.2	108.5	111.3	111.2		102.4
1984	137.6	121.6	111.8	110.1	113.0	112.9		101.5
1985	149.6	132.2	121.5	119.7	122.8	122.7		108.7
1986	156.3	138.1	127.0	125.1	128.3	128.2		104.5
1987	169.1	149.5	137.4	135.4	138.8	138.7		108.2
1988	200.7	177.4	163.1	160.7	164.8	164.7		118.7
1989	235.5	208.1	191.3	188.5	193.3	199.1		117.3
1990	243.5	215.2	197.9	194.9	199.9	199.7		103.4
1991	255.4	225.7	207.5	204.4	209.7	209.5	104.9	104.9
1992	272.8	241.1	221.7	218.3	223.9	223.7	112.0	106.8
1993	307.4	271.7	249.8	246.0	252.4	252.2	126.3	112.7
1994	379.4	335.3	308.3	303.6	311.5	311.2	155.8	123.4
1995	446.1	394.3	362.5	357.1	366.3	365.9	183.2	117.6
1996	489.0	432.1	397.3	391.3	401.4	401.1	200.8	109.6
1997	502.6	443.2	408.4	402.3	412.8	412.3	206.4	102.8
1998	499.6	440.5	405.9	399.9	410.3	409.8	205.2	99.4
1999	496.1	437.4	403.1	397.1	407.4	406.9	203.8	99.3
2000	497.1	438.3	403.9	397.9	408.2	407.7	204.2	100.2
2001	506.0	446.2	411.2	405.1	415.5	415.0	207.9	101.8
2002	502.5	443.1	408.3	402.3	412.6	412.1	206.4	99.3
2003	508.0	448.0	412.8	406.7	417.1	416.6	208.7	101.1
2004	526.3	464.1	427.7	421.3	432.1	431.6	216.2	103.6
2005	535.2	472.0	434.9	428.5	439.5	439.0	219.9	101.7
2006	540.6	476.7	439.3	432.8	443.9	443.4	222.1	101.0

7-4 历年城市居民消费价格总指数
Urban Consumer Price Indices from 1953 to 2006

年份 Year	以1930～1936年平均价格为100 Average Price from 1930 to 1936=100	以1950年为100 1950=100	以1952年为100 1952=100	以1957年为100 1957=100	以1965年为100 1965=100	以1970年为100 1970=100	以1978年为100 1978=100	以1990年为100 1990=100	以上年为100 Preceding Year=100
1953	312.2	103.3							103.3
1954	322.8	106.8							103.4
1955	322.5	106.7							99.9
1956	324.8	107.4							100.7
1957	328.0	108.5							101.0
1958	326.7	108.1	99.6						99.6
1959	328.7	108.7	100.2						100.6
1960	330.3	109.2	100.7						100.5
1961	351.2	116.2	107.0						106.3
1962	352.9	116.8	107.6						100.5
1963	348.3	115.2	106.2						98.7
1964	341.0	112.8	104.0						97.8
1965	333.5	110.3	101.7						97.8
1966	329.2	108.9	100.4	98.7					98.7
1967	329.5	109.0	100.5	98.8					100.1
1968	328.8	108.8	100.3	98.6					99.8
1969	328.5	108.7	100.2	98.5					99.9
1970	324.9	107.4	99.1	97.4					98.9
1971	324.6	107.4	99.0	97.3	99.9				99.9
1972	324.6	107.4	99.0	97.3	99.9				100.0
1973	323.9	107.2	98.8	97.1	99.7				99.8
1974	323.6	107.1	99.7	97.0	99.6				99.9
1975	324.2	107.3	99.9	97.2	99.8				100.2
1976	324.9	107.5	100.1	97.4	100.0				100.2
1977	324.3	107.3	99.9	97.2	99.8				99.8
1978	325.2	107.6	100.2	97.5	100.1				100.3
1979	329.7	109.1	101.6	98.9	101.5	101.4			101.4
1980	339.3	112.3	104.5	101.7	104.4	104.3			102.9
1981	346.4	114.6	106.7	103.9	106.6	106.5	102.1		102.1
1982	347.4	115.0	107.0	104.2	107.0	106.9	102.4		100.3
1983	345.3	114.3	106.4	103.6	106.3	106.2	101.8		99.4
1984	350.5	116.0	108.0	105.1	107.9	107.8	103.3		101.5
1985	381.4	126.2	117.5	114.4	117.4	117.3	112.4		108.8
1986	400.5	132.5	123.3	120.1	123.3	123.2	118.0		105.0
1987	436.9	144.6	134.6	131.0	134.5	134.4	128.8		109.1
1988	526.9	174.4	162.3	158.0	162.2	162.1	155.3		120.6
1989	609.6	201.7	187.8	182.8	187.7	187.5	179.7		115.7
1990	625.5	207.0	192.7	187.5	192.5	192.4	184.4		102.6
1991	664.3	219.8	224.6	199.2	204.5	204.3	195.8	106.2	106.2
1992	721.4	238.7	222.2	216.3	222.1	221.9	212.6	115.3	108.6
1993	826.7	273.6	254.7	247.9	254.5	254.3	243.7	132.1	114.6
1994	1036.7	343.1	319.4	310.8	319.1	318.9	305.6	165.7	125.4
1995	1210.9	400.7	373.0	363.1	392.7	372.5	356.9	193.6	116.8
1996	1338.0	442.8	412.2	401.2	411.9	411.6	394.4	213.9	110.5
1997	1380.8	457.0	425.4	414.0	425.1	424.8	407.0	220.7	103.2
1998	1376.7	455.6	424.1	412.8	423.8	423.5	405.8	220.0	99.7
1999	1376.7	455.6	424.1	412.8	423.8	423.5	405.8	220.0	100.0
2000	1393.2	461.1	429.2	417.8	428.9	428.6	410.7	222.6	101.2
2001	1408.5	466.2	433.9	422.4	433.6	433.3	415.2	225.0	101.1
2002	1390.2	460.1	428.3	416.9	428.0	427.7	409.8	222.1	98.7
2003	1399.9	463.3	431.3	419.8	431.0	430.7	412.7	223.7	100.7
2004	1439.1	476.3	443.3	431.6	443.0	442.7	424.2	230.0	102.8
2005	1454.9	481.5	448.2	436.3	447.9	447.6	428.9	232.5	101.1
2006	1469.5	486.3	452.7	440.7	452.4	452.1	433.2	234.8	101.0

7-5 历年农村居民消费价格总指数
Rural Consumer Price Indices from 1978 to 2006

年份 Year	以1978年为100 1978=100	以1980年为100 1980=100	以1985年为100 1985=100	以1990年为100 1990=100	以1995年为100 1995=100	以上年为100 Preceding Year=100
1978						100.3
1979	100.4					100.4
1980	106.2					105.8
1981	107.9	101.6				101.6
1982	109.1	102.7				101.1
1983	113.0	106.4				103.6
1984	114.7	108.0				101.5
1985	124.7	117.4				108.7
1986	129.8	122.2	104.1			104.1
1987	139.4	131.2	111.8			107.4
1988	163.1	153.5	130.8			117.0
1989	194.0	182.5	155.5			118.9
1990	201.7	189.8	161.7			104.0
1991	209.8	197.4	168.2	104.0		104.0
1992	219.5	206.5	175.9	108.8		104.6
1993	242.9	228.6	194.7	120.4		110.7
1994	295.7	278.2	236.9	146.5		121.7
1995	348.6	328.0	279.3	172.7		117.9
1996	379.9	357.5	304.4	188.2	109.0	109.0
1997	389.1	366.1	311.7	192.7	111.6	102.4
1998	385.2	362.4	308.6	190.8	110.5	99.0
1999	379.8	357.3	304.3	188.1	109.0	98.6
2000	377.1	354.8	302.2	186.8	108.2	99.3
2001	386.2	363.3	309.5	191.3	110.8	102.4
2002	385.8	362.9	309.2	191.1	110.7	99.9
2003	391.6	368.3	313.8	194.0	112.4	101.5
2004	409.6	385.2	328.2	202.9	117.5	104.6
2005	419.4	394.5	336.1	207.8	120.3	102.4
2006	423.6	398.4	339.5	209.9	121.6	101.0

7-6 历年全省商品零售价格总指数
Entire Province Retail Price Index from 1953 to 2006

年份 Year	1930～1936年平均价格为100 Average Price from 1930 to 1936=100	以1952年为100 1952=100	以1957年为100 1957=100	以1965年为100 1965=100	以1970年为100 1970=100	以1978年为100 1978=100	以1980年为100 1980=100	以1990年为100 1990=100	以上年为100 Preceding Year=100
1953	315.2	103.8							103.8
1954	325.0	107.0							103.1
1955	325.6	107.2							100.2
1956	327.9	108.0							100.7
1957	333.5	109.8							101.7
1958	333.8	109.9	100.1						100.1
1959	337.1	111.0	101.1						101.0
1960	338.8	111.6	101.6						100.5
1961	358.4	118.1	107.4						105.8
1962	359.9	118.5	107.9						100.4
1963	362.7	119.5	108.8						100.8
1964	358.0	117.9	107.3						98.7
1965	349.4	115.1	104.8						97.6
1966	347.7	114.5	103.7	99.5					99.5
1967	348.0	114.7	103.8	99.6					100.1
1968	348.0	114.7	103.8	99.6					100.0
1969	346.6	114.2	103.4	99.2					99.6
1970	343.8	113.3	102.6	98.4					99.2
1971	343.5	113.2	102.5	98.3	99.9				99.9
1972	342.5	112.8	102.2	98.0	99.6				99.7
1973	342.2	112.7	102.1	97.9	99.5				99.9
1974	341.8	112.6	101.2	97.8	99.4				99.9
1975	342.2	112.7	102.1	97.9	99.5				100.1
1976	342.5	112.8	102.2	98.0	99.6				100.1
1977	342.2	112.7	102.1	97.9	99.5				99.9
1978	343.5	113.2	102.5	98.3	99.9				100.4
1979	349.0	115.0	104.1	99.9	101.5	101.6			101.6
1980	359.5	118.5	107.2	102.9	104.5	104.6			103.0
1981	365.6	120.5	109.0	104.6	106.3	106.4	101.7		101.7
1982	367.8	121.2	109.7	105.2	106.9	107.1	102.3		100.6
1983	363.0	119.7	108.3	103.9	105.6	105.6	101.0		98.7
1984	367.0	121.0	109.5	105.1	106.7	106.8	102.1		101.1
1985	398.2	131.3	118.8	114.0	115.8	115.9	110.8		108.5
1986	416.1	137.2	124.1	119.1	121.0	121.1	115.8		104.5
1987	450.6	148.6	134.4	129.0	131.0	131.2	125.4		108.3
1988	536.3	176.8	160.0	153.5	155.9	156.1	149.2		119.0
1989	626.9	206.7	187.0	179.5	182.3	182.5	174.4		116.9
1990	636.9	210.0	190.0	181.4	185.2	185.4	177.2		101.6
1991	668.1	220.3	199.3	190.2	194.3	194.5	185.9	104.9	104.9
1992	709.5	233.9	211.7	202.0	206.3	206.6	197.4	111.4	106.2
1993	782.6	258.0	233.5	222.8	227.6	227.8	217.7	122.9	110.3
1994	941.5	310.4	280.9	268.1	273.8	274.1	261.9	147.8	120.3
1995	1075.2	354.5	320.7	306.2	312.6	313.0	299.1	168.8	114.2
1996	1150.6	378.9	345.1	329.3	334.6	334.9	320.1	180.6	107.0
1997	159.8	381.9	347.9	331.9	337.3	337.6	322.7	182.0	100.8
1998	1126.2	370.8	337.8	322.3	327.5	327.8	313.3	176.7	97.1
1999	1093.5	360.0	328.0	313.0	318.0	318.3	304.2	171.6	97.1
2000	1078.2	355.0	323.4	308.6	313.5	313.8	299.9	169.2	98.6
2001	1078.2	355.0	323.4	308.6	313.5	313.8	299.9	169.2	100.0
2002	1065.3	350.7	319.5	304.9	309.7	310.0	296.3	167.2	98.8
2003	1067.4	351.4	320.2	305.5	310.4	310.7	296.9	167.5	100.2
2004	1097.3	361.3	329.1	314.1	319.0	319.4	305.2	172.2	102.8
2005	1103.9	363.4	331.1	315.9	321.0	321.3	307.0	173.2	100.6
2006	1110.5	365.6	333.1	317.8	322.9	323.2	308.9	174.3	100.6

注：本表已根据先行价格调查统计制度予以调整，均不包括农业生产资料部分。

Notice:This Table Has Acted to Adjust According to the Advance Price Investigation Statistical System, Not Including Agricultural Means of Production Part。

7-7 历年城市商品零售价格总指数
Urban Retail Price Index from 1953 to 2006

年份 Year	以1950年为100 1950=100	以1952年为100 1952=100	以1957年为100 1957=100	以1965年为100 1965=100	以1970年为100 1970=100	以1978年为100 1978=100	以1990年为100 1990=100	以上年为100 Preceding Year=100
1953	114.9	103.7						103.7
1954	119.3	107.6						103.8
1955	118.8	107.2						99.6
1956	120.0	108.3						101.0
1957	121.7	109.8						101.4
1958	121.0	109.1	99.4					99.4
1959	121.7	109.8	100.0					100.6
1960	122.4	110.5	100.6					100.6
1961	129.6	117.0	106.5					105.9
1962	130.2	117.6	107.0					100.5
1963	129.5	117.0	106.5					99.5
1964	130.7	114.6	104.4					98.0
1965	128.1	112.3	102.3					98.0
1966	126.4	110.9	101.0	98.7				98.7
1967	126.4	110.9	101.0	98.7				100.0
1968	126.1	110.7	100.8	98.5				99.8
1969	126.0	110.5	100.7	98.4				99.9
1970	124.6	109.3	99.6	97.3				98.9
1971	124.6	109.3	99.6	97.3	100.0			100.0
1972	124.6	109.3	99.6	97.3	100.0			100.0
1973	124.5	109.2	99.5	97.2	99.9			99.9
1974	124.4	109.1	99.4	97.1	99.8			99.9
1975	124.6	109.3	99.6	97.3	100.0			100.2
1976	124.8	109.5	99.8	97.5	100.2			100.2
1977	124.6	109.3	99.6	97.3	100.0			99.8
1978	125.0	109.7	99.9	97.6	100.3			100.3
1979	126.8	111.2	101.3	99.0	101.7	101.4		101.4
1980	130.7	114.6	104.4	102.1	104.9	104.5		103.1
1981	133.6	117.2	106.7	104.3	107.2	106.8		102.2
1982	134.0	117.5	107.0	104.6	107.5	107.1		100.3
1983	133.1	116.7	106.3	103.9	106.7	106.4		99.3
1984	134.7	118.1	107.6	105.1	108.0	107.7		101.2
1985	146.7	128.6	117.2	114.5	117.6	117.3		108.9
1986	153.9	134.9	122.9	120.1	123.4	123.0		104.9
1987	168.4	147.6	134.5	131.4	135.0	134.6		109.4
1988	204.1	178.9	146.9	159.3	163.6	163.1		121.2
1989	235.1	206.1	169.2	183.5	188.5	187.9		115.2
1990	238.9	209.3	171.9	186.4	191.5	190.9		101.6
1991	253.5	222.1	182.4	197.8	203.2	202.5	106.1	106.1
1992	274.0	240.1	197.2	213.8	219.7	218.9	114.7	108.1
1993	307.7	269.6	221.5	240.1	246.7	245.8	128.8	112.3
1994	371.1	325.2	267.1	289.6	297.5	296.4	155.3	120.6
1995	420.1	368.1	302.4	327.8	336.8	335.5	175.8	113.2
1996	448.2	392.8	322.7	349.8	359.4	358.0	187.6	106.7
1997	451.8	395.9	325.3	352.6	362.3	360.9	189.1	100.8
1998	438.7	384.4	315.9	342.4	351.8	350.4	183.6	97.1
1999	426.0	373.3	306.7	332.5	341.6	340.2	178.3	97.1
2000	420.9	368.8	303.0	328.5	337.5	336.1	176.2	98.8
2001	418.8	367.0	301.5	326.9	335.8	334.4	175.3	99.5
2002	412.5	361.5	297.0	322.0	330.8	329.4	172.7	98.5
2003	410.9	360.0	295.8	320.7	329.4	328.1	172.0	99.6
2004	420.3	368.3	302.6	328.1	337.0	335.6	175.9	102.3
2005	422.0	369.8	303.8	329.4	338.4	337.0	176.6	100.4
2006	424.1	371.7	305.3	331.0	340.1	338.6	177.5	100.5

7-8 历年农村商品零售价格总指数
Rural Retail Price Index from 1953 to 2006

年份 Year	以1950年为100 1950=100	以1952年为100 1952=100	以1957年为100 1957=100	以1965年为100 1965=100	以1970年为100 1970=100	以1978年为100 1978=100	以1990年为100 1990=100	以上年为100 Preceding Year=100
1953	103.9							103.9
1954	106.4							102.4
1955	106.6							100.2
1956	107.1							100.5
1957	109.1							101.9
1958	109.2	100.1						100.1
1959	110.7	101.5						101.4
1960	111.1	101.9						100.4
1961	116.1	106.5						104.5
1962	116.4	106.8						100.3
1963	118.3	108.5						101.6
1964	116.9	107.2						98.8
1965	114.1	104.6						97.6
1966	113.6	104.2	99.6					99.6
1967	113.7	104.3	99.7					100.1
1968	113.7	104.3	99.7					100.0
1969	113.1	103.7	99.1					99.4
1970	112.4	103.1	98.5					99.4
1971	112.3	103.0	98.4	99.9				99.9
1972	111.9	102.6	98.0	99.5				99.6
1973	111.8	102.5	97.9	99.4				99.9
1974	111.7	102.4	97.8	99.3				99.9
1975	111.7	102.4	97.8	99.3				100.0
1976	111.7	102.4	97.8	99.3				100.0
1977	111.7	102.4	97.8	99.3				100.0
1978	112.1	102.8	98.2	99.7				100.4
1979	114.0	104.5	99.9	101.4	101.7			101.7
1980	117.3	107.5	102.8	104.3	104.6			102.9
1981	118.7	108.8	104.0	105.6	105.9			101.2
1982	119.6	109.7	104.8	106.4	106.7			100.8
1983	117.8	108.1	103.2	104.8	105.1			98.5
1984	119.1	109.3	104.3	106.0	106.3			101.1
1985	129.0	118.4	113.0	114.8	115.1			108.3
1986	134.5	123.5	117.9	119.7	120.0			104.3
1987	144.5	132.6	126.6	128.6	128.9			107.4
1988	169.4	155.4	148.4	150.7	151.1			117.2
1989	200.7	184.1	175.9	178.6	179.1			118.5
1990	203.9	187.0	178.7	181.5	181.9			101.6
1991	212.3	194.7	186.0	188.9	189.4	104.1		104.1
1992	220.4	202.1	193.1	196.1	196.6	108.1		103.8
1993	238.7	218.9	209.1	212.4	212.9	117.1		108.3
1994	286.4	262.7	250.9	254.9	255.5	140.5		120.0
1995	332.8	305.3	291.5	296.2	296.9	163.3		116.2
1996	357.4	327.9	313.1	318.1	318.9	175.4	107.4	107.4
1997	359.9	330.2	315.3	320.3	321.1	176.6	108.2	100.7
1998	349.8	321.0	306.5	311.3	312.1	171.7	105.2	97.2
1999	340.0	311.7	297.6	302.3	303.0	166.7	102.1	97.1
2000	334.2	306.4	292.5	297.2	297.8	163.9	100.4	98.3
2001	336.5	308.5	294.5	299.3	299.9	165.0	101.1	100.7
2002	335.5	307.6	293.6	298.4	299.0	164.5	100.8	99.7
2003	338.8	310.7	296.6	301.4	302.0	166.2	101.8	101.0
2004	351.4	322.1	307.5	312.5	313.2	172.3	105.6	103.7
2005	355.6	326.0	311.2	316.3	316.9	174.4	106.8	101.2
2006	358.8	328.9	314.0	319.1	319.8	175.9	107.8	100.9

7-9 历年全省农业生产资料价格总指数
Entire Province Price Indices of Means of Agricultural Production from 1953 to 2006

年份 Year	以1950年为100 1950=100	以1952年为100 1952=100	以1957年为100 1957=100	以1965年为100 1965=100	以1970年为100 1970=100	以1978年为100 1978=100	以1990年为100 1990=100	以上年为100 Preceding Year=100
1953	99.5	102.6						102.6
1954	110.3	113.7						110.8
1955	103.8	107.0						94.1
1956	103.7	107.0						100.0
1957	103.4	106.7						99.7
1958	100.2	103.4	96.9					96.9
1959	100.0	103.2	96.7					99.8
1960	100.9	104.1	97.6					100.9
1961	107.5	110.9	103.9					106.5
1962	106.8	110.1	103.2					99.3
1963	100.4	103.5	97.0					94.0
1964	95.8	98.7	92.5					95.4
1965	92.7	95.5	89.5					96.8
1966	90.8	93.5	87.6	97.9				97.9
1967	85.6	88.2	82.6	92.3				94.3
1968	85.1	87.7	82.1	91.7				99.4
1969	84.3	86.9	81.4	90.9				99.1
1970	84.2	86.8	81.3	90.8				99.9
1971	80.9	83.4	78.1	87.3	96.1			96.1
1972	80.3	82.7	77.5	86.6	95.3			99.2
1973	79.9	82.2	77.1	86.1	94.8			99.5
1974	79.2	81.6	76.4	85.3	94.0			99.1
1975	79.2	81.6	76.4	85.3	94.0			100.0
1976	79.2	81.6	76.4	85.3	94.0			100.0
1977	79.2	81.6	76.4	85.3	94.0			100.0
1978	78.5	80.9	75.7	84.3	93.2			99.1
1979	78.6	81.0	75.8	84.4	93.3	100.1		100.1
1980	78.6	81.0	75.8	84.4	93.3	100.1		100.0
1981	79.9	82.4	77.1	85.8	94.9	101.8		101.7
1982	80.8	83.3	77.9	86.7	95.9	102.9		101.1
1983	82.9	85.5	79.9	89.0	98.4	105.6		102.6
1984	88.9	91.7	85.7	95.4	105.5	113.2		107.2
1985	92.5	95.5	89.2	99.3	109.8	117.8		104.1
1986	94.4	97.5	91.1	101.4	112.1	120.3		102.1
1987	99.9	103.2	96.4	107.3	118.6	127.3		105.8
1988	114.6	118.4	110.6	123.1	136.0	146.0		114.7
1989	135.5	139.9	130.7	145.5	160.8	172.6		118.2
1990	139.8	144.4	134.9	150.2	165.9	178.1		103.2
1991	142.6	147.3	137.6	153.2	169.2	181.7	102.0	102.0
1992	144.6	149.4	139.5	155.3	171.6	184.2	103.4	101.4
1993	161.4	166.7	155.7	173.3	191.5	205.6	115.4	111.6
1994	200.3	206.9	193.2	215.1	237.7	255.1	143.2	124.1
1995	267.0	275.8	257.5	286.7	316.9	340.1	190.9	133.3
1996	281.7	291.0	271.7	302.5	334.3	358.8	201.4	105.5
1997	272.1	281.1	262.5	292.2	322.9	346.6	194.6	96.6
1998	261.8	270.4	252.5	281.1	310.6	336.5	187.2	96.2
1999	249.0	257.2	240.1	267.3	295.4	320.0	178.0	95.1
2000	245.8	253.9	237.0	263.8	291.6	315.8	175.7	98.7
2001	250.2	258.5	241.3	268.5	296.8	321.5	178.9	101.8
2002	251.0	259.3	242.0	269.3	297.7	322.5	179.4	100.3
2003	257.0	265.5	247.8	275.8	304.8	330.2	183.7	102.4
2004	283.2	292.6	273.1	303.9	335.9	363.9	202.5	110.2
2005	300.7	310.7	290.0	322.7	356.8	386.4	215.0	106.2
2006	309.8	320.0	298.7	332.4	367.5	398.0	221.5	103.0

7-10 全省居民消费价格（定基）指数
Entire Province Consumer Price Indices

（以2005年平均价格为100）

商品类别及品名	Commodity Category and Commodity Name	1月 January	2月 February	3月 March	4月 April	5月 May	6月 June	7月 July	8月 August	9月 September	10月 October	11月 November	12月 December
居民消费价格总指数	**General Consumer Price Index**	**101.8**	**101.8**	**101.1**	**101.2**	**100.9**	**100.1**	**99.7**	**100.2**	**100.8**	**100.5**	**101.1**	**102.8**
非食品价格指数	**No-food**	**100.4**	**100.2**	**100.1**	**100.3**	**100.3**	**100.4**	**100.5**	**100.5**	**100.6**	**100.8**	**101.0**	**101.2**
服务项目价格指数	**Services**	**100.9**	**100.9**	**100.9**	**101.4**	**101.6**	**101.5**	**101.9**	**102.2**	**102.3**	**102.4**	**102.4**	**102.6**
工业品价格指数	**Industrial Products**	**100.2**	**100.0**	**99.8**	**99.9**	**99.9**	**100.0**	**100.0**	**100.0**	**100.1**	**100.3**	**100.5**	**100.6**
扣除食品和能源价格指数	**Deducting Foods and Energy**	**100.2**	**100.0**	**99.9**	**100.1**	**100.1**	**100.2**	**100.2**	**100.3**	**100.3**	**100.5**	**100.7**	**100.8**
扣除鲜菜鲜果总指数	**Deducting Fresh, Vegetables and Fruits**	**100.1**	**99.9**	**99.5**	**99.5**	**99.6**	**99.7**	**100.0**	**100.6**	**100.9**	**101.0**	**101.6**	**102.5**
消费品价格指数	**Consumer**	**102.0**	**102.0**	**101.2**	**101.2**	**100.7**	**99.8**	**99.3**	**99.7**	**100.5**	**100.1**	**100.9**	**102.8**
一、食品	**Food**	**105.1**	**105.5**	**103.5**	**103.6**	**102.2**	**99.5**	**98.0**	**99.3**	**101.2**	**99.8**	**101.5**	**106.6**
1.粮食	Grain	99.9	100.2	100.2	100.4	100.9	101.1	102.2	103.0	103.9	104.5	107.5	110.0
大米	Rice	102.7	102.5	102.7	103.3	105.2	106.5	109.6	112.8	113.8	114.7	114.2	116.3
面粉	Flour	97.2	97.8	97.6	97.6	97.3	96.6	97.3	96.2	97.0	97.6	104.5	107.9
粮食制品	Grain Products	99.7	100.0	100.1	100.3	100.4	100.4	100.6	101.3	101.4	101.6	104.3	106.1
其他	Others	103.3	103.2	103.0	103.4	103.7	104.4	105.2	105.3	109.6	111.8	111.4	113.6
2.淀粉	Starches	100.3	99.5	99.7	100.3	100.5	100.8	102.3	103.6	104.4	104.5	104.4	107.3
淀粉	Starches	100.3	99.5	99.7	100.3	100.5	100.8	102.3	103.6	104.4	104.5	104.4	107.3
3.干豆类及豆制品	Beans and Beans Products	99.3	99.7	98.8	98.9	99.3	99.8	100.9	101.1	100.7	100.3	100.2	100.9
干豆	Beans	97.3	98.8	98.8	99.8	101.0	103.2	106.2	106.6	104.6	102.8	102.0	103.1
豆制品	Beans Products	100.0	100.0	98.7	98.5	98.6	98.5	98.8	98.9	99.2	99.4	99.5	100.0
4.油脂	Oil and Fat	97.5	97.6	97.0	96.8	97.5	97.6	97.8	98.7	99.3	100.0	104.2	109.8
食用植物油	Edible Vegetable Oil	97.8	98.2	97.8	97.7	98.0	98.1	98.3	99.3	100.2	100.7	104.7	110.1
植物油制品	Plant Oil Products	98.9	98.7	98.7	98.5	103.1	103.0	102.6	102.8	103.0	103.0	106.0	114.2
其他	Others	89.4	85.7	81.1	79.0	77.9	79.4	80.4	80.7	77.7	82.6	91.3	94.3
5.肉禽及其制品	Meal,Poultry and Their Products	96.4	96.1	92.9	90.4	88.9	89.4	92.0	96.5	98.3	98.6	102.4	108.3
（1）食用畜肉及副产品	Edible Livestock Meat and Their By-products	97.3	96.3	91.7	87.3	85.4	86.3	89.2	94.8	97.2	97.7	103.2	110.9
猪肉	Pork	94.5	92.7	86.9	81.0	78.7	79.9	84.1	91.6	94.6	95.0	101.9	111.1
牛肉	Beef	105.3	106.1	104.8	104.8	103.5	103.8	104.1	103.8	104.5	105.1	106.9	110.3
羊肉	Mutton	107.1	107.8	105.8	105.9	106.2	105.9	105.8	106.7	107.7	109.5	111.1	116.3
畜肉副产品	Livestock Meat By-products	97.7	98.6	95.1	91.4	89.0	90.9	91.2	93.5	96.0	96.4	100.3	107.0
其他	Others	100.6	99.9	97.6	94.6	93.7	92.9	94.1	99.2	100.5	101.1	104.2	107.6
（2）禽	Poultry	90.3	92.1	91.6	93.3	92.3	92.7	96.8	100.9	101.8	101.6	102.0	105.2
鸡	Chicken	89.1	91.5	91.3	93.4	92.5	93.3	98.4	102.5	103.9	103.5	103.5	106.7
鸭	Duck	95.0	93.6	93.6	94.0	94.1	91.5	88.9	92.1	91.0	91.5	94.7	97.5
其他	Others	93.1	94.2	91.8	92.4	90.5	90.9	93.4	98.2	98.0	98.3	98.8	102.0
（3）加工肉禽	Meal and Poultry processing products	98.6	98.8	98.2	98.9	98.1	97.3	97.4	98.5	98.8	98.7	100.2	102.0
畜肉制品	Livestock Meat Products	99.3	99.5	99.4	98.9	98.3	97.9	98.3	99.4	99.6	99.8	100.8	102.4
禽制品	Poultry Products	97.5	97.9	96.5	98.9	97.9	96.6	96.1	97.3	97.7	97.2	99.3	101.4

7-10 续表 1 continued

商品类别及品名	Commodity Category and Commodity Name	1月 January	2月 February	3月 March	4月 April	5月 May	6月 June	7月 July	8月 August	9月 September	10月 October	11月 November	12月 December
		（以2005年平均价格为100）											
6.蛋	Eggs	93.9	89.2	86.7	86.6	88.2	89.0	90.3	98.9	105.0	104.5	105.9	110.3
鲜蛋	Fresh Eggs	92.9	87.8	85.1	85.1	86.8	87.5	89.0	98.5	105.3	104.6	106.0	110.7
蛋制品	Egg Products	102.2	101.2	100.8	100.4	101.0	102.0	101.7	102.1	102.8	103.8	104.9	106.9
7.水产品	Aquatic Product	102.5	104.1	102.8	103.2	103.1	104.0	105.4	105.2	102.5	102.8	102.7	102.4
（1）鱼	Fish	99.6	99.7	97.9	98.4	99.7	101.4	103.2	103.9	103.0	101.9	101.2	100.5
淡水鱼	Freshwater Fish	97.1	95.7	93.8	93.3	95.7	98.5	101.1	101.8	101.1	98.9	97.5	96.1
海水鱼	Seawater Fish	102.1	103.8	102.2	103.6	103.8	104.4	105.3	106.1	105.1	105.0	105.0	105.1
（2）其他水产品	Other Aquatic Product	107.1	111.0	110.5	110.7	108.4	108.1	108.8	107.4	101.6	104.2	105.2	105.4
虾蟹类	Shrimp and Crab	107.7	112.4	111.6	111.8	109.0	108.9	109.2	107.5	100.3	103.5	104.7	105.1
其他	Others	104.8	105.6	106.2	106.2	105.9	105.2	107.4	107.0	106.6	106.9	107.2	106.5
8.菜	Vegetable	140.6	141.2	128.5	124.3	106.3	86.5	82.6	90.5	104.5	88.5	88.4	110.2
鲜菜	Fresh Vegetable	145.2	145.7	131.2	126.2	105.4	84.0	79.6	88.6	104.5	86.8	86.5	110.5
干菜及菜制品	Dried Vegetable and Vegetable Products	101.5	101.8	101.7	101.9	101.4	101.5	101.4	102.1	103.0	104.1	105.5	109.9
薯类	Potato	111.3	116.0	123.4	128.8	144.8	118.1	117.0	113.7	109.8	96.2	96.7	104.1
9.调味品	Flavoring	101.9	101.7	101.8	102.0	102.0	101.9	102.3	102.3	102.4	102.6	103.3	104.1
盐	Salt	105.5	105.0	105.5	105.7	105.7	106.1	106.9	106.7	107.0	107.1	107.1	107.0
酱油	Soy Sauce	100.6	100.6	100.6	100.8	100.7	100.4	100.7	100.9	100.7	100.9	101.1	102.0
醋	Vinegar	101.0	101.0	100.9	101.3	101.2	101.3	101.9	101.8	101.9	102.0	102.0	103.3
味精	Aginomoto	100.2	100.2	100.2	100.4	100.6	100.4	100.9	100.8	100.8	101.2	101.0	101.4
其他	Others	100.8	100.5	100.5	100.2	100.3	99.6	99.5	99.5	99.5	100.1	104.2	105.6
10.糖	Carbohydrate	102.3	106.6	108.0	108.9	109.8	110.3	110.8	111.0	111.1	111.2	111.3	112.1
食糖	Sugar	105.0	115.7	119.4	121.2	123.4	124.5	125.3	126.0	126.3	126.0	126.1	128.0
糖果	Sweet	100.9	101.5	101.6	102.2	102.3	102.4	102.8	102.8	102.8	103.2	103.3	102.3
巧克力制品	Chocolate Products	100.6	100.5	100.5	100.5	100.3	100.2	100.3	100.2	100.2	100.4	100.3	102.9
糖类小食品	Little Carbohydrate Food	100.3	100.7	100.8	100.8	101.1	101.1	101.2	101.6	101.5	101.5	102.0	103.0
11.茶及饮料	Tea and Beverages	100.1	100.3	101.1	101.1	101.1	101.3	101.4	101.6	101.6	101.7	101.7	102.2
（1）茶叶	Tea	99.8	100.1	100.6	100.6	100.3	100.4	100.6	100.7	100.7	101.0	101.0	101.4
茶叶	Tea	99.8	100.1	100.6	100.6	100.3	100.4	100.6	100.7	100.7	101.0	101.0	101.4
（2）饮料	Beverages	100.3	100.4	101.4	101.5	101.7	102.0	102.0	102.3	102.2	102.2	102.2	102.7
固体饮料	Solid Beverages	100.7	101.0	100.8	100.6	100.9	101.1	101.1	101.0	100.9	101.0	100.9	100.7
液体饮料	Liquid Beverages	100.0	100.1	100.9	101.1	101.3	101.0	101.1	101.4	101.4	101.4	101.4	101.9
冷冻饮品	Frozen Beverages	100.2	100.3	102.9	103.0	103.2	104.7	104.6	105.3	105.2	105.4	105.3	106.2
12.干鲜瓜果	Dried and Fresh Melons and Fruits	121.1	128.4	130.0	140.8	147.6	136.2	113.5	99.3	96.0	97.9	101.0	106.3
鲜瓜果	Fresh Fruits	126.1	135.6	137.5	151.5	160.4	145.2	115.4	96.5	92.2	93.9	97.2	104.0
干（坚）果	Dried Fruits	105.4	105.3	106.1	106.5	106.9	107.4	107.5	108.1	108.3	110.6	113.0	114.0
13.糕点饼干面包	Cake, Biscuit and Bread	100.5	100.5	100.3	100.5	100.5	100.5	100.7	100.9	100.9	100.8	100.7	101.7
糕点	Cake	100.6	100.6	100.4	100.4	100.4	100.3	100.3	100.0	100.0	99.8	100.0	101.2
饼干	Biscuit	100.3	100.2	100.2	100.6	100.9	101.0	101.4	102.3	102.2	102.1	101.6	102.7
面包	Bread	100.6	100.4	100.4	100.4	100.4	100.3	100.6	100.8	100.9	101.3	100.9	101.3
14.液体乳及乳制品	Liquid Milk and Their Products	100.2	100.3	100.7	100.9	100.9	101.0	101.1	101.5	102.4	102.4	102.4	103.2

7-10 续表 2 continued

商品类别及品名	Commodity Category and Commodity Name	1月 January	2月 February	3月 March	4月 April	5月 May	6月 June	7月 July	8月 August	9月 September	10月 October	11月 November	12月 December
		（以2005年平均价格为100）											
巴氏杀菌奶或消毒奶	Pasteurization Milk or Disinfection Milk	99.7	99.7	100.4	100.5	100.5	100.7	100.8	101.2	102.3	102.3	102.2	103.4
酸奶	Leben	100.2	100.2	100.3	101.0	101.1	101.2	100.9	100.9	102.0	102.0	101.7	101.3
奶粉	Milk Powder	100.9	101.0	101.0	101.3	101.2	101.2	101.6	102.4	102.4	102.2	102.4	103.5
其他	Others	102.3	102.3	102.2	102.2	102.2	102.2	102.2	102.2	104.5	104.1	104.2	104.0
15.在外用膳食品	Outward Dinner	100.2	100.2	100.3	100.3	100.4	100.7	100.7	100.9	100.9	100.8	101.5	103.5
主食	Staple Food	100.0	99.6	99.7	99.6	99.6	100.0	99.9	100.0	100.1	100.1	101.9	105.9
炒菜	Hot Dish	100.4	100.5	100.7	100.6	100.7	101.0	101.0	101.0	101.1	101.0	101.1	102.1
地方小吃	Local Snack	100.3	100.2	100.4	100.5	101.1	101.3	101.7	102.5	102.2	101.7	101.8	103.7
16.其他食品	Other Foods	100.7	100.6	100.9	100.9	101.0	101.1	101.2	101.2	101.3	101.0	101.0	101.6
其他食品	Other foods	100.7	100.6	100.9	100.9	101.0	101.1	101.2	101.2	101.3	101.0	101.0	101.6
二、烟酒及用品	**Tobacco,Liquor and Their Appliances**	**100.2**	**100.1**	**100.2**	**100.5**	**100.5**	**100.6**	**100.7**	**101.0**	**101.1**	**101.1**	**101.2**	**102.1**
1.烟草	Tobacco	100.0	100.2	100.2	100.5	100.6	100.5	100.4	100.3	100.2	100.3	100.3	100.9
国产卷烟	Domestic Cigarette	100.1	100.4	100.3	100.7	100.8	100.7	100.6	100.6	100.5	100.5	100.5	101.2
进口卷烟	Import Cigarette	99.6	98.5	98.4	98.5	98.1	98.1	97.8	97.9	98.0	97.8	98.4	98.6
其他	Others	99.8	99.8	99.8	99.8	99.8	99.8	99.8	99.7	99.7	99.7	99.7	99.7
2.酒	Liquor	100.2	100.0	100.2	100.5	100.5	100.7	101.0	101.5	101.8	101.9	102.0	103.2
白酒	White Spirit	100.6	100.2	100.4	100.8	100.8	101.1	101.2	102.0	102.1	102.4	102.5	104.2
葡萄酒	Grape	101.2	101.3	101.4	101.6	101.6	102.8	103.4	103.4	103.6	103.7	104.1	104.2
啤酒	Beer	99.5	99.6	99.6	99.9	99.7	99.7	100.1	100.4	101.0	100.8	100.8	101.3
其他	Others	100.1	100.1	100.1	100.2	100.2	100.3	100.5	100.5	100.5	100.5	100.5	100.6
3.吸烟、饮酒用品	Appliances for Smoking and Drinking	100.2	100.2	100.2	100.2	100.3	100.3	100.3	100.3	100.0	100.1	100.1	99.9
吸烟用品	Appliances for Smoking	100.2	100.2	100.2	100.3	100.3	100.3	100.3	100.3	100.1	100.4	100.4	100.3
饮酒用品	Appliances for Drinking	100.2	100.2	100.1	100.2	100.3	100.3	100.3	100.3	99.9	99.9	99.9	99.6
三、衣着	**Clothing**	**99.7**	**98.6**	**98.2**	**97.9**	**97.4**	**97.4**	**96.8**	**96.3**	**96.4**	**97.1**	**97.6**	**97.7**
1.服装	Garments	99.1	97.6	97.0	96.6	96.1	96.1	95.8	95.4	95.5	96.5	97.3	97.4
（1）男式服装	Men's Garments	98.6	97.5	96.7	96.3	95.6	95.5	95.2	94.7	94.9	96.0	96.9	97.0
大衣	Topcoat	96.3	94.4	93.5	92.3	92.3	91.6	91.5	91.5	91.4	91.3	91.2	92.0
毛线衣	Woollen Sweater	100.0	95.8	92.2	91.6	90.0	89.8	89.6	89.3	89.8	91.6	92.2	93.1
夹克衫	Jacket	98.2	97.3	96.2	95.8	95.7	95.6	95.4	95.5	95.4	97.4	99.1	99.3
衬衫	Shirt	95.2	94.5	94.5	94.1	93.4	93.9	92.9	92.2	92.5	93.2	93.4	94.3
T恤衫	T-shirt	100.8	101.2	100.9	100.9	99.9	98.3	96.1	94.8	95.4	95.8	96.6	96.7
裤子	Trousers	97.5	95.2	95.1	94.9	94.5	94.2	94.0	93.6	93.1	95.4	95.9	95.4
西服	Western-style Clothes	99.3	99.7	98.7	99.0	98.6	98.5	99.0	97.4	98.4	99.6	99.8	99.6
运动衫裤	Gym Suit	98.7	98.7	98.7	98.4	95.2	95.4	95.1	95.5	95.5	96.0	97.2	97.7
内衣	Underwaist	101.9	101.7	102.2	101.8	101.4	101.6	101.4	101.5	101.3	101.7	101.8	101.7
羽绒衣	Eider Down Outer-wear	99.9	98.1	97.5	95.9	95.9	95.9	95.5	95.2	94.8	96.8	100.5	99.6
其他	Others	97.5	96.4	95.6	95.1	95.3	95.4	95.3	95.0	95.0	95.0	97.6	97.6
（2）女式服装	Women's Garments	99.4	97.6	96.9	96.4	95.8	95.9	95.7	95.3	95.6	96.7	97.4	97.6
大衣	Topcoat	98.8	92.4	90.8	90.2	90.1	90.1	90.0	90.0	89.8	89.8	90.5	93.0
毛线衣	Woollen Sweater	100.1	93.9	92.0	91.7	89.7	89.9	89.9	89.9	90.7	92.5	93.5	94.6

7-10 续表 3 continued

商品类别及品名	Commodity Category and Commodity Name	1月 January	2月 February	3月 March	4月 April	5月 May	6月 June	7月 July	8月 August	9月 September	10月 October	11月 November	12月 December
		（以2005年平均价格为100）											
羽绒衣	Eider Down Outer-wear	98.6	97.4	96.7	96.6	96.6	96.4	96.2	96.0	95.5	98.0	101.1	100.4
套装	Coordinates	100.7	100.4	100.3	98.4	98.8	98.0	98.3	96.6	99.0	100.0	99.5	99.7
衬衫	Shirt	98.4	99.3	99.6	98.3	98.0	98.2	98.7	97.2	97.0	97.3	97.1	96.0
T恤衫	T-shirt	99.7	100.0	99.8	99.3	98.7	99.2	97.9	97.3	98.7	102.3	102.6	102.5
裙子	Skirt	99.4	98.9	98.6	97.8	98.1	98.6	98.2	97.7	97.3	97.6	98.2	97.8
裤子	Trousers	100.9	99.2	98.1	97.5	96.9	97.1	96.5	96.3	96.6	96.5	97.5	97.0
运动衫裤	Gym Suit	99.9	100.4	99.4	99.9	95.9	96.2	96.0	95.9	95.8	97.4	97.3	98.5
内衣	Underwaist	97.8	97.3	98.0	98.7	98.9	99.1	98.9	99.0	99.7	100.4	101.6	101.5
其他	Others	99.6	99.4	99.7	100.1	99.8	99.9	99.9	100.3	100.1	100.5	100.8	100.7
（3）儿童服装	Children's Garments	98.9	98.3	98.1	98.3	98.7	98.8	98.2	97.8	97.2	97.5	98.0	98.0
套装	Coordinates	98.8	98.3	97.9	98.1	97.4	97.1	97.2	96.9	96.6	96.9	97.5	97.6
裤子	Trousers	100.1	99.3	99.1	98.9	100.0	100.0	99.0	99.0	99.0	99.8	100.4	100.7
裙子	Skirt	97.5	97.2	97.6	98.4	100.2	100.8	99.5	98.6	96.5	96.5	96.6	96.4
其他	Others	100.2	98.3	97.2	96.5	96.4	96.7	96.6	96.6	96.0	96.0	96.3	96.0
2.衣着材料	Clothing Materials	100.1	100.1	99.9	100.0	100.4	100.4	100.5	100.5	100.2	100.6	100.7	100.9
棉布	Cotton Cloth	99.5	99.5	99.5	99.7	100.4	100.5	100.5	100.6	100.4	100.8	100.8	100.8
棉混纺布	Cotton Textiles Cloth	99.9	100.1	100.1	100.1	100.1	100.1	100.2	100.3	100.1	100.5	100.8	100.9
化纤布	Chemical Fiber Cloth	100.1	100.3	100.2	100.2	101.0	101.0	101.1	101.0	100.5	101.1	101.3	101.4
毛线	Knitting Wool	100.9	100.3	99.7	99.7	99.6	99.6	99.7	99.6	99.6	99.6	99.7	100.2
3.鞋袜帽	Shoes,Socks and Hats	101.1	100.4	100.7	100.3	99.6	99.5	97.8	96.8	97.1	97.1	97.3	96.9
（1）鞋	Shoes	101.3	100.5	100.9	100.4	99.6	99.5	97.4	96.3	96.7	96.7	97.0	96.5
男鞋	Men's Shoes	100.0	99.4	100.1	99.9	99.0	99.4	97.2	96.5	96.6	96.6	96.9	96.6
女鞋	Women's Shoes	102.3	101.2	101.5	100.7	99.5	99.2	96.8	95.0	95.8	95.7	96.0	95.3
童鞋	Children's Shoes	100.9	100.6	100.4	100.5	100.8	100.5	100.2	99.9	99.5	99.8	100.0	100.0
（2）袜子	Socks	100.2	100.1	99.7	100.0	99.7	99.7	99.7	99.7	99.4	99.7	99.1	99.0
男袜	Men's Socks	100.0	99.8	99.8	100.0	99.8	99.7	99.6	99.6	99.4	99.6	98.6	98.3
女袜	Women's Socks	100.3	100.2	99.7	100.0	99.7	99.8	99.7	99.7	99.4	99.7	99.5	99.5
（3）帽子	Hats	99.9	99.7	99.6	99.6	99.6	99.6	99.7	99.6	99.5	99.8	100.2	100.3
男帽	Men's Hats	99.9	99.7	99.5	99.5	99.7	99.8	99.9	99.8	99.6	99.8	100.6	100.7
女帽	Women's Hats	99.9	99.6	99.6	99.6	99.6	99.5	99.5	99.5	99.4	99.9	100.0	100.0
4.衣着加工服务费	Clothing Manufacturing Services	100.1	99.9	99.9	99.8	99.8	99.8	99.9	99.9	99.9	99.9	99.9	101.2
缝纫	Sewing	100.1	99.7	99.8	99.8	99.8	99.8	99.8	99.8	99.8	99.8	99.8	101.8
清洗	Washing	100.1	100.2	100.2	100.0	100.0	100.0	100.0	100.2	100.2	100.2	100.2	100.2
四、家庭设备用品及维修服务	**Household Facilities, Articles and Services**	**100.2**	**100.2**	**100.2**	**100.3**	**100.3**	**101.1**	**101.3**	**101.5**	**101.6**	**101.9**	**102.0**	**102.4**
1.耐用消费品	Durable Consumer Goods	100.0	99.9	100.0	100.1	100.2	101.5	102.0	102.2	102.1	102.5	102.6	102.7
（1）家具	Furniture	100.0	99.9	99.9	100.1	100.0	100.1	100.1	100.2	100.3	101.0	101.3	101.3
柜	Cabinet	100.3	100.1	99.9	99.8	99.9	100.0	99.9	100.1	100.2	101.0	101.1	101.3
床	Bed	100.0	100.1	100.1	100.8	100.7	100.6	100.8	100.9	100.9	101.7	101.7	101.9
桌	Desk	99.9	100.0	100.0	100.0	99.8	99.7	99.5	99.4	99.3	99.8	100.2	100.5
椅	Chair	100.3	99.4	99.5	99.5	99.5	99.5	99.4	99.5	100.2	101.2	101.3	101.3
沙发	Sofa	99.5	99.6	99.6	100.1	99.9	100.1	100.2	100.3	100.4	101.0	101.4	101.4

7-10 续表 4 continued

(以2005年平均价格为100)

商品类别及品名	Commodity Category and Commodity Name	1月 January	2月 February	3月 March	4月 April	5月 May	6月 June	7月 July	8月 August	9月 September	10月 October	11月 November	12月 December
其他	Others	100.4	100.4	100.5	100.2	100.0	100.6	101.0	101.0	101.5	101.8	101.9	101.9
(2)家庭设备	Household Appliances	100.0	100.0	100.1	100.0	100.4	102.4	103.2	103.3	103.2	103.3	103.4	103.5
洗衣机	Washing Machine	99.5	99.6	99.6	98.9	99.3	100.1	100.7	100.7	100.9	101.0	101.0	101.0
电风扇	Electric Fan	100.1	99.4	99.4	100.2	100.6	101.3	102.3	102.4	102.1	102.2	102.2	103.6
电冰箱(柜)	Refrigerator	102.0	101.8	102.0	102.4	103.2	105.5	106.7	106.6	106.5	107.0	106.7	106.7
吸排油烟机	Kitchen Ventilato	101.0	100.9	100.7	100.7	100.5	102.3	103.8	104.6	104.2	104.0	104.2	104.8
空调器	Air-conditioning	99.9	100.1	100.1	99.9	100.5	104.9	105.9	106.3	105.9	106.0	106.2	106.3
热水器	Water Heater	98.9	99.2	99.7	99.5	99.0	99.4	99.4	99.2	99.5	99.7	99.7	99.2
微波炉	Microwave Oven	97.8	97.4	97.5	97.0	96.9	97.3	97.3	97.3	97.2	97.3	97.7	97.2
电炊具	Electric Cooking Appliance	99.3	99.3	99.1	99.6	99.7	99.9	99.8	99.9	99.6	99.8	99.9	100.1
2.室内装饰品	Interior Decorations	99.9	99.9	99.9	99.8	99.5	99.4	99.4	99.6	99.6	99.8	99.9	100.0
纺织装饰品	Textile Process Decorations	99.6	99.6	99.6	99.4	99.4	99.1	99.0	99.1	99.0	99.3	99.3	99.4
装饰灯具	Architectural Lamps and Lanterns	100.3	100.3	100.3	100.2	99.5	99.4	99.8	99.7	100.0	100.1	99.9	100.1
其他	Others	100.1	100.1	100.0	99.9	99.9	99.9	99.8	100.5	100.2	100.4	101.2	101.2
3.床上用品	Bedclothes	99.2	99.7	99.9	100.1	99.4	99.8	99.6	99.4	99.4	99.7	99.7	100.3
毛毯	Woollen Blanket	100.0	99.9	100.1	100.7	99.5	99.9	99.4	99.2	99.5	100.4	100.1	101.7
被子	Quilt	99.0	99.3	99.4	99.3	98.8	99.3	99.0	98.6	98.5	98.3	98.4	99.0
床上套件	Bed Articles	98.8	99.5	99.7	99.8	99.4	99.7	99.7	99.6	99.5	99.9	100.0	100.0
其他	Others	99.1	101.2	101.4	101.5	101.2	101.0	101.0	101.0	100.9	101.1	101.2	101.3
4.日用杂品	Sundry Articles	100.1	100.1	100.2	100.3	100.4	100.2	99.9	100.2	100.4	100.7	100.7	101.3
茶具	Tea Set	98.0	98.0	98.1	98.5	98.1	99.9	99.9	99.9	101.2	103.6	103.4	103.6
餐具	Tableware	99.9	99.9	99.6	99.6	100.0	100.1	98.1	98.4	98.5	98.5	98.5	98.7
厨具	Kitchen Utensils	100.4	100.4	100.4	101.5	101.5	100.8	100.9	101.0	101.9	101.9	102.0	102.6
家用手工工具	Domestic Handwork Tools	100.7	100.7	100.7	100.7	100.6	101.0	101.2	101.5	101.5	101.5	101.1	103.2
洗涤用品	Washing Articles	100.7	100.8	100.8	100.7	100.8	100.1	100.1	100.5	100.3	100.3	100.4	101.1
其他	Others	100.0	100.0	100.3	100.3	100.4	100.1	99.9	100.3	100.4	100.5	100.5	101.1
5.家庭服务及加工维修服务	Household Service and Manufacturing Upkeep	103.6	102.8	102.8	102.8	102.8	102.9	103.2	104.9	105.2	105.4	106.5	107.7
家庭服务	Household Service	106.6	105.0	105.0	105.0	105.0	105.0	105.5	108.6	109.3	109.7	111.3	112.0
加工维修服务	Manufacturing Upkeep	100.9	100.9	100.9	100.8	100.8	101.0	101.1	101.5	101.5	101.5	102.1	103.7
五、医疗保健和个人用品	**Health Care and Personal Articles**	**100.2**	**100.4**	**100.4**	**100.5**	**100.9**	**100.9**	**100.9**	**101.0**	**101.0**	**100.9**	**101.0**	**101.1**
1.医疗保健	Health Care	100.0	100.1	100.0	100.0	100.1	100.2	100.2	100.2	100.2	100.1	100.2	100.3
(1)医疗器具及用品	Medical Facilities and Goods	96.8	97.3	97.0	96.6	96.3	96.3	96.3	96.3	96.9	95.0	95.0	93.8
医疗器具及用品	Medical Facilities and Goods	96.8	97.3	97.0	96.6	96.3	96.3	96.3	96.3	96.9	95.0	95.0	93.8
(2)中药材及中成药	Herbs and Ready-made Traditional Chinese Medicine	100.9	101.4	100.9	101.0	101.0	101.5	101.3	101.5	101.7	102.7	102.9	103.1
中药材	Herbs	101.3	102.2	101.0	101.3	102.1	103.3	103.0	103.0	103.7	105.2	105.7	105.9
中成药	Ready-made Traditional Chinese Medicine	100.4	100.5	100.8	100.6	99.9	99.7	99.6	100.0	99.6	100.1	100.0	100.3
(3)西药	Western Medicine	99.4	99.5	99.4	99.5	99.8	99.6	99.6	99.5	99.5	98.9	98.9	99.1
抗微生物药	Anti-microorganism Medicine	97.5	97.5	97.6	97.6	97.7	98.0	99.2	98.8	99.0	97.6	97.8	98.2

7-10 续表 5 continued

商品类别及品名	Commodity Category and Commodity Name	1月 January	2月 February	3月 March	4月 April	5月 May	6月 June	7月 July	8月 August	9月 September	10月 October	11月 November	12月 December
		（以2005年平均价格为100）											
消化系统用药	Alimentary System Medicine	99.5	99.6	99.8	99.9	100.1	100.1	100.1	100.1	100.0	100.0	99.6	100.0
呼吸系统用药	Respiratory System Medicine	99.0	99.0	99.1	99.5	99.3	99.9	99.9	99.9	100.7	100.2	100.5	100.5
解热镇痛及非甾体抗炎药	Allays a Fever the Analgesia and the Non-steroid Body Anti-in flammatory Agent	101.4	101.3	101.0	100.8	101.2	100.1	99.7	99.6	99.4	100.0	100.1	100.8
抗肿瘤药	Antineoplastic Drug	99.8	99.7	99.5	99.4	102.3	100.2	100.3	99.7	98.7	98.4	98.8	98.7
激素及调节内分泌功能药	Hormone and Adjustment Internal Secretion Function Medicine	99.2	99.4	99.2	99.2	99.2	99.0	98.1	98.1	98.7	96.3	96.8	96.0
循环系统用药	Circulating System Medicine	99.3	99.2	99.2	99.3	99.3	99.7	99.4	99.4	99.7	100.4	99.5	99.9
神经系统用药	Nerve System Medicine	100.4	100.6	100.4	100.8	100.8	100.6	100.6	100.4	100.8	98.9	98.9	99.4
专科用药	Junior Medicine	99.6	99.4	99.7	99.7	99.8	100.0	99.8	99.9	98.7	96.8	96.9	96.6
其他	Others	99.8	99.8	99.2	99.3	98.9	98.8	98.8	98.7	98.7	98.1	97.9	97.8
（4）保健品及器具	Healthcare Equipment	99.6	99.3	99.2	99.5	99.4	99.6	99.4	99.5	99.7	99.4	99.6	99.5
保健器具	Health Protection Equipment	100.0	99.5	99.4	99.5	99.4	99.9	99.8	99.8	99.8	99.2	99.3	99.0
滋补保健用品	Tonic and Health Products	99.4	99.2	99.1	99.5	99.5	99.5	99.3	99.4	99.7	99.6	99.8	99.8
（5）医疗保健服务	Health Care Services	100.4	100.5	100.5	100.4	100.4	100.5	100.6	100.6	100.7	100.5	100.6	100.7
挂号费	Registration	100.1	100.2	100.3	100.3	100.3	100.3	100.4	100.4	100.4	100.4	100.4	100.4
注射费	Injection Expenses	100.0	100.0	100.0	100.0	100.0	100.0	100.0	100.0	100.0	100.0	100.0	100.0
检查费	Examination Expenses	100.8	100.9	100.9	100.9	100.9	101.0	101.0	101.0	101.4	101.4	101.5	101.5
手术费	Operation Expenses	100.1	100.1	100.1	100.1	100.1	100.1	100.1	100.1	100.1	100.1	100.1	100.6
住院费	Hospitalization Expenses	101.2	101.2	101.2	101.0	101.0	101.4	101.9	101.9	101.7	101.0	101.4	101.4
理疗费	Physiotherapy Expenses	100.0	100.0	100.0	100.0	100.0	100.0	100.0	100.0	100.0	100.0	100.0	100.0
化验费	Analysis Expenses	100.1	100.1	100.1	100.1	100.1	100.1	100.1	100.1	100.1	100.0	100.0	100.0
其他	Others	100.0	100.0	100.0	100.0	100.0	100.0	100.0	100.0	100.0	100.0	100.0	100.0
2.个人用品及服务	Personal Articles and Services	100.7	101.0	101.2	101.5	102.4	102.4	102.3	102.5	102.4	102.6	102.5	102.6
（1）化妆美容用品	Cosmetics	99.4	99.4	99.4	99.4	99.4	99.4	99.3	99.5	99.2	99.6	99.3	99.4
化妆美容器具	Cosmetics Appliances	99.6	99.6	99.7	99.8	99.9	100.2	100.1	100.4	100.1	100.2	100.2	100.2
美容化妆品	Facial Beautifiers	99.5	99.6	99.6	99.6	99.6	99.6	99.8	99.8	99.8	99.9	100.0	100.2
护肤品	Protects Skin Products	99.7	99.8	99.7	99.8	99.9	99.7	99.7	99.9	98.5	100.0	99.3	99.0
护发美容品	Protects Sends the Beauty Products	98.8	98.8	98.6	98.6	98.5	98.6	97.6	98.1	98.1	98.2	97.5	97.5
（2）清洁化妆用品	Cleaning Toiletware	100.2	100.2	100.3	100.3	100.4	100.7	100.4	100.7	100.4	100.6	100.6	100.9
洗发用品	Hairdressing Articles	100.3	100.3	100.4	100.3	100.2	100.6	100.3	100.6	99.9	100.5	100.2	99.4
洗浴用品	Bathing Articles	100.2	100.2	100.0	100.1	100.2	100.3	100.1	100.5	100.4	100.3	100.5	100.7
其他	Others	100.0	100.2	100.4	100.5	101.6	101.8	101.6	101.6	101.5	101.5	101.7	104.7

7-10 续表 6 continued

商品类别及品名	Commodity Category and Commodity Name	1月 January	2月 February	3月 March	4月 April	5月 May	6月 June	7月 July	8月 August	9月 September	10月 October	11月 November	12月 December
		（以2005年平均价格为100）											
（3）个人饰品	Personal Decoraions	102.1	103.1	104.0	105.7	109.3	109.2	109.2	109.5	109.6	109.7	109.6	109.6
首饰	Ornaments	105.0	107.4	109.4	114.0	122.4	122.4	122.9	123.6	123.5	123.3	123.2	123.5
皮件	Leather Appliance	100.0	100.0	100.3	98.0	97.5	97.5	96.4	97.1	97.1	97.6	97.3	96.9
手表	Watch	99.4	99.3	99.3	99.2	99.2	98.6	98.4	98.4	98.5	98.9	99.0	99.4
领带	Necktie	100.4	100.2	100.0	100.5	100.3	100.2	99.8	99.3	100.0	100.0	100.1	99.4
其他	Others	98.1	98.1	98.4	98.3	98.4	98.4	98.4	98.6	98.4	98.5	98.5	98.7
（4）个人服务	Personal Services	101.4	101.5	101.5	101.5	101.4	101.4	101.4	101.4	101.5	101.5	101.6	101.8
美容	Cosmetology	101.2	101.2	101.2	101.2	101.2	101.2	101.2	101.2	101.2	101.2	101.2	101.2
理（烫）发	Haircut(permanent wave)	101.0	101.1	101.1	101.1	101.1	101.1	101.1	101.2	101.4	101.4	101.4	101.9
洗浴	Bathe	102.0	102.0	102.0	102.0	101.6	101.6	101.6	101.6	101.6	101.6	101.9	102.2
其他	Others	102.7	102.7	102.7	102.7	102.7	102.7	102.7	102.7	102.7	102.7	102.7	102.7
六、交通和通信	**Transportation and Communication**	**99.2**	**99.3**	**98.8**	**98.7**	**98.7**	**99.0**	**98.9**	**98.7**	**98.5**	**98.2**	**98.3**	**98.3**
1.交通	Transportation	101.6	102.1	101.8	102.1	102.7	103.4	103.5	103.6	103.5	103.5	103.5	103.4
（1）交通工具	Transportation Facility	99.4	99.8	99.7	99.3	99.0	98.6	98.3	98.1	97.7	97.6	97.5	97.1
摩托车	Motorcycle	99.7	101.4	101.4	101.4	101.6	101.7	101.5	101.7	101.7	101.7	101.7	101.2
自行车	Bicycle	100.1	100.0	99.7	99.2	99.1	98.5	97.7	97.5	97.6	97.7	97.7	97.8
轿车	Car	98.4	98.3	98.2	98.0	97.3	96.6	96.5	96.0	94.8	94.7	94.3	93.4
其他	Others	100.7	100.7	100.7	98.6	97.8	97.7	97.5	97.5	97.5	96.5	96.5	96.5
（2）车用燃料及零配件	Fuels and Parts	104.2	104.1	104.7	108.2	110.5	115.6	116.2	116.3	116.4	116.6	116.7	116.7
汽油	Gasoline	105.5	105.5	106.2	111.4	114.6	121.7	122.0	122.0	122.1	122.1	122.1	122.1
柴油	Diesel Oil	106.2	106.2	107.1	110.1	113.4	119.7	120.3	120.3	120.4	120.8	121.0	121.2
零配件	Parts	99.4	99.4	99.5	99.9	99.9	99.9	101.1	101.2	101.4	101.8	101.9	101.7
其他	Others	100.3	100.2	100.8	102.5	101.8	103.2	103.2	103.7	103.9	103.6	103.6	103.6
（3）车辆使用及维修费	Using and Upkeep Fare	100.2	99.6	100.0	99.8	100.1	100.3	100.4	100.9	100.9	100.8	100.6	101.0
驾驶证	Driving License	100.3	100.1	99.4	98.3	100.0	100.9	101.3	101.9	101.9	101.0	100.1	99.3
保险费	Insurance Expenses	99.8	99.8	99.6	99.6	99.6	99.6	99.6	99.8	99.9	99.9	99.9	99.9
停车费	Parking Expenses	100.4	100.4	100.4	100.4	100.4	100.4	100.4	104.2	104.2	104.2	104.2	104.2
车辆修理服务费	Vehicle Upkeep Service Fare	100.4	98.9	100.3	100.3	100.3	100.4	100.4	100.4	100.4	100.4	100.4	101.9
其他	Others	100.7	100.7	100.7	100.8	100.8	100.8	100.8	100.6	100.6	100.6	100.6	100.6
（4）市区公共交通费	Incity Traffic Fare	102.6	102.9	102.9	102.9	104.2	104.3	105.6	105.9	105.9	105.9	106.3	106.4
公共汽车票	Bus Ticket	101.5	102.1	102.1	102.1	102.1	102.1	102.5	102.5	102.5	102.5	102.5	102.7
出租汽车	Taxi	103.9	104.0	104.0	104.0	106.8	106.9	109.2	109.7	109.7	109.7	110.6	110.6
其他	Others	101.3	101.3	101.3	101.5	101.5	101.5	101.5	103.5	103.5	103.5	103.5	103.3
（5）城市间交通费	Intercity Traffic Fare	104.8	106.9	105.1	105.2	105.7	106.9	106.9	107.0	107.2	107.3	107.6	107.6
飞机票	Airplane Ticket	102.0	99.0	99.1	102.5	104.9	102.0	102.1	104.0	104.9	105.6	105.1	105.1
火车票	Train Ticket	101.2	100.7	100.5	100.5	100.5	100.6	100.6	100.6	100.7	100.7	100.8	100.8
长途汽车	Intertown Bus	106.4	109.8	107.2	107.2	107.2	109.0	109.0	109.2	109.4	109.4	109.9	109.9
其他	Others	101.6	102.1	101.1	101.1	110.8	111.2	111.2	111.3	111.3	111.3	111.3	111.3
2.通信	Communication	96.5	96.0	95.4	94.6	94.2	93.8	93.5	93.0	92.6	92.2	92.4	92.4
（1）通信工具	Communication Facility	89.7	88.4	86.6	84.3	83.0	81.8	80.9	79.4	78.5	77.2	76.5	75.4
固定电话机	Telephone	98.0	97.5	96.5	96.2	94.9	94.8	94.7	94.5	94.5	94.5	94.4	94.0
移动电话机	Mobile Phone	85.8	84.2	82.0	78.8	77.4	75.7	74.5	72.3	71.0	69.1	68.0	66.6
其他	Others	96.7	95.8	94.8	94.3	93.8	93.6	93.3	93.0	92.9	92.9	92.8	92.8

7-10 续表 7 continued

商品类别及品名	Commodity Category and Commodity Name	1月 January	2月 February	3月 March	4月 April	5月 May	6月 June	7月 July	8月 August	9月 September	10月 October	11月 November	12月 December
		（以2005年平均价格为100）											
（2）通信服务	Communication Service	99.9	99.9	99.9	99.9	99.9	99.9	99.9	99.9	99.9	99.9	100.6	101.2
移动通信费	Mobile Communication Fee	99.5	99.5	99.5	99.5	99.5	99.5	99.5	99.5	99.5	99.5	99.5	99.5
市内电话费	Incity Telephone Fee	100.0	100.0	100.0	100.0	100.0	100.0	100.0	100.0	100.0	100.0	100.0	100.0
长途电话费	Long Distance Call Fee	100.0	100.0	100.0	100.0	100.0	100.0	100.0	100.0	100.0	100.0	100.0	100.0
月租费	Month Hiring Fee	100.0	100.0	100.0	100.0	100.0	100.0	100.0	100.0	100.0	100.0	100.0	100.0
上网费	Net Play Fee	100.8	100.6	100.6	100.6	100.6	100.6	100.6	100.6	100.6	100.6	100.6	100.6
信件邮寄	Letter Post	100.0	100.0	100.0	100.0	100.0	100.0	100.0	100.0	100.0	100.0	115.5	128.7
包裹邮寄	Package Post	100.0	100.0	100.0	100.0	100.0	100.0	100.0	100.0	100.0	100.0	100.5	100.5
其他	Others	100.0	100.0	100.0	100.0	100.0	100.0	100.0	100.0	100.0	100.0	100.0	100.0
七、娱乐教育文化用品及服务	**Recreation,Education and Culture Articles**	**100.0**	**99.8**	**99.7**	**100.2**	**100.2**	**99.9**	**100.1**	**100.2**	**100.1**	**100.1**	**99.8**	**99.7**
1.文娱用耐用消费品及服务	Durable Consumer Goods For Cultural and Recreational Use and Service	97.3	96.9	96.7	96.2	96.0	95.8	95.6	95.1	94.4	94.2	94.0	93.7
电视机	Television	95.7	95.0	94.8	93.9	94.0	93.7	93.4	92.8	92.1	91.5	91.3	91.4
激光视盘机	Laser Video Disc Machine	98.6	97.6	97.6	97.4	97.0	97.3	97.4	97.3	96.8	96.3	95.9	93.5
摄像机	Pickup Camera	98.6	98.2	97.6	97.1	96.9	96.1	95.8	95.7	95.0	94.9	94.5	94.2
照相机	Camera	96.5	96.1	95.5	94.8	94.7	94.9	94.9	94.9	95.2	95.1	95.3	94.7
家用音响	Acoustic Equipment	100.2	99.9	99.6	98.7	98.5	98.5	98.9	98.9	98.6	98.7	98.6	98.1
便携式音响	Portable Acoustics	99.6	99.1	99.0	98.9	98.9	98.9	98.9	98.8	98.7	98.7	98.7	98.6
电脑	Computer	97.2	97.0	97.0	96.9	96.3	95.7	95.3	94.4	93.2	93.2	93.0	92.9
修理服务	Repair Service	102.2	102.2	102.1	102.1	102.1	102.0	102.6	102.6	102.7	102.8	102.8	102.8
其他	Others	98.7	100.1	99.9	99.7	99.5	99.5	99.4	99.0	97.2	97.5	97.2	97.2
2.教育	Education	101.1	101.2	101.2	101.4	101.4	101.4	101.4	101.5	101.8	101.8	101.8	101.8
（1）教材及参考书	Teaching Material and Reference Books	101.0	101.0	101.1	101.2	101.2	101.1	101.1	101.6	101.6	101.4	101.4	101.5
工具书	Tool Book	101.1	101.1	101.1	101.1	101.1	101.1	101.1	101.1	101.1	101.1	101.1	101.2
教材	Teaching Material	100.6	100.6	100.7	100.8	100.8	100.8	100.8	101.3	100.3	100.0	100.0	100.0
参考书	Reference Book	102.2	102.2	102.3	102.3	102.3	102.0	102.0	103.2	104.8	104.8	104.8	104.8
教育软件	Educational Software	99.8	99.8	99.7	99.7	99.7	99.7	99.7	99.7	99.7	99.7	99.7	99.7
（2）学杂托幼费	Tuition and Child Care	101.2	101.3	101.3	101.5	101.5	101.5	101.5	101.5	101.9	101.9	101.9	101.9
义务教育杂费	Incidental Expenses of Compulcory Education	100.8	100.8	100.8	100.8	100.8	100.8	100.8	100.8	100.8	100.8	100.8	100.8
非义务教育学杂费	Tuition of Non-compulsory Education	100.9	100.9	100.9	100.9	100.9	100.9	100.9	100.9	101.6	101.6	101.6	101.6
技能培训学费	Skill Train Tuition	101.4	101.4	101.4	100.5	100.5	100.5	100.5	100.5	100.3	100.3	100.3	100.3
托幼费	Child care	102.7	103.8	103.8	106.2	106.2	106.2	106.2	106.7	106.8	106.8	106.8	107.3
其他	Others	101.6	101.6	101.6	103.4	103.4	103.4	103.4	103.4	104.2	104.2	104.2	104.2
3.文化娱乐类	Recreation and Culture	100.8	100.5	100.5	102.1	102.2	101.8	102.3	102.3	101.8	102.4	102.1	102.2
（1）文化娱乐用品	Culture Articles	100.2	100.0	99.9	99.8	99.8	99.8	99.7	99.7	99.6	99.7	99.6	99.7
乐器	Musical Instrument	100.2	100.2	100.2	100.2	100.2	100.4	100.3	100.1	100.3	100.5	100.3	100.2
音响光盘和磁带	Audio,Disk and Tap	99.9	99.1	98.9	98.9	99.0	99.0	99.0	99.0	98.9	99.0	99.0	98.9
照相胶卷和存储卡	Roll Film and Memorizing Card	100.0	100.0	100.0	99.7	99.6	99.5	99.5	99.2	98.9	98.3	98.7	98.9
录像磁带和视盘	Video Tape and Disk	99.8	99.7	99.8	99.9	99.6	99.8	99.3	99.2	99.2	99.3	99.1	99.1
儿童玩具	Children's Toy	100.5	100.5	100.0	99.6	99.7	99.7	99.8	99.6	99.5	99.6	99.6	99.5

7-10 续表 8 continued

商品类别及品名	Commodity Category and Commodity Name	1月 January	2月 February	3月 March	4月 April	5月 May	6月 June	7月 July	8月 August	9月 September	10月 October	11月 November	12月 December
		（以2005年平均价格为100）											
纸张本册	Paper and Volume	101.3	100.8	100.8	100.8	100.8	101.0	101.0	101.6	101.7	102.0	102.1	102.1
文具	Stationery	99.8	99.9	99.9	99.8	99.8	99.5	99.0	99.1	98.8	98.9	98.9	98.9
体育用品	Sports Goods	99.5	99.5	99.5	99.5	99.4	99.2	99.4	99.4	99.2	99.4	99.1	99.1
其他	Others	99.8	99.8	99.8	99.7	99.7	99.5	99.6	99.6	99.0	99.4	99.4	99.4
（2）书报杂志	Books,Newspapers, Magazines	102.1	102.1	102.2	102.2	102.2	102.2	102.2	102.2	102.2	102.2	102.2	102.2
书籍	Books	100.8	100.8	101.0	101.0	101.0	101.0	101.0	101.0	101.0	101.0	101.0	101.1
报纸	Newspapers	105.1	105.1	105.1	105.1	105.1	105.1	105.1	105.1	105.1	105.1	105.1	105.1
杂志	Magazines	100.6	100.6	100.6	100.6	100.6	100.6	100.6	100.6	100.6	100.6	100.6	100.6
（3）文娱费	Expenditure of Culture and Recreation	100.4	99.8	99.7	106.2	106.7	105.3	107.3	107.2	105.4	107.5	106.5	106.8
电影票	Film Ticket	106.1	102.9	102.0	101.0	99.3	100.3	100.0	99.8	100.1	101.5	100.4	101.0
景点门票	Scene Spot Ticket	93.9	93.9	94.3	107.9	112.6	102.8	115.3	115.3	104.0	114.8	110.1	111.3
有线电视	Cable Television	100.0	100.0	100.0	110.5	110.5	110.5	110.5	110.5	110.5	110.6	110.6	110.6
健身活动	Exercise	100.6	100.6	101.0	101.7	101.7	101.7	101.7	101.7	101.6	101.6	101.6	101.6
其他	Others	101.6	101.6	101.6	101.6	101.6	101.6	101.7	101.7	101.7	101.7	101.7	101.4
4.旅游	Tourism	99.3	97.9	97.2	100.5	100.1	98.1	99.9	102.4	101.4	101.3	98.8	99.0
旅行社收费	Travel Agency Charge	98.8	96.4	95.3	100.1	99.2	96.1	98.4	102.2	101.8	101.9	97.4	97.7
宾馆住宿	Guesthouse Stay	100.2	99.8	99.9	101.0	101.0	100.7	101.2	101.7	101.0	101.1	100.9	100.8
其他住宿	Other Stay	99.6	99.3	99.3	100.6	101.2	100.3	102.5	104.4	100.7	99.9	99.8	100.0
八、居住	**Residence**	**102.7**	**102.7**	**102.8**	**103.3**	**103.6**	**103.9**	**104.3**	**104.9**	**105.6**	**105.9**	**106.5**	**106.7**
1.建房及装修材料	Building and Building Decoration Materials	101.4	101.4	102.0	102.6	102.7	103.3	103.8	104.5	105.0	105.5	106.7	106.9
木材	Wood	102.8	102.9	103.3	103.8	103.6	104.6	105.5	108.1	109.4	110.8	114.1	114.4
木地板	Wood Floor	101.2	101.2	100.8	97.6	98.0	98.3	98.4	98.6	98.1	99.5	100.8	100.9
砖	Brick	102.2	102.7	104.4	105.9	106.3	107.9	108.2	109.4	109.3	109.4	109.7	109.8
水泥	Cement	101.1	100.3	100.4	102.5	102.9	102.6	102.5	102.4	102.6	102.5	103.4	103.4
涂料	Coating Material	101.1	101.1	100.9	100.7	99.9	100.5	100.6	100.7	100.4	100.7	101.1	101.5
胶合板	Plywood	101.4	101.5	102.4	103.4	102.4	103.1	104.2	105.1	106.1	105.3	107.9	108.6
玻璃	Glass	99.4	98.9	99.7	99.9	100.7	100.9	101.8	102.4	102.9	104.1	104.9	105.1
粘胶	Rayon	101.0	101.0	101.0	100.9	101.0	101.3	101.3	102.2	102.8	103.3	103.6	104.7
油漆	Paint	102.0	102.2	102.2	102.1	102.6	103.0	103.2	103.3	105.1	105.1	105.0	105.4
其他	Others	98.6	98.1	100.4	101.0	102.2	101.7	102.5	101.5	101.5	103.7	103.8	102.5
2.租房	Renting	100.6	100.6	102.8	102.8	103.1	103.4	105.9	106.6	107.2	107.2	107.6	107.6
公房房租	Public House Rent	100.0	100.0	100.0	100.0	100.0	100.0	100.1	103.0	103.0	103.0	103.1	103.1
私房房租	Private House Rent	100.5	100.5	101.1	101.1	101.6	102.3	105.3	105.3	106.5	106.6	107.3	107.3
其他费用	Other Fare	101.4	101.4	108.5	108.5	108.5	108.5	112.2	112.2	112.2	112.2	112.2	112.2
3.自有住房	Private Housing	100.5	100.5	100.7	100.7	102.4	103.5	103.5	104.1	105.1	105.1	106.4	106.4
房屋贷款利率	Houses Loans Interest Rate	102.4	102.4	102.4	102.4	105.5	106.3	106.3	108.8	110.0	110.0	110.0	110.0
物业管理费用	Propety Management Fee	101.2	101.2	102.2	102.2	102.2	102.2	101.4	101.4	102.1	102.1	102.1	102.1
维护修理费用	Upkeep and Repair Fee	98.6	98.7	98.7	98.7	100.7	102.9	103.0	103.0	104.1	104.1	107.3	107.3
其他	Others	101.5	101.8	101.8	101.8	101.8	101.8	101.9	101.6	101.9	101.8	101.8	101.9
4.水、电、燃料	Water,Electricity and Fuels	104.6	104.6	104.1	104.6	104.8	104.5	104.9	105.3	106.2	106.2	106.3	106.6
水	Water	107.1	107.1	108.2	110.7	111.2	111.2	111.2	111.2	111.2	111.2	111.2	111.2
电	Electricity	101.3	101.6	101.6	101.6	101.6	101.6	103.0	103.4	103.4	103.4	103.4	103.4
液化石油气	Liquefiled Petroleum Gas	116.8	116.3	110.8	110.3	111.2	109.6	108.1	109.5	115.9	115.4	115.5	115.7
管道燃气	Pipelined Gas	100.1	100.1	100.1	100.1	100.2	100.2	100.2	100.2	100.2	100.2	100.2	100.2
其他燃料	Other Fuels	102.4	102.2	102.1	102.2	102.0	101.8	101.9	102.1	102.4	103.1	103.5	104.9

7-11 城市居民消费价格（定基）指数
Urban Consumer Price Indices

（以2005年平均价格为100）

商品类别及品名	Commodity Category and Commodity Name	1月 January	2月 February	3月 March	4月 April	5月 May	6月 June	7月 July	8月 August	9月 September	10月 October	11月 November	12月 December
居民消费价格总指数	**General Consumer Price Index**	**102.3**	**102.2**	**101.5**	**101.5**	**101.0**	**100.2**	**99.6**	**99.9**	**100.5**	**100.3**	**100.9**	**102.4**
非食品价格指数	**No-food**	**100.7**	**100.4**	**100.1**	**100.2**	**100.2**	**100.4**	**100.3**	**100.4**	**100.5**	**100.7**	**100.8**	**100.8**
服务项目价格指数	**Services**	**101.0**	**100.8**	**100.7**	**101.2**	**101.4**	**101.2**	**101.8**	**102.3**	**102.4**	**102.5**	**102.2**	**102.4**
工业品价格指数	**Industrial Products**	**100.5**	**100.2**	**99.9**	**99.9**	**99.8**	**100.0**	**99.8**	**99.7**	**99.7**	**100.0**	**100.2**	**100.3**
扣除食品和能源价格指数	**Deducting Foods and Energy**	**100.4**	**100.1**	**99.9**	**100.0**	**99.9**	**100.1**	**100.1**	**100.1**	**100.1**	**100.3**	**100.4**	**100.4**
扣除鲜菜鲜果总指数	**Deducting Fresh,Vegetables and Fruits**	**100.4**	**100.1**	**99.8**	**99.8**	**99.7**	**99.9**	**100.1**	**100.6**	**100.7**	**101.0**	**101.4**	**102.1**
消费品价格指数	**Consumer Goods**	**102.6**	**102.5**	**101.6**	**101.6**	**100.9**	**99.9**	**99.1**	**99.3**	**100.0**	**99.8**	**100.6**	**102.4**
一、食品	**Food**	**106.0**	**106.4**	**104.5**	**104.4**	**102.7**	**99.8**	**97.9**	**98.8**	**100.5**	**99.6**	**101.2**	**106.0**
1.粮食	Grain	99.8	99.9	100.1	100.2	100.6	101.1	101.7	102.6	102.7	103.3	107.0	109.3
大米	Rice	101.4	101.4	101.7	101.9	103.4	105.0	106.7	109.5	109.8	110.7	111.8	114.2
面粉	Flour	97.5	97.9	97.9	97.6	97.4	97.0	97.2	96.3	96.1	96.6	104.1	107.2
粮食制品	Grain Products	99.4	99.6	100.0	100.3	100.4	100.6	100.9	101.8	101.9	102.2	105.0	106.7
其他	Others	105.3	104.1	104.1	104.7	105.1	106.0	106.7	107.7	108.8	109.6	112.0	114.0
2.淀粉	Starches	97.1	97.3	97.4	97.6	97.6	97.8	97.6	98.4	99.4	99.5	99.8	103.7
淀粉	Starches	97.1	97.3	97.4	97.6	97.6	97.8	97.6	98.4	99.4	99.5	99.8	103.7
3.干豆类及豆制品	Beans and Beans Products	100.4	100.3	100.8	100.4	100.9	101.4	102.4	102.5	102.2	102.1	102.3	102.8
干豆	Beans	98.4	98.3	98.0	97.9	99.7	103.0	106.7	108.1	104.9	102.9	102.6	102.4
豆制品	Beans Products	100.8	100.8	101.4	101.0	101.2	101.0	101.4	101.3	101.6	101.9	102.2	102.9
4.油脂	Oil and Fat	99.1	99.0	98.7	98.9	98.8	99.3	99.3	99.8	100.1	100.0	101.9	107.6
食用植物油	Edible Vegetable Oil	99.2	99.2	98.9	99.4	99.3	99.8	99.9	100.4	100.6	100.5	102.2	106.7
植物油制品	Plant Oil Products	99.2	98.6	98.4	97.7	97.8	97.9	97.1	97.0	97.2	97.3	99.4	115.2
其他	Others	96.3	93.5	89.6	83.8	81.9	81.9	82.9	85.4	90.0	90.7	103.4	113.4
5.肉禽及其制品	Meal,Poultry and Their Products	97.6	97.3	94.2	91.7	89.8	90.4	93.3	97.2	98.6	99.1	102.5	107.9
（1）食用畜肉及副产品	Edible Livestock Meat and Their By-products	98.3	97.6	93.2	89.3	87.2	88.0	90.8	95.6	97.9	98.1	102.9	109.8
猪肉	Pork	95.3	94.5	88.8	82.7	80.1	81.3	85.6	92.5	95.6	95.5	102.2	110.6
牛肉	Beef	105.8	106.1	104.3	104.1	102.3	102.7	103.2	103.0	104.1	104.2	106.3	109.6
羊肉	Mutton	106.3	105.7	103.2	104.7	104.5	104.4	104.0	104.2	104.9	105.9	106.0	108.8
畜肉副产品	Livestock Meat By-products	99.7	99.3	96.6	94.5	93.0	93.1	95.0	96.4	97.4	98.2	100.2	108.2
其他	Others	100.5	99.7	98.8	98.2	97.1	97.0	96.2	99.0	100.6	101.7	103.2	106.6
（2）禽	Poultry	93.8	94.3	94.1	94.8	92.8	92.9	98.0	101.3	99.8	101.7	101.9	104.3
鸡	Chicken	92.5	93.4	93.4	94.6	92.0	92.2	98.7	102.6	100.9	103.4	103.5	106.1
鸭	Duck	97.0	96.6	96.2	93.7	95.7	96.0	94.6	94.1	92.2	92.2	92.0	93.7
其他	Others	98.6	97.8	96.6	96.3	95.1	94.8	96.2	98.2	97.9	97.9	98.5	100.3
（3）加工肉禽	Meal and Poultry Processing Products	99.6	99.9	99.8	99.8	99.6	99.6	99.7	100.1	100.4	100.8	101.2	102.9
畜肉制品	Livestock Meat Products	99.9	100.3	100.0	100.1	99.6	99.6	99.6	99.8	99.9	100.3	101.0	102.9
禽制品	Poultry Products	99.0	99.3	99.4	99.2	99.6	99.6	99.8	100.6	101.6	101.7	101.8	102.8

7-11 续表 1 continued

商品类别及品名	Commodity Category and Commodity Name	（以2005年平均价格为100）											
		1月 January	2月 February	3月 March	4月 April	5月 May	6月 June	7月 July	8 月 August	9 月 September	10 月 October	11月 November	12月 December
6.蛋	Eggs	93.6	89.3	86.7	86.5	88.0	89.1	90.1	100.0	105.5	104.1	105.5	110.5
鲜蛋	Fresh Eggs	92.8	88.2	85.4	85.2	86.8	88.1	89.1	99.8	105.7	104.1	105.6	110.8
蛋制品	Egg Products	103.6	103.3	102.6	103.1	102.7	101.8	102.0	102.5	102.8	104.1	104.1	107.1
7.水产品	Aquatic Product	104.5	106.3	105.0	105.6	104.5	105.3	106.5	105.9	101.5	102.8	102.4	101.9
（1）鱼	Fish	100.3	100.2	97.8	98.8	99.9	102.2	104.4	105.3	103.6	102.4	100.3	99.8
淡水鱼	Freshwater Fish	95.2	94.1	91.6	89.8	91.9	96.2	100.1	101.8	101.2	98.6	95.6	94.7
海水鱼	Seawater Fish	103.6	104.3	101.9	104.8	105.3	106.2	107.3	107.5	105.3	104.9	103.4	103.2
（2）其他水产品	Other Aquatic Product	109.1	112.8	112.7	113.0	109.4	108.6	108.8	106.5	99.2	103.2	104.6	104.2
虾蟹类	Shrimp and Crab	110.1	114.8	114.3	114.7	110.1	109.6	109.2	106.4	97.0	102.2	103.9	103.7
其他	Others	105.7	106.6	107.4	107.3	107.0	105.0	107.6	106.7	106.3	106.6	106.9	105.9
8.菜	Vegetable	142.2	141.4	127.7	122.3	103.6	87.0	83.1	88.9	103.6	89.3	91.2	112.8
鲜菜	Fresh Vegetable	145.4	144.4	129.4	123.3	102.6	84.7	80.4	86.9	103.2	87.7	89.7	112.5
干菜及菜制品	Dried Vegetable and Vegetable Products	102.7	103.4	103.3	104.7	104.6	104.9	105.4	106.1	107.9	110.3	111.2	117.7
薯类	Potato	112.7	118.6	121.8	130.9	144.6	137.5	137.7	130.6	110.0	100.4	100.3	111.8
9.调味品	Flavoring	101.7	101.3	101.1	101.4	101.4	101.5	101.3	101.2	101.1	101.6	103.0	103.6
盐	Salt	102.9	101.7	101.1	101.6	101.6	102.5	101.5	100.5	100.1	100.2	100.2	100.3
酱油	Soy Sauce	101.6	101.6	101.5	101.8	101.6	101.1	101.0	101.4	101.0	101.4	101.7	101.7
醋	Vinegar	101.6	101.6	101.5	102.2	102.0	102.3	102.4	102.4	102.6	102.7	102.6	103.1
味精	Aginomoto	100.1	100.1	99.9	100.5	100.8	100.4	100.4	100.2	100.3	100.4	100.0	100.4
其他	Others	101.4	100.7	100.7	100.3	100.2	100.5	100.9	100.8	101.1	102.6	109.5	112.1
10.糖	Carbohydrate	103.6	105.6	107.7	108.5	109.1	109.5	109.3	109.6	109.7	109.9	109.9	110.9
食糖	Sugar	109.5	114.2	120.2	122.3	123.6	124.6	124.2	125.3	125.5	125.1	124.6	127.4
糖果	Sweet	100.5	101.8	102.1	102.5	102.9	103.2	103.2	103.2	103.0	104.0	104.2	104.3
巧克力制品	Chocolate Products	101.0	101.0	100.8	100.8	100.6	100.5	100.2	100.0	100.0	100.3	100.3	100.3
糖类小食品	Little Carbohydrate Food	100.5	100.8	100.9	100.9	101.6	101.5	101.5	101.6	101.6	101.5	102.0	102.2
11.茶及饮料	Tea and Beverages	100.0	100.3	101.5	101.6	101.6	101.9	101.9	102.0	102.0	102.2	102.2	102.4
（1）茶叶	Tea	99.6	100.1	101.0	101.0	100.5	100.7	101.1	101.0	101.1	101.5	101.5	102.2
茶叶	Tea	99.6	100.1	101.0	101.0	100.5	100.7	101.1	101.0	101.1	101.5	101.5	102.2
（2）饮料	Beverages	100.2	100.3	101.9	101.9	102.2	102.7	102.4	102.6	102.6	102.6	102.6	102.6
固体饮料	Solid Beverages	100.9	101.1	100.9	100.5	101.0	101.3	101.3	101.0	100.9	100.9	100.9	100.2
液体饮料	Liquid Beverages	99.8	99.9	101.2	101.4	101.6	101.2	100.6	100.9	100.9	100.8	100.9	101.3
冷冻饮品	Frozen Beverages	100.3	100.3	104.7	104.9	105.2	107.6	107.5	108.7	108.5	108.8	108.6	108.5
12.干鲜瓜果	Dried and Fresh Melons and Fruits	120.0	126.8	128.8	137.9	143.3	126.2	103.5	92.3	90.6	95.3	99.7	104.2
鲜瓜果	Fresh Fruits	124.3	133.1	135.4	147.0	153.9	131.4	101.6	87.0	84.8	90.2	95.0	100.6
干（坚）果	Dried Fruits	106.5	106.7	107.8	108.7	109.3	109.7	109.5	109.1	109.3	111.6	114.5	115.7
13.糕点饼干面包	Cake,Biscuit and Bread	100.8	100.6	100.5	100.6	100.8	100.6	100.6	100.4	100.4	100.3	100.2	100.8
糕点	Cake	100.7	100.7	100.4	100.3	100.3	100.1	100.0	99.5	99.5	99.0	99.4	100.4
饼干	Biscuit	100.6	100.5	100.5	101.2	101.7	101.6	101.6	101.8	101.5	101.4	100.8	101.1
面包	Bread	101.0	100.6	100.6	100.7	100.6	100.5	100.5	100.8	101.0	101.7	101.1	101.5
14.液体乳及乳制品	Liquid Milk and Their Products	100.3	100.3	100.8	101.0	101.0	101.2	101.3	101.8	103.0	103.0	102.9	102.9
巴氏杀菌奶或消毒奶	Pasteurization Milk or Disinfection Milk	99.7	99.7	100.5	100.6	100.5	100.8	101.0	101.4	102.7	102.8	102.6	102.5
酸奶	Leben	100.7	100.7	100.8	101.4	101.6	101.6	101.3	101.3	102.7	102.7	102.3	102.5

7-11 续表 2 continued

商品类别及品名	Commodity Category and Commodity Name	1月 January	2月 February	3月 March	4月 April	5月 May	6月 June	7月 July	8月 August	9月 September	10月 October	11月 November	12月 December
		（以2005年平均价格为100）											
奶粉	Milk Powder	101.3	101.5	101.4	102.1	101.8	101.8	102.1	103.6	103.6	103.1	103.5	103.9
其他	Others	102.5	102.5	102.5	102.5	102.5	102.5	102.5	102.5	105.6	105.1	105.2	105.0
15.在外用膳食品	Outward Dinner	100.0	99.9	100.0	100.1	100.1	100.6	100.6	100.8	100.9	100.8	101.3	103.5
主食	Staple Food	100.0	99.5	99.5	99.5	99.5	100.0	100.0	100.2	100.3	100.3	101.5	105.7
炒菜	Hot Dish	100.0	100.0	100.2	100.3	100.4	100.9	100.8	100.9	101.0	100.8	101.0	102.2
地方小吃	Local Snack	100.1	100.1	100.5	100.5	100.5	100.5	100.9	102.1	101.7	101.7	102.4	104.1
16.其他食品	Other Foods	100.8	100.6	101.0	101.1	101.2	101.2	101.1	101.0	101.2	100.8	100.8	101.5
其他食品	Other Foods	100.8	100.6	101.0	101.1	101.2	101.2	101.1	101.0	101.2	100.8	100.8	101.5
二、烟酒及用品	**Tobacco,Liquor and Their Appliances**	**100.5**	**100.4**	**100.4**	**100.9**	**101.0**	**101.4**	**101.5**	**101.7**	**101.8**	**101.9**	**101.9**	**102.2**
1.烟草	Tobacco	99.9	99.6	99.5	100.1	100.0	100.2	100.1	100.1	99.8	99.8	99.9	100.0
国产卷烟	Domestic Cigarette	100.0	99.8	99.8	100.4	100.4	100.6	100.6	100.5	100.2	100.2	100.2	100.3
进口卷烟	Import Cigarette	99.6	98.1	98.1	98.2	97.7	97.7	97.7	97.8	97.9	97.7	98.1	98.3
其他	Others	99.8	99.8	99.8	99.8	99.8	99.8	99.8	99.3	99.3	99.3	99.3	99.3
2.酒	Liquor	100.9	100.9	101.0	101.6	101.7	102.3	102.5	103.0	103.5	103.5	103.5	104.0
白酒	White Spirit	101.4	101.3	101.6	102.1	102.2	102.9	103.0	103.5	103.9	104.0	104.1	104.8
葡萄酒	Grape	102.9	103.2	103.3	103.7	103.7	106.3	106.9	107.0	107.5	107.6	107.5	107.5
啤酒	Beer	99.8	99.9	99.7	100.5	100.6	100.7	101.1	101.5	102.0	102.0	101.9	102.1
其他	Others	99.0	99.0	99.0	99.8	99.9	100.8	100.9	100.7	100.9	100.9	101.0	101.0
3.吸烟、饮酒用品	Appliances For Smoking and Drinking	100.3	100.3	100.2	100.3	100.4	100.4	100.4	100.4	100.0	100.2	100.1	99.9
吸烟用品	Appliances for Smoking	100.4	100.3	100.3	100.4	100.4	100.4	100.4	100.4	100.2	100.6	100.6	100.4
饮酒用品	Appliances For Drinking	100.2	100.2	100.1	100.2	100.4	100.4	100.4	100.4	99.8	99.9	99.7	99.5
三、衣着	**Clothing**	**100.7**	**99.5**	**99.0**	**98.5**	**98.0**	**98.0**	**96.9**	**96.1**	**96.4**	**97.4**	**98.0**	**98.1**
1.服装	Garments	100.2	98.6	97.7	97.3	96.8	96.8	96.4	95.8	96.0	97.4	98.2	98.5
（1）男式服装	Men's Garments	99.9	98.7	97.6	97.1	96.2	96.1	95.6	94.9	95.0	96.5	97.4	97.7
大衣	Topcoat	96.6	95.0	94.2	92.6	92.6	91.8	91.7	91.7	91.3	91.1	91.2	92.5
毛线衣	Woollen Sweater	104.1	98.0	93.2	92.8	91.7	91.9	90.7	90.1	90.4	93.0	94.7	96.1
夹克衫	Jacket	98.5	97.6	95.5	94.9	94.8	94.8	94.4	94.5	94.4	97.6	98.0	98.5
衬衫	Shirt	96.4	95.2	95.3	94.6	93.7	94.4	92.9	91.8	92.4	93.1	92.9	94.3
T恤衫	T-shirt	101.6	102.3	101.7	101.7	100.4	97.7	94.5	92.0	92.5	92.6	93.2	93.2
裤子	Trousers	99.0	96.9	95.9	95.6	95.0	94.6	94.4	93.8	93.0	96.2	96.7	96.6
西服	Western-style Clothes	100.3	101.3	99.8	100.4	99.9	99.7	100.3	97.9	99.5	101.1	100.7	100.4
运动衫裤	Gym Suit	98.4	98.4	98.3	98.0	93.9	94.2	93.7	94.3	94.3	94.5	95.5	96.2
内衣	Underwaist	103.1	103.0	104.1	103.8	103.3	103.7	103.3	103.5	103.1	103.5	103.2	103.4
羽绒衣	Eider Down Outerwear	101.4	99.5	98.9	96.6	96.6	96.5	96.0	95.7	95.1	97.8	102.9	101.5
其他	Others	98.0	97.1	96.0	95.3	95.6	95.7	95.6	95.1	95.1	95.1	98.6	98.6
（2）女式服装	Women's Garments	100.5	98.3	97.6	97.1	96.6	96.8	96.6	96.1	96.6	98.0	98.9	99.2
大衣	Topcoat	100.3	93.4	91.0	90.1	90.0	90.0	89.9	89.9	89.5	89.5	90.3	93.9
毛线衣	Woollen Sweater	101.8	94.0	92.7	92.4	91.3	91.6	91.6	91.6	92.7	95.3	96.6	98.3
羽绒衣	Eider Down Outerwear	99.4	98.5	97.4	97.3	97.3	97.0	96.6	96.5	95.7	99.8	104.8	103.6
套装	Coordinates	100.8	100.1	100.1	100.0	100.7	99.4	99.8	97.1	101.3	102.4	101.0	101.4
衬衫	Shirt	98.9	100.0	100.4	98.7	98.4	98.7	99.3	97.5	98.2	98.6	98.4	97.0

7-11 续表 3 continued

商品类别及品名	Commodity Category and Commodity Name	1月 January	2月 February	3月 March	4月 April	5月 May	6月 June	7月 July	8月 August	9月 September	10月 October	11月 November	12月 December
		（以2005年平均价格为100）											
T恤衫	T-shirt	99.8	100.4	100.0	99.3	99.6	100.3	98.6	97.8	99.6	104.0	104.0	103.9
裙子	Skirt	102.6	101.8	101.5	100.2	101.8	102.0	101.4	101.3	101.0	101.3	102.2	101.9
裤子	Trousers	102.1	99.4	97.7	97.6	97.0	97.3	96.9	96.6	97.0	97.4	98.5	97.6
运动衫裤	Gym Suit	100.0	100.5	99.6	100.0	94.5	94.9	94.7	94.5	94.4	96.0	95.0	96.7
内衣	Underwaist	98.4	98.4	99.9	101.0	100.7	101.3	100.9	101.1	100.4	101.3	102.9	102.8
其他	Others	100.0	99.7	100.2	101.0	100.4	100.9	100.9	101.4	101.2	101.8	102.1	101.9
（3）儿童服装	Children's Garments	99.7	99.4	99.0	99.2	99.7	99.7	98.6	97.9	97.3	97.9	98.4	98.4
套装	Coordinates	99.6	99.6	98.7	98.7	97.7	97.7	97.8	97.3	96.6	97.1	97.7	97.7
裤子	Trousers	99.5	98.7	98.3	98.0	98.5	98.5	96.6	96.6	96.5	97.7	98.2	98.7
裙子	Skirt	99.4	99.6	100.0	101.4	104.3	104.4	102.2	100.5	99.2	99.7	99.9	99.6
其他	Others	104.0	102.1	99.3	97.5	96.3	96.0	95.7	95.7	96.5	96.5	97.4	96.6
2.衣着材料	Clothing Materials	99.7	99.8	99.6	99.8	99.7	99.8	99.7	99.9	99.5	99.9	100.0	100.6
棉布	Cotton Cloth	99.9	99.8	99.9	100.6	100.4	100.5	100.8	101.1	100.6	101.6	101.5	101.5
棉混纺布	Cotton Textiles Cloth	99.6	99.7	99.7	99.7	99.6	99.6	99.3	99.6	99.0	99.4	99.7	100.0
化纤布	Chemical Fiber Cloth	99.8	100.1	99.8	99.8	99.7	100.0	99.7	99.8	99.6	99.7	99.8	99.9
毛线	Knitting Wool	99.4	99.3	99.2	99.2	99.1	99.1	99.2	99.1	98.8	99.0	99.1	101.0
3.鞋袜帽	Shoes,Socks and Hats	102.5	101.9	102.4	101.7	100.8	100.7	97.8	96.2	96.7	96.8	97.1	96.4
（1）鞋	Shoes	102.8	102.1	102.7	101.9	101.0	100.9	97.5	95.6	96.2	96.3	96.7	95.9
男鞋	Men's Shoes	100.8	100.0	101.2	100.7	99.8	100.5	96.8	95.7	95.9	95.8	96.3	95.7
女鞋	Women's Shoes	104.5	103.8	104.3	103.0	101.6	101.1	97.2	94.6	95.8	95.7	96.1	95.0
童鞋	Children's Shoes	101.1	101.1	100.6	100.7	101.4	101.1	100.5	99.7	98.9	99.8	100.3	100.3
（2）袜子	Socks	100.9	101.0	100.3	100.8	99.9	100.0	99.8	99.8	99.4	99.9	98.9	98.7
男袜	Men's Socks	101.4	101.4	101.2	101.6	101.3	101.1	100.9	100.9	100.5	100.9	98.7	98.2
女袜	Women's Socks	100.7	100.7	99.8	100.4	99.2	99.4	99.3	99.3	98.8	99.3	99.0	99.0
（3）帽子	Hats	100.3	99.9	99.7	99.8	99.8	99.8	99.8	99.8	99.6	100.1	100.7	100.8
男帽	Men's Hats	100.2	99.8	99.4	99.4	99.7	99.9	100.0	99.9	99.5	99.8	101.3	101.4
女帽	Women's Hats	100.3	99.9	99.9	99.9	99.8	99.8	99.8	99.7	99.6	100.3	100.4	100.4
4.衣着加工服务费	Clothing Manufacturing Services	100.1	100.2	100.2	100.0	100.0	100.0	100.1	100.3	100.3	100.3	100.3	100.3
缝纫	Sewing	100.1	100.1	100.2	100.2	100.2	100.2	100.2	100.3	100.3	100.3	100.3	100.3
清洗	Washing	100.1	100.2	100.3	99.9	99.9	99.9	100.0	100.2	100.3	100.3	100.3	100.3
四、家庭设备用品及维修服务	**Household Facilities, Articles and Services**	**100.4**	**100.5**	**100.6**	**100.6**	**100.7**	**101.8**	**102.2**	**102.5**	**102.5**	**102.6**	**102.7**	**102.9**
1.耐用消费品	Durable Consumer Goods	100.3	100.4	100.5	100.4	100.6	102.4	103.0	103.2	103.1	103.3	103.4	103.4
（1）家具	Furniture	100.4	100.4	100.4	100.1	100.0	100.1	100.1	100.4	100.7	100.8	100.8	100.9
柜	Cabinet	101.0	101.0	101.0	100.1	100.2	100.4	100.3	100.9	101.2	100.9	101.2	101.1
床	Bed	100.3	100.5	100.6	100.5	100.3	100.2	100.5	100.7	100.8	101.3	100.6	100.6
桌	Desk	100.0	100.2	100.0	100.1	99.7	99.5	99.2	99.5	99.7	99.7	100.0	100.4
椅	Chair	100.4	99.9	100.0	99.9	99.9	100.0	99.9	100.1	101.1	101.7	101.9	101.8
沙发	Sofa	100.1	100.2	100.2	100.0	99.7	100.0	100.1	100.3	100.5	100.4	100.4	100.4
其他	Others	100.4	100.2	100.3	100.3	99.4	100.3	100.9	101.0	101.7	101.3	101.3	101.4
（2）家庭设备	Household Appliances	100.2	100.4	100.5	100.5	100.9	103.5	104.4	104.6	104.3	104.5	104.7	104.7
洗衣机	Washing Machine	100.0	100.1	100.0	99.0	99.6	100.9	101.8	101.7	101.3	101.2	101.5	101.4

7-11 续表 4 continued

商品类别及品名	Commodity Category and Commodity Name	1月 January	2月 February	3月 March	4月 April	5月 May	6月 June	7月 July	8月 August	9月 September	10月 October	11月 November	12月 December
		（以2005年平均价格为100）											
电风扇	Electric Fan	99.7	99.8	99.9	99.5	99.9	100.3	99.8	100.1	99.3	99.6	99.7	99.7
电冰箱（柜）	Refrigerator	102.4	102.4	102.6	103.2	104.3	107.6	109.2	109.0	109.0	109.7	109.4	109.6
吸排油烟机	Kitchen Ventilato	102.4	102.4	102.3	102.4	102.1	105.0	107.1	108.5	107.9	107.7	108.1	108.3
空调器	Air-conditioning	99.9	100.2	100.3	100.0	100.7	105.1	106.2	106.7	106.2	106.3	106.6	106.8
热水器	Water Heater	98.8	99.3	99.9	100.7	100.1	100.6	100.6	100.3	100.8	101.0	101.0	101.0
微波炉	Microwave Oven	97.4	97.4	97.3	97.3	97.2	97.9	97.7	97.7	97.5	97.7	98.1	97.5
电炊具	Electric Cooking Appliance	99.8	99.7	99.8	100.9	101.1	101.0	101.0	101.1	100.6	101.0	101.0	101.1
2.室内装饰品	Interior Decorations	100.1	100.1	100.1	99.9	99.5	99.6	99.6	99.9	99.7	100.0	100.1	100.2
纺织装饰品	Textile Process Decorations	99.5	99.5	99.5	99.3	99.3	99.3	99.0	99.3	98.6	99.2	99.2	99.2
装饰灯具	Architectural Lamps and Lanterns	101.2	101.2	101.2	101.0	99.8	99.8	100.5	100.3	100.9	101.0	100.7	100.7
其他	Others	100.1	100.1	100.0	99.9	99.9	99.9	99.7	100.7	100.4	100.6	101.8	101.8
3.床上用品	Bedclothes	98.6	99.7	100.0	99.9	99.2	99.8	99.5	99.2	98.8	99.0	98.9	99.6
毛毯	Woollen Blanket	100.5	101.1	101.5	101.4	100.5	101.5	100.5	100.3	100.1	100.5	99.6	101.2
被子	Quilt	98.2	98.7	98.8	98.6	97.6	98.5	98.2	97.4	97.1	96.7	96.6	97.5
床上套件	Bed Articles	97.7	98.8	99.3	99.2	98.7	99.2	99.1	99.1	98.4	99.0	99.2	99.5
其他	Others	99.1	102.0	102.3	102.5	102.4	102.1	102.1	102.1	102.0	102.3	102.4	102.7
4.日用杂品	Sundry Articles	100.2	100.3	100.4	100.5	100.7	101.0	100.9	101.1	101.0	101.2	101.2	101.3
茶具	Tea Set	99.1	99.2	99.5	100.1	100.0	100.0	100.0	100.1	100.0	100.3	99.9	100.3
餐具	Tableware	98.8	98.8	98.8	98.8	100.0	100.1	99.4	100.3	100.3	100.5	100.5	100.8
厨具	Kitchen Utensils	100.2	100.2	100.2	101.2	101.2	101.9	102.0	101.9	101.9	101.9	102.1	101.9
家用手工工具	Domestic Handwork Tools	101.7	101.7	101.7	101.6	101.4	101.4	101.1	101.6	101.6	101.6	100.9	100.9
洗涤用品	Washing Articles	101.4	101.6	101.6	101.4	101.6	101.7	101.6	102.3	101.9	102.0	102.1	102.4
其他	Others	99.8	99.9	99.8	99.9	100.0	100.6	100.5	100.2	100.2	100.6	100.6	100.6
5.家庭服务及加工维修服务	Household Service and Manufacturing Upkeep	105.3	104.0	104.0	104.0	104.0	104.1	104.6	107.6	108.2	108.3	108.8	109.8
家庭服务	Household Service	110.7	107.8	107.8	107.8	107.8	107.8	108.7	114.5	115.9	116.0	117.2	117.3
加工维修服务	Manufacturing Upkeep	101.0	101.0	101.0	101.0	101.0	101.2	101.4	102.1	102.1	102.1	102.1	103.9
五、医疗保健和个人用品	**Health Care and Personal Articles**	**100.1**	**100.1**	**100.2**	**100.3**	**100.4**	**100.5**	**100.5**	**100.5**	**100.2**	**100.5**	**100.5**	**100.6**
1.医疗保健	Health Care	99.9	99.7	99.7	99.7	99.6	99.7	99.7	99.7	99.2	99.5	99.5	99.6
（1）医疗器具及用品	Medical Facilities and Goods	97.5	97.6	97.3	97.3	97.4	97.3	97.2	97.2	97.2	94.9	94.9	94.9
医疗器具及用品	Medical Facilities and Goods	97.5	97.6	97.3	97.3	97.4	97.3	97.2	97.2	97.2	94.9	94.9	94.9
（2）中药材及中成药	Herbs and Ready-made Traditional Chinese Medicine	100.1	99.6	100.0	99.7	99.3	100.1	99.4	99.5	98.9	101.0	101.1	101.2
中药材	Herbs	98.9	98.2	98.4	98.2	98.4	100.7	99.9	100.1	99.9	103.6	103.9	104.3
中成药	Ready-made Traditinonal Chinese Medicine	101.0	100.8	101.2	100.8	100.0	99.5	99.1	99.1	98.0	98.8	98.8	98.8
（3）西药	Western Medicine	99.7	99.6	99.5	99.4	99.5	99.3	99.5	99.4	98.7	98.4	98.3	98.4
抗微生物药	Anti-microorganism Medicine	99.9	99.9	100.0	100.0	100.1	100.7	103.0	102.5	101.5	100.9	101.2	100.9

7-11 续表 5 continued

商品类别及品名	Commodity Category and Commodity Name	（以2005年平均价格为100）											
		1月 January	2月 February	3月 March	4月 April	5月 May	6月 June	7月 July	8月 August	9月 September	10月 October	11月 November	12月 December
消化系统用药	Alimentary System Medicine	98.8	98.8	99.1	99.3	99.7	99.6	99.6	99.6	99.1	99.5	98.6	99.4
呼吸系统用药	Respiratory System Medicine	99.5	99.5	99.2	99.2	99.2	100.1	100.1	100.1	100.0	100.2	100.2	100.2
解热镇痛及非甾体抗炎药	Allays a Fever the Analgesia and the Non-steroid Body Anti-inflammatory Agent	100.2	99.9	99.7	99.5	99.4	98.2	97.5	97.4	96.5	98.0	98.3	98.4
抗肿瘤药	Antineoplastic Drug	100.2	100.1	99.8	99.7	99.7	97.7	97.5	97.4	97.4	94.7	94.7	94.7
激素及调节内分泌功能药	Hormone and Adjustment Internal Secretion Function Medicine	99.1	99.0	98.5	98.5	98.5	97.8	97.8	97.5	95.5	92.9	94.1	93.9
循环系统用药	Circulating System Medicine	99.5	99.4	99.1	98.8	98.9	99.8	99.3	99.1	99.5	100.7	99.1	99.9
神经系统用药	Nerve System Medicine	100.9	100.9	100.2	100.2	100.2	99.4	99.4	98.6	97.7	94.2	94.2	94.2
专科用药	Junior Medicine	100.1	100.1	100.2	100.0	100.0	100.4	100.0	100.1	97.7	95.2	95.5	95.5
其他	Others	99.7	99.7	98.8	98.8	98.2	97.9	97.9	97.9	97.7	96.9	96.5	96.3
（4）保健品及器具	Healthcare Equipment	100.5	100.3	100.1	100.1	100.0	100.0	99.6	99.7	99.7	99.9	100.0	99.9
保健器具	Health Protection Equipment	100.1	99.6	99.4	99.4	99.2	99.2	98.8	98.8	98.8	98.8	98.8	98.4
滋补保健用品	Tonic and Health Products	100.7	100.6	100.4	100.4	100.4	100.4	99.9	100.1	100.0	100.4	100.6	100.5
（5）医疗保健服务	Health Care Services	100.1	100.2	100.2	100.3	100.3	100.3	100.5	100.5	100.5	100.4	100.5	100.5
挂号费	Registration	100.3	100.4	100.6	100.6	100.6	100.6	100.8	100.8	100.8	100.8	100.8	100.8
注射费	Injection Expenses	100.0	100.0	100.1	100.1	100.1	100.1	100.1	100.1	100.1	100.1	100.1	100.1
检查费	Examination Expenses	99.9	100.0	100.0	100.0	100.0	100.2	100.2	100.2	100.7	100.7	100.8	100.9
手术费	Operation Expenses	100.3	100.3	100.3	100.3	100.3	100.3	100.3	100.3	100.3	100.3	100.3	100.3
住院费	Hospitalization Expenses	100.3	100.3	100.3	100.7	100.7	100.7	101.8	101.8	101.3	100.7	100.7	100.8
理疗费	Physiotherapy Expenses	99.9	99.9	99.9	99.9	99.9	99.9	99.9	99.9	99.9	99.9	99.9	99.9
化验费	Analysis Expenses	100.1	100.1	100.3	100.3	100.3	100.3	100.3	100.3	100.3	100.1	100.1	100.1
其他	Others	100.3	100.3	100.3	100.3	100.3	100.3	100.3	100.3	100.3	100.3	100.3	100.3
2.个人用品及服务	Personal Articles and Services	100.6	100.9	100.9	101.3	101.9	102.0	101.8	102.1	102.0	102.4	102.3	102.4
（1）化妆美容用品	Cosmetics	98.8	98.9	98.9	99.0	98.9	99.0	98.7	99.0	98.6	99.2	98.8	98.6
化妆美容器具	Cosmetics Appliances	100.1	100.1	100.1	100.5	100.6	101.0	101.0	101.3	100.8	101.0	100.9	100.9
美容化妆品	Facial Beautifiers	98.7	98.8	98.8	98.9	98.8	98.8	99.1	99.1	99.1	99.3	99.4	99.3
护肤品	Protects Skin Products	99.4	99.6	99.5	99.6	99.6	99.6	99.5	99.9	97.5	100.1	98.9	98.3
护发美容品	Protects Sends the Beauty Products	98.2	98.3	98.3	98.3	98.1	98.1	96.9	97.6	97.5	97.7	96.8	96.7
（2）清洁化妆用品	Cleaning Toiletware	100.3	100.3	100.3	100.2	100.5	100.8	100.4	100.7	100.5	100.6	100.7	100.6
洗发用品	Hairdressing Articles	100.3	100.3	100.3	100.2	100.1	100.7	100.3	100.5	100.3	100.5	100.0	99.7
洗浴用品	Bathing Articles	100.3	100.3	100.1	99.7	99.8	99.8	99.5	100.0	99.9	99.9	100.3	100.5
其他	Others	100.2	100.6	101.1	101.4	103.5	104.0	103.6	103.6	103.3	103.4	103.8	103.7

7-11 续表 6 continued

商品类别及品名	Commodity Category and Commodity Name	（以2005年平均价格为100）											
		1月 January	2月 February	3月 March	4月 April	5月 May	6月 June	7月 July	8 月 August	9 月 September	10 月 October	11月 November	12月 December
（3）个人饰品	Personal Decoraions	102.6	103.7	104.1	106.3	109.0	109.1	109.3	109.7	110.1	110.7	110.9	111.2
首饰	Ornaments	105.2	107.2	107.9	112.1	117.2	117.7	119.1	119.6	119.8	120.2	120.5	121.8
皮件	Leather Appliance	99.5	99.7	100.3	100.3	100.1	100.0	97.4	99.3	99.3	100.5	100.7	99.6
手表	Watch	98.2	98.0	98.0	98.4	98.4	96.5	95.9	95.9	96.1	97.4	97.8	97.8
领带	Necktie	100.9	100.7	100.3	99.4	98.9	98.6	97.8	96.8	98.7	98.6	98.6	96.5
其他	Others	97.6	97.7	98.6	98.3	98.6	98.7	98.6	99.1	98.5	99.0	98.9	99.4
（4）个人服务	Personal Services	102.2	102.2	102.2	102.2	102.2	102.2	102.2	102.2	102.4	102.4	102.4	102.9
美容	Cosmetology	103.0	103.0	103.0	103.0	103.0	103.0	103.0	103.0	103.0	103.0	103.0	103.0
理（烫）发	Haircut(permanent wave)	100.8	100.8	100.8	100.8	100.8	100.8	100.8	100.8	101.3	101.3	101.3	102.2
洗浴	Bathe	107.5	107.5	107.5	107.5	107.5	107.5	107.7	107.7	107.7	107.7	107.7	108.1
其他	Others	102.7	102.7	102.7	102.7	102.7	102.7	102.7	102.7	102.7	102.7	102.7	102.7
六、交通和通信	**Transportation and Communication**	**98.8**	**98.6**	**98.0**	**97.7**	**97.8**	**98.1**	**98.0**	**97.7**	**97.4**	**97.0**	**96.9**	**96.7**
1.交通	Transportation	102.0	102.1	101.7	102.2	102.7	103.9	104.2	104.2	104.0	104.0	103.9	103.6
（1）交通工具	Transportation Facility	99.7	99.6	99.5	99.4	98.9	98.9	98.8	98.4	97.6	97.5	97.2	96.4
摩托车	Motorcycle	99.7	99.7	99.7	99.7	100.1	100.3	100.3	100.7	100.8	100.9	100.7	99.7
自行车	Bicycle	100.4	100.3	100.2	100.2	99.9	100.0	100.5	100.1	100.2	100.4	100.4	99.9
轿车	Car	99.2	99.1	99.0	98.7	97.9	97.8	97.4	96.7	95.0	94.8	94.4	93.3
其他	Others	101.1	101.1	101.1	100.9	99.2	99.1	99.1	99.1	99.1	97.1	97.1	97.1
（2）车用燃料及零配件	Fuels and Parts	104.1	104.1	104.5	108.1	110.1	115.8	115.9	115.9	116.2	116.2	116.2	116.3
汽油	Gasoline	105.6	105.6	106.1	111.8	114.6	122.4	122.5	122.5	122.6	122.6	122.6	122.6
柴油	Diesel Oil	106.3	106.2	106.8	110.3	112.5	120.7	121.0	121.0	121.2	121.2	121.4	121.7
零配件	Parts	99.7	99.6	99.6	99.6	99.7	99.7	99.7	99.8	100.2	100.2	100.3	100.3
其他	Others	100.5	100.1	100.1	100.1	100.2	100.2	100.2	100.2	100.9	100.9	100.9	100.9
（3）车辆使用及维修费	Using and Upkeep Fare	99.7	99.7	99.6	99.6	99.6	99.7	99.7	100.6	100.7	100.7	100.7	100.7
驾驶证	Driving License	97.2	97.2	97.2	97.2	97.2	97.2	97.3	97.3	97.3	97.3	97.3	97.3
保险费	Insurance Expenses	99.9	99.9	99.7	99.6	99.6	99.6	99.5	100.1	100.2	100.3	100.3	100.3
停车费	Parking Expenses	100.5	100.5	100.5	100.5	100.5	100.5	100.5	105.8	105.8	105.8	105.8	105.8
车辆修理服务费	Vehicle Upkeep Service Fare	99.9	99.9	99.9	99.9	99.9	100.2	100.2	100.2	100.1	100.1	100.1	100.1
其他	Others	100.0	100.0	100.0	100.2	100.2	100.2	100.2	99.8	99.8	99.8	99.8	99.8
（4）市区公共交通费	Incity Traffic Fare	102.8	102.8	102.8	102.8	104.5	104.6	106.1	106.5	106.5	106.5	106.5	106.6
公共汽车票	Bus Ticket	101.5	101.6	101.6	101.6	101.6	101.6	102.1	102.1	102.1	102.1	102.1	102.2
出租汽车	Taxi	104.0	104.0	104.0	104.0	107.3	107.5	110.2	110.7	110.7	110.8	110.8	110.8
其他	Others	103.9	103.9	103.9	104.4	104.4	104.4	104.4	110.6	110.6	110.6	110.6	110.1
（5）城市间交通费	Intercity Traffic Fare	105.5	105.7	103.5	103.7	104.5	106.1	106.2	106.3	106.6	106.7	106.7	106.7
飞机票	Airplane Ticket	99.8	99.8	99.0	101.7	103.4	102.0	102.2	104.2	105.2	106.0	105.4	105.4
火车票	Train Ticket	101.7	101.0	100.7	100.7	100.7	100.8	100.8	100.8	100.9	100.9	101.0	101.0
长途汽车	Intertown Bus	108.3	109.1	105.7	105.7	105.6	108.5	108.5	108.5	108.9	108.9	108.9	108.9
其他	Others	103.5	103.2	101.1	101.1	120.8	120.9	120.9	121.1	121.1	121.1	121.1	121.1
2.通信	Communication	95.7	95.3	94.5	93.5	93.1	92.6	92.2	91.5	91.1	90.4	90.3	90.2
（1）通信工具	Communication Facility	88.6	87.5	85.3	82.6	81.4	80.0	78.9	77.1	75.9	74.2	73.3	72.3
固定电话机	Telephone	98.4	97.9	96.7	96.2	95.8	95.8	95.4	94.9	94.7	94.6	94.6	93.5
移动电话机	Mobile Phone	85.9	84.7	82.2	78.9	77.5	75.7	74.4	72.2	70.7	68.6	67.5	66.4
其他	Others	97.3	97.3	97.1	96.6	95.7	95.6	95.5	95.5	95.3	95.2	95.1	95.1

7-11 续表 7 continued

商品类别及品名	Commodity Category and Commodity Name	1月 January	2月 February	3月 March	4月 April	5月 May	6月 June	7月 July	8月 August	9月 September	10月 October	11月 November	12月 December
		（以2005年平均价格为100）											
（2）通信服务	Communication Service	99.9	99.9	99.9	99.9	99.9	99.9	99.9	99.9	99.9	99.9	100.3	100.6
移动通信费	Mobile Communication Fee	99.5	99.5	99.5	99.5	99.5	99.5	99.5	99.5	99.5	99.5	99.5	99.5
市内电话费	Incity Telephone Fee	100.0	100.0	100.0	100.0	100.0	100.0	100.0	100.0	100.0	100.0	100.0	100.0
长途电话费	Long Distance Call Fee	100.0	100.0	100.0	100.0	100.0	100.0	100.0	100.0	100.0	100.0	100.0	100.0
月租费	Month Hiring Fee	100.0	100.0	100.0	100.0	100.0	100.0	100.0	100.0	100.0	100.0	100.0	100.0
上网费	Net Play Fee	101.4	101.1	101.1	101.1	101.1	101.1	101.1	101.1	101.4	101.4	101.4	101.4
信件邮寄	Letter Post	100.0	100.0	100.0	100.0	100.0	100.0	100.0	100.0	100.0	100.0	115.9	133.1
包裹邮寄	Package Post	100.0	100.0	100.0	100.0	100.0	100.0	100.0	100.0	100.0	100.0	102.1	102.1
其他	Others	100.0	100.0	100.0	100.0	100.0	100.0	100.0	100.0	100.0	100.0	100.0	100.0
七、娱乐教育文化用品及服务	**Recreation,Education and Culture Articles**	**100.1**	**99.8**	**99.6**	**100.0**	**99.9**	**99.4**	**99.7**	**100.1**	**99.7**	**99.7**	**99.2**	**99.2**
1.文娱用耐用消费品及服务	Durable Consumer Goods For Cultural and Recreational Use and Service	97.7	97.5	97.2	96.7	96.3	95.8	95.5	94.8	93.5	93.1	92.9	92.6
电视机	Television	96.7	96.6	96.3	94.8	94.8	94.3	93.9	92.6	91.0	89.9	89.5	88.9
激光视盘机	Laser Video Disc Machine	99.9	99.2	98.9	98.6	98.4	98.4	98.4	98.4	97.2	96.3	96.3	96.2
摄像机	Pickup Camera	98.2	97.8	97.0	96.3	96.0	95.0	94.5	94.5	93.5	93.3	92.9	92.4
照相机	Camera	98.0	97.3	96.0	94.7	94.5	94.4	94.3	94.3	93.5	93.3	93.7	93.8
家用音响	Acoustic Equipment	99.7	99.7	99.6	99.4	99.2	99.3	99.3	99.2	98.7	98.8	98.8	98.7
便携式音响	Portable Acoustics	99.5	97.7	97.1	96.9	96.8	96.8	96.8	96.6	96.1	96.3	96.3	96.3
电脑	Computer	97.2	97.1	97.0	97.0	96.2	95.6	95.1	94.3	92.9	92.9	92.6	92.4
修理服务	Repair Service	100.5	100.5	100.5	100.5	100.5	100.5	100.7	100.7	100.7	100.7	100.7	100.7
其他	Others	98.2	100.2	99.8	99.5	99.3	99.3	99.1	98.7	96.2	96.6	96.2	96.2
2.教育	Education	101.1	101.1	101.2	101.0	101.0	101.0	101.0	101.2	101.6	101.6	101.6	101.7
（1）教材及参考书	Teaching Material and Reference Books	101.3	101.3	101.5	101.5	101.5	101.4	101.4	102.4	102.2	102.0	102.0	102.0
工具书	Tool Book	101.6	101.6	101.6	101.6	101.6	101.6	101.6	101.6	101.6	101.6	101.6	101.7
教材	Teaching Material	100.5	100.5	100.8	100.8	100.8	100.8	100.8	102.0	100.8	100.3	100.3	100.3
参考书	Reference Book	102.8	102.8	102.9	102.9	102.9	102.6	102.6	104.4	105.4	105.4	105.4	105.4
教育软件	Educational Software	100.0	99.9	99.9	99.9	99.9	99.9	99.9	99.9	99.9	99.9	99.9	99.9
（2）学杂托幼费	Tuition and Child Care	101.1	101.1	101.1	100.9	100.9	100.9	100.9	100.9	101.5	101.5	101.5	101.6
义务教育杂费	Incidental Expenses of Compulcory Education	101.8	101.8	101.8	101.8	101.8	101.8	101.8	101.8	101.8	101.8	101.8	101.8
非义务教育学杂费	Tuition of Non-compulsory Education	100.0	100.0	100.0	100.0	100.0	100.0	100.0	100.0	101.3	101.3	101.3	101.3
技能培训学费	Skill Train Tuition	102.7	102.7	102.7	101.0	101.0	101.0	101.0	101.0	100.6	100.6	100.6	100.6
托幼费	Child care	102.3	102.3	102.3	102.3	102.3	102.3	102.3	102.3	102.4	102.4	102.4	103.5
其他	Others	100.0	100.0	100.0	100.0	100.0	100.0	100.0	100.0	101.5	101.5	101.5	101.5
3.文化娱乐类	Recreation and Culture	100.9	100.6	100.5	101.3	101.5	100.9	101.8	101.7	100.8	101.8	101.0	101.2
（1）文化娱乐用品	Culture Articles	100.1	99.9	99.7	99.5	99.5	99.6	99.6	99.6	99.3	99.4	99.3	99.3
乐器	Musical Instrument	100.3	100.3	100.3	100.4	100.3	100.4	100.3	100.3	100.4	100.5	100.6	100.8
音响光盘和磁带	Audio,Disk and Tape	99.7	98.0	97.5	97.7	97.7	97.7	97.7	97.7	97.5	97.7	97.7	97.7
照相胶卷和存储卡	Roll Film and Memorizing Card	100.6	100.5	100.5	100.0	99.9	99.6	99.6	99.5	99.0	98.0	97.5	97.3
录像磁带和视盘	Video Tape and Disk	99.7	99.5	99.6	99.8	100.1	100.3	100.3	100.3	100.3	100.4	100.1	100.1
儿童玩具	Children's Toy	101.1	101.0	100.2	99.7	99.8	99.9	100.0	99.9	99.6	99.7	99.7	99.7

7-11 续表 8 continued

商品类别及品名	Commodity Category and Commodity Name	1月 January	2月 February	3月 March	4月 April	5月 May	6月 June	7月 July	8月 August	9月 September	10月 October	11月 November	12月 December
		（以2005年平均价格为100）											
纸张本册	Paper and Volume	100.6	100.6	100.6	100.6	100.6	100.5	100.4	100.4	100.5	101.0	100.9	100.9
文具	Stationery	98.8	98.9	98.9	98.8	98.8	98.8	98.8	98.8	98.3	98.5	98.5	98.5
体育用品	Sports Goods	99.1	99.1	99.1	99.1	98.9	99.0	99.3	99.3	99.0	99.3	98.8	98.9
其他	Others	100.1	100.1	100.1	99.9	99.8	99.5	99.7	99.7	98.7	99.4	99.4	99.4
（2）书报杂志	Books,Newspapers, Magazines	102.7	102.7	102.9	102.9	102.9	102.9	102.9	102.9	102.9	102.9	102.9	103.0
书籍	Books	101.3	101.3	101.7	101.7	101.7	101.7	101.7	101.7	101.7	101.7	101.7	101.9
报纸	Newspapers	106.5	106.5	106.5	106.5	106.5	106.5	106.5	106.5	106.5	106.5	106.5	106.5
杂志	Magazines	100.1	100.1	100.1	100.1	100.1	100.1	100.1	100.1	100.1	100.1	100.1	100.2
（3）文娱费	Expenditure of Culture and Recreation	100.6	99.7	99.6	102.5	103.1	101.2	104.0	103.9	101.2	104.2	101.9	102.3
电影票	Film Ticket	110.5	105.0	103.5	101.8	98.8	100.5	100.1	99.6	100.1	102.7	100.8	101.8
景点门票	Scene Spot Ticket	93.2	93.2	93.6	108.5	113.8	102.8	116.8	116.8	103.2	115.3	105.9	107.2
有线电视	Cable Television	100.0	100.0	100.0	100.0	100.0	100.0	100.0	100.0	100.0	100.2	100.2	100.2
健身活动	Exercise	100.7	100.7	101.2	101.9	101.9	101.9	101.9	101.9	101.8	101.8	101.8	101.8
其他	Others	101.9	101.9	101.9	101.9	101.9	101.9	102.0	102.0	102.0	102.0	102.0	101.7
4.旅游	Tourism	99.1	96.7	95.2	100.4	99.7	96.6	99.5	103.6	102.0	101.9	97.8	98.0
旅行社收费	Travel Agency Charge	99.0	96.2	94.3	99.8	98.7	95.2	97.8	102.1	101.7	101.9	96.8	97.1
宾馆住宿	Guesthouse Stay	100.2	98.7	99.0	103.1	103.2	101.9	103.9	105.7	103.3	103.5	102.9	102.5
其他住宿	Other Stay	98.7	97.8	97.8	102.0	104.0	101.0	108.4	114.7	102.3	99.6	99.5	99.9
八、居住	**Residence**	**103.3**	**103.3**	**103.1**	**103.7**	**104.1**	**104.2**	**104.6**	**105.1**	**106.1**	**106.3**	**106.8**	**106.9**
1.建房及装修材料	Building and Building Decoration Materials	101.6	101.6	101.7	101.9	102.2	102.8	103.3	103.8	105.0	105.6	107.3	107.7
木材	Wood	102.7	102.9	102.7	102.5	102.1	102.9	103.4	104.6	106.0	106.6	111.0	111.8
木地板	Wood Floor	103.5	103.5	102.5	105.3	105.8	106.6	107.0	107.4	108.8	109.2	111.4	111.5
砖	Brick	102.8	102.4	102.8	102.3	103.4	104.2	104.9	106.9	106.8	106.7	108.1	108.8
水泥	Cement	98.7	98.7	99.1	99.4	99.8	100.4	100.5	99.9	100.3	100.9	102.3	102.5
涂料	Coating Material	100.7	100.8	100.8	100.9	100.9	102.6	102.9	102.8	101.9	102.0	102.3	102.4
胶合板	Plywood	100.8	101.0	101.2	101.7	101.6	102.1	102.9	103.1	105.1	105.7	108.1	108.7
玻璃	Glass	101.1	100.9	101.4	101.4	102.3	102.3	102.8	102.8	103.9	104.6	104.8	104.9
粘胶	Rayon	100.8	100.8	100.8	100.8	100.9	101.8	102.0	102.5	103.4	104.3	105.2	105.8
油漆	Paint	100.4	100.6	100.8	100.9	101.2	101.3	102.1	102.1	107.4	107.4	107.0	107.0
其他	Others	102.8	102.6	102.6	102.6	102.6	102.8	102.8	103.0	103.6	106.7	106.8	107.3
2.租房	Renting	100.3	100.3	103.1	103.1	103.4	103.9	106.6	107.5	108.2	108.3	108.3	108.4
公房房租	Public House Rent	100.0	100.0	100.0	100.0	100.0	100.0	100.1	103.4	103.4	103.4	103.5	103.5
私房房租	Private House Rent	100.7	100.7	101.7	101.7	102.4	103.4	106.9	106.9	108.6	108.9	108.9	108.9
其他费用	Other Fare	100.0	100.0	107.8	107.8	107.8	107.8	111.9	111.9	111.9	111.9	111.9	111.9
3.自有住房	Private Housing	101.6	101.7	102.0	102.0	103.2	103.6	103.4	104.3	105.2	105.2	105.2	105.2
房屋贷款利率	Houses Loans Interest Rate	102.5	102.5	102.5	102.5	105.8	106.7	106.7	109.3	110.5	110.5	110.5	110.5
物业管理费用	Propety Management Fee	101.3	101.3	102.2	102.2	102.2	102.2	101.4	101.4	102.2	102.2	102.2	102.2
维护修理费用	Upkeep and Repair Fee	100.1	100.3	100.3	100.3	100.4	100.4	100.4	100.4	100.8	100.8	100.8	100.8
其他	Others	104.5	104.5	104.5	104.5	104.4	104.5	104.7	104.0	104.8	104.5	104.5	104.6
4.水、电、燃料	Water,Electricity and Fuels	104.7	104.7	104.0	104.8	105.2	104.9	105.1	105.5	106.6	106.6	106.6	106.7
水	Water	107.2	107.2	107.8	110.6	111.2	111.2	111.2	111.2	111.2	111.2	111.2	111.2
电	Electricity	101.3	101.3	101.3	101.3	101.3	101.3	102.7	103.0	103.0	103.0	103.0	103.0
液化石油气	Liquefiled Petroleum Gas	116.6	116.2	109.8	109.8	111.2	109.4	106.8	108.7	116.3	116.0	116.1	116.2
管道燃气	Pipelined Gas	100.0	100.0	100.0	100.0	100.0	100.0	100.0	100.0	100.0	100.0	100.0	100.0
其他燃料	Other Fuels	102.4	102.3	102.2	103.1	103.2	102.8	102.9	102.9	104.7	105.0	105.1	105.6

7-12　农村居民消费价格（定基）指数
Rural Consumer Price Indices

（以2005年平均价格为100）

商品类别及品名	Commodity Category and Commodity Name	1月 January	2月 February	3月 March	4月 April	5月 May	6月 June	7月 July	8 月 August	9 月 September	10 月 October	11月 November	12月 December
居民消费价格总指数	**General Consumer Price Index**	**101.1**	**101.3**	**100.7**	**100.9**	**100.7**	**100.1**	**99.9**	**100.6**	**101.3**	**100.8**	**101.5**	**103.2**
非食品价格指数	**No-food**	**100.1**	**100.0**	**100.1**	**100.3**	**100.4**	**100.5**	**100.6**	**100.8**	**100.9**	**101.0**	**101.3**	**101.6**
服务项目价格指数	**Services**	**100.8**	**101.1**	**101.1**	**101.6**	**101.8**	**102.0**	**102.0**	**102.1**	**102.2**	**102.2**	**102.7**	**103.0**
工业品价格指数	**Industrial Products**	**99.8**	**99.6**	**99.7**	**99.9**	**99.9**	**100.0**	**100.1**	**100.3**	**100.4**	**100.6**	**100.9**	**101.1**
扣除食品和能源价格指数	**Deducting Foods and Energy**	**99.8**	**99.8**	**99.9**	**100.1**	**100.2**	**100.3**	**100.4**	**100.5**	**100.6**	**100.7**	**101.1**	**101.3**
扣除鲜菜鲜果总指数	**Deducting Fresh,Vegetables and Fruits**	**99.6**	**99.5**	**99.2**	**99.2**	**99.3**	**99.4**	**99.8**	**100.6**	**101.1**	**101.1**	**102.0**	**103.0**
消费品价格指数	**Consumer Goods**	**101.2**	**101.3**	**100.6**	**100.7**	**100.5**	**99.7**	**99.4**	**100.2**	**101.1**	**100.4**	**101.2**	**103.3**
一、食品	**Food**	**103.8**	**104.4**	**102.1**	**102.3**	**101.4**	**99.1**	**98.2**	**100.0**	**102.2**	**100.2**	**101.8**	**107.4**
1.粮食	Grain	100.1	100.4	100.2	100.7	101.2	101.1	102.8	103.3	105.1	105.9	108.1	110.7
大米	Rice	104.1	103.7	103.6	104.7	107.1	108.0	112.5	116.0	117.8	118.7	116.7	118.5
面粉	Flour	96.9	97.6	97.3	97.7	97.3	96.2	97.3	96.1	97.8	98.5	104.8	108.4
粮食制品	Grain Products	100.1	100.5	100.1	100.2	100.3	100.1	100.2	100.6	100.7	100.7	103.2	105.2
其他	Others	101.4	102.3	102.1	102.3	102.4	103.0	103.9	103.1	110.3	113.7	110.9	113.2
2.淀粉	Starches	105.8	103.4	103.5	104.9	105.6	106.0	110.3	112.7	113.1	113.3	112.3	113.4
淀粉	Starches	105.8	103.4	103.5	104.9	105.6	106.0	110.3	112.7	113.1	113.3	112.3	113.4
3.干豆类及豆制品	Beans and Beans Products	98.0	99.0	96.6	97.2	97.6	98.2	99.3	99.6	99.1	98.4	97.9	98.8
干豆	Beans	96.8	99.1	99.2	100.7	101.6	103.3	105.9	105.8	104.4	102.7	101.6	103.5
豆制品	Beans Products	98.9	98.9	94.8	94.9	94.9	94.9	94.9	95.5	95.7	95.6	95.5	95.7
4.油脂	Oil and Fat	96.5	96.7	96.0	95.5	96.7	96.6	96.9	98.1	98.8	100.0	105.6	111.1
食用植物油	Edible Vegetable Oil	96.9	97.5	97.0	96.6	97.1	96.8	97.1	98.6	99.9	100.9	106.6	112.6
植物油制品	Plant Oil Products	98.8	98.8	98.8	98.9	105.6	105.3	105.1	105.5	105.7	105.6	109.0	113.7
其他	Others	88.2	84.3	79.6	78.2	77.2	79.0	80.0	79.9	75.6	81.2	89.2	91.0
5.肉禽及其制品	Meal,Poultry and Their Products	95.2	94.9	91.5	89.2	88.0	88.4	90.7	95.8	98.0	98.0	102.4	108.8
（1）食用畜肉及副产品	Edible Livestock Meat and Their By-products	96.4	95.0	90.1	85.1	83.6	84.5	87.5	93.9	96.5	97.3	103.6	112.1
猪肉	Pork	93.7	91.0	85.0	79.2	77.4	78.4	82.6	90.7	93.7	94.4	101.6	111.5
牛肉	Beef	104.6	106.1	105.6	105.7	105.0	105.2	105.3	104.9	105.0	106.1	107.7	111.3
羊肉	Mutton	108.0	110.4	109.1	107.5	108.4	107.8	108.2	109.9	111.3	114.0	117.5	125.7
畜肉副产品	Livestock Meat By-products	95.9	97.9	93.8	88.6	85.5	89.0	87.7	90.8	94.7	94.8	100.5	105.8
其他	Others	100.8	100.4	94.9	86.8	86.1	83.7	89.3	99.7	100.1	99.8	106.4	109.7
（2）禽	Poultry	86.3	89.5	88.8	91.7	91.8	92.6	95.3	100.4	104.0	101.4	102.1	106.1
鸡	Chicken	85.2	89.2	88.9	92.1	93.0	94.5	98.0	102.4	107.3	103.5	103.5	107.4
鸭	Duck	93.5	91.3	91.7	94.2	92.9	88.3	84.7	90.6	90.1	91.1	96.8	100.2
其他	Others	86.4	89.7	86.0	87.5	84.9	86.1	90.0	98.2	98.2	98.7	99.1	104.2
（3）加工肉禽	Meal and Poultry Processing Products	98.0	98.2	97.3	98.4	97.4	96.0	96.1	97.7	97.9	97.5	99.6	101.5
畜肉制品	Livestock Meat Products	98.9	99.0	99.0	98.1	97.5	96.7	97.4	99.2	99.5	99.4	100.7	102.1
禽制品	Poultry Products	96.8	97.2	95.2	98.7	97.2	95.3	94.5	95.9	96.0	95.2	98.2	100.8

7-12 续表 1 continued

商品类别及品名	Commodity Category and Commodity Name	（以2005年平均价格为100）											
		1月 January	2月 February	3月 March	4月 April	5月 May	6月 June	7月 July	8 月 August	9 月 September	10 月 October	11月 November	12月 December
6.蛋	Eggs	94.1	89.1	86.7	86.7	88.4	88.9	90.4	97.9	104.6	104.9	106.3	110.2
鲜蛋	Fresh Eggs	93.1	87.5	84.8	84.9	86.7	87.0	88.8	97.3	104.9	105.1	106.4	110.7
蛋制品	Egg Products	101.4	100.1	99.8	99.1	100.1	102.1	101.5	101.9	102.7	103.6	105.3	106.8
7.水产品	Aquatic Product	99.6	100.9	99.6	99.6	101.0	102.2	103.6	104.4	104.0	102.8	103.3	103.1
（1）鱼	Fish	98.8	99.2	98.1	97.9	99.4	100.5	101.8	102.5	102.4	101.4	102.1	101.2
淡水鱼	Freshwater Fish	98.4	96.8	95.3	95.7	98.2	100.0	101.7	101.8	101.0	99.2	98.7	97.0
海水鱼	Seawater Fish	99.6	103.1	102.7	101.8	101.3	101.4	102.1	103.7	104.8	105.0	107.8	108.3
（2）其他水产品	Other Aquatic Product	101.7	105.8	104.3	104.3	105.5	107.0	108.8	109.8	108.5	107.0	106.7	108.8
虾蟹类	Shrimp and Crab	101.9	106.7	104.9	104.8	106.3	107.2	109.2	110.0	108.6	106.8	106.4	108.6
其他	Others	100.3	100.5	100.6	101.0	100.4	106.1	106.7	108.1	108.1	108.3	108.7	109.9
8.菜	Vegetable	138.3	140.9	129.6	127.2	110.3	85.9	81.9	92.7	105.7	87.3	84.4	106.5
鲜菜	Fresh Vegetable	145.0	147.8	133.9	131.0	109.9	83.0	78.4	91.3	106.4	85.2	81.5	107.3
干菜及菜制品	Dried Vegetable and Vegetable Products	100.6	100.6	100.5	99.7	99.1	99.0	98.3	99.2	99.3	99.5	101.2	104.0
薯类	Potato	110.4	114.4	124.4	127.5	145.0	106.0	104.1	103.1	109.7	93.6	94.4	99.4
9.调味品	Flavoring	102.2	102.2	102.5	102.6	102.6	102.3	103.3	103.4	103.6	103.6	103.6	104.5
盐	Salt	107.2	107.2	108.3	108.3	108.3	108.3	110.4	110.7	111.5	111.5	111.5	111.4
酱油	Soy Sauce	99.7	99.7	99.8	99.9	99.8	99.8	100.5	100.5	100.5	100.5	100.5	102.3
醋	Vinegar	100.3	100.3	100.3	100.3	100.3	100.3	101.3	101.3	101.3	101.3	101.3	103.7
味精	Aginomoto	100.3	100.3	100.3	100.3	100.3	100.3	101.3	101.3	101.3	101.9	101.9	102.3
其他	Others	100.1	100.1	100.1	100.1	100.5	98.5	97.5	97.6	97.2	96.5	96.5	96.5
10.糖	Carbohydrate	101.4	107.3	108.3	109.2	110.3	110.8	111.8	112.0	112.2	112.1	112.4	113.0
食糖	Sugar	102.4	116.6	119.0	120.6	123.3	124.5	126.0	126.4	126.8	126.5	127.0	128.4
糖果	Sweet	101.2	101.3	101.3	102.0	102.0	102.0	102.6	102.6	102.7	102.8	102.8	101.1
巧克力制品	Chocolate Products	99.8	99.8	99.8	99.8	99.8	99.8	100.5	100.5	100.5	100.5	100.5	107.7
糖类小食品	Little Carbohydrate Food	100.1	100.6	100.6	100.6	100.6	100.6	100.9	101.5	101.5	101.5	102.0	103.9
11.茶及饮料	Tea and Beverages	100.2	100.2	100.3	100.4	100.3	100.3	100.7	100.9	100.9	100.9	100.9	101.6
（1）茶叶	Tea	100.1	100.1	100.1	100.1	99.9	99.9	99.9	100.0	100.0	100.0	100.0	100.0
茶叶	Tea	100.1	100.1	100.1	100.1	99.9	99.9	99.9	100.0	100.0	100.0	100.0	100.0
（2）饮料	Beverages	100.3	100.4	100.4	100.6	100.5	100.5	101.3	101.5	101.5	101.5	101.5	102.8
固体饮料	Solid Beverages	100.1	100.4	100.6	101.0	100.8	100.8	100.7	101.1	101.1	101.1	101.1	102.1
液体饮料	Liquid Beverages	100.5	100.5	100.4	100.6	100.6	100.6	102.1	102.4	102.4	102.4	102.5	103.2
冷冻饮品	Frozen Beverages	100.2	100.2	100.2	100.2	100.2	100.2	100.2	100.2	100.2	100.2	100.2	102.7
12.干鲜瓜果	Dried and Fresh Melons and Fruits	123.2	131.3	132.3	146.3	155.9	155.0	132.3	112.5	106.3	102.8	103.4	110.4
鲜瓜果	Fresh Fruits	129.5	140.3	141.5	160.0	172.7	171.3	141.3	114.5	106.2	100.9	101.3	110.3
干（坚）果	Dried Fruits	103.4	102.8	102.9	102.4	102.6	103.2	103.7	106.1	106.4	108.9	110.1	110.7
13.糕点饼干面包	Cake,Biscuit and Bread	100.2	100.2	100.2	100.2	100.3	100.3	101.0	101.6	101.6	101.5	101.4	102.9
糕点	Cake	100.5	100.5	100.5	100.5	100.5	100.5	100.9	100.9	100.9	100.9	100.9	102.3
饼干	Biscuit	99.9	99.9	99.8	100.0	100.1	100.2	101.2	103.0	103.0	102.8	102.6	104.6
面包	Bread	100.0	100.0	100.0	100.0	100.0	100.0	100.7	100.7	100.7	100.7	100.7	100.9
14.液体乳及乳制品	Liquid Milk and Their Products	99.9	100.0	100.0	100.2	100.2	100.2	100.4	100.4	100.4	100.4	100.4	104.1
巴氏杀菌奶或消毒奶	Pasteurization Milk or Disinfection Milk	99.7	99.7	99.9	99.9	99.9	99.9	99.9	99.9	99.9	99.9	99.9	108.7
酸奶	Leben	98.0	98.0	98.0	99.4	99.4	99.4	99.4	99.4	99.4	99.4	99.4	96.6

7-12 续表 2 continued

（以2005年平均价格为100）

商品类别及品名	Commodity Category and Commodity Name	1月 January	2月 February	3月 March	4月 April	5月 May	6月 June	7月 July	8月 August	9月 September	10月 October	11月 November	12月 December
奶粉	Milk Powder	100.3	100.5	100.3	100.3	100.3	100.3	100.8	100.8	100.8	101.0	101.0	103.0
其他	Others	101.8	102.0	101.7	101.7	101.7	101.7	101.7	101.7	101.7	101.7	101.7	101.7
15.在外用膳食品	Outward Dinner	100.7	101.0	101.0	100.7	101.0	101.1	101.1	101.1	101.1	100.8	101.7	103.6
主食	Staple Food	99.9	99.9	100.0	99.8	99.8	99.8	99.7	99.7	99.7	99.7	102.5	106.2
炒菜	Hot Dish	101.4	102.0	102.0	101.5	101.5	101.5	101.4	101.4	101.4	101.4	101.5	101.7
地方小吃	Local Snack	100.6	100.5	100.2	100.4	102.0	102.6	103.0	103.0	103.0	101.6	100.9	103.0
16.其他食品	Other Foods	100.6	100.6	100.6	100.6	100.7	100.8	101.6	101.7	101.7	101.6	101.3	101.9
其他食品	Other Foods	100.6	100.6	100.6	100.6	100.7	100.8	101.6	101.7	101.7	101.6	101.3	101.9
二、烟酒及用品	**Tobacco,Liquor and Their Appliances**	**100.0**	**99.9**	**100.1**	**100.3**	**100.2**	**100.1**	**100.2**	**100.5**	**100.6**	**100.7**	**100.8**	**102.0**
1.烟草	Tobacco	100.1	100.5	100.5	100.7	100.9	100.6	100.5	100.5	100.5	100.5	100.5	101.4
国产卷烟	Domestic Cigarette	100.2	100.6	100.6	100.9	101.0	100.8	100.6	100.6	100.6	100.6	100.6	101.7
进口卷烟	Import Cigarette	99.9	99.8	99.7	99.7	99.7	99.7	98.4	98.4	98.4	98.4	99.7	99.7
其他	Others	99.8	99.8	99.8	99.8	99.8	99.8	99.8	99.8	99.8	99.8	99.8	99.8
2.酒	Liquor	99.8	99.5	99.7	99.8	99.7	99.7	100.0	100.6	100.7	100.9	101.0	102.6
白酒	White Spirit	100.1	99.5	99.8	100.0	100.0	100.0	100.2	101.1	101.1	101.4	101.6	103.8
葡萄酒	Grape	99.7	99.7	99.7	99.7	99.7	99.7	100.2	100.2	100.2	100.3	101.0	101.2
啤酒	Beer	99.2	99.2	99.5	99.4	99.0	98.8	99.3	99.5	100.1	99.8	99.8	100.6
其他	Others	100.3	100.3	100.3	100.3	100.3	100.3	100.5	100.5	100.5	100.5	100.5	100.6
3.吸烟、饮酒用品	Appliances For Smoking and Drinking	100.1	100.0	100.0	100.0	100.0	100.0	100.0	100.0	100.0	100.0	100.1	99.8
吸烟用品	Appliances for Smoking	99.9	99.9	100.0	99.9	99.9	99.9	99.9	99.9	99.9	99.9	99.9	100.0
饮酒用品	Appliances For Drinking	100.2	100.1	100.0	100.0	100.0	100.0	100.0	100.0	100.0	100.0	100.2	99.7
三、衣着	**Clothing**	**98.1**	**97.2**	**97.0**	**96.8**	**96.5**	**96.5**	**96.6**	**96.5**	**96.4**	**96.6**	**97.0**	**97.1**
1.服装	Garments	97.0	95.9	95.6	95.3	94.9	94.8	94.8	94.7	94.6	94.9	95.6	95.5
（1）男式服装	Men's Garments	96.1	95.0	94.8	94.6	94.2	94.1	94.3	94.3	94.4	95.0	95.8	95.7
大衣	Topcoat	95.6	93.2	92.0	91.7	91.7	91.0	91.0	91.0	91.6	91.6	91.1	91.1
毛线衣	Woollen Sweater	92.3	91.6	90.2	89.3	86.7	85.9	87.7	87.7	88.5	88.9	87.4	87.5
夹克衫	Jacket	97.8	97.0	97.0	96.9	96.7	96.6	96.6	96.5	96.5	97.2	100.4	100.2
衬衫	Shirt	92.9	92.9	92.9	92.9	92.9	92.9	92.9	92.9	92.9	93.5	94.2	94.2
T恤衫	T-shirt	99.3	99.4	99.5	99.6	99.1	99.2	99.0	99.8	100.5	101.6	102.6	102.8
裤子	Trousers	94.7	92.1	93.7	93.6	93.6	93.6	93.3	93.3	93.3	93.9	94.5	93.3
西服	Western-style Clothes	97.4	96.5	96.5	96.3	96.2	96.3	96.3	96.3	96.3	96.7	98.0	98.0
运动衫裤	Gym Suit	100.1	100.1	100.1	100.1	100.1	100.1	100.0	100.0	100.1	101.8	103.5	103.5
内衣	Underwaist	98.3	98.0	96.4	96.1	95.8	95.8	95.8	95.8	95.8	96.5	97.5	96.9
羽绒衣	Eider Down Outerwear	96.5	94.6	94.4	94.4	94.4	94.4	94.4	94.1	94.0	94.4	95.2	95.4
其他	Others	96.1	94.5	94.5	94.5	94.5	94.5	94.5	94.5	94.5	94.5	94.5	94.5
（2）女式服装	Women's Garments	97.3	96.1	95.6	95.0	94.1	94.2	94.1	93.8	93.7	93.9	94.5	94.4
大衣	Topcoat	95.5	90.4	90.4	90.4	90.4	90.4	90.4	90.4	90.4	90.4	90.8	90.8
毛线衣	Woollen Sweater	96.3	93.9	90.4	90.1	86.1	86.1	86.1	86.1	86.1	86.1	86.2	86.1
羽绒衣	Eider Down Outerwear	97.5	96.0	95.8	95.8	95.8	95.7	95.7	95.3	95.2	95.7	96.1	96.1
套装	Coordinates	100.7	100.7	100.7	96.0	96.0	96.0	96.0	95.9	95.9	96.6	97.3	97.3
衬衫	Shirt	96.2	96.0	96.0	96.0	96.5	96.1	96.1	96.1	91.2	91.3	91.3	91.3

7-12 续表 3 continued

商品类别及品名	Commodity Category and Commodity Name	1月 January	2月 February	3月 March	4月 April	5月 May	6月 June	7月 July	8月 August	9月 September	10月 October	11月 November	12月 December
		（以2005年平均价格为100）											
T恤衫	T-shirt	99.4	98.7	99.0	99.3	95.6	95.6	95.6	95.6	95.6	96.9	98.1	98.2
裙子	Skirt	93.5	93.5	93.4	93.4	91.5	92.4	92.4	91.1	90.6	91.0	91.0	90.5
裤子	Trousers	98.8	98.8	98.8	97.3	96.8	96.7	95.8	95.8	95.8	94.9	95.8	95.8
运动衫裤	Gym Suit	99.8	100.1	99.1	99.7	99.1	99.1	99.1	99.1	99.1	100.6	102.6	102.6
内衣	Underwaist	97.2	96.1	96.0	96.1	96.9	96.8	96.7	96.6	99.0	99.5	100.0	100.2
其他	Others	98.9	98.8	98.8	98.8	98.8	98.4	98.4	98.4	98.4	98.4	98.8	98.8
（3）儿童服装	Children's Garments	98.1	97.1	97.2	97.3	97.8	97.8	97.8	97.8	97.1	97.1	97.6	97.6
套装	Coordinates	98.1	97.2	97.2	97.5	97.2	96.6	96.6	96.6	96.7	96.8	97.4	97.5
裤子	Trousers	100.8	100.0	100.0	99.9	101.7	101.7	101.7	101.7	101.7	102.2	102.8	102.9
裙子	Skirt	94.8	94.0	94.2	94.3	94.7	95.9	95.9	95.9	93.0	92.2	92.2	92.2
其他	Others	97.8	95.9	95.9	95.9	96.5	97.1	97.1	97.1	95.6	95.6	95.6	95.6
2.衣着材料	Clothing Materials	100.3	100.2	100.0	100.0	100.6	100.6	100.8	100.7	100.5	100.8	101.0	101.0
棉布	Cotton Cloth	99.4	99.4	99.4	99.4	100.4	100.4	100.4	100.4	100.3	100.4	100.4	100.5
棉混纺布	Cotton Textiles Cloth	100.1	100.3	100.3	100.3	100.3	100.3	100.6	100.6	100.6	100.9	101.2	101.2
化纤布	Chemical Fiber Cloth	100.1	100.3	100.3	100.3	101.3	101.3	101.5	101.3	100.8	101.6	101.8	101.8
毛线	Knitting Wool	101.5	100.7	99.9	99.9	99.9	99.9	99.9	99.9	99.9	99.9	99.9	99.9
3.鞋袜帽	Shoes,Socks and Hats	99.0	98.1	98.1	98.2	97.7	97.6	97.7	97.7	97.7	97.6	97.7	97.8
（1）鞋	Shoes	99.0	98.0	98.0	98.1	97.4	97.3	97.4	97.4	97.3	97.3	97.4	97.5
男鞋	Men's Shoes	98.5	98.4	98.4	98.5	97.8	97.8	97.8	97.7	97.7	97.7	97.7	98.0
女鞋	Women's Shoes	98.4	96.6	96.6	96.6	95.6	95.6	95.9	95.8	95.7	95.7	95.9	95.9
童鞋	Children's Shoes	100.7	100.1	100.2	100.3	100.3	100.0	100.0	100.0	100.1	99.8	99.8	99.8
（2）袜子	Socks	99.2	99.0	99.0	99.0	99.5	99.5	99.5	99.5	99.5	99.5	99.5	99.5
男袜	Men's Socks	98.7	98.4	98.4	98.4	98.4	98.4	98.4	98.4	98.4	98.4	98.4	98.4
女袜	Women's Socks	99.7	99.4	99.4	99.4	100.4	100.4	100.4	100.4	100.4	100.4	100.4	100.4
（3）帽子	Hats	99.3	99.3	99.3	99.3	99.4	99.4	99.4	99.4	99.4	99.4	99.4	99.4
男帽	Men's Hats	99.6	99.6	99.6	99.6	99.7	99.7	99.7	99.7	99.7	99.7	99.7	99.7
女帽	Women's Hats	99.2	99.0	99.0	99.0	99.0	99.0	99.0	99.0	99.0	99.1	99.2	99.2
4.衣着加工服务费	Clothing Manufacturing Services	100.1	99.7	99.7	99.7	99.7	99.7	99.7	99.7	99.7	99.7	99.7	102.0
缝纫	Sewing	100.1	99.6	99.6	99.6	99.6	99.6	99.6	99.6	99.6	99.6	99.6	102.6
清洗	Washing	100.0	100.0	100.0	100.0	100.0	100.0	100.0	100.0	100.0	100.0	100.0	100.0
四、家庭设备用品及维修服务	**Household Facilities, Articles and Services**	**99.7**	**99.5**	**99.5**	**99.8**	**99.8**	**99.8**	**99.8**	**99.8**	**100.1**	**100.7**	**100.9**	**101.5**
1.耐用消费品	Durable Consumer Goods	99.4	99.1	99.0	99.4	99.5	100.0	100.3	100.2	100.2	100.9	101.2	101.4
（1）家具	Furniture	99.4	99.1	99.0	100.0	100.0	100.1	100.0	99.8	99.7	101.4	101.9	102.1
柜	Cabinet	99.2	98.7	98.3	99.3	99.3	99.3	99.2	98.9	98.9	101.1	101.1	101.4
床	Bed	99.5	99.5	99.5	101.2	101.2	101.2	101.2	101.2	101.1	102.3	103.3	103.6
桌	Desk	99.8	99.8	99.8	99.9	99.9	100.1	100.1	99.3	98.6	99.9	100.6	100.7
椅	Chair	100.1	98.6	98.6	98.6	98.6	98.6	98.4	98.5	98.6	100.3	100.4	100.4
沙发	Sofa	98.8	98.8	98.8	100.2	100.2	100.2	100.2	100.2	100.2	101.7	102.7	102.7
其他	Others	100.5	100.7	100.8	100.2	101.0	101.1	101.1	101.2	101.2	102.8	102.9	103.0
（2）家庭设备	Household Appliances	99.5	99.1	99.0	99.0	99.1	99.9	100.5	100.4	100.6	100.6	100.6	100.8
洗衣机	Washing Machine	98.7	98.9	98.8	98.7	98.6	98.7	98.8	99.0	100.1	100.6	100.2	100.4

7-12 续表 4 continued

商品类别及品名	Commodity Category and Commodity Name	1月 January	2月 February	3月 March	4月 April	5月 May	6月 June	7月 July	8月 August	9月 September	10月 October	11月 November	12月 December
		（以2005年平均价格为100）											
电风扇	Electric Fan	100.4	99.0	99.0	100.8	101.3	102.1	104.4	104.4	104.4	104.4	104.4	106.9
电冰箱（柜）	Refrigerator	101.1	100.3	100.7	100.8	100.8	100.8	101.0	100.9	100.6	100.7	100.5	100.2
吸排油烟机	Kitchen Ventilato	98.6	98.4	98.0	97.7	97.7	97.9	98.2	98.0	97.8	97.8	97.8	99.0
空调器	Air-conditioning	99.4	99.3	99.0	99.4	99.9	103.7	104.2	104.1	104.3	104.3	104.1	103.8
热水器	Water Heater	99.0	99.0	99.4	96.4	96.1	96.4	96.3	96.2	96.1	96.1	96.4	94.6
微波炉	Microwave Oven	98.3	97.3	97.7	96.5	96.5	96.5	96.7	96.8	96.8	96.8	97.2	96.6
电炊具	Electric Cooking Appliance	98.8	98.8	98.4	98.2	98.2	98.6	98.5	98.5	98.5	98.5	98.5	98.9
2.室内装饰品	Interior Decorations	99.5	99.5	99.5	99.5	99.5	99.1	99.1	99.1	99.5	99.5	99.5	99.6
纺织装饰品	Textile Process Decorations	99.8	99.8	99.8	99.8	99.8	98.9	98.9	98.8	99.8	99.8	99.8	99.8
装饰灯具	Architectural Lamps and Lanterns	99.2	99.2	99.2	99.2	99.1	99.0	99.0	99.0	99.0	99.0	99.0	99.3
其他	Others	100.0	100.0	100.0	100.0	100.0	100.0	100.0	100.0	100.0	100.0	100.0	100.0
3.床上用品	Bedclothes	99.9	99.8	99.8	100.3	99.7	99.7	99.6	99.6	100.0	100.4	100.6	101.0
毛毯	Woollen Blanket	99.7	99.0	99.0	100.2	98.7	98.7	98.5	98.3	99.0	100.4	100.4	102.1
被子	Quilt	100.0	100.1	100.2	100.2	100.3	100.3	100.0	100.0	100.3	100.3	100.9	100.9
床上套件	Bed Articles	100.3	100.3	100.3	100.6	100.3	100.3	100.4	100.4	101.1	101.1	101.1	100.7
其他	Others	99.1	99.9	99.9	99.9	99.1	99.1	99.1	99.1	99.1	99.1	99.1	99.1
4.日用杂品	Sundry Articles	99.9	99.9	99.9	100.1	100.0	99.1	98.6	98.9	99.6	100.1	100.1	101.3
茶具	Tea Set	96.5	96.5	96.4	96.4	95.8	99.8	99.7	99.7	102.6	107.8	107.8	107.8
餐具	Tableware	101.2	101.2	100.6	100.6	100.0	100.0	96.5	96.2	96.2	96.2	96.2	96.2
厨具	Kitchen Utensils	100.7	100.7	100.7	101.9	101.9	99.8	99.8	100.2	101.9	101.9	101.9	103.2
家用手工工具	Domestic Handwork Tools	100.0	100.0	100.0	100.0	100.0	100.7	101.3	101.3	101.3	101.3	101.3	104.9
洗涤用品	Washing Articles	99.6	99.6	99.6	99.6	99.6	97.9	97.9	97.9	98.0	98.0	98.0	99.2
其他	Others	100.3	100.3	101.6	101.6	101.6	98.4	98.3	100.7	100.7	100.5	100.4	102.4
5.家庭服务及加工维修服务	Household Service and Manufacturing Upkeep	101.3	101.3	101.3	101.3	101.3	101.3	101.3	101.3	101.3	101.6	103.4	104.8
家庭服务	Household Service	101.9	101.9	101.9	101.9	101.9	101.9	101.9	101.9	101.9	102.5	104.6	106.0
加工维修服务	Manufacturing Upkeep	100.6	100.6	100.6	100.6	100.6	100.6	100.6	100.6	100.6	100.6	102.1	103.5
五、医疗保健和个人用品	**Health Care and Personal Articles**	**100.3**	**100.6**	**100.6**	**100.8**	**101.4**	**101.4**	**101.4**	**101.4**	**101.8**	**101.4**	**101.5**	**101.7**
1.医疗保健	Health Care	100.1	100.5	100.2	100.3	100.6	100.6	100.7	100.7	101.3	100.7	100.9	101.1
（1）医疗器具及用品	Medical Facilities and Goods	96.4	97.2	96.9	96.3	95.8	95.8	95.8	95.8	96.8	95.0	95.0	93.2
医疗器具及用品	Medical Facilities and Goods	96.4	97.2	96.9	96.3	95.8	95.8	95.8	95.8	96.8	95.0	95.0	93.2
（2）中药材及中成药	Herbs and Ready-made Traditional Chinese Medicine	101.8	103.5	102.0	102.5	103.0	103.3	103.5	103.9	105.0	104.7	105.1	105.4
中药材	Herbs	103.7	106.1	103.4	104.2	105.6	105.7	105.9	105.8	107.2	106.7	107.4	107.5
中成药	Ready-made Traditinonal Chinese Medicine	99.4	100.0	100.3	100.2	99.6	100.1	100.4	101.3	102.0	101.9	101.9	102.6
（3）西药	Western Medicine	99.1	99.2	99.3	99.5	100.1	99.8	99.8	99.7	100.5	99.6	99.7	100.1
抗微生物药	Anti-microorganism Medicine	94.6	94.7	94.7	94.8	94.8	94.7	94.7	94.5	96.1	93.6	93.6	94.9

7-12 续表 5 continued

商品类别及品名	Commodity Category and Commodity Name	1月 January	2月 February	3月 March	4月 April	5月 May	6月 June	7月 July	8月 August	9月 September	10月 October	11月 November	12月 December
		（以2005年平均价格为100）											
消化系统用药	Alimentary System Medicine	100.4	100.9	100.9	100.8	100.8	100.8	100.8	100.9	101.4	100.8	101.1	100.8
呼吸系统用药	Respiratory System Medicine	98.3	98.3	99.0	99.8	99.5	99.7	99.7	99.7	101.7	100.2	100.8	100.8
解热镇痛及非甾体抗炎药	Allays a Fever the Analgesia and the Nonsteroid Body Anti-inflammatory Agent	103.2	103.4	102.8	102.8	103.8	102.8	102.8	102.8	103.5	102.9	102.5	104.2
抗肿瘤药	Antineoplastic Drug	99.1	99.1	98.9	98.9	106.6	104.2	104.9	103.5	101.0	104.4	105.4	105.4
激素及调节内分泌功能药	Hormone and Adjustment Internal Secretion Function Medicine	99.3	99.7	99.7	99.7	99.7	99.8	98.3	98.5	100.7	98.5	98.5	97.3
循环系统用药	Circulating System Medicine	99.0	99.0	99.4	99.9	99.8	99.7	99.6	99.6	100.0	100.0	100.0	100.1
神经系统用药	Nerve System Medicine	100.1	100.5	100.5	101.1	101.1	101.1	101.1	101.1	102.1	100.8	100.8	101.5
专科用药	Junior Medicine	99.0	98.5	99.1	99.3	99.5	99.6	99.6	99.6	99.9	98.6	98.6	98.0
其他	Others	99.8	99.9	99.9	100.0	99.9	100.0	100.0	99.9	100.2	99.7	99.8	99.8
（4）保健品及器具	Healthcare Equipment	99.0	98.6	98.6	99.0	99.0	99.3	99.3	99.4	99.8	99.1	99.3	99.3
保健器具	Health Protection Equipment	100.0	99.5	99.5	99.6	99.6	100.3	100.3	100.3	100.3	99.5	99.6	99.3
滋补保健用品	Tonic and Health Products	98.4	98.1	98.1	98.7	98.7	98.7	98.8	98.9	99.5	98.9	99.2	99.2
（5）医疗保健服务	Health Care Services	100.7	100.7	100.7	100.6	100.6	100.7	100.7	100.7	100.8	100.6	100.7	100.9
挂号费	Registration	100.0	100.0	100.0	100.0	100.0	100.0	100.0	100.0	100.0	100.0	100.0	100.0
注射费	Injection Expenses	100.0	100.0	100.0	100.0	100.0	100.0	100.0	100.0	100.0	100.0	100.0	100.0
检查费	Examination Expenses	102.0	102.0	102.0	102.0	102.0	102.0	102.0	102.0	102.2	102.2	102.2	102.2
手术费	Operation Expenses	100.0	100.0	100.0	100.0	100.0	100.0	100.0	100.0	100.0	100.0	100.0	100.9
住院费	Hospitalization Expenses	101.8	101.8	101.8	101.2	101.2	102.0	102.0	102.0	102.0	101.2	101.8	101.8
理疗费	Physiotherapy Expenses	100.0	100.0	100.0	100.0	100.0	100.0	100.0	100.0	100.0	100.0	100.0	100.0
化验费	Analysis Expenses	100.0	100.0	100.0	100.0	100.0	100.0	100.0	100.0	100.0	100.0	100.0	100.0
其他	Others	99.9	99.9	99.9	99.9	99.9	99.9	99.9	99.9	99.9	99.9	99.9	99.9
2.个人用品及服务	Personal Articles and Services	100.8	101.1	101.5	101.8	103.0	102.9	102.9	103.0	102.8	102.8	102.7	103.0
（1）化妆美容用品	Cosmetics	100.6	100.5	100.4	100.4	100.5	100.5	100.5	100.5	100.5	100.5	100.5	100.9
化妆美容器具	Cosmetics Appliances	98.9	98.9	99.2	99.0	99.2	99.2	99.2	99.3	99.3	99.3	99.3	99.3
美容化妆品	Facial Beautifiers	101.2	101.2	101.2	101.2	101.2	101.2	101.2	101.2	101.2	101.2	101.2	102.2
护肤品	Protects Skin Products	100.0	100.0	100.0	100.0	100.3	100.0	100.0	100.0	100.0	100.0	99.9	99.9
护发美容品	Protects Sends the Beauty Products	101.7	101.2	100.2	100.2	100.7	100.7	100.7	100.7	100.7	100.7	100.7	101.0
（2）清洁化妆用品	Cleaning Toiletware	100.1	100.0	100.2	100.4	100.4	100.5	100.5	100.7	100.1	100.5	100.5	101.3
洗发用品	Hairdressing Articles	100.3	100.2	100.6	100.3	100.3	100.3	100.3	100.6	99.1	100.6	100.6	98.9
洗浴用品	Bathing Articles	99.9	99.9	99.9	101.0	100.9	101.2	101.2	101.4	101.4	101.0	101.0	100.9
其他	Others	99.8	99.8	99.8	99.8	99.8	99.8	99.8	99.8	99.8	99.8	99.8	105.5

7-12 续表 6 continued

商品类别及品名	Commodity Category and Commodity Name	1月 January	2月 February	3月 March	4月 April	5月 May	6月 June	7月 July	8月 August	9月 September	10月 October	11月 November	12月 December
		（以2005年平均价格为100）											
（3）个人饰品	Personal Decoraions	101.6	102.6	103.9	105.2	109.6	109.4	109.1	109.4	109.1	108.8	108.5	108.2
首饰	Ornaments	104.8	107.6	111.4	116.6	129.5	128.9	128.2	129.2	128.4	127.6	127.0	125.8
皮件	Leather Appliance	100.3	100.3	100.3	96.2	95.6	95.6	95.6	95.3	95.3	95.3	94.7	94.7
手表	Watch	100.0	100.0	100.0	99.6	99.6	99.6	99.6	99.6	99.6	99.6	99.6	100.2
领带	Necktie	100.0	99.9	99.8	101.3	101.3	101.2	101.1	100.9	100.9	100.9	101.1	101.3
其他	Others	98.3	98.3	98.3	98.3	98.3	98.3	98.3	98.3	98.3	98.3	98.3	98.3
（4）个人服务	Personal Services	100.8	100.9	100.9	100.9	100.8	100.8	100.8	100.8	100.8	100.8	100.9	100.9
美容	Cosmetology	100.0	100.0	100.0	100.0	100.0	100.0	100.0	100.0	100.0	100.0	100.0	100.0
理（烫）发	Haircut(permanent wave)	101.2	101.6	101.6	101.6	101.6	101.6	101.6	101.6	101.6	101.6	101.6	101.6
洗浴	Bathe	100.3	100.3	100.3	100.3	99.7	99.7	99.7	99.7	99.7	99.7	100.1	100.4
其他	Others	102.7	102.7	102.7	102.7	102.7	102.7	102.7	102.7	102.7	102.7	102.7	102.7
六、交通和通信	**Transportation and Communication**	**99.8**	**100.3**	**100.1**	**100.0**	**100.1**	**100.3**	**100.1**	**100.1**	**100.0**	**100.0**	**100.4**	**100.6**
1.交通	Transportation	101.0	102.1	102.0	102.1	102.6	102.9	102.8	102.8	102.8	102.8	103.0	103.1
（1）交通工具	Transportation Facility	99.2	100.0	99.8	99.3	99.2	98.4	97.8	97.7	97.8	97.8	97.7	97.7
摩托车	Motorcycle	99.7	102.5	102.5	102.6	102.6	102.6	102.3	102.3	102.3	102.3	102.3	102.2
自行车	Bicycle	99.9	99.9	99.6	98.8	98.8	97.9	96.5	96.5	96.6	96.6	96.6	97.0
轿车	Car	96.6	96.6	96.6	96.5	95.9	94.2	94.7	94.6	94.5	94.5	94.0	93.6
其他	Others	100.2	100.2	100.3	96.2	96.2	96.2	95.9	95.9	95.9	95.9	95.9	95.9
（2）车用燃料及零配件	Fuels and Parts	104.2	104.1	105.1	108.2	111.1	115.5	116.6	116.7	116.7	117.1	117.2	117.1
汽油	Gasoline	105.4	105.2	106.3	110.8	114.5	120.6	121.3	121.3	121.3	121.3	121.3	121.3
柴油	Diesel Oil	106.2	106.2	107.2	109.9	114.1	119.0	119.8	119.8	119.8	120.6	120.7	120.8
零配件	Parts	98.9	98.9	99.4	100.4	100.4	100.4	103.4	103.4	103.4	104.4	104.4	104.1
其他	Others	100.2	100.2	101.2	103.8	102.7	104.7	104.7	105.4	105.4	105.0	105.0	105.0
（3）车辆使用及维修费	Using and Upkeep Fare	100.7	99.5	100.3	99.9	100.5	100.8	100.9	101.1	101.1	100.8	100.5	101.3
驾驶证	Driving License	101.6	101.4	100.4	98.7	101.2	102.4	103.0	103.8	103.8	102.6	101.3	100.2
保险费	Insurance Expenses	99.6	99.6	99.6	99.6	99.6	99.6	99.6	99.6	99.6	99.6	99.6	99.6
停车费	Parking Expenses	100.0	100.0	100.0	100.0	100.0	100.0	100.0	100.0	100.0	100.0	100.0	100.0
车辆修理服务费	Vehicle Upkeep Service Fare	100.8	98.0	100.6	100.6	100.6	100.6	100.6	100.6	100.6	100.6	100.6	103.2
其他	Others	101.5	101.5	101.5	101.5	101.5	101.5	101.5	101.5	101.5	101.5	101.5	101.5
（4）市区公共交通费	Incity Traffic Fare	101.5	103.3	103.3	103.3	103.3	103.3	103.3	103.3	103.3	103.3	105.3	105.3
公共汽车票	Bus Ticket	101.2	104.7	104.7	104.7	104.7	104.7	104.7	104.7	104.7	104.7	104.7	104.7
出租汽车	Taxi	102.8	103.5	103.5	103.5	103.5	103.5	103.5	103.5	103.5	103.5	109.2	109.2
其他	Others	100.0	100.0	100.0	100.0	100.0	100.0	100.0	100.0	100.0	100.0	100.0	100.0
（5）城市间交通费	Intercity Traffic Fare	104.0	108.4	107.0	107.1	107.2	107.8	107.8	108.0	108.0	108.0	108.7	108.7
飞机票	Airplane Ticket	130.5	89.2	101.0	112.8	124.6	101.0	101.0	101.0	101.0	101.0	101.0	101.0
火车票	Train Ticket	100.0	100.0	100.0	100.0	100.0	100.0	100.0	100.0	100.0	100.0	100.0	100.0
长途汽车	Intertown Bus	104.7	110.5	108.6	108.6	108.6	109.6	109.6	109.8	109.8	109.8	110.7	110.7
其他	Others	99.7	101.0	101.0	101.0	101.0	101.8	101.8	101.8	101.8	101.8	101.8	101.8
2.通信	Communication	97.9	97.4	97.1	96.8	96.3	96.1	96.0	95.8	95.7	95.6	96.4	96.7
（1）通信工具	Communication Facility	92.5	90.7	89.8	88.6	86.8	86.3	85.9	85.1	84.8	84.5	84.2	83.1
固定电话机	Telephone	97.7	97.1	96.4	96.2	94.1	94.1	94.1	94.1	94.3	94.3	94.3	94.3
移动电话机	Mobile Phone	85.3	82.2	81.2	78.6	76.9	75.8	74.9	72.9	71.9	71.3	70.6	67.9
其他	Others	95.8	93.3	91.2	90.7	90.9	90.4	89.7	89.2	89.2	89.2	89.2	89.2

7-12 续表 7 continued

商品类别及品名	Commodity Category and Commodity Name	1月 January	2月 February	3月 March	4月 April	5月 May	6月 June	7月 July	8月 August	9月 September	10月 October	11月 November	12月 December
		（以2005年平均价格为100）											
（2）通信服务	Communication Service	100.0	100.0	100.0	100.0	100.0	100.0	100.0	100.0	100.0	100.0	101.2	102.1
移动通信费	Mobile Communication Fee	100.0	100.0	100.0	100.0	100.0	100.0	100.0	100.0	100.0	100.0	100.0	100.0
市内电话费	Incity Telephone Fee	100.0	100.0	100.0	100.0	100.0	100.0	100.0	100.0	100.0	100.0	100.0	100.0
长途电话费	Long Distance Call Fee	100.0	100.0	100.0	100.0	100.0	100.0	100.0	100.0	100.0	100.0	100.0	100.0
月租费	Month Hiring Fee	100.0	100.0	100.0	100.0	100.0	100.0	100.0	100.0	100.0	100.0	100.0	100.0
上网费	Net Play Fee	100.0	100.0	100.0	100.0	100.0	100.0	100.0	100.0	99.5	99.5	99.5	99.5
信件邮寄	Letter Post	100.0	100.0	100.0	100.0	100.0	100.0	100.0	100.0	100.0	100.0	115.3	126.6
包裹邮寄	Package Post	100.0	100.0	100.0	100.0	100.0	100.0	100.0	100.0	100.0	100.0	100.0	100.0
其他	Others	100.0	100.0	100.0	100.0	100.0	100.0	100.0	100.0	100.0	100.0	100.0	100.0
七、娱乐教育文化用品及服务	**Recreation,Education and Culture Articles**	**99.9**	**99.8**	**99.9**	**100.5**	**100.5**	**100.5**	**100.5**	**100.5**	**100.5**	**100.5**	**100.5**	**100.4**
1.文娱用耐用消费品及服务	Durable Consumer Goods For Cultural and Recreational Use and Service	96.8	96.1	96.1	95.7	95.7	95.7	95.7	95.4	95.5	95.4	95.3	94.9
电视机	Television	95.0	93.9	93.9	93.3	93.5	93.3	93.1	92.9	92.8	92.7	92.6	93.1
激光视盘机	Laser Video Disc Machine	97.8	96.6	96.7	96.7	96.2	96.6	96.8	96.6	96.6	96.3	95.6	91.8
摄像机	Pickup Camera	99.7	99.7	99.7	99.7	99.7	99.7	99.7	99.7	99.7	99.7	99.7	99.7
照相机	Camera	94.9	94.9	94.9	94.9	94.9	95.5	95.5	95.5	97.1	97.1	97.1	95.7
家用音响	Acoustic Equipment	100.6	100.0	99.5	98.1	97.9	97.9	98.5	98.6	98.6	98.6	98.5	97.6
便携式音响	Portable Acoustics	99.6	99.6	99.6	99.6	99.6	99.6	99.6	99.6	99.6	99.6	99.6	99.4
电脑	Computer	96.8	96.7	96.6	96.5	96.5	96.5	96.3	94.9	94.9	94.9	94.9	94.9
修理服务	Repair Service	104.6	104.5	104.3	104.2	104.3	104.1	105.3	105.2	105.5	105.7	105.7	105.7
其他	Others	100.0	100.0	100.0	100.0	100.0	100.0	100.0	100.0	100.0	100.0	100.0	100.0
2.教育	Education	101.1	101.3	101.3	101.9	101.9	101.9	101.9	102.0	102.0	102.0	102.0	102.0
（1）教材及参考书	Teaching Material and Reference Books	100.4	100.4	100.4	100.6	100.6	100.6	100.6	100.1	100.4	100.4	100.4	100.4
工具书	Tool Book	99.6	99.6	99.6	99.6	99.6	99.6	99.6	99.6	99.6	99.6	99.6	99.6
教材	Teaching Material	100.7	100.7	100.7	101.0	101.0	101.0	101.0	100.3	99.6	99.6	99.6	99.6
参考书	Reference Book	100.8	100.8	100.8	100.8	100.8	100.8	100.8	100.5	103.3	103.3	103.3	103.3
教育软件	Educational Software	99.4	99.4	99.2	99.2	99.2	99.2	99.2	99.2	99.2	99.2	99.2	99.2
（2）学杂托幼费	Tuition and Child Care	101.2	101.5	101.5	102.1	102.1	102.1	102.1	102.2	102.2	102.2	102.2	102.2
义务教育杂费	Incidental Expenses of Compulcory Education	100.0	100.0	100.0	100.0	100.0	100.0	100.0	100.0	100.0	100.0	100.0	100.0
非义务教育学杂费	Tuition of Non-compulsory Education	102.1	102.1	102.1	102.1	102.1	102.1	102.1	102.1	102.1	102.1	102.1	102.1
技能培训学费	Skill Train Tuition	100.0	100.0	100.0	100.0	100.0	100.0	100.0	100.0	100.0	100.0	100.0	100.0
托幼费	Child care	103.0	105.0	105.0	109.2	109.2	109.2	109.2	110.2	110.2	110.2	110.2	110.2
其他	Others	103.7	103.7	103.7	107.8	107.8	107.8	107.8	107.8	107.8	107.8	107.8	107.8
3.文化娱乐类	Recreation and Culture	100.5	100.4	100.4	103.3	103.3	103.2	103.1	103.2	103.3	103.3	103.8	103.8
（1）文化娱乐用品	Culture Articles	100.3	100.2	100.2	100.2	100.1	100.0	99.8	99.9	99.9	100.0	100.1	100.2
乐器	Musical Instrument	99.9	99.9	99.9	99.9	99.9	100.4	100.4	99.6	99.9	100.4	99.5	98.8
音响光盘和磁带	Audio,Disk and Tap	100.0	100.0	100.0	100.0	100.1	100.1	100.1	100.1	100.1	100.1	100.1	100.0
照相胶卷和存储卡	Roll Film and Memorizing Card	99.0	99.2	99.2	99.2	99.2	99.2	99.2	98.8	98.8	98.8	100.6	101.2
录像磁带和视盘	Video Tape and Disk	100.0	100.0	100.0	100.0	99.1	99.1	97.9	97.9	97.9	97.9	97.9	97.9
儿童玩具	Children's Toy	99.3	99.5	99.5	99.5	99.5	99.5	99.5	99.2	99.2	99.2	99.2	99.2

7-12 续表 8 continued

商品类别及品名	Commodity Category and Commodity Name	（以2005年平均价格为100）											
		1月 January	2月 February	3月 March	4月 April	5月 May	6月 June	7月 July	8月 August	9月 September	10月 October	11月 November	12月 December
纸张本册	Paper and Volume	101.7	100.9	100.9	100.9	100.9	101.4	101.4	102.4	102.6	102.7	102.9	103.0
文具	Stationery	101.1	101.1	101.1	101.1	101.1	100.4	99.4	99.5	99.5	99.5	99.5	99.5
体育用品	Sports Goods	100.1	100.1	100.1	100.1	100.1	99.4	99.4	99.5	99.5	99.5	99.5	99.4
其他	Others	99.4	99.4	99.4	99.4	99.4	99.4	99.4	99.4	99.4	99.4	99.4	99.4
（2）书报杂志	Books,Newspapers, Magazines	101.2	101.2	101.2	101.2	101.2	101.2	101.2	101.2	101.2	101.2	101.2	101.2
书籍	Books	100.0	100.0	100.0	100.0	100.0	100.0	100.0	100.0	100.0	100.0	100.0	100.0
报纸	Newspapers	103.0	103.0	103.0	103.0	103.0	103.0	103.0	103.0	103.0	103.0	103.0	103.0
杂志	Magazines	101.3	101.3	101.3	101.3	101.3	101.3	101.3	101.3	101.3	101.3	101.3	101.3
（3）文娱费	Expenditure of Culture and Recreation	100.0	100.0	100.0	115.3	115.3	115.3	115.3	115.3	115.8	115.8	117.9	117.9
电影票	Film Ticket	100.0	100.0	100.0	100.0	100.0	100.0	100.0	100.0	100.0	100.0	100.0	100.0
景点门票	Scene Spot Ticket	100.0	100.0	100.0	102.8	102.8	102.8	102.8	102.8	110.9	110.9	145.9	145.9
有线电视	Cable Television	100.0	100.0	100.0	127.9	127.9	127.9	127.9	127.9	127.9	127.9	127.9	127.9
健身活动	Exercise	100.0	100.0	100.0	100.0	100.0	100.0	100.0	100.0	100.0	100.0	100.0	100.0
其他	Others	100.0	100.0	100.0	100.0	100.0	100.0	100.0	100.0	100.0	100.0	100.0	100.0
4.旅游	Tourism	99.7	99.8	100.4	100.5	100.6	100.5	100.6	100.5	100.5	100.5	100.5	100.5
旅行社收费	Travel Agency Charge	97.4	98.0	101.7	102.2	102.6	102.4	102.6	102.5	102.5	102.3	102.0	102.0
宾馆住宿	Guesthouse Stay	100.2	100.2	100.2	100.2	100.2	100.2	100.2	100.2	100.2	100.2	100.2	100.2
其他住宿	Other Stay	100.0	100.0	100.0	100.0	100.0	100.0	100.0	100.0	100.0	100.0	100.0	100.0
八、居住	**Residence**	**102.0**	**102.0**	**102.5**	**102.8**	**103.0**	**103.6**	**104.1**	**104.7**	**105.0**	**105.4**	**106.3**	**106.6**
1.建房及装修材料	Building and Building Decoration Materials	101.3	101.3	102.2	102.8	103.0	103.5	104.0	104.9	105.0	105.5	106.4	106.5
木材	Wood	102.9	103.0	103.6	104.5	104.4	105.5	106.6	109.9	111.1	113.0	115.8	115.8
木地板	Wood Floor	99.9	99.9	99.9	93.2	93.4	93.6	93.5	93.5	91.9	93.9	94.6	94.8
砖	Brick	102.1	102.8	104.7	106.8	107.1	108.9	109.0	110.0	110.0	110.1	110.1	110.0
水泥	Cement	101.7	100.7	100.7	103.3	103.7	103.2	103.1	103.1	103.2	102.9	103.7	103.7
涂料	Coating Material	101.3	101.2	101.0	100.7	99.3	99.3	99.3	99.6	99.6	100.0	100.4	101.0
胶合板	Plywood	101.9	101.9	103.5	104.7	103.2	103.8	105.3	106.7	106.8	105.0	107.7	108.5
玻璃	Glass	98.7	98.2	99.1	99.3	100.1	100.4	101.4	102.3	102.5	103.9	104.9	105.2
粘胶	Rayon	101.1	101.2	101.1	101.0	101.0	101.0	101.0	102.1	102.4	102.8	102.8	104.1
油漆	Paint	102.7	102.8	102.7	102.6	103.1	103.6	103.7	103.8	104.1	104.1	104.1	104.8
其他	Others	94.3	93.4	98.2	99.4	101.7	100.6	102.2	100.0	99.3	100.6	100.7	97.5
2.租房	Renting	101.7	101.7	101.7	101.7	101.7	101.7	103.3	103.3	103.3	103.3	105.0	105.0
公房房租	Public House Rent	100.0	100.0	100.0	100.0	100.0	100.0	100.2	100.2	100.2	100.2	100.3	100.3
私房房租	Private House Rent	100.0	100.0	100.0	100.0	100.0	100.0	102.1	102.1	102.1	102.1	104.3	104.3
其他费用	Other Fare	115.8	115.8	115.8	115.8	115.8	115.8	115.8	115.8	115.8	115.8	115.8	115.8
3.自有住房	Private Housing	98.3	98.4	98.4	98.4	100.7	103.5	103.7	103.7	104.9	104.9	108.8	108.8
房屋贷款利率	Houses Loans Interest Rate	100.8	100.8	100.8	100.8	101.3	101.3	101.3	102.8	103.2	103.2	103.2	103.2
物业管理费用	Propety Management Fee	100.0	100.0	100.0	100.0	100.0	100.0	100.0	100.0	100.0	100.0	100.0	100.0
维护修理费用	Upkeep and Repair Fe	97.7	97.7	97.7	97.7	100.8	104.5	104.7	104.7	106.2	106.2	111.4	111.4
其他	Others	99.7	100.2	100.2	100.2	100.2	100.2	100.2	100.2	100.2	100.2	100.2	100.2
4.水、电、燃料	Water,Electricity and Fuels	104.4	104.5	104.4	104.0	103.9	103.7	104.4	104.8	105.1	105.4	105.6	106.4
水	Water	106.4	106.4	110.9	110.9	110.9	110.9	110.9	110.9	110.9	110.9	110.9	110.9
电	Electricity	101.3	102.2	102.2	102.3	102.3	102.3	103.7	104.3	104.3	104.3	104.3	104.3
液化石油气	Liquefiled Petroleum Gas	117.1	116.4	113.0	111.3	111.3	110.2	110.7	111.1	114.9	114.3	114.2	114.5
管道燃气	Pipelined Gas	104.4	104.4	104.4	104.4	106.6	106.6	106.6	106.6	106.6	106.6	106.6	106.6
其他燃料	Other Fuels	102.4	102.2	102.1	101.7	101.3	101.2	101.4	101.6	101.1	102.0	102.6	104.5

7-13 全省居民消费价格指数
Entire Province Consumer Price Indices

（以2005年同期价格为100）

商品类别及品名	Commodity Category and Commodity Name	全年 Annural	1月 January	2月 February	3月 March	4月 April	5月 May	6月 June	7月 July	8月 August	9月 September	10月 October	11月 November	12月 December
居民消费价格总指数	**General Consumer Price Index**	**101.0**	**101.8**	**100.7**	**100.7**	**101.1**	**101.0**	**100.9**	**100.0**	**100.3**	**100.8**	**100.8**	**101.5**	**102.5**
非食品价格指数	**No-food**	**100.5**	**100.2**	**100.3**	**100.4**	**100.5**	**100.5**	**100.6**	**100.6**	**100.6**	**100.5**	**100.6**	**100.7**	**100.7**
服务项目价格指数	**Services**	**101.8**	**101.7**	**101.5**	**101.5**	**101.6**	**101.8**	**101.9**	**102.0**	**102.0**	**101.7**	**101.7**	**101.9**	**102.0**
工业品价格指数	**Industrial Products**	**100.1**	**99.7**	**99.9**	**100.0**	**100.1**	**100.0**	**100.2**	**100.1**	**100.1**	**100.1**	**100.2**	**100.3**	**100.3**
扣除食品和能源价格指数	**Deducting Foods and Energy**	**100.3**	**99.9**	**99.9**	**100.1**	**100.2**	**100.2**	**100.3**	**100.3**	**100.4**	**100.3**	**100.4**	**100.6**	**100.6**
扣除鲜菜鲜果总指数	**Deducting Fresh, Vegetables and Fruits**	**100.4**	**99.8**	**99.3**	**99.5**	**99.6**	**99.5**	**99.7**	**100.0**	**100.6**	**100.7**	**101.3**	**102.1**	**102.9**
消费品价格指数	**Consumer Goods**	**100.8**	**101.8**	**100.5**	**100.6**	**101.0**	**100.8**	**100.7**	**99.6**	**99.9**	**100.6**	**100.6**	**101.4**	**102.6**
一、食品	**Food**	**102.1**	**105.4**	**101.5**	**101.5**	**102.5**	**102.0**	**101.7**	**98.7**	**99.6**	**101.5**	**101.2**	**103.4**	**106.7**
1.粮食	Grain	102.8	98.1	98.1	98.4	99.4	101.1	102.0	103.5	104.3	105.0	105.5	108.3	110.5
大米	Rice	108.7	101.0	100.8	101.4	102.9	106.5	108.1	111.2	114.2	114.1	114.9	114.3	115.4
面粉	Flour	98.7	93.6	93.2	93.8	95.6	96.8	97.4	98.6	98.1	99.7	100.6	107.7	110.9
粮食制品	Grain Products	101.3	99.3	99.3	99.3	99.3	100.1	100.7	101.2	102.0	102.0	102.2	104.5	106.3
其他	Others	106.5	103.4	105.3	104.3	104.9	106.2	106.8	107.7	107.0	108.2	107.0	106.6	110.3
2.淀粉	Starches	102.3	102.6	98.9	98.6	100.7	98.4	99.3	99.8	100.9	105.8	107.4	108.4	107.4
淀粉	Starches	102.3	102.6	98.9	98.6	100.7	98.4	99.3	99.8	100.9	105.8	107.4	108.4	107.4
3.干豆类及豆制品	Beans and Beans Products	100.0	99.8	99.0	98.5	98.5	99.3	100.0	100.3	100.7	100.1	100.1	101.3	102.4
干豆	Beans	102.0	98.7	98.4	97.6	99.4	101.3	103.5	104.0	104.9	103.1	102.9	104.0	106.6
豆制品	Beans Products	99.2	100.2	99.2	98.8	98.2	98.6	98.6	98.8	99.0	98.9	99.1	100.2	100.7
4.油脂	Oil and Fat	99.5	94.7	94.0	94.1	94.8	97.3	98.0	98.5	100.3	101.1	102.7	107.0	112.7
食用植物油	Edible Vegetable Oil	100.1	95.4	94.9	95.2	95.9	98.1	98.8	99.1	100.9	101.7	102.8	107.0	112.3
植物油制品	Plant Oil Products	102.7	98.4	98.2	98.1	97.7	102.4	102.6	103.0	103.4	103.7	103.7	106.7	115.0
其他	Others	83.3	78.5	74.2	70.7	72.8	74.9	76.5	79.7	84.2	84.3	97.4	109.3	114.6
5.肉禽及其制品	Meal,Poultry and Their Products	95.8	94.6	91.2	89.3	88.4	87.1	88.1	90.9	95.9	97.9	102.5	110.8	117.5
（1）食用畜肉及副产品	Edible Livestock Meat and Their By-products	94.8	94.2	90.0	87.3	85.5	84.7	85.6	88.2	93.9	96.8	102.8	113.1	120.8
猪肉	Pork	91.0	89.5	84.5	80.9	78.2	77.4	78.6	82.6	90.7	94.6	102.6	117.0	126.4
牛肉	Beef	105.2	110.3	106.1	106.1	107.2	105.6	105.0	103.7	102.9	102.3	103.8	103.9	106.3
羊肉	Mutton	108.0	110.8	108.0	108.3	108.6	109.1	108.7	108.4	105.8	105.1	105.8	106.8	110.8
畜肉副产品	Livestock Meat By-products	95.6	95.1	94.0	91.3	90.3	88.4	90.0	90.4	93.1	96.3	99.2	106.4	115.3
其他	Others	98.8	98.3	96.4	95.9	92.7	92.5	92.2	93.1	98.9	100.0	104.7	110.8	112.3
（2）禽	Poultry	96.7	92.0	88.3	88.4	88.4	85.0	88.3	94.8	101.0	101.9	106.1	112.9	121.3
鸡	Chicken	97.5	90.6	86.4	87.0	87.6	83.8	88.3	96.6	103.4	104.9	109.6	115.8	126.6
鸭	Duck	93.1	96.3	93.4	92.8	93.0	91.6	89.3	87.2	91.3	90.3	90.2	101.4	102.0
其他	Others	95.1	96.3	95.8	92.9	89.7	87.0	87.9	90.7	95.2	94.3	99.4	105.7	109.3
（3）加工肉禽	Meal and Poultry Processing Products	98.8	98.4	98.4	98.0	98.9	97.9	97.1	97.1	98.1	98.1	98.4	101.6	103.7
畜肉制品	Livestock Meat Products	99.5	98.9	98.9	99.2	99.2	98.5	97.9	98.3	99.3	99.0	99.5	101.9	103.2
禽制品	Poultry Products	97.8	97.6	97.6	96.2	98.5	97.2	96.0	95.5	96.5	96.9	96.7	101.2	104.3
6.蛋	Eggs	95.7	93.4	85.8	89.4	90.3	88.1	86.5	89.2	96.0	98.8	105.6	110.0	117.5
鲜蛋	Fresh Eggs	94.9	92.4	84.2	88.0	89.0	86.6	84.7	87.7	95.3	98.5	106.0	110.8	119.0

7-13 续表 1 continued

商品类别及品名	Commodity Category and Commodity Name	（以2005年同期价格为100）												
		全年 Annural	1月 January	2月 February	3月 March	4月 April	5月 May	6月 June	7月 July	8 月 August	9 月 September	10 月 October	11月 November	12月 December
蛋制品	Egg Products	102.5	103.1	100.8	101.6	101.9	102.0	102.8	102.8	102.8	101.3	102.2	103.1	105.1
7.水产品	Aquatic Product	103.4	102.1	99.7	100.1	100.9	102.2	103.8	105.7	106.2	104.1	106.2	106.0	104.2
（1）鱼	Fish	100.9	99.9	97.1	96.9	97.6	98.7	100.8	101.9	102.9	103.4	104.1	103.8	103.6
淡水鱼	Freshwater Fish	97.6	96.8	92.8	92.4	92.9	94.9	97.6	100.2	101.5	101.2	100.1	101.0	99.9
海水鱼	Seawater Fish	104.3	103.1	101.6	101.7	102.4	102.8	104.1	103.8	104.3	105.8	108.4	106.8	107.3
（2）其他水产品	Other Aquatic Product	107.4	105.5	103.5	104.8	106.0	107.7	108.7	111.9	111.7	105.1	109.4	109.6	105.3
虾蟹类	Shrimp and Crab	107.7	105.9	103.8	104.8	106.1	107.9	109.3	112.8	112.5	104.3	110.0	109.9	105.6
其他	Others	106.3	104.3	102.2	105.0	105.5	107.0	106.6	108.7	108.7	108.0	107.4	108.4	104.1
8.菜	Vegetable	107.7	149.7	119.6	117.0	120.4	112.9	105.8	85.8	91.9	107.4	88.5	90.2	101.1
鲜菜	Fresh Vegetable	107.9	155.7	121.1	118.1	121.7	113.6	105.6	83.2	90.3	107.6	86.6	88.4	100.2
干菜及菜制品	Dried Vegetable and Vegetable Products	103.0	100.9	100.9	101.2	101.9	102.1	101.1	101.2	102.3	103.6	104.8	105.8	110.0
薯类	Potato	115.0	116.3	118.4	127.4	129.0	122.3	122.6	117.1	109.5	111.8	99.3	101.7	103.2
9.调味品	Flavoring	102.4	104.1	102.7	102.4	102.3	102.4	102.5	102.8	102.3	102.0	101.3	101.7	102.2
盐	Salt	106.3	114.0	108.3	107.5	105.9	107.2	108.2	108.7	106.7	105.3	102.4	101.6	101.0
酱油	Soy Sauce	100.8	100.9	100.9	100.9	101.0	100.6	100.5	100.7	100.9	100.8	100.8	100.8	101.5
醋	Vinegar	101.6	101.7	101.6	100.9	101.6	101.3	101.3	101.9	101.8	101.9	101.6	101.4	102.4
味精	Aginomoto	100.7	100.3	100.3	100.3	100.6	100.6	100.3	100.8	100.7	100.8	101.1	100.9	101.5
其他	Others	100.9	100.5	100.1	100.3	100.6	100.5	100.0	99.9	99.6	99.5	100.0	104.1	105.5
10.糖	Carbohydrate	109.5	102.9	107.3	108.7	109.5	110.2	110.6	110.9	110.7	110.8	110.6	110.6	110.5
食糖	Sugar	122.3	106.5	117.4	120.9	122.8	124.5	125.5	125.9	125.0	125.5	124.3	124.0	124.3
糖果	Sweet	102.3	100.8	101.3	101.8	102.1	102.4	102.5	102.9	102.9	102.9	103.4	103.5	101.7
巧克力制品	Chocolate Products	100.6	101.3	101.5	101.0	100.8	100.2	100.0	100.0	99.8	99.8	100.0	100.0	102.5
糖类小食品	Little Carbohydrate Food	101.3	100.4	101.0	100.9	100.8	101.2	101.2	101.4	101.7	101.5	101.4	101.7	102.6
11.茶及饮料	Tea and Beverages	101.3	100.1	100.1	101.0	101.3	101.4	101.5	101.3	101.6	101.7	101.6	101.7	102.0
（1）茶叶	Tea	100.6	99.5	99.9	100.6	101.1	100.8	100.6	100.4	100.4	100.8	101.0	100.8	101.3
茶叶	Tea	100.6	99.5	99.9	100.6	101.1	100.8	100.6	100.4	100.4	100.8	101.0	100.8	101.3
（2）饮料	Beverages	101.7	100.5	100.3	101.2	101.4	101.7	102.1	101.9	102.3	102.3	102.0	102.3	102.5
固体饮料	Solid Beverages	100.9	101.2	100.9	100.5	100.8	101.1	101.4	100.9	101.3	101.3	100.6	100.9	100.1
液体饮料	Liquid Beverages	101.1	100.0	99.8	100.7	101.0	101.4	101.3	101.3	101.5	101.3	101.4	101.5	102.1
冷冻饮品	Frozen Beverages	103.9	100.9	100.8	102.8	103.0	103.1	104.5	104.4	105.1	105.5	105.0	105.3	106.2
12.干鲜瓜果	Dried and Fresh Melons and Fruits	118.2	124.8	125.9	129.4	137.7	142.8	149.7	120.5	102.5	99.5	99.8	95.4	94.4
鲜瓜果	Fresh Fruits	121.3	129.5	131.4	135.5	146.3	153.4	164.8	125.3	101.2	96.9	96.9	91.1	89.9
干（坚）果	Dried Fruits	108.3	109.6	107.6	109.2	108.6	107.4	107.4	106.4	106.4	107.3	108.8	109.9	110.8
13.糕点饼干面包	Cake,Biscuit and Bread	100.7	101.0	101.0	101.1	100.9	100.4	100.4	100.6	100.9	100.5	100.3	100.2	101.2
糕点	Cake	100.3	101.3	101.4	101.7	101.3	100.2	100.2	100.2	100.0	99.3	99.0	99.1	100.4
饼干	Biscuit	101.3	101.1	101.0	100.7	100.6	100.8	100.7	101.1	102.1	101.9	101.7	101.5	102.5
面包	Bread	100.7	100.1	100.3	100.2	100.3	100.4	100.2	100.9	101.3	101.0	101.5	101.0	101.0
14.液体乳及乳制品	Liquid Milk and Their Products	101.4	101.0	101.2	101.7	100.8	100.6	100.6	100.7	101.2	102.1	102.1	102.1	102.7
巴氏杀菌奶或消毒奶	Pasteurization Milk or Disinfection Milk	101.1	100.6	100.6	101.5	100.1	100.0	100.2	100.4	101.0	102.1	102.0	102.2	103.3
酸奶	Leben	101.1	100.6	100.6	100.7	101.1	101.1	100.9	100.7	100.7	101.8	101.9	101.4	101.2
奶粉	Milk Powder	101.8	101.6	101.7	101.6	101.8	101.5	101.1	101.2	102.0	101.9	101.8	102.2	102.7
其他	Others	102.9	103.1	104.8	104.8	103.2	102.2	102.0	101.7	101.5	103.6	103.5	103.1	101.7
15.在外用膳食品	Outward Dinner	100.9	100.4	100.1	100.3	100.3	100.3	100.7	100.6	100.8	100.9	100.9	101.6	103.6

7-13 续表 2 continued

商品类别及品名	Commodity Category and Commodity Name	（以2005年同期价格为100）												
		全年 Annural	1月 January	2月 February	3月 March	4月 April	5月 May	6月 June	7月 July	8 月 August	9 月 September	10 月 October	11月 November	12月 December
炒菜	Hot Dish	100.9	100.7	100.5	100.6	100.7	100.5	100.9	100.8	100.9	101.1	101.0	101.2	102.1
地方小吃	Local Snack	101.4	100.4	100.2	100.6	100.7	101.0	101.1	101.5	102.2	102.0	101.8	101.9	103.8
16.其他食品	Other Foods	101.0	101.0	101.1	101.2	101.1	101.0	101.0	101.2	101.2	101.3	101.0	100.7	100.7
其他食品	Other Foods	101.0	101.0	101.1	101.2	101.1	101.0	101.0	101.2	101.2	101.3	101.0	100.7	100.7
二、烟酒及用品	**Tobacco,Liquor and Their Appliances**	**100.8**	**100.4**	**100.1**	**100.1**	**100.4**	**100.5**	**100.6**	**100.8**	**101.1**	**101.1**	**101.1**	**101.2**	**102.0**
1.烟草	Tobacco	100.4	100.1	100.0	99.9	100.3	100.3	100.2	100.4	100.5	100.5	100.5	100.5	101.2
国产卷烟	Domestic Cigarette	100.6	100.2	100.1	100.0	100.5	100.6	100.4	100.6	100.7	100.7	100.7	100.7	101.4
进口卷烟	Import Cigarette	98.3	98.9	97.8	98.0	98.4	98.1	98.2	97.9	98.2	98.4	98.3	98.8	98.9
其他	Others	99.8	99.6	99.6	99.6	99.6	99.6	99.8	100.0	99.9	99.7	99.9	99.9	100.0
2.酒	Liquor	101.1	100.6	100.2	100.2	100.5	100.6	100.9	101.1	101.6	101.6	101.6	101.8	102.9
白酒	White Spirit	101.5	100.7	100.3	100.5	100.8	101.0	101.4	101.5	102.1	101.9	102.1	102.2	103.7
葡萄酒	Grape	102.7	101.0	101.1	101.5	101.6	101.7	103.0	103.7	103.6	103.6	103.8	104.0	103.8
啤酒	Beer	100.2	100.2	99.8	99.6	99.8	99.6	99.5	99.9	100.2	100.7	100.6	100.8	101.5
其他	Others	100.3	100.4	100.3	100.2	100.1	100.0	100.0	100.8	100.8	100.2	100.2	100.5	100.5
3.吸烟、饮酒用品	Appliances for Smoking and Drinking	100.2	100.4	100.4	100.5	100.2	100.3	100.3	100.2	100.2	99.9	100.0	99.9	99.7
吸烟用品	Appliances for Smoking	100.3	100.4	100.3	100.4	100.4	100.4	100.4	100.3	100.2	100.0	100.2	100.3	100.1
饮酒用品	Appliances for Drinking	100.1	100.4	100.4	100.6	100.1	100.3	100.3	100.2	100.2	99.9	99.7	99.7	99.4
三、衣着	**Clothing**	**97.6**	**97.0**	**97.2**	**98.1**	**98.2**	**97.7**	**97.9**	**97.6**	**97.4**	**97.3**	**97.7**	**97.6**	**97.2**
1.服装	Garments	96.7	95.8	95.9	96.7	97.0	96.8	96.8	96.6	96.3	96.5	97.3	97.5	97.3
（1）男式服装	Men's Garments	96.2	94.9	95.6	96.3	96.4	96.3	96.4	96.2	95.9	96.1	96.7	97.0	97.0
大衣	Topcoat	92.4	92.3	91.7	93.4	92.7	92.3	92.0	92.3	91.9	92.0	92.0	92.7	93.9
毛线衣	Woollen Sweater	92.1	93.4	90.9	92.0	93.2	92.0	92.6	91.9	90.1	91.8	93.4	90.8	92.7
夹克衫	Jacket	96.7	93.7	94.6	94.3	94.0	97.3	97.0	96.8	97.0	96.7	99.2	101.3	99.7
衬衫	Shirt	93.7	89.8	93.4	95.4	94.6	93.3	94.5	93.6	93.4	93.0	93.3	94.1	96.0
T恤衫	T-shirt	98.1	99.4	100.0	99.4	99.7	100.2	99.2	97.1	95.7	96.2	96.8	98.0	95.8
裤子	Trousers	94.9	95.9	95.2	96.0	94.2	93.9	93.9	93.8	95.4	94.3	95.7	95.1	95.7
西服	Western-style Clothes	99.0	96.0	97.3	96.8	99.2	100.1	99.7	100.4	98.7	99.8	100.6	100.3	99.1
运动衫裤	Gym Suit	96.9	93.4	96.4	99.2	98.9	95.7	96.0	96.1	96.6	96.9	97.2	98.5	97.9
内衣	Underwaist	101.7	101.6	102.1	102.9	102.7	103.2	102.8	102.5	102.8	102.2	99.0	99.2	99.3
羽绒衣	Eider Down Outerwear	97.1	95.6	96.4	96.2	95.3	96.1	97.0	97.3	97.1	97.8	99.0	100.1	97.9
其他	Others	95.9	96.2	94.8	94.0	95.7	96.0	94.8	95.0	94.9	94.8	96.0	99.4	99.3
（2）女式服装	Women's Garments	96.7	96.1	95.8	96.7	97.1	96.5	96.5	96.5	96.2	96.5	97.7	97.7	97.3
大衣	Topcoat	91.3	92.1	89.0	92.1	91.6	90.7	92.4	92.0	91.2	91.0	91.2	90.3	91.9
毛线衣	Woollen Sweater	92.4	93.4	91.7	94.1	94.6	93.1	92.1	90.5	89.4	90.6	92.4	93.1	93.7
羽绒衣	Eider Down Outerwear	97.5	93.6	95.2	94.9	95.5	96.0	96.9	98.8	98.8	98.5	100.4	101.3	100.3
套装	Coordinates	99.1	100.5	100.0	100.1	99.8	99.7	98.4	98.9	97.0	99.0	99.9	98.0	98.3
衬衫	Shirt	97.9	95.3	96.8	97.2	98.8	98.8	99.5	99.7	98.6	98.0	98.9	98.3	95.7
T恤衫	T-shirt	99.8	97.9	98.2	97.9	98.5	98.4	99.1	97.8	97.9	100.1	104.4	105.0	102.9
裙子	Skirt	98.2	98.0	97.8	97.7	98.6	98.1	97.3	97.6	98.5	97.9	99.3	99.4	98.1
裤子	Trousers	97.5	98.9	98.6	99.5	98.9	97.4	96.4	96.5	97.2	96.6	96.8	97.2	96.3
运动衫裤	Gym Suit	97.7	98.6	99.7	98.8	99.8	96.5	96.2	96.4	96.6	97.1	97.4	97.0	98.5
内衣	Underwaist	99.2	96.5	96.2	97.7	98.2	98.7	98.8	98.6	99.0	100.4	101.0	103.0	102.9
其他	Others	100.1	99.3	98.8	99.0	99.8	99.4	100.0	100.4	100.5	100.9	100.6	101.3	100.8
（3）儿童服装	Children's Garments	98.2	97.4	97.4	97.8	98.6	99.0	98.8	98.1	98.2	97.8	98.0	98.2	98.6

7-13 续表 3 continued

商品类别及品名	Commodity Category and Commodity Name	全年 Annural	1月 January	2月 February	3月 March	4月 April	5月 May	6月 June	7月 July	8月 August	9月 September	10月 October	11月 November	12月 December
		（以2005年同期价格为100）												
套装	Coordinates	97.5	97.2	96.9	97.3	98.0	97.8	97.7	98.0	97.8	97.2	96.8	97.4	98.4
裤子	Trousers	99.6	96.9	97.4	97.8	99.5	100.7	100.9	100.0	100.5	100.1	101.4	100.5	99.9
裙子	Skirt	98.0	98.1	97.6	98.2	98.6	99.6	98.8	96.9	97.2	97.2	97.3	97.8	98.4
其他	Others	96.9	98.7	99.7	99.8	99.2	98.0	96.7	96.2	95.5	94.4	94.6	95.5	94.6
2.衣着材料	Clothing Materials	100.4	100.0	100.4	100.2	100.2	100.4	100.4	100.5	100.5	100.0	100.3	100.5	100.9
棉布	Cotton Cloth	100.3	100.0	99.8	99.7	99.6	100.1	100.3	100.4	100.4	100.4	100.5	100.7	101.3
棉混纺布	Cotton Textiles Cloth	100.3	99.7	99.9	99.9	100.2	100.2	100.2	100.2	100.2	100.2	100.5	100.8	101.2
化纤布	Chemical Fiber Cloth	100.8	99.2	100.5	100.4	100.4	101.1	100.9	101.0	101.0	100.6	101.2	101.3	101.4
毛线	Knitting Wool	99.8	101.9	101.2	100.5	100.5	99.7	99.9	99.9	99.9	98.4	98.5	98.7	99.3
3.鞋袜帽	Shoes,Socks and Hats	98.7	99.3	99.6	100.8	100.4	99.1	99.7	99.3	98.8	98.2	97.6	96.7	95.2
（1）鞋	Shoes	98.5	99.2	99.6	101.0	100.4	99.0	99.7	99.1	98.6	97.8	97.3	96.3	94.5
男鞋	Men's Shoes	98.2	98.6	99.4	99.9	100.1	97.5	98.5	97.7	98.2	97.8	97.7	96.9	95.8
女鞋	Women's Shoes	98.3	99.7	99.8	102.1	100.6	99.5	100.3	99.6	98.1	96.8	95.9	94.6	92.3
童鞋	Children's Shoes	100.3	98.8	99.2	100.0	100.5	100.9	100.8	100.8	101.3	101.0	100.6	100.5	98.8
（2）袜子	Socks	99.7	99.8	100.1	99.9	100.3	100.1	100.0	99.9	99.9	100.1	99.0	98.5	98.6
男袜	Men's Socks	99.5	99.1	99.0	99.0	100.8	100.7	100.5	100.4	99.8	99.9	99.1	98.0	98.0
女袜	Women's Socks	99.8	100.2	100.8	100.5	99.9	99.6	99.6	99.6	99.9	100.2	99.0	98.8	99.0
（3）帽子	Hats	99.8	99.8	99.5	99.5	99.5	99.5	99.4	99.8	99.7	100.0	100.0	100.1	100.3
男帽	Men's Hats	99.9	99.5	99.3	99.3	99.3	99.6	99.8	100.2	100.1	100.2	100.1	100.7	100.6
女帽	Women's Hats	99.7	100.1	99.6	99.7	99.6	99.4	99.0	99.5	99.5	99.9	99.9	99.7	100.1
4.衣着加工服务费	Clothing Manufacturing Services	100.0	99.1	98.8	100.1	100.1	100.1	100.1	100.1	100.2	100.2	100.2	100.0	101.2
缝纫	Sewing	100.0	98.4	98.1	100.1	100.2	100.2	100.2	100.2	100.2	100.2	100.2	99.8	101.9
清洗	Washing	100.1	100.4	100.2	100.1	99.9	99.9	99.9	100.0	100.1	100.1	100.2	100.2	100.2
四、家庭设备用品及维修服务	**Household Facilities, Articles and Services**	**101.1**	**100.4**	**100.4**	**100.4**	**100.2**	**100.2**	**100.9**	**101.1**	**101.4**	**101.7**	**101.8**	**101.9**	**102.3**
1.耐用消费品	Durable Consumer Goods	101.3	100.4	100.4	100.2	99.8	100.0	101.3	101.8	101.9	102.2	102.4	102.6	102.7
（1）家具	Furniture	100.3	99.7	99.7	99.5	99.7	100.0	100.2	100.3	100.4	100.7	101.2	101.4	101.4
柜	Cabinet	100.3	100.3	100.2	99.6	99.4	100.0	100.1	100.0	100.3	100.4	101.2	101.0	101.0
床	Bed	100.8	99.4	99.9	99.5	100.2	100.8	100.9	101.0	101.1	101.3	102.0	102.2	102.0
桌	Desk	99.8	100.0	100.2	99.7	99.7	99.5	99.5	99.7	99.6	99.4	99.8	100.5	100.5
椅	Chair	100.0	100.5	99.9	99.9	99.7	99.6	99.7	99.3	99.2	99.8	100.9	101.0	100.9
沙发	Sofa	100.3	98.5	98.6	98.6	99.3	99.8	100.1	100.7	100.9	101.4	101.6	102.1	101.9
其他	Others	100.9	101.1	100.6	100.5	100.4	99.8	100.7	101.0	101.1	102.0	101.3	101.2	101.7
（2）家庭设备	Household Appliances	101.9	100.8	100.8	100.7	100.0	100.1	102.0	102.6	102.8	103.0	103.1	103.3	103.5
洗衣机	Washing Machine	100.2	99.6	99.9	99.4	98.8	99.1	100.0	101.0	100.3	100.6	101.0	101.2	101.3
电风扇	Electric Fan	101.3	101.6	101.3	101.4	98.7	98.6	100.9	101.9	102.4	102.0	101.9	101.9	103.2
电冰箱（柜）	Refrigerator	104.8	105.0	104.6	104.9	104.8	104.7	105.2	105.1	103.9	104.5	105.1	104.8	104.6
吸排油烟机	Kitchen Ventilato	102.6	102.3	102.4	101.8	100.4	100.3	101.7	103.2	103.9	104.0	103.9	103.9	103.8
空调器	Air-conditioning	103.5	100.8	100.7	100.3	99.6	99.9	104.3	105.3	106.2	106.1	105.9	106.1	106.5
热水器	Water Heater	99.4	98.8	99.2	99.6	98.8	98.8	98.9	98.9	99.0	99.9	99.8	100.3	100.5
微波炉	Microwave Oven	97.3	95.7	95.6	96.2	95.6	95.5	96.5	96.8	98.7	99.2	99.4	99.9	99.3
电炊具	Electric Cooking Appliance	99.7	99.1	99.0	98.9	99.4	99.6	99.7	99.6	99.6	99.5	99.8	100.7	101.0
2.室内装饰品	Interior Decorations	99.7	100.2	100.1	100.1	99.6	99.4	99.2	99.2	99.4	100.1	99.5	99.7	100.0
纺织装饰品	Textile Process Decorations	99.3	100.0	99.9	99.9	99.0	99.2	98.8	98.6	98.9	99.6	99.1	99.2	99.8
装饰灯具	Architectural Lamps and Lanterns	100.0	100.5	100.5	100.5	100.1	99.4	99.4	99.8	99.6	100.6	99.5	99.6	99.8

7-13 续表 4 continued

商品类别及品名	Commodity Category and Commodity Name	（以2005年同期价格为100）												
		全年 Annural	1月 January	2月 February	3月 March	4月 April	5月 May	6月 June	7月 July	8月 August	9月 September	10月 October	11月 November	12月 December
其他	Others	100.3	100.0	100.0	99.9	99.9	100.0	99.9	99.8	100.4	100.5	100.5	101.1	101.1
3.床上用品	Bedclothes	99.7	98.2	99.1	99.9	100.0	99.4	100.1	99.9	99.7	99.9	99.9	99.5	100.5
毛毯	Woollen Blanket	100.0	96.9	98.1	101.0	101.0	100.1	100.4	100.1	100.0	100.4	100.8	100.1	101.4
被子	Quilt	98.9	98.4	98.8	98.8	98.7	98.1	99.7	99.4	99.0	99.2	98.6	98.7	99.4
床上套件	Bed Articcles	99.6	98.8	99.4	99.6	99.8	99.5	99.9	99.9	99.5	99.7	100.1	99.2	100.2
其他	Others	101.0	98.9	101.2	101.3	101.4	101.1	100.8	100.9	100.9	101.0	101.0	101.1	102.1
4.日用杂品	Sundry Articles	100.4	100.1	100.1	100.3	100.2	100.1	100.1	100.0	100.4	100.8	100.8	100.7	101.4
茶具	Tea Set	100.2	97.6	97.6	98.0	98.0	97.4	99.5	99.0	99.1	100.6	104.7	105.3	105.7
餐具	Tableware	99.2	98.4	99.1	98.8	98.8	99.2	99.9	99.4	100.3	100.7	98.4	98.3	98.8
厨具	Kitchen Utensils	101.3	100.3	100.6	100.9	101.9	102.0	100.8	100.9	100.8	101.6	101.6	101.6	102.3
家用手工工具	Domestic Handwork Tools	101.2	101.3	101.2	101.2	101.2	100.8	101.1	101.3	101.3	101.1	100.8	100.5	102.4
洗涤用品	Washing Articles	100.6	101.3	100.8	101.2	100.5	100.3	100.0	99.9	100.5	100.7	100.6	100.2	100.7
其他	Others	100.3	100.1	100.1	100.5	100.4	100.3	99.8	99.8	100.3	100.5	100.4	100.5	101.1
5.家庭服务及加工维修服务	Household Srvice and Manufacturing Upkeep	104.2	104.3	104.0	103.7	103.8	103.7	103.4	103.0	104.2	104.5	104.7	105.2	106.0
家庭服务	Household Srvice	107.3	107.5	107.1	106.4	106.7	106.4	105.8	105.3	107.2	108.0	108.3	109.5	109.5
加工维修服务	Manufacturing Upkeep	101.4	101.3	101.3	101.3	101.2	101.2	101.1	100.9	101.4	101.4	101.4	101.2	102.9
五、医疗保健和个人用品	**Health Care and Personal Articles**	**100.8**	**100.0**	**100.2**	**100.0**	**100.4**	**100.9**	**101.0**	**101.1**	**101.1**	**101.1**	**101.1**	**101.1**	**101.0**
1.医疗保健	Health Care	100.1	99.6	99.8	99.8	99.9	100.1	100.1	100.4	100.3	100.4	100.4	100.5	100.3
（1）医疗器具及用品	Medical Facilities and Goods	96.1	93.6	94.1	97.3	96.9	96.6	96.8	96.8	96.8	97.7	96.2	96.1	94.8
医疗器具及用品	Medical Facilities and Goods	96.1	93.6	94.1	97.3	96.9	96.6	96.8	96.8	96.8	97.7	96.2	96.1	94.8
（2）中药材及中成药	Herbs and Ready-made Traditional Chinese Medicine	101.7	100.3	100.9	100.6	100.9	100.9	101.3	102.0	102.1	102.4	102.9	103.2	102.5
中药材	Herbs	103.2	100.1	101.1	100.2	101.2	102.0	103.0	104.1	103.7	104.7	106.0	106.8	104.9
中成药	Ready-made Traditional Chinese Medicine	100.1	100.4	100.7	101.1	100.5	99.8	99.6	99.8	100.3	100.1	99.7	99.6	99.9
（3）西药	Western Medicine	99.4	99.1	99.2	99.1	99.1	99.7	99.5	99.7	99.5	99.5	99.4	99.4	99.6
抗微生物药	Anti-microorganism Medicine	98.1	96.4	96.4	96.6	96.7	96.9	97.2	98.5	98.1	98.4	100.4	100.6	100.7
消化系统用药	Alimentary System Medicine	99.9	99.0	99.2	99.4	99.3	99.7	100.1	100.9	100.2	100.2	100.4	100.0	100.4
呼吸系统用药	Respiratory System Medicine	99.8	98.8	98.8	98.9	99.3	99.3	100.0	100.0	99.9	101.0	100.4	100.6	100.6
解热镇痛及非甾体抗炎药	Allays a Fever the Analgesia and the Non-steroid Body Anti-inflammatory Agent	100.4	100.7	100.6	100.3	100.5	101.9	100.4	100.1	100.1	99.7	100.0	100.2	100.9
抗肿瘤药	Antineoplastic Drug	99.6	100.0	100.0	99.8	99.4	102.3	100.1	100.3	99.6	98.7	98.3	98.7	98.2
激素及调节内分泌功能药	Hormone and Adjustment Internal Secretion Function Medicine	98.3	99.2	99.5	99.2	99.2	99.2	99.0	98.2	98.2	98.7	96.0	96.5	96.2
循环系统用药	Circulating System Medicine	99.5	99.3	99.4	99.4	99.0	98.9	99.5	99.4	99.6	100.0	100.6	99.5	100.0

7-13 续表 5 continued

商品类别及品名	Commodity Category and Commodity Name	（以2005年同期价格为100）												
		全年 Annural	1月 January	2月 February	3月 March	4月 April	5月 May	6月 June	7月 July	8月 August	9月 September	10月 October	11月 November	12月 December
神经系统用药	Nerve System Medicine	100.2	100.6	100.9	100.6	101.0	101.0	100.9	100.9	100.0	100.5	98.5	98.5	99.1
专科用药	Junior Medicine	98.9	99.7	99.6	99.8	99.9	99.9	100.3	100.0	99.8	98.8	96.4	96.3	96.3
其他	Others	98.8	99.8	100.1	98.6	98.4	99.1	99.0	98.9	98.8	98.9	98.2	98.0	98.1
（4）保健品及器具	Healthcare Equipment	99.5	99.9	99.6	99.6	99.6	99.5	99.7	99.5	99.5	99.5	99.1	99.3	99.3
保健器具	Health Protection Equipment	99.5	99.8	99.4	99.5	99.6	99.6	99.9	99.9	100.0	99.9	99.0	99.1	98.8
滋补保健用品	Tonic and Health Products	99.5	99.9	99.7	99.6	99.5	99.5	99.6	99.4	99.2	99.3	99.2	99.4	99.6
（5）医疗保健服务	Health Care Services	100.5	100.5	100.6	100.6	100.6	100.6	100.5	100.7	100.7	100.5	100.5	100.6	100.3
挂号费	Registration	100.3	100.1	100.2	100.3	100.3	100.3	100.3	100.4	100.4	100.4	100.4	100.4	100.4
注射费	Injection Expenses	100.0	100.1	100.1	100.1	100.1	99.9	99.9	99.9	100.0	100.0	100.0	100.0	100.0
检查费	Examination Expenses	101.1	101.3	101.4	101.4	101.3	101.3	100.9	101.4	101.4	100.8	100.8	100.9	100.7
手术费	Operation Expenses	100.2	100.2	100.2	100.2	100.2	100.2	100.1	100.1	100.1	100.1	100.1	100.1	100.6
住院费	Hospitalization Expenses	101.4	101.3	101.3	101.3	101.3	101.3	101.3	101.8	101.8	101.6	101.3	101.7	100.2
理疗费	Physiotherapy Expenses	100.0	99.9	99.9	99.9	100.0	100.0	100.0	100.0	100.0	100.0	100.0	100.0	100.0
化验费	Analysis Expenses	100.1	100.0	100.1	100.1	100.1	100.1	100.1	100.1	100.1	100.1	100.1	100.1	100.0
其他	Others	100.0	100.0	100.0	100.0	100.0	100.0	100.0	100.0	100.0	100.0	100.0	100.0	100.0
2.个人用品及服务	Personal Articles and Services	102.0	100.7	101.0	100.5	101.5	102.5	102.7	102.5	102.7	102.5	102.6	102.4	102.3
（1）化妆美容用品	Cosmetics	99.4	100.0	99.9	97.3	99.4	99.6	99.7	99.5	99.6	99.4	99.4	99.3	99.8
化妆美容器具	Cosmetics Appliances	100.0	98.2	98.3	98.4	99.5	99.9	100.9	100.8	101.1	100.9	100.9	100.7	100.5
美容化妆品	Facial Beautifier	99.7	100.5	100.5	100.3	99.2	99.3	99.4	99.5	99.3	99.4	99.2	99.6	100.6
护肤品	Protects Skin Products	99.6	99.8	99.9	99.8	99.9	100.0	99.8	99.7	100.0	98.8	99.5	98.8	99.1
护发美容品	Protects Sends the Beauty Products	98.2	100.2	99.7	89.5	99.6	99.5	99.6	98.4	98.9	98.9	99.0	98.3	98.4
（2）清洁化妆用品	Cleaning Toiletware	100.5	99.8	99.8	100.0	99.9	100.5	101.0	100.8	101.0	100.7	100.8	100.6	100.7
洗发用品	Hairdressing Articles	100.2	100.5	100.1	100.3	100.0	100.0	100.9	100.8	100.9	100.1	100.5	100.0	99.0
洗浴用品	Bathing Articles	100.3	99.3	99.3	99.4	99.5	100.4	100.8	100.6	101.0	100.9	100.8	100.7	100.8
其他	Others	101.4	99.3	100.3	100.5	100.9	101.7	101.7	101.5	101.5	101.6	101.5	101.7	104.7
（3）个人饰品	Personal Decoraions	107.6	101.7	103.0	104.2	106.0	109.6	109.6	109.6	110.1	109.8	109.5	109.2	108.4
首饰	Ornaments	118.4	105.8	108.0	110.1	114.3	122.8	123.0	123.5	124.0	123.7	122.7	122.2	120.4
皮件	Leather Appliance	98.0	97.9	99.1	99.8	98.0	97.6	97.5	96.9	98.1	97.9	98.2	97.7	96.8
手表	Watch	99.0	99.1	99.3	99.2	99.3	99.4	98.7	98.1	97.9	98.4	99.2	99.5	99.8
领带	Necktie	100.0	99.0	99.5	100.1	101.4	100.5	101.0	100.9	101.1	99.9	99.3	98.8	98.8
其他	Others	98.4	97.6	97.5	97.8	98.3	98.4	98.4	98.2	98.5	98.6	98.6	98.5	100.2
（4）个人服	Personal Services	101.5	101.6	101.5	101.5	101.6	101.4	101.4	101.4	101.5	101.3	101.7	101.6	101.3
美容	Cosmetology	101.2	101.3	101.3	101.3	101.3	101.3	101.3	101.3	101.3	101.3	101.3	101.3	100.7
理（烫）发	Haircut (permnaent wave)	101.3	101.2	101.0	100.8	101.3	101.1	101.1	100.9	100.9	101.0	102.0	102.0	102.0
洗浴	Bathe	101.8	101.9	101.9	101.9	102.0	101.5	101.5	101.5	102.2	102.2	101.9	102.1	101.3
其他	Others	102.7	104.0	104.0	104.0	103.5	103.5	103.5	103.5	103.9	101.5	101.5	100.0	100.0

7-13 续表 6 continued

商品类别及品名	Commodity Category and Commodity Name	（以2005年同期价格为100） 全年 Annural	1月 January	2月 February	3月 March	4月 April	5月 May	6月 June	7月 July	8月 August	9月 September	10月 October	11月 November	12月 December
六、交通和通信	**Transportation and Communication**	**98.7**	**98.2**	**98.5**	**98.5**	**98.3**	**98.7**	**99.2**	**98.8**	**98.6**	**98.7**	**98.8**	**99.1**	**99.0**
1.交通	Transportation	102.9	103.0	103.5	103.3	102.9	103.3	104.0	103.1	102.4	102.4	102.4	102.4	102.0
（1）交通工具	Transportation Facility	98.5	98.4	99.5	99.7	99.2	99.0	98.5	98.2	98.1	98.0	98.0	98.2	97.5
摩托车	Motorcycle	101.4	98.9	100.9	101.2	101.2	101.4	101.5	101.4	101.9	102.3	102.5	102.5	101.1
自行车	Bicycle	98.6	99.3	100.2	100.0	99.5	99.3	98.6	97.8	97.4	97.6	97.6	97.6	97.8
轿车	Car	96.4	96.9	97.3	97.7	97.5	97.0	96.3	96.3	96.2	95.3	95.5	95.9	94.7
其他	Others	98.2	101.2	101.0	102.8	99.0	98.1	97.6	97.5	97.0	97.0	95.7	95.7	95.9
（2）车用燃料及零配件	Fuels and Parts	112.2	110.0	110.1	109.1	110.8	113.1	118.4	115.3	111.7	111.6	112.0	112.0	111.9
汽油	Gasoline	116.4	114.6	114.7	112.0	113.4	117.5	126.1	121.0	115.7	115.3	115.7	115.7	115.7
柴油	Diesel Oil	115.6	113.0	113.3	113.8	117.0	118.2	122.6	118.6	113.9	114.0	114.4	114.3	114.1
零配件	Parts	100.6	99.2	99.3	99.4	99.7	99.8	99.8	100.9	101.3	101.5	101.9	102.2	102.1
其他	Others	102.5	99.9	100.1	100.7	102.4	102.4	103.9	103.1	103.5	104.4	104.1	102.5	103.3
（3）车辆使用及维修费	Using and Upkeep Fare	100.4	100.4	99.8	100.2	99.9	100.0	100.2	100.2	100.9	101.0	101.0	100.3	100.7
驾驶证	Driving License	100.4	100.7	100.8	100.0	98.8	99.3	100.1	100.6	102.1	102.1	101.2	99.9	98.8
保险费	Insurance Expenses	99.7	99.4	99.5	99.5	99.6	99.6	99.6	99.5	99.9	100.1	100.1	100.1	100.1
停车费	Parking Expenses	102.0	101.6	101.6	101.6	100.0	100.0	100.0	100.0	103.8	103.8	103.8	103.8	103.8
车辆修理服务费	Vehicle Upkeep Service fare	100.4	100.5	98.9	100.4	100.4	100.4	100.5	100.5	100.5	100.5	100.8	99.9	101.4
其他	Others	100.7	101.3	101.3	101.3	101.4	101.4	101.4	101.4	99.9	99.9	99.9	99.9	99.9
（4）市区公共交通费	Incity Traffic Fare	104.7	103.9	104.2	104.2	103.8	105.1	105.1	106.0	105.4	105.0	104.9	104.3	103.9
公共汽车票	Bus Ticket	102.3	102.2	102.8	102.8	102.6	102.5	102.5	102.2	102.0	102.0	102.0	101.8	101.9
出租汽车	Taxi	107.4	105.8	105.9	105.9	105.3	108.2	108.1	110.4	109.1	108.4	108.3	107.1	106.1
其他	Others	102.2	102.2	102.2	102.2	102.0	102.0	102.0	102.0	103.9	102.2	102.2	102.2	102.0
（5）城市间交通费	Intercity Traffic Fare	106.5	110.2	110.3	109.3	107.0	107.2	108.2	105.1	104.2	104.5	104.2	104.8	104.0
飞机票	Airplane Ticket	103.0	104.2	99.2	100.3	99.3	103.7	102.4	101.7	100.8	105.3	103.8	108.6	107.7
火车票	Train Ticket	100.7	101.2	100.7	100.5	100.5	100.5	100.6	100.6	100.6	100.7	100.7	100.8	100.8
长途汽车	Intertown Bus	108.6	114.3	115.1	113.5	110.2	109.5	111.1	106.5	105.1	105.3	104.9	105.5	104.5
其他	Others	108.0	102.9	100.8	101.8	101.3	111.0	111.3	111.0	111.1	111.1	111.1	111.1	111.1
2.通信	Communication	93.9	93.0	92.9	93.2	93.2	93.4	93.6	93.8	94.1	94.3	94.4	95.1	95.5
（1）通信工具	Communication Facility	81.8	81.3	81.0	81.5	80.8	80.9	81.2	81.7	82.2	82.7	82.8	83.2	83.1
固定电话机	Telephone	95.4	95.8	95.6	94.6	95.7	95.1	95.2	95.0	94.8	95.7	95.8	95.9	95.3
移动电话机	Mobile Phone	75.5	75.2	74.8	75.7	74.2	74.5	74.8	75.3	76.1	76.3	76.1	76.6	76.5
其他	others	93.9	94.2	93.4	93.5	93.9	93.7	93.6	93.6	93.4	93.4	94.3	94.4	95.6
（2）通信服务	Communication Service	100.1	99.6	99.6	99.6	99.9	100.0	100.0	100.0	100.0	100.0	100.0	100.7	101.2
移动通信费	Mobile Communication Fee	99.5	98.4	98.4	98.4	99.3	100.0	100.0	100.0	100.0	100.0	100.0	100.0	100.0
市内电话费	Incity Telephone Fee	100.0	100.0	100.0	100.0	100.0	100.0	100.0	100.0	100.0	100.0	100.0	100.0	100.0
长途电话费	Long Distance Call Fee	100.0	100.0	100.0	100.0	100.0	100.0	100.0	100.0	100.0	100.0	100.0	100.0	100.0
月租费	Month Hiring Fee	100.0	100.0	100.0	100.0	100.0	100.0	100.0	100.0	100.0	100.0	100.0	100.0	100.0
上网费	Net Play Fee	100.6	100.8	100.9	100.7	100.7	100.7	100.7	100.7	100.7	100.6	100.6	100.8	99.8
信件邮寄	Letter Post	103.7	100.0	100.0	100.0	100.0	100.0	100.0	100.0	100.0	100.0	100.0	115.5	128.7
包裹邮寄	Package Post	100.1	100.0	100.0	100.0	100.0	100.0	100.0	100.0	100.0	100.0	100.0	100.5	100.5

7-13 续表 7 continued

（以2005年同期价格为100）

商品类别及品名	Commodity Category and Commodity Name	全年 Annural	1月 January	2月 February	3月 March	4月 April	5月 May	6月 June	7月 July	8月 August	9月 September	10月 October	11月 November	12月 December
其他	Others	100.0	100.0	100.0	100.0	100.0	100.0	100.0	100.0	100.0	100.0	100.0	100.0	100.0
七、娱乐教育文化用品及服务	**Recreation,Education and Culture Articles**	**100.0**	**100.1**	**99.8**	**99.9**	**100.1**	**100.2**	**100.1**	**100.3**	**100.3**	**99.6**	**99.7**	**99.8**	**99.8**
1.文娱用耐用消费品及服务	Durable Consumer Goods for Cultural and Recreational Use and Service	95.5	95.8	95.6	95.5	95.2	95.4	95.2	95.4	95.5	95.2	95.3	95.9	95.8
电视机	Television	93.3	93.3	93.1	93.0	92.4	93.0	92.7	93.1	93.3	93.3	93.4	94.5	94.7
激光视盘机	Laser Video Disc Machine	96.9	97.0	96.7	96.7	96.5	96.4	97.0	97.0	98.0	98.2	97.6	97.1	94.5
摄像机	Pickup Camera	96.2	96.9	97.3	96.8	96.9	96.9	96.2	96.0	95.8	95.5	95.3	95.8	95.3
照相机	Camera	95.2	95.4	94.8	94.0	93.6	93.8	94.6	95.0	96.0	96.5	96.3	96.8	95.9
家用音响	Acoustic Equipment	98.9	99.6	99.3	99.3	98.8	98.9	98.7	99.2	99.1	98.7	98.8	98.7	98.1
便携式音响	Portable Acoustics	98.9	99.5	99.2	99.0	98.8	98.8	98.7	98.7	98.7	98.7	98.8	98.8	99.0
电脑	Computer	95.2	96.1	96.0	96.1	95.9	95.7	95.3	95.1	94.6	93.6	93.8	94.7	95.2
修理服务	Repair Service	102.4	101.6	101.8	101.6	101.8	102.3	102.6	102.5	102.3	102.4	103.3	103.3	103.5
其他	Others	98.7	97.7	99.5	99.5	99.3	99.2	99.3	98.9	98.7	97.2	98.7	98.5	98.5
2.教育	Education	101.5	101.7	101.8	101.8	102.0	102.0	101.9	101.9	101.6	100.9	100.9	100.9	100.7
（1）教材及参考书	Teaching Materials and Reference	101.3	101.6	101.6	101.7	101.8	101.8	101.7	101.7	101.6	100.5	100.3	100.4	100.4
工具书	Tool Book	101.1	101.8	101.8	101.8	101.8	101.7	101.7	101.7	100.8	100.1	100.1	100.1	100.0
教材	Teaching Material	100.6	100.9	100.9	101.0	101.2	101.2	101.1	101.1	101.5	99.7	99.5	99.5	99.5
参考书	Reference Book	103.1	103.3	103.3	103.7	103.7	103.7	103.4	103.4	103.2	102.5	102.5	102.5	102.5
教育软件	Educational Software	99.7	99.9	99.8	99.8	99.8	99.8	99.8	99.8	99.8	99.8	98.9	99.8	99.9
（2）学杂托幼费	Tuition and Child Care	101.5	101.7	101.8	101.8	102.0	102.0	102.0	101.9	101.6	101.0	101.0	101.0	100.7
义务教育杂费	Incidental Expenses of Compulcory Education	100.8	101.4	101.4	101.4	101.4	101.4	101.4	101.4	100.4	100.0	100.0	100.0	100.0
非义务教育学杂费	Tuition of Non-compulsory Education	101.1	101.4	101.4	101.4	101.4	101.4	101.4	101.4	101.4	100.7	100.7	100.7	100.7
技能培训学费	Skill Train Tuition	100.7	101.5	101.5	101.5	100.6	100.6	100.6	100.7	100.7	100.5	100.5	100.5	98.9
托幼费	Child Care	105.8	104.6	105.8	105.6	107.8	107.8	107.3	106.7	107.3	104.3	104.0	104.0	104.4
其他	Others	103.2	101.8	101.8	101.8	103.5	103.5	103.6	103.6	103.6	104.4	104.4	104.4	102.6
3.文化娱乐类	Recreation and Culture	101.7	101.2	101.0	101.0	102.0	102.4	102.1	102.0	101.7	101.7	101.9	101.9	102.0
（1）文化娱乐用品	Culture Articles	99.8	100.3	100.1	100.0	99.9	99.9	99.7	99.6	99.6	99.6	99.6	99.6	99.6
乐器	Musical Instrument	100.3	99.6	100.0	99.9	100.2	100.3	100.3	100.5	100.4	100.7	100.8	100.6	100.2
音响光盘和磁带	Audio,Disk and Tape	99.0	99.4	99.3	98.8	99.0	98.9	98.9	98.9	98.9	99.0	99.0	99.1	99.1
照相胶卷和存储卡	Roll Film and Memorizing Card	99.4	99.9	99.9	100.1	99.9	99.8	99.7	99.5	99.1	98.7	98.1	98.5	99.0
录像磁带和视盘	Video Tape and Disk	99.5	99.3	99.3	99.3	99.7	99.8	100.0	99.5	99.4	99.5	99.5	99.3	99.2
儿童玩具	Children's Toy	99.8	101.5	101.1	100.8	100.2	100.0	99.7	99.5	99.0	98.9	98.9	99.0	99.0
纸张本册	Paper and Volume	101.3	102.8	101.1	101.3	100.9	100.9	100.7	100.7	101.4	101.5	101.6	101.6	101.4
文具	Stationery	99.4	99.3	99.7	99.6	99.7	99.8	99.4	99.1	99.0	99.1	99.1	99.3	99.3
体育用品	Sports Goods	99.4	99.2	99.4	99.4	99.4	99.4	99.1	99.4	99.5	99.5	99.6	99.3	99.2
其他	Others	99.6	99.3	99.4	99.3	99.3	99.3	99.7	99.8	99.8	99.7	99.9	99.6	99.6

7-13　续表 8 continued

商品类别及品名	Commodity Category and Commodity Name	（以2005年同期价格为100）												
		全年 Annural	1月 January	2月 February	3月 March	4月 April	5月 May	6月 June	7月 July	8 月 August	9 月 September	10 月 October	11月 November	12月 December
（2）书报杂志	Books,Newspapers, Magazines	102.2	102.2	102.2	102.3	102.3	102.3	102.3	102.3	102.1	102.1	102.1	102.0	101.9
书籍	Books	101.0	101.1	101.1	101.3	101.3	101.2	101.2	101.2	100.9	100.8	100.8	100.6	100.4
报纸	Newspapers	105.1	105.1	105.1	105.1	105.1	105.1	105.1	105.1	105.1	105.1	105.1	105.1	105.0
杂志	Magazines	100.6	100.6	100.6	100.6	100.6	100.6	100.6	100.6	100.6	100.6	100.6	100.6	100.6
（3）文娱费	Expenditure of Culture and Recreation	104.9	101.8	101.3	101.5	105.5	107.0	106.2	106.2	105.0	105.1	106.1	106.2	106.8
电影票	Film Ticket	101.2	105.3	104.6	103.4	102.1	100.2	101.3	100.6	100.2	99.2	101.9	99.3	96.9
景点门票	Scene Spot ticket	106.4	100.5	98.8	100.5	100.2	113.1	107.2	109.1	104.4	106.6	106.7	111.0	118.5
有线电视	Cable Television	107.9	100.0	100.0	100.0	110.5	110.5	110.5	110.5	110.5	110.5	110.6	110.6	110.6
健身活动	Exercise	101.4	102.9	102.6	103.2	103.3	102.3	101.7	100.4	99.0	98.9	101.3	100.9	101.1
其他	Others	101.6	103.3	103.3	103.3	103.1	101.9	101.4	101.5	101.5	100.1	100.1	100.1	99.8
4.旅游	Tourism	99.7	100.0	97.2	98.2	98.8	99.1	99.1	100.8	102.0	99.9	100.5	99.5	100.9
旅行社收费	Travel Agency Charge	98.8	98.8	94.7	96.4	97.6	97.7	98.1	100.3	102.3	99.0	100.6	98.8	101.0
宾馆住宿	Guesthouse Stay	100.8	102.4	100.6	100.4	100.2	100.8	100.4	100.8	100.5	101.0	100.8	100.7	101.0
其他住宿	Other Stay	100.6	100.2	99.9	99.9	100.1	100.7	100.3	102.5	103.6	100.9	99.7	99.9	100.1
八、居住	**Residence**	**104.4**	**104.8**	**105.0**	**104.8**	**104.9**	**104.4**	**104.0**	**103.9**	**104.1**	**104.3**	**104.0**	**104.3**	**104.4**
1.建房及装修材料	Building and Building Decoration Materials	103.8	102.4	102.4	102.8	103.2	103.5	103.7	103.8	104.6	104.0	104.3	105.4	105.6
木材	Wood	107.0	105.1	104.9	105.3	105.4	104.7	104.5	104.7	107.3	108.4	108.8	112.0	112.1
木地板	Wood Floor	99.5	103.7	103.7	103.3	99.2	99.2	97.1	97.2	97.3	96.8	98.0	99.0	99.6
砖	Brick	107.1	103.3	104.1	105.3	107.4	108.3	110.0	109.5	110.6	106.6	106.7	106.8	106.7
水泥	Cement	102.2	101.6	100.8	100.6	102.9	103.5	103.1	102.9	102.8	102.3	102.1	102.3	102.0
涂料	Coating Material	100.8	101.4	101.9	101.4	100.4	99.8	100.5	100.6	100.8	100.4	100.3	100.7	101.0
胶合板	Plywood	104.3	102.0	102.1	102.4	103.0	102.3	103.0	104.5	105.2	106.0	105.1	107.8	107.9
玻璃	Glass	101.7	98.3	98.0	99.5	99.4	100.6	100.8	102.1	102.7	103.1	103.9	105.4	107.1
粘胶	Rayon	102.0	101.4	101.5	101.4	101.3	101.4	101.8	101.8	101.9	102.3	102.5	102.8	104.0
油漆	Paint	103.4	102.9	103.4	103.3	102.2	102.6	103.0	103.3	103.4	104.3	104.3	104.0	104.4
其他	Others	101.5	99.3	98.7	99.9	101.3	103.6	102.5	101.2	100.4	100.3	103.1	104.0	103.4
2.租房	Renting	104.6	101.2	101.2	103.5	103.5	103.7	103.5	105.6	106.0	106.5	106.6	107.0	107.0
公房房租	Public House Rent	101.3	100.0	100.0	100.0	100.0	100.0	100.0	100.1	103.0	103.0	103.0	103.1	103.1
私房房租	Private House Rent	103.8	101.1	101.1	101.8	101.8	102.3	101.8	104.8	104.8	106.0	106.1	106.8	106.8
其他费用	Other Fare	109.2	102.6	102.6	109.8	109.8	109.8	109.8	112.1	110.7	110.7	110.7	110.7	110.7
3.自有住房	Private Housing	103.3	102.9	103.0	101.4	100.3	101.6	102.8	102.7	103.2	104.7	103.9	106.2	106.2
房屋贷款利率	Houses Loans Interest Rate	106.4	107.3	107.3	103.9	102.0	104.7	105.5	105.5	108.1	109.2	107.7	107.7	107.7
物业管理费用	Property Management Fee	101.9	101.7	101.7	102.6	102.6	102.6	102.6	101.9	101.9	102.6	100.7	100.7	100.9
维护修理费用	Upkeep and Repair Fee	102.3	101.1	101.1	99.2	98.0	99.2	101.4	101.5	101.2	103.6	103.6	108.8	108.8
其他	Others	101.8	101.6	102.2	102.2	101.6	101.6	101.6	101.7	101.6	101.9	101.6	102.0	102.0
4.水、电、燃料	Water,Electricity and Fuels	105.2	108.2	108.4	107.8	107.9	106.0	104.7	104.1	103.6	104.2	103.4	102.5	102.6
水	Water	110.2	114.9	114.1	114.5	115.5	116.0	111.1	107.6	106.8	106.8	106.2	106.2	104.9
电	Electricity	102.5	103.7	104.0	104.0	104.0	100.8	100.6	102.0	102.3	102.1	102.1	102.1	102.1
液化石油气	Liquefiled Petroleum Gas	112.9	123.9	126.8	122.3	121.2	116.3	113.9	110.4	106.7	111.1	107.1	100.7	102.1
管道燃气	Pipelined Gas	100.1	100.1	100.1	100.1	100.1	100.2	100.2	100.2	100.1	100.1	100.1	100.1	100.1
其他燃料	Other Fuels	102.6	104.1	103.8	102.9	102.7	102.3	102.0	102.0	102.1	102.4	102.0	101.7	102.7

7-14 城市居民消费价格指数
Urban Consumer Price Indices

（以2005年同期价格为100）

商品类别及品名	Commodity Category and Commodity Name	全年 Annural	1月 January	2月 February	3月 March	4月 April	5月 May	6月 June	7月 July	8月 August	9月 September	10月 October	11月 November	12月 December
居民消费价格总指数	**General Consumer Price Index**	**101.0**	**102.3**	**101.0**	**101.2**	**101.5**	**101.1**	**101.1**	**99.9**	**100.1**	**100.7**	**100.6**	**101.0**	**101.7**
非食品价格指数	**No-food**	**100.5**	**100.4**	**100.5**	**100.6**	**100.6**	**100.5**	**100.6**	**100.5**	**100.4**	**100.5**	**100.5**	**100.3**	**100.2**
服务项目价格指数	**Services**	**101.7**	**101.6**	**101.3**	**101.3**	**101.2**	**101.6**	**101.6**	**101.9**	**101.9**	**101.9**	**101.9**	**101.8**	**101.9**
工业品价格指数	**Industrial Products**	**100.0**	**99.9**	**100.2**	**100.4**	**100.4**	**100.1**	**100.2**	**100.0**	**99.9**	**99.9**	**99.9**	**99.8**	**99.6**
扣除食品和能源价格指数	**Deducting Foods and Energy**	**100.1**	**100.0**	**100.0**	**100.3**	**100.2**	**100.1**	**100.2**	**100.2**	**100.2**	**100.2**	**100.2**	**100.1**	**100.0**
扣除鲜菜鲜果总指数	**Deducting Fresh, Vegetables and Fruits**	**100.5**	**100.2**	**99.7**	**99.9**	**100.0**	**99.8**	**100.0**	**100.2**	**100.6**	**100.7**	**101.1**	**101.5**	**102.1**
消费品价格指数	**Consumer Goods**	**100.9**	**102.4**	**101.0**	**101.2**	**101.5**	**101.0**	**100.9**	**99.5**	**99.7**	**100.5**	**100.2**	**100.8**	**101.7**
一、食品	**Food**	**102.3**	**106.6**	**102.2**	**102.6**	**103.4**	**102.6**	**102.3**	**98.6**	**99.4**	**101.3**	**100.8**	**102.5**	**105.3**
1.粮食	Grain	102.3	98.6	98.7	98.9	99.4	100.5	101.6	102.6	103.9	103.5	103.8	107.4	109.6
大米	Rice	106.4	99.8	100.3	100.8	101.3	103.5	106.1	107.7	110.9	110.2	110.8	112.2	113.9
面粉	Flour	98.6	95.1	95.3	95.4	96.0	96.7	97.3	98.0	97.9	97.6	98.3	106.2	109.6
粮食制品	Grain Products	101.6	98.9	99.0	99.1	99.5	100.1	100.6	101.6	102.8	102.5	102.8	105.1	106.9
其他	Others	107.3	106.4	105.1	105.4	106.2	106.9	107.8	108.8	109.5	108.3	106.3	107.8	109.5
2.淀粉	Starches	98.6	99.2	97.1	96.9	98.0	96.8	94.8	93.5	94.1	101.6	103.0	103.4	106.0
淀粉	Starches	98.6	99.2	97.1	96.9	98.0	96.8	94.8	93.5	94.1	101.6	103.0	103.4	106.0
3.干豆类及豆制品	Beans and Beans Products	101.5	100.7	99.1	100.6	100.4	101.2	101.9	102.7	102.8	101.9	101.9	102.3	103.0
干豆	Beans	101.9	99.1	98.5	97.4	97.6	99.6	103.0	106.1	107.3	103.9	103.0	103.6	103.8
豆制品	Beans Products	101.5	101.1	99.3	101.3	101.0	101.6	101.6	101.9	101.8	101.5	101.7	102.0	102.8
4.油脂	Oil and Fat	100.2	98.9	98.1	98.0	98.3	98.9	99.5	99.3	100.2	100.2	100.5	102.5	108.1
食用植物油	Edible Vegetable Oil	100.5	99.0	98.2	98.3	98.9	99.5	100.2	100.0	100.8	100.7	100.9	102.6	107.1
植物油制品	Plant Oil Products	99.4	99.9	99.0	98.6	97.0	97.1	97.5	96.8	97.3	97.4	97.6	99.5	115.4
其他	Others	91.1	92.6	89.8	85.2	81.7	80.4	81.1	81.3	85.1	91.6	96.9	109.2	122.9
5.肉禽及其制品	Meal,Poultry and Their Products	96.6	96.2	91.6	90.8	89.9	88.6	89.9	93.3	97.4	98.3	102.0	109.3	115.5
（1）食用畜肉及副产品	Edible Livestock Meat and Their By-products	95.7	95.7	90.9	89.3	88.1	86.8	87.8	90.8	95.8	97.4	101.6	110.5	117.4
猪肉	Pork	92.1	91.3	86.1	83.3	80.8	79.2	80.6	85.2	92.8	95.2	100.7	114.1	123.1
牛肉	Beef	104.6	109.9	104.5	105.5	106.1	103.5	104.6	103.7	103.0	102.3	102.6	103.9	106.1
羊肉	Mutton	105.2	107.5	103.0	104.4	106.7	106.5	107.4	106.3	104.5	103.8	103.8	103.5	105.4
畜肉副产品	Livestock Meat By-products	97.6	98.9	95.3	94.1	93.5	92.6	92.0	94.1	96.1	97.3	101.3	104.3	113.5
其他	Others	99.9	97.4	95.2	96.5	96.7	96.6	96.8	96.1	100.0	101.5	105.5	108.0	109.5
（2）禽	Poultry	97.5	94.8	88.6	90.3	89.4	87.6	90.9	98.2	101.5	100.1	104.6	111.0	118.6
鸡	Chicken	97.8	92.3	85.8	88.4	87.9	85.9	90.0	99.6	103.2	101.9	107.9	115.2	125.0
鸭	Duck	94.5	103.4	99.9	98.5	95.8	94.2	93.9	88.7	91.1	89.2	89.6	94.7	96.6
其他	Others	97.4	103.7	98.1	96.0	94.1	93.4	94.2	96.4	98.2	96.9	96.5	99.6	101.8
（3）加工肉禽	Meal and Poultry Processing Products	100.3	100.2	99.8	99.8	99.8	99.5	99.6	99.5	99.9	100.0	100.4	101.7	103.2
畜肉制品	Livestock Meat Products	100.2	100.5	100.1	100.1	100.1	99.5	99.7	99.5	99.7	99.5	100.1	101.4	102.9
禽制品	Poultry Products	100.4	99.7	99.4	99.4	99.2	99.7	99.2	99.5	100.2	101.0	101.1	102.3	103.7

7-14 续表 1 continued

商品类别及品名	Commodity Category and Commodity Name	（以2005年同期价格为100） 全年 Annural	1月 January	2月 February	3月 March	4月 April	5月 May	6月 June	7月 July	8月 August	9月 September	10月 October	11月 November	12月 December
6.蛋	Eggs	95.7	93.8	86.8	90.2	90.7	86.7	85.9	88.3	96.7	99.5	105.7	109.0	117.5
鲜蛋	Fresh Eggs	95.1	92.9	85.5	89.1	89.6	85.4	84.7	87.2	96.2	99.4	105.9	109.6	118.6
蛋制品	Egg Products	103.3	106.3	104.6	104.3	104.9	103.4	102.6	102.5	102.4	100.7	102.3	101.9	104.3
7.水产品	Aquatic Product	104.3	104.2	100.7	100.7	102.4	103.7	105.3	107.6	108.2	103.9	106.5	106.2	103.3
（1）鱼	Fish	101.3	101.2	97.8	96.8	98.6	99.6	101.8	102.8	104.3	103.7	103.5	102.7	102.6
淡水鱼	Freshwater Fish	95.9	94.0	90.2	89.8	90.1	91.6	95.3	99.1	101.1	101.2	99.7	99.7	99.6
海水鱼	Seawater Fish	104.8	106.1	103.0	101.4	104.1	105.0	106.1	105.2	106.3	105.4	106.0	104.6	104.6
（2）其他水产品	Other Aquatic Product	107.7	107.4	103.7	104.6	106.3	108.1	109.1	113.1	112.7	104.0	110.0	110.2	104.1
虾蟹类	Shrimp and Crab	108.0	108.1	104.0	104.2	106.2	108.1	109.8	114.5	114.0	102.8	111.0	110.8	104.4
其他	Others	106.6	105.1	102.7	106.0	106.5	108.3	106.7	109.0	108.8	108.0	107.2	108.1	103.0
8.菜	Vegetable	107.8	150.4	117.3	116.0	118.2	111.8	107.6	85.7	89.9	106.7	89.7	94.0	104.2
鲜菜	Fresh Vegetable	107.5	154.4	118.2	116.8	119.0	111.8	107.1	83.3	88.0	106.4	87.9	92.4	103.1
干菜及菜制品	Dried Vegetable and Vegetable Products	106.9	101.4	101.3	101.9	103.8	104.5	104.9	105.7	106.7	109.2	111.9	112.5	118.9
薯类	Potato	121.4	121.3	118.4	119.2	120.6	130.9	134.1	133.2	125.0	114.1	108.7	113.7	113.6
9.调味品	Flavoring	101.7	102.5	102.0	102.1	101.9	101.7	101.6	101.2	101.0	100.7	100.9	102.0	102.3
盐	Salt	101.2	106.1	104.7	105.6	103.0	103.1	102.4	100.4	99.4	98.0	98.1	97.1	97.2
酱油	Soy Sauce	101.5	102.2	102.1	102.1	102.2	101.4	101.2	100.9	101.3	101.1	101.2	101.2	100.5
醋	Vinegar	102.2	103.1	103.0	101.5	102.3	102.2	102.5	102.6	102.4	102.6	101.9	101.6	101.5
味精	Aginomoto	100.3	99.4	99.3	99.6	100.5	100.9	100.7	100.7	100.5	100.5	100.5	100.1	100.8
其他	Others	102.6	100.4	99.7	100.4	100.7	100.5	101.0	101.4	101.3	101.4	102.5	109.5	112.0
10.糖	Carbohydrate	108.6	105.0	107.0	108.5	109.2	109.6	109.9	109.3	109.4	109.1	108.8	108.4	108.9
食糖	Sugar	122.2	112.7	117.7	122.4	124.8	125.6	126.0	124.5	125.0	124.3	121.7	120.3	121.6
糖果	Sweet	102.9	101.1	102.0	102.4	102.4	102.6	103.0	102.9	102.9	102.8	104.0	104.5	104.6
巧克力制品	Chocolate Products	100.5	102.1	102.3	101.2	100.9	100.5	100.4	99.9	99.6	99.7	100.0	99.7	99.6
糖类小食品	Little Carbohydrate Food	101.4	100.9	101.2	101.2	100.8	101.7	101.7	101.7	101.8	101.6	101.3	101.4	101.4
11.茶及饮料	Tea and Beverages	101.6	100.0	100.0	101.2	101.7	101.9	102.2	101.8	102.0	102.2	102.1	102.1	102.3
（1）茶叶	Tea	100.9	99.3	99.8	100.8	101.6	101.3	101.1	100.8	100.6	101.2	101.6	101.2	102.0
茶叶	Tea	100.9	99.3	99.8	100.8	101.6	101.3	101.1	100.8	100.6	101.2	101.6	101.2	102.0
（2）饮料	Beverages	102.1	100.5	100.2	101.5	101.8	102.3	102.9	102.4	102.8	102.9	102.4	102.7	102.4
固体饮料	Solid Beverages	100.9	101.4	100.9	100.4	100.6	101.2	101.8	101.2	101.5	101.5	100.4	100.8	99.3
液体饮料	Liquid Beverages	100.9	99.8	99.5	100.8	101.1	101.6	101.4	100.9	101.1	100.9	100.9	101.0	101.5
冷冻饮品	Frozen Beverages	106.1	100.8	100.7	104.6	104.9	105.1	107.5	107.3	108.4	109.1	108.2	108.7	108.4
12.干鲜瓜果	Dried and Fresh Melons and Fruits	114.0	122.9	122.9	128.1	133.2	135.4	136.9	109.2	97.6	97.5	99.0	94.2	92.4
鲜瓜果	Fresh Fruits	115.4	126.9	127.1	133.3	139.8	142.7	146.1	109.4	94.2	93.7	95.4	89.0	86.9
干（坚）果	Dried Fruits	109.9	110.0	108.7	110.7	110.6	109.9	110.2	108.6	107.4	108.4	109.9	111.5	112.3
13.糕点饼干面包	Cake,Biscuit and Bread	100.5	101.0	101.1	101.2	100.8	100.9	100.8	100.8	100.7	100.0	99.8	99.6	100.1
糕点	Cake	100.0	100.8	101.0	101.5	100.9	100.6	100.6	100.3	99.9	98.8	98.2	98.5	99.3
饼干	Biscuit	101.2	101.9	101.8	101.3	100.9	101.5	101.3	101.2	101.4	101.1	100.9	100.4	100.6
面包	Bread	100.9	100.1	100.4	100.3	100.4	100.7	100.3	101.1	101.7	101.2	102.1	101.2	101.1
14.液体乳及乳制品	Liquid Milk and Their Products	101.6	101.2	101.3	101.9	100.9	100.7	100.8	100.9	101.5	102.7	102.6	102.7	102.4
巴氏杀菌奶或消毒奶	Pasteurization Milk or Disinfection Milk	101.2	100.7	100.7	101.6	100.1	100.0	100.3	100.4	101.2	102.4	102.3	102.6	102.4
酸奶	Leben	101.6	101.4	101.4	101.6	101.6	101.6	101.3	101.0	101.0	102.4	102.5	102.0	101.9

7-14 续表 2 continued

商品类别及品名	Commodity Category and Commodity Name	全年 Annural	1月 January	2月 February	3月 March	4月 April	5月 May	6月 June	7月 July	8月 August	9月 September	10月 October	11月 November	12月 December
		（以2005年同期价格为100）												
奶粉	Milk Powder	102.5	101.6	101.8	101.8	102.3	101.9	101.9	102.2	103.6	103.4	103.1	103.4	102.7
其他	Others	103.4	103.3	105.1	105.1	102.9	102.9	102.5	101.8	101.6	104.5	104.2	104.3	102.4
15.在外用膳食品	Outward Dinner	100.7	100.1	99.8	100.0	100.1	100.0	100.6	100.5	100.8	100.9	100.9	101.4	103.6
主食	Staple Food	100.5	99.8	99.3	99.4	99.4	99.5	100.2	100.1	100.2	100.3	100.3	101.6	105.8
炒菜	Hot Dish	100.7	100.2	100.1	100.2	100.3	100.2	100.7	100.5	100.8	101.1	100.9	101.1	102.3
地方小吃	Local Snack	101.3	99.9	99.9	100.5	100.6	100.6	100.6	100.9	102.1	101.7	101.7	102.4	104.2
16.其他食品	Other Foods	101.0	101.3	101.2	101.4	101.2	101.2	101.1	101.1	101.0	101.2	100.6	100.3	100.6
其他食品	Other Foods	101.0	101.3	101.2	101.4	101.2	101.2	101.1	101.1	101.0	101.2	100.6	100.3	100.6
二、烟酒及用品	**Tobacco,Liquor and Their Appliances**	**101.3**	**100.7**	**100.4**	**100.4**	**101.0**	**101.0**	**101.4**	**101.5**	**101.8**	**101.9**	**101.8**	**101.7**	**101.9**
1.烟草	Tobacco	99.9	99.8	99.2	99.1	99.8	99.8	99.9	100.0	100.3	100.3	100.3	100.2	100.4
国产卷烟	Domestic Cigarette	100.2	100.0	99.5	99.3	100.1	100.2	100.3	100.4	100.7	100.7	100.6	100.5	100.7
进口卷烟	Import Cigarette	98.1	98.7	97.2	97.6	98.0	97.7	97.8	97.8	98.2	98.4	98.3	98.5	98.7
其他	Others	99.6	99.7	99.7	99.7	99.7	99.7	99.7	99.7	99.2	99.2	99.2	99.4	99.7
2.酒	Liquor	102.4	101.3	101.3	101.2	101.9	101.9	102.6	102.7	103.0	103.2	103.1	103.0	103.3
白酒	White Spirit	102.9	101.9	101.8	101.9	102.4	102.5	103.3	103.3	103.5	103.6	103.4	103.3	103.7
葡萄酒	Grape	105.6	103.4	103.2	103.9	104.1	104.2	106.9	107.2	106.9	107.0	107.2	106.9	106.3
啤酒	Beer	101.0	100.0	100.0	99.8	100.6	100.6	100.7	101.1	101.5	101.8	101.9	101.7	102.1
其他	Others	100.2	98.7	99.4	99.2	100.0	100.1	100.3	100.4	100.2	100.4	100.1	102.2	102.1
3.吸烟、饮酒用品	Appliances for Smoking and Drinking	100.2	100.6	100.7	100.7	100.3	100.4	100.4	100.3	100.2	99.9	99.9	99.9	99.6
吸烟用品	Appliances for Smoking	100.4	100.6	100.5	100.5	100.6	100.6	100.6	100.4	100.3	100.1	100.4	100.4	100.1
饮酒用品	Appliances for Drinking	100.1	100.6	100.8	100.8	100.0	100.3	100.3	100.2	100.2	99.8	99.6	99.5	99.2
三、衣着	**Clothing**	**98.0**	**97.9**	**98.4**	**99.5**	**99.5**	**98.4**	**98.5**	**98.0**	**97.5**	**97.5**	**97.8**	**97.3**	**96.5**
1.服装	Garments	97.5	97.1	97.4	98.4	98.6	97.8	97.5	97.0	96.6	96.9	97.7	97.5	97.2
（1）男式服装	Men's Garments	96.9	96.7	97.8	98.5	98.1	97.1	96.8	96.3	95.8	96.2	96.6	96.4	96.3
大衣	Topcoat	92.7	93.8	93.9	95.2	93.5	92.7	91.9	91.7	91.1	91.4	91.1	92.4	93.8
毛线衣	Woollen Sweater	93.9	99.4	95.6	96.6	97.7	95.6	94.9	92.4	89.7	90.8	93.0	89.6	91.7
夹克衫	Jacket	96.1	94.0	96.1	95.2	94.9	95.6	95.0	94.7	95.1	95.2	99.5	100.5	98.0
衬衫	Shirt	93.9	91.0	95.3	97.7	96.2	93.1	94.9	93.6	93.3	92.7	92.3	92.6	94.6
T恤衫	T-shirt	97.0	99.2	100.1	99.1	99.5	101.4	99.8	96.4	93.6	93.9	93.6	95.0	91.6
裤子	Trousers	95.6	98.0	98.3	98.7	95.9	93.8	93.7	93.8	96.2	94.6	95.7	93.9	95.6
西服	Western-style Clothes	100.1	97.8	99.7	99.0	100.5	101.3	100.6	101.6	99.0	100.7	101.8	100.5	98.9
运动衫裤	Gym Suit	95.8	91.7	95.4	98.9	98.6	94.5	94.8	95.0	95.6	96.1	95.9	97.1	96.4
内衣	Underwaist	103.4	104.7	104.8	105.6	105.4	105.1	104.3	103.8	104.2	104.5	99.7	99.5	99.9
羽绒衣	Eider Down Outerwear	98.2	97.1	98.8	98.5	97.2	97.3	97.4	97.2	97.0	98.2	100.1	101.3	98.3
其他	Others	96.3	96.8	95.5	94.4	96.7	97.0	94.6	94.9	94.7	94.7	96.0	100.3	100.2
（2）女式服装	Women's Garments	97.7	97.2	96.8	98.1	98.6	97.8	97.5	97.2	96.8	97.4	98.7	98.4	97.8
大衣	Topcoat	91.5	93.5	90.4	94.6	93.4	91.7	92.1	91.6	90.4	90.1	90.0	88.7	91.3
毛线衣	Woollen Sweater	94.2	94.9	92.3	96.9	97.1	96.2	94.3	91.7	90.1	91.8	94.2	95.0	95.9
羽绒衣	Eider Down Outerwear	98.7	94.9	96.7	96.3	96.6	96.8	96.5	99.1	99.5	99.1	101.9	104.0	102.6
套装	Coordinates	100.3	100.4	99.5	99.8	102.6	102.3	100.1	100.9	97.8	101.2	102.3	98.5	98.9
衬衫	Shirt	98.7	96.4	98.3	98.2	99.4	98.9	99.8	100.1	98.7	99.0	100.0	99.3	96.1

7-14 续表 3 continued

商品类别及品名	Commodity Category and Commodity Name	（以2005年同期价格为100）												
		全年 Annural	1月 January	2月 February	3月 March	4月 April	5月 May	6月 June	7月 July	8 月 August	9 月 September	10 月 October	11月 November	12月 December
T恤衫	T-shirt	100.6	97.2	97.8	97.4	98.0	99.6	100.5	98.8	98.9	101.8	106.6	107.1	104.1
裙子	Skirt	101.6	101.2	100.9	100.8	102.0	102.6	101.7	100.7	102.7	102.1	103.0	102.0	99.5
裤子	Trousers	97.9	99.6	98.8	100.3	99.2	97.1	96.7	97.3	98.3	97.3	97.7	97.2	95.7
运动衫裤	Gym Suit	96.7	98.7	100.1	98.6	99.8	95.1	94.8	95.0	95.4	96.1	95.8	94.4	96.6
内衣	Underwaist	100.7	98.4	98.5	99.6	100.5	100.4	100.5	100.0	100.7	101.1	101.6	104.0	103.8
其他	Others	100.9	100.7	99.9	100.2	101.6	100.5	100.1	100.7	100.9	101.6	101.6	102.2	101.4
（3）儿童服装	Children's Garments	98.8	98.2	98.9	99.5	100.4	100.3	99.9	98.5	98.5	97.6	97.6	97.7	98.2
套装	Coordinates	98.0	98.5	98.9	99.1	100.2	99.2	98.4	98.4	98.0	96.7	95.5	95.7	97.6
裤子	Trousers	98.0	94.5	96.2	97.3	98.5	98.8	99.3	97.6	98.6	97.8	99.8	99.4	98.2
裙子	Skirt	100.9	101.1	100.9	101.7	102.2	103.8	103.2	99.8	99.7	99.2	99.3	99.5	99.9
其他	Others	97.8	102.1	103.8	104.1	102.6	98.3	97.7	96.4	94.5	94.0	93.5	94.9	92.7
2.衣着材料	Clothing Materials	99.8	100.0	99.9	99.8	99.9	99.5	99.5	99.4	99.7	99.7	99.9	100.1	100.8
棉布	Cotton Cloth	100.7	101.3	100.6	100.6	100.4	99.4	100.0	100.3	100.5	100.9	101.1	101.6	101.6
棉混纺布	Cotton Textiles Cloth	99.6	99.0	99.2	99.1	100.1	99.9	99.9	99.3	99.5	99.3	99.5	100.0	100.3
化纤布	Chemical Fiber Cloth	99.8	100.2	100.7	100.3	100.3	99.9	99.2	98.9	99.6	99.5	99.7	99.7	99.8
毛线	Knitting Wool	99.3	99.5	98.9	98.8	98.8	98.7	99.1	99.2	99.1	99.4	99.1	99.3	101.6
3.鞋袜帽	Shoes,Socks and Hats	99.2	99.6	100.5	102.5	101.9	100.0	101.2	100.3	99.7	98.5	97.5	95.9	93.6
（1）鞋	Shoes	99.1	99.5	100.6	102.9	102.0	99.9	101.3	100.3	99.5	98.2	97.2	95.5	92.8
男鞋	Men's Shoes	98.3	98.5	99.7	100.5	100.9	97.4	99.1	97.8	98.7	98.0	97.8	96.4	94.3
女鞋	Women's Shoes	99.4	100.5	101.6	105.2	103.2	101.3	102.8	101.7	99.4	97.4	96.0	93.8	90.5
童鞋	Children's Shoes	100.5	98.3	98.6	99.9	100.4	101.3	101.3	101.5	102.6	101.8	100.8	100.4	98.9
（2）袜子	Socks	99.9	99.9	100.7	100.4	101.4	100.6	100.7	100.6	100.5	100.8	98.7	97.6	97.5
男袜	Men's Socks	100.7	99.6	99.6	99.7	103.6	103.2	103.0	102.9	101.6	101.7	99.6	97.4	96.5
女袜	Women's Socks	99.6	100.1	101.3	100.7	100.3	99.3	99.4	99.4	99.9	100.4	98.2	97.8	98.1
（3）帽子	Hats	100.0	100.0	99.7	99.7	99.6	99.6	99.4	100.1	100.0	100.4	100.4	100.6	100.6
男帽	Men's Hats	100.0	99.4	99.1	99.1	99.1	99.5	99.9	100.5	100.4	100.5	100.3	101.4	101.2
女帽	Women's Hats	100.0	100.4	100.0	100.1	100.0	99.6	99.1	99.8	99.8	100.4	100.4	100.1	100.3
4.衣着加工服务费	Clothing Manufacturing Services	100.2	100.3	100.1	100.1	100.0	100.0	100.1	100.1	100.3	100.3	100.3	100.3	100.2
缝纫	Sewing	100.2	99.9	100.0	100.1	100.1	100.1	100.2	100.3	100.4	100.4	100.4	100.3	100.3
清洗	Washing	100.1	100.7	100.2	100.2	99.9	99.9	99.9	100.0	100.2	100.2	100.2	100.2	100.2
四、家庭设备用品及维修服务	**Household Facilities, Articles and Services**	**101.7**	**101.0**	**101.1**	**101.0**	**100.5**	**100.5**	**101.7**	**101.9**	**102.3**	**102.6**	**102.5**	**102.4**	**102.6**
1.耐用消费品	Durable Consumer Goods	102.0	101.0	101.3	101.0	100.3	100.4	102.1	102.5	102.8	103.1	103.1	103.1	103.1
（1）家具	Furniture	100.4	100.7	100.9	100.5	100.1	99.9	100.1	100.1	100.3	100.8	100.7	100.7	100.5
柜	Cabinet	100.8	102.2	102.3	101.5	100.2	100.3	100.2	100.0	100.6	100.8	100.6	100.4	100.2
床	Bed	100.6	100.2	101.0	100.3	100.3	100.1	100.2	100.5	100.6	101.0	101.3	100.9	100.4
桌	Desk	99.8	100.4	100.8	100.0	100.0	99.5	99.4	99.2	99.5	99.4	99.4	100.2	100.1
椅	Chair	100.6	100.6	100.5	100.4	100.3	100.2	100.3	99.9	99.8	100.7	101.3	101.4	101.3
沙发	Sofa	100.2	99.7	99.8	99.9	99.7	99.5	100.1	100.2	100.5	101.3	100.6	100.6	100.4
其他	Others	100.7	101.2	100.4	100.3	100.3	99.1	100.5	101.0	101.1	102.4	100.6	100.5	101.2
（2）家庭设备	Household Appliances	102.8	101.2	101.4	101.3	100.4	100.7	103.2	103.7	104.0	104.3	104.3	104.4	104.5
洗衣机	Washing Machine	100.7	99.7	100.4	100.2	99.3	99.7	101.0	101.8	101.3	101.2	101.2	101.3	101.3

7-14 续表 4 continued

商品类别及品名	Commodity Category and Commodity Name	（以2005年同期价格为100）												
		全年 Annural	1月 January	2月 February	3月 March	4月 April	5月 May	6月 June	7月 July	8月 August	9月 September	10月 October	11月 November	12月 December
电风扇	Electric Fan	99.8	100.6	101.5	101.6	96.2	96.8	100.6	100.0	100.3	100.1	100.0	100.0	99.9
电冰箱（柜）	Refrigerator	106.5	106.4	106.3	105.9	105.8	106.2	107.2	106.9	105.8	106.7	107.4	106.9	106.8
吸排油烟机	Kitchen Ventilato	105.4	105.0	105.0	104.1	102.0	101.8	104.3	106.5	107.5	107.4	107.1	107.2	106.2
空调器	Air-conditioning	103.8	100.9	100.9	100.6	99.7	100.0	104.5	105.6	106.5	106.5	106.2	106.5	107.0
热水器	Water Heater	100.3	98.6	99.2	99.8	99.9	99.9	100.2	100.2	100.2	101.3	101.2	101.6	102.1
微波炉	Microwave Oven	97.6	94.8	95.1	95.8	95.7	95.4	96.8	97.5	99.8	100.0	100.3	100.4	99.6
电炊具	Electric Cooking Appliance	100.7	99.6	99.6	99.6	100.8	101.0	101.0	100.9	101.0	100.7	101.3	101.3	101.4
2.室内装饰品	Interior Decorations	99.9	100.6	100.6	100.5	99.7	99.4	99.3	99.4	99.7	100.6	99.4	99.5	100.0
纺织装饰品	Textile Process Decorations	99.2	100.1	100.0	100.0	98.7	99.0	98.7	98.5	98.9	99.5	98.8	98.8	99.7
装饰灯具	Architectural Lamps and Lanterns	100.7	101.8	101.9	101.9	101.1	99.8	100.0	100.7	100.4	102.1	99.7	99.4	99.6
其他	Others	100.4	100.0	100.0	99.9	99.8	100.0	99.9	99.7	100.7	100.7	100.7	101.7	101.7
3.床上用品	Bedclothes	99.4	98.2	99.3	99.8	99.6	99.0	100.1	99.8	99.4	99.5	99.5	98.4	99.8
毛毯	Woollen Blanket	100.7	100.3	101.1	103.1	101.7	101.1	101.5	100.8	100.4	100.5	100.0	98.6	99.7
被子	Quilt	97.8	97.2	97.8	97.8	97.6	96.5	99.2	98.9	98.1	98.2	97.6	97.0	98.2
床上套件	Bed Articcles	98.9	97.6	98.5	99.0	99.1	98.7	99.4	99.1	99.0	99.1	99.7	98.0	100.1
其他	Others	102.0	98.8	102.1	102.3	102.4	102.5	102.0	102.1	102.1	102.2	102.3	102.5	102.9
4.日用杂品	Sundry Articles	100.8	100.5	100.5	100.7	100.3	100.5	100.8	100.6	101.0	101.2	101.2	101.0	101.2
茶具	Tea Set	99.9	98.9	99.0	99.9	99.9	99.9	100.3	99.6	99.6	100.1	99.6	100.4	101.2
餐具	Tableware	99.7	98.2	99.0	98.2	98.3	99.5	99.6	99.1	100.3	100.9	101.2	100.9	102.0
厨具	Kitchen Utensils	101.4	100.0	100.3	100.3	101.2	101.8	102.0	102.1	101.7	101.7	101.7	101.9	101.7
家用手工工具	Domestic Handwork Tools	101.4	103.0	102.9	102.9	102.9	101.9	101.6	101.4	101.2	100.9	100.1	99.3	99.2
洗涤用品	Washing Articles	101.8	102.5	101.7	102.4	101.1	101.0	101.6	101.3	102.3	102.4	102.3	101.5	101.5
其他	Others	100.2	99.9	99.9	100.0	99.8	99.8	100.3	100.3	100.2	100.5	100.6	100.7	100.8
5.家庭服务及加工维修服务	Household Srvice and Manufacturing Upkeep	106.1	105.5	105.2	104.6	104.8	104.6	104.5	104.8	107.4	108.0	108.1	107.6	107.9
家庭服务	Household Srvice	111.6	110.9	110.2	108.8	109.3	108.8	108.4	108.8	113.7	115.1	115.2	115.6	114.1
加工维修服务	Manufacturing Upkeep	101.7	101.2	101.2	101.2	101.2	101.2	101.4	101.6	102.3	102.3	102.3	101.1	102.8
五、医疗保健和个人用品	**Health Care and Personal Articles**	**100.4**	**99.9**	**99.9**	**99.7**	**100.1**	**100.4**	**100.6**	**100.8**	**100.8**	**100.5**	**100.7**	**100.5**	**100.5**
1.医疗保健	Health Care	99.6	99.4	99.4	99.6	99.5	99.5	99.6	100.0	100.0	99.6	99.7	99.6	99.6
（1）医疗器	Medical Facilities	96.7	89.1	89.3	98.7	98.8	99.1	99.1	98.9	98.9	98.9	97.5	97.1	97.1
医疗器具及用品	Medical Facilities and Goods	96.7	89.1	89.3	98.7	98.8	99.1	99.1	98.9	98.9	98.9	97.5	97.1	97.1
（2）中药材及中成药	Herbs and Ready-made Traditional Chinese Medicine	100.0	99.1	98.9	99.4	99.4	98.9	99.5	100.1	100.6	100.0	101.4	101.3	101.4
中药材	Herbs	100.4	96.8	96.3	96.7	97.8	97.8	99.7	100.9	101.7	101.3	105.1	105.4	105.6
中成药	Ready-made Traditional Chinese Medicine	99.7	101.1	101.1	101.6	100.7	99.9	99.3	99.4	99.8	98.9	98.4	98.1	98.0
（3）西药	Western Medicine	99.1	99.6	99.5	99.2	99.0	99.4	99.4	99.9	99.5	98.9	98.5	98.4	98.4
抗微生物药	Anti-microorganism Medicine	100.9	99.9	99.9	99.9	99.9	100.0	100.6	102.9	102.5	101.6	101.0	101.3	101.0
消化系统用药	Alimentary System Medicine	99.3	98.3	98.2	98.5	98.2	98.9	99.6	100.8	99.7	99.5	100.1	99.3	100.1
呼吸系统用药	Respiratory System Medicine	99.8	99.4	99.4	99.1	99.1	99.1	100.2	100.2	100.1	100.6	100.5	100.5	99.5

7-14 续表 5 continued

商品类别及品名	Commodity Category and Commodity Name	全年 Annural	1月 January	2月 February	3月 March	4月 April	5月 May	6月 June	7月 July	8月 August	9月 September	10月 October	11月 November	12月 December
		（以2005年同期价格为100）												
解热镇痛及非留体抗炎药	Allays a Fever the Analgesia and the Non-steroid Body Anti-inflammatory Agent	98.6	99.5	99.1	98.9	99.1	100.4	98.6	98.1	97.9	96.8	97.9	98.3	98.4
抗肿瘤药	Antineoplastic Drug	97.8	100.6	100.5	100.3	99.7	99.7	97.7	97.5	97.3	97.3	94.7	94.7	93.8
激素及调节内分泌功能药	Hormone and Adjustment Internal Secretion Function Medicine	96.9	98.8	99.0	98.2	98.2	98.2	97.6	97.8	97.5	95.5	92.8	94.1	95.2
循环系统用药	Circulating System Medicine	99.4	99.4	99.6	99.2	98.1	97.9	99.1	99.5	99.7	100.1	101.2	99.3	100.0
神经系统用药	Nerve System Medicine	98.3	101.7	101.7	100.9	100.8	100.8	100.4	100.4	97.5	96.6	93.1	93.1	93.4
专科用药	Junior Medicine	98.7	100.4	100.6	100.6	100.4	100.0	100.7	100.3	99.8	97.7	94.9	94.7	94.8
其他	Others	98.0	99.7	100.3	97.6	97.3	98.5	98.2	98.1	98.1	97.9	97.1	96.7	96.7
（4）保健品及器具	Healthcare Equipment	100.0	100.7	100.6	100.5	100.4	100.3	100.3	99.9	99.7	99.4	99.5	99.5	99.3
保健器具	Health Protection Equipment	99.1	99.7	99.4	99.5	99.7	99.5	99.3	99.2	99.3	99.0	98.3	98.3	97.9
滋补保健用品	Tonic and Health Products	100.4	101.2	101.1	100.8	100.6	100.6	100.7	100.1	99.8	99.5	99.9	100.0	99.9
（5）医疗保健服务	Health Care Services	100.4	100.2	100.3	100.3	100.3	100.3	100.2	100.5	100.5	100.5	100.4	100.4	100.4
挂号费	Registration	100.7	100.3	100.4	100.6	100.6	100.6	100.6	100.8	100.8	100.8	100.8	100.8	100.8
注射费	Injection Expenses	100.1	100.2	100.2	100.3	100.3	99.9	99.9	99.9	99.9	100.0	100.0	100.0	100.0
检查费	Examination Expenses	100.3	100.1	100.2	100.2	99.9	99.9	100.1	100.1	100.1	100.6	100.6	100.8	100.8
手术费	Operation Expenses	100.3	100.5	100.5	100.5	100.5	100.5	100.2	100.2	100.2	100.2	100.2	100.2	100.1
住院费	Hospitalization Expenses	100.8	100.4	100.4	100.4	100.6	100.6	100.6	101.8	101.8	101.2	100.6	100.6	100.5
理疗费	Physiotherapy Expenses	99.9	99.7	99.7	99.7	100.0	100.0	100.0	100.0	100.0	100.0	100.0	100.0	100.0
化验费	Analysis Expenses	100.2	100.0	100.2	100.3	100.3	100.3	100.3	100.3	100.3	100.3	100.1	100.1	100.0
其他	Others	100.3	100.3	100.3	100.3	100.3	100.3	100.3	100.3	100.3	100.3	100.3	100.1	100.0
2.个人用品及服务	Personal Articles and Services	101.7	100.7	100.9	99.8	101.3	102.0	102.3	102.1	102.4	102.2	102.4	102.2	102.2
（1）化妆美容用品	Cosmetics	98.9	99.8	99.8	96.0	99.0	99.0	99.2	98.8	99.0	98.8	98.9	98.8	99.5
化妆美容器具	Cosmetics Appliances	100.7	99.9	99.9	100.0	100.4	100.6	101.1	101.0	101.4	101.2	101.3	100.9	100.7
美容化妆品	Facial Beautifiers	99.0	100.1	100.0	99.7	98.1	98.4	98.5	98.6	98.3	98.6	98.3	99.1	100.4
护肤品	Protects Skin Products	99.3	99.7	99.8	99.7	99.8	99.8	99.6	99.6	100.0	98.0	99.1	97.9	98.4
护发美容品	Protects Sends the Beauty Products	97.7	99.3	99.3	87.5	99.3	99.2	99.3	98.0	98.6	98.7	98.8	97.9	98.2
（2）清洁化妆用品	Cleaning Toiletware	100.5	99.7	99.6	100.0	99.7	100.6	101.3	101.0	101.1	101.0	100.9	100.5	100.4
洗发用品	Hairdressing Articles	100.3	100.2	99.8	100.4	100.1	100.2	101.1	100.8	100.9	100.4	100.5	99.7	99.2
洗浴用品	Bathing Articles	100.0	99.1	99.1	99.2	98.7	100.1	100.7	100.3	100.7	100.6	100.6	100.4	100.6
其他	Others	102.7	100.2	100.8	101.2	101.3	103.5	103.8	103.5	103.5	103.6	103.5	103.7	103.6
（3）个人饰	Personal Decoraions	108.1	101.7	103.5	104.3	107.0	109.6	109.8	110.1	110.6	110.1	110.2	110.0	109.8
首饰	Ornaments	115.7	105.6	107.9	108.5	112.6	117.9	118.5	119.9	119.7	119.5	119.3	119.5	119.2
皮件	Leather Appliance	99.7	96.7	98.3	99.8	101.0	100.6	100.5	98.1	101.1	100.7	101.0	100.2	98.9

7-14 续表 6 continued

商品类别及品名	Commodity Category and Commodity Name	(以2005年同期价格为100)												
		全年 Annural	1月 January	2月 February	3月 March	4月 April	5月 May	6月 June	7月 July	8月 August	9月 September	10月 October	11月 November	12月 December
手表	Watch	97.4	97.0	97.4	97.4	98.4	98.8	96.5	95.7	95.2	95.9	98.3	99.0	99.1
领带	Necktie	98.8	98.0	99.6	101.0	101.4	98.9	100.2	100.5	101.3	98.2	96.8	95.4	94.9
其他	Others	98.6	96.6	96.4	97.3	98.5	98.9	98.9	98.5	99.3	99.6	99.4	99.2	100.6
(4)个人服务	Personal Services	102.3	102.4	101.9	101.9	102.3	102.1	102.1	101.9	102.2	102.3	103.3	102.9	102.1
美容	Cosmetology	103.0	103.1	103.1	103.1	103.1	103.1	103.1	103.1	103.1	103.1	103.1	103.1	101.6
理(烫)发	Haircut (permnaent wave)	101.0	101.1	100.3	100.3	101.1	100.7	100.7	100.4	100.4	100.6	102.4	102.4	102.3
洗浴	Bathe	107.6	106.8	106.5	106.5	106.8	106.8	106.8	106.7	110.1	109.9	109.9	109.9	104.9
其他	Others	102.7	103.8	103.8	103.8	102.7	102.7	102.7	102.6	103.6	103.6	103.6	100.0	100.0
六、交通和通信	**Transportation and Communication**	**97.7**	**96.9**	**97.0**	**97.2**	**97.1**	**97.7**	**98.3**	**98.1**	**98.0**	**98.0**	**98.0**	**98.2**	**98.0**
1.交通	Transportation	103.2	103.2	103.4	103.1	102.9	103.6	104.7	104.0	103.2	102.9	102.9	102.7	102.1
(1)交通工具	Transportation Facility	98.5	98.3	99.0	99.6	99.3	99.0	98.9	98.9	98.6	97.9	97.9	97.9	96.6
摩托车	Motorcycle	100.2	98.2	99.2	99.7	99.6	100.0	100.2	100.5	101.0	101.1	101.7	101.5	99.7
自行车	Bicycle	100.2	99.8	100.4	100.6	100.7	100.4	100.5	100.8	99.7	100.2	100.0	99.8	99.4
轿车	Car	97.0	97.4	98.0	98.5	98.3	97.9	97.7	97.4	97.2	95.5	95.7	95.8	94.1
其他	Others	99.3	101.6	101.2	104.8	101.8	100.1	99.1	99.2	98.2	98.2	95.6	95.7	96.1
(2)车用燃料及零配件	Fuels and Parts	112.0	110.2	110.2	108.7	110.6	112.5	118.8	115.2	111.3	111.2	111.5	111.6	111.6
汽油	Gasoline	116.8	114.9	114.9	111.8	114.0	117.6	127.1	121.6	116.0	115.5	116.1	116.1	116.1
柴油	Diesel Oil	115.9	113.4	113.2	113.6	117.6	117.3	124.1	119.4	114.3	114.4	114.4	114.4	114.6
零配件	Parts	99.9	99.7	99.8	99.6	99.6	99.7	99.7	99.7	99.7	100.2	100.2	100.3	100.3
其他	Others	100.4	99.8	100.4	100.0	100.2	100.3	100.6	100.6	100.5	100.8	100.8	100.5	100.5
(3)车辆使用及维修费	Using and Upkeep Fare	100.1	99.7	99.6	99.6	99.3	99.3	99.4	99.4	100.8	100.8	101.0	101.0	101.0
驾驶证	Driving License	97.2	95.6	95.6	95.5	95.5	95.5	95.6	95.7	98.9	98.9	100.1	100.1	100.0
保险费	Insurance Expenses	99.9	99.6	99.6	99.5	99.7	99.7	99.7	99.6	100.2	100.3	100.3	100.3	100.3
停车费	Parking Expenses	102.7	102.2	102.2	102.2	100.0	100.0	100.0	100.0	105.2	105.2	105.2	105.2	105.2
车辆修理服务费	Vehicle Upkeep Service fare	100.1	100.0	99.9	99.9	99.9	99.9	100.2	100.2	100.2	100.1	100.1	100.1	100.2
其他	Others	100.0	100.0	100.0	100.0	100.2	100.2	100.2	100.2	99.8	99.8	99.8	99.8	99.8
(4)市区公共交通费	Incity Traffic Fare	104.9	104.2	104.2	104.2	103.7	105.3	105.3	106.5	106.0	105.5	105.5	104.3	104.2
公共汽车票	Bus Ticket	101.8	102.1	102.1	102.1	101.9	101.9	101.9	101.7	101.7	101.7	101.7	101.5	101.6
出租汽车	Taxi	107.9	106.2	106.2	106.2	105.5	108.8	108.7	111.4	110.0	109.3	109.2	106.9	106.5
其他	Others	106.9	106.9	106.9	106.9	106.0	106.0	106.0	106.0	112.1	106.4	106.4	106.4	106.0
(5)城市间交通费	Intercity Traffic Fare	105.7	109.2	108.6	106.5	105.2	106.2	107.7	104.9	103.9	104.5	103.9	104.2	104.0
飞机票	Airplane Ticket	102.8	102.1	100.1	99.4	98.4	102.2	102.5	101.8	100.8	105.7	104.1	109.3	108.3
火车票	Train Ticket	100.9	101.7	101.0	100.7	100.7	100.7	100.8	100.8	100.8	100.9	100.9	101.0	101.0
长途汽车	Intertown Bus	107.9	114.5	114.1	110.8	108.7	108.6	111.2	106.4	104.7	105.1	104.3	104.3	104.0
其他	Others	114.8	105.2	104.4	102.4	101.3	121.0	120.7	120.1	120.3	120.3	120.3	120.3	120.3
2.通信	Communication	92.5	91.3	91.3	91.8	91.7	92.2	92.3	92.6	93.0	93.2	93.3	93.8	94.0
(1)通信工具	Communication Facility	79.8	78.9	78.8	79.6	78.6	79.1	79.3	79.7	80.5	80.8	80.7	81.1	80.9
固定电话机	Telephone	95.7	94.9	94.6	93.4	95.9	96.6	96.6	96.2	95.7	96.6	96.6	96.6	95.0
移动电话机	Mobile Phone	75.4	74.9	74.7	75.8	74.1	74.6	74.7	75.2	76.1	76.3	76.0	76.5	76.4
其他	others	96.0	96.7	96.8	96.7	96.2	95.3	95.2	95.2	95.2	95.0	95.8	95.8	97.7
(2)通信服务	Communication Service	100.0	99.4	99.4	99.4	99.8	100.0	100.0	100.0	100.0	100.0	100.0	100.4	100.8
移动通信费	Mobile Communication Fee	99.5	98.2	98.2	98.2	99.2	100.0	100.0	100.0	100.0	100.0	100.0	100.0	100.0
市内电话费	Incity Telephone Fee	100.0	100.0	100.0	100.0	100.0	100.0	100.0	100.0	100.0	100.0	100.0	100.0	100.0

7-14 续表 7 continued

商品类别及品名	Commodity Category and Commodity Name	（以2005年同期价格为100）												
		全年 Annural	1月 January	2月 February	3月 March	4月 April	5月 May	6月 June	7月 July	8月 August	9月 September	10月 October	11月 November	12月 December
长途电话费	Long Distance Call Fee	100.0	100.0	100.0	100.0	100.0	100.0	100.0	100.0	100.0	100.0	100.0	100.0	100.0
月租费	Month Hiring Fee	100.0	100.0	100.0	100.0	100.0	100.0	100.0	100.0	100.0	100.0	100.0	100.0	100.0
上网费	Net Play Fee	101.2	101.5	101.6	101.2	101.2	101.2	101.2	101.2	101.2	101.5	101.5	101.7	100.0
信件邮寄	Letter Post	104.1	100.0	100.0	100.0	100.0	100.0	100.0	100.0	100.0	100.0	100.0	115.9	133.1
包裹邮寄	Package Post	100.4	100.0	100.0	100.0	100.0	100.0	100.0	100.0	100.0	100.0	100.0	102.1	102.1
其他	Others	100.0	100.0	100.0	100.0	100.0	100.0	100.0	100.0	100.0	100.0	100.0	100.0	100.0
七、娱乐教育文化用品及服务	**Recreation,Education and Culture Articles**	**99.7**	**100.1**	**99.8**	**99.9**	**99.7**	**99.9**	**99.8**	**100.0**	**99.9**	**99.3**	**99.4**	**99.3**	**99.4**
1.文娱用耐用消费品及服务	Durable Consumer Goods for Cultural and Recreational Use and Service	95.3	95.9	96.1	96.0	95.6	95.7	95.4	95.4	95.3	94.4	94.3	94.9	94.6
电视机	Television	93.3	93.5	94.4	94.1	93.3	94.1	93.6	93.6	93.6	92.6	92.3	92.6	91.4
激光视盘机	Laser Video Disc Machine	98.0	98.2	98.4	98.2	97.9	98.3	98.8	98.9	98.9	97.9	97.1	97.0	96.5
摄像机	Pickup Camera	95.1	96.2	96.6	96.0	96.1	96.1	95.1	94.8	94.5	94.1	93.8	94.4	93.7
照相机	Camera	94.8	96.0	95.6	94.2	93.4	93.8	93.7	94.7	95.7	95.3	94.7	95.4	95.3
家用音响	Acoustic Equipment	99.2	98.6	98.7	99.0	99.6	99.2	99.3	99.7	99.7	99.2	99.3	99.3	98.9
便携式音响	Portable Acoustics	96.9	99.0	97.4	96.9	96.6	96.7	96.6	96.7	96.6	96.3	97.0	96.9	96.5
电脑	Computer	95.0	96.1	95.9	96.0	95.8	95.5	95.0	94.9	94.5	93.4	93.5	94.6	95.0
修理服务	Repair Service	100.6	100.5	100.5	100.5	100.5	100.5	100.5	100.7	100.7	100.7	100.7	100.7	100.7
其他	Others	98.3	96.8	99.3	99.3	99.0	98.9	99.0	98.5	98.2	96.1	98.2	98.0	98.0
2.教育	Education	101.2	101.7	101.7	101.7	101.5	101.5	101.5	101.4	100.9	100.9	100.8	100.8	100.5
（1）教材及参考书	Teaching Materials and Reference Books	101.7	102.1	102.1	102.2	102.2	102.2	102.1	102.1	102.3	100.9	100.7	100.7	100.7
工具书	Tool Book	101.6	102.5	102.5	102.5	102.5	102.5	102.5	102.5	101.2	100.2	100.2	100.2	100.3
教材	Teaching Material	100.7	100.8	100.8	101.0	101.0	101.0	101.0	101.0	101.9	100.3	99.9	99.9	99.9
参考书	Reference Book	103.8	104.4	104.4	104.6	104.6	104.6	104.2	104.2	104.7	102.5	102.5	102.5	102.6
教育软件	Educational Software	99.9	100.0	99.9	99.9	99.9	99.9	99.9	99.9	99.9	99.9	99.9	99.9	99.9
（2）学杂托幼费	Tuition and Child Care	101.1	101.6	101.6	101.6	101.3	101.3	101.3	101.2	100.6	100.9	100.8	100.8	100.5
义务教育杂费	Incidental Expenses of Compulcory Education	101.8	103.1	103.1	103.1	103.1	103.1	103.1	103.1	100.8	100.0	100.0	100.0	100.0
非义务教育学杂费	Tuition of Non-compulsory Education	100.4	100.0	100.0	100.0	100.0	100.0	100.0	100.0	100.0	101.3	101.3	101.3	101.3
技能培训学费	Skill Train Tuition	101.3	102.9	102.9	102.9	101.1	101.1	101.2	101.3	101.3	101.0	101.0	101.0	98.0
托幼费	Child Care	102.4	104.2	104.2	103.7	103.4	103.4	103.4	102.1	102.0	100.9	100.3	100.3	101.2
其他	Others	100.5	100.0	100.0	100.0	100.0	100.0	100.1	100.1	100.1	101.5	101.5	101.5	101.5
3.文化娱乐类	Recreation and Culture	101.2	101.6	101.4	101.4	101.2	101.8	101.3	101.3	100.7	100.6	101.0	100.7	100.9
（1）文化娱乐用品	Culture Articles	99.6	100.2	100.1	99.9	99.8	99.7	99.5	99.5	99.3	99.3	99.2	99.1	99.1
乐器	Musical Instrument	100.4	99.5	100.0	99.9	100.3	100.4	100.3	100.5	100.6	100.9	100.9	101.0	100.6
音响光盘和磁带	Audio,Disk and Tape	97.9	98.7	98.5	97.4	97.8	97.6	97.6	97.6	97.6	97.7	97.7	97.9	97.9
照相胶卷和存储卡	Roll Film and Memorizing Card	99.3	100.7	100.5	100.7	100.4	100.3	100.0	99.8	99.2	98.7	97.7	97.2	96.9
录像磁带和视盘	Video Tape and Disk	100.1	98.8	98.9	98.9	99.6	100.4	100.7	100.7	100.5	100.7	100.8	100.5	100.3
儿童玩具	Children's Toy	100.0	102.7	102.1	101.5	100.7	100.3	99.9	99.5	99.0	98.8	98.7	98.5	98.6

7-14 续表 8 continued

商品类别及品名	Commodity Category and Commodity Name	（以2005年同期价格为100）												
		全年 Annural	1月 January	2月 February	3月 March	4月 April	5月 May	6月 June	7月 July	8月 August	9月 September	10月 October	11月 November	12月 December
纸张本册	Paper and Volume	100.6	102.4	101.9	101.8	100.9	100.9	99.8	99.8	100.0	100.0	100.0	99.8	100.5
文具	Stationery	98.7	98.1	98.4	98.3	98.5	98.7	98.6	98.9	98.6	98.7	98.6	99.2	99.5
体育用品	Sports Goods	99.1	98.8	98.9	98.9	98.8	98.7	98.8	99.3	99.5	99.6	99.7	99.1	99.2
其他	Others	99.7	99.8	99.9	99.9	99.8	99.9	99.4	99.6	99.6	99.4	99.7	99.4	99.4
（2）书报杂志	Books,Newspapers, Magazines	102.8	102.9	102.9	103.1	103.1	103.0	103.0	103.0	102.8	102.7	102.7	102.6	102.3
书籍	Books	101.7	101.8	101.8	102.2	102.2	102.1	102.1	102.1	101.5	101.3	101.3	101.1	100.6
报纸	Newspapers	106.5	106.5	106.5	106.5	106.5	106.5	106.5	106.5	106.5	106.5	106.5	106.5	106.4
杂志	Magazines	100.1	100.1	100.1	100.1	100.1	100.1	100.1	100.1	100.1	100.1	100.1	100.1	100.2
（3）文娱费	Expenditure of Culture and Recreation	102.0	102.6	101.9	102.1	101.6	103.6	102.4	102.5	101.0	100.8	102.3	101.5	102.3
电影票	Film Ticket	102.1	109.0	108.0	105.9	103.7	100.3	102.2	101.0	100.3	98.6	103.3	98.8	94.8
景点门票	Scene Spot ticket	105.9	100.5	98.6	100.6	100.0	114.3	107.7	109.8	104.5	106.1	106.3	106.9	115.0
有线电视	Cable Television	100.1	100.0	100.0	100.0	100.0	100.0	100.0	100.0	100.0	100.0	100.2	100.2	100.2
健身活动	Exercise	101.6	103.3	102.9	103.6	103.7	102.5	102.0	100.4	98.9	98.8	101.4	101.1	101.2
其他	Others	102.0	104.0	104.0	104.0	103.8	102.3	101.7	101.8	101.8	100.1	100.1	100.1	99.8
4.旅游	Tourism	99.2	99.5	95.6	96.8	97.8	98.3	98.3	101.1	103.0	99.5	100.6	98.9	101.1
旅行社收费	Travel Agency Charge	98.4	99.0	94.2	95.7	97.0	97.1	97.4	100.0	102.3	98.5	100.4	98.3	100.8
宾馆住宿	Guesthouse Stay	102.3	101.7	102.1	101.5	100.6	103.0	101.6	102.8	101.8	103.8	102.8	102.5	103.7
其他住宿	Other Stay	102.1	100.5	99.7	99.7	100.4	102.3	101.1	108.3	111.6	102.9	98.9	99.5	100.4
八、居住	**Residence**	**104.8**	**106.0**	**106.3**	**105.8**	**106.0**	**105.2**	**104.2**	**103.8**	**103.7**	**104.6**	**104.1**	**103.9**	**103.9**
1.建房及装修材料	Building and Building Decoration Materials	103.7	102.7	103.2	103.1	103.1	103.3	103.0	102.9	103.4	104.3	104.2	105.4	105.9
木材	Wood	104.9	103.2	103.1	103.7	103.9	103.6	103.6	103.9	105.2	106.1	104.8	108.9	109.0
木地板	Wood Floor	106.9	109.6	109.7	108.5	110.6	110.1	103.3	103.8	104.1	105.4	104.8	106.0	107.6
砖	Brick	105.0	105.0	105.5	104.6	103.1	104.5	104.6	104.5	106.1	106.1	105.5	105.0	105.7
水泥	Cement	100.2	98.4	98.2	98.5	99.3	99.9	101.2	100.9	100.2	100.5	101.2	102.0	102.3
涂料	Coating Material	101.8	100.7	102.2	101.7	101.4	101.2	102.7	103.0	102.8	101.7	100.9	101.2	101.5
胶合板	Plywood	103.5	100.8	101.4	102.0	102.0	101.9	102.4	102.9	103.1	104.8	105.1	107.4	107.9
玻璃	Glass	102.8	102.1	101.8	102.1	101.6	102.1	102.2	103.0	103.0	103.8	103.8	103.8	103.9
粘胶	Rayon	102.4	100.7	100.7	101.2	101.1	101.2	102.2	102.6	103.0	103.6	103.5	104.4	105.0
油漆	Paint	103.2	99.1	102.0	102.5	100.9	101.1	101.2	102.1	102.1	106.9	106.9	106.6	106.6
其他	Others	103.9	105.3	105.4	104.8	105.3	105.9	104.0	101.0	101.2	101.4	103.9	103.9	104.4
2.租房	Renting	105.1	100.7	100.7	103.5	103.5	103.9	103.6	106.3	107.2	107.9	108.0	108.0	108.0
公房房租	Public House Rent	101.4	100.0	100.0	100.0	100.0	100.0	100.0	100.1	103.4	103.4	103.4	103.5	103.5
私房房租	Private House Rent	105.0	101.7	101.7	102.7	102.7	103.4	102.7	106.1	106.1	107.9	108.1	108.1	108.1
其他费用	Other Fare	108.5	100.0	100.0	107.8	107.8	107.8	107.8	111.9	111.9	111.9	111.9	111.9	111.9
3.自有住房	Private Housing	103.6	103.6	103.7	102.7	102.0	103.1	103.4	103.2	104.2	105.1	103.9	103.8	103.9
房屋贷款利率	Houses Loans Interest Rate	106.7	107.5	107.5	104.1	102.1	105.0	105.9	105.9	108.5	109.7	108.1	108.1	108.1
物业管理费用	Property Management Fee	101.9	101.7	101.7	102.7	102.7	102.7	102.7	101.9	101.9	102.7	100.7	100.7	100.9
维护修理费用	Upkeep and Repair Fee	100.5	100.1	100.4	100.4	100.4	100.4	100.4	100.4	100.4	100.9	100.9	100.7	100.7
其他	Others	104.5	104.7	104.6	104.5	104.4	104.3	104.4	104.6	104.3	105.0	104.4	104.4	104.5
4.水、电、燃料	Water,Electricity and Fuels	105.4	108.6	109.0	108.0	108.4	106.6	104.9	104.0	103.3	104.3	103.7	102.7	102.7
水	Water	110.2	114.9	114.6	114.4	115.7	116.3	110.8	107.4	106.5	106.5	106.5	106.5	105.1
电	Electricity	102.2	103.8	103.8	103.8	103.8	100.3	100.2	101.6	101.7	101.7	101.7	101.7	101.7
液化石油气	Liquefiled Petroleum Gas	112.8	123.5	127.4	121.3	121.1	116.7	114.0	109.4	105.1	111.6	107.0	100.9	102.7
管道燃气	Pipelined Gas	100.0	100.0	100.0	100.0	100.0	100.0	100.0	100.0	100.0	100.0	100.0	100.0	100.0
其他燃料	Other Fuels	103.5	104.8	104.5	102.6	103.3	103.4	103.0	103.0	102.7	104.6	104.2	102.7	103.2

7-15 农村居民消费价格指数
Rural Consumer Price Indices

（以2005年同期价格为100）

商品类别及品名	Commodity Category and Commodity Name	全年 Annural	1月 January	2月 February	3月 March	4月 April	5月 May	6月 June	7月 July	8月 August	9月 September	10月 October	11月 November	12月 December
居民消费价格总指数	**General Consumer Price Index**	**101.0**	**101.1**	**100.2**	**100.1**	**100.7**	**100.8**	**100.8**	**100.2**	**100.5**	**101.0**	**101.1**	**102.2**	**103.5**
非食品价格指数	**No-food**	**100.6**	**100.1**	**100.1**	**100.2**	**100.4**	**100.6**	**100.7**	**100.8**	**100.8**	**100.7**	**100.8**	**101.2**	**101.4**
服务项目价格指数	**Services**	**101.9**	**101.7**	**101.7**	**101.7**	**102.0**	**102.1**	**102.2**	**102.0**	**102.0**	**101.5**	**101.5**	**102.1**	**102.1**
工业品价格指数	**Industrial Products**	**100.2**	**99.5**	**99.5**	**99.6**	**99.8**	**100.0**	**100.1**	**100.3**	**100.4**	**100.4**	**100.6**	**100.9**	**101.2**
扣除食品和能源价格指数	**Deducting Foods and Energy**	**100.4**	**99.7**	**99.7**	**99.8**	**100.1**	**100.3**	**100.4**	**100.5**	**100.6**	**100.5**	**100.6**	**101.2**	**101.3**
扣除鲜菜鲜果总指数	**Deducting Fresh, Vegetables and Fruits**	**100.3**	**99.3**	**98.8**	**98.9**	**99.1**	**99.2**	**99.4**	**99.8**	**100.5**	**100.8**	**101.5**	**102.8**	**103.8**
消费品价格指数	**Consumer Goods**	**100.8**	**101.0**	**99.9**	**99.7**	**100.4**	**100.5**	**100.4**	**99.8**	**100.2**	**100.9**	**101.0**	**102.2**	**103.8**
一、食品	**Food**	**101.9**	**103.8**	**100.6**	**99.8**	**101.4**	**101.3**	**101.0**	**98.7**	**99.8**	**101.8**	**101.8**	**104.5**	**108.7**
1.粮食	Grain	103.3	97.7	97.5	97.8	99.5	101.9	102.5	104.4	104.8	106.6	107.3	109.2	111.5
大米	Rice	110.9	102.1	101.4	102.0	104.4	109.6	110.0	114.7	117.5	118.1	119.1	116.4	116.8
面粉	Flour	98.8	92.3	91.5	92.4	95.3	96.8	97.4	99.0	98.4	101.6	102.5	109.0	112.0
粮食制品	Grain Products	101.0	99.8	99.8	99.7	99.0	100.1	100.9	100.6	100.7	101.2	101.5	103.5	105.4
其他	Others	105.7	100.7	105.5	103.4	103.7	105.6	105.8	106.7	104.7	108.1	107.7	105.4	111.1
2.淀粉	Starches	108.7	108.4	101.9	101.4	105.4	101.1	107.5	111.4	113.2	113.1	114.9	117.1	109.8
淀粉	Starches	108.7	108.4	101.9	101.4	105.4	101.1	107.5	111.4	113.2	113.1	114.9	117.1	109.8
3.干豆类及豆制品	Beans and Beans Products	98.3	98.7	98.8	96.2	96.5	97.3	98.0	97.8	98.4	98.1	98.2	100.1	101.7
干豆	Beans	102.1	98.5	98.3	97.7	100.2	102.1	103.7	103.0	103.7	102.7	102.8	104.2	107.9
豆制品	Beans Products	95.8	98.9	99.2	95.2	94.1	94.2	94.3	94.3	94.9	95.1	95.2	97.3	97.6
4.油脂	Oil and Fat	99.0	92.1	91.5	91.7	92.5	96.4	97.0	98.0	100.4	101.6	104.1	110.1	115.7
食用植物油	Edible Vegetable Oil	99.8	92.9	92.6	93.1	93.8	97.2	97.8	98.5	101.0	102.4	104.3	110.1	116.1
植物油制品	Plant Oil Products	104.2	97.7	97.8	97.9	97.9	104.8	104.9	105.8	106.2	106.5	106.6	110.1	114.9
其他	Others	81.9	76.3	71.8	68.4	71.3	74.0	75.7	79.5	84.1	82.9	97.5	109.4	113.0
5.肉禽及其制品	Meal,Poultry and Their Products	95.1	93.1	90.7	87.9	86.9	85.7	86.4	88.7	94.4	97.5	103.1	112.3	119.5
（1）食用畜肉及副产品	Edible Livestock Meat and Their By-products	93.8	92.5	89.0	85.1	82.7	82.5	83.2	85.5	91.9	96.2	104.2	116.1	124.6
猪肉	Pork	89.9	87.8	83.0	78.5	75.6	75.6	76.6	80.0	88.7	94.1	104.7	119.9	129.9
牛肉	Beef	106.0	110.8	108.3	106.9	108.8	108.3	105.5	103.8	102.7	102.3	105.4	103.9	106.6
羊肉	Mutton	111.5	115.1	114.6	113.3	111.2	112.5	110.3	111.1	107.4	106.7	108.2	110.7	117.2
畜肉副产品	Livestock Meat By-products	93.7	91.8	92.8	88.8	87.4	84.7	88.1	87.0	90.3	95.4	97.3	108.5	117.1
其他	Others	96.5	100.1	99.1	94.5	84.0	83.7	82.1	86.8	96.6	96.8	102.9	117.4	118.8
（2）禽	Poultry	95.8	88.8	88.1	86.2	87.2	82.1	85.4	91.1	100.3	103.8	107.8	115.1	124.5
鸡	Chicken	97.1	88.5	87.0	85.3	87.2	81.6	86.3	93.2	103.5	108.4	111.7	116.6	128.6
鸭	Duck	92.1	91.6	88.9	88.7	91.1	89.8	86.0	86.1	91.5	91.1	90.5	106.7	106.1
其他	Others	92.4	87.6	92.8	89.0	84.4	79.4	80.6	84.2	91.7	91.3	103.2	114.4	119.8
（3）加工肉禽	Meal and Poultry Processing Products	98.0	97.4	97.6	96.9	98.4	97.0	95.7	95.8	97.2	97.1	97.2	101.5	103.9
畜肉制品	Livestock Meat Products	99.0	97.9	98.2	98.7	98.6	97.8	96.7	97.4	99.0	98.6	99.2	102.2	103.4
禽制品	Poultry Products	96.8	96.7	96.9	94.9	98.2	96.2	94.6	93.8	95.0	95.2	94.8	100.7	104.6

7-15 续表 1 continued

商品类别及品名	Commodity Category and Commodity Name	（以2005年同期价格为100）												
		全年 Annural	1月 January	2月 February	3月 March	4月 April	5月 May	6月 June	7月 July	8月 August	9月 September	10月 October	11月 November	12月 December
6.蛋	Eggs	95.7	93.1	84.9	88.7	89.9	89.4	86.9	90.0	95.4	98.1	105.6	110.9	117.5
鲜蛋	Fresh Eggs	94.8	91.9	83.0	87.0	88.4	87.6	84.7	88.2	94.3	97.7	106.1	112.0	119.4
蛋制品	Egg Products	102.0	101.5	98.9	100.3	100.5	101.4	103.0	103.0	103.0	101.7	102.2	103.7	105.6
7.水产品	Aquatic Product	102.0	99.0	98.0	99.1	98.7	100.0	101.8	103.0	103.4	104.4	105.6	105.8	105.6
（1）鱼	Fish	100.4	98.5	96.3	97.0	96.5	97.8	99.7	101.1	101.5	103.2	104.8	105.0	104.5
淡水鱼	Freshwater Fish	98.6	98.6	94.5	94.0	94.7	97.0	99.2	100.9	101.7	101.2	100.4	101.8	100.1
海水鱼	Seawater Fish	103.5	98.2	99.3	102.1	99.6	99.1	100.7	101.5	101.1	106.4	112.6	110.4	112.0
（2）其他水产品	Other Aquatic Product	106.5	100.5	103.1	105.4	105.1	106.6	107.7	108.6	109.1	107.9	107.9	108.0	108.6
虾蟹类	Shrimp and Crab	106.8	100.5	103.5	106.2	105.8	107.6	108.0	108.8	109.2	107.9	107.8	107.7	108.5
其他	Others	104.9	100.4	99.9	100.2	101.0	100.5	106.1	106.8	108.2	108.0	108.3	109.9	109.5
8.菜	Vegetable	107.5	148.6	123.1	118.5	123.6	114.6	103.1	85.9	94.8	108.3	86.8	84.9	96.7
鲜菜	Fresh Vegetable	108.4	157.9	125.9	120.0	126.1	116.4	103.2	83.0	94.0	109.5	84.7	82.2	95.8
干菜及菜制品	Dried Vegetable and Vegetable Products	100.1	100.4	100.6	100.7	100.5	100.3	98.3	97.8	98.9	99.4	99.5	100.9	103.5
薯类	Potato	111.0	113.2	118.5	132.9	135.1	117.5	114.7	106.4	99.7	110.5	93.9	95.0	96.9
9.调味品	Flavoring	103.0	105.5	103.3	102.7	102.6	103.0	103.3	104.3	103.5	103.1	101.6	101.4	102.1
盐	Salt	109.6	119.5	110.6	108.6	107.8	109.9	112.1	114.2	111.5	110.1	105.1	104.3	103.4
酱油	Soy Sauce	100.3	99.7	99.7	99.8	100.0	99.8	99.8	100.5	100.5	100.5	100.5	100.5	102.5
醋	Vinegar	101.0	100.2	100.2	100.4	100.8	100.5	100.2	101.2	101.2	101.2	101.2	101.1	103.4
味精	Aginomoto	101.0	101.1	101.1	100.8	100.6	100.3	100.0	101.0	101.0	101.0	101.6	101.6	102.0
其他	Others	98.5	100.5	100.5	100.2	100.5	100.4	98.5	97.6	97.2	96.8	96.4	96.4	96.4
10.糖	Carbohydrate	110.1	101.4	107.4	108.8	109.7	110.7	111.2	112.2	111.6	112.1	112.0	112.2	111.7
食糖	Sugar	122.3	102.9	117.3	120.1	121.6	123.9	125.2	126.8	125.0	126.2	125.9	126.3	126.0
糖果	Sweet	102.0	100.7	100.8	101.4	101.9	102.4	102.2	102.9	102.9	102.9	103.1	102.9	100.1
巧克力制品	Chocolate Products	100.7	99.7	100.2	100.6	100.5	99.7	99.4	100.1	100.1	100.1	100.1	100.4	108.0
糖类小食品	Little Carbohydrate Food	101.2	99.9	100.7	100.7	100.7	100.7	100.7	100.9	101.5	101.5	101.5	102.0	103.9
11.茶及饮料	Tea and Beverages	100.6	100.3	100.3	100.5	100.5	100.3	100.3	100.5	100.8	100.7	100.8	100.8	101.6
（1）茶叶	Tea	100.0	99.9	99.9	100.4	100.2	99.9	99.8	99.8	100.0	100.0	100.0	100.0	99.9
茶叶	Tea	100.0	99.9	99.9	100.4	100.2	99.9	99.8	99.8	100.0	100.0	100.0	100.0	99.9
（2）饮料	Beverages	101.1	100.6	100.7	100.5	100.6	100.6	100.5	101.0	101.4	101.3	101.4	101.4	102.8
固体饮料	Solid Beverages	100.9	100.6	100.9	101.0	101.3	100.9	100.3	100.1	100.8	100.9	101.0	101.0	102.1
液体饮料	Liquid Beverages	101.5	100.4	100.4	100.6	100.7	100.8	100.9	102.0	102.4	102.2	102.3	102.4	103.1
冷冻饮品	Frozen Beverages	100.4	100.9	100.9	100.0	100.0	100.0	100.0	100.0	100.0	100.0	100.0	100.0	102.7
12.干鲜瓜果	Dried and Fresh Melons and Fruits	126.0	128.5	131.8	131.9	146.6	158.0	175.1	142.3	111.2	102.8	101.3	97.7	98.3
鲜瓜果	Fresh Fruits	132.5	134.6	139.8	139.6	159.4	175.7	202.4	156.4	113.3	102.1	99.6	95.0	95.6
干（坚）果	Dried Fruits	105.3	108.7	105.6	106.2	104.9	102.6	102.1	102.2	104.4	105.2	106.7	106.9	107.9
13.糕点饼干面包	Cake,Biscuit and Bread	100.9	101.0	101.0	100.9	101.1	99.8	99.9	100.5	101.2	101.2	101.1	101.1	102.7
糕点	Cake	100.8	102.1	102.0	102.0	102.1	99.6	99.7	100.1	100.1	100.1	100.1	100.1	101.9
饼干	Biscuit	101.4	100.1	100.1	100.0	100.3	100.0	100.1	101.0	102.9	102.9	102.7	102.7	104.7
面包	Bread	100.4	100.0	100.0	100.0	100.0	100.0	100.0	100.7	100.7	100.7	100.7	100.7	100.9
14.液体乳及乳制品	Liquid Milk and Their Products	100.6	100.4	100.6	100.7	100.6	100.2	100.0	100.0	100.0	100.0	100.1	100.1	104.1
巴氏杀菌奶或消毒奶	Pasteurization Milk or Disinfection Milk	100.6	99.6	99.6	100.5	99.9	99.9	99.8	99.9	99.9	100.0	99.9	99.9	108.7
酸奶	Leben	98.8	97.7	97.7	97.2	99.1	99.1	99.4	99.7	99.4	99.4	99.4	99.1	98.6

7-15 续表 2 continued

商品类别及品名	Commodity Category and Commodity Name	(以2005年同期价格为100)												
		全年 Annural	1月 January	2月 February	3月 March	4月 April	5月 May	6月 June	7月 July	8月 August	9月 September	10月 October	11月 November	12月 December
奶粉	Milk Powder	100.8	101.6	101.5	101.2	101.1	100.9	100.2	99.9	99.9	99.9	100.1	100.6	102.7
其他	Others	101.8	102.6	104.3	104.0	103.7	100.5	100.6	101.4	101.4	101.4	101.7	100.1	99.9
15.在外用膳食品	Outward Dinner	101.2	101.2	100.9	100.9	100.9	101.0	100.9	100.9	100.9	100.9	100.9	102.0	103.5
主食	Staple Food	100.6	99.9	99.9	100.0	99.9	99.9	99.5	99.6	99.6	99.6	99.9	102.9	106.5
炒菜	Hot Dish	101.6	102.2	101.6	101.6	101.7	101.7	101.5	101.5	101.4	101.3	101.3	101.6	101.4
地方小吃	Local Snack	101.7	101.3	100.7	100.8	101.0	101.7	102.0	102.4	102.4	102.4	102.0	101.2	103.0
16.其他食品	Other Foods	101.1	100.5	100.8	100.8	100.7	100.7	100.7	101.6	101.7	101.6	101.8	101.6	101.2
其他食品	Other Foods	101.1	100.5	100.8	100.8	100.7	100.7	100.7	101.6	101.7	101.6	101.8	101.6	101.2
二、烟酒及用品	**Tobacco,Liquor and Their Appliances**	**100.4**	**100.2**	**99.9**	**99.9**	**100.1**	**100.1**	**100.1**	**100.3**	**100.6**	**100.6**	**100.6**	**100.8**	**102.1**
1.烟草	Tobacco	100.6	100.2	100.3	100.3	100.6	100.6	100.4	100.6	100.6	100.6	100.6	100.6	101.5
国产卷烟	Domestic Cigarette	100.7	100.3	100.5	100.4	100.7	100.8	100.5	100.7	100.7	100.7	100.7	100.8	101.8
进口卷烟	Import Cigarette	99.3	99.9	99.8	99.7	99.7	99.7	99.8	98.3	98.3	98.3	98.3	99.7	99.8
其他	Others	99.8	99.6	99.6	99.6	99.6	99.6	99.8	100.0	100.0	99.7	100.0	100.0	100.0
2.酒	Liquor	100.3	100.1	99.5	99.6	99.7	99.7	99.8	100.1	100.7	100.6	100.7	101.0	102.7
白酒	White Spirit	100.7	100.1	99.5	99.6	99.9	100.1	100.3	100.5	101.4	100.9	101.3	101.5	103.8
葡萄酒	Grape	100.1	98.9	99.2	99.4	99.4	99.5	99.6	100.5	100.5	100.5	100.6	101.3	101.5
啤酒	Beer	99.5	100.3	99.5	99.4	99.2	98.8	98.6	99.0	99.2	99.8	99.5	100.0	101.0
其他	Others	100.4	100.7	100.5	100.3	100.2	100.0	100.0	100.9	100.9	100.2	100.2	100.2	100.3
3.吸烟、饮酒用品	Appliances for Smoking and Drinking	100.0	99.8	99.6	100.2	100.2	100.1	100.0	100.1	100.0	100.0	100.0	100.1	99.8
吸烟用品	Appliances for Smoking	99.9	99.8	99.7	100.0	99.9	99.9	99.9	99.9	99.9	99.9	99.9	100.0	100.1
饮酒用品	Appliances for Drinking	100.1	99.8	99.6	100.3	100.3	100.2	100.1	100.2	100.1	100.1	100.1	100.2	99.6
三、衣着	**Clothing**	**96.9**	**95.8**	**95.6**	**95.9**	**96.2**	**96.7**	**96.9**	**97.2**	**97.1**	**97.0**	**97.5**	**98.1**	**98.2**
1.服装	Garments	95.3	93.4	93.2	93.6	94.3	94.9	95.5	95.9	95.9	95.8	96.6	97.5	97.5
(1)男式服装	Men's Garments	94.9	91.3	91.1	91.9	92.9	94.7	95.5	96.0	96.0	96.0	97.0	98.3	98.3
大衣	Topcoat	91.9	89.1	87.4	89.8	91.0	91.5	92.3	93.7	93.7	93.3	93.9	93.5	94.3
毛线衣	Woollen Sweater	88.6	82.8	82.7	84.3	85.6	85.5	88.2	90.9	90.9	93.9	94.2	93.4	94.8
夹克衫	Jacket	97.4	93.3	92.9	93.2	93.1	99.3	99.3	99.2	99.1	98.3	99.0	102.1	101.7
衬衫	Shirt	93.2	87.4	89.9	90.9	91.6	93.6	93.6	93.6	93.5	93.6	95.3	97.3	99.1
T恤衫	T-shirt	100.2	99.7	99.8	99.8	99.9	98.1	98.2	98.2	99.3	100.2	102.3	103.3	103.6
裤子	Trousers	93.6	92.0	89.7	91.3	91.2	94.1	94.2	94.0	93.8	93.9	95.6	97.4	95.9
西服	Western-style Clothes	96.8	92.5	92.7	92.7	96.7	97.8	97.9	97.9	97.9	97.9	98.3	99.8	99.6
运动衫裤	Gym Suit	100.8	100.1	100.2	100.2	100.2	100.2	100.2	100.1	100.1	100.0	101.8	103.5	103.4
内衣	Underwaist	96.6	93.3	94.5	95.0	94.9	97.7	98.3	98.7	98.7	95.5	96.8	98.4	97.4
羽绒衣	Eider Down Outerwear	94.7	92.1	91.0	91.0	91.4	93.3	96.1	97.5	97.1	96.9	96.7	97.3	97.0
其他	Others	94.6	94.3	92.7	92.7	92.7	92.7	95.3	95.3	95.3	95.3	95.9	96.4	96.4
(2)女式服装	Women's Garments	94.7	93.9	93.8	94.0	94.3	93.9	94.6	95.0	94.8	94.7	95.4	96.3	96.3
大衣	Topcoat	90.9	89.0	85.9	86.8	87.7	88.8	93.1	93.1	93.1	93.1	93.9	93.9	93.5
毛线衣	Woollen Sweater	88.3	89.9	90.4	88.1	89.2	86.1	87.1	87.8	87.8	87.8	88.0	88.4	88.3
羽绒衣	Eider Down Outerwear	95.9	92.0	93.1	93.1	94.0	94.9	97.4	98.3	97.8	97.8	98.2	97.6	97.2
套装	Coordinates	97.4	100.7	100.7	100.7	96.0	96.0	96.0	96.0	95.9	95.9	96.6	97.3	97.3
衬衫	Shirt	94.5	90.1	90.0	92.5	95.9	98.6	98.2	98.2	98.2	93.2	93.3	93.4	93.6

7-15 续表 3 continued

商品类别及品名	Commodity Category and Commodity Name	全年 Annural	1月 January	2月 February	3月 March	4月 April	5月 May	6月 June	7月 July	8月 August	9月 September	10月 October	11月 November	12月 December
		（以2005年同期价格为100）												
T恤衫	T-shirt	97.3	100.1	99.3	99.6	100.0	94.8	94.8	94.8	94.8	94.8	97.6	98.8	98.9
裙子	Skirt	92.0	92.2	92.2	92.1	92.6	90.2	89.6	91.9	90.9	90.4	92.6	94.5	95.3
裤子	Trousers	96.8	97.6	98.1	98.0	98.4	97.9	96.0	95.2	95.2	95.2	95.1	97.2	97.2
运动衫裤	Gym Suit	100.0	98.5	98.9	99.3	100.0	99.5	99.3	99.3	99.3	99.3	100.9	102.8	102.8
内衣	Underwaist	97.6	94.4	93.8	95.6	95.7	96.9	96.9	97.0	97.1	99.6	100.5	101.9	102.0
其他	Others	98.7	97.1	97.0	97.0	97.0	97.8	99.9	99.9	99.9	99.9	99.1	99.9	99.9
（3）儿童服装	Children's Garments	97.5	96.6	95.8	96.1	96.7	97.7	97.6	97.8	98.0	98.1	98.4	98.7	99.0
套装	Coordinates	97.1	96.1	95.2	95.7	96.0	96.5	97.0	97.6	97.6	97.7	98.0	98.9	99.0
裤子	Trousers	101.4	99.6	98.8	98.4	100.5	102.8	102.7	102.6	102.6	102.6	103.3	101.7	101.7
裙子	Skirt	94.1	94.2	93.4	93.6	93.7	94.1	93.1	93.1	93.8	94.4	94.5	95.4	96.3
其他	Others	96.3	96.6	97.2	97.2	97.2	97.8	96.1	96.1	96.1	94.7	95.3	95.9	95.9
2.衣着材料	Clothing Materials	100.5	100.1	100.5	100.4	100.4	100.8	100.8	100.9	100.8	100.1	100.5	100.7	100.9
棉布	Cotton Cloth	100.1	99.4	99.4	99.4	99.3	100.4	100.4	100.4	100.4	100.2	100.3	100.3	101.1
棉混纺布	Cotton Textiles Cloth	100.6	100.0	100.2	100.2	100.2	100.3	100.3	100.6	100.6	100.6	100.9	101.2	101.5
化纤布	Chemical Fiber Cloth	101.1	98.9	100.5	100.5	100.5	101.5	101.5	101.7	101.4	100.9	101.6	101.8	101.9
毛线	Knitting Wool	100.1	102.9	102.1	101.2	101.2	100.2	100.2	100.2	100.2	98.0	98.2	98.4	98.4
3.鞋袜帽	Shoes,Socks and Hats	97.9	98.8	98.2	98.3	98.1	97.9	97.6	97.7	97.6	97.6	97.7	97.9	97.7
（1）鞋	Shoes	97.7	98.6	98.0	98.1	97.9	97.6	97.3	97.4	97.3	97.3	97.4	97.6	97.3
男鞋	Men's Shoes	98.0	98.6	99.0	98.8	98.7	97.7	97.5	97.5	97.4	97.4	97.7	97.8	98.3
女鞋	Women's Shoes	96.2	98.4	96.5	96.5	96.0	96.2	95.7	95.9	95.8	95.7	95.7	95.9	95.9
童鞋	Children's Shoes	100.1	99.3	99.6	100.1	100.6	100.6	100.3	100.3	100.2	100.4	100.4	100.7	98.7
（2）袜子	Socks	99.3	99.5	99.3	99.3	98.8	99.4	99.1	99.1	99.1	99.2	99.4	99.6	100.0
男袜	Men's Socks	98.5	98.6	98.4	98.4	98.4	98.4	98.2	98.2	98.2	98.3	98.6	98.6	99.5
女袜	Women's Socks	100.1	100.4	100.1	100.1	99.2	100.2	100.0	100.0	100.0	100.0	100.2	100.5	100.5
（3）帽子	Hats	99.3	99.5	99.2	99.2	99.2	99.3	99.3	99.3	99.3	99.3	99.3	99.4	99.8
男帽	Men's Hats	99.7	99.6	99.6	99.6	99.6	99.7	99.7	99.7	99.7	99.7	99.7	99.7	99.7
女帽	Women's Hats	99.1	99.5	98.9	98.9	98.9	98.9	98.9	98.9	98.9	98.9	99.0	99.1	99.9
4.衣着加工服务费	Clothing Manufacturing Services	99.9	98.2	97.8	100.1	100.1	100.1	100.1	100.1	100.1	100.1	100.1	99.7	102.1
缝纫	Sewing	99.9	97.7	97.2	100.2	100.2	100.2	100.2	100.2	100.2	100.2	100.2	99.6	102.7
清洗	Washing	100.0	100.0	100.0	100.0	100.0	100.0	100.0	100.0	100.0	100.0	100.0	100.0	100.0
四、家庭设备用品及维修服务	**Household Facilities, Articles and Services**	**100.1**	**99.4**	**99.3**	**99.4**	**99.7**	**99.7**	**99.7**	**99.9**	**99.9**	**100.2**	**100.7**	**101.1**	**101.8**
1.耐用消费品	Durable Consumer Goods	100.0	99.2	98.8	98.7	99.0	99.3	99.8	100.4	100.3	100.4	101.2	101.6	102.0
（1）家具	Furniture	100.2	98.2	98.0	97.9	99.0	100.2	100.3	100.7	100.5	100.5	102.1	102.6	102.7
柜	Cabinet	99.6	97.6	97.1	96.9	98.2	99.6	100.0	100.1	99.7	99.7	101.9	101.9	102.2
床	Bed	101.2	98.4	98.4	98.4	100.1	101.8	101.8	101.8	101.8	101.7	102.9	103.8	104.1
桌	Desk	99.9	99.2	99.2	99.2	99.3	99.5	99.8	100.7	99.9	99.2	100.5	101.1	101.1
椅	Chair	99.1	100.3	98.9	98.9	98.7	98.7	98.6	98.3	98.3	98.4	100.1	100.3	100.2
沙发	Sofa	100.4	96.9	97.0	97.0	98.7	100.1	100.1	101.4	101.5	101.5	103.0	104.0	104.0
其他	Others	101.4	100.8	100.9	101.0	100.4	101.1	101.2	101.1	101.1	101.1	102.7	102.6	102.6
（2）家庭设备	Household Appliances	99.9	100.0	99.5	99.4	99.0	98.7	99.4	100.1	100.1	100.3	100.5	100.8	101.4
洗衣机	Washing Machine	99.3	99.3	99.0	98.1	98.0	98.1	98.4	99.7	98.7	99.7	100.6	100.9	101.2

7-15 续表 4 continued

商品类别及品名	Commodity Category and Commodity Name	（以2005年同期价格为100） 全年 Annural	1月 January	2月 February	3月 March	4月 April	5月 May	6月 June	7月 July	8月 August	9月 September	10月 October	11月 November	12月 December
电风扇	Electric Fan	102.6	102.5	101.2	101.2	100.9	100.2	101.2	103.5	104.2	103.5	103.5	103.5	106.0
电冰箱（柜）	Refrigerator	100.7	101.7	101.0	102.4	102.5	101.3	100.6	100.9	99.5	99.5	99.8	99.8	99.5
吸排油烟机	Kitchen Ventilato	98.1	98.0	98.1	97.9	97.6	97.6	97.5	97.7	97.7	98.4	98.4	98.2	99.8
空调器	Air-conditioning	102.1	100.1	99.8	98.8	99.3	99.5	103.3	103.7	104.4	104.3	104.3	103.9	104.2
热水器	Water Heater	96.8	99.4	99.1	99.1	96.1	95.8	95.5	95.4	95.8	96.2	96.4	97.0	96.3
微波炉	Microwave Oven	97.0	97.2	96.3	96.7	95.5	95.5	96.1	95.8	97.0	98.0	98.0	99.0	99.0
电炊具	Electric Cooking Appliance	98.5	98.5	98.3	98.1	97.9	98.1	98.2	98.3	98.1	98.2	98.1	100.1	100.6
2.室内装饰品	Interior Decorations	99.4	99.5	99.4	99.4	99.4	99.4	99.0	99.0	99.0	99.4	99.7	100.0	100.1
纺织装饰品	Textile Process Decorations	99.5	99.9	99.7	99.7	99.7	99.7	98.8	98.8	98.7	99.7	99.8	100.0	100.0
装饰灯具	Architectural Lamps and Lanterns	99.1	99.0	99.0	99.0	99.0	98.9	98.8	98.8	98.8	98.9	99.4	99.9	100.1
其他	Others	100.0	100.0	100.0	100.0	100.0	100.0	100.0	100.0	100.0	100.0	100.0	100.0	100.0
3.床上用品	Bedclothes	100.0	98.3	98.9	100.0	100.4	99.9	100.0	100.0	99.9	100.3	100.4	100.8	101.3
毛毯	Woollen Blanket	99.5	94.5	95.9	99.5	100.5	99.3	99.7	99.5	99.7	100.4	101.4	101.2	102.8
被子	Quilt	100.3	100.0	100.1	100.2	100.2	100.3	100.3	100.1	100.1	100.4	99.8	101.0	101.0
床上套件	Bed Articcles	100.6	100.4	100.5	100.5	100.8	100.5	100.5	100.8	100.2	100.5	100.6	100.9	100.5
其他	Others	99.3	99.0	99.7	99.7	99.7	99.0	99.0	99.0	99.0	99.0	99.0	99.0	100.8
4.日用杂品	Sundry Articles	99.8	99.3	99.5	99.8	100.0	99.6	99.0	98.9	99.4	100.1	100.2	100.2	101.6
茶具	Tea Set	100.6	95.8	95.8	95.6	95.6	94.2	98.5	98.3	98.3	101.2	111.5	111.8	111.8
餐具	Tableware	98.4	98.6	99.2	99.4	99.4	98.8	100.4	99.8	100.4	100.4	95.2	95.2	95.0
厨具	Kitchen Utensils	101.2	100.6	100.9	101.6	102.7	102.2	99.7	99.7	99.9	101.6	101.6	101.3	102.9
家用手工工具	Domestic Handwork Tools	101.0	100.0	100.0	100.0	100.0	100.0	100.7	101.3	101.3	101.3	101.3	101.3	104.9
洗涤用品	Washing Articles	98.8	99.5	99.5	99.4	99.5	99.4	97.7	97.9	97.9	98.2	98.2	98.2	99.6
其他	Others	100.6	100.7	100.6	101.8	102.1	101.6	98.5	98.3	100.7	100.7	99.9	99.8	102.1
5.家庭服务及加工维修服务	Household Srvice and Manufacturing Upkeep	101.8	102.6	102.6	102.6	102.6	102.6	101.8	100.7	100.0	100.0	100.3	102.1	103.5
家庭服务	Household Srvice	102.5	103.7	103.7	103.7	103.7	103.7	102.9	101.3	100.0	100.0	100.6	102.7	104.1
加工维修服务	Manufacturing Upkeep	101.0	101.4	101.4	101.4	101.4	101.4	100.7	100.0	100.0	100.0	100.0	101.5	102.9
五、医疗保健和个人用品	**Health Care and Personal Articles**	**101.2**	**100.2**	**100.5**	**100.5**	**100.7**	**101.4**	**101.4**	**101.4**	**101.4**	**101.7**	**101.6**	**101.8**	**101.5**
1.医疗保健	Health Care	100.6	99.8	100.2	100.0	100.3	100.7	100.6	100.7	100.6	101.2	101.1	101.4	101.0
（1）医疗器具及用品	Medical Facilities and Goods	95.8	96.2	96.9	96.6	95.9	95.4	95.6	95.8	95.8	97.0	95.5	95.5	93.7
医疗器具及用品	Medical Facilities and Goods	95.8	96.2	96.9	96.6	95.9	95.4	95.6	95.8	95.8	97.0	95.5	95.5	93.7
（2）中药材及中成药	Herbs and Ready-made Traditional Chinese Medicine	103.7	101.6	103.3	102.1	102.7	103.3	103.6	104.2	103.8	105.4	104.8	105.5	103.7
中药材	Herbs	105.8	103.3	105.7	103.5	104.5	106.0	106.2	107.1	105.7	107.9	106.9	108.1	104.4
中成药	Ready-made Traditional Chinese Medicine	100.8	99.4	100.0	100.2	100.2	99.6	100.0	100.4	101.2	102.0	101.9	101.9	102.9
（3）西药	Western Medicine	99.7	98.5	98.7	98.8	99.1	100.0	99.7	99.6	99.4	100.3	100.5	100.7	101.1
抗微生物药	Anti-microorganism Medicine	94.6	92.3	92.4	92.6	92.9	93.2	93.2	93.2	92.9	94.5	99.7	99.7	100.4
消化系统用药	Alimentary System Medicine	100.9	100.2	100.8	100.8	100.9	101.0	101.0	101.0	101.0	101.3	100.7	101.1	100.7
呼吸系统用药	Respiratory System Medicine	99.8	98.0	98.0	98.7	99.5	99.5	99.7	99.7	99.7	101.6	100.2	100.8	102.1

7-15 续表 5 continued

商品类别及品名	Commodity Category and Commodity Name	（以2005年同期价格为100）												
		全年 Annural	1月 January	2月 February	3月 March	4月 April	5月 May	6月 June	7月 July	8月 August	9月 September	10月 October	11月 November	12月 December
解热镇痛及非甾体抗炎药	Allays a Fever the Analgesia and the Non-steroid Body Anti-inflammatory Agent	103.1	102.4	102.7	102.2	102.4	104.1	103.0	103.0	103.0	103.8	103.1	102.8	104.6
抗肿瘤药	Antineoplastic Drug	102.6	99.1	99.1	98.9	98.9	106.6	104.2	104.9	103.5	101.0	104.4	105.4	105.4
激素及调节内分泌功能药	Hormone and Adjustment Internal Secretion Function Medicine	99.1	99.4	99.8	99.8	99.9	99.9	99.9	98.4	98.6	100.9	98.1	98.1	96.9
循环系统用药	Circulating System Medicine	99.7	99.1	99.1	99.5	100.1	100.1	99.9	99.4	99.4	99.8	99.8	99.8	99.9
神经系统用药	Nerve System Medicine	101.0	100.1	100.5	100.5	101.1	101.1	101.1	101.1	101.1	102.1	100.8	100.8	101.5
专科用药	Junior Medicine	99.1	98.9	98.4	98.9	99.4	99.8	99.9	99.8	99.8	100.1	98.1	98.1	98.1
其他	Others	99.9	99.8	99.9	99.9	100.0	99.9	100.0	100.0	99.9	100.2	99.7	99.8	99.8
（4）保健品及器具	Healthcare Equipment	99.1	99.2	98.9	98.9	99.0	99.0	99.3	99.3	99.3	99.6	98.9	99.1	99.3
保健器具	Health Protection Equipment	99.8	99.9	99.4	99.5	99.6	99.6	100.3	100.3	100.3	100.3	99.5	99.6	99.4
滋补保健用品	Tonic and Health Products	98.8	98.8	98.6	98.6	98.6	98.6	98.6	98.7	98.7	99.1	98.5	98.9	99.3
（5）医疗保健服务	Health Care Services	100.7	100.8	100.8	100.8	100.8	100.8	100.7	100.8	100.8	100.5	100.5	100.7	100.3
挂号费	Registration	100.0	100.0	100.0	100.0	100.0	100.0	100.0	100.0	100.0	100.0	100.0	100.0	100.0
注射费	Injection Expenses	100.0	100.0	100.0	100.0	100.0	100.0	100.0	100.0	100.0	100.0	100.0	100.0	100.0
检查费	Examination Expenses	102.1	102.8	102.8	102.8	102.8	102.8	101.7	102.8	102.8	101.0	101.0	101.0	100.5
手术费	Operation Expenses	100.1	100.0	100.0	100.0	100.0	100.0	100.0	100.0	100.0	100.0	100.0	100.0	100.9
住院费	Hospitalization Expenses	101.7	101.8	101.8	101.8	101.8	101.8	101.8	101.8	101.8	101.8	101.8	102.5	100.0
理疗费	Physiotherapy Expenses	100.0	100.0	100.0	100.0	100.0	100.0	100.0	100.0	100.0	100.0	100.0	100.0	100.0
化验费	Analysis Expenses	100.0	100.0	100.0	100.0	100.0	100.0	100.0	100.0	100.0	100.0	100.0	100.0	100.0
其他	Others	99.9	99.9	99.9	99.9	99.9	99.9	99.9	99.9	99.9	99.9	99.9	99.9	100.0
2.个人用品及服务	Personal Articles and Services	102.4	100.9	101.1	101.4	101.9	103.0	103.1	103.0	103.2	102.9	102.8	102.6	102.5
（1）化妆美容用品	Cosmetics	100.5	100.5	100.2	100.1	100.4	100.7	100.9	100.8	100.8	100.7	100.6	100.4	100.4
化妆美容器具	Cosmetics Appliances	99.1	96.3	96.3	96.6	98.4	99.0	100.6	100.6	100.7	100.5	100.4	100.3	100.3
美容化妆品	Facial Beautifiers	101.3	101.4	101.5	101.5	101.5	101.5	101.4	101.4	101.4	101.2	101.2	100.7	100.9
护肤品	Protects Skin Products	100.0	100.0	99.9	99.9	99.9	100.2	99.9	99.9	100.0	100.0	100.0	100.0	100.0
护发美容品	Protects Sends the Beauty Products	100.7	104.4	101.6	100.6	100.7	101.1	101.1	100.2	100.2	100.0	100.0	100.0	99.3
（2）清洁化妆用品	Cleaning Toiletware	100.4	100.0	100.1	99.9	100.4	100.2	100.6	100.6	100.9	100.2	100.6	100.7	101.2
洗发用品	Hairdressing Articles	100.2	101.1	100.6	100.0	99.7	99.7	100.7	100.7	101.0	99.4	100.6	100.6	98.5
洗浴用品	Bathing Articles	100.8	99.8	99.7	99.8	101.0	100.9	101.1	101.1	101.5	101.5	101.2	101.2	101.0
其他	Others	100.3	98.5	99.8	99.8	100.4	100.1	99.8	99.8	99.8	99.8	99.8	100.0	105.7
（3）个人饰品	Personal Decoraions	107.1	101.7	102.6	104.1	105.1	109.6	109.4	109.1	109.6	109.6	108.9	108.4	107.3
首饰	Ornaments	122.1	106.2	108.1	112.4	116.6	129.6	129.0	128.3	129.9	129.5	127.3	125.9	121.9
皮件	Leather Appliance	96.6	98.8	99.8	99.8	95.8	95.3	95.3	95.9	95.8	95.8	96.1	95.7	95.1

7-15 续表 6 continued

商品类别及品名	Commodity Category and Commodity Name	（以2005年同期价格为100）												
		全年 Annual	1月 January	2月 February	3月 March	4月 April	5月 May	6月 June	7月 July	8月 August	9月 September	10月 October	11月 November	12月 December
手表	Watch	99.8	100.1	100.2	100.1	99.7	99.7	99.7	99.3	99.2	99.6	99.6	99.7	100.2
领带	Necktie	100.8	99.7	99.4	99.4	101.4	101.6	101.5	101.1	101.0	101.0	101.0	101.1	101.3
其他	Others	98.3	98.1	98.1	98.1	98.1	98.1	98.1	98.1	98.1	98.1	98.1	98.1	100.0
（4）个人服务	Personal Services	100.8	101.0	101.2	101.1	101.1	100.9	100.9	100.9	100.9	100.5	100.4	100.5	100.6
美容	Cosmetology	100.0	100.0	100.0	100.0	100.0	100.0	100.0	100.0	100.0	100.0	100.0	100.0	100.0
理（烫）发	Haircut (permnaent wave)	101.6	101.4	101.8	101.5	101.5	101.5	101.5	101.5	101.5	101.5	101.5	101.5	101.5
洗浴	Bathe	100.0	100.4	100.4	100.4	100.4	99.8	99.8	99.8	99.8	99.8	99.4	99.7	100.1
其他	Others	102.7	104.1	104.1	104.1	104.1	104.1	104.1	104.1	104.1	100.0	100.0	100.0	100.0
六、交通和通信	**Transportation and Communication**	**100.1**	**100.1**	**100.6**	**100.6**	**100.2**	**100.2**	**100.4**	**99.8**	**99.5**	**99.7**	**99.8**	**100.3**	**100.4**
1.交通	Transportation	102.5	102.6	103.6	103.6	102.9	103.0	103.3	102.1	101.6	101.8	101.9	102.1	101.8
（1）交通工具	Transportation Facility	98.5	98.5	99.9	99.7	99.1	98.9	98.1	97.5	97.7	98.1	98.1	98.4	98.2
摩托车	Motorcycle	102.2	99.3	102.1	102.1	102.3	102.3	102.3	102.0	102.5	103.1	103.1	103.1	102.1
自行车	Bicycle	97.9	99.1	100.1	99.8	99.0	98.8	97.9	96.6	96.6	96.7	96.7	96.7	97.1
轿车	Car	95.2	95.8	96.0	95.9	95.8	95.2	93.4	94.0	94.3	94.8	95.1	96.2	95.9
其他	Others	97.1	100.8	100.8	100.8	96.1	96.1	96.1	95.7	95.7	95.7	95.7	95.7	95.7
（2）车用燃料及零配件	Fuels and Parts	112.5	109.8	110.1	109.6	111.0	113.8	117.9	115.4	112.1	112.1	112.6	112.5	112.4
汽油	Gasoline	115.9	114.1	114.3	112.2	112.6	117.3	124.6	120.1	115.2	115.1	115.1	115.1	115.0
柴油	Diesel Oil	115.4	112.7	113.3	113.9	116.6	118.8	121.6	118.0	113.7	113.6	114.4	114.2	113.8
零配件	Parts	101.8	98.5	98.5	98.9	99.9	99.9	99.9	102.9	103.8	103.8	104.8	105.5	105.2
其他	Others	103.6	100.0	100.0	101.0	103.6	103.5	105.6	104.4	105.1	106.3	105.8	103.6	104.7
（3）车辆使用及维修费	Using and Upkeep Fare	100.6	100.9	99.9	100.7	100.3	100.5	100.8	100.9	101.0	101.1	101.0	99.8	100.5
驾驶证	Driving License	101.7	102.9	103.0	102.0	100.2	100.9	102.1	102.7	103.5	103.5	101.7	99.9	98.3
保险费	Insurance Expenses	99.6	99.2	99.4	99.5	99.5	99.5	99.5	99.5	99.6	100.0	100.0	100.0	100.0
停车费	Parking Expenses	100.0	100.0	100.0	100.0	100.0	100.0	100.0	100.0	100.0	100.0	100.0	100.0	100.0
车辆修理服务费	Vehicle Upkeep Service Fare	100.6	100.9	98.1	100.7	100.7	100.7	100.7	100.7	100.7	100.7	101.4	99.7	102.2
其他	Others	101.5	102.6	102.6	102.6	102.6	102.6	102.6	102.6	100.0	100.0	100.0	100.0	100.0
（4）市区公共交通费	Incity Traffic Fare	103.5	102.5	104.3	104.3	104.3	104.1	104.1	103.6	102.8	102.6	102.4	104.4	102.8
公共汽车票	Bus Ticket	104.4	102.5	106.0	106.0	106.0	105.6	105.6	104.5	103.4	103.4	103.4	103.4	103.4
出租汽车	Taxi	104.4	104.0	104.7	104.7	104.7	104.7	104.7	104.7	103.8	103.0	102.6	108.2	103.6
其他	Others	100.0	100.0	100.0	100.0	100.0	100.0	100.0	100.0	100.0	100.0	100.0	100.0	100.0
（5）城市间交通费	Intercity Traffic Fare	107.6	111.5	112.6	112.9	109.3	108.5	108.9	105.4	104.5	104.5	104.5	105.5	104.0
飞机票	Airplane Ticket	105.4	129.2	88.3	113.2	111.7	123.3	100.0	100.0	100.0	100.0	100.0	100.0	100.0
火车票	Train Ticket	100.0	100.0	100.0	100.0	100.0	100.0	100.0	100.0	100.0	100.0	100.0	100.0	100.0
长途汽车	Intertown Bus	109.3	114.2	116.0	116.0	111.5	110.3	110.9	106.5	105.4	105.4	105.4	106.6	104.9
其他	Others	101.4	100.8	97.6	101.3	101.3	101.3	102.0	102.0	102.0	102.0	102.0	102.0	102.0
2.通信	Communication	96.5	96.3	96.1	96.0	96.1	95.8	96.0	96.2	96.2	96.4	96.6	97.5	98.3
（1）通信工具	Communication Facility	86.9	87.5	86.7	86.4	86.4	85.5	86.0	86.6	86.5	87.2	87.7	88.0	88.2
固定电话机	Telephone	95.1	96.5	96.4	95.6	95.5	93.9	94.1	94.0	94.2	95.0	95.2	95.4	95.5
移动电话机	Mobile Phone	75.8	76.7	75.3	75.2	74.7	74.3	74.9	76.2	75.7	76.1	76.8	77.1	77.1
其他	Others	90.7	90.6	88.4	88.8	90.3	91.1	90.9	91.1	90.5	90.7	91.7	92.2	92.2
（2）通信服务	Communication Service	100.3	100.0	100.0	100.0	100.0	100.0	100.0	100.0	100.0	100.0	100.0	101.2	102.1
移动通信费	Mobile Communication Fee	100.0	100.0	100.0	100.0	100.0	100.0	100.0	100.0	100.0	100.0	100.0	100.0	100.0
市内电话费	Incity Telephone Fee	100.0	100.0	100.0	100.0	100.0	100.0	100.0	100.0	100.0	100.0	100.0	100.0	100.0

7-15 续表 7 continued

商品类别及品名	Commodity Category and Commodity Name	（以2005年同期价格为100）												
		全年 Annural	1月 January	2月 February	3月 March	4月 April	5月 May	6月 June	7月 July	8月 August	9月 September	10月 October	11月 November	12月 December
长途电话费	Long Distance Call Fee	100.0	100.0	100.0	100.0	100.0	100.0	100.0	100.0	100.0	100.0	100.0	100.0	100.0
月租费	Month Hiring Fee	100.0	100.0	100.0	100.0	100.0	100.0	100.0	100.0	100.0	100.0	100.0	100.0	100.0
上网费	Net Play Fee	99.8	100.0	100.0	100.0	100.0	100.0	100.0	100.0	100.0	99.5	99.5	99.5	99.5
信件邮寄	Letter Post	103.5	100.0	100.0	100.0	100.0	100.0	100.0	100.0	100.0	100.0	100.0	115.3	126.6
包裹邮寄	Package Post	100.0	100.0	100.0	100.0	100.0	100.0	100.0	100.0	100.0	100.0	100.0	100.0	100.0
其他	Others	100.0	100.0	100.0	100.0	100.0	100.0	100.0	100.0	100.0	100.0	100.0	100.0	100.0
七、娱乐教育文化用品及服务	**Recreation,Education and Culture Articles**	**100.3**	**100.0**	**99.9**	**99.9**	**100.5**	**100.6**	**100.6**	**100.7**	**100.8**	**100.1**	**100.2**	**100.4**	**100.4**
1.文娱用耐用消费品及服务	Durable Consumer Goods for Cultural and Recreational Use and Service	95.7	95.6	95.1	95.0	94.6	94.9	95.0	95.4	95.7	96.2	96.4	97.1	97.2
电视机	Television	93.3	93.1	92.3	92.2	91.7	92.2	92.0	92.8	93.2	93.8	94.2	95.8	97.0
激光视盘机	Laser Video Disc Machine	96.2	96.3	95.6	95.7	95.7	95.3	95.9	95.9	97.4	98.4	98.0	97.1	93.3
摄像机	Pickup Camera	99.7	99.2	99.3	99.3	99.4	99.5	99.5	100.0	100.0	100.0	100.0	100.0	100.0
照相机	Camera	95.7	94.8	93.8	93.8	93.8	93.9	95.6	95.2	96.2	97.9	98.0	98.4	96.6
家用音响	Acoustic Equipment	98.7	100.4	99.8	99.4	98.2	98.6	98.2	98.7	98.7	98.4	98.3	98.3	97.5
便携式音响	Portable Acoustics	99.6	99.7	99.9	99.8	99.6	99.5	99.5	99.5	99.5	99.5	99.5	99.5	99.8
电脑	Computer	95.9	96.4	96.3	96.3	96.1	96.3	96.6	96.4	94.9	95.0	95.0	95.0	96.2
修理服务	Repair Service	104.9	103.0	103.7	103.1	103.6	104.8	105.6	105.0	104.5	104.7	106.9	106.9	107.5
其他	Others	100.0	100.0	100.0	100.0	100.0	100.0	100.0	100.0	100.0	100.0	100.0	100.0	100.0
2.教育	Education	101.8	101.7	101.9	101.9	102.5	102.5	102.4	102.4	102.4	101.0	101.0	101.0	100.8
（1）教材及参考书	Teaching Materials and Reference Books	100.4	100.7	100.7	100.8	101.0	101.0	101.0	101.0	100.2	99.9	99.6	99.9	99.8
工具书	Tool Book	99.6	99.7	99.7	99.7	99.7	99.7	99.7	99.7	99.7	99.7	99.7	99.7	99.0
教材	Teaching Material	100.4	101.0	101.1	101.0	101.3	101.3	101.3	101.3	100.7	98.9	98.9	98.9	98.9
参考书	Reference Book	101.6	100.9	100.9	101.7	101.7	101.7	101.7	101.7	99.6	102.5	102.5	102.5	102.5
教育软件	Educational Software	99.2	99.6	99.6	99.4	99.4	99.4	99.4	99.4	99.4	99.4	96.7	99.4	99.7
（2）学杂托幼费	Tuition and Child Care	102.0	101.8	102.1	102.1	102.7	102.7	102.6	102.6	102.7	101.2	101.2	101.2	101.0
义务教育杂费	Incidental Expenses of Compulcory Education	100.0	100.0	100.0	100.0	100.0	100.0	100.0	100.0	100.0	100.0	100.0	100.0	100.0
非义务教育学杂费	Tuition of Non-compulsory Education	102.1	103.1	103.1	103.1	103.1	103.1	103.1	103.1	103.1	100.0	100.0	100.0	100.0
技能培训学费	Skill Train Tuition	100.0	100.0	100.0	100.0	100.0	100.0	100.0	100.0	100.0	100.0	100.0	100.0	100.0
托幼费	Child Care	108.4	104.9	107.0	107.0	111.2	111.2	110.3	110.3	111.4	106.9	106.9	106.9	106.9
其他	Others	106.7	104.1	104.1	104.1	108.1	108.1	108.1	108.1	108.1	108.1	108.1	108.1	103.9
3.文化娱乐类	Recreation and Culture	102.6	100.6	100.4	100.4	103.3	103.2	103.2	103.1	103.1	103.3	103.3	103.8	103.8
（1）文化娱乐用品	Culture Articles	100.1	100.4	100.1	100.1	100.1	100.1	100.0	99.8	99.9	99.9	100.1	100.3	100.1
乐器	Musical Instrument	99.9	99.7	99.8	99.8	99.8	100.0	100.4	100.4	99.7	100.0	100.4	99.6	98.9
音响光盘和磁带	Audio,Disk and Tape	100.1	100.0	100.0	100.0	100.0	100.1	100.1	100.1	100.1	100.1	100.1	100.1	100.1
照相胶卷和存储卡	Roll Film and Memorizing Card	99.4	98.7	98.9	99.1	99.2	99.2	99.2	99.2	98.8	98.8	98.8	100.6	102.2
录像磁带和视盘	Video Tape and Disk	98.8	99.9	99.9	100.0	100.0	99.2	99.2	97.9	97.9	97.9	97.9	97.9	97.9

7-15 续表 8 continued

商品类别及品名	Commodity Category and Commodity Name	（以2005年同期价格为100）												
		全年 Annural	1月 January	2月 February	3月 March	4月 April	5月 May	6月 June	7月 July	8月 August	9月 September	10月 October	11月 November	12月 December
儿童玩具	Children's Toy	99.4	99.2	99.3	99.3	99.3	99.3	99.3	99.5	99.1	99.1	99.5	99.9	99.9
纸张本册	Paper and Volume	101.8	103.2	100.6	100.9	100.9	100.9	101.4	101.4	102.4	102.6	102.7	102.9	102.1
文具	Stationery	100.2	100.9	101.3	101.2	101.2	101.2	100.4	99.4	99.5	99.6	99.6	99.5	98.9
体育用品	Sports Goods	99.7	99.8	100.2	100.2	100.2	100.2	99.5	99.5	99.5	99.5	99.5	99.5	99.4
其他	Others	99.4	98.7	98.7	98.7	98.7	98.7	100.0	100.0	100.0	100.0	100.0	100.0	100.0
（2）书报杂志	Books,Newspapers, Magazines	101.2	101.2	101.2	101.2	101.2	101.2	101.2	101.2	101.2	101.2	101.2	101.2	101.2
书籍	Books	100.0	100.0	100.0	100.0	100.0	100.0	100.0	100.0	100.0	100.0	100.0	100.0	100.0
报纸	Newspapers	103.0	103.0	103.0	103.0	103.0	103.0	103.0	103.0	103.0	103.0	103.0	103.0	103.0
杂志	Magazines	101.3	101.3	101.3	101.3	101.3	101.3	101.3	101.3	101.3	101.3	101.3	101.3	101.3
（3）文娱费	Expenditure of Culture and Recreation	112.0	100.0	100.0	100.0	115.3	115.3	115.3	115.3	115.3	115.8	115.8	117.9	117.9
电影票	Film Ticket	100.0	100.0	100.0	100.0	100.0	100.0	100.0	100.0	100.0	100.0	100.0	100.0	100.0
景点门票	Scene Spot ticket	110.6	100.0	100.0	100.0	102.8	102.8	102.8	102.8	102.8	110.9	110.9	145.9	145.9
有线电视	Cable Television	120.9	100.0	100.0	100.0	127.9	127.9	127.9	127.9	127.9	127.9	127.9	127.9	127.9
健身活动	Exercise	100.0	100.0	100.0	100.0	100.0	100.0	100.0	100.0	100.0	100.0	100.0	100.0	100.0
其他	Others	100.0	100.0	100.0	100.0	100.0	100.0	100.0	100.0	100.0	100.0	100.0	100.0	100.0
4.旅游	Tourism	100.4	100.9	99.6	100.3	100.3	100.4	100.4	100.4	100.5	100.5	100.4	100.4	100.5
旅行社收费	Travel Agency Charge	101.5	97.4	97.9	101.7	102.0	102.2	102.4	102.5	102.6	102.6	102.1	102.1	102.6
宾馆住宿	Guesthouse Stay	100.2	102.6	100.0	100.0	100.0	100.0	100.0	100.0	100.0	100.0	100.0	100.0	100.0
其他住宿	Other Stay	100.0	100.0	100.0	100.0	100.0	100.0	100.0	100.0	100.0	100.0	100.0	100.0	100.0
八、居住	**Residence**	**104.0**	**103.6**	**103.5**	**103.7**	**103.7**	**103.6**	**103.9**	**104.1**	**104.5**	**103.8**	**103.9**	**104.7**	**104.9**
1.建房及装修材料	Building and Building Decoration Materials	103.9	102.2	102.1	102.7	103.3	103.6	104.0	104.2	105.1	103.9	104.4	105.3	105.4
木材	Wood	108.0	106.0	105.9	106.1	106.1	105.3	104.9	105.1	108.5	109.6	110.8	113.6	113.6
木地板	Wood Floor	95.2	100.4	100.4	100.4	92.9	93.2	93.3	93.3	93.3	91.7	93.9	94.7	94.9
砖	Brick	107.6	102.9	103.7	105.4	108.5	109.3	111.4	110.8	111.7	106.7	107.1	107.2	106.9
水泥	Cement	102.7	102.4	101.4	101.2	103.8	104.4	103.5	103.4	103.4	102.8	102.3	102.4	101.9
涂料	Coating Material	100.2	101.8	101.8	101.2	99.8	99.0	99.3	99.4	99.7	99.7	100.1	100.5	100.8
胶合板	Plywood	104.9	103.0	102.7	102.8	103.8	102.6	103.5	105.8	106.9	107.0	105.1	108.2	107.8
玻璃	Glass	101.3	96.9	96.6	98.5	98.6	100.0	100.3	101.8	102.6	102.8	104.0	106.0	108.3
粘胶	Rayon	101.8	101.8	101.9	101.5	101.4	101.5	101.5	101.5	101.3	101.7	102.0	101.9	103.4
油漆	Paint	103.5	104.5	103.9	103.7	102.8	103.2	103.7	103.8	103.9	103.2	103.2	103.0	103.5
其他	Others	99.0	93.4	92.0	95.0	97.3	101.3	100.8	101.5	99.6	99.2	102.2	104.1	102.2
2.租房	Renting	102.8	103.2	103.2	103.2	103.2	103.2	103.2	103.2	101.6	101.6	101.6	103.2	103.2
公房房租	Public House Rent	100.1	100.0	100.0	100.0	100.0	100.0	100.0	100.2	100.2	100.2	100.2	100.3	100.3
私房房租	Private House Rent	101.4	100.0	100.0	100.0	100.0	100.0	100.0	102.1	102.1	102.1	102.1	104.3	104.3
其他费用	Other Fare	115.8	133.6	133.6	133.6	133.6	133.6	133.6	114.4	100.0	100.0	100.0	100.0	100.0
3.自有住房	Private Housing	102.7	101.5	101.6	99.1	97.3	98.9	101.5	101.7	101.4	104.1	104.1	110.7	110.7
房屋贷款利率	Houses Loans Interest Rate	101.9	104.3	104.3	101.1	100.0	100.5	100.5	100.5	102.0	102.4	102.4	102.4	102.4
物业管理费用	Property Management Fee	100.0	100.0	100.0	100.0	100.0	100.0	100.0	100.0	100.0	100.0	100.0	100.0	100.0
维护修理费用	Upkeep and Repair Fee	103.4	101.8	101.6	98.5	96.5	98.4	102.0	102.2	101.7	105.3	105.3	114.1	114.1
其他	Others	100.2	99.7	100.8	100.8	100.0	100.0	100.0	100.0	100.0	100.0	100.0	100.5	100.5
4.水、电、燃料	Water,Electricity and Fuels	104.7	107.3	107.2	107.4	106.6	104.6	104.2	104.3	104.3	103.8	102.9	101.9	102.5
水	Water	110.1	115.3	110.5	115.2	114.2	113.7	113.4	109.5	109.5	109.4	104.2	104.2	104.2
电	Electricity	103.1	103.3	104.2	104.2	104.3	101.9	101.6	103.0	103.6	102.9	102.9	102.9	102.9
液化石油气	Liquefiled Petroleum Gas	113.3	124.9	125.6	124.5	121.4	115.5	113.6	112.5	110.2	110.1	107.3	100.2	100.8
管道燃气	Pipelined Gas	105.9	105.5	105.5	105.5	105.5	107.8	107.8	106.2	105.4	105.4	105.4	105.4	105.4
其他燃料	Other Fuels	102.0	103.7	103.4	103.2	102.4	101.7	101.4	101.5	101.7	101.1	100.8	101.0	102.4

7-16 全省居民消费价格（环比）指数
Entire Province Consumer Price Indices

（以上月价格为100）

商品类别及品名	Commodity Category and Commodity Name	1月 January	2月 February	3月 March	4月 April	5月 May	6月 June	7月 July	8月 August	9月 September	10月 October	11月 November	12月 December
居民消费价格总指数	**General Consumer Price Index**	**101.5**	**100.0**	**99.3**	**100.1**	**99.6**	**99.3**	**99.6**	**100.4**	**100.6**	**99.7**	**100.6**	**101.6**
非食品价格指数	**No-food**	**100.0**	**99.8**	**99.9**	**100.2**	**100.0**	**100.1**	**100.0**	**100.1**	**100.1**	**100.2**	**100.2**	**100.1**
服务项目价格指数	**Services**	**100.3**	**100.0**	**100.0**	**100.5**	**100.2**	**100.0**	**100.3**	**100.3**	**100.1**	**100.1**	**100.1**	**100.2**
工业品价格指数	**Industrial Products**	**99.9**	**99.7**	**99.9**	**100.0**	**100.0**	**100.2**	**99.9**	**100.0**	**100.1**	**100.2**	**100.2**	**100.1**
扣除食品和能源价格指数	**Deducting Foods and Energy**	**99.9**	**99.8**	**100.0**	**100.1**	**100.0**	**100.1**	**100.1**	**100.1**	**100.0**	**100.2**	**100.2**	**100.1**
扣除鲜菜鲜果总指数	**Deducting Fresh,Vegetables and Fruits**	**100.4**	**99.8**	**99.7**	**100.0**	**100.0**	**100.2**	**100.3**	**100.6**	**100.3**	**100.2**	**100.6**	**100.9**
消费品价格指数	**Consumer Goods**	**101.8**	**100.0**	**99.2**	**100.0**	**99.5**	**99.1**	**99.4**	**100.5**	**100.8**	**99.6**	**100.8**	**101.9**
一、食品	**Food**	**105.2**	**100.4**	**98.1**	**100.0**	**98.7**	**97.4**	**98.5**	**101.3**	**102.0**	**98.6**	**101.6**	**105.0**
1.粮食	Grain	100.4	100.2	100.0	100.3	100.5	100.2	101.2	100.7	100.9	100.7	102.8	102.3
大米	Rice	101.8	99.8	100.1	100.6	101.9	101.2	102.9	102.9	100.9	100.8	99.6	101.8
面粉	Flour	99.9	100.6	99.8	100.1	99.7	99.2	100.7	98.9	100.9	100.6	107.0	103.3
粮食制品	Grain Products	99.8	100.3	100.1	100.2	100.1	100.1	100.2	100.7	100.1	100.2	102.6	101.7
其他	Others	100.3	99.9	99.9	100.4	100.3	100.7	100.8	100.0	104.1	101.9	99.7	101.9
2.淀粉	Starches	100.4	99.2	100.1	100.6	100.2	100.3	101.5	101.3	100.8	100.1	99.9	102.7
淀粉	Starches	100.4	99.2	100.1	100.6	100.2	100.3	101.5	101.3	100.8	100.1	99.9	102.7
3.干豆类及豆制品	Beans and Beans Products	100.7	100.4	99.1	100.1	100.5	100.5	101.0	100.2	99.6	99.6	99.9	100.7
干豆	Beans	100.5	101.5	100.0	100.9	101.2	102.2	102.9	100.4	98.1	98.3	99.2	101.2
豆制品	Beans Products	100.7	100.0	98.7	99.8	100.2	99.9	100.3	100.2	100.3	100.1	100.1	100.5
4.油脂	Oil and Fat	100.1	100.1	99.4	99.8	100.7	100.1	100.2	100.9	100.6	100.7	104.2	105.4
食用植物油	Edible Vegetable Oil	99.8	100.4	99.6	99.9	100.3	100.0	100.2	101.1	100.8	100.5	104.0	105.1
植物油制品	Plant Oil Products	99.6	99.8	99.9	99.8	104.7	99.9	99.6	100.2	100.2	100.0	102.9	107.8
其他	Others	108.6	95.9	94.6	97.5	98.6	101.9	101.3	100.4	96.3	106.3	110.4	103.4
5.肉禽及其制品	Meal,Poultry and Their Products	104.6	99.7	96.7	97.3	98.3	100.6	102.9	104.9	101.9	100.3	103.9	105.8
（1）食用畜肉及副产品	Edible Livestock Meat and Their By-products	106.0	99.0	95.2	95.2	97.9	101.1	103.4	106.2	102.6	100.5	105.6	107.5
猪肉	Pork	107.6	98.1	93.7	93.2	97.3	101.5	105.3	109.0	103.3	100.3	107.3	109.0
牛肉	Beef	101.5	100.8	98.8	99.9	98.8	100.3	100.3	99.7	100.7	100.5	101.8	103.2
羊肉	Mutton	102.0	100.6	98.2	100.1	100.3	99.7	99.9	100.8	100.9	101.6	101.5	104.7
畜肉副产品	Livestock Meat By-products	105.4	100.9	96.5	96.1	97.4	102.1	100.3	102.5	102.7	100.4	104.1	106.6
其他	Others	105.0	99.4	97.6	97.0	99.0	99.1	101.3	105.5	101.2	100.6	103.0	103.3
（2）禽	Poultry	104.1	102.0	99.5	101.9	98.9	100.5	104.3	104.3	100.9	99.8	100.4	103.1
鸡	Chicken	105.8	102.6	99.8	102.3	99.0	100.9	105.5	104.2	101.3	99.6	100.0	103.1
鸭	Duck	99.5	98.5	100.1	100.4	100.1	97.3	97.1	103.6	98.8	100.6	103.5	102.9
其他	Others	99.7	101.1	97.5	100.6	98.0	100.4	102.8	105.1	99.8	100.3	100.5	103.3
（3）加工肉禽	Meal and Poultry Processing Products	100.2	100.3	99.4	100.7	99.2	99.2	100.1	101.2	100.3	99.9	101.5	101.8
畜肉制品	Livestock Meat Products	100.1	100.2	99.9	99.5	99.4	99.5	100.5	101.1	100.2	100.1	101.1	101.6
禽制品	Poultry Products	100.3	100.4	98.6	102.5	99.0	98.6	99.5	101.3	100.4	99.5	102.2	102.2

7-16 续表 1 continued

商品类别及品名	Commodity Category and Commodity Name	(以上月价格为100)											
		1月 January	2月 February	3月 March	4月 April	5月 May	6月 June	7月 July	8月 August	9月 September	10月 October	11月 November	12月 December
6.蛋	Eggs	99.9	95.0	97.2	99.9	101.9	100.9	101.4	109.5	106.2	99.5	101.4	104.2
鲜蛋	Fresh Eggs	99.9	94.5	96.9	99.9	102.0	100.9	101.7	110.7	106.9	99.3	101.4	104.4
蛋制品	Egg Products	100.5	99.1	99.6	99.7	100.5	101.0	99.7	100.4	100.6	101.0	101.1	101.9
7.水产品	Aquatic Product	104.3	101.6	98.8	100.3	99.9	100.9	101.3	99.9	97.4	100.3	99.9	99.7
（1）鱼	Fish	102.6	100.1	98.2	100.4	101.3	101.7	101.8	100.7	99.2	98.9	99.3	99.3
淡水鱼	Freshwater Fish	101.0	98.6	98.0	99.5	102.6	102.9	102.7	100.7	99.3	97.9	98.5	98.6
海水鱼	Seawater Fish	104.2	101.7	98.4	101.4	100.1	100.6	100.9	100.7	99.0	99.9	100.1	100.1
（2）其他水产品	Other Aquatic Product	107.0	103.6	99.5	100.2	97.9	99.8	100.6	98.7	94.7	102.5	100.9	100.2
虾蟹类	Shrimp and Crab	108.3	104.3	99.3	100.2	97.5	99.9	100.2	98.4	93.4	103.2	101.1	100.4
其他	Others	102.4	100.8	100.6	100.0	99.7	99.3	102.1	99.6	99.7	100.3	100.3	99.4
8.菜	Vegetable	128.9	100.4	91.0	96.7	85.5	81.4	95.4	109.6	115.5	84.7	99.9	124.7
鲜菜	Fresh Vegetable	131.8	100.3	90.0	96.3	83.5	79.7	94.8	111.2	117.9	83.1	99.8	127.7
干菜及菜制品	Dried Vegetable and Vegetable Products	101.6	100.3	99.9	100.1	99.6	100.1	99.9	100.7	100.8	101.1	101.3	104.2
薯类	Potato	110.3	104.2	106.4	104.4	112.4	81.6	99.1	97.1	96.6	87.6	100.5	107.7
9.调味品	Flavoring	100.1	99.8	100.1	100.2	100.0	99.9	100.4	100.0	100.1	100.2	100.7	100.8
盐	Salt	99.7	99.5	100.5	100.2	100.0	100.4	100.8	99.8	100.3	100.1	100.0	99.9
酱油	Soy Sauce	100.1	100.0	100.0	100.2	99.9	99.7	100.3	100.2	99.8	100.2	100.1	100.9
醋	Vinegar	100.0	100.0	99.9	100.4	99.9	100.1	100.6	100.0	100.1	100.1	100.0	101.3
味精	Aginomoto	100.3	100.0	99.9	100.3	100.1	99.8	100.5	99.9	100.1	100.4	99.8	100.4
其他	Others	100.8	99.6	100.0	99.7	100.1	99.3	99.8	100.0	100.0	100.6	104.1	101.4
10.糖	Carbohydrate	100.9	104.1	101.4	100.8	100.8	100.4	100.4	100.2	100.1	100.0	100.1	100.7
食糖	Sugar	102.0	110.2	103.2	101.5	101.8	100.9	100.7	100.5	100.3	99.7	100.1	101.5
糖果	Sweet	100.3	100.5	100.1	100.6	100.1	100.1	100.4	100.0	100.0	100.4	100.1	99.0
巧克力制品	Chocolate Products	100.2	100.0	99.9	100.0	99.9	99.9	100.1	99.9	100.0	100.2	100.0	102.6
糖类小食品	Little Carbohydrate Food	99.9	100.4	100.1	100.0	100.3	100.0	100.1	100.3	100.0	99.9	100.5	101.0
11.茶及饮料	Tea and Beverages	99.9	100.2	100.8	100.0	100.0	100.2	100.1	100.2	100.0	100.1	100.0	100.4
（1）茶叶	Tea	99.6	100.4	100.5	100.0	99.6	100.1	100.2	100.0	100.0	100.3	100.0	100.4
茶叶	Tea	99.6	100.4	100.5	100.0	99.6	100.1	100.2	100.0	100.0	100.3	100.0	100.4
（2）饮料	Beverages	100.1	100.1	101.0	100.1	100.2	100.3	100.0	100.3	99.9	100.0	100.0	100.4
固体饮料	Solid Beverages	100.0	100.3	99.9	99.8	100.3	100.2	100.0	99.9	99.9	100.1	100.0	99.8
液体饮料	Liquid Beverages	100.1	100.1	100.8	100.2	100.1	99.8	100.1	100.3	100.0	100.0	100.0	100.5
冷冻饮品	Frozen Beverages	100.2	100.0	102.7	100.1	100.2	101.4	99.9	100.7	99.9	100.1	99.9	100.9
12.干鲜瓜果	Dried and Fresh Melons and Fruits	107.6	106.0	101.3	108.3	104.9	92.2	83.3	87.5	96.7	101.9	103.2	105.3
鲜瓜果	Fresh Fruits	109.0	107.6	101.4	110.2	105.9	90.5	79.5	83.7	95.5	101.8	103.5	106.9
干（坚）果	Dried Fruits	102.4	100.0	100.8	100.4	100.4	100.5	100.0	100.6	100.2	102.2	102.1	100.9
13.糕点饼干面包	Cake,Biscuit and Bread	100.0	99.9	99.9	100.1	100.1	100.0	100.2	100.2	100.0	99.9	99.9	101.0
糕点	Cake	99.9	100.0	99.8	99.9	100.0	99.9	100.1	99.7	100.0	99.7	100.2	101.2
饼干	Biscuit	100.1	99.9	99.9	100.4	100.3	100.1	100.5	100.9	99.8	99.9	99.6	101.1
面包	Bread	100.3	99.8	100.0	100.0	100.0	99.9	100.3	100.2	100.1	100.4	99.6	100.3
14.液体乳及乳制品	Liquid Milk and Their Products	99.8	100.0	100.4	100.2	100.0	100.2	100.1	100.4	101.0	100.0	99.9	100.8
巴氏杀菌奶或消毒奶	Pasteurization Milk or Disinfection Milk	99.6	100.0	100.7	100.0	100.0	100.2	100.2	100.4	101.0	100.1	99.9	101.2
酸奶	Leben	100.1	100.0	100.1	100.7	100.2	100.1	99.7	100.0	101.1	100.0	99.7	99.6

7-16 续表 2 continued

商品类别及品名	Commodity Category and Commodity Name	1月 January	2月 February	3月 March	4月 April	5月 May	6月 June	7月 July	8月 August	9月 September	10月 October	11月 November	12月 December
		(以上月价格为100)											
奶粉	Milk Powder	100.1	100.1	99.9	100.4	99.8	100.0	100.4	100.8	100.0	99.8	100.2	101.1
其他	Others	100.0	100.0	99.9	100.0	100.0	100.0	100.0	100.0	102.2	99.7	100.1	99.8
15.在外用膳食品	Outward Dinner	100.3	100.0	100.1	100.0	100.1	100.3	100.0	100.1	100.0	99.9	100.7	102.0
主食	Staple Food	100.1	99.7	100.1	99.9	100.0	100.3	100.0	100.1	100.1	100.0	101.8	103.9
炒菜	Hot Dish	100.3	100.2	100.1	100.0	100.0	100.4	99.9	100.0	100.1	99.9	100.1	101.0
地方小吃	Local Snack	100.3	99.9	100.2	100.1	100.6	100.2	100.4	100.7	99.7	99.5	100.1	101.9
16.其他食品	Other Foods	99.9	99.9	100.2	100.1	100.1	100.1	100.1	100.0	100.1	99.7	99.9	100.6
其他食品	Other Foods	99.9	99.9	100.2	100.1	100.1	100.1	100.1	100.0	100.1	99.7	99.9	100.6
二、烟酒及用品	**Tobacco,Liquor and Their Appliances**	**100.1**	**100.0**	**100.1**	**100.3**	**100.0**	**100.1**	**100.1**	**100.3**	**100.1**	**100.1**	**100.1**	**100.9**
1.烟草	Tobacco	100.3	100.2	100.0	100.3	100.0	99.9	99.9	100.0	99.9	100.0	100.0	100.6
国产卷烟	Domestic Cigarette	100.3	100.3	100.0	100.4	100.1	99.9	99.9	100.0	99.9	100.0	100.0	100.7
进口卷烟	Import Cigarette	100.0	98.8	100.0	100.1	99.6	100.0	99.7	100.1	100.0	99.9	100.6	100.2
其他	Others	100.0	100.0	100.0	100.0	100.0	100.0	100.0	100.0	100.0	100.0	100.0	100.0
2.酒	Liquor	100.0	99.8	100.2	100.3	100.0	100.2	100.3	100.5	100.3	100.1	100.1	101.2
白酒	White Spirit	100.1	99.6	100.3	100.3	100.0	100.3	100.2	100.7	100.1	100.2	100.1	101.6
葡萄酒	Grape	100.9	100.1	100.0	100.2	100.0	101.2	100.5	100.0	100.2	100.1	100.3	100.1
啤酒	Beer	99.6	100.1	100.0	100.3	99.8	100.0	100.4	100.3	100.6	99.8	100.0	100.5
其他	Others	100.0	100.0	100.0	100.1	100.0	100.1	100.2	100.0	100.0	100.0	100.0	100.1
3.吸烟、饮酒用品	Appliances For Smoking and Drinking	100.0	100.0	100.0	100.1	100.1	100.0	100.0	100.0	99.7	100.2	100.0	99.7
吸烟用品	Appliances for Smoking	100.1	100.0	100.0	100.1	100.0	100.0	100.0	100.0	99.9	100.3	100.0	99.8
饮酒用品	Appliances For Drinking	100.0	99.9	100.0	100.1	100.1	100.1	100.0	100.0	99.6	100.1	100.0	99.7
三、衣着	**Clothing**	**99.2**	**98.9**	**99.6**	**99.6**	**99.5**	**100.0**	**99.4**	**99.5**	**100.1**	**100.7**	**100.6**	**100.1**
1.服装	Garments	98.9	98.6	99.3	99.6	99.5	100.0	99.7	99.5	100.1	101.1	100.8	100.2
(1)男式服装	Men's Garments	98.6	98.8	99.2	99.6	99.3	99.9	99.7	99.5	100.2	101.2	100.9	100.2
大衣	Topcoat	98.2	98.1	99.1	98.7	99.9	99.3	99.9	100.0	99.9	99.8	99.9	100.9
毛线衣	Woollen Sweater	99.6	95.8	96.2	99.4	98.2	99.8	99.8	99.6	100.6	102.0	100.7	101.0
夹克衫	Jacket	98.6	99.1	98.9	99.6	99.9	99.9	99.8	100.0	99.9	102.1	101.8	100.2
衬衫	Shirt	97.0	99.2	100.1	99.5	99.4	100.5	98.9	99.2	100.4	100.8	100.1	101.0
T恤衫	T-shirt	99.9	100.5	99.7	100.0	99.0	98.4	97.8	98.6	100.7	100.4	100.8	100.1
裤子	Trousers	97.8	97.7	99.9	99.7	99.6	99.7	99.7	99.6	99.4	102.5	100.6	99.5
西服	Western-style Clothes	98.8	100.3	99.0	100.3	99.6	99.9	100.4	98.4	101.1	101.2	100.2	99.8
运动衫裤	Gym Suit	98.9	100.0	100.0	99.7	96.7	100.2	99.6	100.5	100.0	100.5	101.3	100.5
内衣	Underwaist	99.4	99.8	100.4	99.7	99.6	100.2	99.7	100.2	99.8	100.4	100.1	99.9
羽绒衣	Eider Down Outerwear	98.2	98.1	99.5	98.4	100.0	100.0	99.6	99.7	99.5	102.2	103.9	99.1
其他	Others	99.2	98.9	99.1	99.5	100.3	100.0	99.9	99.6	100.0	100.0	102.8	100.0
(2)女式服装	Women's Garments	99.1	98.1	99.3	99.4	99.4	100.1	99.8	99.5	100.3	101.1	100.8	100.2
大衣	Topcoat	97.7	93.5	98.3	99.3	99.9	100.0	99.9	100.0	99.7	100.0	100.8	102.8
毛线衣	Woollen Sweater	99.1	93.9	97.9	99.7	97.8	100.3	100.0	100.0	100.8	102.0	101.0	101.2
羽绒衣	Eider Down Outerwear	98.6	98.8	99.3	99.9	100.0	99.8	99.8	99.8	99.5	102.6	103.1	99.3
套装	Coordinates	99.3	99.6	100.0	98.1	100.4	99.2	100.3	98.3	102.6	101.0	99.5	100.2
衬衫	Shirt	98.1	100.9	100.4	98.6	99.8	100.2	100.5	98.5	99.7	100.4	99.8	98.8

7-16 续表 3 continued

商品类别及品名	Commodity Category and Commodity Name	1月 January	2月 February	3月 March	4月 April	5月 May	6月 June	7月 July	8月 August	9月 September	10月 October	11月 November	12月 December
		（以上月价格为100）											
T恤衫	T-shirt	100.0	100.3	99.7	99.5	99.4	100.5	98.7	99.4	101.4	103.7	100.3	99.9
裙子	Skirt	99.6	99.5	99.7	99.2	100.3	100.5	99.6	99.5	99.6	100.3	100.6	99.6
裤子	Trousers	100.1	98.3	98.9	99.4	99.4	100.1	99.4	99.8	100.3	99.9	101.1	99.4
运动衫裤	Gym Suit	99.9	100.5	99.1	100.5	96.0	100.3	99.8	99.9	99.9	101.6	99.9	101.2
内衣	Underwaist	99.1	99.5	100.8	100.7	100.2	100.3	99.8	100.0	100.8	100.7	101.1	100.0
其他	Others	99.7	99.7	100.3	100.5	99.7	100.1	100.0	100.3	99.8	100.4	100.4	99.9
（3）儿童服装	Children's Garments	99.5	99.4	99.8	100.2	100.5	100.0	99.4	99.6	99.3	100.4	100.5	100.0
套装	Coordinates	99.6	99.5	99.6	100.2	99.4	99.7	100.1	99.7	99.7	100.3	100.6	100.0
裤子	Trousers	99.3	99.2	99.8	99.8	101.1	100.0	99.0	100.0	100.0	100.9	100.6	100.3
裙子	Skirt	99.5	99.8	100.4	100.8	101.8	100.6	98.7	99.1	97.9	100.0	100.1	99.8
其他	Others	98.8	98.1	98.9	99.3	99.9	100.3	99.9	100.0	99.4	100.0	100.4	99.7
2.衣着材料	Clothing Materials	100.1	100.0	99.8	100.0	100.4	100.0	100.1	100.0	99.7	100.4	100.1	100.2
棉布	Cotton Cloth	100.0	100.0	100.0	100.2	100.7	100.0	100.1	100.1	99.7	100.4	100.0	100.0
棉混纺布	Cotton Textiles Cloth	100.2	100.2	100.0	100.0	100.0	100.0	100.1	100.1	99.8	100.4	100.3	100.1
化纤布	Chemical Fiber Cloth	100.1	100.2	99.9	100.0	100.8	100.1	100.1	99.9	99.6	100.6	100.2	100.1
毛线	Knitting Wool	100.0	99.4	99.4	100.0	100.0	100.0	100.0	100.0	99.9	100.1	100.0	100.6
3.鞋袜帽	Shoes,Socks and Hats	99.3	99.3	100.3	99.6	99.3	99.9	98.3	99.0	100.3	100.0	100.2	99.6
（1）鞋	Shoes	99.2	99.2	100.4	99.5	99.2	99.9	98.0	98.8	100.4	100.0	100.3	99.5
男鞋	Men's Shoes	99.2	99.4	100.8	99.7	99.2	100.4	97.7	99.3	100.2	99.9	100.3	99.7
女鞋	Women's Shoes	99.1	98.9	100.3	99.2	98.8	99.7	97.6	98.2	100.8	99.9	100.3	99.3
童鞋	Children's Shoes	99.6	99.7	99.8	100.1	100.3	99.7	99.7	99.7	99.6	100.3	100.2	100.0
（2）袜子	Socks	99.8	99.9	99.6	100.3	99.7	100.0	99.9	100.0	99.8	100.3	99.4	99.9
男袜	Men's Socks	99.7	99.8	99.9	100.2	99.8	99.9	99.9	100.0	99.8	100.2	99.0	99.7
女袜	Women's Socks	99.8	99.9	99.4	100.4	99.6	100.1	99.9	100.0	99.7	100.3	99.8	100.0
（3）帽子	Hats	100.0	99.7	99.9	100.0	100.1	100.0	100.0	100.0	99.9	100.3	100.4	100.0
男帽	Men's Hats	99.8	99.8	99.7	100.0	100.2	100.1	100.0	100.0	99.8	100.2	100.9	100.0
女帽	Women's Hats	100.1	99.7	100.0	100.0	99.9	100.0	100.0	100.0	99.9	100.4	100.1	100.0
4.衣着加工服务费	Clothing Manufacturing Services	100.1	99.8	100.0	99.9	100.0	100.0	100.0	100.1	100.0	100.0	100.0	101.3
缝纫	Sewing	100.1	99.6	100.0	100.0	100.0	100.0	100.0	100.0	100.0	100.0	100.0	102.0
清洗	Washing	100.0	100.1	100.0	99.8	100.0	100.0	100.1	100.1	100.0	100.0	100.0	100.0
四、家庭设备用品及维修服务	**Household Facilities, Articles and Services**	**100.1**	**100.0**	**100.0**	**100.1**	**100.0**	**100.7**	**100.2**	**100.2**	**100.0**	**100.3**	**100.1**	**100.3**
1.耐用消费品	Durable Consumer Goods	100.0	99.9	100.0	100.1	100.2	101.3	100.5	100.1	100.0	100.4	100.1	100.1
（1）家具	Furniture	100.0	99.9	100.0	100.2	99.9	100.1	100.0	100.1	100.2	100.7	100.2	100.1
柜	Cabinet	100.0	99.8	99.9	99.9	100.1	100.1	99.9	100.2	100.1	100.8	100.1	100.1
床	Bed	100.1	100.1	100.0	100.7	99.9	100.0	100.1	100.1	100.1	100.8	100.0	100.1
桌	Desk	99.9	100.1	99.9	100.0	99.8	99.9	99.8	99.9	99.9	100.5	100.4	100.3
椅	Chair	99.9	99.2	100.1	99.9	100.0	100.0	99.9	100.1	100.6	101.0	100.1	99.9
沙发	Sofa	100.1	100.0	100.0	100.5	99.8	100.2	100.0	100.1	100.1	100.6	100.4	100.0
其他	Others	100.2	100.0	100.1	99.8	99.7	100.6	100.4	100.1	100.5	100.3	100.0	100.1
（2）家庭设备	Household Appliances	100.0	100.0	100.1	100.0	100.3	102.1	100.7	100.1	99.8	100.2	100.1	100.1
洗衣机	Washing Machine	99.7	100.2	100.0	99.3	100.4	100.8	100.6	100.0	100.1	100.1	100.0	100.0

7-16 续表 4 continued

（以上月价格为100）

商品类别及品名	Commodity Category and Commodity Name	1月 January	2月 February	3月 March	4月 April	5月 May	6月 June	7月 July	8月 August	9月 September	10月 October	11月 November	12月 December
电风扇	Electric Fan	99.7	99.3	100.0	100.8	100.4	100.7	101.0	100.1	99.7	100.1	100.0	101.3
电冰箱（柜）	Refrigerator	100.0	99.8	100.2	100.4	100.8	102.2	101.1	99.9	99.9	100.5	99.8	100.0
吸排油烟机	Kitchen Ventilato	100.1	99.9	99.8	100.0	99.8	101.9	101.4	100.7	99.6	99.9	100.2	100.5
空调器	Air-conditioning	100.1	100.2	100.0	99.8	100.6	104.3	100.9	100.3	99.6	100.1	100.2	100.1
热水器	Water Heater	100.2	100.3	100.5	99.8	99.5	100.4	100.0	99.7	100.3	100.1	100.1	99.5
微波炉	Microwave Oven	100.0	99.6	100.1	99.5	99.9	100.4	100.0	100.0	99.9	100.1	100.4	99.4
电炊具	Electric Cooking Appliance	100.3	100.0	99.9	100.5	100.1	100.2	100.0	100.1	99.7	100.2	100.0	100.2
2.室内装饰品	Interior Decorations	100.0	100.0	100.0	99.9	99.7	99.9	100.0	100.1	100.0	100.2	100.1	100.1
纺织装饰品	Textile Process Decorations	100.0	100.0	100.0	99.9	100.0	99.7	99.8	100.2	99.9	100.4	100.0	100.0
装饰灯具	Architectural Lamps and Lanterns	100.0	100.0	100.0	99.9	99.3	100.0	100.4	99.9	100.4	100.0	99.8	100.2
其他	Others	100.0	100.0	99.9	99.9	100.0	100.0	99.8	100.7	99.8	100.2	100.8	100.0
3.床上用品	Bedclothes	99.4	100.6	100.2	100.2	99.4	100.3	99.8	99.8	100.0	100.3	100.0	100.6
毛毯	Woollen Blanket	99.8	99.9	100.2	100.6	98.8	100.4	99.5	99.8	100.3	100.9	99.6	101.7
被子	Quilt	99.4	100.4	100.1	99.9	99.5	100.5	99.7	99.6	99.9	99.8	100.2	100.5
床上套件	Bed Articles	99.0	100.7	100.3	100.1	99.6	100.3	100.0	100.0	99.9	100.3	100.2	100.0
其他	Others	99.9	102.1	100.2	100.1	99.7	99.8	100.0	100.0	99.9	100.1	100.1	100.1
4.日用杂品	Sundry Articles	100.1	100.0	100.1	100.1	100.1	99.9	99.7	100.3	100.2	100.3	100.0	100.6
茶具	Tea Set	100.0	100.0	100.1	100.3	99.7	101.8	100.0	100.0	101.3	102.4	99.8	100.2
餐具	Tableware	100.0	100.0	99.7	100.0	100.4	100.1	98.0	100.4	100.0	100.1	100.0	100.2
厨具	Kitchen Utensils	100.2	100.0	100.0	101.1	100.0	99.3	100.1	100.1	100.8	100.0	100.1	100.6
家用手工工具	Domestic Handwork Tools	100.0	100.0	100.0	100.0	99.9	100.4	100.2	100.2	100.0	100.0	99.7	102.0
洗涤用品	Washing Articles	100.3	100.1	100.0	99.9	100.1	99.4	100.0	100.4	99.8	100.1	100.1	100.7
其他	Others	100.0	100.0	100.3	100.0	100.1	99.7	99.9	100.4	100.0	100.2	100.0	100.5
5.家庭服务及加工维修服务	Household Service and Manufacturing Upkeep	102.0	99.3	100.0	100.0	100.0	100.1	100.3	101.7	100.3	100.2	101.0	101.1
家庭服务	Household Service	104.1	98.5	100.0	100.0	100.0	100.0	100.5	102.9	100.7	100.3	101.5	100.6
加工维修服务	Manufacturing Upkeep	100.0	100.0	100.0	100.0	100.0	100.2	100.1	100.4	100.0	100.0	100.6	101.6
五、医疗保健和个人用品	**Health Care and Personal Articles**	**100.1**	**100.2**	**100.0**	**100.1**	**100.4**	**100.1**	**100.0**	**100.1**	**100.0**	**100.0**	**100.0**	**100.1**
1.医疗保健	Health Care	99.9	100.1	99.9	100.0	100.1	100.1	100.0	100.0	100.1	99.9	100.1	100.1
（1）医疗器具及用品	Medical Facilities and Goods	97.9	100.5	99.7	99.6	99.7	100.0	100.0	100.0	100.7	98.0	100.0	98.8
医疗器具及用品	Medical Facilities and Goods	97.9	100.5	99.7	99.6	99.7	100.0	100.0	100.0	100.7	98.0	100.0	98.8
（2）中药材及中成药	Herbs and Ready-made Traditional Chinese Medicine	100.2	100.5	99.5	100.1	100.0	100.5	99.8	100.2	100.2	101.0	100.3	100.2
中药材	Herbs	100.4	100.9	98.8	100.4	100.8	101.2	99.7	100.1	100.6	101.5	100.5	100.2
中成药	Ready-made Traditional Chinese Medicine	100.0	100.1	100.4	99.8	99.3	99.9	99.9	100.4	99.7	100.4	100.0	100.2
（3）西药	Western Medicine	99.9	100.0	99.9	100.1	100.3	99.8	100.1	99.9	100.0	99.4	100.0	100.2
抗微生物药	Anti-microorganism Medicine	100.0	100.0	100.1	100.0	100.1	100.3	101.3	99.6	100.2	98.5	100.2	100.4

7-16 续表 5 continued

商品类别及品名	Commodity Category and Commodity Name	1月 January	2月 February	3月 March	4月 April	5月 May	6月 June	7月 July	8月 August	9月 September	10月 October	11月 November	12月 December
		（以上月价格为100）											
消化系统用药	Alimentary System Medicine	99.9	100.2	100.2	100.1	100.2	100.0	100.0	100.0	99.9	100.0	99.6	100.4
呼吸系统用药	Respiratory System Medicine	99.1	100.0	100.1	100.4	99.9	100.6	100.0	100.0	100.8	99.5	100.3	100.0
解热镇痛及非甾体抗炎药	Allays a Fever the Analgesia and the Non-steroid Body Anti-in flammatory Agent	101.6	99.9	99.6	99.9	100.4	98.9	99.6	100.0	99.7	100.6	100.1	100.7
抗肿瘤药	Antineoplastic Drug	99.2	99.9	99.8	99.9	102.9	97.9	100.1	99.4	99.0	99.6	100.4	100.0
激素及调节内分泌功能药	Hormone and Adjustment Internal Secretion Function Medicine	99.5	100.2	99.8	100.0	100.0	99.8	99.1	100.0	100.6	97.6	100.5	99.2
循环系统用药	Circulating System Medicine	99.3	99.9	100.0	100.0	100.0	100.4	99.7	99.9	100.4	100.6	99.1	100.5
神经系统用药	Nerve System Medicine	100.1	100.3	99.8	100.4	100.0	99.8	100.0	99.8	100.4	98.1	100.0	100.5
专科用药	Junior Medicine	99.3	99.8	100.3	100.0	100.1	100.3	99.8	100.0	98.8	98.0	100.2	99.7
其他	Others	100.0	100.0	99.5	100.0	99.6	99.9	100.0	100.0	100.0	99.3	99.8	99.9
（4）保健品及器具	Healthcare Equipment	99.4	99.7	99.9	100.2	100.0	100.2	99.8	100.1	100.2	99.7	100.2	99.9
保健器具	Health Protection Equipment	99.9	99.5	99.9	100.1	99.9	100.5	99.9	100.0	100.0	99.4	100.1	99.7
滋补保健用品	Tonic and Health Products	99.2	99.8	99.9	100.3	100.0	100.0	99.8	100.2	100.3	99.8	100.3	100.0
（5）医疗保健服务	Health Care Services	100.0	100.0	100.0	100.0	100.0	100.1	100.1	100.0	100.0	99.9	100.1	100.1
挂号费	Registration	100.1	100.1	100.1	100.0	100.0	100.0	100.1	100.0	100.0	100.0	100.0	100.0
注射费	Injection Expenses	100.0	100.0	100.0	100.0	100.0	100.0	100.0	100.0	100.0	100.0	100.0	100.0
检查费	Examination Expense	100.0	100.1	100.0	100.0	100.0	100.1	100.0	100.0	100.4	100.0	100.1	100.0
手术费	Operation Expenses	100.1	100.0	100.0	100.0	100.0	100.0	100.0	100.0	100.0	100.0	100.0	100.5
住院费	Hospitalization Expenses	100.0	100.0	100.0	99.8	100.0	100.5	100.5	100.0	99.8	99.3	100.4	100.1
理疗费	Physiotherapy Expenses	100.0	100.0	100.0	100.0	100.0	100.0	100.0	100.0	100.0	100.0	100.0	100.0
化验费	Analysis Expenses	100.0	100.0	100.1	100.0	100.0	100.0	100.0	100.0	100.0	99.9	100.0	100.0
其他	Others	100.0	100.0	100.0	100.0	100.0	100.0	100.0	100.0	100.0	100.0	100.0	100.0
2.个人用品及服务	Personal Articles and Services	100.4	100.3	100.2	100.4	100.8	100.0	99.9	100.2	99.9	100.2	99.9	100.1
（1）化妆美容用品	Cosmetics	99.8	100.1	100.0	100.0	100.0	100.0	99.8	100.2	99.7	100.4	99.7	100.0
化妆美容器具	Cosmetics Appliances	99.9	100.0	100.1	100.1	100.1	100.2	100.0	100.3	99.7	100.1	100.0	100.0
美容化妆品	Facial Beautifiers	99.8	100.1	100.0	100.1	100.0	99.9	100.2	100.0	100.0	100.1	100.1	100.2
护肤品	Protects Skin Products	99.8	100.1	99.9	100.1	100.1	99.9	100.0	100.2	98.6	101.5	99.3	99.6
护发美容品	Protects Sends the Beauty Products	99.7	100.0	99.8	100.0	99.9	100.1	99.0	100.6	99.9	100.2	99.2	100.0
（2）清洁化妆用品	Cleaning Toiletware	100.1	100.0	100.0	100.0	100.2	100.2	99.8	100.3	99.7	100.2	100.0	100.3
洗发用品	Hairdressing Articles	99.9	100.0	100.1	99.9	99.9	100.4	99.7	100.2	99.3	100.7	99.7	99.2
洗浴用品	Bathing Articles	100.3	100.0	99.9	100.1	100.1	100.1	99.8	100.4	99.9	99.9	100.2	100.1
其他	Others	100.0	100.2	100.2	100.1	101.0	100.2	99.8	100.0	99.9	100.0	100.2	103.0

7-16 续表 6 continued

商品类别及品名	Commodity Category and Commodity Name	（以上月价格为100）											
		1月 January	2月 February	3月 March	4月 April	5月 May	6月 June	7月 July	8月 August	9月 September	10月 October	11月 November	12月 December
（3）个人饰品	Personal Decoraions	100.9	101.0	100.9	101.6	103.4	99.9	100.0	100.3	100.0	100.1	100.0	100.0
首饰	Ornaments	102.3	102.2	101.9	104.2	107.4	100.0	100.4	100.6	99.9	99.9	99.9	100.2
皮件	Leather Appliance	99.8	100.1	100.2	97.7	99.5	100.0	98.9	100.7	100.0	100.6	99.7	99.5
手表	Watch	99.8	99.9	100.0	99.9	100.0	99.4	99.8	100.0	100.1	100.4	100.1	100.4
领带	Necktie	99.7	99.9	99.8	100.5	99.8	99.8	99.7	99.5	100.7	100.0	100.1	99.3
其他	Others	99.6	100.0	100.3	99.9	100.1	100.0	100.0	100.2	99.8	100.2	100.0	100.2
（4）个人服务	Personal Services	100.8	100.1	100.0	100.0	99.9	100.0	100.0	100.0	100.1	100.0	100.0	100.3
美容	Cosmetology	100.7	100.0	100.0	100.0	100.0	100.0	100.0	100.0	100.0	100.0	100.0	100.0
理（烫）发	Haircut(permanent wave)	101.0	100.2	100.0	100.0	100.0	100.0	100.0	100.0	100.2	100.0	100.0	100.5
洗浴	Bathe	101.0	100.0	100.0	100.0	99.6	100.0	100.0	100.0	100.0	100.0	100.3	100.4
其他	Others	100.0	100.0	100.0	100.0	100.0	100.0	100.0	100.0	100.0	100.0	100.0	100.0
六、交通和通信	**Transportation and Communication**	**99.9**	**100.1**	**99.6**	**99.8**	**100.1**	**100.2**	**99.9**	**99.8**	**99.8**	**99.8**	**100.1**	**100.0**
1.交通	Transportation	100.1	100.5	99.7	100.3	100.5	100.8	100.1	100.1	99.9	100.0	100.0	99.9
（1）交通工具	Transportation Facility	99.8	100.4	99.9	99.6	99.7	99.6	99.6	99.8	99.6	99.9	99.8	99.6
摩托车	Motorcycle	99.6	101.7	100.0	100.0	100.2	100.1	99.8	100.1	100.1	100.0	99.9	99.6
自行车	Bicycle	100.0	100.0	99.7	99.5	99.9	99.4	99.1	99.9	100.1	100.1	100.0	100.2
轿车	Car	99.6	100.0	99.9	99.8	99.3	99.3	99.9	99.5	98.8	99.9	99.5	99.1
其他	Others	100.0	100.0	100.0	98.0	99.1	100.0	99.8	100.0	100.0	99.0	100.0	100.0
（2）车用燃料及零配件	Fuels and Parts	99.9	100.0	100.6	103.3	102.2	104.6	100.5	100.0	100.1	100.2	100.1	100.0
汽油	Gasoline	100.0	100.0	100.6	104.9	102.9	106.2	100.3	100.0	100.1	100.0	100.0	100.0
柴油	Diesel Oil	100.0	100.0	100.8	102.8	103.0	105.5	100.5	100.0	100.1	100.4	100.2	100.1
零配件	Parts	99.8	100.0	100.2	100.4	100.0	100.0	101.1	100.1	100.3	100.4	100.1	99.9
其他	Others	100.1	99.8	100.7	101.7	99.3	101.3	100.0	100.5	100.2	99.7	100.0	100.0
（3）车辆使用及维修费	Using and Upkeep Fare	99.9	99.3	100.4	99.8	100.3	100.2	100.1	100.5	100.0	99.8	99.8	100.4
驾驶证	Driving License	99.8	99.9	99.3	98.8	101.8	100.8	100.4	100.6	100.0	99.2	99.1	99.2
保险费	Insurance Expenses	100.0	100.0	99.9	100.0	100.0	100.0	99.9	100.3	100.1	100.0	100.0	100.0
停车费	Parking Expenses	100.0	100.0	100.0	100.0	100.0	100.0	100.0	103.8	100.0	100.0	100.0	100.0
车辆修理服务费	Vehicle Upkeep Service Fare	99.9	98.4	101.5	100.0	100.0	100.1	100.0	100.0	100.0	100.0	100.0	101.5
其他	Others	100.0	100.0	100.0	100.1	100.0	100.0	100.0	99.8	100.0	100.0	100.0	100.0
（4）市区公共交通费	Incity Traffic Fare	100.2	100.3	100.0	100.0	101.3	100.1	101.2	100.3	100.0	100.0	100.4	100.1
公共汽车票	Bus Ticket	100.8	100.6	100.0	100.0	100.0	100.0	100.4	100.0	100.0	100.0	100.0	100.1
出租汽车	Taxi	99.6	100.1	100.0	100.0	102.7	100.2	102.1	100.4	100.0	100.1	100.7	100.0
其他	Others	100.0	100.0	100.0	100.2	100.0	100.0	100.0	102.0	100.0	100.0	100.0	99.8
（5）城市间交通费	Intercity Traffic Fare	101.3	102.0	98.3	100.1	100.5	101.1	100.0	100.2	100.2	100.0	100.3	100.0
飞机票	Airplane Ticket	104.5	97.1	100.1	103.4	102.4	97.2	100.1	101.8	100.9	100.7	99.5	100.0
火车票	Train Ticket	101.2	99.5	99.8	100.0	100.0	100.0	100.0	100.0	100.1	100.0	100.1	100.0
长途汽车	Intertown Bus	101.2	103.2	97.6	100.0	100.0	101.7	100.0	100.1	100.2	100.0	100.4	100.0
其他	Others	101.4	100.5	99.0	100.0	109.6	100.4	100.0	100.1	100.0	100.0	100.0	100.0
2.通信	Communication	99.6	99.5	99.4	99.2	99.5	99.6	99.7	99.5	99.7	99.5	100.2	100.0
（1）通信工具	Communication Facility	98.8	98.6	98.0	97.4	98.4	98.6	98.9	98.1	98.8	98.4	99.1	98.6
固定电话机	Telephone	99.4	99.4	99.0	99.7	98.6	100.0	99.8	99.8	100.0	99.9	100.0	99.5
移动电话机	Mobile Phone	98.5	98.1	97.4	96.1	98.2	97.9	98.4	97.1	98.1	97.3	98.5	98.0
其他	Others	99.6	99.0	99.0	99.5	99.5	99.7	99.6	99.7	99.9	99.9	99.9	100.0

7-16 续表 7 continued

商品类别及品名	Commodity Category and Commodity Name	（以上月价格为100）											
		1月 January	2月 February	3月 March	4月 April	5月 May	6月 June	7月 July	8月 August	9月 September	10月 October	11月 November	12月 December
（2）通信服务	Communication Service	100.0	100.0	100.0	100.0	100.0	100.0	100.0	100.0	100.0	100.0	100.7	100.6
移动通信费	Mobile Communication Fee	100.0	100.0	100.0	100.0	100.0	100.0	100.0	100.0	100.0	100.0	100.0	100.0
市内电话费	Incity Telephone Fee	100.0	100.0	100.0	100.0	100.0	100.0	100.0	100.0	100.0	100.0	100.0	100.0
长途电话费	Long Distance Call Fee	100.0	100.0	100.0	100.0	100.0	100.0	100.0	100.0	100.0	100.0	100.0	100.0
月租费	Month Hiring Fee	100.0	100.0	100.0	100.0	100.0	100.0	100.0	100.0	100.0	100.0	100.0	100.0
上网费	Net Play Fee	100.0	99.8	100.0	100.0	100.0	100.0	100.0	100.0	100.0	100.0	100.0	100.0
信件邮寄	Letter Post	100.0	100.0	100.0	100.0	100.0	100.0	100.0	100.0	100.0	100.0	115.5	111.4
包裹邮寄	Package Post	100.0	100.0	100.0	100.0	100.0	100.0	100.0	100.0	100.0	100.0	100.5	100.0
其他	Others	100.0	100.0	100.0	100.0	100.0	100.0	100.0	100.0	100.0	100.0	100.0	100.0
七、娱乐教育文化用品及服务	**Recreation,Education and Culture Articles**	**100.1**	**99.8**	**99.9**	**100.5**	**99.9**	**99.7**	**100.2**	**100.2**	**99.8**	**100.0**	**99.7**	**100.0**
1.文娱用耐用消费品及服务	Durable Consumer Goods For Cultural and Recreational Use and Service	99.5	99.6	99.8	99.5	99.8	99.7	99.8	99.5	99.3	99.7	99.8	99.7
电视机	Television	99.2	99.3	99.8	99.0	100.1	99.7	99.7	99.3	99.3	99.4	99.8	100.1
激光视盘机	Laser Video Disc Machine	99.7	99.0	99.9	99.8	99.6	100.3	100.1	99.9	99.5	99.4	99.6	97.5
摄像机	Pickup Camera	99.7	99.7	99.4	99.5	99.8	99.2	99.6	100.0	99.2	99.9	99.7	99.6
照相机	Camera	97.7	99.6	99.3	99.3	99.9	100.3	99.9	100.0	100.4	99.9	100.2	99.3
家用音响	Acoustic Equipment	100.2	99.7	99.7	99.1	99.8	100.0	100.3	100.0	99.8	100.0	100.0	99.4
便携式音响	Portable Acoustics	99.9	99.6	99.8	99.9	100.0	100.0	100.0	99.9	99.9	100.0	100.0	99.8
电脑	Computer	99.6	99.9	99.9	99.9	99.4	99.4	99.6	99.1	98.8	100.0	99.8	99.8
修理服务	Repair Service	103.0	100.0	99.9	100.0	100.0	99.9	100.6	100.0	100.1	100.1	100.0	100.0
其他	Others	100.0	101.5	99.8	99.8	99.8	100.0	99.8	99.7	98.2	100.3	99.7	100.0
2.教育	Education	100.0	100.1	100.0	100.2	100.0	100.0	100.0	100.1	100.3	100.0	100.0	100.0
（1）教材及参考书	Teaching Material and Reference Books	100.0	100.0	100.1	100.1	100.0	99.9	100.0	100.5	99.9	99.9	100.0	100.0
工具书	Tool Book	99.9	100.0	100.0	100.0	100.0	100.0	100.0	100.0	100.0	100.0	100.0	100.1
教材	Teaching Material	100.0	100.0	100.2	100.1	100.0	100.0	100.0	100.5	99.0	99.7	100.0	100.0
参考书	Reference Book	100.0	100.0	100.1	100.0	100.0	99.8	100.0	101.2	101.5	100.0	100.0	100.0
教育软件	Educational Software	100.0	100.0	99.9	100.0	100.0	100.0	100.0	100.0	100.0	100.0	100.0	100.0
（2）学杂托幼费	Tuition and Child Care	100.0	100.1	100.0	100.2	100.0	100.0	100.0	100.1	100.3	100.0	100.0	100.0
义务教育杂费	Incidental Expenses of Compulcory Education	100.0	100.0	100.0	100.0	100.0	100.0	100.0	100.0	100.0	100.0	100.0	100.0
非义务教育学杂费	Tuition of Non-compulsory Education	100.0	100.0	100.0	100.0	100.0	100.0	100.0	100.0	100.7	100.0	100.0	100.0
技能培训学费	Skill Train Tuition	100.0	100.0	100.0	99.1	100.0	100.0	100.0	100.0	99.8	100.0	100.0	100.0
托幼费	Child care	100.0	101.1	100.0	102.2	100.0	100.0	100.0	100.5	100.1	100.0	100.0	100.4
其他	Others	100.0	100.0	100.0	101.7	100.0	100.0	100.0	100.0	100.8	100.0	100.0	100.0
3.文化娱乐类	Recreation and Culture	100.6	99.8	100.0	101.6	100.1	99.6	100.5	100.0	99.5	100.6	99.7	100.1
（1）文化娱乐用品	Culture Articles	100.1	99.8	99.9	99.9	100.0	100.0	99.9	100.0	99.9	100.1	100.0	100.0
乐器	Musical Instrument	100.2	100.0	100.0	100.0	100.0	100.1	100.0	99.8	100.1	100.2	99.8	99.9
音响光盘和磁带	Audio,Disk and Tape	100.0	99.2	99.8	100.1	100.1	100.0	100.0	100.0	99.9	100.1	100.0	100.0
照相胶卷和存储卡	Roll Film and Memorizing Card	100.1	100.0	100.0	99.7	99.9	99.9	100.0	99.8	99.7	99.4	100.4	100.1
录像磁带和视盘	Video Tape and Disk	100.0	99.9	100.0	100.1	99.8	100.2	99.4	100.0	100.0	100.1	99.8	100.0
儿童玩具	Children's Toy	100.0	100.0	99.5	99.6	100.1	100.1	100.1	99.8	99.8	100.1	100.0	100.0

7-16 续表 8 continued

商品类别及品名	Commodity Category and Commodity Name	（以上月价格为100）											
		1月 January	2月 February	3月 March	4月 April	5月 May	6月 June	7月 July	8月 August	9月 September	10月 October	11月 November	12月 December
纸张本册	Paper and Volume	100.6	99.5	100.0	100.0	100.0	100.3	100.0	100.6	100.1	100.3	100.0	100.1
文具	Stationery	100.1	100.1	100.0	99.9	100.0	99.7	99.5	100.0	99.7	100.1	100.0	100.0
体育用品	Sports Goods	99.6	100.0	100.0	100.0	99.9	99.7	100.2	100.1	99.8	100.2	99.7	100.0
其他	Others	100.0	100.0	100.0	99.9	100.0	99.8	100.1	100.0	99.5	100.4	100.0	100.0
（2）书报杂志	Books,Newspapers, Magazines	101.7	100.0	100.1	100.0	100.0	100.0	100.0	100.0	100.0	100.0	100.0	100.0
书籍	Books	100.1	100.0	100.2	100.0	100.0	100.0	100.0	100.0	100.0	100.0	100.0	100.1
报纸	Newspapers	105.0	100.0	100.0	100.0	100.0	100.0	100.0	100.0	100.0	100.0	100.0	100.0
杂志	Magazines	100.6	100.0	100.0	100.0	100.0	100.0	100.0	100.0	100.0	100.0	100.0	100.1
（3）文娱费	Expenditure of Culture and Recreation	100.4	99.4	99.9	106.5	100.4	98.7	101.9	99.9	98.3	102.0	99.1	100.3
电影票	Film Ticket	101.7	97.0	99.1	99.0	98.3	101.0	99.8	99.7	100.3	101.5	98.9	100.6
景点门票	Scene Spot Ticket	100.0	100.0	100.4	114.4	104.4	91.3	112.2	100.0	90.2	110.4	95.9	101.1
有线电视	Cable Television	100.0	100.0	100.0	110.5	100.0	100.0	100.0	100.0	100.0	100.1	100.0	100.0
健身活动	Exercise	100.0	100.1	100.4	100.7	100.0	100.0	100.0	100.0	99.9	100.0	100.0	100.0
其他	Others	100.0	100.0	100.0	100.0	100.0	100.0	100.1	100.0	100.0	100.0	100.0	99.7
4.旅游	Tourism	101.3	98.5	99.4	103.3	99.6	98.1	101.8	102.5	99.0	99.9	97.5	100.1
旅行社收费	Travel Agency Charge	102.2	97.6	98.8	105.1	99.1	96.9	102.4	103.8	99.7	100.1	95.6	100.3
宾馆住宿	Guesthouse Stay	100.4	99.6	100.1	101.1	100.0	99.6	100.5	100.5	99.4	100.1	99.8	99.9
其他住宿	Other Stay	99.7	99.7	100.0	101.3	100.6	99.1	102.2	101.9	96.4	99.2	100.0	100.1
八、居住	**Residence**	**100.4**	**100.0**	**100.2**	**100.4**	**100.3**	**100.3**	**100.4**	**100.6**	**100.7**	**100.3**	**100.6**	**100.2**
1.建房及装修材料	Building and Building Decoration Materials	100.2	100.0	100.6	100.5	100.2	100.6	100.4	100.8	100.4	100.5	101.1	100.2
木材	Wood	100.7	100.1	100.3	100.5	99.8	100.9	100.8	102.5	101.1	101.3	103.0	100.2
木地板	Wood Floor	100.0	100.0	99.6	96.8	100.4	100.4	100.1	100.2	99.5	101.4	101.3	100.1
砖	Brick	99.4	100.5	101.6	101.5	100.4	101.5	100.2	101.1	100.0	100.1	100.2	100.1
水泥	Cement	99.7	99.3	100.1	102.1	100.4	99.8	99.9	99.9	100.2	99.9	100.9	100.0
涂料	Coating Material	100.6	99.9	99.9	99.8	99.2	100.6	100.1	100.1	99.7	100.3	100.4	100.4
胶合板	Plywood	100.7	100.1	100.9	100.9	99.1	100.6	101.1	100.8	100.9	99.3	102.5	100.7
玻璃	Glass	101.2	99.5	100.8	100.1	100.8	100.2	100.9	100.6	100.4	101.2	100.7	100.3
粘胶	Rayon	100.3	100.1	100.0	99.9	100.1	100.3	100.1	100.9	100.5	100.6	100.3	101.0
油漆	Paint	101.0	100.2	100.0	100.0	100.4	100.4	100.2	100.1	101.7	100.0	99.9	100.4
其他	Others	99.4	99.5	102.4	100.6	101.1	99.5	100.8	99.0	100.0	102.2	100.1	98.7
2.租房	Renting	100.0	100.0	102.2	100.0	100.2	100.3	102.4	100.7	100.5	100.1	100.3	100.0
公房房租	Public House Rent	100.0	100.0	100.0	100.0	100.0	100.0	100.1	102.9	100.0	100.0	100.1	100.0
私房房租	Private House Rent	100.0	100.0	100.7	100.0	100.5	100.7	102.9	100.0	101.1	100.1	100.7	100.0
其他费用	Other Fare	100.0	100.0	107.0	100.0	100.0	100.0	103.4	100.0	100.0	100.0	100.0	100.0
3.自有住房	Private Housing	100.2	100.1	100.2	100.0	101.6	101.2	99.9	100.6	100.9	100.0	101.3	100.0
房屋贷款利率	Houses Loans Interest Rate	100.3	100.0	100.0	100.0	103.0	100.8	100.0	102.4	101.1	100.0	100.0	100.0
物业管理费用	Propety Management Fee	100.0	100.0	100.9	100.0	100.0	100.0	99.3	100.0	100.7	100.0	100.0	100.0
维护修理费用	Upkeep and Repair Fee	100.0	100.1	100.0	100.0	101.9	102.2	100.2	100.0	101.1	100.0	103.1	100.0
其他	Others	101.6	100.3	100.0	100.0	100.0	100.0	100.1	99.8	100.3	99.9	100.0	100.0
4.水、电、燃料	Water,Electricity and Fuels	100.7	100.0	99.5	100.4	100.2	99.8	100.4	100.3	100.8	100.1	100.1	100.3
水	Water	101.1	100.0	101.0	102.3	100.5	100.0	100.0	100.0	100.0	100.0	100.0	100.0
电	Electricity	100.0	100.3	100.0	100.0	100.0	100.0	101.4	100.4	100.0	100.0	100.0	100.0
液化石油气	Liquefiled Petroleum Gas	103.1	99.5	95.3	99.5	100.9	98.6	98.6	101.3	105.8	99.6	100.1	100.2
管道燃气	Pipelined Gas	100.1	100.0	100.0	100.0	100.1	100.0	100.0	100.0	100.0	100.0	100.0	100.0
其他燃料	Other Fuels	100.3	99.8	99.9	100.1	99.8	99.8	100.1	100.2	100.3	100.7	100.4	101.4

7-17 城市居民消费价格（环比）指数
Urban Consumer Price Indices

（以上月价格为100）

商品类别及品名	Commodity Category and Commodity Name	1月 January	2月 February	3月 March	4月 April	5月 May	6月 June	7月 July	8月 August	9月 September	10月 October	11月 November	12月 December
居民消费价格总指数	**General Consumer Price Index**	**101.7**	**99.9**	**99.3**	**100.0**	**99.5**	**99.2**	**99.4**	**100.3**	**100.6**	**99.9**	**100.6**	**101.5**
非食品价格指数	**No-food**	**100.0**	**99.7**	**99.8**	**100.1**	**100.0**	**100.1**	**100.0**	**100.0**	**100.1**	**100.2**	**100.1**	**100.1**
服务项目价格指数	**Services**	**100.5**	**99.8**	**99.9**	**100.5**	**100.2**	**99.8**	**100.5**	**100.6**	**100.1**	**100.1**	**99.7**	**100.2**
工业品价格指数	**Industrial Products**	**99.9**	**99.7**	**99.7**	**100.0**	**99.9**	**100.2**	**99.8**	**99.9**	**100.1**	**100.3**	**100.2**	**100.0**
扣除食品和能源价格指数	**Deducting Foods and Energy**	**100.0**	**99.7**	**99.9**	**100.0**	**99.9**	**100.1**	**100.0**	**100.0**	**100.0**	**100.2**	**100.1**	**100.1**
扣除鲜菜鲜果总指数	**Deducting Fresh,Vegetables and Fruits**	**100.4**	**99.7**	**99.7**	**100.0**	**99.9**	**100.2**	**100.2**	**100.4**	**100.2**	**100.2**	**100.4**	**100.7**
消费品价格指数	**Consumer Goods**	**101.9**	**99.9**	**99.2**	**100.0**	**99.3**	**99.1**	**99.2**	**100.2**	**100.7**	**99.8**	**100.8**	**101.8**
一、食品	**Food**	**105.3**	**100.4**	**98.3**	**99.9**	**98.3**	**97.1**	**98.1**	**100.9**	**101.8**	**99.0**	**101.7**	**104.7**
1.粮食	Grain	100.1	100.1	100.2	100.1	100.4	100.4	100.6	100.9	100.1	100.6	103.6	102.2
大米	Rice	101.1	100.0	100.3	100.2	101.5	101.5	101.6	102.7	100.2	100.9	101.0	102.1
面粉	Flour	99.6	100.4	100.0	99.6	99.8	99.6	100.1	99.1	99.8	100.5	107.8	103.0
粮食制品	Grain Products	99.6	100.2	100.4	100.3	100.1	100.2	100.3	100.9	100.0	100.4	102.7	101.6
其他	Others	101.2	98.9	100.0	100.6	100.4	100.8	100.6	100.9	101.1	100.7	102.1	101.8
2.淀粉	Starches	99.2	100.2	100.1	100.2	99.9	100.2	99.8	100.7	101.1	100.1	100.4	103.9
淀粉	Starches	99.2	100.2	100.1	100.2	99.9	100.2	99.8	100.7	101.1	100.1	100.4	103.9
3.干豆类及豆制品	Beans and Beans Products	100.5	99.9	100.5	99.6	100.5	100.4	101.0	100.2	99.7	99.9	100.2	100.5
干豆	Beans	99.8	99.9	99.7	99.8	101.9	103.3	103.7	101.3	97.1	98.1	99.7	99.8
豆制品	Beans Products	100.7	100.0	100.7	99.6	100.2	99.8	100.4	99.9	100.3	100.3	100.3	100.7
4.油脂	Oil and Fat	99.6	99.9	99.7	100.2	99.9	100.4	100.0	100.5	100.3	99.9	101.9	105.5
食用植物油	Edible Vegetable Oil	99.6	100.0	99.7	100.5	100.0	100.5	100.1	100.5	100.2	99.9	101.6	104.4
植物油制品	Plant Oil Products	99.3	99.4	99.8	99.3	100.2	100.1	99.2	99.9	100.1	100.1	102.3	115.9
其他	Others	104.3	97.1	95.8	93.6	97.7	100.0	101.2	103.0	105.4	100.8	114.0	109.7
5.肉禽及其制品	Meal,Poultry and Their Products	104.5	99.7	96.9	97.3	98.0	100.7	103.2	104.1	101.4	100.6	103.4	105.3
（1）食用畜肉及副产品	Edible Livestock Meat and Their By-products	105.0	99.3	95.5	95.8	97.7	101.0	103.2	105.2	102.4	100.2	104.8	106.7
猪肉	Pork	106.1	99.1	94.0	93.2	96.8	101.6	105.2	108.1	103.3	100.0	107.0	108.2
牛肉	Beef	102.5	100.2	98.3	99.8	98.3	100.4	100.4	99.8	101.1	100.1	102.0	103.1
羊肉	Mutton	103.0	99.4	97.7	101.4	99.8	100.0	99.6	100.2	100.6	100.9	100.2	102.6
畜肉副产品	Livestock Meat By-products	104.6	99.6	97.3	97.8	98.4	100.2	102.0	101.5	101.0	100.8	102.1	108.0
其他	Others	103.2	99.3	99.1	99.4	98.9	99.9	99.2	102.9	101.6	101.1	101.4	103.3
（2）禽	Poultry	106.6	100.6	99.8	100.8	97.9	100.1	105.5	103.3	98.6	101.9	100.1	102.4
鸡	Chicken	108.9	101.0	100.0	101.3	97.3	100.2	107.1	103.9	98.4	102.4	100.1	102.6
鸭	Duck	100.1	99.6	99.6	97.4	102.1	100.3	98.6	99.5	98.0	99.9	99.8	101.9
其他	Others	100.1	99.2	98.7	99.7	98.7	99.7	101.5	102.1	99.7	100.0	100.6	101.7
（3）加工肉禽	Meal and Poultry Processing Products	99.9	100.3	99.8	100.0	99.8	100.0	100.1	100.4	100.4	100.3	100.5	101.6
畜肉制品	Livestock Meat Products	99.9	100.4	99.7	100.1	99.4	100.0	100.0	100.1	100.1	100.4	100.7	101.9
禽制品	Poultry Products	99.8	100.3	100.1	99.8	100.4	100.0	100.3	100.8	100.9	100.1	100.1	101.0

7-17 续表 1 continued

商品类别及品名	Commodity Category and Commodity Name	(以上月价格为100)											
		1月 January	2月 February	3月 March	4月 April	5月 May	6月 June	7月 July	8月 August	9月 September	10月 October	11月 November	12月 December
6.蛋	Eggs	99.5	95.4	97.1	99.8	101.7	101.3	101.1	111.0	105.5	98.6	101.4	104.7
鲜蛋	Fresh Eggs	99.3	95.0	96.9	99.7	101.9	101.5	101.2	111.9	105.9	98.4	101.5	104.8
蛋制品	Egg Products	100.9	99.8	99.3	100.4	99.7	99.1	100.2	100.5	100.3	101.2	100.0	102.9
7.水产品	Aquatic Product	106.0	101.7	98.8	100.6	98.9	100.8	101.2	99.4	95.9	101.3	99.6	99.6
(1)鱼	Fish	103.1	100.0	97.6	101.0	101.1	102.3	102.1	100.8	98.4	98.8	97.9	99.6
淡水鱼	Freshwater Fish	100.1	98.9	97.3	98.0	102.3	104.7	104.1	101.7	99.3	97.5	96.9	99.1
海水鱼	Seawater Fish	104.9	100.7	97.7	102.8	100.5	100.9	101.0	100.3	97.9	99.7	98.5	99.9
(2)其他水产品	Other Aquatic Product	109.0	103.4	99.9	100.2	96.8	99.2	100.2	97.9	93.1	104.1	101.4	99.5
虾蟹类	Shrimp and Crab	111.0	104.2	99.6	100.3	96.0	99.6	99.6	97.4	91.1	105.4	101.7	99.7
其他	Others	102.9	100.9	100.7	100.0	99.7	98.1	102.5	99.2	99.6	100.3	100.3	99.0
8.菜	Vegetable	131.3	99.4	90.3	95.8	84.7	84.0	95.5	107.0	116.6	86.2	102.1	123.7
鲜菜	Fresh Vegetable	133.2	99.3	89.6	95.2	83.2	82.6	94.9	108.1	118.8	85.0	102.3	125.4
干菜及菜制品	Dried Vegetable and Vegetable Products	103.8	100.6	100.0	101.3	99.9	100.3	100.5	100.6	101.7	102.2	100.8	105.9
薯类	Potato	114.6	105.2	102.7	107.5	110.4	95.1	100.2	94.8	84.2	91.3	100.0	111.4
9.调味品	Flavoring	100.4	99.6	99.8	100.3	100.0	100.1	99.9	99.9	99.9	100.5	101.4	100.6
盐	Salt	99.8	98.8	99.5	100.5	100.0	100.9	98.9	99.1	99.5	100.1	100.0	100.1
酱油	Soy Sauce	100.4	100.0	99.9	100.3	99.9	99.5	99.9	100.4	99.6	100.4	100.3	100.0
醋	Vinegar	100.1	100.0	99.9	100.7	99.8	100.3	100.1	99.9	100.2	100.1	99.9	100.4
味精	Aginomoto	100.5	100.1	99.8	100.6	100.3	99.6	100.0	99.8	100.1	100.0	99.6	100.4
其他	Others	101.3	99.4	100.0	99.6	99.9	100.2	100.4	100.0	100.3	101.5	106.8	102.3
10.糖	Carbohydrate	101.8	101.9	102.0	100.8	100.6	100.4	99.8	100.3	100.0	100.2	100.0	100.9
食糖	Sugar	104.5	104.3	105.2	101.7	101.1	100.8	99.7	100.9	100.2	99.7	99.6	102.2
糖果	Sweet	100.7	101.3	100.3	100.4	100.3	100.3	100.0	100.0	99.8	100.9	100.3	100.1
巧克力制品	Chocolate Products	100.3	100.0	99.9	100.0	99.8	99.9	99.8	99.8	100.0	100.3	100.0	100.1
糖类小食品	Little Carbohydrate Food	99.7	100.2	100.1	100.0	100.6	100.0	100.0	100.1	100.0	99.9	100.6	100.2
11.茶及饮料	Tea and Beverages	99.8	100.3	101.3	100.0	100.0	100.3	99.9	100.2	100.0	100.2	100.0	100.3
(1)茶叶	Tea	99.4	100.6	100.8	100.0	99.5	100.2	100.3	100.0	100.0	100.4	100.0	100.7
茶叶	Tea	99.4	100.6	100.8	100.0	99.5	100.2	100.3	100.0	100.0	100.4	100.0	100.7
(2)饮料	Beverages	100.1	100.1	101.5	100.0	100.3	100.4	99.7	100.3	99.9	100.1	100.0	100.0
固体饮料	Solid Beverages	100.1	100.2	99.8	99.6	100.6	100.3	100.0	99.7	99.8	100.1	99.9	99.3
液体饮料	Liquid Beverages	100.0	100.1	101.3	100.3	100.2	99.6	99.4	100.2	100.0	100.0	100.0	100.4
冷冻饮品	Frozen Beverages	100.3	100.0	104.4	100.1	100.3	102.3	99.9	101.1	99.9	100.2	99.8	99.9
12.干鲜瓜果	Dried and Fresh Melons and Fruits	106.5	105.7	101.6	107.0	103.9	88.1	82.0	89.2	98.2	105.1	104.6	104.5
鲜瓜果	Fresh Fruits	107.3	107.1	101.7	108.6	104.7	85.4	77.4	85.7	97.4	106.4	105.4	105.9
干(坚)果	Dried Fruits	103.4	100.2	101.1	100.8	100.5	100.4	99.8	99.7	100.2	102.0	102.6	101.0
13.糕点饼干面包	Cake,Biscuit and Bread	100.0	99.9	99.8	100.2	100.1	99.9	99.9	99.9	99.9	99.9	99.9	100.7
糕点	Cake	99.7	100.0	99.7	99.9	100.0	99.8	99.9	99.5	100.0	99.5	100.4	101.0
饼干	Biscuit	100.1	99.9	100.0	100.7	100.4	100.0	100.0	100.1	99.7	99.9	99.4	100.3
面包	Bread	100.5	99.6	100.0	100.0	99.9	99.9	100.0	100.3	100.2	100.7	99.4	100.4
14.液体乳及乳制品	Liquid Milk and Their Products	99.8	100.0	100.5	100.2	100.0	100.2	100.1	100.4	101.2	100.0	99.9	100.0
巴氏杀菌奶或消毒奶	Pasteurization Milk or Disinfection Milk	99.6	100.0	100.8	100.0	100.0	100.3	100.2	100.4	101.2	100.1	99.9	99.9
酸奶	Leben	100.1	100.0	100.1	100.5	100.2	100.1	99.6	100.0	101.4	100.0	99.7	100.1

7-17 续表 2 continued

商品类别及品名	Commodity Category and Commodity Name	1月 January	2月 February	3月 March	4月 April	5月 May	6月 June	7月 July	8月 August	9月 September	10月 October	11月 November	12月 December
		（以上月价格为100）											
奶粉	Milk Powder	100.2	100.1	100.0	100.7	99.7	100.0	100.3	101.4	100.0	99.5	100.4	100.4
其他	Others	99.9	100.0	100.0	100.0	100.0	100.0	100.0	100.0	103.1	99.5	100.1	99.7
15.在外用膳食品	Outward Dinner	100.1	99.9	100.2	100.1	100.0	100.5	100.0	100.2	100.0	99.9	100.5	102.1
主食	Staple Food	100.1	99.5	100.1	100.0	100.0	100.5	100.0	100.1	100.1	100.0	101.2	104.1
炒菜	Hot Dish	100.1	100.0	100.2	100.1	100.1	100.5	99.9	100.0	100.1	99.9	100.2	101.2
地方小吃	Local Snack	100.2	100.0	100.5	100.0	100.0	100.0	100.4	101.2	99.6	100.0	100.7	101.7
16.其他食品	Other Foods	99.9	99.8	100.3	100.1	100.1	100.0	99.9	99.9	100.2	99.6	100.0	100.7
其他食品	Other Foods	99.9	99.8	100.3	100.1	100.1	100.0	99.9	99.9	100.2	99.6	100.0	100.7
二、烟酒及用品	**Tobacco,Liquor and Their Appliances**	**100.2**	**99.9**	**100.0**	**100.5**	**100.0**	**100.4**	**100.1**	**100.2**	**100.1**	**100.0**	**100.0**	**100.3**
1.烟草	Tobacco	100.3	99.7	100.0	100.6	99.9	100.2	99.9	99.9	99.8	100.0	100.0	100.1
国产卷烟	Domestic Cigarette	100.3	99.9	99.9	100.7	100.0	100.2	99.9	99.9	99.7	100.0	100.0	100.1
进口卷烟	Import Cigarette	100.0	98.5	100.0	100.1	99.5	100.0	100.0	100.2	100.0	99.8	100.4	100.2
其他	Others	100.2	100.0	100.0	100.0	100.0	100.0	100.0	99.5	100.0	100.0	100.0	100.0
2.酒	Liquor	100.2	100.0	100.1	100.6	100.1	100.6	100.2	100.5	100.4	100.0	100.0	100.5
白酒	White Spirit	100.3	99.9	100.3	100.5	100.1	100.7	100.1	100.6	100.4	100.0	100.1	100.7
葡萄酒	Grape	101.8	100.3	100.1	100.3	100.1	102.5	100.5	100.1	100.5	100.1	99.9	100.0
啤酒	Beer	99.7	100.2	99.7	100.8	100.1	100.2	100.3	100.5	100.5	100.0	99.9	100.2
其他	Others	100.0	100.0	100.0	100.9	100.1	100.8	100.1	99.8	100.2	100.0	100.0	100.0
3.吸烟、饮酒用品	Appliances For Smoking and Drinking	100.0	100.0	100.0	100.1	100.1	100.0	100.0	100.0	99.6	100.2	99.9	99.8
吸烟用品	Appliances for Smoking	100.1	100.0	100.0	100.1	100.0	100.0	100.0	100.0	99.8	100.4	100.0	99.7
饮酒用品	Appliances For Drinking	99.9	100.0	100.0	100.1	100.1	100.1	100.0	100.0	99.4	100.1	99.9	99.8
三、衣着	**Clothing**	**99.1**	**98.8**	**99.5**	**99.5**	**99.4**	**100.0**	**98.9**	**99.1**	**100.3**	**101.0**	**100.7**	**100.1**
1.服装	Garments	98.9	98.4	99.2	99.6	99.5	100.0	99.6	99.4	100.3	101.4	100.8	100.3
（1）男式服装	Men's Garments	98.5	98.8	98.9	99.5	99.1	99.9	99.5	99.3	100.2	101.5	100.9	100.3
大衣	Topcoat	97.9	98.3	99.2	98.3	99.9	99.2	99.8	100.0	99.6	99.8	100.1	101.3
毛线衣	Woollen Sweater	99.4	94.1	95.1	99.6	98.8	100.2	98.7	99.4	100.3	102.9	101.9	101.4
夹克衫	Jacket	98.1	99.0	97.9	99.3	99.9	100.0	99.6	100.1	99.9	103.4	100.4	100.5
衬衫	Shirt	96.6	98.8	100.1	99.3	99.0	100.7	98.4	98.9	100.6	100.8	99.8	101.5
T恤衫	T-shirt	99.8	100.6	99.5	100.0	98.7	97.4	96.7	97.3	100.6	100.1	100.6	100.0
裤子	Trousers	98.0	97.9	98.9	99.7	99.4	99.6	99.8	99.4	99.1	103.5	100.5	99.8
西服	Western-style Clothes	98.8	101.0	98.5	100.5	99.6	99.8	100.7	97.6	101.7	101.5	99.7	99.7
运动衫裤	Gym Suit	98.6	100.0	100.0	99.6	95.8	100.3	99.6	100.6	99.9	100.2	101.1	100.7
内衣	Underwaist	99.6	99.9	101.1	99.6	99.6	100.3	99.6	100.2	99.7	100.3	99.8	100.1
羽绒衣	Eider Down Outerwear	98.3	98.1	99.3	97.7	100.0	100.0	99.4	99.7	99.3	102.9	105.2	98.6
其他	Others	99.5	99.1	98.9	99.3	100.3	100.1	99.9	99.5	100.0	100.0	103.7	100.0
（2）女式服装	Women's Garments	99.0	97.8	99.3	99.5	99.5	100.2	99.8	99.4	100.5	101.5	100.9	100.4
大衣	Topcoat	97.5	93.1	97.5	99.0	99.9	100.0	99.9	100.0	99.6	100.0	100.9	104.0
毛线衣	Woollen Sweater	99.3	92.4	98.6	99.7	98.8	100.4	100.0	100.0	101.2	102.8	101.4	101.7
羽绒衣	Eider Down Outerwear	98.5	99.0	98.9	99.8	100.0	99.7	99.6	99.9	99.2	104.2	105.0	98.8
套装	Coordinates	98.4	99.3	99.9	100.0	100.7	98.7	100.4	97.2	104.3	101.1	98.6	100.4
衬衫	Shirt	98.0	101.1	100.4	98.3	99.6	100.3	100.7	98.1	100.8	100.4	99.7	98.6

7-17 续表 3 continued

商品类别及品名	Commodity Category and Commodity Name	（以上月价格为100）											
		1月 January	2月 February	3月 March	4月 April	5月 May	6月 June	7月 July	8月 August	9月 September	10月 October	11月 November	12月 December
T恤衫	T-shirt	100.0	100.7	99.6	99.2	100.4	100.7	98.3	99.2	101.9	104.4	100.1	99.9
裙子	Skirt	100.2	99.2	99.7	98.8	101.5	100.3	99.4	99.9	99.7	100.3	100.9	99.7
裤子	Trousers	100.1	97.4	98.3	99.9	99.4	100.2	99.6	99.7	100.4	100.4	101.2	99.1
运动衫裤	Gym Suit	99.9	100.5	99.1	100.4	94.5	100.4	99.7	99.9	99.9	101.7	98.9	101.8
内衣	Underwaist	99.3	100.0	101.5	101.2	99.7	100.6	99.6	100.2	99.4	100.8	101.6	99.9
其他	Others	99.5	99.6	100.5	100.8	99.5	100.4	100.0	100.5	99.8	100.6	100.3	99.8
（3）儿童服装	Children's Garments	99.5	99.8	99.5	100.2	100.5	100.0	98.9	99.3	99.3	100.7	100.5	100.0
套装	Coordinates	99.5	100.0	99.1	100.0	99.0	99.9	100.2	99.4	99.3	100.5	100.6	100.0
裤子	Trousers	99.0	99.2	99.7	99.7	100.5	100.0	98.1	100.0	99.9	101.3	100.5	100.4
裙子	Skirt	99.8	100.2	100.4	101.4	102.8	100.2	97.8	98.4	98.6	100.5	100.2	99.7
其他	Others	99.8	98.2	97.3	98.2	98.8	99.7	99.6	100.0	100.9	100.0	101.0	99.1
2.衣着材料	Clothing Materials	99.9	100.1	99.9	100.2	99.9	100.1	99.9	100.1	99.6	100.4	100.1	100.5
棉布	Cotton Cloth	100.0	99.9	100.0	100.7	99.8	100.1	100.3	100.3	99.5	101.0	99.9	100.0
棉混纺布	Cotton Textiles Cloth	99.9	100.1	100.0	100.0	99.8	100.0	99.7	100.3	99.4	100.5	100.3	100.2
化纤布	Chemical Fiber Cloth	99.8	100.3	99.7	100.0	99.9	100.3	99.7	100.1	99.8	100.1	100.1	100.1
毛线	Knitting Wool	100.0	99.9	99.8	100.0	99.9	100.0	100.1	99.9	99.7	100.2	100.1	101.9
3.鞋袜帽	Shoes,Socks and Hats	99.5	99.4	100.4	99.3	99.1	99.9	97.1	98.3	100.5	100.1	100.3	99.3
（1）鞋	Shoes	99.5	99.4	100.6	99.2	99.1	99.9	96.6	98.1	100.7	100.0	100.4	99.2
男鞋	Men's Shoes	99.4	99.1	101.2	99.5	99.2	100.6	96.3	98.9	100.3	99.9	100.5	99.3
女鞋	Women's Shoes	99.5	99.4	100.4	98.8	98.7	99.5	96.2	97.3	101.3	99.9	100.4	98.9
童鞋	Children's Shoes	99.8	100.0	99.5	100.1	100.7	99.7	99.4	99.2	99.1	101.0	100.4	100.0
（2）袜子	Socks	99.8	100.0	99.3	100.5	99.1	100.0	99.9	100.0	99.6	100.5	99.0	99.8
男袜	Men's Socks	99.6	99.9	99.8	100.4	99.7	99.8	99.8	100.0	99.7	100.4	97.9	99.4
女袜	Women's Socks	99.8	100.0	99.1	100.6	98.8	100.2	99.9	100.0	99.5	100.5	99.6	100.0
（3）帽子	Hats	100.1	99.6	99.8	100.0	100.0	100.0	100.0	100.0	99.8	100.5	100.6	100.0
男帽	Men's Hats	100.0	99.6	99.6	100.1	100.3	100.2	100.1	100.0	99.6	100.3	101.5	100.1
女帽	Women's Hats	100.2	99.6	100.0	100.0	99.9	100.0	100.0	99.9	99.9	100.7	100.1	100.0
4.衣着加工服务费	Clothing Manufacturing Services	100.0	100.1	100.1	99.8	100.0	100.0	100.1	100.1	100.0	100.0	100.0	100.0
缝纫	Sewing	100.1	100.0	100.1	100.0	100.0	100.0	100.1	100.1	100.0	100.0	100.0	100.0
清洗	Washing	100.0	100.2	100.0	99.7	100.0	100.0	100.1	100.2	100.1	100.0	100.0	100.0
四、家庭设备用品及维修服务	**Household Facilities, Articles and Services**	**100.2**	**100.1**	**100.1**	**100.0**	**100.1**	**101.2**	**100.3**	**100.4**	**99.9**	**100.2**	**100.1**	**100.2**
1.耐用消费品	Durable Consumer Goods	100.0	100.1	100.1	99.9	100.2	101.7	100.6	100.2	99.9	100.2	100.1	100.1
（1）家具	Furniture	100.0	100.0	100.0	99.7	99.8	100.1	100.0	100.3	100.3	100.1	100.0	100.0
柜	Cabinet	100.0	100.0	100.0	99.1	100.1	100.2	99.9	100.6	100.2	99.8	100.2	100.0
床	Bed	100.1	100.1	100.1	99.9	99.8	99.9	100.2	100.2	100.1	100.4	99.3	100.0
桌	Desk	99.8	100.1	99.9	100.0	99.7	99.7	99.7	100.3	100.2	100.0	100.2	100.4
椅	Chair	99.9	99.6	100.1	99.9	100.0	100.0	100.0	100.2	100.9	100.7	100.2	99.8
沙发	Sofa	100.1	100.1	100.1	99.8	99.7	100.3	100.1	100.2	100.2	99.9	100.0	100.0
其他	Others	100.2	99.8	100.1	100.0	99.2	100.9	100.5	100.1	100.7	99.6	100.0	100.0
（2）家庭设备	Household Appliances	100.0	100.2	100.1	100.0	100.4	102.6	100.8	100.2	99.7	100.2	100.1	100.1
洗衣机	Washing Machine	99.9	100.1	100.0	99.0	100.6	101.3	100.9	99.9	99.6	99.9	100.3	99.9

7-17 续表 4 continued

（以上月价格为100）

商品类别及品名	Commodity Category and Commodity Name	1月 January	2月 February	3月 March	4月 April	5月 May	6月 June	7月 July	8 月 August	9 月 September	10 月 October	11月 November	12月 December
电风扇	Electric Fan	100.0	100.1	100.1	99.6	100.4	100.5	99.5	100.3	99.2	100.3	100.0	100.0
电冰箱（柜）	Refrigerator	99.8	100.0	100.2	100.6	101.1	103.2	101.5	99.9	100.0	100.6	99.8	100.1
吸排油烟机	Kitchen Ventilato	100.5	100.0	99.9	100.1	99.7	102.8	102.1	101.3	99.5	99.8	100.3	100.2
空调器	Air-conditioning	100.1	100.3	100.0	99.7	100.7	104.4	101.1	100.4	99.5	100.1	100.2	100.2
热水器	Water Heater	99.9	100.4	100.6	100.8	99.4	100.5	100.1	99.7	100.5	100.2	100.0	100.0
微波炉	Microwave Oven	99.5	100.0	99.9	99.9	99.9	100.7	99.8	100.0	99.8	100.2	100.4	99.4
电炊具	Electric Cooking Appliance	100.1	99.9	100.1	101.2	100.1	99.9	100.0	100.2	99.5	100.4	100.0	100.0
2.室内装饰品	Interior Decorations	100.0	100.0	100.0	99.8	99.6	100.0	100.1	100.2	99.8	100.3	100.1	100.0
纺织装饰品	Textile Process Decorations	100.0	100.0	99.9	99.8	100.0	100.0	99.8	100.2	99.4	100.5	100.0	100.0
装饰灯具	Architectural Lamps and Lanterns	100.1	100.0	100.0	99.9	98.7	100.0	100.7	99.8	100.7	100.0	99.7	100.0
其他	Others	100.0	100.0	99.9	99.9	100.0	100.0	99.8	101.0	99.7	100.2	101.2	100.0
3.床上用品	Bedclothes	98.7	101.1	100.3	99.9	99.4	100.6	99.7	99.7	99.6	100.2	99.9	100.7
毛毯	Woollen Blanket	99.0	100.6	100.5	99.9	99.2	100.9	99.0	99.8	99.8	100.4	99.2	101.6
被子	Quilt	98.9	100.5	100.1	99.7	99.0	100.9	99.7	99.2	99.7	99.6	99.8	101.0
床上套件	Bed Articles	98.2	101.2	100.4	99.9	99.5	100.4	100.0	99.9	99.3	100.6	100.3	100.2
其他	Others	99.3	103.0	100.3	100.1	100.0	99.7	100.0	100.0	99.9	100.2	100.2	100.2
4.日用杂品	Sundry Articles	100.2	100.1	100.1	100.1	100.2	100.3	99.9	100.3	99.9	100.2	100.0	100.2
茶具	Tea Set	100.0	100.1	100.3	100.6	99.9	100.0	100.0	100.1	100.0	100.2	99.6	100.4
餐具	Tableware	100.0	100.0	100.0	100.0	101.2	100.1	99.3	100.9	100.1	100.1	100.0	100.3
厨具	Kitchen Utensils	100.0	100.0	100.0	101.0	100.0	100.7	100.1	99.9	100.0	100.0	100.2	99.8
家用手工工具	Domestic Handwork Tools	100.0	100.0	100.0	100.0	99.7	100.0	99.8	100.5	100.0	100.0	99.3	100.0
洗涤用品	Washing Articles	100.5	100.2	100.1	99.8	100.1	100.1	99.9	100.7	99.6	100.1	100.1	100.3
其他	Others	99.9	100.0	100.0	100.0	100.1	100.7	99.9	99.7	100.0	100.3	100.0	100.0
5.家庭服务及加工维修服务	Household Service and Manufacturing Upkeep	103.5	98.8	100.0	100.0	100.0	100.1	100.5	102.9	100.6	100.0	100.5	100.9
家庭服务	Household Service	107.8	97.3	100.0	100.0	100.0	100.0	100.8	105.4	101.2	100.1	101.0	100.1
加工维修服务	Manufacturing Upkeep	100.0	100.0	100.0	100.0	100.0	100.3	100.1	100.7	100.0	100.0	100.0	101.7
五、医疗保健和个人用品	**Health Care and Personal Articles**	**100.1**	**100.0**	**100.0**	**100.1**	**100.2**	**100.1**	**99.9**	**100.1**	**99.7**	**100.3**	**100.0**	**100.1**
1.医疗保健	Health Care	99.9	99.9	100.0	99.9	99.9	100.1	100.0	100.0	99.5	100.3	100.0	100.1
（1）医疗器具及用品	Medical Facilities and Goods	99.8	100.1	99.7	100.0	100.1	100.0	99.9	100.0	100.0	97.6	100.0	100.0
医疗器具及用品	Medical Facilities and Goods	99.8	100.1	99.7	100.0	100.1	100.0	99.9	100.0	100.0	97.6	100.0	100.0
（2）中药材及中成药	Herbs and Ready-made Traditional Chinese Medicine	100.2	99.6	100.3	99.7	99.6	100.8	99.4	100.1	99.4	102.1	100.1	100.1
中药材	Herbs	100.1	99.3	100.3	99.8	100.2	102.3	99.2	100.2	99.9	103.7	100.3	100.3
中成药	Ready-made Traditinonal Chinese Medicine	100.2	99.8	100.4	99.6	99.2	99.5	99.5	100.1	98.9	100.8	100.0	100.0
（3）西药	Western Medicine	99.7	99.9	99.8	100.0	100.0	99.9	100.2	99.8	99.3	99.7	99.9	100.1
抗微生物药	Anti-microorganism Medicine	100.0	100.0	100.1	100.0	100.1	100.6	102.3	99.5	99.1	99.4	100.3	99.6

7-17 续表 5 continued

商品类别及品名	Commodity Category and Commodity Name	（以上月价格为100）											
		1月 January	2月 February	3月 March	4月 April	5月 May	6月 June	7月 July	8月 August	9月 September	10月 October	11月 November	12月 December
消化系统用药	Alimentary System Medicine	99.6	100.0	100.3	100.2	100.4	99.9	100.0	100.0	99.5	100.4	99.1	100.8
呼吸系统用药	Respiratory System Medicine	98.9	100.0	99.7	100.1	100.0	100.9	100.0	100.0	99.9	100.2	100.0	100.0
解热镇痛及非甾体抗炎药	Allays a Fever the Analgesia and the Non-steroid Body Anti-in flammatory Agent	100.2	99.7	99.8	99.8	99.9	98.8	99.2	100.0	99.0	101.6	100.4	100.1
抗肿瘤药	Antineoplastic Drug	99.3	99.9	99.7	99.9	100.0	98.1	99.8	99.9	100.0	97.3	100.0	100.0
激素及调节内分泌功能药	Hormone and Adjustment Internal Secretion Function Medicine	100.4	99.9	99.5	100.0	100.0	99.3	100.0	99.7	97.9	97.3	101.4	99.8
循环系统用药	Circulating System Medicine	99.7	99.9	99.7	99.7	100.1	100.9	99.6	99.8	100.4	101.2	98.4	100.8
神经系统用药	Nerve System Medicine	100.0	100.0	99.3	100.0	100.0	99.3	100.0	99.2	99.0	96.4	100.0	100.0
专科用药	Junior Medicine	99.4	100.1	100.0	99.9	99.9	100.4	99.7	100.1	97.6	97.5	100.4	99.9
其他	Others	100.1	100.0	99.1	100.0	99.5	99.7	99.9	100.0	99.8	99.2	99.6	99.9
（4）保健品及器具	Healthcare Equipment	99.9	99.8	99.8	100.0	99.9	100.0	99.5	100.2	100.0	100.2	100.1	99.9
保健器具	Health Protection Equipment	99.6	99.5	99.8	100.0	99.8	100.0	99.6	100.0	100.0	100.0	100.0	99.6
滋补保健用品	Tonic and Health Products	100.1	99.9	99.8	100.0	100.0	100.0	99.5	100.2	99.9	100.3	100.2	99.9
（5）医疗保健服务	Health Care Services	100.0	100.0	100.0	100.1	100.0	100.0	100.2	100.0	100.0	99.9	100.0	100.0
挂号费	Registration	100.3	100.1	100.3	100.0	100.0	100.0	100.1	100.0	100.0	100.0	100.0	100.0
注射费	Injection Expenses	100.0	100.0	100.0	100.0	100.0	100.0	100.0	100.0	100.0	100.0	100.0	100.0
检查费	Examination Expenses	99.8	100.2	100.0	100.0	100.0	100.2	100.0	100.0	100.5	100.0	100.2	100.0
手术费	Operation Expenses	100.1	100.0	100.0	100.0	100.0	100.1	100.0	100.0	100.0	100.0	100.0	99.9
住院费	Hospitalization Expenses	100.0	100.0	100.0	100.4	100.0	100.0	101.2	100.0	99.4	99.4	100.0	100.2
理疗费	Physiotherapy Expenses	100.0	100.0	100.0	100.0	100.0	100.0	100.0	100.0	100.0	100.0	100.0	100.0
化验费	Analysis Expenses	100.0	100.0	100.1	100.0	100.0	100.0	100.0	100.0	100.0	99.8	100.0	100.0
其他	Others	100.0	100.0	100.0	100.0	100.0	100.0	100.0	100.0	100.0	100.0	100.0	100.0
2.个人用品及服务	Personal Articles and Services	100.4	100.2	100.1	100.4	100.6	100.1	99.9	100.3	99.9	100.3	99.9	100.1
（1）化妆美容用品	Cosmetics	99.7	100.1	100.0	100.1	99.9	100.0	99.8	100.3	99.5	100.6	99.6	99.8
化妆美容器具	Cosmetics Appliances	99.9	100.0	100.0	100.3	100.1	100.4	100.0	100.4	99.5	100.2	100.0	100.0
美容化妆品	Facial Beautifiers	99.8	100.1	100.0	100.1	100.0	99.9	100.3	100.1	100.0	100.2	100.1	99.9
护肤品	Protects Skin Products	99.6	100.2	99.9	100.1	100.0	100.0	100.0	100.3	97.6	102.7	98.8	99.4
护发美容品	Protects Sends the Beauty Products	99.7	100.1	100.0	100.0	99.8	100.1	98.7	100.7	99.9	100.2	99.1	99.9
（2）清洁化妆用品	Cleaning Toiletware	100.1	100.0	100.0	99.8	100.3	100.3	99.6	100.3	99.8	100.1	100.0	99.9
洗发用品	Hairdressing Articles	99.9	100.0	100.0	99.9	99.9	100.6	99.6	100.2	99.8	100.2	99.5	99.7
洗浴用品	Bathing Articles	100.4	100.0	99.8	99.6	100.1	100.0	99.7	100.5	99.9	100.1	100.4	100.2
其他	Others	100.0	100.4	100.4	100.3	102.1	100.5	99.6	100.0	99.8	100.0	100.5	99.9

7-17 续表 6 continued

商品类别及品名	Commodity Category and Commodity Name	1月 January	2月 February	3月 March	4月 April	5月 May	6月 June	7月 July	8月 August	9月 September	10月 October	11月 November	12月 December
		（以上月价格为100）											
（3）个人饰品	Personal Decoraions	101.2	101.1	100.4	102.1	102.6	100.0	100.2	100.4	100.3	100.5	100.2	100.3
首饰	Ornaments	102.9	101.9	100.6	103.9	104.6	100.4	101.2	100.4	100.2	100.3	100.3	101.1
皮件	Leather Appliance	98.8	100.2	100.6	100.0	99.8	99.9	97.5	102.0	100.0	101.2	100.1	99.0
手表	Watch	99.5	99.8	100.0	100.5	99.9	98.2	99.3	100.0	100.2	101.3	100.5	100.0
领带	Necktie	99.3	99.8	99.6	99.0	99.5	99.7	99.2	99.0	101.9	100.0	100.0	97.9
其他	Others	98.7	100.1	100.9	99.6	100.4	100.0	99.9	100.5	99.4	100.5	100.0	100.5
（4）个人服务	Personal Services	101.3	100.0	100.0	100.0	100.0	100.0	100.0	100.0	100.2	100.0	100.0	100.5
美容	Cosmetology	101.6	100.0	100.0	100.0	100.0	100.0	100.0	100.0	100.0	100.0	100.0	100.0
理（烫）发	Haircut(permanent wave)	100.9	100.0	100.0	100.0	100.0	100.0	100.0	100.0	100.4	100.0	100.0	100.9
洗浴	Bathe	104.3	100.0	100.0	100.0	100.0	100.0	100.2	100.0	100.0	100.0	100.0	100.4
其他	Others	100.0	100.0	100.0	100.0	100.0	100.0	100.0	100.0	100.0	100.0	100.0	100.0
六、交通和通信	**Transportation and Communication**	**100.1**	**99.8**	**99.4**	**99.7**	**100.1**	**100.3**	**99.9**	**99.7**	**99.7**	**99.6**	**99.9**	**99.8**
1.交通	Transportation	100.6	100.0	99.6	100.5	100.6	101.1	100.3	100.0	99.8	100.0	99.9	99.7
（1）交通工具	Transportation Facility	99.9	100.0	99.9	99.8	99.5	100.0	99.9	99.6	99.2	99.8	99.7	99.1
摩托车	Motorcycle	99.7	100.0	100.0	99.9	100.5	100.2	100.0	100.3	100.2	100.1	99.8	99.0
自行车	Bicycle	99.9	99.9	99.9	100.0	99.7	100.1	100.5	99.6	100.1	100.2	100.0	99.6
轿车	Car	100.0	100.0	99.9	99.7	99.2	99.9	99.6	99.3	98.3	99.8	99.5	98.9
其他	Others	100.0	100.0	100.0	99.8	98.3	99.9	100.0	100.0	100.0	98.0	100.0	100.0
（2）车用燃料及零配件	Fuels and Parts	99.9	100.0	100.4	103.5	101.8	105.2	100.1	100.0	100.2	100.0	100.1	100.0
汽油	Gasoline	100.0	100.0	100.4	105.4	102.5	106.8	100.1	100.0	100.1	100.0	100.0	100.0
柴油	Diesel Oil	100.1	99.9	100.6	103.3	102.0	107.3	100.2	100.0	100.2	100.0	100.2	100.2
零配件	Parts	99.6	99.9	100.0	100.0	100.1	100.0	100.0	100.1	100.4	100.0	100.1	100.0
其他	Others	100.2	99.5	100.0	100.0	100.2	100.0	100.0	100.0	100.7	100.0	100.0	100.0
（3）车辆使用及维修费	Using and Upkeep Fare	100.0	100.0	99.9	100.0	100.0	100.1	100.0	101.0	100.0	100.0	100.0	100.0
驾驶证	Driving License	100.0	100.0	99.9	100.0	100.0	100.0	100.1	100.0	100.0	100.0	100.0	100.0
保险费	Insurance Expenses	100.0	100.0	99.7	100.0	100.0	100.0	99.9	100.6	100.1	100.0	100.0	100.0
停车费	Parking Expenses	100.0	100.0	100.0	100.0	100.0	100.0	100.0	105.2	100.0	100.0	100.0	100.0
车辆修理服务费	Vehicle Upkeep Service Fare	100.0	100.0	100.0	100.0	100.0	100.2	100.0	100.0	100.0	100.0	100.0	100.0
其他	Others	100.0	100.0	100.0	100.2	100.0	100.0	100.0	99.6	100.0	100.0	100.0	100.0
（4）市区公共交通费	Incity Traffic Fare	100.4	100.0	100.0	100.0	101.6	100.1	101.5	100.4	100.0	100.0	100.0	100.1
公共汽车票	Bus Ticket	100.9	100.0	100.0	100.0	100.0	100.0	100.5	100.0	100.0	100.0	100.0	100.2
出租汽车	Taxi	100.0	100.0	100.0	100.0	103.2	100.2	102.5	100.5	100.0	100.1	100.0	100.0
其他	Others	100.0	100.0	100.0	100.5	100.0	100.0	100.0	105.9	100.0	100.0	100.0	99.6
（5）城市间交通费	Intercity Traffic Fare	102.8	100.2	97.9	100.2	100.8	101.5	100.0	100.1	100.3	100.0	100.0	100.0
飞机票	Airplane Ticket	102.5	100.0	99.2	102.8	101.7	98.7	100.1	102.0	100.9	100.7	99.5	100.0
火车票	Train Ticket	101.7	99.3	99.8	100.0	100.0	100.1	100.0	100.0	100.1	100.0	100.1	100.0
长途汽车	Intertown Bus	103.4	100.7	96.9	100.0	99.9	102.7	100.0	100.0	100.4	100.0	100.0	100.0
其他	Others	102.8	99.7	98.0	100.0	119.5	100.1	100.0	100.1	100.0	100.0	100.0	100.0
2.通信	Communication	99.7	99.6	99.2	98.9	99.5	99.5	99.6	99.3	99.5	99.3	99.9	99.9
（1）通信工具	Communication Facility	99.1	98.8	97.5	96.8	98.5	98.3	98.6	97.7	98.4	97.7	98.8	98.6
固定电话机	Telephone	100.0	99.5	98.8	99.5	99.6	100.0	99.6	99.5	99.8	99.9	99.9	98.9
移动电话机	Mobile Phone	98.9	98.5	97.1	96.0	98.2	97.8	98.3	97.1	97.9	97.0	98.3	98.4
其他	Others	100.0	100.0	99.8	99.5	99.1	99.9	99.9	99.9	99.8	99.9	99.9	100.0

7-17 续表 7 continued

（以上月价格为100）

商品类别及品名	Commodity Category and Commodity Name	1月 January	2月 February	3月 March	4月 April	5月 May	6月 June	7月 July	8月 August	9月 September	10月 October	11月 November	12月 December
（2）通信服务	Communication Service	100.0	100.0	100.0	100.0	100.0	100.0	100.0	100.0	100.0	100.0	100.4	100.4
移动通信费	Mobile Communication Fee	100.0	100.0	100.0	100.0	100.0	100.0	100.0	100.0	100.0	100.0	100.0	100.0
市内电话费	Incity Telephone Fee	100.0	100.0	100.0	100.0	100.0	100.0	100.0	100.0	100.0	100.0	100.0	100.0
长途电话费	Long Distance Call Fee	100.0	100.0	100.0	100.0	100.0	100.0	100.0	100.0	100.0	100.0	100.0	100.0
月租费	Month Hiring Fee	100.0	100.0	100.0	100.0	100.0	100.0	100.0	100.0	100.0	100.0	100.0	100.0
上网费	Net Play Fee	100.0	99.7	100.0	100.0	100.0	100.0	100.0	100.0	100.3	100.0	100.0	100.0
信件邮寄	Letter Post	100.0	100.0	100.0	100.0	100.0	100.0	100.0	100.0	100.0	100.0	115.9	114.8
包裹邮寄	Package Post	100.0	100.0	100.0	100.0	100.0	100.0	100.0	100.0	100.0	100.0	102.1	100.0
其他	Others	100.0	100.0	100.0	100.0	100.0	100.0	100.0	100.0	100.0	100.0	100.0	100.0
七、娱乐教育文化用品及服务	**Recreation,Education and Culture Articles**	**100.3**	**99.7**	**99.8**	**100.4**	**99.9**	**99.5**	**100.4**	**100.3**	**99.6**	**100.0**	**99.4**	**100.0**
1.文娱用耐用消费品及服务	Durable Consumer Goods For Cultural and Recreational Use and Service	99.8	99.8	99.7	99.4	99.6	99.5	99.7	99.2	98.7	99.6	99.8	99.7
电视机	Television	99.5	99.9	99.7	98.5	99.9	99.5	99.6	98.5	98.3	98.7	99.7	99.3
激光视盘机	Laser Video Disc Machine	100.3	99.2	99.8	99.6	99.8	100.0	100.0	100.0	98.8	99.1	99.9	99.9
摄像机	Pickup Camera	99.6	99.6	99.2	99.3	99.7	98.9	99.5	100.0	99.0	99.8	99.5	99.5
照相机	Camera	99.5	99.3	98.7	98.7	99.7	99.9	99.9	100.0	99.1	99.8	100.4	100.1
家用音响	Acoustic Equipment	100.0	100.0	100.0	99.8	99.8	100.1	100.0	99.9	99.5	100.1	100.0	99.8
便携式音响	Portable Acoustics	99.8	98.2	99.3	99.9	99.8	100.0	100.0	99.8	99.5	100.2	100.0	100.0
电脑	Computer	99.9	99.9	99.9	99.9	99.2	99.3	99.5	99.2	98.6	99.9	99.8	99.8
修理服务	Repair Service	100.5	100.0	100.0	100.0	100.0	100.0	100.2	100.0	100.0	100.0	100.0	100.0
其他	Others	100.0	102.0	99.7	99.7	99.8	100.0	99.8	99.6	97.5	100.4	99.6	100.0
2.教育	Education	100.0	100.0	100.0	99.8	100.0	100.0	100.0	100.2	100.4	100.0	100.0	100.1
（1）教材及参考书	Teaching Material and Reference Books	100.1	100.0	100.1	100.0	100.0	99.9	100.0	101.0	99.8	99.8	100.0	100.0
工具书	Tool Book	100.2	100.0	100.0	100.0	100.0	100.0	100.0	100.0	100.0	100.0	100.0	100.1
教材	Teaching Material	100.0	100.0	100.3	100.0	100.0	100.0	100.0	101.3	98.8	99.5	100.0	100.0
参考书	Reference Book	100.0	100.0	100.1	100.0	100.0	99.7	100.0	101.8	100.9	100.0	100.0	100.0
教育软件	Educational Software	100.0	99.9	100.0	100.0	100.0	100.0	100.0	100.0	100.0	100.0	100.0	100.0
（2）学杂托幼费	Tuition and Child Care	100.0	100.0	100.0	99.8	100.0	100.0	100.0	100.0	100.6	100.0	100.0	100.1
义务教育杂费	Incidental Expenses of Compulcory Education	100.0	100.0	100.0	100.0	100.0	100.0	100.0	100.0	100.0	100.0	100.0	100.0
非义务教育学杂费	Tuition of Non-compulsory Education	100.0	100.0	100.0	100.0	100.0	100.0	100.0	100.0	101.3	100.0	100.0	100.0
技能培训学费	Skill Train Tuition	100.0	100.0	100.0	98.4	100.0	100.0	100.0	100.0	99.6	100.0	100.0	100.0
托幼费	Child care	100.0	100.0	100.0	100.0	100.0	100.0	100.0	100.0	100.2	100.0	100.0	101.0
其他	Others	100.0	100.0	100.0	100.0	100.0	100.0	100.0	100.0	101.5	100.0	100.0	100.0
3.文化娱乐类	Recreation and Culture	100.7	99.7	99.9	100.8	100.2	99.4	100.9	100.0	99.1	100.9	99.3	100.1
（1）文化娱乐用品	Culture Articles	100.0	99.8	99.8	99.8	100.0	100.0	100.1	99.9	99.7	100.1	99.9	100.0
乐器	Musical Instrument	100.2	100.0	100.0	100.1	100.0	100.0	100.0	100.0	100.1	100.1	100.1	100.2
音响光盘和磁带	Audio,Disk and Tape	100.0	98.2	99.5	100.1	100.0	100.0	100.0	100.0	99.9	100.1	100.0	100.0
照相胶卷和存储卡	Roll Film and Memorizing Card	100.2	99.9	100.0	99.5	99.9	99.8	100.0	99.8	99.5	99.0	99.5	99.8
录像磁带和视盘	Video Tape and Disk	99.9	99.8	100.1	100.3	100.2	100.3	100.0	100.0	100.0	100.2	99.7	100.0
儿童玩具	Children's Toy	100.0	99.8	99.2	99.4	100.1	100.1	100.1	99.9	99.7	100.1	100.0	100.0

7-17 续表 8 continued

商品类别及品名	Commodity Category and Commodity Name	1月 January	2月 February	3月 March	4月 April	5月 May	6月 June	7月 July	8月 August	9月 September	10月 October	11月 November	12月 December
		（以上月价格为100）											
纸张本册	Paper and Volume	100.2	100.0	100.0	100.0	100.0	99.9	99.9	99.9	100.1	100.6	99.9	100.0
文具	Stationery	99.9	100.2	100.0	99.9	100.0	100.0	100.0	100.0	99.5	100.2	100.0	100.0
体育用品	Sports Goods	99.3	100.1	100.0	100.0	99.8	100.1	100.3	100.0	99.7	100.3	99.5	100.1
其他	Others	100.0	100.0	100.0	99.9	99.9	99.7	100.2	100.0	99.0	100.7	100.0	100.0
（2）书报杂志	Books,Newspapers, Magazines	102.0	100.0	100.2	100.0	100.0	100.0	100.0	100.0	100.0	100.0	100.0	100.1
书籍	Books	100.1	100.0	100.4	100.0	100.0	100.0	100.0	100.1	100.0	100.0	100.0	100.1
报纸	Newspapers	106.4	100.0	100.0	100.0	100.0	100.0	100.0	100.0	100.0	100.0	100.0	100.0
杂志	Magazines	100.1	100.0	100.0	100.0	100.0	100.0	100.0	100.0	100.0	100.0	100.0	100.1
（3）文娱费	Expenditure of Culture and Recreation	100.5	99.1	99.9	102.9	100.6	98.1	102.8	99.9	97.4	103.0	97.8	100.4
电影票	Film Ticket	102.8	95.1	98.5	98.3	97.1	101.7	99.6	99.5	100.5	102.6	98.2	101.0
景点门票	Scene Spot Ticket	100.0	100.0	100.4	115.9	104.9	90.4	113.6	100.0	88.3	111.8	91.8	101.2
有线电视	Cable Television	100.0	100.0	100.0	100.0	100.0	100.0	100.0	100.0	100.0	100.2	100.0	100.0
健身活动	Exercise	100.0	100.1	100.4	100.7	100.0	100.0	100.0	100.0	99.9	100.0	100.0	100.0
其他	Others	100.0	100.0	100.0	100.0	100.0	100.0	100.1	100.0	100.0	100.0	100.0	99.7
4.旅游	Tourism	102.3	97.5	98.5	105.5	99.3	96.8	103.0	104.2	98.4	99.9	96.0	100.2
旅行社收费	Travel Agency Charge	102.8	97.2	98.0	105.8	98.9	96.5	102.7	104.4	99.6	100.1	95.0	100.3
宾馆住宿	Guesthouse Stay	101.4	98.5	100.3	104.2	100.1	98.7	102.0	101.7	97.7	100.3	99.4	99.6
其他住宿	Other Stay	99.2	99.1	100.0	104.3	102.0	97.1	107.4	105.8	89.2	97.4	99.9	100.4
八、居住	**Residence**	**100.5**	**100.0**	**99.9**	**100.5**	**100.4**	**100.1**	**100.4**	**100.5**	**101.0**	**100.2**	**100.4**	**100.1**
1.建房及装修材料	Building and Building Decoration Materials	99.9	100.0	100.0	100.3	100.2	100.6	100.4	100.5	101.1	100.6	101.6	100.4
木材	Wood	100.2	100.2	99.8	99.8	99.6	100.8	100.5	101.2	101.3	100.6	104.1	100.7
木地板	Wood Floor	100.0	100.0	99.0	102.7	100.5	100.7	100.4	100.4	101.2	100.4	102.0	100.0
砖	Brick	99.9	99.6	100.4	99.5	101.1	100.7	100.8	101.9	99.9	99.9	101.3	100.7
水泥	Cement	98.6	99.9	100.5	100.3	100.4	100.6	100.1	99.5	100.3	100.6	101.5	100.1
涂料	Coating Material	99.9	100.0	100.0	100.1	100.1	101.7	100.3	99.9	99.1	100.1	100.3	100.1
胶合板	Plywood	100.0	100.2	100.2	100.5	99.9	100.6	100.7	100.2	101.9	100.5	102.3	100.5
玻璃	Glass	100.1	99.8	100.5	100.1	100.9	100.0	100.5	100.0	101.0	100.7	100.2	100.0
粘胶	Rayon	100.0	100.0	100.0	99.9	100.2	100.9	100.2	100.5	100.9	100.9	100.8	100.6
油漆	Paint	100.0	100.2	100.2	100.1	100.3	100.1	100.8	100.0	105.2	100.0	99.7	100.0
其他	Others	100.0	99.8	100.0	100.0	100.0	100.1	100.0	100.2	100.6	103.1	100.1	100.4
2.租房	Renting	100.0	100.0	102.8	100.0	100.3	100.4	102.6	100.8	100.7	100.1	100.0	100.0
公房房租	Public House Rent	100.0	100.0	100.0	100.0	100.0	100.0	100.1	103.3	100.0	100.0	100.1	100.0
私房房租	Private House Rent	100.0	100.0	101.0	100.0	100.7	101.0	103.3	100.0	101.7	100.2	100.0	100.0
其他费用	Other Fare	100.0	100.0	107.8	100.0	100.0	100.0	103.8	100.0	100.0	100.0	100.0	100.0
3.自有住房	Private Housing	100.4	100.1	100.3	100.0	101.2	100.4	99.8	100.9	100.8	100.0	100.0	100.0
房屋贷款利率	Houses Loans Interest Rate	100.3	100.0	100.0	100.0	103.2	100.9	100.0	102.5	101.1	100.0	100.0	100.0
物业管理费用	Propety Management Fee	100.0	100.0	100.9	100.0	100.0	100.0	99.2	100.0	100.7	100.0	100.0	100.0
维护修理费用	Upkeep and Repair Fee	100.0	100.3	100.0	100.0	100.0	100.0	100.0	100.0	100.5	100.0	100.0	100.0
其他	Others	104.3	100.0	100.0	100.0	99.9	100.1	100.2	99.4	100.7	99.8	100.0	100.1
4.水、电、燃料	Water,Electricity and Fuels	100.8	99.9	99.4	100.8	100.3	99.7	100.2	100.3	101.1	100.0	100.0	100.1
水	Water	101.3	100.0	100.6	102.6	100.5	100.0	100.0	100.0	100.0	100.0	100.0	100.0
电	Electricity	100.0	100.0	100.0	100.0	100.0	100.0	101.4	100.3	100.0	100.0	100.0	100.0
液化石油气	Liquefiled Petroleum Gas	103.1	99.6	94.5	100.0	101.3	98.3	97.6	101.8	106.9	99.7	100.1	100.1
管道燃气	Pipelined Gas	100.0	100.0	100.0	100.0	100.0	100.0	100.0	100.0	100.0	100.0	100.0	100.0
其他燃料	Other Fuels	100.1	99.9	99.9	100.9	100.1	99.7	100.0	100.0	101.8	100.3	100.1	100.5

7-18 农村居民消费价格（环比）指数
Rural Consumer Price Indices

商品类别及品名	Commodity Category and Commodity Name	（以上月价格为100）											
		1月 January	2月 February	3月 March	4月 April	5月 May	6月 June	7月 July	8月 August	9月 September	10月 October	11月 November	12月 December
居民消费价格总指数	**General Consumer Price Index**	**101.4**	**100.1**	**99.4**	**100.2**	**99.8**	**99.4**	**99.8**	**100.6**	**100.7**	**99.5**	**100.7**	**101.8**
非食品价格指数	**No-food**	**99.9**	**100.0**	**100.1**	**100.2**	**100.1**	**100.1**	**100.1**	**100.1**	**100.1**	**100.1**	**100.3**	**100.2**
服务项目价格指数	**Services**	**100.0**	**100.3**	**100.0**	**100.5**	**100.1**	**100.2**	**100.1**	**100.1**	**100.1**	**100.0**	**100.5**	**100.2**
工业品价格指数	**Industrial Products**	**99.9**	**99.8**	**100.1**	**100.1**	**100.1**	**100.1**	**100.1**	**100.2**	**100.1**	**100.1**	**100.3**	**100.2**
扣除食品和能源价格指数	**Deducting Foods and Energy**	**99.9**	**100.0**	**100.1**	**100.2**	**100.1**	**100.1**	**100.1**	**100.1**	**100.1**	**100.1**	**100.3**	**100.2**
扣除鲜菜鲜果总指数	**Deducting Fresh,Vegetables and Fruits**	**100.4**	**99.9**	**99.7**	**100.0**	**100.1**	**100.1**	**100.4**	**100.7**	**100.5**	**100.1**	**100.8**	**101.0**
消费品价格指数	**Consumer Goods**	**101.7**	**100.1**	**99.3**	**100.2**	**99.7**	**99.2**	**99.8**	**100.8**	**100.9**	**99.4**	**100.7**	**102.1**
一、食品	**Food**	**105.0**	**100.6**	**97.8**	**100.2**	**99.1**	**97.7**	**99.1**	**101.8**	**102.2**	**98.0**	**101.6**	**105.5**
1.粮食	Grain	100.8	100.3	99.8	100.5	100.5	99.9	101.7	100.5	101.7	100.7	102.1	102.4
大米	Rice	102.6	99.6	99.9	101.0	102.2	100.9	104.1	103.1	101.6	100.8	98.3	101.6
面粉	Flour	100.1	100.7	99.7	100.4	99.5	98.9	101.2	98.7	101.8	100.7	106.4	103.4
粮食制品	Grain Products	100.3	100.4	99.6	100.0	100.1	99.8	100.1	100.3	100.1	100.0	102.5	101.9
其他	Others	99.5	100.8	99.8	100.2	100.1	100.6	100.9	99.2	107.0	103.0	97.6	102.0
2.淀粉	Starches	102.5	97.6	100.2	101.3	100.7	100.3	104.0	102.2	100.3	100.2	99.2	100.9
淀粉	Starches	102.5	97.6	100.2	101.3	100.7	100.3	104.0	102.2	100.3	100.2	99.2	100.9
3.干豆类及豆制品	Beans and Beans Products	100.9	101.0	97.6	100.6	100.4	100.7	101.1	100.3	99.5	99.3	99.5	100.9
干豆	Beans	100.9	102.3	100.2	101.5	100.9	101.7	102.6	99.9	98.6	98.4	99.0	101.9
豆制品	Beans Products	100.8	100.1	95.8	100.1	100.0	99.9	100.1	100.6	100.2	99.9	99.9	100.2
4.油脂	Oil and Fat	100.5	100.2	99.2	99.5	101.3	99.9	100.3	101.3	100.7	101.2	105.6	105.3
食用植物油	Edible Vegetable Oil	99.9	100.7	99.5	99.5	100.6	99.7	100.3	101.5	101.3	101.0	105.7	105.6
植物油制品	Plant Oil Products	99.8	100.0	100.0	100.1	106.7	99.8	99.8	100.4	100.2	99.9	103.2	104.4
其他	Others	109.4	95.6	94.4	98.2	98.8	102.2	101.3	99.9	94.7	107.4	109.7	102.1
5.肉禽及其制品	Meal,Poultry and Their Products	104.6	99.7	96.5	97.4	98.7	100.5	102.6	105.6	102.3	100.0	104.5	106.2
（1）食用畜肉及副产品	Edible Livestock Meat and Their By-products	107.1	98.6	94.8	94.5	98.1	101.2	103.5	107.3	102.8	100.8	106.4	108.3
猪肉	Pork	109.2	97.1	93.4	93.2	97.7	101.3	105.3	109.9	103.3	100.7	107.6	109.8
牛肉	Beef	100.2	101.4	99.6	100.1	99.3	100.2	100.1	99.6	100.1	101.1	101.5	103.3
羊肉	Mutton	100.7	102.2	98.9	98.5	100.9	99.4	100.4	101.5	101.3	102.4	103.1	107.0
畜肉副产品	Livestock Meat By-products	106.2	102.0	95.9	94.4	96.5	104.1	98.6	103.5	104.3	100.1	106.0	105.3
其他	Others	109.2	99.6	94.5	91.4	99.2	97.2	106.7	111.6	100.4	99.7	106.7	103.1
（2）禽	Poultry	101.2	103.7	99.2	103.3	100.2	100.8	103.0	105.3	103.6	97.5	100.7	104.0
鸡	Chicken	102.0	104.7	99.6	103.6	101.0	101.6	103.7	104.4	104.8	96.5	100.0	103.8
鸭	Duck	99.1	97.6	100.4	102.7	98.6	95.0	95.9	107.0	99.5	101.1	106.2	103.6
其他	Others	99.2	103.9	95.9	101.8	96.9	101.4	104.5	109.1	100.0	100.5	100.4	105.2
（3）加工肉禽	Meal and Poultry Processing Products	100.3	100.2	99.1	101.1	98.9	98.7	100.1	101.7	100.2	99.6	102.1	101.9
畜肉制品	Livestock Meat Products	100.2	100.1	100.0	99.1	99.4	99.2	100.8	101.8	100.3	100.0	101.3	101.3
禽制品	Poultry Products	100.5	100.4	98.0	103.7	98.4	98.0	99.2	101.5	100.1	99.2	103.1	102.7

7-18 续表 1 continued

商品类别及品名	Commodity Category and Commodity Name	（以上月价格为100）											
		1月 January	2月 February	3月 March	4月 April	5月 May	6月 June	7月 July	8月 August	9月 September	10月 October	11月 November	12月 December
6.蛋	Eggs	100.4	94.7	97.3	100.0	102.0	100.6	101.7	108.3	106.8	100.3	101.3	103.7
鲜蛋	Fresh Eggs	100.4	94.0	96.9	100.1	102.1	100.3	102.1	109.5	107.8	100.2	101.3	104.0
蛋制品	Egg Products	100.3	98.7	99.7	99.3	101.0	102.0	99.5	100.4	100.8	100.9	101.7	101.4
7.水产品	Aquatic Product	101.9	101.3	98.8	99.9	101.4	101.2	101.4	100.7	99.6	98.9	100.5	99.9
（1）鱼	Fish	102.1	100.3	98.9	99.9	101.5	101.1	101.4	100.6	99.9	99.0	100.8	99.1
淡水鱼	Freshwater Fish	101.5	98.4	98.4	100.4	102.7	101.7	101.7	100.1	99.2	98.2	99.6	98.2
海水鱼	Seawater Fish	103.0	103.5	99.6	99.1	99.6	100.1	100.7	101.6	101.1	100.3	102.6	100.5
（2）其他水产品	Other Aquatic Product	101.5	104.1	98.6	100.0	101.2	101.4	101.7	100.9	98.9	98.6	99.7	102.0
虾蟹类	Shrimp and Crab	101.8	104.7	98.3	99.9	101.4	100.8	101.9	100.8	98.7	98.4	99.6	102.1
其他	Others	100.0	100.2	100.1	100.4	99.5	105.6	100.6	101.3	100.0	100.2	100.3	101.1
8.菜	Vegetable	125.5	101.9	92.0	98.1	86.7	77.9	95.3	113.2	114.0	82.5	96.7	126.3
鲜菜	Fresh Vegetable	129.5	102.0	90.6	97.8	83.9	75.5	94.5	116.4	116.6	80.1	95.6	131.6
干菜及菜制品	Dried Vegetable and Vegetable Products	100.1	100.1	99.9	99.2	99.4	99.9	99.4	100.9	100.1	100.2	101.7	102.7
薯类	Potato	107.7	103.6	108.8	102.4	113.7	73.1	98.2	99.0	106.4	85.3	100.8	105.3
9.调味品	Flavoring	99.8	100.0	100.3	100.0	100.0	99.7	101.0	100.1	100.2	100.0	100.0	100.9
盐	Salt	99.6	99.9	101.1	100.0	100.0	100.0	101.9	100.3	100.7	100.0	100.0	99.8
酱油	Soy Sauce	99.9	100.0	100.0	100.1	99.9	100.0	100.7	100.0	100.0	100.0	100.0	101.8
醋	Vinegar	100.0	100.0	100.0	100.0	100.0	100.0	101.0	100.0	100.0	100.0	100.0	102.3
味精	Aginomoto	100.0	100.0	100.0	100.0	100.0	100.0	100.9	100.0	100.0	100.6	100.0	100.4
其他	Others	100.0	100.0	100.0	100.0	100.3	98.0	99.0	100.0	99.7	99.3	100.0	100.0
10.糖	Carbohydrate	100.2	105.8	100.9	100.9	101.0	100.4	100.9	100.2	100.2	99.9	100.2	100.6
食糖	Sugar	100.5	113.9	102.1	101.3	102.2	101.0	101.2	100.3	100.3	99.7	100.4	101.1
糖果	Sweet	100.1	100.1	100.0	100.7	100.0	100.0	100.6	100.0	100.1	100.1	100.0	98.4
巧克力制品	Chocolate Products	100.0	100.0	100.0	100.0	100.0	100.0	100.7	100.0	100.0	100.0	100.0	107.2
糖类小食品	Little Carbohydrate Food	100.0	100.6	100.0	100.0	100.0	100.0	100.3	100.6	100.0	100.0	100.5	101.9
11.茶及饮料	Tea and Beverages	100.2	100.0	100.0	100.1	99.9	100.0	100.4	100.2	100.0	100.0	100.0	100.7
（1）茶叶	Tea	100.0	100.0	100.0	100.0	99.8	100.0	100.0	100.1	100.0	100.0	100.0	100.0
茶叶	Tea	100.0	100.0	100.0	100.0	99.8	100.0	100.0	100.1	100.0	100.0	100.0	100.0
（2）饮料	Beverages	100.2	100.1	100.0	100.2	100.0	100.0	100.7	100.3	100.0	100.0	100.0	101.3
固体饮料	Solid Beverages	100.0	100.4	100.2	100.3	99.8	100.1	99.9	100.4	100.0	100.0	100.0	101.0
液体饮料	Liquid Beverages	100.4	100.0	100.0	100.2	100.0	100.0	101.5	100.3	99.9	100.0	100.1	100.7
冷冻饮品	Frozen Beverages	100.1	100.0	100.0	100.0	100.0	100.0	100.0	100.0	100.0	100.0	100.0	102.5
12.干鲜瓜果	Dried and Fresh Melons and Fruits	109.7	106.6	100.7	110.6	106.6	99.4	85.4	85.0	94.5	96.8	100.6	106.7
鲜瓜果	Fresh Fruits	112.2	108.4	100.8	113.1	107.9	99.2	82.5	81.0	92.8	95.0	100.4	108.8
干（坚）果	Dried Fruits	100.7	99.5	100.1	99.5	100.2	100.6	100.5	102.3	100.3	102.4	101.1	100.5
13.糕点饼干面包	Cake,Biscuit and Bread	100.0	100.0	100.0	100.0	100.0	100.0	100.6	100.6	100.0	99.9	99.9	101.4
糕点	Cake	100.1	100.0	100.0	100.0	100.0	100.0	100.4	100.0	100.0	100.0	100.0	101.5
饼干	Biscuit	100.0	100.0	99.9	100.1	100.1	100.1	101.0	101.7	100.0	99.8	99.8	102.0
面包	Bread	100.0	100.0	100.0	100.0	100.0	100.0	100.6	100.0	100.0	100.0	100.0	100.2
14.液体乳及乳制品	Liquid Milk and Their Products	99.9	100.1	100.0	100.2	100.0	100.0	100.1	100.0	100.0	100.1	100.0	103.6
巴氏杀菌奶或消毒奶	Pasteurization Milk or Disinfection Milk	99.8	100.0	100.2	100.0	100.0	100.0	100.0	100.0	100.0	100.0	100.0	108.7
酸奶	Leben	100.0	100.0	100.0	101.4	100.0	100.0	100.0	100.0	100.0	100.0	100.0	97.2

7-18 续表 2 continued

商品类别及品名	Commodity Category and Commodity Name	（以上月价格为100）											
		1月 January	2月 February	3月 March	4月 April	5月 May	6月 June	7月 July	8月 August	9月 September	10月 October	11月 November	12月 December
奶粉	Milk Powder	100.0	100.2	99.9	100.0	100.0	100.0	100.4	100.0	100.0	100.2	100.0	102.0
其他	Others	100.0	100.2	99.7	100.0	100.0	100.0	100.0	100.0	100.0	100.0	100.0	100.0
15.在外用膳食品	Outward Dinner	100.7	100.3	100.0	99.8	100.3	100.1	100.0	100.0	100.0	99.8	100.9	101.8
主食	Staple Food	100.2	100.0	100.1	99.8	100.0	100.0	99.9	100.0	100.0	100.0	102.8	103.6
炒菜	Hot Dish	101.2	100.6	100.0	99.5	100.0	100.0	99.9	100.0	100.0	100.0	100.1	100.2
地方小吃	Local Snack	100.6	99.9	99.7	100.2	101.6	100.6	100.4	100.0	100.0	98.7	99.3	102.1
16.其他食品	Other Foods	99.9	100.1	100.0	100.0	100.1	100.1	100.8	100.2	99.9	99.9	99.7	100.5
其他食品	Other Foods	99.9	100.1	100.0	100.0	100.1	100.1	100.8	100.2	99.9	99.9	99.7	100.5
二、烟酒及用品	**Tobacco,Liquor and Their Appliances**	**100.1**	**100.0**	**100.1**	**100.2**	**100.0**	**99.9**	**100.1**	**100.3**	**100.1**	**100.1**	**100.1**	**101.2**
1.烟草	Tobacco	100.3	100.4	100.0	100.2	100.1	99.8	99.8	100.0	100.0	100.0	100.0	100.9
国产卷烟	Domestic Cigarette	100.3	100.5	100.0	100.3	100.1	99.7	99.9	100.0	100.0	100.0	100.0	101.0
进口卷烟	Import Cigarette	100.0	99.9	99.9	100.0	100.0	100.0	98.6	100.0	100.0	100.0	101.4	100.0
其他	Others	100.0	100.0	100.0	100.0	100.0	100.0	100.0	100.0	100.0	100.0	100.0	100.0
2.酒	Liquor	99.9	99.6	100.2	100.1	99.9	100.0	100.3	100.6	100.2	100.1	100.1	101.6
白酒	White Spirit	100.0	99.4	100.3	100.3	100.0	100.0	100.2	100.9	100.0	100.3	100.2	102.2
葡萄酒	Grape	100.0	100.0	100.0	100.0	100.0	100.0	100.5	100.0	100.0	100.1	100.7	100.2
啤酒	Beer	99.6	100.0	100.2	99.9	99.6	99.8	100.5	100.2	100.7	99.7	100.0	100.8
其他	Others	100.0	100.0	100.0	100.0	100.0	100.0	100.2	100.0	100.0	100.0	100.0	100.1
3.吸烟、饮酒用品	Appliances For Smoking and Drinking	100.1	99.9	100.0	100.0	100.0	100.0	100.0	100.0	100.0	100.0	100.1	99.7
吸烟用品	Appliances for Smoking	100.0	100.0	100.1	100.0	100.0	100.0	100.0	100.0	100.0	100.0	100.0	100.1
饮酒用品	Appliances For Drinking	100.2	99.8	100.0	100.0	100.0	100.0	100.0	100.0	100.0	100.0	100.2	99.5
三、衣着	**Clothing**	**99.2**	**99.1**	**99.8**	**99.8**	**99.7**	**100.0**	**100.0**	**99.9**	**99.9**	**100.2**	**100.4**	**100.1**
1.服装	Garments	99.1	98.8	99.7	99.7	99.5	100.0	100.0	99.9	99.9	100.3	100.7	99.9
（1）男式服装	Men's Garments	98.8	98.9	99.8	99.8	99.6	99.9	100.2	100.0	100.2	100.6	100.9	99.8
大衣	Topcoat	98.9	97.5	98.8	99.6	100.0	99.3	100.0	100.0	100.6	100.0	99.5	100.0
毛线衣	Woollen Sweater	100.0	99.2	98.5	98.9	97.2	99.0	102.1	100.0	101.0	100.4	98.3	100.0
夹克衫	Jacket	99.3	99.2	99.9	99.9	99.9	99.9	99.9	100.0	100.0	100.7	103.3	99.8
衬衫	Shirt	97.8	100.0	100.0	100.0	100.0	100.0	100.0	100.0	100.0	100.6	100.7	100.0
T恤衫	T-shirt	100.0	100.1	100.0	100.1	99.5	100.1	99.8	100.7	100.8	101.0	101.0	100.2
裤子	Trousers	97.4	97.2	101.8	99.9	100.0	100.0	99.7	100.0	100.0	100.7	100.7	98.7
西服	Western-style Clothes	98.9	99.1	100.0	99.8	99.8	100.2	100.0	100.0	100.0	100.4	101.4	100.0
运动衫裤	Gym Suit	100.0	100.0	100.0	100.0	100.0	100.0	99.9	100.0	100.1	101.8	101.7	100.0
内衣	Underwaist	98.8	99.6	98.4	99.7	99.7	100.0	100.0	100.0	100.0	100.8	101.1	99.4
羽绒衣	Eider Down Outerwear	98.1	98.1	99.8	100.0	100.0	100.0	100.0	99.6	99.9	100.5	100.8	100.2
其他	Others	98.1	98.3	100.0	100.0	100.0	100.0	100.0	100.0	100.0	100.0	100.0	100.0
（2）女式服装	Women's Garments	99.2	98.7	99.5	99.4	99.1	100.0	99.9	99.8	99.8	100.3	100.6	99.9
大衣	Topcoat	98.3	94.6	100.0	100.0	100.0	100.0	100.0	100.0	100.0	100.0	100.5	100.0
毛线衣	Woollen Sweater	98.7	97.5	96.3	99.7	95.5	100.0	100.0	100.0	100.0	100.0	100.2	99.9
羽绒衣	Eider Down Outerwear	98.6	98.4	99.8	100.0	100.0	100.0	100.0	99.5	99.9	100.5	100.5	100.0
套装	Coordinates	100.7	100.0	100.0	95.4	100.0	100.0	100.0	99.8	100.0	100.8	100.8	100.0
衬衫	Shirt	98.6	99.8	100.0	100.0	100.5	99.6	100.0	100.0	94.9	100.1	100.1	100.0

7-18 续表 3 continued

商品类别及品名	Commodity Category and Commodity Name	（以2005年平均价格为100）											
		1月 January	2月 February	3月 March	4月 April	5月 May	6月 June	7月 July	8月 August	9月 September	10月 October	11月 November	12月 December
T恤衫	T-shirt	100.1	99.2	100.3	100.4	96.3	100.0	100.0	100.0	100.0	101.3	101.2	100.1
裙子	Skirt	98.5	100.0	99.9	100.0	97.9	101.0	100.0	98.6	99.5	100.5	100.0	99.4
裤子	Trousers	100.2	100.0	100.0	98.5	99.5	100.0	99.1	100.0	100.0	99.1	100.9	100.0
运动衫裤	Gym Suit	100.0	100.4	99.0	100.6	99.4	100.0	100.0	100.0	100.0	101.5	101.9	100.0
内衣	Underwaist	98.9	98.9	99.9	100.1	100.8	99.9	99.9	99.9	102.4	100.5	100.6	100.2
其他	Others	100.0	99.9	100.0	100.0	100.0	99.6	100.0	100.0	100.0	100.0	100.4	100.0
（3）儿童服装	Children's Garments	99.4	99.0	100.1	100.1	100.5	100.0	100.0	100.0	99.3	100.0	100.5	100.1
套装	Coordinates	99.7	99.1	100.0	100.3	99.7	99.4	100.0	100.0	100.1	100.1	100.6	100.1
裤子	Trousers	99.7	99.2	100.0	99.9	101.8	100.0	99.9	100.0	100.1	100.5	100.6	100.1
裙子	Skirt	99.1	99.1	100.3	100.1	100.4	101.3	100.0	100.0	96.9	99.2	100.0	100.0
其他	Others	98.1	98.1	100.0	100.0	100.6	100.6	100.0	100.0	98.5	100.0	100.0	100.0
2.衣着材料	Clothing Materials	100.1	99.9	99.8	100.0	100.6	100.0	100.1	99.9	99.8	100.4	100.1	100.0
棉布	Cotton Cloth	100.0	100.0	100.0	100.0	101.1	100.0	100.0	100.0	99.8	100.2	100.0	100.0
棉混纺布	Cotton Textiles Cloth	100.3	100.2	100.0	100.0	100.1	100.0	100.2	100.0	100.0	100.3	100.3	100.0
化纤布	Chemical Fiber Cloth	100.2	100.2	100.0	100.0	101.0	100.0	100.2	99.8	99.5	100.7	100.2	100.0
毛线	Knitting Wool	100.0	99.2	99.2	100.0	100.0	100.0	100.0	100.0	100.0	100.0	100.0	100.0
3.鞋袜帽	Shoes,Socks and Hats	99.0	99.1	100.0	100.1	99.5	99.9	100.1	100.0	100.0	99.9	100.1	100.1
（1）鞋	Shoes	98.8	99.0	100.0	100.1	99.3	99.9	100.1	99.9	100.0	99.9	100.1	100.1
男鞋	Men's Shoes	98.8	99.9	100.0	100.2	99.2	100.0	100.0	100.0	100.0	100.0	100.0	100.3
女鞋	Women's Shoes	98.5	98.1	100.0	100.0	99.0	100.0	100.3	99.9	99.9	100.0	100.2	100.0
童鞋	Children's Shoes	99.6	99.4	100.1	100.1	100.0	99.7	100.0	100.0	100.0	99.7	100.0	100.0
（2）袜子	Socks	99.8	99.8	100.0	100.0	100.5	100.0	100.0	100.0	100.0	100.0	100.0	100.0
男袜	Men's Socks	99.8	99.8	100.0	100.0	100.0	100.0	100.0	100.0	100.0	100.0	100.0	100.0
女袜	Women's Socks	99.8	99.7	100.0	100.0	101.0	100.0	100.0	100.0	100.0	100.0	100.0	100.0
（3）帽子	Hats	99.7	99.9	100.0	100.0	100.1	100.0	100.0	100.0	100.0	100.0	100.0	100.0
男帽	Men's Hats	99.6	100.0	100.0	100.0	100.2	100.0	100.0	100.0	100.0	100.0	100.0	100.0
女帽	Women's Hats	99.9	99.9	100.0	100.0	100.0	100.0	100.0	100.0	100.0	100.1	100.1	100.0
4.衣着加工服务费	Clothing Manufacturing Services	100.1	99.6	100.0	100.0	100.0	100.0	100.0	100.0	100.0	100.0	100.0	102.4
缝纫	Sewing	100.2	99.4	100.0	100.0	100.0	100.0	100.0	100.0	100.0	100.0	100.0	103.1
清洗	Washing	100.0	100.0	100.0	100.0	100.0	100.0	100.0	100.0	100.0	100.0	100.0	100.0
四、家庭设备用品及维修服务	**Household Facilities, Articles and Services**	**100.0**	**99.8**	**100.0**	**100.3**	**99.9**	**100.0**	**100.0**	**100.0**	**100.2**	**100.6**	**100.3**	**100.6**
1.耐用消费品	Durable Consumer Goods	100.0	99.6	100.0	100.4	100.1	100.5	100.3	99.9	100.0	100.7	100.2	100.2
（1）家具	Furniture	100.0	99.7	99.9	101.0	100.0	100.0	99.9	99.8	99.9	101.6	100.6	100.2
柜	Cabinet	100.0	99.4	99.7	101.0	100.0	100.0	99.9	99.6	100.0	102.2	100.0	100.3
床	Bed	100.0	100.0	100.0	101.7	100.0	100.0	100.0	100.0	99.9	101.2	101.0	100.2
桌	Desk	100.1	100.0	100.0	100.1	100.0	100.2	100.0	99.2	99.3	101.3	100.7	100.1
椅	Chair	99.8	98.6	100.0	100.0	100.0	100.0	99.8	100.1	100.1	101.7	100.1	100.1
沙发	Sofa	100.0	100.0	100.0	101.4	100.0	100.0	100.0	100.0	100.0	101.4	101.0	100.0
其他	Others	100.1	100.2	100.1	99.5	100.8	100.1	100.0	100.0	100.1	101.6	100.1	100.1
（2）家庭设备	Household Appliances	100.0	99.6	100.0	99.9	100.1	100.9	100.5	100.0	100.1	100.1	100.0	100.2
洗衣机	Washing Machine	99.4	100.3	99.9	99.9	99.9	100.0	100.1	100.2	101.1	100.5	99.6	100.2

7-18 续表 4 continued

商品类别及品名	Commodity Category and Commodity Name	（以上月价格为100）											
		1月 January	2月 February	3月 March	4月 April	5月 May	6月 June	7月 July	8月 August	9月 September	10月 October	11月 November	12月 December
电风扇	Electric Fan	99.5	98.6	100.0	101.8	100.4	100.9	102.2	100.0	100.0	100.0	100.0	102.4
电冰箱（柜）	Refrigerator	100.4	99.2	100.4	100.1	100.0	100.0	100.2	99.9	99.7	100.0	99.8	99.7
吸排油烟机	Kitchen Ventilato	99.4	99.8	99.5	99.7	100.0	100.2	100.3	99.8	99.8	100.0	100.0	101.2
空调器	Air-conditioning	99.8	99.9	99.7	100.5	100.5	103.8	100.4	100.0	100.1	100.0	99.9	99.7
热水器	Water Heater	100.9	100.0	100.3	97.0	99.6	100.4	99.9	99.8	99.9	100.0	100.3	98.0
微波炉	Microwave Oven	100.7	99.0	100.4	98.8	100.0	100.0	100.2	100.0	100.0	100.0	100.4	99.4
电炊具	Electric Cooking Appliance	100.5	100.0	99.6	99.8	100.0	100.4	99.9	100.0	100.0	100.0	100.0	100.4
2.室内装饰品	Interior Decorations	100.0	100.0	100.0	100.0	100.0	99.6	100.0	100.0	100.4	100.0	100.0	100.1
纺织装饰品	Textile Process Decorations	100.0	100.0	100.0	100.0	100.0	99.1	100.0	100.0	100.9	100.0	100.0	100.0
装饰灯具	Architectural Lamps and Lanterns	100.0	100.0	100.0	100.0	99.9	99.9	100.0	100.0	100.0	100.0	100.0	100.3
其他	Others	100.0	100.0	100.0	100.0	100.0	100.0	100.0	100.0	100.0	100.0	100.0	100.0
3.床上用品	Bedclothes	100.2	99.9	100.0	100.5	99.4	100.0	99.9	100.0	100.5	100.4	100.2	100.4
毛毯	Woollen Blanket	100.4	99.3	100.0	101.2	98.5	100.0	99.8	99.8	100.7	101.3	100.0	101.7
被子	Quilt	100.1	100.1	100.0	100.1	100.1	100.0	99.7	100.0	100.3	100.0	100.6	100.0
床上套件	Bed Articles	100.1	100.1	100.0	100.3	99.7	100.0	100.0	100.0	100.7	100.0	100.0	99.6
其他	Others	100.8	100.7	100.0	100.0	99.3	100.0	100.0	100.0	100.0	100.0	100.0	100.0
4.日用杂品	Sundry Articles	100.1	100.0	100.1	100.2	99.8	99.2	99.4	100.4	100.6	100.6	100.0	101.2
茶具	Tea Set	100.0	100.0	99.9	100.0	99.3	104.2	99.9	100.0	102.9	105.1	100.0	100.0
餐具	Tableware	100.0	100.0	99.4	100.0	99.4	100.0	96.4	99.7	100.0	100.0	100.0	100.0
厨具	Kitchen Utensils	100.4	100.0	100.0	101.2	100.0	97.9	100.0	100.4	101.7	100.0	100.0	101.3
家用手工工具	Domestic Handwork Tools	100.0	100.0	100.0	100.0	100.0	100.7	100.6	100.0	100.0	100.0	100.0	103.5
洗涤用品	Washing Articles	100.0	100.0	100.0	100.0	100.0	98.3	100.0	100.0	100.1	100.0	100.0	101.2
其他	Others	100.0	100.0	101.2	100.0	100.0	96.9	99.9	102.4	100.0	99.9	99.9	101.9
5.家庭服务及加工维修服务	Household Service and Manufacturing Upkeep	100.0	100.0	100.0	100.0	100.0	100.0	100.0	100.0	100.0	100.3	101.8	101.4
家庭服务	Household Service	100.0	100.0	100.0	100.0	100.0	100.0	100.0	100.0	100.0	100.6	102.1	101.4
加工维修服务	Manufacturing Upkeep	100.0	100.0	100.0	100.0	100.0	100.0	100.0	100.0	100.0	100.0	101.5	101.4
五、医疗保健和个人用品	**Health Care and Personal Articles**	**100.1**	**100.4**	**99.9**	**100.2**	**100.6**	**100.0**	**100.0**	**100.1**	**100.4**	**99.6**	**100.1**	**100.2**
1.医疗保健	Health Care	100.0	100.4	99.7	100.1	100.3	100.0	100.0	100.0	100.6	99.4	100.2	100.2
（1）医疗器具及用品	Medical Facilities and Goods	96.9	100.8	99.7	99.4	99.5	100.0	100.0	100.0	101.1	98.2	100.0	98.1
医疗器具及用品	Medical Facilities and Goods	96.9	100.8	99.7	99.4	99.5	100.0	100.0	100.0	101.1	98.2	100.0	98.1
（2）中药材及中成药	Herbs and Ready-made Traditional Chinese Medicine	100.2	101.6	98.6	100.5	100.5	100.3	100.2	100.3	101.1	99.7	100.4	100.3
中药材	Herbs	100.7	102.3	97.5	100.8	101.3	100.2	100.1	100.0	101.3	99.5	100.7	100.0
中成药	Ready-made Traditional Chinese Medicine	99.6	100.6	100.3	100.0	99.4	100.5	100.4	100.8	100.8	99.9	100.0	100.7
（3）西药	Western Medicine	100.2	100.1	100.1	100.2	100.6	99.7	99.9	99.9	100.9	99.1	100.1	100.3
抗微生物药	Anti-microorganism Medicine	100.1	100.1	100.1	100.0	100.0	100.0	100.0	99.7	101.7	97.5	100.0	101.4

7-18 续表 5 continued

商品类别及品名	Commodity Category and Commodity Name	1月 January	2月 February	3月 March	4月 April	5月 May	6月 June	7月 July	8月 August	9月 September	10月 October	11月 November	12月 December
		(以上月价格为100)											
消化系统用药	Alimentary System Medicine	100.3	100.5	100.0	100.0	100.0	100.0	100.0	100.0	100.5	99.4	100.3	99.7
呼吸系统用药	Respiratory System Medicine	99.4	100.0	100.7	100.8	99.7	100.2	100.1	100.0	101.9	98.5	100.7	100.0
解热镇痛及非甾体抗炎药	Allays a Fever the Analgesia and the Non-steroid Body Anti-inflammatory Agent	103.6	100.2	99.4	100.0	101.0	99.0	100.0	100.0	100.7	99.4	99.7	101.6
抗肿瘤药	Antineoplastic Drug	99.1	100.0	99.9	100.0	107.8	97.8	100.7	98.7	97.5	103.4	101.0	100.0
激素及调节内分泌功能药	Hormone and Adjustment Internal Secretion Function Medicine	98.9	100.4	100.0	100.0	100.0	100.1	98.5	100.2	102.3	97.8	100.0	98.8
循环系统用药	Circulating System Medicine	98.9	100.0	100.4	100.5	100.0	99.8	99.9	100.0	100.4	100.0	100.0	100.1
神经系统用药	Nerve System Medicine	100.1	100.4	100.0	100.6	100.0	100.0	100.0	100.0	101.0	98.7	100.0	100.7
专科用药	Junior Medicine	99.1	99.5	100.6	100.2	100.2	100.1	100.0	100.0	100.3	98.7	100.0	99.4
其他	Others	99.8	100.0	100.0	100.1	99.9	100.1	100.1	99.9	100.3	99.5	100.1	100.0
(4) 保健品及器具	Healthcare Equipment	99.0	99.6	100.0	100.4	100.0	100.3	100.0	100.1	100.4	99.3	100.3	99.9
保健器具	Health Protection Equipment	100.0	99.5	100.0	100.1	100.0	100.8	100.0	100.0	100.0	99.1	100.1	99.8
滋补保健用品	Tonic and Health Products	98.5	99.7	100.0	100.6	100.0	100.0	100.1	100.1	100.6	99.4	100.3	100.0
(5) 医疗保健服务	Health Care Services	100.0	100.0	100.0	99.9	100.0	100.2	100.0	100.0	100.0	99.8	100.1	100.2
挂号费	Registration	100.0	100.0	100.0	100.0	100.0	100.0	100.0	100.0	100.0	100.0	100.0	100.0
注射费	Injection Expenses	100.0	100.0	100.0	100.0	100.0	100.0	100.0	100.0	100.0	100.0	100.0	100.0
检查费	Examination Expenses	100.3	100.0	100.0	100.0	100.0	100.0	100.0	100.0	100.2	100.0	100.0	100.0
手术费	Operation Expenses	100.0	100.0	100.0	100.0	100.0	100.0	100.0	100.0	100.0	100.0	100.0	100.9
住院费	Hospitalization Expenses	100.0	100.0	100.0	99.3	100.0	100.8	100.0	100.0	100.0	99.2	100.7	100.0
理疗费	Physiotherapy Expenses	100.0	100.0	100.0	100.0	100.0	100.0	100.0	100.0	100.0	100.0	100.0	100.0
化验费	Analysis Expenses	100.0	100.0	100.0	100.0	100.0	100.0	100.0	100.0	100.0	100.0	100.0	100.0
其他	Others	100.0	100.0	100.0	100.0	100.0	100.0	100.0	100.0	100.0	100.0	100.0	100.0
2.个人用品及服务	Personal Articles and Services	100.3	100.3	100.4	100.4	101.2	99.9	99.9	100.1	99.8	100.0	99.9	100.2
(1) 化妆美容用品	Cosmetics	100.0	99.9	99.9	100.0	100.2	99.9	100.0	100.0	100.0	100.0	100.0	100.5
化妆美容器具	Cosmetics Appliances	100.0	100.0	100.2	99.8	100.2	100.0	100.0	100.1	100.0	100.0	100.0	100.0
美容化妆品	Facial Beautifiers	100.0	100.0	100.0	100.0	100.0	100.0	100.0	100.0	100.0	100.0	100.0	100.9
护肤品	Protects Skin Products	100.1	100.0	100.0	100.0	100.3	99.7	100.0	100.0	100.0	100.0	100.0	100.0
护发美容品	Protects Sends the Beauty Products	100.0	99.6	98.9	100.0	100.5	100.0	100.0	100.0	100.0	100.0	100.0	100.3
(2) 清洁化妆用品	Cleaning Toiletware	100.0	100.0	100.1	100.3	100.0	100.1	100.0	100.2	99.4	100.4	100.0	100.8
洗发用品	Hairdressing Articles	99.9	99.9	100.4	99.7	100.0	100.0	100.0	100.3	98.5	101.5	100.0	98.3
洗浴用品	Bathing Articles	100.1	100.0	100.0	101.0	100.0	100.2	100.0	100.3	100.0	99.5	100.0	100.0
其他	Others	100.0	100.0	100.0	100.0	100.0	100.0	100.0	100.0	100.0	100.0	100.0	105.7

7-18 续表 6 continued

商品类别及品名	Commodity Category and Commodity Name	1月 January	2月 February	3月 March	4月 April	5月 May	6月 June	7月 July	8月 August	9月 September	10月 October	11月 November	12月 December
		（以上月价格为100）											
（3）个人饰品	Personal Decoraions	100.7	100.9	101.3	101.2	104.2	99.8	99.8	100.2	99.8	99.7	99.7	99.8
首饰	Ornaments	101.5	102.6	103.6	104.7	111.1	99.5	99.4	100.8	99.4	99.4	99.5	99.1
皮件	Leather Appliance	100.6	100.0	100.0	95.9	99.3	100.0	100.0	99.8	100.0	100.0	99.4	100.0
手表	Watch	100.0	100.0	100.0	99.6	100.0	100.0	100.0	100.0	100.0	100.0	100.0	100.6
领带	Necktie	100.0	99.9	99.9	101.5	100.0	99.9	100.0	99.7	100.0	100.0	100.2	100.2
其他	Others	100.0	100.0	100.0	100.0	100.0	100.0	100.0	100.0	100.0	100.0	100.0	100.0
（4）个人服务	Personal Services	100.4	100.1	100.0	100.0	99.9	100.0	100.0	100.0	100.0	100.0	100.1	100.1
美容	Cosmetology	100.0	100.0	100.0	100.0	100.0	100.0	100.0	100.0	100.0	100.0	100.0	100.0
理（烫）发	Haircut(permanent wave)	101.1	100.4	100.0	100.0	100.0	100.0	100.0	100.0	100.0	100.0	100.0	100.0
洗浴	Bathe	100.0	100.0	100.0	100.0	99.4	100.0	100.0	100.0	100.0	100.0	100.3	100.3
其他	Others	100.0	100.0	100.0	100.0	100.0	100.0	100.0	100.0	100.0	100.0	100.0	100.0
六、交通和通信	**Transportation and Communication**	**99.6**	**100.5**	**99.8**	**99.9**	**100.1**	**100.2**	**99.9**	**99.9**	**100.0**	**100.0**	**100.4**	**100.2**
1.交通	Transportation	99.7	101.1	99.9	100.1	100.4	100.3	99.9	100.1	100.0	100.0	100.1	100.1
（1）交通工具	Transportation Facility	99.7	100.8	99.8	99.5	99.9	99.2	99.4	100.0	100.0	100.0	99.9	100.1
摩托车	Motorcycle	99.5	102.8	100.0	100.1	100.0	100.0	99.7	100.0	100.0	100.0	100.0	99.9
自行车	Bicycle	100.0	100.0	99.6	99.3	100.0	99.1	98.6	100.0	100.1	100.0	100.0	100.4
轿车	Car	99.0	100.0	100.0	99.9	99.4	98.2	100.6	99.9	99.9	100.0	99.5	99.7
其他	Others	100.0	100.0	100.0	96.0	100.0	100.0	99.6	100.0	100.0	100.0	100.0	100.0
（2）车用燃料及零配件	Fuels and Parts	100.0	100.0	100.9	102.9	102.7	103.9	101.0	100.0	100.0	100.4	100.0	100.0
汽油	Gasoline	99.9	99.9	101.0	104.2	103.4	105.4	100.6	100.0	100.0	100.0	100.0	100.0
柴油	Diesel Oil	100.0	100.0	101.0	102.5	103.8	104.3	100.7	100.0	100.0	100.6	100.1	100.1
零配件	Parts	100.0	100.0	100.5	100.9	100.0	100.0	103.1	100.0	100.0	101.0	100.0	99.7
其他	Others	100.0	100.0	101.0	102.6	98.9	102.0	100.0	100.7	100.0	99.6	100.0	100.0
（3）车辆使用及维修费	Using and Upkeep Fare	99.9	98.8	100.8	99.6	100.6	100.3	100.1	100.2	100.0	99.7	99.7	100.8
驾驶证	Driving License	99.7	99.8	99.0	98.3	102.6	101.1	100.6	100.8	100.0	98.8	98.7	98.9
保险费	Insurance Expenses	100.0	100.0	100.0	100.0	100.0	100.0	100.0	100.0	100.0	100.0	100.0	100.0
停车费	Parking Expenses	100.0	100.0	100.0	100.0	100.0	100.0	100.0	100.0	100.0	100.0	100.0	100.0
车辆修理服务费	Vehicle Upkeep Service Fare	99.9	97.2	102.6	100.0	100.0	100.0	100.0	100.0	100.0	100.0	100.0	102.6
其他	Others	100.0	100.0	100.0	100.0	100.0	100.0	100.0	100.0	100.0	100.0	100.0	100.0
（4）市区公共交通费	Incity Traffic Fare	99.1	101.7	100.0	100.0	100.0	100.0	100.0	100.0	100.0	100.0	101.9	100.0
公共汽车票	Bus Ticket	100.0	103.4	100.0	100.0	100.0	100.0	100.0	100.0	100.0	100.0	100.0	100.0
出租汽车	Taxi	97.6	100.7	100.0	100.0	100.0	100.0	100.0	100.0	100.0	100.0	105.4	100.0
其他	Others	100.0	100.0	100.0	100.0	100.0	100.0	100.0	100.0	100.0	100.0	100.0	100.0
（5）城市间交通费	Intercity Traffic Fare	99.5	104.3	98.7	100.1	100.1	100.6	100.0	100.2	100.0	100.0	100.7	100.0
飞机票	Airplane Ticket	129.2	68.4	113.2	111.7	110.5	81.1	100.0	100.0	100.0	100.0	100.0	100.0
火车票	Train Ticket	100.0	100.0	100.0	100.0	100.0	100.0	100.0	100.0	100.0	100.0	100.0	100.0
长途汽车	Intertown Bus	99.2	105.5	98.3	100.0	100.0	100.8	100.0	100.2	100.0	100.0	100.8	100.0
其他	Others	100.0	101.3	100.0	100.0	100.0	100.8	100.0	100.0	100.0	100.0	100.0	100.0
2.通信	Communication	99.5	99.5	99.7	99.7	99.5	99.8	99.9	99.8	99.9	99.9	100.8	100.3
（1）通信工具	Communication Facility	98.2	98.1	98.9	98.7	98.0	99.4	99.5	99.0	99.7	99.7	99.7	98.7
固定电话机	Telephone	98.9	99.4	99.2	99.9	97.8	100.0	100.0	100.0	100.2	100.0	100.0	100.0
移动电话机	Mobile Phone	96.9	96.5	98.8	96.7	97.9	98.5	98.8	97.4	98.6	99.1	99.0	96.1
其他	Others	99.0	97.4	97.8	99.4	100.1	99.5	99.2	99.4	100.0	100.0	100.0	100.0

7-18 续表 7 continued

商品类别及品名	Commodity Category and Commodity Name	（以上月价格为100）											
		1月 January	2月 February	3月 March	4月 April	5月 May	6月 June	7月 July	8月 August	9月 September	10月 October	11月 November	12月 December
（2）通信服务	Communication Service	100.0	100.0	100.0	100.0	100.0	100.0	100.0	100.0	100.0	100.0	101.2	100.9
移动通信费	Mobile Communication Fee	100.0	100.0	100.0	100.0	100.0	100.0	100.0	100.0	100.0	100.0	100.0	100.0
市内电话费	Incity Telephone Fee	100.0	100.0	100.0	100.0	100.0	100.0	100.0	100.0	100.0	100.0	100.0	100.0
长途电话费	Long Distance Call Fee	100.0	100.0	100.0	100.0	100.0	100.0	100.0	100.0	100.0	100.0	100.0	100.0
月租费	Month Hiring Fee	100.0	100.0	100.0	100.0	100.0	100.0	100.0	100.0	100.0	100.0	100.0	100.0
上网费	Net Play Fee	100.0	100.0	100.0	100.0	100.0	100.0	100.0	100.0	99.5	100.0	100.0	100.0
信件邮寄	Letter Post	100.0	100.0	100.0	100.0	100.0	100.0	100.0	100.0	100.0	100.0	115.3	109.8
包裹邮寄	Package Post	100.0	100.0	100.0	100.0	100.0	100.0	100.0	100.0	100.0	100.0	100.0	100.0
其他	Others	100.0	100.0	100.0	100.0	100.0	100.0	100.0	100.0	100.0	100.0	100.0	100.0
七、娱乐教育文化用品及服务	**Recreation,Education and Culture Articles**	**99.8**	**99.9**	**100.0**	**100.6**	**100.0**	**100.0**	**100.0**	**100.0**	**100.1**	**100.0**	**100.0**	**99.9**
1.文娱用耐用消费品及服务	Durable Consumer Goods For Cultural and Recreational Use and Service	99.2	99.3	99.9	99.6	100.0	100.0	100.0	99.8	100.1	99.9	99.9	99.6
电视机	Television	98.9	98.9	99.9	99.4	100.2	99.8	99.8	99.8	99.9	99.8	99.9	100.6
激光视盘机	Laser Video Disc Machine	99.3	98.8	100.1	100.0	99.5	100.5	100.2	99.8	100.0	99.6	99.3	96.0
摄像机	Pickup Camera	100.0	100.0	100.0	100.0	100.0	100.0	100.0	100.0	100.0	100.0	100.0	100.0
照相机	Camera	95.8	100.0	100.0	100.0	100.0	100.6	100.0	100.0	101.8	100.0	100.0	98.5
家用音响	Acoustic Equipment	100.4	99.5	99.5	98.6	99.8	100.0	100.6	100.1	100.0	100.0	99.9	99.1
便携式音响	Portable Acoustics	100.0	100.1	100.0	100.0	100.0	100.0	100.0	100.0	100.0	100.0	100.0	99.8
电脑	Computer	98.1	99.8	99.9	99.9	100.0	100.0	99.8	98.5	100.0	100.0	100.0	100.0
修理服务	Repair Service	106.3	99.9	99.8	100.0	100.0	99.8	101.2	99.9	100.3	100.2	100.0	100.0
其他	Others	100.0	100.0	100.0	100.0	100.0	100.0	100.0	100.0	100.0	100.0	100.0	100.0
2.教育	Education	100.0	100.2	100.0	100.6	100.0	100.0	100.0	100.0	100.0	100.0	100.0	100.0
（1）教材及参考书	Teaching Material and Reference Books	99.9	100.0	100.0	100.1	100.0	100.0	100.0	99.6	100.3	100.0	100.0	100.0
工具书	Tool Book	99.0	100.0	100.0	100.0	100.0	100.0	100.0	100.0	100.0	100.0	100.0	100.0
教材	Teaching Material	100.0	100.0	100.0	100.3	100.0	100.0	100.0	99.3	99.3	100.0	100.0	100.0
参考书	Reference Book	100.0	100.0	100.0	100.0	100.0	100.0	100.0	99.6	102.8	100.0	100.0	100.0
教育软件	Educational Software	100.0	100.0	99.7	100.0	100.0	100.0	100.0	100.0	100.0	100.0	100.0	100.0
（2）学杂托幼费	Tuition and Child Care	100.0	100.2	100.0	100.6	100.0	100.0	100.0	100.1	100.0	100.0	100.0	100.0
义务教育杂费	Incidental Expenses of Compulcory Education	100.0	100.0	100.0	100.0	100.0	100.0	100.0	100.0	100.0	100.0	100.0	100.0
非义务教育学杂费	Tuition of Non-compulsory Education	100.0	100.0	100.0	100.0	100.0	100.0	100.0	100.0	100.0	100.0	100.0	100.0
技能培训学费	Skill Train Tuition	100.0	100.0	100.0	100.0	100.0	100.0	100.0	100.0	100.0	100.0	100.0	100.0
托幼费	Child care	100.0	101.9	100.0	103.9	100.0	100.0	100.0	100.9	100.0	100.0	100.0	100.0
其他	Others	100.0	100.0	100.0	103.9	100.0	100.0	100.0	100.0	100.0	100.0	100.0	100.0
3.文化娱乐类	Recreation and Culture	100.5	99.9	100.0	102.8	100.0	100.0	99.9	100.1	100.1	100.0	100.5	100.0
（1）文化娱乐用品	Culture Articles	100.2	99.9	100.0	100.0	99.9	99.9	99.7	100.1	100.1	100.0	100.2	100.0
乐器	Musical Instrument	100.0	100.0	100.0	100.0	100.0	100.4	100.0	99.3	100.3	100.4	99.2	99.3
音响光盘和磁带	Audio,Disk and Tape	100.0	100.0	100.0	100.0	100.1	100.0	100.0	100.0	100.0	100.0	100.0	100.0
照相胶卷和存储卡	Roll Film and Memorizing Card	100.0	100.2	100.0	100.0	100.0	100.0	100.0	99.6	100.0	100.0	101.7	100.6
录像磁带和视盘	Video Tape and Disk	100.0	100.0	100.0	100.0	99.2	100.0	98.8	100.0	100.0	100.0	100.0	100.0
儿童玩具	Children's Toy	100.0	100.2	100.0	100.0	100.0	100.0	100.0	99.7	100.0	100.0	100.0	100.0

7-18 续表 8 continued

商品类别及品名	Commodity Category and Commodity Name	（以上月价格为100） 1月 January	2月 February	3月 March	4月 April	5月 May	6月 June	7月 July	8月 August	9月 September	10月 October	11月 November	12月 December
纸张本册	Paper and Volume	100.8	99.2	100.0	100.0	100.0	100.5	100.0	101.0	100.2	100.1	100.2	100.1
文具	Stationery	100.5	100.0	100.0	100.0	100.0	99.4	99.0	100.1	100.0	100.0	100.0	100.0
体育用品	Sports Goods	100.0	100.0	100.0	100.0	100.0	99.3	100.0	100.2	100.0	100.0	100.0	99.9
其他	Others	100.0	100.0	100.0	100.0	100.0	100.0	100.0	100.0	100.0	100.0	100.0	100.0
（2）书报杂志	Books,Newspapers, Magazines	101.2	100.0	100.0	100.0	100.0	100.0	100.0	100.0	100.0	100.0	100.0	100.0
书籍	Books	100.0	100.0	100.0	100.0	100.0	100.0	100.0	100.0	100.0	100.0	100.0	100.0
报纸	Newspapers	103.0	100.0	100.0	100.0	100.0	100.0	100.0	100.0	100.0	100.0	100.0	100.0
杂志	Magazines	101.3	100.0	100.0	100.0	100.0	100.0	100.0	100.0	100.0	100.0	100.0	100.0
（3）文娱费	Expenditure of Culture and Recreation	100.0	100.0	100.0	115.3	100.0	100.0	100.0	100.0	100.4	100.0	101.8	100.0
电影票	Film Ticket	100.0	100.0	100.0	100.0	100.0	100.0	100.0	100.0	100.0	100.0	100.0	100.0
景点门票	Scene Spot Ticket	100.0	100.0	100.0	102.8	100.0	100.0	100.0	100.0	107.9	100.0	131.6	100.0
有线电视	Cable Television	100.0	100.0	100.0	127.9	100.0	100.0	100.0	100.0	100.0	100.0	100.0	100.0
健身活动	Exercise	100.0	100.0	100.0	100.0	100.0	100.0	100.0	100.0	100.0	100.0	100.0	100.0
其他	Others	100.0	100.0	100.0	100.0	100.0	100.0	100.0	100.0	100.0	100.0	100.0	100.0
4.旅游	Tourism	99.7	100.1	100.7	100.1	100.1	100.0	100.0	100.0	100.0	100.0	99.9	100.0
旅行社收费	Travel Agency Charge	98.0	100.6	103.9	100.5	100.3	99.9	100.2	99.9	100.0	99.8	99.7	100.0
宾馆住宿	Guesthouse Stay	100.0	100.0	100.0	100.0	100.0	100.0	100.0	100.0	100.0	100.0	100.0	100.0
其他住宿	Other Stay	100.0	100.0	100.0	100.0	100.0	100.0	100.0	100.0	100.0	100.0	100.0	100.0
八、居住	**Residence**	**100.4**	**100.0**	**100.5**	**100.3**	**100.2**	**100.5**	**100.5**	**100.6**	**100.2**	**100.4**	**100.9**	**100.3**
1.建房及装修材料	Building and Building Decoration Materials	100.3	100.0	100.9	100.7	100.1	100.6	100.4	100.8	100.1	100.5	100.8	100.1
木材	Wood	100.9	100.1	100.6	100.9	99.9	101.0	101.0	103.2	101.1	101.7	102.5	100.0
木地板	Wood Floor	100.0	100.0	100.0	93.3	100.2	100.2	99.9	100.0	98.3	102.1	100.8	100.1
砖	Brick	99.2	100.7	101.9	101.9	100.3	101.7	100.1	100.9	100.0	100.1	100.0	99.9
水泥	Cement	99.9	99.1	100.0	102.6	100.4	99.6	99.9	100.0	100.1	99.7	100.7	100.0
涂料	Coating Material	101.1	99.9	99.8	99.7	98.7	100.0	100.0	100.3	100.0	100.4	100.4	100.6
胶合板	Plywood	101.3	100.0	101.5	101.2	98.5	100.6	101.5	101.3	100.1	98.3	102.6	100.7
玻璃	Glass	101.6	99.5	100.9	100.1	100.8	100.3	101.1	100.8	100.2	101.4	100.9	100.4
粘胶	Rayon	100.4	100.1	99.9	99.9	100.0	100.0	100.0	101.1	100.3	100.4	100.0	101.3
油漆	Paint	101.4	100.1	99.9	99.9	100.5	100.5	100.0	100.1	100.3	100.0	100.0	100.6
其他	Others	98.8	99.1	105.1	101.3	102.3	98.9	101.6	97.9	99.3	101.2	100.1	96.9
2.租房	Renting	100.0	100.0	100.0	100.0	100.0	100.0	101.6	100.0	100.0	100.0	101.6	100.0
公房房租	Public House Rent	100.0	100.0	100.0	100.0	100.0	100.0	100.2	100.0	100.0	100.0	100.2	100.0
私房房租	Private House Rent	100.0	100.0	100.0	100.0	100.0	100.0	102.1	100.0	100.0	100.0	102.1	100.0
其他费用	Other Fare	100.0	100.0	100.0	100.0	100.0	100.0	100.0	100.0	100.0	100.0	100.0	100.0
3.自有住房	Private Housing	100.0	100.1	100.0	100.0	102.4	102.7	100.2	100.1	101.1	100.0	103.7	100.0
房屋贷款利率	Houses Loans Interest Rate	100.0	100.0	100.0	100.0	100.5	100.0	100.0	101.4	100.4	100.0	100.0	100.0
物业管理费用	Propety Management Fee	100.0	100.0	100.0	100.0	100.0	100.0	100.0	100.0	100.0	100.0	100.0	100.0
维护修理费用	Upkeep and Repair Fee	100.0	100.0	100.0	100.0	103.2	103.6	100.2	100.0	101.4	100.0	104.9	100.0
其他	Others	100.0	100.5	100.0	100.0	100.0	100.0	100.0	100.0	100.0	100.0	100.0	100.0
4.水、电、燃料	Water,Electricity and Fuels	100.6	100.1	99.9	99.7	99.9	99.8	100.7	100.4	100.3	100.3	100.2	100.7
水	Water	100.0	100.0	104.2	100.0	100.0	100.0	100.0	100.0	100.0	100.0	100.0	100.0
电	Electricity	100.0	100.9	100.0	100.1	100.0	100.0	101.4	100.5	100.0	100.0	100.0	100.0
液化石油气	Liquefiled Petroleum Gas	103.1	99.4	97.1	98.5	100.0	99.0	100.5	100.4	103.4	99.4	99.9	100.3
管道燃气	Pipelined Gas	103.2	100.0	100.0	100.0	102.2	100.0	100.0	100.0	100.0	100.0	100.0	100.0
其他燃料	Other Fuels	100.3	99.7	99.9	99.6	99.7	99.9	100.2	100.3	99.5	100.9	100.6	101.8

7-19 全省商品零售价格（定基）指数
Entire Province Retail Price Index

商品类别及品名	Commodity Category and Commodity Name	（以2005年平均价格为100）											
		1月 January	2月 February	3月 March	4月 April	5月 May	6月 June	7月 July	8月 August	9月 September	10月 October	11月 November	12月 December
商品零售价格总指数	**Genaral Retail Price Index**	**101.5**	**101.5**	**100.9**	**100.9**	**100.6**	**100.0**	**99.5**	**99.8**	**100.3**	**100.1**	**100.6**	**102.0**
一、食品	**Food**	**105.7**	**106.3**	**104.2**	**104.3**	**102.8**	**99.8**	**98.3**	**99.3**	**101.3**	**100.0**	**101.5**	**106.7**
1.粮食	Grain	99.8	99.9	99.9	100.0	100.5	100.7	102.0	102.8	103.7	104.4	107.4	109.7
大米	Rice	102.9	102.6	102.8	103.1	105.2	106.4	109.7	112.7	113.7	114.8	114.4	116.4
面粉	Flour	97.0	97.4	97.1	97.0	96.7	96.2	97.0	96.5	97.3	97.9	104.3	107.4
粮食制品	Grain Products	99.7	99.9	100.0	100.2	100.2	100.5	101.0	101.6	101.8	102.0	104.5	106.0
其他	Others	103.2	103.2	103.2	103.6	103.9	104.9	105.5	105.6	109.0	110.8	111.6	113.5
2.淀粉	Starches	99.5	99.4	99.6	100.2	100.2	100.8	101.3	102.1	102.7	103.0	103.5	106.1
淀粉	Starches	99.5	99.4	99.6	100.2	100.2	100.8	101.3	102.1	102.7	103.0	103.5	106.1
3.干豆类及豆制品	Beans and Beans Products	99.4	99.7	99.4	99.2	99.6	100.2	101.4	101.8	101.4	101.0	101.1	102.1
干豆	Beans	98.1	98.9	98.7	98.9	99.8	101.5	105.1	105.8	104.1	102.5	102.3	103.4
豆制品	Beans Products	100.0	100.0	99.6	99.4	99.6	99.6	99.8	100.0	100.2	100.3	100.5	101.5
4.油脂	Oil and Fat	98.3	98.2	97.7	97.4	97.8	98.0	98.2	99.0	99.6	100.1	102.9	108.8
食用植物油	Edible Vegetable Oil	98.5	98.7	98.4	98.4	98.6	98.7	99.1	100.0	100.8	101.3	103.9	109.1
植物油制品	Plant Oil Products	99.1	98.9	98.7	98.6	100.7	100.6	100.2	100.3	100.5	100.5	103.2	113.4
其他	Others	92.0	89.6	85.2	80.1	78.4	79.3	79.5	80.5	79.6	82.1	87.7	92.0
5.肉禽及其制品	Meal,Poultry and Their Products	96.9	96.7	94.1	92.1	90.8	91.2	93.5	97.0	98.6	98.9	102.1	107.6
（1）食用畜肉及副产品	Edible Livestock Meat and Their By-products	97.4	96.5	92.4	88.5	86.7	87.7	90.3	95.0	97.4	97.9	102.8	110.5
猪肉	Pork	94.4	92.6	87.3	82.2	80.0	81.2	85.1	91.6	94.5	94.8	101.1	110.1
牛肉	Beef	105.7	106.6	105.6	105.4	104.3	104.6	105.1	104.8	105.6	106.1	107.7	111.5
羊肉	Mutton	107.2	108.4	106.6	106.5	106.6	106.3	106.2	106.5	107.9	109.7	111.3	117.7
畜肉副产品	Livestock Meat By-products	97.6	98.1	95.8	92.7	90.5	92.3	92.5	94.8	96.6	97.2	100.4	106.9
其他	Others	100.5	100.4	96.8	92.7	92.3	91.9	93.7	99.1	99.9	100.2	103.8	107.2
（2）禽	Poultry	91.2	92.7	92.3	93.4	92.4	92.7	96.6	100.1	101.1	101.0	101.6	104.9
鸡	Chicken	90.1	92.1	91.9	93.2	92.2	92.9	98.0	101.4	102.8	102.7	103.0	106.5
鸭	Duck	95.3	94.1	94.1	94.3	94.3	92.0	89.2	92.1	90.9	91.4	94.2	97.0
其他	Others	94.8	95.8	93.7	93.8	92.2	92.6	94.7	98.9	98.5	98.6	99.0	101.7
（3）肉禽加工制品	Meal and Poultry Processing Products	99.3	99.7	99.1	99.6	99.0	98.4	98.6	99.4	99.7	99.7	100.8	102.4
畜肉制品	Livestock Meat Products	99.9	100.3	100.0	99.7	99.2	98.9	99.3	100.0	100.1	100.3	101.2	102.8
禽制品	Poultry Products	98.3	98.5	97.5	99.4	98.6	97.5	97.4	98.4	98.9	98.7	100.1	101.8
6.蛋	Eggs	93.9	89.2	86.7	86.4	88.3	89.1	90.4	98.4	105.0	105.0	106.5	111.1
鲜蛋	Fresh Eggs	92.6	87.4	84.5	84.3	86.3	87.1	88.8	97.9	105.2	105.0	106.6	111.6
蛋制品	Egg Products	102.9	102.4	101.8	101.5	102.4	102.8	101.4	102.0	103.4	104.5	105.3	107.5
7.水产品	Aquatic Product	101.5	102.9	101.6	102.0	102.7	103.6	104.9	105.1	103.6	103.3	102.6	102.9
（1）鱼	Fish	99.8	99.9	97.6	98.3	99.3	101.5	103.3	104.5	103.2	102.2	100.7	100.5
淡水鱼	Freshwater Fish	97.0	95.6	93.0	92.1	94.2	97.3	100.0	101.6	100.8	98.6	96.6	95.8
海水鱼	Seawater Fish	102.6	104.4	102.3	104.5	104.6	105.8	106.7	107.5	105.8	105.9	105.0	105.2
（2）其他水产品	Other Aquatic Product	104.3	107.8	108.2	108.1	108.1	107.0	107.6	106.2	104.2	105.1	105.7	106.8
虾蟹类	Shrimp and Crab	104.5	109.2	108.8	108.8	108.9	107.2	107.3	105.5	102.7	104.0	104.8	106.6

7-19 续表 1 continued

商品类别及品名	Commodity Category and Commodity Name	1月 January	2月 February	3月 March	4月 April	5月 May	6月 June	7月 July	8月 August	9月 September	10月 October	11月 November	12月 December
		（以2005年平均价格为100）											
其他	Others	103.9	104.7	107.0	106.5	106.4	106.4	108.1	107.9	107.3	107.4	107.7	107.4
8.菜	Vegetable	140.4	140.6	128.4	124.7	107.0	88.6	83.7	91.3	104.2	89.2	89.7	110.6
鲜菜	Fresh Vegetable	146.7	146.6	132.0	127.4	105.8	85.1	79.3	88.3	103.9	86.6	87.1	110.6
干菜及菜制品	Dried Vegetable and Vegetable Products	101.4	101.9	102.1	102.2	101.8	101.7	101.9	102.7	103.7	104.9	106.3	110.6
薯类	Potato	112.4	117.6	123.0	128.1	144.2	128.4	126.3	123.8	112.7	101.6	101.6	109.4
9.调味品	Flavoring	102.1	102.1	102.1	102.4	102.5	102.6	103.1	103.1	103.2	103.4	104.1	104.9
盐	Salt	105.2	105.4	105.9	106.5	106.5	107.2	107.7	107.5	107.7	107.8	107.8	107.9
酱油	Soy Sauce	101.5	101.5	101.5	101.7	101.6	101.2	101.6	101.9	101.8	102.0	102.1	102.8
醋	Vinegar	101.2	101.2	101.1	101.3	101.2	101.4	102.0	102.0	102.1	102.1	102.1	103.2
味精	Aginomoto	100.2	100.2	100.1	100.4	100.5	100.3	100.6	100.5	100.5	100.7	100.6	101.0
其他	Others	100.7	100.5	100.5	100.7	101.5	101.5	102.1	102.0	102.2	102.8	107.4	109.1
10.糖	Carbohydrate	102.5	105.4	106.8	107.5	108.2	108.6	109.3	109.6	110.0	110.1	110.3	111.1
食糖	Sugar	106.4	115.1	120.2	122.2	124.1	125.5	127.1	128.4	129.3	129.3	129.4	131.6
糖果	Sweet	101.3	102.3	102.5	102.8	103.0	103.1	103.8	103.7	103.9	104.2	104.4	103.9
巧克力制品	Chocolate Products	100.6	100.5	100.3	100.2	100.0	99.8	99.7	99.4	99.4	99.7	99.7	101.1
糖类小食品	Little Carbohydrate Food	100.9	101.3	101.3	101.3	102.0	102.0	102.2	102.4	102.4	102.4	102.8	103.4
11.干鲜瓜果	Dried and Fresh Melons and Fruits	123.3	131.5	131.8	142.2	147.2	132.8	111.8	97.7	95.3	98.5	101.9	107.6
鲜瓜果	Fresh Fruits	128.5	138.9	139.1	152.2	158.5	140.0	113.2	94.9	91.7	95.2	98.9	105.9
干（坚）果	Dried Fruits	104.6	105.0	105.6	106.2	106.7	106.8	106.9	107.6	107.9	110.3	112.6	113.9
12.糕点饼干面包	Cake,Biscuit and Bread	100.7	100.6	100.5	100.7	100.8	100.7	100.9	101.0	101.0	100.7	100.6	101.5
糕点	Cake	100.7	100.7	100.5	100.5	100.5	100.3	100.2	99.9	99.9	99.2	99.4	100.5
饼干	Biscuit	100.3	100.2	100.3	100.8	101.3	101.4	101.8	102.6	102.2	102.1	101.6	102.5
面包	Bread	101.0	100.8	100.8	100.8	100.8	100.6	100.9	101.4	101.6	102.1	101.6	102.2
13.液体乳及乳制品	Liquid Milk and Their Products	100.5	100.6	100.9	101.1	101.1	101.2	101.3	101.6	102.7	102.6	102.6	103.4
巴氏杀菌奶或消毒奶	Pasteurization Milk or Disinfection Milk	100.0	100.0	100.8	100.8	100.7	100.9	101.0	101.2	102.3	102.3	102.2	103.6
酸奶	Leben	100.1	100.1	100.1	100.4	100.8	100.9	100.7	100.6	102.2	102.2	101.9	101.8
奶粉	Milk Powder	101.7	101.8	101.7	102.2	101.9	102.0	102.5	103.4	103.6	103.3	103.5	104.2
其他	Others	102.4	102.4	102.3	102.3	102.3	102.3	102.3	102.3	104.4	104.2	104.3	104.2
14.在外用膳食品	Outward Dinner	100.2	100.3	100.3	100.4	100.5	100.8	100.9	101.0	101.1	101.0	101.5	103.6
主食	Staple Food	100.0	99.7	99.8	99.8	99.8	100.2	100.2	100.3	100.4	100.4	102.1	105.9
炒菜	Hot Dish	100.4	100.6	100.7	100.7	100.8	101.1	101.0	101.0	101.3	101.1	101.2	102.3
地方小吃	Local Snack	100.2	100.2	100.2	100.3	100.7	100.9	101.7	102.2	102.0	101.6	101.7	103.5
15.其他食品	Other Foods	100.4	100.3	100.5	100.5	100.6	100.6	100.6	100.7	100.7	100.6	100.5	101.2
其他食品	Other Foods	100.4	100.3	100.5	100.5	100.6	100.6	100.6	100.7	100.7	100.6	100.5	101.2
二、饮料、烟酒	**Beverages,Tobacco,Liquor**	**100.3**	**100.3**	**100.5**	**100.7**	**100.7**	**100.9**	**101.1**	**101.3**	**101.4**	**101.5**	**101.6**	**102.3**
1.茶及饮料	Tea and Beverages	99.8	100.0	100.5	100.5	100.7	100.9	101.2	101.3	101.3	101.4	101.3	101.8
（1）茶叶	Tea	99.9	100.2	100.4	100.4	100.4	100.5	100.6	100.5	100.5	100.6	100.6	100.9
茶叶	Tea	99.9	100.2	100.4	100.4	100.4	100.5	100.6	100.5	100.5	100.6	100.6	100.9
（2）饮料	Beverages	99.7	99.8	100.5	100.6	100.8	101.1	101.5	101.8	101.7	101.8	101.7	102.3
固体饮料	Solid Beverages	100.6	100.9	100.9	100.8	101.0	101.0	101.0	100.9	100.8	100.8	100.8	100.4
液体饮料	Liquid Beverages	99.7	99.8	100.3	100.5	100.6	100.7	101.5	101.6	101.7	101.7	101.7	102.3

7-19 续表 2 continued

商品类别及品名	Commodity Category and Commodity Name	1月 January	2月 February	3月 March	4月 April	5月 May	6月 June	7月 July	8月 August	9月 September	10月 October	11月 November	12月 December
		(以2005年平均价格为100)											
冷冻饮品	Frozen Beverages	99.0	99.0	100.5	100.7	101.0	101.8	101.8	102.8	102.6	102.7	102.6	103.9
2.烟草	Tobacco	100.2	100.2	100.1	100.4	100.5	100.4	100.3	100.3	100.2	100.2	100.2	100.7
国产卷烟	Domestic Cigarette	100.3	100.4	100.3	100.7	100.8	100.8	100.7	100.6	100.5	100.6	100.5	101.0
进口卷烟	Import Cigarette	99.5	98.5	98.4	98.5	98.2	98.2	97.8	97.8	97.8	97.7	98.2	98.8
其他	Others	99.5	99.5	99.3	99.1	99.1	99.1	99.1	98.9	98.9	98.9	98.9	98.9
3.酒	Liquor	100.8	100.7	100.8	101.1	101.0	101.3	101.6	102.0	102.4	102.7	102.9	103.9
白酒	White Spirit	101.0	100.8	101.1	101.5	101.5	101.9	102.0	102.6	102.9	103.4	103.7	105.2
葡萄酒	Grape	103.2	103.3	103.2	103.4	103.3	103.9	104.7	104.8	105.1	105.1	106.0	106.0
啤酒	Beer	100.0	100.0	99.7	99.9	99.8	99.8	100.2	100.5	101.0	101.0	100.9	101.4
其他	Others	100.0	100.0	100.0	100.2	100.2	100.4	100.6	100.5	100.6	100.6	100.6	100.7
三、服装、鞋帽	**Garments,Footgearand and Hats**	**99.9**	**98.8**	**98.5**	**98.2**	**97.7**	**97.7**	**96.9**	**96.3**	**96.5**	**97.3**	**97.9**	**97.7**
1.服装	Garments	99.3	97.9	97.3	96.9	96.5	96.5	96.1	95.7	95.8	97.0	97.7	97.8
（1）男式服装	Men's Garments	98.9	97.8	97.0	96.6	96.0	95.7	95.4	94.8	94.9	96.2	97.0	97.0
大衣	Topcoat	96.6	95.2	94.4	93.3	93.3	92.6	92.4	92.4	92.2	92.0	92.0	92.3
毛线衣	Woollen Sweater	100.8	96.1	91.1	90.7	89.6	89.5	89.6	89.4	89.4	91.1	91.9	92.9
夹克衫	Jacket	98.0	96.7	94.7	94.3	94.2	94.1	94.0	94.0	94.1	96.5	97.8	98.0
衬衫	Shirt	94.5	94.3	94.4	93.9	93.4	94.0	93.0	92.2	92.7	93.3	93.5	94.3
T恤衫	T-shirt	102.1	102.3	101.6	101.6	100.2	98.1	95.9	94.4	95.4	95.6	96.4	96.5
裤子	Trousers	97.0	95.0	95.4	95.3	95.0	94.5	94.0	93.5	92.8	95.2	95.7	95.0
西服	Western-style Clothes	99.6	100.3	99.8	100.3	99.9	99.7	100.5	98.2	99.7	101.3	101.2	100.9
运动衫裤	Gym Suit	99.6	99.6	99.7	99.2	96.6	96.8	96.3	96.9	96.6	97.1	98.3	98.5
内衣	Underwaist	101.6	101.6	102.3	102.1	101.8	102.0	101.5	101.6	101.4	101.9	101.8	101.9
羽绒衣	Eider Down Outerwear	101.4	100.2	99.7	96.9	96.8	96.8	96.3	96.1	95.5	97.5	101.5	100.1
其他	Others	96.6	95.3	94.3	93.6	93.7	93.6	93.4	93.3	93.3	93.3	96.1	95.9
（2）女式服装	Women's Garments	99.7	97.8	97.2	96.7	96.2	96.3	96.1	95.7	96.1	97.3	98.0	98.3
大衣	Topcoat	100.1	94.4	92.8	92.2	92.1	92.1	91.9	91.9	91.7	91.7	92.4	94.8
毛线衣	Woollen Sweater	99.7	94.0	91.6	91.6	89.9	90.2	90.2	90.2	90.7	92.9	92.7	93.8
羽绒衣	Eider Down Outerwear	99.1	97.8	96.7	96.5	96.5	96.3	96.0	95.8	95.3	97.6	101.7	100.6
套装	Coordinates	101.0	101.1	100.8	98.9	99.3	98.3	98.8	96.6	99.5	100.7	99.9	100.2
衬衫	Shirt	99.1	100.2	100.5	98.5	98.6	98.9	99.1	97.8	96.7	96.9	96.7	95.7
T恤衫	T-shirt	101.0	101.2	101.1	100.3	99.7	100.0	99.1	98.8	101.8	107.8	108.2	108.2
裙子	Skirt	101.3	100.7	100.3	98.5	99.1	99.4	99.3	99.0	98.6	99.0	99.8	99.7
裤子	Trousers	99.1	97.5	96.9	96.6	96.1	96.5	95.7	95.9	95.8	95.8	96.8	95.7
运动衫裤	Gym Suit	98.2	98.8	98.2	98.8	94.1	94.5	94.2	94.1	94.0	96.0	95.3	96.9
内衣	Underwaist	98.0	97.9	99.3	100.4	100.0	100.5	100.1	100.1	100.1	101.1	102.3	102.3
其他	Others	100.1	99.6	99.9	100.7	100.2	100.5	100.6	101.2	101.1	101.6	102.0	101.8
（3）儿童服装	Children's Garments	99.1	98.5	98.5	98.8	99.4	99.5	98.7	98.5	97.7	98.2	98.7	98.6
套装	Coordinates	99.2	98.6	98.4	98.6	98.2	98.0	97.7	97.4	97.1	97.5	98.1	98.1
裤子	Trousers	100.4	99.9	99.9	99.9	101.2	101.1	99.9	100.0	99.7	100.6	101.2	101.5
裙子	Skirt	96.9	96.6	97.3	98.6	100.8	101.5	100.0	99.8	97.4	97.4	97.5	96.9
其他	Others	100.6	98.4	97.0	95.8	95.4	95.5	95.3	95.3	95.2	95.2	95.6	95.2

7-19 续表 3 continued

商品类别及品名	Commodity Category and Commodity Name	1月 January	2月 February	3月 March	4月 April	5月 May	6月 June	7月 July	8月 August	9月 September	10月 October	11月 November	12月 December
		（以2005年平均价格为100）											
2.鞋袜帽	Shoes,Socks and Hats	101.3	100.7	101.1	100.7	100.0	99.9	98.1	97.1	97.5	97.6	97.8	97.3
（1）鞋	Shoes	101.6	100.8	101.4	100.8	100.1	99.9	97.8	96.6	97.1	97.2	97.4	96.8
男鞋	Men's Shoes	100.3	100.0	101.0	100.7	100.0	100.3	98.0	96.9	97.2	97.2	97.4	97.0
女鞋	Women's Shoes	102.3	101.1	101.5	100.5	99.4	98.8	96.2	94.6	95.5	95.6	95.8	94.9
童鞋	Children's Shoes	102.3	102.0	101.9	101.9	102.3	102.1	101.7	101.6	101.1	101.6	101.9	101.9
（2）袜子	Socks	100.1	100.0	99.7	100.1	99.9	100.0	99.8	99.8	99.6	99.9	99.6	99.3
男袜	Men's Socks	99.9	99.8	99.7	100.0	99.9	99.8	99.7	99.7	99.5	99.8	99.2	98.6
女袜	Women's Socks	100.2	100.2	99.7	100.2	99.9	100.1	99.9	99.9	99.7	100.0	99.8	99.8
（3）帽子	Hats	99.8	99.5	99.5	99.5	99.6	99.7	99.7	99.7	99.4	99.7	100.0	100.1
男帽	Men's Hats	100.1	99.9	99.7	99.7	100.0	100.2	100.2	100.5	99.8	100.1	100.6	100.8
女帽	Women's Hats	99.6	99.3	99.3	99.3	99.4	99.3	99.3	99.2	99.1	99.5	99.6	99.5
3.其他	Others	99.0	99.7	99.3	100.3	100.2	100.2	99.9	99.4	100.0	100.3	100.3	99.3
领带	Necktie	99.0	99.7	99.3	100.3	100.2	100.2	99.9	99.4	100.0	100.3	100.3	99.3
四、纺织品	**Textiles**	**99.0**	**99.3**	**99.3**	**99.3**	**99.2**	**99.4**	**99.3**	**99.2**	**99.0**	**99.3**	**99.3**	**99.6**
1.衣着材料	Clothing Materials	99.0	99.0	98.8	98.8	99.2	99.2	99.3	99.2	99.1	99.5	99.7	99.8
棉布	Cotton Cloth	97.1	97.0	97.4	97.9	98.6	98.6	98.8	98.8	99.2	99.6	99.5	99.5
棉混纺布	Cotton Textiles Cloth	97.5	97.7	97.7	97.7	97.7	97.8	97.8	97.8	97.6	98.0	98.4	98.6
化纤布	Chemical Fiber Cloth	100.9	101.0	100.5	100.2	100.7	100.7	100.7	100.6	100.1	100.8	100.9	101.0
毛线	Knitting Wool	100.0	99.4	98.8	98.8	98.8	98.8	98.8	98.7	98.8	98.9	99.0	99.6
2.床上用品	Bedclothes	98.9	99.5	99.7	99.7	99.2	99.6	99.3	99.2	98.9	99.1	98.9	99.3
毛毯	Woollen Blanket	99.5	99.7	100.0	100.2	99.3	99.9	99.2	99.1	99.0	99.6	99.5	101.0
被子	Quilt	98.1	98.5	98.5	98.4	97.7	98.2	97.9	97.6	96.8	96.5	95.8	96.2
床上套件	Bed Articcles	98.7	99.4	99.7	99.7	99.4	99.6	99.6	99.6	99.4	99.7	99.9	99.6
其他	Others	100.0	101.5	101.8	101.9	101.7	101.5	101.5	101.5	101.5	101.7	101.8	101.9
五、家用电器及音像器材	**Household Appliances,Music and Video Equipments**	**99.0**	**98.7**	**98.7**	**98.3**	**98.4**	**99.3**	**99.6**	**99.5**	**99.1**	**99.0**	**99.0**	**98.9**
1.家庭设备	Household Appliances	100.1	99.9	100.0	100.0	100.2	102.1	102.8	103.0	103.1	103.2	103.3	103.4
洗衣机	Washing Machine	99.7	99.7	99.7	98.7	99.2	100.1	100.6	100.2	100.7	101.0	101.1	101.0
电风扇	Electric Fan	100.1	99.2	99.2	102.0	102.2	103.6	105.4	105.9	105.3	105.4	105.4	106.8
电冰箱（柜）	Refrigerator	102.0	101.5	101.7	101.8	102.3	103.9	105.0	104.9	104.9	105.5	105.2	105.2
吸排油烟机	Kitchen Ventilato	101.2	101.1	101.0	101.0	100.9	102.7	104.2	105.0	104.7	104.6	104.8	105.0
空调器	Air-conditioning	99.7	99.6	99.6	99.6	100.0	103.8	104.8	105.2	105.5	105.5	105.8	105.8
热水器	Water Heater	99.0	99.5	100.2	99.1	98.5	98.8	98.8	98.9	98.9	99.1	99.1	98.7
微波炉	Microwave Oven	98.2	97.9	98.0	97.3	97.3	97.7	97.7	97.7	97.5	97.7	98.2	97.9
电炊具	Electric Cooking Appliance	99.8	99.7	99.6	100.2	100.2	100.2	100.1	100.2	99.9	100.1	100.1	100.4
2.文娱用耐用消费品	Durable Consumer Goods for Recreational use	97.5	97.0	96.8	96.1	96.0	95.6	95.5	95.0	93.9	93.4	93.3	93.0
电视机	Television	96.0	95.4	95.3	94.4	94.3	93.9	93.7	92.8	91.5	91.0	90.9	90.6
激光视盘机	Laser Video Disc Machine	98.4	97.5	97.2	96.8	96.5	96.6	96.5	96.5	94.7	93.4	93.2	92.5

7-19 续表 4 continued

商品类别及品名	Commodity Category and Commodity Name	（以2005年平均价格为100）											
		1月 January	2月 February	3月 March	4月 April	5月 May	6月 June	7月 July	8 月 August	9 月 September	10 月 October	11月 November	12月 December
摄像机	Pickup Camera	99.4	99.2	98.7	97.7	97.2	96.2	95.9	95.8	94.6	94.4	94.1	93.4
家用音响设备	Acoustic Equipment	99.9	99.8	99.5	98.9	98.7	98.7	99.0	99.0	98.7	98.8	98.8	98.6
便携式音响	Portable Acoustics	99.3	98.9	98.6	98.4	98.3	98.3	98.4	98.3	98.1	98.2	98.2	97.9
其他	Others	99.9	100.0	100.0	99.9	99.9	99.9	99.9	99.4	99.2	99.3	99.2	99.2
3.音像器材	Music and Video Equipment	99.3	99.1	99.0	98.9	98.9	98.9	98.9	98.9	98.9	98.9	98.9	98.9
专业音响器材	Specialized Acoustic Apparatus	100.0	99.9	99.8	99.7	99.7	99.8	99.8	99.8	99.8	99.8	99.8	99.8
专业声像器材	Specialized Acoustic Image Apparatus	98.4	97.9	97.9	97.7	97.8	97.7	97.7	97.7	97.7	97.7	97.7	97.7
六、文化办公用品	**Cultural and Office Applicances**	**98.0**	**97.9**	**97.8**	**97.7**	**97.5**	**97.3**	**97.1**	**96.6**	**96.2**	**96.2**	**96.1**	**96.1**
纸张本册	Paper and Volume	100.5	100.1	100.1	100.1	100.1	100.2	100.2	100.5	100.8	101.1	101.2	101.2
文具	Stationery	99.8	99.9	99.9	99.8	99.8	99.8	99.6	99.6	99.3	99.5	99.5	99.5
电脑及配件	Computer and its Fitting	96.2	96.1	95.9	95.8	95.3	94.6	94.3	92.9	91.8	91.7	91.6	91.5
打印机及配件	Printer and its Fitting	97.1	97.0	96.9	96.8	96.7	96.9	96.6	95.8	95.8	95.7	95.5	95.5
扫描仪	Scanner	98.3	98.3	98.1	98.1	98.0	98.1	98.1	98.0	98.0	98.0	97.9	97.9
复印机	Xerox Machine	97.0	97.0	97.0	96.8	96.8	96.7	96.6	96.1	96.0	95.9	94.9	94.7
电子辞典	Electronic Dictionary	99.6	99.5	99.3	98.9	98.9	98.7	98.0	96.8	97.0	97.2	97.3	97.3
计算器	Calculator	98.4	98.5	98.5	98.4	98.4	98.5	98.3	98.2	98.1	98.2	98.5	98.6
教学设备	Teaching Equipment	99.4	99.4	99.4	99.4	99.6	99.5	99.4	100.5	100.4	100.5	100.5	100.6
其他	Others	100.1	100.1	100.1	100.1	100.1	100.0	99.9	99.9	100.0	100.2	100.2	100.2
七、日用品	**Articles for Daily use**	**100.3**	**100.3**	**100.4**	**100.4**	**100.6**	**100.6**	**100.4**	**100.6**	**100.5**	**100.8**	**100.8**	**101.0**
1.日用百货	General Merchandise for Daily use	100.1	100.1	100.1	100.2	100.3	100.3	100.3	100.3	100.2	100.3	100.3	100.8
自行车	Bicycle	100.5	100.4	100.4	100.2	100.1	100.0	100.0	99.9	100.0	100.1	100.2	100.2
雨具	Rain Gear	99.8	99.8	99.8	99.8	99.9	99.5	99.4	99.8	99.0	98.6	98.3	98.4
剃须刀具	Shaver	100.1	100.2	100.5	100.9	101.0	102.9	102.9	102.9	102.7	102.6	102.7	102.9
电池	Battery	98.9	99.1	99.1	99.0	99.5	97.7	97.9	97.8	97.5	97.6	97.8	97.9
卫生纸	Tissue Paper	101.1	101.1	101.4	101.9	102.1	102.7	102.7	103.1	103.0	103.1	102.9	105.0
卫生巾	Sanitary Towel	98.6	98.4	98.4	98.4	98.9	98.6	98.2	98.2	97.8	98.3	98.2	98.1
其他	Others	100.4	100.4	100.4	100.4	100.4	100.4	100.4	100.4	100.3	100.5	101.5	101.9
2.日用杂品	Sundry Articles	99.8	99.9	99.9	100.1	100.1	100.2	100.0	100.1	100.6	101.1	101.1	101.3
茶具	Tea Set	98.3	98.3	98.3	98.4	98.2	99.6	99.6	99.7	100.5	102.6	102.5	102.6
餐具	Tableware	100.1	100.2	100.2	100.2	100.6	100.6	99.8	100.1	100.1	100.2	100.2	100.6
厨具	Kitchen Utensils	100.3	100.3	100.3	100.8	100.8	100.1	100.2	100.3	101.2	101.3	101.4	101.7
其他	Others	100.2	100.5	100.7	100.5	100.5	100.5	100.4	100.4	100.3	100.1	100.0	100.0
3.洗涤用品	Washing Articles	100.9	101.0	101.0	101.0	101.2	101.4	101.2	101.5	101.2	101.4	101.4	101.6
洗衣粉	Washing Powder	101.7	101.6	101.7	101.8	101.6	102.2	102.2	102.8	102.7	102.8	102.7	103.0
肥皂类	Soap	100.0	100.1	100.0	99.9	99.9	99.9	99.9	100.7	99.9	100.1	100.2	100.3
牙膏	Toothpaste	101.0	101.3	101.1	101.2	102.1	102.1	101.3	101.2	101.0	101.2	101.4	101.7
清洁洗涤剂	Cleaning Agent	100.5	100.6	100.7	100.8	100.7	100.7	100.6	100.5	100.3	100.4	100.4	100.5
4.其他日用品	Other Articles for Daily use	100.3	100.3	100.5	100.4	100.5	100.5	100.2	100.4	99.9	100.4	100.5	100.3
燃气灶具	Gas-oven	101.4	101.4	102.1	102.4	102.4	102.9	103.3	103.5	103.3	103.4	103.4	103.4
儿童玩具	Children's Toy	100.8	100.7	100.4	99.9	100.0	100.1	100.3	100.2	99.8	100.1	100.1	100.0
照明器具	Illumination Utensil	99.6	99.6	99.7	99.8	99.8	99.8	99.8	99.8	99.8	99.9	99.8	99.8

7-19 续表 5 continued

商品类别及品名	Commodity Category and Commodity Name	1月 January	2月 February	3月 March	4月 April	5月 May	6月 June	7月 July	8月 August	9月 September	10月 October	11月 November	12月 December
		（以2005年平均价格为100）											
钟表眼镜及配件	Clocks,Glasses and Their Fittings	98.7	98.6	98.6	98.9	98.9	99.0	99.1	99.1	98.6	98.9	99.1	99.1
日用普通饰品	Common Ornament for Daily use	100.0	100.4	100.1	98.8	100.3	99.4	100.1	99.6	98.8	99.8	99.8	99.8
日用皮革制品	Leatherware for Daily use	100.3	100.5	101.1	101.1	100.9	100.7	97.7	98.8	97.9	99.6	100.0	98.7
其他	Others	99.9	100.0	100.6	100.6	100.4	100.5	97.9	98.9	98.3	99.2	99.6	98.8
八、体育娱乐用品	**Sports and Recreation Articles**	**99.6**	**99.6**	**99.5**	**99.5**	**99.3**	**99.2**	**99.1**	**99.2**	**98.8**	**99.0**	**99.0**	**99.0**
1.体育用品	Sports Articles	99.9	99.9	99.8	99.8	99.6	99.4	99.4	99.3	99.1	99.3	99.3	99.3
球类	Ball	99.4	99.2	99.1	99.0	98.8	98.4	98.3	98.4	98.2	98.4	98.4	98.4
棋牌	Chess and Cards	101.1	101.2	101.2	101.0	100.9	100.5	100.5	100.5	100.5	100.7	100.7	100.7
健身器材	Exercise Machine	99.5	99.6	99.6	99.6	99.4	99.5	99.5	99.3	98.9	99.2	99.1	99.1
2.娱乐用品	Recreation Articles	99.3	99.3	99.3	99.2	99.1	99.1	98.9	99.0	98.6	98.7	98.7	98.8
游艺器材	Entertainment Apparatus	99.5	99.4	99.2	98.8	98.6	98.3	97.9	98.3	97.4	97.7	97.6	97.8
照相器材	Photographic Apparatus	98.4	98.5	98.5	98.5	98.5	98.5	98.5	98.5	98.1	98.2	98.3	98.4
乐器	Musical Instrument	100.6	100.6	100.6	100.6	100.6	100.7	100.7	100.6	100.4	100.7	100.5	100.5
九、交通、通信用品	**Transportation and Communication Appliances**	**96.4**	**96.1**	**95.5**	**94.6**	**94.1**	**93.8**	**93.4**	**92.8**	**92.0**	**91.6**	**91.2**	**90.6**
1.交通运输机械	Transportation Machine	99.3	99.5	99.3	99.1	99.0	99.0	98.8	98.6	98.0	97.8	97.5	97.1
轿车	Car	98.9	98.8	98.7	98.4	98.0	97.7	97.4	96.7	95.2	95.1	94.5	93.8
客车	Bus	98.6	98.6	98.4	98.3	98.3	98.4	98.3	98.3	97.2	97.2	97.1	97.1
货车	Truck	100.4	100.4	99.9	99.6	99.6	99.6	99.5	99.5	99.4	98.7	98.6	98.6
摩托车	Motorcycle	99.6	100.4	100.4	100.4	100.6	100.6	100.6	100.7	100.8	100.8	100.6	100.0
其他	Others	99.1	99.1	99.1	98.3	98.3	98.3	98.2	98.2	98.2	98.2	98.2	98.2
2.通信器材	Telecommunications Facilities	91.2	90.1	88.7	86.7	85.5	84.7	84.0	82.6	81.6	80.8	80.1	79.1
固定电话机	Telephone	98.2	97.7	97.0	96.7	95.8	95.8	95.7	95.6	95.7	95.7	95.6	95.4
移动电话机	Mobile Phone	86.0	84.5	82.3	79.0	77.4	76.1	74.9	73.0	71.2	69.9	68.8	67.1
传真机	Fax Machine	99.7	99.5	99.7	99.5	99.5	99.5	99.5	98.1	98.0	98.0	97.8	97.8
其他	Others	97.9	97.4	97.1	96.6	95.7	95.7	95.5	95.5	95.5	95.5	95.5	95.5
十、家具	**Furniture**	**100.1**	**100.0**	**100.0**	**100.1**	**100.0**	**100.1**	**100.2**	**100.2**	**100.5**	**101.2**	**101.4**	**101.5**
柜	Cabinet	100.4	100.2	100.1	99.9	100.0	100.1	100.0	100.1	100.2	101.2	101.3	101.5
床	Bed	100.7	100.8	100.8	101.2	101.1	101.2	101.3	101.4	101.5	102.2	102.3	102.3
桌	Desk	100.5	100.6	100.5	100.6	100.5	100.3	100.4	100.2	100.1	100.6	100.9	101.0
椅	Chair	100.4	99.9	100.0	99.9	99.9	100.0	99.9	100.1	101.0	102.0	102.2	102.2
沙发	Sofa	99.1	99.1	99.1	99.2	99.0	99.2	99.1	99.2	99.3	100.0	100.2	100.3
其他	Others	99.4	99.4	99.6	99.7	99.5	100.7	101.7	101.7	102.8	103.2	103.3	103.4
十一、化妆品	**Cosmetics**	**99.0**	**99.1**	**99.0**	**99.1**	**99.1**	**99.1**	**99.0**	**99.0**	**99.0**	**99.2**	**99.0**	**98.9**
护肤品	Skincare Products	99.5	99.7	99.6	99.8	99.8	99.7	99.7	99.7	99.4	99.9	99.4	99.1
美容化妆品	Facial Beautifiers	97.4	97.4	97.4	97.5	97.5	97.4	97.6	97.7	97.6	97.8	97.9	97.9
护发美容品	Protects Sends the Beauty Products	99.4	99.4	99.2	99.1	99.0	99.1	98.9	99.0	98.9	99.1	98.9	98.9
清洁化妆用品	Cleaning Toiletware	99.7	99.7	99.8	99.9	100.0	99.8	99.7	99.5	99.9	99.9	99.8	99.8
药物美容用品	Medicinal Cosmetics	99.6	99.6	99.4	99.6	99.5	99.5	99.4	99.3	99.3	99.4	99.4	99.4
十二、金银珠宝	**Gold,Silver and Jewelry**	**103.7**	**105.5**	**108.5**	**111.7**	**119.2**	**122.4**	**122.5**	**123.8**	**123.1**	**122.9**	**123.2**	**123.6**
金饰品	Gold	106.5	109.4	113.3	118.1	129.9	131.2	130.5	132.3	131.5	130.4	130.6	131.0

7-19 续表 6 continued

商品类别及品名	Commodity Category and Commodity Name	1月 January	2月 February	3月 March	4月 April	5月 May	6月 June	7月 July	8月 August	9月 September	10月 October	11月 November	12月 December
		（以2005年平均价格为100）											
银饰品	Silver	100.8	101.0	106.7	107.2	112.5	121.8	123.6	126.3	126.6	127.6	127.5	128.2
铂金饰品	Platinum	102.4	103.8	105.0	108.5	113.4	117.3	117.6	118.0	116.9	117.3	118.2	118.6
其他	Others	99.9	100.0	101.1	101.2	101.4	102.0	102.0	102.2	102.0	102.3	102.3	102.2
十三、中西药品及医疗保健用品	**Traditional Chinese and Western Medicines and Health Care Articles**	**99.9**	**99.9**	**99.7**	**99.7**	**99.9**	**100.0**	**100.0**	**99.9**	**99.8**	**99.7**	**99.8**	**99.9**
1.医疗器具及用品	Medical Facilities and Goods	98.2	98.3	98.0	97.6	97.4	97.4	97.4	97.4	97.6	94.2	94.3	93.8
医疗器具及用品	Medical Facilities and Goods	98.2	98.3	98.0	97.6	97.4	97.4	97.4	97.4	97.6	94.2	94.3	93.8
2.中药材及中成药	Herbs and Ready-made Traditional Chinese Medicine	100.5	100.8	100.6	100.6	100.5	101.1	100.8	101.0	100.9	102.2	102.4	102.7
中药材	Herbs	100.5	101.1	100.5	100.7	101.3	103.1	102.7	102.9	103.3	105.6	106.1	106.4
中成药	Ready-made Traditional Chinese Medicine	100.6	100.6	100.7	100.5	99.9	99.5	99.2	99.5	99.0	99.4	99.4	99.6
3.西药	Western Medicine	99.6	99.6	99.5	99.5	99.8	99.6	99.8	99.7	99.4	98.8	98.8	99.0
抗微生物药	Anti-microorganism Medicine	98.4	98.3	98.4	98.4	98.4	98.7	100.8	100.3	100.2	99.1	99.3	99.5
消化系统用药	Alimentary System Medicine	99.2	99.3	99.5	99.6	99.8	99.7	99.7	99.7	99.6	99.7	99.4	99.7
呼吸系统用药	Respiratory System Medicine	99.1	99.1	99.1	99.3	99.0	99.5	99.6	99.6	100.0	99.5	99.9	99.8
解热镇痛及非甾体抗炎药	Allays a Fever the Analgesia and the Non-steroid Body Anti-inflammatory Agent	101.3	101.3	100.7	100.6	101.0	99.9	99.4	99.5	99.1	99.9	99.8	100.4
抗肿瘤药	Antineoplastic Drug	100.0	100.0	99.7	99.7	102.3	100.6	100.7	100.1	99.2	99.0	99.3	99.3
激素及调节内分泌功能药	Hormone and Adjustment Internal Secretion Function Medicine	99.5	99.5	99.0	99.1	99.1	98.6	98.1	97.8	97.0	94.8	95.5	95.0
循环系统用药	Circulating System Medicine	99.5	99.5	99.5	99.5	99.6	100.1	99.7	99.7	100.1	101.0	100.2	100.6
神经系统用药	Nerve System Medicine	100.7	100.8	100.4	100.6	100.6	100.3	100.3	99.9	99.6	96.6	96.6	96.8
专科用药	Junior Medicine	99.8	99.6	99.9	99.8	99.9	100.3	100.2	100.2	98.7	96.8	97.0	96.7
其他	Others	99.9	99.9	99.2	99.2	98.9	98.6	98.5	98.5	98.5	98.0	97.9	97.7
4.保健品及器具	Healthcare Equipment	100.1	99.9	99.7	99.8	99.8	100.1	99.6	99.8	99.9	99.9	100.1	100.0
保健器具	Health Protection Equipment	100.1	99.7	99.5	99.6	99.5	99.8	99.6	99.5	99.5	99.2	99.3	99.0
滋补保健用品	Tonic and Health Product	100.1	100.0	99.8	99.9	99.9	100.2	99.6	99.9	100.0	100.2	100.4	100.4
十四、书报杂志及电子出版物	**Books,Newspapers,Magazines and Electronic Publications**	**101.2**	**101.1**	**101.1**	**101.2**	**101.2**	**101.2**	**101.2**	**101.3**	**101.3**	**101.3**	**101.2**	**101.2**
1.教材及参考书	Teaching Materials and Reference Books	101.4	101.4	101.5	101.5	101.5	101.5	101.5	101.9	101.8	101.7	101.7	101.7
工具书	Tool Book	101.0	101.0	101.0	101.0	101.0	101.0	101.0	101.0	101.0	101.0	101.0	101.0
教材	Teaching Material	100.6	100.6	100.9	101.0	101.0	101.0	101.0	101.2	100.1	99.9	99.9	99.9
参考书	Reference Book	103.4	103.4	103.5	103.5	103.5	103.4	103.4	104.3	106.0	106.0	106.0	106.1
教育软件	Educational Software	99.8	99.7	99.2	99.2	99.2	99.2	99.2	99.2	99.2	99.2	99.2	99.2
2.书报杂志	Books,Newspapers, Magazines	102.2	102.2	102.3	102.3	102.3	102.3	102.3	102.4	102.4	102.4	102.4	102.4

7-19 续表 7 continued

（以2005年平均价格为100）

商品类别及品名	Commodity Category and Commodity Name	1月 January	2月 February	3月 March	4月 April	5月 May	6月 June	7月 July	8月 August	9月 September	10月 October	11月 November	12月 December
书籍	Books	100.7	100.7	101.0	101.0	101.0	101.0	101.0	101.0	101.0	101.0	101.0	101.1
报纸	Newspapers	105.5	105.5	105.5	105.5	105.5	105.5	105.5	105.5	105.5	105.5	105.5	105.5
杂志	Magazines	100.4	100.4	100.4	100.4	100.4	100.4	100.4	100.4	100.4	100.4	100.4	100.5
3.电子音像制品	Electronic Publications	99.6	99.3	99.1	99.3	99.3	99.3	99.2	99.2	99.2	99.3	99.0	99.0
音响光盘和磁带	Acoustic Light Disk and Tape	99.7	98.9	98.8	99.1	99.1	99.1	99.1	99.1	99.0	99.1	99.1	99.1
录像磁带和视盘	Video Tape and Disk	100.1	100.0	100.0	100.3	100.3	100.4	100.2	100.2	100.0	100.3	100.2	100.1
计算机软件	Computer Software	98.9	98.9	98.6	98.5	98.4	98.4	98.4	98.4	98.5	98.5	97.7	97.7
十五、燃料	**Fuels**	**105.7**	**105.8**	**105.4**	**107.3**	**108.6**	**111.1**	**111.1**	**111.4**	**112.4**	**113.0**	**113.4**	**113.7**
1.煤炭及制品	Coal and Related Products	104.0	103.8	103.9	104.1	104.3	103.8	103.8	103.9	104.3	106.4	107.0	108.0
原煤	Raw Coal	103.8	103.6	103.9	103.3	103.6	103.2	103.2	103.5	103.7	107.2	108.1	109.0
煤制品	Coal Products	104.2	104.1	104.0	105.1	105.0	104.6	104.5	104.5	105.1	105.5	105.7	106.6
2.石油及制品	Petroleum and Related Products	106.6	106.7	106.1	108.8	110.6	114.4	114.5	114.8	116.2	116.1	116.3	116.4
液化石油气	Liquefiled Petroleum Gas	116.4	117.4	112.0	111.4	111.8	110.1	109.2	111.0	117.6	116.8	116.8	117.0
管道燃气	Pipelined Gas	100.3	100.3	100.3	100.3	100.4	100.4	100.4	100.4	100.4	100.4	100.4	100.4
汽油	Gasoline	105.5	105.5	106.1	111.6	114.5	121.8	122.1	122.2	122.3	122.3	122.3	122.3
柴油	Diesel Oil	106.5	106.4	107.2	110.7	113.7	120.5	120.8	120.8	121.0	121.4	122.4	122.6
其他	Others	100.5	100.5	100.6	102.0	101.9	102.9	103.3	103.3	103.9	103.7	103.8	104.3
十六、建筑材料及五金电料	**Building Materials and Hardware**	**100.5**	**100.5**	**101.0**	**101.6**	**102.2**	**102.9**	**103.2**	**103.9**	**104.7**	**105.0**	**105.8**	**106.0**
1.建筑装璜材料	Building and Decoration Materials	100.4	100.4	100.9	101.8	102.3	103.1	103.5	104.0	104.7	105.1	106.0	106.1
木材	Wood	101.8	102.0	102.4	103.0	103.0	104.0	104.9	107.4	108.6	110.0	112.7	112.7
木地板	Wood Floor	102.0	102.0	101.4	101.9	102.4	103.2	103.9	104.3	105.2	105.9	107.5	107.7
钢材	Steel Products	92.1	92.3	93.2	94.8	96.9	99.3	98.4	97.0	97.0	97.0	96.9	96.6
砖	Brick	102.1	102.2	103.7	105.7	106.7	107.9	108.2	109.3	109.5	109.6	109.8	109.8
水泥	Cement	100.7	100.0	100.2	101.8	102.2	102.2	102.3	102.0	102.7	102.7	103.6	103.6
涂料	Coating Material	101.0	101.1	100.9	100.8	100.2	100.6	100.6	100.7	100.3	100.5	100.9	101.3
胶合板	Plywood	101.1	101.3	102.0	102.7	102.0	102.8	103.9	104.7	106.0	105.4	108.1	108.5
玻璃	Glass	99.3	99.0	99.5	99.6	100.3	100.7	101.7	102.3	102.9	103.9	104.5	104.6
粘胶	Rayon	100.8	100.8	100.8	100.7	100.9	101.4	101.7	102.5	103.2	103.7	104.0	105.2
油漆	Paint	101.6	101.8	101.9	101.9	102.3	102.8	103.3	103.4	105.7	105.7	105.5	105.9
其他	Others	101.6	101.7	103.5	103.9	104.3	102.7	104.5	104.5	104.9	107.4	107.5	105.8
2.五金电料	Hardware	100.6	100.9	101.0	101.1	102.0	102.6	102.7	103.5	104.7	104.9	105.2	105.6
五金工具	Hardware Tools	101.4	101.4	101.0	100.5	100.4	101.1	101.1	101.4	102.6	102.6	102.4	102.7
电工电料	Electrical Engineering and Electrical Materials	99.9	100.7	100.8	101.1	102.8	103.1	103.1	104.7	105.5	105.5	105.5	105.6
水暖器材	Heating Equipment	100.7	100.7	101.1	101.3	102.5	102.8	102.7	102.9	104.4	104.9	106.0	106.6
其他	Others	100.4	101.2	101.8	101.7	101.7	104.8	106.4	107.2	108.8	108.8	108.8	109.5

7-20 城市商品零售价格（定基）指数
Urban Retail Price Index

（以2005年平均价格为100）

商品类别及品名	Commodity Category and Commodity Name	1月 January	2月 February	3月 March	4月 April	5月 May	6月 June	7月 July	8 月 August	9 月 September	10 月 October	11月 November	12月 December
商品零售价格总指数	**Genaral Retail Price Index**	**101.6**	**101.7**	**101.0**	**101.0**	**100.6**	**100.0**	**99.4**	**99.5**	**99.9**	**99.8**	**100.3**	**101.5**
一、食品	**Food**	**106.1**	**106.6**	**104.7**	**104.8**	**103.0**	**100.0**	**98.2**	**98.8**	**100.7**	**99.8**	**101.4**	**106.0**
1.粮食	Grain	100.0	100.0	100.1	100.1	100.6	101.3	101.9	102.8	103.0	103.6	107.1	109.4
大米	Rice	102.0	102.0	102.3	102.2	103.9	105.8	107.2	109.8	110.1	111.1	112.3	114.8
面粉	Flour	97.5	97.6	97.3	96.8	96.8	96.6	96.8	96.2	96.2	96.6	103.6	107.0
粮食制品	Grain Products	99.5	99.7	100.0	100.3	100.3	100.9	101.2	102.2	102.4	102.7	105.1	106.6
其他	Others	105.6	104.9	105.0	105.7	106.2	107.5	107.6	108.4	109.2	110.4	113.4	115.2
2.淀粉	Starches	97.5	97.9	98.0	98.1	98.0	98.7	98.2	98.8	99.5	99.9	100.8	104.3
淀粉	Starches	97.5	97.9	98.0	98.1	98.0	98.7	98.2	98.8	99.5	99.9	100.8	104.3
3.干豆类及豆制品	Beans and Beans Products	100.3	100.2	100.4	100.1	100.4	100.9	101.8	102.1	101.7	101.5	101.8	102.8
干豆	Beans	99.1	99.1	98.5	98.3	99.2	101.5	104.7	105.8	103.2	101.5	101.9	102.3
豆制品	Beans Products	100.6	100.5	101.0	100.5	100.7	100.8	101.1	101.0	101.3	101.4	101.7	103.0
4.油脂	Oil and Fat	99.4	99.2	98.8	98.6	98.6	98.9	98.8	99.2	99.6	99.5	101.4	107.4
食用植物油	Edible Vegetable Oil	99.6	99.4	99.2	99.4	99.5	99.9	99.8	100.3	100.6	100.5	102.1	106.5
植物油制品	Plant Oil Products	99.4	99.0	98.7	98.4	98.6	98.8	98.0	97.8	98.0	98.0	100.6	114.8
其他	Others	95.3	95.8	90.1	80.8	77.6	79.2	78.5	80.6	82.6	83.6	89.6	95.7
5.肉禽及其制品	Meal,Poultry and Their Products	97.9	97.6	95.3	93.2	91.6	92.1	94.3	97.3	98.5	99.0	101.7	106.7
（1）食用畜肉及副产品	Edible Livestock Meat and Their By-products	98.0	97.0	93.3	89.7	87.6	88.3	91.0	95.2	97.4	97.8	102.0	109.1
猪肉	Pork	95.1	93.9	89.1	83.9	81.3	82.2	86.0	92.0	95.0	95.2	101.0	109.2
牛肉	Beef	106.5	106.5	105.1	104.7	103.2	103.8	104.5	104.3	105.7	105.5	106.9	110.5
羊肉	Mutton	106.8	106.2	104.2	105.0	104.8	104.7	104.9	104.5	105.3	106.1	106.5	110.6
畜肉副产品	Livestock Meat By-products	99.3	99.0	97.0	94.9	93.2	93.5	95.0	96.8	97.7	98.5	100.5	107.8
其他	Others	99.0	98.7	97.1	96.0	95.6	95.8	95.4	97.8	98.7	99.4	101.1	104.5
（2）禽	Poultry	93.5	94.3	93.9	94.0	92.1	92.2	96.7	99.6	98.5	100.1	100.6	103.8
鸡	Chicken	92.2	93.2	93.0	93.4	91.1	91.2	96.9	100.3	99.3	101.3	101.9	105.6
鸭	Duck	97.0	96.8	96.3	94.1	95.4	95.6	93.5	93.3	91.1	91.1	90.9	92.8
其他	Others	100.4	99.7	98.5	97.8	96.7	96.5	97.6	99.5	98.8	98.6	99.0	100.4
（3）肉禽加工制品	Meal and Poultry Processing Products	100.1	100.6	100.3	100.3	100.1	100.1	100.3	100.6	100.8	101.1	101.6	103.0
畜肉制品	Livestock Meat Products	100.6	101.2	100.7	100.7	100.3	100.3	100.5	100.6	100.6	100.9	101.6	103.2
禽制品	Poultry Products	99.1	99.6	99.5	99.3	99.6	99.7	99.9	100.6	101.4	101.5	101.6	102.7
6.蛋	Eggs	93.6	89.5	86.8	86.5	87.8	89.1	89.8	99.0	104.7	103.8	105.2	109.9
鲜蛋	Fresh Eggs	92.2	87.6	84.6	84.2	85.8	87.4	88.2	98.6	104.8	103.7	105.3	110.3
蛋制品	Egg Products	103.7	103.8	103.3	103.5	102.9	102.4	102.0	102.6	103.3	104.1	104.4	107.2
7.水产品	Aquatic Product	102.2	103.8	102.4	103.0	103.4	104.1	105.5	105.4	103.4	103.4	102.4	102.7
（1）鱼	Fish	100.1	100.2	97.1	98.3	99.3	101.9	103.9	105.3	103.5	102.4	100.0	99.9
淡水鱼	Freshwater Fish	96.1	94.9	91.4	89.7	91.4	95.7	99.0	101.5	100.8	98.1	95.3	95.0
海水鱼	Seawater Fish	103.4	104.6	101.9	105.4	105.7	107.1	108.0	108.5	105.7	106.0	103.9	104.1

7-20 续表 1 continued

商品类别及品名	Commodity Category and Commodity Name	1月 January	2月 February	3月 March	4月 April	5月 May	6月 June	7月 July	8月 August	9月 September	10月 October	11月 November	12月 December
		(以2005年平均价格为100)											
(2)其他水产品	Other Aquatic Product	105.0	108.5	109.3	109.2	108.9	107.0	107.5	105.6	103.2	104.8	105.6	106.4
虾蟹类	Shrimp and Crab	105.0	109.6	109.5	109.5	109.3	107.0	106.9	104.4	101.3	103.5	104.5	106.0
其他	Others	105.0	106.0	108.9	108.3	108.1	107.0	109.1	108.4	107.7	107.7	108.0	107.2
8.菜	Vegetable	141.4	140.5	127.9	123.4	105.3	90.1	84.5	90.6	103.8	89.9	92.2	112.3
鲜菜	Fresh Vegetable	146.8	145.4	130.8	125.1	103.6	86.2	79.7	86.8	102.9	87.0	89.7	111.7
干菜及菜制品	Dried Vegetable and Vegetable Products	102.5	103.4	103.5	104.6	104.6	104.4	105.4	106.1	107.8	110.1	111.6	117.0
薯类	Potato	112.7	118.0	120.6	127.7	142.6	143.1	141.1	136.5	114.7	105.3	104.4	114.5
9.调味品	Flavoring	101.9	101.8	101.7	102.2	102.4	102.6	102.6	102.5	102.5	102.9	104.1	104.7
盐	Salt	103.0	102.6	102.6	103.7	103.8	105.0	103.8	102.9	102.5	102.7	102.7	102.8
酱油	Soy Sauce	102.6	102.6	102.5	102.7	102.6	102.1	102.1	102.5	102.3	102.6	102.8	103.0
醋	Vinegar	101.7	101.7	101.6	101.9	101.8	102.0	102.1	102.0	102.1	102.2	102.2	102.7
味精	Aginomoto	100.1	100.1	99.9	100.4	100.6	100.2	100.3	100.0	100.1	100.1	99.9	100.4
其他	Others	101.2	100.9	100.9	101.2	102.2	103.2	104.4	104.5	105.1	106.4	113.3	115.9
10.糖	Carbohydrate	102.7	104.6	105.9	106.3	107.1	107.6	107.4	107.6	107.8	108.0	108.1	109.0
食糖	Sugar	108.3	114.0	120.4	121.7	124.6	126.5	126.3	127.5	128.0	127.6	127.4	130.9
糖果	Sweet	101.7	103.2	103.4	103.7	104.1	104.3	104.2	104.2	104.4	104.8	105.2	105.4
巧克力制品	Chocolate Products	100.8	100.7	100.5	100.4	100.0	99.8	99.5	99.2	99.2	99.5	99.5	99.5
糖类小食品	Little Carbohydrate Food	101.1	101.5	101.6	101.5	102.5	102.4	102.4	102.5	102.6	102.5	103.0	103.1
11.干鲜瓜果	Dried and Fresh Melons and Fruits	122.3	130.7	131.2	140.6	144.2	124.5	104.7	91.8	91.0	97.0	101.3	106.1
鲜瓜果	Fresh Fruits	127.0	137.6	138.0	149.7	154.1	128.9	103.6	87.3	86.1	93.2	97.8	103.7
干(坚)果	Dried Fruits	105.2	105.7	106.5	107.6	108.3	108.4	108.4	108.4	108.7	110.9	113.7	115.0
12.糕点饼干面包	Cake,Biscuit and Bread	100.9	100.7	100.7	100.8	101.0	100.9	100.7	100.7	100.6	100.3	100.1	100.7
糕点	Cake	100.8	100.8	100.6	100.5	100.5	100.2	99.9	99.4	99.4	98.5	98.8	99.5
饼干	Biscuit	100.5	100.3	100.6	101.2	101.9	102.0	101.9	102.2	101.6	101.5	100.8	101.0
面包	Bread	101.4	101.0	101.0	101.1	101.0	100.9	100.8	101.4	101.7	102.4	101.8	102.4
13.液体乳及乳制品	Liquid Milk and Their Products	100.7	100.7	101.2	101.4	101.3	101.5	101.6	101.9	103.3	103.2	103.2	103.2
巴氏杀菌奶或消毒奶	Pasteurization Milk or Disinfection Milk	100.1	100.1	100.9	101.0	100.8	101.1	101.2	101.5	102.7	102.8	102.7	102.7
酸奶	Leben	100.5	100.5	100.5	100.7	101.1	101.3	101.0	100.9	102.7	102.7	102.5	102.6
奶粉	Milk Powder	102.6	102.7	102.7	103.5	103.1	103.3	103.6	105.2	105.4	104.9	105.2	105.5
其他	Others	102.3	102.3	102.3	102.3	102.3	102.3	102.3	102.3	105.1	104.8	105.0	104.8
14.在外用膳食品	Outward Dinner	99.9	99.9	100.0	100.2	100.2	100.7	100.7	100.9	101.1	100.9	101.5	103.7
主食	Staple Food	100.0	99.6	99.8	99.8	99.8	100.3	100.4	100.5	100.6	100.6	101.8	105.7
炒菜	Hot Dish	99.9	100.0	100.1	100.4	100.4	100.9	100.8	100.8	101.3	100.9	101.0	102.5
地方小吃	Local Snack	100.0	100.0	100.3	100.3	100.3	100.3	101.2	101.9	101.7	101.7	102.2	103.7
15.其他食品	Other Foods	100.4	100.3	100.5	100.5	100.5	100.5	100.3	100.2	100.3	100.1	100.1	100.6
其他食品	Other Foods	100.4	100.3	100.5	100.5	100.5	100.5	100.3	100.2	100.3	100.1	100.1	100.6
二、饮料、烟酒	**Beverages,Tobacco,Liquor**	**100.5**	**100.4**	**100.6**	**100.9**	**100.9**	**101.3**	**101.3**	**101.6**	**101.7**	**101.7**	**101.7**	**102.0**
1.茶及饮料	Tea and Beverages	99.6	99.8	100.6	100.7	100.9	101.2	101.1	101.3	101.2	101.3	101.3	101.5
(1)茶叶	Tea	99.8	100.2	100.6	100.6	100.7	100.9	101.1	100.9	100.9	101.0	101.0	101.5

7-20 续表 2 continued

商品类别及品名	Commodity Category and Commodity Name	（以2005年平均价格为100）											
		1月 January	2月 February	3月 March	4月 April	5月 May	6月 June	7月 July	8月 August	9月 September	10月 October	11月 November	12月 December
茶叶	Tea	99.8	100.2	100.6	100.6	100.7	100.9	101.1	100.9	100.9	101.0	101.0	101.5
（2）饮料	Beverages	99.5	99.6	100.6	100.7	100.9	101.3	101.1	101.5	101.4	101.5	101.4	101.5
固体饮料	Solid Beverages	100.9	101.0	100.8	100.5	100.9	100.9	100.9	100.6	100.4	100.5	100.4	99.8
液体饮料	Liquid Beverages	99.4	99.6	100.4	100.6	100.7	100.8	100.2	100.4	100.5	100.5	100.5	101.0
冷冻饮品	Frozen Beverages	98.3	98.3	100.8	101.0	101.5	102.7	102.7	104.2	104.0	104.2	104.0	104.0
2.烟草	Tobacco	99.8	99.5	99.3	99.8	99.7	99.8	99.8	99.6	99.4	99.5	99.5	99.7
国产卷烟	Domestic Cigarette	99.8	99.7	99.6	100.1	100.1	100.3	100.2	100.1	99.8	99.9	99.9	100.0
进口卷烟	Import Cigarette	99.4	98.2	98.1	98.2	97.8	97.8	97.7	97.6	97.7	97.6	97.9	98.6
其他	Others	99.3	99.3	98.9	98.4	98.4	98.4	98.4	97.5	97.5	97.5	97.5	97.5
3.酒	Liquor	101.5	101.6	101.5	101.9	101.9	102.4	102.6	103.3	103.7	103.8	103.7	104.2
白酒	White Spirit	101.7	101.6	101.9	102.4	102.4	103.2	103.2	104.1	104.6	104.8	104.8	105.6
葡萄酒	Grape	105.7	105.9	105.7	106.0	105.8	106.9	107.2	107.5	107.9	108.0	107.9	107.9
啤酒	Beer	100.4	100.5	99.8	100.2	100.2	100.2	100.7	101.0	101.4	101.4	101.2	101.4
其他	Others	99.5	99.5	99.5	100.0	100.1	100.5	100.6	100.5	100.6	100.6	100.7	100.7
三、服装、鞋帽	**Garments,Footgearand and Hats**	**100.8**	**99.8**	**99.4**	**99.0**	**98.4**	**98.4**	**97.2**	**96.4**	**96.8**	**97.8**	**98.4**	**98.2**
1.服装	Garments	100.3	98.9	98.1	97.8	97.3	97.3	96.8	96.3	96.5	97.9	98.7	98.9
（1）男式服装	Men's Garments	100.1	99.1	98.0	97.5	96.8	96.5	96.0	95.1	95.3	96.7	97.5	97.5
大衣	Topcoat	97.0	96.1	95.6	94.2	94.3	93.5	93.3	93.3	92.8	92.5	92.7	93.1
毛线衣	Woollen Sweater	104.1	97.9	91.5	91.4	90.5	90.7	90.2	90.0	89.6	91.7	93.4	94.6
夹克衫	Jacket	98.3	96.9	93.8	93.2	93.2	93.1	93.0	93.1	93.3	96.7	97.1	97.5
衬衫	Shirt	95.8	95.4	95.6	94.8	94.1	95.0	93.6	92.5	93.2	93.8	93.7	94.8
T恤衫	T-shirt	103.0	103.3	102.3	102.2	100.4	97.4	94.5	92.1	92.7	92.5	93.2	93.2
裤子	Trousers	98.0	96.3	96.3	96.1	95.7	95.1	94.5	93.9	93.0	95.8	96.2	95.6
西服	Western-style Clothes	100.8	102.3	101.5	102.3	101.9	101.6	102.6	99.4	101.5	103.5	102.9	102.4
运动衫裤	Gym Suit	99.5	99.5	99.6	99.0	96.0	96.2	95.6	96.3	95.9	96.2	97.2	97.5
内衣	Underwaist	102.7	102.8	103.9	103.8	103.2	103.5	102.9	103.0	102.7	103.1	102.7	102.9
羽绒衣	Eider Down Outerwear	103.2	102.6	102.0	98.1	98.1	98.0	97.4	97.3	96.4	98.9	104.0	102.1
其他	Others	97.3	96.2	94.8	93.9	94.0	93.9	93.6	93.5	93.5	93.5	97.3	97.0
（2）女式服装	Women's Garments	100.6	98.5	97.9	97.6	97.1	97.2	97.0	96.6	97.1	98.6	99.4	99.8
大衣	Topcoat	101.2	95.4	93.4	92.7	92.6	92.6	92.3	92.3	92.2	92.1	92.9	95.8
毛线衣	Woollen Sweater	101.0	94.2	92.7	92.6	91.8	92.2	92.1	92.1	92.8	95.7	95.4	96.9
羽绒衣	Eider Down Outerwear	100.1	99.2	97.7	97.5	97.4	97.2	96.8	96.6	95.9	99.1	105.0	103.3
套装	Coordinates	101.0	101.2	100.8	100.8	101.5	100.0	100.8	97.5	101.9	103.1	101.6	101.9
衬衫	Shirt	100.4	101.9	102.2	99.5	99.5	100.0	100.4	98.6	99.2	99.5	99.2	97.8
T恤衫	T-shirt	101.4	101.7	101.5	100.2	100.4	100.8	99.5	99.1	103.2	110.9	111.0	110.9
裙子	Skirt	104.4	103.6	103.1	100.6	101.7	101.9	101.8	101.7	101.3	101.6	102.8	102.7
裤子	Trousers	99.3	97.0	96.1	96.3	95.7	96.3	95.4	95.6	95.5	96.2	97.3	95.6
运动衫裤	Gym Suit	97.8	98.5	97.9	98.5	92.7	93.2	92.7	92.7	92.5	94.6	93.2	95.3
内衣	Underwaist	98.5	98.7	100.5	101.9	101.2	101.8	101.3	101.4	100.6	101.6	103.0	102.9
其他	Others	100.4	99.7	100.2	101.3	100.6	101.1	101.2	102.1	101.9	102.6	103.0	102.8

7-20 续表 3 continued

商品类别及品名	Commodity Category and Commodity Name	(以2005年平均价格为100)											
		1月 January	2月 February	3月 March	4月 April	5月 May	6月 June	7月 July	8月 August	9月 September	10月 October	11月 November	12月 December
(3) 儿童服装	Children's Garments	100.0	99.8	99.7	100.2	100.8	100.9	99.5	99.3	98.6	99.3	99.9	99.6
套装	Coordinates	100.3	100.1	99.7	99.8	99.4	99.3	98.8	98.3	97.7	98.2	99.0	98.8
裤子	Trousers	99.9	99.7	99.7	99.7	100.0	100.0	98.0	98.2	97.6	98.8	99.4	99.8
裙子	Skirt	98.7	98.9	99.8	101.9	105.1	105.7	103.5	103.1	101.7	102.4	102.7	101.6
其他	Others	104.5	102.5	99.4	97.0	95.7	95.3	95.0	95.0	95.9	95.9	96.8	95.9
2.鞋袜帽	Shoes,Socks and Hats	102.4	102.0	102.7	101.9	101.2	101.0	98.2	96.7	97.3	97.5	97.7	96.9
(1) 鞋	Shoes	102.7	102.3	103.2	102.2	101.4	101.2	97.9	96.1	96.9	97.1	97.4	96.5
男鞋	Men's Shoes	101.3	101.2	102.7	102.2	101.4	101.9	98.4	96.7	97.3	97.3	97.6	96.8
女鞋	Women's Shoes	104.1	103.4	104.0	102.5	101.3	100.5	96.6	94.3	95.7	95.8	96.1	94.9
童鞋	Children's Shoes	101.7	101.6	101.3	101.1	101.9	101.8	101.1	100.9	100.0	101.1	101.6	101.6
(2) 袜子	Socks	100.6	100.5	100.0	100.8	100.0	100.1	99.8	99.8	99.4	100.0	99.4	98.8
男袜	Men's Socks	100.5	100.4	100.2	100.8	100.5	100.4	100.2	100.2	99.9	100.4	99.4	98.2
女袜	Women's Socks	100.7	100.7	99.9	100.7	99.6	99.8	99.5	99.5	99.1	99.7	99.4	99.4
(3) 帽子	Hats	100.0	99.6	99.5	99.5	99.7	99.8	99.8	99.8	99.3	99.8	100.3	100.4
男帽	Men's Hats	100.3	99.9	99.6	99.6	100.0	100.3	100.4	100.9	99.7	100.2	101.1	101.6
女帽	Women's Hats	99.8	99.4	99.4	99.4	99.5	99.4	99.4	99.2	99.1	99.7	99.8	99.6
3.其他	Others	98.5	99.6	99.1	98.4	98.2	98.4	97.9	97.1	98.0	98.6	98.5	96.8
领带	Necktie	98.5	99.6	99.1	98.4	98.2	98.4	97.9	97.1	98.0	98.6	98.5	96.8
四、纺织品	**Textiles**	**98.1**	**98.6**	**98.7**	**98.6**	**98.2**	**98.5**	**98.4**	**98.3**	**97.9**	**98.1**	**98.0**	**98.4**
1.衣着材料	Clothing Materials	98.0	98.0	97.8	97.8	97.7	97.7	97.7	97.7	97.8	98.1	98.2	98.5
棉布	Cotton Cloth	94.1	94.0	94.8	95.9	95.8	95.9	96.3	96.3	97.4	98.0	97.7	97.6
棉混纺布	Cotton Textiles Cloth	95.0	95.3	95.3	95.3	95.2	95.2	95.1	95.2	94.8	95.1	95.5	95.7
化纤布	Chemical Fiber Cloth	101.5	101.5	100.6	99.9	99.6	99.7	99.4	99.5	99.3	99.4	99.5	99.5
毛线	Knitting Wool	99.4	99.2	99.1	99.1	99.0	99.0	99.1	98.8	99.0	99.1	99.3	100.6
2.床上用品	Bedclothes	98.2	99.2	99.5	99.4	98.7	99.2	98.9	98.7	98.0	98.2	97.9	98.2
毛毯	Woollen Blanket	99.5	100.1	100.6	100.4	99.4	100.4	99.4	99.1	98.7	99.1	98.9	99.8
被子	Quilt	97.0	97.6	97.6	97.2	96.1	97.0	96.6	96.2	94.8	94.4	93.1	93.7
床上套件	Bed Articcles	97.6	98.8	99.3	99.2	98.7	99.2	99.1	99.1	98.4	99.0	99.2	99.2
其他	Others	100.0	101.9	102.2	102.4	102.3	102.1	102.1	102.1	102.0	102.2	102.4	102.5
五、家用电器及音像器材	**Household Appliances,Music and Video Equipments**	**99.4**	**99.4**	**99.3**	**98.9**	**99.0**	**100.0**	**100.4**	**100.2**	**99.5**	**99.3**	**99.4**	**99.2**
1.家庭设备	Household Appliances	100.3	100.4	100.5	100.4	100.7	102.9	103.8	104.0	103.9	104.1	104.3	104.3
洗衣机	Washing Machine	100.0	100.1	100.0	98.7	99.4	100.8	101.5	100.9	100.5	100.5	100.8	100.5
电风扇	Electric Fan	100.5	100.7	100.8	100.4	100.8	101.3	100.7	101.0	99.0	99.3	99.3	99.3
电冰箱(柜)	Refrigerator	102.3	102.4	102.6	102.7	103.4	105.8	107.3	107.2	107.2	108.0	107.6	107.8
吸排油烟机	Kitchen Ventilato	102.5	102.4	102.5	102.6	102.4	105.2	107.4	108.8	108.4	108.2	108.5	108.4
空调器	Air-conditioning	99.7	99.7	99.7	99.5	99.9	103.6	104.7	105.2	105.5	105.5	105.9	106.0
热水器	Water Heater	99.2	99.9	100.9	101.3	100.5	100.8	100.8	100.9	100.9	101.2	101.2	101.4
微波炉	Microwave Oven	98.2	98.2	98.1	97.9	97.8	98.5	98.3	98.3	98.0	98.3	98.9	98.7
电炊具	Electric Cooking Appliance	100.1	100.0	100.1	101.1	101.2	101.1	101.1	101.3	100.7	101.0	101.0	101.0
2.文娱用耐用消费品	Durable Consumer Goods For Recreational Use	98.1	97.9	97.6	96.6	96.5	96.1	95.8	95.0	93.3	92.4	92.3	91.8

7-20 续表 4 continued

商品类别及品名	Commodity Category and Commodity Name	（以2005年平均价格为100）											
		1月 January	2月 February	3月 March	4月 April	5月 May	6月 June	7月 July	8月 August	9月 September	10月 October	11月 November	12月 December
电视机	Television	97.0	96.9	96.6	95.4	95.3	94.9	94.6	93.1	91.0	89.9	89.7	89.1
激光视盘机	Laser Video Disc Machine	98.6	97.9	97.5	96.8	96.6	96.6	96.0	96.0	93.0	91.4	91.3	91.3
摄像机	Pickup Camera	99.3	99.1	98.5	97.3	96.8	95.6	95.2	95.1	93.7	93.4	93.1	92.3
家用音响设备	Acoustic Equipment	99.7	99.7	99.6	99.4	99.2	99.2	99.2	99.2	98.8	98.9	98.9	98.8
便携式音响	Portable Acoustics	99.5	98.8	98.2	97.8	97.8	97.8	97.8	97.8	97.3	97.4	97.4	97.4
其他	Others	99.9	100.0	100.0	99.9	99.8	99.8	99.8	99.2	98.8	99.0	98.9	98.9
3.音像器材	Music and Video Equipments	99.5	99.5	99.5	99.3	99.3	99.3	99.3	99.3	99.3	99.3	99.3	99.3
专业音响器材	Specialized Acoustic Apparatus	100.0	99.9	99.9	99.8	99.8	99.8	99.8	99.8	99.8	99.8	99.8	99.8
专业声像器材	Specialized Acoustic Image Apparatus	98.9	98.9	98.9	98.7	98.7	98.6	98.6	98.6	98.6	98.6	98.6	98.6
六、文化办公用品	**Cultural and Office Applicances**	**97.4**	**97.3**	**97.3**	**97.2**	**96.9**	**96.6**	**96.3**	**95.8**	**95.2**	**95.2**	**95.0**	**94.9**
纸张本册	Paper and Volume	99.6	99.6	99.6	99.6	99.6	99.6	99.5	99.5	99.7	100.1	100.0	100.1
文具	Stationery	98.7	98.9	98.9	98.9	98.9	98.8	98.8	98.8	98.3	98.6	98.6	98.6
电脑及配件	Computer and its Fitting	95.6	95.5	95.3	95.2	94.5	93.6	93.3	92.5	91.0	90.9	90.7	90.6
打印机及配件	Printer and its Fitting	97.1	97.1	96.9	96.8	96.6	96.9	96.6	95.6	95.5	95.4	95.1	95.1
扫描仪	Scanner	99.2	99.2	99.2	99.2	99.1	99.1	99.0	98.9	98.9	98.9	98.8	98.8
复印机	Xerox Machine	96.9	96.9	96.9	96.9	96.9	96.8	96.7	96.3	96.0	95.9	94.7	94.4
电子辞典	Electronic Dictionary	99.5	99.4	99.2	98.6	98.5	98.5	97.7	96.1	96.3	96.7	96.8	96.8
计算器	Calculator	97.6	97.9	97.8	97.8	97.8	97.7	97.7	97.5	97.4	97.5	97.7	97.9
教学设备	Teaching Equipment	98.4	98.5	98.4	98.4	98.4	98.3	98.2	98.2	98.0	98.1	98.1	98.1
其他	Others	100.2	100.2	100.2	100.2	100.2	100.1	99.8	99.8	100.0	100.3	100.3	100.4
七、日用品	**Articles for Daily Use**	**100.2**	**100.3**	**100.4**	**100.4**	**100.6**	**100.7**	**100.6**	**100.7**	**100.5**	**100.8**	**100.9**	**100.9**
1.日用百货	General Merchandise for Daily Use	100.2	100.1	100.3	100.5	100.7	100.6	100.7	100.7	100.6	100.8	100.9	100.8
自行车	Bicycle	101.0	100.9	100.9	100.9	100.7	100.8	101.6	101.4	101.6	101.8	101.9	101.6
雨具	Rain Gear	99.1	99.1	99.1	99.1	99.1	99.4	99.4	100.0	100.2	100.3	99.9	100.0
剃须刀具	Shaver	100.2	100.4	100.8	101.4	101.5	101.9	101.7	101.7	101.4	101.3	101.1	101.2
电池	Battery	98.4	98.7	98.6	98.6	99.3	96.5	96.9	96.7	96.3	96.4	96.8	96.9
卫生纸	Tissue Paper	101.4	101.3	101.8	102.6	102.9	103.7	103.7	103.8	103.8	103.9	103.8	104.0
卫生巾	Sanitary Towel	98.7	98.4	98.4	98.3	99.1	98.7	98.2	98.1	97.6	98.3	98.1	98.0
其他	Others	100.6	100.7	100.7	100.7	100.7	100.7	100.7	100.7	100.5	100.8	102.4	102.4
2.日用杂品	Sundry Articles	99.9	99.9	100.0	100.1	100.3	100.4	100.4	100.5	100.5	100.6	100.6	100.8
茶具	Tea Set	99.4	99.4	99.5	99.6	99.5	99.4	99.3	99.4	99.2	99.5	99.3	99.5
餐具	Tableware	99.4	99.4	99.5	99.6	100.1	100.1	99.8	100.3	100.2	100.4	100.4	101.0
厨具	Kitchen Utensils	100.3	100.3	100.3	100.8	100.8	101.2	101.3	101.3	101.4	101.5	101.7	101.6
其他	Others	100.2	100.5	100.8	100.6	100.6	100.6	100.5	100.5	100.4	100.1	99.9	100.0
3.洗涤用品	Washing Articles	100.6	100.7	100.7	100.7	100.7	101.0	101.0	101.3	101.1	101.3	101.4	101.7

7-20 续表 5 continued

商品类别及品名	Commodity Category and Commodity Name	（以2005年平均价格为100）											
		1月 January	2月 February	3月 March	4月 April	5月 May	6月 June	7月 July	8月 August	9月 September	10月 October	11月 November	12月 December
洗衣粉	Washing Powder	100.7	100.8	100.9	101.0	100.8	101.7	101.7	102.6	102.4	102.6	102.5	103.0
肥皂类	Soap	100.2	100.3	100.2	99.9	99.9	100.0	100.0	100.2	100.0	100.2	100.4	100.5
牙膏	Toothpaste	100.6	101.0	100.7	100.8	101.0	101.0	101.0	100.9	100.7	100.7	101.2	101.5
清洁洗涤剂	Cleaning Agent	100.7	100.8	100.9	101.0	101.0	100.9	100.9	100.8	100.6	100.8	100.8	100.8
4.其他日用品	Other Articles for Daily Use	100.3	100.3	100.5	100.4	100.6	100.6	100.2	100.4	99.8	100.5	100.7	100.3
燃气灶具	Gas-Oven	101.9	101.8	102.8	103.2	103.2	104.0	104.5	104.7	104.5	104.7	104.7	104.7
儿童玩具	Children's Toy	101.3	101.1	100.7	100.1	100.2	100.3	100.6	100.5	99.9	100.3	100.3	100.3
照明器具	Illumination Utensil	99.2	99.2	99.3	99.5	99.5	99.5	99.5	99.5	99.4	99.6	99.4	99.3
钟表眼镜及配件	Clocks,Glasses and Their Rittings	98.3	98.1	98.1	98.5	98.5	98.7	98.8	98.9	98.1	98.7	99.0	99.0
日用普通饰品	Common Ornament for Daily Use	100.2	100.9	100.4	98.5	100.8	99.4	100.4	99.6	98.4	99.9	99.9	99.9
日用皮革制品	Leatherware for Daily Use	99.2	99.6	100.4	100.4	100.1	99.8	95.4	97.0	95.7	98.1	98.9	97.0
其他	Others	99.6	99.9	100.7	100.7	100.4	100.6	96.6	98.1	97.3	98.6	99.2	98.0
八、体育娱乐用品	**Sports and Recreation Articles**	**99.5**	**99.5**	**99.4**	**99.3**	**99.2**	**99.1**	**99.0**	**99.1**	**98.6**	**98.9**	**98.9**	**98.9**
1.体育用品	Sports Articles	99.6	99.6	99.5	99.5	99.2	99.3	99.2	99.1	98.7	99.1	99.0	99.0
球类	Ball	99.1	98.7	98.5	98.5	98.2	98.5	98.4	98.4	98.1	98.4	98.3	98.3
棋牌	Chess and Ccards	101.7	101.9	101.9	101.6	101.4	100.6	100.6	100.6	100.5	100.9	100.9	100.9
健身器材	Exercise Machine	99.1	99.2	99.2	99.2	98.9	99.2	99.1	98.9	98.4	98.8	98.6	98.6
2.娱乐用品	Recreation Articles	99.4	99.4	99.3	99.2	99.1	99.0	98.9	99.0	98.5	98.7	98.8	98.9
游艺器材	Entertainment Apparatus	99.4	99.2	98.9	98.3	98.1	97.7	97.1	97.6	96.7	97.1	97.0	97.2
照相器材	Photographic Apparatus	98.6	98.6	98.7	98.7	98.7	98.7	98.7	98.7	98.3	98.3	98.4	98.5
乐器	Musical Instrument	100.9	100.9	100.9	100.9	100.9	100.9	100.9	100.9	100.6	100.9	101.0	101.1
九、交通、通信用品	**Transportation and Communication Appliances**	**96.5**	**96.2**	**95.5**	**94.5**	**94.1**	**93.8**	**93.4**	**92.8**	**91.9**	**91.4**	**90.9**	**90.3**
1.交通运输机械	Transportation Machine	99.4	99.4	99.1	98.9	98.8	98.8	98.6	98.4	97.5	97.3	97.0	96.5
轿车	Car	99.0	99.0	98.8	98.5	98.2	98.0	97.6	96.8	95.3	95.1	94.6	93.7
客车	Bus	98.7	98.7	98.4	98.4	98.4	98.4	98.3	98.3	96.9	96.9	96.9	96.9
货车	Truck	100.4	100.4	99.8	99.5	99.5	99.5	99.4	99.4	99.3	98.5	98.3	98.3
摩托车	Motorcycle	99.7	99.7	99.7	99.5	100.0	100.0	100.2	100.5	100.6	100.7	100.2	99.2
其他	Others	99.0	99.0	99.0	98.9	98.9	98.9	98.8	98.8	98.8	98.8	98.8	98.8
2.通信器材	Telecommunications Facilities	90.3	89.4	87.6	85.1	83.9	82.9	82.1	80.7	79.7	78.6	77.7	76.9
固定电话机	Telephone	99.3	98.7	98.3	98.1	97.6	97.5	97.3	97.1	96.8	96.8	96.7	96.2
移动电话机	Mobile Phone	85.3	84.1	81.4	77.7	76.0	74.6	73.3	71.4	69.9	68.2	66.9	65.9
传真机	Fax Machine	99.8	99.5	99.8	99.6	99.6	99.6	99.5	99.0	98.9	98.9	98.7	98.7
其他	Others	99.2	99.2	99.2	98.2	96.3	96.3	96.2	96.2	96.2	96.2	96.2	96.2
十、家具	**Furniture**	**100.4**	**100.3**	**100.4**	**100.0**	**99.9**	**100.1**	**100.2**	**100.4**	**100.9**	**101.0**	**101.0**	**101.0**
柜	Cabinet	101.0	101.0	101.0	100.1	100.3	100.4	100.3	100.8	101.1	101.0	101.1	101.1
床	Bed	101.4	101.4	101.5	101.4	101.3	101.3	101.6	101.8	101.9	102.3	102.0	101.8
桌	Desk	100.7	100.8	100.7	100.7	100.5	100.2	100.4	100.8	101.1	101.2	101.4	101.5

7-20 续表 6 continued

商品类别及品名	Commodity Category and Commodity Name	（以2005年平均价格为100）											
		1月 January	2月 February	3月 March	4月 April	5月 May	6月 June	7月 July	8 月 August	9 月 September	10 月 October	11月 November	12月 December
椅	Chair	100.6	100.1	100.2	100.2	100.2	100.3	100.3	100.4	101.7	102.2	102.4	102.3
沙发	Sofa	99.1	99.2	99.2	98.7	98.5	98.7	98.5	98.7	98.9	98.9	98.9	99.0
其他	Others	98.6	98.3	98.6	98.8	98.2	100.0	101.5	101.5	103.1	102.8	102.9	102.9
十一、化妆品	**Cosmetics**	**98.5**	**98.7**	**98.6**	**98.8**	**98.7**	**98.6**	**98.6**	**98.7**	**98.5**	**98.8**	**98.6**	**98.4**
护肤品	Skincare Products	99.3	99.7	99.5	99.7	99.7	99.6	99.6	99.6	99.2	99.9	99.3	98.8
美容化妆品	Facial Beautifiers	95.5	95.6	95.7	95.8	95.8	95.6	96.0	96.0	96.0	96.2	96.4	96.1
护发美容品	Protects Sends the Beauty Products	99.4	99.5	99.6	99.5	99.2	99.4	99.0	99.2	99.1	99.4	99.1	99.0
清洁化妆用品	Cleaning Toiletware	99.3	99.3	99.4	99.5	99.7	99.5	99.3	99.3	99.4	99.5	99.5	99.4
药物美容用品	Medicinal Cosmetics	99.5	99.4	99.1	99.4	99.3	99.3	99.2	99.0	99.0	99.1	99.1	99.1
十二、金银珠宝	**Gold,Silver and Jewelry**	**103.9**	**105.3**	**106.0**	**108.9**	**113.8**	**115.6**	**116.2**	**117.6**	**117.0**	**117.2**	**117.4**	**118.0**
金饰品	Gold	107.6	110.2	111.1	115.0	123.0	123.9	124.2	125.8	124.7	124.0	124.4	124.9
银饰品	Silver	100.6	100.9	101.5	102.0	103.1	103.8	106.4	110.6	111.1	112.8	112.5	114.1
铂金饰品	Platinum	102.3	103.3	103.6	107.6	112.1	116.0	116.3	116.8	116.5	116.9	117.1	117.6
其他	Others	99.8	99.9	100.6	100.3	99.8	100.3	100.4	100.7	100.4	100.8	100.8	100.9
十三、中西药品及医疗保健用品	**Traditional Chinese andWestern Medicines and Health Care Articles**	**100.0**	**99.8**	**99.7**	**99.6**	**99.5**	**99.7**	**99.7**	**99.6**	**99.0**	**99.2**	**99.2**	**99.3**
1.医疗器具及用品	Medical Facilities and Goods	98.6	98.7	98.3	97.9	98.0	98.0	97.9	97.9	97.9	93.3	93.3	93.3
医疗器具及用品	Medical Facilities and Goods	98.6	98.7	98.3	97.9	98.0	98.0	97.9	97.9	97.9	93.3	93.3	93.3
2.中药材及中成药	Herbs and Ready-made Traditional Chinese Medicine	100.2	99.8	100.0	99.8	99.6	100.3	99.7	99.8	99.1	101.3	101.3	101.4
中药材	Herbs	98.8	98.4	98.7	98.6	98.7	101.6	100.9	101.2	101.1	105.2	105.4	105.8
中成药	Ready-made Traditional Chinese Medicine	101.1	100.9	101.0	100.7	100.1	99.3	98.8	98.8	97.7	98.4	98.4	98.3
3.西药	Western Medicine	99.9	99.8	99.6	99.6	99.6	99.5	99.9	99.7	98.9	98.5	98.5	98.5
抗微生物药	Anti-microorganism Medicine	99.9	99.9	99.9	99.9	100.0	100.4	103.6	102.9	101.9	101.5	101.8	101.5
消化系统用药	Alimentary System Medicine	98.8	98.7	99.0	99.2	99.4	99.4	99.4	99.3	98.9	99.3	98.7	99.4
呼吸系统用药	Respiratory System Medicine	99.7	99.7	99.4	99.4	99.4	100.0	100.0	100.1	99.8	100.0	100.0	99.9
解热镇痛及非甾体抗炎药	Allays a Fever the Analgesia and the Non-steroid Body anti-inflammatory Agent	100.6	100.4	100.0	99.9	99.8	98.7	97.9	97.9	96.7	98.5	98.8	99.1
抗肿瘤药	AntineopLastic Drug	100.2	100.2	99.9	99.8	99.8	98.6	98.6	98.3	98.3	96.5	96.5	96.4
激素及调节内分泌功能药	Hormone and Adjustment Internal Secretion Function Medicine	99.4	99.3	98.7	98.7	98.7	98.0	98.0	97.6	95.5	93.4	94.3	94.0
循环系统用药	Circulating System Medicine	99.8	99.7	99.4	99.2	99.3	100.2	99.7	99.7	100.0	101.6	100.3	100.9
神经系统用药	Nerve System Medicine	101.1	101.1	100.5	100.5	100.5	100.2	100.2	99.6	98.6	94.9	94.9	94.9
专科用药	Junior Medicine	99.9	100.0	100.0	99.8	99.8	100.2	100.1	100.1	97.9	95.9	96.1	96.0
其他	Others	100.0	100.0	98.9	98.9	98.5	98.1	98.0	98.0	97.9	97.6	97.3	97.1
4.保健品及器具	Healthcare Equipment	100.6	100.4	100.1	100.1	100.1	100.3	99.6	99.8	99.7	100.1	100.2	100.1
保健器具	Health Protection Equipment	100.2	99.7	99.5	99.5	99.3	99.3	98.9	98.8	98.8	98.8	98.8	98.5
滋补保健用品	Tonic and Health Products	100.7	100.7	100.3	100.4	100.3	100.7	99.9	100.2	100.1	100.6	100.8	100.7
十四、书报杂志及电子出版物	**Books,Newspapers,Magazines and Electronic Publications**	**101.4**	**101.3**	**101.4**	**101.5**	**101.5**	**101.4**	**101.4**	**101.7**	**101.6**	**101.6**	**101.5**	**101.6**

7-20 续表 7 continued

商品类别及品名	Commodity Category and Commodity Name	（以2005年平均价格为100）											
		1月 January	2月 February	3月 March	4月 April	5月 May	6月 June	7月 July	8月 August	9月 September	10月 October	11月 November	12月 December
1.教材及参考书	Teaching Materials and Reference Books	102.1	102.1	102.3	102.3	102.3	102.2	102.2	103.0	102.9	102.7	102.7	102.8
工具书	Tool Book	101.6	101.6	101.6	101.6	101.6	101.6	101.6	101.6	101.6	101.6	101.6	101.6
教材	Teaching Material	100.8	100.8	101.2	101.2	101.2	101.2	101.2	101.9	100.9	100.6	100.6	100.6
参考书	Reference Book	104.9	104.9	105.0	105.0	105.0	104.9	104.9	106.4	107.5	107.5	107.5	107.6
教育软件	Educational Software	100.0	100.0	100.0	100.0	100.0	100.0	100.0	100.0	100.0	100.0	100.0	100.0
2.书报杂志	Books,Newspapers, Magazines	102.3	102.3	102.5	102.5	102.5	102.5	102.5	102.5	102.5	102.5	102.5	102.7
书籍	Books	101.0	101.0	101.4	101.4	101.4	101.4	101.4	101.5	101.5	101.5	101.5	101.6
报纸	Newspapers	105.8	105.8	105.8	105.8	105.8	105.8	105.8	105.8	105.8	105.8	105.8	105.8
杂志	Magazines	100.1	100.1	100.1	100.1	100.1	100.1	100.1	100.1	100.1	100.1	100.1	100.3
3.电子音像制品	Electronic Publications	99.6	99.2	99.0	99.2	99.2	99.2	99.2	99.2	99.1	99.3	98.9	98.9
音响光盘和磁带	Acoustic Light Disk and Tape	99.6	98.5	98.3	98.7	98.7	98.7	98.7	98.7	98.5	98.7	98.7	98.7
录像磁带和视盘	Video Tape and Disk	100.1	100.0	100.1	100.5	100.6	100.8	100.8	100.7	100.5	100.8	100.7	100.6
计算机软件	Computer Software	99.0	99.0	98.7	98.7	98.6	98.4	98.4	98.4	98.5	98.5	97.5	97.5
十五、燃料	**Fuels**	**105.6**	**105.6**	**105.1**	**107.4**	**108.6**	**111.3**	**111.2**	**111.6**	**112.9**	**113.0**	**113.4**	**113.8**
1.煤炭及制品	Coal and Related Products	104.8	104.3	104.6	105.2	105.3	104.8	104.7	104.9	105.9	106.4	107.1	108.3
原煤	Raw Coal	105.6	104.7	105.3	104.1	104.6	104.1	104.1	104.5	105.2	105.9	107.0	108.0
煤制品	Coal Products	103.9	103.8	103.8	106.3	106.2	105.6	105.4	105.4	106.6	107.0	107.3	108.6
2.石油及制品	Petroleum and Related Products	105.8	106.1	105.3	108.2	109.7	113.5	113.4	113.8	115.3	115.2	115.5	115.6
液化石油气	Liquefiled Petroleum Gas	115.7	117.2	110.5	111.2	111.9	109.6	108.4	111.1	118.9	118.1	118.3	118.3
管道燃气	Pipelined Gas	100.0	100.0	100.0	100.0	100.0	100.0	100.0	100.0	100.0	100.0	100.0	100.0
汽油	Gasoline	105.6	105.7	106.2	112.1	114.7	122.6	122.8	122.8	123.0	123.0	123.0	123.0
柴油	Diesel Oil	106.6	106.5	107.4	111.0	113.5	120.9	121.1	121.1	121.4	121.4	123.1	123.3
其他	Others	100.8	100.8	100.8	101.5	101.6	102.2	102.8	102.8	103.6	103.6	103.6	104.2
十六、建筑材料及五金电料	**Building Materials and Hardware**	**100.4**	**100.7**	**100.8**	**101.2**	**101.8**	**102.6**	**102.8**	**103.4**	**104.7**	**105.1**	**106.0**	**106.3**
1.建筑装璜材料	Building and Decoration Materials	100.3	100.5	100.7	101.2	101.7	102.6	103.0	103.4	104.6	105.1	106.2	106.4
木材	Wood	101.0	101.3	101.4	101.4	101.4	102.2	102.8	104.5	105.7	106.5	109.3	109.7
木地板	Wood Floor	103.0	103.1	102.1	104.7	105.2	106.4	107.3	107.9	109.6	110.1	112.3	112.5
钢材	Steel Products	95.0	95.8	96.1	96.9	98.3	100.6	100.3	99.9	100.2	100.2	100.1	100.0
砖	Brick	102.0	101.6	102.7	103.5	104.9	105.7	106.0	107.6	108.3	108.3	108.9	109.3
水泥	Cement	98.5	98.6	99.1	99.5	99.6	100.3	100.7	99.9	101.5	102.1	103.3	103.4
涂料	Coating Material	100.8	100.9	100.9	101.0	101.1	101.8	101.7	101.6	100.8	100.9	101.3	101.4
胶合板	Plywood	100.7	101.0	101.2	101.7	101.5	102.3	103.1	103.3	105.2	105.6	108.0	108.5
玻璃	Glass	101.2	101.1	101.6	101.7	102.4	102.5	103.1	103.1	104.2	104.8	105.0	105.0
粘胶	Rayon	100.8	100.8	100.8	100.8	101.1	102.1	102.2	102.5	103.6	104.3	105.0	105.6
油漆	Paint	100.1	100.4	100.7	100.8	101.0	101.3	102.4	102.4	106.5	106.5	106.2	106.2
其他	Others	102.6	102.6	102.6	102.7	102.7	102.8	102.8	103.0	103.6	106.5	106.7	106.8
2.五金电料	Hardware	100.5	101.1	101.1	101.1	102.1	102.6	102.5	103.5	104.9	105.1	105.6	106.2
五金工具	Hardware Tools	102.1	102.1	101.3	100.5	100.4	100.7	100.2	100.5	102.5	102.6	102.2	102.7
电工电料	Dlectrical Engineering and Electrical Materials	98.9	100.3	100.4	100.8	102.9	102.8	102.5	105.3	106.2	106.2	106.2	106.3
水暖器材	Heating Equipment	100.9	100.9	101.0	101.4	102.6	103.0	102.9	103.2	104.2	104.8	106.4	107.4
其他	Others	100.3	101.4	102.5	102.2	102.2	104.9	106.5	106.6	109.2	109.2	109.2	110.3

7-21 农村商品零售价格（定基）指数
Rural Retail Price Index

（以2005年平均价格为100）

商品类别及品名	Commodity Category and Commodity Name	1月 January	2月 February	3月 March	4月 April	5月 May	6月 June	7月 July	8月 August	9月 September	10月 October	11月 November	12月 December
商品零售价格总指数	**Genaral Retail Price Index**	**101.1**	**101.2**	**100.6**	**100.8**	**100.7**	**100.1**	**99.9**	**100.3**	**101.0**	**100.6**	**101.2**	**102.9**
一、食品	**Food**	**104.9**	**105.6**	**103.2**	**103.5**	**102.3**	**99.5**	**98.5**	**100.2**	**102.5**	**100.4**	**101.8**	**107.8**
1.粮食	Grain	99.6	99.8	99.6	99.9	100.4	100.0	102.2	102.9	104.5	105.4	107.8	110.1
大米	Rice	104.3	103.6	103.6	104.5	107.0	107.2	113.2	116.7	118.7	120.0	117.5	118.8
面粉	Flour	96.5	97.1	96.9	97.1	96.7	95.8	97.1	96.8	98.2	99.0	104.8	107.9
粮食制品	Grain Products	100.0	100.3	100.0	100.0	100.1	99.9	100.4	100.6	100.8	100.8	103.4	105.1
其他	Others	100.5	101.4	101.2	101.3	101.4	102.2	103.1	102.6	108.8	111.3	109.6	111.7
2.淀粉	Starches	103.9	102.9	103.3	105.0	105.1	105.5	108.2	109.5	109.9	110.1	109.6	110.2
淀粉	Starches	103.9	102.9	103.3	105.0	105.1	105.5	108.2	109.5	109.9	110.1	109.6	110.2
3.干豆类及豆制品	Beans and Beans Products	97.8	98.6	97.3	97.6	98.1	98.6	100.6	101.2	100.8	100.1	99.7	100.6
干豆	Beans	97.1	98.8	98.9	99.5	100.4	101.5	105.5	105.9	104.9	103.5	102.8	104.5
豆制品	Beans Products	98.4	98.5	95.8	95.9	96.2	96.1	96.2	97.0	97.2	97.1	97.0	97.2
4.油脂	Oil and Fat	96.9	97.1	96.5	96.0	96.9	96.8	97.4	98.7	99.6	100.9	104.6	110.4
食用植物油	Edible Vegetable Oil	97.2	97.9	97.5	97.1	97.6	97.3	98.1	99.6	101.1	102.4	106.1	112.3
植物油制品	Plant Oil Products	98.7	98.8	98.7	98.8	103.1	102.9	102.9	103.2	103.4	103.4	106.3	111.7
其他	Others	90.2	86.2	82.5	79.8	78.8	79.4	80.0	80.5	77.9	81.2	86.6	89.9
5.肉禽及其制品	Meal,Poultry and Their Products	95.4	95.3	92.3	90.5	89.5	90.0	92.2	96.6	98.6	98.7	102.8	108.9
（1）食用畜肉及副产品	Edible Livestock Meat and Their By-products	96.6	95.7	91.0	86.7	85.3	86.7	89.3	94.9	97.3	98.2	104.1	112.8
猪肉	Pork	93.3	90.6	84.6	79.5	77.9	79.5	83.6	90.9	93.7	94.3	101.3	111.5
牛肉	Beef	104.7	106.7	106.3	106.3	105.6	105.7	105.7	105.5	105.6	107.0	108.7	112.8
羊肉	Mutton	107.9	111.5	110.2	108.8	109.3	108.7	108.1	109.5	111.7	115.0	118.4	128.3
畜肉副产品	Livestock Meat By-products	94.8	96.8	93.8	89.1	86.2	90.4	88.5	91.4	95.0	95.1	100.2	105.4
其他	Others	103.3	103.5	96.3	86.7	86.2	84.8	90.5	101.5	102.2	101.7	108.8	112.0
（2）禽	Poultry	88.5	91.0	90.5	92.7	92.8	93.4	96.6	100.8	104.0	102.1	102.8	106.1
鸡	Chicken	87.5	90.7	90.4	92.9	93.6	94.9	99.2	102.8	107.1	104.4	104.4	107.6
鸭	Duck	93.8	91.7	92.1	94.5	93.3	88.9	85.5	91.1	90.7	91.6	97.2	100.7
其他	Others	89.7	92.2	89.5	90.1	88.1	89.0	92.0	98.3	98.3	98.7	99.0	103.0
（3）肉禽加工制品	Meal and Poultry Processing Products	98.0	98.0	97.1	98.4	97.2	95.5	95.7	97.3	97.5	97.3	99.5	101.4
畜肉制品	Livestock Meat Products	98.7	98.7	98.8	97.8	97.1	96.3	97.1	98.8	99.2	99.1	100.6	102.1
禽制品	Poultry Products	97.0	96.9	94.5	99.4	97.2	94.2	93.6	95.0	95.1	94.5	97.8	100.4
6.蛋	Eggs	94.3	88.9	86.5	86.4	88.9	89.0	91.0	97.7	105.3	106.4	108.0	112.5
鲜蛋	Fresh Eggs	93.2	87.1	84.4	84.4	86.9	86.8	89.6	97.1	105.6	106.6	108.2	113.2
蛋制品	Egg Products	102.0	100.9	100.2	99.3	101.8	103.3	100.7	101.3	103.6	104.8	106.2	107.8
7.水产品	Aquatic Product	99.7	100.8	99.7	99.6	100.8	102.2	103.6	104.4	104.1	103.0	103.3	103.3
（1）鱼	Fish	99.1	99.4	98.4	98.2	99.5	100.7	102.1	102.8	102.7	101.8	102.2	101.5
淡水鱼	Freshwater Fish	98.2	96.8	95.3	95.7	98.1	99.7	101.5	101.6	100.7	99.3	98.5	97.0
海水鱼	Seawater Fish	100.5	103.7	103.3	102.1	101.7	102.2	103.1	104.7	105.9	105.7	108.0	108.4
（2）其他水产品	Other Aquatic Product	101.5	104.8	103.5	103.6	104.6	106.7	107.8	108.9	108.1	106.5	106.2	108.5
虾蟹类	Shrimp and Crab	102.2	107.4	105.3	105.2	107.0	108.1	109.5	110.4	109.1	106.6	105.9	108.9
其他	Others	100.3	100.4	100.4	100.8	100.4	104.3	104.9	106.3	106.3	106.4	106.7	107.8

7-21 续表 1 continued

商品类别及品名	Commodity Category and Commodity Name	1月 January	2月 February	3月 March	4月 April	5月 May	6月 June	7月 July	8月 August	9月 September	10月 October	11月 November	12月 December
		（以2005年平均价格为100）											
8.菜	Vegetable	138.7	140.8	129.2	127.1	109.9	86.1	82.2	92.5	104.8	88.1	85.6	107.7
鲜菜	Fresh Vegetable	146.4	148.7	134.0	131.5	109.9	83.2	78.6	90.9	105.6	85.9	82.5	108.8
干菜及菜制品	Dried Vegetable and Vegetable Products	100.2	100.2	100.6	99.5	98.7	98.6	98.0	98.9	99.0	99.1	100.3	103.4
薯类	Potato	111.9	117.1	127.0	128.9	146.7	104.2	102.0	102.9	109.4	95.6	97.1	101.2
9.调味品	Flavoring	102.2	102.4	102.8	102.8	102.8	102.6	103.8	104.0	104.1	104.1	104.1	105.1
盐	Salt	107.7	108.4	109.5	109.5	109.5	109.5	111.9	112.6	113.4	113.4	113.4	113.6
酱油	Soy Sauce	99.8	99.8	99.8	100.0	99.8	99.8	100.9	100.9	100.9	100.9	100.9	102.6
醋	Vinegar	100.2	100.2	100.2	100.2	100.2	100.2	101.9	101.9	101.9	101.9	101.9	104.1
味精	Aginomoto	100.4	100.4	100.4	100.4	100.4	100.4	101.1	101.1	101.1	101.6	101.6	102.1
其他	Others	99.8	99.8	99.8	99.8	100.1	98.3	97.6	97.1	96.4	95.8	95.8	95.8
10.糖	Carbohydrate	102.2	106.7	108.3	109.5	109.9	110.3	112.4	112.9	113.5	113.6	113.8	114.4
食糖	Sugar	104.9	116.0	120.1	122.7	123.8	124.6	127.8	129.1	130.4	130.7	131.2	132.2
糖果	Sweet	100.8	101.0	101.1	101.4	101.4	101.4	103.1	103.1	103.1	103.2	103.2	101.8
巧克力制品	Chocolate Products	99.8	99.8	99.8	99.8	99.8	99.8	100.3	100.3	100.3	100.3	100.3	107.8
糖类小食品	Little Carbohydrate Food	100.0	100.4	100.4	100.4	100.4	100.4	101.6	101.9	101.9	101.9	102.3	104.2
11.干鲜瓜果	Dried and Fresh Melons and Fruits	125.5	133.2	133.3	145.9	154.0	151.8	128.3	111.1	105.0	101.7	103.4	111.1
鲜瓜果	Fresh Fruits	131.8	141.7	141.8	158.1	168.6	165.6	135.3	112.5	104.7	99.6	101.4	111.0
干（坚）果	Dried Fruits	103.3	103.3	103.4	103.0	102.9	103.3	103.6	105.9	106.3	108.9	110.1	111.4
12.糕点饼干面包	Cake,Biscuit and Bread	100.2	100.2	100.2	100.2	100.3	100.3	101.2	101.8	101.8	101.7	101.7	103.3
糕点	Cake	100.5	100.5	100.5	100.5	100.5	100.5	100.9	100.9	100.9	100.9	100.9	102.7
饼干	Biscuit	100.0	100.0	99.9	99.9	100.1	100.2	101.5	103.3	103.3	103.2	103.1	105.2
面包	Bread	100.0	100.0	100.0	100.0	100.0	100.0	101.2	101.2	101.2	101.2	101.2	101.5
13.液体乳及乳制品	Liquid Milk and Their Products	100.0	100.0	100.0	100.2	100.2	100.2	100.4	100.4	100.4	100.4	100.4	104.2
巴氏杀菌奶或消毒奶	Pasteurization Milk or Disinfection Milk	99.9	99.9	100.1	100.1	100.1	100.1	100.1	100.1	100.1	100.1	100.1	108.3
酸奶	Leben	97.7	97.7	97.7	99.2	99.2	99.2	99.2	99.2	99.2	99.2	99.2	97.9
奶粉	Milk Powder	100.3	100.3	100.1	100.1	100.1	100.1	100.8	100.8	100.8	100.9	100.9	102.3
其他	Others	102.6	102.7	102.4	102.4	102.4	102.4	102.4	102.4	102.4	102.4	102.4	102.4
14.在外用膳食品	Outward Dinner	100.9	101.2	101.1	100.9	101.1	101.2	101.2	101.2	101.2	101.0	101.8	103.4
主食	Staple Food	99.9	99.9	100.0	99.9	99.9	99.9	99.8	99.8	99.8	99.8	102.7	106.6
炒菜	Hot Dish	101.5	102.0	101.9	101.6	101.6	101.6	101.5	101.5	101.5	101.5	101.6	101.9
地方小吃	Local Snack	100.6	100.5	100.1	100.3	101.7	102.5	102.9	102.9	102.9	101.4	100.5	102.9
15.其他食品	Other Foods	100.4	100.5	100.4	100.4	100.7	100.9	101.6	102.1	101.8	101.9	101.5	102.5
其他食品	Other Foods	100.4	100.5	100.4	100.4	100.7	100.9	101.6	102.1	101.8	101.9	101.5	102.5
二、饮料、烟酒	**Beverages,Tobacco,Liquor**	**100.2**	**100.2**	**100.3**	**100.5**	**100.5**	**100.4**	**100.7**	**100.8**	**100.9**	**101.2**	**101.5**	**102.6**
1.茶及饮料	Tea and Beverages	100.2	100.2	100.2	100.4	100.3	100.3	101.4	101.4	101.4	101.4	101.4	102.4
（1）茶叶	Tea	100.1	100.1	100.1	100.1	99.9	99.9	99.9	100.0	100.0	100.0	100.0	100.0
茶叶	Tea	100.1	100.1	100.1	100.1	99.9	99.9	99.9	100.0	100.0	100.0	100.0	100.0
（2）饮料	Beverages	100.2	100.3	100.3	100.5	100.5	100.5	102.3	102.3	102.3	102.3	102.3	103.9

7-21 续表 2 continued

（以2005年平均价格为100）

商品类别及品名	Commodity Category and Commodity Name	1月 January	2月 February	3月 March	4月 April	5月 May	6月 June	7月 July	8月 August	9月 September	10月 October	11月 November	12月 December
固体饮料	Solid Beverages	100.2	100.7	101.0	101.4	101.1	101.2	101.2	101.6	101.6	101.6	101.6	101.8
液体饮料	Liquid Beverages	100.3	100.2	100.2	100.3	100.5	100.5	104.1	104.1	104.0	104.0	104.1	104.8
冷冻饮品	Frozen Beverages	100.1	100.1	100.1	100.1	100.1	100.1	100.1	100.1	100.1	100.1	100.1	103.9
2.烟草	Tobacco	100.7	100.9	100.9	101.2	101.4	101.1	101.0	101.0	101.0	101.0	101.1	101.9
国产卷烟	Domestic Cigarette	100.8	101.1	101.1	101.4	101.6	101.3	101.3	101.3	101.3	101.3	101.3	102.2
进口卷烟	Import Cigarette	99.9	99.8	99.8	99.8	99.8	99.8	98.4	98.4	98.4	98.4	99.8	99.8
其他	Others	99.6	99.6	99.6	99.6	99.6	99.6	99.6	99.6	99.6	99.6	99.6	99.6
3.酒	Liquor	99.8	99.6	99.9	100.0	99.9	99.9	100.2	100.4	100.6	101.2	101.8	103.4
白酒	White Spirit	100.0	99.7	100.0	100.3	100.3	100.3	100.5	100.7	100.7	101.7	102.4	104.8
葡萄酒	Grape	99.7	99.7	99.7	99.7	99.7	99.7	101.1	101.1	101.1	101.2	103.2	103.4
啤酒	Beer	99.4	99.4	99.5	99.5	99.2	99.1	99.5	99.7	100.4	100.5	100.5	101.4
其他	Others	100.3	100.3	100.3	100.3	100.3	100.3	100.6	100.6	100.6	100.6	100.6	100.7
三、服装、鞋帽	**Garments,Footgearand and Hats**	**97.8**	**96.6**	**96.5**	**96.4**	**96.1**	**96.1**	**96.1**	**96.0**	**95.9**	**96.1**	**96.6**	**96.6**
1.服装	Garments	96.6	95.4	95.1	94.7	94.4	94.3	94.3	94.3	94.2	94.5	95.2	95.2
（1）男式服装	Men's Garments	95.5	94.2	94.2	94.0	93.8	93.6	93.7	93.7	94.1	94.7	95.6	95.5
大衣	Topcoat	95.1	92.3	90.6	90.3	90.3	89.4	89.4	89.4	90.2	90.2	89.7	89.7
毛线衣	Woollen Sweater	91.3	90.8	89.8	88.9	87.1	85.9	87.6	87.6	88.8	89.1	87.7	87.8
夹克衫	Jacket	97.4	96.4	96.3	96.1	95.8	95.7	95.6	95.5	95.4	96.2	98.9	98.8
衬衫	Shirt	91.5	91.5	91.5	91.5	91.5	91.5	91.5	91.5	91.5	92.2	93.1	93.2
T恤衫	T-shirt	99.6	99.8	99.8	100.0	99.8	100.0	99.8	100.6	102.5	103.7	104.9	105.1
裤子	Trousers	93.9	91.0	92.9	92.8	92.8	92.7	92.5	92.5	92.5	93.2	94.0	93.2
西服	Western-style Clothes	96.7	95.4	95.4	95.3	95.2	95.3	95.3	95.3	95.3	95.8	97.1	97.2
运动衫裤	Gym Suit	100.1	100.1	100.1	100.1	100.1	100.1	100.0	100.0	100.0	102.1	104.2	104.2
内衣	Underwaist	97.6	97.4	96.5	96.2	96.7	96.7	96.7	96.7	96.7	97.7	98.9	98.5
羽绒衣	Eider Down Outerwear	96.2	93.6	93.3	93.2	93.2	93.2	93.2	92.9	92.9	93.5	94.3	94.5
其他	Others	94.5	92.7	92.7	92.7	92.7	92.7	92.7	92.7	92.7	92.7	92.7	92.7
（2）女式服装	Women's Garments	97.1	95.8	95.2	94.3	93.6	93.6	93.5	93.4	93.2	93.5	94.1	94.1
大衣	Topcoat	95.1	90.0	90.0	90.0	90.0	90.0	90.0	90.0	90.0	90.0	90.4	90.4
毛线衣	Woollen Sweater	95.7	93.1	88.4	88.2	84.3	84.3	84.3	84.3	84.3	84.3	84.4	84.4
羽绒衣	Eider Down Outerwear	97.1	95.1	94.8	94.7	94.7	94.6	94.6	94.3	94.2	94.8	95.3	95.3
套装	Coordinates	100.9	100.9	100.9	94.9	94.9	94.9	94.9	94.7	94.7	95.6	96.5	96.5
衬衫	Shirt	95.6	95.4	95.4	95.4	96.0	95.6	95.6	95.6	89.5	89.6	89.7	89.7
T恤衫	T-shirt	100.0	99.6	100.1	100.7	98.1	98.1	98.1	98.1	98.1	99.5	100.8	101.0
裙子	Skirt	92.6	92.6	92.5	92.5	91.6	92.3	92.3	91.5	91.1	91.4	91.4	91.1
裤子	Trousers	98.7	98.7	98.7	97.3	97.0	97.0	96.3	96.3	96.3	94.8	95.7	95.7
运动衫裤	Gym Suit	99.7	99.9	99.2	99.6	99.2	99.2	99.2	99.2	99.2	100.8	102.7	102.7
内衣	Underwaist	95.9	94.4	94.3	94.3	94.9	94.7	94.6	94.4	98.1	98.7	99.4	99.6
其他	Others	99.2	99.1	99.1	99.1	99.1	98.9	98.9	98.9	98.9	98.9	99.1	99.1
（3）儿童服装	Children's Garments	97.7	96.6	96.7	96.8	97.4	97.4	97.4	97.4	96.6	96.5	96.9	97.0
套装	Coordinates	97.8	96.7	96.7	96.9	96.7	96.3	96.3	96.3	96.4	96.6	97.0	97.2

7-21 续表 3 continued

商品类别及品名	Commodity Category and Commodity Name	（以2005年平均价格为100）											
		1月 January	2月 February	3月 March	4月 April	5月 May	6月 June	7月 July	8月 August	9月 September	10月 October	11月 November	12月 December
裤子	Trousers	101.1	100.3	100.3	100.2	103.0	103.0	102.9	102.9	103.0	103.5	104.1	104.2
裙子	Skirt	93.5	92.6	92.8	92.8	93.1	94.0	94.0	94.0	89.6	88.5	88.5	88.5
其他	Others	97.0	94.8	94.8	94.8	95.2	95.6	95.6	95.6	94.6	94.6	94.6	94.6
2.鞋袜帽	Shoes,Socks and Hats	99.4	98.3	98.3	98.4	97.9	97.9	97.9	97.9	97.8	97.8	97.8	97.9
（1）鞋	Shoes	99.4	98.1	98.1	98.2	97.5	97.5	97.5	97.5	97.4	97.3	97.4	97.5
男鞋	Men's Shoes	98.4	97.8	97.7	97.9	97.2	97.2	97.2	97.1	97.1	97.1	97.1	97.3
女鞋	Women's Shoes	98.3	96.0	96.0	96.0	95.1	95.1	95.3	95.1	95.0	95.0	95.1	95.1
童鞋	Children's Shoes	103.1	102.5	102.6	102.7	102.7	102.4	102.4	102.5	102.5	102.2	102.3	102.3
（2）袜子	Socks	99.5	99.3	99.3	99.3	99.8	99.8	99.8	99.8	99.8	99.8	99.8	99.8
男袜	Men's Socks	99.2	99.0	99.0	99.0	99.0	99.0	99.0	99.0	99.0	99.0	99.0	99.0
女袜	Women's Socks	99.7	99.5	99.5	99.5	100.4	100.4	100.4	100.4	100.4	100.4	100.4	100.4
（3）帽子	Hats	99.5	99.4	99.4	99.4	99.5	99.5	99.5	99.5	99.5	99.6	99.6	99.6
男帽	Men's Hats	99.8	99.8	99.8	99.8	100.0	100.0	100.0	100.0	100.0	100.0	100.0	100.0
女帽	Women's Hats	99.3	99.1	99.1	99.1	99.1	99.1	99.1	99.1	99.1	99.2	99.3	99.3
3.其他	Others	99.8	99.8	99.7	103.5	103.5	103.4	103.4	103.3	103.3	103.3	103.3	103.4
领带	Necktie	99.8	99.8	99.7	103.5	103.5	103.4	103.4	103.3	103.3	103.3	103.3	103.4
四、纺织品	**Textiles**	**100.1**	**100.1**	**100.0**	**100.1**	**100.5**	**100.5**	**100.5**	**100.5**	**100.4**	**100.8**	**100.9**	**101.1**
1.衣着材料	Clothing Materials	100.1	100.1	99.9	99.9	100.8	100.8	100.9	100.8	100.4	101.0	101.2	101.2
棉布	Cotton Cloth	99.7	99.7	99.7	99.7	101.1	101.1	101.1	101.1	100.8	101.1	101.1	101.1
棉混纺布	Cotton Textiles Cloth	100.1	100.3	100.3	100.3	100.4	100.4	100.6	100.6	100.6	101.1	101.6	101.6
化纤布	Chemical Fiber Cloth	100.2	100.5	100.5	100.5	101.9	101.9	102.1	101.9	101.0	102.3	102.6	102.6
毛线	Knitting Wool	100.7	99.6	98.5	98.5	98.5	98.5	98.5	98.5	98.5	98.5	98.5	98.5
2.床上用品	Bedclothes	100.0	100.1	100.1	100.3	100.1	100.1	100.0	100.0	100.3	100.5	100.6	100.9
毛毯	Woollen Blanket	99.6	99.3	99.3	99.9	99.1	99.1	99.1	99.0	99.3	100.3	100.3	102.5
被子	Quilt	100.1	100.3	100.3	100.5	100.6	100.6	100.5	100.5	100.6	100.6	100.9	100.9
床上套件	Bed Articcles	100.2	100.3	100.3	100.4	100.3	100.3	100.4	100.4	100.7	100.7	100.7	100.1
其他	Others	100.0	100.4	100.4	100.4	100.0	100.0	100.0	100.0	100.0	100.0	100.0	100.0
五、家用电器及音像器材	**Household Appliances,Music and Video Equipments**	**98.2**	**97.4**	**97.3**	**97.3**	**97.3**	**97.7**	**98.1**	**98.1**	**98.2**	**98.4**	**98.3**	**98.3**
1.家庭设备	Household Appliances	99.6	99.0	98.9	99.1	99.2	100.3	100.9	100.9	101.2	101.4	101.3	101.5
洗衣机	Washing Machine	99.1	99.1	99.0	98.9	98.7	98.7	98.8	98.9	101.0	102.0	101.8	102.0
电风扇	Electric Fan	99.9	98.6	98.6	102.6	102.8	104.6	107.4	108.0	108.0	108.0	108.0	110.0
电冰箱（柜）	Refrigerator	101.3	99.6	99.7	99.8	99.8	99.9	100.2	100.2	100.1	100.1	100.0	99.8
吸排油烟机	Kitchen Ventilato	99.0	98.8	98.5	98.4	98.4	98.6	98.8	98.7	98.6	98.6	98.6	99.6
空调器	Air-conditioning	99.5	99.3	99.1	99.8	100.6	104.9	105.4	105.4	105.5	105.5	105.3	105.1
热水器	Water Heater	98.6	98.6	98.7	94.7	94.6	94.7	94.8	94.7	94.7	94.7	94.9	93.4
微波炉	Microwave Oven	98.2	97.5	97.7	96.2	96.2	96.2	96.4	96.4	96.5	96.5	96.7	96.2
电炊具	Electric Cooking Appliance	99.4	99.3	99.1	99.1	99.1	99.1	99.1	99.1	99.1	99.1	99.1	99.7
2.文娱用耐用消费品	Durable Consumer Goods For Recreational Use	96.5	95.6	95.6	95.2	95.2	94.9	95.0	94.9	94.9	95.1	95.0	94.8
电视机	Television	94.5	93.3	93.3	92.9	92.9	92.4	92.3	92.2	92.1	92.7	92.6	92.9
激光视盘机	Laser Video Disc Machine	98.1	96.8	96.9	96.8	96.4	96.7	97.2	97.1	97.1	96.4	96.0	94.3
摄像机	Pickup Camera	99.7	99.6	99.6	99.6	99.6	99.6	99.6	99.6	99.6	99.6	99.6	99.6
家用音响设备	Acoustic Equipment	100.1	99.8	99.2	98.1	97.9	97.9	98.6	98.6	98.6	98.6	98.6	98.3

7-21 续表 4 continued

商品类别及品名	Commodity Category and Commodity Name	1月 January	2月 February	3月 March	4月 April	5月 May	6月 June	7月 July	8月 August	9月 September	10月 October	11月 November	12月 December
		（以2005年平均价格为100）											
便携式音响	Portable Acoustics	99.0	99.0	99.0	99.0	99.0	99.0	99.0	99.0	99.0	99.0	99.0	98.5
其他	Others	100.0	100.0	100.0	100.0	100.0	100.0	100.0	100.0	100.0	100.0	100.0	100.0
3.音像器材	Music and Video Equipments	98.5	97.5	97.2	97.1	97.1	97.3	97.3	97.3	97.3	97.3	97.3	97.3
专业音响器材	Specialized Acoustic Apparatus	100.0	100.0	99.5	99.3	99.3	99.7	99.7	99.7	99.7	99.7	99.6	99.6
专业声像器材	Specialized Acoustic Image Apparatus	96.7	94.5	94.5	94.5	94.5	94.5	94.5	94.5	94.5	94.5	94.5	94.5
六、文化办公用品	**Cultural and Office Applicances**	**99.3**	**99.1**	**99.1**	**99.0**	**99.0**	**99.0**	**98.8**	**98.2**	**98.3**	**98.3**	**98.4**	**98.4**
纸张本册	Paper and Volume	101.5	100.8	100.8	100.8	100.8	101.1	101.1	101.8	102.1	102.3	102.5	102.7
文具	Stationery	101.4	101.4	101.4	101.4	101.4	101.2	100.8	100.8	100.8	100.8	100.8	100.8
电脑及配件	Computer and its Fitting	98.2	97.9	97.9	97.8	97.8	97.8	97.6	94.4	94.4	94.4	94.4	94.4
打印机及配件	Printer and its Fitting	97.1	97.0	96.9	96.8	96.8	96.8	96.5	96.4	96.3	96.2	96.2	96.2
扫描仪	Scanner	95.3	95.3	94.9	94.8	94.7	94.7	95.0	94.8	95.0	95.1	95.1	95.1
复印机	Xerox Machine	97.3	97.4	97.3	96.6	96.3	96.3	96.3	95.8	95.8	95.7	95.7	95.7
电子辞典	Electronic Dictionary	99.6	99.6	99.6	99.6	99.6	99.1	98.7	98.3	98.3	98.3	98.3	98.3
计算器	Calculator	99.2	99.2	99.2	99.2	99.2	99.4	99.0	99.0	99.0	99.0	99.5	99.4
教学设备	Teaching Equipment	100.8	100.8	100.8	100.8	101.2	101.2	101.2	103.9	103.9	103.9	103.9	104.1
其他	Others	100.0	100.0	100.0	100.0	100.0	100.0	100.0	100.0	100.0	100.0	100.0	100.0
七、日用品	**Articles for Daily Use**	**100.5**	**100.5**	**100.4**	**100.4**	**100.6**	**100.6**	**100.2**	**100.4**	**100.5**	**100.6**	**100.6**	**101.1**
1.日用百货	General Merchandise for Daily Use	99.9	99.9	99.9	99.8	99.8	99.9	99.6	99.7	99.6	99.5	99.4	100.7
自行车	Bicycle	99.8	99.8	99.6	99.3	99.3	98.9	97.9	97.9	97.9	97.9	97.9	98.3
雨具	Rain Gear	100.7	100.8	100.8	100.8	100.9	99.6	99.4	99.4	97.5	96.2	96.2	96.1
剃须刀具	Shaver	99.9	99.9	99.9	99.9	99.9	105.0	105.3	105.3	105.3	105.3	105.9	106.1
电池	Battery	100.0	100.0	100.0	100.0	100.0	100.0	100.0	100.0	100.0	100.0	100.0	100.0
卫生纸	Tissue Paper	100.6	100.6	100.6	100.8	100.8	100.8	101.0	101.7	101.7	101.7	101.4	106.7
卫生巾	Sanitary Towel	98.4	98.4	98.4	98.4	98.4	98.4	98.4	98.4	98.4	98.4	98.4	98.4
其他	Others	100.0	100.0	100.0	100.0	100.0	100.0	100.0	100.0	100.0	100.0	100.0	100.9
2.日用杂品	Sundry Articles	99.8	99.8	99.7	99.9	99.8	99.5	98.8	99.1	101.0	102.5	102.5	103.0
茶具	Tea Set	95.0	95.0	95.0	95.0	94.7	100.4	100.3	100.3	104.3	111.6	111.6	111.6
餐具	Tableware	102.0	102.0	101.9	101.9	101.7	101.7	99.8	99.7	99.7	99.7	99.7	99.7
厨具	Kitchen Utensils	100.3	100.3	100.3	100.7	100.7	96.9	96.9	97.6	100.7	100.7	100.7	101.9
其他	Others	100.0	100.0	100.0	100.0	100.0	100.0	100.0	100.0	100.0	100.0	100.0	100.0
3.洗涤用品	Washing Articles	101.6	101.6	101.6	101.6	102.1	102.1	101.5	102.0	101.4	101.4	101.4	101.5
洗衣粉	Washing Powder	103.3	103.2	103.2	103.2	103.2	103.2	103.2	103.2	103.1	103.1	103.1	102.9
肥皂类	Soap	99.8	99.8	99.8	99.8	99.8	99.8	99.8	101.4	99.8	99.8	99.9	99.9
牙膏	Toothpaste	101.9	101.9	101.9	101.9	104.2	104.2	101.9	101.9	101.6	101.9	101.9	102.1
清洁洗涤剂	Cleaning Agent	100.0	100.0	100.0	100.1	100.0	99.9	99.8	99.6	99.5	99.4	99.0	99.8
4.其他日用品	Other Articles for Daily Use	100.3	100.3	100.3	100.3	100.3	100.3	100.3	100.2	100.2	100.2	100.2	100.2
燃气灶具	Gas-Oven	100.3	100.3	100.3	100.3	100.3	100.3	100.3	100.3	100.3	100.3	100.3	100.3
儿童玩具	Children's Toy	99.3	99.4	99.4	99.4	99.4	99.4	99.4	99.2	99.2	99.2	99.2	99.2

7-21 续表 5 continued

商品类别及品名	Commodity Category and Commodity Name	1月 January	2月 February	3月 March	4月 April	5月 May	6月 June	7月 July	8月 August	9月 September	10月 October	11月 November	12月 December
		（以2005年平均价格为100）											
照明器具	Illumination Utensil	100.6	100.6	100.6	100.6	100.6	100.6	100.6	100.6	100.6	100.6	100.6	100.8
钟表眼镜及配件	Clocks,Glasses and Their Rittings	99.5	99.5	99.5	99.5	99.5	99.5	99.5	99.5	99.5	99.3	99.3	99.3
日用普通饰品	Common Ornamentfor Daily Use	99.5	99.5	99.5	99.5	99.5	99.5	99.3	99.5	99.5	99.5	99.5	99.5
日用皮革制品	Leatherware for Daily Use	102.6	102.6	102.6	102.6	102.6	102.6	102.6	102.6	102.6	102.6	102.3	102.3
其他	Others	100.4	100.4	100.4	100.4	100.4	100.4	100.4	100.4	100.4	100.4	100.4	100.4
八、体育娱乐用品	**Sports and Recreation Articles**	**99.8**	**99.8**	**99.8**	**99.8**	**99.8**	**99.5**	**99.4**	**99.4**	**99.3**	**99.3**	**99.3**	**99.3**
1.体育用品	Sports Articles	100.4	100.4	100.4	100.3	100.3	99.7	99.7	99.8	99.8	99.8	99.8	99.8
球类	Ball	100.0	100.0	100.0	99.8	99.7	98.2	98.2	98.4	98.4	98.4	98.4	98.4
棋牌	Chess and Ccards	100.4	100.4	100.4	100.4	100.4	100.4	100.4	100.4	100.4	100.4	100.4	100.4
健身器材	Exercise Machine	100.9	100.9	100.9	100.9	101.1	101.0	100.8	100.8	100.8	100.8	100.9	101.0
2.娱乐用品	Recreation Articles	99.1	99.1	99.1	99.1	99.1	99.1	99.0	98.9	98.8	98.8	98.5	98.6
游艺器材	Entertainment Apparatus	100.0	100.0	100.0	100.0	100.0	100.0	100.0	100.0	99.2	99.2	99.2	99.2
照相器材	Photographic Apparatus	98.0	97.9	97.9	97.9	98.0	98.0	97.7	97.7	97.7	97.7	97.7	98.1
乐器	Musical Instrument	99.9	99.9	99.9	99.9	99.9	100.1	100.1	99.8	99.9	100.1	99.2	98.9
九、交通、通信用品	**Transportation and Communication Appliances**	**96.0**	**95.9**	**95.5**	**94.7**	**94.1**	**93.8**	**93.5**	**92.8**	**92.3**	**92.1**	**92.0**	**91.2**
1.交通运输机械	Transportation Machine	99.1	100.1	100.1	99.8	99.7	99.6	99.4	99.4	99.4	99.4	99.3	99.3
轿车	Car	97.2	97.2	97.2	97.1	96.1	94.5	94.7	94.6	94.6	94.6	94.3	94.2
客车	Bus	98.3	98.3	98.3	98.2	98.2	98.5	98.4	98.4	98.4	98.4	98.4	98.5
货车	Truck	100.2	100.2	100.2	100.2	100.2	100.2	100.2	100.2	100.2	100.2	100.2	100.1
摩托车	Motorcycle	99.4	101.1	101.1	101.2	101.2	101.2	100.9	100.9	100.9	100.9	100.9	100.8
其他	Others	99.4	99.4	99.4	97.0	97.0	97.0	96.8	96.8	96.8	96.8	96.8	96.8
2.通信器材	Telecommunications Facilities	92.7	91.4	90.5	89.2	88.0	87.6	87.1	85.7	84.6	84.4	84.0	82.6
固定电话机	Telephone	97.3	96.8	96.0	95.7	94.4	94.4	94.4	94.4	94.9	94.9	94.9	94.9
移动电话机	Mobile Phone	87.5	85.3	84.3	81.8	80.3	79.5	78.5	76.4	74.0	73.5	72.8	69.9
传真机	Fax Machine	99.7	99.6	99.4	99.4	99.4	99.4	99.3	95.8	95.6	95.6	95.6	95.5
其他	Others	96.6	95.7	95.1	95.1	95.1	95.1	94.8	94.8	94.8	94.8	94.8	94.8
十、家具	**Furniture**	**99.6**	**99.5**	**99.4**	**100.1**	**100.2**	**100.2**	**100.2**	**99.9**	**99.7**	**101.6**	**102.0**	**102.3**
柜	Cabinet	99.4	99.1	98.8	99.6	99.6	99.6	99.5	99.0	99.0	101.5	101.5	102.1
床	Bed	99.7	99.7	99.7	100.9	100.9	100.9	100.9	100.9	100.7	102.2	102.7	103.2
桌	Desk	100.2	100.3	100.3	100.3	100.4	100.5	100.5	99.0	97.8	99.4	99.8	99.9
椅	Chair	100.1	99.4	99.4	99.4	99.4	99.4	99.2	99.4	99.6	101.7	101.8	101.9
沙发	Sofa	99.1	99.1	99.1	100.1	100.1	100.1	100.1	100.1	100.1	101.9	102.7	102.7
其他	Others	100.9	101.2	101.4	101.1	101.8	102.0	102.0	102.1	102.2	103.9	104.0	104.2
十一、化妆品	**Cosmetics**	**100.0**	**100.0**	**99.8**	**99.8**	**100.0**	**99.9**	**99.9**	**99.8**	**99.9**	**99.9**	**99.9**	**100.0**
护肤品	Skincare Products	99.9	99.9	99.9	99.9	100.2	99.9	99.9	99.9	99.9	99.8	99.8	99.8
美容化妆品	Facial Beautifiers	100.3	100.3	100.3	100.3	100.3	100.3	100.3	100.3	100.3	100.3	100.3	100.7

7-21 续表 6 continued

商品类别及品名	Commodity Category and Commodity Name	1月 January	2月 February	3月 March	4月 April	5月 May	6月 June	7月 July	8月 August	9月 September	10月 October	11月 November	12月 December
		（以2005年平均价格为100）											
护发美容品	Protects Sends the Beauty Products	99.4	99.2	98.4	98.4	98.7	98.7	98.7	98.7	98.7	98.7	98.7	98.8
清洁化妆用品	Cleaning Toiletware	100.8	100.8	100.9	101.0	100.9	100.9	100.9	100.1	101.2	101.2	100.9	100.9
药物美容用品	Medicinal Cosmetics	100.0	100.0	100.0	100.0	100.0	100.0	100.0	100.0	100.0	100.0	100.0	100.0
十二、金银珠宝	**Gold,Silver and Jewelry**	**103.3**	**105.7**	**114.6**	**118.5**	**132.6**	**138.9**	**137.8**	**138.9**	**137.8**	**136.8**	**137.7**	**137.5**
金饰品	Gold	104.5	107.8	117.6	123.7	142.7	144.6	142.3	144.4	144.1	142.3	142.2	142.3
银饰品	Silver	101.2	101.2	116.0	116.3	129.0	153.6	154.0	154.0	154.0	154.0	154.0	153.2
铂金饰品	Platinum	102.8	105.6	109.8	111.5	118.0	121.9	122.2	122.2	118.5	118.5	122.2	122.2
其他	Others	100.2	100.2	103.6	106.3	110.5	112.0	110.9	110.9	110.9	110.9	110.9	109.4
十三、中西药品及医疗保健用品	**Traditional Chinese and Western Medicines and Hea lth Care Articles**	**99.6**	**100.1**	**99.8**	**100.0**	**100.5**	**100.5**	**100.5**	**100.5**	**101.4**	**100.7**	**100.9**	**101.2**
1.医疗器具及用品	Medical Facilities and Goods	97.5	97.8	97.5	96.9	96.4	96.6	96.6	96.6	97.1	96.0	95.9	94.7
医疗器具及用品	Medical Facilities and Goods	97.5	97.8	97.5	96.9	96.4	96.6	96.6	96.6	97.1	96.0	95.9	94.7
2.中药材及中成药	Herbs and Ready-made Traditional Chinese Medicine	101.2	102.7	101.7	102.1	102.4	102.8	102.9	103.2	104.4	104.1	104.6	105.0
中药材	Herbs	102.9	105.3	103.1	103.9	105.2	105.4	105.4	105.3	106.7	106.2	107.2	107.3
中成药	Ready-made Traditional Chinese Medicine	99.3	99.9	100.1	100.1	99.3	99.9	100.3	100.9	101.9	101.7	101.7	102.6
3.西药	Western Medicine	99.1	99.1	99.2	99.3	100.2	99.8	99.7	99.6	100.3	99.4	99.6	99.9
抗微生物药	Anti-microorganism Medicine	95.3	95.2	95.3	95.3	95.3	95.3	95.3	95.1	96.8	94.3	94.3	95.6
消化系统用药	Alimentary System Medicine	100.3	100.7	100.6	100.6	100.6	100.5	100.6	100.7	101.2	100.6	101.1	100.7
呼吸系统用药	Respiratory System Medicine	97.7	97.6	98.4	98.9	98.2	98.3	98.4	98.4	100.3	98.5	99.7	99.7
解热镇痛及非甾体抗炎药	Allays a Fever the Analgesia and the Non-steroid Body anti-inflammatory Agent	102.2	102.5	101.8	101.8	102.8	101.8	101.8	101.8	102.6	102.0	101.3	102.3
抗肿瘤药	AntineopLastic Drug	99.5	99.5	99.3	99.3	108.3	105.5	105.9	104.5	101.2	105.2	106.3	106.3
激素及调节内分泌功能药	Hormone and Adjustment Internal Secretion Function Medicine	99.7	99.9	99.9	100.0	99.9	100.1	98.4	98.5	101.1	98.5	98.5	97.8
循环系统用药	Circulating System Medicine	99.2	99.3	99.7	100.1	100.0	99.8	99.7	99.7	100.2	99.9	99.9	100.1
神经系统用药	Nerve System Medicine	99.9	100.2	100.2	100.8	100.7	100.7	100.7	100.7	101.8	100.4	100.4	101.0
专科用药	Junior Medicine	99.4	98.8	99.5	99.8	100.2	100.5	100.4	100.4	100.7	99.2	99.2	98.4
其　他	Others	99.8	99.8	99.9	100.0	99.8	99.8	99.8	99.7	99.8	99.2	99.3	99.3
4.保健品及器具	Healthcare Equipment	99.1	98.8	98.8	99.2	99.2	99.6	99.7	99.8	100.1	99.5	99.8	99.7
保健器具	Health Protection Equipment	99.9	99.5	99.6	99.7	99.7	100.7	100.7	100.7	100.7	99.9	100.0	99.9
滋补保健用品	Tonic and Health Products	98.6	98.4	98.4	98.9	98.9	99.0	99.1	99.2	99.8	99.3	99.6	99.6
十四、书报杂志及电子出版物	**Books,Newspapers,Magazines and Electronic Publications**	**100.7**	**100.7**	**100.6**	**100.7**	**100.7**	**100.7**	**100.7**	**100.5**	**100.5**	**100.5**	**100.5**	**100.5**
1.教材及参考书	Teaching Materials and Reference Books	100.3	100.3	100.1	100.3	100.3	100.3	100.3	100.0	100.0	100.0	100.0	100.0
工具书	Tool Book	99.6	99.6	99.6	99.6	99.6	99.6	99.6	99.6	99.6	99.6	99.6	99.6

7-21 续表 7 continued

商品类别及品名	Commodity Category and Commodity Name	1月 January	2月 February	3月 March	4月 April	5月 May	6月 June	7月 July	8月 August	9月 September	10月 October	11月 November	12月 December
		（以2005年平均价格为100）											
教材	Teaching Material	100.4	100.4	100.4	100.8	100.8	100.8	100.8	100.3	98.9	98.9	98.9	98.9
参考书	Reference Book	100.6	100.6	100.6	100.6	100.6	100.6	100.6	100.4	103.2	103.2	103.2	103.2
教育软件	Educational Software	99.4	99.4	97.8	97.8	97.8	97.8	97.8	97.8	97.8	97.8	97.8	97.8
2.书报杂志	Books,Newspapers, Magazines	102.0	102.0	102.0	102.0	102.0	102.0	102.0	102.0	102.0	102.0	102.0	102.0
书籍	Books	100.0	100.0	100.0	100.0	100.0	100.0	100.0	100.0	100.0	100.0	100.0	100.0
报纸	Newspapers	104.9	104.9	104.9	104.9	104.9	104.9	104.9	104.9	104.9	104.9	104.9	104.9
杂志	Magazines	101.1	101.1	101.1	101.1	101.1	101.1	101.1	101.1	101.1	101.1	101.1	101.1
3.电子音像制品	Electronic Publications	99.6	99.6	99.4	99.4	99.3	99.4	99.3	99.3	99.3	99.3	99.2	99.2
音响光盘和磁带	Acoustic Light Disk and Tape	100.0	100.0	100.0	100.0	100.2	100.2	100.2	100.2	100.2	100.2	100.2	100.1
录像磁带和视盘	Video Tape and Disk	100.0	100.0	100.0	99.9	99.4	99.4	98.8	98.8	98.8	98.8	98.8	98.8
计算机软件	Computer Software	98.7	98.6	98.0	98.0	98.0	98.3	98.5	98.5	98.5	98.5	98.5	98.5
十五、燃料	**Fuels**	**106.0**	**106.1**	**105.9**	**107.1**	**108.5**	**110.7**	**110.9**	**111.0**	**111.5**	**113.2**	**113.4**	**113.7**
1.煤炭及制品	Coal and Related Products	103.1	103.3	103.3	103.0	103.1	102.8	102.8	102.9	102.7	106.4	107.0	107.6
原煤	Raw Coal	102.1	102.6	102.6	102.5	102.8	102.3	102.3	102.4	102.3	108.3	109.1	110.0
煤制品	Coal Products	104.6	104.4	104.2	103.8	103.6	103.5	103.4	103.5	103.3	103.7	103.9	104.4
2.石油及制品	Petroleum and Related Products	108.2	108.2	107.9	110.2	112.6	116.6	117.0	117.1	118.2	118.3	118.2	118.3
液化石油气	Liquefiled Petroleum Gas	117.6	117.7	114.3	111.6	111.6	110.8	110.6	110.8	115.4	114.8	114.4	114.9
管道燃气	Pipelined Gas	105.1	105.1	105.1	105.1	107.3	107.3	107.3	107.3	107.3	107.3	107.3	107.3
汽油	Gasoline	105.3	105.1	105.9	110.5	114.0	120.1	120.8	120.8	120.8	120.9	120.9	120.9
柴油	Diesel Oil	106.3	106.3	107.0	110.4	114.0	119.8	120.5	120.5	120.5	121.4	121.4	121.5
其他	Others	99.7	99.7	100.0	103.6	102.6	105.2	104.9	104.9	104.9	104.2	104.7	104.4
十六、建筑材料及五金电料	**Building Materials and Hardware**	**100.5**	**100.4**	**101.1**	**102.1**	**102.6**	**103.3**	**103.7**	**104.3**	**104.7**	**105.0**	**105.6**	**105.6**
1.建筑装璜材料	Building and Decoration Materials	100.5	100.3	101.2	102.4	102.9	103.5	103.9	104.6	104.8	105.1	105.9	105.9
木材	Wood	102.6	102.6	103.3	104.4	104.4	105.5	106.6	109.9	111.0	113.0	115.5	115.3
木地板	Wood Floor	99.8	99.8	99.8	96.1	96.4	96.7	96.6	96.6	95.7	96.8	97.4	97.6
钢材	Steel Products	87.7	87.1	89.0	91.8	95.0	97.4	95.5	92.7	92.3	92.3	92.1	91.6
砖	Brick	102.1	102.5	104.2	106.9	107.6	109.0	109.2	110.1	110.1	110.2	110.2	110.1
水泥	Cement	101.9	100.8	100.7	103.1	103.5	103.3	103.1	103.1	103.3	103.0	103.8	103.8
涂料	Coating Material	101.3	101.3	100.9	100.5	99.3	99.3	99.2	99.6	99.6	99.9	100.5	101.2
胶合板	Plywood	101.7	101.7	103.3	104.3	102.9	103.8	105.2	107.1	107.3	105.0	108.2	108.5
玻璃	Glass	97.9	97.3	97.9	97.9	98.6	99.4	100.7	101.7	101.9	103.3	104.1	104.3
粘胶	Rayon	100.9	100.9	100.8	100.7	100.7	100.7	101.1	102.6	102.7	102.9	102.9	104.7
油漆	Paint	103.0	103.1	103.0	102.9	103.5	104.2	104.2	104.4	104.9	104.9	104.9	105.7
其他	Others	100.2	100.4	104.5	105.5	106.4	102.5	106.6	106.6	106.6	108.6	108.6	104.4
2.五金电料	Hardware	100.7	100.7	101.0	101.0	101.8	102.7	103.2	103.5	104.5	104.6	104.7	104.7
五金工具	Hardware Tools	100.5	100.5	100.5	100.5	100.5	101.7	102.3	102.6	102.6	102.6	102.6	102.6
电工电料	Electrical Engineering and Electrical Materials	101.2	101.2	101.4	101.4	102.6	103.4	103.8	104.0	104.7	104.7	104.7	104.7
水暖器材	Heating Equipment	100.4	100.4	101.1	101.2	102.3	102.3	102.3	102.3	104.8	105.1	105.4	105.4
其他	Others	100.7	100.7	100.7	100.7	100.7	104.4	106.3	108.2	108.2	108.2	108.2	108.2

7-22 全省商品零售价格指数
Entire Province Retail Price Index

（以2005年同期价格为100）

商品类别及品名	Commodity Category and Commodity Name	全年 Annural	1月 January	2月 February	3月 March	4月 April	5月 May	6月 June	7月 July	8月 August	9月 September	10月 October	11月 November	12月 December
商品零售价格总指数	**Genaral Retail Price Index**	**100.6**	**100.9**	**100.2**	**100.2**	**100.6**	**100.7**	**100.8**	**99.9**	**100.1**	**100.7**	**100.7**	**101.1**	**101.9**
一、食品	**Food**	**102.5**	**105.9**	**102.4**	**102.1**	**103.2**	**102.8**	**102.3**	**99.1**	**99.8**	**101.8**	**101.3**	**103.2**	**106.3**
1.粮食	Grain	102.6	97.6	97.5	97.9	98.9	100.8	101.7	103.3	104.3	105.0	105.5	108.3	110.4
大米	Rice	108.7	100.7	100.4	101.5	102.8	107.0	108.3	111.4	114.5	114.3	115.0	114.3	115.2
面粉	Flour	98.5	93.3	93.0	93.4	95.0	96.3	96.8	98.2	98.3	99.8	100.7	107.5	110.6
粮食制品	Grain Products	101.5	98.9	99.0	99.0	99.0	99.9	100.9	101.6	102.4	102.7	103.0	104.8	106.5
其他	Others	106.5	103.0	104.6	104.1	104.7	106.3	107.2	108.0	107.5	107.8	107.1	107.0	110.3
2.淀粉	Starches	101.5	100.7	98.7	98.5	99.9	98.9	99.8	99.8	100.2	104.1	105.2	106.2	106.8
淀粉	Starches	101.5	100.7	98.7	98.5	99.9	98.9	99.8	99.8	100.2	104.1	105.2	106.2	106.8
3.干豆类及豆制品	Beans and Beans Products	100.5	100.3	99.1	99.0	98.8	99.6	100.2	100.8	101.3	100.8	100.9	102.0	103.3
干豆	Beans	101.6	99.9	100.1	97.6	97.7	100.0	101.5	103.2	104.5	102.8	102.6	103.8	105.9
豆制品	Beans Products	100.0	100.4	98.8	99.7	99.3	99.5	99.7	99.7	99.9	100.0	100.2	101.2	102.2
4.油脂	Oil and Fat	99.7	96.2	95.6	95.7	96.0	97.8	98.3	98.7	100.1	100.7	102.0	104.9	110.7
食用植物油	Edible Vegetable Oil	100.5	96.5	96.1	96.5	97.1	99.0	99.5	99.8	101.2	101.9	102.9	105.5	110.4
植物油制品	Plant Oil Products	101.2	99.0	98.6	98.4	97.9	100.0	100.2	100.5	100.8	101.0	101.0	103.6	113.9
其他	Others	83.8	84.1	81.2	78.8	76.2	76.2	77.4	78.4	81.7	82.6	91.0	99.8	105.2
5.肉禽及其制品	Meal, Poultry and their Products	96.6	95.4	92.6	91.1	90.4	89.5	90.0	92.4	96.4	98.1	102.2	109.2	115.2
（1）食用畜肉及副产品	Edible Livestock Meat and their By-products	95.3	94.3	90.6	88.2	86.8	86.3	86.8	89.2	94.3	96.9	102.9	112.1	119.6
猪肉	Pork	91.2	89.5	85.0	81.6	79.6	79.0	79.6	83.3	90.7	94.2	102.2	115.4	124.5
牛肉	Beef	106.1	110.6	107.1	107.1	108.1	106.7	105.6	104.7	103.9	103.6	104.7	104.1	107.3
羊肉	Mutton	108.4	109.6	108.1	108.8	108.9	109.8	109.3	108.7	105.9	106.0	106.7	107.1	112.3
畜肉副产品	Livestock Meat By-products	96.3	95.4	93.4	92.0	90.8	89.6	91.3	91.9	94.7	97.1	100.3	106.8	114.6
其他	Others	98.2	97.2	96.5	94.8	90.2	90.8	91.5	93.1	99.4	99.8	103.7	110.9	113.1
（2）禽	Poultry	96.7	93.0	89.9	89.6	89.0	86.0	88.5	94.5	99.7	100.9	104.3	111.5	119.6
鸡	Chicken	97.2	91.7	88.2	88.2	87.9	84.8	88.1	95.7	101.5	103.5	107.2	114.2	124.4
鸭	Duck	93.2	96.4	93.8	93.2	93.5	92.3	90.5	87.7	91.3	89.7	89.7	100.3	101.4
其他	Others	96.2	97.9	97.3	95.2	91.9	89.3	90.1	92.3	96.0	94.8	99.2	104.6	107.5
（3）肉禽加工制品	Meal and Poultry Processing Products	99.7	99.3	99.2	98.9	99.5	99.0	98.4	98.4	99.2	99.2	99.6	101.8	103.4
畜肉制品	Livestock Meat Products	100.2	99.7	99.7	99.8	99.8	99.4	99.1	99.3	100.0	99.7	100.3	102.0	103.3
禽制品	Poultry Products	98.8	98.6	98.5	97.3	99.1	98.2	97.0	97.0	97.9	98.4	98.3	101.4	103.6
6.蛋	Eggs	95.8	93.4	85.9	89.2	90.0	87.9	86.7	89.2	95.6	99.3	106.2	110.6	118.0
鲜蛋	Fresh Eggs	94.8	91.9	83.6	87.2	88.1	85.8	84.3	87.3	94.8	99.0	106.8	111.7	120.0
蛋制品	Egg Products	103.2	104.9	102.8	103.1	103.3	103.6	104.4	102.6	101.6	101.0	102.3	103.0	105.1
7.水产品	Aquatic Product	103.1	100.5	99.0	98.6	99.7	102.4	103.7	105.0	105.7	105.5	106.7	105.7	104.9
（1）鱼	Fish	100.9	100.1	97.4	96.4	97.4	98.8	100.8	101.8	103.3	104.0	104.3	103.4	103.5
淡水鱼	Freshwater Fish	96.9	96.7	92.7	91.4	91.8	93.6	96.2	99.1	101.0	101.5	99.8	99.9	99.5
海水鱼	Seawater Fish	105.0	103.7	102.4	101.6	103.1	104.1	105.6	104.5	105.6	106.6	109.0	106.9	107.5

7-22 续表 1 continued

（以2005年同期价格为100）

商品类别及品名	Commodity Category and Commodity Name	全年 Annural	1月 January	2月 February	3月 March	4月 April	5月 May	6月 June	7月 July	8月 August	9月 September	10月 October	11月 November	12月 December
（2）其他水产品	Other Aquatic Product	106.6	101.0	101.4	102.1	103.3	108.3	108.5	110.5	109.9	108.1	110.8	109.6	107.1
虾蟹类	Shrimp and Crab	106.5	100.6	100.6	100.1	102.0	109.0	108.5	111.0	110.4	108.3	112.5	110.0	107.9
其他	Others	106.7	101.9	103.1	106.9	106.2	106.7	108.3	109.6	108.7	107.7	107.4	108.8	105.6
8.菜	Vegetable	108.2	147.7	120.3	116.9	120.7	113.6	107.8	87.2	93.0	107.1	89.3	91.9	101.2
鲜菜	Fresh Vegetable	108.3	155.4	122.4	118.2	122.6	114.3	107.6	83.4	90.4	107.1	86.4	89.1	99.7
干菜及菜制品	Dried Vegetable and Vegetable Products	103.4	100.7	100.8	101.5	102.1	102.3	101.3	101.6	102.8	104.5	105.9	106.9	111.0
薯类	Potato	119.1	117.9	118.8	125.0	126.5	126.4	128.7	123.5	118.9	114.4	107.0	109.9	109.8
9.调味品	Flavoring	103.0	104.0	103.1	102.8	102.9	103.0	103.3	103.4	102.8	102.6	102.0	102.5	103.0
盐	Salt	106.9	112.4	108.6	108.0	107.1	108.2	109.5	109.0	106.7	105.7	103.6	102.8	102.6
酱油	Soy Sauce	101.8	102.5	102.4	102.4	102.5	101.8	101.6	101.5	101.6	101.4	101.0	101.1	101.5
醋	Vinegar	101.7	102.2	102.2	101.3	101.7	101.5	101.5	102.0	101.8	101.9	101.4	101.3	102.1
味精	Aginomoto	100.5	100.1	100.0	100.1	100.5	100.6	100.4	100.7	100.5	100.5	100.6	100.5	101.2
其他	Others	102.6	99.8	99.7	100.0	100.9	101.5	102.0	102.6	102.2	102.4	103.0	107.6	109.3
10.糖	Carbohydrate	108.3	103.5	106.5	107.8	108.2	108.7	108.6	109.2	109.1	109.6	109.4	109.5	109.2
食糖	Sugar	124.1	108.4	117.3	122.3	124.4	125.9	125.6	127.1	126.9	128.9	127.6	127.3	126.2
糖果	Sweet	103.2	102.0	102.9	103.2	103.1	103.2	103.2	103.5	103.3	103.3	103.8	104.1	103.1
巧克力制品	Chocolate Products	100.0	101.1	101.3	100.7	100.5	99.8	99.7	99.4	99.1	99.1	99.5	99.5	100.9
糖类小食品	Little Carbohydrate Food	102.0	101.5	102.0	101.8	101.4	102.2	102.1	102.3	102.4	102.2	101.9	102.0	102.3
11.干鲜瓜果	Dried and Fresh Melons and Fruits	118.5	126.0	128.3	130.9	137.9	142.7	146.6	119.4	102.3	99.2	100.5	96.5	94.9
鲜瓜果	Fresh Fruits	121.4	131.3	134.1	137.0	145.9	152.4	159.4	123.5	101.1	96.7	98.0	92.6	90.8
干（坚）果	Dried Fruits	107.8	107.0	106.6	107.9	107.5	106.4	106.4	105.8	106.4	107.7	109.5	110.8	111.7
12.糕点饼干面包	Cake, Biscuit and Bread	100.8	100.9	101.0	101.1	101.0	100.7	100.6	100.9	101.1	100.7	100.4	100.2	100.9
糕点	Cake	100.2	101.2	101.3	101.7	101.5	100.4	100.4	100.1	99.8	99.2	98.5	98.6	99.6
饼干	Biscuit	101.4	101.0	100.9	100.8	100.8	101.3	101.2	101.4	102.3	101.9	101.7	101.3	102.2
面包	Bread	101.2	99.9	100.5	100.3	100.4	100.6	100.3	101.6	102.3	102.1	102.8	102.1	101.7
13.液体乳及乳制品	Liquid Milk and their Products	101.6	101.3	101.5	102.0	101.2	100.9	101.0	101.1	101.3	102.3	102.1	102.1	102.7
巴氏杀菌奶或消毒奶	Pasteurization Milk or Disinfection Milk	101.3	101.1	101.1	102.0	100.6	100.4	100.6	100.7	100.8	101.9	101.7	101.9	103.2
酸奶	Leben	101.0	100.3	100.3	100.3	100.6	100.8	100.7	100.6	100.5	101.9	102.1	101.7	101.9
奶粉	Milk Powder	102.6	102.5	102.5	102.5	102.7	102.3	102.3	102.6	103.3	103.2	102.7	102.7	102.6
其他	Others	103.0	102.8	105.2	105.1	103.6	101.8	101.7	102.0	101.7	103.5	103.6	103.4	101.7
14.在外用膳食品	Outward Dinner	101.0	100.4	100.2	100.3	100.4	100.4	100.7	100.7	100.9	101.2	101.0	101.7	103.6
主食	Staple Food	100.7	99.9	99.6	99.8	99.8	99.8	100.2	100.3	100.3	100.4	100.5	102.2	106.1
炒菜	Hot Dish	101.0	100.7	100.6	100.7	100.7	100.6	101.0	100.8	100.9	101.4	101.2	101.3	102.3
地方小吃	Local Snack	101.3	100.3	100.2	100.4	100.5	100.6	100.8	101.5	102.0	101.8	101.7	101.8	103.5
15.其他食品	Other Foods	100.6	100.8	100.8	100.8	100.6	100.6	100.5	100.6	100.8	100.7	100.4	100.2	100.5
其他食品	Other Foods	100.6	100.8	100.8	100.8	100.6	100.6	100.5	100.6	100.8	100.7	100.4	100.2	100.5
二、饮料、烟酒	**Beverages, Tobacco, Liquor**	**101.0**	**100.5**	**100.4**	**100.4**	**100.7**	**100.8**	**101.0**	**101.1**	**101.3**	**101.3**	**101.4**	**101.5**	**102.2**
1.茶及饮料	Tea and Beverages	100.9	99.9	99.8	100.3	100.5	100.7	100.9	101.1	101.3	101.3	101.3	101.5	102.0
（1）茶叶	Tea	100.5	99.8	100.0	100.5	100.6	100.7	100.6	100.5	100.4	100.6	100.7	100.6	100.9

7-22 续表 2 continued

商品类别及品名	Commodity Category and Commodity Name	（以2005年同期价格为100）												
		全年 Annural	1月 January	2月 February	3月 March	4月 April	5月 May	6月 June	7月 July	8月 August	9月 September	10月 October	11月 November	12月 December
茶叶	Tea	100.5	99.8	100.0	100.5	100.6	100.7	100.6	100.5	100.4	100.6	100.7	100.6	100.9
（2）饮料	Beverages	101.1	100.0	99.7	100.1	100.4	100.7	101.1	101.4	101.8	101.7	101.7	101.9	102.7
固体饮料	Solid Beverages	100.8	101.2	101.0	100.8	101.0	101.1	101.0	100.6	101.1	101.1	100.5	100.7	99.8
液体饮料	Liquid Beverages	101.0	99.5	99.3	99.9	100.1	100.6	100.9	101.8	101.9	101.8	101.8	102.0	102.7
冷冻饮品	Frozen Beverages	101.5	99.8	99.2	100.1	100.4	100.6	101.5	101.4	102.4	102.3	102.4	103.1	105.1
2.烟草	Tobacco	100.3	100.0	99.8	99.7	100.1	100.2	100.2	100.3	100.6	100.6	100.5	100.6	101.0
国产卷烟	Domestic Cigarette	100.6	100.2	100.1	100.0	100.5	100.6	100.5	100.6	100.9	100.9	100.9	100.8	101.3
进口卷烟	Import Cigarette	98.3	98.7	97.7	97.9	98.3	98.1	98.2	97.9	98.1	98.4	98.3	98.7	99.3
其他	Others	99.1	98.9	98.9	98.8	98.6	98.8	99.1	99.5	99.3	99.1	99.3	99.4	99.4
3.酒	Liquor	101.8	101.3	101.1	101.0	101.3	101.3	101.6	101.8	101.9	102.0	102.2	102.4	103.3
白酒	White Spirit	102.3	101.5	101.2	101.3	101.7	101.8	102.4	102.2	102.5	102.5	102.8	103.1	104.4
葡萄酒	Grape	104.3	103.5	103.5	103.7	103.8	103.8	104.6	105.4	105.0	104.7	104.5	104.9	104.9
啤酒	Beer	100.3	100.7	100.4	99.9	100.0	99.8	99.7	100.2	100.3	100.5	100.6	100.6	101.2
其他	Others	100.4	100.3	100.4	100.1	100.2	100.1	100.1	100.6	100.6	100.2	100.2	100.7	100.7
三、服装、鞋帽	**Garments, Footgearand and Hats**	**97.8**	**96.9**	**97.2**	**98.2**	**98.6**	**98.1**	**98.1**	**97.9**	**97.7**	**97.8**	**98.2**	**97.8**	**96.8**
1.服装	Garments	97.1	95.9	96.1	96.9	97.5	97.3	97.1	97.0	96.8	97.1	97.9	97.8	97.4
（1）男式服装	Men's Garments	96.4	95.2	96.1	96.6	96.8	96.8	96.7	96.4	96.0	96.3	96.9	96.9	96.5
大衣	Topcoat	93.2	93.2	93.1	94.4	93.7	93.7	93.1	93.0	92.6	92.6	92.4	93.2	93.7
毛线衣	Woollen Sweater	91.8	94.1	91.5	91.8	93.3	91.8	92.5	91.8	89.9	91.2	92.7	89.6	91.6
夹克衫	Jacket	95.5	93.2	94.5	93.2	93.0	95.7	95.3	95.1	95.2	95.2	98.1	100.0	98.3
衬衫	Shirt	93.6	89.7	93.9	95.5	94.7	93.1	94.5	93.5	93.1	92.7	93.1	93.9	96.1
T恤衫	T-shirt	98.4	100.1	100.6	99.4	100.2	101.5	99.9	97.6	95.8	96.5	96.4	97.7	94.5
裤子	Trousers	94.9	95.5	95.3	96.6	94.6	93.9	93.5	93.4	95.6	94.4	95.5	94.5	95.7
西服	Western-style Clothes	100.1	95.6	97.4	97.3	100.2	102.0	101.3	102.3	99.9	101.5	102.7	101.9	99.7
运动衫裤	Gym Suit	97.9	95.0	97.9	99.9	99.4	96.9	97.0	97.3	97.9	98.2	98.3	99.7	98.0
内衣	Underwaist	101.8	101.6	102.1	103.0	103.1	103.9	103.2	102.4	102.6	102.2	99.2	99.2	99.6
羽绒衣	Eider down Outerwear	98.2	96.2	98.7	98.6	97.0	97.9	98.5	98.4	98.3	98.9	99.6	100.5	96.4
其他	Others	94.4	94.8	93.2	92.2	93.6	93.7	93.1	93.3	93.6	93.5	94.9	98.6	98.3
（2）女式服装	Women's Garments	97.1	96.1	95.8	96.8	97.6	97.0	96.8	96.9	96.9	97.3	98.5	98.3	97.7
大衣	Topcoat	93.2	93.7	91.0	94.6	94.0	93.2	94.3	93.8	93.1	93.0	93.1	91.7	92.9
毛线衣	Woollen Sweater	92.3	93.5	92.0	94.0	94.4	93.0	92.1	90.5	89.4	90.6	92.7	92.1	93.1
羽绒衣	Eider down Outerwear	97.5	94.2	95.7	95.2	95.8	96.3	96.9	98.5	98.6	98.3	99.5	101.4	99.9
套装	Coordinates	99.6	100.9	100.8	100.6	100.9	100.5	98.9	99.6	97.1	99.5	100.4	97.9	98.0
衬衫	Shirt	98.2	94.0	95.7	96.4	100.1	100.5	101.2	101.1	100.0	98.5	99.2	98.6	94.3
T恤衫	T-shirt	102.3	98.4	98.5	98.5	100.3	100.4	100.8	99.9	99.9	103.6	109.9	110.5	107.2
裙子	Skirt	99.6	98.5	98.4	98.2	99.8	100.1	99.2	99.4	100.8	99.8	101.4	101.0	98.2
裤子	Trousers	96.5	96.4	95.8	97.4	96.6	95.4	94.4	95.9	97.9	97.1	97.5	97.6	96.4
运动衫裤	Gym Suit	96.1	94.4	95.4	94.4	97.6	94.7	94.4	95.6	96.6	97.4	97.7	96.5	98.6
内衣	Underwaist	100.2	97.5	97.4	99.0	99.9	99.8	99.8	99.3	100.0	101.1	101.7	103.4	103.2
其他	Others	100.8	100.0	99.2	99.5	101.0	100.1	100.2	100.8	101.2	101.9	101.7	102.4	101.3

7-22 续表 3 continued

商品类别及品名	Commodity Category and Commodity Name	全年 Annural	1月 January	2月 February	3月 March	4月 April	5月 May	6月 June	7月 July	8月 August	9月 September	10月 October	11月 November	12月 December
		（以2005年同期价格为100）												
（3）儿童服装	Children's Garments	98.7	97.6	97.5	98.3	99.2	99.8	99.8	98.8	99.0	98.4	98.3	98.4	98.8
套装	Coordinates	98.1	98.3	97.8	98.6	99.3	99.3	99.1	98.5	98.1	97.0	96.1	96.7	98.3
裤子	Trousers	100.4	96.7	97.6	98.3	100.4	101.5	102.0	101.2	102.1	101.5	102.7	101.5	100.4
裙子	Skirt	98.4	96.9	96.3	97.3	97.8	99.8	99.7	97.8	98.5	98.8	98.8	99.3	99.6
其他	Others	96.2	98.8	100.1	100.4	99.2	96.5	95.4	94.8	94.2	93.5	93.8	94.8	93.4
2.鞋袜帽	Shoes, Socks and Hats	99.1	98.9	99.3	101.1	100.7	99.5	100.0	99.6	99.4	99.2	98.7	97.6	95.1
（1）鞋	Shoes	99.0	98.8	99.3	101.4	100.9	99.4	100.0	99.5	99.2	98.9	98.4	97.3	94.4
男鞋	Men's Shoes	98.8	98.5	99.7	100.7	100.9	98.2	99.2	98.6	99.1	99.0	98.8	97.6	95.7
女鞋	Women's Shoes	98.0	98.9	98.8	102.0	100.5	99.3	99.8	99.0	97.7	97.2	96.5	95.0	91.7
童鞋	Children's Shoes	101.9	99.4	99.6	101.2	101.8	102.4	102.4	103.0	104.0	103.5	103.2	103.0	99.1
（2）袜子	Socks	99.8	99.3	99.5	99.7	100.1	99.9	99.9	100.1	100.4	100.7	99.9	99.5	98.8
男袜	Men's Socks	99.6	99.0	98.8	99.2	100.4	100.1	100.0	100.2	100.2	100.4	100.0	99.3	98.2
女袜	Women's Socks	100.0	99.5	100.1	100.2	99.9	99.8	99.8	100.0	100.5	101.0	99.8	99.6	99.3
（3）帽子	Hats	99.7	99.8	99.4	99.6	99.5	99.6	99.3	99.5	99.6	99.9	99.9	100.0	100.2
男帽	Men's Hats	100.1	99.3	99.0	99.4	99.4	99.9	100.3	100.5	100.9	100.8	100.6	100.9	100.7
女帽	Women's Hats	99.4	100.2	99.7	99.7	99.6	99.3	98.6	98.7	98.7	99.3	99.3	99.4	99.8
3.其他	Others	99.8	98.2	99.5	99.0	100.3	100.4	100.8	100.3	99.9	99.9	100.1	99.7	99.6
领带	Necktie	99.8	98.2	99.5	99.0	100.3	100.4	100.8	100.3	99.9	99.9	100.1	99.7	99.6
四、纺织品	**Textiles**	**99.3**	**98.5**	**98.9**	**99.1**	**99.0**	**98.7**	**99.4**	**99.3**	**99.4**	**99.3**	**99.6**	**99.6**	**100.2**
1.衣着材料	Clothing Materials	99.2	99.0	99.3	99.1	98.7	98.6	98.6	98.7	99.1	99.0	99.6	100.2	100.7
棉布	Cotton Cloth	98.5	98.5	98.0	98.4	97.1	96.0	96.5	97.0	97.9	99.0	100.3	101.5	102.1
棉混纺布	Cotton Textiles Cloth	97.9	96.5	96.7	96.5	96.9	97.1	97.3	97.5	97.8	98.1	99.0	100.1	100.9
化纤布	Chemical Fiber Cloth	100.7	100.2	101.8	101.4	101.0	101.5	100.8	100.7	100.8	99.8	100.0	100.2	100.2
毛线	Knitting Wool	99.0	100.5	99.4	98.8	98.8	98.4	98.9	98.9	98.8	98.7	98.6	98.8	99.6
2.床上用品	Bedclothes	99.3	97.9	98.5	99.1	99.3	98.8	100.2	99.9	99.7	99.6	99.7	99.0	99.6
毛毯	Woollen Blanket	99.7	97.5	97.9	100.2	100.2	99.8	100.2	99.8	99.8	99.9	100.1	99.7	100.9
被子	Quilt	97.5	96.1	96.6	96.5	96.4	95.7	99.7	99.4	99.1	98.6	98.1	97.1	97.4
床上套件	Bed Articles	99.5	98.7	99.1	99.4	99.7	99.4	99.9	99.7	99.6	99.7	100.1	99.1	99.9
其他	Others	101.5	99.7	101.5	102.2	102.6	102.5	102.0	101.6	101.1	101.2	101.2	101.3	101.4
五、家用电器及音像器材	**Household Appliances, Music and Video Equipments**	**99.0**	**98.4**	**98.4**	**98.3**	**97.8**	**98.1**	**98.9**	**99.3**	**99.6**	**99.6**	**99.7**	**99.9**	**99.7**
1.家庭设备	Household Appliances	101.8	100.8	100.7	100.5	99.8	99.9	101.6	102.4	102.6	103.1	103.2	103.3	103.3
洗衣机	Washing Machine	100.1	99.7	100.3	99.5	98.6	99.0	99.9	100.6	99.9	100.6	101.1	101.2	101.1
电风扇	Electric Fan	103.4	101.5	100.7	100.8	101.7	101.0	102.9	104.7	105.7	105.2	105.1	105.0	106.3
电冰箱（柜）	Refrigerator	103.7	104.9	104.3	104.3	103.8	103.7	103.8	103.6	102.3	103.2	103.8	103.4	103.1
吸排油烟机	Kitchen Ventilato	103.0	102.5	102.5	102.2	100.8	100.7	102.1	103.6	104.4	104.5	104.4	104.3	104.0
空调器	Air-Conditioning	102.9	100.4	100.0	99.6	98.8	99.1	103.1	104.2	105.4	106.1	105.8	106.2	106.4
热水器	Water Heater	99.0	98.5	98.9	99.7	97.8	97.9	98.1	99.3	99.5	99.7	99.7	99.7	99.9
微波炉	Microwave Oven	97.8	96.1	96.3	96.9	96.4	96.2	97.0	97.4	98.8	99.4	99.6	100.0	99.3
电炊具	Electric Cooking Appliance	100.0	99.7	99.5	99.6	100.1	100.3	100.2	100.1	100.2	99.8	100.0	100.3	100.7
2.文娱用耐用消费品	Durable Consumer Goods For Recreational Use	95.3	95.2	95.5	95.4	95.0	95.5	95.2	95.3	95.6	94.9	95.1	95.5	94.9

7-22 续表 4 continued

商品类别及品名	Commodity Category and Commodity Name	（以2005年同期价格为100）												
		全年 Annural	1月 January	2月 February	3月 March	4月 April	5月 May	6月 June	7月 July	8月 August	9月 September	10月 October	11月 November	12月 December
电视机	Television	93.3	92.9	93.3	93.1	92.6	93.6	93.1	93.2	93.6	92.9	93.5	94.3	93.7
激光视盘机	Laser Video Disc Machine	95.8	96.5	96.4	96.2	95.9	95.8	96.5	96.6	97.3	95.9	94.7	94.5	93.6
摄像机	Pickup Camera	96.4	97.3	98.4	98.0	97.5	97.3	96.4	96.2	96.0	95.2	95.0	95.4	93.7
家用音响设备	Acoustic Equipment	99.0	99.0	98.9	99.0	99.0	99.0	98.9	99.3	99.3	99.1	99.1	99.1	98.8
便携式音响	Portable Acoustics	98.4	98.7	98.6	98.4	98.1	98.3	98.3	98.3	98.4	98.2	98.5	98.4	98.6
其他	Others	99.7	99.7	100.0	100.0	99.9	99.9	99.9	99.9	99.5	99.3	99.4	99.3	99.3
3.音像器材	Music and Video Equipments	99.0	99.2	98.8	98.7	98.5	98.7	99.0	99.0	99.2	99.1	99.0	99.1	99.3
专业音响器材	Specialized Acoustic Apparatus	99.8	99.8	99.9	99.8	99.6	99.7	99.7	99.9	100.0	99.9	99.8	99.8	99.7
专业声像器材	Specialized Acoustic Image Apparatus	97.8	98.3	97.2	97.3	97.0	97.2	98.0	97.8	98.1	98.0	97.8	98.1	98.7
六、文化办公用品	**Cultural and Office Applicances**	**97.0**	**96.6**	**96.4**	**96.5**	**96.5**	**97.3**	**97.4**	**97.4**	**96.9**	**96.8**	**97.3**	**97.5**	**97.9**
纸张本册	Paper and Volume	100.5	101.9	100.3	100.4	100.1	100.1	99.8	99.9	100.4	100.8	100.7	100.7	101.1
文具	Stationery	99.7	99.4	99.8	99.7	99.8	99.9	99.7	99.6	99.3	99.6	99.7	100.0	99.6
电脑及配件	Computer and its Fitting	94.0	93.7	93.5	93.6	93.4	94.9	94.9	94.8	93.6	92.6	93.6	94.4	94.8
打印机及配件	Printer and its Fitting	96.3	96.0	95.5	95.4	95.4	96.0	96.7	96.8	96.1	96.7	96.8	96.9	98.1
扫描仪	Scanner	98.1	96.2	96.2	97.2	97.5	98.0	98.3	98.5	98.7	98.8	98.9	98.9	99.5
复印机	Xerox Machine	96.3	94.3	94.4	94.5	94.4	97.0	97.4	97.5	97.1	97.0	98.1	97.1	97.2
电子辞典	Electronic Dictionary	98.2	98.2	98.5	98.4	99.1	99.0	98.8	98.2	97.2	97.8	97.7	97.8	97.8
计算器	Calculator	98.4	97.8	97.9	97.9	97.8	97.8	97.9	97.7	97.6	99.1	99.2	99.6	100.2
教学设备	Teaching Equipment	99.9	96.8	97.7	98.8	98.8	99.5	99.7	100.1	101.3	101.2	101.8	101.6	101.5
其他	Others	100.1	100.1	100.2	100.1	100.2	100.2	100.1	99.9	99.8	100.0	100.1	100.1	100.1
七、日用品	**Articles for Daily Use**	**100.6**	**100.4**	**100.6**	**100.5**	**100.5**	**100.6**	**100.5**	**100.4**	**100.7**	**100.7**	**100.7**	**100.5**	**100.7**
1.日用百货	General Merchandise for Daily Use	100.3	99.8	100.3	100.2	100.1	100.3	100.0	100.2	100.6	100.4	100.3	100.3	100.8
自行车	Bicycle	100.2	99.8	100.8	100.8	100.6	100.5	100.3	100.2	99.6	100.0	99.9	99.8	99.7
雨具	Rain Gear	99.3	99.2	99.9	99.5	99.3	99.7	99.3	99.9	100.3	99.0	98.7	98.5	98.7
剃须刀具	Shaver	101.9	100.1	100.2	100.6	100.8	100.9	102.8	102.8	103.0	102.9	102.8	102.6	102.8
电池	Battery	98.3	99.0	99.2	99.4	97.7	98.2	95.9	97.5	98.7	98.3	98.4	98.6	98.9
卫生纸	Tissue Paper	102.5	102.4	102.3	102.1	102.3	102.3	102.4	101.6	103.4	102.2	102.2	102.4	104.4
卫生巾	Sanitary Towel	98.4	96.6	97.5	97.2	97.4	98.8	97.6	98.8	99.3	99.2	99.6	99.0	99.4
其他	Others	100.6	100.8	100.8	100.6	100.4	100.2	100.2	100.2	100.2	100.8	100.3	101.2	101.9
2.日用杂品	Sundry Articles	100.4	99.5	99.8	99.8	99.9	100.0	100.0	100.1	100.4	101.2	101.0	101.0	101.5
茶具	Tea Set	99.9	98.1	98.1	98.0	98.0	97.6	99.0	98.8	98.9	100.2	103.6	104.0	104.3
餐具	Tableware	100.2	99.1	99.6	99.3	99.5	99.9	100.5	101.1	101.9	102.0	99.9	99.7	100.5
厨具	Kitchen Utensils	100.7	100.4	100.6	100.9	101.1	101.3	100.0	100.0	100.0	101.0	100.9	101.1	101.4
其他	Others	100.3	100.5	100.7	100.9	100.4	100.5	100.5	100.2	100.4	101.2	99.5	99.4	99.7
3.洗涤用品	Washing Articles	101.2	101.6	101.6	101.2	101.1	101.1	101.3	101.1	101.5	101.3	101.2	101.0	100.6

7-22 续表 5 continued

（以2005年同期价格为100）

商品类别及品名	Commodity Category and Commodity Name	全年 Annural	1月 January	2月 February	3月 March	4月 April	5月 May	6月 June	7月 July	8月 August	9月 September	10月 October	11月 November	12月 December
洗衣粉	Washing Powder	102.2	103.1	102.7	101.8	101.6	101.5	102.2	102.2	102.8	102.8	102.5	102.3	101.3
肥皂类	Soap	100.1	100.4	100.3	100.3	100.0	99.6	99.7	99.7	100.6	100.1	100.1	100.1	99.9
牙膏	Toothpaste	101.4	101.3	102.0	101.4	101.4	102.4	102.2	101.3	101.1	101.0	101.2	100.9	100.7
清洁洗涤剂	Cleaning Agent	100.6	100.8	100.9	101.0	101.1	100.8	100.8	100.5	100.5	100.4	100.2	99.9	100.0
4.其他日用品	Other Articles for Daily Use	100.3	100.5	100.4	100.7	100.6	100.9	100.4	100.0	100.2	100.2	100.3	100.0	99.9
燃气灶具	Gas-oven	102.8	102.6	102.6	103.4	102.6	103.1	102.3	102.8	102.8	102.7	102.9	102.3	102.9
儿童玩具	Children's Toy	100.2	102.0	101.6	101.5	100.8	100.5	100.1	99.8	99.4	99.3	99.3	99.1	99.2
照明器具	Illumination Utensil	99.8	100.3	100.6	99.6	100.2	100.2	99.7	99.1	99.2	100.0	99.3	99.2	99.9
钟表眼镜及配件	Clocks, Glasses and their Fittings	98.9	97.9	98.0	98.2	98.6	98.7	98.9	99.0	99.0	99.2	99.4	99.7	99.9
日用普通饰品	Common Ornament for Daily Use	99.7	98.9	99.6	99.6	98.8	100.3	99.4	100.3	100.0	100.3	100.0	99.6	99.9
日用皮革制品	Leatherware for Daily Use	99.8	99.0	98.4	100.5	101.6	102.0	101.2	98.2	100.0	98.9	100.4	99.7	97.3
其他	Others	99.6	100.7	99.4	99.8	100.5	100.5	100.2	98.0	99.9	99.2	99.7	98.8	98.2
八、体育娱乐用品	**Sports and Recreation Articles**	**99.2**	**99.0**	**99.1**	**99.0**	**99.1**	**99.2**	**99.1**	**99.2**	**99.4**	**99.4**	**99.5**	**99.4**	**99.5**
1.体育用品	Sports Articles	99.5	99.4	99.5	99.5	99.6	99.4	99.3	99.4	99.5	99.6	99.6	99.4	99.5
球类	Ball	98.7	98.8	98.9	98.7	98.7	98.5	98.2	98.3	98.7	98.7	98.8	98.9	98.8
棋牌	Chess and Cards	100.8	101.4	101.5	101.4	101.2	101.1	100.6	100.6	100.5	100.3	100.5	100.3	100.0
健身器材	Exercise Machine	99.4	98.7	98.9	99.1	99.4	99.1	99.4	99.5	99.6	99.9	99.7	99.4	99.6
2.娱乐用品	Recreation Articles	99.0	98.7	98.7	98.6	98.7	99.0	98.9	98.9	99.3	99.2	99.4	99.3	99.5
游艺器材	Entertainment Apparatus	98.4	99.4	99.4	99.3	98.7	98.4	98.1	97.4	97.6	97.4	98.3	98.1	98.3
照相器材	Photographic Apparatus	98.4	97.7	97.3	97.2	97.6	98.2	98.2	98.6	99.3	99.0	99.0	99.1	99.8
乐器	Musical Instrument	100.6	99.7	100.5	100.5	100.6	100.9	100.7	100.8	100.8	101.0	100.9	100.7	99.9
九、交通、通信用品	**Transportation and Communication Appliances**	**93.5**	**92.7**	**93.0**	**93.4**	**93.1**	**93.3**	**93.6**	**93.6**	**94.0**	**93.9**	**94.1**	**94.1**	**93.6**
1.交通运输机械	Transportation Machine	98.6	98.1	98.6	98.9	98.8	98.9	99.0	98.8	98.9	98.6	98.6	98.4	97.6
轿车	Car	96.9	96.4	97.3	98.1	97.9	97.6	97.5	97.1	97.0	96.3	96.7	96.4	94.7
客车	Bus	98.0	96.5	96.6	97.4	98.1	98.1	98.9	98.8	98.9	98.0	98.0	98.4	98.5
货车	Truck	99.5	100.5	100.2	99.4	99.4	99.8	99.8	99.7	99.7	99.7	98.7	98.6	98.2
摩托车	Motorcycle	100.5	98.8	100.0	100.4	100.4	100.7	100.7	100.4	100.9	101.0	101.3	101.0	99.9
其他	Others	98.4	99.4	98.8	98.8	98.0	98.2	98.2	98.0	98.4	98.4	98.4	98.4	98.5
2.通信器材	Telecommunications Facilities	84.6	83.9	83.7	84.1	83.3	83.5	84.2	84.6	85.1	85.3	85.8	86.1	86.0
固定电话机	Telephone	96.2	96.1	96.2	95.5	96.0	95.6	95.9	95.8	95.8	96.8	97.1	97.2	96.9
移动电话机	Mobile Phone	75.9	75.6	75.3	75.9	74.3	74.5	75.2	75.7	76.7	76.4	77.0	77.3	77.1
传真机	Fax Machine	98.9	99.0	99.1	99.1	99.0	99.7	99.9	99.8	98.3	98.4	98.3	98.1	98.0
其他	Others	96.1	96.2	95.7	96.1	96.1	95.4	95.7	95.9	95.9	96.0	96.6	96.8	97.0
十、家具	**Furniture**	**10.04**	**99.9**	**100.0**	**99.8**	**99.8**	**100.1**	**100.2**	**100.3**	**100.4**	**100.7**	**101.3**	**101.4**	**101.4**
柜	Cabinet	100.4	100.5	100.5	100.0	99.8	100.3	100.2	100.0	100.1	100.3	101.2	101.0	101.1
床	Bed	101.4	100.3	100.9	100.6	101.0	101.4	101.5	101.7	101.6	101.8	102.4	102.1	101.6
桌	Desk	100.5	100.6	100.9	100.4	100.5	100.3	100.3	100.7	100.5	100.2	100.6	100.9	100.5
椅	Chair	100.6	100.7	100.5	100.5	100.3	100.3	100.3	99.9	99.7	100.6	101.5	101.7	101.6
沙发	Sofa	99.4	98.2	98.2	98.3	98.5	98.6	99.0	99.2	99.6	100.3	100.6	101.1	101.2
其他	Others	101.2	101.4	99.2	99.3	99.6	99.5	100.7	101.7	101.6	102.9	102.3	102.2	103.9

7-22 续表 6 continued

商品类别及品名	Commodity Category and Commodity Name	（以2005年同期价格为100）												
		全年 Annural	1月 January	2月 February	3月 March	4月 April	5月 May	6月 June	7月 July	8月 August	9月 September	10月 October	11月 November	12月 December
十一、化妆品	**Cosmetics**	**99.1**	**99.2**	**98.9**	**98.7**	**98.8**	**98.9**	**99.0**	**98.9**	**99.0**	**99.1**	**99.3**	**99.4**	**99.6**
护肤品	Skincare Products	99.6	99.7	99.8	99.7	99.8	99.8	99.5	99.6	99.6	99.5	100.0	99.4	99.1
美容化妆品	Facial Beautifiers	97.6	98.1	97.0	96.7	96.6	96.7	97.2	97.3	97.5	97.5	97.7	98.6	100.4
护发美容品	Protects Sends the Beauty Products	99.1	99.5	99.1	98.7	98.9	98.8	99.1	98.8	98.8	99.1	99.5	99.4	99.3
清洁化妆用品	Cleaning Toiletware	99.8	99.4	99.2	99.3	99.7	99.9	99.8	99.9	99.8	100.2	100.2	100.1	100.0
药物美容用品	Medicinal Cosmetics	99.5	99.4	99.3	99.0	99.3	99.6	99.5	99.4	99.3	99.7	99.6	99.6	99.8
十二、金银珠宝	**Gold, Silver and Jewelry**	**117.5**	**103.8**	**105.6**	**108.8**	**112.2**	**119.5**	**122.4**	**122.5**	**124.1**	**123.7**	**123.0**	**122.8**	**121.5**
金饰品	Gold	124.6	107.1	109.9	114.1	118.8	130.2	131.4	130.7	133.1	132.5	130.5	128.9	127.3
银饰品	Silver	117.5	100.2	100.8	106.8	107.4	112.8	121.8	123.6	126.3	126.8	127.7	127.5	128.0
铂金饰品	Platinum	113.1	102.4	103.8	104.9	108.8	113.7	117.2	117.5	118.2	117.3	117.5	118.9	116.9
其他	Others	101.5	99.4	99.4	101.3	101.5	101.5	102.1	101.7	102.3	102.3	102.4	102.4	102.2
十三、中西药品及医疗保健用品	**Traditional Chinese and Western Medicines and Healthcare Articles**	**99.8**	**99.5**	**99.7**	**99.6**	**99.6**	**99.8**	**99.9**	**100.2**	**100.1**	**100.0**	**99.9**	**100.0**	**99.9**
1.医疗器具及用品	Medical Facilities and Goods	96.8	95.8	96.5	97.8	97.7	97.8	97.8	97.8	97.8	98.0	95.3	95.1	94.5
医疗器具及用品	Medical Facilities and Goods	96.8	95.8	96.5	97.8	97.7	97.8	97.8	97.8	97.8	98.0	95.3	95.1	94.5
2.中药材及中成药	Herbs and Ready-made Traditional Chinese Medicine	101.2	99.9	100.4	100.3	100.6	100.5	100.8	101.4	101.6	101.7	102.3	102.5	102.3
中药材	Herbs	102.9	99.2	100.0	99.6	100.5	101.1	102.4	103.7	103.7	104.4	106.5	107.2	106.2
中成药	Ready-made Traditional Chinese Medicine	99.8	100.6	100.8	101.0	100.6	99.9	99.4	99.5	99.9	99.5	98.9	98.7	99.1
3.西药	Western Medicine	99.4	99.4	99.5	99.3	99.2	99.7	99.6	100.0	99.5	99.4	99.1	99.1	99.3
抗微生物药	Anti-microorganism Medicine	99.2	97.5	97.5	97.6	97.7	97.9	98.2	100.3	99.9	99.8	101.1	101.3	101.2
消化系统用药	Alimentary System Medicine	99.6	98.7	98.8	99.0	98.7	99.1	99.7	100.5	99.6	100.0	100.3	100.1	100.4
呼吸系统用药	Respiratory System Medicine	99.5	99.0	98.9	98.9	99.1	99.0	99.6	99.6	99.5	100.3	99.6	99.9	100.0
解热镇痛及非甾体抗炎药	Allays a Fever the Analgesia and the Non-steroid Body Anti-inflammatory Agent	100.2	101.0	100.9	100.5	100.3	101.7	100.2	99.8	99.7	99.2	99.8	99.7	100.1
抗肿瘤药	Anti-neoplastic Drug	100.0	100.4	100.4	100.2	99.7	102.4	100.5	100.6	99.9	99.0	98.9	99.2	98.7
激素及调节内分泌功能药	Hormone and Adjustment Internal Secretion Function Medicine	97.7	99.3	99.5	98.9	98.9	98.9	98.5	98.2	97.9	97.1	94.7	95.4	95.5
循环系统用药	Circulating System Medicine	99.9	99.8	99.9	99.7	99.1	99.0	99.7	99.7	100.0	100.4	101.1	100.1	100.5
神经系统用药	Nerve System Medicine	99.4	101.4	101.4	101.0	101.1	101.0	101.1	101.1	99.1	98.7	95.7	95.7	96.2
专科用药	Junior Medicine	99.1	99.9	99.8	100.0	100.0	100.0	100.5	100.3	100.1	98.8	96.6	96.4	96.5
其他	Others	98.7	100.1	100.3	98.7	98.5	99.0	98.8	98.5	98.5	98.5	98.1	97.9	97.8
4.保健品及器具	Healthcare Equipment	99.9	100.4	100.2	100.0	100.0	99.9	100.2	99.8	99.8	99.7	99.5	99.6	99.5
保健器具	Health Protection Equipment	99.5	100.1	99.8	99.7	99.7	99.6	99.9	99.8	99.8	99.6	98.8	98.8	98.6
滋补保健用品	Tonic and Health Products	100.0	100.5	100.4	100.1	100.1	100.1	100.4	99.8	99.9	99.7	99.8	99.9	99.9

7-22 续表 7 continued

商品类别及品名	Commodity Category and Commodity Name	全年 Annural	1月 January	2月 February	3月 March	4月 April	5月 May	6月 June	7月 July	8月 August	9月 September	10月 October	11月 November	12月 December
		（以2005年同期价格为100）												
十四、书报杂志及电子出版物	**Books, Newspapers, Magazines and Electronic Publications**	**101.2**	**101.3**	**101.4**	**101.3**	**101.5**	**101.5**	**101.5**	**101.5**	**101.5**	**100.8**	**100.8**	**100.8**	**100.7**
1.教材及参考书	Teaching Materials and Reference Books	101.6	102.1	102.1	102.3	102.3	102.3	102.3	102.3	102.2	100.4	100.3	100.3	100.3
工具书	Tool Book	101.0	101.6	101.6	101.6	101.6	101.5	101.5	101.5	101.0	100.0	100.0	100.0	100.0
教材	Teaching Material	100.6	101.0	101.0	101.2	101.3	101.3	101.3	101.3	101.4	99.5	99.3	99.3	99.3
参考书	Reference Book	104.4	105.2	105.2	105.5	105.5	105.5	105.4	105.4	105.3	102.5	102.5	102.5	102.6
教育软件	Educational Software	99.3	99.8	99.8	99.2	99.2	99.2	99.2	99.2	99.2	99.2	98.8	99.2	99.4
2.书报杂志	Books, Newspapers, Magazines	102.3	102.3	102.3	102.5	102.5	102.4	102.4	102.4	102.3	102.3	102.3	102.2	102.1
书籍	Books	101.0	100.9	100.9	101.2	101.2	101.1	101.1	101.1	100.9	100.8	100.8	100.7	100.5
报纸	Newspapers	105.5	105.5	105.5	105.5	105.5	105.5	105.5	105.5	105.5	105.5	105.5	105.5	105.4
杂志	Magazines	100.4	100.4	100.4	100.4	100.4	100.4	100.4	100.4	100.4	100.4	100.4	100.4	100.5
3.电子音像制品	Electronic Publications	99.2	98.7	99.1	98.7	99.1	99.3	99.3	99.4	99.4	99.5	99.6	99.4	99.2
音响光盘和磁带	Acoustic Light Disk and Tape	99.1	98.9	99.5	98.5	99.2	99.1	99.1	99.1	99.1	99.1	99.1	99.3	99.4
录像磁带和视盘	Video Tape and Disk	100.2	99.1	99.5	99.6	100.2	100.5	100.6	100.5	100.4	100.6	100.5	100.6	100.0
计算机软件	Computer Software	98.4	98.2	98.2	97.9	98.0	98.3	98.3	98.8	98.7	98.9	99.2	98.5	98.2
十五、燃料	**Fuels**	**109.9**	**110.6**	**111.0**	**109.5**	**110.2**	**110.7**	**113.0**	**110.8**	**108.6**	**109.3**	**109.2**	**108.1**	**108.3**
1.煤炭及制品	Coal and Related Products	104.8	106.6	106.3	105.1	104.8	104.9	103.9	103.7	104.0	104.1	105.4	104.4	104.3
原煤	Raw Coal	104.7	105.0	104.6	104.9	103.9	104.1	103.5	103.3	103.9	103.7	107.0	106.5	105.7
煤制品	Coal Products	104.9	108.6	108.4	105.3	106.0	105.8	104.5	104.2	104.1	104.5	103.5	102.0	102.6
2.石油及制品	Petroleum and Related Products	112.3	112.4	113.2	111.7	112.8	113.5	117.2	114.1	110.7	111.7	110.9	109.7	110.1
液化石油气	Liquefiled Petroleum Gas	113.9	124.1	127.8	123.6	122.2	116.8	113.9	111.4	108.1	112.8	108.3	101.7	103.8
管道燃气	Pipelined Gas	100.4	100.3	100.3	100.3	100.3	100.5	100.5	100.4	100.4	100.4	100.4	100.4	100.4
汽油	Gasoline	116.5	114.4	114.6	112.4	113.5	117.4	126.1	120.8	115.8	115.7	115.9	115.9	115.9
柴油	Diesel Oil	116.2	113.3	113.4	113.6	117.5	118.2	123.5	119.2	114.6	114.7	115.1	115.8	115.4
其他	Others	102.6	99.9	101.1	101.1	102.4	102.3	103.4	103.0	102.8	103.9	103.7	103.1	104.0
十六、建筑材料及五金电料	**Building Materials and Hardware**	**103.1**	**101.0**	**101.3**	**101.4**	**101.9**	**102.5**	**102.9**	**103.1**	**103.8**	**104.2**	**104.5**	**105.2**	**105.6**
1.建筑装璜材料	Building and Decoration Materials	103.2	100.9	101.0	101.1	102.0	102.9	103.4	103.6	104.0	103.9	104.4	105.3	105.8
木材	Wood	106.0	103.3	103.2	103.8	104.1	103.7	103.8	104.3	106.8	107.7	108.8	111.3	111.3
木地板	Wood Floor	103.9	105.7	105.7	105.1	104.6	104.4	101.4	102.0	102.2	103.1	103.3	104.5	105.6
钢材	Steel Products	96.0	89.8	89.7	88.0	90.9	95.5	99.4	98.4	97.0	98.0	100.9	101.5	104.7
砖	Brick	107.0	103.1	103.6	104.6	107.2	108.6	110.0	109.5	110.5	106.7	106.9	106.9	107.0
水泥	Cement	102.0	101.3	100.4	100.4	102.0	102.7	102.5	102.4	102.3	102.5	102.4	102.7	102.4
涂料	Coating Material	100.7	101.2	101.9	101.4	100.6	100.2	100.7	100.8	100.9	100.2	99.8	100.3	100.8
胶合板	Plywood	104.0	101.5	101.7	102.2	102.6	102.2	103.0	104.0	104.7	105.8	105.0	107.7	107.8
玻璃	Glass	101.5	98.6	98.4	99.4	99.3	100.3	100.7	102.0	102.5	103.0	103.5	104.7	106.1
粘胶	Rayon	102.1	100.8	100.8	101.0	101.1	101.3	101.9	102.3	102.6	103.0	103.0	103.3	104.5
油漆	Paint	103.5	101.5	102.9	103.1	102.0	102.4	102.9	103.6	103.7	105.0	104.9	104.7	105.1
其他	Others	104.3	103.2	103.5	105.0	105.3	105.8	103.2	103.4	103.5	103.5	105.7	105.9	104.2
2.五金电料	Hardware	102.9	101.3	102.0	101.9	101.5	101.7	102.0	102.0	103.1	104.8	104.6	105.0	105.0
五金工具	Hardware Tools	101.5	101.6	102.1	101.5	101.0	100.7	101.5	101.3	101.4	102.3	102.2	101.8	101.2
电工电料	Electrical Engineering and Electrical Materials	103.2	100.9	102.3	102.0	101.4	101.9	101.3	101.0	104.1	106.4	105.4	105.9	105.9
水暖器材	Heating Equipment	103.0	101.5	101.6	101.8	101.9	102.2	102.3	102.3	102.6	104.0	104.6	105.6	105.9
其他	Others	105.1	101.5	102.0	102.7	101.5	101.2	104.4	106.1	106.9	108.5	108.5	108.5	109.1

7-23 城市商品零售价格指数
Urban Retail Price Index

（以2005年同期价格为100）

商品类别及品名	Commodity Category and Commodity Name	全年 Annural	1月 January	2月 February	3月 March	4月 April	5月 May	6月 June	7月 July	8月 August	9月 September	10月 October	11月 November	12月 December
商品零售价格总指数	**Genaral Retail Price Index**	**100.5**	**101.0**	**100.3**	**100.4**	**100.7**	**100.6**	**100.8**	**99.8**	**99.9**	**100.5**	**100.4**	**100.7**	**101.2**
一、食品	**Food**	**102.5**	**106.2**	**102.7**	**102.7**	**103.5**	**103.1**	**102.7**	**99.1**	**99.6**	**101.6**	**101.0**	**102.6**	**105.2**
1.粮食	Grain	102.5	98.1	98.3	98.5	99.1	100.7	102.2	103.1	104.3	104.0	104.3	107.6	109.7
大米	Rice	106.9	99.9	100.4	101.4	101.7	104.7	107.5	108.4	111.6	110.9	111.3	112.1	113.8
面粉	Flour	98.2	94.5	94.6	94.4	95.2	96.6	97.2	98.1	97.9	97.7	98.3	105.9	109.3
粮食制品	Grain Products	101.8	98.5	98.7	98.7	99.2	100.0	101.3	102.1	103.3	103.4	103.7	105.4	107.1
其他	Others	108.2	106.3	105.6	105.9	106.9	108.5	109.8	110.4	110.9	108.8	107.4	108.5	110.0
2.淀粉	Starches	99.1	98.2	96.7	96.6	97.4	97.1	96.8	96.0	96.2	101.7	103.1	103.9	106.4
淀粉	Starches	99.1	98.2	96.7	96.6	97.4	97.1	96.8	96.0	96.2	101.7	103.1	103.9	106.4
3.干豆类及豆制品	Beans and Beans Products	101.2	100.8	98.8	100.2	100.3	100.7	101.4	101.9	102.2	101.4	101.3	101.9	103.0
干豆	Beans	101.3	99.9	99.2	98.0	98.1	99.5	102.1	104.3	105.6	102.3	101.0	102.1	102.8
豆制品	Beans Products	101.1	101.0	98.7	100.8	100.9	101.0	101.3	101.2	101.2	101.2	101.4	101.8	103.1
4.油脂	Oil and Fat	99.9	99.0	98.0	98.3	98.2	98.7	99.2	98.8	99.6	99.6	100.1	102.0	107.9
食用植物油	Edible Vegetable Oil	100.6	99.3	98.3	98.7	99.1	99.8	100.2	100.0	100.7	100.6	100.8	102.5	106.7
植物油制品	Plant Oil Products	100.0	100.1	99.3	99.0	98.0	98.1	98.6	97.8	98.1	98.2	98.0	100.3	114.6
其他	Others	85.8	87.8	88.2	86.8	78.8	76.4	78.3	77.2	80.2	82.9	91.6	98.9	106.3
5.肉禽及其制品	Meal, Poultry and their Products	97.1	96.5	93.1	92.3	91.5	91.0	91.4	94.0	97.4	98.2	101.5	107.4	112.8
（1）食用畜肉及副产品	Edible Livestock Meat and their By-products	95.5	95.0	90.8	89.2	88.2	87.6	87.8	90.7	95.7	97.1	101.6	109.5	116.3
猪肉	Pork	92.0	90.9	86.3	83.7	81.9	80.9	81.2	85.3	92.4	94.5	100.5	112.2	120.5
牛肉	Beef	105.6	110.6	105.8	106.3	107.0	105.0	105.4	104.8	104.1	103.8	103.6	104.1	106.9
羊肉	Mutton	105.8	106.4	103.3	105.0	106.7	107.6	108.1	107.4	105.1	105.0	104.4	103.9	107.0
畜肉副产品	Livestock Meat By-products	97.8	98.2	94.3	93.8	92.7	92.4	92.5	94.5	97.3	97.9	102.3	105.9	113.2
其他	Others	98.3	94.6	93.1	93.9	93.7	95.1	95.9	95.9	100.3	100.5	103.1	106.1	108.6
（2）禽	Poultry	96.6	94.9	89.8	90.7	89.1	87.3	89.7	95.7	98.7	98.6	102.2	109.9	118.3
鸡	Chicken	96.6	92.7	87.4	88.8	87.4	85.5	88.2	96.2	99.6	100.1	104.8	113.5	124.0
鸭	Duck	94.0	102.0	99.2	97.9	95.7	94.5	94.7	88.6	90.5	87.7	88.3	93.9	96.2
其他	Others	98.6	106.1	100.1	98.7	96.6	95.8	96.5	98.0	99.2	97.0	96.3	99.0	100.8
（3）肉禽加工制品	Meal and Poultry Processing Products	100.7	100.4	100.3	100.1	100.2	100.3	100.1	100.1	100.5	100.5	101.0	102.1	103.3
畜肉制品	Livestock Meat Products	100.9	100.7	100.6	100.5	100.6	100.6	100.6	100.4	100.6	100.4	101.0	101.9	103.2
禽制品	Poultry Products	100.4	99.7	99.7	99.3	99.3	99.7	99.2	99.5	100.3	100.9	101.0	102.4	103.5
6.蛋	Eggs	95.5	93.6	86.8	89.7	90.5	86.6	86.4	88.2	95.8	99.0	105.4	109.3	116.6
鲜蛋	Fresh Eggs	94.4	91.8	84.4	87.6	88.4	84.4	84.2	86.3	95.1	98.8	105.9	110.3	118.4
蛋制品	Egg Products	103.6	107.2	105.3	105.2	105.5	103.6	104.1	103.4	101.3	99.9	101.7	102.1	104.3
7.水产品	Aquatic Product	103.5	101.0	99.2	98.4	100.1	103.4	104.4	105.9	106.7	105.9	107.1	105.7	104.6
（1）鱼	Fish	101.0	100.9	97.8	95.9	97.7	99.2	101.3	102.0	104.1	104.2	103.8	102.5	102.9
淡水鱼	Freshwater Fish	95.7	95.7	91.6	89.7	89.7	91.3	94.1	97.9	100.6	101.7	99.2	98.7	99.1
海水鱼	Seawater Fish	105.4	105.3	103.1	101.1	104.2	105.7	107.3	105.4	106.9	106.3	107.7	105.5	106.0

7-23 续表 1 continued

商品类别及品名	Commodity Category and Commodity Name	（以2005年同期价格为100）												
		全年 Annural	1月 January	2月 February	3月 March	4月 April	5月 May	6月 June	7月 July	8月 August	9月 September	10月 October	11月 November	12月 December
（2）其他水产品	Other Aquatic Product	106.8	101.0	101.0	101.6	103.1	109.0	108.7	111.4	110.3	108.4	111.8	110.1	106.9
虾蟹类	Shrimp and Crab	106.4	100.4	99.8	98.8	101.2	109.2	108.3	111.5	110.7	108.4	113.7	110.5	107.7
其他	Others	107.6	102.3	104.1	108.9	107.8	108.6	109.6	111.0	109.5	108.2	107.7	109.1	105.0
8.菜	Vegetable	108.5	147.1	118.4	116.0	119.3	113.3	111.1	87.8	92.1	107.0	90.0	95.0	103.1
鲜菜	Fresh Vegetable	108.0	153.4	120.0	117.1	120.8	113.3	110.3	83.4	88.6	106.3	86.8	92.2	101.1
干菜及菜制品	Dried Vegetable and Vegetable Products	106.8	101.1	101.3	102.1	103.7	104.4	104.6	105.7	106.9	109.2	111.6	112.9	117.9
薯类	Potato	123.4	119.8	117.5	119.1	121.3	131.4	137.4	134.3	130.5	117.5	114.4	117.6	116.5
9.调味品	Flavoring	102.7	102.9	102.8	102.8	103.0	102.9	103.2	102.5	102.2	102.1	101.8	102.7	103.2
盐	Salt	103.2	105.7	105.2	106.0	105.2	105.3	106.0	103.0	101.8	101.0	100.3	99.6	99.7
酱油	Soy Sauce	102.5	104.1	104.0	104.0	104.1	103.0	102.6	101.8	102.0	101.7	101.1	101.3	100.8
醋	Vinegar	102.0	103.3	103.2	101.8	102.1	102.0	102.3	102.1	101.8	101.9	101.2	101.0	101.1
味精	Aginomoto	100.2	99.4	99.3	99.6	100.3	100.7	100.6	100.6	100.3	100.3	100.1	100.0	100.9
其他	Others	104.9	99.8	99.7	100.3	101.4	102.5	103.9	105.0	105.0	105.5	106.6	113.5	116.2
10.糖	Carbohydrate	106.8	104.1	106.0	106.9	107.0	107.5	107.8	107.4	107.3	107.1	106.8	106.9	107.3
食糖	Sugar	123.6	110.7	116.8	122.6	124.0	126.5	127.9	127.4	127.5	127.0	123.9	122.9	125.6
糖果	Sweet	104.1	103.1	104.5	104.5	104.3	104.2	104.2	103.8	103.4	103.4	104.1	104.7	104.6
巧克力制品	Chocolate Products	99.9	101.5	101.6	100.7	100.4	99.8	99.7	99.2	98.8	98.9	99.4	99.3	99.1
糖类小食品	Little Carbohydrate Food	102.2	102.0	102.4	102.2	101.7	102.7	102.7	102.5	102.6	102.3	101.9	102.0	101.8
11.干鲜瓜果	Dried and Fresh Melons and Fruits	115.5	124.5	126.6	130.3	134.7	137.3	136.1	111.2	97.6	97.6	100.5	95.9	93.6
鲜瓜果	Fresh Fruits	117.3	129.5	131.7	136.2	141.5	144.8	144.7	112.4	94.7	94.2	97.6	91.6	88.9
干（坚）果	Dried Fruits	108.9	106.6	106.9	108.5	108.5	108.2	108.4	107.5	107.3	108.9	110.6	112.2	113.1
12.糕点饼干面包	Cake, Biscuit and Bread	100.7	100.8	100.9	101.2	101.0	101.2	100.9	101.0	101.1	100.4	100.1	99.7	99.9
糕点	Cake	99.9	100.8	100.9	101.6	101.1	100.8	100.7	100.2	99.6	98.9	97.7	97.9	98.5
饼干	Biscuit	101.3	101.5	101.3	101.2	101.0	102.0	101.8	101.5	101.9	101.2	101.1	100.4	100.6
面包	Bread	101.4	99.9	100.6	100.4	100.5	100.8	100.4	101.7	102.7	102.4	103.3	102.4	101.8
13.液体乳及乳制品	Liquid Milk and their Products	101.9	101.6	101.8	102.4	101.4	101.2	101.3	101.4	101.6	102.9	102.7	102.7	102.3
巴氏杀菌奶或消毒奶	Pasteurization Milk or Disinfection Milk	101.5	101.3	101.3	102.3	100.7	100.5	100.7	100.9	101.0	102.3	102.0	102.3	102.1
酸奶	Leben	101.4	100.9	100.9	101.0	100.9	101.1	101.1	100.8	100.8	102.5	102.7	102.3	102.2
奶粉	Milk Powder	104.0	103.2	103.4	103.5	104.2	103.6	103.8	104.1	105.3	105.1	104.3	104.1	103.0
其他	Others	103.2	102.2	104.4	104.4	102.6	102.4	102.3	102.3	102.0	104.4	104.3	104.6	102.3
14.在外用膳食品	Outward Dinner	100.8	99.9	99.8	100.0	100.1	100.1	100.6	100.6	100.8	101.3	101.1	101.6	103.8
主食	Staple Food	100.7	99.9	99.5	99.6	99.7	99.7	100.5	100.5	100.6	100.7	100.7	101.9	105.7
炒菜	Hot Dish	100.8	100.0	100.0	100.1	100.3	100.2	100.8	100.5	100.7	101.5	101.2	101.3	102.7
地方小吃	Local Snack	101.1	100.0	100.0	100.3	100.3	100.4	100.3	101.2	101.9	101.7	101.7	102.2	103.7
15.其他食品	Other Foods	100.4	100.8	100.7	100.8	100.6	100.5	100.4	100.3	100.3	100.3	100.0	99.7	99.9
其他食品	Other Foods	100.4	100.8	100.7	100.8	100.6	100.5	100.4	100.3	100.3	100.3	100.0	99.7	99.9
二、饮料、烟酒	**Beverages, Tobacco, Liquor**	**101.2**	**100.7**	**100.5**	**100.5**	**100.9**	**101.0**	**101.4**	**101.3**	**101.6**	**101.7**	**101.6**	**101.6**	**101.8**
1.茶及饮料	Tea and Beverages	100.9	99.8	99.6	100.2	100.5	100.9	101.2	101.0	101.3	101.3	101.3	101.5	101.8
（1）茶叶	Tea	100.8	99.7	100.1	100.5	100.7	101.1	101.0	100.9	100.6	101.0	101.2	101.0	101.4

7-23 续表 2 continued

商品类别及品名	Commodity Category and Commodity Name	全年 Annural	1月 January	2月 February	3月 March	4月 April	5月 May	6月 June	7月 July	8月 August	9月 September	10月 October	11月 November	12月 December
		（以2005年同期价格为100）												
茶叶	Tea	100.8	99.7	100.1	100.5	100.7	101.1	101.0	100.9	100.6	101.0	101.2	101.0	101.4
（2）饮料	Beverages	100.9	99.8	99.3	100.0	100.4	100.8	101.4	101.1	101.6	101.5	101.4	101.7	102.1
固体饮料	Solid Beverages	100.6	101.3	100.9	100.4	100.7	101.0	101.2	100.7	101.1	100.9	100.1	100.3	99.0
液体饮料	Liquid Beverages	100.4	99.4	98.9	99.8	100.1	100.6	100.9	100.6	100.8	100.6	100.7	100.8	101.6
冷冻饮品	Frozen Beverages	102.1	99.3	98.5	100.1	100.7	101.0	102.3	102.2	103.7	103.6	103.8	104.8	105.8
2.烟草	Tobacco	99.6	99.4	98.9	98.8	99.3	99.4	99.5	99.6	100.1	100.2	100.1	100.0	100.2
国产卷烟	Domestic Cigarette	99.9	99.6	99.2	99.0	99.6	99.7	99.9	100.0	100.5	100.6	100.5	100.4	100.4
进口卷烟	Import Cigarette	98.0	98.4	97.2	97.4	97.9	97.7	97.8	97.7	98.0	98.4	98.3	98.5	99.2
其他	Others	98.2	98.7	98.7	98.4	97.7	98.2	98.2	98.5	98.0	98.0	98.0	98.1	98.2
3.酒	Liquor	102.7	102.4	102.2	102.0	102.4	102.4	102.9	102.9	103.0	103.1	103.0	102.8	103.1
白酒	White Spirit	103.4	102.6	102.4	102.5	103.0	103.0	103.8	103.5	103.7	104.0	103.8	103.8	104.1
葡萄酒	Grape	106.9	106.6	106.5	106.7	106.9	106.8	108.1	108.3	107.6	107.0	106.6	105.9	105.8
啤酒	Beer	100.7	101.0	101.0	100.3	100.6	100.4	100.3	100.8	100.9	100.8	100.8	100.5	100.8
其他	Others	100.2	99.6	100.0	99.8	100.2	100.3	100.2	100.2	100.1	100.2	100.0	101.2	101.1
三、服装、鞋帽	**Garments, Footgearand and Hats**	**98.4**	**97.6**	**98.3**	**99.7**	**99.8**	**98.9**	**98.9**	**98.4**	**98.2**	**98.3**	**98.6**	**97.8**	**96.4**
1.服装	Garments	97.9	97.1	97.6	98.5	99.0	98.4	98.0	97.6	97.4	97.7	98.4	97.9	97.3
（1）男式服装	Men's Garments	97.2	96.9	98.4	98.7	98.4	97.8	97.3	96.8	96.2	96.4	96.9	96.4	95.8
大衣	Topcoat	94.0	95.0	95.5	96.3	94.8	94.6	93.8	93.3	92.8	92.8	92.4	93.4	93.9
毛线衣	Woollen Sweater	93.0	99.2	95.6	95.3	96.7	94.3	93.8	92.0	89.4	89.8	91.7	88.0	90.3
夹克衫	Jacket	94.9	93.4	95.9	93.8	93.5	94.1	93.5	93.4	93.6	93.8	98.0	99.5	96.9
衬衫	Shirt	94.4	91.3	96.1	98.0	96.6	93.6	95.5	94.2	93.7	93.1	92.7	92.9	95.0
T恤衫	T-shirt	97.2	100.1	100.8	99.2	100.1	102.4	100.1	96.9	94.1	94.3	93.5	94.8	90.4
裤子	Trousers	95.5	97.0	97.6	98.8	96.0	94.0	93.6	93.4	96.5	94.9	95.7	93.7	95.5
西服	Western-style Clothes	101.9	97.4	100.1	100.2	102.0	104.0	103.0	104.5	101.1	103.3	104.7	103.0	100.0
运动衫裤	Gym Suit	97.4	94.1	97.5	99.8	99.3	96.3	96.5	96.7	97.5	97.8	97.6	98.9	96.8
内衣	Underwaist	103.1	104.4	104.7	105.5	105.6	105.3	104.3	103.1	103.4	103.7	99.3	98.9	99.5
羽绒衣	Eider down Outerwear	99.8	97.7	101.8	101.8	99.5	99.8	99.8	99.2	99.1	100.1	101.1	101.9	96.6
其他	Others	94.9	95.8	94.3	92.9	94.8	95.0	92.6	93.0	93.4	93.3	94.9	99.6	99.2
（2）女式服装	Women's Garments	98.1	96.9	96.5	97.9	99.0	98.2	97.8	97.8	97.8	98.5	99.8	99.1	98.2
大衣	Topcoat	93.8	94.7	92.2	96.6	95.5	94.1	94.8	94.2	93.3	93.2	93.1	91.3	92.9
毛线衣	Woollen Sweater	94.1	95.1	92.9	96.7	96.9	96.1	94.3	91.8	90.5	92.0	94.7	93.8	95.1
羽绒衣	Eider down Outerwear	98.8	95.3	97.5	96.9	97.2	97.5	97.3	99.3	99.7	99.2	100.8	103.6	101.7
套装	Coordinates	101.0	100.9	100.7	100.5	103.9	103.3	100.9	102.0	98.2	101.8	102.8	98.6	98.6
衬衫	Shirt	99.8	96.1	98.5	98.2	101.7	101.2	102.3	102.1	100.6	100.7	101.6	100.8	94.9
T恤衫	T-shirt	103.4	97.8	98.1	97.8	100.1	101.4	101.9	100.7	100.7	105.9	113.9	114.2	109.4
裙子	Skirt	102.3	101.0	100.9	100.7	102.8	103.8	102.6	102.2	104.4	103.2	104.4	103.0	98.7
裤子	Trousers	96.4	95.8	94.9	97.2	95.7	94.0	93.7	96.2	99.0	97.8	98.6	97.8	96.0
运动衫裤	Gym Suit	95.0	93.5	94.6	93.0	97.0	93.4	92.9	94.4	95.7	96.8	96.7	94.7	97.3
内衣	Underwaist	101.1	98.8	98.9	100.3	101.4	101.0	101.0	100.4	101.1	101.6	102.0	103.7	103.4
其他	Others	101.4	100.9	99.7	100.1	102.2	100.8	100.3	101.1	101.6	102.6	102.5	103.3	101.8

7-23　续表 3 continued

商品类别及品名	Commodity Category and Commodity Name	（以2005年同期价格为100）												
		全年 Annural	1月 January	2月 February	3月 March	4月 April	5月 May	6月 June	7月 July	8 月 August	9 月 September	10 月 October	11月 November	12月 December
（3）儿童服装	Children's Garments	99.8	98.8	99.3	100.6	101.5	101.7	101.5	99.8	99.9	98.7	98.3	98.5	99.1
套装	Coordinates	99.1	100.3	100.2	101.4	102.5	101.8	100.8	99.6	98.7	96.7	94.8	95.2	98.0
裤子	Trousers	99.2	95.2	97.0	98.4	99.8	99.8	100.5	99.2	100.7	99.6	101.2	100.9	99.0
裙子	Skirt	102.1	99.8	99.3	100.7	101.6	104.4	104.6	101.7	102.5	102.4	102.4	102.7	102.8
其他	Others	97.4	102.5	105.2	106.0	103.5	97.1	96.0	94.8	93.4	93.2	92.9	94.4	91.6
2.鞋袜帽	Shoes, Socks and Hats	99.6	98.8	99.8	102.6	102.1	100.2	101.1	100.6	100.3	99.9	99.1	97.4	93.9
（1）鞋	Shoes	99.6	98.7	99.8	103.1	102.4	100.3	101.3	100.6	100.2	99.7	98.9	97.0	93.1
男鞋	Men's Shoes	99.6	98.6	100.4	102.0	102.5	98.8	100.4	99.6	100.3	100.2	99.6	97.7	94.7
女鞋	Women's Shoes	99.1	99.2	100.1	104.8	102.9	101.0	101.9	100.8	98.9	98.2	97.1	94.9	90.2
童鞋	Children's Shoes	101.3	97.4	97.5	100.0	100.5	101.7	101.9	103.1	104.9	103.9	103.3	102.6	99.4
（2）袜子	Socks	99.9	98.9	99.5	99.8	100.8	100.1	100.2	100.5	101.0	101.6	99.9	99.1	97.9
男袜	Men's Socks	100.1	98.8	98.8	99.3	101.4	100.9	100.9	101.2	101.2	101.4	100.6	99.3	97.3
女袜	Women's Socks	99.8	98.9	100.1	100.2	100.4	99.5	99.7	99.9	100.9	101.7	99.4	99.0	98.5
（3）帽子	Hats	99.8	99.8	99.4	99.7	99.6	99.6	99.2	99.4	99.6	100.2	100.1	100.3	100.3
男帽	Men's Hats	100.3	98.8	98.4	99.0	99.0	99.8	100.6	101.0	101.6	101.4	101.2	101.7	101.2
女帽	Women's Hats	99.5	100.5	100.1	100.1	100.0	99.5	98.4	98.5	98.4	99.5	99.5	99.5	99.8
3.其他	Others	98.3	97.5	99.7	98.9	98.5	98.4	99.1	98.6	97.8	97.8	98.0	97.5	97.3
领带	Necktie	98.3	97.5	99.7	98.9	98.5	98.4	99.1	98.6	97.8	97.8	98.0	97.5	97.3
四、纺织品	**Textiles**	**98.3**	**97.8**	**98.1**	**98.3**	**98.0**	**97.3**	**98.4**	**98.2**	**98.4**	**98.5**	**98.8**	**98.6**	**99.4**
1.衣着材料	Clothing Materials	97.9	98.5	98.3	98.1	97.4	96.5	96.5	96.6	97.4	97.9	98.4	99.4	100.1
棉布	Cotton Cloth	96.1	96.9	96.0	96.8	94.2	90.7	91.6	92.6	94.4	97.0	99.7	102.2	102.9
棉混纺布	Cotton Textiles Cloth	95.2	93.2	93.3	93.1	93.8	94.1	94.5	94.5	95.2	95.8	97.0	98.7	99.9
化纤布	Chemical Fiber Cloth	100.0	102.2	102.7	101.9	101.1	100.9	99.5	99.2	99.7	98.6	97.9	97.9	98.0
毛线	Knitting Wool	99.2	99.6	98.4	98.3	98.3	98.2	99.2	99.2	99.0	100.0	99.5	99.7	101.2
2.床上用品	Bedclothes	98.7	97.3	97.9	98.5	98.6	98.0	100.1	99.7	99.3	99.1	99.1	97.9	98.8
毛毯	Woollen Blanket	99.6	99.0	98.4	100.8	100.4	99.8	100.4	99.9	99.7	99.6	99.4	98.7	99.2
被子	Quilt	95.9	94.1	94.8	94.5	94.3	93.2	99.2	98.8	98.3	97.4	96.8	95.0	95.5
床上套件	Bed Articles	98.9	97.6	98.3	98.7	99.1	98.7	99.6	99.1	99.1	99.1	99.8	97.9	99.8
其他	Others	102.0	100.2	102.4	102.8	103.3	103.3	102.6	102.1	101.3	101.5	101.5	101.6	101.7
五、家用电器及音像器材	**Household Appliances, Music and Video Equipments**	**99.5**	**98.7**	**99.1**	**99.0**	**98.3**	**98.6**	**99.7**	**100.1**	**100.5**	**100.2**	**100.0**	**100.2**	**99.7**
1.家庭设备	Household Appliances	102.5	101.0	101.2	101.1	100.1	100.3	102.4	103.3	103.7	104.1	104.2	104.2	104.1
洗衣机	Washing Machine	100.3	99.5	100.4	100.3	98.9	99.5	100.8	101.4	100.5	100.5	100.7	100.8	100.4
电风扇	Electric Fan	100.3	100.8	101.4	101.5	98.8	99.7	101.6	100.9	101.2	99.7	99.5	99.3	98.9
电冰箱（柜）	Refrigerator	105.3	105.9	105.9	105.7	104.9	104.9	105.8	105.4	104.2	105.2	106.0	105.4	105.0
吸排油烟机	Kitchen Ventilato	105.6	104.9	104.9	104.4	102.2	102.1	104.4	106.8	107.9	107.9	107.7	107.6	106.2
空调器	Air-Conditioning	102.9	100.3	100.0	99.8	98.5	98.9	102.8	104.0	105.4	106.3	105.9	106.4	106.7
热水器	Water Heater	100.7	98.4	99.3	100.2	99.4	99.6	100.0	101.9	102.1	102.3	102.1	101.9	102.1
微波炉	Microwave Oven	98.3	95.6	96.1	97.0	96.9	96.6	97.6	98.3	100.0	100.2	100.5	100.8	99.9
电炊具	Electric Cooking Appliance	100.8	100.1	100.0	100.1	101.1	101.3	101.2	101.1	101.2	100.5	101.0	101.0	101.1
2.文娱用耐用消费品	Durable Consumer Goods For Recreational Use	95.3	95.2	96.1	95.9	95.4	96.0	95.8	95.8	96.1	94.8	94.2	94.6	93.3

7-23 续表 4 continued

商品类别及品名	Commodity Category and Commodity Name	（以2005年同期价格为100）												
		全年 Annural	1月 January	2月 February	3月 March	4月 April	5月 May	6月 June	7月 July	8月 August	9月 September	10月 October	11月 November	12月 December
电视机	Television	93.6	93.1	94.3	94.1	93.5	94.6	94.1	94.3	94.8	93.3	92.6	93.1	91.4
激光视盘机	Laser Video Disc Machine	95.3	96.1	96.5	96.1	95.6	95.8	96.7	96.5	97.1	94.3	92.7	92.9	92.5
摄像机	Pickup Camera	95.8	97.0	98.2	97.8	97.2	96.9	95.8	95.5	95.2	94.3	94.1	94.6	92.6
家用音响设备	Acoustic Equipment	99.2	98.5	98.6	98.9	99.5	99.5	99.5	99.6	99.6	99.4	99.4	99.4	99.1
便携式音响	Portable Acoustics	97.9	98.6	98.1	97.8	97.4	97.8	97.8	97.8	98.0	97.7	98.2	98.1	97.7
其他	Others	99.5	99.5	100.0	100.0	99.9	99.8	99.9	99.8	99.2	99.0	99.1	99.0	99.0
3.音像器材	Music and Video Equipments	99.4	99.5	99.2	99.2	98.9	99.0	99.4	99.5	99.6	99.5	99.3	99.5	99.7
专业音响器材	Specialized Acoustic Apparatus	99.8	99.8	99.8	99.8	99.6	99.8	99.7	99.9	100.1	100.0	99.8	99.8	99.8
专业声像器材	Specialized Acoustic Image Apparatus	98.7	99.0	98.2	98.2	97.8	98.0	98.9	98.8	99.0	98.8	98.6	99.0	99.6
六、文化办公用品	**Cultural and Office Applicances**	**96.2**	**95.5**	**95.3**	**95.5**	**95.4**	**96.6**	**96.7**	**96.7**	**96.2**	**96.0**	**96.7**	**97.0**	**97.4**
纸张本册	Paper and Volume	99.7	101.2	100.2	100.1	99.5	99.6	98.8	99.0	99.3	99.7	99.4	99.2	100.5
文具	Stationery	98.7	98.3	98.6	98.5	98.6	98.8	98.6	98.8	98.3	98.7	98.8	99.4	99.6
电脑及配件	Computer and its Fitting	93.2	92.5	92.3	92.3	92.2	94.0	94.0	93.9	93.3	92.0	93.4	94.3	94.8
打印机及配件	Printer and its Fitting	96.2	95.8	95.0	94.9	95.0	95.8	96.8	97.0	96.0	96.7	97.0	97.1	97.9
扫描仪	Scanner	99.0	97.2	97.3	98.7	98.9	99.1	99.6	99.6	99.6	99.6	99.5	99.6	99.6
复印机	Xerox Machine	96.3	94.0	94.0	94.0	94.0	97.4	97.9	97.8	97.3	97.1	98.5	97.1	96.9
电子辞典	Electronic Dictionary	97.8	98.0	98.2	97.9	98.9	98.8	98.7	97.9	96.5	97.3	97.2	97.3	97.3
计算器	Calculator	97.7	96.6	96.9	96.8	96.7	96.8	96.7	96.7	96.6	99.5	99.4	99.5	100.2
教学设备	Teaching Equipment	98.3	95.6	95.9	97.6	97.6	98.2	98.6	98.7	98.8	99.0	99.7	99.7	99.8
其他	Others	100.1	100.2	100.4	100.2	100.2	100.3	100.1	99.8	99.7	100.1	100.2	100.1	100.2
七、日用品	**Articles for Daily Use**	**100.6**	**100.5**	**100.6**	**100.6**	**100.5**	**100.7**	**100.5**	**100.4**	**100.7**	**100.8**	**100.7**	**100.5**	**100.6**
1.日用百货	General Merchandise for Daily Use	100.6	100.0	100.6	100.4	100.2	100.6	100.2	100.4	101.0	100.8	100.8	100.8	100.9
自行车	Bicycle	101.3	100.5	101.4	101.5	101.6	101.3	101.4	101.9	100.9	101.6	101.3	101.1	100.6
雨具	Rain Gear	99.6	99.5	99.5	98.7	98.6	98.5	98.8	99.1	99.9	100.5	100.6	100.5	100.8
剃须刀具	Shaver	101.2	100.2	100.2	101.0	101.3	101.4	101.7	101.5	101.8	101.7	101.6	101.0	101.1
电池	Battery	97.5	98.2	98.9	99.1	96.7	97.4	94.0	96.3	98.1	97.5	97.7	97.9	98.4
卫生纸	Tissue Paper	103.1	102.7	102.8	102.9	103.2	103.2	103.6	102.1	104.4	102.6	102.6	103.1	103.4
卫生巾	Sanitary Towel	98.3	96.8	98.2	96.5	96.7	98.7	98.2	98.6	99.3	99.1	99.7	98.9	99.2
其他	Others	101.0	101.3	101.2	100.9	100.6	100.3	100.3	100.3	100.3	101.2	100.4	102.0	102.5
2.日用杂品	Sundry Articles	100.3	99.8	100.1	100.1	100.1	100.4	100.3	100.2	100.3	100.7	100.4	100.4	100.9
茶具	Tea Set	99.4	99.4	99.4	99.5	99.5	99.3	99.3	99.0	99.1	99.5	99.3	99.6	100.0
餐具	Tableware	100.0	99.0	99.5	99.1	99.4	99.9	99.9	99.8	100.4	100.6	100.7	100.5	101.6
厨具	Kitchen Utensils	101.1	100.4	100.7	100.8	101.0	101.4	101.2	101.2	100.9	101.2	101.1	101.3	101.3
其他	Others	100.4	100.6	100.9	101.1	100.5	100.6	100.5	100.2	100.5	101.5	99.4	99.3	99.7
3.洗涤用品	Washing Articles	101.0	101.3	101.4	100.9	100.7	100.6	101.0	100.9	101.2	101.2	101.1	100.8	101.0

7-23 续表 5 continued

商品类别及品名	Commodity Category and Commodity Name	全年 Annural	1月 January	2月 February	3月 March	4月 April	5月 May	6月 June	7月 July	8月 August	9月 September	10月 October	11月 November	12月 December
		（以2005年同期价格为100）												
洗衣粉	Washing Powder	101.7	103.0	102.4	101.1	100.6	100.4	101.4	101.4	102.3	102.3	101.9	101.6	102.3
肥皂类	Soap	100.2	100.5	100.3	100.6	100.1	99.8	99.9	99.9	100.3	100.3	100.2	100.2	100.0
牙膏	Toothpaste	100.9	100.0	101.0	100.8	100.8	101.4	101.3	101.2	100.9	100.9	101.0	100.7	100.9
清洁洗涤剂	Cleaning Agent	100.8	101.0	101.2	101.2	101.3	101.1	101.0	100.7	100.7	100.7	100.7	100.3	100.0
4.其他日用品	Other Articles for Daily Use	100.4	100.7	100.3	100.8	100.7	101.1	100.4	99.9	100.3	100.3	100.3	99.9	99.8
燃气灶具	Gas-oven	103.7	103.6	103.6	104.7	103.5	104.3	103.2	103.8	103.9	103.7	104.0	103.2	103.2
儿童玩具	Children's Toy	100.5	102.9	102.3	102.2	101.3	100.9	100.3	100.0	99.5	99.4	99.2	98.9	98.9
照明器具	Illumination Utensil	99.4	99.3	99.8	98.4	99.2	99.2	99.2	99.2	99.3	100.5	99.4	99.3	100.2
钟表眼镜及配件	Clocks, Glasses and their Fittings	98.6	97.2	97.2	97.5	98.2	98.3	98.5	98.8	98.7	99.1	99.4	99.7	100.1
日用普通饰品	Common Ornament for Daily Use	99.9	99.1	100.2	100.1	98.5	100.8	99.2	100.6	100.1	100.5	100.1	99.6	99.8
日用皮革制品	Leatherware for Daily Use	98.5	98.7	96.4	99.4	101.0	101.5	100.3	96.0	98.6	97.0	98.8	97.9	96.2
其他	Others	99.1	100.1	98.2	99.5	100.5	100.8	100.3	96.9	99.8	98.7	99.5	98.2	97.2
八、体育娱乐用品	**Sports and Recreation Articles**	**99.1**	**98.8**	**98.8**	**98.7**	**98.9**	**98.9**	**98.9**	**99.0**	**99.4**	**99.4**	**99.6**	**99.5**	**99.5**
1.体育用品	Sports Articles	99.2	99.0	98.9	99.0	99.2	98.9	99.0	99.1	99.3	99.5	99.7	99.4	99.5
球类	Ball	98.5	98.6	98.1	97.8	97.9	97.7	98.1	98.3	98.7	98.7	99.2	99.2	99.1
棋牌	Chess and Cards	101.1	102.1	102.2	102.2	101.9	101.7	100.9	100.7	100.6	100.6	100.6	100.2	99.8
健身器材	Exercise Machine	98.9	98.0	98.2	98.5	98.9	98.5	98.9	99.0	99.2	99.6	99.7	99.3	99.6
2.娱乐用品	Recreation Articles	99.0	98.6	98.6	98.5	98.6	99.0	98.8	98.9	99.4	99.3	99.5	99.5	99.6
游艺器材	Entertainment Apparatus	97.9	99.2	99.2	99.0	98.2	97.8	97.4	96.4	96.7	96.8	97.9	97.6	98.0
照相器材	Photographic Apparatus	98.6	97.8	97.2	97.0	97.5	98.3	98.3	98.9	99.8	99.4	99.4	99.5	99.9
乐器	Musical Instrument	100.9	99.7	100.9	100.8	101.0	101.2	101.0	101.1	101.2	101.4	101.2	101.3	100.2
九、交通、通信用品	**Transportation and Communication Appliances**	**93.5**	**92.4**	**92.7**	**93.3**	**93.0**	**93.3**	**93.6**	**93.6**	**94.2**	**94.0**	**94.0**	**94.1**	**93.3**
1.交通运输机械	Transportation Machine	98.3	97.9	98.2	98.6	98.6	98.8	98.9	98.7	98.7	98.2	98.1	98.0	96.9
轿车	Car	97.1	96.4	97.4	98.2	98.0	97.8	97.8	97.4	97.2	96.5	96.8	96.5	94.6
客车	Bus	97.9	96.3	96.4	97.3	98.2	98.2	99.1	99.0	99.0	97.7	97.7	98.1	98.2
货车	Truck	99.4	100.5	100.2	99.3	99.3	99.8	99.7	99.6	99.7	99.6	98.5	98.3	97.9
摩托车	Motorcycle	100.0	98.5	99.2	99.9	99.7	100.4	100.3	100.0	100.8	100.6	101.1	100.6	98.9
其他	Others	98.9	99.5	98.7	98.7	98.7	99.0	98.9	98.9	98.8	98.8	98.8	98.8	99.0
2.通信器材	Telecommunications Facilities	82.9	81.5	81.6	82.5	81.4	81.8	82.2	82.7	83.9	84.3	84.5	84.9	84.7
固定电话机	Telephone	97.5	96.9	97.0	96.5	98.1	97.8	97.7	97.6	97.4	98.2	98.3	98.2	96.9
移动电话机	Mobile Phone	74.6	73.6	73.7	74.6	72.6	73.1	73.5	74.0	75.7	76.0	76.1	76.6	76.4
传真机	Fax Machine	99.3	99.0	98.9	99.2	99.1	99.9	99.9	99.9	99.3	99.3	99.1	98.9	98.9
其他	Others	97.1	98.8	98.8	98.9	97.9	96.1	96.1	96.1	96.1	96.2	96.7	96.7	96.9
十、家具	**Furniture**	**100.5**	**100.6**	**100.8**	**100.4**	**100.1**	**99.9**	**100.1**	**100.1**	**100.3**	**101.0**	**100.8**	**100.8**	**100.6**
柜	Cabinet	100.8	102.0	102.2	101.6	100.5	100.5	100.2	99.9	100.4	100.7	100.6	100.4	100.1
床	Bed	101.6	101.2	102.1	101.6	101.5	101.5	101.7	102.0	101.8	102.1	102.2	101.5	100.4
桌	Desk	100.8	101.0	101.5	100.7	100.8	100.5	100.3	100.5	100.9	101.0	100.9	101.2	100.8
椅	Chair	100.9	100.8	100.9	100.8	100.7	100.7	100.8	100.3	99.9	101.2	101.6	101.7	101.6
沙发	Sofa	98.9	98.5	98.6	98.6	98.2	98.0	98.5	98.3	98.8	99.8	99.4	99.7	99.9
其他	Others	100.6	101.3	97.9	98.0	98.6	98.1	100.0	101.5	101.5	103.4	101.6	101.5	104.1

7-23 续表 6 continued

商品类别及品名	Commodity Category and Commodity Name	(以2005年同期价格为100)												
		全年 Annural	1月 January	2月 February	3月 March	4月 April	5月 May	6月 June	7月 July	8月 August	9月 September	10月 October	11月 November	12月 December
十一、化妆品	**Cosmetics**	**98.6**	**98.7**	**98.3**	**98.2**	**98.4**	**98.4**	**98.5**	**98.4**	**98.5**	**98.6**	**98.9**	**99.0**	**99.5**
护肤品	Skincare Products	99.5	99.5	99.9	99.6	99.7	99.6	99.4	99.3	99.4	99.3	100.1	99.3	98.6
美容化妆品	Facial Beautifiers	95.9	96.4	95.0	94.4	94.4	94.5	95.4	95.5	95.7	95.8	96.0	97.6	100.3
护发美容品	Protects Sends the Beauty Products	99.3	99.6	99.0	99.6	99.7	99.6	99.4	98.9	99.0	98.9	99.4	99.3	99.2
清洁化妆用品	Cleaning Toiletware	99.4	98.7	98.4	98.8	99.2	99.6	99.5	99.6	99.8	99.8	99.8	99.8	100.0
药物美容用品	Medicinal Cosmetics	99.2	99.5	99.4	99.0	99.4	99.3	99.2	99.1	98.9	99.2	98.9	98.9	99.6
十二、金银珠宝	**Gold, Silver and Jewelry**	**113.1**	**103.7**	**105.3**	**106.2**	**109.6**	**114.3**	**115.8**	**116.3**	**117.9**	**117.6**	**117.4**	**117.1**	**115.6**
金饰品	Gold	119.9	108.1	111.0	111.9	116.1	123.9	124.5	124.7	126.2	125.4	124.1	122.7	120.1
银饰品	Silver	106.6	99.6	100.5	101.6	102.3	103.6	103.9	106.5	110.7	111.4	112.9	112.6	113.9
铂金饰品	Platinum	112.2	101.9	102.8	103.4	108.0	112.5	115.8	116.1	117.0	117.0	117.4	118.0	116.1
其他	Others	100.4	99.1	99.2	100.8	100.7	99.9	100.4	100.2	100.8	100.8	101.0	100.9	101.0
十三、中西药品及医疗保健用品	**Traditional Chinese and Western Medicines and Healthcare Articles**	**99.5**	**99.6**	**99.6**	**99.6**	**99.5**	**99.5**	**99.6**	**100.1**	**99.9**	**99.4**	**99.3**	**99.2**	**99.2**
1.医疗器具及用品	Medical Facilities and Goods	96.9	94.9	95.7	97.9	98.2	98.6	98.6	98.5	98.6	98.5	94.7	94.5	94.3
医疗器具及用品	Medical Facilities and Goods	96.9	94.9	95.7	97.9	98.2	98.6	98.6	98.5	98.6	98.5	94.7	94.5	94.3
2.中药材及中成药	Herbs and Ready-made Traditional Chinese Medicine	100.2	99.4	99.3	99.6	99.7	99.4	99.7	100.2	100.8	100.1	101.4	101.3	101.4
中药材	Herbs	101.2	97.0	96.7	97.3	98.2	98.2	100.4	101.8	102.7	102.4	106.5	106.8	107.1
中成药	Ready-made Traditional Chinese Medicine	99.5	101.2	101.2	101.3	100.8	100.2	99.2	99.1	99.5	98.5	97.8	97.4	97.4
3.西药	Western Medicine	99.3	99.9	99.9	99.6	99.3	99.5	99.5	100.2	99.6	99.0	98.5	98.4	98.4
抗微生物药	Anti-microorganism Medicine	101.1	99.8	99.8	99.8	99.8	99.9	100.4	103.5	103.0	102.0	101.6	101.9	101.6
消化系统用药	Alimentary System Medicine	99.1	98.1	98.1	98.3	97.9	98.5	99.3	100.4	99.1	99.6	100.3	99.7	100.3
呼吸系统用药	Respiratory System Medicine	99.8	99.7	99.6	99.3	99.3	99.3	100.2	100.2	100.0	100.3	100.1	100.1	99.3
解热镇痛及非甾体抗炎药	Allays a Fever the Analgesia and the Non-steroid Body Anti-inflammatory Agent	99.0	100.7	100.4	100.0	99.6	100.7	98.8	98.1	98.1	96.7	98.0	98.4	98.6
抗肿瘤药	Anti-neoplastic Drug	98.6	100.9	100.8	100.6	99.9	99.9	98.4	98.4	98.1	98.1	96.3	96.3	95.6
激素及调节内分泌功能药	Hormone and Adjustment Internal Secretion Function Medicine	97.1	99.0	99.3	98.5	98.5	98.5	97.8	98.0	97.7	95.5	93.4	94.3	94.8
循环系统用药	Circulating System Medicine	100.0	100.1	100.2	99.7	98.4	98.3	99.6	99.7	100.3	100.6	101.9	100.3	100.8
神经系统用药	Nerve System Medicine	98.9	102.0	102.0	101.3	101.2	101.2	101.3	101.3	98.3	97.3	93.7	93.7	94.0
专科用药	Junior Medicine	98.8	100.2	100.3	100.2	100.0	99.8	100.3	100.2	99.9	97.9	95.8	95.6	95.6
其他	Others	98.3	100.3	100.5	98.3	97.9	98.7	98.4	98.0	98.0	98.0	97.6	97.3	97.2
4.保健品及器具	Healthcare Equipment	100.1	100.8	100.8	100.4	100.3	100.3	100.5	99.9	99.9	99.6	99.6	99.6	99.4
保健器具	Health Protection Equipment	99.2	100.3	100.0	99.8	99.7	99.6	99.4	99.2	99.3	99.0	98.1	98.1	97.8
滋补保健用品	Tonic and Health Products	100.5	101.1	101.1	100.7	100.6	100.6	101.0	100.2	100.1	99.8	100.1	100.2	100.1

7-23 续表 7 continued

商品类别及品名	Commodity Category and Commodity Name	（以2005年同期价格为100）												
		全年 Annural	1月 January	2月 February	3月 March	4月 April	5月 May	6月 June	7月 July	8月 August	9月 September	10月 October	11月 November	12月 December
十四、书报杂志及电子出版物	**Books, Newspapers, Magazines and Electronic Publications**	**101.5**	**101.5**	**101.7**	**101.7**	**101.8**	**101.9**	**101.9**	**101.9**	**101.9**	**101.0**	**101.0**	**100.9**	**100.8**
1.教材及参考书	Teaching Materials and Reference Books	102.5	103.2	103.2	103.4	103.4	103.4	103.3	103.3	103.6	100.9	100.7	100.7	100.8
工具书	Tool Book	101.6	102.5	102.5	102.5	102.5	102.3	102.3	102.3	101.5	100.2	100.2	100.2	100.3
教材	Teaching Material	101.0	101.2	101.2	101.6	101.6	101.6	101.6	101.6	102.1	100.2	99.9	99.9	99.9
参考书	Reference Book	105.9	107.6	107.6	107.8	107.8	107.8	107.6	107.6	108.3	102.5	102.5	102.5	102.6
教育软件	Educational Software	100.0	100.0	100.0	100.0	100.0	100.0	100.0	100.0	100.0	100.0	100.0	100.0	100.0
2.书报杂志	Books, Newspapers, Magazines	102.5	102.5	102.5	102.7	102.7	102.6	102.6	102.6	102.5	102.4	102.4	102.3	102.2
书籍	Books	101.4	101.4	101.4	101.7	101.7	101.6	101.6	101.6	101.4	101.2	101.2	101.0	100.7
报纸	Newspapers	105.8	105.8	105.8	105.8	105.8	105.8	105.8	105.8	105.8	105.8	105.8	105.8	105.7
杂志	Magazines	100.1	100.1	100.1	100.1	100.1	100.1	100.1	100.1	100.1	100.1	100.1	100.1	100.3
3.电子音像制品	Electronic Publications	99.2	98.6	99.1	98.6	99.1	99.3	99.3	99.3	99.3	99.5	99.6	99.4	99.0
音响光盘和磁带	Acoustic Light Disk and Tape	98.7	98.4	99.3	97.9	98.9	98.6	98.6	98.6	98.6	98.7	98.7	98.9	99.0
录像磁带和视盘	Video Tape and Disk	100.5	98.9	99.4	99.5	100.3	100.9	101.1	101.1	101.0	101.3	101.2	101.3	100.4
计算机软件	Computer Software	98.4	98.5	98.6	98.4	98.3	98.5	98.3	98.5	98.5	98.7	99.0	98.1	97.7
十五、燃料	**Fuels**	**110.0**	**110.4**	**110.8**	**109.0**	**110.1**	**110.6**	**113.3**	**110.9**	**108.7**	**109.9**	**109.2**	**108.2**	**108.6**
1.煤炭及制品	Coal and Related Products	105.5	108.3	107.5	105.4	105.5	105.5	105.0	104.7	105.0	105.8	105.8	104.0	104.1
原煤	Raw Coal	105.3	107.4	106.1	106.7	104.9	105.0	104.6	104.2	105.1	105.4	105.8	104.6	103.6
煤制品	Coal Products	105.8	109.4	109.2	103.8	106.2	106.1	105.5	105.3	104.9	106.2	105.8	103.4	104.7
2.石油及制品	Petroleum and Related Products	111.4	111.2	112.0	110.3	111.8	112.4	116.2	113.0	109.9	111.2	110.3	109.5	110.0
液化石油气	Liquefiled Petroleum Gas	114.1	122.8	128.2	121.4	122.0	117.3	113.9	110.7	107.2	114.3	108.6	103.1	106.0
管道燃气	Pipelined Gas	100.0	100.0	100.0	100.0	100.0	100.0	100.0	100.0	100.0	100.0	100.0	100.0	100.0
汽油	Gasoline	117.0	114.8	114.9	112.6	114.2	117.8	127.0	121.3	116.2	116.1	116.4	116.4	116.4
柴油	Diesel Oil	116.4	113.5	112.8	113.4	117.8	118.0	124.1	119.3	115.0	115.3	115.3	116.7	116.1
其他	Others	102.3	99.8	101.4	101.3	101.9	102.0	102.6	102.8	102.6	103.4	103.4	103.1	103.7
十六、建筑材料及五金电料	**Building Materials and Hardware**	**103.0**	**100.9**	**101.6**	**101.6**	**101.6**	**102.0**	**102.2**	**102.3**	**103.1**	**104.6**	**104.7**	**105.4**	**105.7**
1.建筑装璜材料	Building and Decoration Materials	103.0	100.7	101.2	101.3	101.5	102.3	102.6	102.9	103.1	104.3	104.6	105.4	105.8
木材	Wood	103.9	101.4	101.4	102.0	102.2	102.1	102.3	102.9	104.5	105.3	105.8	108.5	108.7
木地板	Wood Floor	107.0	108.2	108.3	107.3	109.1	108.6	103.7	104.8	105.0	106.7	106.2	107.7	109.2
钢材	Steel Products	98.6	92.4	93.3	92.0	92.9	96.7	100.7	101.4	100.3	102.0	104.2	104.2	104.8
砖	Brick	105.7	103.6	103.9	104.1	103.8	105.7	106.1	105.9	107.0	107.8	107.4	106.5	107.0
水泥	Cement	100.6	97.9	98.0	98.6	99.5	100.0	100.8	100.4	100.1	102.0	102.6	103.3	103.6
涂料	Coating Material	101.2	100.9	102.2	101.9	101.6	101.4	101.9	102.0	101.8	100.6	99.6	100.0	100.4
胶合板	Plywood	103.5	100.8	101.4	101.9	102.0	101.9	102.5	103.1	103.4	104.9	105.1	107.1	107.6
玻璃	Glass	103.0	102.2	102.1	102.3	102.1	102.5	102.5	103.3	103.3	103.9	103.9	103.8	103.8
粘胶	Rayon	102.4	100.5	100.5	101.2	101.1	101.4	102.4	102.9	103.0	103.8	103.5	104.2	104.8
油漆	Paint	102.9	98.0	101.4	102.3	100.8	100.9	101.2	102.7	102.6	106.3	106.3	106.0	106.0
其他	Others	103.8	105.2	105.4	105.0	105.3	105.5	103.9	101.1	101.3	101.3	103.6	104.0	104.1
2.五金电料	Hardware	103.0	101.3	102.4	102.2	101.8	101.7	101.6	101.3	103.0	105.1	104.8	105.4	105.5
五金工具	Hardware Tools	101.5	102.0	103.1	102.2	101.3	100.9	101.3	100.5	100.5	102.2	102.0	101.2	100.6
电工电料	Electrical Engineering and Electrical Materials	103.2	100.1	102.6	101.9	101.5	101.6	99.9	99.1	104.3	107.9	106.1	107.0	107.0
水暖器材	Heating Equipment	103.2	101.9	102.0	102.2	102.2	102.1	102.4	102.4	102.8	103.7	104.4	105.9	106.4
其他	Others	105.4	100.9	101.6	102.7	102.4	101.9	104.8	106.3	106.5	109.1	109.1	109.0	110.1

7-24 农村商品零售价格指数
Rural Retail Price Index

商品类别及品名	Commodity Category and Commodity Name	（以2005年同期价格为100）												
		全年 Annural	1月 January	2月 February	3月 March	4月 April	5月 May	6月 June	7月 July	8月 August	9月 September	10月 October	11月 November	12月 December
商品零售价格总指数	**Genaral Retail Price Index**	**100.9**	**100.9**	**100.0**	**99.8**	**100.4**	**100.7**	**100.8**	**100.1**	**100.3**	**101.0**	**101.2**	**102.0**	**103.3**
一、食品	**Food**	**102.5**	**105.2**	**101.9**	**101.0**	**102.5**	**102.2**	**101.6**	**99.1**	**100.1**	**102.3**	**101.8**	**104.3**	**108.3**
1.粮食	Grain	102.7	96.9	96.6	97.1	98.6	100.8	101.1	103.6	104.2	106.2	107.1	109.4	111.4
大米	Rice	111.3	101.8	100.4	101.6	104.5	110.2	109.5	115.7	118.6	119.0	120.2	117.2	117.2
面粉	Flour	98.7	92.3	91.6	92.4	94.7	96.0	96.5	98.4	98.6	101.8	103.0	109.1	111.9
粮食制品	Grain Products	101.0	99.7	99.7	99.6	98.7	99.8	100.3	100.8	100.8	101.4	101.7	103.8	105.4
其他	Others	104.6	99.6	103.6	102.2	102.3	103.9	104.4	105.4	103.9	106.8	106.8	105.4	110.5
2.淀粉	Starches	106.9	106.5	103.2	102.7	105.6	102.9	106.6	108.4	109.5	109.1	109.8	111.2	107.7
淀粉	Starches	106.9	106.5	103.2	102.7	105.6	102.9	106.6	108.4	109.5	109.1	109.8	111.2	107.7
3.干豆类及豆制品	Beans and Beans Products	99.3	99.2	99.8	96.7	96.0	97.7	97.9	98.7	99.7	99.7	100.0	102.1	103.9
干豆	Beans	101.9	99.9	100.8	97.2	97.3	100.4	100.9	102.3	103.5	103.2	104.1	105.2	108.7
豆制品	Beans Products	96.9	98.6	98.9	96.3	94.9	95.3	95.3	95.3	96.2	96.5	96.5	99.3	99.6
4.油脂	Oil and Fat	99.3	92.9	92.7	92.7	93.4	96.7	97.3	98.5	100.7	102.1	104.3	108.5	114.2
食用植物油	Edible Vegetable Oil	100.4	93.1	93.3	93.8	94.6	97.8	98.5	99.5	101.8	103.6	105.5	109.4	115.3
植物油制品	Plant Oil Products	102.7	97.8	97.7	97.6	97.7	102.1	102.1	103.7	104.1	104.4	104.6	107.5	113.0
其他	Others	82.7	82.0	77.4	74.7	74.8	76.2	76.9	79.1	82.6	82.5	90.6	100.4	104.6
5.肉禽及其制品	Meal, Poultry and their Products	95.9	93.7	91.8	89.2	88.6	87.2	87.8	90.0	95.0	98.0	103.4	111.9	118.9
（1）食用畜肉及副产品	Edible Livestock Meat and their	94.9	93.2	90.3	86.5	84.6	84.3	85.1	86.8	92.3	96.6	104.9	116.2	124.9
猪肉	Pork	90.0	87.5	82.9	78.3	76.2	76.0	77.2	80.2	88.0	93.7	105.0	120.6	131.0
牛肉	Beef	106.7	110.5	108.8	108.1	109.4	108.8	105.9	104.5	103.6	103.3	106.2	104.2	107.8
羊肉	Mutton	112.3	114.7	115.7	114.6	112.2	113.0	111.0	110.6	107.2	107.4	109.9	111.6	119.8
畜肉副产品	Livestock Meat By-products	93.9	91.0	92.0	89.3	87.7	85.1	89.4	87.7	90.6	95.6	97.3	108.3	117.0
其他	Others	98.1	102.1	102.9	96.5	83.9	83.2	83.7	88.1	97.7	98.6	104.7	120.0	121.6
（2）禽	Poultry	96.8	90.7	90.0	88.3	88.9	84.6	87.3	93.1	100.9	103.6	106.8	113.4	121.0
鸡	Chicken	97.9	90.5	89.3	87.5	88.6	83.9	87.9	95.1	103.8	107.7	110.3	115.1	125.0
鸭	Duck	92.6	91.8	89.2	89.4	91.6	90.4	86.8	86.9	92.1	91.5	91.0	106.3	106.0
其他	Others	94.0	90.8	94.8	92.0	87.7	83.7	84.6	87.4	93.3	92.9	102.0	110.1	114.1
（3）肉禽加工制品	Meal and Poultry Processing Products	97.8	97.4	97.4	96.7	98.4	96.8	95.2	95.5	96.9	96.9	97.1	101.2	103.7
畜肉制品	Livestock Meat Products	98.7	97.7	97.9	98.4	98.2	97.2	96.2	97.1	98.6	98.4	99.0	102.2	103.6
禽制品	Poultry Products	96.3	96.9	96.6	94.2	98.8	96.1	93.6	93.1	94.3	94.5	94.2	99.9	103.7
6.蛋	Eggs	96.2	93.3	84.9	88.6	89.5	89.6	87.0	90.3	95.4	99.6	107.2	112.1	119.7
鲜蛋	Fresh Eggs	95.3	91.9	82.7	86.7	87.7	87.5	84.4	88.6	94.4	99.3	107.9	113.4	122.0
蛋制品	Egg Products	102.7	102.6	100.2	100.9	101.0	103.5	104.8	101.7	102.0	102.2	102.9	104.0	106.1
7.水产品	Aquatic Product	102.0	99.2	98.3	99.1	98.8	99.9	101.9	102.9	103.4	104.6	105.7	105.7	105.5
（1）鱼	Fish	100.7	98.6	96.7	97.4	96.9	98.0	100.0	101.3	101.7	103.7	105.2	105.1	104.6
淡水鱼	Freshwater Fish	98.5	98.1	94.3	93.7	94.8	96.9	99.2	100.9	101.6	101.2	100.6	101.5	100.1
海水鱼	Seawater Fish	104.1	99.5	100.4	103.1	100.2	99.8	101.2	102.0	101.9	107.6	112.7	110.7	111.6

7-24 续表 1 continued

商品类别及品名	Commodity Category and Commodity Name	（以2005年同期价格为100）												
		全年 Annural	1月 January	2月 February	3月 March	4月 April	5月 May	6月 June	7月 July	8 月 August	9 月 September	10 月 October	11月 November	12月 December
（2）其他水产品	Other Aquatic Product	105.9	101.0	102.9	104.2	104.2	105.3	107.5	107.3	108.1	107.2	107.2	107.5	108.2
虾蟹类	Shrimp and Crab	107.1	101.3	104.7	106.6	106.1	108.2	109.3	108.7	109.1	107.9	107.7	107.4	108.6
其他	Others	103.7	100.4	99.9	100.2	100.8	100.4	104.4	105.0	106.3	106.1	106.4	107.7	107.4
8.菜	Vegetable	107.7	148.7	123.5	118.4	122.8	114.1	102.4	86.2	94.5	107.3	88.0	86.7	98.0
鲜菜	Fresh Vegetable	108.8	159.2	126.8	120.3	125.7	116.2	102.8	83.4	93.5	108.6	85.7	83.8	97.1
干菜及菜制品	Dried Vegetable and Vegetable Products	99.7	100.2	100.2	100.8	100.3	99.9	97.6	97.0	98.2	99.2	99.6	100.3	103.3
薯类	Potato	112.0	114.7	121.1	135.5	135.9	119.2	112.8	104.4	99.6	109.4	95.7	98.6	99.1
9.调味品	Flavoring	103.4	105.6	103.5	102.9	102.9	103.2	103.5	104.9	103.8	103.3	102.3	102.1	102.8
盐	Salt	111.0	120.6	112.2	110.0	109.2	111.3	113.5	115.9	112.2	110.8	107.0	106.3	105.7
酱油	Soy Sauce	100.5	99.8	99.8	99.8	100.0	99.8	99.8	100.9	100.9	100.9	100.9	100.9	102.7
醋	Vinegar	101.3	100.2	100.2	100.3	100.8	100.4	100.2	101.8	101.8	101.8	101.8	101.7	103.9
味精	Aginomoto	100.9	101.2	101.2	100.9	100.7	100.3	100.0	100.8	100.8	100.8	101.3	101.3	101.7
其他	Others	98.0	99.9	99.9	99.3	99.9	99.7	98.2	97.8	96.9	96.2	96.0	96.0	96.0
10.糖	Carbohydrate	110.6	102.7	107.2	109.2	110.3	110.7	110.0	112.1	112.1	113.6	113.7	113.9	112.3
食糖	Sugar	124.5	106.4	117.8	122.2	124.8	125.4	123.7	126.8	126.5	130.6	130.9	131.2	126.8
糖果	Sweet	102.1	100.5	100.7	101.3	101.5	101.7	101.6	103.2	103.2	103.2	103.4	103.3	101.1
巧克力制品	Chocolate Products	100.7	99.6	100.1	100.6	100.5	99.7	99.4	100.0	100.0	100.0	100.0	100.3	108.1
糖类小食品	Little Carbohydrate Food	101.3	99.9	100.4	100.4	100.4	100.4	100.4	101.6	101.9	101.9	101.9	102.3	104.1
11.干鲜瓜果	Dried and Fresh Melons and Fruits	125.3	129.4	132.5	132.1	145.5	155.9	171.5	138.3	112.6	102.7	100.6	97.7	97.9
鲜瓜果	Fresh Fruits	131.0	135.4	139.7	139.0	156.6	171.5	195.2	149.9	114.9	102.1	98.8	95.0	95.2
干（坚）果	Dried Fruits	105.5	108.0	106.0	106.6	105.3	102.4	102.1	102.1	104.6	105.0	106.9	107.8	108.8
12.糕点饼干面包	Cake, Biscuit and Bread	101.1	101.0	101.0	101.0	101.1	99.8	99.9	100.7	101.3	101.3	101.3	101.3	103.1
糕点	Cake	100.8	102.1	102.1	102.0	102.2	99.6	99.7	100.0	100.0	100.0	100.0	100.0	102.2
饼干	Biscuit	101.6	100.1	100.2	100.1	100.4	99.9	100.1	101.3	103.1	103.1	103.0	103.1	105.2
面包	Bread	100.6	100.0	100.0	100.0	100.0	100.0	100.0	101.2	101.2	101.2	101.2	101.2	101.5
13.液体乳及乳制品	Liquid Milk and their Products	100.6	100.4	100.7	100.8	100.7	99.9	99.8	100.0	100.0	100.1	100.1	100.0	104.2
巴氏杀菌奶或消毒奶	Pasteurization Milk or Disinfection Milk	100.7	99.8	99.8	100.5	100.0	100.0	100.0	100.0	100.1	100.2	100.1	100.0	108.3
酸奶	Leben	98.7	97.5	97.5	97.0	99.0	99.0	99.1	99.2	99.0	99.0	99.0	98.8	100.2
奶粉	Milk Powder	100.6	101.3	101.2	101.0	100.5	100.3	99.9	100.2	100.2	100.2	100.2	100.5	101.9
其他	Others	102.4	104.3	107.5	107.2	106.7	100.1	100.1	100.9	100.9	100.9	101.3	100.0	99.8
14.在外用膳食品	Outward Dinner	101.3	101.6	101.2	101.2	101.0	101.1	101.0	101.0	101.0	100.9	101.0	101.9	103.2
主食	Staple Food	100.7	99.9	99.9	100.0	99.9	99.9	99.5	99.6	99.6	99.6	100.0	103.1	106.9
炒菜	Hot Dish	101.6	102.5	102.0	102.0	101.6	101.6	101.5	101.5	101.4	101.3	101.3	101.5	101.4
地方小吃	Local Snack	101.6	101.3	100.7	100.7	100.9	101.3	101.8	102.2	102.2	102.2	101.8	100.8	102.9
15.其他食品	Other Foods	101.2	100.9	101.0	100.7	100.5	100.7	100.8	101.6	102.0	101.7	101.5	101.5	102.0
其他食品	Other Foods	101.2	100.9	101.0	100.7	100.5	100.7	100.8	101.6	102.0	101.7	101.5	101.5	102.0
二、饮料、烟酒	**Beverages, Tobacco, Liquor**	**100.8**	**100.3**	**100.2**	**100.3**	**100.4**	**100.5**	**100.4**	**100.8**	**100.9**	**100.9**	**101.2**	**101.5**	**102.7**
1.茶及饮料	Tea and Beverages	100.9	100.2	100.2	100.4	100.4	100.3	100.3	101.3	101.4	101.3	101.4	101.4	102.3
（1）茶叶	Tea	100.0	100.0	100.0	100.5	100.2	99.9	99.9	99.9	99.9	99.9	99.9	99.9	99.9

7-24 续表 2 continued

商品类别及品名	Commodity Category and Commodity Name	全年 Annural	1月 January	2月 February	3月 March	4月 April	5月 May	6月 June	7月 July	8月 August	9月 September	10月 October	11月 November	12月 December
		（以2005年同期价格为100）												
茶叶	Tea	100.0	100.0	100.0	100.5	100.2	99.9	99.9	99.9	99.9	99.9	99.9	99.9	99.9
（2）饮料	Beverages	101.5	100.3	100.4	100.4	100.5	100.6	100.6	102.1	102.3	102.2	102.3	102.3	103.9
固体饮料	Solid Beverages	101.2	100.9	101.4	101.5	101.8	101.3	100.7	100.5	101.1	101.3	101.3	101.4	101.6
液体饮料	Liquid Beverages	102.2	99.9	99.9	100.0	100.2	100.6	100.8	104.2	104.2	104.0	104.1	104.2	104.9
冷冻饮品	Frozen Beverages	100.4	100.5	100.5	100.0	100.0	100.0	100.0	100.0	100.0	100.0	100.0	100.0	103.9
2.烟草	Tobacco	101.1	100.7	100.8	100.8	101.1	101.2	101.0	101.1	101.1	101.1	101.1	101.2	102.0
国产卷烟	Domestic Cigarette	101.3	100.9	101.1	101.0	101.4	101.5	101.2	101.3	101.3	101.3	101.3	101.3	102.3
进口卷烟	Import Cigarette	99.4	99.9	99.8	99.8	99.8	99.8	99.9	98.4	98.4	98.4	98.4	99.8	99.9
其他	Others	99.6	99.1	99.1	99.1	99.1	99.1	99.5	100.0	100.0	99.7	100.0	100.0	100.0
3.酒	Liquor	100.6	100.0	99.7	99.7	99.8	99.9	99.9	100.3	100.5	100.5	101.1	101.8	103.5
白酒	White Spirit	101.0	100.0	99.7	99.9	100.2	100.4	100.6	100.7	101.0	100.6	101.6	102.3	104.7
葡萄酒	Grape	100.8	99.2	99.3	99.5	99.5	99.6	99.7	101.4	101.4	101.4	101.4	103.5	103.6
啤酒	Beer	99.8	100.2	99.6	99.4	99.3	99.0	98.9	99.3	99.4	100.1	100.3	100.8	101.7
其他	Others	100.5	100.9	100.7	100.5	100.2	100.0	100.0	101.0	101.0	100.3	100.3	100.3	100.4
三、服装、鞋帽	**Garments, Footgearand and Hats**	**96.4**	**95.4**	**94.8**	**95.1**	**95.8**	**96.3**	**96.5**	**96.7**	**96.6**	**96.7**	**97.3**	**97.9**	**97.8**
1.服装	Garments	94.8	92.9	92.5	92.9	93.6	94.5	95.0	95.3	95.3	95.4	96.3	97.3	97.4
（1）男式服装	Men's Garments	94.4	90.4	90.0	90.9	92.2	94.2	95.0	95.4	95.5	95.8	97.0	98.4	98.6
大衣	Topcoat	90.5	87.6	85.6	88.4	90.2	91.0	90.9	91.8	91.8	91.9	92.7	92.5	93.0
毛线衣	Woollen Sweater	88.5	80.6	80.6	82.9	84.5	85.1	88.6	91.3	91.3	95.6	95.9	94.9	96.2
夹克衫	Jacket	96.5	93.0	92.2	92.4	92.2	98.3	98.2	98.0	98.0	97.4	98.2	100.8	100.6
衬衫	Shirt	91.8	85.8	88.6	89.5	90.2	91.9	91.9	91.9	91.8	91.9	94.1	96.6	99.0
T恤衫	T-shirt	101.3	99.9	100.1	100.1	100.3	99.2	99.3	99.2	100.3	102.1	104.1	105.3	105.6
裤子	Trousers	92.8	91.1	88.4	90.3	90.2	93.3	93.4	93.2	93.1	93.1	95.1	97.2	96.3
西服	Western-style Clothes	95.8	91.3	90.9	90.7	95.8	97.1	97.2	97.2	97.2	97.1	97.7	99.2	99.0
运动衫裤	Gym Suit	100.9	100.1	100.1	100.2	100.1	100.1	100.1	100.0	100.0	100.0	102.1	104.1	104.1
内衣	Underwaist	97.2	91.9	93.2	94.3	94.3	98.7	99.3	99.7	99.8	96.9	98.6	100.6	100.0
羽绒衣	Eider down Outerwear	93.7	92.1	90.1	89.6	90.2	92.7	95.0	96.1	95.8	95.5	95.6	96.3	95.9
其他	Others	92.8	91.7	89.9	89.9	89.9	89.9	94.4	94.4	94.4	94.4	95.0	95.6	95.6
（2）女式服装	Women's Garments	94.3	93.8	93.5	93.6	93.7	93.5	94.0	94.3	94.2	94.1	94.9	96.0	96.0
大衣	Topcoat	90.5	89.5	86.1	86.7	87.8	89.1	92.1	92.1	92.1	92.1	93.1	93.5	93.0
毛线衣	Woollen Sweater	86.7	88.9	89.5	86.4	87.3	84.1	85.3	86.1	86.1	86.1	86.3	86.7	86.7
羽绒衣	Eider down Outerwear	95.0	92.2	92.2	91.9	93.1	94.2	96.2	96.9	96.5	96.5	97.1	96.9	96.5
套装	Coordinates	96.7	100.9	100.9	100.9	94.9	94.9	94.9	94.9	94.7	94.7	95.6	96.5	96.5
衬衫	Shirt	93.6	88.4	88.2	91.2	95.2	98.5	98.1	98.1	98.1	91.8	92.0	92.2	92.4
T恤衫	T-shirt	99.3	100.2	99.8	100.3	100.9	97.8	97.8	97.8	97.8	97.8	99.8	101.0	101.2
裙子	Skirt	91.9	91.3	91.3	91.2	91.6	90.2	89.8	91.6	91.1	90.7	93.1	95.2	96.6
裤子	Trousers	96.9	97.8	98.0	97.8	99.0	98.6	96.0	95.4	95.4	95.4	95.0	97.2	97.2
运动衫裤	Gym Suit	100.1	98.0	98.2	99.5	99.9	99.7	99.5	99.5	99.5	99.5	101.2	103.0	103.0
内衣	Underwaist	96.1	92.1	91.1	93.7	93.7	94.7	94.8	94.9	95.1	99.1	100.4	102.2	102.3
其他	Others	99.0	97.8	97.8	97.8	97.8	98.3	100.0	100.0	100.0	100.0	99.5	100.0	100.0

7-24 续表 3 continued

商品类别及品名	Commodity Category and Commodity Name	（以2005年同期价格为100） 全年 Annural	1月 January	2月 February	3月 March	4月 April	5月 May	6月 June	7月 July	8月 August	9月 September	10月 October	11月 November	12月 December
（3）儿童服装	Children's Garments	97.0	95.9	95.0	95.2	96.0	97.2	97.4	97.5	97.6	97.8	98.2	98.2	98.5
套装	Coordinates	96.7	95.8	94.8	95.1	95.3	96.1	96.9	97.3	97.3	97.4	97.8	98.6	98.8
裤子	Trousers	102.4	99.2	98.4	98.1	101.4	104.4	104.4	104.3	104.3	104.3	105.1	102.4	102.6
裙子	Skirt	91.8	92.1	91.1	91.3	91.3	91.7	91.1	91.1	91.5	92.3	92.0	93.0	93.7
其他	Others	95.1	95.4	95.6	95.6	95.6	96.1	94.9	94.9	94.9	93.8	94.5	95.2	95.2
2.鞋袜帽	Shoes, Socks and Hats	98.1	99.2	98.4	98.4	98.3	98.1	97.9	97.9	97.8	97.9	98.0	98.1	97.5
（1）鞋	Shoes	97.8	99.0	98.1	98.2	98.1	97.8	97.5	97.6	97.4	97.5	97.6	97.8	96.9
男鞋	Men's Shoes	97.4	98.3	98.2	98.0	97.9	97.0	96.8	96.9	96.7	96.9	97.2	97.3	97.8
女鞋	Women's Shoes	95.6	98.2	95.9	95.9	95.5	95.6	95.2	95.3	95.2	95.1	95.1	95.2	95.2
童鞋	Children's Shoes	102.5	101.7	102.2	102.7	103.3	103.3	103.0	103.0	102.9	103.1	103.1	103.4	98.7
（2）袜子	Socks	99.6	99.8	99.6	99.6	99.1	99.7	99.5	99.5	99.5	99.5	99.8	99.9	100.1
男袜	Men's Socks	99.0	99.2	99.0	99.0	99.0	99.0	98.8	98.8	98.8	98.9	99.2	99.3	99.6
女袜	Women's Socks	100.1	100.4	100.2	100.2	99.2	100.3	100.1	100.1	100.1	100.1	100.3	100.5	100.5
（3）帽子	Hats	99.5	99.7	99.4	99.4	99.4	99.5	99.5	99.5	99.5	99.5	99.5	99.6	99.9
男帽	Men's Hats	99.9	99.8	99.8	99.8	99.8	100.0	100.0	100.0	100.0	100.0	100.0	100.0	100.0
女帽	Women's Hats	99.2	99.6	99.0	99.0	99.0	99.0	99.0	99.0	99.0	99.0	99.1	99.2	99.8
3.其他	Others	102.5	99.4	99.3	99.3	103.5	103.8	103.7	103.1	103.5	103.5	103.5	103.5	103.6
领带	Necktie	102.5	99.4	99.3	99.3	103.5	103.8	103.7	103.1	103.5	103.5	103.5	103.5	103.6
四、纺织品	**Textiles**	**100.4**	**99.3**	**100.0**	**100.1**	**100.2**	**100.6**	**100.6**	**100.7**	**100.6**	**100.3**	**100.7**	**100.9**	**101.2**
1.衣着材料	Clothing Materials	100.6	99.6	100.4	100.1	100.1	100.8	100.8	101.0	100.9	100.2	100.8	101.0	101.3
棉布	Cotton Cloth	100.6	99.8	99.8	99.7	99.7	101.0	101.0	101.0	101.0	100.8	100.9	100.8	101.4
棉混纺布	Cotton Textiles Cloth	100.7	100.1	100.3	100.3	100.3	100.4	100.4	100.6	100.6	100.6	101.1	101.5	101.8
化纤布	Chemical Fiber Cloth	101.5	98.0	100.8	100.8	100.8	102.2	102.2	102.4	102.1	101.1	102.3	102.7	102.7
毛线	Knitting Wool	98.8	101.6	100.5	99.4	99.4	98.6	98.6	98.6	98.6	97.4	97.7	97.9	97.8
2.床上用品	Bedclothes	100.2	98.9	99.4	100.2	100.4	100.3	100.3	100.4	100.3	100.5	100.6	100.8	101.0
毛毯	Woollen Blanket	99.7	95.6	97.2	99.5	100.0	99.7	99.9	99.8	99.9	100.2	101.1	101.0	103.1
被子	Quilt	100.5	100.0	100.2	100.3	100.4	100.5	100.5	100.5	100.6	100.7	100.4	101.0	101.0
床上套件	Bed Articles	100.4	100.3	100.4	100.4	100.5	100.4	100.4	100.6	100.3	100.5	100.5	100.6	100.0
其他	Others	100.1	98.2	99.1	100.7	100.7	100.4	100.4	100.4	100.4	100.4	100.4	100.4	100.4
五、家用电器及音像器材	**Household Appliances, Music and Video Equipments**	**97.9**	**97.9**	**97.2**	**97.0**	**96.9**	**96.9**	**97.2**	**97.6**	**97.7**	**98.3**	**98.9**	**99.3**	**99.7**
1.家庭设备	Household Appliances	100.3	100.3	99.6	99.2	99.2	99.0	99.8	100.5	100.4	101.0	101.2	101.3	101.8
洗衣机	Washing Machine	99.8	100.2	100.0	98.2	98.1	98.2	98.4	99.1	98.7	100.8	101.9	102.2	102.5
电风扇	Electric Fan	104.7	101.7	100.5	100.5	103.0	101.6	103.4	106.4	107.6	107.4	107.4	107.4	109.4
电冰箱（柜）	Refrigerator	100.0	102.8	101.1	101.3	101.4	101.0	99.5	99.8	98.1	98.8	99.0	99.0	98.8
吸排油烟机	Kitchen Ventilato	98.7	98.6	98.6	98.6	98.4	98.4	98.3	98.5	98.5	98.9	99.0	98.8	100.1
空调器	Air-Conditioning	103.0	100.4	100.1	99.0	99.7	100.0	104.3	104.9	105.5	105.5	105.5	105.2	105.3
热水器	Water Heater	95.6	98.7	98.3	98.5	94.5	94.3	94.2	94.2	94.5	94.6	94.9	95.3	95.4
微波炉	Microwave Oven	96.7	97.2	96.6	96.8	95.4	95.4	95.7	95.6	96.2	97.8	97.8	98.2	98.0
电炊具	Electric Cooking Appliance	99.2	99.3	98.9	99.0	98.9	99.1	99.1	99.1	99.0	99.0	98.9	99.6	100.3
2.文娱用耐用消费品	Durable Consumer Goods For Recreational Use	95.2	95.2	94.6	94.5	94.2	94.6	94.3	94.5	94.7	95.2	96.5	97.1	97.5

7-24 续表 4 continued

商品类别及品名	Commodity Category and Commodity Name	（以2005年同期价格为100） 全年 Annural	1月 January	2月 February	3月 March	4月 April	5月 May	6月 June	7月 July	8月 August	9月 September	10月 October	11月 November	12月 December
电视机	Television	92.8	92.6	91.7	91.6	91.3	92.0	91.5	91.5	91.7	92.4	94.8	96.1	97.2
激光视盘机	Laser Video Disc Machine	96.6	97.0	96.1	96.3	96.2	95.9	96.3	96.7	97.6	98.2	97.5	96.8	95.1
摄像机	Pickup Camera	99.6	99.2	99.3	99.3	99.3	99.5	99.5	99.9	99.9	99.9	99.9	99.9	99.9
家用音响设备	Acoustic Equipment	98.7	99.7	99.5	99.1	98.1	98.3	98.1	98.7	98.7	98.6	98.6	98.6	98.3
便携式音响	Portable Acoustics	98.9	98.9	99.2	99.1	98.9	98.8	98.8	98.8	98.8	98.8	98.8	98.8	99.5
其他	Others	100.0	100.0	100.0	100.0	100.0	100.0	100.0	100.0	100.0	100.0	100.0	100.0	100.0
3.音像器材	Music and Video Equipments	97.4	97.9	97.1	97.0	97.0	97.2	97.4	97.4	97.5	97.5	97.5	97.5	97.7
专业音响器材	Specialized Acoustic Apparatus	99.7	99.6	100.1	99.6	99.5	99.3	99.7	99.7	99.7	99.7	99.7	99.6	99.6
专业声像器材	Specialized Acoustic Image Apparatus	94.7	95.8	93.6	93.9	94.1	94.6	94.6	94.6	94.9	94.9	94.9	94.9	95.5
六、文化办公用品	**Cultural and Office Applicances**	**98.8**	**98.9**	**98.8**	**98.8**	**98.8**	**98.9**	**99.0**	**98.9**	**98.4**	**98.5**	**98.6**	**98.7**	**98.9**
纸张本册	Paper and Volume	101.5	102.9	100.5	100.8	100.8	100.8	101.1	101.1	101.8	102.1	102.2	102.5	101.9
文具	Stationery	101.1	101.2	101.7	101.5	101.5	101.5	101.3	100.8	100.9	101.0	101.0	100.9	99.7
电脑及配件	Computer and its Fitting	96.4	97.8	97.7	97.6	97.5	97.5	97.9	97.7	94.5	94.5	94.5	94.5	94.8
打印机及配件	Printer and its Fitting	96.6	96.3	96.6	96.5	96.4	96.5	96.5	96.3	96.3	96.5	96.4	96.4	98.8
扫描仪	Scanner	95.0	93.0	92.9	92.5	93.2	94.4	94.4	94.8	95.9	96.4	97.0	97.0	98.9
复印机	Xerox Machine	96.4	95.2	95.7	96.0	95.6	95.7	95.9	96.7	96.7	96.7	96.9	96.9	98.3
电子辞典	Electronic Dictionary	99.0	98.6	99.2	99.5	99.5	99.5	99.0	98.7	98.7	98.7	98.7	98.7	98.7
计算器	Calculator	99.2	99.2	99.2	99.2	99.2	99.1	99.3	98.9	98.9	98.7	98.9	99.8	100.2
教学设备	Teaching Equipment	102.2	98.6	100.4	100.4	100.7	101.3	101.3	102.1	104.8	104.2	104.8	104.2	103.8
其他	Others	100.0	100.0	100.0	100.0	100.0	100.0	100.0	100.0	100.0	100.0	100.0	100.0	100.0
七、日用品	**Articles for Daily Use**	**100.5**	**100.2**	**100.5**	**100.4**	**100.5**	**100.5**	**100.4**	**100.4**	**100.6**	**100.6**	**100.7**	**100.7**	**100.7**
1.日用百货	General Merchandise for Daily Use	99.8	99.4	99.8	100.0	99.9	99.9	99.6	99.8	99.9	99.6	99.5	99.5	100.8
自行车	Bicycle	98.7	98.8	99.9	99.8	99.4	99.3	98.9	97.9	97.9	97.9	98.0	98.0	98.5
雨具	Rain Gear	99.0	98.9	100.4	100.6	100.4	101.3	100.1	101.0	101.0	97.1	96.0	95.9	95.8
剃须刀具	Shaver	103.1	99.9	100.1	99.6	99.8	99.9	105.0	105.3	105.3	105.3	105.3	105.9	106.2
电池	Battery	100.0	100.5	100.0	100.0	100.0	100.0	100.0	100.0	100.0	100.0	100.0	100.0	100.0
卫生纸	Tissue Paper	101.5	101.8	101.5	100.8	100.8	100.6	100.4	100.8	101.5	101.5	101.5	101.2	106.1
卫生巾	Sanitary Towel	98.4	96.0	95.9	99.0	99.2	99.0	95.9	99.3	99.2	99.3	99.3	99.3	100.0
其他	Others	100.1	100.0	100.0	100.0	100.1	100.1	100.0	100.0	100.0	100.0	100.0	100.0	100.9
2.日用杂品	Sundry Articles	100.5	98.7	99.0	99.0	99.1	98.7	99.2	100.0	100.6	102.6	102.7	102.8	103.2
茶具	Tea Set	101.2	94.6	94.5	93.6	93.6	92.6	98.3	98.3	98.3	102.2	116.8	117.4	117.4
餐具	Tableware	100.8	99.3	99.8	99.9	99.9	99.7	102.1	104.8	106.0	106.0	97.8	97.8	97.7
厨具	Kitchen Utensils	99.8	100.1	100.4	101.1	101.3	100.8	96.8	96.8	97.4	100.4	100.4	100.4	101.7
其他	Others	100.0	100.0	100.0	100.0	100.0	100.0	100.0	100.0	100.0	100.0	100.0	100.0	100.0
3.洗涤用品	Washing Articles	101.6	102.2	102.1	101.7	101.8	102.1	102.1	101.6	102.0	101.5	101.5	101.5	99.9

7-24 续表 5 continued

商品类别及品名	Commodity Category and Commodity Name	全年 Annural	1月 January	2月 February	3月 March	4月 April	5月 May	6月 June	7月 July	8月 August	9月 September	10月 October	11月 November	12月 December
		（以2005年同期价格为100）												
洗衣粉	Washing Powder	103.2	103.3	103.1	103.2	103.3	103.6	103.7	103.7	103.7	103.6	103.6	103.6	99.7
肥皂类	Soap	99.9	100.3	100.3	99.8	99.7	99.3	99.4	99.5	101.1	99.8	99.9	100.1	99.8
牙膏	Toothpaste	102.3	103.7	103.7	102.5	102.5	104.3	103.7	101.4	101.4	101.1	101.4	101.4	100.3
清洁洗涤剂	Cleaning Agent	99.7	100.0	100.0	100.2	100.4	99.8	100.0	99.9	99.7	99.7	98.8	98.5	99.8
4.其他日用品	Other Articles for Daily Use	100.3	100.1	100.5	100.4	100.5	100.5	100.3	100.0	100.0	100.0	100.2	100.3	100.2
燃气灶具	Gas-oven	100.3	100.1	100.1	100.1	100.1	100.1	100.1	100.1	100.1	100.1	100.1	100.1	102.4
儿童玩具	Children's Toy	99.3	99.1	99.2	99.2	99.2	99.2	99.2	99.4	99.0	99.0	99.5	99.9	99.9
照明器具	Illumination Utensil	100.6	102.6	102.6	102.6	102.6	102.6	100.7	99.0	99.0	99.0	99.0	99.0	99.1
钟表眼镜及配件	Clocks, Glasses and their Fittings	99.4	99.3	99.3	99.3	99.3	99.5	99.5	99.5	99.5	99.5	99.6	99.6	99.6
日用普通饰品	Common Ornament for Daily Use	99.4	98.6	98.6	98.6	99.4	99.4	99.8	99.7	99.8	99.8	99.8	99.8	100.0
日用皮革制品	Leatherware for Daily Use	102.6	99.6	103.0	103.0	103.0	103.1	103.1	103.1	103.1	103.1	103.7	103.9	99.7
其他	Others	100.4	101.7	101.7	100.4	100.5	100.0	100.0	100.0	100.0	100.0	100.0	100.0	100.0
八、体育娱乐用品	**Sports and Recreation Articles**	**99.5**	**99.7**	**99.9**	**99.9**	**99.8**	**99.9**	**99.6**	**99.5**	**99.5**	**99.3**	**99.1**	**99.1**	**99.3**
1.体育用品	Sports Articles	100.0	100.3	100.7	100.6	100.5	100.5	99.9	99.8	99.9	99.8	99.4	99.4	99.5
球类	Ball	99.0	99.1	100.1	100.1	100.0	99.8	98.3	98.3	98.5	98.5	98.3	98.3	98.4
棋牌	Chess and Cards	100.4	100.7	100.7	100.6	100.4	100.4	100.4	100.4	100.4	100.1	100.4	100.4	100.3
健身器材	Exercise Machine	100.9	101.3	101.5	101.3	101.3	101.4	101.3	101.1	101.1	101.0	99.6	99.8	99.8
2.娱乐用品	Recreation Articles	98.9	98.9	98.8	98.9	99.0	99.1	99.2	99.1	99.0	98.8	98.8	98.6	99.2
游艺器材	Entertainment Apparatus	99.7	100.0	100.0	100.0	100.0	100.0	100.0	100.0	100.0	99.2	99.2	99.2	99.2
照相器材	Photographic Apparatus	97.9	97.6	97.6	97.8	97.9	97.9	97.9	97.7	97.7	97.7	97.7	97.7	99.3
乐器	Musical Instrument	99.8	99.7	99.7	99.7	99.7	100.0	100.2	100.2	99.9	100.0	100.2	99.3	99.0
九、交通、通信用品	**Transportation and Communication Appliances**	**93.7**	**93.5**	**93.6**	**93.4**	**93.2**	**93.0**	**93.5**	**93.7**	**93.5**	**93.6**	**94.2**	**94.3**	**94.3**
1.交通运输机械	Transportation Machine	99.5	98.8	99.7	99.8	99.5	99.4	99.3	99.1	99.5	99.9	99.9	100.0	99.7
轿车	Car	95.5	96.2	96.3	96.7	96.6	95.6	94.0	94.2	94.4	95.0	95.5	95.9	95.8
客车	Bus	98.4	97.6	97.9	97.6	97.5	97.5	97.8	97.7	98.1	99.4	99.4	100.0	100.1
货车	Truck	100.2	100.2	100.2	100.2	100.2	100.2	100.2	100.2	100.2	100.3	100.3	100.2	100.3
摩托车	Motorcycle	100.9	99.1	100.8	100.8	101.0	101.0	101.0	100.8	101.0	101.4	101.4	101.4	100.8
其他	Others	97.5	99.1	99.1	99.1	96.5	96.5	96.5	96.2	97.4	97.4	97.4	97.5	97.5
2.通信器材	Telecommunications Facilities	87.3	88.0	87.4	86.9	86.6	86.3	87.3	87.7	87.0	86.8	87.8	88.0	88.1
固定电话机	Telephone	95.2	95.5	95.5	94.7	94.4	94.0	94.5	94.4	94.6	95.8	96.2	96.5	96.8
移动电话机	Mobile Phone	78.6	80.4	79.0	78.6	78.0	77.6	78.8	79.5	78.7	77.2	78.6	78.7	78.4
传真机	Fax Machine	97.9	98.9	99.5	98.9	98.7	99.3	99.9	99.5	95.8	96.1	96.2	96.0	95.8
其他	Others	95.1	93.6	92.8	93.3	94.4	94.7	95.3	95.8	95.8	95.9	96.5	96.8	97.1
十、家具	**Furniture**	**100.4**	**98.8**	**98.6**	**98.6**	**99.4**	**100.3**	**100.4**	**100.7**	**100.4**	**100.3**	**102.2**	**102.5**	**102.7**
柜	Cabinet	99.9	98.1	97.9	97.6	98.7	99.9	100.1	100.2	99.7	99.7	102.2	102.1	102.7
床	Bed	101.0	98.9	98.9	98.9	100.1	101.3	101.3	101.3	101.3	101.1	102.6	103.1	103.6
桌	Desk	99.9	99.8	99.8	99.8	99.9	100.1	100.2	101.0	99.5	98.3	99.9	100.1	100.0
椅	Chair	100.1	100.6	99.8	99.9	99.5	99.5	99.4	99.0	99.1	99.3	101.4	101.7	101.6
沙发	Sofa	100.4	97.5	97.5	97.6	98.9	99.9	100.0	101.0	101.2	101.2	103.0	103.8	103.7
其他	Others	102.2	101.5	101.7	101.7	101.5	102.0	102.1	102.0	101.9	101.9	103.6	103.4	103.5

7-24 续表 6 continued

商品类别及品名	Commodity Category and Commodity Name	（以2005年同期价格为100）												
		全年 Annural	1月 January	2月 February	3月 March	4月 April	5月 May	6月 June	7月 July	8 月 August	9 月 September	10 月 October	11月 November	12月 December
十一、化妆品	**Cosmetics**	**99.9**	**100.2**	**99.9**	**99.5**	**99.6**	**99.7**	**99.8**	**99.9**	**99.8**	**100.2**	**100.2**	**100.1**	**100.0**
护肤品	Skincare Products	99.9	100.1	99.7	99.8	99.9	100.2	99.8	100.0	100.0	99.9	99.7	99.6	100.0
美容化妆品	Facial Beautifiers	100.3	100.6	100.3	100.3	100.2	100.3	100.3	100.2	100.2	100.2	100.2	100.2	100.4
护发美容品	Protects Sends the Beauty Products	98.7	99.5	99.1	97.2	97.6	97.5	98.6	98.7	98.5	99.6	99.6	99.6	99.5
清洁化妆用品	Cleaning Toiletware	100.9	101.5	101.5	100.9	101.1	100.8	100.7	100.8	100.0	101.2	101.3	100.9	100.0
药物美容用品	Medicinal Cosmetics	100.0	99.0	99.0	99.1	99.0	100.2	100.2	100.2	100.1	100.9	101.1	101.1	100.1
十二、金银珠宝	**Gold, Silver and Jewelry**	**128.3**	**104.0**	**106.1**	**115.1**	**118.6**	**132.2**	**138.6**	**137.4**	**139.6**	**138.6**	**136.8**	**136.7**	**136.1**
金饰品	Gold	133.2	105.2	107.7	118.0	123.8	141.9	144.0	141.7	145.8	145.7	142.6	140.6	141.1
银饰品	Silver	136.7	101.3	101.3	116.1	116.5	129.0	153.6	153.9	153.9	153.9	153.9	153.9	152.8
铂金饰品	Platinum	116.3	103.9	107.1	110.2	111.6	118.1	121.9	122.3	122.3	118.4	118.0	121.7	119.7
其他	Others	108.1	100.9	100.9	104.3	106.1	110.2	111.7	110.7	110.7	110.7	110.7	110.7	109.1
十三、中西药品及医疗保健用品	**Traditional Chinese and Western Medicines and Healthcare Articles**	**100.5**	**99.2**	**99.8**	**99.6**	**99.8**	**100.5**	**100.5**	**100.6**	**100.4**	**101.3**	**101.2**	**101.5**	**101.4**
1.医疗器具及用品	Medical Facilities and Goods	96.6	97.5	97.9	97.6	96.8	96.4	96.5	96.4	96.4	97.2	96.2	96.0	94.8
医疗器具及用品	Medical Facilities and Goods	96.6	97.5	97.9	97.6	96.8	96.4	96.5	96.4	96.4	97.2	96.2	96.0	94.8
2.中药材及中成药	Herbs and Ready-made Traditional Chinese Medicine	103.1	101.0	102.5	101.7	102.2	102.5	102.9	103.5	103.1	104.7	104.1	104.9	104.0
中药材	Herbs	105.3	102.5	105.0	103.2	104.0	105.4	105.6	106.5	105.1	107.4	106.4	107.9	105.0
中成药	Ready-made Traditional Chinese Medicine	100.6	99.3	99.9	100.1	100.1	99.3	99.9	100.3	100.8	101.7	101.6	101.7	102.9
3.西药	Western Medicine	99.6	98.4	98.5	98.6	98.9	100.0	99.7	99.5	99.4	100.1	100.4	100.6	101.0
抗微生物药	Anti-microorganism Medicine	95.3	92.9	92.9	93.2	93.5	94.0	94.1	94.0	93.8	95.5	99.9	99.9	100.5
消化系统用药	Alimentary System Medicine	100.7	100.0	100.6	100.6	100.7	100.7	100.7	100.8	100.8	101.2	100.5	101.0	100.6
呼吸系统用药	Respiratory System Medicine	98.7	97.4	97.2	98.0	98.5	98.1	98.3	98.3	98.3	100.2	98.5	99.6	101.6
解热镇痛及非甾体抗炎药	Allays a Fever the Analgesia and the Non-steroid Body Anti-inflammatory Agent	102.0	101.4	101.6	101.1	101.4	103.2	102.2	102.2	102.2	103.0	102.4	101.6	102.4
抗肿瘤药	Anti-neoplastic Drug	103.4	99.5	99.5	99.3	99.3	108.3	105.5	105.9	104.5	101.2	105.2	106.3	106.3
激素及调节内分泌功能药	Hormone and Adjustment Internal Secretion Function Medicine	99.3	99.8	100.0	100.0	100.1	100.1	100.2	98.5	98.6	101.2	98.1	98.1	97.4
循环系统用药	Circulating System Medicine	99.8	99.2	99.3	99.7	100.2	100.2	100.0	99.6	99.6	100.1	99.8	99.8	100.1
神经系统用药	Nerve System Medicine	100.6	99.9	100.2	100.2	100.8	100.7	100.7	100.7	100.7	101.8	100.4	100.4	101.0
专科用药	Junior Medicine	99.7	99.3	98.8	99.3	99.8	100.5	100.8	100.6	100.6	101.0	98.6	98.6	98.6
其他	Others	99.7	99.8	99.8	99.9	100.0	99.8	99.8	99.8	99.7	99.8	99.2	99.3	99.3
4.保健品及器具	Healthcare Equipment	99.4	99.4	99.1	99.1	99.2	99.2	99.6	99.7	99.7	99.9	99.3	99.5	99.7
保健器具	Health Protection Equipment	100.1	99.9	99.5	99.5	99.7	99.7	100.7	100.7	100.7	100.7	99.9	100.1	100.0
滋补保健用品	Tonic and Health Products	99.1	99.1	98.9	98.8	98.9	98.9	99.0	99.1	99.1	99.4	98.9	99.2	99.5

7-24 续表 7 continued

（以2005年同期价格为100）

商品类别及品名	Commodity Category and Commodity Name	全年 Annural	1月 January	2月 February	3月 March	4月 April	5月 May	6月 June	7月 July	8月 August	9月 September	10月 October	11月 November	12月 December
十四、书报杂志及电子出版物	**Books, Newspapers, Magazines and Electronic Publications**	**100.6**	**100.6**	**100.6**	**100.6**	**100.7**	**100.8**	**100.8**	**100.9**	**100.6**	**100.4**	**100.4**	**100.5**	**100.4**
1.教材及参考书	Teaching Materials and Reference Books	100.2	100.4	100.4	100.4	100.6	100.6	100.6	100.6	100.0	99.6	99.5	99.6	99.6
工具书	Tool Book	99.6	99.6	99.6	99.6	99.6	99.6	99.6	99.6	99.6	99.6	99.6	99.6	99.2
教材	Teaching Material	100.0	100.6	100.6	100.6	101.0	101.0	101.0	101.0	100.6	98.5	98.5	98.5	98.5
参考书	Reference Book	101.5	100.6	100.6	101.3	101.3	101.3	101.3	101.3	99.7	102.5	102.5	102.5	102.5
教育软件	Educational Software	98.1	99.4	99.4	97.8	97.8	97.8	97.8	97.8	97.8	97.8	96.9	97.8	98.4
2.书报杂志	Books, Newspapers, Magazines	102.0	102.0	102.0	102.0	102.0	102.0	102.0	102.0	102.0	102.0	102.0	102.0	102.0
书籍	Books	100.0	100.0	100.0	100.0	100.0	100.0	100.0	100.0	100.0	100.0	100.0	100.0	100.0
报纸	Newspapers	104.9	104.9	104.9	104.9	104.9	104.9	104.9	104.9	104.9	104.9	104.9	104.9	104.9
杂志	Magazines	101.1	101.1	101.1	101.1	101.1	101.1	101.1	101.1	101.1	101.1	101.1	101.1	101.1
3.电子音像制品	Electronic Publications	99.4	99.1	99.1	98.9	99.0	99.2	99.4	99.6	99.5	99.6	99.6	99.6	99.6
音响光盘和磁带	Acoustic Light Disk and Tape	100.1	100.1	100.1	100.0	100.0	100.2	100.2	100.2	100.2	100.2	100.3	100.3	100.2
录像磁带和视盘	Video Tape and Disk	99.3	99.7	99.8	99.9	99.9	99.5	99.5	98.9	98.9	98.9	98.9	98.9	98.9
计算机软件	Computer Software	98.4	97.1	96.9	96.3	96.7	97.6	98.3	99.7	99.4	99.7	99.7	99.7	99.8
十五、燃料	**Fuels**	**109.8**	**110.7**	**111.2**	**110.5**	**110.4**	**110.9**	**112.3**	**110.6**	**108.5**	**108.4**	**109.3**	**107.9**	**107.8**
1.煤炭及制品	Coal and Related Products	104.0	104.9	105.0	104.8	104.1	104.2	102.8	102.7	102.8	102.3	105.0	104.9	104.5
原煤	Raw Coal	104.1	102.8	103.2	103.2	102.9	103.2	102.5	102.5	102.6	102.0	108.1	108.3	107.8
煤制品	Coal Products	103.9	107.8	107.6	107.1	105.8	105.5	103.3	102.9	103.1	102.7	100.9	100.3	100.1
2.石油及制品	Petroleum and Related Products	114.2	115.4	116.1	115.1	115.3	116.0	119.7	116.6	112.6	112.7	112.4	110.0	110.2
液化石油气	Liquefiled Petroleum Gas	113.7	126.2	127.2	126.9	122.5	116.0	113.9	112.6	109.6	110.3	107.9	99.5	100.5
管道燃气	Pipelined Gas	106.5	105.6	105.6	105.6	105.6	107.7	107.7	107.1	106.7	106.7	106.7	106.7	106.7
汽油	Gasoline	115.5	113.6	113.9	111.8	112.2	116.6	124.1	119.7	115.0	114.8	114.8	114.8	114.7
柴油	Diesel Oil	115.8	113.0	114.2	113.8	117.1	118.6	122.6	118.9	114.1	113.9	114.8	114.6	114.3
其他	Others	103.2	100.1	100.1	100.5	104.1	103.1	105.6	103.5	103.5	105.4	104.7	103.3	104.9
十六、建筑材料及五金电料	**Building Materials and Hardware**	**103.2**	**101.2**	**100.9**	**101.1**	**102.2**	**103.0**	**103.7**	**103.9**	**104.5**	**103.7**	**104.3**	**105.0**	**105.4**
1.建筑装璜材料	Building and Decoration Materials	103.4	101.1	100.8	101.0	102.6	103.4	104.1	104.2	104.9	103.5	104.2	105.2	105.8
木材	Wood	107.8	105.0	104.9	105.4	105.8	105.0	105.0	105.5	108.7	109.8	111.3	113.8	113.6
木地板	Wood Floor	97.4	100.6	100.6	100.6	95.7	95.9	96.2	96.1	96.1	95.3	97.0	97.5	97.7
钢材	Steel Products	92.1	86.0	84.3	82.1	88.0	93.8	97.5	94.1	92.1	92.2	96.0	97.4	104.5
砖	Brick	107.7	102.9	103.5	104.9	109.0	110.1	112.1	111.3	112.2	106.1	106.7	107.1	107.0
水泥	Cement	102.8	103.1	101.8	101.4	103.4	104.1	103.4	103.4	103.4	102.8	102.3	102.4	101.9
涂料	Coating Material	100.2	101.6	101.6	100.9	99.5	98.9	99.4	99.3	99.7	99.7	100.1	100.6	101.2
胶合板	Plywood	104.9	102.6	102.3	102.8	103.6	102.7	103.8	105.5	107.0	107.2	104.9	108.6	108.1
玻璃	Glass	100.4	95.9	95.6	97.1	97.2	98.6	99.4	101.0	102.0	102.2	103.3	105.4	107.9
粘胶	Rayon	101.8	101.1	101.2	100.9	101.0	101.3	101.3	101.7	102.1	102.2	102.3	102.3	104.1
油漆	Paint	104.1	105.0	104.4	103.9	103.2	103.7	104.4	104.5	104.7	103.7	103.7	103.5	104.1
其他	Others	105.1	100.8	101.0	104.9	105.4	106.1	102.3	106.4	106.3	106.3	108.4	108.5	104.4
2.五金电料	Hardware	102.7	101.4	101.3	101.5	101.0	101.6	102.5	103.0	103.3	104.2	104.3	104.4	104.3
五金工具	Hardware Tools	101.6	101.0	100.7	100.6	100.5	100.5	101.7	102.3	102.6	102.5	102.5	102.5	102.1
电工电料	Electrical Engineering and Electrical Materials	103.1	101.9	101.9	102.1	101.3	102.3	103.1	103.6	103.8	104.4	104.4	104.4	104.4
水暖器材	Heating Equipment	102.8	100.9	100.9	101.1	101.4	102.3	102.2	102.2	102.2	104.7	105.0	105.2	105.0
其他	Others	104.6	102.7	102.7	102.7	100.0	100.0	103.7	105.6	107.5	107.5	107.5	107.5	107.5

7-25 全省商品零售价格（环比）指数

Entire Province Retail Price Index

商品类别及品名	Commodity Category and Commodity Name	（以上月价格为100） 1月 January	2月 February	3月 March	4月 April	5月 May	6月 June	7月 July	8月 August	9月 September	10月 October	11月 November	12月 December
商品零售价格总指数	**Genaral Retail Price Index**	**101.4**	**100.0**	**99.4**	**100.1**	**99.7**	**99.4**	**99.5**	**100.2**	**100.5**	**99.8**	**100.5**	**101.4**
一、食品	**Food**	**105.3**	**100.5**	**98.1**	**100.1**	**98.5**	**97.1**	**98.5**	**101.0**	**102.0**	**98.7**	**101.5**	**105.0**
1.粮食	Grain	100.5	100.1	100.0	100.1	100.5	100.3	101.3	100.8	100.8	100.7	102.9	102.1
大米	Rice	101.8	99.7	100.2	100.3	102.0	101.1	103.1	102.7	100.9	101.0	99.7	101.7
面粉	Flour	99.9	100.4	99.7	99.9	99.8	99.4	100.8	99.5	100.8	100.6	106.5	103.1
粮食制品	Grain Products	100.1	100.2	100.1	100.2	100.1	100.3	100.4	100.6	100.2	100.2	102.4	101.5
其他	Others	100.2	100.1	100.0	100.4	100.3	101.0	100.5	100.2	103.2	101.7	100.7	101.7
2.淀粉	Starches	100.1	100.0	100.2	100.6	100.0	100.6	100.5	100.8	100.6	100.3	100.5	102.5
淀粉	Starches	100.1	100.0	100.2	100.6	100.0	100.6	100.5	100.8	100.6	100.3	100.5	102.5
3.干豆类及豆制品	Beans and Beans Products	100.6	100.2	99.7	99.9	100.4	100.5	101.3	100.3	99.6	99.6	100.1	101.0
干豆	Beans	100.4	100.9	99.8	100.2	100.9	101.7	103.5	100.7	98.3	98.5	99.8	101.1
豆制品	Beans Products	100.7	100.0	99.7	99.7	100.2	100.0	100.2	100.2	100.2	100.1	100.2	100.9
4.油脂	Oil and Fat	100.0	100.0	99.5	99.7	100.4	100.1	100.2	100.8	100.6	100.6	102.7	105.7
食用植物油	Edible Vegetable Oil	99.8	100.2	99.7	100.0	100.2	100.1	100.3	100.9	100.8	100.5	102.5	105.0
植物油制品	Plant Oil Products	99.5	99.8	99.9	99.9	102.1	100.0	99.6	100.1	100.2	100.0	102.7	109.9
其他	Others	105.2	97.5	95.0	94.1	97.8	101.2	100.2	101.3	98.8	103.2	106.8	104.9
5.肉禽及其制品	Meal, Poultry and their Products	103.8	99.8	97.3	97.9	98.5	100.5	102.5	103.7	101.6	100.3	103.3	105.3
（1）食用畜肉及副产品	Edible Livestock Meat and their By-products	105.4	99.0	95.7	95.8	98.0	101.1	103.1	105.2	102.5	100.5	105.0	107.5
猪肉	Pork	106.7	98.0	94.3	94.1	97.3	101.5	104.8	107.6	103.2	100.4	106.6	108.9
牛肉	Beef	101.8	100.8	99.0	99.8	98.9	100.3	100.5	99.8	100.8	100.5	101.5	103.5
羊肉	Mutton	102.2	101.1	98.4	99.9	100.1	99.8	99.9	100.3	101.3	101.7	101.4	105.8
畜肉副产品	Livestock Meat By-products	104.6	100.6	97.6	96.7	97.7	102.0	100.2	102.4	102.0	100.6	103.3	106.5
其他	Others	106.1	99.9	96.4	95.7	99.6	99.6	102.0	105.8	100.8	100.3	103.6	103.2
（2）禽	Poultry	103.9	101.7	99.5	101.1	99.0	100.4	104.2	103.6	100.9	99.9	100.6	103.2
鸡	Chicken	105.2	102.2	99.8	101.4	98.9	100.7	105.5	103.5	101.4	99.8	100.3	103.4
鸭	Duck	99.6	98.7	100.0	100.3	99.9	97.6	97.0	103.2	98.6	100.6	103.1	102.9
其他	Others	100.1	101.1	97.8	100.0	98.3	100.4	102.3	104.5	99.7	100.1	100.4	102.7
（3）肉禽加工制品	Meal and Poultry Processing Products	100.3	100.4	99.4	100.5	99.4	99.4	100.2	100.8	100.3	100.1	101.1	101.6
畜肉制品	Livestock Meat Products	100.4	100.4	99.7	99.7	99.5	99.7	100.4	100.6	100.1	100.2	100.9	101.6
禽制品	Poultry Products	100.1	100.3	98.9	101.9	99.2	98.9	99.8	101.0	100.5	99.8	101.5	101.6
6.蛋	Eggs	99.8	95.0	97.1	99.7	102.2	100.9	101.5	108.9	106.6	100.0	101.4	104.4
鲜蛋	Fresh Eggs	99.6	94.3	96.7	99.7	102.4	101.0	101.9	110.2	107.4	99.9	101.5	104.7
蛋制品	Egg Products	100.6	99.5	99.5	99.7	100.9	100.5	98.6	100.6	101.4	101.0	100.8	102.1
7.水产品	Aquatic Product	103.5	101.4	98.7	100.4	100.7	100.9	101.3	100.2	98.5	99.7	99.3	100.2
（1）鱼	Fish	102.7	100.2	97.6	100.7	101.1	102.2	101.8	101.1	98.8	99.0	98.6	99.7
淡水鱼	Freshwater Fish	100.7	98.6	97.2	99.1	102.2	103.3	102.8	101.5	99.2	97.8	98.0	99.2
海水鱼	Seawater Fish	104.8	101.7	98.0	102.2	100.1	101.1	100.8	100.7	98.4	100.2	99.1	100.3

7-25 续表 1 continued

商品类别及品名	Commodity Category and Commodity Name	（以上月价格为100）											
		1月 January	2月 February	3月 March	4月 April	5月 May	6月 June	7月 July	8月 August	9月 September	10月 October	11月 November	12月 December
（2）其他水产品	Other Aquatic Product	104.6	103.3	100.4	99.9	100.0	98.9	100.6	98.7	98.0	100.9	100.5	101.1
虾蟹类	Shrimp and Crab	105.8	104.4	99.6	100.0	100.1	98.5	100.1	98.3	97.4	101.3	100.7	101.7
其他	Others	102.2	100.8	102.2	99.6	99.8	100.1	101.6	99.8	99.5	100.1	100.2	99.7
8.菜	Vegetable	128.4	100.1	91.3	97.2	85.8	82.9	94.4	109.1	114.1	85.6	100.6	123.2
鲜菜	Fresh Vegetable	132.1	99.9	90.0	96.6	83.1	80.4	93.2	111.4	117.6	83.4	100.5	127.0
干菜及菜制品	Dried Vegetable and Vegetable Products	101.8	100.5	100.2	100.1	99.6	99.9	100.2	100.8	100.9	101.2	101.3	104.1
薯类	Potato	112.7	104.7	104.6	104.2	112.5	89.0	98.4	98.0	91.1	90.1	100.0	107.7
9.调味品	Flavoring	100.3	100.0	100.1	100.3	100.1	100.1	100.5	100.0	100.0	100.2	100.7	100.8
盐	Salt	100.1	100.1	100.5	100.6	100.0	100.6	100.5	99.9	100.1	100.1	100.0	100.1
酱油	Soy Sauce	100.2	100.0	99.9	100.2	99.9	99.7	100.4	100.3	99.9	100.2	100.1	100.7
醋	Vinegar	100.0	100.0	99.9	100.2	99.9	100.1	100.6	100.0	100.1	100.1	100.0	101.1
味精	Aginomoto	100.4	100.0	99.9	100.3	100.2	99.7	100.3	99.9	100.0	100.2	99.9	100.4
其他	Others	101.0	99.8	100.0	100.2	100.8	100.0	100.6	99.9	100.2	100.6	104.4	101.6
10.糖	Carbohydrate	100.8	102.8	101.4	100.6	100.6	100.4	100.7	100.3	100.3	100.2	100.2	100.7
食糖	Sugar	102.1	108.1	104.5	101.7	101.6	101.1	101.3	101.0	100.7	100.0	100.1	101.7
糖果	Sweet	100.6	101.0	100.1	100.3	100.2	100.1	100.6	100.0	100.1	100.3	100.2	99.6
巧克力制品	Chocolate Products	100.3	100.0	99.8	99.9	99.7	99.8	99.9	99.7	100.0	100.3	100.0	101.5
糖类小食品	Little Carbohydrate Food	99.9	100.4	100.0	100.0	100.7	100.0	100.2	100.2	100.1	100.0	100.4	100.5
11.干鲜瓜果	Dried and Fresh Melons and Fruits	108.7	106.7	100.2	107.9	103.5	90.2	84.2	87.3	97.5	103.4	103.5	105.6
鲜瓜果	Fresh Fruits	110.1	108.1	100.2	109.4	104.1	88.3	80.9	83.8	96.7	103.7	104.0	107.1
干（坚）果	Dried Fruits	102.6	100.4	100.5	100.6	100.4	100.2	100.1	100.7	100.3	102.2	102.1	101.2
12.糕点饼干面包	Cake, Biscuit and Bread	100.1	99.9	100.0	100.1	100.1	99.9	100.2	100.2	99.9	99.8	99.8	100.9
糕点	Cake	99.9	100.0	99.9	100.0	100.0	99.8	100.0	99.6	100.0	99.3	100.2	101.1
饼干	Biscuit	100.1	99.9	100.1	100.5	100.5	100.2	100.4	100.8	99.6	99.9	99.5	100.9
面包	Bread	100.6	99.7	100.0	100.0	100.0	99.9	100.2	100.5	100.2	100.5	99.5	100.6
13.液体乳及乳制品	Liquid Milk and their Products	99.8	100.0	100.4	100.2	99.9	100.2	100.1	100.2	101.1	100.0	100.0	100.8
巴氏杀菌奶或消毒奶	Pasteurization Milk or Disinfection Milk	99.6	100.0	100.7	100.0	99.9	100.2	100.2	100.2	101.0	100.1	99.9	101.4
酸奶	Leben	100.1	100.0	100.0	100.4	100.3	100.2	99.8	99.9	101.5	100.0	99.8	99.9
奶粉	Milk Powder	100.1	100.1	99.9	100.5	99.8	100.1	100.4	100.9	100.2	99.7	100.1	100.7
其他	Others	100.0	100.0	99.9	100.0	100.0	100.0	100.0	100.0	102.0	99.8	100.2	99.8
14.在外用膳食品	Outward Dinner	100.3	100.0	100.1	100.0	100.1	100.3	100.1	100.1	100.2	99.8	100.6	102.0
主食	Staple Food	100.1	99.7	100.1	100.0	100.0	100.4	100.0	100.1	100.1	100.0	101.7	103.8
炒菜	Hot Dish	100.4	100.2	100.1	100.1	100.0	100.3	99.9	100.0	100.3	99.8	100.1	101.1
地方小吃	Local Snack	100.2	100.0	100.1	100.0	100.4	100.2	100.8	100.5	99.8	99.6	100.1	101.7
15.其他食品	Other Foods	99.8	99.9	100.1	100.0	100.1	100.0	100.0	100.1	100.0	99.9	99.9	100.7
其他食品	Other Foods	99.8	99.9	100.1	100.0	100.1	100.0	100.0	100.1	100.0	99.9	99.9	100.7
二、饮料、烟酒	**Beverages, Tobacco, Liquor**	**100.2**	**100.0**	**100.1**	**100.3**	**100.0**	**100.2**	**100.1**	**100.2**	**100.1**	**100.1**	**100.1**	**100.7**
1.茶及饮料	Tea and Beverages	100.0	100.2	100.5	100.1	100.1	100.2	100.3	100.2	100.0	100.1	100.0	100.5
（1）茶叶	Tea	99.9	100.2	100.3	100.0	100.0	100.1	100.1	99.9	100.0	100.1	100.0	100.3

7-25 续表 2 continued

商品类别及品名	Commodity Category and Commodity Name	（以上月价格为100）											
		1月 January	2月 February	3月 March	4月 April	5月 May	6月 June	7月 July	8月 August	9月 September	10月 October	11月 November	12月 December
茶叶	Tea	99.9	100.2	100.3	100.0	100.0	100.1	100.1	99.9	100.0	100.1	100.0	100.3
（2）饮料	Beverages	100.1	100.1	100.7	100.1	100.2	100.3	100.4	100.3	100.0	100.1	100.0	100.6
固体饮料	Solid Beverages	100.0	100.3	100.0	99.9	100.2	100.0	100.0	99.9	99.9	100.0	100.0	99.7
液体饮料	Liquid Beverages	100.1	100.1	100.5	100.2	100.1	100.1	100.9	100.1	100.1	100.0	100.0	100.6
冷冻饮品	Frozen Beverages	100.1	100.0	101.6	100.2	100.3	100.8	100.0	101.0	99.9	100.1	99.9	101.3
2.烟草	Tobacco	100.5	100.0	99.9	100.3	100.0	100.0	99.9	99.9	99.9	100.0	100.0	100.5
国产卷烟	Domestic Cigarette	100.6	100.1	99.9	100.4	100.1	100.0	99.9	99.9	99.9	100.0	100.0	100.5
进口卷烟	Import Cigarette	100.0	99.0	100.0	100.1	99.7	100.0	99.7	99.9	100.1	99.9	100.5	100.6
其他	Others	100.0	100.0	99.8	99.8	100.0	100.0	100.0	99.7	100.0	100.0	100.0	100.0
3.酒	Liquor	100.2	99.9	100.0	100.3	100.0	100.3	100.3	100.4	100.3	100.3	100.2	101.0
白酒	White Spirit	100.2	99.8	100.3	100.4	100.0	100.4	100.1	100.6	100.2	100.5	100.3	101.4
葡萄酒	Grape	102.1	100.1	99.9	100.2	99.9	100.6	100.7	100.2	100.2	100.1	100.8	100.1
啤酒	Beer	99.7	100.1	99.7	100.2	99.9	100.0	100.4	100.3	100.5	100.1	99.9	100.5
其他	Others	100.0	100.0	100.0	100.2	100.0	100.2	100.2	100.0	100.1	100.0	100.0	100.1
三、服装、鞋帽	**Garments, Footgearand and Hats**	**98.9**	**98.9**	**99.7**	**99.7**	**99.5**	**99.9**	**99.2**	**99.4**	**100.2**	**100.8**	**100.5**	**99.9**
1.服装	Garments	98.8	98.6	99.4	99.6	99.6	100.0	99.6	99.6	100.1	101.2	100.8	100.1
（1）男式服装	Men's Garments	98.4	99.0	99.1	99.6	99.4	99.7	99.6	99.4	100.2	101.3	100.8	100.0
大衣	Topcoat	98.0	98.6	99.2	98.8	100.1	99.2	99.8	100.0	99.9	99.7	100.0	100.4
毛线衣	Woollen Sweater	99.4	95.3	94.8	99.6	98.8	99.8	100.1	99.8	100.0	101.9	100.9	101.1
夹克衫	Jacket	98.3	98.7	98.0	99.6	99.9	99.9	99.9	100.0	100.2	102.5	101.4	100.1
衬衫	Shirt	96.3	99.8	100.1	99.4	99.5	100.7	98.9	99.1	100.5	100.7	100.2	100.8
T恤衫	T-shirt	99.9	100.3	99.3	100.0	98.7	97.9	97.8	98.4	101.0	100.2	100.9	100.1
裤子	Trousers	97.7	97.9	100.5	99.9	99.7	99.5	99.5	99.5	99.3	102.5	100.5	99.3
西服	Western-style Clothes	98.4	100.7	99.4	100.5	99.7	99.8	100.7	97.8	101.6	101.5	100.0	99.7
运动衫裤	Gym Suit	99.1	100.0	100.0	99.6	97.4	100.2	99.5	100.6	99.7	100.6	101.2	100.2
内衣	Underwaist	99.3	100.0	100.7	99.8	99.7	100.2	99.6	100.1	99.8	100.5	99.9	100.1
羽绒衣	Eider down Outerwear	97.6	98.9	99.5	97.1	99.9	99.9	99.5	99.8	99.3	102.1	104.1	98.7
其他	Others	98.9	98.7	98.9	99.2	100.1	99.9	99.8	99.9	100.0	100.0	103.1	99.8
（2）女式服装	Women's Garments	99.0	98.2	99.4	99.5	99.4	100.1	99.8	99.7	100.3	101.3	100.7	100.3
大衣	Topcoat	98.1	94.3	98.3	99.4	99.9	100.0	99.7	100.0	99.9	100.0	100.7	102.6
毛线衣	Woollen Sweater	99.0	94.3	97.5	99.9	98.2	100.4	100.0	100.0	100.6	102.4	99.8	101.2
羽绒衣	Eider down Outerwear	98.4	98.7	98.9	99.8	99.9	99.9	99.7	99.8	99.5	102.5	104.1	98.9
套装	Coordinates	98.7	100.1	99.7	98.1	100.4	99.0	100.5	97.7	103.1	101.1	99.2	100.3
衬衫	Shirt	97.7	101.1	100.2	98.0	100.1	100.3	100.3	98.6	98.9	100.2	99.8	98.9
T恤衫	T-shirt	100.0	100.1	99.9	99.3	99.4	100.3	99.1	99.7	103.0	105.8	100.4	100.0
裙子	Skirt	99.8	99.5	99.6	98.2	100.6	100.4	99.9	99.7	99.6	100.4	100.9	99.9
裤子	Trousers	99.9	98.3	99.4	99.8	99.4	100.4	99.2	100.2	99.9	100.0	101.1	98.8
运动衫裤	Gym Suit	99.9	100.6	99.4	100.6	95.3	100.4	99.6	99.9	99.9	102.1	99.2	101.8
内衣	Underwaist	98.9	99.9	101.5	101.1	99.5	100.5	99.6	100.0	100.0	100.9	101.2	99.9
其他	Others	99.6	99.5	100.4	100.8	99.5	100.3	100.0	100.7	99.9	100.5	100.3	99.9

7-25 续表 3 continued

商品类别及品名	Commodity Category and Commodity Name	(以上月价格为100)											
		1月 January	2月 February	3月 March	4月 April	5月 May	6月 June	7月 July	8 月 August	9 月 September	10 月 October	11月 November	12月 December
（3）儿童服装	Children's Garments	99.4	99.4	100.0	100.3	100.7	100.1	99.2	99.9	99.2	100.4	100.5	99.9
套装	Coordinates	99.4	99.4	99.8	100.2	99.7	99.8	99.7	99.7	99.7	100.4	100.7	100.0
裤子	Trousers	99.2	99.5	100.0	99.9	101.3	100.0	98.8	100.2	99.6	101.0	100.6	100.3
裙子	Skirt	99.6	99.7	100.7	101.4	102.2	100.7	98.6	99.8	97.6	100.0	100.2	99.3
其他	Others	98.7	97.9	98.5	98.8	99.6	100.0	99.9	100.0	99.9	100.0	100.4	99.6
2.鞋袜帽	Shoes, Socks and Hats	99.1	99.4	100.4	99.5	99.4	99.9	98.2	99.0	100.4	100.1	100.2	99.5
（1）鞋	Shoes	99.0	99.3	100.6	99.4	99.3	99.8	97.9	98.8	100.5	100.1	100.3	99.4
男鞋	Men's Shoes	99.0	99.7	101.0	99.7	99.2	100.3	97.7	98.9	100.4	100.0	100.2	99.5
女鞋	Women's Shoes	98.8	98.8	100.5	99.0	98.9	99.4	97.3	98.3	101.0	100.1	100.3	99.1
童鞋	Children's Shoes	99.5	99.7	99.9	100.0	100.4	99.8	99.6	99.9	99.5	100.5	100.3	100.0
（2）袜子	Socks	99.7	99.9	99.7	100.4	99.8	100.0	99.9	100.0	99.8	100.3	99.6	99.7
男袜	Men's Socks	99.6	99.9	99.9	100.4	99.8	100.0	99.9	100.0	99.8	100.3	99.4	99.3
女袜	Women's Socks	99.7	99.9	99.5	100.5	99.7	100.1	99.9	100.0	99.7	100.4	99.8	100.0
（3）帽子	Hats	99.9	99.7	99.9	100.0	100.2	100.0	100.0	100.0	99.7	100.3	100.3	100.1
男帽	Men's Hats	99.9	99.8	99.8	100.0	100.3	100.1	100.1	100.3	99.4	100.2	100.5	100.3
女帽	Women's Hats	99.9	99.7	100.0	100.0	100.1	100.0	99.9	99.9	99.9	100.4	100.1	99.9
3.其他	Others	99.4	100.7	99.7	100.9	99.9	100.1	99.7	99.5	100.5	100.4	100.0	99.0
领带	Necktie	99.4	100.7	99.7	100.9	99.9	100.1	99.7	99.5	100.5	100.4	100.0	99.0
四、纺织品	**Textiles**	**99.6**	**100.3**	**100.0**	**100.0**	**99.9**	**100.2**	**99.9**	**99.9**	**99.8**	**100.3**	**100.0**	**100.2**
1.衣着材料	Clothing Materials	99.9	100.0	99.8	100.0	100.4	100.0	100.0	100.0	99.9	100.4	100.1	100.2
棉布	Cotton Cloth	99.6	99.9	100.4	100.5	100.7	100.1	100.2	100.0	100.4	100.4	99.9	100.0
棉混纺布	Cotton Textiles Cloth	99.7	100.3	100.0	100.0	100.0	100.0	100.0	100.1	99.8	100.4	100.5	100.1
化纤布	Chemical Fiber Cloth	100.1	100.1	99.5	99.7	100.6	100.0	100.0	99.9	99.5	100.6	100.2	100.1
毛线	Knitting Wool	100.0	99.4	99.4	100.0	100.0	100.0	100.0	99.9	100.1	100.1	100.1	100.7
2.床上用品	Bedclothes	99.2	100.6	100.2	100.0	99.5	100.3	99.8	99.9	99.6	100.2	99.9	100.3
毛毯	Woollen Blanket	99.5	100.2	100.3	100.2	99.2	100.6	99.4	99.8	99.9	100.7	99.9	101.5
被子	Quilt	99.3	100.4	100.1	99.8	99.3	100.6	99.7	99.7	99.1	99.7	99.3	100.4
床上套件	Bed Articles	99.0	100.8	100.3	100.0	99.7	100.3	100.0	100.0	99.7	100.4	100.2	99.7
其他	Others	99.5	101.5	100.2	100.1	99.9	99.8	100.0	100.0	99.9	100.2	100.1	100.1
五、家用电器及音像器材	**Household Appliances, Music and Video Equipments**	**99.8**	**99.7**	**99.9**	**99.7**	**100.1**	**100.9**	**100.4**	**99.9**	**99.6**	**99.9**	**100.0**	**99.9**
1.家庭设备	Household Appliances	100.0	99.9	100.1	99.9	100.2	101.9	100.8	100.2	100.0	100.2	100.1	100.1
洗衣机	Washing Machine	99.8	100.0	99.9	99.1	100.4	100.9	100.5	99.7	100.5	100.3	100.1	99.9
电风扇	Electric Fan	99.6	99.1	100.0	102.7	100.3	101.3	101.8	100.5	99.4	100.1	100.0	101.3
电冰箱（柜）	Refrigerator	99.9	99.5	100.2	100.1	100.5	101.6	101.0	99.9	100.0	100.5	99.8	100.0
吸排油烟机	Kitchen Ventilato	100.1	99.9	99.9	100.0	99.9	101.8	101.4	100.8	99.7	99.9	100.1	100.3
空调器	Air-Conditioning	100.2	100.0	100.0	99.9	100.5	103.8	101.0	100.4	100.3	100.0	100.3	100.0
热水器	Water Heater	100.2	100.4	100.7	98.9	99.4	100.3	100.0	100.1	100.0	100.2	100.1	99.6
微波炉	Microwave Oven	99.6	99.7	100.0	99.4	99.9	100.5	99.9	100.0	99.9	100.2	100.5	99.7
电炊具	Electric Cooking Appliance	100.1	99.9	100.0	100.5	100.0	100.0	100.0	100.1	99.7	100.2	100.0	100.3
2.文娱用耐用消费品	Durable Consumer Goods For Recreational Use	99.6	99.5	99.8	99.3	99.9	99.7	99.9	99.5	98.8	99.5	99.9	99.6

7-25 续表 4 continued

商品类别及品名	Commodity Category and Commodity Name	（以上月价格为100）											
		1月 January	2月 February	3月 March	4月 April	5月 May	6月 June	7月 July	8 月 August	9 月 September	10 月 October	11月 November	12月 December
电视机	Television	99.3	99.4	99.8	99.0	100.0	99.5	99.8	99.0	98.6	99.5	99.9	99.7
激光视盘机	Laser Video Disc Machine	99.5	99.0	99.8	99.6	99.7	100.1	99.9	99.9	98.1	98.7	99.8	99.2
摄像机	Pickup Camera	99.7	99.8	99.5	99.0	99.6	99.0	99.6	100.0	98.7	99.8	99.7	99.3
家用音响设备	Acoustic Equipment	100.1	99.9	99.7	99.4	99.8	100.0	100.3	100.0	99.8	100.1	100.0	99.8
便携式音响	Portable Acoustics	99.9	99.6	99.7	99.8	100.0	100.0	100.0	100.0	99.8	100.1	100.0	99.7
其他	Others	100.0	100.1	99.9	100.0	100.0	100.0	100.0	99.6	99.7	100.1	99.9	100.0
3.音像器材	Music and Video Equipments	99.8	99.8	99.9	99.9	100.0	100.0	100.0	100.0	100.0	100.0	100.0	100.0
专业音响器材	Specialized Acoustic Apparatus	100.0	100.0	99.9	99.9	100.0	100.1	100.0	100.0	100.0	100.0	100.0	100.0
专业声像器材	Specialized Acoustic Image Apparatus	99.5	99.5	100.0	99.8	100.0	99.9	100.0	100.0	100.0	100.0	100.0	100.0
六、文化办公用品	**Cultural and Office Applicances**	**99.9**	**99.9**	**99.9**	**99.9**	**99.8**	**99.8**	**99.8**	**99.4**	**99.6**	**100.0**	**99.9**	**100.0**
纸张本册	Paper and Volume	100.4	99.7	100.0	100.0	100.0	100.1	100.0	100.3	100.3	100.3	100.1	100.1
文具	Stationery	100.0	100.1	100.0	100.0	100.0	99.9	99.8	100.0	99.7	100.2	100.0	100.0
电脑及配件	Computer and its Fitting	99.7	99.8	99.9	99.9	99.4	99.3	99.7	98.5	98.8	99.9	99.8	99.9
打印机及配件	Printer and its Fitting	99.8	100.0	99.8	99.9	99.9	100.2	99.7	99.2	99.9	99.9	99.8	100.0
扫描仪	Scanner	99.8	100.0	99.9	100.0	99.9	100.0	100.0	99.9	100.0	100.0	99.9	100.0
复印机	Xerox Machine	99.6	100.0	100.0	99.8	99.9	99.9	99.9	99.5	99.8	99.9	99.0	99.8
电子辞典	Electronic Dictionary	100.0	99.9	99.8	99.6	99.9	99.8	99.3	98.8	100.2	100.3	100.1	100.0
计算器	Calculator	100.0	100.1	100.0	100.0	100.0	100.1	99.8	99.9	99.9	100.0	100.3	100.1
教学设备	Teaching Equipment	100.2	100.1	100.0	100.0	100.2	99.9	99.9	101.1	99.9	100.1	100.0	100.1
其他	Others	100.0	100.0	100.0	100.0	100.0	99.9	99.9	100.0	100.1	100.2	100.0	100.1
七、日用品	**Articles for Daily Use**	**100.0**	**100.0**	**100.1**	**100.0**	**100.1**	**100.1**	**99.8**	**100.2**	**99.8**	**100.3**	**100.0**	**100.2**
1.日用百货	General Merchandise for Daily Use	100.1	100.0	100.1	100.1	100.1	100.0	100.0	100.0	99.9	100.1	100.0	100.4
自行车	Bicycle	100.0	100.0	99.9	99.9	99.9	99.8	100.0	99.9	100.1	100.2	100.0	100.0
雨具	Rain Gear	100.1	100.0	100.0	100.0	100.0	99.6	100.0	100.3	99.3	99.5	99.8	100.1
剃须刀具	Shaver	100.0	100.1	100.3	100.4	100.1	101.9	100.0	100.0	99.8	99.9	100.0	100.2
电池	Battery	100.0	100.2	100.0	100.0	100.5	98.1	100.2	99.9	99.7	100.1	100.2	100.0
卫生纸	Tissue Paper	100.5	100.0	100.3	100.5	100.2	100.5	100.0	100.3	100.0	100.1	99.9	102.0
卫生巾	Sanitary Towel	99.9	99.8	100.0	99.9	100.6	99.7	99.6	99.9	99.6	100.5	99.9	99.9
其他	Others	100.5	100.0	100.0	100.0	100.0	100.0	100.0	100.0	99.9	100.2	101.0	100.3
2.日用杂品	Sundry Articles	100.0	100.0	100.0	100.2	100.1	100.0	99.8	100.2	100.5	100.4	100.0	100.3
茶具	Tea Set	100.0	100.0	100.0	100.1	99.9	101.4	99.9	100.1	100.9	102.0	99.9	100.1
餐具	Tableware	100.0	100.0	100.0	100.0	100.3	100.0	99.2	100.3	100.0	100.2	100.0	100.4
厨具	Kitchen Utensils	100.0	100.0	100.0	100.4	100.0	99.3	100.1	100.1	100.9	100.0	100.1	100.3
其他	Others	99.9	100.3	100.2	99.8	100.0	100.0	100.0	100.0	99.9	99.7	99.9	100.0
3.洗涤用品	Washing Articles	99.9	100.1	100.0	100.0	100.2	100.2	99.8	100.3	99.7	100.1	100.0	100.2

7-25 续表 5 continued

商品类别及品名	Commodity Category and Commodity Name	（以上月价格为100）											
		1月 January	2月 February	3月 March	4月 April	5月 May	6月 June	7月 July	8月 August	9月 September	10月 October	11月 November	12月 December
洗衣粉	Washing Powder	100.0	100.0	100.1	100.1	99.9	100.6	100.0	100.6	99.8	100.1	99.9	100.3
肥皂类	Soap	99.7	100.1	99.9	99.9	100.0	100.1	100.0	100.7	99.3	100.1	100.2	100.0
牙膏	Toothpaste	100.0	100.2	99.8	100.0	100.9	100.0	99.2	99.9	99.8	100.1	100.3	100.3
清洁洗涤剂	Cleaning Agent	100.0	100.1	100.0	100.1	100.0	99.9	99.9	99.9	99.8	100.1	99.9	100.1
4.其他日用品	Other Articles for Daily Use	99.9	100.0	100.2	99.9	100.1	100.0	99.7	100.2	99.6	100.5	100.1	99.8
燃气灶具	Gas-oven	100.9	99.9	100.7	100.3	100.0	100.5	100.4	100.1	99.8	100.1	100.0	100.0
儿童玩具	Children's Toy	99.9	99.9	99.7	99.5	100.1	100.1	100.2	99.9	99.6	100.3	100.0	99.9
照明器具	Illumination Utensil	99.8	100.0	100.1	100.1	100.0	100.0	100.0	100.0	99.9	100.1	99.9	100.0
钟表眼镜及配件	Clocks, Glasses and their Fittings	99.6	99.9	100.0	100.3	100.0	100.1	100.1	100.1	99.5	100.3	100.2	99.9
日用普通饰品	Common Ornament for Daily Use	100.1	100.5	99.6	98.7	101.6	99.1	100.7	99.5	99.2	101.0	100.0	100.0
日用皮革制品	Leatherware for Daily Use	98.9	100.2	100.6	100.0	99.8	99.8	97.0	101.1	99.1	101.7	100.4	98.7
其他	Others	99.2	100.2	100.6	100.0	99.8	100.1	97.4	101.0	99.5	100.9	100.4	99.2
八、体育娱乐用品	**Sports and Recreation Articles**	**100.0**	**100.0**	**100.0**	**99.9**	**99.9**	**99.9**	**99.9**	**100.0**	**99.7**	**100.2**	**100.0**	**100.1**
1.体育用品	Sports Articles	100.1	100.0	99.9	99.9	99.8	99.9	99.9	100.0	99.8	100.2	100.0	100.0
球类	Ball	99.9	99.8	99.8	100.0	99.7	99.6	99.9	100.1	99.8	100.2	99.9	100.0
棋牌	Chess and Cards	100.4	100.1	100.0	99.8	99.9	99.6	100.0	100.0	99.9	100.2	100.0	100.0
健身器材	Exercise Machine	100.0	100.1	100.0	100.0	99.8	100.2	99.9	99.8	99.6	100.3	99.9	100.0
2.娱乐用品	Recreation Articles	99.9	100.0	100.0	99.9	100.0	99.9	99.9	100.1	99.6	100.2	100.0	100.1
游艺器材	Entertainment Apparatus	100.1	99.9	99.8	99.6	99.9	99.7	99.6	100.4	99.1	100.3	100.0	100.1
照相器材	Photographic Apparatus	99.8	100.0	100.0	100.0	100.0	100.0	99.9	100.0	99.7	100.0	100.1	100.2
乐器	Musical Instrument	100.0	100.0	100.0	100.0	100.0	100.0	100.0	99.9	99.8	100.2	99.8	100.0
九、交通、通信用品	**Transportation and Communication Appliances**	**99.6**	**99.7**	**99.3**	**99.1**	**99.5**	**99.6**	**99.6**	**99.3**	**99.2**	**99.6**	**99.5**	**99.3**
1.交通运输机械	Transportation Machine	99.8	100.2	99.8	99.8	99.9	99.9	99.8	99.8	99.3	99.8	99.7	99.6
轿车	Car	99.9	99.9	99.9	99.7	99.6	99.7	99.7	99.3	98.5	99.9	99.4	99.2
客车	Bus	100.0	100.0	99.8	100.0	100.0	100.1	99.9	100.0	98.9	100.0	100.0	100.0
货车	Truck	100.0	100.0	99.5	99.7	100.0	100.0	99.9	100.0	99.9	99.3	99.8	100.0
摩托车	Motorcycle	99.4	100.8	100.0	99.9	100.3	100.0	99.9	100.2	100.0	100.0	99.8	99.4
其他	Others	99.5	100.0	100.0	99.2	100.0	100.0	99.9	100.0	100.0	100.0	100.0	100.0
2.通信器材	Telecommunications Facilities	99.2	98.8	98.4	97.7	98.6	99.1	99.1	98.4	98.8	99.0	99.1	98.7
固定电话机	Telephone	99.6	99.5	99.3	99.7	99.0	100.0	99.9	99.9	100.1	100.0	100.0	99.8
移动电话机	Mobile Phone	98.8	98.2	97.4	96.0	97.9	98.3	98.4	97.4	97.6	98.1	98.4	97.6
传真机	Fax Machine	100.0	99.8	100.1	99.9	100.0	100.0	100.0	98.6	99.9	100.0	99.9	100.0
其他	Others	99.5	99.5	99.7	99.5	99.1	100.0	99.8	100.0	100.0	100.0	100.0	100.0
十、家具	**Furniture**	**100.0**	**99.9**	**100.0**	**100.0**	**99.9**	**100.1**	**100.0**	**100.1**	**100.2**	**100.8**	**100.2**	**100.1**
柜	Cabinet	100.0	99.9	99.9	99.8	100.1	100.0	99.9	100.1	100.2	100.9	100.1	100.2
床	Bed	100.0	100.0	100.0	100.4	99.9	100.0	100.2	100.1	100.1	100.8	100.0	100.1
桌	Desk	100.0	100.1	99.9	100.1	99.9	99.9	100.1	99.8	99.9	100.5	100.3	100.1
椅	Chair	99.9	99.5	100.1	99.9	100.0	100.1	99.9	100.1	101.0	101.0	100.1	100.0
沙发	Sofa	100.1	100.0	100.0	100.0	99.8	100.2	99.9	100.1	100.1	100.7	100.3	100.0
其他	Others	99.9	99.9	100.2	100.1	99.8	101.2	101.0	100.0	101.1	100.5	100.1	100.1

7-25 续表 6 continued

商品类别及品名	Commodity Category and Commodity Name	1月 January	2月 February	3月 March	4月 April	5月 May	6月 June	7月 July	8月 August	9月 September	10月 October	11月 November	12月 December
		(以上月价格为100)											
十一、化妆品	**Cosmetics**	**99.7**	**100.1**	**99.9**	**100.1**	**100.0**	**99.9**	**100.0**	**100.0**	**100.0**	**100.2**	**99.8**	**99.9**
护肤品	Skincare Products	99.4	100.3	99.9	100.1	100.1	99.9	100.0	100.0	99.7	100.4	99.6	99.7
美容化妆品	Facial Beautifiers	99.8	100.1	100.0	100.1	100.0	99.9	100.2	100.0	100.0	100.1	100.1	100.0
护发美容品	Protects Sends the Beauty Products	99.7	100.0	99.7	100.0	99.9	100.1	99.8	100.2	99.9	100.2	99.8	100.0
清洁化妆用品	Cleaning Toiletware	99.9	100.0	100.1	100.1	100.1	99.8	99.9	99.8	100.3	100.1	99.9	100.0
药物美容用品	Medicinal Cosmetics	100.0	99.9	99.8	100.2	100.0	99.9	99.9	99.9	99.9	100.1	100.0	100.0
十二、金银珠宝	**Gold, Silver and Jewelry**	**101.9**	**101.7**	**102.9**	**103.0**	**106.7**	**102.6**	**100.1**	**101.1**	**99.4**	**99.9**	**100.3**	**100.3**
金饰品	Gold	103.5	102.7	103.6	104.2	110.0	101.0	99.5	101.4	99.4	99.2	100.2	100.3
银饰品	Silver	100.6	100.2	105.7	100.4	104.9	108.3	101.5	102.2	100.2	100.9	99.9	100.6
铂金饰品	Platinum	100.9	101.4	101.1	103.3	104.6	103.4	100.3	100.3	99.1	100.3	100.8	100.3
其他	Others	99.9	100.1	101.1	100.1	100.2	100.6	99.9	100.3	99.8	100.3	100.1	99.9
十三、中西药品及医疗保健用品	**Traditional Chinese and Western Medicines and Healthcare Articles**	**99.9**	**100.1**	**99.8**	**100.0**	**100.1**	**100.1**	**100.0**	**100.0**	**99.9**	**99.9**	**100.1**	**100.1**
1.医疗器具及用品	Medical Facilities and Goods	98.9	100.2	99.7	99.5	99.8	100.0	100.0	100.0	100.2	96.6	100.0	99.5
医疗器具及用品	Medical Facilities and Goods	98.9	100.2	99.7	99.5	99.8	100.0	100.0	100.0	100.2	96.6	100.0	99.5
2.中药材及中成药	Herbs and Ready-made Traditional Chinese Medicine	100.1	100.3	99.8	100.0	99.9	100.6	99.7	100.2	99.9	101.3	100.2	100.2
中药材	Herbs	100.3	100.7	99.3	100.2	100.6	101.8	99.6	100.1	100.4	102.2	100.5	100.2
中成药	Ready-made Traditional Chinese Medicine	100.0	100.0	100.1	99.8	99.4	99.6	99.7	100.2	99.5	100.4	100.0	100.2
3.西药	Western Medicine	99.9	100.0	99.9	100.0	100.3	99.8	100.2	99.8	99.7	99.4	100.0	100.1
抗微生物药	Anti-microorganism Medicine	100.0	100.0	100.0	100.0	100.0	100.3	102.1	99.5	99.9	98.9	100.2	100.2
消化系统用药	Alimentary System Medicine	99.9	100.1	100.2	100.1	100.2	100.0	100.0	100.0	99.9	100.1	99.7	100.4
呼吸系统用药	Respiratory System Medicine	99.3	99.9	100.0	100.2	99.8	100.5	100.0	100.0	100.4	99.6	100.3	99.9
解热镇痛及非甾体抗炎药	Allays a Fever the Analgesia and the Non-steroid Body Anti-inflammatory Agent	101.1	100.0	99.5	99.9	100.4	98.9	99.5	100.0	99.6	100.9	99.9	100.5
抗肿瘤药	Anti-neoplastic Drug	99.4	99.9	99.8	100.0	102.6	98.4	100.1	99.4	99.0	99.8	100.3	100.0
激素及调节内分泌功能药	Hormone and Adjustment Internal Secretion Function Medicine	100.0	100.0	99.6	100.0	100.0	99.5	99.5	99.7	99.2	97.7	100.7	99.5
循环系统用药	Circulating System Medicine	99.5	100.0	100.0	100.0	100.1	100.5	99.6	100.0	100.3	100.9	99.2	100.4
神经系统用药	Nerve System Medicine	100.0	100.1	99.6	100.2	100.0	99.8	100.0	99.6	99.7	97.0	100.0	100.3
专科用药	Junior Medicine	99.5	99.9	100.2	100.0	100.1	100.4	99.9	100.0	98.5	98.1	100.2	99.7
其他	Others	100.0	100.0	99.3	100.0	99.7	99.8	99.9	100.0	100.0	99.6	99.8	99.8
4.保健品及器具	Healthcare Equipment	99.7	99.8	99.8	100.1	100.0	100.3	99.5	100.2	100.1	100.1	100.1	99.9
保健器具	Health Protection Equipment	99.7	99.5	99.8	100.0	99.9	100.4	99.7	99.9	100.0	99.7	100.1	99.8
滋补保健用品	Tonic and Health Products	99.6	99.9	99.8	100.2	100.0	100.3	99.4	100.3	100.1	100.2	100.2	100.0

7-25 续表 7 continued

商品类别及品名	Commodity Category and Commodity Name	（以上月价格为100） 1月 January	2月 February	3月 March	4月 April	5月 May	6月 June	7月 July	8月 August	9月 September	10月 October	11月 November	12月 December
十四、书报杂志及电子出版物	**Books, Newspapers, Magazines and Electronic Publications**	**100.6**	**99.9**	**100.0**	**100.1**	**100.0**	**100.0**	**100.0**	**100.1**	**100.0**	**100.0**	**99.9**	**100.0**
1.教材及参考书	Teaching Materials and Reference Books	100.0	100.0	100.1	100.1	100.0	100.0	100.0	100.3	99.9	99.9	100.0	100.0
工具书	Tool Book	100.0	100.0	100.0	100.0	100.0	100.0	100.0	100.0	100.0	100.0	100.0	100.0
教材	Teaching Material	100.0	100.0	100.2	100.1	100.0	100.0	100.0	100.2	98.9	99.8	100.0	100.0
参考书	Reference Book	100.0	100.0	100.1	100.0	100.0	99.9	100.0	100.9	101.7	100.0	100.0	100.0
教育软件	Educational Software	100.0	100.0	99.4	100.0	100.0	100.0	100.0	100.0	100.0	100.0	100.0	100.0
2.书报杂志	Books, Newspapers, Magazines	101.9	100.0	100.1	100.0	100.0	100.0	100.0	100.0	100.0	100.0	100.0	100.1
书籍	Books	100.1	100.0	100.3	100.0	100.0	100.0	100.0	100.1	100.0	100.0	100.0	100.1
报纸	Newspapers	105.4	100.0	100.0	100.0	100.0	100.0	100.0	100.0	100.0	100.0	100.0	100.0
杂志	Magazines	100.4	100.0	100.0	100.0	100.0	100.0	100.0	100.0	100.0	100.0	100.0	100.2
3.电子音像制品	Electronic Publications	99.8	99.7	99.8	100.2	100.0	100.0	99.9	100.0	99.9	100.1	99.7	100.0
音响光盘和磁带	Acoustic Light Disk and Tape	100.0	99.2	99.8	100.3	100.1	100.0	100.0	100.0	99.9	100.1	100.0	100.0
录像磁带和视盘	Video Tape and Disk	99.9	99.9	100.0	100.3	100.0	100.1	99.8	100.0	99.8	100.2	99.9	99.9
计算机软件	Computer Software	99.4	100.0	99.6	100.0	99.9	99.9	100.0	100.0	100.1	100.0	99.2	100.0
十五、燃料	**Fuels**	**100.7**	**100.1**	**99.6**	**101.8**	**101.2**	**102.3**	**100.0**	**100.3**	**100.9**	**100.6**	**100.3**	**100.3**
1.煤炭及制品	Coal and Related Products	100.5	99.9	100.1	100.2	100.1	99.6	99.9	100.2	100.4	102.0	100.6	100.9
原煤	Raw Coal	100.7	99.8	100.3	99.4	100.3	99.6	100.0	100.2	100.3	103.3	100.9	100.8
煤制品	Coal Products	100.2	99.9	99.9	101.1	99.9	99.6	99.9	100.0	100.5	100.4	100.2	100.9
2.石油及制品	Petroleum and Related Products	100.8	100.2	99.4	102.5	101.6	103.5	100.1	100.3	101.2	99.9	100.2	100.1
液化石油气	Liquefiled Petroleum Gas	103.3	100.9	95.4	99.5	100.4	98.5	99.2	101.6	105.9	99.4	99.9	100.2
管道燃气	Pipelined Gas	100.3	100.0	100.0	100.0	100.1	100.0	100.0	100.0	100.0	100.0	100.0	100.0
汽油	Gasoline	100.0	100.0	100.6	105.1	102.6	106.4	100.3	100.0	100.1	100.0	100.0	100.0
柴油	Diesel Oil	100.3	99.9	100.8	103.3	102.7	105.9	100.3	100.0	100.2	100.3	100.9	100.1
其他	Others	100.3	100.0	100.1	101.4	99.8	101.1	100.4	100.0	100.6	99.8	100.1	100.4
十六、建筑材料及五金电料	**Building Materials and Hardware**	**100.1**	**100.1**	**100.4**	**100.6**	**100.6**	**100.7**	**100.3**	**100.6**	**100.8**	**100.3**	**100.7**	**100.2**
1.建筑装璜材料	Building and Decoration Materials	100.1	100.0	100.5	100.9	100.5	100.8	100.4	100.5	100.6	100.4	100.9	100.1
木材	Wood	100.6	100.2	100.4	100.6	100.0	100.9	100.9	102.4	101.1	101.3	102.4	100.1
木地板	Wood Floor	100.0	100.0	99.4	100.5	100.4	100.9	100.6	100.4	100.9	100.6	101.5	100.2
钢材	Steel Products	99.7	100.2	101.0	101.7	102.2	102.4	99.0	98.6	100.0	100.0	99.9	99.7
砖	Brick	99.4	100.2	101.5	102.0	100.9	101.2	100.2	101.0	100.2	100.0	100.2	100.0
水泥	Cement	99.5	99.4	100.1	101.7	100.3	100.1	100.0	99.7	100.7	100.0	100.9	100.0
涂料	Coating Material	100.5	100.0	99.9	99.9	99.5	100.4	100.0	100.1	99.6	100.2	100.4	100.4
胶合板	Plywood	100.5	100.1	100.7	100.7	99.4	100.8	101.0	100.8	101.2	99.5	102.6	100.4
玻璃	Glass	100.7	99.6	100.5	100.1	100.7	100.4	101.0	100.6	100.6	101.0	100.5	100.1
粘胶	Rayon	100.2	100.0	99.9	99.9	100.2	100.5	100.3	100.8	100.7	100.4	100.4	101.1
油漆	Paint	100.8	100.2	100.1	100.0	100.4	100.5	100.5	100.1	102.2	100.0	99.8	100.4
其他	Others	100.1	100.1	101.8	100.4	100.4	98.4	101.8	100.1	100.3	102.4	100.1	98.4
2.五金电料	Hardware	100.1	100.3	100.1	100.0	100.9	100.7	100.1	100.7	101.2	100.2	100.3	100.4
五金工具	Hardware Tools	100.0	100.0	99.6	99.5	99.9	100.7	99.9	100.3	101.2	100.1	99.8	100.3
电工电料	Electrical Engineering and Electrical Materials	100.2	100.8	100.1	100.2	101.7	100.3	100.0	101.6	100.8	100.0	100.0	100.1
水暖器材	Heating Equipment	100.0	100.0	100.3	100.2	101.2	100.3	99.9	100.2	101.5	100.5	101.0	100.6
其他	Others	100.0	100.7	100.6	99.9	100.0	103.0	101.6	100.7	101.5	100.0	100.0	100.6

7-26 城市商品零售价格（环比）指数

Urban Retail Price Index

（以上月价格为100）

商品类别及品名	Commodity Category and Commodity Name	1月 January	2月 February	3月 March	4月 April	5月 May	6月 June	7月 July	8月 August	9月 September	10月 October	11月 November	12月 December
商品零售价格总指数	**Genaral Retail Price Index**	**101.3**	**100.0**	**99.4**	**100.0**	**99.6**	**99.4**	**99.4**	**100.1**	**100.4**	**99.9**	**100.5**	**101.3**
一、食品	**Food**	**105.2**	**100.5**	**98.2**	**100.0**	**98.3**	**97.1**	**98.2**	**100.6**	**101.9**	**99.1**	**101.6**	**104.6**
1.粮食	Grain	100.2	100.0	100.1	100.0	100.5	100.7	100.6	100.9	100.2	100.6	103.4	102.2
大米	Rice	101.1	100.0	100.3	99.9	101.7	101.8	101.3	102.5	100.2	100.9	101.0	102.2
面粉	Flour	99.6	100.1	99.7	99.5	99.9	99.8	100.2	99.4	100.0	100.5	107.2	103.2
粮食制品	Grain Products	100.0	100.2	100.3	100.3	100.0	100.6	100.3	100.9	100.3	100.3	102.3	101.4
其他	Others	101.0	99.3	100.1	100.7	100.5	101.2	100.2	100.7	100.7	101.1	102.7	101.6
2.淀粉	Starches	99.5	100.4	100.1	100.1	99.9	100.7	99.5	100.6	100.7	100.3	100.9	103.5
淀粉	Starches	99.5	100.4	100.1	100.1	99.9	100.7	99.5	100.6	100.7	100.3	100.9	103.5
3.干豆类及豆制品	Beans and Beans Products	100.5	99.9	100.2	99.6	100.4	100.5	100.9	100.2	99.6	99.8	100.3	101.0
干豆	Beans	99.6	100.0	99.4	99.7	101.0	102.3	103.1	101.1	97.5	98.4	100.4	100.4
豆制品	Beans Products	100.7	99.9	100.5	99.6	100.2	100.0	100.3	100.0	100.2	100.2	100.3	101.2
4.油脂	Oil and Fat	99.9	99.7	99.6	99.8	100.0	100.4	99.8	100.4	100.4	100.0	101.9	105.9
食用植物油	Edible Vegetable Oil	99.8	99.7	99.8	100.3	100.0	100.4	100.0	100.5	100.3	99.9	101.5	104.3
植物油制品	Plant Oil Products	99.3	99.5	99.7	99.7	100.2	100.1	99.2	99.9	100.1	100.1	102.6	114.2
其他	Others	105.8	100.6	94.0	89.7	96.1	102.0	99.1	102.8	102.4	101.3	107.2	106.8
5.肉禽及其制品	Meal, Poultry and their Products	103.6	99.7	97.6	97.8	98.4	100.5	102.5	103.1	101.3	100.5	102.7	104.9
（1）食用畜肉及副产品	Edible Livestock Meat and their By-products	104.5	99.0	96.1	96.1	97.7	100.8	103.1	104.6	102.4	100.3	104.4	106.9
猪肉	Pork	105.0	98.6	94.9	94.2	96.9	101.2	104.6	106.9	103.2	100.2	106.1	108.1
牛肉	Beef	103.1	100.0	98.6	99.7	98.6	100.5	100.7	99.8	101.3	99.8	101.3	103.3
羊肉	Mutton	103.3	99.5	98.1	100.7	99.8	100.0	100.2	99.6	100.8	100.8	100.4	103.8
畜肉副产品	Livestock Meat By-products	104.2	99.7	98.1	97.8	98.3	100.3	101.6	101.9	100.9	100.9	101.9	107.3
其他	Others	102.9	99.7	98.3	98.8	99.6	100.2	99.6	102.5	100.9	100.7	101.7	103.4
（2）禽	Poultry	106.6	100.8	99.7	100.1	98.0	100.1	104.9	103.0	99.0	101.6	100.5	103.3
鸡	Chicken	108.3	101.1	99.8	100.4	97.4	100.1	106.3	103.5	99.1	102.0	100.6	103.6
鸭	Duck	100.5	99.7	99.5	97.8	101.3	100.2	97.8	99.8	97.7	100.0	99.7	102.1
其他	Others	100.8	99.3	98.7	99.4	98.9	99.8	101.1	102.0	99.3	99.8	100.4	101.4
（3）肉禽加工制品	Meal and Poultry Processing Products	100.4	100.6	99.6	100.0	99.8	100.0	100.2	100.3	100.3	100.3	100.5	101.4
畜肉制品	Livestock Meat Products	100.6	100.6	99.5	100.1	99.6	99.9	100.3	100.0	100.0	100.3	100.6	101.6
禽制品	Poultry Products	99.9	100.5	99.9	99.9	100.2	100.2	100.1	100.7	100.8	100.1	100.2	101.0
6.蛋	Eggs	99.2	95.6	97.0	99.6	101.5	101.6	100.8	110.2	105.7	99.2	101.4	104.5
鲜蛋	Fresh Eggs	99.0	95.0	96.6	99.5	101.9	101.9	100.9	111.7	106.4	98.9	101.5	104.8
蛋制品	Egg Products	100.8	100.1	99.6	100.2	99.4	99.5	99.6	100.6	100.6	100.8	100.3	102.7
7.水产品	Aquatic Product	104.1	101.5	98.7	100.6	100.4	100.7	101.3	100.0	98.0	100.0	99.0	100.3
（1）鱼	Fish	103.0	100.1	96.9	101.2	101.0	102.7	101.9	101.4	98.3	99.0	97.6	100.0
淡水鱼	Freshwater Fish	100.2	98.7	96.4	98.1	102.0	104.6	103.5	102.5	99.3	97.3	97.1	99.7
海水鱼	Seawater Fish	105.3	101.2	97.4	103.5	100.3	101.3	100.8	100.5	97.5	100.3	98.0	100.2

7-26 续表 1 continued

商品类别及品名	Commodity Category and Commodity Name	（以上月价格为100）											
		1月 January	2月 February	3月 March	4月 April	5月 May	6月 June	7月 July	8月 August	9月 September	10月 October	11月 November	12月 December
（2）其他水产品	Other Aquatic Product	105.5	103.3	100.8	99.8	99.8	98.2	100.5	98.2	97.7	101.5	100.8	100.8
虾蟹类	Shrimp and Crab	106.7	104.3	100.0	100.0	99.8	97.9	99.9	97.7	97.0	102.1	101.0	101.5
其他	Others	102.8	101.0	102.7	99.4	99.9	99.0	101.9	99.4	99.3	100.1	100.3	99.3
8.菜	Vegetable	129.8	99.4	91.1	96.4	85.3	85.6	93.8	107.2	114.6	86.5	102.6	121.7
鲜菜	Fresh Vegetable	132.9	99.0	90.0	95.6	82.8	83.2	92.5	108.9	118.5	84.6	103.0	124.6
干菜及菜制品	Dried Vegetable and Vegetable Products	103.3	100.9	100.1	101.1	100.0	99.9	100.9	100.7	101.7	102.1	101.4	104.8
薯类	Potato	114.7	104.7	102.2	105.9	111.7	100.3	98.6	96.7	84.0	91.7	99.2	109.7
9.调味品	Flavoring	100.4	99.9	99.9	100.5	100.2	100.3	100.0	99.9	100.0	100.3	101.1	100.7
盐	Salt	99.9	99.7	100.0	101.1	100.1	101.2	98.9	99.2	99.6	100.2	100.0	100.1
酱油	Soy Sauce	100.4	100.0	99.9	100.2	99.9	99.5	100.0	100.5	99.8	100.3	100.2	100.2
醋	Vinegar	100.1	100.0	99.9	100.3	99.9	100.2	100.1	100.0	100.1	100.1	100.0	100.5
味精	Aginomoto	100.6	100.0	99.8	100.4	100.3	99.6	100.0	99.8	100.1	99.9	99.8	100.5
其他	Others	101.4	99.6	100.0	100.3	101.0	101.0	101.2	100.1	100.6	101.2	106.5	102.4
10.糖	Carbohydrate	101.2	101.8	101.3	100.3	100.8	100.4	99.9	100.2	100.2	100.1	100.2	100.8
食糖	Sugar	103.9	105.2	105.7	101.0	102.4	101.6	99.8	100.9	100.4	99.8	99.8	102.8
糖果	Sweet	100.8	101.5	100.2	100.3	100.3	100.2	100.0	100.0	100.2	100.4	100.3	100.2
巧克力制品	Chocolate Products	100.4	100.0	99.7	99.9	99.7	99.8	99.7	99.7	100.0	100.3	100.0	99.9
糖类小食品	Little Carbohydrate Food	99.9	100.4	100.1	100.0	100.9	100.0	99.9	100.1	100.1	100.0	100.4	100.1
11.干鲜瓜果	Dried and Fresh Melons and Fruits	107.8	106.9	100.3	107.2	102.6	86.3	84.1	87.7	99.1	106.6	104.3	104.8
鲜瓜果	Fresh Fruits	108.9	108.3	100.2	108.5	103.0	83.7	80.4	84.2	98.7	108.2	104.9	106.0
干（坚）果	Dried Fruits	103.4	100.5	100.7	101.1	100.7	100.0	100.0	100.0	100.3	102.1	102.5	101.2
12.糕点饼干面包	Cake, Biscuit and Bread	100.1	99.9	100.0	100.2	100.2	99.9	99.9	100.0	99.9	99.7	99.8	100.6
糕点	Cake	99.7	100.0	99.8	99.9	100.0	99.7	99.8	99.5	100.0	99.0	100.3	100.8
饼干	Biscuit	100.1	99.8	100.2	100.7	100.7	100.2	99.9	100.2	99.4	100.0	99.3	100.3
面包	Bread	100.8	99.7	100.0	100.0	100.0	99.8	99.9	100.6	100.3	100.6	99.4	100.7
13.液体乳及乳制品	Liquid Milk and their Products	99.8	100.0	100.5	100.2	99.9	100.2	100.1	100.3	101.4	99.9	99.9	100.0
巴氏杀菌奶或消毒奶	Pasteurization Milk or Disinfection Milk	99.6	100.0	100.9	100.1	99.8	100.2	100.2	100.2	101.2	100.1	99.9	100.0
酸奶	Leben	100.2	100.0	100.0	100.2	100.4	100.2	99.7	99.9	101.8	100.0	99.7	100.1
奶粉	Milk Powder	100.2	100.1	100.0	100.8	99.6	100.2	100.3	101.5	100.3	99.5	100.2	100.3
其他	Others	99.9	100.0	100.0	100.0	100.0	100.0	100.0	100.0	102.7	99.7	100.2	99.8
14.在外用膳食品	Outward Dinner	100.1	100.0	100.1	100.1	100.0	100.4	100.1	100.1	100.2	99.8	100.5	102.2
主食	Staple Food	100.1	99.6	100.1	100.0	100.0	100.5	100.1	100.1	100.1	100.0	101.2	103.7
炒菜	Hot Dish	100.1	100.1	100.1	100.3	100.0	100.5	99.9	100.0	100.4	99.7	100.1	101.5
地方小吃	Local Snack	100.1	100.0	100.3	100.0	100.0	100.0	100.9	100.7	99.8	100.0	100.5	101.5
15.其他食品	Other Foods	99.7	99.9	100.2	100.0	100.0	100.0	99.8	100.0	100.1	99.8	100.0	100.6
其他食品	Other Foods	99.7	99.9	100.2	100.0	100.0	100.0	99.8	100.0	100.1	99.8	100.0	100.6
二、饮料、烟酒	**Beverages, Tobacco, Liquor**	**100.2**	**100.0**	**100.1**	**100.3**	**100.0**	**100.4**	**100.0**	**100.3**	**100.1**	**100.1**	**100.0**	**100.3**
1.茶及饮料	Tea and Beverages	99.9	100.2	100.8	100.1	100.2	100.3	99.9	100.2	100.0	100.1	100.0	100.2
（1）茶叶	Tea	99.8	100.4	100.4	100.0	100.1	100.1	100.2	99.8	100.0	100.1	100.0	100.5

7-26 续表 2 continued

商品类别及品名	Commodity Category and Commodity Name	1月 January	2月 February	3月 March	4月 April	5月 May	6月 June	7月 July	8月 August	9月 September	10月 October	11月 November	12月 December
		（以上月价格为100）											
茶叶	Tea	99.8	100.4	100.4	100.0	100.1	100.1	100.2	99.8	100.0	100.1	100.0	100.5
（2）饮料	Beverages	100.0	100.1	101.0	100.1	100.3	100.4	99.7	100.4	100.0	100.1	99.9	100.1
固体饮料	Solid Beverages	100.0	100.2	99.8	99.7	100.4	100.0	100.0	99.7	99.8	100.1	99.9	99.4
液体饮料	Liquid Beverages	100.0	100.1	100.8	100.2	100.1	100.1	99.5	100.1	100.1	100.0	100.0	100.5
冷冻饮品	Frozen Beverages	100.1	100.0	102.5	100.3	100.4	101.3	99.9	101.5	99.8	100.2	99.8	99.9
2.烟草	Tobacco	100.2	99.7	99.9	100.4	99.9	100.1	99.9	99.9	99.8	100.0	100.0	100.2
国产卷烟	Domestic Cigarette	100.3	99.9	99.9	100.5	100.0	100.2	99.9	99.9	99.7	100.1	100.0	100.1
进口卷烟	Import Cigarette	100.0	98.7	100.0	100.1	99.6	100.0	99.9	99.9	100.1	99.9	100.3	100.7
其他	Others	100.0	100.0	99.5	99.5	100.0	100.0	100.0	99.1	100.0	100.0	100.0	100.0
3.酒	Liquor	100.4	100.0	99.9	100.4	100.0	100.5	100.2	100.6	100.4	100.1	100.0	100.5
白酒	White Spirit	100.3	99.9	100.3	100.4	100.0	100.8	100.1	100.9	100.4	100.2	100.1	100.7
葡萄酒	Grape	103.6	100.2	99.8	100.3	99.9	101.0	100.3	100.3	100.4	100.0	100.0	100.0
啤酒	Beer	99.8	100.1	99.3	100.4	100.0	100.0	100.4	100.3	100.4	100.0	99.8	100.2
其他	Others	100.0	100.0	100.0	100.5	100.1	100.4	100.1	99.9	100.1	100.0	100.0	100.0
三、服装、鞋帽	**Garments, Footgearand and Hats**	**98.9**	**99.0**	**99.6**	**99.5**	**99.5**	**99.9**	**98.9**	**99.2**	**100.4**	**101.1**	**100.6**	**99.8**
1.服装	Garments	98.8	98.6	99.2	99.7	99.5	100.0	99.5	99.4	100.2	101.5	100.8	100.2
（1）男式服装	Men's Garments	98.3	99.1	98.9	99.5	99.3	99.7	99.5	99.1	100.1	101.5	100.8	100.0
大衣	Topcoat	97.9	99.1	99.4	98.5	100.1	99.3	99.7	100.0	99.6	99.7	100.1	100.5
毛线衣	Woollen Sweater	99.3	94.1	93.4	99.9	99.1	100.2	99.5	99.7	99.5	102.4	101.8	101.4
夹克衫	Jacket	97.8	98.6	96.8	99.4	99.9	100.0	99.9	100.1	100.3	103.6	100.5	100.3
衬衫	Shirt	96.0	99.7	100.2	99.2	99.3	101.0	98.5	98.8	100.7	100.6	99.9	101.1
T恤衫	T-shirt	99.8	100.3	99.0	99.9	98.2	97.0	97.0	97.5	100.7	99.7	100.8	100.0
裤子	Trousers	97.9	98.3	100.0	99.9	99.6	99.4	99.4	99.3	99.0	103.0	100.4	99.3
西服	Western-style Clothes	98.4	101.5	99.2	100.8	99.6	99.7	101.0	96.9	102.2	101.9	99.4	99.6
运动衫裤	Gym Suit	98.9	100.0	100.0	99.5	96.9	100.2	99.4	100.8	99.6	100.3	101.1	100.2
内衣	Underwaist	99.3	100.1	101.1	99.8	99.5	100.2	99.4	100.1	99.7	100.4	99.6	100.2
羽绒衣	Eider down Outerwear	97.6	99.4	99.5	96.2	99.9	99.9	99.4	99.9	99.1	102.6	105.1	98.2
其他	Others	99.4	98.9	98.6	99.0	100.2	99.8	99.7	99.8	100.0	100.0	104.1	99.8
（2）女式服装	Women's Garments	99.0	98.0	99.4	99.6	99.4	100.2	99.7	99.6	100.5	101.6	100.8	100.4
大衣	Topcoat	98.1	94.2	97.9	99.2	99.9	100.0	99.6	100.0	99.9	100.0	100.8	103.1
毛线衣	Woollen Sweater	99.2	93.3	98.4	99.9	99.0	100.5	99.9	100.0	100.7	103.1	99.7	101.6
羽绒衣	Eider down Outerwear	98.5	99.1	98.5	99.7	100.0	99.8	99.5	99.8	99.3	103.4	105.9	98.4
套装	Coordinates	97.7	100.2	99.6	100.0	100.6	98.6	100.8	96.7	104.6	101.2	98.5	100.4
衬衫	Shirt	97.5	101.5	100.3	97.4	100.0	100.5	100.3	98.2	100.6	100.3	99.7	98.6
T恤衫	T-shirt	100.0	100.3	99.7	98.8	100.2	100.4	98.8	99.6	104.1	107.4	100.1	99.9
裙子	Skirt	100.3	99.3	99.5	97.6	101.1	100.2	99.9	99.9	99.6	100.4	101.2	99.9
裤子	Trousers	99.7	97.7	99.1	100.2	99.3	100.6	99.1	100.2	99.9	100.7	101.2	98.3
运动衫裤	Gym Suit	99.8	100.7	99.5	100.6	94.0	100.6	99.5	99.9	99.9	102.2	98.5	102.3
内衣	Underwaist	99.0	100.2	101.8	101.4	99.3	100.7	99.5	100.1	99.2	101.0	101.4	99.9
其他	Others	99.4	99.3	100.5	101.1	99.3	100.5	100.0	100.9	99.8	100.7	100.4	99.8

7-26 续表 3 continued

商品类别及品名	Commodity Category and Commodity Name	（以上月价格为100）											
		1月 January	2月 February	3月 March	4月 April	5月 May	6月 June	7月 July	8月 August	9月 September	10月 October	11月 November	12月 December
（3）儿童服装	Children's Garments	99.5	99.8	99.9	100.4	100.6	100.1	98.7	99.8	99.3	100.7	100.6	99.7
套装	Coordinates	99.4	99.8	99.6	100.1	99.6	99.9	99.5	99.5	99.4	100.6	100.8	99.8
裤子	Trousers	99.1	99.7	100.0	99.9	100.4	100.0	98.0	100.3	99.3	101.3	100.6	100.5
裙子	Skirt	99.9	100.1	101.0	102.1	103.1	100.6	97.9	99.6	98.7	100.6	100.3	99.0
其他	Others	99.8	98.1	97.0	97.5	98.7	99.6	99.7	100.0	100.9	100.0	100.9	99.1
2.鞋袜帽	Shoes, Socks and Hats	99.2	99.6	100.7	99.3	99.3	99.8	97.2	98.5	100.6	100.2	100.2	99.1
（1）鞋	Shoes	99.1	99.6	100.8	99.1	99.2	99.8	96.7	98.2	100.8	100.2	100.3	99.0
男鞋	Men's Shoes	99.1	99.9	101.5	99.5	99.2	100.5	96.6	98.3	100.6	99.9	100.3	99.2
女鞋	Women's Shoes	99.0	99.2	100.7	98.5	98.9	99.2	96.1	97.7	101.5	100.1	100.3	98.7
童鞋	Children's Shoes	99.5	99.9	99.7	99.8	100.8	99.9	99.3	99.8	99.1	101.1	100.5	100.0
（2）袜子	Socks	99.6	100.0	99.5	100.7	99.2	100.1	99.8	100.0	99.6	100.6	99.3	99.5
男袜	Men's Socks	99.5	99.9	99.8	100.6	99.7	99.9	99.8	100.0	99.7	100.5	99.0	98.9
女袜	Women's Socks	99.7	100.0	99.2	100.9	98.8	100.2	99.8	100.0	99.5	100.7	99.7	100.0
（3）帽子	Hats	100.0	99.6	99.9	100.0	100.2	100.1	100.0	100.1	99.5	100.5	100.4	100.1
男帽	Men's Hats	100.0	99.6	99.7	100.0	100.5	100.3	100.1	100.5	98.8	100.4	100.9	100.5
女帽	Women's Hats	99.9	99.6	100.0	100.0	100.1	99.9	99.9	99.8	99.9	100.6	100.1	99.9
3.其他	Others	99.0	101.1	99.5	99.2	99.8	100.1	99.5	99.2	100.9	100.6	100.0	98.3
领带	Necktie	99.0	101.1	99.5	99.2	99.8	100.1	99.5	99.2	100.9	100.6	100.0	98.3
四、纺织品	**Textiles**	**99.1**	**100.6**	**100.1**	**99.9**	**99.6**	**100.3**	**99.8**	**99.9**	**99.7**	**100.2**	**99.9**	**100.3**
1.衣着材料	Clothing Materials	99.6	100.0	99.8	100.0	99.8	100.1	100.0	100.0	100.1	100.3	100.1	100.3
棉布	Cotton Cloth	99.2	99.9	100.8	101.2	99.9	100.2	100.3	100.1	101.1	100.6	99.7	100.0
棉混纺布	Cotton Textiles Cloth	99.1	100.4	100.0	100.0	99.9	100.0	99.8	100.1	99.6	100.3	100.5	100.2
化纤布	Chemical Fiber Cloth	99.9	100.0	99.0	99.3	99.7	100.0	99.8	100.0	99.9	100.1	100.0	100.1
毛线	Knitting Wool	100.0	99.8	99.9	100.0	99.9	100.0	100.1	99.8	100.2	100.2	100.2	101.3
2.床上用品	Bedclothes	98.7	101.0	100.3	99.9	99.3	100.6	99.7	99.8	99.2	100.2	99.7	100.3
毛毯	Woollen Blanket	98.9	100.6	100.5	99.8	99.1	101.0	99.0	99.8	99.5	100.4	99.8	100.9
被子	Quilt	98.8	100.6	100.0	99.6	98.9	100.9	99.6	99.5	98.6	99.5	98.7	100.6
床上套件	Bed Articles	98.2	101.2	100.5	99.9	99.5	100.5	100.0	100.0	99.3	100.6	100.3	99.9
其他	Others	99.3	101.9	100.3	100.1	100.0	99.7	100.0	100.0	99.9	100.2	100.2	100.1
五、家用电器及音像器材	**Household Appliances, Music and Video Equipments**	**99.9**	**99.9**	**100.0**	**99.5**	**100.1**	**101.0**	**100.4**	**99.8**	**99.3**	**99.8**	**100.0**	**99.8**
1.家庭设备	Household Appliances	100.1	100.1	100.1	99.8	100.3	102.2	100.9	100.2	99.9	100.2	100.2	100.0
洗衣机	Washing Machine	99.9	100.0	99.9	98.7	100.8	101.3	100.7	99.4	99.7	99.9	100.3	99.7
电风扇	Electric Fan	100.1	100.2	100.1	99.6	100.4	100.5	99.4	100.3	98.0	100.3	100.0	100.0
电冰箱（柜）	Refrigerator	99.7	100.0	100.2	100.1	100.7	102.3	101.4	99.9	100.0	100.7	99.7	100.1
吸排油烟机	Kitchen Ventilato	100.5	100.0	100.0	100.1	99.8	102.7	102.1	101.3	99.7	99.8	100.2	99.9
空调器	Air-Conditioning	100.3	100.0	100.0	99.8	100.4	103.7	101.1	100.5	100.3	100.0	100.3	100.1
热水器	Water Heater	99.9	100.7	101.0	100.4	99.2	100.3	100.0	100.1	100.0	100.3	100.0	100.2
微波炉	Microwave Oven	99.4	99.9	99.9	99.8	99.9	100.7	99.8	100.0	99.8	100.3	100.6	99.8
电炊具	Electric Cooking Appliance	100.1	99.9	100.1	101.0	100.1	99.9	100.0	100.2	99.4	100.3	100.0	100.0
2.文娱用耐用消费品	Durable Consumer Goods For Recreational Use	99.7	99.7	99.7	99.0	99.9	99.6	99.7	99.2	98.1	99.1	99.9	99.5

7-26 续表 4 continued

商品类别及品名	Commodity Category and Commodity Name	（以上月价格为100） 1月 January	2月 February	3月 March	4月 April	5月 May	6月 June	7月 July	8月 August	9月 September	10月 October	11月 November	12月 December
电视机	Television	99.6	99.9	99.8	98.7	99.9	99.6	99.7	98.5	97.7	98.7	99.8	99.3
激光视盘机	Laser Video Disc Machine	99.9	99.3	99.6	99.3	99.8	100.0	99.4	100.0	96.8	98.3	100.0	100.0
摄像机	Pickup Camera	99.7	99.8	99.4	98.8	99.5	98.8	99.6	99.9	98.5	99.8	99.6	99.1
家用音响设备	Acoustic Equipment	100.0	100.0	99.9	99.8	99.8	100.0	100.0	99.9	99.7	100.1	100.0	99.9
便携式音响	Portable Acoustics	99.9	99.2	99.4	99.6	100.0	100.0	100.0	100.0	99.5	100.1	100.0	99.9
其他	Others	100.0	100.1	99.9	99.9	99.9	100.0	100.0	99.4	99.6	100.2	99.9	100.0
3.音像器材	Music and Video Equipments	100.0	100.0	100.0	99.8	100.0	100.0	100.0	100.0	100.0	100.0	100.0	100.0
专业音响器材	Specialized Acoustic Apparatus	99.9	100.0	100.0	99.9	100.0	100.0	100.0	100.0	100.0	100.0	100.0	100.0
专业声像器材	Specialized Acoustic Image Apparatus	100.0	99.9	100.0	99.8	100.0	99.9	100.0	100.0	100.0	100.0	100.0	100.0
六、文化办公用品	**Cultural and Office Applicances**	**99.9**	**100.0**	**99.9**	**99.9**	**99.7**	**99.7**	**99.8**	**99.4**	**99.4**	**100.1**	**99.8**	**100.0**
纸张本册	Paper and Volume	100.0	100.0	100.0	100.0	100.0	100.0	99.9	100.0	100.3	100.4	99.9	100.0
文具	Stationery	99.8	100.2	100.0	99.9	100.0	100.0	100.0	100.0	99.5	100.3	100.0	100.0
电脑及配件	Computer and its Fitting	100.0	99.9	99.8	99.9	99.2	99.1	99.7	99.1	98.4	99.9	99.8	99.9
打印机及配件	Printer and its Fitting	99.8	100.0	99.8	99.9	99.8	100.3	99.7	98.9	99.9	99.9	99.7	100.0
扫描仪	Scanner	100.0	100.0	100.0	100.0	99.9	100.0	99.9	99.9	100.0	99.9	99.9	100.0
复印机	Xerox Machine	99.5	100.0	100.0	100.0	100.0	99.9	99.9	99.5	99.8	99.9	98.7	99.7
电子辞典	Electronic Dictionary	100.1	99.9	99.8	99.4	99.9	100.0	99.1	98.4	100.2	100.4	100.1	100.0
计算器	Calculator	100.0	100.2	100.0	99.9	100.0	100.0	100.0	99.9	99.9	100.1	100.2	100.2
教学设备	Teaching Equipment	100.0	100.1	99.9	100.0	100.0	99.9	99.9	100.0	99.8	100.1	100.0	100.0
其他	Others	100.0	100.0	100.0	100.0	100.0	99.9	99.8	100.0	100.2	100.2	100.0	100.1
七、日用品	**Articles for Daily Use**	**100.0**	**100.0**	**100.1**	**100.0**	**100.1**	**100.1**	**99.9**	**100.2**	**99.7**	**100.3**	**100.1**	**100.0**
1.日用百货	General Merchandise for Daily Use	100.2	100.0	100.1	100.2	100.2	99.9	100.2	100.0	99.9	100.3	100.1	100.0
自行车	Bicycle	100.0	99.9	100.0	100.0	99.8	100.1	100.8	99.9	100.1	100.3	100.0	99.7
雨具	Rain Gear	99.9	100.0	100.0	100.0	100.0	100.3	100.1	100.6	100.2	100.1	99.6	100.1
剃须刀具	Shaver	100.1	100.2	100.4	100.6	100.2	100.3	99.9	100.0	99.7	99.9	99.8	100.1
电池	Battery	100.0	100.2	100.0	99.9	100.7	97.2	100.3	99.8	99.6	100.2	100.4	100.1
卫生纸	Tissue Paper	100.8	99.9	100.5	100.7	100.3	100.8	100.0	100.1	100.0	100.1	100.0	100.2
卫生巾	Sanitary Towel	99.9	99.7	100.0	99.9	100.8	99.6	99.4	99.9	99.5	100.7	99.9	99.9
其他	Others	100.7	100.0	100.0	100.0	100.0	100.0	100.0	100.0	99.8	100.3	101.6	100.0
2.日用杂品	Sundry Articles	100.0	100.1	100.1	100.2	100.1	100.1	99.9	100.1	100.0	100.1	100.0	100.2
茶具	Tea Set	100.0	100.0	100.0	100.1	99.9	99.9	99.9	100.1	99.8	100.2	99.9	100.1
餐具	Tableware	100.0	100.0	100.1	100.1	100.5	100.0	99.7	100.4	100.0	100.2	100.0	100.6
厨具	Kitchen Utensils	100.0	100.0	100.0	100.4	100.0	100.4	100.1	99.9	100.2	100.1	100.2	100.0
其他	Others	99.9	100.3	100.3	99.7	100.0	100.0	100.0	100.0	99.9	99.7	99.9	100.0
3.洗涤用品	Washing Articles	99.9	100.1	100.0	100.0	100.0	100.3	100.0	100.3	99.8	100.2	100.1	100.3

7-26 续表 5 continued

商品类别及品名	Commodity Category and Commodity Name	（以上月价格为100）											
		1月 January	2月 February	3月 March	4月 April	5月 May	6月 June	7月 July	8月 August	9月 September	10月 October	11月 November	12月 December
洗衣粉	Washing Powder	100.0	100.0	100.1	100.1	99.8	100.9	100.0	100.9	99.8	100.2	99.8	100.5
肥皂类	Soap	99.7	100.1	99.9	99.8	100.0	100.1	100.0	100.2	99.8	100.2	100.2	100.1
牙膏	Toothpaste	100.0	100.4	99.7	100.1	100.2	100.1	99.9	99.9	99.8	100.1	100.4	100.3
清洁洗涤剂	Cleaning Agent	100.0	100.1	100.1	100.0	100.0	99.9	99.9	99.9	99.8	100.2	100.0	99.9
4.其他日用品	Other Articles for Daily Use	99.8	100.0	100.3	99.8	100.2	100.0	99.5	100.2	99.4	100.7	100.1	99.7
燃气灶具	Gas-oven	100.4	99.9	101.0	100.5	100.0	100.7	100.5	100.2	99.8	100.2	100.0	100.0
儿童玩具	Children's Toy	99.9	99.8	99.6	99.4	100.1	100.1	100.3	99.9	99.4	100.4	100.0	99.9
照明器具	Illumination Utensil	100.1	100.0	100.1	100.2	100.0	100.0	100.0	100.0	99.9	100.2	99.8	99.9
钟表眼镜及配件	Clocks, Glasses and their Fittings	99.4	99.8	100.1	100.4	100.0	100.2	100.1	100.1	99.2	100.6	100.3	99.9
日用普通饰品	Common Ornament for Daily Use	100.1	100.7	99.5	98.1	102.4	98.6	101.1	99.2	98.8	101.5	100.0	100.0
日用皮革制品	Leatherware for Daily Use	98.5	100.3	100.9	100.0	99.7	99.7	95.6	101.7	98.6	102.6	100.7	98.1
其他	Others	98.8	100.2	100.9	100.0	99.7	100.2	96.0	101.5	99.2	101.3	100.6	98.8
八、体育娱乐用品	**Sports and Recreation Articles**	**100.1**	**100.0**	**99.9**	**99.9**	**99.8**	**100.0**	**99.9**	**100.0**	**99.5**	**100.3**	**100.0**	**100.1**
1.体育用品	Sports Articles	100.1	100.0	99.9	100.0	99.7	100.1	99.9	99.9	99.6	100.4	99.9	100.0
球类	Ball	99.8	99.7	99.7	100.1	99.7	100.3	99.9	100.0	99.8	100.3	99.9	100.0
棋牌	Chess and Cards	100.6	100.2	100.0	99.7	99.8	99.2	100.0	100.0	99.9	100.4	100.0	100.0
健身器材	Exercise Machine	100.1	100.1	100.0	100.0	99.7	100.3	100.0	99.8	99.5	100.4	99.9	100.0
2.娱乐用品	Recreation Articles	100.0	100.0	99.9	99.9	100.0	99.9	99.9	100.1	99.5	100.2	100.1	100.1
游艺器材	Entertainment Apparatus	100.2	99.8	99.7	99.4	99.8	99.6	99.4	100.6	99.0	100.4	100.0	100.2
照相器材	Photographic Apparatus	100.0	100.1	100.0	100.0	100.0	100.0	100.0	100.0	99.6	100.1	100.1	100.1
乐器	Musical Instrument	100.0	100.0	100.0	100.0	100.0	100.0	100.0	100.0	99.7	100.3	100.1	100.1
九、交通、通信用品	**Transportation and Communication Appliances**	**99.7**	**99.7**	**99.2**	**99.0**	**99.6**	**99.6**	**99.6**	**99.4**	**99.1**	**99.5**	**99.4**	**99.4**
1.交通运输机械	Transportation Machine	99.8	100.0	99.8	99.7	100.0	99.9	99.8	99.7	99.2	99.8	99.7	99.5
轿车	Car	99.9	99.9	99.8	99.6	99.7	99.8	99.6	99.2	98.4	99.8	99.4	99.1
客车	Bus	100.1	99.9	99.7	100.0	100.0	100.0	99.9	100.0	98.6	100.0	100.0	100.0
货车	Truck	99.9	100.0	99.4	99.7	100.0	100.0	99.9	100.0	99.9	99.2	99.8	100.0
摩托车	Motorcycle	99.5	99.9	100.0	99.8	100.6	100.0	100.2	100.4	100.0	100.1	99.5	99.0
其他	Others	99.2	100.0	100.0	100.0	100.0	100.0	99.9	100.0	100.0	100.0	99.9	100.0
2.通信器材	Telecommunications Facilities	99.4	99.0	98.0	97.2	98.6	98.8	98.9	98.3	98.8	98.6	98.8	99.0
固定电话机	Telephone	100.0	99.4	99.6	99.8	99.5	99.9	99.8	99.8	99.6	100.0	99.9	99.6
移动电话机	Mobile Phone	99.0	98.6	96.8	95.5	97.8	98.0	98.3	97.4	98.0	97.6	98.0	98.4
传真机	Fax Machine	100.0	99.8	100.2	99.8	100.0	100.0	100.0	99.5	99.9	100.0	99.8	100.0
其他	Others	100.0	100.0	100.0	99.0	98.1	99.9	100.0	100.0	100.0	100.0	100.0	100.0
十、家具	**Furniture**	**100.0**	**100.0**	**100.0**	**99.7**	**99.9**	**100.2**	**100.1**	**100.3**	**100.4**	**100.1**	**100.0**	**100.0**
柜	Cabinet	100.0	100.0	100.0	99.2	100.2	100.1	99.9	100.5	100.3	99.9	100.1	100.0
床	Bed	100.0	100.0	100.1	99.9	99.9	100.1	100.3	100.2	100.2	100.3	99.7	99.8
桌	Desk	99.9	100.1	99.9	100.0	99.8	99.7	100.1	100.4	100.3	100.0	100.2	100.2
椅	Chair	99.9	99.6	100.1	99.9	100.0	100.1	100.0	100.1	101.3	100.5	100.2	99.9
沙发	Sofa	100.1	100.0	100.0	99.5	99.7	100.3	99.8	100.2	100.2	100.1	100.0	100.0
其他	Others	99.8	99.7	100.3	100.2	99.4	101.8	101.5	100.0	101.6	99.8	100.0	100.0

7-26 续表 6 continued

商品类别及品名	Commodity Category and Commodity Name	（以上月价格为100）											
		1月 January	2月 February	3月 March	4月 April	5月 May	6月 June	7月 July	8月 August	9月 September	10月 October	11月 November	12月 December
十一、化妆品	**Cosmetics**	**99.6**	**100.2**	**99.9**	**100.1**	**100.0**	**99.9**	**100.0**	**100.1**	**99.9**	**100.3**	**99.8**	**99.8**
护肤品	Skincare Products	99.1	100.4	99.8	100.2	99.9	100.0	99.9	100.1	99.6	100.6	99.4	99.5
美容化妆品	Facial Beautifiers	99.7	100.1	100.0	100.1	100.0	99.9	100.3	100.1	100.0	100.2	100.1	99.7
护发美容品	Protects Sends the Beauty Products	99.6	100.1	100.0	100.0	99.7	100.1	99.7	100.2	99.9	100.3	99.7	99.9
清洁化妆用品	Cleaning Toiletware	99.8	100.0	100.1	100.1	100.2	99.8	99.9	100.0	100.1	100.1	100.0	100.0
药物美容用品	Medicinal Cosmetics	99.9	99.9	99.7	100.3	99.9	99.9	99.9	99.9	99.9	100.1	100.0	100.0
十二、金银珠宝	**Gold, Silver and Jewelry**	**101.8**	**101.4**	**100.6**	**102.8**	**104.5**	**101.6**	**100.5**	**101.2**	**99.5**	**100.1**	**100.1**	**100.5**
金饰品	Gold	103.5	102.4	100.8	103.6	107.0	100.7	100.2	101.3	99.1	99.4	100.3	100.4
银饰品	Silver	100.4	100.3	100.7	100.5	101.1	100.6	102.5	104.0	100.4	101.5	99.7	101.5
铂金饰品	Platinum	101.0	101.0	100.3	103.9	104.2	103.5	100.3	100.4	99.7	100.4	100.1	100.4
其他	Others	99.8	100.1	100.7	99.7	99.5	100.5	100.1	100.3	99.7	100.3	100.1	100.1
十三、中西药品及医疗保健用品	**Traditional Chinese and Western Medicines and Healthcare Articles**	**99.9**	**99.9**	**99.9**	**99.9**	**99.9**	**100.2**	**99.9**	**100.0**	**99.4**	**100.2**	**100.0**	**100.0**
1.医疗器具及用品	Medical Facilities and Goods	99.8	100.0	99.7	99.6	100.0	100.0	99.9	100.0	100.0	95.3	100.1	99.9
医疗器具及用品	Medical Facilities and Goods	99.8	100.0	99.7	99.6	100.0	100.0	99.9	100.0	100.0	95.3	100.1	99.9
2.中药材及中成药	Herbs and Ready-made Traditional Chinese Medicine	100.1	99.7	100.2	99.8	99.7	100.7	99.4	100.2	99.3	102.2	100.1	100.1
中药材	Herbs	100.0	99.5	100.4	99.8	100.2	102.9	99.3	100.3	99.9	104.1	100.1	100.4
中成药	Ready-made Traditional Chinese Medicine	100.2	99.8	100.1	99.7	99.4	99.2	99.4	100.1	98.9	100.7	100.0	99.9
3.西药	Western Medicine	99.8	100.0	99.8	100.0	100.0	99.9	100.4	99.8	99.2	99.6	100.0	100.1
抗微生物药	Anti-microorganism Medicine	100.0	100.0	100.0	100.0	100.0	100.5	103.1	99.4	99.0	99.7	100.3	99.7
消化系统用药	Alimentary System Medicine	99.7	100.0	100.3	100.2	100.3	100.0	100.0	99.9	99.6	100.4	99.3	100.7
呼吸系统用药	Respiratory System Medicine	99.2	100.0	99.7	100.0	100.0	100.6	100.0	100.0	99.8	100.1	100.0	99.9
解热镇痛及非甾体抗炎药	Allays a Fever the Analgesia and the Non-steroid Body Anti-inflammatory	100.2	99.8	99.6	99.8	100.0	98.9	99.2	100.0	98.8	101.9	100.3	100.2
抗肿瘤药	Anti-neoplastic Drug	99.4	99.9	99.7	99.9	100.0	98.8	100.0	99.7	100.0	98.1	100.0	100.0
激素及调节内分泌功能药	Hormone and Adjustment Internal Secretion Function Medicine	100.2	100.0	99.4	100.0	100.0	99.3	100.0	99.6	97.8	97.8	101.0	99.6
循环系统用药	Circulating System Medicine	99.6	99.9	99.7	99.8	100.1	100.9	99.4	100.1	100.2	101.6	98.8	100.6
神经系统用药	Nerve System Medicine	100.1	100.0	99.4	100.0	100.0	99.7	100.0	99.4	99.0	96.2	100.0	100.1
专科用药	Junior Medicine	99.5	100.0	100.0	99.9	100.0	100.4	99.9	100.1	97.8	97.9	100.3	99.9
其他	Others	100.1	100.0	98.9	100.0	99.6	99.7	99.9	100.0	99.9	99.6	99.7	99.8
4.保健品及器具	Healthcare Equipment	99.9	99.8	99.7	100.0	99.9	100.3	99.3	100.2	99.9	100.4	100.1	99.9
保健器具	Health Protection Equipment	99.5	99.5	99.7	100.0	99.9	100.0	99.5	99.9	100.0	100.0	100.0	99.7
滋补保健用品	Tonic and Health Products	100.1	100.0	99.7	100.0	100.0	100.4	99.2	100.4	99.9	100.5	100.1	100.0

7-26 续表 7 continued

商品类别及品名	Commodity Category and Commodity Name	（以上月价格为100）											
		1月 January	2月 February	3月 March	4月 April	5月 May	6月 June	7月 July	8月 August	9月 September	10月 October	11月 November	12月 December
十四、书报杂志及电子出版物	**Books, Newspapers, Magazines and Electronic Publications**	**100.6**	**99.9**	**100.1**	**100.1**	**100.0**	**100.0**	**100.0**	**100.3**	**100.0**	**100.0**	**99.9**	**100.0**
1.教材及参考书	Teaching Materials and Reference Books	100.1	100.0	100.2	100.0	100.0	99.9	100.0	100.7	99.9	99.9	100.0	100.0
工具书	Tool Book	100.3	100.0	100.0	100.0	100.0	100.0	100.0	100.0	99.9	100.0	100.0	100.1
教材	Teaching Material	100.0	100.0	100.4	100.0	100.0	100.0	100.0	100.7	99.1	99.7	100.0	100.0
参考书	Reference Book	100.0	100.0	100.2	100.0	100.0	99.8	100.0	101.4	101.1	100.0	100.0	100.0
教育软件	Educational Software	100.0	100.0	100.0	100.0	100.0	100.0	100.0	100.0	100.0	100.0	100.0	100.0
2.书报杂志	Books, Newspapers, Magazines	101.9	100.0	100.2	100.0	100.0	100.0	100.0	100.0	100.0	100.0	100.0	100.1
书籍	Books	100.1	100.0	100.4	100.0	100.0	100.0	100.0	100.1	100.0	100.0	100.0	100.1
报纸	Newspapers	105.7	100.0	100.0	100.0	100.0	100.0	100.0	100.0	100.0	100.0	100.0	100.0
杂志	Magazines	100.1	100.0	100.0	100.0	100.0	100.0	100.0	100.0	100.0	100.0	100.0	100.2
3.电子音像制品	Electronic Publications	99.7	99.6	99.8	100.3	100.0	100.0	100.0	100.0	99.9	100.2	99.6	100.0
音响光盘和磁带	Acoustic Light Disk and Tape	100.0	98.9	99.8	100.4	100.0	100.0	100.0	100.0	99.8	100.2	100.0	100.0
录像磁带和视盘	Video Tape and Disk	99.9	99.9	100.1	100.4	100.1	100.2	100.0	100.0	99.8	100.3	99.9	99.9
计算机软件	Computer Software	99.3	100.0	99.7	100.0	99.9	99.8	100.0	100.0	100.2	100.0	98.9	100.0
十五、燃料	**Fuels**	**100.7**	**100.1**	**99.5**	**102.2**	**101.1**	**102.5**	**99.9**	**100.3**	**101.2**	**100.0**	**100.4**	**100.3**
1.煤炭及制品	Coal and Related Products	100.7	99.5	100.3	100.5	100.2	99.5	99.9	100.2	100.9	100.5	100.7	101.1
原煤	Raw Coal	101.3	99.2	100.5	98.9	100.4	99.6	100.0	100.4	100.7	100.7	101.0	100.9
煤制品	Coal Products	100.1	100.0	100.0	102.4	99.9	99.4	99.8	100.0	101.2	100.4	100.2	101.3
2.石油及制品	Petroleum and Related Products	100.7	100.2	99.3	102.7	101.4	103.4	99.9	100.4	101.3	99.9	100.3	100.1
液化石油气	Liquefiled Petroleum Gas	103.6	101.3	94.3	100.6	100.6	98.0	98.9	102.5	107.0	99.4	100.1	100.0
管道燃气	Pipelined Gas	100.0	100.0	100.0	100.0	100.0	100.0	100.0	100.0	100.0	100.0	100.0	100.0
汽油	Gasoline	100.0	100.0	100.5	105.5	102.4	106.9	100.1	100.0	100.2	100.0	100.0	100.0
柴油	Diesel Oil	100.4	99.9	100.8	103.3	102.3	106.5	100.1	100.0	100.3	100.0	101.4	100.2
其他	Others	100.3	100.0	100.0	100.7	100.1	100.6	100.6	100.0	100.8	100.0	100.0	100.6
十六、建筑材料及五金电料	**Building Materials and Hardware**	**99.8**	**100.3**	**100.1**	**100.4**	**100.7**	**100.8**	**100.2**	**100.6**	**101.2**	**100.4**	**100.8**	**100.3**
1.建筑装璜材料	Building and Decoration Materials	99.8	100.2	100.2	100.6	100.5	100.9	100.4	100.4	101.2	100.5	101.0	100.2
木材	Wood	100.0	100.3	100.1	100.0	100.0	100.8	100.6	101.6	101.2	100.7	102.7	100.4
木地板	Wood Floor	100.0	100.0	99.1	102.5	100.5	101.1	100.9	100.5	101.6	100.4	101.9	100.2
钢材	Steel Products	99.5	100.8	100.3	100.8	101.4	102.4	99.7	99.6	100.3	100.0	99.9	99.9
砖	Brick	99.8	99.7	101.0	100.8	101.4	100.7	100.3	101.5	100.7	99.9	100.6	100.4
水泥	Cement	98.6	100.1	100.5	100.4	100.1	100.8	100.3	99.3	101.6	100.6	101.2	100.1
涂料	Coating Material	99.8	100.1	100.1	100.1	100.1	100.7	100.0	99.9	99.2	100.1	100.3	100.1
胶合板	Plywood	100.0	100.2	100.2	100.5	99.8	100.8	100.8	100.2	101.8	100.4	102.3	100.4
玻璃	Glass	100.1	99.9	100.4	100.1	100.7	100.0	100.6	100.0	101.1	100.6	100.2	100.0
粘胶	Rayon	100.0	100.0	100.0	100.0	100.3	101.0	100.1	100.3	101.1	100.7	100.7	100.5
油漆	Paint	100.0	100.3	100.3	100.2	100.2	100.3	101.0	100.0	104.0	100.0	99.7	100.0
其他	Others	100.0	100.0	100.0	100.0	100.0	100.1	100.0	100.2	100.6	102.8	100.2	100.1
2.五金电料	Hardware	99.9	100.5	100.0	100.0	101.0	100.5	99.9	101.0	101.3	100.2	100.4	100.6
五金工具	Hardware Tools	100.0	100.0	99.2	99.2	99.8	100.4	99.4	100.3	102.1	100.1	99.6	100.5
电工电料	Electrical Engineering and Electrical Materials	99.5	101.4	100.1	100.4	102.0	99.9	99.7	102.7	100.8	100.0	100.0	100.2
水暖器材	Heating Equipment	100.0	100.0	100.1	100.3	101.2	100.5	99.9	100.3	101.0	100.6	101.5	100.9
其他	Others	100.1	101.2	101.0	99.8	100.0	102.6	101.5	100.2	102.4	100.0	100.0	101.0

7-27 农村商品零售价格（环比）指数
Rural Retail Price Index

（以上月价格为100）

商品类别及品名	Commodity Category and Commodity Name	1月 January	2月 February	3月 March	4月 April	5月 May	6月 June	7月 July	8月 August	9月 September	10月 October	11月 November	12月 December
商品零售价格总指数	**Genaral Retail Price Index**	**101.5**	**100.0**	**99.4**	**100.2**	**99.9**	**99.4**	**99.8**	**100.5**	**100.7**	**99.6**	**100.5**	**101.7**
一、食品	**Food**	**105.5**	**100.6**	**97.8**	**100.3**	**98.8**	**97.3**	**99.0**	**101.7**	**102.3**	**98.0**	**101.4**	**105.8**
1.粮食	Grain	100.7	100.2	99.8	100.3	100.5	99.7	102.2	100.7	101.6	100.8	102.3	102.1
大米	Rice	102.8	99.3	100.0	100.9	102.5	100.1	105.7	103.1	101.7	101.1	97.9	101.1
面粉	Flour	100.1	100.6	99.7	100.2	99.6	99.1	101.3	99.6	101.5	100.8	105.9	102.9
粮食制品	Grain Products	100.3	100.3	99.7	100.0	100.1	99.8	100.6	100.2	100.2	100.0	102.6	101.6
其他	Others	99.4	100.9	99.8	100.1	100.1	100.7	100.9	99.5	106.0	102.3	98.5	101.9
2.淀粉	Starches	101.5	99.0	100.4	101.6	100.1	100.4	102.6	101.2	100.4	100.2	99.6	100.5
淀粉	Starches	101.5	99.0	100.4	101.6	100.1	100.4	102.6	101.2	100.4	100.2	99.6	100.5
3.干豆类及豆制品	Beans and Beans Products	101.0	100.8	98.6	100.4	100.5	100.5	102.0	100.6	99.7	99.3	99.6	100.9
干豆	Beans	101.1	101.7	100.1	100.6	100.9	101.1	103.9	100.3	99.1	98.7	99.3	101.7
豆制品	Beans Products	100.9	100.1	97.3	100.1	100.3	99.9	100.1	100.8	100.2	99.9	99.9	100.2
4.油脂	Oil and Fat	100.2	100.3	99.3	99.5	101.0	99.8	100.7	101.3	101.0	101.3	103.7	105.6
食用植物油	Edible Vegetable Oil	99.8	100.7	99.6	99.7	100.4	99.8	100.8	101.5	101.4	101.3	103.7	105.8
植物油制品	Plant Oil Products	99.8	100.1	100.0	100.0	104.4	99.8	100.0	100.3	100.2	100.0	102.8	105.1
其他	Others	104.9	95.7	95.6	96.7	98.8	100.8	100.8	100.6	96.8	104.2	106.6	103.8
5.肉禽及其制品	Meal, Poultry and their Products	104.2	99.9	96.8	98.1	98.8	100.6	102.4	104.8	102.2	100.1	104.1	106.0
（1）食用畜肉及副产品	Edible Livestock Meat and their By-products	106.9	99.0	95.1	95.3	98.4	101.6	103.0	106.2	102.6	100.9	106.0	108.4
猪肉	Pork	109.5	97.1	93.4	94.0	97.9	102.1	105.1	108.7	103.1	100.6	107.4	110.1
牛肉	Beef	100.1	101.9	99.6	100.0	99.4	100.0	100.1	99.8	100.1	101.3	101.6	103.8
羊肉	Mutton	100.7	103.4	98.8	98.7	100.5	99.5	99.5	101.3	102.0	103.0	102.9	108.4
畜肉副产品	Livestock Meat By-products	105.3	102.1	96.9	94.9	96.8	104.9	97.9	103.2	103.9	100.1	105.4	105.1
其他	Others	112.1	100.2	93.1	90.0	99.4	98.4	106.7	112.1	100.7	99.5	107.0	102.9
（2）禽	Poultry	100.9	102.8	99.4	102.4	100.1	100.7	103.5	104.3	103.1	98.2	100.7	103.2
鸡	Chicken	101.6	103.7	99.7	102.7	100.8	101.4	104.6	103.6	104.2	97.4	100.0	103.0
鸭	Duck	98.8	97.8	100.4	102.6	98.7	95.3	96.2	106.6	99.5	101.0	106.1	103.6
其他	Others	99.4	102.8	97.0	100.7	97.8	101.1	103.4	106.8	100.0	100.4	100.3	104.0
（3）肉禽加工制品	Meal and Poultry Processing Products	100.2	100.0	99.1	101.4	98.7	98.3	100.2	101.7	100.2	99.7	102.3	101.9
畜肉制品	Livestock Meat Products	100.2	100.1	100.0	99.0	99.3	99.2	100.8	101.8	100.3	100.0	101.5	101.5
禽制品	Poultry Products	100.2	99.9	97.5	105.2	97.8	96.9	99.4	101.5	100.1	99.3	103.6	102.6
6.蛋	Eggs	100.4	94.3	97.3	99.8	103.0	100.1	102.3	107.3	107.8	101.0	101.5	104.2
鲜蛋	Fresh Eggs	100.4	93.5	96.9	99.9	103.0	99.8	103.2	108.4	108.7	101.0	101.5	104.6
蛋制品	Egg Products	100.4	98.9	99.4	99.1	102.5	101.5	97.4	100.7	102.2	101.2	101.3	101.5
7.水产品	Aquatic Product	101.9	101.1	98.9	99.9	101.2	101.4	101.3	100.8	99.7	99.0	100.2	100.0
（1）鱼	Fish	102.2	100.3	99.0	99.8	101.3	101.2	101.5	100.7	99.9	99.1	100.4	99.3
淡水鱼	Freshwater Fish	101.4	98.5	98.5	100.5	102.5	101.7	101.8	100.1	99.1	98.6	99.3	98.5

7-27 续表 1 continued

商品类别及品名	Commodity Category and Commodity Name	（以上月价格为100）											
		1月 January	2月 February	3月 March	4月 April	5月 May	6月 June	7月 July	8月 August	9月 September	10月 October	11月 November	12月 December
海水鱼	Seawater Fish	103.4	103.2	99.7	98.8	99.6	100.5	100.9	101.6	101.1	99.9	102.2	100.4
（2）其他水产品	Other Aquatic Product	101.2	103.2	98.8	100.1	100.9	102.0	101.0	101.0	99.3	98.6	99.7	102.1
虾蟹类	Shrimp and Crab	101.9	105.1	98.1	100.0	101.7	101.0	101.3	100.9	98.8	97.7	99.4	102.8
其他	Others	100.0	100.1	100.1	100.3	99.6	103.9	100.6	101.3	100.0	100.2	100.2	101.0
8.菜	Vegetable	126.1	101.5	91.7	98.4	86.5	78.4	95.4	112.6	113.3	84.1	97.1	125.9
鲜菜	Fresh Vegetable	130.8	101.5	90.1	98.1	83.5	75.7	94.5	115.7	116.1	81.4	96.1	131.8
干菜及菜制品	Dried Vegetable and Vegetable Products	100.0	100.1	100.4	98.9	99.2	99.9	99.3	100.9	100.1	100.2	101.2	103.1
薯类	Potato	109.6	104.6	108.5	101.5	113.9	71.1	97.9	100.8	106.4	87.4	101.6	104.2
9.调味品	Flavoring	100.0	100.2	100.3	100.0	100.0	99.8	101.3	100.1	100.1	100.0	100.0	101.0
盐	Salt	100.2	100.6	101.1	100.0	100.0	100.0	102.2	100.6	100.7	100.0	100.0	100.2
酱油	Soy Sauce	99.9	100.0	100.0	100.2	99.8	100.0	101.1	100.0	100.0	100.0	100.0	101.7
醋	Vinegar	100.0	100.0	100.0	100.0	100.0	100.0	101.7	100.0	100.0	100.0	100.0	102.2
味精	Aginomoto	100.0	100.0	100.0	100.0	100.0	100.0	100.8	100.0	100.0	100.5	100.0	100.4
其他	Others	100.0	100.0	100.0	100.0	100.3	98.2	99.4	99.5	99.3	99.4	100.0	100.0
10.糖	Carbohydrate	100.3	104.4	101.5	101.1	100.4	100.3	101.9	100.5	100.5	100.2	100.2	100.5
食糖	Sugar	100.6	110.6	103.5	102.2	100.8	100.7	102.5	101.0	101.0	100.2	100.3	100.8
糖果	Sweet	100.2	100.2	100.0	100.4	100.0	100.0	101.6	100.0	100.0	100.1	100.0	98.6
巧克力制品	Chocolate Products	100.0	100.0	100.0	100.0	100.0	100.0	100.6	100.0	100.0	100.0	100.0	107.5
糖类小食品	Little Carbohydrate Food	100.0	100.3	100.0	100.0	100.0	100.0	101.3	100.3	100.0	100.0	100.3	101.9
11.干鲜瓜果	Dried and Fresh Melons and Fruits	110.5	106.2	100.0	109.5	105.6	98.5	84.5	86.6	94.6	96.8	101.6	107.5
鲜瓜果	Fresh Fruits	113.0	107.6	100.0	111.5	106.6	98.2	81.7	83.2	93.0	95.2	101.8	109.5
干（坚）果	Dried Fruits	100.9	100.1	100.1	99.6	99.8	100.4	100.3	102.2	100.3	102.4	101.1	101.2
12.糕点饼干面包	Cake, Biscuit and Bread	100.0	100.0	100.0	100.0	100.1	100.1	100.8	100.6	100.0	100.0	100.0	101.6
糕点	Cake	100.1	100.0	100.0	100.0	100.0	100.0	100.4	100.0	100.0	100.0	100.0	101.8
饼干	Biscuit	100.0	100.0	99.9	100.1	100.2	100.1	101.3	101.7	100.0	99.9	99.9	102.1
面包	Bread	100.0	100.0	100.0	100.0	100.0	100.0	101.2	100.0	100.0	100.0	100.0	100.3
13.液体乳及乳制品	Liquid Milk and their Products	99.9	100.0	100.0	100.2	100.0	100.0	100.2	100.0	100.0	100.0	100.0	103.8
巴氏杀菌奶或消毒奶	Pasteurization Milk or Disinfection Milk	99.8	100.0	100.2	100.0	100.0	100.0	100.0	100.0	100.0	100.0	100.0	108.3
酸奶	Leben	100.0	100.0	100.0	101.5	100.0	100.0	100.0	100.0	100.0	100.0	100.0	98.7
奶粉	Milk Powder	99.9	100.1	99.8	100.0	100.0	100.0	100.6	100.0	100.0	100.1	100.0	101.4
其他	Others	100.0	100.1	99.7	100.0	100.0	100.0	100.0	100.0	100.0	100.0	100.0	100.0
14.在外用膳食品	Outward Dinner	100.7	100.3	100.0	99.8	100.2	100.1	100.0	100.0	100.0	99.8	100.8	101.6
主食	Staple Food	100.2	100.0	100.1	99.9	100.0	100.0	99.9	100.0	100.0	100.0	103.0	103.8
炒菜	Hot Dish	101.0	100.5	100.0	99.7	100.0	100.0	99.9	100.0	100.0	100.0	100.1	100.3
地方小吃	Local Snack	100.6	99.8	99.7	100.2	101.4	100.7	100.4	100.0	100.0	98.6	99.1	102.4
15.其他食品	Other Foods	99.9	100.1	99.9	100.0	100.3	100.2	100.7	100.4	99.8	100.1	99.6	100.9
其他食品	Other Foods	99.9	100.1	99.9	100.0	100.3	100.2	100.7	100.4	99.8	100.1	99.6	100.9
二、饮料、烟酒	**Beverages, Tobacco, Liquor**	**100.3**	**100.0**	**100.1**	**100.2**	**100.0**	**99.9**	**100.3**	**100.1**	**100.1**	**100.3**	**100.3**	**101.2**

7-27 续表 2 continued

商品类别及品名	Commodity Category and Commodity Name	（以上月价格为100）											
		1月 January	2月 February	3月 March	4月 April	5月 May	6月 June	7月 July	8月 August	9月 September	10月 October	11月 November	12月 December
1.茶及饮料	Tea and Beverages	100.1	100.1	100.0	100.1	99.9	100.0	101.1	100.1	100.0	100.0	100.0	100.9
（1）茶叶	Tea	100.0	100.0	100.0	100.0	99.8	100.0	100.0	100.1	100.0	100.0	100.0	100.0
茶叶	Tea	100.0	100.0	100.0	100.0	99.8	100.0	100.0	100.1	100.0	100.0	100.0	100.0
（2）饮料	Beverages	100.2	100.1	100.0	100.2	100.0	100.0	101.7	100.1	100.0	100.0	100.0	101.5
固体饮料	Solid Beverages	100.0	100.5	100.3	100.4	99.7	100.1	100.0	100.4	100.0	100.0	100.0	100.2
液体饮料	Liquid Beverages	100.3	100.0	100.0	100.2	100.2	100.0	103.6	100.0	99.9	100.0	100.1	100.7
冷冻饮品	Frozen Beverages	100.1	100.0	100.0	100.0	100.0	100.0	100.0	100.0	100.0	100.0	100.0	103.8
2.烟草	Tobacco	100.8	100.3	100.0	100.3	100.1	99.8	99.9	100.0	100.0	100.0	100.1	100.8
国产卷烟	Domestic Cigarette	100.9	100.3	100.0	100.3	100.2	99.7	99.9	100.0	100.0	100.0	100.0	100.9
进口卷烟	Import Cigarette	100.0	99.9	100.0	100.0	100.0	100.0	98.6	100.0	100.0	100.0	101.4	100.0
其他	Others	100.0	100.0	100.0	100.0	100.0	100.0	100.0	100.0	100.0	100.0	100.0	100.0
3.酒	Liquor	99.9	99.8	100.2	100.2	99.9	100.0	100.4	100.2	100.2	100.6	100.6	101.6
白酒	White Spirit	100.0	99.7	100.3	100.3	100.0	100.0	100.1	100.3	100.0	100.9	100.7	102.3
葡萄酒	Grape	100.0	100.0	100.0	100.0	100.0	100.0	101.4	100.0	100.0	100.1	102.0	100.1
啤酒	Beer	99.7	100.0	100.2	100.0	99.7	99.9	100.5	100.1	100.7	100.2	100.0	100.9
其他	Others	100.0	100.0	100.0	100.0	100.0	100.0	100.3	100.0	100.0	100.0	100.0	100.1
三、服装、鞋帽	**Garments, Footgearand and Hats**	**99.0**	**98.9**	**99.8**	**100.0**	**99.7**	**99.9**	**100.0**	**99.9**	**99.9**	**100.2**	**100.4**	**100.0**
1.服装	Garments	98.9	98.7	99.7	99.5	99.7	99.9	100.0	99.9	99.9	100.4	100.7	100.0
（1）男式服装	Men's Garments	98.5	98.7	99.9	99.8	99.7	99.8	100.1	100.0	100.3	100.7	100.9	99.9
大衣	Topcoat	98.6	97.1	98.1	99.7	100.0	99.0	100.0	100.0	100.9	100.0	99.5	100.0
毛线衣	Woollen Sweater	100.0	99.4	98.9	99.0	97.9	98.6	102.0	100.0	101.4	100.4	98.5	100.1
夹克衫	Jacket	99.1	99.0	99.9	99.8	99.7	99.9	99.9	99.9	99.9	100.8	102.8	99.9
衬衫	Shirt	97.1	100.0	100.0	100.0	100.0	100.0	100.0	100.0	100.0	100.8	101.0	100.1
T恤衫	T-shirt	100.1	100.1	100.0	100.2	99.8	100.2	99.8	100.9	101.8	101.2	101.1	100.3
裤子	Trousers	97.0	96.9	102.1	99.9	100.0	100.0	99.7	100.0	100.0	100.8	100.8	99.2
西服	Western-style Clothes	98.5	98.7	100.0	99.9	99.9	100.1	100.0	100.0	100.0	100.5	101.4	100.0
运动衫裤	Gym Suit	100.0	100.0	100.0	100.0	100.0	100.0	99.9	100.0	100.1	102.1	102.0	100.0
内衣	Underwaist	99.1	99.7	99.1	99.7	100.5	100.0	100.0	100.0	100.0	101.0	101.2	99.6
羽绒衣	Eider down Outerwear	97.6	97.3	99.6	100.0	100.0	100.0	100.0	99.7	99.9	100.6	100.9	100.2
其他	Others	97.5	98.1	100.0	100.0	100.0	100.0	100.0	100.0	100.0	100.0	100.0	100.0
（2）女式服装	Women's Garments	99.1	98.7	99.3	99.1	99.2	100.0	99.9	99.8	99.9	100.3	100.6	100.0
大衣	Topcoat	97.9	94.6	100.0	100.0	100.0	100.0	100.0	100.0	100.0	100.0	100.4	100.0
毛线衣	Woollen Sweater	98.4	97.3	95.0	99.8	95.5	100.0	100.0	100.0	100.0	100.0	100.2	100.0
羽绒衣	Eider down Outerwear	98.3	97.9	99.7	100.0	99.9	100.0	100.0	99.6	99.9	100.6	100.6	100.0
套装	Coordinates	100.9	100.0	100.0	94.1	100.0	100.0	100.0	99.9	100.0	100.9	100.9	100.0
衬衫	Shirt	98.6	99.8	100.0	100.0	100.6	99.6	100.0	100.0	93.6	100.1	100.1	100.0
T恤衫	T-shirt	100.2	99.7	100.5	100.6	97.4	100.0	100.0	100.0	100.0	101.5	101.3	100.2
裙子	Skirt	98.2	100.0	99.9	100.0	99.0	100.8	100.0	99.2	99.6	100.3	100.0	99.7
裤子	Trousers	100.2	100.0	100.0	98.7	99.6	100.0	99.4	100.0	100.0	98.4	101.0	100.0
运动衫裤	Gym Suit	100.0	100.2	99.4	100.4	99.6	100.0	100.0	100.0	100.0	101.6	101.8	100.0
内衣	Underwaist	98.5	98.5	99.8	100.0	100.6	99.8	99.9	99.9	103.9	100.6	100.7	100.1
其他	Others	100.0	100.0	100.0	100.0	100.0	99.8	100.0	100.0	100.0	100.0	100.2	100.0
（3）儿童服装	Children's Garments	99.2	98.9	100.0	100.1	100.7	100.0	100.0	100.0	99.1	100.0	100.4	100.1
套装	Coordinates	99.4	98.9	100.0	100.2	99.8	99.6	100.0	100.0	100.1	100.1	100.5	100.2

7-27 续表 3 continued

商品类别及品名	Commodity Category and Commodity Name	1月 January	2月 February	3月 March	4月 April	5月 May	6月 June	7月 July	8月 August	9月 September	10月 October	11月 November	12月 December
		（以上月价格为100）											
裤子	Trousers	99.5	99.2	100.0	99.9	102.7	100.0	100.0	100.0	100.0	100.5	100.6	100.1
裙子	Skirt	99.0	99.0	100.2	100.0	100.4	101.0	100.0	100.0	95.4	98.8	100.0	100.0
其他	Others	97.7	97.7	100.0	100.0	100.4	100.4	100.0	100.0	98.9	100.0	100.0	100.0
2.鞋袜帽	Shoes, Socks and Hats	99.0	98.9	100.0	100.1	99.5	99.9	100.1	99.9	100.0	99.9	100.1	100.1
（1）鞋	Shoes	98.8	98.7	100.0	100.1	99.3	99.9	100.1	99.9	100.0	99.9	100.1	100.1
男鞋	Men's Shoes	98.8	99.4	100.0	100.2	99.3	100.0	100.0	99.9	100.0	100.0	100.0	100.2
女鞋	Women's Shoes	98.4	97.7	100.0	100.0	99.0	100.0	100.2	99.8	99.9	100.0	100.1	100.0
童鞋	Children's Shoes	99.5	99.5	100.1	100.1	100.0	99.7	100.0	100.1	100.1	99.7	100.1	100.0
（2）袜子	Socks	99.8	99.8	100.0	100.0	100.5	100.0	100.0	100.0	100.0	100.0	100.0	100.0
男袜	Men's Socks	99.8	99.8	100.0	100.0	100.0	100.0	100.0	100.0	100.0	100.0	100.0	100.0
女袜	Women's Socks	99.8	99.8	100.0	100.0	101.0	100.0	100.0	100.0	100.0	100.0	100.0	100.0
（3）帽子	Hats	99.8	99.9	100.0	100.0	100.1	100.0	100.0	100.0	100.0	100.0	100.0	100.0
男帽	Men's Hats	99.8	100.0	100.0	100.0	100.2	100.0	100.0	100.0	100.0	100.0	100.0	100.0
女帽	Women's Hats	99.8	99.8	100.0	100.0	100.0	100.0	100.0	100.0	100.0	100.1	100.1	100.0
3.其他	Others	100.0	99.9	99.9	103.8	100.0	99.9	100.0	99.9	100.0	100.0	100.0	100.0
领带	Necktie	100.0	99.9	99.9	103.8	100.0	99.9	100.0	99.9	100.0	100.0	100.0	100.0
四、纺织品	**Textiles**	**100.2**	**100.0**	**99.9**	**100.1**	**100.4**	**100.0**	**100.0**	**100.0**	**99.9**	**100.4**	**100.1**	**100.1**
1.衣着材料	Clothing Materials	100.2	99.9	99.8	100.0	100.9	100.0	100.1	99.9	99.6	100.6	100.2	100.0
棉布	Cotton Cloth	100.0	100.0	100.0	100.0	101.4	100.0	100.0	100.0	99.8	100.2	100.0	100.1
棉混纺布	Cotton Textiles Cloth	100.4	100.2	100.0	100.0	100.1	100.0	100.2	100.0	100.0	100.5	100.5	100.0
化纤布	Chemical Fiber Cloth	100.3	100.3	100.0	100.0	101.5	100.0	100.2	99.8	99.1	101.2	100.3	100.1
毛线	Knitting Wool	100.0	98.9	98.9	100.0	100.0	100.0	100.0	100.0	100.0	100.0	100.0	100.0
2.床上用品	Bedclothes	100.2	100.0	100.0	100.2	99.8	100.0	100.0	100.0	100.2	100.2	100.1	100.3
毛毯	Woollen Blanket	100.2	99.7	100.0	100.6	99.3	100.0	99.9	99.9	100.3	101.0	100.0	102.2
被子	Quilt	100.2	100.2	100.1	100.2	100.1	100.0	99.9	100.0	100.1	100.0	100.3	100.0
床上套件	Bed Articles	100.1	100.1	100.0	100.1	99.9	100.0	100.0	100.0	100.3	100.0	100.0	99.4
其他	Others	100.4	100.4	100.0	100.0	99.6	100.0	100.0	100.0	100.0	100.0	100.0	100.0
五、家用电器及音像器材	**Household Appliances, Music and Video Equipments**	**99.6**	**99.2**	**99.9**	**99.9**	**100.0**	**100.5**	**100.3**	**100.0**	**100.1**	**100.2**	**99.9**	**100.0**
1.家庭设备	Household Appliances	99.9	99.4	100.0	100.1	100.1	101.1	100.6	100.1	100.3	100.1	100.0	100.2
洗衣机	Washing Machine	99.6	100.0	99.9	99.9	99.8	100.0	100.1	100.1	102.1	100.9	99.8	100.2
电风扇	Electric Fan	99.4	98.7	100.0	104.1	100.2	101.7	102.8	100.6	100.0	100.0	100.0	101.8
电冰箱（柜）	Refrigerator	100.4	98.3	100.2	100.0	100.0	100.1	100.3	100.0	99.9	100.0	99.9	99.8
吸排油烟机	Kitchen Ventilato	99.5	99.8	99.7	99.8	100.0	100.3	100.2	99.9	99.9	100.0	100.0	101.0
空调器	Air-Conditioning	99.7	99.8	99.8	100.7	100.7	104.3	100.5	100.0	100.1	100.0	99.9	99.7
热水器	Water Heater	100.7	100.0	100.2	96.0	99.8	100.2	100.1	99.9	100.0	100.0	100.2	98.3
微波炉	Microwave Oven	100.0	99.3	100.2	98.5	100.0	100.0	100.2	100.0	100.1	100.0	100.2	99.6
电炊具	Electric Cooking Appliance	100.0	99.9	99.8	99.9	100.0	100.1	99.9	100.0	100.0	100.0	100.0	100.6
2.文娱用耐用消费品	Durable Consumer Goods For Recreational Use	99.3	99.1	99.9	99.7	99.9	99.7	100.1	99.9	100.0	100.2	99.9	99.8
电视机	Television	98.9	98.7	100.0	99.6	100.0	99.4	99.9	99.9	99.9	100.6	99.9	100.3
激光视盘机	Laser Video Disc Machine	99.0	98.7	100.0	99.9	99.6	100.3	100.6	99.9	100.0	99.3	99.6	98.2

7-27 续表 4 continued

商品类别及品名	Commodity Category and Commodity Name	（以上月价格为100）											
		1月 January	2月 February	3月 March	4月 April	5月 May	6月 June	7月 July	8月 August	9月 September	10月 October	11月 November	12月 December
摄像机	Pickup Camera	100.0	100.0	100.0	100.0	100.0	100.0	100.0	100.0	100.0	100.0	100.0	100.0
家用音响设备	Acoustic Equipment	100.1	99.7	99.4	98.9	99.8	100.0	100.7	100.0	100.0	100.0	100.0	99.7
便携式音响	Portable Acoustics	100.0	100.0	100.0	100.0	100.0	100.0	100.0	100.0	100.0	100.0	100.0	99.5
其他	Others	100.0	100.0	100.0	100.0	100.0	100.0	100.0	100.0	100.0	100.0	100.0	100.0
3.音像器材	Music and Video Equipments	98.9	99.0	99.7	99.9	100.0	100.2	100.0	100.0	100.0	100.0	100.0	100.0
专业音响器材	Specialized Acoustic Apparatus	100.0	100.0	99.5	99.8	100.0	100.4	100.0	100.0	100.0	100.0	99.9	100.0
专业声像器材	Specialized Acoustic Image Apparatus	97.7	97.7	100.0	100.0	100.0	100.0	100.0	100.0	100.0	100.0	100.0	100.0
六、文化办公用品	**Cultural and Office Applicances**	**99.8**	**99.8**	**99.9**	**99.9**	**100.0**	**100.0**	**99.8**	**99.4**	**100.1**	**100.0**	**100.1**	**100.0**
纸张本册	Paper and Volume	100.8	99.3	100.0	100.0	100.0	100.3	100.0	100.7	100.3	100.1	100.3	100.1
文具	Stationery	100.2	100.0	100.0	100.0	100.0	99.8	99.6	100.1	100.0	100.0	100.0	100.0
电脑及配件	Computer and its Fitting	98.7	99.8	99.9	99.9	100.0	100.0	99.8	96.7	100.0	100.0	100.0	100.0
打印机及配件	Printer and its Fitting	99.7	99.9	99.9	99.9	100.0	100.0	99.7	99.8	100.0	99.9	100.0	100.0
扫描仪	Scanner	99.2	100.0	99.5	99.9	100.0	100.0	100.3	99.7	100.2	100.1	100.0	100.0
复印机	Xerox Machine	100.0	100.1	99.8	99.3	99.8	100.0	100.0	99.5	100.0	100.0	100.0	100.0
电子辞典	Electronic Dictionary	100.0	100.0	100.0	100.0	100.0	99.5	99.6	99.6	100.0	100.0	100.0	100.0
计算器	Calculator	100.0	100.0	100.0	100.0	100.0	100.2	99.6	100.0	100.0	100.0	100.5	99.9
教学设备	Teaching Equipment	100.5	100.0	100.0	100.0	100.4	100.0	100.0	102.7	100.0	100.0	100.0	100.2
其他	Others	100.0	100.0	100.0	100.0	100.0	100.0	100.0	100.0	100.0	100.0	100.0	100.0
七、日用品	**Articles for Daily Use**	**100.1**	**100.0**	**100.0**	**100.0**	**100.1**	**100.0**	**99.6**	**100.2**	**100.1**	**100.2**	**100.0**	**100.5**
1.日用百货	General Merchandise for Daily Use	100.0	100.0	99.9	99.9	100.0	100.1	99.7	100.1	99.9	99.9	100.0	101.3
自行车	Bicycle	100.0	100.0	99.8	99.6	100.0	99.6	99.0	100.0	100.1	100.0	100.0	100.4
雨具	Rain Gear	100.4	100.0	100.0	100.0	100.1	98.7	99.8	100.0	98.1	98.7	100.0	99.9
剃须刀具	Shaver	99.9	100.0	100.0	100.0	100.0	105.1	100.3	100.0	100.0	100.0	100.5	100.3
电池	Battery	100.0	100.0	100.0	100.0	100.0	100.0	100.0	100.0	100.0	100.0	100.0	100.0
卫生纸	Tissue Paper	100.1	100.0	100.0	100.2	100.0	100.0	100.2	100.8	100.0	100.0	99.7	105.2
卫生巾	Sanitary Towel	100.0	100.0	100.0	100.0	100.0	100.0	100.0	100.0	100.0	100.0	100.0	100.0
其他	Others	100.0	100.0	100.0	100.0	100.0	100.0	100.0	100.0	100.0	100.0	100.0	100.9
2.日用杂品	Sundry Articles	100.0	100.0	99.9	100.1	99.9	99.8	99.3	100.2	102.0	101.5	100.0	100.4
茶具	Tea Set	100.0	100.0	99.9	100.0	99.7	106.0	99.9	100.0	104.0	107.0	100.0	100.0
餐具	Tableware	100.0	100.0	99.9	100.0	99.8	100.0	98.1	99.9	100.0	100.0	100.0	100.0
厨具	Kitchen Utensils	100.1	100.0	100.0	100.4	100.0	96.3	100.0	100.7	103.1	100.0	100.0	101.2
其他	Others	100.0	100.0	100.0	100.0	100.0	100.0	100.0	100.0	100.0	100.0	100.0	100.0
3.洗涤用品	Washing Articles	99.9	100.0	100.0	100.0	100.5	100.0	99.5	100.4	99.4	100.0	100.0	100.1
洗衣粉	Washing Powder	100.0	99.9	100.0	100.0	99.9	100.1	100.0	100.0	99.9	100.0	100.0	99.9
肥皂类	Soap	99.7	100.0	100.0	100.0	100.0	100.0	100.0	101.6	98.4	100.0	100.2	99.9
牙膏	Toothpaste	100.1	100.0	100.0	100.0	102.2	100.0	97.8	100.0	99.7	100.3	100.0	100.2
清洁洗涤剂	Cleaning Agent	100.0	100.0	100.0	100.2	99.8	99.9	99.9	99.8	99.9	99.8	99.6	100.8
4.其他日用品	Other Articles for Daily Use	100.3	100.0	100.0	100.0	100.0	100.0	100.0	100.0	100.0	100.0	100.0	100.0
燃气灶具	Gas-oven	102.4	100.0	100.0	100.0	100.0	100.0	100.0	100.0	100.0	100.0	100.0	100.0
儿童玩具	Children's Toy	100.0	100.2	100.0	100.0	100.0	100.0	100.0	99.8	100.0	100.0	100.0	100.0

7-27 续表 5 continued

商品类别及品名	Commodity Category and Commodity Name	(以上月价格为100)											
		1月 January	2月 February	3月 March	4月 April	5月 May	6月 June	7月 July	8月 August	9月 September	10月 October	11月 November	12月 December
照明器具	Illumination Utensil	99.0	100.0	100.0	100.0	100.0	100.0	100.0	100.0	100.0	100.0	100.0	100.2
钟表眼镜及配件	Clocks, Glasses and their Fittings	99.8	100.0	100.0	100.0	100.0	100.0	100.0	100.0	100.0	99.8	100.1	99.9
日用普通饰品	Common Ornament for Daily Use	100.0	100.0	100.0	100.0	100.0	100.0	99.9	100.1	100.0	100.0	100.0	100.0
日用皮革制品	Leatherware for Daily Use	100.0	100.0	100.0	100.0	100.0	100.0	100.0	100.0	100.0	100.0	99.7	100.0
其他	Others	100.0	100.0	100.0	100.0	100.0	100.0	100.0	100.0	100.0	100.0	100.0	100.0
八、体育娱乐用品	**Sports and Recreation Articles**	**99.9**	**100.0**	**100.0**	**100.0**	**100.0**	**99.7**	**99.9**	**100.0**	**99.9**	**100.0**	**99.9**	**100.1**
1.体育用品	Sports Articles	100.1	100.0	100.0	99.9	100.0	99.4	99.9	100.1	100.0	100.0	100.0	100.0
球类	Ball	100.0	100.0	100.0	99.8	99.8	98.5	100.0	100.2	100.0	100.0	100.0	100.0
棋牌	Chess and Cards	100.3	100.0	100.0	100.0	100.0	100.0	100.0	100.0	100.0	100.0	100.0	100.0
健身器材	Exercise Machine	99.8	100.0	100.0	100.0	100.1	99.9	99.8	100.0	100.0	100.0	100.2	100.0
2.娱乐用品	Recreation Articles	99.6	100.0	100.0	100.0	100.0	100.1	99.9	99.9	99.8	100.0	99.7	100.1
游艺器材	Entertainment Apparatus	100.0	100.0	100.0	100.0	100.0	100.0	100.0	100.0	99.2	100.0	100.0	100.0
照相器材	Photographic Apparatus	99.2	99.9	100.0	100.0	100.0	100.0	99.8	100.0	100.0	100.0	100.0	100.5
乐器	Musical Instrument	100.0	100.0	100.0	100.0	100.0	100.2	100.0	99.7	100.1	100.2	99.1	99.7
九、交通、通信用品	**Transportation and Communication Appliances**	**99.3**	**99.8**	**99.6**	**99.2**	**99.3**	**99.7**	**99.6**	**99.3**	**99.4**	**99.9**	**99.8**	**99.2**
1.交通运输机械	Transportation Machine	99.6	100.9	100.0	99.8	99.9	99.8	99.8	100.0	100.0	100.0	100.0	99.9
轿车	Car	98.8	100.0	100.0	100.0	99.0	98.3	100.3	99.9	99.9	100.0	99.7	99.9
客车	Bus	99.9	100.0	100.0	99.9	100.0	100.3	99.9	100.0	100.0	100.0	100.0	100.1
货车	Truck	100.4	100.0	100.0	100.0	100.0	100.0	100.0	100.0	100.0	100.0	100.0	99.9
摩托车	Motorcycle	99.4	101.7	100.0	100.1	100.0	100.0	99.7	100.0	100.0	100.0	100.0	99.9
其他	Others	100.1	100.0	100.0	97.6	100.0	100.0	99.8	100.0	100.0	100.0	100.0	100.0
2.通信器材	Telecommunications Facilities	98.9	98.6	99.1	98.5	98.7	99.5	99.4	98.4	98.7	99.7	99.6	98.3
固定电话机	Telephone	99.3	99.5	99.2	99.7	98.7	100.0	100.0	100.0	100.5	100.0	100.0	100.0
移动电话机	Mobile Phone	98.3	97.4	98.9	97.1	98.2	98.9	98.7	97.4	96.8	99.3	99.1	96.0
传真机	Fax Machine	100.0	99.9	99.9	100.0	100.0	100.0	100.0	96.5	99.8	100.0	100.0	99.9
其他	Others	98.9	99.1	99.4	100.0	100.0	100.0	99.7	100.0	100.0	100.0	100.0	100.0
十、家具	**Furniture**	**100.1**	**99.9**	**99.9**	**100.7**	**100.0**	**100.0**	**99.9**	**99.7**	**99.9**	**101.9**	**100.4**	**100.3**
柜	Cabinet	100.0	99.7	99.7	100.8	100.0	100.0	99.9	99.5	100.0	102.6	100.0	100.5
床	Bed	100.0	100.0	100.0	101.2	100.0	100.0	100.0	100.0	99.9	101.5	100.5	100.5
桌	Desk	100.3	100.1	100.0	100.1	100.0	100.1	100.0	98.5	98.8	101.6	100.4	100.1
椅	Chair	99.8	99.3	100.0	100.0	100.0	100.0	99.8	100.2	100.2	102.1	100.1	100.1
沙发	Sofa	100.1	100.0	100.0	101.0	100.0	100.0	100.0	100.0	100.0	101.8	100.8	100.0
其他	Others	100.2	100.3	100.2	99.8	100.6	100.2	100.0	100.1	100.1	101.7	100.1	100.1
十一、化妆品	**Cosmetics**	**100.0**	**100.0**	**99.9**	**100.0**	**100.1**	**99.9**	**100.0**	**99.9**	**100.1**	**100.0**	**99.9**	**100.1**
护肤品	Skincare Products	100.1	100.0	100.0	100.0	100.3	99.7	100.0	100.0	100.0	99.9	99.9	100.0
美容化妆品	Facial Beautifiers	100.0	100.0	100.0	100.0	100.0	100.0	100.0	100.0	100.0	100.0	100.0	100.4
护发美容品	Protects Sends the Beauty Products	100.0	99.8	99.3	100.0	100.2	100.0	100.0	100.0	100.0	100.0	100.0	100.2
清洁化妆用品	Cleaning Toiletware	99.9	100.0	100.1	100.1	99.9	100.0	100.0	99.2	101.1	100.0	99.7	99.9
药物美容用品	Medicinal Cosmetics	100.1	100.0	100.0	99.9	100.0	100.0	100.0	100.0	100.0	100.1	100.0	100.0

7-27 续表 6 continued

商品类别及品名	Commodity Category and Commodity Name	1月 January	2月 February	3月 March	4月 April	5月 May	6月 June	7月 July	8月 August	9月 September	10月 October	11月 November	12月 December
		（以上月价格为100）											
十二、金银珠宝	**Gold, Silver and Jewelry**	**102.2**	**102.4**	**108.4**	**103.4**	**111.9**	**104.7**	**99.2**	**100.8**	**99.2**	**99.3**	**100.6**	**99.9**
金饰品	Gold	103.6	103.2	109.0	105.2	115.3	101.4	98.4	101.5	99.7	98.7	99.9	100.1
银饰品	Silver	101.0	100.0	114.6	100.3	110.9	119.0	100.2	100.0	100.0	100.0	100.0	99.5
铂金饰品	Platinum	100.7	102.7	104.0	101.5	105.9	103.3	100.3	100.0	96.9	100.0	103.2	100.0
其他	Others	100.0	100.0	103.3	102.7	103.9	101.4	99.0	100.0	100.0	100.0	100.0	98.6
十三、中西药品及医疗保健用品	**Traditional Chinese and Western Medicines and Healthcare Articles**	**99.9**	**100.5**	**99.7**	**100.2**	**100.5**	**100.0**	**100.0**	**100.0**	**100.8**	**99.3**	**100.3**	**100.2**
1.医疗器具及用品	Medical Facilities and Goods	97.5	100.4	99.7	99.4	99.5	100.1	100.1	99.9	100.6	98.8	99.9	98.8
医疗器具及用品	Medical Facilities and Goods	97.5	100.4	99.7	99.4	99.5	100.1	100.1	99.9	100.6	98.8	99.9	98.8
2.中药材及中成药	Herbs and Ready-made Traditional Chinese Medicine	100.2	101.5	99.0	100.4	100.3	100.4	100.2	100.3	101.1	99.7	100.5	100.4
中药材	Herbs	100.7	102.3	97.9	100.8	101.3	100.2	100.0	99.9	101.3	99.5	100.9	100.1
中成药	Ready-made Traditional Chinese	99.7	100.6	100.2	100.0	99.2	100.6	100.3	100.6	100.9	99.9	100.0	100.8
3.西药	Western Medicine	100.2	100.1	100.0	100.2	100.8	99.6	99.9	99.9	100.8	99.1	100.2	100.3
抗微生物药	Anti-microorganism Medicine	100.1	99.9	100.1	100.0	100.0	100.0	100.0	99.8	101.8	97.5	100.0	101.4
消化系统用药	Alimentary System Medicine	100.2	100.3	100.0	100.0	100.0	100.0	100.1	100.1	100.6	99.3	100.5	99.6
呼吸系统用药	Respiratory System Medicine	99.7	99.8	100.8	100.5	99.3	100.2	100.0	100.0	101.9	98.2	101.1	100.0
解热镇痛及非甾体抗炎药	Allays a Fever the Analgesia and the Non-steroid Body Anti-inflammatory Agent	102.4	100.3	99.3	100.0	101.0	99.0	100.0	100.0	100.8	99.4	99.3	101.0
抗肿瘤药	Anti-neoplastic Drug	99.5	100.0	99.8	100.0	109.1	97.4	100.4	98.7	96.8	103.9	101.0	100.0
激素及调节内分泌功能药	Hormone and Adjustment Internal Secretion Function Medicine	99.3	100.2	100.0	100.0	100.0	100.1	98.3	100.1	102.7	97.4	100.0	99.3
循环系统用药	Circulating System Medicine	99.3	100.1	100.3	100.4	100.0	99.8	99.9	100.0	100.5	99.7	100.0	100.1
神经系统用药	Nerve System Medicine	99.9	100.3	100.0	100.5	99.9	100.0	100.0	100.0	101.1	98.6	100.0	100.6
专科用药	Junior Medicine	99.5	99.5	100.7	100.2	100.4	100.3	99.9	100.0	100.3	98.5	100.0	99.3
其他	Others	99.8	100.0	100.0	100.1	99.9	100.0	100.0	99.9	100.1	99.3	100.1	100.0
4.保健品及器具	Healthcare Equipment	99.1	99.7	100.0	100.4	100.0	100.4	100.1	100.1	100.3	99.4	100.3	99.9
保健器具	Health Protection Equipment	100.0	99.6	100.0	100.1	100.0	101.0	100.0	100.0	100.0	99.2	100.2	99.9
滋补保健用品	Tonic and Health Products	98.6	99.7	100.0	100.5	100.0	100.1	100.1	100.1	100.5	99.5	100.3	100.0
十四、书报杂志及电子出版物	**Books, Newspapers, Magazines and Electronic Publications**	**100.7**	**100.0**	**99.9**	**100.1**	**100.0**	**100.0**	**100.0**	**99.9**	**100.0**	**100.0**	**100.0**	**100.0**
1.教材及参考书	Teaching Materials and Reference Books	99.9	100.0	99.9	100.2	100.0	100.0	100.0	99.7	100.0	100.0	100.0	100.0

7-27 续表 7 continued

商品类别及品名	Commodity Category and Commodity Name	（以上月价格为100）											
		1月 January	2月 February	3月 March	4月 April	5月 May	6月 June	7月 July	8月 August	9月 September	10月 October	11月 November	12月 December
工具书	Tool Book	99.2	100.0	100.0	100.0	100.0	100.0	100.0	100.0	100.0	100.0	100.0	100.0
教材	Teaching Material	100.0	100.0	100.0	100.3	100.0	100.0	100.0	99.5	98.6	100.0	100.0	100.0
参考书	Reference Book	100.0	100.0	100.0	100.0	100.0	100.0	100.0	99.7	102.8	100.0	100.0	100.0
教育软件	Educational Software	100.0	100.0	98.4	100.0	100.0	100.0	100.0	100.0	100.0	100.0	100.0	100.0
2.书报杂志	Books, Newspapers, Magazines	102.0	100.0	100.0	100.0	100.0	100.0	100.0	100.0	100.0	100.0	100.0	100.0
书籍	Books	100.0	100.0	100.0	100.0	100.0	100.0	100.0	100.0	100.0	100.0	100.0	100.0
报纸	Newspapers	104.9	100.0	100.0	100.0	100.0	100.0	100.0	100.0	100.0	100.0	100.0	100.0
杂志	Magazines	101.1	100.0	100.0	100.0	100.0	100.0	100.0	100.0	100.0	100.0	100.0	100.0
3.电子音像制品	Electronic Publications	100.0	100.0	99.8	100.0	99.9	100.1	99.9	100.0	100.0	100.0	100.0	100.0
音响光盘和磁带	Acoustic Light Disk and Tape	100.1	100.1	100.0	100.0	100.2	100.0	100.0	100.0	100.0	100.0	99.9	99.9
录像磁带和视盘	Video Tape and Disk	100.0	100.0	100.0	99.9	99.6	100.0	99.4	100.0	100.0	100.0	100.0	100.0
计算机软件	Computer Software	100.0	99.9	99.4	100.0	100.0	100.3	100.2	100.0	100.0	100.0	100.0	100.0
十五、燃料	**Fuels**	**100.6**	**100.1**	**99.8**	**101.1**	**101.3**	**102.0**	**100.2**	**100.1**	**100.5**	**101.5**	**100.2**	**100.3**
1.煤炭及制品	Coal and Related Products	100.2	100.2	99.9	99.8	100.1	99.7	100.0	100.1	99.8	103.6	100.5	100.6
原煤	Raw Coal	100.1	100.5	100.0	99.9	100.3	99.6	100.0	100.1	99.9	105.9	100.8	100.8
煤制品	Coal Products	100.3	99.8	99.8	99.6	99.8	99.8	99.9	100.1	99.7	100.5	100.2	100.4
2.石油及制品	Petroleum and Related Products	100.8	100.0	99.7	102.1	102.2	103.5	100.4	100.1	100.9	100.1	99.9	100.1
液化石油气	Liquefiled Petroleum Gas	102.9	100.1	97.1	97.6	100.0	99.3	99.8	100.2	104.1	99.5	99.6	100.4
管道燃气	Pipelined Gas	104.6	100.0	100.0	100.0	102.1	100.0	100.0	100.0	100.0	100.0	100.0	100.0
汽油	Gasoline	99.9	99.9	100.7	104.3	103.2	105.4	100.6	100.0	100.0	100.0	100.0	100.0
柴油	Diesel Oil	100.0	100.0	100.7	103.1	103.3	105.1	100.6	100.0	100.0	100.8	100.0	100.0
其他	Others	100.1	100.0	100.3	103.5	99.1	102.5	99.8	100.0	100.0	99.3	100.5	99.8
十六、建筑材料及五金电料	**Building Materials and Hardware**	**100.4**	**99.9**	**100.7**	**100.9**	**100.5**	**100.7**	**100.4**	**100.6**	**100.4**	**100.3**	**100.6**	**100.0**
1.建筑装璜材料	Building and Decoration Materials	100.4	99.8	100.9	101.2	100.4	100.6	100.4	100.7	100.2	100.3	100.7	100.0
木材	Wood	101.1	100.0	100.7	101.0	100.0	101.1	101.1	103.1	101.0	101.8	102.2	99.8
木地板	Wood Floor	100.0	100.0	100.0	96.3	100.3	100.3	99.9	100.0	99.1	101.1	100.6	100.2
钢材	Steel Products	100.1	99.3	102.2	103.1	103.5	102.5	98.0	97.1	99.5	100.0	99.8	99.4
砖	Brick	99.3	100.4	101.7	102.5	100.6	101.4	100.2	100.8	100.0	100.1	100.0	99.9
水泥	Cement	100.0	99.0	99.9	102.3	100.5	99.7	99.9	100.0	100.2	99.7	100.8	100.0
涂料	Coating Material	101.4	99.9	99.7	99.6	98.8	100.0	99.9	100.3	100.0	100.3	100.6	100.7
胶合板	Plywood	101.4	100.0	101.5	101.0	98.7	100.8	101.3	101.8	100.2	97.9	103.0	100.3
玻璃	Glass	101.3	99.4	100.6	100.0	100.7	100.8	101.3	101.0	100.2	101.3	100.8	100.2
粘胶	Rayon	100.3	100.0	99.9	99.9	100.0	100.0	100.4	101.5	100.1	100.1	100.0	101.7
油漆	Paint	101.5	100.1	99.9	99.9	100.5	100.7	100.0	100.2	100.4	100.0	100.0	100.8
其他	Others	100.1	100.2	104.1	101.0	100.8	96.4	104.0	100.0	100.0	101.9	100.0	96.2
2.五金电料	Hardware	100.3	100.0	100.3	100.0	100.8	100.9	100.4	100.3	101.0	100.1	100.1	100.0
五金工具	Hardware Tools	100.0	100.0	100.0	100.0	100.0	101.2	100.6	100.4	100.0	100.0	100.0	100.0
电工电料	Electrical Engineering and Electrical Materials	101.0	100.0	100.2	100.0	101.2	100.8	100.4	100.2	100.6	100.0	100.0	100.0
水暖器材	Heating Equipment	100.1	100.0	100.7	100.1	101.1	100.0	100.0	100.0	102.4	100.3	100.3	100.0
其他	Others	100.0	100.0	100.0	100.0	100.0	103.7	101.8	101.8	100.0	100.0	100.0	100.0

7-28 全省农业生产资料价格（定基）指数

Entire Province Price Indices of Means of Agricultural Production

商品类别及品名	Commodity Category and Commodity Name	（以2005年平均价格为100 middle price in 2005=100）											
		1月 January	2月 February	3月 March	4月 April	5月 May	6月 June	7月 July	8月 August	9月 September	10月 October	11月 November	12月 December
农业生产资料价格指数	**Price Indices of Means of Agricultural Production**	**100.2**	**100.9**	**101.0**	**101.1**	**101.8**	**103.9**	**103.9**	**104.1**	**104.3**	**104.3**	**104.8**	**105.8**
一、农用手工工具	**Agricultural Handwork Tools**	**102.4**	**102.1**	**101.8**	**101.9**	**101.9**	**108.8**	**109.5**	**109.5**	**109.4**	**109.3**	**108.8**	**108.8**
农用手工工具	Agricultural Handwork Tools	102.4	102.1	101.8	101.9	101.9	108.8	109.5	109.5	109.4	109.3	108.8	108.8
二、饲料	**Forage**	**100.0**	**100.1**	**100.5**	**101.0**	**101.3**	**101.7**	**104.0**	**105.9**	**108.2**	**107.8**	**109.8**	**110.9**
混合饲料	Mixed Forage	100.0	99.8	100.0	99.8	99.8	100.0	100.3	100.2	100.3	100.2	101.0	101.4
其他	Others	99.9	100.4	101.1	102.6	103.3	103.8	109.1	113.5	118.7	117.9	121.5	123.6
三、产品畜	**Production Livestock**	**88.0**	**93.2**	**89.9**	**85.5**	**82.0**	**82.3**	**83.5**	**89.6**	**91.4**	**94.0**	**96.9**	**105.4**
幼禽家畜	Young Fowls and Livestock	88.0	93.2	89.9	85.5	82.0	82.3	83.5	89.6	91.4	94.0	96.9	105.4
四、半机械化农具	**Semi-mechanized Farm Tools**	**101.2**	**101.2**	**101.5**	**102.6**	**103.1**	**103.5**	**103.6**	**104.0**	**104.0**	**104.0**	**103.8**	**104.0**
半机械化农具	Semi-mechanized Farm Tools	101.2	101.2	101.5	102.6	103.1	103.5	103.6	104.0	104.0	104.0	103.8	104.0
五、机械化农具	**Mechanized Farm Tools**	**101.3**	**101.3**	**101.3**	**101.4**	**101.9**	**102.6**	**102.5**	**104.2**	**105.2**	**105.1**	**105.1**	**105.2**
农用机械	Agricultural Machinery	101.3	101.3	101.3	101.4	101.9	102.6	102.5	104.2	105.2	105.1	105.1	105.2
六、化学肥料	**Chemical Fertilizer**	**99.1**	**99.8**	**100.0**	**100.6**	**101.1**	**103.5**	**102.1**	**100.7**	**99.3**	**99.1**	**98.2**	**98.6**
氮肥	Nitrogenous Fertilizer	96.5	97.3	97.7	98.7	99.7	104.1	101.0	97.8	95.3	95.0	94.3	94.8
磷肥	Phosphate Fertilizer	101.0	101.7	102.2	100.3	100.4	101.8	102.4	101.7	99.8	100.1	97.3	97.8
钾肥	Potassic Fertilizer	104.3	104.4	104.4	106.5	106.6	107.1	106.9	107.2	106.9	107.1	106.7	107.0
复合肥料	Compound Fertilizer	100.4	101.2	100.8	101.7	101.8	102.3	102.0	102.5	102.8	102.4	101.8	102.2
七、农药及农药械	**Pesticide and its Appliances**	**102.8**	**103.7**	**104.9**	**104.3**	**106.4**	**105.9**	**106.1**	**105.7**	**106.5**	**106.1**	**106.2**	**106.2**
1.化学农药	Chemical Pesticide	103.0	104.1	104.7	104.0	106.5	105.9	106.1	105.6	106.5	106.1	106.2	106.2
杀虫剂	Insecticide	103.4	105.2	106.0	104.7	108.9	107.7	108.6	108.0	109.3	108.9	109.4	109.5
杀菌剂	Fungicide	101.4	101.8	102.5	102.6	103.4	103.4	103.4	103.4	104.3	103.6	103.6	103.6
除草剂	Weeding Pesticide	104.2	104.2	104.4	104.2	104.5	104.6	103.5	102.6	102.5	102.5	101.5	101.5
2.农药器械	Pesticide Appliances	101.6	101.6	106.1	106.1	106.1	106.1	106.1	106.1	106.1	106.1	106.1	106.1
农药器械	Pesticide Appliances	101.6	101.6	106.1	106.1	106.1	106.1	106.1	106.1	106.1	106.1	106.1	106.1
八、农用机油	**Oil for Farm Machinery**	**104.6**	**104.7**	**104.9**	**107.5**	**110.6**	**113.7**	**115.6**	**115.6**	**115.6**	**116.3**	**116.9**	**117.4**
农用机油	Oil for Farm Machinery	104.6	104.7	104.9	107.5	110.6	113.7	115.6	115.6	115.6	116.3	116.9	117.4
九、其他农业生产资料	**Other Means of Agricultural Production**	**103.2**	**102.8**	**102.4**	**101.2**	**100.4**	**100.4**	**100.2**	**100.1**	**101.9**	**101.5**	**103.7**	**104.4**
1.农用种子	Agricultural Seed	103.2	102.7	102.1	100.2	98.8	97.5	96.9	96.9	98.8	97.6	100.0	100.0
农用种子	Agricultural Seed	103.2	102.7	102.1	100.2	98.8	97.5	96.9	96.9	98.8	97.6	100.0	100.0
2.其他	Others	103.2	102.9	102.8	102.5	102.4	103.9	104.2	104.0	105.7	106.1	108.0	109.8
农用薄膜	Agricultural Film	103.6	103.2	102.9	102.7	102.5	104.4	104.7	104.5	106.6	107.1	109.4	111.2
其他	Others	101.2	101.7	102.0	101.7	101.9	101.8	101.9	101.9	101.8	102.0	102.6	103.7
十、农业生产服务	**Agricultural Production Service**	**101.9**	**101.9**	**103.4**	**105.3**	**108.2**	**121.3**	**122.9**	**123.8**	**124.2**	**123.9**	**128.8**	**128.8**
排灌费	Drain and Irrigate Fee	101.3	101.3	102.5	106.5	112.6	117.0	118.1	118.1	118.1	118.1	129.6	129.6
机械作业费	Mechanical Manipulation Fee	102.8	102.8	105.0	105.0	105.0	132.5	132.7	135.0	136.0	135.0	133.6	133.6
其他	Others	101.8	101.8	101.8	101.8	101.8	103.5	110.9	110.9	110.9	112.0	112.0	112.0

7-29 全省农业生产资料价格指数
Entire Province Price Indices of Means of Agricultural Production

商品类别及品名	Commodity Category and Commodity Name	（以2005年同期价格为100 2005=100）												
		全年 Annural	1月 January	2月 February	3月 March	4月 April	5月 May	6月 June	7月 July	8月 August	9月 September	10月 October	11月 November	12月 December
农业生产资料价格指数	**Price Indices of Means of Agricultural Production**	**103.0**	**102.6**	**102.5**	**102.1**	**101.4**	**101.4**	**102.7**	**102.2**	**102.8**	**103.4**	**103.9**	**104.9**	**106.2**
一、农用手工工具	**Agricultural Handwork Tools**	**106.2**	**105.3**	**105.0**	**103.2**	**103.1**	**102.9**	**108.4**	**108.8**	**108.8**	**108.7**	**107.0**	**106.4**	**106.3**
农用手工工具	Agricultural Handwork Tools	106.2	105.3	105.0	103.2	103.1	102.9	108.4	108.8	108.8	108.7	107.0	106.4	106.3
二、饲料	**Forage**	**104.3**	**99.6**	**98.8**	**100.5**	**101.2**	**102.1**	**101.6**	**103.4**	**105.6**	**107.8**	**107.4**	**110.5**	**112.7**
混合饲料	Mixed Forage	100.2	100.2	99.6	99.9	99.7	99.8	100.0	100.3	100.3	100.5	99.9	101.1	101.7
其他	Others	109.6	98.9	97.8	101.4	103.3	105.2	103.8	107.5	112.6	117.5	117.4	123.2	127.9
三、产品畜	**Production Livestock**	**90.1**	**89.6**	**90.8**	**85.4**	**78.3**	**73.7**	**75.9**	**77.2**	**86.5**	**92.3**	**104.5**	**115.6**	**131.0**
幼禽家畜	Young Fowls and Livestock	90.1	89.6	90.8	85.4	78.3	73.7	75.9	77.2	86.5	92.3	104.5	115.6	131.0
四、半机械化农具	**Semi-mechanized Farm Tools**	**103.1**	**101.3**	**101.3**	**101.7**	**103.0**	**103.6**	**104.0**	**104.5**	**104.0**	**103.8**	**103.4**	**103.0**	**102.9**
半机械化农具	Semi-mechanized Farm Tools	103.1	101.3	101.3	101.7	103.0	103.6	104.0	104.5	104.0	103.8	103.4	103.0	102.9
五、机械化农具	**Mechanized Farm Tools**	**103.1**	**101.6**	**101.6**	**101.7**	**101.7**	**102.2**	**102.8**	**102.3**	**104.0**	**104.8**	**104.8**	**104.8**	**104.8**
农用机械	Agricultural Machinery	103.1	101.6	101.6	101.7	101.7	102.2	102.8	102.3	104.0	104.8	104.8	104.8	104.8
六、化学肥料	**Chemical Fertilizer**	**100.2**	**101.8**	**101.7**	**100.9**	**101.2**	**100.8**	**101.8**	**99.8**	**99.4**	**98.6**	**98.8**	**98.3**	**99.2**
氮肥	Nitrogenous Fertilizer	97.7	98.5	99.0	99.5	99.8	99.3	101.3	96.8	95.7	94.6	95.3	95.6	96.7
磷肥	Phosphate Fertilizer	100.5	102.9	102.2	101.4	99.4	99.7	101.7	102.8	101.6	100.8	99.8	96.8	97.4
钾肥	Potassic Fertilizer	106.2	110.8	109.6	106.4	106.6	104.5	106.7	106.3	106.6	104.7	104.6	104.4	104.6
复合肥料	Compound Fertilizer	101.8	103.3	102.8	101.0	102.5	102.4	100.9	100.9	101.5	101.7	101.7	101.3	102.1
七、农药及农药械	**Pesticide and its Appliances**	**105.4**	**108.0**	**109.0**	**109.8**	**106.0**	**106.9**	**103.7**	**104.2**	**103.5**	**104.1**	**103.9**	**103.2**	**103.2**
1.化学农药	Chemical Pesticide	105.4	108.6	109.8	110.0	105.9	106.9	103.4	104.0	103.2	103.8	103.7	103.3	103.3
杀虫剂	Insecticide	107.5	109.9	111.1	112.3	107.3	109.1	104.9	106.2	105.1	106.2	106.2	106.2	106.2
杀菌剂	Fungicide	103.1	103.0	105.3	105.8	104.1	103.5	102.0	102.0	102.2	103.0	102.2	102.2	102.1
除草剂	Weeding Pesticide	103.4	113.3	112.8	109.9	104.9	106.1	101.4	101.0	99.7	99.1	99.3	97.8	97.8
2.农药器械	Pesticide Appliances	105.4	103.9	103.9	108.4	106.8	106.8	106.0	106.0	105.8	105.8	105.8	102.8	102.9
农药器械	Pesticide Appliances	105.4	103.9	103.9	108.4	106.8	106.8	106.0	106.0	105.8	105.8	105.8	102.8	102.9
八、农用机油	**Oil for Farm Machinery**	**112.0**	**109.7**	**110.0**	**110.0**	**112.2**	**113.6**	**115.8**	**114.5**	**111.0**	**110.8**	**111.6**	**111.5**	**112.4**
农用机油	Oil for Farm Machinery	112.0	109.7	110.0	110.0	112.2	113.6	115.8	114.5	111.0	110.8	111.6	111.5	112.4
九、其他农业生产资料	**Other Means of Agricultural Production**	**101.9**	**106.9**	**105.3**	**104.0**	**101.9**	**100.8**	**100.9**	**99.8**	**99.7**	**101.4**	**99.9**	**100.9**	**101.2**
1.农用种子	Agricultural Seed	99.6	106.5	103.9	102.7	100.4	98.9	97.7	96.4	98.2	99.7	97.1	96.9	96.9
农用种子	Agricultural Seed	99.6	106.5	103.9	102.7	100.4	98.9	97.7	96.4	98.2	99.7	97.1	96.9	96.9
2.其他	Others	104.6	107.5	107.0	105.6	103.6	103.2	104.8	103.8	101.4	103.3	103.2	105.7	106.4
农用薄膜	Agricultural Film	105.2	109.1	108.3	106.5	104.1	103.5	105.5	104.2	101.3	103.7	103.5	106.4	107.4
其他	Others	102.0	101.4	101.9	102.2	101.7	102.0	101.9	102.0	102.0	102.0	102.1	102.7	102.4
十、农业生产服务	**Agricultural Production Service**	**116.2**	**102.5**	**102.5**	**104.0**	**105.9**	**108.8**	**121.8**	**123.4**	**124.3**	**124.7**	**122.1**	**127.0**	**127.0**
排灌费	Drain and Irrigate Fee	114.4	101.7	101.7	102.9	107.0	113.1	117.5	118.6	118.6	118.6	116.6	128.0	128.0
机械作业费	Mechanical Manip-	121.6	103.5	103.5	105.8	105.8	105.8	133.4	133.6	135.9	137.0	132.3	130.9	130.9
其他	Others	106.7	102.5	102.5	102.5	102.5	102.5	103.0	110.3	110.3	110.3	111.4	111.4	111.4

7-30 全省农业生产资料价格（环比）指数

Entire Province Price Indices of Means of Agricultural Production

商品类别及品名	Commodity Category and Commodity Name	1月 January	2月 February	3月 March	4月 April	5月 May	6月 June	7月 July	8月 August	9月 September	10月 October	11月 November	12月 December
		（以上月价格为100 preceding month=100）											
农业生产资料价格指数	**Price Indices of Means of Agricultural Production**	**100.6**	**100.7**	**100.1**	**100.2**	**100.6**	**102.1**	**100.0**	**100.2**	**100.2**	**100.0**	**100.5**	**100.9**
一、农用手工工具	**Agricultural Handwork Tools**	**100.1**	**99.7**	**99.7**	**100.1**	**100.0**	**106.7**	**100.6**	**100.0**	**99.9**	**99.9**	**99.6**	**100.0**
农用手工工具	Agricultural Handwork Tools	100.1	99.7	99.7	100.1	100.0	106.7	100.6	100.0	99.9	99.9	99.6	100.0
二、饲料	**Forage**	**101.6**	**100.1**	**100.4**	**100.5**	**100.3**	**100.4**	**102.3**	**101.8**	**102.2**	**99.6**	**101.9**	**101.1**
混合饲料	Mixed Forage	100.3	99.8	100.2	99.8	100.0	100.2	100.2	99.9	100.2	99.8	100.8	100.5
其他	Others	103.3	100.5	100.7	101.5	100.7	100.5	105.1	104.0	104.6	99.3	103.1	101.7
三、产品畜	**Production Livestock**	**109.3**	**106.0**	**96.5**	**95.1**	**95.8**	**100.4**	**101.4**	**107.3**	**102.0**	**102.9**	**103.1**	**108.8**
幼禽家畜	Young Fowls and Livestock	109.3	106.0	96.5	95.1	95.8	100.4	101.4	107.3	102.0	102.9	103.1	108.8
四、半机械化农具	**Semi-mechanized Farm Tools**	**100.1**	**100.0**	**100.4**	**101.0**	**100.5**	**100.3**	**100.2**	**100.4**	**100.0**	**100.0**	**99.8**	**100.2**
半机械化农具	Semi-mechanized Farm Tools	100.1	100.0	100.4	101.0	100.5	100.3	100.2	100.4	100.0	100.0	99.8	100.2
五、机械化农具	**Mechanized Farm Tools**	**100.8**	**100.0**	**100.0**	**100.1**	**100.5**	**100.6**	**100.0**	**101.7**	**100.9**	**99.9**	**100.0**	**100.1**
农用机械	Agricultural Machinery	100.8	100.0	100.0	100.1	100.5	100.6	100.0	101.7	100.9	99.9	100.0	100.1
六、化学肥料	**Chemical Fertilizer**	**99.7**	**100.7**	**100.2**	**100.6**	**100.5**	**102.4**	**98.7**	**98.6**	**98.7**	**99.8**	**99.1**	**100.4**
氮肥	Nitrogenous Fertilizer	98.4	100.8	100.5	101.0	101.1	104.4	97.1	96.8	97.4	99.7	99.3	100.5
磷肥	Phosphate Fertilizer	100.5	100.7	100.5	98.1	100.0	101.4	100.6	99.3	98.2	100.3	97.2	100.5
钾肥	Potassic Fertilizer	102.0	100.0	100.0	102.0	100.1	100.5	99.8	100.2	99.8	100.1	99.7	100.3
复合肥料	Compound Fertilizer	100.4	100.7	99.7	100.9	100.1	100.5	99.8	100.4	100.3	99.6	99.4	100.4
七、农药及农药械	**Pesticide and its Appliances**	**100.0**	**100.9**	**101.1**	**99.4**	**102.1**	**99.5**	**100.2**	**99.6**	**100.7**	**99.7**	**100.1**	**100.0**
1.化学农药	Chemical Pesticide	100.2	101.0	100.6	99.4	102.4	99.4	100.2	99.5	100.9	99.6	100.1	100.0
杀虫剂	Insecticide	100.2	101.8	100.7	98.8	104.0	98.9	100.8	99.5	101.2	99.6	100.5	100.0
杀菌剂	Fungicide	100.0	100.3	100.7	100.1	100.8	100.0	100.0	100.0	100.8	99.4	100.0	99.9
除草剂	Weeding Pesticide	100.4	100.0	100.2	99.8	100.4	100.1	98.9	99.0	100.0	99.9	99.1	100.0
2.农药器械	Pesticide Appliances	98.6	100.0	104.4	100.0	100.0	100.0	100.0	100.0	100.0	100.0	100.0	100.0
农药器械	Pesticide Appliances	98.6	100.0	104.4	100.0	100.0	100.0	100.0	100.0	100.0	100.0	100.0	100.0
八、农用机油	**Oil for Farm Machinery**	**100.2**	**100.0**	**100.3**	**102.5**	**102.9**	**102.8**	**101.6**	**100.0**	**100.0**	**100.6**	**100.5**	**100.4**
农用机油	Oil for Farm Machinery	100.2	100.0	100.3	102.5	102.9	102.8	101.6	100.0	100.0	100.6	100.5	100.4
九、其他农业生产资料	**Other Means of Agricultural Production**	**100.0**	**99.6**	**99.6**	**98.9**	**99.2**	**100.0**	**99.8**	**99.9**	**101.8**	**99.6**	**102.1**	**100.7**
1.农用种子	Agricultural Seed	100.0	99.5	99.4	98.2	98.5	98.7	99.4	100.0	101.9	98.8	102.5	100.0
农用种子	Agricultural Seed	100.0	99.5	99.4	98.2	98.5	98.7	99.4	100.0	101.9	98.8	102.5	100.0
2.其他	Others	100.0	99.8	99.8	99.7	99.9	101.5	100.3	99.8	101.6	100.4	101.8	101.6
农用薄膜	Agricultural Film	100.1	99.6	99.7	99.7	99.8	101.9	100.3	99.8	102.0	100.5	102.1	101.7
其他	Others	100.0	100.5	100.3	99.6	100.3	99.9	100.1	100.0	99.9	100.2	100.6	101.1
十、农业生产服务	**Agricultural Production Service**	**100.4**	**100.0**	**101.4**	**101.9**	**102.7**	**112.1**	**101.3**	**100.7**	**100.3**	**99.8**	**104.0**	**100.0**
排灌费	Drain and Irrigate Fee	100.0	100.0	101.1	104.0	105.7	103.9	100.9	100.0	100.0	100.0	109.8	100.0
机械作业费	Mechanical Manipulation Fee	100.7	100.0	102.2	100.0	100.0	126.1	100.2	101.7	100.8	99.2	99.0	100.0
其他	Others	101.2	100.0	100.0	100.0	100.0	101.7	107.1	100.0	100.0	101.0	100.0	100.0

7-31 分市、县居民消费价格指数
Consumer Price Indices by Each City and County

（以2005年价格为100 2005=100）

市县名称	Name of City and County	居民消费价格总指数 General Consumer Price Index	非食品价格指数 No-food Price Index	服务项目价格指数 Services Price Index	工业品价格指数 Industrial Products Price Index	扣除食品和能源价格指数 Deducting Foods and Energy Price Index	扣除鲜菜鲜果总指数 Deducting Fresh, Vegetables and Fruits Price Index	消费品价格指数 Consumer Goods Price Index
济南市	Jinan	100.9	100.2	100.9	99.8	99.8	100.2	100.8
青岛市	Qingdao	100.9	100.5	100.8	100.4	100.3	100.6	101.0
淄博市	Zibo	101.1	100.1	102.1	99.1	99.7	100.4	100.8
枣庄市	Zaozhuang	101.3	100.4	102.9	99.3	100.3	100.8	100.9
东营市	Dongying	100.5	100.7	104.4	99.1	100.6	100.5	99.4
利津县	Lijin	100.9	100.9	100.0	101.2	100.5	100.6	101.1
烟台市	Yantai	101.6	100.8	102.2	100.1	100.5	100.9	101.5
潍坊市	Weifang	101.0	100.1	101.3	99.7	99.9	100.3	100.9
青州市	Qingzhou	100.3	99.2	102.1	98.0	98.7	99.5	99.8
诸城市	Zhucheng	100.5	100.5	102.9	99.6	100.2	99.9	100.0
济宁市	Jining	100.9	100.3	100.5	100.2	100.0	100.3	101.0
微山县	Weishan	101.4	101.1	100.5	101.4	100.8	100.8	101.6
泰安市	Taian	101.3	100.7	101.0	100.5	100.4	101.0	101.3
威海市	Weihai	101.0	100.1	101.2	99.5	99.7	100.2	100.9
文登市	Wendeng	101.4	100.7	100.9	100.7	100.0	100.9	101.5
日照市	Rizhao	101.1	100.6	102.2	99.9	100.3	100.0	100.8
莱芜市	Laiwu	100.3	99.0	100.8	98.3	98.8	99.3	100.1
临沂市	Linyi	100.6	100.3	102.5	99.3	99.9	100.3	100.1
费县	Feixian	101.5	100.7	99.7	101.2	100.6	100.4	102.0
德州市	Dezhou	101.1	100.2	101.2	99.7	99.8	100.2	101.0
武城县	Wucheng	101.3	101.3	102.3	101.0	100.9	100.7	101.1
聊城市	Liaocheng	101.4	99.5	102.0	98.0	99.3	100.1	101.2
东阿县	Donge	102.1	102.8	104.7	101.9	102.5	101.5	101.4
临清市	Linqing	101.6	100.4	100.7	100.4	100.2	100.1	101.9
滨州市	Binzhou	100.7	99.4	100.5	98.9	99.1	100.0	100.7
菏泽市	Heze	101.2	100.7	101.1	100.5	100.2	100.6	101.2
巨野县	Juye	101.2	100.7	101.5	100.4	100.4	100.4	101.1

7-31 续表 1 continued

市县名称	Name of City and County	一、食品 Food	二、烟酒及用品 Tobacco, Liquor and their Appliances	三、衣着 Clothing	四、家庭设备用品及维修服务 Household Facilities, Articles and Services	五、医疗保健和个人用品 Healthcare and Personal Articles	六、交通和通信 Transportation and Communication	七、娱乐教育文化用品及服务 Recreation, Education and Culture Article	八、居住 Residence
		（以2005年价格为100 2005=100）							
济南市	Jinan	102.4	102.5	100.4	102.0	100.8	97.9	98.4	103.1
青岛市	Qingdao	101.7	102.7	99.4	101.9	101.7	98.9	98.2	103.9
淄博市	Zibo	103.2	102.0	95.6	101.5	100.6	98.4	100.1	104.4
枣庄市	Zaozhuang	103.4	98.4	97.1	101.2	101.2	99.5	101.0	104.7
东营市	Dongying	99.9	99.4	93.6	101.8	101.1	100.0	101.7	108.8
利津县	Lijin	100.9	100.0	99.6	100.0	100.2	101.6	100.1	103.9
烟台市	Yantai	103.5	99.9	98.6	101.1	97.6	103.3	101.4	103.6
潍坊市	Weifang	102.7	98.7	99.0	101.4	100.2	98.0	100.9	101.9
青州市	Qingzhou	102.8	101.3	87.1	100.8	99.6	100.1	100.0	103.6
诸城市	Zhucheng	100.7	100.1	97.0	100.3	102.2	98.4	100.5	103.8
济宁市	Jining	102.3	99.7	98.2	98.8	100.2	98.6	100.1	106.0
微山县	Weishan	102.0	100.3	100.1	99.9	101.4	100.0	99.7	104.8
泰安市	Taian	102.6	99.9	100.4	102.5	99.8	100.6	100.2	101.7
威海市	Weihai	103.2	105.2	95.7	102.0	99.1	100.1	100.2	104.6
文登市	Wendeng	103.0	102.4	97.4	100.0	100.2	100.6	99.5	104.1
日照市	Rizhao	102.2	99.9	97.9	99.8	99.8	103.3	100.3	103.0
莱芜市	Laiwu	103.1	99.6	91.7	100.0	99.0	100.2	99.9	105.7
临沂市	Linyi	101.3	101.0	95.5	103.1	98.8	99.8	101.3	104.9
费县	Feixian	103.5	100.0	99.0	99.9	99.3	99.1	99.7	105.6
德州市	Dezhou	103.0	100.4	98.3	101.6	100.9	99.1	97.4	107.2
武城县	Wucheng	101.4	101.1	101.2	101.5	102.8	99.5	99.9	103.5
聊城市	Liaocheng	105.1	102.5	96.9	99.8	101.2	99.4	98.6	102.9
东阿县	Donge	100.4	100.2	104.5	99.5	102.5	100.7	105.7	102.0
临清市	Linqing	104.5	101.4	95.2	98.6	103.2	95.1	99.5	108.0
滨州市	Binzhou	103.8	101.4	100.9	98.3	100.6	96.2	97.9	104.2
菏泽市	Heze	102.2	100.9	100.1	101.4	99.7	99.5	99.6	105.5
巨野县	Juye	102.3	96.6	100.7	100.7	100.3	104.3	98.4	102.0

7-32 分市、县商品零售价格指数
Retail Price Indices by Each City and County

（以2005年价格为100 2005=100）

市县名称	Name of City and County	商品零售价格总指数 General Retail Price Index	一、食品 Food	二、饮料、烟酒 Beverages, Tobacco, Liquor	三、服装、鞋帽 Garments, Footgear and Hats	四、纺织品 Textiles	五、家用电器及音像器材 Household Appliances, Music and Video Equipments	六、文化办公用品 Cultural and Office Applicances	七、日用品 Articles for Daily Use	八、体育娱乐用品 Sports and Recreation Articles
济南市	Jinan	100.3	102.4	101.7	100.4	97.9	100.8	95.1	101.1	99.1
青岛市	Qingdao	99.7	101.5	102.9	99.8	100.3	96.9	88.7	100.7	99.2
淄博市	Zibo	99.9	103.3	102.4	96.2	97.5	98.8	98.4	101.5	100.0
枣庄市	Zaozhuang	100.7	103.5	98.3	97.0	100.7	101.4	99.4	100.1	100.1
东营市	Dongying	99.1	99.7	99.7	93.7	98.7	100.0	99.2	99.6	93.9
利津县	Lijin	100.9	101.9	100.2	99.7	100.0	100.0	100.0	100.0	100.0
烟台市	Yantai	100.7	103.4	99.9	98.7	99.5	100.6	99.8	100.7	99.8
潍坊市	Weifang	100.5	103.0	98.6	98.9	100.0	101.4	100.0	100.0	100.0
青州市	Qingzhou	100.1	102.9	101.0	86.9	103.6	93.6	98.8	102.3	100.3
诸城市	Zhucheng	100.2	100.8	100.0	97.5	98.9	98.3	97.8	100.5	98.8
济宁市	Jining	100.4	101.8	99.6	98.1	97.5	99.3	98.4	99.7	99.7
微山县	Weishan	101.2	102.2	100.3	99.7	101.5	100.1	99.9	99.3	101.7
泰安市	Taian	101.3	102.6	101.0	100.7	106.1	99.3	100.2	99.4	100.4
威海市	Weihai	102.2	103.5	103.9	96.1	100.0	101.4	100.3	102.0	100.2
文登市	Wendeng	101.7	103.5	102.2	99.2	99.6	97.9	98.5	100.4	97.4
日照市	Rizhao	100.8	102.6	100.1	97.9	98.1	99.7	99.9	100.1	100.0
莱芜市	Laiwu	99.9	103.2	99.6	92.1	100.0	97.7	100.0	100.1	100.0
临沂市	Linyi	100.1	101.2	103.4	95.3	101.7	100.6	100.1	100.6	99.2
费县	Feixian	101.4	104.7	100.1	98.9	100.0	101.2	97.7	99.9	99.9
德州市	Dezhou	100.9	103.1	100.5	99.4	99.0	96.6	90.2	100.0	99.6
武城县	Wucheng	101.1	101.4	101.5	101.0	102.2	99.7	100.3	99.8	99.5
聊城市	Liaocheng	101.1	104.8	101.8	97.2	99.2	94.7	89.5	101.6	99.0
东阿县	Donge	101.1	100.0	101.0	104.4	102.2	97.8	103.1	100.0	100.6
临清市	Linqing	101.3	105.5	101.1	94.3	98.8	96.3	96.4	97.8	98.0
滨州市	Binzhou	100.9	103.4	99.7	99.5	89.0	96.4	88.7	99.7	94.8
菏泽市	Heze	100.5	102.2	100.9	100.0	99.5	102.3	97.9	100.5	100.0
巨野县	Juye	101.2	103.2	97.2	100.2	100.1	98.4	97.6	99.6	100.0

7-32 续表 1 continued

市县名称	Name of City and County	（以2005年价格为100 2005=100）							
		九、交通、通信用品 Transportation and Communication Appliances	十、家具 Furniture	十一、化妆品 Cosmetics	十二、金银珠宝 Gold, Silver and Jewelry	十三、中西药品及医疗保健用品 Traditional Chinese and Western Medicines and Healthcare Articles	十四、书报杂志及电子出版物 Books, Newspapers, Magazines and Electronic Publications	十五、燃料 Fuels	十六、建筑材料及五金电料 Building Materials and Hardware
济南市	Jinan	91.0	99.9	99.7	109.4	101.4	101.2	108.9	102.3
青岛市	Qingdao	92.9	100.7	97.5	107.1	101.7	101.8	110.4	106.5
淄博市	Zibo	89.6	100.2	99.7	121.5	99.3	99.6	110.1	102.6
枣庄市	Zaozhuang	96.9	101.9	101.8	105.2	98.8	101.7	104.7	101.6
东营市	Dongying	95.3	106.0	99.6	117.0	99.9	100.7	110.4	100.5
利津县	Lijin	100.0	100.0	100.0	100.0	101.4	101.4	108.4	100.0
烟台市	Yantai	98.9	100.2	96.4	105.0	93.1	100.8	107.2	102.3
潍坊市	Weifang	93.7	99.9	100.0	100.0	100.0	99.5	108.8	100.7
青州市	Qingzhou	94.9	102.5	100.6	139.0	97.9	100.5	109.4	102.9
诸城市	Zhucheng	90.8	101.1	99.1	126.3	102.1	99.7	109.4	103.2
济宁市	Jining	96.7	100.0	100.0	119.8	99.9	99.9	106.7	99.8
微山县	Weishan	94.9	98.0	100.3	127.2	101.2	99.2	109.4	101.9
泰安市	Taian	92.7	100.1	97.9	114.0	97.9	99.5	108.8	101.6
威海市	Weihai	98.7	100.0	100.0	110.2	95.8	101.2	111.9	101.8
文登市	Wendeng	96.6	99.0	98.6	115.9	99.6	102.8	111.8	101.0
日照市	Rizhao	97.7	99.0	98.7	104.7	98.8	102.5	112.6	102.7
莱芜市	Laiwu	96.8	99.9	100.0	103.0	98.1	100.0	108.5	106.9
临沂市	Linyi	91.7	100.4	100.1	132.6	94.7	105.7	113.1	103.2
费县	Feixian	98.1	99.9	100.4	101.1	99.0	100.3	102.0	102.9
德州市	Dezhou	94.0	99.3	100.1	120.8	100.7	100.0	113.0	104.7
武城县	Wucheng	86.8	105.0	100.4	125.4	101.0	100.5	114.0	104.7
聊城市	Liaocheng	96.7	95.2	100.7	128.7	101.1	100.4	109.6	103.5
东阿县	Donge	97.2	99.2	104.4	133.1	99.2	103.4	108.0	100.3
临清市	Linqing	85.2	98.5	99.9	120.9	104.5	100.2	110.8	108.7
滨州市	Binzhou	95.1	102.2	99.1	129.0	99.4	104.4	112.2	103.3
菏泽市	Heze	93.3	92.3	100.9	116.7	96.3	101.8	113.7	102.0
巨野县	Juye	94.5	100.0	100.0	122.6	99.8	100.4	110.6	105.2

8

企业集团统计资料
Statistical Data of Enterprise Groups

简要说明

一、企业集团是指以母子公司为主体，通过投资及生产经营协作等多种方式，与众多的企事业单位共同组成的经济联合体。企业集团内部统计范围包括：企业集团的母公司、在中国境内和境外的全资子公司（单位）、绝对控股子公司（单位）和相对控股子公司（单位）；不包括参股和协作企业（单位）。

二、企业集团的调查范围包括：一是中央企业；二是由国务院批准的国家试点企业集团；三是国家重点企业（包括520户和重组为集团公司的原512户国家重点企业）；四是国务院确定的建立现代企业制度原百户试点企业；五是由国务院主管部门批准的企业集团；六是由省、自治区、直辖市人民政府批准的企业集团；七是省政府确定的重点企业（集团）和其他各类企业集团。

三、企业集团财务指标按财政部门有关“合并会计报表”的规定填报。但是，部分企业集团由于内部财务制度尚未完善，采用相加汇总的方法填报。

Brief Introduction

Ⅰ. The enterprise group is the economical unified body which takes the mother and child company as a main body and is composed together with the multitudinous enterprises and institutions by the investment and the production management cooperation and so on many kinds of ways. Interior statistics scope of the enterprise group includes: Enterprise group's parent company, entire capital subsidiary company (unit) within the boundaries of Chinese and beyond the border, the subsidiary company (unit) of controlling stock absolutely and the relative holding subsidiary company (unit); no including share-holding and cooperation enterprise (unit).

Ⅱ. Enterprise group's field of investigation includes: One is the central enterprise; Two is site enterprise group of the national experiment which was authorized by the State Council; Three is National Key Enterprise (including 520 and reorganization for group company's original 512 national key Enterprises); Four is original hundred household experiment site enterprises which the State Council determined to establish modern enterprise system; Five is the enterprise group which is authorized by State Council Department; Six is the enterprise group which was authorized by the province, the autonomous region, the municipality people's government; Seven is the key enterprise group which the provincial government determined and other each kind of enterprise group.

Ⅲ. The enterprise group financial is filled according to "merged accountant form" about the finance department. Because the internal finance system is not yet consummated, partial enterprise group uses the method of adding together for compiling to fill.

8-1　企业集团构成情况（2006年）
Constitution of Enterprise Groups(2006)

分组	Groups	集团个数（个）Number of Enterprise Groups	占集团总数的比重（%）The Proportion of Enterprise Groups	集团所属成员企业个数（个）Respective Member of Enterprise Groups	占成员企业总数的比重（%）The Proportion of Respective Member
总计	Total	726	100	4463	100.0
按集团审批部门分	Grouped by Examining Department				
国务院	The State Council	4	0.6	47	1.1
国务院主管部门	Governing Departments of the State Council	8	1.1	57	1.3
省级人民政府	Provincial Government	215	29.6	1578	35.3
省级人民政府主管部门	Governing Departments of Provincial Government	154	21.2	846	19.0
其他	Others	345	47.5	1935	43.3
按控股情况分	Grouped by Controlling Shares				
国有控股	State-holding	233	32.1	1534	34.4
集体控股	Collective-owned Absolute Holding	159	21.9	1100	24.6
私人控股	Private Holding	315	43.4	1744	39.1
港澳台商控股	Holding by Traders from Hong Kong, Macao and Taiwan	4	0.6	4	0.1
外商控股	Holding by Foreign Traders	15	2.1	81	1.8
按主营行业分	Grouped by Sector				
第一产业合计	Primary Industry	1	0.1	9	0.2
农、林、牧、渔业	Farming, Forestry, Animal Husbandry and Fishery	1	0.1	9	0.2
第二产业合计	Secondary Industry	602	82.9	3514	78.7
工业小计	Industry	549	75.6	3173	71.1
采矿业	Mining	34	4.7	218	4.9
制造业	Manufacturing	493	67.9	2808	62.9
电力、燃气及水的生产和供应业	Production and Supply of Electricity	22	3	147	3.3
建筑业	Construction	53	7.3	341	7.6
第三产业合计	Tertiary-industry	123	16.9	940	21.1
交通运输、仓储和邮政业	Transportation, Storage and Telecommunications	17	2.3	121	2.7
信息传输、计算机服务和软件业	Information Transmission, Computer Services and Software	5	0.7	27	0.6
批发和零售业	Wholesale and Retail Trade	66	9.1	588	13.2

8-1 续表 1 continued

分组	Groups	集团个数（个）Number of Enterprise Groups	占集团总数的比重（%）The Proportion of Enterprise Groups	集团所属成员企业个数（个）Respective Member of Enterprise Groups	占成员企业总数的比重（%）The Proportion of Respective Member
住宿和餐饮业	Hotel and Catering Services	1	0.1	5	0.1
金融业	Financial Intermediation	0	0		
房地产业	Real Estate	23	3.2	128	2.9
其他合计	Others	11	1.5	71	1.6
租赁和商务服务业	Leasing and Business Services	7	1	37	0.8
科学研究、技术服务和地质勘查业	Scientific Research, Technical Service and Geologic Prospecting	0	0		
水利、环境和公共设施管理业	Management of Water Conservancy, Environment and Public Facilities	1	0.1	6	0.1
居民服务和其他服务业	Services to Household and Other Services	2	0.3	11	0.3
教育	Education	0	0		
卫生、社会保障和社会福利业	Health, Social Security and Social Welfare	0	0		
文化、体育和娱乐业	Culture, Sports and Entertainment	1	0.1	17	0.4
公共管理和社会组织	Public Management and Social Organization	0	0		
国际组织	International Organization	0	0		
按登记注册类型分	By Status of Registration				
国有企业	State-owned Enterprises	59	8.1	339	7.6
公司制企业小计	Corporation	626	86.2	3847	86.2
国有独资企业	Sole State-funded Corporation	71	9.8	676	15.2
其他有限责任公司	Other Limited Liability Corporation	374	51.5	2210	49.5
股份有限公司	Share-holding Corporations Limited	134	18.5	737	16.5
中外合资企业	Joint-venture Enterprises	22	3	100	2.2
外商投资股份有限公司	Share-holding Corporations Limited with Foreign Investment	8	1.1	41	0.9
港澳台合资企业	Enterprises with Funds from Hong kong, Macao and Taiwan	13	1.8	79	1.8
港澳台商投资股份有限公司	Share-holding Corporations Limited with Investment from Hong kong, Macao and Taiwan	4	0.6	4	0.1
其他	Others	41	5.6	277	6.2

8-2 企业集团主要经济指标
Main Economic Norms of Enterprise Groups

单位：万元 unit:10 000yuan

分组	Groups	年末资产总计 Year-end Total Assets	固定资产原价 Original Value of Fixed Assets	累计折旧 Accumulated Depreciation	本年折旧 Accumulated Depreciation of Current Year
总计	Total	190967802	116134972	40813386	7670702
按集团审批部门分	Grouped by Examining Department				
国务院	The State Council	9210379	5026027	1712346	306042
国务院主管部门	Governing Departments of the State Council	9483693	8554429	3066356	572188
省级人民政府	Provincial Government	105813012	64366389	20413401	4633904
省级人民政府主管部门	Governing Departments of Provincial Government	19156714	7383562	2216215	405803
其他	Others	47304004	30804565	13405068	1752765
按控股情况分	Grouped by Controlling Shares				
国有控股	State-holding	105910381	74565965	28856760	5073070
集体控股	Collective-owned Absolute Holding	39638302	17082027	3881785	919368
私人控股	Private Holding	37378800	14768502	3836015	909622
港澳台商控股	Holding by Traders from Hong Kong, Macao and Taiwan	3813177	6298504	2947269	499842
外商控股	Holding by Foreign Traders	4227142	3419974	1291557	268800
按主营行业分	Grouped by Sector				
第一产业合计	Primary Industry	139104	81016	36597	1638
农、林、牧、渔业	Farming, Forestry, Animal Husbandry and Fishery	139104	81016	36597	1638
第二产业合计	Secondary Industry	156408742	95710770	33299340	6261285
工业小计	Industry	151446295	94956878	33025984	6208944
采矿业	Mining	23530233	23237493	10923793	1333097
制造业	Manufacturing	102805265	53478380	16219395	3952433
电力、燃气及水的生产和供应业	Production and Supply of Electricity	25110797	18241005	5882796	923414
建筑业	Construction	4962447	753892	273356	52341
第三产业合计	Tertiary-industry	34419956	20343186	7477449	1407779
交通运输、仓储和邮政业	Transportation, Storage and Telecommunications	10469879	6400276	1539574	317479
信息传输、计算机服务和软件业	Information Transmission, Computer Services and Software	6836777	10444810	5061646	901069
批发和零售业	Wholesale and Retail Trade	9385995	2711757	655938	142000

续表 continued

分组	Groups	年末资产总计 Year-end Total Assets	固定资产原价 Original Value of Fixed Assets	累计折旧 Accumulated Depreciation	本年折旧 Accumulated Depreciation of Current Year
住宿和餐饮业	Hotel and Catering Services	23032	11073	5268	428
金融业	Financial Intermediation	0	0	0	0
房地产业	Real Estate	3137432	213657	49771	9108
其他合计	Others	4566841	561613	165252	37695
租赁和商务服务业	Leasing and Business Services	4023642	326184	92272	16355
科学研究、技术服务和地质勘查业	Scientific Research, Technical Service and Geologic Prospecting	0	0	0	0
水利、环境和公共设施管理业	Management of Water Conservancy, Environment and Public Facilities	6758	1118	397	35
居民服务和其他服务业	Services to Household and Other Services	307553	91123	29525	5608
教育	Education	0	0	0	0
卫生、社会保障和社会福利业	Health, Social Security and Social Welfare	0	0	0	0
文化、体育和娱乐业	Culture, Sports and Entertainment	228888	143188	43058	15697
公共管理和社会组织	Public Management and Social Organization	0	0	0	0
国际组织	International Organization	0	0	0	0
按登记注册类型分	By Status of Registration				
国有企业	State-owned Enterprises	19383066	12745746	4553364	726058
公司制企业小计	Corporation	165126916	99457232	34709374	6657752
国有独资企业	Sole State-funded Corporation	46882813	23452141	7170684	1423335
其他有限责任公司	Other Limited Liability Corporation	71108368	41456152	14746639	2382926
股份有限公司	Share-holding Corporations Limited	27889182	17664275	6897248	1849785
中外合资企业	Joint-venture Enterprises	10043824	7174115	1974331	386884
外商投资股份有限公司	Share-holding Corporations Limited with Foreign Investment	2317973	1701450	671981	81480
港澳台合资企业	Enterprises with Funds from Hong kong, Macao and Taiwan	6611871	7847779	3195191	522367
港澳台商投资股份有限公司	Share-holding Corporations Limited with Investment from Hong kong,Macao and Taiwan	272885	161320	53300	10975
其他	Others	6457820	3931994	1550648	286892

8-2 续表 1

单位：万元 unit:10 000yuan

分组	Groups	累计对外投资 Accumulative Outside Investment	本年对外投资 Outside Investment of Current Year	本年对境外投资 Overseas Investment of Current Year	存货 Stock	流动资产年平均余额 Average Balance of Circulating Funds
总计	Total	5908703	740748	15741	21980202	79257914
按集团审批部门分	Grouped by Examining Department					
国务院	The State Council	358555	19761	0	926949	3944626
国务院主管部门	Governing Departments of the State Council	449188	31710	0	131504	1611583
省级人民政府	Provincial Government	3186732	400462	14328	11938669	42341521
省级人民政府主管部门	Governing Departments of Provincial Government	697422	93397	1257	2424401	10483750
其他	Others	1216806	195418	156	6558679	20876434
按控股情况分	Grouped by Controlling Shares					
国有控股	State-holding	3824271	488980	10505	9442733	38975573
集体控股	Collective-owned Absolute Holding	1091613	74396	3519	5946318	19533163
私人控股	Private Holding	982021	171554	1717	6042083	18818540
港澳台商控股	Holding by Traders from Hong Kong, Macao and Taiwan	624	0	0	49162	232549
外商控股	Holding by Foreign Traders	10174	5818	0	499906	1698089
按主营行业分	Grouped by Sector					
第一产业合计	Primary Industry	7452	0	0	10737	84681
农、林、牧、渔业	Farming, Forestry, Animal Husbandry and Fishery	7452	0	0	10737	84681
第二产业合计	Secondary Industry	4233533	454241	15701	18460357	64862983
工业小计	Industry	4046104	425131	15701	17740681	61362362
采矿业	Mining	753505	121958	7146	1309724	7607403
制造业	Manufacturing	2100190	215413	5192	14489847	46760058
电力、燃气及水的生产和供应业	Production and Supply of Electricity	1192409	87760	3363	1941110	6994901
建筑业	Construction	187429	29110	0	719676	3500621
第三产业合计	Tertiary-industry	1667718	286507	40	3509108	14310250
交通运输、仓储和邮政业	Transportation, Storage and Telecommunications	349755	154176	0	244434	2977685
信息传输、计算机服务和软件业	Information Transmission, Computer Services and Software	18069	1240	40	29884	926612
批发和零售业	Wholesale and Retail Trade	415497	79310	0	1776294	5520531

续表 continued

分组	Groups	累计对外投资 Accumulative Outside Investment	本年对外投资 Outside Investment of Current Year	本年对境外投资 Overseas Investment of Current Year	存货 Stock	流动资产年平均余额 Average Balance of Circulating Funds
住宿和餐饮业	Hotel and Catering Services	11435	0	0	241	0
金融业	Financial Intermediation	0	0	0	0	0
房地产业	Real Estate	280249	9576	0	1322783	2134831
其他合计	Others	592713	42205	0	135472	2750591
租赁和商务服务业	Leasing and Business Services	544875	42205	0	97605	2547917
科学研究、技术服务和地质勘查业	Scientific Research, Technical Service and Geologic Prospecting	0	0	0	0	0
水利、环境和公共设施管理业	Management of Water Conservancy, Environment and Public Facilities	627	0	0	1138	3424
居民服务和其他服务业	Services to Household and Other Services	47211	0	0	30897	121651
教育	Education	0	0	0	0	0
卫生、社会保障和社会福利业	Health, Social Security and Social Welfare	0	0	0	0	0
文化、体育和娱乐业	Culture,Sports and Entertainment	0	0	0	5832	77599
公共管理和社会组织	Public Management and Social Organization	0	0	0	0	0
国际组织	International Organization	0	0	0	0	0
按登记注册类型分	By Status of Registration					
国有企业	State-owned Enterprises	809298	31549	0	1736100	7253324
公司制企业小计	Corporation	4840330	756284	15741	19508245	68994565
国有独资企业	Sole State-funded Corporation	1948388	354639	10465	4576697	19781810
其他有限责任公司	Other Limited Liability Corporation	1916095	248188	3828	9879349	31480484
股份有限公司	Share-holding Corporations Limited	570056	123808	540	3670834	12813639
中外合资企业	Joint-venture Enterprises	297017	10578	908	514221	2481564
外商投资股份有限公司	Share-holding Corporations Limited with Foreign Investment	71153	10280	0	461415	1019476
港澳台合资企业	Enterprises with Funds from Hong kong, Macao and Taiwan	32649	8791	0	340789	1306971
港澳台商投资股份有限公司	Share-holding Corporations Limited with Investment from Hong kong, Macao and Taiwan	4972	0	0	64940	110621
其他	Others	259075	-47085	0	735857	3010025

8-2 续表 2

单位：万元 unit:10 000yuan

分组	Groups	应收帐款 Accounts Receivable	年末负债合计 Year-end Total Liabilities	流动负债 Current Liabilities	银行借款 Bank Loan
总计	Total	12270827	120442156	90400438	39218150
按集团审批部门分	Grouped by Examining Department				
国务院	The State Council	251661	6339395	4352947	3087349
国务院主管部门	Governing Departments of the State Council	244824	5353919	3173941	450737
省级人民政府	Provincial Government	6041628	67835725	49792108	26143323
省级人民政府主管部门	Governing Departments of Provincial Government	1766871	12847472	9524647	2456702
其他	Others	3965843	28065645	23556795	7080039
按控股情况分	Grouped by Controlling Shares				
国有控股	State-holding	5300967	64763545	46784455	18779550
集体控股	Collective-owned Absolute Holding	3014308	26264716	19987580	11697727
私人控股	Private Holding	3292196	24321033	19792327	7283721
港澳台商控股	Holding by Traders from Hong Kong, Macao and Taiwan	142560	2804882	2397744	992784
外商控股	Holding by Foreign Traders	520796	2287980	1438332	464368
按主营行业分	Grouped by Sector				
第一产业合计	Primary Industry	5615	177157	165184	882
农、林、牧、渔业	Farming, Forestry, Animal Husbandry and Fishery	5615	177157	165184	882
第二产业合计	Secondary Industry	10866395	96795126	72963544	32076233
工业小计	Industry	9329501	93031154	69863473	31700650
采矿业	Mining	629582	12914934	9462331	4953115
制造业	Manufacturing	7904238	63328923	50812031	19204339
电力、燃气及水的生产和供应业	Production and Supply of Electricity	795681	16787297	9589111	7543196
建筑业	Construction	1536894	3763972	3100071	375583
第三产业合计	Tertiary-industry	1398817	23469873	17271710	7141035
交通运输、仓储和邮政业	Transportation, Storage and Telecommunications	262743	6647582	4518238	2372829
信息传输、计算机服务和软件业	Information Transmission, Computer Services and Software	262723	3912196	3093732	995611
批发和零售业	Wholesale and Retail Trade	740411	7422428	6746274	2093747

续表 continued

分组	Groups	应收帐款 Accounts Receivable	年末负债合计 Year-end Total Liabilities	流动负债 Current Liabilities	银行借款 Bank Loan
住宿和餐饮业	Hotel and Catering Services	93	9068	9067	0
金融业	Financial Intermediation	0	0	0	0
房地产业	Real Estate	42872	2542534	1968804	1106950
其他合计	Others	89975	2936065	935595	571898
租赁和商务服务业	Leasing and Business Services	76079	2598923	626088	558698
科学研究、技术服务和地质勘查业	Scientific Research, Technical Service and Geologic Prospecting	0	0	0	0
水利、环境和公共设施管理业	Management of Water Conservancy, Environment and Public Facilities	393	4329	4329	0
居民服务和其他服务业	Services to Household and Other Services	6631	209529	195590	13200
教育	Education	0	0	0	0
卫生、社会保障和社会福利业	Health, Social Security and Social Welfare	0	0	0	0
文化、体育和娱乐业	Culture,Sports and Entertainment	6872	123284	109588	0
公共管理和社会组织	Public Management and Social Organization	0	0	0	0
国际组织	International Organization	0	0	0	0
按登记注册类型分	By Status of Registration				
国有企业	State-owned Enterprises	1088629	12150478	9032305	3379576
公司制企业小计	Corporation	10623994	104417602	78235821	34873342
国有独资企业	Sole State-funded Corporation	2267092	31223607	22063313	10249275
其他有限责任公司	Other Limited Liability Corporation	4664966	45371121	34992686	18032813
股份有限公司	Share-holding Corporations Limited	2505489	15821303	12908283	3969079
中外合资企业	Joint-venture Enterprises	734271	6424285	3721570	537993
外商投资股份有限公司	Share-holding Corporations Limited with Foreign Investment	214447	1174072	1068461	316376
港澳台合资企业	Enterprises with Funds from Hong kong, Macao and Taiwan	204305	4223269	3331273	1717139
港澳台商投资股份有限公司	Share-holding Corporations Limited with Investment from Hong kong, Macao and Taiwan	33424	179945	150235	50667
其他	Others	558204	3874076	3132312	965232

8-2 续表 3

单位：万元　　　　unit:10 000yuan

分组	Groups	年末股东权益总计 Total Creditors's Equity	年末少数股东权益 Few Creditors's Equity	年末股东（所有者）权益 Creditors's Equity	股本（实收资本） Paid-in Capital
总计	Total	70049459	8836294	61213165	23613637
按集团审批部门分	Grouped by Examining Department				
国务院	The State Council	2870984	1120069	1750915	554516
国务院主管部门	Governing Departments of the State Council	4129774	217558	3912216	1702557
省级人民政府	Provincial Government	37977287	5637883	32339404	11333071
省级人民政府主管部门	Governing Departments of Provincial Government	6309242	505721	5803521	2455599
其他	Others	18762172	1355063	17407109	7567894
按控股情况分	Grouped by Controlling Shares				
国有控股	State-holding	41146836	5888966	35257870	15503500
集体控股	Collective-owned Absolute Holding	13373586	1857780	11515806	3706138
私人控股	Private Holding	13057767	1074451	11983316	4037521
港澳台商控股	Holding by Traders from Hong Kong, Macao and Taiwan	1008295	538	1007757	25097
外商控股	Holding by Foreign Traders	1462975	14559	1448416	341381
按主营行业分	Grouped by Sector				
第一产业合计	Primary Industry	-38053	-742	-37311	78647
农、林、牧、渔业	Farming, Forestry, Animal Husbandry and Fishery	-38053	-742	-37311	78647
第二产业合计	Secondary Industry	59137429	7691556	51445873	19034656
工业小计	Industry	57938954	7646980	50291974	18285984
采矿业	Mining	10615299	1770671	8844628	2981151
制造业	Manufacturing	39476342	4794165	34682177	11745083
电力、燃气及水的生产和供应业	Production and Supply of Electricity	7847313	1082144	6765169	3559750
建筑业	Construction	1198475	44576	1153899	748672
第三产业合计	Tertiary-industry	10950083	1145480	9804603	4500334
交通运输、仓储和邮政业	Transportation, Storage and Telecommunications	3822297	790559	3031738	1030809
信息传输、计算机服务和软件业	Information Transmission, Computer Services and Software	2924581	-996	2925577	640246
批发和零售业	Wholesale and Retail Trade	1963567	98333	1865234	1305605

续表 continued

分组	Groups	年末股东权益总计 Total Creditors's Equity	年末少数股东权益 Few Creditors's Equity	年末股东（所有者）权益 Creditors's Equity	股本（实收资本） Paid-in Capital
住宿和餐饮业	Hotel and Catering Services	13964	0	13964	19215
金融业	Financial Intermediation	0	0	0	0
房地产业	Real Estate	594898	170921	423977	423247
其他合计	Others	1630776	86663	1544113	1081212
租赁和商务服务业	Leasing and Business Services	1424719	72926	1351793	1007325
科学研究、技术服务和地质勘查业	Scientific Research, Technical Service and Geologic Prospecting	0	0	0	0
水利、环境和公共设施管理业	Management of Water Conservancy, Environment and Public Facilities	2429	0	2429	2003
居民服务和其他服务业	Services to Household and Other Services	98024	5881	92143	61884
教育	Education	0	0	0	0
卫生、社会保障和社会福利业	Health, Social Security and Social Welfare	0	0	0	0
文化、体育和娱乐业	Culture,Sports and Entertainment	105604	7856	97748	10000
公共管理和社会组织	Public Management and Social Organization	0	0	0	0
国际组织	International Organization	0	0	0	0
按登记注册类型分	By Status of Registration				
国有企业	State-owned Enterprises	7232588	1146453	6086135	2801558
公司制企业小计	Corporation	60233127	7593725	52639402	20101744
国有独资企业	Sole State-funded Corporation	15659206	3823255	11835951	5175955
其他有限责任公司	Other Limited Liability Corporation	25737247	2242417	23494830	9195458
股份有限公司	Share-holding Corporations Limited	11591692	1195453	10396239	3789363
中外合资企业	Joint-venture Enterprises	3619539	239041	3380498	1355351
外商投资股份有限公司	Share-holding Corporations Limited with Foreign Investment	1143901	79316	1064585	333736
港澳台合资企业	Enterprises with Funds from Hong kong, Macao and Taiwan	2388602	9388	2379214	201784
港澳台商投资股份有限公司	Share-holding Corporations Limited with Investment from Hong kong, Macao and Taiwan	92940	4855	88085	50097
其他	Others	2583744	96116	2487628	710335

8-2　续表 4

单位：万元　　　　unit:10 000yuan

分组	Groups	营业收入（主营业务收入+其他业务收入） Operating Income	主营业务收入 Prime Operating Revenue	其他业务收入 Other Operating Revenue	主营业务成本 Operating Costs	主营业务税金及附加 Tax and Associate Charge
总计	Total	201408833	195263766	6145067	162887632	2462518
按集团审批部门分	Grouped by Examining Department					
国务院	The State Council	7513015	6878759	634256	5473219	63490
国务院主管部门	Governing Departments of the State Council	3618738	3578123	40615	1832975	78185
省级人民政府	Provincial Government	113803482	110673443	3130039	96071236	844858
省级人民政府主管部门	Governing Departments of Provincial Government	23314770	22738906	575864	19347959	271871
其他	Others	53158828	51394535	1764293	40162243	1204114
按控股情况分	Grouped by Controlling Shares					
国有控股	State-holding	105269017	100783649	4485368	81272771	1891602
集体控股	Collective-owned Absolute Holding	43994730	43556140	438590	38516112	223699
私人控股	Private Holding	44279231	43127401	1151830	37100260	278157
港澳台商控股	Holding by Traders from Hong Kong, Macao and Taiwan	1831879	1799666	32213	1008971	43052
外商控股	Holding by Foreign Traders	6033976	5996910	37066	4989518	26008
按主营行业分	Grouped by Sector					
第一产业合计	Primary Industry	21779	21468	311	21486	144
农、林、牧、渔业	Farming, Forestry, Animal Husbandry and Fishery	21779	21468	311	21486	144
第二产业合计	Secondary Industry	174906575	169269625	5636950	141397608	2139100
工业小计	Industry	171039125	165595567	5443558	138121680	2025303
采矿业	Mining	20463989	18172718	2291271	9716539	844087
制造业	Manufacturing	136845614	133758737	3086877	116284311	1087975
电力、燃气及水的生产和供应业	Production and Supply of Electricity	13729522	13664112	65410	12120830	93241
建筑业	Construction	3867450	3674058	193392	3275928	113797
第三产业合计	Tertiary-industry	26480479	25972673	507806	21468538	323274
交通运输、仓储和邮政业	Transportation, Storage and Telecommunications	3684737	3401251	283486	2479592	130190
信息传输、计算机服务和软件业	Information Transmission, Computer Services and Software	3913675	3861927	51748	1559354	106563
批发和零售业	Wholesale and Retail Trade	17794219	17634257	159962	16629020	41272

续表 continued

分组	Groups	营业收入（主营业务收入+其他业务收入） Operating Income	主营业务收入 Prime Operating Revenue	其他业务收入 Other Operating Revenue	主营业务成本 Operating Costs	主营业务税金及附加 Tax and Associate Charge
住宿和餐饮业	Hotel and Catering Services	2891	2891	0	2892	160
金融业	Financial Intermediation	0	0	0	0	0
房地产业	Real Estate	578262	573185	5077	427783	29821
其他合计	Others	506695	499162	7533	369897	15268
租赁和商务服务业	Leasing and Business Services	329054	321664	7390	258597	6907
科学研究、技术服务和地质勘查业	Scientific Research, Technical Service and Geologic Prospecting	0	0	0	0	0
水利、环境和公共设施管理业	Management of Water Conservancy, Environment and Public Facilities	2631	2581	50	2154	90
居民服务和其他服务业	Services to Household and Other Services	41914	41821	93	30017	1229
教育	Education	0	0	0	0	0
卫生、社会保障和社会福利业	Health, Social Security and Social Welfare	0	0	0	0	0
文化、体育和娱乐业	Culture, Sports and Entertainment	133096	133096	0	79129	7042
公共管理和社会组织	Public Management and Social Organization	0	0	0	0	0
国际组织	International Organization	0	0	0	0	0
按登记注册类型分	By Status of Registration					
国有企业	State-owned Enterprises	19671720	19346015	325705	17076917	175806
公司制企业小计	Corporation	175215224	169422129	5793095	140156016	2237649
国有独资企业	Sole State-funded Corporation	34244177	31962866	2281311	25924243	403844
其他有限责任公司	Other Limited Liability Corporation	77626969	75426457	2200512	61394817	1184065
股份有限公司	Share-holding Corporations Limited	48737661	47779650	958011	42061770	380240
中外合资企业	Joint-venture Enterprises	8250915	7976407	274508	6377397	99098
外商投资股份有限公司	Share-holding Corporations Limited with Foreign Investment	2429335	2407409	21926	1681785	118269
港澳台合资企业	Enterprises with Funds from Hong kong, Macao and Taiwan	3532847	3498605	34242	2378664	51674
港澳台商投资股份有限公司	Share-holding Corporations Limited with Investment from Hong kong, Macao and Taiwan	393320	370735	22585	337340	459
其他	Others	6521889	6495622	26267	5654699	49063

8-2 续表 5

单位：万元 unit:10 000yuan

分组	Groups	新产品销售收入 Sales Revenue of New Products	出口销售总额 Total Volume Export Sales	营业费用 Operating Expenses	管理费用 General and Administrative Expense	税金 Tax
总计	Total	29142809	17569444	8794851	7402225	345318
按集团审批部门分	Grouped by Examining Department					
国务院	The State Council	1335807	881317	236440	487366	11014
国务院主管部门	Governing Departments of the State Council	63	0	386092	199697	3942
省级人民政府	Provincial Government	19670410	8919151	5945646	3932863	166988
省级人民政府主管部门	Governing Departments of Provincial Government	3346959	3060818	829854	820259	45841
其他	Others	4789570	4708158	1396819	1962040	117533
按控股情况分	Grouped by Controlling Shares					
国有控股	State-holding	15190044	6238467	5772838	4649403	177743
集体控股	Collective-owned Absolute Holding	8285086	4819008	1160890	1189722	71456
私人控股	Private Holding	5483372	5210236	1186103	1219186	83208
港澳台商控股	Holding by Traders from Hong Kong, Macao and Taiwan	0	14873	225964	153478	5230
外商控股	Holding by Foreign Traders	184307	1286860	449056	190436	7681
按主营行业分	Grouped by Sector					
第一产业合计	Primary Industry	0	0	1075	-12800	0
农、林、牧、渔业	Farming, Forestry, Animal Husbandry and Fishery	0	0	1075	-12800	0
第二产业合计	Secondary Industry	28879735	15448011	7441007	6184351	300288
工业小计	Industry	28878875	15442226	7421512	6041668	290872
采矿业	Mining	401342	636190	276453	1672826	40891
制造业	Manufacturing	28471702	14768716	7084799	4075629	229906
电力、燃气及水的生产和供应业	Production and Supply of Electricity	5831	37320	60260	293213	20075
建筑业	Construction	860	5785	19495	142683	9416
第三产业合计	Tertiary-industry	263074	2121433	1352769	1230674	45030
交通运输、仓储和邮政业	Transportation, Storage and Telecommunications	0	0	50129	348933	13449
信息传输、计算机服务和软件业	Information Transmission, Computer Services and Software	134480	2624	769351	312247	8183
批发和零售业	Wholesale and Retail Trade	71121	2005996	491132	447391	19091

续表 continued

分组	Groups	新产品销售收入 Sales Revenue of New Products	出口销售总额 Total Volume Export Sales	营业费用 Operating Expenses	管理费用 General and Administrative Expense	税金 Tax
住宿和餐饮业	Hotel and Catering Services	0	0	885	1106	0
金融业	Financial Intermediation	0	0	0	0	0
房地产业	Real Estate	0	0	15733	51968	2615
其他合计	Others	57473	112813	25539	69029	1692
租赁和商务服务业	Leasing and Business Services	57473	112813	24131	35581	1124
科学研究、技术服务和地质勘查业	Scientific Research, Technical Service and Geologic Prospecting	0	0	0	0	0
水利、环境和公共设施管理业	Management of Water Conservancy, Environment and Public Facilities	0	0	0	478	10
居民服务和其他服务业	Services to Household and Other Services	0	0	1408	9931	558
教育	Education	0	0	0	0	0
卫生、社会保障和社会福利业	Health, Social Security and Social Welfare	0	0	0	0	0
文化、体育和娱乐业	Culture, Sports and Entertainment	0	0	0	23039	0
公共管理和社会组织	Public Management and Social Organization	0	0	0	0	0
国际组织	International Organization	0	0	0	0	0
按登记注册类型分	By Status of Registration					
国有企业	State-owned Enterprises	1554120	1563311	352358	717604	33222
公司制企业小计	Corporation	27061220	15768793	8147698	6417710	303986
国有独资企业	Sole State-funded Corporation	6596116	4186597	4045877	2330492	76103
其他有限责任公司	Other Limited Liability Corporation	7703286	5959961	1357298	2151979	133334
股份有限公司	Share-holding Corporations Limited	10944627	3280202	1702096	1378923	65436
中外合资企业	Joint-venture Enterprises	1724648	1749096	459697	230271	8989
外商投资股份有限公司	Share-holding Corporations Limited with Foreign Investment	60396	370244	278637	134042	7815
港澳台合资企业	Enterprises with Funds from Hong kong, Macao and Taiwan	32147	182693	297733	180450	11430
港澳台商投资股份有限公司	Share-holding Corporations Limited with Investment from Hong kong, Macao and Taiwan	0	40000	6360	11553	879
其他	Others	527469	237340	294795	266911	8110

8-2 续表 6

单位：万元 unit:10 000yuan

分组	Groups	劳动、待业保险费 Labour and Unemployment Insurance	职工教育费 Worker Education Fee	财务费用 Finance Expense	利息支出 Interest Exchange	投资收益 Investment Income
总计	Total	753616	85903	2692064	2478445	397413
按集团审批部门分	Grouped by Examining Department					
国务院	The State Council	89219	5194	154760	140735	4041
国务院主管部门	Governing Departments of the State Council	14490	1615	68897	83196	5909
省级人民政府	Provincial Government	456912	47280	1559357	1455697	249740
省级人民政府主管部门	Governing Departments of Provincial Government	62022	9414	256443	226403	42781
其他	Others	130973	22400	652607	572414	94942
按控股情况分	Grouped by Controlling Shares					
国有控股	State-holding	557160	50944	1265331	1168298	184163
集体控股	Collective-owned Absolute Holding	85228	18254	609213	567126	137878
私人控股	Private Holding	74903	12829	688013	615264	73627
港澳台商控股	Holding by Traders from Hong Kong, Macao and Taiwan	22565	2189	69340	70790	1758
外商控股	Holding by Foreign Traders	13760	1687	60167	56967	-13
按主营行业分	Grouped by Sector					
第一产业合计	Primary Industry	0	0	3066	107	64
农、林、牧、渔业	Farming, Forestry, Animal Husbandry and Fishery	0	0	3066	107	64
第二产业合计	Secondary Industry	635272	77041	2345726	2178317	320357
工业小计	Industry	614711	73660	2317335	2151605	311385
采矿业	Mining	280228	17037	280482	238006	46990
制造业	Manufacturing	302214	53435	1682773	1554166	244266
电力、燃气及水的生产和供应业	Production and Supply of Electricity	32269	3188	354080	359433	20129
建筑业	Construction	20561	3381	28391	26712	8972
第三产业合计	Tertiary-industry	118344	8862	343272	300021	76992
交通运输、仓储和邮政业	Transportation, Storage and Telecommunications	48431	2077	76741	50061	11419
信息传输、计算机服务和软件业	Information Transmission, Computer Services and Software	34423	3446	68501	77467	115
批发和零售业	Wholesale and Retail Trade	30771	2536	147588	134241	6904

续表 continued

分组	Groups	劳动、待业保险费 Labour and Unemployment Insurance	职工教育费 Worker Education Fee	财务费用 Finance Expense	利息支出 Interest Exchange	投资收益 Investment Income
住宿和餐饮业	Hotel and Catering Services	0	0	0	0	0
金融业	Financial Intermediation	0	0	0	0	0
房地产业	Real Estate	2085	219	31053	28817	20123
其他合计	Others	2634	584	19389	9435	38431
租赁和商务服务业	Leasing and Business Services	2228	536	9521	8469	33895
科学研究、技术服务和地质勘查业	Scientific Research, Technical Service and Geologic Prospecting	0	0	0	0	0
水利、环境和公共设施管理业	Management of Water Conservancy, Environment and Public Facilities	86	6	50	18	20
居民服务和其他服务业	Services to Household and Other Services	320	42	6775	948	4516
教育	Education	0	0	0	0	0
卫生、社会保障和社会福利业	Health, Social Security and Social Welfare	0	0	0	0	0
文化、体育和娱乐业	Culture,Sports and Entertainment	0	0	3043	0	0
公共管理和社会组织	Public Management and Social Organization	0	0	0	0	0
国际组织	International Organization	0	0	0	0	0
按登记注册类型分	By Status of Registration					
国有企业	State-owned Enterprises	96419	6695	210279	201938	28571
公司制企业小计	Corporation	633702	77316	2393573	2201427	335589
国有独资企业	Sole State-funded Corporation	359055	29377	552442	525631	119641
其他有限责任公司	Other Limited Liability Corporation	134177	22364	1250788	1089472	147533
股份有限公司	Share-holding Corporations Limited	96775	18384	337477	326309	61763
中外合资企业	Joint-venture Enterprises	14324	2458	125516	128553	9489
外商投资股份有限公司	Share-holding Corporations Limited with Foreign Investment	4249	2151	20258	24266	-4866
港澳台合资企业	Enterprises with Funds from Hong kong, Macao and Taiwan	24269	2500	98606	99334	194
港澳台商投资股份有限公司	Share-holding Corporations Limited with Investment from Hong kong, Macao and Taiwan	853	82	8486	7862	1835
其他	Others	23495	1892	88212	75080	33253

8-2 续表 7

单位：万元 unit:10 000yuan

分组	Groups	利润总额 Total Profit	应交所得税 Income Tax Payable	应交增值税 Value Added Tax Payable	固定资产投资完成额 Total Investment In Fixed Assets	研究开发（R&D）费用 Research and Development Expenses
总计	Total	14080329	4491595	6271466	15817908	2381513
按集团审批部门分	Grouped by Examining Department					
国务院	The State Council	488156	157344	264891	867560	248617
国务院主管部门	Governing Departments of the State Council	939619	311923	171536	2447221	2144
省级人民政府	Provincial Government	5382683	1829684	3087146	8372978	1692233
省级人民政府主管部门	Governing Departments of Provincial Government	1235890	306209	668817	1118526	184981
其他	Others	6033981	1886435	2079076	3011623	253538
按控股情况分	Grouped by Controlling Shares					
国有控股	State-holding	9055204	3201724	4017904	9713530	1025275
集体控股	Collective-owned Absolute Holding	1942038	555626	1166282	2534219	855148
私人控股	Private Holding	2531148	570687	962676	2657313	466647
港澳台商控股	Holding by Traders from Hong Kong, Macao and Taiwan	310773	78343	1146	446379	270
外商控股	Holding by Foreign Traders	241166	85215	123458	466467	34173
按主营行业分	Grouped by Sector					
第一产业合计	Primary Industry	9845	205	0	0	0
农、林、牧、渔业	Farming, Forestry, Animal Husbandry and Fishery	9845	205	0	0	0
第二产业合计	Secondary Industry	12456194	3867820	6130861	13490208	2359405
工业小计	Industry	12351238	3839568	6122962	13440637	2357596
采矿业	Mining	5276773	1797429	1633668	2604705	114462
制造业	Manufacturing	6370270	1776104	3750660	6797239	2225285
电力、燃气及水的生产和供应业	Production and Supply of Electricity	704195	266035	738634	4038693	17849
建筑业	Construction	104956	28252	7899	49571	1809
第三产业合计	Tertiary-industry	1614290	623570	140605	2327700	22108
交通运输、仓储和邮政业	Transportation, Storage and Telecommunications	341007	120426	6668	848998	8800
信息传输、计算机服务和软件业	Information Transmission, Computer Services and Software	978369	335130	746	1180613	5417
批发和零售业	Wholesale and Retail Trade	217980	143526	123743	215035	7367

续表 continued

分组	Groups	利润总额 Total Profit	应交所得税 Income Tax Payable	应交增值税 Value Added Tax Payable	固定资产投资完成额 Total Investment In Fixed Assets	研究开发(R&D)费用 Research and Development Expenses
住宿和餐饮业	Hotel and Catering Services	-486	2	0	0	0
金融业	Financial Intermediation	0	0	0	0	0
房地产业	Real Estate	43701	16406	458	60852	234
其他合计	Others	33719	8080	8990	22202	290
租赁和商务服务业	Leasing and Business Services	26857	7196	7572	17535	290
科学研究、技术服务和地质勘查业	Scientific Research, Technical Service and Geologic Prospecting	0	0	0	0	0
水利、环境和公共设施管理业	Management of Water Conservancy, Environment and Public Facilities	5	2	0	0	0
居民服务和其他服务业	Services to Household and Other Services	-3171	435	1418	4667	0
教育	Education	0	0	0	0	0
卫生、社会保障和社会福利业	Health, Social Security and Social Welfare	0	0	0	0	0
文化、体育和娱乐业	Culture, Sports and Entertainment	10028	447	0	0	0
公共管理和社会组织	Public Management and Social Organization	0	0	0	0	0
国际组织	International Organization	0	0	0	0	0
按登记注册类型分	By Status of Registration					
国有企业	State-owned Enterprises	912728	287314	619885	1510250	149029
公司制企业小计	Corporation	13001483	4093435	5550420	13868625	2191435
国有独资企业	Sole State-funded Corporation	1734683	613811	1200290	2714343	529989
其他有限责任公司	Other Limited Liability Corporation	7671053	2301077	2887307	5250417	624146
股份有限公司	Share-holding Corporations Limited	2212612	894486	960053	2695186	872303
中外合资企业	Joint-venture Enterprises	682482	143995	345891	2406221	149276
外商投资股份有限公司	Share-holding Corporations Limited with Foreign Investment	172321	33962	125715	171404	9445
港澳台合资企业	Enterprises with Funds from Hong kong, Macao and Taiwan	517694	104779	27730	628696	4420
港澳台商投资股份有限公司	Share-holding Corporations Limited with Investment from Hong kong, Macao and Taiwan	10638	1325	3434	2358	1856
其他	Others	166118	110846	101161	439033	41049

8-3 企业集团劳动工资指标
Labour and Wage Norms of Enterprise Groups

分组	Groups	从业人员年末人数（人）Year-end Employed Persons	在岗职工（人）Fully-employed Staff and Workers	其他从业人员（人）Other Employed Persons	研究开发（R&D）人员（人）Persons of Research and Development	从业人员劳动报酬（万元）Labour Payment for Year-end Employed Persons	在岗职工劳动报酬（万元）Labour Payment for Fully-employed Staff and Workers	其他从业人员劳动报酬（万元）Labour Payment for Other Employed Persons	研究开发（R&D）人员劳动报酬（万元）Labour Payment for Persons of Research and Development
总计	Total	3016589	2847832	168757	102113	5864903	5642263	222640	272940
按集团审批部门分	Grouped by Examining Department								
国务院	The State Council	133432	125591	7841	1847	385941	372516	13425	7424
国务院主管部门	Governing Departments of the State Council	59163	39623	19540	59	150757	128859	21898	203
省级人民政府	Provincial Government	1479616	1404138	75478	61036	2975226	2866181	109045	179255
省级人民政府主管部门	Governing Departments of Provincial Government	393798	382405	11393	8698	615361	602975	12386	22896
其他	Others	950580	896075	54505	30473	1737618	1671732	65886	63162
按控股情况分	Grouped by Controlling Shares								
国有控股	State-holding	1440900	1325447	115453	55611	3586387	3428789	157598	157675
集体控股	Collective-owned Absolute Holding	664127	632764	31363	19908	986900	945694	41206	56581
私人控股	Private Holding	829970	810108	19862	25507	1045931	1024454	21477	54931
港澳台商控股	Holding by Traders from Hong Kong, Macao and Taiwan	26598	26398	200	75	128165	128125	40	140
外商控股	Holding by Foreign Traders	54994	53115	1879	1012	117520	115201	2319	3613
按主营行业分	Grouped by Sector								
第一产业合计	Primary Industry	759	759	0	0	880	880	0	0
农、林、牧、渔业	Farming, Forestry, Animal Husbandry and Fishery	759	759	0	0	880	880	0	0
第二产业合计	Secondary Industry	2709536	2588588	120948	99465	5178611	5014422	164189	265520
工业小计	Industry	2502294	2410202	92092	98629	4829329	4709901	119428	263900
采矿业	Mining	472264	435414	36850	12548	1379549	1321793	57756	31357
制造业	Manufacturing	1906659	1852648	54011	84968	2991129	2930648	60481	228615
电力、燃气及水的生产和供应业	Production and Supply of Electricity	123371	122140	1231	1113	458651	457460	1191	3928
建筑业	Construction	207242	178386	28856	836	349282	304521	44761	1620
第三产业合计	Tertiary-industry	306294	258485	47809	2648	685412	626961	58451	7420
交通运输、仓储和邮政业	Transportation, Storage and Telecommunications	94409	92869	1540	969	254855	252398	2457	3388
信息传输、计算机服务和软件业	Information Transmission, Computer Services and Software	51205	33131	18074	136	181285	161404	19881	780
批发和零售业	Wholesale and Retail Trade	138108	111009	27099	1379	196227	160996	35231	2740

续表 continued

分组	Groups	从业人员年末人数（人）Year-end Employed Persons	在岗职工（人）Fully-employed Staff and Workers	其他从业人员（人）Other Employed Persons	研究开发（R&D）人员（人）Persons of Research and Development	从业人员劳动报酬（万元）Labour Payment for Year-end Employed Persons	在岗职工劳动报酬（万元）Labour Payment for Fully-employed Staff and Workers	其他从业人员劳动报酬（万元）Labour Payment for Other Employed Persons	研究开发（R&D）人员劳动报酬（万元）Labour Payment for Persons of Research and Development
住宿和餐饮业	Hotel and Catering Services	590	590	0	0	729	729	0	0
金融业	Financial Intermediation	0	0	0	0	0	0	0	0
房地产业	Real Estate	10395	9342	1053	132	18158	17286	872	355
其他合计	Others	11587	11544	43	32	34158	34148	10	157
租赁和商务服务业	Leasing and Business Services	4618	4617	1	32	19150	19146	4	157
科学研究、技术服务和地质勘查业	Scientific Research, Technical Service and Geologic Prospecting	0	0	0	0	0	0	0	0
水利、环境和公共设施管理业	Management of Water Conservancy,Environment and Public Facilities	146	146	0	0	235	235	0	0
居民服务和其他服务业	Services to Household and Other Services	2034	1992	42	0	2377	2371	6	0
教育	Education	0	0	0	0	0	0	0	0
卫生、社会保障和社会福利业	Health, Social Security and Social Welfare	0	0	0	0	0	0	0	0
文化、体育和娱乐业	Culture, Sports and Entertainment	4789	4789	0	0	12396	12396	0	0
公共管理和社会组织	Public Management and Social Organization	0	0	0	0	0	0	0	0
国际组织	International Organization	0	0	0	0	0	0	0	0
按登记注册类型分	By Status of Registration								
国有企业	State-owned Enterprises	254755	237242	17513	7153	715251	693226	22025	25324
公司制企业小计	Corporation	2642735	2495574	147161	91940	4960795	4764167	196628	240647
国有独资企业	Sole State-funded Corporation	663791	619070	44721	22839	1600693	1536887	63806	72512
其他有限责任公司	Other Limited Liability Corporation	1296998	1256707	40291	43144	2154490	2103662	50828	91413
股份有限公司	Share-holding Corporations Limited	449964	389440	60524	19542	744071	664408	79663	61696
中外合资企业	Joint-venture Enterprises	95834	94485	1349	4099	146988	144887	2101	9259
外商投资股份有限公司	Share-holding Corporations Limited with Foreign Investment	53812	53751	61	755	95449	95373	76	2148
港澳台合资企业	Enterprises with Funds from Hong kong, Macao and Taiwan	79675	79660	15	1423	213401	213287	114	3096
港澳台商投资股份有限公司	Share-holding Corporations Limited with Investment from Hong kong, Macao and Taiwan	2661	2461	200	138	5703	5663	40	523
其他	Others	119099	115016	4083	3020	188857	184870	3987	6969

8-4 企业集团主要经济效益指标

Main Economic Efficiency Norms of Enterprise Groups

单位：% unit:%

分组	Groups	净资产收益率 Ratio of Interests to Net Assets	总资产报酬率 Ratio of Reward to Total Assets	销售利润率 Ratio of Selling Profit	资本保值增值率 Ratio of Capital Value-preserved and Value-added	劳动生产率（万元/人） Rátio of Labour Productiv-ity	成本费用利润率 Ratio of Profits to Cost
总计	Total	13.7	8.7	7.0	111.7	66.8	7.7
按集团审批部门分	Grouped by Examining Department						
国务院	The State Council	11.5	6.8	6.5	122.4	56.3	7.7
国务院主管部门	Governing Departments of the State Council	15.2	10.8	26.0	101.1	61.2	37.8
省级人民政府	Provincial Government	9.4	6.5	4.7	114.8	76.9	5.0
省级人民政府主管部门	Governing Departments of Provincial Government	14.7	7.6	5.3	122.1	59.2	5.8
其他	Others	22.1	14.0	11.4	104.0	55.9	13.7
按控股情况分	Grouped by Controlling Shares						
国有控股	State-holding	14.2	9.7	8.6	107.9	73.1	9.7
集体控股	Collective-owned Absolute Holding	10.4	6.3	4.4	119.3	66.2	4.7
私人控股	Private Holding	15.0	8.4	5.7	122.5	53.4	6.3
港澳台商控股	Holding by Traders from Hong Kong, Macao and Taiwan	23.1	10.0	17.0	100.3	68.9	21.3
外商控股	Holding by Foreign Traders	10.7	7.1	4.0	85.4	109.7	4.2
按主营行业分	Grouped by Sector						
第一产业合计	Primary Industry	-25.3	7.2	45.2	80.0	28.7	76.8
农、林、牧、渔业	Farming, Forestry, Animal Husbandry and Fishery	-25.3	7.2	45.2	80.0	28.7	76.8
第二产业合计	Secondary Industry	14.5	9.4	7.1	113.3	64.6	7.9
工业小计	Industry	14.7	9.6	7.2	113.5	68.4	8.0
采矿业	Mining	32.8	23.4	25.8	109.9	43.3	44.2
制造业	Manufacturing	11.6	7.7	4.7	115.5	71.8	4.9
电力、燃气及水的生产和供应业	Production and Supply of Electricity	5.6	4.2	5.1	108.9	111.3	5.5
建筑业	Construction	6.4	2.7	2.7	105.0	18.7	3.0
第三产业合计	Tertiary-industry	9.0	5.6	6.1	103.3	86.5	6.6
交通运输、仓储和邮政业	Transportation, Storage and Telecommunications	5.8	3.7	9.3	120.7	39.0	11.5
信息传输、计算机服务和软件业	Information Transmission, Computer Services and Software	22.0	15.4	25.0	113.9	76.4	36.1
批发和零售业	Wholesale and Retail Trade	3.8	3.8	1.2	91.3	128.8	1.2

续表 continued

分组	Groups	净资产收益率 Ratio of Interests to Net Assets	总资产报酬率 Ratio of Reward to Total Assets	销售利润率 Ratio of Selling Profit	资本保值增值率 Ratio of Capital Value-preserved and Value-added	劳动生产率（万元/人） Ratio of Labour Productivity	成本费用利润率 Ratio of Profits to Cost
住宿和餐饮业	Hotel and Catering Services	-3.5	-2.1	-16.8	94.6	4.9	-10.0
金融业	Financial Intermediation	0.0	0.0	0.0	0.0	0.0	0.0
房地产业	Real Estate	4.6	2.3	7.6	95.6	55.6	8.3
其他合计	Others	1.6	0.9	6.7	78.5	43.7	7.0
租赁和商务服务业	Leasing and Business Services	1.4	0.9	8.2	75.7	71.3	8.2
科学研究、技术服务和地质勘查业	Scientific Research, Technical Service and Geologic Prospecting	0.0	0.0	0.0	0.0	0.0	0.0
水利、环境和公共设施管理业	Management of Water Conservancy, Environment and Public Facilities	0.1	0.3	0.2	135.4	18.0	0.2
居民服务和其他服务业	Services to Household and Other Services	-3.7	-0.7	-7.6	96.5	20.6	-6.6
教育	Education	0.0	0.0	0.0	0.0	0.0	0.0
卫生、社会保障和社会福利业	Health, Social Security and Social Welfare	0.0	0.0	0.0	0.0	0.0	0.0
文化、体育和娱乐业	Culture, Sports and Entertainment	9.1	4.4	7.5	114.5	27.8	9.5
公共管理和社会组织	Public Management and Social Organization	0.0	0.0	0.0	0.0	0.0	0.0
国际组织	International Organization	0.0	0.0	0.0	0.0	0.0	0.0
按登记注册类型分	By Status of Registration						
国有企业	State-owned Enterprises	8.6	5.8	4.6	109.3	77.2	5.0
公司制企业小计	Corporation	14.8	9.2	7.4	112.9	66.3	8.3
国有独资企业	Sole State-funded Corporation	7.2	4.8	5.1	117.0	51.6	5.3
其他有限责任公司	Other Limited Liability Corporation	20.9	12.3	9.9	112.9	59.9	11.6
股份有限公司	Share-holding Corporations Limited	11.4	9.1	4.5	108.2	108.3	4.9
中外合资企业	Joint-venture Enterprises	14.9	8.1	8.3	114.4	86.1	9.5
外商投资股份有限公司	Share-holding Corporations Limited with Foreign Investment	12.1	8.5	7.1	116.3	45.1	8.1
港澳台合资企业	Enterprises with Funds from Hong kong, Macao and Taiwan	17.3	9.3	14.7	108.5	44.3	17.5
港澳台商投资股份有限公司	Share-holding Corporations Limited with Investment from Hong kong, Macao and Taiwan	10.0	6.8	2.7	107.8	147.8	2.9
其他	Others	2.1	3.7	2.5	92.9	54.8	2.6

8-4 续表 1

单位：% unit:%

分组	Groups	资产利税率 Ratio of Pre-tax Profits to Assets	总资产使用率 Assets Using Rate	流动资产比率 Ratio of Circulating Funds	资金利润率 Current Assets Ratio	资产负债率 Assets Liabilities Ratio	长期负债与资产总计比率 Ratio of Long Term Liability
总计	Total	11.9	102.2	41.5	9.1	63.1	15.7
按集团审批部门分	Grouped by Examining Department						
国务院	The State Council	8.9	74.7	42.8	6.7	68.8	21.6
国务院主管部门	Governing Departments of the State Council	12.5	37.7	17.0	13.2	56.5	23.0
省级人民政府	Provincial Government	8.8	104.6	40.0	6.2	64.1	17.1
省级人民政府主管部门	Governing Departments of Provincial Government	11.4	118.7	54.7	7.9	67.1	17.3
其他	Others	19.7	108.6	44.1	15.8	59.3	9.5
按控股情况分	Grouped by Controlling Shares						
国有控股	State-holding	14.1	95.2	36.8	10.7	61.1	17.0
集体控股	Collective-owned Absolute Holding	8.4	109.9	49.3	5.9	66.3	15.8
私人控股	Private Holding	10.1	115.4	50.3	8.5	65.1	12.1
港澳台商控股	Holding by Traders from Hong Kong, Macao and Taiwan	9.3	47.2	6.1	8.7	73.6	10.7
外商控股	Holding by Foreign Traders	9.2	141.9	40.2	6.3	54.1	20.1
按主营行业分	Grouped by Sector						
第一产业合计	Primary Industry	7.2	15.4	60.9	7.6	127.4	8.6
农、林、牧、渔业	Farming, Forestry, Animal Husbandry and Fishery	7.2	15.4	60.9	7.6	127.4	8.6
第二产业合计	Secondary Industry	13.3	108.2	41.5	9.8	61.9	15.2
工业小计	Industry	13.5	109.3	40.5	10.0	61.4	15.3
采矿业	Mining	33.0	77.2	32.3	26.5	54.9	14.7
制造业	Manufacturing	10.9	130.1	45.5	7.6	61.6	12.2
电力、燃气及水的生产和供应业	Production and Supply of Electricity	6.1	54.4	27.9	3.6	66.9	28.7
建筑业	Construction	4.6	74.0	70.5	2.6	75.8	13.4
第三产业合计	Tertiary-industry	6.0	75.5	41.6	5.9	68.2	18.0
交通运输、仓储和邮政业	Transportation, Storage and Telecommunications	4.6	32.5	28.4	4.4	63.5	20.3
信息传输、计算机服务和软件业	Information Transmission, Computer Services and Software	15.9	56.5	13.6	15.5	57.2	12.0
批发和零售业	Wholesale and Retail Trade	4.1	187.9	58.8	2.9	79.1	7.2

续表 continued

分组	Groups	资产利税率 Ratio of Pre-tax Profits to Assets	总资产使用率 Assets Using Rate	流动资产比率 Ratio of Circulating Funds	资金利润率 Current Assets Ratio	资产负债率 Assets Liabilities Ratio	长期负债与资产总计比率 Ratio of Long Term Liability
住宿和餐饮业	Hotel and Catering Services	-1.4	12.6	0.0	-8.4	39.4	0.0
金融业	Financial Intermediation	0.0	0.0	0.0	0.0	0.0	0.0
房地产业	Real Estate	2.4	18.3	68.0	1.9	81.0	18.3
其他合计	Others	1.3	10.9	60.2	1.1	64.3	43.8
租赁和商务服务业	Leasing and Business Services	1.0	8.0	63.3	1.0	64.6	49.0
科学研究、技术服务和地质勘查业	Scientific Research, Technical Service and Geologic Prospecting	0.0	0.0	0.0	0.0	0.0	0.0
水利、环境和公共设施管理业	Management of Water Conservancy, Environment and Public Facilities	1.4	38.2	50.7	0.1	64.1	0.0
居民服务和其他服务业	Services to Household and Other Services	-0.2	13.6	39.6	-1.7	68.1	4.5
教育	Education	0.0	0.0	0.0	0.0	0.0	0.0
卫生、社会保障和社会福利业	Health, Social Security and Social Welfare	0.0	0.0	0.0	0.0	0.0	0.0
文化、体育和娱乐业	Culture, Sports and Entertainment	7.5	58.1	33.9	5.6	53.9	6.0
公共管理和社会组织	Public Management and Social Organization	0.0	0.0	0.0	0.0	0.0	0.0
国际组织	International Organization	0.0	0.0	0.0	0.0	0.0	0.0
按登记注册类型分	By Status of Registration						
国有企业	State-owned Enterprises	8.8	99.8	37.4	5.9	62.7	16.1
公司制企业小计	Corporation	12.6	102.6	41.8	9.7	63.2	15.9
国有独资企业	Sole State-funded Corporation	7.1	68.2	42.2	4.8	66.6	19.5
其他有限责任公司	Other Limited Liability Corporation	16.5	106.1	44.3	13.2	63.8	14.6
股份有限公司	Share-holding Corporations Limited	12.7	171.3	45.9	9.4	56.7	10.4
中外合资企业	Joint-venture Enterprises	11.2	79.4	24.7	8.9	64.0	26.9
外商投资股份有限公司	Share-holding Corporations Limited with Foreign Investment	18.0	103.9	44.0	8.4	50.7	4.6
港澳台合资企业	Enterprises with Funds from Hong kong, Macao and Taiwan	9.0	52.9	19.8	8.7	63.9	13.5
港澳台商投资股份有限公司	Share-holding Corporations Limited with Investment from Hong kong, Macao and Taiwan	5.3	135.9	40.5	4.9	65.9	10.9
其他	Others	4.9	100.6	46.6	3.1	60.0	11.5

8-4 续表 2

单位：% unit:%

分组	Groups	已获利息倍数（倍）The Attained Interest Multiple	流动比率 Current Ratio	速动比率 Quick Ratio	新产品销售收入与营业收入比率 Ratio of Sales Revenue of New Products and Operating Income	研究开发费用与营业收入比率 Ratio of R&D and Operating Income	研究开发费用与主营业务收入比率 Ratio of R&D and Prime Operating Revenue
总计	Total	6.7	87.7	63.4	14.5	1.2	1.2
按集团审批部门分	Grouped by Examining Department						
国务院	The State Council	4.5	90.6	69.3	17.8	3.3	3.6
国务院主管部门	Governing Departments of the State Council	12.3	50.8	46.6	0.0	0.1	0.1
省级人民政府	Provincial Government	4.7	85.0	61.1	17.3	1.5	1.5
省级人民政府主管部门	Governing Departments of Provincial Government	6.5	110.1	84.6	14.4	0.8	0.8
其他	Others	11.5	88.6	60.8	9.0	0.5	0.5
按控股情况分	Grouped by Controlling Shares						
国有控股	State-holding	8.8	83.3	63.1	14.4	1.0	1.0
集体控股	Collective-owned Absolute Holding	4.4	97.7	68.0	18.8	1.9	2.0
私人控股	Private Holding	5.1	95.1	64.6	12.4	1.1	1.1
港澳台商控股	Holding by Traders from Hong Kong, Macao and Taiwan	5.4	9.7	7.6	0.0	0.0	0.0
外商控股	Holding by Foreign Traders	5.2	118.1	83.3	3.1	0.6	0.6
按主营行业分	Grouped by Sector						
第一产业合计	Primary Industry	93.0	51.3	44.8	0.0	0.0	0.0
农、林、牧、渔业	Farming, Forestry, Animal Husbandry and Fishery	93.0	51.3	44.8	0.0	0.0	0.0
第二产业合计	Secondary Industry	6.7	88.9	63.6	16.5	1.3	1.4
工业小计	Industry	6.7	87.8	62.4	16.9	1.4	1.4
采矿业	Mining	23.2	80.4	66.6	2.0	0.6	0.6
制造业	Manufacturing	5.1	92.0	63.5	20.8	1.6	1.7
电力、燃气及水的生产和供应业	Production and Supply of Electricity	3.0	72.9	52.7	0.0	0.1	0.1
建筑业	Construction	4.9	112.9	89.7	0.0	0.0	0.0
第三产业合计	Tertiary-industry	6.4	82.9	62.5	1.0	0.1	0.1
交通运输、仓储和邮政业	Transportation, Storage and Telecommunications	7.8	65.9	60.5	0.0	0.2	0.3
信息传输、计算机服务和软件业	Information Transmission, Computer Services and Software	13.6	30.0	29.0	3.4	0.1	0.1
批发和零售业	Wholesale and Retail Trade	2.6	81.8	55.5	0.4	0.0	0.0

续表 continued

分组	Groups	已获利息倍数（倍）The Attained Interest Multiple	流动比率 Current Ratio	速动比率 Quick Ratio	新产品销售收入与营业收入比率 Ratio of Sales Revenue of New Products and Operating Income	研究开发费用与营业收入比率 Ratio of R&D and Operating Income	研究开发费用与主营业务收入比率 Ratio of R&D and Prime Operating Revenue
住宿和餐饮业	Hotel and Catering Services	0.0	0.0	-2.7	0.0	0.0	0.0
金融业	Financial Intermediation	0.0	0.0	0.0	0.0	0.0	0.0
房地产业	Real Estate	2.5	108.4	41.2	0.0	0.0	0.0
其他合计	Others	4.6	294.0	279.5	11.3	0.1	0.1
租赁和商务服务业	Leasing and Business Services	4.2	407.0	391.4	17.5	0.1	0.1
科学研究、技术服务和地质勘查业	Scientific Research, Technical Service and Geologic Prospecting	0.0	0.0	0.0	0.0	0.0	0.0
水利、环境和公共设施管理业	Management of Water Conservancy, Environment and Public Facilities	1.3	79.1	52.8	0.0	0.0	0.0
居民服务和其他服务业	Services to Household and Other Services	-2.3	62.2	46.4	0.0	0.0	0.0
教育	Education	0.0	0.0	0.0	0.0	0.0	0.0
卫生、社会保障和社会福利业	Health, Social Security and Social Welfare	0.0	0.0	0.0	0.0	0.0	0.0
文化、体育和娱乐业	Culture, Sports and Entertainment	0.0	70.8	65.5	0.0	0.0	0.0
公共管理和社会组织	Public Management and Social Organization	0.0	0.0	0.0	0.0	0.0	0.0
国际组织	International Organization	0.0	0.0	0.0	0.0	0.0	0.0
按登记注册类型分	By Status of Registration						
国有企业	State-owned Enterprises	5.5	80.3	61.1	7.9	0.8	0.8
公司制企业小计	Corporation	6.9	88.2	63.3	15.4	1.3	1.3
国有独资企业	Sole State-funded Corporation	4.3	89.7	68.9	19.3	1.5	1.7
其他有限责任公司	Other Limited Liability Corporation	8.0	90.0	61.7	9.9	0.8	0.8
股份有限公司	Share-holding Corporations Limited	7.8	99.3	70.8	22.5	1.8	1.8
中外合资企业	Joint-venture Enterprises	6.3	66.7	52.9	20.9	1.8	1.9
外商投资股份有限公司	Share-holding Corporations Limited with Foreign Investment	8.1	95.4	52.2	2.5	0.4	0.4
港澳台合资企业	Enterprises with Funds from Hong kong, Macao and Taiwan	6.2	39.2	29.0	0.9	0.1	0.1
港澳台商投资股份有限公司	Share-holding Corporations Limited with Investment from Hong kong, Macao and Taiwan	2.4	73.6	30.4	0.0	0.5	0.5
其他	Others	3.2	96.1	72.6	8.1	0.6	0.6

8-5 企业集团按规模分组主要指标
Major Norms of Enterprise Groups by Size of Enterprises

分组	Groups	单位数（个）Unit Number		年末资产总计（万元）Year-end Assets	固定资产原价（万元）Original Value of Fixed Assets
		单位数 Unit Number	比重（%）Proportion		
总 计	Total	726	100.0	190967802	116134972
按营业收入和资产总计分	Grouped by Operating Income and Property				
50亿元及以上	50 Hundred Million Yuan and Above	56	7.7	106661532	78798766
10亿元及以上	10 Hundred Million Yuan and Above	263	36.2	164077649	105861941
5亿元及以上	5 Hundred Million Yuan and Above	379	52.2	175097219	110904525
按资产总计分	Grouped by Total Assets				
1000亿元及以上	1000 Hundred Million Yuan and Above	0	0.0	0	0
500～1000亿元	500～1000 Hundred Million Yuan	6	0.8	36516573	33683823
100～500亿元	100～500 Hundred Million Yuan	28	3.9	57091887	35128741
50～100亿元	50～100 hundred million Yuan	38	5.2	26787548	15561647
5～50亿元	5～50 Hundred Million Yuan	377	51.9	63810610	28854791
按营业收入分	Grouped by Operating Revenue				
100亿元及以上	100 Hundred Million Yuan and Above	40	5.5	85848590	67661085
50～100亿元	50～100 Hundred Million Yuan	49	6.7	32191706	16931277
5～50亿元	5～50 Hundred Million Yuan	332	45.7	58473266	26984206
按利润总额分	Grouped by Profit				
10亿元及以上	10 Hundred Million Yuan and Above	25	3.4	74203173	62553370
5～10亿元	5～10 Hundred Million Yuan	23	3.2	17319794	8767440
1～5亿元	1～5 Hundred Million Yuan	127	17.5	43114417	19752355
0.5～1亿元	0.5～1 Hundred Million Yuan	94	12.9	18254307	8378501
0.1～0.5亿元	0.1～0.5 Hundred Million Yuan	198	27.3	17107207	7341567
按从业人员分	Grouped by Employed Persons				
10万人及以上	100 Thousand Persons and Above	1	0.1	3727686	2480533
5～10万人	50～100 Thousand Persons	5	0.7	20370569	20316429
1～5万人	10～50 Thousand Persons	53	7.3	74504140	51485294
0.5～1万人	5～10 Thousand Persons	70	9.6	25125638	13337177

8-5 续表 1 continued

分组	Groups	营业收入（万元） Operating Revenue	利润总额（万元） Total Profits	从业人员年末人数（人） Year-end Employed Persons
总 计	Total	201408833	14080329	3016589
按营业收入和资产总计分	Grouped by Operating Income and Property			
50亿元及以上	50 Hundred Million Yuan and Above	109943321	9957207	1243135
10亿元及以上	10 Hundred Million Yuan and above	178698798	13076337	2245023
5亿元及以上	5 Hundred Million Yuan and Above	191245314	13700867	2550474
按资产总计分	Grouped by Total Assets			
1000亿元及以上	1000 Hundred Million Yuan and Above	0	0	0
500～1000亿元	500～1000 Hundred Million Yuan	23963740	5282354	250084
100～500亿元	100～500 Hundred Million Yuan	58686290	3465238	738122
50～100亿元	50～100 hundred million Yuan	31999398	1391196	362664
5～50亿元	5～50 Hundred Million Yuan	78698920	3656371	1315356
按营业收入分	Grouped by Operating Revenue			
100亿元及以上	100 Hundred Million Yuan and Above	104863495	9165802	1093284
50～100亿元	50～100 Hundred Million Yuan	33972850	1741784	351952
5～50亿元	5～50 Hundred Million Yuan	56006889	2935066	1191513
按利润总额分	Grouped by Profit			
10亿元及以上	10 Hundred Million Yuan and Above	73368779	9103509	796883
5～10亿元	5～10 Hundred Million Yuan	24274747	1514628	256109
1～5亿元	1～5 Hundred Million Yuan	49057761	2840796	778980
0.5～1亿元	0.5～1 Hundred Million Yuan	18885950	696894	323608
0.1～0.5亿元	0.1～0.5 Hundred Million Yuan	16279383	512430	456971
按从业人员分	Grouped by Employed Persons			
10万人及以上	100 Thousand Persons and Above	5058322	336624	148328
5～10万人	50～100 Thousand Persons	26350661	4833606	342191
1～5万人	10～50 Thousand Persons	72241889	4261217	994117
0.5～1万人	5～10 Thousand Persons	27924218	1653432	486167

8-6 营业收入和资产总计均过五亿元的企业集团主要经济指标

Main Economy Target of Enterprise Groups Whose Operating Income and Total Assets are Greater than 5 Hundred Million Yuan

集团名称	Name of Groups	营业收入（万元）Operating Income (Ten Thousand Yuan)	位次 Precedence	资产总计（万元）Total Assets(Ten Thousand Yuan)	位次 Precedence	从业人员（人）Employed Persons (Persons)	位次 Precedence
海尔集团	Haier Group	10801576	1	4375304	7	53996	6
中国石化胜利油田有限公司	The Victory Oil Field Limited Company of SINOPEC	9148740	2	6218764	2	60210	4
山东电力集团	Shandong Power Group	6535027	3	5870013	3	31350	12
山东魏桥创业集团有限公司	Shandong Wei Qiao Pioneering Group Limited Company	5058322	4	3727686	10	148328	1
中国石油化工股份有限公司山东石油分公司	Shandong Petroleum Subsidiary Company of SINOPEC	4911662	5	794462	47	18203	28
海信集团	Haixin Group	4657965	6	2178726	16	12924	44
中国石油化工股份有限公司齐鲁分公司	Qi Lu Subsidiary Company of SINOPEC	4606303	7	884805	39	10449	57
济南钢铁集团	Jinan Iron and Steel Group	4433354	8	3770710	9	42169	7
莱芜钢铁集团有限公司	Laiwu Iron and Steel Group Limited Company	4422641	9	3812582	8	39057	8
兖矿集团	Yanzhou Deposit Group	3131072	10	5194120	5	96048	2
山东鲁能集团有限公司	Shandong Luneng Group Limited Company	2675393	11	8760348	1	34890	9
潍坊柴油机厂	Weifang Crude Oil Engine Factory	2490943	12	1936744	19	32406	11
青岛钢铁控股集团有限责任公司	Qingdao Iron and Steel Stockholder Group Limited Liability Corporation	2441373	13	1352938	26	14321	37
中国重型汽车集团有限公司	Chinese Heavy Automobile Group Limited Company	2323204	14	2321029	14	17086	30
中国石化齐鲁股份有限公司	Qilu Share-holding Corporation Limited of Sinopec	2268621	15	1151633	29	9316	64
山东晨鸣纸业集团	Shandong Chenming Paper Group	1893178	16	2026178	18	16231	32
山东海化集团	Shandong Haihua Group	1866511	17	1624957	21	19098	26
新华锦集团	Xin Hua Jin Group	1805624	18	425787	85	2875	237
新汶矿业集团	Xin Wen Deposit Group	1760067	19	2844478	12	76332	3
中国移动通信集团山东有限公司	China Mobile Communication Group Shandong Limited Company	1680921	20	2300699	15	22762	19
山东金锣企业集团总公司	Shandong Jin Luo Enterprise Group Controlling Company	1566910	21	456983	81	25063	15
中国网通（集团）有限公司山东省分公司	China Netcom (group) Limited Company Shandong Province Subsidiary Company	1555991	22	3677713	11	24547	16
山东信发铝电集团	ShanDong Xin Fa Aluminium And Electricity Group	1539528	23	1431518	24	13340	42
华电国际电力股份有限公司	China International Electric Power Share-holding Corporation Limited	1521034	24	5401509	4	13710	40
浪潮集团有限公司	Tide Group Limited Company	1520376	25	369926	101	4100	164
枣庄矿业（集团）有限责任公司	Zaozhuang Mining Industry (gr-oup) Limited Liability Company	1509206	26	1737903	20	55605	5

8-6 续表 1 continued

集团名称	Name of Groups	营业收入（万元）Operating Income (Ten Thousand Yuan)	位次 Precedence	资产总计（万元）Total Assets(Ten Thousand Yuan)	位次 Precedence	从业人员（人）Employed Persons (Persons)	位次 Precedence
中国石油化工股份有限公司济南分公司	Jinan Subsidiary Company of Sinopec	1487530	27	253648	145	1906	357
山东滨化集团	Shandong Bin Hua Group	1448855	28	453675	82	3001	228
山东时风集团	Shandong Shi Feng Group	1419579	29	356066	105	26905	14
南山集团	Nanshan Group	1360517	30	2028076	17	34246	10
山东如意科技集团	Shandong Ruyi Science and Technology Group	1260192	31	893681	38	16983	31
青岛啤酒集团	Qing Dao Beer Group	1175999	32	1154358	28	27627	13
三联集团	Sanlian Group	1150521	33	1002234	34	5342	119
日照钢铁控股集团有限公司	Rizhao Iron and Steel Stockholder Group Limited Company	1103291	34	971538	35	5996	106
山东鲁北企业集团总公司	Shandong Lubei Enterprise Group Controlling Company	1065516	35	706231	51	3394	198
山东六和集团有限公司	Shandong Liuhe Group Limited Company	1029582	36	200982	178	19000	27
北汽福田汽车股份有限公司诸城汽车厂	North Steam Fukuda Automobile Limited Liability Company Various City Automotive Factory	1025087	37	271141	138	3046	224
华泰集团有限公司	Huatai Group Limited Company	1024520	38	1137776	31	6062	103
华盛江泉集团	Huasheng Jiangquan Group	1014799	39	795205	45	18000	29
山东石横特钢集团有限公司	Shandong Shiheng Tegang Group Limited Company	988418	40	397178	91	5106	121
山东省高速公路集团有限公司	Shandong Province Highway Group Limited Company	952474	41	5071819	6	13876	39
中国石化集团青岛石油化工有限责任公司	Qingdao Petroleum Chemical Industry Limited Liability Company of Sinopec	928835	42	360913	104	2005	341
南金兆集团有限公司	Nanjinzhao Group Limited Company	915662	43	936554	36	4691	145
福田雷沃国际重工股份有限公司	Fukuda Thunder Fertile International Heavy Industry Share-holding Corporation Limited	897290	44	310907	118	9458	62
三星电子（山东）数码打印机有限公司	Tristar Electron (Shandong) Digital Printer Limited Company	881211	45	210531	170	958	499
双星集团	Double Star Group	862560	46	662141	55	19156	25
山东太阳纸业集团	Shandong Sun Paper Group	858437	47	719466	49	6610	92
上海通用东岳汽车有限公司	Shanghai Generaland Dongyue Automobile Limited Company	849133	48	389867	93	2275	298
利华益集团	Lihuayi Group	828288	49	512298	69	3180	213
山东淄博付山企业集团有限公司	Shandong Zibo Fushan Enterprise Group Limited Company	800778	50	339045	109	6550	94
科达集团股份有限公司	Keda Share-holding Corporation Limited	791732	51	509360	70	11125	53
山东京博控股发展有限公司	Beijing Jingbo Stockholder Limited Company	782312	52	473486	74	3056	222

8-6 续表 2 continued

集团名称	Name of Groups	营业收入（万元）Operating Income (Ten Thousand Yuan)	位次 Precedence	资产总计（万元）Total Assets(Ten Thousand Yuan)	位次 Precedence	从业人员（人）Employed Persons (Persons)	位次 Precedence
万达集团股份有限公司	Wanda Group Share-holding Corporation Limited	779394	53	499312	71	6040	104
诸城外贸有限责任公司	Various City Foreign Trade Limited Liability Company	757468	54	794719	46	7481	82
山东省商业集团总公司	Shandong Province Commercial Group Main Corporation	750303	55	813591	41	13200	43
三角集团	Triangle Group	747405	56	478597	73	6582	93
山东工程机械集团	Shandong Engineering and Machinery Group	742021	57	525796	66	5733	112
淄博矿业集团有限责任公司	Zibo Mining Industry Group Limited Liability Company	736260	58	1171779	27	19429	24
利群集团	Liqun Group	731616	59	327029	113	4927	129
山东东明石化集团	Shandong Dongming Petroleum and Chemistry Group	728191	60	388915	94	2117	316
山东泰山钢铁集团	Shandong Taishan Iron and Steel Group	713939	61	411091	88	7816	77
山东招金集团	Shandong Zhaoyuan Mining Group	709000	62	800096	43	9128	65
青岛港集团	Qingdao Harbour Group	708161	63	1614514	22	14530	36
一汽解放青岛汽车厂	Steam Liberates Qingdao Automotive Factory	700444	64	385286	97	3579	187
山东华星石油化工集团有限公司	Shandong Huaxing Petroleum and Chemistry Group Limited Company	660231	65	458367	80	1099	478
山东玲珑橡胶有限公司	Shandong Linglong Rubber Limited Company	659729	66	472924	75	4918	130
山东西王集团有限公司	Shandong Xiwang Group Limited Company	650206	67	653398	56	5400	117
山东铝业股份有限公司	Shandong Aluminium Share-holding Corporation Limited	632154	68	491397	72	6292	100
山东五征集团	Shandong Wuzheng Group	628957	69	133387	249	8167	73
山东山水水泥集团有限公司	Shandong Shanshui Cement Group Limited Company	615777	70	462231	78	7124	85
山东博汇集团有限公司	Shandong Bohui Group Limited Company	614487	71	645785	57	9700	60
华鲁控股集团有限公司	Hualu Stockholder Group Limited Company	609263	72	1122391	32	15648	34
山东垦利石化有限责任公司	Shandong Kenli Petroleum and Chemistry Limited Company	602061	73	265208	139	3103	221
山东泉林纸业有限责任公司	Shandong Quanlin Paper Limited Liability Corporation	597788	74	552525	64	8884	68
青岛建设集团	Qingdao Construction Group	595178	75	718636	50	9495	61
山东寿光巨能控股集团有限公司	Shandong Shouguang Juneng Sto-ckholder Group Limited Company	592645	76	411216	87	2544	269

8-6 续表 3 continued

集团名称	Name of Groups	营业收入（万元）Operating Income (Ten Thousand Yuan)	位次 Precedence	资产总计（万元）Total Assets(Ten Thousand Yuan)	位次 Precedence	从业人员（人）Employed Persons (Persons)	位次 Precedence
正和集团股份有限公司	Zhenghe Stockholder Group Share-holding corporation Limited	561977	77	211150	169	2018	333
山东黄金集团	Shandong Gold Group	532913	78	926028	37	22786	18
山东西水橡胶集团有限公司	Shandong Xishui Rubber Group Limited Company	528770	79	327816	111	7500	81
山东家家悦超市有限公司	Shandong Jiajiayue Supermarket Limited Company	528085	80	69657	374	10845	56
山东石大科技集团	Shandong Shida Science and Technology Group	525938	81	145267	232	1506	410
山东金升有色集团有限公司	Shandong Jinsheng Coloured Group Limited Company	524191	82	169779	208	620	589
日照港（集团）有限公司	Rizhao Harbour(group) Limited Company	523819	83	1429494	25	7703	79
烟台万华合成革集团	Yantai Wanhua Synthesis Leather Group	520602	84	678037	53	3380	199
中国联通有限公司山东分公司	Chinaunite Communication Limited Company Shandong Subsidiary Company	516548	85	796834	44	2950	231
潍坊钢铁集团公司	Weifang Iron and Steel group Enterprise	516050	86	635467	58	4891	133
力诺集团有限责任公司	Linuo Group Limited Company	511544	87	792954	48	11123	54
青岛泰发集团	Qingdao Taifa Group	486993	88	105560	291	9000	67
山东潍坊百货集团股份有限公司	Shandong Weifang Department Group Share-holding Corporation Limited	478565	89	134393	247	6820	89
青岛海湾集团	Qingdao Bay Group	469138	90	611312	60	12848	45
斗山工程机械（中国）有限公司	Doushan Engineering and Machinery Limited Company (China)	468011	91	298723	123	1052	484
肥城矿业集团	feicheng deposit group	460876	92	804618	42	20601	23
山东聊城鲁西化工集团	Shandong Liaocheng Luxibei Chemistry Industry	460514	93	522348	67	8194	72
山东胜通集团股份有限公司	Shandong Shengtong Group Share-holding Corporation Limited	458026	94	247514	148	2360	287
山东省机械进出口集团	Shandong Province Mechanical Import and Export Group	453246	95	239370	150	576	606
青岛即发集团	Qingdao Jifa Group	451231	96	256863	143	12357	48
山东临清彩虹集团	Shandong Linqing Rainbow Group	451098	97	365049	102	2338	289
山东鲁花集团	Shandong Luhua Group	446428	98	348838	107	5106	122
山东省供销社集团总公司	Shandong Province Supply and Marketing Cooperative Group Main Corporation	442434	99	546745	65	980	497
山东航空集团	Shandong Aviation Group	438612	100	668963	54	4285	158

8-6 续表 4 continued

集团名称	Name of Groups	营业收入（万元）Operating Income (Ten Thousand Yuan)	位次 Precedence	资产总计（万元）Total Assets(Ten Thousand Yuan)	位次 Precedence	从业人员（人）Employed Persons (Persons)	位次 Precedence
华能国际电力股份有限公司德州电厂	Huaneng International Electric Power Limited Liability Company Dezhou Power Plant	423208	101	514654	68	2161	308
山东泸河集团有限公司	Shandong Luriver Group Limited Company	421398	102	164726	210	4314	156
烟台有色金属集团	Yantai non-ferrous Metal Group	419543	103	201825	177	1472	417
龙口矿业集团	Longkou Deposit Group	418030	104	460980	79	15717	33
山东只楚集团	Shandong Zhichu Group	412849	105	194705	183	4760	141
孚日集团股份有限公司	Furi Group Share-holding Corporation Limited	409195	106	402372	89	15550	35
小松山推工程机械有限公司	Xiaosong Shantui Project Machinery Limited Company	408016	107	176471	202	486	620
天元建设集团	Tianyuan Construction Group	405766	108	380031	98	21330	20
山东东辰实业集团有限公司	Shandong Dongchen Industrial Group Limited Company	389562	110	150960	227	680	573
烟台张裕集团	Yantai Zhangyu Group	385198	111	324912	114	3112	219
烟台市振华百货集团股份有限公司	Yantai Zhenhua Department Group Share-holding Corporation Limited	373605	112	290922	126	3771	177
山东大海集团有限公司	Shandong Sea Group Limited Company	367162	113	217634	162	4450	153
得利斯集团有限公司	Delisi Group Limited Company	364131	114	316316	116	4515	150
淄博商厦股份有限公司	Zibo Commerce Edificeshare-holding Corporation Limited	360660	115	117253	272	2855	240
欧美投资集团	Europe and America Investment Group	360337	116	188550	187	2571	267
鲁泰集团	Lutai Group	354918	117	611912	59	13962	38
山东东岳集团	Shandong Dongyue Group	351082	118	284838	131	3330	203
青岛变压器集团	Qingdao Transformer Group	345964	119	315400	117	7251	84
山东凤祥集团	Shandong Fengxiang Group	338600	120	374869	100	11989	50
龙大食品集团	Longda Food Group	333250	121	212001	167	23040	17
山东丛林集团	Shandong Conglin Group	333194	122	428544	84	4236	161
南车四方机车车辆股份有限公司	South Vehicle Sifang Rolling Stock Share-holding Corporation Limited	323343	123	289139	127	6124	102
润华集团股份有限公司	Rubhua Group Share-holding Corporation Limited	322036	124	286722	129	786	548
山东渤海实业股份有限公司	Shandong Bohai Industrial Share-Holding Corporation Limited	319857	125	183274	192	1600	392
山东（临清）银河纸业集团	Shandong (linqing) Yinhe Paper Group	318697	126	261389	142	4976	127

8-6 续表 5 continued

集团名称	Name of Groups	营业收入（万元）Operating Income (Ten Thousand Yuan)	位次 Precedence	资产总计（万元）Total Assets(Ten Thousand Yuan)	位次 Precedence	从业人员（人）Employed Persons (Persons)	位次 Precedence
中国石化集团齐鲁石油化工公司	QiLu Petroleum Chemical Industry Company of Sinopec	315052	127	472434	76	8423	70
山东海丰国际航运集团有限公司	Shandong Haifeng International Shipping Group Limited Company	311752	128	91279	318	370	644
临沂矿业集团有限责任公司	Linyi Deposit Group Limited Liability Corporation	309247	129	424796	86	12845	46
青岛喜盈门集团	Qingdao Xiyingmen Group	307019	130	327057	112	4856	135
青岛汉缆集团	Qingdao Hanlan Group	305087	131	99690	301	1885	358
青岛市胶州建设集团有限公司	Qingdao Jiaozhou Construction Group Limited Company	294735	133	185905	188	11861	51
银河德普胶带有限公司	Yinhe Depu Adhesive Tape Limited Company	288282	134	284736	132	1940	353
山东九羊集团有限公司	Shandong Jiuyang Group Limited Company	287099	135	393258	92	4000	166
山东隆基集团有限公司	Shandong Longji Group Limited Company	285593	136	81571	338	3500	189
齐星集团	Qixing Group	285481	137	610472	61	3605	184
青岛澳柯玛集团	Qingdao Aucma Group	280420	138	1103342	33	4185	162
山东沂州水泥集团总公司	Shandong Yizhou Cement Group Main Corporation	278676	139	216615	164	4951	128
山东德棉集团	Shandong Dezhou Cotton Group	274602	140	300395	122	13634	41
山东联盟化工集团有限公司	Shandong Alliance Chemical Industry Group Limited Company	274555	141	210154	171	3181	212
山东九发集团	Shandong Jiufa Group	268833	142	294726	125	3412	194
山东冠洲集团	Shandong Guanzhou Group	261518	143	211966	168	1288	453
青岛万福集团	Qingdao Wanfu Group	257444	144	77029	353	3112	220
山东省建设建工（集团）有限责任公司	Shandong Province Construction Construction Work (group) Limited Liability Company	256000	145	432748	83	20677	22
山东省高唐蓝山集团	Shandong Province Gaotang Lanshan Group	253460	146	119181	265	2061	326
山东里能集团	Shandong Lineng Group	252038	147	1145681	30	3748	179
山东阳谷电缆集团	Shandong Yanggu Cable Group	251469	148	169916	207	2005	342
山东香驰豆业集团	Shandong Xiangchi Beans Group	250606	149	132356	252	626	587
山东冠鲁集团	Shandong Guanlu Group	249850	150	229676	153	21080	21
山东华乐实业集团公司	Shandong Huale Industrial Group Company	249532	151	112001	282	3600	185
山东省塑料工业有限公司	Shandong Province Plastic Industry Limited Company	246815	152	132359	251	188	674

8-6 续表 6 continued

集团名称	Name of Groups	营业收入（万元）Operating Income (Ten Thousand Yuan)	位次 Precedence	资产总计（万元）Total Assets(Ten Thousand Yuan)	位次 Precedence	从业人员（人）Employed Persons (Persons)	位次 Precedence
山东海龙股份有限公司	Shandong Hailong Share-holding Corporation Limited	245131	153	362803	103	8232	71
山东北金集团有限公司	Shandong Beijin Group Limited Company	242914	154	219421	161	3000	229
山东恒源石油化工集团	Shandong Hengyuan Petroleum Chemical Industry Group	241632	155	174580	204	2798	246
济宁矿业集团	Jining Deposit Group	240918	156	562042	63	10408	58
青岛九联集团股份有限公司	Qingdao Jiulian Group Share-holding Corporation Limited	240169	157	84711	332	8100	74
山东德齐龙化工集团	Shandong Deqilong Chemical Industry Group	237891	158	182603	195	2700	255
青岛黄海橡胶集团	Qingdao Yellow Sea Rubber Group	237107	159	583328	62	8070	75
山东省冠县冠星纺织集团	Sahndong Province Guanxian Guanxing Spinning and Weaving Group	234771	160	99971	300	3160	216
四方机车车辆有限责任公司	Sifang Rolling Stock Limited Liability Company	232408	161	305368	120	4896	132
山东齐鲁增塑剂股份有限公司	Shandong Qilu Plasticizer Share-holding Corporation Limited	230727	162	77329	352	486	621
山东翔龙实业集团	Shandong Xianglong Industrial Group	229902	163	145704	231	3116	218
好当家集团	Haodangjia Group	225601	164	272879	136	3447	191
青岛维客集团	Qingdao Weike Group	220611	165	118663	269	1980	347
山东省交通工业集团总公司	Shandong Province Transportation Industry Group Main Corporation	218488	166	308862	119	5488	115
黄海粮油工业（山东）有限公司	Yellow Sea Cooking Oil Industry (Shandong) Limited Company	218020	167	76067	360	585	604
烟台冰轮集团	Yantai Binglun Group	216284	168	220475	160	4828	137
菱花集团	Lenghua Group	215451	169	148630	228	6500	96
山东雪花生物化工股份有限公司	Shandong Snowflake Organisms Chemical Industry Share-holding Corporation Limited	214564	170	112962	281	2532	271
华纺股份有限公司	Huafang Share-holding Corporation Limited	214242	171	136524	242	4705	144
鲁能泰山电缆电器有限责任公司	Luneng Taishan Electric Cable Electric Appliance Limited Liability Company	213530	172	462761	77	2804	243
山东新郎希努尔集团股份有限公司	Shandong Bridegroom Sinor Group Share-holding Corporation Limited	213527	173	188973	186	6428	97
山东铝业公司	Shandong Aluminium Company	213217	174	248583	147	4275	159
济南华联商厦集团股份有限公司	Jinan Hualian Commerce Edifice Group Share-holding Corporation Limited	210656	175	90908	319	848	531

8-6 续表 7 continued

集团名称	name of groups	营业收入（万元）Operating Income (Ten Thousand Yuan)	位次 Precedence	资产总计（万元）Total Assets(Ten Thousand Yuan)	位次 Precedence	从业人员（人）Employed Persons (Persons)	位次 Precedence
山东省棉麻公司	Shandong Province Cotton and Kapok Hemp Company	209869	176	401450	90	119	691
泰丰纺织集团	Taifeng Spinning and Weaving Group	209022	177	152346	226	6400	98
烟建集团	Yantai Construction Group	208960	178	182711	194	1777	373
山东照东方纸业集团	Shandong Rizhao Dongfang Paper Group	207459	179	183655	191	2800	244
山东华金集团	Shandong Huajin Group	206283	180	185475	189	4478	152
青岛益佳国际贸易集团	Qingdao Yijia International Trade Group	204256	181	225379	156	544	609
胜利油田胜利工程建设集团	Victory Oil Field Victory Engineering Construction Group	203442	182	263613	140	7906	76
史丹利化肥有限公司	Shidanli Fertilizer Limited Company	201743	183	129019	254	2400	281
山东恒通化工股份有限公司	Shandong Hengtong Chemical Industry Share-holding Corporation Limited	200863	184	196858	180	2693	256
山东成山橡胶集团	Shandong Chengshan Rubber Group	199775	185	199883	179	732	557
中国石化胜利油田大明（集团）股份有限公司	Victory Oil Field Ming Dynasty (group) Share-holding Corporation Limited of Sinopec	193634	186	352784	106	4076	165
山东岱银纺织集团	Shandong Daiyin Spinning and Weaving Group	193096	187	93737	315	6210	101
山东长星集团有限公司	Shandong Changxing Group Limited Company	192228	188	70273	372	1200	459
信义集团公司	Xinyi Group Company	191253	189	169727	209	2066	325
山东百年电力发展股份有限公司	Shandong One Hundred Year Power Development Share-holding Corporation Limited	189804	190	209011	172	2415	279
青岛星火纺机纺织集团股份有限公司	Qingdao Xinghuo Spinning and Weaving Group Share-holding Corporation Limited	188589	191	75294	362	2108	320
齐鲁制药有限公司（集团）	QiLu Manufactures Drugs the Limited Company (group)	186875	192	261560	141	3651	181
泰开电气集团有限公司	Taikai Electrical Group Limited Company	184408	193	154115	224	3201	209
泰山玻璃纤维股份有限公司	Taishan Glass Fibre Share-holding Corporations Limited	181869	194	288610	128	2268	299
青岛康大外贸集团有限公司	Qingdao Kangda Foreign Trade Group Limited Company	181810	195	73525	365	1213	457
滨州盟威集团有限公司	Bingzhou Mengwei Group Limited Company	180128	196	178099	201	4737	143
潍坊亚星集团	Weifang Yaxing Group	179556	197	281145	134	2730	252

8-6 续表 8 continued

集团名称	Name of Groups	营业收入（万元）Operating Income (Ten Thousand Yuan)	位次 Precedence	资产总计（万元）Total Assets(Ten Thousand Yuan)	位次 Precedence	从业人员（人）Employed Persons (Persons)	位次 Precedence
山东大洋食品集团有限公司	Shandong Dayang Food Group Limited Company	177777	198	53317	420	5020	125
山东蓝星玻璃集团	Shandong Lanxing Glass Group	177020	199	228909	154	4398	155
山东绮丽集团	Shandong Qili Group	176521	200	97448	308	2204	305
济南华达企业集团总公司	Shandonghuada Enterprise Group Main Corporation	175798	201	193631	184	1549	399
山东银鹰化纤有限公司	Shandong Yinying Chemical Fiber Limited Company	175274	202	116769	274	3128	217
济南四建（集团）有限责任公司	Jinan Forth Construction(group) Limited Liability Corporation	172331	203	180752	197	11139	52
日照兴业集团有限公司	Rizhao Xingye Group Limited Company	172131	204	157950	219	2581	265
山东华力电机集团	Shandong Huali Electrical Machinery Group	171987	205	72602	367	2190	307
山东鲁州食品集团有限公司	Shandong Luzhou Food Group Limited Company	171825	206	120276	264	4558	149
富海集团有限公司	Fuhai Group Limited Company	170693	207	126426	258	793	546
兰雁集团	Lanyan Group	169738	208	193194	185	5353	118
济南锅炉集团有限公司	Jinan Boiler Group Limited Company	167141	209	305084	121	2001	343
山东同济万鑫集团有限公司	Shandong Tongji Wanxin Group Limited Company	166810	210	76309	357	3560	188
青岛广源发集团	Qingdao Guangyuanfa Group	166370	211	255512	144	3746	180
金晶（集团）有限公司	Jinjing(group) Limited Company	165517	212	328841	110	1954	350
烟台港集团有限公司	Yantai Harbour Group Limited Company	165321	213	686273	52	9921	59
山东桑莎制衣集团	Shandong Sangsha Clothing Group	165053	214	139096	238	2136	312
山东华夏集团	Shandong Huaxia Group	165001	215	74878	363	1500	411
山东墨龙石油机械股份有限公司	Shandong Molong Petroleum Machinery Share-holding Corporations Limited	163622	216	172276	205	2688	257
山东金沂蒙集团有限公司	Shandong Jinyimeng Group Limited Company	162873	217	104278	294	2008	338
山东天府集团公司	Shandong Tianfu Group Enterprise	161955	218	123289	261	2100	323
山东汽车工业集团有限公司	Shandong Automobile Industry Group Limited Company	161660	219	162222	211	7041	86
山东德州百货大楼（集团）有限责任公司	Shandong Dezhou Department Store(group) Limited Liability Company	161023	220	63050	393	2108	321

8-6 续表 9 continued

集团名称	Name of Groups	营业收入（万元）Operating Income (Ten Thousand Yuan)	位次 Precedence	资产总计（万元）Total Assets(Ten Thousand Yuan)	位次 Precedence	从业人员（人）Employed Persons (Persons)	位次 Precedence
山东亚太森博浆纸有限公司	Shandong Yatai Senbo Paper Mode Limited Company	160897	221	374994	99	893	517
临清三和纺织集团	Linqing Sanhe Spinning and Weaving Group	160275	222	130209	253	12000	49
鲁丽集团有限公司	Luli Group Limited Company	159321	223	105276	292	3500	190
山东滨州亚光毛巾有限公司	Shandong Binzhou Yaguang Towel Limited Company	159141	224	234771	151	6758	90
山东中创软件工程股份有限公司	Shandong Zhongchuang Software Engineering Share-holding Corporations Limited	158315	225	56630	411	721	558
山东东大化学工业有限公司	Shandong Dongda Chemical Industry Limited Company	158287	226	96858	311	1984	346
青岛中集集装箱制造有限公司	Qingdao Zhongji Container Making Limited Company	158163	227	109722	286	411	634
青岛三恩集团有限公司	Qingdao Sanen Group Limited Company	156548	228	66841	383	2021	331
威高集团	Weigao Group	154852	229	194826	182	6005	105
威海建设集团	Weihai Construction Group	153906	230	156019	223	2585	264
青岛红星化工集团	Qingdao Hongxing Chemical Industry Group	153160	231	342520	108	5732	113
东营市天信纺织有限公司	Dongying Tianxin Spinning and Weaving Limited Company	152676	232	118320	271	3600	186
菏泽交通集团总公司	Heze Transportation Group Main Corporation	152183	233	127184	256	6986	87
山东金顺达集团有限公司	Shandong Jinshunda Group Limited Company	151497	234	220745	159	2316	294
泰山集团股份有限公司	Taishan Group Share-holding Corporation Limited	151193	235	160330	214	2412	280
山东华丰企业集团	Shandong Huafeng Enterprise Group	150833	236	159347	216	4665	147
山东恒联投资有限公司	Shandong Henglian Investment Limited Company	150684	237	125321	259	5223	120
山东金岭集团公司	Shandong Jinling Group Company	150547	238	147991	230	2500	272
烟台市首钢东星集团	Yantai Capital Iron and Steel Dongxing Group	150183	239	212468	166	2375	284
山东中大空调集团	Shandong Zhongda Air-conditioning Group	147943	240	106610	290	2160	309
山东永泰化工集团有限公司	Shandong Yongtai Chemical Industry Group Limited Company	147420	241	98483	303	2000	344
赤山集团	Chishan Group	147376	242	285658	130	3200	211
山东红日阿康化工股份有限公司	Shandong Hongri Akang Chemical Industry Share-holding Corporation limited	145954	243	161687	213	2918	234

8-6 续表 10 continued

集团名称	Name of Groups	营业收入（万元）Operating Income (Ten Thousand Yuan)	位次 Precedence	资产总计（万元）Total Assets(Ten Thousand Yuan)	位次 Precedence	从业人员（人）Employed Persons (Persons)	位次 Precedence
青特集团有限公司	Qingte Group Limited Company	145257	244	203107	175	2009	337
烟台东方电子信息产业集团	Yantai East Electronic Information Industry Group	143376	245	220848	158	2016	334
山东金麒麟集团	Shandong Jinqilin Group	143345	246	86819	330	1980	348
日照市水产集团总公司	Rizhao Aquatic Product Group Main Corporation	140138	247	104134	295	3849	173
山东省鲁信投资控股集团有限公司	Shandong Province Lu Xin Invests the Holding Group Limited Company	139057	248	2387304	13	427	630
威海北洋电气集团	Weihai Beiyang Electricity Group	138281	249	97110	310	2778	249
青岛纺联集团	Qingdao Spinning and Weaving Unite Group	136433	250	207786	173	9121	66
鲁南制药集团	Lunan Drugs Manufacture Group	136298	251	272239	137	2867	238
正海集团	Zhenghai Group	135240	252	244397	149	1739	375
山东华阳农药化工集团	Shandong Huayang Pesticide Chemical Industry Group	134678	253	252027	146	9411	63
大众报业集团	The People Newspapers Group	133096	254	228888	155	4789	140
山东大成化工集团有限公司	Shandong Dacheng Chemical Industry Group Limited Company	130467	255	224210	157	3616	182
德州晶华集团	Dezhou Jinghua Group	130418	256	387818	95	8832	69
青岛宏大纺织机械有限责任公司	Qingdao Great Textile Machinery Limited Liability Company	128124	257	54540	415	1331	445
山东华瑞集团	Shandong Huarui Group	127952	258	107589	288	2130	313
威海市金猴集团	Weihai Gold Monkey Group	126845	259	96302	312	2780	248
山东常林机械集团	Shandong Changlin Machinery Group	124850	260	80581	341	4307	157
华润东阿阿胶有限公司	Huarun Donge Donkey-hide Gelatin Limited Company	121724	261	175540	203	3426	192
邹平怡康集团有限公司	Zouping Yikang Group Limited Company	120126	262	157424	222	1633	389
泰山体育产业集团	Taishan Sports Property Group	119316	263	115279	277	2325	291
青岛伟东置业集团	Qingdao Weidong Zhiye Group	116762	264	205773	174	146	684
青岛正进集团	Qingdao Zhengjin Group	116422	265	157500	221	6900	88
谷神生物科技集团	Valley God Biotechnology Group	115724	266	95242	313	1268	454
方圆集团	Circumference Group	115159	267	79581	345	3410	195
荣成华泰汽车有限公司	Rongcheng Huatai Automobile Limited Company	115078	268	216210	165	2020	332
山东明水化工有限公司	Shandong Mingshui Chemical Industry Limited Company	114326	269	182880	193	3918	169
皇明太阳能集团	Huangming Solar Energy Group	113604	271	86902	329	2350	288

8-6 续表 11 continued

集团名称	Name of Groups	营业收入（万元）Operating Income (Ten Thousand Yuan)	位次 Precedence	资产总计（万元）Total Assets(Ten Thousand Yuan)	位次 Precedence	从业人员（人）Employed Persons (Persons)	位次 Precedence
烟台恒邦集团	Yantai Hengbang Group	111895	272	111670	283	2474	276
济南玫德铸造有限公司	Jinan Meide Foundry Limited Company	111046	274	57258	407	3758	178
山东乐悟集团	Shandong Lewu Group	110972	275	122023	262	1800	368
烟台氨纶集团	Yantai Spandex Group	109651	276	148583	229	950	504
山东凤阳集团股份有限公司	Shandong Fengyang Group Share-holding Corporation Limited	108933	277	97713	307	567	607
青岛金王集团	Qingdao Jinwang Group	108148	278	114174	279	2031	328
耶莉娅集团	Yealia Group	108112	279	57241	408	3375	200
济南二机床集团有限公司	Jinan Second Engine Bed group Limited Company	107337	280	138495	239	4667	146
潍坊昌大建设集团	Weifang Changda Construction Group	105817	282	185360	190	1782	372
山东崔军集团公司	Shandong Cuijun Group Enterprise	105253	284	71730	368	3910	170
山东齐鲁味精集团	Shandong Qilu Aginomoto Group	104431	286	79441	347	2723	253
山东滨州环宇纺织集团有限责任公司	Shandong Binzhou World Spinning and Weaving Group Limited Liability Company	103483	287	121773	263	3900	171
翔宇实业集团有限公司	Xiangyu Industry Group Limited Company	103405	288	99287	302	639	583
山东胜利股份有限公司	Shandong Victory Share-holding Corporation Limited	102558	289	172178	206	1686	384
山东达驰电气股份有限公司	Shandong Dachi Electric Share-holding Corporation Limited	102406	290	90504	320	781	550
山东齐峰集团有限公司	Shandong Chifeng Group Limited Company	101800	291	138174	240	833	534
济南一建集团	Jinan First Construction Group	100793	293	202832	176	7701	80
山东滨州印染集团有限责任公司	Shandong Binzhou Printing Group Limited Liability Company	100630	294	134655	246	2604	261
威海光威集团	Weihai Guangwei Group	100569	295	107067	289	4404	154
山东贺友集团	Shandong Heyou Group	100035	297	102038	299	1490	415
山东靖海实业集团	Shandong Jinghai Industry Group	100002	298	74601	364	3400	197
山东丰源煤电股份有限公司	Shandong Fengyuan Coal and Electricity Share-holding Corporation Limited	99210	299	217444	163	6398	99
特变电工山东鲁能泰山电缆有限公司	Especially Changes the Electrician Shandong Luneng Taishan Electric Cable Limited Company	97434	300	118717	268	1860	362
鲁中冶金矿业集团公司	Luzhong Metallurgy Mining Industry Group Company	95926	301	180396	198	7278	83

8-6 续表 12 continued

集团名称	Name of Groups	营业收入（万元）Operating Income (Ten Thousand Yuan)	位次 Precedence	资产总计（万元）Total Assets(Ten Thousand Yuan)	位次 Precedence	从业人员（人）Employed Persons (Persons)	位次 Precedence
烟台三环锁业集团	Yantai Three Ring Lock Industry Groups	95758	302	56799	410	4578	148
山东东佳集团	Shandong Dongjia Group	94773	303	136336	243	2025	330
山东樱花纺织集团	Shandong Sakura Spinning and Weaving Group	93998	304	178976	200	5795	111
青岛交运集团	Qingdao Communications and Transportation Group	93448	305	118776	267	4798	139
山东宏河矿业集团有限公司	Shandong Hong River Mining Industry Group Limited Company	91762	307	158687	217	7748	78
青岛红领集团有限公司	Qingdao Hongling Group Limited Company	91621	308	118453	270	3862	172
海马集团公司	Hippocampus Japonicus Group Enterprise	88778	310	98039	305	2709	254
山东齐天化学集团	Shandong Qitian Chemical Industry Group	87733	311	69662	373	1557	398
青岛东生集团公司	Qingdao Dongsheng Group Enterprise	87654	312	88125	327	2452	278
山东辰龙纸业股份有限公司	Shandong Chenlong Paper Share-holding Corporation Limited	86222	313	134696	245	1812	367
威海市山花地毯集团	Weihai Wild Flower Rug Group	83971	316	63311	392	2333	290
山东省药用玻璃股份有限公司	Shandong Province for Medicinal Purposes Glass Share-holding Corporation Limited	82671	318	160011	215	5859	110
烟台交运集团	Yantai Communications and Transportation Group	82489	319	84452	334	3996	168
山东明兴矿业集团	Shandong Mingxing Mining Industry Group	82000	320	98099	304	3374	201
山东佳宝集团有限公司	Shandong Jiabao Group Limited Company	81856	321	88990	323	2202	306
山东省医药集团有限公司	Shandong Province Medicine Group Limited Company	81580	322	61475	400	2367	285
青岛市市政工程集团有限公司	Qingdao Municipal Works Group Limited Company	81007	325	134874	244	1460	420
青岛公交集团	Qingdao Transit Group	80373	326	143371	233	12741	47
青岛泰能燃气集团	Qingdao Taineng Gas Group	80261	327	297209	124	1949	351
临沂医药集团有限公司	Linyi Medicine Group Limited Company	79745	329	57643	406	2647	259
临沂桃源集团有限责任公司	Linyi Taoyuan Group Limited Liability Company	78873	330	104621	293	2864	239
青岛中泰集团有限责任公司	Qingdao Zhongtai Group Limited Liability Company	78608	331	57773	405	1397	434
山东高虹电力集团	Shandong Gaohong Power Group	78339	332	52284	426	2215	304
山东鲁泰煤业有限公司	Shandong Lutai Coal Industry Limited Company	78122	333	180310	199	4904	131

8-6 续表 13 continued

集团名称	Name of Groups	营业收入（万元）Operating Income (Ten Thousand Yuan)	位次 Precedence	资产总计（万元）Total Assets(Ten Thousand Yuan)	位次 Precedence	从业人员（人）Employed Persons (Persons)	位次 Precedence
山东裕隆矿业集团	Shandong Yulong Mining Industry Group	77498	334	116762	275	4854	136
烟台市钢铁企业集团	Yantai Iron and Steel Enterprise Group	77136	335	56371	412	907	515
山东莱动内燃机有限公司	Shandong Laidong Internal-combustion Engine Limited Company	76052	336	67740	378	3305	205
山东英克莱集团	Shandong Yongkelai Group	75930	337	55443	413	2317	293
石岛集团有限公司	Shidao Group Limited Company	74215	339	136752	241	2600	263
青岛天泰集团	Qingdao Tiantai Group	74008	340	182026	196	863	526
山东凯银集团股份有限公司	Shandong Kaiyin Group Shareholding Corporation Limited	70629	342	79863	343	1585	396
潍坊市临朐燃气热力集团	Weifang Linqu Gas and Heating Power Group	70560	343	54196	416	1331	446
山东矿机集团有限公司	Shandong Mineral Machine Group Limited Company	69066	346	88115	328	1082	480
青岛海润自来水集团	Qingdao Hairun Running Water Group	67865	347	233793	152	2114	317
山东鲁信高新技术产业股份有限公司	Shandong Luxin High and New Technology Property Shareholding Corporation Limited	67784	348	124485	260	1537	401
青岛福日集团	Qingdao Furi Group	66461	350	71197	371	279	662
山东机械设备进出口集团公司	Shandong Mechanical Equipment Import and Export Group Company	63696	354	50991	431	252	666
菏泽睿鹰制药集团	Heze Ruiying Manufactures Drugs Group	63107	355	111646	284	2014	335
山东新光实业集团有限公司	Shandong Xinguang Industrial Group Limited Company	62897	356	103076	297	3023	227
山东潍坊外贸实业集团公司	Shandong Weifang Foreign Trade Industrial Group Corporation	62777	357	51884	429	1186	466
山东洪业化工集团	Shandong Hongye Chemical Industry Group	62632	358	79727	344	1734	378
山东省物资集团总公司	Shandong Province Commodity Group Main Corporation	62331	359	88645	325	832	535
山东鲁通集团	Shandong Lutong Group	61536	361	141358	236	2276	297
海汇集团	Haihui Group	61460	362	50363	433	1516	407
寿光市新龙电化有限责任公司	Shouguang Xinlong Electrification Limited Liability Corporation	60456	363	66757	384	1086	479
山东龙喜集团	Shandong Longxi Group	60455	364	115217	278	2458	277
山东华盛中天机械集团有限公司	Shandong Huasheng Zhongtian Machinery Group Limited Company	60372	365	71549	370	1871	361
青岛三元集团股份有限公司	Qingdao Sanyuan Group Shareholding Corporation Limited	60251	367	53868	417	605	592

8-6 续表 14 continued

集团名称	Name of Groups	营业收入（万元）Operating Income (Ten Thousand Yuan)	位次 Precedence	资产总计（万元）Total Assets(Ten Thousand Yuan)	位次 Precedence	从业人员（人）Employed Persons (Persons)	位次 Precedence
山东环日集团	Shandong Huanri Group	60164	368	53471	419	3201	210
山东金马工业集团股份有限公司	Shandong Jinma Chemical Industry Group Share-holding Corporation Limited	60108	369	71683	369	1727	379
山东华龙纺织有限公司	Shandong Hualong Spinning and Weaving Limited Company	58997	370	51979	428	4251	160
山东聊建集团总公司	Shandong Liaocheng Construction Group Main Company	57562	372	158466	218	3788	176
济南志友集团股份有限公司	Jinan Zhiyou Group Share-holding Corporation Limited	56890	373	68563	376	795	544
东安黑豹股份有限公司	Dongan Heibao Share-holding Corporation Limited	56732	374	78164	349	1841	363
山东省潍坊生建集团	Shandong Weifang Shengjian Group	56083	375	64735	387	1294	451
青岛麦迪绅集团股份有限公司	Qingdao Maidishen Share-holding Corporation Limited	55333	378	72747	366	104	693
青岛信达荣昌置业集团股份有限公司	Qingdao Xinda Rongchang Zhiye Group Share-holding Corporation Limited	54716	381	103740	296	150	682
枣庄泉兴矿业集团公司	Zaozhuang Quanxing Deposit Group	54639	382	86217	331	3810	174
山东鲁强电缆集团	Shandong Luqiang Cable Group	54457	384	52512	423	950	505
青岛热电集团	Qingdao Pyroelectricity Group	54260	386	153291	225	2031	329
山东世纪泰华集团有限公司	Shandong Century Taihua Group Limited Company	54220	387	54839	414	1727	380
山东王晁煤电集团有限公司	Shandong Wangchao Coal and Electricity Group Limited Company	53561	389	82111	336	2851	241
济南华诚元首集团有限公司	Jinan Huacheng Chief Executive Group Limited Company	53317	390	79207	348	6693	91
山东贵和纸业集团有限公司	Shandong Guihe Paper Group Limited Company	53109	392	88720	324	908	514
中外合资淄博工陶耐火材料有限公司	Chinese-foreign Joint Venture Zibo Labor Ceramic Fire-proof Material Limited Company	52637	394	81212	339	1524	405
山东省微山湖矿业集团	Shandong Weishan Lake Deposit Group	52576	395	132382	250	3792	175
山东奥宝化工集团	Shandong Aobao Chemical Industry Group	52507	396	67430	380	1498	414
淄博华辰集团有限责任公司	Zibo Huachen Limited Liability Corporation	51327	398	67442	379	2242	302
天润曲轴有限公司	Tianrun Crank Axle Limited Company	51217	400	76869	354	1873	360
山东新华医疗器械集团	Shandong Xinhua Medical Equipment Group	50917	402	97933	306	1821	366
山东金宇建筑集团	Shandong Jinyu Construction Group	50457	403	61539	399	3402	196

9

企业景气调查资料

Investigation Material of Business Climate

编辑单位：统计监测处
编　　委：仝义贵
责任编辑：李东法　游海涛
校　　对：李东法　游海涛
电　　话：86197913

Editorial Unit: the Statistical Monitoring Office
Editorial Board: Tong Yigui 、
Executive Editor-in-Chief: Li Dongfa You Haitao
Proofreader: Li Dongfa You Haitao
Telephone: 86197913

简要说明

企业景气调查是适应我国社会主义市场经济发展的新形势，借鉴市场经济国家的成功经验而建立起来的一项新的统计调查制度。它是通过对样本企业的企业家定期进行意向性问卷调查，并根据企业家对企业经营状况及宏观经济形势的判断和预期来编制景气指数。企业景气指数不仅能够及时反映企业经营状况，当前宏观经济运行态势，而且能够预测未来经济发展趋势。

景气指数又称景气度，它是对企业景气调查中的定性指标通过定量方法加工汇总，综合反映某一特定调查群体或某一社会经济现象所处的状态或发展趋势的一种指标。景气指数的数值范围介于0～200之间，100为景气指数的临界值；当景气指数大于100时，表明经济状况趋于上升或改善，处于景气状态；当景气指数小于100时，表明经济状况趋于下降或恶化，处于不景气状况。

景气指数根据其调查对象和反映内容的不同，有宏观和微观等不同分类。企业家信心指数是根据企业家对宏观经济环境信心预期的判断而编制的；企业景气指数是根据企业家对本企业当前综合经营状况的判断和未来发展的预计而编制的指数。

企业景气调查包括工业；建筑业；交通运输、仓储和邮政业；批发和零售业；房地产业；信息传输、计算机服务和软件业；住宿和餐饮业；社会服务业八大行业门类。我省于1998年正式开展企业景气调查，2006年全省每季度进行调查的企业近3000家，基本涵盖全部大型及特大型企业、省重点企业、上市公司和部分中小企业，具有较强的代表性。

Brief Introduction

Business survey is a new statistical investigation system that adopts new situation of our country socialist market economy development and profits from the success experience of the market economy countries. It is through carrying on the intent questionnaire survey regularly to the sample enterprise's entrepreneurs, according to judgment and anticipation of the enterprise management condition and the macroscopic economic situation for the entrepreneurs to establish the booming index. Not only the enterprise booming index can reflect the enterprise management condition promptly, current macroscopic economical movement situation, but also will be able to forecast the future economy trend of development.

The booming index is called the scenery extent, it is the target that is compiled to stationary index through the quantitative method processing in the enterprise booming investigation and reflects some specific investigation community or locating condition or development trend of some social economy phenomenon. The value scope of booming index is situated between 0～200, 100 is marginal value of booming index; When the booming index is bigger than 100, indicates the financial circumstance tends to the rise or the improvement, is at the booming condition; When the booming index is smaller than 100, indicates the financial circumstance tends to the drop or the worsening, is in not the booming condition.

According to its investigation object and the difference of reflection content, the booming index has the different classifications of macroscopic and microscopic. The confidence index of entrepreneurs is established according to the judgment of entrepreneurs to the macroscopic economic environment confidence anticipation; the business climate index is established according to judgment of current comprehensive management condition and the estimate of future development.

Business survey includes industry; construction; transportation, storage and telecommunications; whole sale and retail trade; real estate; information transmission, computer services and software; hotel and catering services; social service eight big profession classes. Shandong business survey was developed in 1998 officially, there are 3000 investigation enterprises that are carried on each quarter in entire province in 2005, cover completely large-scale and the extra large type enterprise, the province key enterprises, listed company and the partial small and medium -sized enterprises basically, have the strong representation.

9-1 企业景气调查主要景气指数
Main Climate Index of Business Climate Investigation

时间序列	Time	企业家信心指数 Confidence Index of Entrepreneurs	企业景气指数 Business Climate Index	生产总量景气指数 Climate Index of Total Output	盈利（亏损）变化景气指数 Climate Index of Profit (loss) Variation	流动资金景气指数 Climate Index of Liquid Capital	货款拖欠景气指数 Climate Index on Overdue Obligations to Suppliers	劳动力需求景气指数 Climate Index of Labor Demand	固定资产投资景气指数 Climate Index on Fixed Assets Investment
1999年1季度	Quarter1, 1999	110.69	118.07	102.65	84.82	46.06	92.93	69.20	96.13
1999年2季度	Quarter2, 1999	109.79	121.19	114.96	90.28	44.38	96.01	74.96	103.98
1999年3季度	Quarter3, 1999	111.56	119.33	115.08	86.99	45.22	96.66	77.22	106.78
1999年4季度	Quarter4, 1999	113.56	122.35	122.69	99.60	46.16	95.58	76.55	108.45
2000年1季度	Quarter1, 2000	122.14	117.15	111.61	91.58	56.74	108.81	86.19	106.98
2000年2季度	Quarter2, 2000	127.86	128.18	135.27	100.98	59.22	106.01	94.37	117.66
2000年3季度	Quarter3, 2000	128.53	125.36	124.53	100.57	61.88	103.71	94.33	119.48
2000年4季度	Quarter4, 2000	128.05	125.22	125.76	103.96	63.86	107.34	90.32	117.28
2001年1季度	Quarter1, 2001	133.64	129.24	116.28	102.10	72.93	110.13	91.00	107.62
2001年2季度	Quarter2, 2001	133.93	137.68	127.66	117.59	73.17	106.53	99.94	119.25
2001年3季度	Quarter3, 2001	129.86	131.59	124.77	106.61	72.97	107.41	96.98	115.56
2001年4季度	Quarter4, 2001	130.27	130.76	120.66	109.44	71.15	107.75	92.82	113.75
2002年1季度	Quarter1, 2002	130.04	127.64	115.03	99.60	75.48	111.26	92.49	108.31
2002年2季度	Quarter2, 2002	133.94	134.21	133.52	122.07	76.20	107.31	99.47	117.67
2002年3季度	Quarter3, 2002	130.44	136.07	132.44	120.42	76.88	105.56	101.43	123.83
2002年4季度	Quarter4, 2002	135.95	136.39	128.91	120.61	76.35	108.53	98.76	121.83
2003年1季度	Quarter1, 2003	139.29	133.85	120.20	114.26	83.20	108.99	105.53	114.24
2003年2季度	Quarter2, 2003	124.77	121.57	118.35	106.17	82.96	106.88	98.73	124.57
2003年3季度	Quarter3, 2003	136.36	139.60	133.00	121.46	86.53	106.59	106.72	125.10
2003年4季度	Quarter4, 2003	138.83	139.64	133.24	122.35	87.28	108.27	105.24	122.71
2004年1季度	Quarter1, 2004	142.12	140.26	129.73	124.35	82.45	112.27	112.75	117.72

9-1 续表 1 continued

时间序列	Time	企业家信心指数 Confidence Index of Entrepreneurs	企业景气指数 Business Climate Index	生产总量景气指数 Climate Index of Total Output	盈利（亏损）变化景气指数 Climate Index of Profit (loss) Variation	流动资金景气指数 Climate Index of Liquid Capital	货款拖欠景气指数 Climate Index on Overdue Obligations to Suppliers	劳动力需求景气指数 Climate Index of Labor Demand	固定资产投资景气指数 Climate Index on Fixed Assets Investment
2004年2季度	Quarter2, 2004	137.40	138.18	134.90	123.30	82.77	110.72	113.41	121.74
2004年3季度	Quarter3, 2004	135.05	137.97	133.47	123.98	81.13	104.87	113.17	119.65
2004年4季度	Quarter4, 2004	137.72	139.99	132.58	125.50	76.88	106.48	108.77	122.26
2005年1季度	Quarter1, 2005	140.79	139.58	117.10	119.63	80.21	111.78	111.15	110.63
2005年2季度	Quarter2, 2005	137.34	140.81	133.21	123.11	76.84	107.41	116.66	123.41
2005年3季度	Quarter3, 2005	133.03	137.76	131.77	121.41	79.89	107.74	116.63	123.32
2005年4季度	Quarter4, 2005	132.95	139.33	133.17	118.74	79.48	107.15	112.78	121.76
2006年1季度	Quarter1, 2006	140.58	141.92	118.85	118.67	82.34	108.58	117.83	108.97
2006年2季度	Quarter2, 2006	141.54	144.75	136.48	129.09	87.14	109.33	118.94	121.33
2006年3季度	Quarter3, 2006	140.35	143.37	132.89	126.91	84.37	106.50	118.97	125.33
2006年4季度	Quarter4, 2006	143.06	145.85	134.74	130.29	89.07	109.87	115.47	120.00

9-2 工业企业景气调查主要景气指数
Main Climate Index of Industrial Enterprise Climate Investigation

时间序列	Time	企业家信心指数 Confidence Index of Entrepreneurs	企业景气指数 Business Climate Index	生产总量景气指数 Climate Index of Total Output	盈利（亏损）变化景气指数 Climate Index of Profit (loss) Variation	流动资金景气指数 Climate Index of Liquid Capital	货款拖欠景气指数 Climate Index on Overdue Obligations to Suppliers	劳动力需求景气指数 Climate Index of Labor Demand	固定资产投资景气指数 Climate Index on Fixed Assets Investment
1999年1季度	Quarter1, 1999	112.44	123.91	106.45	87.68	42.85	93.25	70.94	96.73
1999年2季度	Quarter2, 1999	111.28	125.96	119.82	95.40	43.91	98.20	73.67	107.59
1999年3季度	Quarter3, 1999	113.77	123.60	118.27	89.03	43.77	97.52	75.40	111.87
1999年4季度	Quarter4, 1999	117.25	130.12	131.17	108.64	46.56	97.61	78.47	113.40
2000年1季度	Quarter1, 2000	125.91	126.41	120.49	96.29	57.36	112.39	91.56	108.90
2000年2季度	Quarter2, 2000	131.34	135.11	142.25	105.52	62.09	109.56	95.16	120.38
2000年3季度	Quarter3, 2000	131.67	130.92	127.66	102.59	65.98	108.01	93.93	122.55

9-2 续表 1 continued

时间序列	Time	企业家信心指数 Confidence Index of Entrepreneurs	企业景气指数 Business Climate Index	生产总量景气指数 Climate Index of Total Output	盈利（亏损）变化景气指数 Climate Index of Profit (loss) Variation	流动资金景气指数 Climate Index of Liquid Capital	货款拖欠景气指数 Climate Index on Overdue Obligations to Suppliers	劳动力需求景气指数 Climate Index of Labor Demand	固定资产投资景气指数 Climate Index on Fixed Assets Investment
2000年4季度	Quarter4, 2000	130.93	133.18	131.18	109.20	67.25	112.21	91.72	120.62
2001年1季度	Quarter1, 2001	136.41	139.88	126.00	104.31	79.51	114.79	95.76	109.50
2001年2季度	Quarter2, 2001	137.74	144.06	129.20	119.87	80.54	111.73	99.68	123.12
2001年3季度	Quarter3, 2001	129.62	134.90	123.22	105.16	78.50	112.08	92.41	114.87
2001年4季度	Quarter4, 2001	131.63	134.04	122.77	110.98	74.61	111.21	93.31	114.77
2002年1季度	Quarter1, 2002	129.13	130.39	119.92	100.48	80.35	113.87	95.51	110.94
2002年2季度	Quarter2, 2002	136.04	138.68	136.32	127.32	84.51	112.11	97.63	119.34
2002年3季度	Quarter3, 2002	129.20	141.32	134.81	121.06	81.76	109.46	100.62	129.56
2002年4季度	Quarter4, 2002	138.31	142.81	131.71	123.26	81.89	112.44	102.04	129.17
2003年1季度	Quarter1, 2003	142.58	140.95	129.65	120.88	92.35	112.42	113.84	119.27
2003年2季度	Quarter2, 2003	130.16	130.70	127.97	115.48	92.11	112.97	105.06	129.80
2003年3季度	Quarter3, 2003	139.20	146.52	131.79	128.14	94.07	113.82	107.39	128.13
2003年4季度	Quarter4, 2003	141.89	147.54	138.02	133.32	94.45	117.14	112.49	128.55
2004年1季度	Quarter1, 2004	144.55	147.08	138.28	130.10	89.89	115.07	119.80	122.62
2004年2季度	Quarter2, 2004	136.40	140.44	137.68	122.00	88.09	116.84	114.91	125.59
2004年3季度	Quarter3, 2004	133.21	141.20	134.99	125.93	85.96	108.33	116.40	125.09
2004年4季度	Quarter4, 2004	137.23	143.11	135.89	128.72	78.34	109.84	114.38	127.93
2005年1季度	Quarter1, 2005	139.37	142.66	121.75	125.23	81.85	113.90	117.95	114.78
2005年2季度	Quarter2, 2005	136.11	142.92	135.23	127.51	77.11	110.81	119.12	129.06
2005年3季度	Quarter3, 2005	130.29	139.95	131.80	124.07	80.93	112.15	118.14	127.76
2005年4季度	Quarter4, 2005	130.90	141.99	135.80	119.99	81.65	110.38	117.30	125.37
2006年1季度	Quarter1, 2006	139.43	145.81	121.30	122.18	83.53	108.09	125.97	110.34
2006年2季度	Quarter2, 2006	141.82	148.25	139.05	134.17	90.26	113.00	121.74	125.15
2006年3季度	Quarter3, 2006	140.14	146.50	134.54	131.72	85.28	109.95	121.61	129.33
2006年4季度	Quarter4, 2006	143.51	149.68	139.04	136.20	92.13	115.20	119.45	125.44

9-3 交通运输、仓储和邮政业企业景气调查主要景气指数
Main Climate Index of Transportation, Storage and Telecommunications Enterprise Climate Investigation

时间序列	Time	企业家信心指数 Confidence Index of Entrepreneurs	企业景气指数 Business Climate Index	生产总量景气指数 Climate Index of Total Output	盈利（亏损）变化景气指数 Climate Index of Profit (loss) Variation	流动资金景气指数 Climate Index of Liquid Capital	货款拖欠景气指数 Climate Index on Overdue Obligations to Suppliers	劳动力需求景气指数 Climate Index of Labor Demand	固定资产投资景气指数 Climate Index on Fixed Assets Investment
1999年1季度	Quarter1, 1999	85.48	91.28	96.73	70.06	36.77	83.19	45.05	106.51
1999年2季度	Quarter2, 1999	98.01	105.11	100.78	81.74	40.28	83.07	49.25	106.34
1999年3季度	Quarter3, 1999	101.21	109.94	116.30	96.05	44.99	93.76	60.58	103.31
1999年4季度	Quarter4, 1999	109.31	102.59	117.67	86.63	41.61	82.64	60.84	105.01
2000年1季度	Quarter1, 2000	109.77	99.26	112.55	84.76	50.68	98.47	64.04	114.65
2000年2季度	Quarter2, 2000	120.11	108.51	132.55	97.02	48.62	102.55	72.21	128.58
2000年3季度	Quarter3, 2000	124.16	102.11	114.49	86.26	48.71	88.61	81.54	125.76
2000年4季度	Quarter4, 2000	123.46	106.95	124.59	89.83	54.05	101.71	71.92	119.48
2001年1季度	Quarter1, 2001	121.99	109.85	102.76	107.82	53.25	95.55	77.24	109.75
2001年2季度	Quarter2, 2001	126.09	122.99	124.99	119.03	53.09	97.79	80.12	120.84
2001年3季度	Quarter3, 2001	133.24	129.17	127.03	115.22	59.43	101.27	97.55	130.69
2001年4季度	Quarter4, 2001	129.93	123.90	111.97	99.34	61.44	109.37	86.08	124.32
2002年1季度	Quarter1, 2002	129.35	126.58	121.83	105.89	61.80	106.51	84.46	105.69
2002年2季度	Quarter2, 2002	126.02	126.69	131.41	117.44	56.71	106.01	79.78	112.20
2002年3季度	Quarter3, 2002	132.04	126.37	125.33	124.84	59.50	108.58	88.95	118.83
2002年4季度	Quarter4, 2002	130.78	118.90	124.10	107.36	55.49	112.60	87.97	117.99
2003年1季度	Quarter1, 2003	122.02	116.48	107.69	91.48	55.00	109.95	87.30	110.45
2003年2季度	Quarter2, 2003	94.17	83.98	72.95	70.37	50.20	92.21	72.69	115.02
2003年3季度	Quarter3, 2003	125.16	126.90	129.80	114.25	62.44	102.75	94.87	131.59
2003年4季度	Quarter4, 2003	123.19	120.14	111.56	103.47	59.09	94.59	87.35	122.40
2004年1季度	Quarter1, 2004	127.85	126.98	123.82	113.46	50.84	104.74	94.77	114.12
2004年2季度	Quarter2, 2004	138.58	129.64	126.79	126.66	67.15	98.52	93.63	118.51
2004年3季度	Quarter3, 2004	134.54	128.45	123.44	115.83	64.47	102.61	90.89	119.35

9-3 续表 1 continued

时间序列	Time	企业家信心指数 Confidence Index of Entrepreneurs	企业景气指数 Business Climate Index	生产总量景气指数 Climate Index of Total Output	盈利（亏损）变化景气指数 Climate Index of Profit (loss) Variation	流动资金景气指数 Climate Index of Liquid Capital	货款拖欠景气指数 Climate Index on Overdue Obligations to Suppliers	劳动力需求景气指数 Climate Index of Labor Demand	固定资产投资景气指数 Climate Index on Fixed Assets Investment
2004年4季度	Quarter4, 2004	134.36	127.23	121.94	112.51	60.55	103.59	94.11	122.97
2005年1季度	Quarter1, 2005	131.63	125.36	116.55	112.96	64.62	96.69	95.87	105.71
2005年2季度	Quarter2, 2005	131.70	134.97	118.33	116.07	69.24	102.60	93.26	111.87
2005年3季度	Quarter3, 2005	126.60	124.59	117.95	103.92	65.50	99.16	100.39	110.92
2005年4季度	Quarter4, 2005	126.54	123.03	119.99	91.12	65.83	101.04	101.87	116.44
2006年1季度	Quarter1, 2006	134.44	122.90	121.75	114.17	64.20	98.52	98.43	114.50
2006年2季度	Quarter2, 2006	135.67	125.20	127.26	113.67	68.13	94.81	95.78	115.96
2006年3季度	Quarter3, 2006	132.39	130.39	124.49	113.35	74.98	100.41	103.16	131.77
2006年4季度	Quarter4, 2006	131.45	130.76	116.73	111.57	71.46	97.18	101.02	112.20

9-4 批发和零售业企业景气调查主要景气指数 Main Climate Index of Wholesale, Retail Trade and Cater Services Enterprise Climate Investigation

时间序列	Time	企业家信心指数 Confidence Index of Entrepreneurs	企业景气指数 Business Climate Index	生产总量景气指数 Climate Index of Total Output	盈利（亏损）变化景气指数 Climate Index of Profit (loss) Variation	流动资金景气指数 Climate Index of Liquid Capital	货款拖欠景气指数 Climate Index on Overdue Obligations to Suppliers	劳动力需求景气指数 Climate Index of Labor Demand	固定资产投资景气指数 Climate Index on Fixed Assets Investment
1999年1季度	Quarter1, 1999	101.01	109.46	92.85	80.28	49.40	119.58	58.80	79.30
1999年2季度	Quarter2, 1999	95.42	107.36	87.05	71.39	44.73	121.60	63.22	81.53
1999年3季度	Quarter3, 1999	97.18	104.44	90.76	67.43	45.63	123.30	61.54	85.47
1999年4季度	Quarter4, 1999	90.62	103.94	97.19	74.41	49.00	119.80	60.33	89.16
2000年1季度	Quarter1, 2000	102.34	114.98	111.60	93.32	59.14	130.10	79.57	100.50
2000年2季度	Quarter2, 2000	106.82	113.43	104.32	85.44	56.56	131.42	79.03	104.05
2000年3季度	Quarter3, 2000	111.85	114.42	105.22	89.73	60.73	128.50	79.29	104.35
2000年4季度	Quarter4, 2000	110.66	110.68	108.30	86.17	56.70	125.04	78.80	107.86
2001年1季度	Quarter1, 2001	116.65	119.10	113.99	103.81	67.52	120.82	82.06	100.56

9-4 续表 1 continued

时间序列	Time	企业家信心指数 Confidence Index of Entrepreneurs	企业景气指数 Business Climate Index	生产总量景气指数 Climate Index of Total Output	盈利（亏损）变化景气指数 Climate Index of Profit (loss) Variation	流动资金景气指数 Climate Index of Liquid Capital	货款拖欠景气指数 Climate Index on Overdue Obligations to Suppliers	劳动力需求景气指数 Climate Index of Labor Demand	固定资产投资景气指数 Climate Index on Fixed Assets Investment
2001年2季度	Quarter2, 2001	113.31	117.77	96.37	91.30	70.56	123.19	75.98	106.29
2001年3季度	Quarter3, 2001	110.59	109.94	105.06	88.99	68.72	122.37	80.14	106.92
2001年4季度	Quarter4, 2001	111.74	111.13	101.98	93.71	71.18	123.49	79.40	108.45
2002年1季度	Quarter1, 2002	118.62	119.38	107.46	101.50	71.78	117.90	80.56	96.81
2002年2季度	Quarter2, 2002	115.23	113.26	100.06	92.36	60.81	114.03	79.29	103.31
2002年3季度	Quarter3, 2002	114.91	113.45	115.20	108.47	69.54	110.18	84.21	102.56
2002年4季度	Quarter4, 2002	120.84	117.24	123.29	114.65	69.93	115.90	84.87	101.37
2003年1季度	Quarter1, 2003	126.68	120.99	113.70	112.82	80.32	120.32	89.16	106.66
2003年2季度	Quarter2, 2003	117.58	114.12	96.00	100.60	78.49	122.11	83.00	112.28
2003年3季度	Quarter3, 2003	121.34	123.22	120.26	108.58	72.83	113.37	96.63	105.17
2003年4季度	Quarter4, 2003	124.46	130.93	130.10	122.77	73.60	118.80	99.55	105.46
2004年1季度	Quarter1, 2004	131.61	128.99	123.14	118.75	80.90	117.51	95.78	101.99
2004年2季度	Quarter2, 2004	124.43	128.56	101.31	111.97	77.09	120.04	89.13	103.25
2004年3季度	Quarter3, 2004	126.44	125.97	118.90	113.70	76.28	121.12	96.76	102.88
2004年4季度	Quarter4, 2004	128.80	129.98	127.37	116.67	83.95	117.78	96.46	105.38
2005年1季度	Quarter1, 2005	141.85	140.05	123.39	115.85	86.27	118.07	101.37	93.94
2005年2季度	Quarter2, 2005	136.87	134.34	118.82	111.21	92.19	117.32	90.98	104.23
2005年3季度	Quarter3, 2005	135.61	129.82	126.83	114.04	87.56	115.08	102.54	109.22
2005年4季度	Quarter4, 2005	133.80	132.25	124.00	123.01	86.30	121.15	97.25	108.77
2006年1季度	Quarter1, 2006	142.14	140.57	123.21	122.84	97.74	123.43	105.26	101.19
2006年2季度	Quarter2, 2006	135.36	135.85	113.16	122.22	94.88	120.36	98.46	105.94
2006年3季度	Quarter3, 2006	137.10	139.85	119.96	121.21	95.32	116.49	105.49	112.59
2006年4季度	Quarter4, 2006	142.34	144.77	130.95	125.30	95.11	111.97	105.96	107.73

9-5 房地产业企业景气调查主要景气指数
Main Climate Index of Real Estate Enterprise Climate Investigation

时间序列	Time	企业家信心指数 Confidence Index of Entrepreneurs	企业景气指数 Business Climate Index	生产总量景气指数 Climate Index of Total Output	盈利（亏损）变化景气指数 Climate Index of Profit (loss) Variation	流动资金景气指数 Climate Index of Liquid Capital	货款拖欠景气指数 Climate Index on Overdue Obligations to Suppliers	劳动力需求景气指数 Climate Index of Labor Demand	固定资产投资景气指数 Climate Index on Fixed Assets Investment
1999年1季度	Quarter1, 1999	138.54	127.60	120.09	94.74	66.45	112.86	91.63	117.19
1999年2季度	Quarter2, 1999	127.24	123.92	125.51	80.25	54.64	122.13	91.60	105.75
1999年3季度	Quarter3, 1999	132.58	123.24	123.67	81.75	58.12	118.67	90.90	109.60
1999年4季度	Quarter4, 1999	135.61	125.91	127.34	88.09	49.75	114.50	88.46	105.57
2000年1季度	Quarter1, 2000	140.31	109.23	86.42	90.81	62.23	113.57	91.54	95.41
2000年2季度	Quarter2, 2000	137.84	128.34	133.82	99.89	66.54	111.84	101.10	116.94
2000年3季度	Quarter3, 2000	137.75	126.98	126.75	101.57	63.22	118.99	98.25	115.51
2000年4季度	Quarter4, 2000	151.79	130.47	132.73	107.99	75.20	118.13	97.17	120.81
2001年1季度	Quarter1, 2001	154.41	126.27	105.93	104.25	62.23	117.56	98.21	95.01
2001年2季度	Quarter2, 2001	149.76	130.60	136.45	117.01	60.97	115.20	112.22	111.19
2001年3季度	Quarter3, 2001	153.12	137.88	145.85	115.82	67.83	123.01	109.82	121.06
2001年4季度	Quarter4, 2001	155.33	138.01	135.77	126.51	72.59	115.40	93.63	115.33
2002年1季度	Quarter1, 2002	147.15	132.35	110.81	110.19	76.82	124.36	87.75	109.04
2002年2季度	Quarter2, 2002	150.38	128.85	134.51	116.91	68.02	109.61	101.22	118.27
2002年3季度	Quarter3, 2002	153.51	130.68	136.31	114.02	77.52	111.16	102.68	121.86
2002年4季度	Quarter4, 2002	149.27	133.16	129.70	116.06	74.92	119.26	95.58	119.35
2003年1季度	Quarter1, 2003	152.24	137.88	105.77	119.78	77.31	121.43	101.37	109.09
2003年2季度	Quarter2, 2003	143.46	147.58	138.76	126.86	85.91	123.31	104.89	122.74
2003年3季度	Quarter3, 2003	150.00	141.56	137.15	125.88	82.10	114.03	107.71	128.60
2003年4季度	Quarter4, 2003	154.34	146.88	133.49	128.79	84.25	115.05	100.03	117.16
2004年1季度	Quarter1, 2004	165.01	140.78	114.01	134.31	93.12	129.88	113.18	115.33

9-5 续表 1 continued

时间序列	Time	企业家信心指数 Confidence Index of Entrepreneurs	企业景气指数 Business Climate Index	生产总量景气指数 Climate Index of Total Output	盈利（亏损）变化景气指数 Climate Index of Profit (loss) Variation	流动资金景气指数 Climate Index of Liquid Capital	货款拖欠景气指数 Climate Index on Overdue Obligations to Suppliers	劳动力需求景气指数 Climate Index of Labor Demand	固定资产投资景气指数 Climate Index on Fixed Assets Investment
2004年2季度	Quarter2, 2004	160.76	146.24	132.22	129.78	92.66	124.93	113.40	130.97
2004年3季度	Quarter3, 2004	162.03	144.18	140.21	127.68	89.25	124.46	117.05	121.01
2004年4季度	Quarter4, 2004	165.06	146.89	130.84	135.34	86.55	127.74	98.84	118.59
2005年1季度	Quarter1, 2005	158.82	142.12	99.80	118.54	82.67	127.56	103.24	109.72
2005年2季度	Quarter2, 2005	140.23	137.31	123.57	108.69	78.73	120.11	107.43	114.50
2005年3季度	Quarter3, 2005	137.76	131.11	120.93	117.68	77.81	128.80	108.27	119.41
2005年4季度	Quarter4, 2005	140.14	141.87	125.75	122.59	76.51	119.31	96.86	119.59
2006年1季度	Quarter1, 2006	150.52	144.89	111.71	114.34	78.82	118.92	109.32	112.30
2006年2季度	Quarter2, 2006	146.05	142.03	128.16	126.07	81.81	118.59	112.40	118.29
2006年3季度	Quarter3, 2006	147.81	135.25	123.46	121.71	72.84	117.07	110.28	110.93
2006年4季度	Quarter4, 2006	147.64	137.73	122.85	123.22	78.49	121.69	103.08	111.17

9-6 社会服务业企业景气调查主要景气指数
Main Climate Index of Social Services Enterprise Climate Investigation

时间序列	Time	企业家信心指数 Confidence Index of Entrepreneurs	企业景气指数 Business Climate Index	生产总量景气指数 Climate Index of Total Output	盈利（亏损）变化景气指数 Climate Index of Profit (loss) Variation	流动资金景气指数 Climate Index of Liquid Capital	货款拖欠景气指数 Climate Index on Overdue Obligations to Suppliers	劳动力需求景气指数 Climate Index of Labor Demand	固定资产投资景气指数 Climate Index on Fixed Assets Investment
1999年1季度	Quarter1, 1999	122.86	93.94	88.24	77.14	61.76	67.74	97.14	106.45
1999年2季度	Quarter2, 1999	128.57	125.71	122.86	102.94	57.14	69.70	94.29	111.76
1999年3季度	Quarter3, 1999	103.03	100.00	81.82	60.61	56.25	73.33	75.76	93.33
1999年4季度	Quarter4, 1999	111.76	115.15	111.76	82.35	58.82	70.59	82.35	109.09
2000年1季度	Quarter1, 2000	129.41	100.00	85.29	69.70	60.61	96.43	91.18	112.50
2000年2季度	Quarter2, 2000	135.29	102.94	81.82	66.67	62.50	82.76	82.35	103.13
2000年3季度	Quarter3, 2000	123.53	106.06	97.06	87.88	59.38	93.33	93.94	106.25

9-6 续表 1 continued

时间序列	Time	企业家信心指数 Confidence Index of Entrepreneurs	企业景气指数 Business Climate Index	生产总量景气指数 Climate Index of Total Output	盈利（亏损）变化景气指数 Climate Index of Profit (loss) Variation	流动资金景气指数 Climate Index of Liquid Capital	货款拖欠景气指数 Climate Index on Overdue Obligations to Suppliers	劳动力需求景气指数 Climate Index of Labor Demand	固定资产投资景气指数 Climate Index on Fixed Assets Investment
2000年4季度	Quarter4, 2000	135.29	87.50	63.64	75.76	56.25	100.00	79.41	100.00
2001年1季度	Quarter1, 2001	148.15	109.68	114.52	103.23	77.05	107.47	85.25	111.83
2001年2季度	Quarter2, 2001	157.53	127.87	142.47	127.42	82.26	83.91	112.02	97.81
2001年3季度	Quarter3, 2001	151.61	134.43	140.32	120.43	89.25	80.23	121.31	109.14
2001年4季度	Quarter4, 2001	138.17	125.14	110.22	96.77	75.81	92.66	91.26	120.77
2002年1季度	Quarter1, 2002	141.38	122.21	118.68	94.11	85.57	105.88	102.67	111.04
2002年2季度	Quarter2, 2002	149.28	137.17	143.30	119.13	102.94	100.26	120.43	119.72
2002年3季度	Quarter3, 2002	161.69	141.68	121.01	114.03	89.32	113.53	117.81	131.26
2002年4季度	Quarter4, 2002	145.69	124.76	92.31	93.62	85.32	120.14	86.49	112.61
2003年1季度	Quarter1, 2003	150.78	124.44	120.35	100.58	74.12	99.63	108.99	106.93
2003年2季度	Quarter2, 2003	90.92	54.69	58.44	47.98	55.45	87.72	56.18	99.83
2003年3季度	Quarter3, 2003	134.67	119.82	136.16	126.72	72.88	95.14	124.47	100.30
2003年4季度	Quarter4, 2003	142.28	109.71	94.76	88.74	74.02	102.12	82.93	103.99
2004年1季度	Quarter1, 2004	135.59	125.46	110.47	103.44	68.84	109.24	105.79	111.58
2004年2季度	Quarter2, 2004	142.41	130.92	132.65	128.42	80.20	95.45	118.63	121.20
2004年3季度	Quarter3, 2004	145.86	137.96	127.28	119.42	75.73	93.27	114.15	110.59
2004年4季度	Quarter4, 2004	133.73	122.00	97.62	88.34	67.67	97.82	90.93	109.54
2005年1季度	Quarter1, 2005	139.98	128.92	122.90	101.40	76.37	111.85	105.88	108.89
2005年2季度	Quarter2, 2005	149.16	137.30	133.84	116.07	59.13	99.78	112.85	109.39
2005年3季度	Quarter3, 2005	158.00	139.31	147.03	128.70	79.18	88.13	122.49	124.16
2005年4季度	Quarter4, 2005	143.13	128.84	113.28	111.74	71.96	91.16	92.55	116.89
2006年1季度	Quarter1, 2006	146.45	121.29	115.78	92.54	72.86	104.22	100.00	111.24
2006年2季度	Quarter2, 2006	144.87	146.72	137.55	119.83	88.67	86.25	124.46	109.00
2006年3季度	Quarter3, 2006	142.81	136.29	131.12	107.63	83.90	89.58	115.70	122.27
2006年4季度	Quarter4, 2006	146.67	138.68	117.34	110.32	79.67	100.73	104.05	112.86

9-7 信息传输、计算机服务和软件业企业景气调查主要景气指数
Main Climate Index of Information Transmission, Computer Services and Software Enterprise Climate Investigation

时间序列	Time	企业家信心指数 Confidence Index of Entrepreneurs	企业景气指数 Business Climate Index	生产总量景气指数 Climate Index of Total Output	盈利（亏损）变化景气指数 Climate Index of Profit (loss) Variation	流动资金景气指数 Climate Index of Liquid Capital	货款拖欠景气指数 Climate Index on Overdue Obligations to Suppliers	劳动力需求景气指数 Climate Index of Labor Demand	固定资产投资景气指数 Climate Index on Fixed Assets Investment
1999年1季度	Quarter1, 1999	147.83	147.83	160.87	116.85	39.33	66.85	104.40	142.61
1999年2季度	Quarter2, 1999	149.52	162.56	179.95	136.47	43.67	81.82	99.96	146.87
1999年3季度	Quarter3, 1999	149.52	145.17	147.83	109.63	50.68	86.36	82.61	162.56
1999年4季度	Quarter4, 1999	147.22	156.32	167.18	128.68	54.65	81.86	95.45	158.09
2000年1季度	Quarter1, 2000	157.80	164.14	164.39	125.58	75.57	99.53	105.08	157.12
2000年2季度	Quarter2, 2000	168.06	174.87	179.65	131.04	74.34	111.05	82.82	176.31
2000年3季度	Quarter3, 2000	162.90	169.04	187.54	147.80	61.40	84.68	92.34	164.08
2000年4季度	Quarter4, 2000	158.64	164.78	173.99	133.14	72.39	99.57	105.31	150.97
2001年1季度	Quarter1, 2001	176.16	170.51	160.19	124.21	97.80	119.41	99.11	160.05
2001年2季度	Quarter2, 2001	159.99	161.18	158.60	120.71	65.31	96.91	95.48	115.83
2001年3季度	Quarter3, 2001	153.30	154.70	157.38	99.80	75.21	114.71	116.94	118.47
2001年4季度	Quarter4, 2001	158.58	156.47	162.65	112.96	79.91	104.23	103.04	92.40
2002年1季度	Quarter1, 2002	147.34	157.64	155.06	124.33	85.61	98.20	75.16	73.31
2002年2季度	Quarter2, 2002	137.84	144.56	148.35	116.66	71.07	123.06	82.01	111.01
2002年3季度	Quarter3, 2002	147.35	151.33	155.78	127.76	83.50	105.20	97.86	105.17
2002年4季度	Quarter4, 2002	150.99	157.78	156.04	138.92	78.56	115.74	102.44	120.40
2003年1季度	Quarter1, 2003	159.48	158.28	155.20	136.81	96.83	107.82	123.58	117.35
2003年2季度	Quarter2, 2003	151.37	151.73	145.59	124.95	108.13	117.51	98.40	139.64
2003年3季度	Quarter3, 2003	149.98	160.70	162.68	129.68	104.96	102.31	117.06	132.02
2003年4季度	Quarter4, 2003	152.81	162.57	164.04	138.40	99.02	114.34	119.26	146.15
2004年1季度	Quarter1, 2004	156.49	157.41	147.36	128.98	106.03	98.89	93.25	113.13
2004年2季度	Quarter2, 2004	157.05	160.92	152.96	123.92	120.33	108.89	104.69	119.60
2004年3季度	Quarter3, 2004	166.57	161.49	161.54	146.95	120.02	108.30	110.42	115.10

9-7 续表 1 continued

时间序列	Time	企业家信心指数 Confidence Index of Entrepreneurs	企业景气指数 Business Climate Index	生产总量景气指数 Climate Index of Total Output	盈利（亏损）变化景气指数 Climate Index of Profit (loss) Variation	流动资金景气指数 Climate Index of Liquid Capital	货款拖欠景气指数 Climate Index on Overdue Obligations to Suppliers	劳动力需求景气指数 Climate Index of Labor Demand	固定资产投资景气指数 Climate Index on Fixed Assets Investment
2004年4季度	Quarter4, 2004	160.30	152.42	156.56	139.60	115.53	105.39	102.49	133.29
2005年1季度	Quarter1, 2005	167.15	163.66	145.41	140.66	122.32	118.29	116.86	121.05
2005年2季度	Quarter2, 2005	163.25	171.01	156.62	127.22	114.37	114.89	116.82	124.88
2005年3季度	Quarter3, 2005	159.94	163.56	161.64	138.69	117.57	101.87	120.21	121.92
2005年4季度	Quarter4, 2005	153.73	162.57	157.94	138.93	116.86	106.11	105.17	126.34
2006年1季度	Quarter1, 2006	158.62	158.93	144.83	128.38	119.23	126.27	113.15	130.71
2006年2季度	Quarter2, 2006	151.57	153.16	148.74	138.94	109.16	118.14	114.95	142.00
2006年3季度	Quarter3, 2006	154.98	154.05	162.67	124.65	126.20	100.00	108.35	117.77
2006年4季度	Quarter4, 2006	156.75	153.78	145.08	122.62	111.96	112.46	116.91	110.56

9-8 住宿和餐饮业企业景气调查主要景气指数
Main Climate Index of Hotel and Catering Services Enterprise Climate Investigation

时间序列	Time	企业家信心指数 Confidence Index of Entrepreneurs	企业景气指数 Business Climate Index	生产总量景气指数 Climate Index of Total Output	盈利（亏损）变化景气指数 Climate Index of Profit (loss) Variation	流动资金景气指数 Climate Index of Liquid Capital	货款拖欠景气指数 Climate Index on Overdue Obligations to Suppliers	劳动力需求景气指数 Climate Index of Labor Demand	固定资产投资景气指数 Climate Index on Fixed Assets Investment
1999年1季度	Quarter1, 1999	94.75	91.79	85.43	56.05	47.24	87.52	64.64	90.97
1999年2季度	Quarter2, 1999	93.12	95.85	92.82	80.88	57.10	67.66	72.96	87.20
1999年3季度	Quarter3, 1999	108.38	110.71	112.39	84.95	57.63	64.73	92.84	99.27
1999年4季度	Quarter4, 1999	100.38	101.27	95.96	69.79	51.60	74.51	67.14	92.42
2000年1季度	Quarter1, 2000	117.96	86.43	81.38	72.67	53.35	90.91	76.65	106.06
2000年2季度	Quarter2, 2000	128.59	124.91	139.94	102.42	61.78	95.98	102.07	104.13
2000年3季度	Quarter3, 2000	132.00	112.14	112.72	100.11	57.15	87.75	102.76	114.03
2000年4季度	Quarter4, 2000	118.79	89.94	94.38	77.53	55.20	91.81	79.04	97.77
2001年1季度	Quarter1, 2001	132.84	102.58	98.71	86.02	70.56	80.12	88.22	101.23

9-8 续表 1 continued

时间序列	Time	企业家信心指数 Confidence Index of Entrepreneurs	企业景气指数 Business Climate Index	生产总量景气指数 Climate Index of Total Output	盈利（亏损）变化景气指数 Climate Index of Profit (loss) Variation	流动资金景气指数 Climate Index of Liquid Capital	货款拖欠景气指数 Climate Index on Overdue Obligations to Suppliers	劳动力需求景气指数 Climate Index of Labor Demand	固定资产投资景气指数 Climate Index on Fixed Assets Investment
2001年2季度	Quarter2, 2001	125.85	122.56	119.79	117.64	74.95	87.63	104.13	112.16
2001年3季度	Quarter3, 2001	135.37	135.26	133.64	121.63	81.90	87.31	109.63	118.14
2001年4季度	Quarter4, 2001	121.28	114.64	95.55	87.75	75.73	92.68	88.05	106.27
2002年1季度	Quarter1, 2002	125.89	108.79	90.91	85.07	66.37	97.37	94.07	102.15
2002年2季度	Quarter2, 2002	125.00	114.14	114.28	103.77	75.30	83.32	108.11	116.10
2002年3季度	Quarter3, 2002	130.88	127.54	133.49	119.01	81.86	88.89	107.88	121.16
2002年4季度	Quarter4, 2002	132.46	125.58	113.45	103.13	83.52	97.44	96.20	110.39
2003年1季度	Quarter1, 2003	133.55	129.23	107.91	100.00	80.45	85.16	104.43	99.18
2003年2季度	Quarter2, 2003	64.30	37.56	23.78	25.42	47.28	98.88	39.26	83.86
2003年3季度	Quarter3, 2003	137.62	128.54	142.95	122.93	79.49	84.34	124.59	118.60
2003年4季度	Quarter4, 2003	138.13	127.10	116.34	113.55	78.31	88.98	99.55	112.55
2004年1季度	Quarter1, 2004	142.38	122.22	107.00	109.35	83.54	100.45	105.15	111.06
2004年2季度	Quarter2, 2004	144.69	140.36	130.46	138.52	88.14	86.00	116.69	110.98
2004年3季度	Quarter3, 2004	149.14	144.03	136.66	139.15	91.62	80.53	117.14	112.30
2004年4季度	Quarter4, 2004	146.38	140.12	113.69	125.49	96.22	99.58	102.36	105.69
2005年1季度	Quarter1, 2005	139.40	127.97	105.61	98.27	79.82	87.37	108.42	102.93
2005年2季度	Quarter2, 2005	140.82	130.49	122.81	117.96	85.38	79.77	119.53	108.76
2005年3季度	Quarter3, 2005	143.90	147.29	138.32	128.93	97.85	91.07	121.45	103.24
2005年4季度	Quarter4, 2005	136.22	134.44	105.80	105.34	90.08	86.05	100.52	111.28
2006年1季度	Quarter1, 2006	141.01	139.34	122.72	119.09	84.41	95.03	113.12	110.77
2006年2季度	Quarter2, 2006	139.98	135.99	132.60	122.85	94.37	86.43	117.45	112.31
2006年3季度	Quarter3, 2006	147.35	138.12	132.80	125.97	93.47	81.05	118.64	107.85
2006年4季度	Quarter4, 2006	149.14	140.96	114.66	114.73	91.21	95.19	108.61	105.99

9-9 企业家信心指数（2006年）
Confidence Index of Entrepreneurs (2006)

类别	Classification	一季度 Quarter1	二季度 Quarter2	三季度 Quarter3	四季度 Quarter4
总体状况	**Overall**	**140.58**	**141.54**	**140.35**	**143.06**
一、按行业门类分	**Grouped by Sector**				
（一）工业	Industry	139.43	141.82	140.14	143.51
采矿业	Mining	174.87	168.52	174.38	173.72
制造业	Manufacturing	135.41	139.02	136.70	140.28
电力、燃气及水的生产和供应业	Production and Supply of Electricity	138.82	139.46	135.31	143.27
（二）建筑业	Construction	142.29	146.96	142.89	141.24
房屋和土木工程建筑业	Construction of Buildings and Civil Engineering	142.70	148.67	144.89	142.16
建筑安装业	Building Installation	144.60	138.58	141.36	136.91
建筑装饰业	Building Decoration	116.67	100.00	83.33	116.67
其他建筑业	Other Constrction	200.00	200.00	100.00	200.00
（三）交通运输、仓储及邮政业	Transportation, Storage and Telecommunications	134.44	135.67	132.39	131.45
铁路运输业	Railway Transport	150.00	150.00	150.00	150.00
道路运输业	Road Transport	132.39	132.61	128.37	127.40
城市公共交通业	Urban Public Transport	129.67	116.66	140.78	113.00
水上运输业	Water Transport	116.69	127.22	121.95	121.95
航空运输业	Air Transport	200.00	200.00	200.00	200.00
管道运输业	Transport Via Pipelines	100.00	100.00	100.00	100.00
装卸搬运和其他运输服务业	Loading, Unloading and Other Transport Services	100.00	100.00	125.00	150.00
仓储业	Storage	150.00	150.00	100.00	100.00
邮政业	Post	130.38	130.38	115.90	134.23
（四）批发和零售业	Wholesale and Retail Trade	142.14	135.25	136.99	142.21
批发业	Wholesale Trade	141.43	129.92	133.60	141.20
零售业	Retail Trade	143.13	140.69	140.99	143.45
（五）房地产业	Real Estate	150.52	146.05	147.81	147.64
（六）社会服务业	Social Services	146.45	144.87	142.81	146.67
租赁业	Leasing	144.44	150.00	150.00	162.50
商务服务业	Business Services	155.94	147.98	146.30	149.27
环境资源管理业	Environmental Management	100.00	166.67	166.67	166.67
公共设施管理业	Management of Public Facilities	154.55	150.00	150.00	150.00
居民服务业	Services to Household	60.00	80.00	60.00	80.00
其他服务业	Other Services	100.00	100.00	100.00	100.00
（七）信息传输、计算机服务和软件业	Information Transmission, Computer Services and Software	158.62	151.57	154.98	156.75
信息传输业	Information Transmission	161.39	150.90	155.53	159.64
计算机服务业	Computer Services	155.56	166.67	155.56	144.44
软件业	Software	150.00	142.77	153.85	153.85
（八）住宿和餐饮业	Hotel and Catering Services	141.01	140.22	147.64	149.44
住宿业	Hotels	138.32	143.61	149.17	153.36
餐饮业	Catering Services	144.85	134.12	143.86	137.84
二、按企业登记注册类型分	**by Status of Registration**				

9-9 续表 1 continued

类别	Classification	一季度 Quarter1	二季度 Quarter2	三季度 Quarter3	四季度 Quarter4
国有企业	State-owned Enterprises	138.10	137.33	135.48	145.36
集体企业	Collective-owned Enterprises	132.04	134.48	138.00	134.35
股份合作企业	Cooperative Enterprises	134.07	129.06	131.53	127.48
联营企业	Joint Ownership Enterprises	150.63	142.51	153.58	140.27
有限责任公司	Limited Liability Corporations	146.37	142.40	140.94	142.95
股份有限公司	Share-holding Corporations Limited	138.74	148.33	148.14	153.75
私营企业	Private Enterprises	140.94	145.50	135.22	136.92
其它内资企业	Other Domestic Funded	150.42	135.04	127.35	135.04
外商及港、澳、台投资企业	Enterprises with Funds from Foreign Contry, Hongkong, Macao and Taiwan	145.45	142.94	144.20	143.11
三、按企业规模分	**Grouped by Size of Enterprises**				
大型及以上	Large-sized and Higher	147.13	155.68	152.96	163.97
中型	Medium-sized	139.53	136.38	134.27	133.91
小型	Small-sized	130.96	127.32	130.62	128.84
四、特殊分组	**Special Group**				
省重点企业	Province key Enterprises	151.55	163.16	157.70	172.64
乡镇企业	Township Enterprises	158.58	154.86	154.71	154.62
上市公司	Companies Listed in Stock Exchange	138.87	155.64	152.28	161.90
国有控股企业	Stateholding Enterprises	142.80	142.60	138.93	148.44

9-10 企业景气指数（2006年）
Business Climate Index (2006)

类别	Classification	一季度 Quarter1	二季度 Quarter2	三季度 Quarter3	四季度 Quarter4
总体状况	**Overall**	**141.92**	**144.75**	**143.37**	**145.85**
一、按行业门类分	**Grouped by Sector**				
（一）工业	Industry	145.81	148.25	146.50	149.68
采矿业	Mining	171.77	171.52	168.95	171.32
制造业	Manufacturing	143.57	146.09	144.59	148.20
电力、燃气及水的生产和供应业	Production and Supply of Electricity	143.34	147.59	143.17	145.12
（二）建筑业	Construction	128.67	144.13	137.64	133.27
房屋和土木工程建筑业	Construction of Buildings and Civil Engineering	129.80	146.54	139.36	134.17
建筑安装业	Building Installation	129.65	115.65	123.34	127.20
建筑装饰业	Building Decoration	100.00	100.00	83.33	83.33
其他建筑业	Other Constrction	100.00	200.00	200.00	200.00
（三）交通运输、仓储及邮政业	Transportation, Storage and Telecommunications	122.90	125.20	130.39	130.76
铁路运输业	Railway Transport	100.00	200.00	150.00	150.00
道路运输业	Road Transport	120.71	121.03	118.66	121.05
城市公共交通业	Urban Public Transport	100.00	103.65	127.78	116.67
水上运输业	Water Transport	135.67	116.69	126.02	130.78
航空运输业	Air Transport	200.00	122.28	200.00	145.78

9-10 续表 1 continued

类别	Classification	一季度 Quarter1	二季度 Quarter2	三季度 Quarter3	四季度 Quarter4
管道运输业	Transport Via Pipelines	100.00	100.00	100.00	100.00
装卸搬运和其他运输服务业	Loading, Unloading and Other Transport Services	125.00	125.00	150.00	175.00
仓储业	Storage	100.00	125.00	175.00	125.00
邮政业	Post	121.95	126.02	119.21	137.79
（四）批发和零售业	Wholesale and Retail Trade	140.57	136.04	140.04	144.63
批发业	Wholesale Trade	137.92	134.35	134.36	137.97
零售业	Retail Trade	143.72	137.26	146.01	151.77
（五）房地产业	Real Estate	144.89	142.03	135.25	137.73
（六）社会服务业	Social Services	121.29	146.72	136.29	138.68
租赁业	Leasing	100.00	150.00	125.00	125.00
商务服务业	Business Services	124.80	152.98	145.08	155.95
环境资源管理业	Environmental Management	133.33	100.00	100.00	100.00
公共设施管理业	Management of Public Facilities	131.82	145.45	140.91	127.27
居民服务业	Services to Household	80.00	120.00	80.00	80.00
其他服务业	Other Services	100.00	100.00	100.00	100.00
（七）信息传输、计算机服务和软件业	Information Transmission, Computer Services and Software	158.93	153.16	154.05	153.78
信息传输业	Information Transmission	164.04	159.62	159.09	162.07
计算机服务业	Computer Services	177.78	144.44	144.44	111.11
软件业	Software	124.57	127.39	138.46	146.15
（八）住宿和餐饮业	Hotel and Catering Services	139.34	135.61	137.75	141.21
住宿业	Hotels	136.34	135.80	134.70	141.59
餐饮业	Catering Services	144.51	136.50	143.86	138.79
二、按企业登记注册类型分	**by Status of Registration**				
国有企业	State-owned Enterprises	134.57	139.12	135.29	141.62
集体企业	Collective-owned Enterprises	129.98	123.67	125.31	129.91
股份合作企业	Cooperative Enterprises	117.30	127.69	119.50	131.90
联营企业	Joint Ownership Enterprises	125.34	135.39	143.52	139.30
有限责任公司	Limited Liability Corporations	142.76	145.05	142.43	144.53
股份有限公司	Share-holding Corporations Limited	157.58	161.09	162.74	164.21
私营企业	Private Enterprises	149.45	143.59	137.43	138.58
其它内资企业	Other Domestic Funded	176.92	176.92	153.85	146.15
外商及港、澳、台投资企业	Enterprises with Funds from Foreign Contry, Hongkong, Macao and Taiwan	146.63	144.75	144.61	146.77
三、按企业规模分	**Grouped by Size of Enterprises**				
大型及以上	Large-sized and Higher	166.97	172.37	167.47	175.73
中型	Medium-sized	131.81	133.67	132.09	134.36
小型	Small-sized	122.54	121.89	124.61	120.80
四、特殊分组	**Special Group**				
省重点企业	Province key Enterprises	174.07	179.53	173.04	185.82
乡镇企业	Township Enterprises	152.83	155.60	154.04	149.38
上市公司	Companies Listed in Stock Exchange	173.36	179.88	173.25	179.21
国有控股企业	Stateholding Enterprises	142.62	147.92	142.57	148.60

9-11 工业企业生产总量景气指数（2006年）
Climate Index on Total Output of Industrial Enterprise (2006)

类别	Classification	一季度 Quarter1	二季度 Quarter2	三季度 Quarter3	四季度 Quarter4
工业企业总体状况	**Overall**	**121.30**	**139.05**	**134.54**	**139.04**
一、按行业门类分	**Grouped by Sector**				
采矿业	Mining	103.07	149.35	110.75	131.71
制造业	Manufacturing	124.29	138.51	135.77	140.84
电力、燃气及水的生产和供应业	Production and Supply of Electricity	115.94	136.18	150.97	137.20
二、按企业登记注册类型分	**by Status of Registration**				
国有企业	State-owned Enterprises	113.78	141.41	143.85	145.45
集体企业	Collective-owned Enterprises	122.69	143.09	150.75	122.72
股份合作企业	Cooperative Enterprises	105.60	116.73	94.60	135.06
联营企业	Joint Ownership Enterprises	89.37	185.71	144.69	100.00
有限责任公司	Limited Liability Corporations	116.59	134.77	127.89	137.26
股份有限公司	Share-holding Corporations Limited	134.98	150.88	141.96	149.99
私营企业	Private Enterprises	132.52	134.79	124.96	119.85
其它内资企业	Other Domestic Funded	122.22	144.44	133.33	144.44
外商及港、澳、台投资企业	Enterprises with Funds from Foreign Contry, Hongkong, Macao and Taiwan	116.87	126.48	128.23	124.76
三、按企业规模分	**Grouped by Size of Enterprises**				
大型及以上	Large-sized and Higher	126.71	154.51	146.38	158.67
中型	Medium-sized	120.36	132.03	125.98	128.71
小型	Small-sized	111.54	118.99	124.93	116.12

9-12 工业企业盈利（亏损）变化景气指数（2006年）
Climate Index on Profit(loss) Variation of Industrial Enterprise (2006)

类别	Classification	一季度 Quarter1	二季度 Quarter2	三季度 Quarter3	四季度 Quarter4
工业企业总体状况	**Overall**	**122.18**	**134.17**	**131.72**	**136.20**
一、按行业门类分	**Grouped by Sector**				
采矿业	Mining	142.84	151.20	154.12	137.90
制造业	Manufacturing	120.13	133.86	128.16	138.30
电力、燃气及水的生产和供应业	Production and Supply of Electricity	115.99	122.11	136.43	125.23
二、按企业登记注册类型分	**by Status of Registration**				
国有企业	State-owned Enterprises	104.69	128.80	114.96	142.28
集体企业	Collective-owned Enterprises	115.99	106.39	127.16	114.01
股份合作企业	Cooperative Enterprises	94.64	108.60	107.71	105.85
联营企业	Joint Ownership Enterprises	99.43	116.11	87.54	114.29
有限责任公司	Limited Liability Corporations	119.17	133.24	131.79	138.32
股份有限公司	Share-holding Corporations Limited	145.16	149.67	146.17	143.65
私营企业	Private Enterprises	120.71	122.08	123.83	121.11
其它内资企业	Other Domestic Funded	155.56	133.33	133.33	122.22

9-12　续表 1 continued

类别	Classification	一季度 Quarter1	二季度 Quarter2	三季度 Quarter3	四季度 Quarter4
外商及港、澳、台投资企业	Enterprises with Funds from Foreign Contry, Hongkong, Macao and Taiwan	115.46	133.40	128.81	125.50
三、按企业规模分	**Grouped by Size of Enterprises**				
大型及以上	Large-sized and Higher	131.82	154.18	144.85	156.96
中型	Medium-sized	117.77	124.39	124.84	125.94
小型	Small-sized	109.76	109.50	116.32	110.75

9-13　工业企业流动资金景气指数（2006年）
Climate Index on Liquid Capital of Industrial Enterprise (2006)

类别	Classification	一季度 Quarter1	二季度 Quarter2	三季度 Quarter3	四季度 Quarter4
工业企业总体状况	**Overall**	**83.53**	**90.26**	**85.28**	**92.13**
一、按行业门类分	**Grouped by Sector**				
采矿业	Mining	114.35	131.04	132.20	134.78
制造业	Manufacturing	79.18	84.47	78.98	87.49
电力、燃气及水的生产和供应业	Production and Supply of Electricity	92.14	95.91	87.70	88.21
二、按企业登记注册类型分	**by Status of Registration**				
国有企业	State-owned Enterprises	81.66	76.70	72.74	100.35
集体企业	Collective-owned Enterprises	61.44	71.13	63.08	71.51
股份合作企业	Cooperative Enterprises	77.08	74.88	77.86	72.43
联营企业	Joint Ownership Enterprises	42.86	57.14	44.69	44.69
有限责任公司	Limited Liability Corporations	82.45	87.13	85.11	88.32
股份有限公司	Share-holding Corporations Limited	90.94	108.60	100.13	104.47
私营企业	Private Enterprises	89.91	97.09	76.58	76.95
其它内资企业	Other Domestic Funded	72.83	93.01	74.88	93.01
外商及港、澳、台投资企业	Enterprises with Funds from Foreign Contry, Hongkong, Macao and Taiwan	91.38	91.36	95.19	92.25
三、按企业规模分	**Grouped by Size of Enterprises**				
大型及以上	Large-sized and Higher	95.43	108.58	101.38	118.80
中型	Medium-sized	75.77	78.05	74.35	74.55
小型	Small-sized	72.49	73.59	70.92	67.46

9-14　工业企业货款拖欠景气指数（2006年）
Climate Index on Overdue Obligations to Suppliers about Industrial Enterprise (2006)

类别	Classification	一季度 Quarter1	二季度 Quarter2	三季度 Quarter3	四季度 Quarter4
工业企业总体状况	**Overall**	**108.09**	**113.00**	**109.95**	**115.20**
一、按行业门类分	**Grouped by Sector**				
采矿业	Mining	98.49	118.20	107.10	101.96
制造业	Manufacturing	109.29	112.01	110.14	116.46

9-14 续表 1 continued

类别	Classification	一季度 Quarter1	二季度 Quarter2	三季度 Quarter3	四季度 Quarter4
电力、燃气及水的生产和供应业	Production and Supply of Electricity	113.98	120.08	112.37	112.99
二、按企业登记注册类型分	**by Status of Registration**				
国有企业	State-owned Enterprises	101.62	107.22	106.34	110.66
集体企业	Collective-owned Enterprises	101.52	98.23	106.89	98.05
股份合作企业	Cooperative Enterprises	94.14	95.28	101.99	93.39
联营企业	Joint Ownership Enterprises	116.68	114.29	101.26	73.26
有限责任公司	Limited Liability Corporations	101.54	111.51	107.88	117.93
股份有限公司	Share-holding Corporations Limited	126.29	128.03	116.25	126.19
私营企业	Private Enterprises	112.42	117.46	102.55	108.26
其它内资企业	Other Domestic Funded	79.83	124.27	74.88	151.44
外商及港、澳、台投资企业	Enterprises with Funds from Foreign Contry, Hongkong, Macao and Taiwan	99.10	101.07	113.47	95.76
三、按企业规模分	**Grouped by Size of Enterprises**				
大型及以上	Large-sized and Higher	112.46	122.85	113.23	127.25
中型	Medium-sized	105.65	105.86	111.11	110.60
小型	Small-sized	103.25	105.04	100.89	97.91

9-15 工业企业劳动力需求景气指数（2006年）
Climate Index on Labor Demand of Industrial Enterprise (2006)

类别	Classification	一季度 Quarter1	二季度 Quarter2	三季度 Quarter3	四季度 Quarter4
工业企业总体状况	**Overall**	**125.97**	**121.74**	**121.61**	**119.45**
一、按行业门类分	**Grouped by Sector**				
采矿业	Mining	112.53	106.66	109.97	113.41
制造业	Manufacturing	131.65	127.09	125.47	122.34
电力、燃气及水的生产和供应业	Production and Supply of Electricity	99.09	94.17	103.62	102.82
二、按企业登记注册类型分	**by Status of Registration**				
国有企业	State-owned Enterprises	106.33	100.98	104.96	102.76
集体企业	Collective-owned Enterprises	127.00	115.36	118.11	105.42
股份合作企业	Cooperative Enterprises	113.73	110.43	114.16	101.33
联营企业	Joint Ownership Enterprises	171.43	172.00	142.29	114.29
有限责任公司	Limited Liability Corporations	124.24	124.40	119.84	119.27
股份有限公司	Share-holding Corporations Limited	138.66	130.64	133.18	131.62
私营企业	Private Enterprises	133.22	119.76	125.65	123.27
其它内资企业	Other Domestic Funded	166.67	128.39	113.16	90.94
外商及港、澳、台投资企业	Enterprises with Funds from Foreign Contry, Hongkong, Macao and Taiwan	133.20	135.30	126.20	133.88
三、按企业规模分	**Grouped by Size of Enterprises**				
大型及以上	Large-sized and Higher	130.36	126.48	125.25	129.16
中型	Medium-sized	124.72	122.44	121.41	115.01
小型	Small-sized	118.93	110.39	114.24	106.87

9-16 工业企业固定资产投资景气指数（2006年）
Climate Index on Fixed Assets Investment of Industrial Enterprise (2006)

类别	Classification	一季度 Quarter1	二季度 Quarter2	三季度 Quarter3	四季度 Quarter4
工业企业总体状况	**Overall**	**110.34**	**125.15**	**129.33**	**125.44**
一、按行业门类分	**Grouped by Sector**				
采矿业	Mining	106.27	126.91	150.65	137.27
制造业	Manufacturing	110.81	124.16	125.05	122.23
电力、燃气及水的生产和供应业	Production and Supply of Electricity	115.69	133.82	143.04	137.27
二、按企业登记注册类型分	**by Status of Registration**				
国有企业	State-owned Enterprises	97.35	116.40	116.10	112.51
集体企业	Collective-owned Enterprises	117.64	122.48	135.35	118.59
股份合作企业	Cooperative Enterprises	110.13	105.32	122.07	118.41
联营企业	Joint Ownership Enterprises	114.85	114.85	142.86	112.46
有限责任公司	Limited Liability Corporations	108.64	124.15	122.15	118.72
股份有限公司	Share-holding Corporations Limited	119.64	139.85	155.60	153.22
私营企业	Private Enterprises	111.31	115.75	118.77	110.52
其它内资企业	Other Domestic Funded	140.32	97.10	76.95	111.11
外商及港、澳、台投资企业	Enterprises with Funds from Foreign Contry, Hongkong, Macao and Taiwan	108.84	122.96	115.88	114.76
三、按企业规模分	**Grouped by Size of Enterprises**				
大型及以上	Large-sized and Higher	109.49	136.53	145.16	142.84
中型	Medium-sized	114.38	121.46	122.88	116.80
小型	Small-sized	104.73	107.72	107.42	104.18

9-17 工业企业产品订货景气指数（2006年）
Climate Index on Product Ordering of Industrial Enterprise (2006)

类别	Classification	一季度 Quarter1	二季度 Quarter2	三季度 Quarter3	四季度 Quarter4
工业企业总体状况	**Overall**	**129.79**	**134.03**	**131.04**	**137.12**
一、按行业门类分	**Grouped by Sector**				
采矿业	Mining	115.39	119.79	120.98	134.44
制造业	Manufacturing	134.09	137.89	133.95	140.63
电力、燃气及水的生产和供应业	Production and Supply of Electricity	111.75	118.24	120.54	116.03
二、按企业登记注册类型分	**by Status of Registration**				
国有企业	State-owned Enterprises	123.02	131.95	114.50	133.63
集体企业	Collective-owned Enterprises	128.69	131.94	138.89	121.02
股份合作企业	Cooperative Enterprises	111.65	115.18	94.15	106.95
联营企业	Joint Ownership Enterprises	102.40	142.86	130.97	114.29
有限责任公司	Limited Liability Corporations	131.15	133.73	130.92	138.85
股份有限公司	Share-holding Corporations Limited	137.86	141.11	146.82	150.59
私营企业	Private Enterprises	128.64	128.55	126.26	126.27
其它内资企业	Other Domestic Funded	144.44	144.44	133.33	155.56

9-17 续表 1 continued

类别	Classification	一季度 Quarter1	二季度 Quarter2	三季度 Quarter3	四季度 Quarter4
外商及港、澳、台投资企业	Enterprises with Funds from Foreign Contry, Hongkong, Macao and Taiwan	130.69	135.45	132.08	131.55
三、按企业规模分	**Grouped by Size of Enterprises**				
大型及以上	Large-sized and Higher	141.93	147.14	142.15	155.33
中型	Medium-sized	123.86	127.68	125.33	127.75
小型	Small-sized	114.71	117.33	117.58	115.20

9-18 工业企业科技创新景气指数（2006年）
Climate Index on Technology Innovation of Industrial Enterprise (2006)

类别	Classification	一季度 Quarter1	二季度 Quarter2	三季度 Quarter3	四季度 Quarter4
工业企业总体状况	**Overall**	**125.57**	**124.97**	**130.37**	**126.13**
一、按行业门类分	**Grouped by Sector**				
采矿业	Mining	131.97	138.59	145.73	134.48
制造业	Manufacturing	126.25	124.04	129.73	125.36
电力、燃气及水的生产和供应业	Production and Supply of Electricity	112.04	118.63	120.44	122.00
二、按企业登记注册类型分	**by Status of Registration**				
国有企业	State-owned Enterprises	111.35	111.40	112.99	120.73
集体企业	Collective-owned Enterprises	122.18	119.34	132.16	117.79
股份合作企业	Cooperative Enterprises	110.06	120.52	120.73	97.27
联营企业	Joint Ownership Enterprises	147.20	131.20	133.33	131.20
有限责任公司	Limited Liability Corporations	125.69	127.55	129.82	126.37
股份有限公司	Share-holding Corporations Limited	144.33	137.15	149.49	140.20
私营企业	Private Enterprises	107.14	114.93	124.00	118.20
其它内资企业	Other Domestic Funded	138.28	138.28	117.28	149.39
外商及港、澳、台投资企业	Enterprises with Funds from Foreign Contry, Hongkong, Macao and Taiwan	116.15	114.08	118.15	111.52
三、按企业规模分	**Grouped by Size of Enterprises**				
大型及以上	Large-sized and Higher	142.18	139.17	150.21	148.04
中型	Medium-sized	115.97	118.08	118.97	114.12
小型	Small-sized	107.06	106.71	107.76	100.92

9-19 建筑业企业建筑工程量景气指数（2006年）
Climate Index on Total Output of Construction Enterprises (2006)

类别	Classification	一季度 Quarter1	二季度 Quarter2	三季度 Quarter3	四季度 Quarter4
建筑业企业总体状况	**Overall**	**85.88**	**155.35**	**141.46**	**134.80**
一、按行业门类分	**Grouped by Sector**				
房屋和土木工程建筑业	Construction of Buildings and Civil Engineering	85.79	159.34	143.14	133.26
建筑安装业	Building Installation	108.83	116.54	124.37	130.29

9-19 续表 1 continued

类别	Classification	一季度 Quarter1	二季度 Quarter2	三季度 Quarter3	四季度 Quarter4
建筑装饰业	Building Decoration	66.67	83.33	100.00	150.00
二、按企业登记注册类型分	by Status of Registration				
国有企业	State-owned Enterprises	74.43	151.93	140.45	139.02
集体企业	Collective-owned Enterprises	102.34	157.27	156.68	119.67
股份合作企业	Cooperative Enterprises	80.00	180.00	120.00	180.00
联营企业	Joint Ownership Enterprises	100.00	100.00	100.00	100.00
有限责任公司	Limited Liability Corporations	74.38	158.37	145.19	135.38
股份有限公司	Share-holding Corporations Limited	123.55	156.42	132.83	139.80
私营企业	Private Enterprises	148.78	183.33	148.78	150.00
其它内资企业	Other Domestic Funded	100.00	100.00	100.00	100.00
外商及港、澳、台投资企业	Enterprises with Funds from Foreign Contry, Hongkong, Macao and Taiwan	0.00	100.00	100.00	100.00
三、按企业规模分	Grouped by Size of Enterprises				
大型及以上	Large-sized and Higher	58.48	155.87	143.96	151.75
中型	Medium-sized	101.92	165.38	140.38	134.62
小型	Small-sized	114.29	147.14	138.57	110.00

9-20 建筑业企业盈利（亏损）变化景气指数（2006年）
Climate Index on Profit(loss) Variation of Construction Enterprises (2006)

类别	Classification	一季度 Quarter1	二季度 Quarter2	三季度 Quarter3	四季度 Quarter4
建筑业企业总体状况	**Overall**	**95.25**	**111.31**	**114.38**	**119.12**
一、按行业门类分	**Grouped by Sector**				
房屋和土木工程建筑业	Construction of Buildings and Civil Engineering	97.16	112.18	113.65	117.08
建筑安装业	Building Installation	91.97	118.72	128.21	141.73
建筑装饰业	Building Decoration	100.00	83.33	116.67	133.33
二、按企业登记注册类型分	**by Status of Registration**				
国有企业	State-owned Enterprises	95.36	119.30	123.48	137.53
集体企业	Collective-owned Enterprises	111.48	106.07	123.73	127.55
股份合作企业	Cooperative Enterprises	80.00	120.00	100.00	100.00
联营企业	Joint Ownership Enterprises	100.00	100.00	100.00	100.00
有限责任公司	Limited Liability Corporations	91.98	117.98	110.50	111.90
股份有限公司	Share-holding Corporations Limited	90.93	88.61	117.37	105.56
私营企业	Private Enterprises	132.11	150.00	150.00	110.69
其它内资企业	Other Domestic Funded	100.00	100.00	100.00	100.00
外商及港、澳、台投资企业	Enterprises with Funds from Foreign Contry, Hongkong, Macao and Taiwan	100.00	100.00	100.00	100.00
三、按企业规模分	**Grouped by Size of Enterprises**				
大型及以上	Large-sized and Higher	80.89	104.32	117.81	119.44
中型	Medium-sized	101.92	128.85	109.62	128.85
小型	Small-sized	111.43	108.57	112.86	111.43

9-21 建筑业企业流动资金景气指数（2006年）
Climate Index on Liquid Capital of Construction Enterprises (2006)

类别	Classification	一季度 Quarter1	二季度 Quarter2	三季度 Quarter3	四季度 Quarter4
建筑业企业总体状况	**Overall**	**63.33**	**60.03**	**63.45**	**72.28**
一、按行业门类分	**Grouped by Sector**				
房屋和土木工程建筑业	Construction of Buildings and Civil Engineering	64.84	61.14	61.65	71.34
建筑安装业	Building Installation	42.60	44.40	84.46	61.49
建筑装饰业	Building Decoration	50.00	50.00	83.33	83.33
二、按企业登记注册类型分	**by Status of Registration**				
国有企业	State-owned Enterprises	53.82	47.08	59.22	64.40
集体企业	Collective-owned Enterprises	72.90	63.39	57.76	67.52
股份合作企业	Cooperative Enterprises	80.00	80.00	60.00	60.00
联营企业	Joint Ownership Enterprises	100.00	100.00	100.00	100.00
有限责任公司	Limited Liability Corporations	61.42	62.80	53.53	65.09
股份有限公司	Share-holding Corporations Limited	80.63	80.98	110.13	107.10
私营企业	Private Enterprises	82.11	65.45	100.00	80.34
其它内资企业	Other Domestic Funded	100.00	100.00	100.00	100.00
外商及港、澳、台投资企业	Enterprises with Funds from Foreign Contry, Hongkong, Macao and Taiwan	0.00	0.00	100.00	100.00
三、按企业规模分	**Grouped by Size of Enterprises**				
大型及以上	Large-sized and Higher	51.93	50.55	56.08	70.51
中型	Medium-sized	55.77	57.69	71.15	73.08
小型	Small-sized	85.71	75.71	68.57	74.29

9-22 建筑业企业货款拖欠景气指数（2006年）
Climate Index on Overdue Obligations to Suppliers about Construction Enterprises (2006)

类别	Classification	一季度 Quarter1	二季度 Quarter2	三季度 Quarter3	四季度 Quarter4
建筑业企业总体状况	**Overall**	**98.52**	**84.05**	**78.30**	**71.77**
一、按行业门类分	**Grouped by Sector**				
房屋和土木工程建筑业	Construction of Buildings and Civil Engineering	97.33	81.45	75.97	68.39
建筑安装业	Building Installation	127.16	110.19	105.67	114.04
建筑装饰业	Building Decoration	50.00	100.00	116.67	100.00
二、按企业登记注册类型分	**by Status of Registration**				
国有企业	State-owned Enterprises	92.66	62.36	76.34	55.54
集体企业	Collective-owned Enterprises	106.26	75.64	65.14	79.40
股份合作企业	Cooperative Enterprises	120.00	60.00	100.00	40.00
联营企业	Joint Ownership Enterprises	100.00	100.00	100.00	100.00
有限责任公司	Limited Liability Corporations	91.66	85.43	74.86	69.04
股份有限公司	Share-holding Corporations Limited	114.56	117.80	85.42	81.23
私营企业	Private Enterprises	144.02	166.67	165.45	183.33
其它内资企业	Other Domestic Funded	100.00	100.00	100.00	100.00

9-22 续表 1 continued

类别	Classification	一季度 Quarter1	二季度 Quarter2	三季度 Quarter3	四季度 Quarter4
外商及港、澳、台投资企业	Enterprises with Funds from Foreign Contry, Hongkong, Macao and Taiwan	0.00	100.00	100.00	100.00
三、按企业规模分	**Grouped by Size of Enterprises**				
大型及以上	Large-sized and Higher	98.71	87.49	76.88	59.70
中型	Medium-sized	103.85	71.15	69.23	67.31
小型	Small-sized	94.29	88.57	87.14	92.86

9-23 建筑业企业劳动力需求景气指数（2006年）
Climate Index on Labor Demand of Construction Enterprises (2006)

类别	Classification	一季度 Quarter1	二季度 Quarter2	三季度 Quarter3	四季度 Quarter4
建筑业企业总体状况	**Overall**	**92.56**	**144.54**	**135.74**	**118.03**
一、按行业门类分	**Grouped by Sector**				
房屋和土木工程建筑业	Construction of Buildings and Civil Engineering	92.06	147.47	137.30	120.21
建筑安装业	Building Installation	85.60	123.25	128.89	61.74
建筑装饰业	Building Decoration	116.67	66.67	66.67	83.33
二、按企业登记注册类型分	**by Status of Registration**				
国有企业	State-owned Enterprises	68.07	151.84	133.93	128.00
集体企业	Collective-owned Enterprises	110.18	155.83	146.71	98.24
股份合作企业	Cooperative Enterprises	100.00	180.00	180.00	140.00
联营企业	Joint Ownership Enterprises	100.00	100.00	100.00	100.00
有限责任公司	Limited Liability Corporations	98.00	146.78	144.12	118.25
股份有限公司	Share-holding Corporations Limited	102.79	111.20	98.31	105.31
私营企业	Private Enterprises	133.33	129.12	166.67	97.56
其它内资企业	Other Domestic Funded	100.00	100.00	100.00	100.00
外商及港、澳、台投资企业	Enterprises with Funds from Foreign Contry, Hongkong, Macao and Taiwan	100.00	100.00	0.00	100.00
三、按企业规模分	**Grouped by Size of Enterprises**				
大型及以上	Large-sized and Higher	63.36	148.75	145.07	129.67
中型	Medium-sized	109.62	148.08	125.00	107.69
小型	Small-sized	122.86	135.71	130.00	108.57

9-24 建筑业企业固定资产投资景气指数（2006年）
Climate Index on Fixed Assets Investment of Construction Enterprises (2006)

类别	Classification	一季度 Quarter1	二季度 Quarter2	三季度 Quarter3	四季度 Quarter4
建筑业企业总体状况	**Overall**	**93.63**	**116.89**	**117.34**	**108.85**
一、按行业门类分	**Grouped by Sector**				
房屋和土木工程建筑业	Construction of Buildings and Civil Engineering	93.99	117.08	117.05	108.68
建筑安装业	Building Installation	58.63	110.99	112.96	116.83
建筑装饰业	Building Decoration	116.67	116.67	133.33	83.33

9-24 续表 1 continued

类别	Classification	一季度 Quarter1	二季度 Quarter2	三季度 Quarter3	四季度 Quarter4
二、按企业登记注册类型分	**by Status of Registration**				
国有企业	State-owned Enterprises	79.54	109.13	92.30	106.82
集体企业	Collective-owned Enterprises	101.82	133.27	134.29	106.36
股份合作企业	Cooperative Enterprises	80.00	120.00	80.00	140.00
联营企业	Joint Ownership Enterprises	100.00	100.00	100.00	100.00
有限责任公司	Limited Liability Corporations	106.80	131.57	121.30	101.99
股份有限公司	Share-holding Corporations Limited	73.17	87.17	153.52	128.79
私营企业	Private Enterprises	100.00	116.67	77.35	98.78
其它内资企业	Other Domestic Funded	100.00	100.00	100.00	100.00
外商及港、澳、台投资企业	Enterprises with Funds from Foreign Contry, Hongkong, Macao and Taiwan	100.00	100.00	100.00	100.00
三、按企业规模分	**Grouped by Size of Enterprises**				
大型及以上	Large-sized and Higher	79.30	114.56	121.38	120.29
中型	Medium-sized	96.15	119.23	109.62	90.38
小型	Small-sized	112.86	118.57	117.14	105.71

9-25 交通运输、仓储及邮政业企业业务需求量景气指数（2006年）
Climate Index on Business Demand of Transportation, Storage and Telecommunications (2006)

类别	Classification	一季度 Quarter1	二季度 Quarter2	三季度 Quarter3	四季度 Quarter4
交通运输、仓储及邮政业企业总体状况	**Overall**	**121.75**	**127.26**	**124.49**	**116.73**
一、按主要行业门类分	**Grouped by Sector**				
铁路运输业	Railway Transport	100.00	150.00	150.00	100.00
道路运输业	Road Transport	116.93	120.35	112.10	115.23
城市公共交通业	Urban Public Transport	103.65	124.12	129.68	92.54
水上运输业	Water Transport	115.03	142.79	144.53	127.22
航空运输业	Air Transport	200.00	161.14	200.00	52.69
管道运输业	Transport Via Pipelines	100.00	100.00	100.00	100.00
装卸搬运和其他运输服务业	Loading, Unloading and Other Transport Services	100.00	75.00	75.00	100.00
仓储业	Storage	100.00	100.00	175.00	100.00
邮政业	Post	122.79	127.66	104.22	142.26
二、按企业登记注册类型分	**by Status of Registration**				
国有企业	State-owned Enterprises	135.38	140.00	131.86	131.98
集体企业	Collective-owned Enterprises	80.00	113.33	100.00	80.00
股份合作企业	Cooperative Enterprises	71.43	100.00	85.71	114.29
联营企业	Joint Ownership Enterprises	200.00	100.00	100.00	100.00
有限责任公司	Limited Liability Corporations	129.32	116.86	124.76	105.79
股份有限公司	Share-holding Corporations Limited	110.00	130.00	131.72	126.55
私营企业	Private Enterprises	100.00	100.00	100.00	100.00

9-25 续表 1 continued

类别	Classification	一季度 Quarter1	二季度 Quarter2	三季度 Quarter3	四季度 Quarter4
其它内资企业	Other Domestic Funded	100.00	100.00	100.00	100.00
外商及港、澳、台投资企业	Enterprises with Funds from Foreign Contry, Hongkong, Macao and Taiwan	94.45	113.89	144.45	113.89
三、按企业规模分	**Grouped by Size of Enterprises**				
大型及以上	Large-sized and Higher	183.57	178.92	176.02	145.73
中型	Medium-sized	111.67	111.67	118.33	103.33
小型	Small-sized	98.00	116.00	102.00	116.00

9-26 交通运输、仓储及邮政业企业盈利（亏损）变化景气指数（2006年）
Climate Index on Profit(loss) Variation of Transportation, Storage and Telecommunications (2006)

类别	Classification	一季度 Quarter1	二季度 Quarter2	三季度 Quarter3	四季度 Quarter4
交通运输、仓储及邮政业企业总体状况	**Overall**	**114.17**	**113.67**	**113.35**	**111.57**
一、按主要行业门类分	**Grouped by Sector**				
铁路运输业	Railway Transport	100.00	200.00	150.00	150.00
道路运输业	Road Transport	108.32	108.40	114.62	106.73
城市公共交通业	Urban Public Transport	98.10	109.21	107.46	70.32
水上运输业	Water Transport	107.91	108.24	111.51	128.19
航空运输业	Air Transport	200.00	122.28	200.00	93.08
管道运输业	Transport Via Pipelines	100.00	100.00	100.00	100.00
装卸搬运和其他运输服务业	Loading, Unloading and Other Transport Services	100.00	50.00	75.00	100.00
仓储业	Storage	100.00	100.00	100.00	100.00
邮政业	Post	99.98	114.49	89.36	118.77
二、按企业登记注册类型分	**by Status of Registration**				
国有企业	State-owned Enterprises	125.77	125.90	109.73	126.62
集体企业	Collective-owned Enterprises	80.00	100.00	80.00	46.67
股份合作企业	Cooperative Enterprises	57.14	71.43	85.71	128.57
联营企业	Joint Ownership Enterprises	100.00	100.00	100.00	100.00
有限责任公司	Limited Liability Corporations	116.32	112.48	125.96	105.63
股份有限公司	Share-holding Corporations Limited	110.00	90.00	131.72	138.28
私营企业	Private Enterprises	100.00	100.00	100.00	100.00
其它内资企业	Other Domestic Funded	100.00	100.00	100.00	100.00
外商及港、澳、台投资企业	Enterprises with Funds from Foreign Contry, Hongkong, Macao and Taiwan	127.78	100.00	144.45	97.22
三、按企业规模分	**Grouped by Size of Enterprises**				
大型及以上	Large-sized and Higher	178.26	165.52	167.45	169.26
中型	Medium-sized	98.33	103.33	106.67	98.33
小型	Small-sized	96.00	96.00	90.00	94.00

9-27 交通运输、仓储及邮政业企业流动资金景气指数（2006年）
Climate Index on Liquid Capital of Transportation, Storage and Telecommunications (2006)

类别	Classification	一季度 Quarter1	二季度 Quarter2	三季度 Quarter3	四季度 Quarter4
交通运输、仓储及邮政业企业总体状况	**Overall**	**64.20**	**68.13**	**74.98**	**71.46**
一、按主要行业门类分	**Grouped by Sector**				
铁路运输业	Railway Transport	150.00	150.00	150.00	100.00
道路运输业	Road Transport	59.29	67.63	67.69	66.90
城市公共交通业	Urban Public Transport	62.87	68.43	68.43	73.98
水上运输业	Water Transport	72.13	87.92	87.92	92.27
航空运输业	Air Transport	145.78	68.06	106.92	100.00
管道运输业	Transport Via Pipelines	100.00	100.00	100.00	100.00
装卸搬运和其他运输服务业	Loading, Unloading and Other Transport Services	50.00	75.00	100.00	100.00
仓储业	Storage	100.00	75.00	125.00	50.00
邮政业	Post	19.23	22.18	38.69	53.17
二、按企业登记注册类型分	**by Status of Registration**				
国有企业	State-owned Enterprises	59.85	62.04	68.88	66.13
集体企业	Collective-owned Enterprises	46.67	60.00	33.33	33.33
股份合作企业	Cooperative Enterprises	57.14	57.14	57.14	57.14
联营企业	Joint Ownership Enterprises	0.00	0.00	100.00	100.00
有限责任公司	Limited Liability Corporations	62.20	78.79	81.42	65.63
股份有限公司	Share-holding Corporations Limited	78.28	60.00	98.28	118.28
私营企业	Private Enterprises	100.00	100.00	100.00	100.00
其它内资企业	Other Domestic Funded	100.00	100.00	100.00	100.00
外商及港、澳、台投资企业	Enterprises with Funds from Foreign Contry, Hongkong, Macao and Taiwan	163.89	102.78	150.00	150.00
三、按企业规模分	**Grouped by Size of Enterprises**				
大型及以上	Large-sized and Higher	118.07	126.55	135.23	121.81
中型	Medium-sized	56.67	61.67	66.67	60.00
小型	Small-sized	42.00	42.00	50.00	56.00

9-28 交通运输、仓储及邮政业企业货款拖欠景气指数（2006年）
Climate Index on Overdue Obligations to Suppliers about Transportation, Storage and Telecommunications (2006)

类别	Classification	一季度 Quarter1	二季度 Quarter2	三季度 Quarter3	四季度 Quarter4
交通运输、仓储及邮政业企业总体状况	**Overall**	**98.52**	**94.81**	**100.41**	**97.18**
一、按主要行业门类分	**Grouped by Sector**				
铁路运输业	Railway Transport	100.00	100.00	150.00	150.00
道路运输业	Road Transport	97.95	89.69	91.73	92.53
城市公共交通业	Urban Public Transport	94.44	100.00	116.67	88.89

9-28 续表 1 continued

类别	Classification	一季度 Quarter1	二季度 Quarter2	三季度 Quarter3	四季度 Quarter4
水上运输业	Water Transport	102.94	101.58	88.12	100.00
航空运输业	Air Transport	154.22	154.22	193.08	138.86
管道运输业	Transport Via Pipelines	100.00	100.00	100.00	100.00
装卸搬运和其他运输服务业	Loading, Unloading and Other Transport Services	50.00	75.00	125.00	100.00
仓储业	Storage	50.00	75.00	125.00	25.00
邮政业	Post	110.98	89.58	100.54	96.91
二、按企业登记注册类型分	**by Status of Registration**				
国有企业	State-owned Enterprises	103.90	95.22	94.40	109.73
集体企业	Collective-owned Enterprises	86.67	100.00	80.00	60.00
股份合作企业	Cooperative Enterprises	100.00	85.71	100.00	85.71
联营企业	Joint Ownership Enterprises	100.00	100.00	100.00	100.00
有限责任公司	Limited Liability Corporations	94.14	76.32	95.34	87.44
股份有限公司	Share-holding Corporations Limited	91.72	131.72	131.72	90.00
私营企业	Private Enterprises	100.00	100.00	100.00	100.00
其它内资企业	Other Domestic Funded	100.00	100.00	100.00	100.00
外商及港、澳、台投资企业	Enterprises with Funds from Foreign Contry, Hongkong, Macao and Taiwan	97.22	113.89	163.89	147.22
三、按企业规模分	**Grouped by Size of Enterprises**				
大型及以上	Large-sized and Higher	110.14	95.82	98.51	103.73
中型	Medium-sized	93.33	90.00	101.67	95.00
小型	Small-sized	98.00	100.00	100.00	96.00

9-29 交通运输、仓储及邮政业企业劳动力需求景气指数（2006年）
Climate Index on Labor Demand of Transportation, Storage and Telecommunications (2006)

类别	Classification	一季度 Quarter1	二季度 Quarter2	三季度 Quarter3	四季度 Quarter4
交通运输、仓储及邮政业企业总体状况	**Overall**	**98.43**	**95.78**	**103.16**	**101.02**
一、按主要行业门类分	**Grouped by Sector**				
铁路运输业	Railway Transport	100.00	50.00	50.00	50.00
道路运输业	Road Transport	96.56	94.63	94.51	95.45
城市公共交通业	Urban Public Transport	83.33	113.01	124.12	122.22
水上运输业	Water Transport	95.32	85.63	100.83	93.00
航空运输业	Air Transport	145.78	200.00	200.00	106.92
管道运输业	Transport Via Pipelines	100.00	100.00	100.00	100.00
装卸搬运和其他运输服务业	Loading, Unloading and Other Transport Services	125.00	100.00	100.00	100.00
仓储业	Storage	75.00	100.00	125.00	125.00
邮政业	Post	107.27	107.49	107.49	107.49
二、按企业登记注册类型分	**by Status of Registration**				
国有企业	State-owned Enterprises	107.58	91.18	106.71	104.78
集体企业	Collective-owned Enterprises	73.33	86.67	86.67	80.00

9-29 续表 1 continued

类别	Classification	一季度 Quarter1	二季度 Quarter2	三季度 Quarter3	四季度 Quarter4
股份合作企业	Cooperative Enterprises	100.00	114.29	100.00	128.57
联营企业	Joint Ownership Enterprises	100.00	100.00	100.00	100.00
有限责任公司	Limited Liability Corporations	87.53	90.59	95.69	93.98
股份有限公司	Share-holding Corporations Limited	90.00	101.72	121.72	130.00
私营企业	Private Enterprises	100.00	100.00	100.00	100.00
其它内资企业	Other Domestic Funded	100.00	100.00	100.00	100.00
外商及港、澳、台投资企业	Enterprises with Funds from Foreign Contry, Hongkong, Macao and Taiwan	150.00	133.33	113.89	83.33
三、按企业规模分	**Grouped by Size of Enterprises**				
大型及以上	Large-sized and Higher	106.27	97.03	115.17	101.46
中型	Medium-sized	93.33	91.67	98.33	103.33
小型	Small-sized	100.00	100.00	102.00	98.00

9-30 交通运输、仓储及邮政业企业固定资产投资景气指数（2006年）
Climate Index on Business Demand of Transportation, Storage and Telecommunications (2006)

类别	Classification	一季度 Quarter1	二季度 Quarter2	三季度 Quarter3	四季度 Quarter4
交通运输、仓储及邮政业企业总体状况	**Overall**	**114.50**	**115.96**	**131.77**	**112.20**
一、按主要行业门类分	**Grouped by Sector**				
铁路运输业	Railway Transport	100.00	100.00	150.00	100.00
道路运输业	Road Transport	109.33	123.45	131.00	109.78
城市公共交通业	Urban Public Transport	129.68	125.88	140.79	111.11
水上运输业	Water Transport	109.80	115.50	127.80	110.23
航空运输业	Air Transport	145.78	138.86	200.00	106.92
管道运输业	Transport Via Pipelines	100.00	100.00	100.00	100.00
装卸搬运和其他运输服务业	Loading, Unloading and Other Transport Services	125.00	100.00	100.00	100.00
仓储业	Storage	75.00	75.00	75.00	100.00
邮政业	Post	129.45	99.46	115.06	133.76
二、按企业登记注册类型分	**by Status of Registration**				
国有企业	State-owned Enterprises	122.85	103.18	140.07	114.97
集体企业	Collective-owned Enterprises	106.67	126.67	113.33	93.33
股份合作企业	Cooperative Enterprises	71.43	100.00	85.71	114.29
联营企业	Joint Ownership Enterprises	200.00	100.00	200.00	100.00
有限责任公司	Limited Liability Corporations	114.12	126.77	133.34	115.99
股份有限公司	Share-holding Corporations Limited	100.00	108.28	110.00	100.00
私营企业	Private Enterprises	100.00	100.00	100.00	100.00
其它内资企业	Other Domestic Funded	100.00	100.00	100.00	100.00
外商及港、澳、台投资企业	Enterprises with Funds from Foreign Contry, Hongkong, Macao and Taiwan	130.56	147.22	147.22	116.67
三、按企业规模分	**Grouped by Size of Enterprises**				

9-30 续表 1 continued

类别	Classification	一季度 Quarter1	二季度 Quarter2	三季度 Quarter3	四季度 Quarter4
大型及以上	Large-sized and Higher	124.68	128.24	183.32	137.80
中型	Medium-sized	116.67	118.33	123.33	108.33
小型	Small-sized	106.00	106.00	112.00	102.00

9-31 批发和零售业企业商品销售景气指数（2006年）
Climate Index on Commodity Selling of Wholesale and Retail Trade Enterprise (2006)

类别	Classification	一季度 Quarter1	二季度 Quarter2	三季度 Quarter3	四季度 Quarter4
批发和零售业企业总体状况	**Overall**	**123.21**	**113.16**	**119.96**	**130.95**
一、按主要行业门类分	**Grouped by Sector**				
批发业	Whole Sale Trade	117.12	113.35	124.17	124.71
零售业	Retail Trade	130.35	112.29	114.79	138.64
二、按企业登记注册类型分	**by Status of Registration**				
国有企业	State-owned Enterprises	100.86	85.81	103.78	122.78
集体企业	Collective-owned Enterprises	121.64	123.84	139.97	133.97
股份合作企业	Cooperative Enterprises	87.59	103.18	116.01	127.57
联营企业	Joint Ownership Enterprises	66.67	133.33	66.67	100.00
有限责任公司	Limited Liability Corporations	139.43	128.48	127.81	132.66
股份有限公司	Share-holding Corporations Limited	137.20	120.43	124.94	140.76
私营企业	Private Enterprises	133.33	133.33	83.33	116.67
其它内资企业	Other Domestic Funded	0.00	100.00	200.00	0.00
外商及港、澳、台投资企业	Enterprises with Funds from Foreign Contry, Hongkong, Macao and Taiwan	119.95	146.94	146.94	136.62
三、按企业规模分	**Grouped by Size of Enterprises**				
大型及以上	Large-sized and Higher	146.13	115.88	143.35	147.96
中型	Medium-sized	106.79	117.50	106.96	125.32
小型	Small-sized	116.67	87.80	97.56	100.00

9-32 批发和零售业企业盈利（亏损）变化景气指数（2006年）
Climate Index on Profit(loss) Variation of Wholesale and Retail Trade Enterprise (2006)

类别	Classification	一季度 Quarter1	二季度 Quarter2	三季度 Quarter3	四季度 Quarter4
批发和零售业企业总体状况	**Overall**	**122.84**	**122.22**	**121.21**	**125.30**
一、按主要行业门类分	**Grouped by Sector**				
批发业	Whole Sale Trade	111.99	120.94	119.35	118.34
零售业	Retail Trade	135.26	123.46	123.28	133.27
二、按企业登记注册类型分	**by Status of Registration**				
国有企业	State-owned Enterprises	109.73	114.20	106.58	109.26
集体企业	Collective-owned Enterprises	94.41	106.57	113.46	127.34
股份合作企业	Cooperative Enterprises	134.26	124.10	131.28	114.32

9-32 续表 1 continued

类别	Classification	一季度 Quarter1	二季度 Quarter2	三季度 Quarter3	四季度 Quarter4
联营企业	Joint Ownership Enterprises	33.33	100.00	66.67	66.67
有限责任公司	Limited Liability Corporations	136.10	133.07	127.71	142.62
股份有限公司	Share-holding Corporations Limited	129.06	123.68	131.84	129.20
私营企业	Private Enterprises	133.33	133.33	66.67	66.67
其它内资企业	Other Domestic Funded	0.00	200.00	200.00	0.00
外商及港、澳、台投资企业	Enterprises with Funds from Foreign Contry, Hongkong, Macao and Taiwan	119.95	96.94	143.66	103.28
三、按企业规模分	**Grouped by Size of Enterprises**				
大型及以上	Large-sized and Higher	153.78	137.69	159.96	152.34
中型	Medium-sized	104.94	112.50	99.37	110.13
小型	Small-sized	97.62	112.20	85.37	100.00

9-33 批发和零售业企业流动资金景气指数（2006年）
Climate Index on Liquid Capital of Wholesale and Retail Trade Enterprise (2006)

类别	Classification	一季度 Quarter1	二季度 Quarter2	三季度 Quarter3	四季度 Quarter4
批发和零售业企业总体状况	**Overall**	**97.74**	**94.88**	**95.32**	**95.11**
一、按主要行业门类分	**Grouped by Sector**				
批发业	Whole Sale Trade	90.91	92.64	92.65	89.02
零售业	Retail Trade	104.89	96.47	97.82	101.91
二、按企业登记注册类型分	**by Status of Registration**				
国有企业	State-owned Enterprises	93.97	87.66	87.11	83.62
集体企业	Collective-owned Enterprises	66.30	79.87	80.55	52.34
股份合作企业	Cooperative Enterprises	91.59	103.82	106.83	102.63
联营企业	Joint Ownership Enterprises	0.00	0.00	0.00	0.00
有限责任公司	Limited Liability Corporations	96.65	96.11	99.59	105.40
股份有限公司	Share-holding Corporations Limited	111.85	99.07	110.03	109.95
私营企业	Private Enterprises	133.33	116.67	50.00	83.33
其它内资企业	Other Domestic Funded	100.00	100.00	100.00	100.00
外商及港、澳、台投资企业	Enterprises with Funds from Foreign Contry, Hongkong, Macao and Taiwan	136.62	136.62	100.22	119.95
三、按企业规模分	**Grouped by Size of Enterprises**				
大型及以上	Large-sized and Higher	120.71	115.12	124.24	122.89
中型	Medium-sized	86.42	85.63	82.17	82.91
小型	Small-sized	71.43	68.29	56.10	56.10

9-34 批发和零售业企业货款拖欠景气指数（2006年）
Climate Index on Overdue Obligations to Suppliers about Wholesale and Retail Trade Enterprise (2006)

类别	Classification	一季度 Quarter1	二季度 Quarter2	三季度 Quarter3	四季度 Quarter4
批发和零售业企业总体状况	**Overall**	**123.43**	**120.36**	**116.49**	**111.97**
一、按主要行业门类分	**Grouped by Sector**				
批发业	Whole Sale Trade	125.93	124.48	118.62	112.50
零售业	Retail Trade	120.53	115.77	114.00	111.42
二、按企业登记注册类型分	**by Status of Registration**				
国有企业	State-owned Enterprises	120.28	120.41	107.51	94.02
集体企业	Collective-owned Enterprises	113.03	125.08	116.01	116.49
股份合作企业	Cooperative Enterprises	150.88	130.38	98.06	121.27
联营企业	Joint Ownership Enterprises	133.33	100.00	100.00	100.00
有限责任公司	Limited Liability Corporations	124.83	132.01	130.01	119.33
股份有限公司	Share-holding Corporations Limited	123.89	111.02	122.02	126.51
私营企业	Private Enterprises	100.00	50.00	83.33	100.00
其它内资企业	Other Domestic Funded	200.00	100.00	0.00	0.00
外商及港、澳、台投资企业	Enterprises with Funds from Foreign Contry, Hongkong, Macao and Taiwan	113.61	113.61	86.39	83.33
三、按企业规模分	**Grouped by Size of Enterprises**				
大型及以上	Large-sized and Higher	142.81	135.27	132.75	132.29
中型	Medium-sized	112.96	111.25	103.82	98.73
小型	Small-sized	104.76	109.76	114.63	100.00

9-35 批发和零售业企业劳动力需求景气指数（2006年）
Climate Index on Labor Demand of Wholesale and Retail Trade Enterprise (2006)

类别	Classification	一季度 Quarter1	二季度 Quarter2	三季度 Quarter3	四季度 Quarter4
批发和零售业企业总体状况	**Overall**	**105.26**	**98.46**	**105.49**	**105.96**
一、按主要行业门类分	**Grouped by Sector**				
批发业	Whole Sale Trade	97.71	97.05	100.09	93.59
零售业	Retail Trade	113.86	99.87	110.57	120.63
二、按企业登记注册类型分	**by Status of Registration**				
国有企业	State-owned Enterprises	94.88	86.11	99.62	87.16
集体企业	Collective-owned Enterprises	93.83	82.49	82.29	97.13
股份合作企业	Cooperative Enterprises	84.76	95.04	105.16	99.23
联营企业	Joint Ownership Enterprises	66.67	66.67	100.00	66.67
有限责任公司	Limited Liability Corporations	111.29	101.22	109.37	111.06
股份有限公司	Share-holding Corporations Limited	119.69	111.34	114.28	124.77
私营企业	Private Enterprises	83.33	116.67	100.00	66.67
其它内资企业	Other Domestic Funded	100.00	100.00	100.00	0.00
外商及港、澳、台投资企业	Enterprises with Funds from Foreign Contry, Hongkong, Macao and Taiwan	100.00	113.61	100.00	113.61

9-35 续表 1 continued

类别	Classification	一季度 Quarter1	二季度 Quarter2	三季度 Quarter3	四季度 Quarter4
三、按企业规模分	**Grouped by Size of Enterprises**				
大型及以上	Large-sized and Higher	116.00	107.06	117.23	120.03
中型	Medium-sized	101.23	98.75	103.16	100.00
小型	Small-sized	88.10	70.73	78.05	85.37

9-36 批发和零售业企业固定资产投资景气指数（2006年）
Climate Index on Fixed Assets Investment of Wholesale and Retail Trade Enterprise (2006)

类别	Classification	一季度 Quarter1	二季度 Quarter2	三季度 Quarter3	四季度 Quarter4
批发和零售业企业总体状况	**Overall**	**101.19**	**105.94**	**112.59**	**107.73**
一、按主要行业门类分	**Grouped by Sector**				
批发业	Whole Sale Trade	95.86	101.71	106.51	108.64
零售业	Retail Trade	107.40	110.99	119.70	106.65
二、按企业登记注册类型分	**by Status of Registration**				
国有企业	State-owned Enterprises	91.42	101.38	97.66	103.45
集体企业	Collective-owned Enterprises	93.47	89.53	77.59	85.75
股份合作企业	Cooperative Enterprises	99.65	76.12	99.65	106.30
联营企业	Joint Ownership Enterprises	66.67	100.00	100.00	66.67
有限责任公司	Limited Liability Corporations	104.23	108.85	116.89	111.12
股份有限公司	Share-holding Corporations Limited	112.11	114.09	135.13	117.76
私营企业	Private Enterprises	100.00	100.00	100.00	50.00
其它内资企业	Other Domestic Funded	0.00	200.00	200.00	200.00
外商及港、澳、台投资企业	Enterprises with Funds from Foreign Contry, Hongkong, Macao and Taiwan	130.27	130.27	113.61	113.61
三、按企业规模分	**Grouped by Size of Enterprises**				
大型及以上	Large-sized and Higher	103.08	112.97	120.52	116.68
中型	Medium-sized	101.85	102.50	110.76	103.16
小型	Small-sized	92.86	97.56	95.12	97.56

9-37 房地产业企业完成投资景气指数（2006年）
Climate Index on Completed Investment of Real Estate Enterprise (2006)

类别	Classification	一季度 Quarter1	二季度 Quarter2	三季度 Quarter3	四季度 Quarter4
房地产业企业总体状况	**Overall**	**111.71**	**128.16**	**123.46**	**122.85**
一、按主要行业门类分	**Grouped by Sector**				
房地产业	Real Estate	111.71	128.16	123.46	122.85
二、按企业登记注册类型分	**by Status of Registration**				
国有企业	State-owned Enterprises	102.67	113.79	116.04	119.81

9-37 续表 1 continued

类别	Classification	一季度 Quarter1	二季度 Quarter2	三季度 Quarter3	四季度 Quarter4
集体企业	Collective-owned Enterprises	77.78	122.22	133.33	111.11
股份合作企业	Cooperative Enterprises	133.33	133.33	133.33	116.67
联营企业	Joint Ownership Enterprises	100.00	100.00	100.00	100.00
有限责任公司	Limited Liability Corporations	110.95	139.22	108.27	123.15
股份有限公司	Share-holding Corporations Limited	118.65	124.42	162.02	137.50
私营企业	Private Enterprises	133.33	133.33	133.33	133.33
其它内资企业	Other Domestic Funded	100.00	100.00	100.00	100.00
外商及港、澳、台投资企业	Enterprises with Funds from Foreign Contry, Hongkong, Macao and Taiwan	154.53	125.47	150.00	95.47
三、按企业规模分	**Grouped by Size of Enterprises**				
大型及以上	Large-sized and Higher	157.66	140.06	176.84	171.54
中型	Medium-sized	107.81	123.44	121.88	115.63
小型	Small-sized	104.00	129.33	112.00	117.33

9-38 房地产业企业盈利（亏损）变化景气指数（2006年）
Climate Index on Profit(loss) Variation of Real Estate Enterprise (2006)

类别	Classification	一季度 Quarter1	二季度 Quarter2	三季度 Quarter3	四季度 Quarter4
房地产业企业总体状况	**Overall**	**114.34**	**126.07**	**121.71**	**123.22**
一、按主要行业门类分	**Grouped by Sector**				
房地产业	Real Estate	114.34	126.07	121.71	123.22
二、按企业登记注册类型分	**by Status of Registration**				
国有企业	State-owned Enterprises	112.61	129.59	114.83	119.53
集体企业	Collective-owned Enterprises	100.00	77.78	111.11	88.89
股份合作企业	Cooperative Enterprises	133.33	150.00	150.00	116.67
联营企业	Joint Ownership Enterprises	100.00	100.00	100.00	100.00
有限责任公司	Limited Liability Corporations	114.82	135.23	131.60	129.82
股份有限公司	Share-holding Corporations Limited	125.48	112.50	118.75	144.33
私营企业	Private Enterprises	133.33	133.33	133.33	100.00
其它内资企业	Other Domestic Funded	100.00	100.00	100.00	100.00
外商及港、澳、台投资企业	Enterprises with Funds from Foreign Contry, Hongkong, Macao and Taiwan	134.53	134.53	100.00	124.53
三、按企业规模分	**Grouped by Size of Enterprises**				
大型及以上	Large-sized and Higher	136.20	132.93	105.99	147.01
中型	Medium-sized	114.06	125.00	137.50	123.44
小型	Small-sized	109.33	125.33	112.00	117.33

9-39 房地产业企业流动资金景气指数（2006年）
Climate Index on Liquid Capital of Real Estate Enterprise (2006)

类别	Classification	一季度 Quarter1	二季度 Quarter2	三季度 Quarter3	四季度 Quarter4
房地产业企业总体状况	**Overall**	**78.82**	**81.81**	**72.84**	**78.49**
一、按主要行业门类分	**Grouped by Sector**				
房地产业	Real Estate	78.82	81.81	72.84	78.49
二、按企业登记注册类型分	**by Status of Registration**				
国有企业	State-owned Enterprises	57.86	70.54	59.75	64.74
集体企业	Collective-owned Enterprises	77.78	77.78	66.67	77.78
股份合作企业	Cooperative Enterprises	66.67	83.33	100.00	116.67
联营企业	Joint Ownership Enterprises	100.00	100.00	100.00	100.00
有限责任公司	Limited Liability Corporations	97.27	102.21	85.18	85.00
股份有限公司	Share-holding Corporations Limited	75.96	50.48	50.48	88.56
私营企业	Private Enterprises	166.67	166.67	166.67	66.67
其它内资企业	Other Domestic Funded	100.00	100.00	100.00	100.00
外商及港、澳、台投资企业	Enterprises with Funds from Foreign Contry, Hongkong, Macao and Taiwan	119.05	104.53	100.00	114.53
三、按企业规模分	**Grouped by Size of Enterprises**				
大型及以上	Large-sized and Higher	54.14	52.50	40.88	73.49
中型	Medium-sized	75.00	73.44	64.06	76.56
小型	Small-sized	88.00	96.00	88.00	81.33

9-40 房地产业企业货款拖欠景气指数（2006年）
Climate Index on Overdue Obligations to Suppliers about Real Estate Enterprise (2006)

类别	Classification	一季度 Quarter1	二季度 Quarter2	三季度 Quarter3	四季度 Quarter4
房地产业企业总体状况	**Overall**	**118.92**	**118.59**	**117.07**	**121.69**
一、按主要行业门类分	**Grouped by Sector**				
房地产业	Real Estate	118.92	118.59	117.07	121.69
二、按企业登记注册类型分	**by Status of Registration**				
国有企业	State-owned Enterprises	107.55	114.83	107.55	111.32
集体企业	Collective-owned Enterprises	144.44	122.22	111.11	133.33
股份合作企业	Cooperative Enterprises	116.67	133.33	116.67	100.00
联营企业	Joint Ownership Enterprises	100.00	100.00	100.00	100.00
有限责任公司	Limited Liability Corporations	116.02	121.96	131.02	123.93
股份有限公司	Share-holding Corporations Limited	131.25	106.25	87.50	118.85
私营企业	Private Enterprises	133.33	133.33	133.33	100.00
其它内资企业	Other Domestic Funded	100.00	100.00	100.00	100.00
外商及港、澳、台投资企业	Enterprises with Funds from Foreign Contry, Hongkong, Macao and Taiwan	154.53	130.00	130.00	160.00
三、按企业规模分	**Grouped by Size of Enterprises**				
大型及以上	Large-sized and Higher	103.90	106.59	98.92	116.97
中型	Medium-sized	115.63	107.81	110.94	118.75
小型	Small-sized	125.33	130.67	126.67	125.33

9-41 房地产业企业劳动力需求景气指数（2006年）
Climate Index on Labor Demand of Real Estate Enterprise (2006)

类别	Classification	一季度 Quarter1	二季度 Quarter2	三季度 Quarter3	四季度 Quarter4
房地产业企业总体状况	**Overall**	**109.32**	**112.40**	**110.28**	**103.08**
一、按主要行业门类分	**Grouped by Sector**				
房地产业	Real Estate	109.32	112.40	110.28	103.08
二、按企业登记注册类型分	**by Status of Registration**				
国有企业	State-owned Enterprises	90.64	98.45	108.81	91.83
集体企业	Collective-owned Enterprises	88.89	100.00	111.11	77.78
股份合作企业	Cooperative Enterprises	116.67	116.67	100.00	116.67
联营企业	Joint Ownership Enterprises	100.00	100.00	100.00	100.00
有限责任公司	Limited Liability Corporations	109.64	119.82	105.59	105.89
股份有限公司	Share-holding Corporations Limited	137.40	111.92	124.42	105.67
私营企业	Private Enterprises	100.00	100.00	100.00	166.67
其它内资企业	Other Domestic Funded	100.00	100.00	100.00	100.00
外商及港、澳、台投资企业	Enterprises with Funds from Foreign Contry, Hongkong, Macao and Taiwan	144.53	120.00	100.00	105.47
三、按企业规模分	**Grouped by Size of Enterprises**				
大型及以上	Large-sized and Higher	125.72	119.26	128.57	126.84
中型	Medium-sized	117.19	109.38	107.81	101.56
小型	Small-sized	98.67	113.33	108.00	98.67

9-42 房地产业企业固定资产投资景气指数（2006年）
Climate Index on Fixed Assets Investment of Real Estate Enterprise (2006)

类别	Classification	一季度 Quarter1	二季度 Quarter2	三季度 Quarter3	四季度 Quarter4
房地产业企业总体状况	**Overall**	**112.30**	**118.29**	**110.93**	**111.17**
一、按主要行业门类分	**Grouped by Sector**				
房地产业	Real Estate	112.30	118.29	110.93	111.17
二、按企业登记注册类型分	**by Status of Registration**				
国有企业	State-owned Enterprises	105.49	107.85	100.70	110.36
集体企业	Collective-owned Enterprises	111.11	133.33	133.33	122.22
股份合作企业	Cooperative Enterprises	100.00	133.33	133.33	116.67
联营企业	Joint Ownership Enterprises	100.00	100.00	100.00	100.00
有限责任公司	Limited Liability Corporations	114.28	121.00	113.33	111.67
股份有限公司	Share-holding Corporations Limited	106.25	106.25	106.25	125.00
私营企业	Private Enterprises	166.67	166.67	166.67	166.67
其它内资企业	Other Domestic Funded	100.00	100.00	100.00	100.00
外商及港、澳、台投资企业	Enterprises with Funds from Foreign Contry, Hongkong, Macao and Taiwan	154.53	140.00	100.00	65.47
三、按企业规模分	**Grouped by Size of Enterprises**				
大型及以上	Large-sized and Higher	112.84	98.40	89.79	108.57
中型	Medium-sized	109.38	110.94	115.63	106.25
小型	Small-sized	114.67	129.33	112.00	116.00

9-43 社会服务业企业业务需求量景气指数（2006年）
Climate Index on Business Demand of Social Services Enterprise (2006)

类别	Classification	一季度 Quarter1	二季度 Quarter2	三季度 Quarter3	四季度 Quarter4
社会服务业企业总体状况	**Overall**	**115.78**	**137.55**	**131.12**	**117.34**
一、按主要行业门类分	**Grouped by Sector**				
租赁业	Leasing	111.11	125.00	125.00	100.00
商务服务业	Business Services	118.12	139.03	130.34	117.32
环境资源管理业	Environmental Management	100.00	66.67	100.00	66.67
公共设施管理业	Management of Public Facilities	122.73	145.45	140.91	131.82
居民服务业	Services to Household	100.00	140.00	120.00	120.00
其他服务业	Other Services	100.00	100.00	100.00	100.00
二、按企业登记注册类型分	**by Status of Registration**				
国有企业	State-owned Enterprises	116.22	130.56	144.44	119.44
集体企业	Collective-owned Enterprises	100.00	200.00	166.67	133.33
股份合作企业	Cooperative Enterprises	200.00	175.00	150.00	50.00
联营企业	Joint Ownership Enterprises	100.00	100.00	100.00	100.00
有限责任公司	Limited Liability Corporations	107.41	129.63	118.52	122.22
股份有限公司	Share-holding Corporations Limited	87.14	87.28	98.92	75.49
私营企业	Private Enterprises	140.00	200.00	140.00	160.00
其它内资企业	Other Domestic Funded	200.00	100.00	100.00	0.00
外商及港、澳、台投资企业	Enterprises with Funds from Foreign Contry, Hongkong, Macao and Taiwan	100.00	100.00	100.00	100.00
三、按企业规模分	**Grouped by Size of Enterprises**				
大型及以上	Large-sized and Higher	106.86	159.01	119.06	159.42
中型	Medium-sized	115.38	144.00	144.00	116.00
小型	Small-sized	116.98	132.08	126.42	113.21

9-44 社会服务业企业盈利（亏损）变化景气指数（2006年）
Climate Index on Profit(loss) Variation of Social Services Enterprise (2006)

类别	Classification	一季度 Quarter1	二季度 Quarter2	三季度 Quarter3	四季度 Quarter4
社会服务业企业总体状况	**Overall**	**92.54**	**119.83**	**107.63**	**110.32**
一、按主要行业门类分	**Grouped by Sector**				
租赁业	Leasing	55.56	50.00	62.50	62.50
商务服务业	Business Services	89.61	130.91	110.53	111.36
环境资源管理业	Environmental Management	100.00	100.00	133.33	100.00
公共设施管理业	Management of Public Facilities	109.09	131.82	122.73	140.91
居民服务业	Services to Household	100.00	80.00	60.00	40.00
其他服务业	Other Services	100.00	100.00	100.00	100.00
二、按企业登记注册类型分	**by Status of Registration**				
国有企业	State-owned Enterprises	110.81	133.33	125.00	119.44
集体企业	Collective-owned Enterprises	100.00	100.00	100.00	100.00
股份合作企业	Cooperative Enterprises	125.00	125.00	150.00	50.00

9-44 续表 1 continued

类别	Classification	一季度 Quarter1	二季度 Quarter2	三季度 Quarter3	四季度 Quarter4
联营企业	Joint Ownership Enterprises	100.00	100.00	100.00	100.00
有限责任公司	Limited Liability Corporations	62.96	114.81	96.30	122.22
股份有限公司	Share-holding Corporations Limited	48.78	36.28	48.56	61.51
私营企业	Private Enterprises	100.00	100.00	20.00	60.00
其它内资企业	Other Domestic Funded	0.00	200.00	200.00	0.00
外商及港、澳、台投资企业	Enterprises with Funds from Foreign Contry, Hongkong, Macao and Taiwan	100.00	100.00	100.00	100.00
三、按企业规模分	**Grouped by Size of Enterprises**				
大型及以上	Large-sized and Higher	144.33	144.33	156.81	144.45
中型	Medium-sized	80.77	144.00	108.00	116.00
小型	Small-sized	92.45	105.66	101.89	103.77

9-45 社会服务业企业流动资金景气指数（2006年）
Climate Index on Liquid Capital of Social Services Enterprise (2006)

类别	Classification	一季度 Quarter1	二季度 Quarter2	三季度 Quarter3	四季度 Quarter4
社会服务业企业总体状况	**Overall**	**72.86**	**88.67**	**83.90**	**79.67**
一、按主要行业门类分	**Grouped by Sector**				
租赁业	Leasing	33.33	37.50	50.00	50.00
商务服务业	Business Services	88.63	103.76	95.05	86.44
环境资源管理业	Environmental Management	66.67	100.00	66.67	66.67
公共设施管理业	Management of Public Facilities	68.18	86.36	90.91	95.45
居民服务业	Services to Household	40.00	40.00	20.00	20.00
其他服务业	Other Services	100.00	100.00	100.00	100.00
二、按企业登记注册类型分	**by Status of Registration**				
国有企业	State-owned Enterprises	78.38	91.67	88.89	80.56
集体企业	Collective-owned Enterprises	66.67	66.67	66.67	66.67
股份合作企业	Cooperative Enterprises	75.00	75.00	75.00	125.00
联营企业	Joint Ownership Enterprises	100.00	100.00	100.00	100.00
有限责任公司	Limited Liability Corporations	62.96	85.19	74.07	77.78
股份有限公司	Share-holding Corporations Limited	124.78	137.28	137.05	137.05
私营企业	Private Enterprises	60.00	40.00	40.00	20.00
其它内资企业	Other Domestic Funded	0.00	0.00	0.00	0.00
外商及港、澳、台投资企业	Enterprises with Funds from Foreign Contry, Hongkong, Macao and Taiwan	100.00	100.00	100.00	100.00
三、按企业规模分	**Grouped by Size of Enterprises**				
大型及以上	Large-sized and Higher	115.52	174.66	174.54	115.39
中型	Medium-sized	69.23	88.00	80.00	88.00
小型	Small-sized	69.81	79.25	75.47	71.70

9-46 社会服务业企业货款拖欠景气指数（2006年） Climate Index on Overdue Obligations to Suppliers about Social Services Enterprise (2006)

类别	Classification	一季度 Quarter1	二季度 Quarter2	三季度 Quarter3	四季度 Quarter4
社会服务业企业总体状况	**Overall**	**104.22**	**86.25**	**89.58**	**100.73**
一、按主要行业门类分	**Grouped by Sector**	**0.00**	**0.00**	**0.00**	**0.00**
租赁业	Leasing	88.89	87.50	87.50	100.00
商务服务业	Business Services	106.44	80.52	85.58	106.53
环境资源管理业	Environmental Management	50.00	66.67	100.00	100.00
公共设施管理业	Management of Public Facilities	113.64	95.45	100.00	95.45
居民服务业	Services to Household	80.00	120.00	80.00	80.00
其他服务业	Other Services	100.00	100.00	100.00	100.00
二、按企业登记注册类型分	**by Status of Registration**	**0.00**	**0.00**	**0.00**	**0.00**
国有企业	State-owned Enterprises	102.78	91.67	94.44	111.11
集体企业	Collective-owned Enterprises	100.00	100.00	100.00	133.33
股份合作企业	Cooperative Enterprises	125.00	50.00	125.00	125.00
联营企业	Joint Ownership Enterprises	100.00	100.00	100.00	100.00
有限责任公司	Limited Liability Corporations	107.41	92.59	88.89	96.30
股份有限公司	Share-holding Corporations Limited	75.00	75.00	87.50	99.37
私营企业	Private Enterprises	80.00	80.00	40.00	60.00
其它内资企业	Other Domestic Funded	100.00	200.00	0.00	200.00
外商及港、澳、台投资企业	Enterprises with Funds from Foreign Contry, Hongkong, Macao and Taiwan	100.00	100.00	100.00	100.00
三、按企业规模分	**Grouped by Size of Enterprises**				
大型及以上	Large-sized and Higher	159.14	40.86	87.39	60.17
中型	Medium-sized	92.31	96.00	64.00	120.00
小型	Small-sized	103.85	86.79	101.89	96.23

9-47 社会服务业企业劳动力需求景气指数（2006年） Climate Index on Labor Demand of Social Services Enterprise (2006)

类别	Classification	一季度 Quarter1	二季度 Quarter2	三季度 Quarter3	四季度 Quarter4
社会服务业企业总体状况	**Overall**	**100.00**	**124.46**	**115.70**	**104.05**
一、按主要行业门类分	**Grouped by Sector**				
租赁业	Leasing	100.00	125.00	112.50	125.00
商务服务业	Business Services	106.52	139.05	121.00	94.19
环境资源管理业	Environmental Management	66.67	33.33	100.00	100.00
公共设施管理业	Management of Public Facilities	90.91	109.09	104.55	118.18
居民服务业	Services to Household	100.00	100.00	120.00	120.00
其他服务业	Other Services	100.00	100.00	100.00	100.00
二、按企业登记注册类型分	**by Status of Registration**				
国有企业	State-owned Enterprises	97.30	108.33	113.89	111.11
集体企业	Collective-owned Enterprises	100.00	100.00	100.00	100.00

9-47 续表 1 continued

类别	Classification	一季度 Quarter1	二季度 Quarter2	三季度 Quarter3	四季度 Quarter4
股份合作企业	Cooperative Enterprises	150.00	125.00	125.00	100.00
联营企业	Joint Ownership Enterprises	100.00	100.00	100.00	100.00
有限责任公司	Limited Liability Corporations	100.00	137.04	107.41	100.00
股份有限公司	Share-holding Corporations Limited	62.50	100.00	111.65	99.41
私营企业	Private Enterprises	140.00	160.00	140.00	120.00
其它内资企业	Other Domestic Funded	100.00	200.00	100.00	0.00
外商及港、澳、台投资企业	Enterprises with Funds from Foreign Contry, Hongkong, Macao and Taiwan	100.00	100.00	100.00	100.00
三、按企业规模分	**Grouped by Size of Enterprises**				
大型及以上	Large-sized and Higher	100.00	159.14	153.12	106.73
中型	Medium-sized	96.15	124.00	116.00	96.00
小型	Small-sized	101.89	120.75	111.32	107.55

9-48 社会服务业企业固定资产投资景气指数（2006年）
Climate Index on Fixed Assets Investment of Social Services Enterprise (2006)

类别	Classification	一季度 Quarter1	二季度 Quarter2	三季度 Quarter3	四季度 Quarter4
社会服务业企业总体状况	**Overall**	**111.24**	**109.00**	**122.27**	**112.86**
一、按主要行业门类分	**Grouped by Sector**				
租赁业	Leasing	100.00	112.50	112.50	100.00
商务服务业	Business Services	102.10	97.76	119.41	113.78
环境资源管理业	Environmental Management	133.33	66.67	166.67	133.33
公共设施管理业	Management of Public Facilities	131.82	131.82	122.73	127.27
居民服务业	Services to Household	100.00	120.00	120.00	40.00
其他服务业	Other Services	100.00	100.00	100.00	100.00
二、按企业登记注册类型分	**by Status of Registration**				
国有企业	State-owned Enterprises	110.81	105.56	116.67	108.33
集体企业	Collective-owned Enterprises	100.00	133.33	133.33	100.00
股份合作企业	Cooperative Enterprises	100.00	100.00	100.00	125.00
联营企业	Joint Ownership Enterprises	100.00	100.00	100.00	100.00
有限责任公司	Limited Liability Corporations	103.70	100.00	122.22	111.11
股份有限公司	Share-holding Corporations Limited	100.22	100.22	124.37	112.72
私营企业	Private Enterprises	140.00	140.00	140.00	100.00
其它内资企业	Other Domestic Funded	100.00	100.00	100.00	100.00
外商及港、澳、台投资企业	Enterprises with Funds from Foreign Contry, Hongkong, Macao and Taiwan	100.00	100.00	100.00	100.00
三、按企业规模分	**Grouped by Size of Enterprises**				
大型及以上	Large-sized and Higher	159.27	159.27	178.46	146.66
中型	Medium-sized	115.38	104.00	124.00	120.00
小型	Small-sized	103.77	105.66	115.09	105.66

9-49 信息传输、计算机服务和软件业企业产品销售（提供服务）景气指数（2006年）

Climate Index on Product Selling of Information Transmission, Computer Services and Software Enterprise (2006)

类别	Classification	一季度 Quarter1	二季度 Quarter2	三季度 Quarter3	四季度 Quarter4
信息传输、计算机服务和软件业企业总体状况	**Overall**	**144.83**	**148.74**	**162.67**	**145.08**
一、按主要行业门类分	**Grouped by Sector**				
信息传输业	Information Transmission	156.33	159.22	167.59	155.32
计算机服务业	Computer Services	166.67	133.33	166.67	177.78
软件业	Software	78.57	107.69	138.46	73.54
二、按企业登记注册类型分	**by Status of Registration**				
国有企业	State-owned Enterprises	150.00	141.67	158.33	158.33
集体企业	Collective-owned Enterprises	100.00	100.00	100.00	100.00
股份合作企业	Cooperative Enterprises	50.00	200.00	200.00	0.00
联营企业	Joint Ownership Enterprises	100.00	100.00	100.00	100.00
有限责任公司	Limited Liability Corporations	144.90	146.67	160.00	126.67
股份有限公司	Share-holding Corporations Limited	152.02	146.53	175.99	159.99
私营企业	Private Enterprises	125.00	100.00	150.00	150.00
其它内资企业	Other Domestic Funded	0.00	0.00	0.00	0.00
外商及港、澳、台投资企业	Enterprises with Funds from Foreign Contry, Hongkong, Macao and Taiwan	138.54	146.62	156.22	132.43
三、按企业规模分	**Grouped by Size of Enterprises**				
大型及以上	Large-sized and Higher	159.21	162.35	176.62	158.18
中型	Medium-sized	137.84	143.24	154.05	148.65
小型	Small-sized	140.91	142.86	161.90	123.81

9-50 信息传输、计算机服务和软件业企业盈利（亏损）变化景气指数（2006年）

Climate Index on Profit(loss) Variation of Information Transmission, Computer Services and Software Enterprise (2006)

类别	Classification	一季度 Quarter1	二季度 Quarter2	三季度 Quarter3	四季度 Quarter4
信息传输、计算机服务和软件业企业总体状况	**Overall**	**128.38**	**138.94**	**124.65**	**122.62**
一、按主要行业门类分	**Grouped by Sector**				
信息传输业	Information Transmission	130.51	144.73	122.93	116.85
计算机服务业	Computer Services	166.67	133.33	100.00	166.67
软件业	Software	96.00	111.08	153.85	123.08
二、按企业登记注册类型分	**by Status of Registration**				
国有企业	State-owned Enterprises	116.67	125.00	100.00	108.33
集体企业	Collective-owned Enterprises	100.00	100.00	100.00	100.00

9-50 续表 1 continued

类别	Classification	一季度 Quarter1	二季度 Quarter2	三季度 Quarter3	四季度 Quarter4
股份合作企业	Cooperative Enterprises	50.00	200.00	200.00	200.00
联营企业	Joint Ownership Enterprises	100.00	100.00	100.00	100.00
有限责任公司	Limited Liability Corporations	141.77	146.67	115.10	100.00
股份有限公司	Share-holding Corporations Limited	148.72	137.85	142.70	141.71
私营企业	Private Enterprises	150.00	100.00	125.00	200.00
其它内资企业	Other Domestic Funded	0.00	100.00	0.00	0.00
外商及港、澳、台投资企业	Enterprises with Funds from Foreign Contry, Hongkong, Macao and Taiwan	129.09	127.20	133.43	129.51
三、按企业规模分	**Grouped by Size of Enterprises**				
大型及以上	Large-sized and Higher	143.97	166.39	121.72	118.94
中型	Medium-sized	113.51	124.32	121.62	108.11
小型	Small-sized	136.36	133.33	133.33	152.38

9-51 信息传输、计算机服务和软件业企业流动资金景气指数（2006年）Climate Index on Liquid Capital of Information Transmission, Computer Services and Software Enterprise (2006)

类别	Classification	一季度 Quarter1	二季度 Quarter2	三季度 Quarter3	四季度 Quarter4
信息传输、计算机服务和软件业企业总体状况	**Overall**	**119.23**	**109.16**	**126.20**	**111.96**
一、按主要行业门类分	**Grouped by Sector**				
信息传输业	Information Transmission	130.87	126.31	136.22	123.51
计算机服务业	Computer Services	77.78	44.44	77.78	33.33
软件业	Software	89.71	73.54	115.38	115.38
二、按企业登记注册类型分	**by Status of Registration**				
国有企业	State-owned Enterprises	116.67	100.00	116.67	91.67
集体企业	Collective-owned Enterprises	100.00	100.00	100.00	100.00
股份合作企业	Cooperative Enterprises	50.00	100.00	100.00	100.00
联营企业	Joint Ownership Enterprises	100.00	100.00	100.00	100.00
有限责任公司	Limited Liability Corporations	126.67	100.00	106.67	106.67
股份有限公司	Share-holding Corporations Limited	128.27	120.67	156.86	128.50
私营企业	Private Enterprises	50.00	25.00	75.00	25.00
其它内资企业	Other Domestic Funded	200.00	200.00	200.00	200.00
外商及港、澳、台投资企业	Enterprises with Funds from Foreign Contry, Hongkong, Macao and Taiwan	103.34	101.51	112.32	107.34
三、按企业规模分	**Grouped by Size of Enterprises**				
大型及以上	Large-sized and Higher	153.99	152.14	164.51	157.54
中型	Medium-sized	102.70	91.89	105.41	91.89
小型	Small-sized	109.09	90.48	119.05	95.24

9-52 信息传输、计算机服务和软件业企业货款拖欠景气指数（2006年）
Climate Index on Overdue Obligations to Suppliers about Information Transmission, Computer Services and Software Enterprise (2006)

类别	Classification	一季度 Quarter1	二季度 Quarter2	三季度 Quarter3	四季度 Quarter4
信息传输、计算机服务和软件业企业总体状况	**Overall**	**126.27**	**118.14**	**100.00**	**112.46**
一、按主要行业门类分	**Grouped by Sector**				
信息传输业	Information Transmission	126.15	116.33	99.49	111.46
计算机服务业	Computer Services	100.00	100.00	100.00	122.22
软件业	Software	142.86	141.85	100.92	115.38
二、按企业登记注册类型分	**by Status of Registration**				
国有企业	State-owned Enterprises	100.00	83.33	91.67	100.00
集体企业	Collective-owned Enterprises	100.00	100.00	100.00	100.00
股份合作企业	Cooperative Enterprises	150.00	0.00	0.00	200.00
联营企业	Joint Ownership Enterprises	100.00	100.00	100.00	100.00
有限责任公司	Limited Liability Corporations	144.90	131.57	113.33	86.67
股份有限公司	Share-holding Corporations Limited	129.57	112.72	94.89	97.28
私营企业	Private Enterprises	75.00	100.00	50.00	150.00
其它内资企业	Other Domestic Funded	0.00	0.00	0.00	200.00
外商及港、澳、台投资企业	Enterprises with Funds from Foreign Contry, Hongkong, Macao and Taiwan	113.81	117.24	108.84	133.61
三、按企业规模分	**Grouped by Size of Enterprises**				
大型及以上	Large-sized and Higher	115.84	120.32	83.35	105.05
中型	Medium-sized	132.43	118.92	100.00	113.51
小型	Small-sized	127.27	114.29	119.05	119.05

9-53 信息传输、计算机服务和软件业企业劳动力需求景气指数（2006年）
Climate Index on Labor Demand of Information Transmission, Computer Services and Software Enterprise (2006)

类别	Classification	一季度 Quarter1	二季度 Quarter2	三季度 Quarter3	四季度 Quarter4
信息传输、计算机服务和软件业企业总体状况	**Overall**	**113.15**	**114.95**	**108.35**	**116.91**
一、按主要行业门类分	**Grouped by Sector**				
信息传输业	Information Transmission	114.43	119.37	105.67	125.31
计算机服务业	Computer Services	133.33	133.33	88.89	100.00
软件业	Software	92.86	77.85	138.46	88.92
二、按企业登记注册类型分	**by Status of Registration**				
国有企业	State-owned Enterprises	100.00	125.00	100.00	116.67
集体企业	Collective-owned Enterprises	100.00	100.00	100.00	100.00
股份合作企业	Cooperative Enterprises	100.00	0.00	200.00	0.00
联营企业	Joint Ownership Enterprises	100.00	100.00	100.00	100.00
有限责任公司	Limited Liability Corporations	118.23	118.23	108.43	104.90

9-53 续表 1 continued

类别	Classification	一季度 Quarter1	二季度 Quarter2	三季度 Quarter3	四季度 Quarter4
股份有限公司	Share-holding Corporations Limited	98.57	91.26	116.45	126.70
私营企业	Private Enterprises	125.00	100.00	100.00	100.00
其它内资企业	Other Domestic Funded	100.00	100.00	0.00	0.00
外商及港、澳、台投资企业	Enterprises with Funds from Foreign Contry, Hongkong, Macao and Taiwan	104.38	108.64	111.30	107.30
三、按企业规模分	**Grouped by Size of Enterprises**				
大型及以上	Large-sized and Higher	137.15	130.24	120.19	145.27
中型	Medium-sized	100.00	108.11	97.30	116.22
小型	Small-sized	109.09	109.52	114.29	85.71

9-54 信息传输、计算机服务和软件业企业固定资产投资景气指数（2006年）

Climate Index on Fixed Assets Investment of Information Transmission, Computer Services and Software Enterprise (2006)

类别	Classification	一季度 Quarter1	二季度 Quarter2	三季度 Quarter3	四季度 Quarter4
信息传输、计算机服务和软件业企业总体状况	**Overall**	**130.71**	**142.00**	**117.77**	**110.56**
一、按主要行业门类分	**Grouped by Sector**				
信息传输业	Information Transmission	140.21	145.54	126.25	117.67
计算机服务业	Computer Services	111.11	122.22	88.89	144.44
软件业	Software	100.00	134.15	99.08	50.46
二、按企业登记注册类型分	**by Status of Registration**				
国有企业	State-owned Enterprises	133.33	125.00	116.67	116.67
集体企业	Collective-owned Enterprises	100.00	100.00	100.00	100.00
股份合作企业	Cooperative Enterprises	50.00	200.00	200.00	0.00
联营企业	Joint Ownership Enterprises	100.00	100.00	100.00	100.00
有限责任公司	Limited Liability Corporations	126.67	144.90	113.33	106.67
股份有限公司	Share-holding Corporations Limited	129.29	115.76	121.37	112.41
私营企业	Private Enterprises	100.00	100.00	100.00	125.00
其它内资企业	Other Domestic Funded	100.00	100.00	0.00	0.00
外商及港、澳、台投资企业	Enterprises with Funds from Foreign Contry, Hongkong, Macao and Taiwan	125.57	161.89	100.89	118.74
三、按企业规模分	**Grouped by Size of Enterprises**				
大型及以上	Large-sized and Higher	152.05	168.49	135.72	98.56
中型	Medium-sized	129.73	135.14	105.41	108.11
小型	Small-sized	109.09	123.81	119.05	128.57

9-55 住宿和餐饮业企业产品销售（提供服务）景气指数（2006年）
Climate Index on Product Selling of Hotel and Catering Services Enterprise (2006)

类别	Classification	一季度 Quarter1	二季度 Quarter2	三季度 Quarter3	四季度 Quarter4
住宿和餐饮业企业总体状况	**Overall**	**122.72**	**132.60**	**132.80**	**114.66**
一、按主要行业门类分	**Grouped by Sector**				
住宿业	Hotels	113.31	137.51	138.50	113.61
餐饮业	Catering Services	135.56	123.37	120.55	110.83
二、按企业登记注册类型分	**by Status of Registration**				
国有企业	State-owned Enterprises	111.86	124.62	121.83	104.64
集体企业	Collective-owned Enterprises	107.14	114.29	121.43	84.62
股份合作企业	Cooperative Enterprises	128.72	108.80	108.80	133.33
联营企业	Joint Ownership Enterprises	100.00	100.00	100.00	100.00
有限责任公司	Limited Liability Corporations	120.49	132.37	147.07	113.19
股份有限公司	Share-holding Corporations Limited	125.32	137.34	99.02	119.16
私营企业	Private Enterprises	140.00	140.00	160.00	140.00
私营企业	Private Enterprises	140.00	140.00	160.00	140.00
其它内资企业	Other Domestic Funded	200.00	200.00	200.00	200.00
外商及港、澳、台投资企业	Enterprises with Funds from Foreign Contry, Hongkong, Macao and Taiwan	140.58	158.51	156.75	118.39
三、按企业规模分	**Grouped by Size of Enterprises**				
大型及以上	Large-sized and Higher	156.24	162.77	168.60	127.56
中型	Medium-sized	115.05	132.61	128.26	116.48
小型	Small-sized	121.57	119.23	125.00	105.77

9-56 住宿和餐饮业企业盈利（亏损）变化景气指数（2006年）
Climate Index on Profit(loss) Variation of Hotel and Catering Services Enterprise (2006)

类别	Classification	一季度 Quarter1	二季度 Quarter2	三季度 Quarter3	四季度 Quarter4
住宿和餐饮业企业总体状况	**Overall**	**119.09**	**122.85**	**125.97**	**114.73**
一、按主要行业门类分	**Grouped by Sector**				
住宿业	Hotels	118.47	126.42	130.72	111.56
餐饮业	Catering Services	121.43	119.54	116.75	112.38
二、按企业登记注册类型分	**by Status of Registration**				
国有企业	State-owned Enterprises	116.78	117.27	118.29	112.19
集体企业	Collective-owned Enterprises	92.86	100.00	107.14	84.62
股份合作企业	Cooperative Enterprises	142.14	119.92	108.80	175.47
联营企业	Joint Ownership Enterprises	100.00	100.00	100.00	100.00
有限责任公司	Limited Liability Corporations	115.78	126.47	131.16	104.95
股份有限公司	Share-holding Corporations Limited	116.23	110.07	107.14	136.36
私营企业	Private Enterprises	160.00	180.00	160.00	140.00
其它内资企业	Other Domestic Funded	200.00	200.00	200.00	100.00
外商及港、澳、台投资企业	Enterprises with Funds from Foreign Contry, Hongkong, Macao and Taiwan	124.87	141.28	151.02	95.95

9-56 续表 1 continued

类别	Classification	一季度 Quarter1	二季度 Quarter2	三季度 Quarter3	四季度 Quarter4
三、按企业规模分	Grouped by Size of Enterprises				
大型及以上	Large-sized and Higher	147.32	131.13	179.86	145.46
中型	Medium-sized	116.13	126.09	119.57	109.89
小型	Small-sized	111.76	113.46	113.46	109.62

9-57 住宿和餐饮业企业流动资金景气指数（2006年）
Climate Index on Liquid Capital of Hotel and Catering Services Enterprise (2006)

类别	Classification	一季度 Quarter1	二季度 Quarter2	三季度 Quarter3	四季度 Quarter4
住宿和餐饮业企业总体状况	**Overall**	**84.41**	**94.37**	**93.47**	**91.21**
一、按主要行业门类分	**Grouped by Sector**				
住宿业	Hotels	80.46	94.41	90.34	88.57
餐饮业	Catering Services	89.86	93.30	100.81	94.86
二、按企业登记注册类型分	**by Status of Registration**				
国有企业	State-owned Enterprises	69.23	87.00	78.24	75.53
集体企业	Collective-owned Enterprises	64.29	78.57	85.71	69.23
股份合作企业	Cooperative Enterprises	68.97	77.78	80.08	131.03
联营企业	Joint Ownership Enterprises	100.00	100.00	100.00	100.00
有限责任公司	Limited Liability Corporations	86.63	96.89	90.90	88.48
股份有限公司	Share-holding Corporations Limited	73.70	90.91	100.98	100.98
私营企业	Private Enterprises	80.00	80.00	60.00	60.00
其它内资企业	Other Domestic Funded	200.00	200.00	200.00	200.00
外商及港、澳、台投资企业	Enterprises with Funds from Foreign Contry, Hongkong, Macao and Taiwan	128.25	118.82	137.63	119.20
三、按企业规模分	**Grouped by Size of Enterprises**				
大型及以上	Large-sized and Higher	117.23	133.05	139.55	162.64
中型	Medium-sized	82.80	93.48	88.04	83.52
小型	Small-sized	72.55	78.85	82.69	73.08

9-58 住宿和餐饮业企业货款拖欠景气指数（2006年）
Climate Index on Overdue Obligations to Suppliers about Hotel and Catering Services Enterprise (2006)

类别	Classification	一季度 Quarter1	二季度 Quarter2	三季度 Quarter3	四季度 Quarter4
住宿和餐饮业企业总体状况	**Overall**	**95.03**	**86.43**	**81.05**	**95.19**
一、按主要行业门类分	**Grouped by Sector**				
住宿业	Hotels	91.82	85.58	76.53	97.58
餐饮业	Catering Services	100.80	86.65	84.91	94.67
二、按企业登记注册类型分	**by Status of Registration**				
国有企业	State-owned Enterprises	72.42	75.82	74.51	97.80

9-58 续表 1 continued

类别	Classification	一季度 Quarter1	二季度 Quarter2	三季度 Quarter3	四季度 Quarter4
集体企业	Collective-owned Enterprises	107.14	107.14	76.92	76.92
股份合作企业	Cooperative Enterprises	91.20	68.97	57.86	88.89
联营企业	Joint Ownership Enterprises	100.00	100.00	100.00	100.00
有限责任公司	Limited Liability Corporations	101.06	88.25	84.37	95.19
股份有限公司	Share-holding Corporations Limited	143.50	116.23	108.12	144.48
私营企业	Private Enterprises	100.00	60.00	60.00	20.00
其它内资企业	Other Domestic Funded	200.00	200.00	200.00	0.00
外商及港、澳、台投资企业	Enterprises with Funds from Foreign Contry, Hongkong, Macao and Taiwan	105.82	95.99	87.02	103.95
三、按企业规模分	Grouped by Size of Enterprises				
大型及以上	Large-sized and Higher	99.06	88.45	57.86	127.81
中型	Medium-sized	94.62	90.22	81.32	91.21
小型	Small-sized	94.00	78.85	90.38	88.24

9-59 住宿和餐饮业企业劳动力需求景气指数（2006年）
Climate Index on Labor Demand of Hotel and Catering Services Enterprise (2006)

类别	Classification	一季度 Quarter1	二季度 Quarter2	三季度 Quarter3	四季度 Quarter4
住宿和餐饮业企业总体状况	**Overall**	**113.12**	**117.45**	**118.64**	**108.61**
一、按主要行业门类分	**Grouped by Sector**				
住宿业	Hotels	113.14	117.29	121.79	98.01
餐饮业	Catering Services	111.56	119.03	111.27	121.46
二、按企业登记注册类型分	**by Status of Registration**				
国有企业	State-owned Enterprises	115.66	109.10	119.15	94.80
集体企业	Collective-owned Enterprises	85.71	107.14	107.14	84.62
股份合作企业	Cooperative Enterprises	111.11	131.03	111.11	111.11
联营企业	Joint Ownership Enterprises	100.00	100.00	100.00	100.00
有限责任公司	Limited Liability Corporations	116.86	124.88	129.70	108.67
股份有限公司	Share-holding Corporations Limited	91.88	119.16	118.18	119.16
私营企业	Private Enterprises	160.00	160.00	120.00	140.00
其它内资企业	Other Domestic Funded	0.00	200.00	200.00	0.00
外商及港、澳、台投资企业	Enterprises with Funds from Foreign Contry, Hongkong, Macao and Taiwan	131.53	122.44	121.59	126.86
三、按企业规模分	**Grouped by Size of Enterprises**				
大型及以上	Large-sized and Higher	103.93	122.39	113.62	118.67
中型	Medium-sized	112.90	116.30	119.57	108.79
小型	Small-sized	117.65	117.31	119.23	103.85

9-60 住宿和餐饮业企业固定资产投资景气指数（2006年）
Climate Index on Fixed Assets Investment of Hotel and Catering Services Enterprise (2006)

类别	Classification	一季度 Quarter1	二季度 Quarter2	三季度 Quarter3	四季度 Quarter4
住宿和餐饮业企业总体状况	**Overall**	**110.77**	**112.31**	**107.85**	**105.99**
一、按主要行业门类分	**Grouped by Sector**				
住宿业	Hotels	102.03	106.99	101.81	96.33
餐饮业	Catering Services	125.72	124.71	118.05	119.29
二、按企业登记注册类型分	**by Status of Registration**				
国有企业	State-owned Enterprises	99.51	109.34	101.64	104.16
集体企业	Collective-owned Enterprises	92.86	107.14	100.00	115.38
股份合作企业	Cooperative Enterprises	139.83	142.14	150.94	111.11
联营企业	Joint Ownership Enterprises	100.00	100.00	100.00	100.00
有限责任公司	Limited Liability Corporations	108.15	102.00	102.27	83.86
股份有限公司	Share-holding Corporations Limited	161.69	117.21	144.48	134.41
私营企业	Private Enterprises	120.00	120.00	100.00	120.00
其它内资企业	Other Domestic Funded	100.00	100.00	100.00	100.00
外商及港、澳、台投资企业	Enterprises with Funds from Foreign Contry, Hongkong, Macao and Taiwan	109.72	117.64	105.42	116.00
三、按企业规模分	**Grouped by Size of Enterprises**				
大型及以上	Large-sized and Higher	126.00	132.84	113.49	134.52
中型	Medium-sized	109.68	115.22	114.13	107.69
小型	Small-sized	105.88	98.08	94.23	90.38

国家统计局山东调查总队
大 事 记

（2005年11月～2006年12月）

编者说明

大事记依据总队每月工作、调研纪实，由办公室进行编纂撰写，总队领导审定。入选大事记的条目主要是：山东省委、省政府领导的批示，重要统计调查项目和活动，总队召开的重要会议，总队正处以上领导职务任免，市、县级调查队长的任免，国家统计局领导（司级以上）在山东视察工作，总队领导外出调研等。

2005年

2005年11月8日 根据《国务院办公厅关于印发国家统计局直属调查队管理体制改革方案的通知》（国办发〔2005〕14号）和中央编办《关于国家统计局各级调查队机构设置和人员编制的批复》（中央编办复字〔2005〕149号），国家统计局下发《关于设立国家统计局山东调查总队的通知》（国统字〔2005〕135号）决定：撤销山东省农村社会经济调查队、山东省城市社会经济调查队、山东省企业调查队，设立国家统计局山东调查总队。山东调查总队为正厅级机构。

同日 国家统计局下发《关于宋志申职务任免的通知》（国统任免〔2005〕34号）：经国家统计局党组会议研究决定，并征得中共山东省委组织部同意，任命宋志申为国家统计局山东调查总队总队长（正厅级），试用期一年，免去其原任行政职务。

2005年11月30日 山东省统计局、原山东省农村社会经济调查队、原山东省城市社会经济调查队、原山东省企业调查队召开全体干部大会。会上，山东省统计局局长杜昌祚宣读了《关于设立国家统计局山东调查总队的通知》和《关于宋志申职务任免的通知》。总队长宋志申作就职讲话，省统计局局长杜昌祚讲话。

2005年12月2日 国家统计局下发《关于娄美芝等职务任免的通知》（国统任免〔2005〕78号），经国家统计局党组会议研究，并征得中共山东省委组织部同意，决定下列人员职务任免：任命娄美芝为国家统计局山东调查总队副总队长（副厅局级），免去其原任行政职务；任命段连芳为国家统计局山东调查总队副总队长（副厅局级），试用期一年，免去其原任行政职务；任命谭杰为国家统计局山东调查总队副总队长（副厅局级），试用期一年。

2005年12月7日 国家统计局党组下发《关于宋志申等同志任职的通知》（统党组任免〔2005〕5号），经国家统计局党组会议研究决定，并征得中共山东省委组织部同意，任命：宋志申同志为中共国家统计局山东调查总队党组书记；娄美芝、段连芳、谭杰同志为中共国家统计局山东调查总队党组成员。

同日 国家统计局下发《关于将国家统计局山东调查总队列入地方中直机关序列进行管理的函》（国统函〔2005〕246号）：要求将山东调查总队列入地方中直机关序列进行管理，通知总队参加有关会议，向总队下发有关文件等。

2005年12月22日 山东省统计局、山东调查总队召开2005年度工作总结大会。会上山东省统计局局长杜昌祚宣读了国家统计局党组《关于宋志申等同志任职的通知》和《关于娄美芝等职务任免的通知》。

同日 山东调查总队党组召开第一次会议。党组书记、总队长宋志申主持会议，党组成员、副总队长娄美芝、段连芳、谭杰出席会议，党组成员分别作了就职发言。会上，总队领导进行了初步分工，并决定成立综合、后勤保障、业务指导三个组，临时负责改革期间各项工作的协调。山东省统计局局长杜昌祚、原山东省农村社会经济调查队队长宋文理列席会议。

2005年12年23日 国家统计局山东调查总队召开第一次全体干部职工会议。党组书记、总队长宋志申等总队领导出席会议，党组成员、副总队长娄美芝、段连芳、谭杰分别在会上作了表态发言。总队长宋志申就总队领导分工和下一步的改革工作作了讲话。原山东省农村社会经济调查队队长宋文理主持了会议。

同日 山东省统计局、山东调查总队召开处以上干部会议。党组书记、总队长宋志申传达全国统计工作会议精神。

2006年

2006年1月5日 国家统计局下发《关于宋文理免职退休的通知》（国统任免〔2006〕1号）决定：免去宋文理山东省农村社会经济调查队队长职务，享受正厅级待遇并办理退休手续。

2006年1月6日 全省统计工作暨经济普查表彰会议在济南召开，会议期间专门召开了全省调查队长会议。国家统计局山东调查总队总队长宋志申作了题为《认清新形势 把握新机遇 努力开创调查队工作新局面》的讲话。

2006年1月7日 山东省统计局局长杜昌祚、国家统计局山东调查总队总队长宋志申，向山东省委副书记、省长韩寓群汇报了国家调查队管理体制改革等情况。韩寓群省长听完汇报后作了重要指示，首先祝贺国家统计局山东调查总队成立，并表示山东省委、省政府对国家调查队体制改革完全赞成，坚决拥护。这是加强国民经济和社会统计重要的改革措施，可以使今后的统计数据更加科学、更加真实，为党中央、国务院宏观决策提供必要依据。国家调查队体制改革，地方也是受益者，国家调查队所获得的数据，完全可以做到与地方资源共享，为地方党委政府决策提供参考，省委省政府完全支持调查队的工作。韩寓群省长还对改革后的局队关系、为地方服务及调查队经费支持等问题作重要批示。

2006年2月7日 山东省统计局局长杜昌祚、国家统计局山东调查总队总队长宋志申，就国家调查队管理体制改革的有关情况、调查总队的管理方式、调查任务、局队关系以及为地方服务需要省政府给予经费支持等问题，向山东省常务副省长林廷生作了汇报。林廷生听取汇报后作出四点指示：1、局队过去是一家，今后仍是一家人；2、统计工作很有成绩，工作超前，对全省的经济社会发展反映得到位，分析得透彻，给省委省政府起到了很好的参谋助手作用；3、调查总队承担为地方政府服务的项目所需经费支持，抓紧与省财政厅商量、落实；4、调查总队的一些重大问题可直接向我报告，一般性问题可与统计局沟通，协商解决。

2006年2月16日 《国家统计局关于印发山东调查总队职能配置、内设机构和人员编制规定的通知》（国统字〔2006〕40号），对国家统计局山东调查总队职能配置、内设机构和人员编制作出规定。

2006年2月28日 国家统计局山东调查总队、山东省统计局在济南联合召开全省规模以下工业抽样调查工作会议，贯彻落实国家制度，布置样本轮换和2006年季报工作。省统计局副局长刘银田主持会议，山东调查总队副总队长谭杰作了讲话。

2006年3月2日 国家统计局山东调查总队召开机构改革动员大会，总队党组成员及全体干部职工参加了大会。党组书记、总队长宋志申作动员讲话。

2006年3月7日 国家统计局山东调查总队下发《关于寇祖传等同志职务任免的通知》（鲁调任免字〔2006〕1号），任命寇祖传、杜敏杰为总队长助理（正处级），刘同星为总统计师（正处级）兼综合处处长，王庆国为办公室主任，刘传云为法规制度处处长，杨晓福为农业调查处处长，王象永为农村住户调查处处长，王志珍为城镇住户调查处处长，孟庆斌为工业调查处处长，姜西海为服务业调查处处长，仝义贵为统计监测处处长，刘敏为生产投资价格调查处处长，宋义贵为消费价格调查处处长，张向春为商业和投资建筑业调查处处长，范坤文为专项调查处处长。

2006年3月9日 国家统计局山东调查总队召开总队长办公会议暨内设机构授印仪式，总队长宋志申向各处室主要负责人授印并进行了集体谈话。

2006年3月10～12日　山东调查总队机关各处室开始调整办公用房，并登记固定资产。

2006年3月13日　《国家统计局关于山东省统计联系协调委员会组成人员的批复》（国统函〔2006〕55号），同意设立山东省统计联系协调委员会，杜昌祚为主任，宋志申为副主任。

同日　《国家统计局党组关于娄美芝同志免职的通知》（统党组任免〔2006〕10号），免去娄美芝国家统计局山东调查总队党组成员职务。

同日　《国家统计局关于娄美芝职务任免的通知》（国统任免〔2006〕54号），任命娄美芝为国家统计局山东调查总队巡视员（正厅级），免去其原任行政职务。

2006年3月13日　全省农产量抽样调查工作会议在济南召开。副总队长段连芳出席并讲话。

2006年3月14日　国家统计局山东调查总队下发《关于胡宗明等同志职务任免的通知》（鲁调任免字〔2006〕4号），任命胡宗明为人事教育处处长，黄成海为财务管理处副处长。

2006年3月22日　上午10时，国家统计局山东调查总队成立大会暨揭牌仪式在济南南郊宾馆俱乐部礼堂隆重举行。国家统计局顾问、原局长李德水，山东省委副书记、省长韩寓群共同为山东调查总队揭牌。李德水和山东省委常委、常务副省长林廷生分别在会上作重要讲话。省人大常委会副主任黄可华、省政协副主席王宗廉出席了会议。国家统计局办公室主任谢鸿光宣读了关于成立国家统计局山东调查总队的决定。省统计局局长杜昌祚、山东调查总队总队长宋志申分别在会上致词。会议由省政府副秘书长韩金峰主持。省委办公厅、省政府办公厅、省人大办公厅、省政协办公厅、省委宣传部、省直机关工委和省发展和改革委员会、省财政厅等四十多个省直部门领导到会祝贺。全省十七市地统计局长、省统计局处长以上领导干部、市县调查队长以及山东调查总队全体人员共300余人参加会议。会后与会领导与会议代表合影留念。新华社山东分社、大众日报、山东电视台等新闻媒体对成立大会和揭牌仪式进行了报道。中午，省长韩寓群在山东大厦会见了李德水一行，总队长宋志申陪同。

2006年3月22～25日　李德水一行在总队长宋志申、省统计局局长杜昌祚的陪同下，赴泰安、菏泽、济宁等市考察调研。泰安市委书记耿文清，市委副书记、市长贾学英，菏泽市委书记陈光，济宁市委书记孙守刚等市领导分别会见了李德水一行。

2006年3月28日　国家统计局山东调查总队下发《关于王洪卫同志职务任免的通知》（鲁调任免字〔2006〕5号），任命王洪卫为纪检监察室主任。

2006年4月3日　中国共产党国家统计局山东调查总队机关第一次党员大会在十三楼会议室召开。大会由总队党组成员、副总队长段连芳主持，党组书记、总队长宋志申讲话。巡视员娄美芝，党组成员、副总队长谭杰出席会议。大会以差额选举、无记名投票方式选举产生了中国共产党国家统计局山东调查总队机关第一届委员会和第一届纪律检查委员会。段连芳代表新当选的党委委员向全体党员作了表态发言。

2006年4月4日　机关党委召开第一次会议，以等额选举、无记名投票方式，选举产生了书记、副书记。段连芳任机关党委书记，李承法、胡宗明任副书记。纪委召开第一次会议，以等额选举、无记名投票方式，选举产生了书记、副书记。李承法任机关纪委书记，王红卫任副书记

2006年4月7日　山东调查总队召开全体干部职工大会，总队长宋志申对前一段工作情况进行了总结，并对今后工作进行了部署。

2006年4月10日　国家统计局山东调查总队下发《关于李承法同志职务任免的通知》（鲁调任免字〔2006〕6号），任命李承法为机关党委专职副书记（正处级）。

2006年4月10～11日　总队在济南召开城市统计年报工作会议。副总队长谭杰、国家统计局城市司赵惠云处长到会并讲话。

2006年4月11～16日　国家统计局城市社会经济调查司赵惠云处长到临沂、泰安两市和所属三县（市），就城市统计年报工作和城市发展评价问题进行调研。

2006年4月12日　以国务院第二次全国农业普查领导小组成员、中宣部副部长欧阳坚为组长的国务院第二次农业普查督查组，到山东督查农业普查工作。山东省委副书记、省长韩寓群会见了督查组一行。省第二次农业普查领导小组组长、

副省长贾万志主持召开农业普查汇报会。副总队长谭杰参加了汇报会。

2006年4月26～28日 总队长宋志申到北京参加全国调查队管理体制改革工作会议。

2006年4月29日 国家统计局山东调查总队党组书记、总队长宋志申主持召开党组扩大会议，传达全国调查队管理体制改革工作会议精神。

2006年4月30日 总队长宋志申主持召开总队长办公会。会议研究通过了《总队公务接待工作办法》、《总队车辆管理规定》、《总队财务管理办法》、《总队固定资产管理办法》、《总队公用经费包干管理办法》。批准了总队2006年公用经费包干定额的意见，研究通过了关于报废、更新、增配、调整计算机、打印机等办公设备的意见。研究通过了《2006年市、县级调查队的经费预算》。会议还听取了总队固定资产清理情况汇报和全国财务基建工作会议精神汇报。

2006年4月29～30日 国家统计局山东调查总队与省统计局共同举行庆“五一”乒乓球友谊赛。

2006年5月8～9日 国家统计局山东调查总队在山东省统计干部培训中心召开座谈会，研究讨论修改《统计法》意见。副总队长谭杰出席会议并讲话。

2006年5月9日 山东省委副书记赵春兰在总队撰写的《“十五”时期山东城乡居民收入差距分析》分析报告，批示：“为贯彻落实科学发展观，构建社会主义和谐社会和建设社会主义新农村，山东调查总队始终注重介绍世界发达国家和全国较先进省份的发展情况，积极提供可供我们借鉴的地方数字，这主要是更好地履行职责，出于对我省政治经济及社会事业形势的关心，把山东各项工作搞得更好，为省领导及时提供信息，当好参谋之目的。当看了这些从理论到具体事例、数字等详细的分析、说明，了解不少东西，学到些新的知识；同志辛苦了，十分感谢您们。望再接再厉，为了山东的发展，一如继往地提供这样高质量的材料。”

2006年5月10日 国家统计局山东调查总队召开总队纪检组长候选人民主推荐大会。

2006年5月9～12日 为推动中央和全省两个农村工作会议及中央和省委两个1号文件精神的贯彻落实，推进山东省社会主义新农村建设，受省委、省政府委托，山东调查总队派员参加以省统计局为主组成的联合调查组。

2006年5月12日 国家统计局山东调查总队召开总队机关工会成立大会。机关党委书记、副总队长段连芳到会并讲话。

同日 国家统计局山东调查总队召开了总队机关第一次妇女大会。党组成员、机关党委书记、副总队长段连芳到会并讲话。

2006年5月16日 国家统计局山东调查总队召开机关团委成立大会。党组成员、机关党委书记、副总队长段连芳到会并讲话。

2006年5月18日 山东省统计局、山东调查总队联合下发了《关于开展农村统计数据质量检查工作的通知》（鲁统字〔2006〕27号），就自查、复查、抽查等工作做出具体规定和要求。

2006年5月25日 山东省自然村基本情况抽样调查培训会议在济南召开。副总队长谭杰到会并讲话。

2006年5月26日 山东调查总队召开了农产品价格、农户固定资产投资调查业务培训会议，全省39个国家调查县农调队的分管队长和业务骨干参加了会议。

2006年5月29日 总队干部职工积极参加“慈心一日捐”活动。总队94名干部职工共筹集善款10028.00元。

2006年5月30日 国家统计局、山东省委组织部联合考察组对山东调查总队纪检组长进行考察。考察组召开由山东调查总队全体干部参加的民主推荐大会，总队党组书记、总队长宋志申主持会议，考察组组长、国家统计局人事司副司长邱小聪作动员讲话，考察组成员、山东省委组织部调研员王智南出席会议。

同日 总队召开“未成年人思想道德建设情况”和“大学生思想政治教育情况”调查工作会议。副总队长谭杰出席会议并讲话。

2006年4～5月 山东调查总队对市县调查队基本情况及管理体制改革进行全面调研。由总队领导带队，与省统计局组成四个调研组，分赴有国家属和省属调查队的17个市、45个县（市、区）进行调研，充分了解市县调查队的基本情况和市县统计局、调查队领导对调查队管理体制改革的意见建议。

2006年5月31日 全省服务业抽样调查工作会议在济南召开，总队长宋志申、巡视员娄美芝出席了会议。

2006年6月4日 总队长宋志申、副总队长段连芳一行赴德州市齐河县调研夏粮生产情况，并到国家农产量抽中村齐河县晏城镇江屯村，收割小麦样本。

同日 国家统计局城市司专项调查处吴军副处长到山东就“未成年人思想道德建设情况”和“大学生思想政治教育情况”调查工作进行巡查督导。

2006年6月5～9日 由国家统计局设计管理司副司长孙庆国率领的百县调研组，圆满完成对山东青州、嘉祥两县市的重点调研工作，并向山东省统计局和山东调查总队反馈调研情况。

2006年6月10日 山东省统计局、国家统计局山东调查总队和山东省农业厅在新泰市联合召开全省夏粮预产工作会议召开。副总队长段连芳出席会议并发表讲话。

2006年6月上旬 山东调查总队积极参加省“先进性教育公开承诺回头看”活动。国家统计局山东调查总队认真践行在《大众日报》的公开承诺，深入基层开展调研，形成了《山东农村低收入群体生产生活情况调查报告》、《山东农村劳动力就业与转移情况调查报告》。两项调研报告受到山东省委先进性教育活动办公室的高度评价：“山东调查总队开展的此项工作为其他中央驻鲁单位带了个好头，建议近期在‘先进性教育活动公开承诺回头看’专栏中，对山东调查总队的此项工作进行一次宣传报道”。

2006年6月13日 按照国家统计局关于百县调研的统一部署，山东省统计局、国家统计局山东调查总队百县调研组开展了为期三天的微山县统计基层基础建设情况调研活动。

2006年6月15日 山东电视台、山东人民广播电台、大众日报等新闻媒体，对国家统计局山东调查总队总队长宋志申进行了专题采访。宋志申介绍了山东调查总队的主要职责以及为国家、地方和社会各界提供服务的情况。

2006年6月19日 山东调查总队召开培训会，部署夏粮卫星遥感测量野外调查工作。

2006年6月21日 非制造业采购经理指数调查座谈会在济南召开，为即将在全国范围内实施的“非制造业PMI调查方案（草案）”向企业征求意见。副总队长谭杰出席会议。

2006年6月22日 国家统计局山东调查总队赴无棣县水湾镇中心小学举行“爱心图书室”挂牌暨捐赠图书仪式。段连芳副总队长代表总队将近2000册图书（其中约400册系总队购买了新书）、500本学习笔记本及一台联想开天奔四—200电脑交给学校，并在捐赠仪式上讲话。

2006年6月23日 山东调查总队总队长宋志申、巡视员娄美芝、副总队长段连芳、谭杰等总队领导及各处室主要负责同志到济南舜耕国际会展中心参观“山东省建设节约型社会成果展节能技术产品博览会”。

2006年6月27日 在纪念中国共产党建党85周年前夕，国家统计局山东调查总队在枣庄市举办了机关党支部书记培训班。

2006年6月30日 山东省经济贸易委员会、山东省统计局、国家统计局山东调查总队在济南珍珠泉宾馆召开新闻发布会，公布“山东省100强企业和山东省工业100强企业”名单。

2006年6月10日 山东省委书记、省人大常委会主任张高丽对山东调查总队撰写的分析报告《农村水利设施存在的问题不容忽视》批示：“请万志同志（山东省副省长）阅示研处”；6月13日，山东省副省长贾万志对该文批示：“请继峰厅长（山东省水利厅厅长）向张书记、韩省长报个简要情况”。

2006年6月28日 山东省委书记、人大常委会主任张高丽在《关于山东部分乡镇财政状况的调查报告》上批示：“调查总队的几次调查报告都很有份量，有针对性。几条建议请省政府分管领导和有关部门认真研究”。

2006年6月 山东调查总队撰写的《山东农村劳动力就业与转移情况调查报告》，6月28日被省委办公厅《今日信息》第119期刊登；6月29日副省长才利民批示：“请省劳动社会保障厅阅研。针对存在问题，采取有效措施，加大就业培训，进一步做好全省就业工作，确保全年目标的完成。”

2006年7月初 山东调查总队参加省直机关工

委纪念中国共产党建党85周年和长征胜利70周年文艺汇演活动，参演的两个节目均获二等奖，并获得组织奖。

2006年7月4日 山东省委常委、常务副省长林廷生在山东调查总队撰写的《农村水利设施存在的问题不容忽视》上批示："这个报告调查得很详实，望有关单位（水利厅、发改委、财政厅）针对报告中提出的问题，采取措施逐步解决。"

2006年7月17日 国家统计局领导在山东省政府副秘书长张德宽、山东省统计局局长杜昌祚、山东调查总队总队长宋志申等领导的陪同下，来到国家统计局山东调查总队检查指导工作，国家统计局领导会见了山东调查总队和山东省统计局全体处级以上干部并发表了讲话。

2006年7月下旬 山东夏粮实割实测抽样调查数据通过国家统计局的核定，全省夏粮总产为1890万吨，单产创历史最好水平。

2006年7月20日 国家统计局山东调查总队党组理论学习中心组成员集体学习胡锦涛总书记在庆祝中国共产党成立85周年暨总结保持共产党员先进性教育活动大会上的重要讲话。党组书记、总队长宋志申讲话。

2006年7月21日 全省及17市农村全面小康实现程度测算结果，分别在大众日报《要闻》栏目和齐鲁晚报《重点新闻》栏目进行了报道，山东电视台新闻栏目对总队领导进行了专访和报道。

2006年7月下旬 山东调查总队与省统计局联合建立统计执法检查员资格培训和考试制度。

2006年8月1～2日 山东省农业中间消耗调查培训会议在威海召开。段连芳副总队长到会并讲话。

2006年8月4日 国家统计局纪检组长章国荣、人事司司长闫岭等一行来山东调查总队和山东省统计局检查指导工作。在听取了山东省统计局局长杜昌祚、山东调查总队总队长宋志申的工作汇报后，章国荣组长对山东省统计局、山东调查总队的工作给予了高度评价，表示非常满意。

2006年8月7日 党组书记、总队长宋志申主持召开办公会，集体学习国家统计局党组成员、副局长林贤郁在全国调查队法制工作培训会议上的讲话。宋志申对加强山东调查队系统法制工作提出五点要求。

2006年8月8日 国家统计局下发《国家统计局党组关于赵兴成同志任职的通知》（统党组任免〔2006〕25号），任命赵兴成同志为国家统计局山东调查总队党组成员、党组纪检组组长（副厅局级，试用期一年）。

2006年8月10日 为加强党风廉政建设，提高拒腐防变能力，山东调查总队开展了警示教育活动，组织全体人员收看警示教育片《忏悔录》。

2006年8月11日 国家统计局下发《关于山东地区国家统计局市级调查队组建方案的批复》（国统字〔2006〕163号），在山东地区组建国家统计局市级调查队。

2006年8月15～25日 山东调查总队圆满完成城市社会经济调查专业数据质量检查与评估工作。巡视员娄美芝、副总队长谭杰分别带队，对济宁、微山、枣庄、临沂、费县、日照、烟台、威海、文登、潍坊等市县统计调查数据质量和基础工作进行认真复查，并对下一步工作提出了指导性意见。

2006年8月18日 山东省人民政府办公厅下发《山东省人民政府办公厅关于支持国家统计局山东调查队系统管理体制改革工作的通知》（鲁政办发〔2006〕70号），对贯彻落实《国务院办公厅关于印发国家统计局直属调查队管理体制改革方案的通知》（国办发〔2005〕14号）精神提出要求。

2006年8月21日 国家统计局第一期赴德国弗莱堡大学学习人员英语强化培训班开班仪式在山东泰安市举行。国家统计局党组成员、纪检组长章国荣出席并讲话，国家统计局山东调查总队总队长宋志申出席并致词。

2006年8月中旬 国家统计局党组成员、纪检组长章国荣一行在山东省统计局局长杜昌祚、山东调查总队总队长宋志申等陪同下，到泰安、滨州、东营三市进行调研。

2006年8月23日 国家统计局山东调查总队巡视员娄美芝陪同国家统计局城市司生产投资价格处处长刘文华、信息技术处副处长（处长级）许福建在山东进行工作调研。

2006年8月24日 副总队长谭杰主持召开专题会议，通报国家统计局各省、市、区总队信息采用情况并研究部署总队重要信息报送工作。

2006年8月29日 总队长宋志申为总队机关全体党员干部作《践行荣辱观，努力推进山东统计调查事业发展》的党课。

2006年8月下旬 山东调查总队根据国家统计局《关于开展城市农民工生活质量状况调查的通知》要求，按照调查方案，积极贯彻落实调查任务。经过近20天的共同努力，圆满完成了调查任务。

2006年8月31日 山东调查总队举办由全体干部职工参加的公文写作知识讲座。

2006年8月 山东调查总队与山东省统计局联合制定《山东省统计法制宣传教育第五个五年规划》，并联合成立山东省统计普法依法治理领导小组，杜昌祚任组长，宋志申任副组长，其他领导同志为成员。办公室由省统计局政策法规处和总队法规制度处组成，负责全省普法和依法治理的日常指导工作。

2006年9月7日 根据总队的统一安排，分三个调研组，到东营、滨州、德州、青岛、潍坊、临沂、聊城、菏泽、济宁等9市18个县市区38个乡镇76个村调研秋粮及全年农牧业生产形势。

2006年9月12日 根据《山东省第二次农业普查领导小组办公室关于开展农村住户调查基础工作检查的通知》（鲁农普办字〔2006〕27号）要求，山东调查总队在9～10月负责组织和实施对全省所有县（市、区）、乡（镇）、调查村、调查户等农村住户调查基础工作和数据质量进行全面检查。

2006年9月16日 “2006中国发达县域经济论坛”在山东省荣成市举行。国务院副总理回良玉出席开幕式并作重要讲话。期间回良玉接见了参加论坛的全国十强县（市、区）主要负责人。国家统计局领导主持开幕式并宣布论坛开幕。山东省委书记张高丽、威海市委书记崔日臣先后在开幕式上致辞。山东调查总队总队长宋志申参加了论坛活动。论坛由国家统计局主办，山东省统计局、国家统计局山东调查总队协办，荣成市委、市政府承办。

2006年9月18日 山东调查总队与山东省统计局联合下发《关于加强秋粮及全年农牧业预计及年报统计工作的通知》（鲁统字〔2006〕58号），布置山东省秋粮及全年农牧业预计及年报统计工作。

2006年9月22日 国家统计局下发《关于设立国家统计局济南调查队的通知》（国统字〔2006〕198号），决定撤销济南市城市社会经济调查队、济南市企业调查队，设立国家统计局济南调查队，济南调查队为副厅局级机构。

同日 国家统计局下发《关于设立国家统计局青岛调查队的通知》（国统字〔2006〕199号），决定撤销青岛市农村社会经济调查队、青岛市城市社会经济调查队、青岛市企业调查队，设立国家统计局青岛调查队，青岛调查队为副厅局级机构。

2006年9月24日 “2006山东嘉祥县域经济发展论坛”隆重举行。副总队长谭杰出席论坛并演讲。论坛由山东省科技厅、山东省发改委、山东省统计局、山东调查总队主办，山东省县域经济研究会协办，嘉祥县委、县政府承办。

2006年9月 山东调查总队生产投资价格处撰写的课题《PPI与CPI关联的理论与实证分析》获山东软科学优秀成果一等奖。

2006年9月25日 山东调查总队在济南召开县级规模以下工业抽样调查方案培训会议。

2006年9月27～28日 山东省农村住户调查基础工作集中检查会议在济南召开。副总队长谭杰主持会议并做总结讲话。

2006年9月28日 山东调查总队召开机关处级以上干部会议，传达全国纪检监察业务知识培训会议、全国基层基础工作经验交流暨表彰会议主要精神。党组书记、总队长宋志申讲话，对全国会议精神提出了贯彻落实意见。

2006年10月17～19日 按照国家统计局的统一部署，山东调查总队邀请山东省统计局和市级地方党委组织部组成三个考察组，分别对市级调查队队长人选进行民主推荐考察。

2006年10月26日 山东调查总队撰写的《全国百强县山东发展最快》和《全国千强镇山东增量第一总量第四》两篇分析报告（请阅件2006－11、2006－12）受到山东省委副书记、省纪委书记赵春兰批示。批示内容：“看了2006－11、12两期后，省统计局和调查总队报的这种请阅件很好。使阅文人既能了解全国局势，也清楚咱们情况，同时对我省情况总是客观、一分为二讲问题，使各级领导能受鼓舞，更加充满前进信心，保持清醒头脑，十分有利指导全省工作，谢谢同志们，您们太辛苦了。”

2006年10月下旬 山东调查总队从总队机关及济南、青岛、东营、烟台、济宁五市城调队共抽选出10名同志参加国家局在大连市开展的创建中国最佳旅游城市试点工作问卷调查，并圆满完成任务，受到国家局和大连市的一致好评。

2006年11月1日 山东调查总队召开《山东调查年鉴》编辑工作座谈会，副总队长谭杰主持会议并讲话。

2006年11月6日 国家统计局山东调查总队下发《关于姜宏济等同志职务任免的通知》（鲁调任免字〔2006〕12号），提任姜宏济为城镇住户调查处处长；提任李常良为服务业调查处处长；提任黄成海为财务管理处处长；提任赵兰香为纪检员（正处长级）。

2006年11月7日 国家统计局下发《关于高军任职的通知》（国统任免〔2006〕99号），任命高军为国家统计局济南调查队队长（副厅局级）。

2006年11月7日 山东调查总队与山东省统计局联合召开农业年报会议。副总队长段连芳出席并讲话。

2006年11月8日 山东调查总队召开党组扩大会议，传达贯彻山东省党员领导干部“勤政廉政、科学发展”教育视频会议精神。党组书记、总队长宋志申出席会议。

2006年11月8～9日 山东省服务业抽样调查工作会议在济南召开，副总队长谭杰出席会议并讲话。

2006年11月10日 山东调查总队机关开展“送温暖、献爱心”活动，97名干部职工捐献善款8100.00元，并送交山东省民政厅救灾捐助办公室。

2006年11月10日 山东省农村住户调查年报暨农业普查住户长表调查方案培训会议在济南召开。副总队长谭杰到会并讲话。

2006年11月15日 山东省规模以下工业抽样调查工作会议在济南召开。巡视员娄美芝到会并讲话。

2006年11月16日 山东调查总队处级以上干部集体收看国家统计局视频会议。国家统计局局长谢伏瞻同志主持会议并讲话，会议邀请国家审计署审计长李金华同志作报告。

同日 中加统计信息管理项目组到青岛实地考察，参观了解有关服务业企业情况。山东调查总队巡视员娄美芝等陪同考察。

2006年11月20～21日 山东生产投资价格调查统计工作会议在济南召开。巡视员娄美芝出席会议并讲话。

2006年11月21日 山东调查总队召开新任正处级干部集体谈话会，党组书记、总队长宋志申主持会议并讲话，总队领导娄美芝、段连芳、赵兴成出席会议并提出希望和要求，7位新任正处级干部参加会议并作表态发言。

2006年11月22日 国家统计局下发《关于毕明星任职的通知》（国统任免〔2006〕102号），任命毕明星为国家统计局青岛调查队队长（副厅局级），试用期一年。

同日 国家统计局下发《关于娄美芝免职退休的通知》（国统任免〔2006〕103号），免去娄美芝国家统计局山东调查总队巡视员职务，办理退休手续。

同日 山东调查总队和山东省统计局联合举办的高级统计知识及计算机知识培训班正式开班。总队、省统计局全体处以上干部和培训班学员参加了学习。

2006年11月23日 山东消费价格统计调查工作会议在济南召开。

2006年11月25日 山东省农普办、山东省统计局、山东调查总队、济南市农普办、商河县政府在商河县鼓子秧歌广场联合举办了依法进行农业普查宣传月、“12·4”统计法制宣传日大型活动。

2006年11月28日 为做好“12·4”全国法制宣传日和《统计法》宣传活动，山东调查总队决定在山东调查队系统开展网上有奖答题活动。

2006年11月30日 山东调查总队参加山东省省直机关“做表率、谋发展、促和谐”职业道德建设成果展，制作了六块展板进行全面宣传。山东调查总队二十名同志参加了大众广播操展演。

2006年12月2日 山东调查总队总队长宋志申

率全体干部职工参观省直机关职业道德建设成果展，并接受山东电视台采访。

2006年12月初 山东调查总队获山东省直机关工委2006年度省直机关“爱心助学先进单位”荣誉称号。

2006年12月6日 山东省城镇住户调查工作及新方案培训会议召开。副总队长谭杰出席会议并作讲话。

2006年12月13日 总队长宋志申、副总队长谭杰参加全国及省第二次农业普查电视电话会议。

2006年12月15日 山东调查总队副总队长、机关党委书记段连芳率机关党委、机关团委，与省直机关团工委书记王树山到总队“爱心图书室”挂牌学校无棣县水湾镇中心小学走访。

2006年12月20日 全省企业景气调查暨采购经理调查工作会议在淄博桓台召开。副总队长谭杰出席会议并讲话。

2006年12月23日 国家统计局山东调查总队下发《关于盛明三任职的通知》（鲁调任免字〔2006〕14号），任命盛明三为国家统计局淄博调查队队长（正处级），试用期一年。

国家统计局山东调查总队下发《关于于书峰职务任免的通知》（鲁调任免字〔2006〕15号），任命于书峰为国家统计局枣庄调查队队长（正处级），试用期一年，免去其原任行政职务。

国家统计局山东调查总队下发《关于蔡保卫任职的通知》（鲁调任免字〔2006〕16号），任命蔡保卫为国家统计局潍坊调查队队长（正处级），试用期一年。

国家统计局山东调查总队下发《关于黄金祥职务任免的通知》（鲁调任免字〔2006〕17号），任命黄金祥为国家统计局济宁调查队队长（正处级），试用期一年，免去其原任行政职务。

国家统计局山东调查总队下发《关于万传友任职的通知》（鲁调任免字〔2006〕18号），任命万传友为国家统计局泰安调查队队长（正处级），试用期一年。

国家统计局山东调查总队下发《关于杨笑娜职务任免的通知》（鲁调任免字〔2006〕19号），任命杨笑娜为国家统计局威海调查队队长（正处级），试用期一年，免去其原任行政职务。

国家统计局山东调查总队下发《关于卢中绪任职的通知》（鲁调任免字〔2006〕20号），任命卢中绪为国家统计局日照调查队队长（正处级），试用期一年。

国家统计局山东调查总队下发《关于崔现顺任职的通知》（鲁调任免字〔2006〕21号），任命崔现顺为国家统计局临沂调查队队长（正处级），试用期一年。

国家统计局山东调查总队下发《关于许洪海职务任免的通知》（鲁调任免字〔2006〕22号），任命许洪海为国家统计局德州调查队队长（正处级），试用期一年，免去其原任行政职务。

国家统计局山东调查总队下发《关于高会峰任职的通知》（鲁调任免字〔2006〕23号），任命高会峰为国家统计局菏泽调查队队长（正处级），试用期一年。

2006年12月30日 山东调查总队总队长宋志申主持召开全体干部职工大会，由各处室主要负责人汇报2006年度工作并述职述廉。

2006年12月 山东省直机关工会工委发出关于表彰省直机关职业道德建设成果展暨广播操、太极拳展演的通报。山东调查总队荣获省直机关职业道德建设成果展优秀组织奖；参展展品荣获二等奖；大众广播操展演荣获优秀表演奖。

图书在版编目（CIP）数据

山东调查年鉴2007/ 国家统计局山东调查总队　编
中国国际文化出版社 2007.10
ISBN 988 — 97358 — 3585 — 6
Ⅰ．山．．．Ⅱ．国．．．Ⅲ．调查资料 – 山东省 –2007– 年鉴
Ⅳ．3Z519.30
中国图书在版编目（CIP）数据核字（2007）第（B–927 号）

山东调查年鉴—2007

国家统计局山东调查总队　编

主　　编／谭　杰
出版发行／中国国际文化出版社
文稿审阅／范文静
编辑校阅／第二编辑室
责任编辑／纪　文　丁瑞虎
排版设计／山东海天国际文化传播有限公司
印　　刷／深圳市佳信达印务有限公司
开　　本／ 890 毫米 ×1240 毫米　1/16
印　　张／ 39.75
字　　数／ 970 千字
印　　数／ 1—1000 册
版　　次／ 2007 年 10 月第一版第一次印刷
书　　号／ ISBN 988 — 97358 — 3585 — 6
定　　价／ 320.00 元